Chambers
Crossword Lists

Over 170,000 solutions to every kind of crossword

D1189178

Chambers

CHAMBERS
An imprint of Chambers Harrap Publishers Ltd
338 Euston Road, London, NW1 3BH

Chambers Harrap Publishers Ltd is an Hachette UK Company

© Chambers Harrap Publishers Ltd 2009
This reprint 2010

Chambers® is a registered trademark of Chambers Harrap Publishers Ltd

This second edition published by Chambers Harrap Publishers Ltd 2009
Previous edition published 2005

Database right Chambers Harrap Publishers Ltd (makers)

A CIP catalogue record for this book is available from the British Library.

ISBN 978 0550 104052

www.chambers.co.uk

Designed and typeset by Chambers Harrap Publishers Ltd
Printed and bound in the UK by Clays Ltd, St Ives plc

Contributors

Editor
Anne Robertson

Consultants
Derek Arthur
Chris Feetenby
Derek Harrison
Brian Head
Tom Johnson
Don Manley
Tim Moorey

Contributors
Kay Cullen
Daphne Day
Christina Gleeson
Lucy Hollingworth
George Robertson
Kate Sleight

Editorial Assistance
Francine Toon
Lianne Vella

Data Management
David Wark

Prepress Controller
Nicolas Echallier

Publishing Manager
Hazel Norris

Editorial Director
Vivian Marr

The editor would like to thank contributors to the previous edition.

Preface

Whether tackling quick or cryptic crosswords, every cruciverbalist has experienced the frustration that comes from staring in vain at those obstinately white squares. Even a clue as simple as 'River (5)' may pose insurmountable problems once the Loire, Rhine, Rhône and Seine have been ruled out and one's mind remains stubbornly blank. This book is designed for exactly those moments. Rather than scurrying for an atlas, or – as the case may be – a biographical dictionary, factfinder or other reference, beleaguered solvers can find a wealth of possible solutions in seconds by reaching for *Chambers Crossword Lists*.

This book draws on material from across the authoritative Chambers reference range, including the *Biographical Dictionary*, *Dictionary of Literary Characters*, *Book of Facts*, *Crossword Dictionary* and *Dictionary of World History*. Furthermore, it contains thousands of terms from *The Chambers Dictionary*, including many of the archaic, literary and obscure words so beloved of cryptic crossword compilers.

Over 170,000 possible solutions to quick or cryptic clues are arranged in 1,650 lists under more than 900 headwords in this second edition. The information is truly diverse, from actors to wizards, political parties to capital cities, deserts to racehorses and landmarks to sieges. Additional information is included for many of the entries, such as nationalities and dates for people, sources for literary characters and locations for geographical features. A detailed contents list and extensive cross-references ensure that the material may be quickly and easily found.

Chambers Crossword Lists makes an ideal companion volume to the popular *Chambers Crossword Dictionary*, and should prove to be an invaluable aid to crossword setters and solvers alike.

We welcome all comments and suggestions from members of the public, which will be considered for incorporation in future editions. These should be sent to The Editor, *Chambers Crossword Lists*, Chambers Harrap Publishers Ltd, 7 Hopetoun Crescent, Edinburgh, EH7 4AY.

Introduction

Chambers Crossword Lists contains more than 170,000 possible solutions to quick and cryptic crossword clues. It draws on *The Chambers Dictionary*, *Chambers Biographical Dictionary*, *Chambers Dictionary of Literary Characters*, *Chambers Crossword Dictionary* and the other authoritative Chambers databases.

Word forms

The forms *-ize* and *-ization* are used throughout; users should be aware that the alternative *-ise* and *-isation* spelling may be required as the solution to some crossword clues.

Organization

Words and phrases have been sorted into more than 1,650 lists. These are arranged under 900 main headwords, each with one or more list.

Each list focuses on a specific category of information; for example, there is not simply one list of cities, but four: capital cities, ancient cities, former names of cities and cities and towns from around the world. This makes locating exact information much easier.

Within the lists, words and phrases are grouped firstly by length, that is by the total number of letters in each word or phrase, and then ordered alphabetically within these word-length sections:

rainbow

Colours of the rainbow:			
03 red	05 green	orange	yellow
04 blue	06 indigo	violet	

Solvers should note that alphabetization of solutions is strictly by letter, and usual stylistic conventions may be disregarded. For example, 'Mc' will be found at 'Mc' rather than mingled with 'Mac'. Items which are prefaced with 'The' will be found at 'T' rather than at the first letter of the second word. 'Saint' is rendered as 'St' throughout except in people's names and, similarly, 'Mount' is rendered as 'Mt'. The number of letters given for items will therefore reflect this.

Alphabetization of headwords, however, is by word so that 'air force' and 'air travel' precede 'aircraft' and 'airport'. Headwords which are prefaced with 'The' are alphabetized by the first letter of the second word so that 'The Americas' is found at 'A' rather than at 'T'.

There are extensive cross-references to assist users in finding the correct solution. There is also a detailed contents list at the start of the volume.

Inclusion

The content of the lists is intended to strike a balance between comprehensiveness and the likelihood of the words and phrases actually occurring as the solutions to crossword clues. Consideration has been given to the differing needs of different kinds of crosswords, from concise to the more advanced cryptics, and nothing has been excluded simply on the grounds of obscurity. An effort has been made to include colourful vocabulary, such as dialect, literary and archaic terms.

witch

Witches, witch doctors and wizards include:

03 hag	mganga	conjurer	**10** besom-rider
hex	shaman	magician	reim-kennar
04 mage	voodoo	marabout	**11** enchantress
05 Hecat	wisard	night-hag	gyre-carline
lamia	zendik	**09** enchanter	medicine man
magus	**07** angekok	galdragon	necromancer
sibyl	carline	occultist	thaumaturge
weird	sangoma	pythoness	**12** Weird Sisters
06 Hecate	warlock	sorceress	**13** thaumaturgist
magian	wise man	wise woman	
	08 angekkok	witch-wife	

Content

The lists include both historical and current information; for example, in the list of actors users will find not only contemporary figures like Sir Ian McKellen and Leonardo DiCaprio, but also notable actors from the past like Richard Burbage and Edward Alleyn.

Similarly, the lists may contain both real and fictional or legendary items. For example, the list of heroes and heroines includes the legendary Robin Hood, the literary D'Artagnan, the historical William Wallace, the cinematic Indiana Jones, and the comic strip Superman.

Common generic terms have been omitted from the items in the lists, to avoid unwieldy and unnecessary repetition. For example, the word 'abbey' has not been included in the names in the list of abbeys, and the word 'saw' has not been included in the list of saws.

Users should be aware that such generic terms may form part of the solution to crossword clues.

saw

Saws include:

03 jig	hand	**06** coping	**08** circular
rip	**05** bench	rabbet	crosscut
04 band	chain	scroll	**09** radial-arm
fret	panel	**07** compass	**11** power-driven
hack	tenon	pruning	

The reference material has been selected to be as wide-ranging in scope as possible. Users should note that:

- variant spellings have been included, for example *topi* and *topee* in the list of hats.

- numbers may be found in solutions in some instances, as numbers may be encountered or referenced in some form in cryptic puzzles. For example, the list of films includes *2001: A Space Odyssey* and *Apollo 13*.

- some items are included under a certain headword on the grounds of usefulness, even if they are not strictly types of the headword. For example, *Washington DC* is included in the list of US states; *tomato* is included in the list of vegetables and *Pluto* is included in the list of planets. Similarly, items which are related to the headword may be included; succulents in the list of cacti, for example.

The size of the standard crossword grid is 15 letters across and down. In order to maximize the number of useful solutions in this edition, a distinction has been made between finite and non-finite lists in the book. In finite lists (ie those involving a closed set of solutions, such as members of the Commonwealth), no limit has been imposed on the length of solutions. In non-finite lists (ie those involving an open set of solutions, such as board games), solutions have been edited to 15 letters.

An exception has been made for lists of artistic works as these are often longer than 15 letters in length, such as fables, films and novels. Another minor exception concerns the lists of twins and pairs of lovers, as each solution in these lists comprises two names. In these exceptional cases, solutions longer than 15 letters have been permitted.

In lists of musical works, long solutions of the variety *Symphony No 6 in F Major* have been edited and listed by nickname or shortened title; solvers may need to investigate the full title of a musical work elsewhere.

In lists of people, death dates were researched at the end of 2008.

Extra information

Some of the lists contain extra information in brackets, following the core information. For example:

- first names or nicknames are given following a listed surname for real people, often with the person's birth and death dates and nationality

- fictional characters have the source given, with the date of publication and author

- for geographical features, buildings and similar items, the location is given in brackets

- musical and literary works have the composer/author and date of first performance/publication

- abbreviations, codes and similar items have the expanded form

- archbishops and popes have the date of accession

- legendary or mythological figures and creatures have the source of the legend or myth given

- gods and goddesses have their domain of power given

- words and expressions from foreign languages have the English term given

- films have date of release given

- battles have dates

- some terms have the thing related to; for example phobias include the thing feared, adjectives relating to eating include the thing eaten, dependencies have the governing country, sporting competitions have the relevant sport, and anniversaries have the number

The exact nature of the extra bracketed material is usually not indicated, but should be clear. Where it differs to that which might be expected, this is indicated in the introductory line to the list.

Some lists may have extra bracketed material for some items but not others. For example, in a list of airports *Gatwick* will have (London), but extra information is not needed for *Glasgow*.

Additional bracketed information is not included in the count of the number of letters, although it may form part of the solution to some crossword clues. The regnal numbers of individual popes, emperors, kings and queens have been omitted from main items, but are given in the brackets.

Reference Lists

A

abbey

aborigine

accessory *see* **fashion; photography**

accommodation

Accommodation includes:

03 cot
hut
inn
kip
pad
04 camp
cell
crib
digs
ferm
flat
gaff
gite
mews
room
tent
tipi
unit
weem
yurt
zeta
05 b and b
block
board
bothy
bower
cabin
condo
hotel
house
igloo
lodge
manse
meuse
motel
rooms
split
squat
suite
tepee
villa

06 bedsit
billet
bothie
camper
duplex
flotel
grange
hostel
hostry
insula
mia-mia
pondok
refuge
shanty
studio
succah
sukkah
teepee
walk-up
wigwam
07 caravan
cottage
flatlet
floatel
hospice
hutment
mansion
parador
pension
shelter
taverna
village
08 barracks
crashpad
hacienda
home unit
hospital
lodgings
minshuku
paradise
quarters

tenement
09 almshouse
apartment
bedsitter
bunkhouse
camper van
dharmsala
dormitory
dosshouse
firehouse
frat house
full board
guest-room
half board
homestead
hospitale
hospitium
houseboat
longhouse
peel-house
peel-tower
pele-house
pele-tower
penthouse
pondokkie
residence
rooming-in
single-end
tanka boat
timeshare
tree house
10 casual ward
dharmshala
earth-house
guardhouse
guest house
habitation
habitaunce
labour camp
mobile home
outlodging

padding-ken
Picts' house
pied-à-terre
quarterage
shantytown
wheelhouse
11 agriturismo
appartement
bachelor pad
bed and board
bridal suite
condominium
duplex house
head-station
pit-dwelling
youth hostel
12 guest-chamber
halfway house
hunting-lodge
lodging house
porter's lodge
private hotel
private house
room and board
rooming house
self-catering
two-up, two-down
13 boarding-house
dwelling-house
habitat module
sponging-house
spunging-house
14 bedsitting-room
loft conversion
15 bed and breakfast
duplex apartment
fraternity house
hall of residence
married quarters

See also **house; tent**

acid

Acids include:

03 DNA
RNA
04 EDTA
thio

uric
wood
05 amino
auric

boric
fatty
folic
Lewis

malic
mucic
osmic
06 acetic

bromic
cholic
citric
domoic
erucic
formic
gallic
lactic
lauric
maleic
marine
nitric
oxalic
pectic
phenol
picric
quinic
sorbic
tannic
toluic

07 acrylic
alginic
benzoic
boracic
butyric
cerotic
chloric
chromic
fumaric
fusidic
malonic

nitrous
nucleic
plumbic
prussic
pteroic
pyruvic
sebacic
silicic
stearic
valeric

08 abscisic
ascorbic
aspartic
butanoic
carbamic
carbolic
carbonic
cinnamic
cresylic
ethanoic
glutamic
iopanoic
itaconic
linoleic
lysergic
manganic
margaric
molybdic
myristic
nonanoic
palmitic

periodic
retinoic
succinic
tantalic
tartaric
telluric
trans fat

09 aqua regia
cevitamic
hydrazoic
linolenic
methanoic
nalidixic
nicotinic
pentanoic
propanoic
propenoic
propionic
salicylic
sulphonic
sulphuric

10 aqua fortis
barbituric
carboxylic
dodecanoic
glutaminic
hyaluronic
margaritic
naphthenic
omega fatty
pelargonic

phosphonic
phosphoric
sulphurous
trans fatty
valerianic

11 arachidonic
ethanedioic
gibberellic
hydrobromic
hydrocyanic
pantothenic
permanganic
phosphorous
ribonucleic

12 alpha-hydroxy
hydrochloric
hydrofluoric
indoleacetic
octadecanoic
orthoboracic
terephthalic

13 indolebutyric
spirits of salt
thiosulphuric
tricarboxylic

14 essential fatty
peptide nucleic

15 acetylsalicylic
pteroylglutamic

See also **amino acid**

Act *see* **law**

acting

Actors include:

03 Cox (Brian; 1946– , Scottish)
Fox (Michael J; 1961– , Canadian)
Fry (Stephen; 1957– , English)
Law (Jude; 1973– , English)
Lee (Bruce; 1940–73, Chinese)
Lee (Christopher; 1922– , English)
Lee (Spike; 1957– , US)
Lom (Herbert; 1917– , Czech)
Sim (Alastair; 1900–76, Scottish)

04 Alda (Alan; 1936– , US)
Caan (James; 1939– , US)
Cage (Nicolas; 1964– , US)
Chan (Jackie; 1954– , Chinese)
Cook (Peter; 1937–95, English)
Dean (James; 1931–55, US)
Depp (Johnny; 1963– , US)
Ford (Harrison; 1942– , US)

Foxx (Jamie; 1967– , US)
Gere (Richard; 1949– , US)
Holm (Sir Ian; 1931– , English)
Hope (Bob; 1903–2003, English/US)
Hurt (John; 1940– , English)
Kean (Edmund; c.1789–1833, English)
Lowe (Rob; 1964– , US)
Marx (Chico; 1891–1961, US)
Marx (Groucho; 1895–1977, US)
Marx (Harpo; 1893–1964, US)
Marx (Zeppo; 1901–79, US)
Peck (Gregory; 1916–2003, US)
Penn (Sean; 1960– , US)
Pitt (Brad; 1963– , US)
Reed (Oliver; 1938–99, English)
Roth (Tim; 1961– , English)
Rush (Geoffrey; 1951– , Australian)

Sher (Sir Antony; 1949– , South African/British)
Tati (Jacques; 1908–82, French)
Thaw (John; 1942–2002, English)
Wood (Elijah; 1981– , US)

05 Allen (Woody; 1935– , US)
Arkin (Alan; 1934– , US)
Bacon (Kevin; 1958– , US)
Bates (Alan; 1934–2003, English)
Boyer (Charles; 1897–1978, French)
Brody (Adrien; 1973– , US)
Caine (Sir Michael; 1933– , English)
Candy (John; 1950–94, Canadian)
Chase (Chevy; 1943– , US)
Clift (Montgomery; 1920–66, US)
Conti (Tom; 1941– , Scottish)
Crowe (Russell; 1964– , Australian)
Dafoe (Willem; 1955– , US)
Damon (Matt; 1970– , US)
Dance (Charles; 1946– , English)
Firth (Colin; 1960– , English)
Flynn (Errol; 1909–59, Australian/US)
Fonda (Henry; 1905–82, US)
Fonda (Peter; 1939– , US)
Gabin (Jean; 1904–76, French)
Gable (Clark; 1901–60, US)
Grant (Cary; 1904–86, English/US)
Grant (Hugh; 1960– , English)
Grant (Richard E; 1957– , Swazi/British)
Hanks (Tom; 1956– , US)
Hardy (Oliver; 1892–1957, US)
Hauer (Rutger; 1944– , Dutch)
Hogan (Paul; 1939– , Australian)
Irons (Jeremy; 1948– , English)
Jet Li (1963– , Chinese)
Jones (Tommy Lee; 1946– , US)
Julia (Raul; 1940–94, Puerto Rican)
Kelly (Gene; 1912–96, US)
Kempe (Will; c.1550–c.1603, English)
Kline (Kevin; 1947– , US)
Leung (Tony; 1962– , Chinese)
Lewis (Jerry; 1926– , US)
Lloyd (Harold; 1893–1971, US)
Mason (James; 1909–84, English)
Miles (Bernard, Lord; 1907–91, English)
Mills (Sir John; 1908–2005, English)
Moore (Dudley; 1935–2002, English)
Moore (Roger; 1927– , English)
Neill (Sam; 1947– , New Zealand)
Niven (David; 1910–83, English)
Nolte (Nick; 1940– , US)
Pesci (Joe; 1943– , US)
Price (Vincent; 1911–93, US)
Quinn (Anthony; 1915–2001, Mexican/US)
Reeve (Christopher; 1952–2004, US)
Sheen (Charlie; 1965– , US)
Sheen (Martin; 1940– , US)
Sheen (Michael; 1969– , Welsh)

Smith (Mel; 1952– , English)
Smith (Will; 1968– , US)
Spall (Timothy; 1957– , English)
Stamp (Terence; 1939– , English)
Sydow (Max von; 1929– , Swedish)
Tracy (Spencer; 1900–67, US)
Wayne (John; 1907–79, US)

06 Alleyn (Edward; 1566–1626, English)
Beatty (Warren; 1937– , US)
Bogart (Humphrey; 1899–1957, US)
Brando (Marlon; 1924–2004, US)
Brooks (Mel; 1926– , US)
Burton (Richard; 1925–84, Welsh)
Cagney (James; 1899–1986, US)
Callow (Simon; 1949– , English)
Carrey (Jim; 1962– , Canadian)
Cleese (John; 1939– , English)
Coburn (James; 1928–2002, US)
Cooper (Gary; 1901–61, US)
Coward (Sir Noël; 1899–1973, English)
Crosby (Bing; 1904–77, US)
Cruise (Tom; 1962– , US)
Culkin (Macaulay; 1980– , US)
Curtis (Tony; 1925– , US)
De Niro (Robert; 1943– , US)
De Sica (Vittorio; 1902–74, Italian)
DeVito (Danny; 1944– , US)
Dillon (Matt; 1964– , US)
Duvall (Robert; 1931– , US)
Fields (W C; 1879–1946, US)
Finney (Albert; 1936– , English)
Gambon (Sir Michael; 1940– , Irish)
Garner (James; 1928– , US)
Gibson (Mel; 1956– , US/Australian)
Glover (Danny; 1947– , US)
Harris (Richard; 1930–2002, Irish)
Heston (Charlton; 1924–2008, US)
Hopper (Dennis; 1936– , US)
Howard (Leslie; 1893–1943, English)
Howard (Trevor; 1916–88, English)
Hudson (Rock; 1925–85, US)
Irving (Sir Henry; 1838–1905, English)
Jacobi (Sir Derek; 1938– , English)
Jolson (Al; 1886–1950, Russian/US)
Keaton (Buster; 1895–1966, US)
Keitel (Harvey; 1941– , US)
Kemble (Charles; 1775–1854, English)
Kemble (John Philip; 1757–1823, English)
Kemble (Stephen; 1758–1822, English)
Laurel (Stan; 1890–1965, English/US)
Ledger (Heath; 1979–2008, Australian)
Lemmon (Jack; 1925–2001, US)
Lugosi (Bela; 1882–1956, Hungarian/US)
Martin (Steve; 1945– , US)
Marvin (Lee; 1924–87, US)
Massey (Raymond; 1896–1983, Canadian/US)
Morley (Robert; 1908–92, English)
Murphy (Eddie; 1961– , US)

Murray (Bill; 1950– , US)
Neeson (Liam; 1952– , Northern Irish)
Newman (Paul; 1925–2008, US)
Oldman (Gary; 1959– , English)
O'Toole (Peter; 1932– , Irish)
Pacino (Al; 1940– , US)
Quayle (Sir Anthony; 1913–89, English)
Reagan (Ronald; 1911–2004, US)
Reeves (Keanu; 1964– , US)
Rooney (Mickey; 1920– , US)
Rourke (Mickey; 1956– , US)
Sharif (Omar; 1932– , Egyptian)
Sinden (Sir Donald; 1923– , English)
Slater (Christian; 1969– , US)
Spacey (Kevin; 1959– , US)
Spader (James; 1960– , US)
Suchet (David; 1946– , English)
Swayze (Patrick; 1954– , US)
Walken (Christopher; 1943– , US)
Welles (Orson; 1915–85, US)
Wilder (Gene; 1935– , US)
Willis (Bruce; 1955– , US)
Wolfit (Sir Donald; 1902–68, English)

07 Astaire (Fred; 1899–1987, US)
Auteuil (Daniel; 1950– , French)
Aykroyd (Dan; 1952– , Canadian)
Baldwin (Alec; 1958– , US)
Benigni (Roberto; 1952– , Italian)
Bennett (Alan; 1934– , English)
Berkoff (Steven; 1937– , English)
Blessed (Brian; 1936– , English)
Bogarde (Sir Dirk; 1921–99, English)
Branagh (Kenneth; 1960– , Northern Irish)
Bridges (Jeff; 1949– , US)
Bridges (Lloyd; 1913–98, US)
Bronson (Charles; 1922–2003, US)
Brosnan (Pierce; 1953– , Irish)
Brynner (Yul; 1915–85, Swiss/Russian/US)
Burbage (Richard; c.1567–1619, English)
Carlyle (Robert; 1961– , Scottish)
Chaplin (Charlie; 1889–1977, English)
Clooney (George; 1962– , US)
Connery (Sir Sean; 1930– , Scottish)
Costner (Kevin; 1955– , US)
Crystal (Billy; 1947– , US)
Cushing (Peter; 1913–94, English)
Douglas (Kirk; 1916– , US)
Douglas (Michael; 1944– , US)
Elliott (Denholm; 1922–92, English)
Everett (Rupert; 1960– , English)
Fiennes (Ralph; 1962– , English)
Freeman (Morgan; 1937– , US)
Garrick (David; 1717–79, English)
Gielgud (Sir John; 1904–2000, English)
Hackman (Gene; 1930– , US)
Hoffman (Dustin; 1937– , US)
Hopkins (Sir Anthony; 1937– , Welsh/US)
Hordern (Sir Michael; 1911–95, English)

Hoskins (Bob; 1942– , English)
Jackson (Samuel L; 1948– , US)
Jenkins (Richard; 1947– , US)
Karloff (Boris; 1887–1969, English)
Marceau (Marcel; 1923–2007, French)
Matthau (Walter; 1920–2000, US)
McQueen (Steve; 1930–80, US)
Mitchum (Robert; 1917–97, US)
Montand (Yves; 1921–91, Italian/French)
Nielsen (Leslie; 1926– , Canadian)
Olivier (Laurence, Lord; 1907–89, English)
Perkins (Anthony; 1932–92, US)
Plummer (Christopher; 1927– , Canadian)
Poitier (Sidney; 1924– , US)
Presley (Elvis; 1935–77, US)
Redford (Robert; 1937– , US)
Rickman (Alan; 1947– , English)
Robbins (Tim; 1958– , US)
Roscius (c.134–62 BC; Roman)
Russell (Kurt; 1951– , US)
Selleck (Tom; 1945– , US)
Sellers (Peter; 1925–80, English)
Shepard (Sam; 1943– , US)
Stewart (James; 1908–97, US)
Tennant (David; 1971– , Scottish)
Ustinov (Sir Peter; 1921–2004, English)
Van Dyke (Dick; 1925– , US)

08 Atkinson (Rowan; 1955– , English)
Barrault (Jean-Louis; 1910–94, French)
Belmondo (Jean-Paul; 1933– , French)
Coltrane (Robbie; 1950– , Scottish)
Crawford (Michael; 1942– , English)
Day-Lewis (Daniel; 1958– , English)
DiCaprio (Leonardo; 1974– , US)
Dreyfuss (Richard; 1947– , US)
Eastwood (Clint; 1930– , US)
Goldblum (Jeff; 1952– , US)
Guinness (Sir Alec; 1914–2000, English)
Harrison (Sir Rex; 1908–90, English)
Kingsley (Ben; 1943– , English)
Langella (Frank; 1938– , US)
Laughton (Charles; 1899–1962, English)
Macready (William Charles; 1793–1873,
  English)
McGregor (Ewan; 1971– , Scottish)
McKellen (Sir Ian; 1939– , English)
Rathbone (Basil; 1892–1967, South African/
  British)
Redgrave (Sir Michael; 1908–85, English)
Reynolds (Burt; 1936– , US)
Robinson (Edward G; 1893–1973,
  Romanian/US)
Scofield (Paul; 1922–2008, English)
Stallone (Sylvester; 1946– , US)
Stroheim (Erich von; 1885–1957, Austrian)
Travolta (John; 1954– , US)
Turturro (John; 1957– , US)
Van Damme (Jean-Claude; 1961– , Belgian)

von Sydow (Max; 1929– , Swedish)
Whitaker (Forest; 1961– , US)
Williams (Michael; 1935–2001, English)
Williams (Robin; 1951– , US)
Woodward (Edward; 1930– , English)

09 Barrymore (John; 1882–1942, US)
Barrymore (Lionel; 1878–1954, US)
Broadbent (Jim; 1949– , English)
Broderick (Matthew; 1963– , US)
Chevalier (Maurice; 1888–1972, French)
Courtenay (Sir Tom; 1937– , English)
Depardieu (Gérard; 1948– , French)
Fairbanks (Douglas, Jnr; 1909–2000, US)
Fairbanks (Douglas, Snr; 1883–1939, US)
Griffiths (Richard; 1947– , English)
Harrelson (Woody; 1961– , US)
Hawthorne (Sir Nigel; 1929–2001, English)
Lancaster (Burt; 1913–94, US)
Malkovich (John; 1953– , US)
Nicholson (Jack; 1937– , US)
Pleasence (Donald; 1919–95, English)

Valentino (Rudolph; 1895–1926, Italian/US)

10 Cassavetes (John; 1929–89, US)
Chow Yun-Fat (1956– , Chinese)
Guttenberg (Steve; 1958– , US)
Sutherland (Donald; 1935– , Canadian)
Sutherland (Kiefer; 1966– , US)
Washington (Denzel; 1954– , US)

11 Mastroianni (Marcello; 1923–96, Italian)
von Stroheim (Erich; 1885–1957, Austrian)
Weissmuller (Johnny; 1903–84, Romanian/US)

12 Attenborough (Richard, Lord; 1923– , English)
Downey Junior (Robert; 1965– , US)
Stanislavsky (Konstantin; 1863–1938, Russian)

14 Schwarzenegger (Arnold; 1947– , Austrian/US)
Seymour Hoffman (Philip; 1967– , US)

Actresses include:

03 Bow (Clara; 1905–65, US)
Cox (Courteney; 1964– , US)
Day (Doris; 1924– , US)
Loy (Myrna; 1905–93, US)

04 Ball (Lucille; 1910–89, US)
Cruz (Penélope; 1974– , Spanish)
Diaz (Cameron; 1972– , US)
Duse (Eleonora; 1859–1924, Italian)
Gish (Lillian; 1893–1993, US)
Gwyn (Nell; c.1650–87, English)
Hawn (Goldie; 1945– , US)
Hird (Dame Thora; 1911–2003, English)
Neal (Patricia; 1926– , US)
Rigg (Dame Diana; 1938– , English)
Ryan (Meg; 1962– , US)
Ward (Dame Geneviève; 1838–1922, US)
West (Mae; 1893–1980, US)
Wood (Natalie; 1938–81, US)
Wray (Fay; 1907–2004, US)
York (Susannah; 1941– , English)

05 Allen (Gracie; 1895–1964, US)
Berry (Halle; 1966– , US)
Brice (Fanny; 1891–1951, US)
Close (Glenn; 1947– , US)
Davis (Bette; 1908–89, US)
Davis (Geena; 1957– , US)
Davis (Judy; 1955– , Australian)
Dench (Dame Judi; 1934– , English)
Derek (Bo; 1956– , US)
Evans (Dame Edith; 1888–1976, English)
Field (Sally; 1946– , US)
Fonda (Jane; 1937– , US)
Gabor (Zsa Zsa; 1918– , Hungarian)

Garbo (Greta; 1905–90, Swedish/US)
Gonne (Maud; 1865–1953, Irish)
Horne (Lena; 1917– , US)
Jolie (Angelina; 1975– , US)
Kelly (Grace; 1929–82, US)
Lange (Jessica; 1949– , US)
Leigh (Janet; 1927–2004, US)
Leigh (Vivien; 1913–67, British)
Lenya (Lotte; 1898–1981, Austrian)
Lewis (Juliette; 1973– , US)
Lopez (Jennifer; 1969– , US)
Loren (Sophia; 1934– , Italian)
Mills (Hayley; 1946– , English)
Moore (Demi; 1962– , US)
Moore (Julianne; 1961– , US)
O'Hara (Maureen; 1920– , Irish)
Ryder (Winona; 1971– , US)
Smith (Dame Maggie; 1934– , English)
Smith (Liz; 1921– , English)
Stone (Sharon; 1958– , US)
Swank (Hilary; 1974– , US)
Tandy (Jessica; 1907–94, English/US)
Terry (Dame Ellen; 1848–1928, English)
Tomei (Marisa; 1964– , US)
Weisz (Rachel; 1971– , English)
Welch (Raquel; 1940– , US)

06 Adjani (Isabelle; 1955– , French)
Arnaud (Yvonne; 1892–1958, French)
Bacall (Lauren; 1924– , US)
Bardot (Brigitte; 1934– , French)
Bening (Annette; 1958– , US)
Bergen (Candice; 1946– , US)
Bisset (Jacqueline; 1944– , English)

Cheung (Maggie; 1964– , Chinese)
Curtis (Jamie Lee; 1958– , US)
Ekland (Britt; 1942– , Swedish)
Farrow (Mia; 1945– , US)
Fisher (Carrie; 1956– , US)
Foster (Jodie; 1962– , US)
Gong Li (1965– , Chinese)
Gordon (Hannah; 1941– , Scottish)
Grable (Betty; 1916–73, US)
Hannah (Daryl; 1960– , US)
Harlow (Jean; 1911–37, US)
Hedren (Tippi; 1931– , US)
Hiller (Dame Wendy; 1912–2003, English)
Hopper (Hedda; 1885–1966, US)
Hunter (Holly; 1958– , US)
Huston (Anjelica; 1951– , US)
Keaton (Diane; 1946– , US)
Kemble (Fanny; 1809–93, English)
Kidman (Nicole; 1967– , US/Australian)
Kinski (Nastassja; 1960– , German)
Kudrow (Lisa; 1963– , US)
Lamarr (Hedy; 1913–2000, Austrian)
Lamour (Dorothy; 1914–96, US)
Lumley (Joanna; 1946– , English)
Midler (Bette; 1945– , US)
Mirren (Helen; 1945– , English)
Monroe (Marilyn; 1926–62, US)
Moreau (Jeanne; 1928– , French)
Robson (Dame Flora; 1902–84, English)
Rogers (Ginger; 1911–95, US)
Spacek (Sissy; 1949– , US)
Streep (Meryl; 1949– , US)
Suzman (Janet; 1939– , South African/
    British)
Tautou (Audrey; 1978– , French)
Taylor (Dame Elizabeth; 1932– , English/
    US)
Temple (Shirley; 1928– , US)
Tomlin (Lily; 1939– , US)
Turner (Kathleen; 1954– , US)
Turner (Lana; 1920–95, US)
Weaver (Sigourney; 1949– , US)
Winger (Debra; 1955– , US)

07 Andress (Ursula; 1936– , Swiss)
Andrews (Dame Julie; 1935– , English)
Aniston (Jennifer; 1969– , US)
Bergman (Ingrid; 1915–82, Swedish)
Binoche (Juliette; 1964– , French)
Bullock (Sandra; 1964– , US)
Colbert (Claudette; 1903–96, French/US)
Deneuve (Catherine; 1943– , French)
Dunaway (Faye; 1941– , US)
Gardner (Ava; 1922–90, US)
Garland (Judy; 1922–69, US)
Grahame (Gloria; 1923–81, US)
Hepburn (Audrey; 1929–93, Belgian)
Hepburn (Katharine; 1907–2003, US)
Huppert (Isabelle; 1955– , French)

Jackson (Glenda; 1936– , English)
Johnson (Dame Celia; 1908–82, English)
Langtry (Lillie; 1853–1929, English)
Lombard (Carole; 1908–42, US)
Madonna (1958– , US)
Magnani (Anna; 1908–73, Italian)
Paltrow (Gwyneth; 1973– , US)
Roberts (Julia; 1967– , US)
Russell (Jane; 1921– , US)
Sevigny (Chloë; 1974– , US)
Seymour (Jane; 1951– , English)
Siddons (Sarah; 1755–1831, English)
Swanson (Gloria; 1897–1983, US)
Swinton (Tilda; 1960– , English)
Tierney (Gene; 1920–91, US)
Ullmann (Liv; 1939– , Norwegian)
Walters (Julie; 1950– , English)
Winslet (Kate; 1975– , English)
Winters (Shelley; 1920–2006, US)

08 Ashcroft (Dame Peggy; 1907–91, English)
Bancroft (Anne; 1931–2005, US)
Bankhead (Tallulah; 1903–68, US)
Basinger (Kim; 1953– , US)
Charisse (Cyd; 1922–2008, US)
Christie (Julie; 1940– , English)
Crawford (Joan; 1906–77, US)
Dietrich (Marlene; 1901–92, German/US)
Fontaine (Joan; 1917– , US)
Goldberg (Whoopi; 1949– , US)
Griffith (Melanie; 1957– , US)
Hathaway (Anne; 1982– , US)
Hayworth (Rita; 1918–87, US)
Lawrence (Gertrude; 1898–1952, English)
Lockwood (Margaret; 1911–90, English)
MacLaine (Shirley; 1934– , US)
Mercouri (Melina; 1923–94, Greek)
Minnelli (Liza; 1946– , US)
Pfeiffer (Michelle; 1958– , US)
Pickford (Mary; 1893–1979, Canadian/
    US)
Rampling (Charlotte; 1946– , English)
Redgrave (Vanessa; 1937– , English)
Sarandon (Susan; 1946– , US)
Shepherd (Cybill; 1950– , US)
Signoret (Simone; 1921–85, French)
Stanwyck (Barbara; 1907–90, US)
Thompson (Emma; 1959– , English)
Whitelaw (Billie; 1932– , English)
Woodward (Joanne; 1930– , US)

09 Barrymore (Drew; 1975– , US)
Bernhardt (Sarah; 1844–1923, French)
Blanchett (Cate; 1969– , Australian)
Cotillard (Marion; 1975– , French)
Johansson (Scarlett; 1984– , US)
Knightley (Keira; 1985– , English)
MacDowell (Andie; 1958– , US)
Mansfield (Jayne; 1933–67, US)

McDormand (Frances; 1957– , US)
Plowright (Joan; 1929– , English)
Streisand (Barbra; 1942– , US)
Thorndike (Dame Sybil; 1882–1976, English)
Zellweger (Renée; 1969– , US)
Zeta-Jones (Catherine; 1969– , Welsh)
10 Richardson (Miranda; 1958– , English)
Rossellini (Isabella; 1952– , US)

See also **comedy**

Rutherford (Dame Margaret; 1892–1972, English)
Woffington (Peg; 1720–60, Irish)
11 de Havilland (Olivia; 1916– , US)
Scott-Thomas (Kristin; 1960– , English)
Witherspoon (Reese; 1976– , US)
12 Bonham Carter (Helena; 1966– , English)
Lollobrigida (Gina; 1927– , Italian)

activist

Activists include:

04 Bono (1960– , Irish)
King (Martin Luther, Jnr; 1929–68, US)
05 Nader (Ralph; 1934– , US)
Parks (Rosa Lee; 1913–2005, US)
06 Gandhi (Mahatma; 1869–1948, Indian)
Geldof (Bob; 1954–, Irish)
07 Angelou (Maya; 1928– , US)
Chomsky (Noam; 1928– , US)
Guevara (Che; 1928–67, Argentine)

See also **aborigine**

Jackson (Jesse; 1941– , US)
Mandela (Nelson; 1918– , South African)
Mandela (Winifred 'Winnie'; 1934– , South African)
08 Malcolm X (1925–65, US)
Silkwood (Karen; 1946–1974, US)
09 Pankhurst (Christabel; 1880–1958, English)
Pankhurst (Emmeline; 1857–1928, English)
Pankhurst (Sylvia; 1882–1960, English)

administrative area

Administrative areas include:

04 city	**06** county		enclave	**09** pergunnah	
town	oblast		pargana	territory	
ward	parish		village	**11** conurbation	
zila	region		**08** district	**12** constituency	
zone	sector		division	municipality	
05 shire	zillah		precinct		
state	**07** borough		province		
theme	commune		township		

See also **Australia; Austria; Belgium; Canada; Czech Republic; Denmark; Finland; France; Germany; Greece; India; Ireland; Italy; The Netherlands; Norway; Portugal; South Africa; Spain; Sweden; Switzerland; United Kingdom**

admiral

Admirals include:

04 Byng (George, Viscount Torrington; 1663–1733, English)
Hood (Samuel, Viscount; 1724–1816, English)
Howe (Richard, Earl; 1726–99, English)
Togo (Heihachiro, Count; 1848–1934, Japanese)
05 Blake (Robert; 1599–1657, English)
Croft (Admiral; *Persuasion*, 1818, Jane Austen)

Dewey (George; 1837–1917, US)
Doria (Andrea; c.1466–1560, Genoese)
Hawke (Edward, Lord; 1705–81, English)
Rooke (Sir George; 1650–1709, English)
Tromp (Maarten; 1598–1653, Dutch)
06 Beatty (David, Earl; 1871–1936, English)
Benbow (John; 1653–1702, English)
Darlan (Jean François; 1881–1942, French)
Dönitz (Karl; 1891–1980, German)
Fisher (John, Lord; 1841–1920, English)

Grasse (François, Comte de; 1722–88, French)
Halsey (William F, Jnr; 1884–1959, US)
Howard (Charles; 1536–1624, English)
Nelson (Horatio, Lord; 1758–1805, English)
Nimitz (Chester; 1885–1966, US)
Raeder (Erich; 1876–1960, German)
Rodney (George, Lord; 1719–92, English)
Ruyter (Michiel de; 1607–76, Dutch)
Vernon (Edward; 1684–1757, English)
07 Kanaris (Constantine; 1790–1877, Greek)
McClure (Sir Robert; 1807–73, Irish)
Tirpitz (Alfred von; 1849–1930, German)

Wrangel (Ferdinand, Baron von; 1794–1870, Russian)
08 Cochrane (Thomas; 1775–1860, Scottish)
Gorshkov (Sergei; 1910–88, Soviet)
Jellicoe (John, Earl; 1859–1935, English)
09 Artemisia (fl.5c BC, Greek)
10 Villeneuve (Pierre Charles; 1763–1806, French)
11 Collingwood (Cuthbert, Lord; 1750–1810, English)
Krusenstern (Adam Johann, Baron von; 1770–1846, Russian)
Mountbatten (Louis, Earl; 1900–79, English)

Africa

Countries in Africa:

04 Chad
Mali
Togo
05 Benin
Congo
Egypt
Gabon
Ghana
Kenya
Libya
Niger
Sudan
06 Angola
Guinea
Malawi
Rwanda
Uganda
Zambia
07 Algeria

Burundi
Comoros
Eritrea
Lesotho
Liberia
Morocco
Namibia
Nigeria
Senegal
Somalia
Tunisia
08 Botswana
Cameroon
Djibouti
Ethiopia
Tanzania
Zimbabwe
09 Cape Verde
Mauritius

Swaziland
The Gambia
10 Madagascar
Mauritania
Mozambique
Seychelles
11 Burkina Faso
Côte d'Ivoire
Sierra Leone
South Africa
12 Guinea-Bissau
13 Western Sahara
16 Equatorial Guinea
18 São Tomé and Príncipe
22 Central African Republic
28 Democratic Republic of the Congo

Cities and notable towns in Africa include:

03 Fez (Morocco)
Ife (Nigeria)
04 Kano (Nigeria)
Lomé (Togo)
Oran (Algeria)
Safi (Morocco)
Sfax (Tunisia)
05 Abuja (Nigeria)
Accra (Ghana)
Beira (Mozambique)
Dakar (Senegal)
Enugu (Nigeria)
Gweru (Zimbabwe)
Harer (Ethiopia)
Kitwe (Zambia)
Lagos (Nigeria)

Mopti (Mali)
Ndola (Zambia)
Oujda (Morocco)
Rabat (Morocco)
Ségou (Mali)
Thiès (Senegal)
Tunis (Tunisia)
Zaria (Nigeria)
Zomba (Malawi)
06 Agadès (Niger)
Agadir (Morocco)
Annaba (Algeria)
Asmara (Eritrea)
Bamako (Mali)
Bangui (Central African Republic)
Banjul (The Gambia)

Benoni (South Africa)
Bissau (Guinea-Bissau)
Bouaké (Côte d'Ivoire)
Butare (Rwanda)
Dodoma (Tanzania)
Douala (Cameroon)
Durban (South Africa)
Gondar (Ethiopia)
Harare (Zimbabwe)
Huambo (Angola)
Ibadan (Nigeria)
Ilesha (Nigeria)
Ilorin (Nigeria)
Kaduna (Nigeria)
Kigali (Rwanda)
Kumasi (Ghana)
Lobito (Angola)
Luanda (Angola)
Lusaka (Zambia)
Maputo (Mozambique)
Maseru (Lesotho)
Mekele (Ethiopia)
Meknès (Morocco)
Mutare (Zimbabwe)
Mwanza (Tanzania)
Nakuru (Kenya)
Niamey (Niger)
Skikda (Algeria)
Sokodé (Togo)
Sousse (Tunisia)
Soweto (South Africa)
Tamale (Ghana)

07 Abidjan (Côte d'Ivoire)
Algiers (Algeria)
Berbera (Somalia)
Calabar (Nigeria)
Conakry (Guinea)
Cotonou (Benin)
Kampala (Uganda)
Kananga (Congo, Democratic Republic of the)
Kenitra (Morocco)
Lobamba (Swaziland)
Maramba (Zambia)
Mbabane (Swaziland)
Mombasa (Kenya)
Moundou (Chad)
Nairobi (Kenya)
Nampula (Mozambique)
Oshogbo (Nigeria)
Tangier (Morocco)
Tétouan (Morocco)
Tlemcen (Algeria)
Yaoundé (Cameroon)

08 Abeokuta (Nigeria)
Bandundu (Congo, Democratic Republic of the)

Benguela (Angola)
Blantyre (Malawi)
Bulawayo (Zimbabwe)
Cape Town (South Africa)
Djibouti (Djibouti)
Freetown (Sierra Leone)
Gabarone (Botswana)
Hargeysa (Somalia)
Kairouan (Tunisia)
Kinshasa (Congo, Democratic Republic of the)
Lilongwe (Malawi)
Mafeteng (Lesotho)
Monrovia (Liberia)
N'Djamena (Chad)
Pretoria (South Africa)
Victoria (Seychelles)
Windhoek (Namibia)
Zanzibar (Tanzania)

09 Bujumbura (Burundi)
Kimberley (South Africa)
Kisangani (Congo, Democratic Republic of the)
Maiduguri (Nigeria)
Marrakesh (Morocco)
Mbuji-Mayi (Congo, Democratic Republic of the)
Mogadishu (Somalia)
Ogbomosho (Nigeria)
Port Louis (Mauritius)
Porto-Novo (Benin)
Toamasina (Madagascar)

10 Addis Ababa (Ethiopia)
Casablanca (Morocco)
Klerksdorp (South Africa)
Libreville (Gabon)
Lubumbashi (Congo, Democratic Republic of the)
Nouakchott (Mauritania)

11 Brazzaville (Congo)
Chitungwiza (Zimbabwe)
Constantine (Algeria)
Dar es Salaam (Tanzania)
Ouagadougou (Burkina Faso)
Pointe-Noire (Congo)
Vereeniging (South Africa)

12 Antananarivo (Madagascar)
Bloemfontein (South Africa)
Johannesburg (South Africa)
Port Harcourt (Nigeria)
Yamoussoukro (Côte d'Ivoire)

13 Bobo-Dioulasso (Burkina Faso)
Port Elizabeth (South Africa)

15 Sekondi-Takoradi (Ghana)

Africans include:

03 Ibo	Libyan	Beninese	Ethiopian
Kru	Malian	Egyptian	Sahrawian
Twi	Somali	Eritrean	Santoméan
04 Boer	Tuareg	Gabonese	São Toméan
Efik	Yoruba	Ghanaian	Tanzanian
Igbo	07 Angolan	Liberian	10 Djiboutian
Kroo	Basotho	Malagasy	Mozambican
Moor	Chadian	Malawian	Sahraouian
Susu	Gambian	Moroccan	Senegalese
Tshi	Guinean	Motswana	Zimbabwean
Zulu	Ivorian	Namibian	
05 Masai	Mosotho	Nigerian	11 Cameroonian
Swazi	Rwandan	Nigerien	Cape Verdean
Temne	Sahrawi	Sahraoui	Mauritanian
Tonga	Swahili	Sudanese	12 South African
06 Griqua	Ugandan	Togolese	13 Equatoguinean
Herero	Zambian	Tunisian	Sierra Leonean
Kenyan	08 Algerian	09 Burkinabé	14 Central African
Kikuyu	Batswana	Burundian	Guinea-Bissauan
		Congolese	

African landmarks include:

04 Giza (Egypt)
Nile (east/north-east Africa)

05 Congo (central/west Africa)
Luxor (Egypt)

06 Karnak (Egypt)
Sahara (north Africa)
Sphinx (Egypt)

07 Zambezi (south-east Africa)

08 Aswan Dam (Egypt)
Kalahari (south-west Africa)
Lake Chad (Cameroon/Chad)
Okavango (Angola/Namibia/Botswana)
Pyramids (Egypt)

09 Lake Nyasa (Malawi/Mozambique/Tanzania)
Masai Mara (Kenya)
River Nile (east/north-east Africa)
Serengeti (Tanzania)
Suez Canal (Egypt)

10 Lake Malawi (Malawi/Mozambique/Tanzania)
Lake Nasser (Egypt)

See also **South Africa**

River Congo (central/west Africa)
River Niger (west Africa)

11 Drakensberg (South Africa)
Great Sphinx (Egypt)
Kilimanjaro (Tanzania)
Luxor Temple (Egypt)

12 Aswan High Dam (Egypt)
Great Pyramid (Egypt)
Lake Victoria (Kenya/Tanzania/Uganda)
Sahara Desert (north Africa)
Zambezi River (south-east Africa)

13 Mt Kilimanjaro (Tanzania)
Okavango Delta (Botswana)
Table Mountain (South Africa)
Victoria Falls (Zimbabwe/Zambia)

14 Atlas Mountains (Algeria/Morocco/Tunisia)
Cape of Good Hope (South Africa)
Kalahari Desert (south-west Africa)
Lake Tanganyika (central/east Africa)

15 Great Rift Valley (east/south-east Africa)

agent *see* **spy**

agreement *see* **treaty**

agriculture

Agricultural equipment includes:

03 ard
ATV
axe
hoe
saw

04 fork
plow
rake
wain

05 baler
drill
flail
gambo
mower
share
spade

06 harrow
plough
ricker

ripple
scythe
shovel
sickle
tanker
tedder

07 combine
draw hoe
grubber
hayfork
hayrake
mattock
scuffle
sprayer
tractor
trailer

08 buckrake
chainsaw
hay knife
haymaker

scuffler
spreader

09 corn drill
drop-drill
harvester
irrigator
pitchfork
power lift
rotary hoe
Rotavator®
Rotovator®
scarifier
seed drill
whetstone

10 cropduster
cultivator
disc harrow
disc plough
earth-board
flail mower

seed-harrow

11 bale wrapper
broadcaster
chaff-cutter
chaff-engine
drill-harrow
hedgecutter
mole drainer
reaping hook
wheelbarrow
wheel plough

12 muckspreader
slurry tanker

13 fork-lift truck
potato planter
slurry sprayer

14 field sprinkler
front end loader
milking machine

Agriculturists include:

04 Coke (Thomas William; 1752–1842, English)
Tull (Jethro; 1674–1741, English)

05 Lawes (Sir John Bennet; 1814–1900, English)
Young (Arthur; 1741–1820, English)

06 Carver (George Washington; 1864–1943, US)
Farrer (William; 1845–1906, English)

07 Borlaug (Norman; 1914– , US)
Burbank (Luther; 1849–1926, US)

Russell (Sir John; 1872–1965, English)
Wallace (Harry; 1866–1924, US)
Wallace (Henry; 1836–1916, US)
Wallace (Henry A; 1888–1965, US)

08 Bakewell (Robert; 1725–95, English)

09 McCormick (Cyrus; 1809–84, US)

12 Boussingault (Jean-Baptiste; 1802–87, French)

See also **cattle**; **farm**

air force *see* military

air travel

Airports in the UK include:

04 Dyce (Aberdeen)
Lydd (Kent)
Wick (Caithness)

05 Luton (Bedfordshire)
Tiree (Hebrides)

06 Dundee
Exeter (Devon)
Jersey (Channel Islands)
Scatsa (Shetlands)
Tresco (Scilly Isles)

07 Bristol (Avon)
Cardiff

Gatwick (London)
Glasgow
Norwich (Norfolk)
Sandown (Isle of Wight)
St Mary's (Scilly Isles)
Swansea
Westray (Orkney)

08 Alderney (Channel Islands)
Coventry (West Midlands)
Fair Isle (Shetlands)
Guernsey (Channel Islands)
Heathrow (London)

Kirkwall (Orkney)
North Bay (Hebrides)
Penzance (Cornwall)
Plymouth (Devon)
Southend (Essex)
Stansted (London)
Sumburgh (Shetlands)
Teesside (Cleveland)
Tingwall (Shetlands)

09 Benbecula (Hebrides)
Blackpool (Lancashire)
Cambridge
Inverness
Newcastle
Prestwick (Ayrshire)
Stornoway (Hebrides)

Turnhouse (Edinburgh)

10 Baltasound (Shetlands)
Biggin Hill (Kent)
Grimsetter (Orkney)
Humberside
John Lennon (Liverpool)
London City
Manchester
Ronaldsway (Isle of Man)

11 Belfast City
Bournemouth (Dorset)
Glenegedale (Islay)
Southampton (Hampshire)

12 West Midlands (Birmingham)

13 Leeds-Bradford

Airports worldwide include:

03 JFK (USA)
Kos (Greece)
Moi (Kenya)
Nis (Serbia)
Zia (Bangladesh)

04 Agno (Switzerland)
Bole (Ethiopia)
Cebu (Philippines)
Cork (Ireland)
Doha (Qatar)
Elat (Israel)
Erie (USA)
Faro (Portugal)
Gaza (Israel)
Guam (Guam)
Hato (Netherlands
Antilles)
Linz (Austria)
Lomé (Togo)
Luqa (Malta)
Male (Maldives)
Nadi (Fiji)
Oran (Algeria)
Orly (France)
Pula (Croatia)
Riem (Germany)
Saab (Sweden)
Sale (Morocco)
Seeb (Oman)
Sfax (Tunisia)
Sola (Norway)
Vigo (Spain)
Yoff (Senegal)

05 Adana (Turkey)
Aminu (Nigeria)
Beira (Mozambique)
Berne (Switzerland)
Brnik (Slovenia)

Cairo (Egypt)
Dubai (United Arab
Emirates)
Elmas (Italy)
Hanoi (Vietnam)
Ibiza (Spain)
Ivato (Madagascar)
Izmir (Turkey)
Kimpo (South Korea)
Liège (Belgium)
Logan (USA)
Luano (Democratic
Republic of the Congo)
Lungi (Sierra Leone)
Luxor (Egypt)
Mahon (Menorca)
McCoy (USA)
Miami (USA)
Nauru (Nauru)
O'Hare (USA)
Osaka (Japan)
Palma (Majorca)
Perth (Australia)
Pleso (Croatia)
Praia (Cape Verde)
Rejon (Mexico)
Sanaa (Yemen)
Senou (Mali)
Sliac (Slovakia)
Sofia (Bulgaria)
Split (Croatia)
Sunan (North Korea)
Tampa (USA)
Turin (Italy)
Turku (Finland)
Vaasa (Finland)
Vagar (Faroe Islands)
Varna (Bulgaria)
Vigie (St Lucia)

06 Abadan (Iran)
Alborg (Denmark)
Asmara (Eritrea)
Balice (Poland)
Beirut (Lebanon)
Benina (Libya)
Bremen (Germany)
Bromma (Sweden)
Butmir (Bosnia and
Herzegovina)
Cairns (Australia)
Cancun (Mexico)
Cannon (USA)
Canton (USA)
Changi (Singapore)
Darwin (Australia)
Deurne (Belgium)
Dorval (Canada)
Douala (Cameroon)
Dublin (Ireland)
Dulles (USA)
El Alto (Bolivia)
El Paso (USA)
Findel (Luxembourg)
Geneva (Switzerland)
Gillot (Réunion)
Hahaya (Comoros)
Hanedi (Japan)
Harare (Zimbabwe)
Hassan (Morocco)
Ivanka (Slovakia)
Kalmar (Sweden)
Kamazu (Malawi)
Kigali (Rwanda)
Kjevik (Norway)
Komaki (Japan)
Košice (Slovakia)
Kotoka (Ghana)
Kuwait (Kuwait)

Lahore (Pakistan)
La Mesa (Honduras)
Linate (Italy)
Lisbon (Portugal)
Luanda (Angola)
Lusaka (Zambia)
Mactan (Philippines)
Malaga (Spain)
Maputo (Mozambique)
Maseru (Lesotho)
Medina (Saudi Arabia)
Melita (Tunisia)
Menara (Morocco)
Midway (USA)
Narita (Japan)
Nassau (The Bahamas)
N'Djili (Democratic
  Republic of the Congo)
Nejrab (Syria)
Newark (USA)
Niamey (Niger)
Odense (Denmark)
Okecie (Poland)
Orebro (Sweden)
Palese (Italy)
Paphos (Cyprus)
Penang (Malaysia)
Piarco (Trinidad)
Regina (Canada)
Riyadh (Saudi Arabia)
Ruzyne (Czech Republic)
Skanes (Morocco)
Skopje (Macedonia)
Snilow (Ukraine)
Spilve (Latvia)
Sturup (Sweden)
Subang (Malaysia)
Tacoma (USA)
Tirana (Albania)
Tucson (USA)
Vantaa (Finland)
V C Bird (Antigua)
Verona (Italy)
Wattay (Laos)
Yangon (Myanmar)
Yundum (The Gambia)
Zürich (Switzerland)

07 Alma Ata (Kazakhstan)
Almeria (Spain)
Arlanda (Sweden)
Atatürk (Turkey)
Baghdad (Iraq)
Bahrain (Bahrain)
Baneasa (Romania)
Bangkok (Thailand)
Barajas (Spain)
Beijing (China)
Billund (Denmark)

Blagnac (France)
Bourgas (Bulgaria)
Bradley (USA)
Buffalo (USA)
Calabar (Nigeria)
Calgary (Canada)
Cotonou (Benin)
Dalaman (Turkey)
D F Malan (South Africa)
Dhahran (Saudi Arabia)
Dresden (Germany)
Entebbe (Uganda)
Esbjerg (Denmark)
Faleolo (Samoa)
Fornebu (Norway)
G'Bessia (Guinea)
Granada (Spain)
Halifax (Canada)
Hopkins (USA)
Houston (USA)
Itazuke (Japan)
Karachi (Pakistan)
Kerkyra (Greece)
Key West (USA)
Kuching (Malaysia)
La Parra (Spain)
Larnaca (Cyprus)
Leipzig (Germany)
Lesquin (France)
Liepaja (Latvia)
Lincoln (USA)
Lubbock (USA)
Managua (Nicaragua)
Maxglan (Austria)
Memphis (USA)
Mirabel (Canada)
Morelos (Mexico)
Norfolk (USA)
Oakland (USA)
Okinawa (Japan)
Orlando (USA)
Otopeni (Romania)
Patenga (Bangladesh)
Polonia (Indonesia)
Pulkovo (Russia)
Roberts (Liberia)
San José (USA)
São Tomé (São Tomé and
  Príncipe)
Satolas (France)
Shannon (Ireland)
Sharjah (United Arab
  Emirates)
Sondica (Spain)
Spokane (USA)
St Louis (USA)
Tamatve (Madagascar)
Timehri (Guyana)

Tripoli (Libya)
Unokovo (Russia)
Uplands (Canada)
Vilnius (Lithuania)
Vitoria (Spain)
Wichita (USA)

08 Abu Dhabi (United Arab
  Emirates)
Adelaide (Australia)
Ain el Bay (Algeria)
Alicante (Spain)
Amarillo (USA)
Amborovy (Madagascar)
Arrecife (Canary Islands)
Ashkabad (Turkmenistan)
Asturias (Spain)
Auckland (New Zealand)
Belgrade (Serbia)
Borispol (Ukraine)
Boulogne (France)
Brasilia (Brazil)
Brisbane (Australia)
Bulawayo (Zimbabwe)
Carrasco (Uruguay)
Carthage (Tunisia)
Ciampino (Italy)
Columbus (USA)
Damascus (Syria)
Djibouti (Djibouti)
Edmonton (Canada)
El Dorado (Colombia)
Entzheim (France)
Esenboga (Turkey)
Ferihegy (Hungary)
Flesland (Norway)
Freeport (The Bahamas)
G Marconi (Italy)
Goleniow (Poland)
Hong Kong (Hong Kong)
Hongqiao (China)
Honolulu (USA)
Inezgane (Morocco)
Keflavik (Iceland)
Khartoum (Sudan)
La Aurora (Guatemala)
La Coruña (Spain)
Le Raizet (Guadeloupe)
Loshitsa (Belarus)
Mais Gate (Haiti)
Malpensa (Italy)
Matsapha (Swaziland)
Maya Maya (Congo)
McCarran (USA)
Mehrabad (Iran)
Merignac (France)
Mohamed V (Morocco)
Murmansk (Russia)
Nagasaki (Japan)

N'Djamena (Chad)
Pago Pago (Samoa)
Pamplona (Spain)
Paradisi (Greece)
Peretola (Italy)
Peshawar (Pakistan)
Portland (USA)
Provence (France)
Richmond (USA)
San Diego (USA)
Sangster (Jamaica)
San Pablo (Spain)
Santiago (Spain)
Schiphol (The Netherlands)
St Thomas (Virgin Islands)
Tontouta (New Caledonia)
Ulemiste (Estonia)
Valencia (Spain)
Victoria (Canada)
Winnipeg (Canada)

09 Anchorage (USA)
Archangel (Russia)
Arnos Vale (St Vincent)
Barcelona (Spain)
Ben Gurion (Israel)
Boukhalef (Morocco)
Bujumbura (Burundi)
Charleroi (Belgium)
Charlotte (USA)
Congonhas (Brazil)
Cuscatlan (El Salvador)
Des Moines (USA)
Dubrovnik (Croatia)
Eindhoven (The
  Netherlands)
Fiumicino (Italy)
Fort Myers (USA)
Guarulhos (Brazil)
Heraklion (Greece)
Hewanorra (St Lucia)
Islamabad (Pakistan)
Isle Verde (Puerto Rico)
James M Cox (USA)
Jose Marti (Cuba)
Kagoshima (Japan)
Kaohsiung (Taiwan)
Karpathos (Greece)
La Guardia (USA)
Las Palmas (Canary Islands)
Lindbergh (USA)
Llabanère (France)
Long Beach (USA)
Marco Polo (Italy)
Maupertus (France)
Mogadishu (Somalia)
Nashville (USA)
Nuremberg (Germany)
Octeville (France)

Peninsula (USA)
Port Bouet (Côte d'Ivoire)
Port Sudan (Sudan)
Queen Alia (Jordan)
Rotterdam (The
  Netherlands)
Sainte Foy (Canada)
San Giusto (Italy)
San Javier (Spain)
Santa Cruz (Canary Islands)
Santander (Spain)
Schwechat (Austria)
Stapleton (USA)
St Eufemia (Italy)
Thalerhof (Austria)
Timisoara (Romania)
Tribhuyan (Nepal)
Vancouver (Canada)
Viracopos (Brazil)
Zakynthos (Greece)

10 Alexandria (Egypt)
Belize City (Belize)
Birmingham (USA)
Charleston (USA)
Copenhagen (Denmark)
Côte d'Azure (France)
Crown Point (Tobago)
Domodedovo (Russia)
Dusseldorf (Germany)
Frejorgues (France)
Golden Rock (St Kitts)
Guararapes (Brazil)
Harrisburg (USA)
Hartsfield (USA)
Hellenikon (Greece)
Kansas City (USA)
Katunayake (Sri Lanka)
Kent County (USA)
King Khaled (Saudi Arabia)
Klagenfurt (Austria)
Kungsangen (Sweden)
Landvetter (Sweden)
Les Angades (Morocco)
Libreville (Gabon)
Little Rock (USA)
Los Angeles (USA)
Louis Botha (South Africa)
Louisville (USA)
Maastricht (The
  Netherlands)
Manchester (USA)
New Orleans (USA)
North Front (Gibraltar)
Nouadhibou (Mauritania)
Nouakchott (Mauritania)
Panama City (Panama)
Pochentong (Cambodia)
Punta Raisi (Sicily)

Rabiechowo (Poland)
Reina Sofia (Canary Islands)
Rochambeau (French
  Guiana)
San Antonio (USA)
Seychelles (Seychelles)
Sky Harbour (USA)
Townsville (Australia)
Trivandrum (India)
Truax Field (USA)
Washington (USA)
Wellington (New Zealand)
Will Rogers (USA)

11 Albuquerque (USA)
Capodichino (Italy)
Cologne-Bonn (Germany)
Dar es Salaam (Tanzania)
Dois de Julho (Brazil)
Ecterdingen (Germany)
Fuhlsbüttel (Germany)
Jorge Chavez (Peru)
Khoramaksar (Yemen)
Kranebitten (Austria)
Las Americas (Dominican
  Republic)
Narssarsuaq (Greenland)
Ninoy Aquino (Philippines)
Ouagadougou (Burkina
  Faso)
Owen Roberts (West
  Indies)
Pointe Noire (Congo)
Poprad Tatry (Slovakia)
Punta Arenas (Chile)
San Salvador (El Salvador)
Santa Isabel (Guinea)
Tallahassee (USA)
Tegucigalpa (Honduras)
Tito Menniti (Italy)
Tullamarine (Australia)
Vilo de Porto (Azores)

12 Albany County (USA)
Benito Juarez (Mexico)
Berline-Tegel (Germany)
Bishkek-Manas (Kyrgyzstan)
Christchurch (New
  Zealand)
Eduardo Gomes (Brazil)
Fontanarossa (Sicily)
Fort de France (Martinique)
Fuenterrabia (Spain)
Hancock Field (USA)
Indianapolis (USA)
Indira Gandhi (India)
Jackson Field (Papua New
  Guinea)
Jacksonville (USA)

Johannesburg (South Africa)
John F Kennedy (USA)
Jomo Kenyatta (Kenya)
Khwaja Rawash
  (Afghanistan)
Kota Kinabalu (Malaysia)
Monroe County (USA)
Norman Manley (Jamaica)
Osvaldo Veira (Guinea-
  Bissau)
Papola Casale (Italy)
Philadelphia (USA)
Point Salines (Grenada)
Ponta Delgado (Azores)
Port Harcourt (Nigeria)
Queen Beatrix (Netherlands
  Antilles)
Ras al Khaimah (United
  Arab Emirates)
Rio de Janeiro (Brazil)
Salgado Filho (Brazil)
Salt Lake City (USA)
San Francisco (USA)
Santos Dumont (Brazil)

Sheremetyevo (Russia)
Simon Bolivar (Ecuador)
Simon Bolivar (Venezuela)
Thessalonika (Greece)
13 Amilcar Cabral (Cape
  Verde)
Basle-Mulhouse
  (Switzerland)
Château Bougon (France)
Chiang Kai Shek (Taiwan)
Costa Smeralda (Sardinia)
Fuerteventura (Canary
  Islands)
Grantley Adams (Barbados)
Ho Chi Minh City
  (Vietnam)
King Abdul Aziz (Saudi
  Arabia)
Mariscal Sucre (Ecuador)
Peterson Field (USA)
Raleigh/Durham (USA)
Santa Caterina (Madeira)
14 Eppley Airfield (USA)

Fort Lauderdale (USA)
Galileo Galilei (Italy)
Henderson Field (Solomon
  Islands)
Juan Santamaria (Costa
  Rica)
Kingsford Smith (Australia)
Lester B Pearson (Canada)
Luis Muñoz Marin (Puerto
  Rico)
Novo-Alexeyevka (Georgia)
15 Augusto C Sandino
  (Nicaragua)
Charles de Gaulle (France)
Dallas/Fort Worth (USA)
Frankfurt am Main
  (Germany)
General Mitchell (USA)
Murtala Muhammed
  (Nigeria)
Sir Seretse Khama
  (Botswana)
Theodore Francis (USA)

Airlines include:

02 BA
  UA
03 BEA
  BMI
  JAL
  KLM
  PIA
  SAS
  TWA
04 BOAC

El Al
05 Flybe
  Pan Am
06 Iberia
  Qantas
07 easyJet
  Ryanair
08 Aer Arann
  Aeroflot

Air India
Alitalia
Emirates
Loganair
09 Aer Lingus
  Air Canada
  Air France
  Lufthansa
10 Air Jamaica
  Iceland Air

11 Continental
13 Air New Zealand
  Cathay Pacific
  Delta Airlines
14 British Airways
  British Midland
  United Airlines
  Virgin Atlantic
15 Turkish Airlines

Air travel terms include:

03 DVT
  ETA
  ETD
  FIM
  hub
  leg
  PIR
  rep
04 APEX
  bags
  bump
  desk
  exit
  fare
  fees
  gate
  IATA
  open

seat
taxi
trip
visa
wait
x-ray
05 aisle
  board
  brace
  cargo
  class
  delay
  fleet
  pilot
  plane
  route
  taxes

06 bumped
  charge
  closed
  divert
  flight
  lounge
  no show
  red-eye
  runway
  ticket
  window
07 airline
  air rage
  airside
  arm rest
  baggage
  booking
  captain

carrier
charges
charter
check-in
co-pilot
customs
delayed
descent
drop off
economy
e-ticket
holding
inbound
landing
layover
legroom
life cot
luggage

net fare
net rate
network
on board
photo ID
standby
steward
take-off
transit
trolley
upgrade
voucher

08 act of god
aircraft
airmiles
airplane
APEX fare
approach
arrivals
boarding
cruising
departed
duty-free
empty leg
landside
life vest
long haul
magazine
manifest
outbound
overwing
passport
seat belt
security

stopover
tail wind
terminal
waitlist

09 aeroplane
aisle seat
cabin crew
club class
code share
concourse
franchise
itinerary
passenger
screening
short haul
surcharge

10 air hostess
air marshal
air steward
allowances
baggage tag
connection
departures
first class
flight deck
gate closed
life jacket
luggage tag
medium haul
on approach
open return
open ticket
red channel
safety card

stewardess
turbulence
window seat

11 airport code
blue channel
code sharing
connections
destination
fast bag drop
hand baggage
hand luggage
left luggage
overbooking
reservation
viewing area

12 baggage check
boarding card
boarding pass
cabin baggage
direct flight
economy class
force majeure
green channel
lost property
luggage label
plane spotter
return ticket
Schengen visa
Schengen zone
single ticket
super economy
trolley dolly
wait in lounge

13 airport lounge

blackout dates
budget airline
business class
emergency exit
excess baggage
frequent flier
frequent flyer
non-stop flight
open jaw ticket
seat row number
standard class
ultra-long haul

14 baggage handler
baggage reclaim
baggage trolley
cabin attendant
customs control
flat-bed service
luggage trolley
outsize baggage
overhead locker
representative

15 baggage carousel
cancellation fee
departure lounge
executive lounge
executive travel
flight attendant
in-flight service
oversize baggage
passport control
proof of identity
scheduled flight
travel documents

aircraft

Aircraft types include:

03 B-52
jet
MiG
Yak

04 Hawk
kite
Moth
STOL
VTOL
Zero

05 blimp
Comet
Eagle
jumbo
Piper
plane
Stuka

06 Airbus®

Boeing
bomber
Cessna
copter
Fokker
glider
Jaguar
Mirage
Nimrod

07 airship
air taxi
all-wing
balloon
biplane
Chinook
chopper
Dornier
fighter

gunship
Halifax
Harrier
Heinkel
Hellcat
jump-jet
Junkers
Learjet
Mustang
prop-jet
Tornado
Tristar
Typhoon

08 airliner
autogiro
autogyro
Blenheim
Catalina

Concorde
Henschel
Hercules
jumbo jet
Mosquito
seaplane
Sikorsky
skiplane
Spitfire
spy plane
superjet
triplane
turbojet
warplane
Zeppelin

09 aeroplane
amphibian
aquaplane

Boeing 747
delta-wing
dirigible
egg beater
fixed-wing
Focke-Wulf
freighter
Gipsy Moth
Helldiver
Hurricane
Lancaster
Lightning
monoplane
Sturmovik
swing-wing

Tiger Moth
turboprop
two-seater
10 Concordski
dive-bomber
hang-glider
helicopter
microlight
multiplane
rotorcraft
rotor plane
Sunderland
Super Sabre
tankbuster

Wellington
whirlybird
11 battleplane
Beaufighter
de Havilland
Flying Tiger
interceptor
rocket plane
Starfighter
taildragger
Thunderbolt
Vickers Vimy
12 air ambulance
Lockheed Vega

single-seater
Sopwith Camel
troop-carrier
13 Avro Lancaster
hot-air balloon
Messerschmitt
Stealth Bomber
Superfortress
14 aerospace-plane
Flying Fortress
Mitsubishi Zero
Stratofortress
15 Bristol Blenheim
Hawker Hurricane

Aircraft parts include:

03 fin
rib
04 cowl
flap
hold
hood
prow
skid
wing
05 cabin
probe
pylon
radar
radio
stick
06 canopy
engine
fan-jet

intake
rudder
07 aileron
ammeter
blister
cockpit
cowling
fairing
hush kit
tail fin
trim tab
winglet
08 elevator
fuselage
gust-lock
intercom
joystick
longeron

main gear
tail boom
tailskid
turbojet
wing flap
09 altimeter
astrodome
autoflare
main plane
nose wheel
outrigger
propeller
tailplane
tail wheel
turboprop
10 boost gauge
flight deck
11 chronometer

gyro horizon
landing flap
landing gear
turbo-ram-jet
vertical fin
12 control stick
equilibrator
radio compass
rudder pedals
vertical tail
13 accelerometer
control column
undercarriage
14 horizontal tail
radar altimeter
15 landing-carriage
magnetic compass

Aircraft include:

04 R101
06 Bell X-1
07 *Voyager*
08 *Enola Gay*
See also **aviation**

09 *Winnie Mae*
10 *Hindenburg*
11 *Lucky Lady II*
Spruce Goose

Wright Flyer
Air Force One
12 *Graf Zeppelin*
Memphis Belle

15 *Spirit of St Louis*

airport *see* **air travel**

Albania *see* **Balkans**

alcohol *see* **drink**

algae

Algae and lichens include:

05 chara	Valonia	cup lichen	manna-lichen
usnea	**08** anabaena	Isokontae	Protococcus
06 archil	conferva	rock tripe	Valoniaceae
corkir	lecanora	spirogyra	**12** Cyanophyceae
crotal	lungwort	stonewort	Heterocontae
desmid	pond scum	**10** brown algae	reindeer moss
diatom	red algae	Charophyta	stromatolite
korkir	Roccella	Conjugatae	Ulotrichales
nostoc	sea ivory	cyanophyte	water flowers
volvox	stonerag	fallen star	**13** chlamydomonas
07 crottle	stoneraw	green algae	Protococcales
cup moss	tree moss	heterocont	Schizophyceae
euglena	Ulothrix	heterokont	witches' butter
Graphis	wall moss	rock violet	**14** blue-green algae
oak lump	wartwort	water bloom	cyanobacterium
parella	**09** Characeae	**11** blanketweed	dinoflagellate
seaweed	chlorella	Iceland moss	

See also **seaweed**

alloy *see* **metal**

alphabet

Alphabets and writing systems include:

03 ABC	runic	futhorc	cuneiform
IPA	**06** Arabic	futhork	ideograph
ITA	Brahmi	Glossic	logograph
04 kana	finger	linear A	syllabary
ogam	Glagol	linear B	**10** Chalcidian
05 Greek	Hebrew	**08** Cyrillic	devanagari
kanji	nagari	Georgian	estrangelo
Kufic	naskhi	Gurmukhi	pictograph
Latin	Pinyin	hiragana	**11** estranghelo
ogham	romaji	katakana	hieroglyphs
Roman	**07** Braille	phonetic	**14** Augmented Roman
runes	futhark	**09** Byzantine	**15** Initial Teaching

Letters of the Arabic alphabet:

02 ba	**03** ayn	mim	zay
fa	dad	nun	**04** alif
ha	dai	qaf	dhai
ra	jim	sad	shin
ta	kaf	sin	**05** ghayn
ya	kha	tha	
za	lam	waw	

Letters of the English alphabet:

02 ar	ef	en	oh
ay	el	es	wy
ee	em	ex	**03** bee

cee	ess	see	**06** haitch
cue	eye	tee	**07** double-u
dee	gee	vee	**09** double-you
eff	jay	you	
eks	kay	zed	
ell	kew	zee	
enn	pee	**05** aitch	

Letters of the Old English alphabet include:

03 ash	wen	ogam	**05** thorn
edh	wyn	wynn	
eth	**04** aesc	yogh	

Letters of the Greek alphabet:

02 mu	rho	delta	**07** digamma
nu	san	gamma	epsilon
pi	tau	kappa	omicron
xi	vau	koppa	upsilon
03 chi	**04** beta	omega	ypsilon
eta	iota	sigma	
phi	zeta	theta	
psi	**05** alpha	**06** lambda	

Letters of the Hebrew alphabet:

02 fe	tav	khaf	lamed
he	taw	koph	sadhe
pe	tet	qoph	tsadi
03 bet	vav	resh	tzade
heh	waw	sade	zayin
het	yod	shin	**06** daleth
kaf	**04** alef	teth	lamedh
mem	ayin	yodh	saddhe
nun	beth	**05** aleph	samech
peh	chaf	cheth	samekh
qof	heth	dalet	
sin	kaph	gimel	

Letters of the NATO phonetic alphabet:

04 echo	zulu	romeo	**07** charlie
golf	**05** alpha	tango	foxtrot
kilo	bravo	**06** juliet	uniform
lima	delta	quebec	whiskey
mike	hotel	sierra	**08** november
papa	india	victor	
xray	oscar	yankee	

American football

National Football League teams:

11 New York Jets	Detroit Lions	Miami Dolphins
St Louis Rams	**13** Dallas Cowboys	New York Giants
12 Buffalo Bills	Denver Broncos	**14** Atlanta Falcons
Chicago Bears	Houston Texans	Oakland Raiders

15 Baltimore Ravens
Cleveland Browns
Green Bay Packers
Seattle Seahawks
Tennessee Titans
16 Arizona Cardinals
Carolina Panthers

Kansas City Chiefs
Minnesota Vikings
New Orleans Saints
San Diego Chargers
17 Cincinnati Bengals
Indianapolis Colts
San Francisco 49ers

18 New England Patriots
Philadelphia Eagles
Pittsburgh Steelers
Tampa Bay Buccaneers
Washington Redskins
19 Jacksonville Jaguars

National Football League team nicknames include:

04 Jets (New York)
Rams (St Louis)
05 Bears (Chicago)
Bills (Buffalo)
Colts (Indianapolis)
Lions (Detroit)
06 Browns (Cleveland)
Chiefs (Kansas City)
Eagles (Philadelphia)
Giants (New York)
Niners (San Francisco)

Ravens (Baltimore)
Saints (New Orleans)
Texans (Houston)
Titans (Tennessee)
07 Bengals (Cincinnati)
Broncos (Denver)
Cowboys (Dallas)
Falcons (Atlanta)
Jaguars (Jacksonville)
Packers (Green Bay)
Raiders (Oakland)

Vikings (Minnesota)
08 Chargers (San Diego)
Dolphins (Miami)
Panthers (Carolina)
Patriots (New England)
Redskins (Washington)
Seahawks (Seattle)
Steelers (Pittsburgh)
09 Cardinals (Arizona)
10 Buccaneers (Tampa Bay)
11 Forty Niners (San Francisco)

American footballers include:

04 Camp (Walter; 1859–1925, US)
Rice (Jerry; 1962– , US)
05 Brown (Jim; 1936– , US)
Brown (Paul; 1908–91, US)
Elway (John; 1960– , US)
Favre (Brett; 1969– , US)
Halas (George; 1895–1983, US)
Owens (Terrell; 1973– , US)
Perry (Joe; 1927– , US)
Perry (William 'The Fridge'; 1962– , US)
Shula (Don; 1930– , US)
Smith (Emmitt; 1969– , US)
06 Blanda (George; 1927– , US)
Butkus (Dick; 1942– , US)
Graham (Otto; 1921–2003, US)
Grange (Red; 1903–91, US)
Hutson (Don; 1913–97, US)
Landry (Tom; 1924–2000, US)

Marino (Dan; 1961– , US)
Namath (Joe; 1943– , US)
Payton (Walter; 1954–99, US)
Rockne (Knute; 1888–1931, Norwegian/US)
Sayers (Gale; 1943– , US)
Taylor (Lawrence; 1959– , US)
Thorpe (Jim; 1888–1953, US)
Unitas (Johnny; 1933–2002, US)
07 Lambeau (Curly; 1898–1965, US)
Montana (Joe; 1956– , US)
Sanders (Barry; 1968– , US)
Sanders (Deion; 1967– , US)
Simpson (O J; 1947– , US)
08 Andersen (Morten; 1960– , Danish)
Harrison (Marvin; 1972– , US)
Lombardi (Vince; 1913–70, US)
Peterson (Adrian; 1985– , US)
09 Tarkenton (Fran; 1940– , US)

American football terms include:

03 AFC
NFC
NFL
04 ball
bomb
clip
down
draw
flag
muff
pass

play
punt
sack
snap
05 blitz
block
drive
field
guard
shift
sneak

spike
zebra
06 all-pro
bullet
center
chains
fumble
huddle
pocket
prayer
punter

safety
spiral
tackle
umpire

07 audible
bootleg
defense
end zone
handoff
holding
lateral
lineman
offense
offside
pigskin
Pro Bowl
quarter
red zone
referee
rushing
shotgun
time out
traffic
X's and O's

08 face mask
fullback
gridiron
hail Mary
halfback
hang time
hash mark
linesman
overtime
pass rush
receiver
scramble
split end

See also **sport**

tailback
tight end
trenches
turnover
weak side

09 backfield
back judge
chain gang
chop block
end around
fair catch
field goal
franchise
line judge
pooch kick
reception
scrimmage
secondary
side judge
Super Bowl
take a knee
touchback
touchdown

10 completion
conversion
cornerback
extra point
field judge
Hall of Fame
linebacker
nickelback
nose tackle
onside kick
option play
play action
point after
screen pass

shovel pass
strong side
wobbly duck

11 all-American
counter play
curl pattern
dime defense
flea flicker
man coverage
neutral zone
post pattern
quarterback
running back

12 complete pass
defensive end
interception
naked bootleg
on the numbers
slant pattern
slot receiver
special teams
wide receiver
zone coverage

13 defensive back
Heisman trophy
nickel defense

14 climb the ladder
hurry-up offense
incomplete pass
outlet receiver
prevent defense

15 franchise player
line of scrimmage
no-huddle offense
primary receiver
thread the needle

The Americas

Countries in North, Central and South America:

04 Cuba
Peru
05 Chile
Haiti
06 Belize
Brazil
Canada
Guyana
Mexico
Panama
07 Bolivia
Ecuador

Grenada
Jamaica
St Lucia
Uruguay
08 Colombia
Dominica
Honduras
Paraguay
Suriname
09 Argentina
Costa Rica
Guatemala

Nicaragua
Venezuela
10 El Salvador
The Bahamas
15 St Kitts and Nevis
17 Antigua and Barbuda
Dominican Republic
Trinidad and Tobago
21 United States of America
25 St Vincent and the
Grenadines

Cities and notable towns in North America include:

04 Léon (Mexico)
05 Miami (USA)
    Omaha (USA)
    Tampa (USA)
    Tulsa (USA)
06 Austin (USA)
    Boston (USA)
    Dallas (USA)
    Denver (USA)
    El Paso (USA)
    Jalapa (Mexico)
    London (Canada)
    Mérida (Mexico)
    Newark (USA)
    Oaxaca (Mexico)
    Ottawa (Canada)
    Puebla (Mexico)
    Québec (Canada)
    St Paul (USA)
    Toledo (USA)
    Tucson (USA)
07 Atlanta (USA)
    Buffalo (USA)
    Calgary (Canada)
    Chicago (USA)
    Detroit (USA)
    Houston (USA)
    Memphis (USA)
    Norfolk (USA)
    Oakland (USA)
    Phoenix (USA)

San José (USA)
Seattle (USA)
St Louis (USA)
Tampico (Mexico)
Toronto (Canada)
Zapopan (Mexico)
08 Acapulco (Mexico)
    Campeche (Mexico)
    Columbus (USA)
    Culiacán (Mexico)
    Edmonton (Canada)
    Hamilton (Canada)
    Hartford (USA)
    Honolulu (USA)
    Mexicali (Mexico)
    Montréal (Canada)
    Portland (USA)
    San Diego (USA)
    Veracruz (Mexico)
    Victoria (Canada)
    Winnipeg (Canada)
09 Baltimore (USA)
    Charlotte (USA)
    Chihuahua (Mexico)
    Cleveland (USA)
    Fort Worth (USA)
    Kitchener (Canada)
    Long Beach (USA)
    Milwaukee (USA)
    Monterrey (Mexico)
    Nashville (USA)

Vancouver (Canada)
10 Cincinnati (USA)
    Hermosillo (Mexico)
    Kansas City (USA)
    Los Angeles (USA)
    Mexico City (Mexico)
    New Orleans (USA)
    Pittsburgh (USA)
    Sacramento (USA)
    Salina Cruz (Mexico)
    San Antonio (USA)
    Valladolid (Mexico)
11 Albuquerque (USA)
    Guadalajara (Mexico)
    Minneapolis (USA)
    New York City (USA)
    Scarborough (Canada)
12 Ciudad Juárez (Mexico)
    Indianapolis (USA)
    Jacksonville (USA)
    Oklahoma City (USA)
    Philadelphia (USA)
    Salt Lake City (USA)
    San Francisco (USA)
    St Catharines (Canada)
    Washington DC (USA)
13 Piedras Negras (Mexico)
    San Luis Potosí (Mexico)
    Virginia Beach (USA)
14 Ciudad Victoria (Mexico)

Cities and notable towns in Central America include:

04 León (Nicaragua)
    Xela (Guatemala)
05 Colón (Panama)
    David (Panama)
    Limón (Costa Rica)
06 Masaya (Nicaragua)
07 Antigua (Guatemala)
    Cartago (Costa Rica)
    Granada (Nicaragua)
    Heredia (Costa Rica)
    La Ceiba (Honduras)
    Liberia (Costa Rica)
    Managua (Nicaragua)
    San José (Costa Rica)
08 Santa Ana (El Salvador)
09 Choluteca (Honduras)

Escuintla (Guatemala)
Matagalpa (Nicaragua)
San Miguel (El Salvador)
10 Belize City (Belize)
    Chinandega (Nicaragua)
    El Progreso (Honduras)
    Panama City (Panama)
    Puntarenas (Costa Rica)
11 Mazatenango (Guatemala)
    San Salvador (El Salvador)
    Tegucigalpa (Honduras)
12 San Pedro Sula (Honduras)
13 Guatemala City (Guatemala)
    Huehuetenango (Guatemala)
14 Quetzaltenango (Guatemala)

Cities and notable towns in South America include:

04 Cali (Colombia)
    Lima (Peru)
05 Belém (Brazil)
    Cuzco (Peru)
La Paz (Bolivia)
Natal (Brazil)

Oruro (Bolivia)
Pisco (Peru)
Quito (Ecuador)
Salto (Uruguay)
Sucre (Bolivia)

06 Bogotá (Colombia)
Callao (Peru)
Campos (Brazil)
Cúcuta (Colombia)
Cuenca (Ecuador)
El Alto (Bolivia)
Ibarra (Ecuador)
Maceio (Brazil)
Manaus (Brazil)
Mérida (Venezuela)
Olinda (Brazil)
Osasco (Brazil)
Potosí (Bolivia)
Recife (Brazil)
Santos (Brazil)
Vargas (Venezuela)

07 Aracajú (Brazil)
Caracas (Venezuela)
Cayenne (French Guiana)
Córdoba (Argentina)
Goiânia (Brazil)
Iquitos (Peru)
La Plata (Argentina)
Maracay (Venezuela)
Mendoza (Argentina)
Niterói (Brazil)
Rosario (Argentina)
Santa Fe (Argentina)

São Luis (Brazil)

08 Arequipa (Peru)
Asunción (Paraguay)
Brasilia (Brazil)
Campinas (Brazil)
Chiclayo (Peru)
Chimbote (Peru)
Contagem (Brazil)
Curitiba (Brazil)
Jaboatão (Brazil)
Londrina (Brazil)
Medellin (Colombia)
Mercedes (Uruguay)
Paysandú (Uruguay)
Riobamba (Ecuador)
Salvador (Brazil)
Santiago (Chile)
São Paulo (Brazil)
Sorocaba (Brazil)
Teresina (Brazil)
Trujillo (Peru)
Valencia (Venezuela)

09 Barcelona (Venezuela)
Cartagena (Colombia)
Fortaleza (Brazil)
Guarulhos (Brazil)
Guayaquil (Ecuador)
Maracaibo (Venezuela)
Ouro Preto (Brazil)
Santa Cruz (Bolivia)

10 Cochabamba (Bolivia)
Concepción (Chile)
Concepción (Paraguay)

Esmeraldas (Ecuador)
Georgetown (Guyana)
João Pessoa (Brazil)
Juiz de Fora (Brazil)
Las Piedras (Uruguay)
Montevideo (Uruguay)
Nova Iguaçu (Brazil)
Paramaribo (Suriname)
Santo André (Brazil)
São Gonçalo (Brazil)
Talcahuano (Chile)
Valparaíso (Chile)
Villarrica (Paraguay)
Vina del Mar (Chile)

11 Antofagasta (Chile)
Bucaramanga (Colombia)
Buenos Aires (Argentina)
Campo Grande (Brazil)
Mar del Plata (Argentina)
Pôrto Alegre (Brazil)
San Fernando (Trinidad and Tobago)

12 Barquisimeto (Venezuela)
Barranquilla (Colombia)
Rio de Janeiro (Brazil)
San Cristobal (Venezuela)

13 Belo Horizonte (Brazil)
Ciudad Bolívar (Venezuela)
Ciudad Guayana (Venezuela)
Duque de Caxias (Brazil)
Ribeirão Preto (Brazil)

14 Feira de Santana (Brazil)

Native American peoples include:

02 Ge	Hupa	Tygh	Huari
03 Fox	Inca	Yahi	Huron
Han	Innu	Yana	Jamul
Hoh	Iowa	Yuit	Jemez
Mam	Ipai	Yuki	Kamia
Ofo	Iswa	Yuma	Kanai
Ona	Itzá	Zuñi	Kansa
Sac	Kato	05 Acoma	Karok
Ute	Koso	Ahtna	Kaska
Wea	Kuna	Aleut	Keres
Zia	Maya	Alsea	Lenca
	Mono	Aztec	Lipan
04 Adai	Pima	Bidai	Maidu
Coos	Piro	Brule	Makah
Cree	Pomo	Caddo	Mayan
Crow	Sauk	Campo	Me-wuk
Dene	Seri	Carib	Miwok
Erie	Suma	Comox	Moche
Hano	Tait	Conoy	Modoc
Hare	Taos	Creek	Nambe
Hopi	Tewa	Haida	Nazca

Olmec
Omaha
Opata
Otomi
Pecos
Petun
Pipil
Sahtu
Sarsi
Sioux
Sooke
Tache
Taino
Talio
Teton
Tigua
Tipai
Twana
Unami
Wappo
Wenro
Wiyot
Yaqui
Yuchi
Yupik
Yurok

6 Ahtena
Apache
Arawak
Atsina
Aymara
Babine
Beaver
Bororo
Calusa
Caniba
Cayapó
Cayuga
Cayuse
Celilo
Chatot
Chetco
Chiaha
Cocopa
Cupeño
Cusabo
Dakota
Dogrib
Galice
Haihai
Haisla
Iquito
Isleta
Jivaro
Jumano
Kiliwa
Kitsai
Klemtu

Konkow
Laguna
Lakota
Lassik
Lenape
Mandan
Micmac
Mi'kmaq
Mixtec
Mocama
Mohave
Mohawk
Mojave
Muisca
Munsee
Nakipa
Nakoda
Natick
Navaho
Navajo
Nisga'a
Nishka
Nootka
Oglala
Ohlone
Ojibwa
Oneida
Ottawa
Paipai
Paiute
Panoan
Papago
Patwin
Pawnee
Peigan
Piegan
Pueblo
Quapaw
Quiché
Salish
Samish
Sandia
Santee
Saponi
Sekani
Seneca
Skagit
Slavey
Stoney
Taensa
Tagish
Tanana
Tawasa
Tenino
Tlicho
Toboso
Tolowa
Toltec

Tongva
Tunica
Tupian
Tutelo
Wikeno
Wintun
Woccon
Yahgan
Yakama
Yamana
Yokuts

07 Abenaki
Akokisa
Anasazi
Aranama
Arapaho
Arikara
Atakapa
Bannock
Beothuk
Chibcha
Chilula
Chinook
Choctaw
Chumash
Ciboney
Clatsop
Cochiti
Esselen
Flatbow
Giamina
Guarani
Hasinai
Hidatsa
Ho-Chunk
Hohokam
Huastec
Huchnom
Huichol
Ingalik
Juaneño
Kitimat
Klallam
Klamath
Koasati
Kolchan
Koskimo
Koyukon
Kutchin
Kutenai
Kwatami
Lucayan
Luiseño
Mahican
Mapuche
Mattole
Mazatec
Mimbres

Mískito
Mohegan
Mohican
Monache
Nanaimo
Naskapi
Natchez
Neutral
Nisenan
Nomlaki
Nongatl
Oji-Cree
Picuris
Puelche
Quechan
Quechua
Quiripi
Saanich
Salinan
Sanpoil
Sechelt
Secotan
Selknam
Serrano
Shawnee
Shipibo
Shuswap
Siksika
Songish
Spokane
Tahltan
Takelma
Tamique
Tanaina
Tekesta
Tesuque
Timucua
Tlingit
Tonkawa
Totonac
Tulalip
Tümpisa
Waicuri
Wailaki
Walapai
Wanapum
Wawenoc
Whilkut
Wyandot
Yamasee
Yankton
Yaquina
Zapotec

08 Achomawi
Alacaluf
Atsugewi
Cahuilla
Calapuya

Chawasha
Chehalis
Chemakum
Cherokee
Cheyenne
Chippewa
Comanche
Cowichan
Delaware
Diaguita
Diegueño
Flathead
Fountain
Guaicuru
Heiltsuk
Hesquiat
Hitchiti
Hualapai
Illinois
Iroquois
Kalapuya
Kawaiisu
Kickapoo
Kimsquit
Kittitas
Konomihu
Kootenay
Kumeyaay
Kwakiutl
Kwantlem
Maliseet
Maricopa
Menomini
Minitari
Musqueam
Nez Percé
Nooksack
Nottoway
Okanagan
Okanagon
Onondaga
Panamint

Paviotso
Pocumtuk
Puyallup
Qahatika
Quileute
Quinault
Sahaptin
Saraguro
Seminole
Shoshone
Sinkyone
Sliammon
Squamish
Tarascan
Tasttine
Tataviam
Tepehuan
Tsetsaut
Tsnungwe
Tsuu T'ina
Tukanoan
Tuskegee
Umatilla
Waccamaw
Yanomamo

09 Algonkian
Antoniaño
Atacameño
Atikamekw
Blackfoot
Calapooia
Chickasaw
Chilcotin
Chilliwak
Chimariko
Chipewyan
Clayoquot
Costanoan
Coushatta
Degexit'an
Havasupai
Jicarilla

Karankawa
Kaweshkar
Kitanemuk
Klickitat
Mascouten
Menominee
Migueleño
Mundurucu
Nanticoke
Nipissing
Niskwalli
Nisqually
Paugusset
Pennacook
Pensacola
Pentlatch
Purepecha
Saulteaux
Snohomish
Suquamish
Swinomish
Tanacross
Tehuelche
Tillamook
Tlaxcalan
Topachula
Tsimshian
Tupinamba
Tuscarora
Unquachog
Wappinger
Winnebago
Yanktonai
Yocha Dehe

10 Algonquian
Anishinabe
Araucanian
Athabescan
Bella Bella
Bella Coola
Besawunena
Chemehuevi

Chiricahua
Chitimacha
Chukchansi
Clatskanie
Fernandeño
Gabrieliño
Gros Ventre
Halkomelem
Holikachuk
Kwalhioqua
Laurentian
Los Luceros
Makiritare
Montagnais
Potawatomi
Shinnecock
Tarahumara
Wallawalla
Wet'suweten

11 Assiniboine
Chasta Costa
Chickamauga
Halchidhoma
Lushootseed
Muckleshoot
Souriquoian
Tubatulabal
Unalachtigo

12 Isleta del Sur
Kavelchadhom
Mississaugas
Narragansett
Nuu-chah-nulth
Pend'Oreilles
Rappahannock

13 Haudenosaunee
Nawathinehena
Ponca Nebraska
Susquehannock
Tlatlasikoala

South American landmarks include:

04 moai

05 Andes
Colca
llano
Plata
Plate
selva

06 Amazon
Iguaçu
Itaipu
Osorno

pampas
Paraná

07 Atacama
Ipanema
Orinoco

08 Cape Horn
Cotopaxi
Titicaca

09 Aconcagua
Cartagena
Galápagos

Gran Chaco
Itaipu Dam
Patagonia

10 Angel Falls
Copacabana
Mato Grosso
River Plate
Salto Ángel

11 Colca Canyon
Iguaçu Falls
Machu Picchu

Mt Aconcagua
Pico Bolívar

12 Easter Island
Lake Titicaca
Perito Moreno
Río de la Plata

13 Atacama Desert
Kaieteur Falls

14 Cristo Redentor
Tierra del Fuego

15 Guiana Highlands

North American words and expressions include:

03 cot (camp bed)
gas (petrol)

04 bill (banknote)
crib (cot)
fall (autumn)
hood (car bonnet)
line (queue)
mono (glandular fever)
semi (articulated lorry)
vest (waistcoat)

05 bangs (fringe)
braid (plait)
broil (grill)
candy (sweets)
check (bill)
chips (crisps)
derby (bowler hat)
fries (chips)
jello (jelly)
jelly (jam)
klutz (stupid/clumsy person)
purse (handbag)
sedan (saloon car)
shade (window blind)
trunk (car boot)

06 box car (goods wagon)
catsup (ketchup)
closet (wardrobe)
cookie (biscuit)
diaper (nappy)
faucet (tap)
honcho (gaffer)
period (full stop)
rotary (roundabout)
subway (underground)
teller (cashier)
wrench (spanner)

07 antenna (aerial)
beltway (ring road)
blowout (puncture)
freeway (motorway)
garters (suspenders)
muffler (car silencer)
off ramp (motorway exit)
realtor (estate agent)
repo man (bailiff)
seltzer (soda water)
trailer (caravan)
zip code (postcode)

08 attorney (lawyer)
cilantro (coriander)
crawfish (crayfish)
eggplant (aubergine)
elevator (lift)

gasoline (petrol)
gas pedal (accelerator)
kerosene (paraffin)
men's room (gents' toilets)
overpass (flyover)
pacifier (baby's dummy)
pie dough (shortcrust pastry)
railroad (railway)
restroom (toilets)
scallion (spring onion)
sidewalk (pavement)
sneakers (trainers)
steerage (economy class)
stroller (pushchair)
trash can (dustbin)
vacation (holiday)
zucchini (courgette)

09 blueberry (bilberry)
cream puff (choux bun)
housecoat (dressing gown)
loose meat (minced meat)
thumbtack (drawing pin)
underpass (subway)

10 cornstarch (cornflour)
expressway (motorway)
flashlight (torch)
gas station (petrol station)
ground meat (minced meat)
heavy cream (double cream)
interstate (motorway)
light cream (single cream)
main street (high street)
nightstick (truncheon)
parking lot (car park)
phone booth (phone box)
pocketbook (handbag)
suspenders (braces)
turtle neck (polo neck)
undershirt (vest)
wading pool (paddling pool)
windshield (windscreen)

11 call collect (reverse the charges)
cotton candy (candy floss)
plastic wrap (cling film)

12 garbanzo bean (chickpea)
intersection (junction)
movie theater (cinema)
railroad ties (railway sleepers)
shopping cart (shopping trolley)
station wagon (estate car)
superhighway (motorway)

13 graham cracker (digestive biscuit)
traffic circle (roundabout)

14 divided highway (dual carriageway)
housing project (housing estate)

15 round trip ticket (return ticket)
school principal (head)

See also **Canada; Mexico; mythology; United States of America**

amino acid

Amino acids include:

04 dopa	leucine	threonine	**12** aspartic acid
06 glycin	proline	**10** asparagine	glutamic acid
leucin	**08** arginine	citrulline	phenylalanin
lysine	cysteine	domoic acid	**13** phenylalanine
serine	tyrosine	isoleucine	**14** glutaminic acid
valine	**09** glutamine	methionine	
07 alanine	histidine	tryptophan	
glycine	ornithine	**11** tryptophane	

amphibian

Amphibians include:

03 ask	**08** bullfrog	**10** alpine newt	midwife toad
eft	cane-toad	Bosca's newt	painted frog
olm	frogling	clawed frog	palmate newt
04 frog	mudpuppy	clawed toad	parsley frog
hyla	platanna	common frog	Surinam toad
newt	polliwig	common toad	walking toad
pipa	polliwog	edible frog	**12** platanna frog
toad	pollywig	flying frog	springkeeper
05 siren	pollywog	hellbender	spring peeper
06 peeper	tree frog	horned toad	**14** common treefrog
taddie	tree toad	marine toad	fire salamander
07 axolotl	**09** caecilian	natterjack	labyrinthodont
froglet	green toad	ophiomorph	mole salamander
paddock	marsh frog	salamander	natterjack toad
puddock	Nototrema	smooth newt	**15** arrow-poison frog
tadpole	pouch-toad	**11** goliath frog	Cape nightingale
	warty newt	leopard frog	common spadefoot
		marbled newt	

See also **animal**

anaesthetic

Anaesthetics include:

03 gas	eucaine	lidocaine	laughing gas
PCP	urethan	Pentothal®	thiopentone
05 ether	**08** ketamine	**10** benzocaine	**12** cyclopropane
trike	metopryl	chloroform	hexobarbital
06 eucain	procaine	lignocaine	nitrous oxide
Evipan®	stovaine	nerve block	**13** hexobarbitone
spinal	urethane	orthocaine	phencyclidine
07 Avertin®	**09** Fluothane®	thiopental	**14** methyl chloride
cocaine	halothane	**11** Dutch liquid	**15** tribromoethanol

analgesic

Analgesics include:

06 Calpol®	Panadol®	**09** Calprofen®	paracetamol
07 aspirin	quinine	co-codamol	pentazocine
codeine	salicin	ibuprofen	
Disprin®	**08** Cuprofen®	pethidine	**12** indomethacin
Disprol®	fentanyl	**10** diclofenac	salicylamide
menthol	ketamine		**13** carbamazepine
metopon	morphine	**11** aminobutene	phencyclidine
morphia	salicine	Distalgesic®	
Nurofen®	stovaine	indometacin	**14** phenylbutazone

anatomy

Anatomists include:

03 His (Wilhelm; 1831–1904, German)

04 Baer (Karl Ernst von; 1792–1876, German)
Bell (Sir Charles; 1774–1842, Scottish)
Dart (Raymond A; 1893–1988, South African)
Knox (Robert; 1791–1862, Scottish)
Roux (Wilhelm; 1850–1924, German)

05 Clark (Sir Wilfred le Gros; 1895–1971, English)
Graaf (Regnier de; 1641–73, Dutch)
Henle (Friedrich; 1809–85, German)
Hyrtl (Joseph; 1810–94, Austrian)
Monro (Alexander 'Primus'; 1697–1767, Scottish)
Monro (Alexander 'Secondus'; 1733–1817, Scottish)

06 Adrian (Edgar, Lord; 1889–1977, English)
Camper (Pieter; 1722–89, Dutch)
Cowper (William; 1666–1709, English)
Cuvier (Georges, Baron; 1769–1832, French)
Flower (Sir William Henry; 1831–99, English)
Hagens (Gunther von; 1945– , German)
Haller (Albrecht von; 1708–77, Swiss)
Harvey (William; 1578–1657, English)

Hunter (William; 1718–83, Scottish)
Pander (Christian Heinrich; 1794–1865, German)
Tobias (Phillip; 1925– , South African)

07 Baillie (Matthew; 1761–1823, Scottish)
Colombo (Matteo Realdo; 1516–59, Italian)
Galvani (Luigi; 1737–98, Italian)
Goodsir (John; 1814–67, Scottish)
Pecquet (Jean; 1622–74, French)

08 Alcmaeon (fl.520 BC; Greek)
Kölliker (Albert von; 1817–1905, Swiss)
Malpighi (Marcello; 1628–94, Italian)
Vesalius (Andreas; 1514–64, Belgian)

09 Bartholin (Caspar the Younger; 1655–1738, Danish)
Eustachio (Bartolommeo; 1520–74, Italian)
Fallopius (Gabriele; 1523–62, Italian)
Gegenbaur (Karl; 1826–1903, German)

10 Herophilus (c.335–c.280 BC, Greek)

11 Cruveilhier (Jean; 1791–1874, French)
Weidenreich (Franz; 1873–1948, German)

12 Papanicolaou (George Nicholas; 1883–1962, US)

13 Waldeyer-Hartz (Wilhelm; 1839–1921, German)

Terms used in anatomy include:

03 arm	chin	neck	chest
ear	crus	nose	digit
eye	foot	oral	elbow
hip	hand	shin	gland
jaw	head	vein	groin
leg	hock	womb	heart
toe	knee	**05** aorta	helix
04 anus	limb	aural	ileum
back	lobe	bowel	joint
bone	lung	brain	liver

lungs
mouth
nasal
navel
nerve
optic
ovary
pedal
penis
renal
spine
thumb
trunk
uvula
volar
vulva
wrist

06 artery
atrium
axilla
biceps
breast
buccal
carpal
carpus
crural
dental
dermal
distal
dorsal
finger
flexor
genial
gullet
kidney
lingua
lumbar
muscle
narial
narine
neural
neuron
ocular
penile
pleura
rectum
rectus
rotula
sacral
septum
soleus
spinal
spleen
temple

tendon
tensor
testis
thenar
throat
thymic
thymus
tongue
tonsil
tragus
uterus
uvular
vagina

07 abdomen
alveary
alveoli
auricle
bladder
buttock
cardiac
cnemial
cochlea
cranial
cranium
gastric
genital
glossal
glottal
glottis
gnathic
gristle
hepatic
jejunal
jejunum
jugular
kneecap
levator
lingual
mammary
membral
neurone
optical
osseous
patella
phalanx
pleural
pyloric
pylorus
ribcage
rotator
sternum
stomach
sublime
thyroid

triceps
urethra
uterine
vaginal
ventral

08 appendix
axillary
brachial
brachium
bronchus
cerebral
cervical
cochlear
coronary
duodenal
duodenum
extensor
foreskin
genitals
gingival
laryngal
ligament
mandible
muscular
opponent
pancreas
parietal
pectoral
perineal
perineum
prostate
proximal
shoulder
temporal
testicle
thoracic
vena cava
vertebra
voice-box
windpipe

09 abdominal
antihelix
bronchial
capillary
cartilage
coccygeal
coccygian
depressor
diaphragm
epidermal
epidermis
funny bone
genitalia

hamstring
labyrinth
lachrymal
lymph node
pulmonary
sartorial
sartorius
sphincter
tendinous
umbilical
umbilicus
ventricle
vertebral

10 Adam's apple
antitragus
cerebellum
encephalic
encephalon
epiglottal
epiglottis
intestinal
intestines
ligamental
mandibular
oesophagal
oesophagus
pancreatic
peritoneal
peritoneum
phalangeal
protractor
quadriceps
trochanter

11 diaphragmal
gall bladder
infracostal
intercostal
pericardium
solar plexus

12 adrenal gland

13 cartilaginous
diaphragmatic
Fallopian tube
gastrocnemius
lachrymal duct

14 Achilles tendon
Fallopian tubes
lachrymal gland
large intestine
pituitary gland
small intestine

See also **artery**; **bone**; **brain**; **ear**; **eye**; **face**; **gland**; **heart**; **hormone**; **immune system**; **mouth**; **muscle**; **nerve**; **organ**; **skin**; **teeth**; **vein**

anchor

Anchors include:

03 car	Bruce®	stream	mushroom
CQR	drift	**07** grapnel	**09** admiralty
ice	kedge	killick	stockless
sea	sheet	killock	yachtsman
04 navy	waist	stocked	**12** double fluked
rond	**06** drogue	weather	
05 bower	plough	**08** Danforth®	

ancient *see* city; festival

Ancient Egypt *see* Egypt

angel

Angels include:

05 Ariel	**06** Abdiel	Moloch	Michael
Eblis	Arioch	Zephon	Raphael
Iblis	Azrael	**07** Gabriel	Zadkiel
Satan	Belial	Israfel	**08** Ithuriel
Uriel	Mammon	Lucifer	**09** Beelzebub

Orders of angel:

05 angel	seraph	**08** dominion	**12** principality
power	throne	**09** archangel	
06 cherub	virtue	**10** domination	

angle

Angle types include:

05 acute	reflex	hour-angle	
right	**08** straight	**13** complementary	
06 obtuse	**09** conjugate	supplementary	

Angle measurements include:

04 hour	minute	arcsecond	minute of arc
05 grade	radian	steradian	second of arc
point	second	**10** revolution	**15** radian per second
06 degree	**09** arcminute	**11** degree of arc	

See also **measurement**

angling *see* fishing

animal

Animals include:

03 ape	eland	gibbon	sealion
cat	horse	impala	wallaby
cow	hyena	jaguar	**08** aardvark
dog	koala	monkey	antelope
elk	lemur	ocelot	elephant
fox	llama	rabbit	hedgehog
gnu	moose	racoon	kangaroo
pig	mouse	walrus	mongoose
rat	otter	weasel	platypus
04 bear	panda	wombat	reindeer
bull	sheep	**07** buffalo	squirrel
deer	skunk	caribou	
goat	tiger	cheetah	**09** armadillo
hare	whale	dolphin	orang-utan
lion	zebra	gazelle	polar bear
mink	**06** baboon	giraffe	wolverine
mole	badger	gorilla	
puma	beaver	hamster	**10** chimpanzee
seal	cougar	leopard	giant panda
wolf	ermine	panther	rhinoceros
05 bison	ferret	polecat	**11** grizzly bear
camel	gerbil	raccoon	**12** hippopotamus

Adjectives relating to animals include:

05 apian (bee)
avian (bird)
avine (bird)
ovine (sheep)

06 bovine (cattle/ox)
canine (dog)
equine (horse)
feline (cat)
hippic (horse)
larine (gull)
lupine (wolf)
murine (mouse)
simian (ape/monkey)
ursine (bear)

07 acarine (mite)
anguine (snake)
asinine (ass/donkey)
caprine (goat)
cervine (deer)
corvine (crow)
hircine (goat)
leonine (lion)
milvine (kite)
otarine (seal)
pardine (leopard)

phocine (seal)
piscine (fish)
porcine (pig)
saurian (lizard)
sebrine (zebra)
taurine (bull)
tigrine (tiger)
turdine (thrush)
vespine (wasp)
vulpine (fox)

08 anserine (goose)
aquiline (eagle)
bubaline (buffalo)
cameline (camel)
elaphine (red deer)
ichthyic (fish)
lemurine (lemur)
leporine (hare)
limacine (slug)
ophidian (snake)
pavonine (peacock)
sciurine (squirrel)
soricine (shrew)
suilline (pig)
viperine (viper)
vituline (calf)

09 caballine (horse)
chelonian (tortoise/turtle)
colubrine (snake)
columbine (dove)
crotaline (rattlesnake)
falconine (falcon)
hirundine (swallow)
ichthyoid (fish)
musteline (badger/otter/
   weasel)
ornithoid (bird)
viverrine (civet/ferret)
volucrine (bird)
vulturine (vulture)

10 psittacine (parrot)
serpentine (snake)

11 accipitrine (hawk)
elephantine (elephant)
fringilline (finch)
lacertilian (lizard)

12 gallinaceous (fowl)
oryctolagine (rabbit)

13 rhopalocerous (butterfly)

14 papilionaceous (butterfly)

Collective nouns for animals include:

03 bed (clams/oysters)
cry (hounds)
gam (whales)
mob (kangaroos)
nid (pheasants)
nye (pheasants)
pod (seals/whales)

04 army (caterpillars/frogs)
bale (turtles)
band (gorillas)
bask (crocodiles)
bevy (larks/pheasants/quail/swans)
bury (rabbits)
cast (hawks)
cete (badgers)
dole (doves/turtles)
down (hares)
dray (squirrels)
erst (bees)
fall (woodcocks)
gang (buffalo/elk)
herd (buffalo/cattle/deer/elephants/goats/
   horses/kangaroos/oxen/seals/whales)
hive (bees)
host (sparrows)
husk (hares)
knot (toads)
leap (leopards)
mute (hares/hounds)
nest (ants/bees/pheasants/vipers)
nide (pheasants)
pace (asses)
pack (dogs/grouse/hounds/wolves)
romp (otters)
rout (wolves)
safe (ducks)
span (mules)
team (ducks/horses)
trip (goats/sheep)
turn (turtles)
wing (plovers)
yoke (oxen)
zeal (zebras)

05 bloat (hippopotami)
brace (ducks)
brood (chickens/hens)
charm (finches/goldfinches)
chirm (goldfinches)
cloud (gnats)
covey (partridges/quail)
crash (rhinoceros)
drift (hogs/swine)
drove (cattle/horses/oxen/sheep)
flock (birds/ducks/geese/sheep)
grist (bees)
horde (gnats)

hover (trout)
leash (foxes)
pride (lions)
route (wolves)
sedge (cranes)
shoal (fish)
siege (cranes/herons)
skein (geese)
skulk (foxes)
sloth (bears)
smack (jellyfish)
stand (flamingos)
stare (owls)
swarm (ants/bees/flies/locusts)
tower (giraffes)
tribe (goats)
troop (baboons/kangaroos/monkeys)
watch (nightingales)
wedge (swans)

06 ambush (tigers)
cackle (hyenas)
clutch (chickens)
colony (ants/bees/penguins/rats)
family (otters)
flight (birds)
gaggle (geese)
kennel (dogs)
kindle (kittens)
labour (moles)
litter (kittens/pigs)
murder (crows)
muster (peacocks/penguins)
parade (elephants)
parcel (penguins)
plague (locusts)
pounce (cats)
rafter (turkeys)
school (dolphins/fish/porpoises/whales)
scurry (squirrels)
shiver (sharks)
sleuth (bears)
spring (teal)
stable (horses)
streak (tigers)
string (horses/ponies)
tiding (magpies)
volery (birds)

07 bouquet (pheasants)
clowder (cats)
company (parrots)
descent (woodpeckers)
draught (fish)
prickle (porcupines)
rookery (rooks/seals)
sounder (swine)
turmoil (porpoises)

08 building (rooks)
  busyness (ferrets/flies)
  paddling (ducks)

09 intrusion (cockroaches)
  mustering (storks)
  obstinacy (buffalo)
  tittering (magpies)

10 exaltation (larks)

  parliament (owls/rooks)
  shrewdness (apes)
  unkindness (ravens)

11 convocation (eagles)
  murmuration (starlings)
  ostentation (peacocks)
  pandemonium (parrots)

12 congregation (plovers)

Male animals include:

03 cob (swan)
  dog (dog/fox/wolf)
  hob (ferret)
  nun (smew)
  ram (sheep)
  tom (cat)
  tup (sheep)

04 boar (pig)
  buck (deer/goat/hare/rabbit)
  bull (cattle/elephant/moose/walrus/whale)
  cock (chicken/crab/lobster/salmon/sparrow)
  hart (deer)
  jack (ass/donkey)
  stag (deer)
  zobo (zho)
  zobu (zho)

05 billy (goat)
  drake (duck)
  drone (honey bee)
  dsobo (zho)

06 gander (goose)
  musket (sparrowhawk)
  old man (kangaroo)
  ramcat (cat)
  tarcel (hawk)
  tarsal (hawk)
  tarsel (hawk)
  tassel (hawk)
  tercel (hawk)

07 tassell (hawk)

08 seecatch (Aleutian fur seal)
  stallion (horse)

09 blackcock (black grouse)

10 turkey cock (guinea fowl/turkey)

11 tassell-gent (peregrine falcon)

12 tassel-gentle (peregrine falcon)
  tercel-gentle (peregrine falcon)
  tercel-jerkin (gerfalcon)
  throstle-cock (song-thrush)

Female animals include:

03 cow (cattle/elephant/elk/whale)
  doe (antelope/deer/hare/kangaroo/rabbit)
  ewe (sheep)
  hen (chicken)
  pen (swan)
  ree (ruff)
  sow (pig/badger)

04 gill (ferret)
  hind (deer)
  jill (ferret)
  jomo (zho)
  mare (horse)

05 bitch (dog/fox/wolf)
  dsomo (zho)
  jenny (ass/donkey)
  nanny (goat)
  queen (cat)

  reeve (ruff)
  vixen (fox)
  zhomo (zho)

06 peahen (peacock)

07 greyhen (black grouse)
  lioness (lion)
  tigress (tiger)

08 water cow (water buffalo)

09 dolphinet (dolphin)
  guinea hen (guinea fowl)
  turkey hen (turkey)

10 leopardess (leopard)
  weasel coot (smew)

12 falcon-gentil (peregrine falcon)
  falcon-gentle (peregrine falcon)

Lairs, nests and homes of animals include:

03 den (bear/lion)
  nid (pheasant)
  pen (sheep)

  sty (pig)
04 bike (wasp/wild bee)
  bink (wasp/wild bee)

  byre (cow)
  cage (squirrel)
  coop (fowl)

drey (squirrel)
fold (sheep)
form (hare)
hive (bee)
hole (mouse)
holt (otter)
nest (bird/mouse/wasp)
sett (badger)

05 earth (fox)
eyrie (eagle)
lodge (beaver)
shell (snail)
06 burrow (rabbit)
warren (rabbit)
wurley (rat)
08 dovecote (pigeon)

fortress (mole)
vespiary (wasp)
09 formicary (ant)
11 formicarium (ant)
termitarium (termite)

Sounds made by animals include:

03 baa
bay
caw
coo
low
mew
moo
yap
04 bark
blat
bray
crow
hiss

hoot
howl
purr
roar
woof
yawp
yelp
yowl
05 bleat
cheep
chirp
cluck
croak

groin
growl
grunt
miaow
neigh
quack
snarl
tweet
06 bellow
cackle
gobble
heehaw
squawk

squeak
warble
whinny
07 chirrup
gruntle
screech
trumpet
twitter
whicker
09 caterwaul

Young animals include:

03 cub (bear/fox/lion/wolf)
elt (female pig)
fry (fish)
kid (antelope/goat)
kit (ferret/fox/polecat)
nit (louse)
04 brit (herring/sprat)
calf (cattle/elephant/whale)
colt (horse)
eyas (hawk)
fawn (deer)
foal (horse)
gilt (female pig)
grig (eel)
guga (gannet)
joey (kangaroo)
lamb (sheep)
maid (skate)
parr (salmon)
peal (sea trout)
peel (sea trout)
quey (cow)
sild (herring)
slip (pig)
yelt (female pig)
05 bunny (rabbit)
chick (chicken)
cuddy (coalfish)
elver (eel)
owlet (owl)

piper (pigeon)
poult (chicken)
puppy (dog/rat/seal)
scrod (cod/haddock)
shoat (pig)
shote (pig)
smolt (salmon)
sprod (salmon)
squab (chicken/pigeon/
rook)
steer (ox)
whelp (dog)
06 alevin (fish)
cuddie (coalfish)
cygnet (swan)
eaglet (eagle)
eirack (hen)
finnac (sea trout)
gimmer (female sheep)
grilse (salmon)
heifer (cow)
hidder (male sheep)
kid-fox (fox)
kitten (cat)
lionet (lion)
mattie (herring)
mousie (mouse)
peeper (bird)
piglet (pig)
podley (coalfish)

pullet (chicken)
samlet (salmon)
scaury (gull)
theave (female sheep)
weaner (pig)
07 bull-pup (bulldog)
cheeper (fowl)
cockney (snapper fish)
codling (cod)
eanling (sheep)
eelfare (eel)
finnack (sea trout)
finnock (sea trout)
gosling (goose)
herling (sea trout)
hirling (sea trout)
leveret (hare)
pigling (pig)
sardine (pilchard)
scourie (gull)
scowrie (gull)
sillock (coalfish)
skegger (salmon)
sounder (boar)
spitter (deer)
tadpole (frog/toad)
wolfkin (wolf)
08 brancher (hawk)
cockerel (cock)
duckling (duck)

goatling (goat)
grey-fish (coalfish)
hernshaw (heron)
heronsew (heron)
jackfish (pike)
moor-poot (grouse)
moor-pout (grouse)
mousekin (mouse)

muir-poot (grouse)
muir-pout (grouse)
nestling (bird)
pea-chick (peafowl)
pickerel (pike)
porkling (pig)
squeaker (bird)
squealer (pig/pigeon)

wolfling (wolf)
yeanling (goat/sheep)

09 calf whale (whale)
fledgling (bird)
heronshaw (heron)
whale calf (whale)

Terms to do with animals include:

03 ear	wild	gizzard	camouflage
egg	wing	habitat	digoneutic
eye	wool	migrate	epimeletic
fin	**05** chine	mimicry	gressorial
fur	crest	pallium	ovipositor
leg	fangs	pteryla	viviparous
paw	feral	segment	webbed feet
pet	moult	withers	**11** compound eye
04 beak	pouch	**08** apatetic	diphycercal
bill	scale	coupling	iteroparous
bite	shell	ditokous	lateral line
claw	snout	domestic	search image
coat	spine	forefoot	semelparous
crop	sting	forewing	swim bladder
dock	teeth	halteres	unguligrade
foot	trunk	hindfoot	waggle dance
gill	udder	hindwing	**12** dibranchiate
gula	venom	predator	etepimeletic
hair	**06** antler	shoulder	forked tongue
hoof	barrel	torquate	longicaudate
horn	dewlap	ungulate	longipennate
hump	forfex	whiskers	micropterous
jowl	jubate	**09** didelphic	**13** electric organ
loin	mantle	gastraeum	metamorphosis
mane	muzzle	marsupium	perissodactyl
mate	thorax	oviparous	semioviparous
nose	tongue	prehallux	solidungulate
prey	ungula	proboscis	solidungulous
ribs	**07** abdomen	pygostyle	synaposematic
rump	antenna	syndactyl	**14** startle colours
tail	feather	taligrade	**15** prehensile thumb
teat	flehmen	**10** alloparent	
tusk	flipper	aposematic	

See also **amphibian**; **ant**; **antelope**; **ape**; **bat**; **bear**; **beetle**; **bird**; **butterfly**; **calendar**; **carnivore**; **cat**; **cattle**; **chicken**; **crustacean**; **deer**; **dinosaur**; **disease**; **dog**; **duck**; **eel**; **falcon**; **farm**; **fish**; **fly**; **fur**; **game:** hunting; **goose**; **horse**; **hybrid**; **insect**; **invertebrate**; **jellyfish**; **lizard**; **mammal**; **marsupial**; **mollusc**; **monkey**; **moth**; **mythology**; **parasite**; **parrot**; **pet**; **pig**; **poison**; **poultry**; **primate**; **rabbit**; **reptile**; **rodent**; **ruminant**; **seal**; **shark**; **sheep**; **snake**; **spaniel**; **spider**; **swan**; **terrier**; **vermin**; **whale**; **worm**

anniversary

Wedding anniversaries:

03 fur (13th)	**04** gold (50th)	jade (35th)
tin (10th)	iron (6th)	lace (8th/13th)

ruby (40th)
silk (12th)
wood (5th/6th)
wool (7th)

05 china (2nd/20th)
coral (35th)
fruit (4th)
glass (3rd)
ivory (14th)
linen (8th/12th)
paper (1st)
pearl (12th/30th)
steel (11th)

See also **festival**; **religion**

sugar (6th)

06 bronze (8th)
clocks (1st)
copper (7th)
cotton (2nd)
silver (25th)
willow (9th)

07 crystal (3rd/15th)
diamond (30th/60th)
emerald (55th)
flowers (4th)
leather (3rd/9th)

pottery (8th/9th)
watches (15th)

08 desk sets (7th)
platinum (20th/70th)
sapphire (45th)
textiles (13th)

09 aluminium (10th)

10 appliances (4th)
silverware (5th)

13 gold jewellery (14th)

16 diamond jewellery (10th)
fashion jewellery (11th)

ant

Ants include:

03 red	**05** black	**07** bulldog	**09** black lawn
04 army	crazy	forager	carpenter
fire	**06** Amazon	pharaoh	harvester
leaf	driver	soldier	**10** leaf-cutter
wood	weaver	**08** honeydew	**12** red harvester

antelope

Antelopes include:

03 bok	oribi	**07** blaubok	steenbok
doe	sable	blesbok	tsessebe
gnu	saiga	bloubok	
kid	sasin	bubalis	**09** blackbuck
kob	serow	chamois	sitatunga
04 kudu	**06** bosbok	chikara	situtunga
oryx	dik-dik	gazelle	springbok
puku	duiker	gemsbok	steinbock
suni	duyker	gerenuk	tragelaph
thar	dzeren	grysbok	waterbuck
topi	impala	madoqua	**10** Alcelaphus
05 addax	inyala	nylghau	hartebeest
bubal	koodoo	sassaby	ox-antelope
chiru	lechwe	**08** Antilope	wildebeest
eland	nilgai	bontebok	**11** zebra duiker
goral	nilgau	boschbok	**12** goat-antelope
nagor	pygarg	bushbuck	klipspringer
nyala	reebok	palebuck	**13** sable antelope
		reedbuck	

anthropology

Anthropologists include:

04 Boas (Franz; 1858–1942, US)
Buck (Sir Peter; 1879–1951, New Zealand)
Mead (Margaret; 1901–78, US)

05 Tylor (Sir Edward; 1832–1917, English)

06 Frazer (Sir J G; 1854–1941, Scottish)
Leakey (Louis; 1903–72, Kenyan/British)
Marett (R R; 1866–1943, British)

07 Goodall (Jane; 1934–   , English)

Métraux (Albert; 1902–63, US)
09 Heyerdahl (Thor; 1914–2002, Norwegian)
10 Malinowski (Bronislaw; 1884–1942, Polish/British)

11 Lévi-Strauss (Claude; 1908–   , French)
14 Radcliffe-Brown (Alfred; 1881–1955, English)

antibiotic

Antibiotics include:

05 Cipro®
08 neomycin
nystatin
09 avoparcin
kanamycin
Neosporin®
polymyxin
quinolone
10 ampicillin
Aureomycin®

bacitracin
gramicidin
lincomycin
meticillin
penicillin
polymyxin B
rifampicin
Terramycin®
vancomycin
11 amoxicillin
amoxycillin

clindamycin
cloxacillin
cycloserine
doxorubicin
doxycycline
fusidic acid
methicillin
12 erythromycin
griseofulvin
streptomycin
tetracycline

trimethoprim
13 cephalosporin
ciprofloxacin
co-trimoxazole
metronidazole
spectinomycin
virginiamycin
15 chloramphenicol
oxytetracycline

antipope *see* **pope**

antique

Antiques terms include:

04 Goss
Ming
ring
T'ang
05 glaze
ivory
06 barock
dealer
empire
Gothic
lustre
patina
period
rococo
07 art deco

auction
barocco
baroque
ceramic
federal
impasto
opaline
pilgrim
pottery
Tiffany
08 filigree
Georgian
Jacobean
majolica
Sheraton

trecento
09 bone china
collector
Delftware
Edwardian
porcelain
Queen Anne
soft paste
stoneware
valuation
Victorian
10 art nouveau
millefiori
11 chinoiserie
Chippendale

cinquecento
haute époque
Hepplewhite
period piece
restoration
12 antiques fair
blanc de Chine
blue and white
reproduction
transitional
13 arts and crafts
willow pattern
15 churrigueresque

See also **furniture**

antiseptic

Antiseptics include:

03 TCP®
05 eupad
eusol
06 cresol
Dettol®
flavin
formol
phenol

Savlon®
thymol
07 benzoin
flavine
08 creasote
creosote
formalin
iodoform

09 cassareep
cassaripe
cetrimide
Germolene®
Listerine®
merbromin
zinc oxide
10 acriflavin

11 acriflavine
12 carbolic acid
   methyl violet
13 chlorhexidine
   crystal violet

flowers of zinc
gentian violet
silver nitrate
14 Dakin's solution
   rubbing alcohol

sodium benzoate
sodium chlorate
15 hexachlorophane
   hexachlorophene

ape

Apes include:

05 chimp
   orang
   pongo
06 bonobo
   gibbon
07 gorilla
09 orang-utan
10 chimpanzee
11 orang-outang
15 pygmy chimpanzee

See also **primate**

Apocrypha *see* Bible

apostle

Apostles of Jesus Christ:

04 John
05 James
   Judas
   Peter
   Simon
06 Andrew

Philip
Thomas
07 Matthew
08 Matthias
   Thaddeus
11 Bartholomew

13 Judas Iscariot
14 Simon the Zealot
15 James of Alphaeus
17 Simon the Canaanite

apparatus *see* laboratory

apple

Apple varieties include:

03 Cox
04 Cox's
   crab
   snow
05 eater
06 biffin
   codlin
   cooker
   eating
   idared

pippin
russet
07 Baldwin
   Bramley
   codling
   cooking
   costard
   crispin
   ribston
   Sturmer
   wine-sap

08 Braeburn
   Jonathan
   McIntosh
   pearmain
   Pink Lady
   queening
   ribstone
   sweeting
09 delicious
   jenneting
   king-apple

nonpareil
Royal gala
11 Granny Smith
   McIntosh red
   russet apple
12 Red Delicious
13 Ribston pippin
   Sturmer Pippin
15 Golden Delicious

See also **fruit**

appliance *see* domestic appliance

aquarium *see* fish

Arab League

Arab League members:

04 Iraq	**06** Jordan	Tunisia
Oman	Kuwait	**08** Djibouti
05 Egypt	**07** Algeria	**09** Palestine
Libya	Bahrain	**10** Mauritania
Qatar	Comoros	**11** Saudi Arabia
Sudan	Lebanon	**18** United Arab Emirates
Syria	Morocco	
Yemen	Somalia	

Arabic *see* **alphabet**

arable *see* **crop**

arachnid *see* **spider**

arch

Arches include:

04 keel	lancet	**08** inverted	**10** proscenium
ogee	Norman	recessed	shouldered
skew	safety	**09** Ctesiphon	**11** discharging
05 round	tented	horseshoe	equilateral
Tudor	**07** pointed	parabolic	four-centred
06 convex	squinch	relieving	**12** basket handle
corbel	stilted	segmental	three-centred
Gothic	trefoil	triumphal	

archaeology

Archaeologists include:

04 Uhle (Max; 1856–1944, German)

05 Aston (Michael; 1946– , English)
Clark (Grahame; 1907–95, English)
Evans (Sir Arthur; 1851–1941, English)

06 Anning (Mary; 1799–1847, English)
Breuil (Henri; 1877–1961, French)
Carter (Howard; 1874–1939, English)
Childe (Gordon; 1892–1957, Australian)
Clarke (David L; 1937–76, English)
Daniel (Glyn; 1914–86, Welsh)
Hawkes (Jacquetta; 1910–96, English)
Kenyon (Dame Kathleen; 1906–78, English)
Kidder (A V; 1885–1963, US)
Layard (Sir Austen; 1817–94, English)
Leakey (Louis; 1903–72, Kenyan/British)
Leakey (Mary; 1913–96, English)
Petrie (Sir Flinders; 1853–1942, English)
Putnam (Frederic Ward; 1839–1915, US)

07 Binford (Lewis; 1930– , US)

Renfrew (Colin, Lord; 1937– , English)
Thomsen (Christian; 1788–1865, Danish)
Wheeler (Sir Mortimer; 1890–1976, English)
Woolley (Sir Leonard; 1880–1960, English)
Worsaae (J J A; 1821–85, Danish)

08 Breasted (J H; 1865–1935, US)
Cunliffe (Barry; 1939– , English)
Fiorelli (Giuseppe; 1823–96, Italian)
Koldewey (Robert; 1855–1925, German)
Mallowan (Sir Max; 1904–78, English)
Mariette (Auguste; 1821–81, French)
Marshall (Sir John; 1876–1958, English)

09 Andersson (Johan Gunnar; 1874–1960, Swedish)

10 Pitt-Rivers (Augustus; 1827–1900, English)
Schliemann (Heinrich; 1822–90, German)

11 Champollion (Jean François; 1790–1832, French)

Terms used in archaeology include:

03 ard
cup
dig
DMV
DNA
jar
jug
SAM
tor
urn

04 adze
berm
bowl
celt
cist
core
dyke
grid
kist
rath
site
tell
term
work

05 agger
armil
auger
blade
burin
cairn
ditch
flake
flask
flint
fogou
henge
hoard
mound
mummy
quoit
shard
sherd
stele
whorl

06 barrow
Beaker
bogman
crater
cursus
dolmen
dromos

dugout
eolith
juglet
kurgan
menhir
midden
mosaic
patina
raggle
strata
syrinx
trench
vallum

07 amphora
anomaly
armilla
Azilian
cave art
crannog
cup mark
geofact
handaxe
horizon
Iron Age
logboat
lynchet
neolith
obelisk
papyrus
rock art
sondage
spindle
stratum
talayot
tumulus

08 artefact
artifact
capstone
carbon-14
Chellean
cistvaen
cromlech
dene-hole
excavate
grattoir
Halstatt
hill fort
kistvaen
knapping
ley lines
megalith

palmette
palstave
post hole
potshard
potshare
potsherd
ring fort
Stone Age
Strepyan
tranchet
typology

09 Acheulean
Acheulian
arrowhead
bracteate
Bronze Age
C14 dating
cartouche
Cro-Magnon
crop-marks
earthwork
enclosure
fieldwork
hut-circle
hypocaust
longhouse
microlith
Neolithic
palafitte
potboiler
shell heap
Solutrean
Solutrian

10 Anglo-Saxon
assemblage
burnt earth
Clactonian
cup-and-ring
excavation
fire-plough
geophysics
grave goods
Gravettian
hieroglyph
inhumation
loom weight
Madelenian
megalithic
Mesolithic
Middle Ages
Mousterian

Neandertal
palaeolith
petroglyph
roundhouse
shadow mark
skeuomorph
tear bottle
wheelhouse

11 Aurignacian
burial mound
cross-dating
horned cairn
Magdalenian
Maglemosian
Neanderthal
New Stone Age
Old Stone Age
Perigordian
Reindeer Age
rock shelter
shell midden
spacer plate
stone circle

12 amphitheatre
archaeometry
carbon dating
field walking
interglacial
lake dwelling
maiden castle
palaeobotany
Palaeolithic
stratigraphy
Tardenoisian

13 kitchen-midden
Neandertal Man
standing stone
treasure trove
vitrified fort
wattle and daub

14 archaeozoology
clearance cairn
conchoidal ring
diatom analysis
extended burial
hunter-gatherer
Neanderthal Man
pollen analysis

15 linear earthwork
occupation level

archbishop

Archbishops of Canterbury, with date of accession:

03 Oda (942)

04 Lang (Cosmo Gordon; 1928)
Laud (William; 1633)
Pole (Reginald; 1556)
Tait (Archibald; 1868)
Wake (William; 1716)

05 Abbot (George; 1611)
Carey (George; 1991)
Deane (Henry; 1501)
Grant (Richard le; 1229)
Islip (Simon; 1349)
Juxon (William; 1660)
Kempe (John; 1452)
Moore (John; 1783)

06 Anselm (1093)
Athelm (914)
Becket (Thomas à; 1162)
Benson (Edward; 1883)
Coggan (Donald; 1974)
Edmund (of Abingdon; 1234)
Fisher (Geoffrey; 1945)
Howley (William; 1828)
Hutton (Matthew; 1757)
Justus (624)
Lyfing (1013)
Morton (John; 1486)
Parker (Matthew; 1559)
Potter (John; 1737)
Ramsey (Michael; 1961)
Robert (of Jumieges; 1051)
Runcie (Robert; 1980)
Secker (Thomas; 1758)
Sumner (John; 1848)
Temple (Frederick; 1896)
Temple (William; 1942)
Walden (Roger; 1398)
Walter (Hubert; 1193)
Warham (William; 1503)

07 Aelfric (995)
Alphege (1005)
Arundel (Thomas; 1396/1399)
Baldwin (1184)
Corbeil (William de; 1123)
Cranmer (Thomas; 1533)
Dunstan (960)
Eadsige (1038)
Grindal (Edmund; 1576)
Herring (Thomas; 1747)
Langham (Simon; 1366)
Langton (Stephen; 1207)
Longley (Charles; 1862)
Meopham (Simon; 1328)

Nothelm (735)
Peckham (John; 1279)
Richard (of Dover; 1174)
Sheldon (Gilbert; 1663)
Sigeric (990)
Stigand (1052)
Sudbury (Simon; 1375)
Tatwine (731)
Tenison (Thomas; 1695)
Wulfred (805)

08 Aelfsige (959)
Bancroft (Richard; 1604)
Boniface (of Savoy; 1245)
Brithelm (959)
Ceolnoth (833)
Chichele (Henry; 1414)
Cuthbert (740)
Davidson (Randall; 1903)
d'Escures (Ralph; 1114)
Ethelgar (c.988)
Ethelred (870)
Honorius (627)
Jaenbert (765)
Lanfranc (1070)
Mellitus (619)
Plegmund (890)
Reynolds (Walter; 1313)
Sancroft (William; 1678)
Stafford (John; 1443)
Theobald (1139)
Theodore (668)
Whitgift (John; 1583)
Williams (Rowan; 2002)
Wulfhelm (923)

09 Augustine (597)
Berhtwald (693)
Bourchier (Thomas; 1454)
Bregowine (761)
Courtenay (William; 1381)
Deusdedit (655)
Ethelhard (793)
Ethelnoth (1020)
Feologeld (832)
Kilwardby (Robert; 1273)
Stratford (John de; 1333)
Tillotson (John; 1691)

10 Cornwallis (Frederick; 1768)
Laurentius (604)
Whittlesey (William; 1368)
Winchelsey (Robert; 1294)

11 Bradwardine (Thomas; 1349)

13 Manners-Sutton (Charles; 1805)

Archbishops of York, with date of accession:

03 Lee (Edward; 1531)

04 Bosa (678)
Chad (644)
Grey (Walter de; 1215)
Hope (David; 1995)
John (of Thoresby; 1352)
John (St, of Beverley; 705)
Lang (Cosmo Gordon; 1908)

05 Booth (Lawrence; 1476)
Booth (William; 1452)
Bowet (Henry; 1407)
Dawes (Sir William; 1714)
Heath (Nicholas; 1555)
Henry (of Newark; 1298)
Kempe (John; 1425)
Magee (William Connor; 1890)
Neile (Richard; 1632)
Piers (John; 1589)
Roger (of Pont-L'Eveque; 1154)
Scott (Thomas; 1480)
Sharp (John; 1691)
Young (Thomas; 1561)

06 Blanch (Stuart; 1975)
Bovill (Sewal de; 1256)
Ceadda (644)
Coggan (Donald; 1961)
Dolben (John; 1683)
Edwald (971)
Egbert (735)
Frewen (Accepted; 1660)
Gerard (1101)
Hutton (Matthew; 1595)
Hutton (Matthew; 1747)
Oswald (972)
Puttoc (Aelfric; 1023)
Ramsey (Michael; 1956)
Romeyn (John le; 1286)
Sandys (Edwin; 1577)
Savage (Thomas; 1501)
Scrope (Richard le; 1398)
Sterne (Richard; 1664)
Temple (William; 1929)
Thomas (I; 1070)
Thomas (II; 1109)
Thomas (of Corbridge; 1300)
Waldby (Robert; 1396)
Wolsey (Thomas; 1514)
Zouche (William le; 1342)

07 Arundel (Thomas; 1388)
Ealdred (1061)
Ealdulf (992)
Eanbald (I; 780)

Eanbald (II; 796)
Garbett (Cyril; 1942)
Giffard (Walter; 1265)
Gilbert (John; 1757)
Godfrey (of Kineton; 1258)
Godfrey (of Ludham; 1258)
Grindal (Edmund; 1570)
Habgood (John; 1983)
Herring (Thomas; 1743)
Holgate (Robert; 1545)
Longley (Charles; 1860)
Markham (William; 1777)
Matthew (Tobias; 1606)
Neville (Alexander; 1374)
Neville (George; 1465)
Oskytel (958)
Romanus (1286)
Sentamu (John; 2005)
Thomson (William; 1862)
Wigmund (837)
Wilfrid (I; 669)
Wilfrid (II; 718)
William (of Melton; 1317)

08 Cynesige (1051)
Drummond (Robert; 1761)
Harcourt (Edward Vernon; 1807)
Harsnett (Samuel; 1628)
Lamplugh (Thomas; 1688)
Lodeward (904)
Maclagan (William; 1891)
Musgrave (Thomas; 1847)
Paulinus (627)
Rotheram (Thomas; 1480)
Thurstan (1119)
Wickwane (William; 1279)
Williams (John; 1641)
Wulfhere (854)
Wulfsige (808)
Wulfstan (I; 931)
Wulfstan (II; 1003)

09 Ethelbald (900)
Ethelbert (767)
Ethelwold (971)
Monteigne (George; 1628)

10 Bainbridge (Christopher; 1508)
Blackburne (Lancelot; 1724)
Greenfield (William; 1306)

11 Fitzherbert (Henry; 1147)
Fitzherbert (William; 1143)
Hrotheweard (904)
Plantagenet (Geoffrey; 1181)

Other archbishops, with date of accession include:

04 Gray (Gordon; 1951)
Hume (Basil; 1976)
Tutu (Desmond; 1986)

05 Beran (Josef; 1946)
Glemp (Jozef; 1981)

06 Beaton (David; 1539)
Heenan (John Carmel; 1963)
Hilary (St; c.350)
Mannix (Daniel; 1917)

Trench (Richard Chenevix; 1864)
Ussher (James; 1625)

07 Mendoza (Pedro Gonzalez de; 1474)
Wiseman (Nicholas; 1850)

08 Adalbert (1043)
Makarios (1948)

10 Damaskinos (Dimitrios Papandreou; 1938)
Huddleston (Trevor; 1978)

archdiocese *see* diocese

archery

Archery types include:

03 run ski	**05** clout field	**06** flight target

Archery terms include:

03 bow
end

04 back
bolt
boss
butt
face
fast
FITA
grip
limb
nock
pile

05 arrow
belly
cable
inner
notch
outer
point
riser
rover
scope
shaft

sight
wheel

06 anchor
archer
bowman
bracer
flight
handle
magpie
quiver
string
target
upshot

07 barebow
bow-hand
bowshot
longbow
nocking
release

08 armguard
bull's-eye
crossbow
draw hand

limb bolt

09 arrowhead
arrow rest
bowstring
finger tab
fletching
lower limb
upper limb

10 cable guard
classic bow
draw weight
recurve bow
stabilizer
target face

11 cock feather
compound bow
shooting peg

12 nocking point
shooting line

14 instinctive bow
marked distance
tensioning wire

15 mounting bracket

archipelago

Archipelagoes include:

04 Cuba (Caribbean Sea)
Fiji (South Pacific)
Sulu (South China Sea/Pacific Ocean)

05 Åland (Baltic Sea)
Gulag (USSR)

Japan (Pacific Ocean)
Malay (Indian Ocean/Pacific Ocean)
Malta (Mediterranean Sea)
Tonga (Pacific Ocean)

06 Arctic (Arctic Ocean)

Azores (Atlantic Ocean)
Chagos (Indian Ocean)
Kosrae (Pacific Ocean)
Tuvalu (Pacific Ocean)

07 Iles d'Or (Mediterranean Sea)
Mayotte (Indian Ocean)
Tuamotu (Pacific Ocean)

08 Bismarck (Papua New Guinea/Pacific
Ocean)
Cyclades (Aegean Sea)
Kiribati (Pacific Ocean)
Maldives (Indian Ocean)
Moluccas (Pacific Ocean)
Svalbard (Arctic Ocean)

09 Alexander (Alaska/Pacific Ocean)
Antarctic (Southern Ocean)
Cape Verde (Atlantic Ocean)
Catherine (Alaska/Pacific Ocean)
Galápagos (Pacific Ocean)
Indonesia (Indian Ocean/Pacific Ocean)
Louisiade (Solomon Sea/Coral Sea)
Marquesas (Pacific Ocean)
North Land (Arctic Ocean)

10 Ahvenanmaa (Baltic Sea)
Seychelles (Indian Ocean)
The Bahamas (Caribbean Sea)
Vesterålen (Norwegian Sea/Arctic Ocean)
West Indies (Caribbean Sea)

11 Iles d'Hyères (Mediterranean Sea)
Line Islands (Pacific Ocean)
Philippines (Pacific Ocean)
Spitsbergen (Arctic Ocean)
Vesteraalen (Norwegian Sea/Arctic Ocean)

12 Kuril Islands (Pacific Ocean)
Novaya Zemlya (Kara Sea/Arctic Ocean)

See also **island**

Pearl Islands (Indian Ocean)
Spice Islands (Pacific Ocean)
Sunda Islands (Celebes Sea/South China Sea)

13 Aegean Islands (Aegean Sea)
Caicos Islands (Atlantic Ocean)
Canary Islands (Atlantic Ocean)
Ellice Islands (Atlantic Ocean)
Ionian Islands (Ionian Sea)
Tubuai Islands (Pacific Ocean)

14 Austral Islands (South Pacific)
Bijagos Islands (Guinea-Bissau/Atlantic
Ocean)
Channel Islands (English Channel)
Franz Josef Land (Arctic Ocean)
Gilbert Islands (Pacific Ocean)
Leeward Islands (Caribbean Sea/Atlantic
Ocean)
Lofoten Islands (Arctic Ocean)
Nicholas II Land (Arctic Ocean)
Oki Archipelago (Sea of Japan)
Papua New Guinea (Pacific Ocean)
Phoenix Islands (Pacific Ocean)
Solomon Islands (Solomon Sea/Pacific
Ocean)
Tierra del Fuego (Atlantic Ocean/Pacific
Ocean/Southern Ocean)
Visayan Islands (Visayan Sea/South China
Sea)

15 Balearic Islands (Mediterranean Sea)
Friendly Islands (South Pacific)
Marshall Islands (Pacific Ocean)
Pitcairn Islands (Pacific Ocean)
Severnaya Zemlya (Arctic Ocean)
Wallis and Futuna (South Pacific)
Windward Islands (Caribbean Sea)

architecture

Architectural features include:

03 orb	neck	hance	torus
web	ogee	helix	tower
04 anta	ribs	mould	truss
apse	vase	nerve	vault
arch	void	ogive	**06** abacus
base	**05** antae	print	atrium
bell	attic	pylon	canton
boss	congé	quirk	caulis
cove	crown	scape	chevet
crop	flute	socle	cinque
cusp	gable	spire	cippus
cyma	gavel	stria	column
dado	glyph	talon	concha
drum	groin	tenia	congee
list	gutta	tondo	coping

corbel
corona
coving
crenel
dentil
façade
fascia
fillet
finial
flèche
fornix
frieze
haunch
impost
lierne
metope
patera
patten
pillar
podium
portal
reglet
regula
rosace
scotia
severy
striae
taenia
turret
wreath

07 aileron
annulet
balloon
bandrol
capital
cavetti
cavetto
conchae
corbeil
cornice
crocket
diglyph

doucine
echinus
fantail
festoon
fronton
fusarol
grecque
larmier
mullion
necking
nervure
pannier
parapet
Persian
pilotis
portico
rosette
solidum
squinch
surbase
tambour
telamon
tondino

08 abutment
accolade
apophyge
astragal
baguette
bandelet
banderol
bannerol
bellcote
buttress
canephor
cartouch
chapiter
chaptrel
ciborium
cincture
crenelle
diastyle
dipteral

dipteros
entresol
epistyle
frontoon
fusarole
gorgerin
imperial
intrados
mascaron
moulding
pediment
pilaster
prostyle
pulpitum
rockwork
sept-foil
skewback
spandrel
spandril
terminus
triglyph
tympanum
voussoir

09 apsidiole
archivolt
balection
banderole
bolection
cartouche
crossette
cul-de-four
decastyle
embrasure
embrazure
foliation
guilloche
hypostyle
mezzanine
modillion
octastyle
octostyle
peristyle

strap work
stylobate
tierceron
triforium
water leaf

10 acroterion
architrave
ball-flower
bratticing
cauliculus
chambranle
clearstory
clerestory
demicupola
ditriglyph
egg-and-dart
eye-catcher
feathering
jerkinhead
pendentive
quatrefoil
subarcuate
water table
weathering

11 brattishing
entablature
paternoster

12 egg-and-anchor
egg-and-tongue
frontispiece

13 chain moulding
Ctesiphon arch
interpilaster
quatrefeuille
vermiculation

14 Catherine-wheel
flying buttress
shouldered arch

Architectural styles include:

04 Adam
05 Greek
Saxon
06 Gothic
Norman
rococo
07 art deco
barocco

baroque
Italian
Lombard
mission
mudéjar
08 baronial
high tech
09 beaux arts

brutalism
Byzantine
Cape Dutch
decorated
Palladian
Queen Anne
10 art nouveau
Corinthian
Romanesque

11 Elizabethan
Renaissance
13 Gothic revival
international
neoclassicism
Perpendicular
post-modernism
15 churrigueresque

Architects include:

03 Ito (Toyo; 1941– , Japanese)
Lin (Maya; 1959– , US)
Oud (J J P; 1890–1963, Dutch)
Pei (I M; 1917– , US)

04 Adam (James; 1730–94, Scottish)
Adam (Robert; 1728–92, Scottish)
Adam (William; 1689–1748, Scottish)
Ando (Tadao; 1941– , Japanese)
Burn (William; 1789–1870, Scottish)
Drew (Dame Jane; 1911–96, English)
Hood (Raymond M; 1881–1934, US)
Hunt (Richard Morris; 1827–95, US)
Jahn (Helmut; 1940– , US)
Kahn (Louis I; 1901–74, US)
Kent (William; 1684–1748, English)
Loos (Adolf; 1870–1933, Austrian)
Nash (John; 1752–1835, English)
Otto (Frei; 1925– , German)
Shaw (Norman; 1831–1912, English)
Webb (Philip; 1831–1915, English)
Webb (Sir Aston; 1849–1930, English)
Wood (John; 1728–82, English)
Wood (John, the Elder; c.1705–54, English)
Wren (Sir Christopher; 1632–1723, English)

05 Aalto (Alvar; 1898–1976, Finnish)
Alsop (Will; 1947– , English)
Baker (Sir Herbert; 1862–1946, English)
Barry (Sir Charles; 1795–1860, English)
Bryce (David; 1803–76, Scottish)
Costa (Lucio; 1902–98, French/Brazilian)
Dance (George; 1700–68, Fnglish)
Dance (George; 1741–1825, English)
Doshi (Balkrishna; 1927– , Indian)
Dudok (Willem; 1884–1974, Dutch)
Engel (Carl Ludwig; 1778–1840, German/
Finnish)
Gaudí (Antoni; 1852–1926, Spanish)
Gehry (Frank; 1929– , Canadian/US)
Gibbs (James; 1682–1754, Scottish)
Gilly (Friedrich; 1772–1800, German)
Hadid (Zaha; 1950– , Iraqi)
Horta (Victor, Baron; 1861–1947, Belgian)
Jones (Inigo; 1573–1652, English)
Levau (Louis; 1612–70, French)
Mayne (Thom; 1944– , US)
McKim (Charles; 1847–1909, US)
Meier (Richard; 1934– , US)
Mills (Robert; 1781–1855, US)
Moore (Charles; 1925–93, US)
Nervi (Pier Luigi; 1891–1979, Italian)
Pelli (César; 1926– , US)
Piano (Renzo; 1937– , Italian)
Pugin (Augustus; 1812–52, English)
Rocha (Paulo Mendes da; 1928– ,
Brazilian)
Scott (M H Baillie; 1865–1945, English)

Scott (Sir George Gilbert; 1811–78, English)
Scott (Sir Giles Gilbert; 1880–1960, English)
Soane (Sir John; 1753–1837, English)
Speer (Albert; 1905–81, German)
Stern (Robert A M; 1939– , US)
Tange (Kenzo; 1913–2005, Japanese)
Utzon (Jørn; 1918– , Danish)
Velde (Henri van de; 1863–1957, Belgian)
Wyatt (James; 1746–1813, English)
Yeang (Ken; 1948– , Malaysian)

06 Breuer (Marcel; 1902–81, Hungarian/US)
Burton (Decimus; 1800–81, English)
Campen (Jacob van; 1595–1657, Dutch)
Casson (Sir Hugh; 1910–99, English)
Coates (Wells; 1895–1958, English)
Foster (Norman, Lord; 1935– , English)
Fowler (Sir Michael; 1929– , New
Zealand)
Fuller (Buckminster; 1895–1983, US)
Geddes (Norman Bel; 1893–1958, US)
Geddes (Sir Patrick; 1854–1932, Scottish)
Giotto (c.1267–1337, Italian)
Graves (Michael; 1934– , US)
Howard (Sir Ebenezer; 1850–1928, English)
Keyser (Hendrik de; 1565–1621, Dutch)
Lasdun (Sir Denys; 1914–2001, English)
Ledoux (Claude Nicolas; 1736–1806,
French)
Lescot (Pierre; c.1510–78, French)
Nouvel (Jean; 1945– , French)
Paxton (Sir Joseph; 1801–65, English)
Perret (Auguste; 1874–1954, French)
Pisano (Giovanni; c.1250–c.1320, Italian)
Pisano (Nicola; c.1225–c.1284, Italian)
Rogers (Richard, Lord; 1933– , English)
Safdie (Moshe; 1938– , Israeli/Canadian)
Serlio (Sebastiano; 1475–1554, Italian)
Smirke (Sir Robert; 1781–1867, English)
Spence (Sir Basil; 1907–76, Scottish)
Street (G E; 1824–81, English)
Stuart (James; 1713–88, English)
Tessin (Nicodemus the Elder; 1615–81,
Swedish)
Tessin (Nicodemus the Younger; 1654–1728,
Swedish)
Voysey (Charles; 1857–1941, English)
Wagner (Otto; 1841–1918, Austrian)
Wright (Frank Lloyd; 1867–1959, US)

07 Alberti (Leon Battista; 1404–72, Italian)
Asplund (Erik Gunnar; 1885–1940, Swedish)
Behrens (Peter; 1868–1940, German)
Berlage (H P; 1856–1934, Dutch)
Bernini (Gian Lorenzo; 1598–1680, Italian)
Bethune (Louise; 1856–1913, US)
Burnham (Daniel; 1846–1912, US)
Candela (Felix; 1910–97, Mexican)

Delorme (Philibert; c.1510–70, French)
Gabriel (Jacques-Ange; 1698–1782, French)
Garnier (Tony; 1869–1948, French)
Gilbert (Cass; 1859–1934, US)
Gropius (Walter; 1883–1969, US)
Guarini (Guarino; 1624–83, Italian)
Guimard (Hector; 1867–1942, French)
Holland (Henry; 1746–1806, English)
Ictinus (5cBC, Greek)
Imhotep (27cBC; Egyptian)
Johnson (Philip; 1906–2005, US)
L'Enfant (Pierre Charles; 1754–1825, US)
Lethaby (William; 1857–1931, English)
Lorimer (Sir Robert; 1864–1929, Scottish)
Lutyens (Sir Edwin; 1869–1944, English)
Maderna (Carlo; 1556–1629, Italian)
Maderno (Carlo; 1556–1629, Italian)
Mansard (François; 1598–1666, French)
Mansard (Jules; 1645–1708, French)
Mansart (François; 1598–1666, French)
Mansart (Jules; 1645–1708, French)
Neumann (Balthasar; 1687–1753,
  German)
Orcagna (c.1308–68, Italian)
Peruzzi (Baldassare; 1481–1536, Italian)
Poelzig (Hans; 1869–1936, German)
Renwick (James; 1818–95, US)
Thomson (Alexander 'Greek'; 1817–75,
  Scottish)
Venturi (Robert; 1925– , US)
Vignola (Giacomo da; 1507–73, Italian)

08 Bramante (Donato; 1444–1514, Italian)
Chambers (Sir William; 1726–96, Scottish)
Cullinan (Edward; 1931– , English)
Eisenman (Peter; 1932– , US)
Erickson (Arthur; 1924– , Canadian)
Figueroa (Leonardo de; c.1650–1730,
  Spanish)
Gwathmey (Charles; 1938– , US)
Hamilton (Thomas; 1784–1858, Scottish)
Hoffmann (Josef; 1870–1956, Austrian)
Jacobsen (Arne; 1902–71, Danish)
Leonardo (da Vinci; 1452–1519, Italian)
Lombardo (Pietro; c.1433–1515, Italian)
Makovecz (Imre; 1935– , Hungarian)
Miralles (Enric, 1955–2000, Spanish)
Niemeyer (Oscar; 1907– , Brazilian)
Palladio (Andrea; 1508–80, Italian)
Piranesi (Giambattista; 1720–78, Italian)
Playfair (William Henry; 1789–1857,
  Scottish)
Rietveld (Gerrit; 1888–1964, Dutch)

Saarinen (Eero; 1910–61, Finnish/US)
Saarinen (Eliel; 1873–1950, Finnish/US)
Schinkel (Karl Friedrich; 1781–1841,
  German)
Smythson (Robert; c.1535–1614, English)
Sottsass (Ettore, Jnr; 1917–2007, Italian)
Soufflot (Jacques Germain; 1709–80,
  French)
Stirling (James; 1926–92, Scottish)
Sullivan (Louis; 1856–1924, US)
Vanbrugh (Sir John; 1664–1726, English)

09 Blomfield (Sir Reginald; 1856–1942,
  English)
Borromini (Francesco; 1599–1667, Italian)
Chowdhury (Eulie; 1923– , Indian)
Cockerell (Charles Robert; 1788–1863,
  English)
Haussmann (Georges, Baron; 1809–91,
  French)
Hawksmoor (Nicholas; 1661–1736, English)
Labrouste (Henri; 1801–75, French)
Libeskind (Daniel; 1946– , US)
Mackmurdo (Arthur; 1851–1942, English)
Sansovino (1460–1529, Italian)
Sansovino (Jacopo; 1486–1570, Italian)
Vitruvius (1cAD, Roman)

10 Andronicus (1cBC, Greek)
Chermayeff (Serge; 1900–96, Russian/US)
Cyrrhestes (1cBC, Greek)
Darbyshire (Jane; 1948– , English)
Mackintosh (Charles Rennie; 1868–1928,
  Scottish)
Mendelsohn (Erich; 1887–1953, US)
Michelozzi (Michelozzo; 1396–1472,
  Italian)
Sanmichele (Michele; c.1484–1559, Italian)
Waterhouse (Alfred; 1830–1905, English)

11 Abercrombie (Sir Patrick; 1879–1957,
  English)
Butterfield (William; 1814–1900, English)
Callicrates (5cBC, Greek)
Churriguera (Don José; 1650–1725, Spanish)
Hertzberger (Herman; 1932– , Dutch)
Le Corbusier (1887–1965, French)

12 Brunelleschi (Filippo; 1377–1446, Italian)
Viollet-Le-Duc (Eugène; 1814–79, French)

14 Mies van der Rohe (Ludwig; 1886–1969,
  US)

15 Leonardo da Vinci (1452–1519, Italian)
Vitruvius Pollio (Marcus; 1cAD, Roman)

Terms used in architecture and building include:

03 CAD	jamb	**05** Doric	groin
04 dado	plan	eaves	Ionic
dome	roof	gable	model

ridge
Tudor
06 alcove
annexe
coving
dormer
duplex
façade
fascia
fillet
finial
frieze
Gothic
lintel
Norman
pagoda
plinth
reveal

rococo
scroll
soffit
stucco
Tuscan
07 baroque
cornice
festoon
fletton
fluting
mullion
pantile
parapet
rafters
Regency
rotunda
08 baluster
capstone

dogtooth
dry-stone
fanlight
gargoyle
Georgian
pinnacle
sacristy
terrazzo
wainscot
09 bas relief
classical
decorated
Edwardian
elevation
gatehouse
Queen Anne
roughcast
10 architrave

barge-board
Corinthian
drawbridge
flamboyant
groundplan
Romanesque
weathering
11 coping stone
cornerstone
Elizabethan
Flemish bond
12 Early English
French window
frontispiece
half-timbered
13 double glazing
14 casement window

See also **building**

area *see* **administrative area**

armour

Armour includes:

04 cush
gear
gere
jack
lame
mail
suit
tace
05 armet
brace
cuish
culet
curat
salet
tasse
visor
06 beaver
byrnie
casque
corium
couter
crinet
cuisse
curiet
faulds
gorget
greave
grille

gusset
helmet
jamber
morion
poleyn
rondel
salade
sallet
shield
taslet
tasset
tonlet
tuille
voider
07 ailette
barding
basinet
besagew
brasset
buckler
cap-à-pie
corslet
cuirass
harness
hauberk
jambeau
jambeux
jambier
lamboys

morrion
palette
placcat
placket
poitrel
puldron
sabaton
surcoat
ventail
08 aventail
bascinet
brassard
brassart
chaffron
chamfron
chausses
corselet
gauntlet
giambeux
jambeaux
jazerant
pauldron
pectoral
placcate
pouldron
shynbald
solleret
spaulder
vambrace

ventaile
ventayle
09 aventaile
backpiece
backplate
chain mail
chamfrain
garniture
habergeon
jesserant
mandilion
mandylion
nosepiece
rerebrace
vantbrace
vantbrass
10 body armour
cataphract
coat-armour
coat of mail
11 breastplate
genouillère
mentonnière
plate armour
scale armour
12 splint armour

army

Armies include:

02 AA	Red	05 Sally	Salvation
SA	USA	06 Church	10 Blue Ribbon
TA	WLA	Tartan	Women's Land
03 AVR		08 New Model	11 Grande Armée
GAR	04 BAOR	09 Eurocorps	Territorial
IRA	INLA		

See also **military**; **regiment**

art

Arts and crafts include:

04 film	08 ceramics	sculpture	psaligraphy
05 batik	graphics	sketching	stitchcraft
video	knitting	woodcraft	watercolour
06 fresco	painting	10 basketwork	woodcarving
mosaic	pencraft	caricature	wood cutting
saikei	spinning	embroidery	12 animatronics
07 carving	tapestry	enamelling	architecture
collage	tsutsumu	needlework	chalcography
crochet	09 animation	xylography	illustration
drawing	cloisonné	11 calligraphy	stained glass
etching	engraving	lithography	13 digital design
ikebana	jewellery	needlecraft	graphic design
origami	marquetry	oil painting	wood engraving
pottery	metalwork	photography	14 relief printing
weaving	modelling	portraiture	screenprinting
	patchwork		

Schools, movements and styles of art include:

02 Op	netPop	Futurism	10 arte povera
03 mec	Purism	graffiti	Automatism
PRB	Rayism	informel	bande noire
YBA	Rococo	Intimism	Biomorphic
04 BMPT	07 Baroque	Japonism	Classicism
Brit	Bauhaus	kakemono	Conceptual
Brut	Dadaism	Luminism	Literalism
Dada	digital	OuPeinPo	Minimalism
Deco	Fauvism	Pont-Aven	Naturalism
funk	Kinetic	Rayonism	New Realism
Madí	New York	Tachisme	Romanesque
Merz	Nouveau	Venetian	Section d'Or
Nabi	Optical	09 Die Brücke	Surrealism
05 Cobra	Orphism	Encaustic	troubadour
Hague	Plastic	Formalism	11 anacronismo
Lyons	Realism	Intimisme	bad painting
Mosan	Tachism	Mannerism	Blaue Reiter
Naïve	08 Abstract	Modernism	Caravaggism
video	Atticism	Nazarenes	Divisionism
Zebra	Barbizon	Rubénisme	Eclecticism
06 Cubism	Concrete	Symbolism	Glasgow Boys
fluxus	Feminist	Tenebrism	Macchiaioli
		Vorticism	Orientalism

Pointillism	Hyperrealism	second empire	Social Realism
Primitivism	Magic Realism	Superrealism	**14** Action Painting
Renaissance	Mir Iskusstva	**13** Arts and Crafts	Constructivism
Romanticism	non-figuratif	Expressionism	Post-Minimalism
spazialismo	Non-objective	Impressionism	Pre-Raphaelites
Suprematism	Photorealism	Neoclassicism	**15** Camden Town
Synchronism	pittura colta	Neo-Plasticism	Group
12 Aestheticism	Quattrocento	Post-Modernism	nouveau réalisme

Artists, craftsmen and craftswomen include:

05 video	designer	**10** blacksmith	portraitist
06 etcher	engraver	cartoonist	silversmith
limner	graffiti	conceptual	web designer
master	pavement	oil painter	**12** caricaturist
potter	sculptor	**11** coppersmith	lithographer
weaver	**09** architect	craftswoman	photographer
07 graphic	carpenter	draughtsman	**13** draughtswoman
painter	colourist	illustrator	screenprinter
printer	craftsman	miniaturist	**14** watercolourist
08 animator	goldsmith	performance	**15** graphic designer

Art materials and art terms include:

03 ink	fusain	torchon	stretcher
04 term	pastel	**08** abstract	**10** delineavit
wash	pencil	alfresco	from nature
05 cameo	relief	charcoal	paintbrush
easel	sketch	gumption	sketchbook
fitch	tusche	intaglio	turpentine
liner	**07** atelier	monotint	**11** perspective
sable	cartoon	paintbox	trompe l'oeil
smock	digital	pastille	wash drawing
turps	grainer	terminus	**12** installation
video	modello	**09** lay-figure	underdrawing
06 badger	organic	maulstick	**13** social realism
crayon	palette	pen and ink	**15** oil of turpentine
	scumble		

See also **cartoon**; **Japan**; **paint**; **photography**

artery

Arteries include:

05 aorta (heart)	hepatic (liver)	**10** innominate (neck)
renal (kidney)	splenic (spleen)	mesenteric (gut)
ulnar (arm)	**08** brachial (arm)	subclavian (upper body)
06 radial (arm)	coronary (heart)	**11** common iliac (groin)
07 carotid (neck)	**09** popliteal (leg)	**14** anterior tibial (leg)
coeliac (gut)	pulmonary (lung)	**15** brachiocephalic (neck)
femoral (thigh)	spermatic (testes)	posterior tibial (leg)

See also **vein**

Arthurian legend *see* **legend**

Asia

Countries in Asia include:

04 Laos	Vietnam	**09** East Timor	Tajikistan
05 China	**08** Cambodia	Indonesia	Uzbekistan
India	Malaysia	Singapore	**11** Afghanistan
Japan	Maldives	**10** Bangladesh	Philippines
Nepal	Mongolia	Kazakhstan	**12** Turkmenistan
06 Bhutan	Pakistan	Kyrgyzstan	
Taiwan	Sri Lanka	North Korea	
07 Myanmar	Thailand	South Korea	

Cities and notable towns in Asia include:

03 Osh (Kyrgyzstan)

04 Agra (India)
Baku (Azerbaijan)
Gifu (Japan)
Jixi (China)
Kobe (Japan)
Kota (India)
Kure (Japan)
Mary (Turkmenistan)
Naha (Japan)
Nara (Japan)
Oita (Japan)
Wuhu (China)
Wuxi (China)
Xian (China)
Zibo (China)

05 Adana (Turkey)
Ajmer (India)
Akita (Japan)
Baoji (China)
Benxi (China)
Bursa (Turkey)
Chiba (Japan)
Delhi (India)
Dhaka (Bangladesh)
Dukou (China)
Fukui (Japan)
Fuxin (China)
Gäncä (Azerbaijan)
Haeju (North Korea)
Hefei (China)
Herat (Afghanistan)
Hubli (India)
Iwaki (Japan)
Izmir (Turkey)
Jilin (China)
Jinan (China)
Kabul (Afghanistan)
Kandy (Sri Lanka)
Kochi (Japan)
Konya (Turkey)
Kyoto (Japan)

Masan (South Korea)
Nampo (North Korea)
Omiya (Japan)
Osaka (Japan)
Patan (Nepal)
Patna (India)
Poona (India)
Pusan (South Korea)
Sakai (Japan)
Semey (Kazakhstan)
Seoul (South Korea)
Surat (India)
Suwon (South Korea)
Taegu (South Korea)
Taraz (Kazakhstan)
Tokyo (Japan)
Ulsan (South Korea)
Urawa (Japan)
Wuhan (China)

06 Almaty (Kazakhstan)
Ankara (Turkey)
Anshan (China)
Anyang (China)
Aqtöbe (Kazakhstan)
Astana (Kazakhstan)
Baotou (China)
Batumi (Georgia)
Bhopal (India)
Cochin (India)
Dalian (China)
Daqing (China)
Datong (China)
Fushun (China)
Fuzhou (China)
Guilin (China)
Guntur (India)
Gyumri (Armenia)
Handan (China)
Harbin (China)
Hegang (China)
Himeji (Japan)
Hohhot (China)

Howrah (India)
Inchon (South Korea)
Indore (India)
Jaffna (Sri Lanka)
Jaipur (India)
Kanpur (India)
Khulna (Bangladesh)
Kulyab (Tajikistan)
Lahore (Pakistan)
Leshan (China)
Meerut (India)
Multan (Pakistan)
Mumbai (India)
Mysore (India)
Nagano (Japan)
Nagoya (Japan)
Nagpur (India)
Ningbo (China)
Quetta (Pakistan)
Raipur (India)
Rajkot (India)
Ranchi (India)
Sendai (Japan)
Sukkur (Pakistan)
Suzhou (China)
Taejon (South Korea)
Tainan (Taiwan)
T'aipei (Taiwan)
Toyama (Japan)
Urumqi (China)
Wonsan (North Korea)
Xiamen (China)
Xining (China)
Xuzhou (China)
Yantai (China)
Yichun (China)
Zigong (China)

07 Aligarh (India)
Andijon (Uzbekistan)
Asansol (India)
Baoding (China)
Beijing (China)

Bishkek (Kyrgyzstan)
Bukhara (Uzbekistan)
Chengdu (China)
Chennai (India)
Chifeng (China)
Chilung (Taiwan)
Chungho (Taiwan)
Colombo (Sri Lanka)
Dandong (China)
Fukuoka (Japan)
Ganzhou (China)
Guiyang (China)
Gwalior (India)
Hamhung (North Korea)
Huaibei (China)
Huainan (China)
Jessore (Bangladesh)
Jiamusi (China)
Jiaozuo (China)
Jinzhou (China)
Jodhpur (India)
Kaesong (North Korea)
Kaifeng (China)
Karachi (Pakistan)
Kayseri (Turkey)
Khoqand (Uzbekistan)
Kolkata (India)
Kunming (China)
Kutaisi (Georgia)
Kwangju (South Korea)
Lanzhou (China)
Liuzhou (China)
Lucknow (India)
Luoyang (China)
Madurai (India)
Matsudo (Japan)
Nanjing (China)
Nanning (China)
Nantong (China)
Niigata (Japan)
Okayama (Japan)
Qingdao (China)
Qiqihar (China)
Rustavi (Georgia)
Sapporo (Japan)
Shantou (China)
Shihezi (China)
Sialkot (Pakistan)
Sinuiju (North Korea)
Taiyuan (China)
Tbilisi (Georgia)
Thimphu (Bhutan)
Tianjin (China)
Tonghua (China)
Weifang (China)
Wenzhou (China)
Yakeshi (China)
Yerevan (Armenia)

Yichang (China)
Yingkou (China)
Zhuzhou (China)

08 Amritsar (India)
Ashgabat (Turkmenistan)
Bareilly (India)
Changsha (China)
Chimkent (Kazakhstan)
Chongjin (North Korea)
Dashoguz (Turkmenistan)
Durgapur (India)
Dushanbe (Tajikistan)
Ferghana (Uzbekistan)
Fukuyama (Japan)
Guwahati (India)
Hachioji (Japan)
Hakodate (Japan)
Hangzhou (China)
Hengyang (China)
Hong Kong (China)
Huangshi (China)
Hunjiang (China)
Ichikawa (Japan)
Istanbul (Turkey)
Jabalpur (India)
Kanazawa (Japan)
Kandahar (Afghanistan)
Kawasaki (Japan)
Khudzand (Tajikistan)
Kimchaek (North Korea)
Kolhapur (India)
Koriyama (Japan)
Kumamoto (Japan)
Kustanay (Kazakhstan)
Liaoyang (China)
Liaoyuan (China)
Ludhiana (India)
Maebashi (Japan)
Miyazaki (Japan)
Nagasaki (Japan)
Namangan (Uzbekistan)
Nanchang (China)
New Delhi (India)
Panchiao (Taiwan)
Pavlodar (Kazakhstan)
Peshawar (Pakistan)
Sargodha (Pakistan)
Shanghai (China)
Shaoguan (China)
Shenyang (China)
Shenzhen (China)
Shizuoka (Japan)
Sholapur (India)
Srinagar (India)
Sumqayit (Azerbaijan)
Taichung (Taiwan)
Tangshan (China)
Tashkent (Uzbekistan)

Vadodara (India)
Vanadzor (Armenia)
Varanasi (India)
Wakayama (Japan)
Warangal (India)
Xiangfan (China)
Xiangtan (China)
Xinxiang (China)
Yamagata (Japan)
Yangquan (China)
Yinchuan (China)
Yokohama (Japan)
Yokosuka (Japan)

09 Ahmadabad (India)
Allahabad (India)
Amagasaki (Japan)
Asahikawa (Japan)
Bangalore (India)
Bhaktapur (Nepal)
Bhavnagar (India)
Changchun (China)
Changzhou (China)
Chongqing (China)
Eskiçehir (Turkey)
Faridabad (India)
Fukushima (Japan)
Funabashi (Japan)
Gaziantep (Turkey)
Gorakhpur (India)
Guangzhou (China)
Hamamatsu (Japan)
Hiroshima (Japan)
Hyderabad (India)
Hyderabad (Pakistan)
Islamabad (Pakistan)
Jalalabad (Afghanistan)
Jalandhar (India)
Kagoshima (Japan)
Kaohsiung (Taiwan)
Karaganda (Kazakhstan)
Kathmandu (Nepal)
Kawaguchi (Japan)
Kyzyl-Kiya (Kyrgyzstan)
Matsuyama (Japan)
Moradabad (India)
Pingxiang (China)
Pyongyang (North Korea)
Samarkand (Uzbekistan)
Takamatsu (Japan)
Tokushima (Japan)
Toyohashi (Japan)
Ulan Bator (Mongolia)
Zhengzhou (China)
Zhenjiang (China)

10 Bahawalpur (Pakistan)
Balkanabat (Turkmenistan)
Chandigarh (India)

Chittagong (Bangladesh)
Coimbatore (India)
Diyarbakir (Turkey)
Faisalabad (Pakistan)
Gujranwala (Pakistan)
Jamshedpur (India)
Jingdezhen (China)
Kitakyushu (Japan)
Liupanshui (China)
Mudanjiang (China)
Przhevalsk (Kyrgyzstan)

Rawalpindi (Pakistan)
Sagamihara (Japan)
Trivandrum (India)
Utsunomiya (Japan)
Vijayawada (India)
11 Bhubaneswar (India)
Gandhinagar (India)
Kurgan-Tyube (Tajikistan)
Lianyungang (China)
Narayanganj (Bangladesh)
Qinhuangdao (China)

Zhangjiakou (China)
12 Higashiosaka (Japan)
Mazar-e-Sharif
(Afghanistan)
Pingdingshan (China)
Shijiazhuang (China)
Shuangyashan (China)
Türkmenbashi
(Turkmenistan)
13 Petropavlovsk (Kazakhstan)
Visakhapatnam (India)

Asians include:

03 Han
Lao
04 Ainu
Cham
Nair
Shan
Sulu
Thai
05 Bajau
Karen
Kazak
Nayar
Tajik
Tamil
Uzbeg
Uzbek
Vedda

06 Afghan
Baluch
Gurkha
Indian
Kazakh
Kyrgyz
Manchu
Mongol
Pathan
Tadjik
Telugu
07 Baluchi
Burmese
Chinese
Goanese
Goorkha
Karenni

Kirghiz
Laotian
Manchoo
Maratha
Russian
Tadzhik
Tagálog
Turkish
Turkmen
08 Bruneian
Canarese
Filipina
Filipino
Japanese
Kanarese
Mahratta
Nepalese

09 Bhutanese
Cambodian
Malaysian
Mongolian
Pakistani
Sri Lankan
Taiwanese
10 Indonesian
Myanmarese
Vietnamese
11 Azerbaijani
Bangladeshi
Kazakhstani
North Korean
Singaporean
South Korean
Tajikistani

Asian landmarks include:

05 Indus (China/India/Pakistan)
06 Mekong (south-east Asia)
07 Everest (China/Nepal)
08 Krakatoa (Indonesia)
Lake Sebu (Philippines)
Red River (China/Vietnam)
09 Angkor Wat (Cambodia)
Annapurna (Nepal)
Himalayas (central Asia)

See also **China**; **India**; **Japan**

Mt Everest (China/Nepal)
10 Gobi Desert (China/Mongolia)
River Indus (China/India/Pakistan)
Sagarmatha (China/Nepal)
11 Mekong River (south-east Asia)
12 Raffles Hotel (Singapore)
13 Kangchenjunga (India/Nepal)
14 Jaganath Temple (Nepal)

assassin *see* **murder**

assembly *see* **parliament**

asteroid

Asteroids include:

04 Eros
Hebe

Iris
Juno

05 Ceres
Flora

Metis
Vesta

06 Apollo	Europa	Pallas	07 Eunomia
Cybele	Hygiea	Psyche	10 Interamnia
Davida	Icarus	Trojan	

astrology

Terms used in astrology include:

02 IC	Libra	Apollon	infortune
MC	metal	destiny	planetary
ox	Pluto	element	spiritual
03 age	snake	equinox	10 astrologer
air	tiger	fortune	birthchart
arc	trine	Jupiter	descendant
dog	Venus	Mercury	dispositor
Leo	Virgo	Neptune	exaltation
orb	water	rooster	numerology
pig	06 apogee	Scorpio	opposition
rat	aspect	sextile	prediction
sun	astral	transit	retrograde
04 aura	Cancer	08 anaretic	11 astrologian
cast	dragon	Aquarius	astrologist
cusp	Gemini	forecast	conjunction
fate	monkey	quartile	Medium Coeli
fire	occult	quincunx	progression
goat	oracle	quintile	Sagittarius
Mars	Pisces	solstice	satellitium
moon	planet	star sign	12 astroanalyst
node	rabbit	synastry	degree of fate
star	Saturn	09 ascendant	planet-struck
wood	spirit	aspectual	significator
05 Aries	Taurus	Capricorn	13 constellation
earth	trigon	celestial	14 acronycal place
horse	Uranus	horoscope	planet-stricken
house	zodiac	Imum Coeli	
	07 Admetos	influence	

See also **birth symbol; zodiac**

astronaut

Astronauts include:

04 Bean (Alan; 1932– , US)
Ride (Sally; 1951– , US)

05 Foale (Michael; 1957– , English)
Glenn (John; 1921– , US)
Irwin (James; 1930–91, US)
Scott (David; 1932– , US)
Titov (Gherman; 1935–2000, Soviet)
White (Edward; 1930–67, US)

06 Aldrin (Edwin 'Buzz'; 1930– , US)
Conrad (Charles 'Pete'; 1930–99, US)
Leonov (Aleksei; 1934– , Russian)
Lovell (James 'Jim'; 1928– , US)

See also **space travel**

07 Chaffee (Roger; 1935–67, US)
Collins (Eileen; 1956– , US)
Collins (Michael; 1930– , US)
Gagarin (Yuri; 1934–68, Soviet)
Grissom (Gus; 1926–67, US)
Schirra (Wally; 1923–2007, US)
Sharman (Helen; 1963– , English)
Shepard (Alan; 1923–98, US)

08 Mitchell (Edgar; 1930– , US)
Williams (Sunita; 1965– , US)

09 Armstrong (Neil; 1930– , US)

10 Tereshkova (Valentina; 1937– , Russian)

astronomy

Astronomers and astrophysicists include:

04 Airy (Sir George; 1801–92, English)
Biot (Jean Baptiste; 1774–1862, French)
Gold (Thomas; 1920–2004, US)
Hale (George; 1868–1938, US)
Lyot (Bernard; 1897–1952, French)
Oort (Jan; 1900–92, Dutch)
Pond (John; 1767–1836, English)
Rees (Sir Martin; 1942–   , English)
Ryle (Sir Martin; 1918–84, English)
Saha (Meghnad; 1894–1956, Indian)
Webb (James E; 1906–92, US)

05 Adams (John Couch; 1819–92, English)
Adams (Walter S; 1876–1956, US)
Baade (Walter; 1893–1960, US)
Baily (Francis; 1774–1844, English)
Bliss (Nathaniel; 1700–64, English)
Brahe (Tycho; 1546–1601, Danish)
Brown (John Campbell; 1947–   , Scottish)
Dyson (Sir Frank; 1868–1939, English)
Gauss (Carl Friedrich; 1777–1855, German)
Hoyle (Sir Fred; 1915–2001, English)
Jeans (Sir James; 1877–1946, English)
Jones (Sir Harold Spencer; 1890–1960, English)
Milne (Edward; 1896–1950, English)
Moore (Sir Patrick; 1923–   , English)
Sagan (Carl; 1934–96, US)
Smith (Sir Francis; 1923–   , English)
Vogel (Hermann; 1841–1907, German)

06 Bessel (Friedrich; 1784–1846, German)
Halley (Edmond; 1656–1742, English)
Hewish (Antony; 1924–   , English)
Hubble (Edwin; 1889–1953, US)
Jansky (Karl; 1905–50, US)
Kepler (Johannes; 1571–1630, German)
Kuiper (Gerard; 1905–73, US)
Lovell (Sir Bernard; 1913–   , English)
Olbers (Heinrich Wilhelm; 1758–1840, German)
Piazzi (Giuseppe; 1746–1826, Italian)
Roemer (Olaus; 1644–1710, Danish)

07 Babcock (Harold D; 1882–1968, US)
Barnard (Edward Emerson; 1857–1923, US)
Bradley (James; 1693–1762, English)
Cassini (Giovanni; 1625–1712, French)
Celsius (Anders; 1701–44, Swedish)
Galilei (Galileo; 1564–1642, Italian)
Galileo (1564–1642, Italian)
Hawking (Stephen; 1942–   , English)
Huggins (Sir William; 1824–1910, English)
Korolev (Sergei; 1907–66, Soviet)

Langley (Samuel; 1834–1906, US)
Laplace (Pierre, Marquis de; 1749–1827, French)
Lockyer (Sir Norman; 1836–1920, English)
Maunder (E W; 1851–1924, English)
Michell (John; 1724–93, English)
Penrose (Sir Roger; 1931–   , English)
Penzias (Arno; 1933–   , US)
Ptolemy (c.90–168 AD, Egyptian)
Russell (Henry Norris; 1877–1957, US)
Sandage (Allan; 1926–   , US)
Schmidt (Maarten; 1929–   , US)
Seyfert (Carl; 1911–60, US)
Shapley (Harlow; 1885–1972, US)
Slipher (Vesto; 1875–1969, US)
Whipple (Fred; 1906–2004, US)
Woolley (Sir Richard; 1906–86, English)

08 Burbidge (Geoffrey; 1925–   , English)
Burbidge (Margaret; 1923–   , English)
Chandler (Seth Carlo; 1846–1913, US)
Christie (Sir William; 1845–1922, English)
Douglass (Andrew Ellicott; 1867–1962, US)
Friedman (Herbert; 1916–2000, US)
Herschel (Caroline; 1750–1848, German/British)
Herschel (Sir John; 1792–1871, English)
Herschel (Sir William; 1738–1822, British)
Lemaître (Georges; 1894–1966, Belgian)
Tombaugh (Clyde W; 1906–97, US)
Trumpler (Robert; 1886–1956, US)

09 Eddington (Sir Arthur; 1882–1944, English)
Fabricius (David; 1564–1617, German)
Flamsteed (John; 1646–1719, English)
Maskelyne (Nevil; 1732–1811, English)
Sosigenes (fl.c.40 BC, Egyptian)

10 Carrington (Richard; 1826–75, English)
Copernicus (Nicolas; 1473–1543, Polish)
Hipparchos (c.180–125 BC, Greek)
Wolfendale (Sir Arnold; 1927–   , English)

11 Bell Burnell (Jocelyn; 1943–   , Northern Irish)
Graham-Smith (Sir Francis; 1923–   , English)
Hertzsprung (Ejnar; 1873–1967, Danish)
Tsiolkovsky (Konstantin; 1857–1935, Russian)

12 Schiaparelli (Giovanni; 1835–1910, Italian)

13 Chandrasekhar (Subrahmanyan; 1910–95, US)
Schwarzschild (Karl; 1873–1916, German)

Terms used in astronomy include:

03 GUT	Metonic	radio star	cosmic string
NEO	nocturn	Roche lobe	Doppler shift
sun	perigee	satellite	event horizon
04 core	transit	shell star	galactic halo
flux	**08** aphelion	supernova	heliocentric
moon	asteroid	telescope	main sequence
node	cosmical	**10** aberration	meteor shower
nova	ecliptic	almacantar	Metonic cycle
star	emersion	astrometry	periselenium
Yagi	evection	binary star	perturbation
05 comet	inferior	black dwarf	shepherd moon
coudé	infrared	brown dwarf	spectral type
epoch	Milky Way	Copernican	spiral galaxy
giant	nutation	cosmic rays	supercluster
orbit	parallax	dark matter	**13** accretion disk
rings	prograde	double star	celestial body
umbra	red dwarf	inequality	constellation
06 apogee	red giant	Kuiper Belt	Olbers' paradox
blazar	red shift	Local Group	Seyfert galaxy
corona	subgiant	luminosity	solar constant
cosmos	sunspots	periastron	synodic period
galaxy	totality	perihelion	X-ray astronomy
jansky	Tychonic	retrograde	**14** celestial poles
lander	universe	Roche limit	Chandler wobble
meteor	**09** astrodome	supergiant	closed universe
nebula	black body	white dwarf	equation of time
parsec	black hole	**11** Baily's beads	Hubble constant
planet	coelostat	bright giant	radar astronomy
pulsar	collapsar	declination	right ascension
quasar	ephemeris	gegenschein	space telescope
spinar	great year	helium flash	**15** armillary sphere
syzygy	hour-angle	neutron star	celestial sphere
07 almanac	hypernova	observatory	Cepheid variable
anomaly	immersion	occultation	eclipsing binary
azimuth	magnitude	singularity	globular cluster
big bang	Oort cloud	solar system	Hubble telescope
eclipse	polar axis	**12** binary pulsar	near-Earth object
	protostar		

See also **asteroid**; **astronaut**; **comet**; **constellation**; **galaxy**; **meteor**; **moon**; **observatory**; **planet**; **satellite**; **space travel**; **star**

astrophysics *see* **astronomy**

athletics

Athletics events include:

04 100m	3,000m	sprint	50km walk
200m	5,000m	**07** hurdles	biathlon
400m	field	javelin	high jump
800m	relay	shot put	long jump
dash	track	**08** 10km walk	marathon
mile	**06** 10,000m	16lb ball	tug-of-war
shot	discus	20km walk	**09** broad jump
05 1,500m	hammer	22lb ball	caber toss

decathlon	pentathlon	400m hurdles	javelin throw
pole vault	tetrathlon	discus throw	steeplechase
sheaf toss	triple jump	fell running	**13** sprint hurdles
triathlon	**11** 100m hurdles	hammer throw	**14** hop, step and jump
10 16lb hammer	110m hurdles	high hurdles	
22lb hammer	4×100m relay	race walking	**15** tossing the caber
heptathlon	4×400m relay	**12** half marathon	

Athletes include:

03 Coe (Sebastian, Lord; 1956– , English)

04 Bolt (Usain; 1986– , Jamaican)
Budd (Zola; 1966– , South African)
Cram (Steve; 1960– , English)
Ewry (Ray; 1873–1937, US)
Koch (Marita; 1957– , German)
Mota (Rosa; 1958– , Portuguese)
Tyus (Wyomia; 1945– , US)

05 Balas (Iolanda; 1936– , Romanian)
Bubka (Sergey; 1963– , Ukrainian)
Defar (Meseret; 1983– , Ethiopian)
Etone (Françoise Mbango; 1976– , Cameroon)
Felix (Allyson; 1985– , US)
Jamal (Maryam Jusuf; 1984– , Bahraini)
Jones (Marion; 1975– , US)
Keino (Kip; 1940– , Kenyan)
Lewis (Carl; 1961– , US)
Lewis (Denise; 1972– , English)
Moses (Ed; 1955– , US)
Nurmi (Paavo; 1897–1973, Finnish)
Ottey (Merlene; 1960– , Jamaican/Slovenian)
Ovett (Steve; 1955– , English)
Owens (Jesse; 1913–80, US)
Pérec (Marie-José; 1968– , French)
Snell (Peter; 1938– , New Zealand)
Viren (Lasse; 1949– , Finnish)
Waitz (Grete; 1953– , Norwegian)
Wells (Allan; 1952– , Scottish)
Xiang (Liu; 1983– , Chinese)

06 Aouita (Said; 1960– , Moroccan)
Barber (Eunice; 1974– , French)
Beamon (Bob; 1946– , US)
Bekele (Kenenisa; 1982– , Ethiopian)
Bikila (Abebe; 1932–73, Ethiopian)
Borzov (Valeri; 1949– , Ukrainian)
Boston (Ralph; 1939– , US)
Clarke (Ron; 1937– , Australian)
Devers (Gail; 1966– , US)
Dibaba (Tirunesh; 1985– , Ethiopian)
Dvořák (Tomáš; 1972– , Czech)
Foster (Brendan; 1948– , English)
Greene (Maurice; 1974– , US)
Holmes (Dame Kelly; 1970– , English)
Kemboi (Ezekiel; 1982– , Kenyan)
Mutola (Maria; 1972– , Mozambican)

Oerter (Al; 1936–2007, US)
Peters (Mary; 1939– , Northern Irish)
Powell (Asafa; 1982– , Jamaican)
Slaney (Mary Decker; 1958– , US)
Wöckel (Bärbel; 1955– , German)
Yifter (Miruts, c.1938– , Ethiopian)

07 Backley (Steve; 1969– , English)
Edwards (Jonathan; 1966– , English)
Elliott (Herb; 1938– , Australian)
Fosbury (Dick; 1947– , US)
Freeman (Cathy; 1973– , Australian)
Gunnell (Sally; 1966– , English)
Jackson (Colin; 1967– , Welsh)
Johnson (Ben; 1961– , Canadian)
Johnson (Michael; 1967– , US)
Liddell (Eric; 1902–45, Scottish)
Rudolph (Wilma; 1940–94, US)
Shorter (Frank; 1947– , US)
Stecher (Renate; 1950– , German)
Wariner (Jeremy; 1984– , US)
Zatopek (Emil; 1922–2000, Czech)
Zelezny (Jan; 1966– , Czech)

08 Christie (Linford; 1960– , English)
Crawford (Shawn 1978– , US)
Cuthbert (Betty; 1938– , Australian)
Guerrouj (Hicham el-; 1974– , Moroccan)
Kipketer (Wilson; 1970– , Kenyan/Danish)
McColgan (Liz; 1964– , Scottish)
Morcelli (Noureddine; 1977– , Algerian)
Ohuruogu (Christine; 1984– , English)
Phillips (Dwight; 1977– , US)
Thompson (Daley; 1958– , English)
Zaharias (Babe; 1914–56, US)

09 Bannister (Sir Roger; 1929– , English)
Boulmerka (Hassiba; 1968– , Algerian)
de la Hunty (Shirley; 1925–2004, Australian)
Drechsler (Heike; 1964– , German)
Jepkosgei (Janeth; 1983– , Kenyan)
Kazankina (Tatyana; 1951– , Russian)
O'Sullivan (Sonia; 1969– , Irish)
Radcliffe (Paula; 1973– , English)
Sanderson (Tessa; 1956– , English)
Špotáková (Babora; 1981– , Czech)
Szewinska (Irena; 1946– , Polish)
Warmerdam (Cornelius 'Dutch'; 1915–2001, US)
Whitbread (Fatima; 1961– , English)

10 Isinbayeva (Yelena; 1982– , Russian)
Wang Junxia (1973– , Chinese)

11 Kristiansen (Ingrid; 1956– , Norwegian)
Newby-Fraser (Paula; 1962– , South
African)
Thorkildsen (Andreas; 1982– , Norwegian)

12 Blankers-Koen (Fanny; 1918–2004, Dutch)

Gebrselassie (Haile; 1973– , Ethiopian)
Grey-Thompson (Dame Tanni; 1969– ,
Welsh)
Joyner-Kersee (Jackie; 1962– , US)

13 Campbell-Brown (Veronica; 1982– ,
Jamaican)

14 Griffith Joyner (Florence; 1959–98, US)

Athletics terms include:

02 PB	race	**07** boxed in	finish line
SB	skip	qualify	plasticine
03 air	step	red flag	**11** Fosbury flop
bar	walk	shot put	photo finish
box	**05** baton	starter	season's best
dip	board	unpaced	track record
hop	break	**08** deselect	western roll
lap	field	distance	**12** back straight
leg	prize	gymkhana	home straight
pit	relay	straight	long distance
04 bend	track	**09** hitch kick	personal best
bore	**06** blocks	pacemaker	reaction time
fail	circle	pancratic	take-over zone
foul	no jump	pole vault	wind-assisted
heat	record	water jump	**13** following wind
jump	runway	white flag	**14** crouching start
kick	spikes	**10** disqualify	middle distance
lane	Tartan®	false start	staggered start

See also **Olympic Games; Paralympic Games; sport**

atmosphere

Atmospheric layers include:

09 exosphere	**10** ionosphere	tropopause	**12** stratosphere
ionopause	mesosphere	**11** stratopause	thermosphere
mesopause	ozone layer	troposphere	

atom

Subatomic particles include:

01 W	preon	nucleon	down quark
X	quark	pi meson	gravitron
Z	sigma	up quark	tau lepton
03 psi	**06** baryon	upsilon	**10** anti-proton
04 J/psi	B-meson	**08** electron	gauge boson
kaon	hadron	neutrino	truth quark
muon	lambda	neutrino (electron)	**11** anti-neutron
pion	lepton	neutrino (muon)	beauty quark
05 boson	parton	neutrino (tau)	bottom quark
gluon	photon	positron	**12** anti-neutrino
meson	proton	top quark	charmed quark
omega	**07** neutron	**09** antiquark	strange quark

aunt

Aunts include:

02 Em (*The Wonderful Wizard of Oz*, 1900, L Frank Baum)

03 Dot (*The Towers of Trebizond*, 1956, Rose Macaulay)

04 Doom (Ada; *Cold Comfort Farm*, 1932, Stella Gibbons)
Gray (Ruth; *Epitaph for George Dillon*, 1954, John Osborne and Anthony Creighton)
Jean (*Tingha and Tucker*, TV)
Monk (Lady; *Can You Forgive Her?*, 1864–65, Anthony Trollope)
Reed (Mrs; *Jane Eyre*, 1847, Charlotte Brontë)
Zita (*Wild Nights*, 1979, Emma Tennant)

05 Glegg (Mrs; *The Mill on the Floss*, 1860, George Eliot)
Hamps (Clara; *Clayhanger*, 1910, Arnold Bennett)
Julia (*Aunt Julia and the Scriptwriter*, 1977, Mario Vargas Llosa)
Livia (*Women Beware Women*, c.1621, Thomas Middleton)
March (*Little Women*, 1868, Louisa M Alcott)
Mildy (*Langton Tetralogy*, 1952–62, Martin Boyd)
Polly (*The Adventures of Tom Sawyer*, 1876, Mark Twain)
Sally
Scott (Vanessa; *Careful, He Might Hear You*, 1963, Sumner Locke Elliott)

06 Agatha (*The Family Reunion*, 1939, T S Eliot)
Baines (Lila; *Careful, He Might Hear You*, 1963, Sumner Locke Elliott)
Dahlia (*Carry On, Jeeves*, 1925, et seq, P G Wodehouse)
Fisher (Sylvie; *Housekeeping*, 1980, Marilynne Robinson)
Lizzie (*Philadelphia, Here I Come!*, 1965, Brian Friel)
Lowder (Mrs; *The Wings of the Dove*, 1902, Henry James)
Maylie (Rose; *Oliver Twist*, 1838, Charles Dickens)
Morton (Jean; *Tingha and Tucker*, TV)
Nellie (*The Dressmaker*, 1973, Beryl Bainbridge)
Poyser (Mrs; *Adam Bede*, 1859, George Eliot)
Pullet (Mrs; *The Mill on the Floss*, 1860, George Eliot)

Rayner (Claire; 1931– , English)
Sophie (*Act of Darkness*, 1983, Francis King)

07 Barbary (Miss; *Bleak House*, 1853, Charles Dickens)
Bertram (Augusta; *Travels with My Aunt*, 1969, Graham Greene)
Failing (Emily; *The Longest Journey*, 1907, E M Forster)
Flowers (Margaret; *The Magic Toyshop*, 1967, Angela Carter)
Forsyte (Ann; *The Forsyte Saga*, 1922, John Galsworthy)
Langton (Mildred; *Langton Tetralogy*, 1952–62, Martin Boyd)
Rickard (Miss; *No Laughing Matter*, 1967, Angus Wilson)
Spenser (Lucy; *Love Always*, 1985, Ann Beattie)

08 Charley's (*Charley's Aunt*, 1892, Brandon Thomas)
de Bourgh (Lady Catherine; *Pride and Prejudice*, 1813, Jane Austen)
Malaprop (Mrs; *The Rivals*, 1775, Richard Brinsley Sheridan)
Pontifex (Alethea; *The Way of All Flesh*, 1903, Samuel Butler)
Slingsby, (Helen; *Prufrock and Other Observations*, 1917, T S Eliot)
Trotwood (Betsey; *David Copperfield*, 1850, Charles Dickens)
Willowes (Lolly; *Lolly Willowes*, 1926, Sylvia Townsend Warner)
Wishfort (Lady; *The Way of the World*, 1700, William Congreve)

09 Bordereau (Miss; *The Aspern Papers*, 1888, Henry James)
Bracknell (Lady; *The Importance of Being Earnest*, 1895, Oscar Wilde)
McPherson (Cathy; *The Tax Inspector*, 1991, Peter Carey)
Poppyseed (Philomela; *Headlong Hall*, 1816, Thomas Love Peacock)
Stansbury (Jemima; *He Knew He Was Right*, 1869, Anthony Trollope)
Stephanie (*Too Late the Phalarope*, 1953, Alan Paton)
Yeobright (Mrs; *The Return of the Native*, 1878, Thomas Hardy)

10 Harrington (Polly; *Pollyanna*, 1913, Eleanor Porter)

12 Lonelyhearts (Miss; *Miss Lonelyhearts*, 1933, Nathanael West)

Austen, Jane (1775–1817)

Significant works include:

04 *Emma* (1816)

08 *Sanditon* (1925)

09 *Lady Susan* (1871)

10 *Persuasion* (1818)

The Watsons (1871)

13 *Mansfield Park* (1814)

15 *Northanger Abbey* (1818)

17 *Pride and Prejudice* (1813)

19 *Sense and Sensibility* (1811)

Significant characters include:

04 Clay (Mrs)

05 Bates (Hetty)
Croft (Admiral)
Croft (Mrs)
Darcy (Mr Fitzwilliam)
Elton (Mr)
Elton (Mrs)
Lucas (Charlotte)
Price (Fanny)
Price (Mrs)
Smith (Harriet)
Smith (Mrs)
Yates (Mr)

06 Bennet (Elizabeth)
Bennet (Jane)
Bennet (Lydia)
Bennet (Mr)
Bennet (Mrs)
Elliot (Anne)
Elliot (Elizabeth)
Elliot (Mary)
Elliot (Sir Walter)
Elliot (William)
Martin (Robert)

Norris (Mrs)
Steele (Lucy)
Taylor (Anne)
Thorpe (Isabella)
Thorpe (John)
Tilney (Captain Frederick)
Tilney (Eleanor)
Tilney (General)
Tilney (Henry)
Weston (Mr)

07 Bertram (Edmund)
Bertram (Julia)
Bertram (Lady)
Bertram (Maria)
Bertram (Sir Thomas)
Bertram (Tom)
Bingley (Charles)
Brandon (Colonel)
Collins (William)
Fairfax (Jane)
Ferrars (Edward)
Ferrars (Mrs)
Ferrars (Robert)
Morland (Catherine)

Morland (James)
Russell (Lady)
Wickham (George)

08 Crawford (Henry)
Crawford (Mary)
Dashwood (Elinor)
Dashwood (Fanny)
Dashwood (John)
Dashwood (Marianne)
Dashwood (Mrs)
de Bourgh (Lady Catherine)
Jennings (Mrs)
Musgrove (Charles)
Musgrove (Henrietta)
Musgrove (Louisa)

09 Churchill (Frank)
Knightley (Mr George)
Rushworth (Mr)
Wentworth (Captain
Frederick)
Woodhouse (Emma)
Woodhouse (Mr Henry)

10 Willoughby (John)

Australasia

Countries in Australasia and Oceania include:

04 Fiji (Melanesia)
Guam (Federated States of Micronesia)
Niue (Polynesia)

05 Nauru (Federated States of Micronesia)
Palau (Federated States of Micronesia)
Samoa (Polynesia)
Tonga (Polynesia)

06 Tuvalu (Polynesia)

07 Tokelau (Polynesia)
Vanuatu (Melanesia)

08 Kiribati (Federated States of Micronesia)
Pitcairn (Polynesia)

09 Australia

10 New Zealand

11 Cook Islands (Polynesia)

12 New Caledonia (Melanesia)

13 American Samoa (Polynesia)
Norfolk Island

14 Papua New Guinea (Melanesia)
Solomon Islands (Melanesia)

15 French Polynesia (Polynesia)
Marshall Islands (Federated States of
Micronesia)

Cities and notable towns in Australasia and Oceania include:

04 Apia (Samoa)
Suva (Fiji)

05 Perth (Australia)

06 Sydney (Australia)

07 Dunedin (New Zealand)
Honiara (Solomon Islands)

Manukau (New Zealand)
08 Adelaide (Australia)
Auckland (New Zealand)
Brisbane (Australia)
Canberra (Australia)
Hamilton (New Zealand)

09 Melbourne (Australia)
Newcastle (Australia)
10 Wellington (New Zealand)
11 Port Moresby (Papua New Guinea)
12 Christchurch (New Zealand)

Australia

Australian states and territories, with abbreviations and regional capitals:

08 Tasmania (TAS; Hobart)
Victoria (VIC; Melbourne)
10 Queensland (QLD; Brisbane)
13 New South Wales (NSW; Sydney)

14 South Australia (SA; Adelaide)
16 Western Australia (WA; Perth)
17 Northern Territory (NT; Darwin)
26 Australian Capital Territory (ACT; Canberra)

Australian state residents' nicknames include:

08 Top Ender (Northern Territory)
09 croweater (South Australia)
gumsucker (Victoria)
Taswegian (Tasmania)
10 sandgroper (Western Australia)
11 Territorian (Northern Territory)

Vandemonian (Tasmania)
12 bananabender (Queensland)
13 Apple Islander (Tasmania)
14 Cabbage Patcher (Victoria)
15 Cabbage Gardener (Victoria)

Cities and notable towns in Australia include:

05 Perth
06 Cairns
Darwin

Hobart
Sydney
08 Adelaide

Brisbane
Canberra
09 Fremantle

Melbourne
12 Alice Springs

Australian electorates:

04 Bass	Lyons	Gwydir	Dickson
Cook	Makin	Hotham	Dunkley
Grey	Moore	Hughes	Fairfax
Holt	Oxley	Hunter	Forrest
Hume	Perth	Isaacs	Gilmore
Indi	Sturt	Lilley	Hasluck
Lowe	Wills	Mallee	Herbert
Lyne	**06** Barker	McEwan	Higgins
Mayo	Barton	Murray	Hinkler
Page	Batman	Parkes	Kennedy
Reid	Bonner	Pearce	Kooyong
Ryan	Bowman	Petrie	La Trobe
Swan	Calare	Rankin	Lindsay
05 Aston	Cowper	Sydney	Longman
Banks	Curtin	Wannon	Maranoa
Blair	Dawson	Watson	Menzies
Brand	Deakin	**07** Bendigo	Moreton
Bruce	Dobell	Berowra	O'Connor
Casey	Fadden	Boothby	Scullin
Corio	Farrer	Braddon	Solomon
Cowan	Fisher	Calwell	Tangney
Forde	Fowler	Canning	Throsby
Groom	Fraser	Chifley	Werriwa
Lalor	Gorton	Denison	Wide Bay

08 Adelaide | McMillan | Macarthur | Gellibrand
Ballarat | Mitchell | Mackellar | Kalgoorlie
Blaxland | Paterson | Macquarie | Leichhardt
Brisbane | Prospect | McPherson | New England
Canberra | Richmond | Melbourne | Parramatta
Charlton | Riverina | Moncrieff | **11** Capricornia
Chisholm | Stirling | Newcastle | Corangamite
Flinders | **09** Bennelong | Robertson | Maribyrnong
Franklin | Bradfield | Shortland | North Sydney
Greenway | Fremantle | Wakefield | **12** Port Adelaide
Griffith | Gippsland | Warringah | **14** Kingsford Smith
Jagajaga | Goldstein | Wentworth | Melbourne Ports
Kingston | Grayndler | **10** Cunningham
Lingiari | Hindmarsh | Eden-Monaro

Australian landmarks include:

05 Uluru | **10** Bondi Beach | Hunter Valley | Simpson Desert
08 Lake Eyre | Yarra River | Rialto Towers | **14** Australian Alps
Shark Bay | **11** Mt Kosciusko | **13** Barossa Valley | Nullarbor Plain
09 Ayers Rock | Murray River | Blue Mountains | Pinnacle Desert
Botany Bay | **12** Darling River | Bungle Bungles | Snowy Mountains
Pinnacles | Fraser Island | Devil's Marbles | Twelve Apostles
Purnululu | Gibson Desert | Flinders Range | Uluru-Kata Tjuta

See also **aborigine**; **Australasia**; **governor**; **prime minister**

Australian rules football

Australian rules football teams include:

07 Carlton | Essendon | Kangaroos | **12** Port Adelaide
Geelong | Hawthorn | Melbourne | **13** Brisbane Lions
St Kilda | Richmond | **11** Collingwood | **15** West Coast Eagles
08 Adelaide | **09** Fremantle | Sydney Swans | Western Bulldogs

Australian rules football team nicknames include:

04 Cats (Geelong) | Swans (Sydney) | Dockers (Fremantle)
05 Blues (Carlton) | **06** Demons (Melbourne) | Magpies (Collingwood)
Crows (Adelaide) | Eagles (West Coast) | **08** Bulldogs (Western
Hawks (Hawthorn) | Saints (St Kilda) | Bulldogs)
Lions (Brisbane) | Tigers (Richmond) | **09** Kangaroos (North
Power (Port Adelaide) | **07** Bombers (Essendon) | Melbourne)

Australian rules football players include:

04 Dyer (Jack; 1913–2003)

05 Carey (Wayne; 1971–)

06 Ablett (Gary, Jnr; 1984–)
Ablett (Gary, Snr; 1961–)
Blight (Malcolm; 1950–)
Bunton (Haydn, Jnr; 1937–)
Bunton (Haydn, Snr; 1911–55)
Capper (Warwick; 1963–)
Cazaly (Roy; 1893–1963)
Farmer (Graham 'Polly'; 1935–)

07 Barassi (Ron; 1936–)
Jackson (Mark 'Jacko'; 1959–)
Lockett (Tony 'Plugger'; 1966–)
Whitten (Ted; 1933–95)

08 Bartlett (Kevin; 1947–)
Brereton (Dermot; 1964–)
Brownlow (Charles 'Chas'; 1861–1924)
Matthews (Leigh; 1952–)
Richards (Lewis 'Lou'; 1923–)

10 Jesaulenko (Alex 'Jezza'; 1945–)

Australian rules football terms include:

04 goal	time on	left wing	half forward
mark	umpire	**09** playfield	**12** boundary line
ruck	**07** dispose	right wing	centre bounce
wing	quarter	ruck rover	centre square
05 rover	ruckman	**10** back pocket	**13** fifty-metre arc
06 ball up	**08** free kick	centre line	forward pocket
behind	full back	goal square	half-back flank
centre	half back	**11** full forward	**14** centre half-back
tackle	handpass		

See also **sport**

Austria

Cities and notable towns in Austria include:

04 Graz	Wien	**08** Salzburg	**10** Klagenfurt
Linz	**06** Vienna	**09** Innsbruck	

Administrative divisions of Austria, with regional capitals:

04 Wien	**08** Salzburg (Salzburg)	Upper Austria (Linz)
05 Tirol (Innsbruck)	**09** Carinthia (Klagenfurt)	**14** Oberösterreich (Linz)
Tyrol (Innsbruck)	**10** Burgenland (Eisenstadt)	**16** Niederösterreich (Sankt
06 Styria (Graz)	Steiermark (Graz)	Pölten)
Vienna	Vorarlberg (Bregenz)	
07 Kärnten (Klagenfurt)	**12** Lower Austria (Sankt Pölten)	

Austrian landmarks include:

07 Hofburg	Untersberg	Zwölferhorn	Neusiedler See
Rathaus	Wienerwald	**12** Mozart's House	Stift Nonnberg
08 Domplatz	**11** Burgtheater	**13** Grossglockner	**14** Mozart-
09 Hellbrunn	Stephansdom	Hohensalzburg	Wohnhaus
10 Opera House	Vienna Woods	Kapuzinerberg	**15** Pasterze Glacier
Schönbrunn	Wolfgangsee	Linz Cathedral	Schloss Mirabell

author *see* **novel**

aviation

Aviators, aviation pioneers and aircraft designers include:

03 Ulm (Charles; 1898–1934, Australian)

04 Ader (Clément; 1841–1926, French)
Byrd (Richard E; 1888–1957, US)
Cody (Samuel; 1862–1913, US/British)
Fysh (Sir Hudson; 1895–1974, Australian)
Post (Wiley; 1900–35, US)
Udet (Ernst; 1896–1941, German)

05 Bader (Sir Douglas; 1910–82, English)
Balbo (Italo, Count; 1896–1940, Italian)
Brown (Sir Arthur; 1886–1948, Scottish)
Johns (Captain W E; 1893–1968, English)

Rolls (Charles; 1877–1910, English)
Scott (Sheila; 1927–88, English)
Smith (Sir Ross; 1892–1922, Australian)

06 Alcock (Sir John; 1892–1919, English)
Arnold (Henry 'Hap'; 1886–1950, US)
Auriol (Jacqueline; 1917–2000, French)
Batten (Jean; 1909–82, New Zealand)
Cayley (Sir George; 1773–1857, English)
Cessna (Clyde; 1879–1954, US)
Farman (Henri; 1874–1958, French)
Gibson (Guy; 1918–44, English)

Göring (Hermann; 1893–1946, German)
Harris (Sir Arthur 'Bomber'; 1892–1984, English)
Hughes (Howard; 1905–76, US)
Nobile (Umberto; 1885–1978, Italian)
Quimby (Harriet; 1882–1912, US)
Taylor (Sir Gordon; 1896–1966, Australian)
Wallis (Barnes; 1887–1979, English)
Wright (Orville; 1871–1948, US)
Wright (Wilbur; 1867–1912, US)
Yeager (Chuck; 1923– , US)

07 Balchen (Bernt; 1899–1973, US)
Bennett (Floyd; 1890–1928, US)
Blériot (Louis; 1872–1936, French)
Branson (Sir Richard; 1950– , English)
Cochran (Jacqueline; 1910–80, US)
Curtiss (Glenn; 1878–1930, US)
Dornier (Claudius; 1884–1969, German)
Douglas (Donald; 1892–1981, US)
Earhart (Amelia; 1897–1937, US)
Fossett (Steve; 1944–2007, US)
Giffard (Henri; 1825–82, French)
Goering (Hermann; 1893–1946, German)
Heinkel (Ernst; 1888–1958, German)
Hinkler (Bert; 1892–1933, Australian)
Johnson (Amy; 1903–41, English)
Korolev (Sergei; 1907–66, Soviet)
Markham (Beryl; 1902–86, English/African)
Piccard (Auguste; 1884–1962, Swiss)
Piccard (Bertrand; 1958– , Swiss)
Piccard (Jean; 1884–1963, Swiss/US)

Sopwith (Sir Thomas; 1888–1989, English)

08 Brabazon (John, Lord; 1884–1964, English)
Cheshire (Leonard, Lord; 1917–92, English)
Dassault (Marcel; 1892–1986, French)
Ilyushin (Sergei; 1894–1977, Russian)
Mitchell (Reginald; 1895–1937, English)
Mitchell (William; 1879–1936, US)
Mollison (James; 1905–59, Scottish)
Zeppelin (Ferdinand, Count von; 1838–1917, German)

09 Blanchard (Jean Pierre; 1753–1809, French)
Doolittle (Jimmy; 1896–1993, US)
Lindbergh (Charles; 1902–74, US)
McDonnell (James; 1899–1980, US)

10 Lindstrand (Per; 1953– , Swedish)
Richthofen (Manfred, Baron von; 1882–1918, German)
Tissandier (Gaston; 1835–99, French)

11 Montgolfier (Jacques; 1745–99, French)
Montgolfier (Joseph; 1740–1810, French)

12 Grahame-White (Claude, 1879–1959, English)
Rickenbacker (Eddie; 1890–1973, US)
Saint-Exupéry (Antoine de; 1900–44, French)
Santos-Dumont (Alberto; 1873–1932, Brazilian)

13 Messerschmitt (Willy; 1898–1978, German)

14 Kingsford Smith (Sir Charles; 1897–1935, Australian)

Terms to do with aviation include:

03 hop

04 dive
drag
flap
taxi

05 fly-by
pilot
plane
prang

06 airway
flight
hangar
runway
thrust

07 airline
air miss
airport
airprox

airship
captain
console
fly-past
landing
lift-off
spoiler
take-off

08 aircraft
airfield
airplane
airspace
airstrip
altitude
black box
nose dive
subsonic
windsock
wingspan

See also **air travel**; **aircraft**; **bomb**

09 aeroplane
aerospace
crash dive
fixed-wing
fly-by-wire
jetstream
overshoot
parachute
sonic boom
test pilot
touchdown

10 air station
chocks away
flight crew
Mach number
solo flight
supersonic
test flight
undershoot

11 aeronautics
ground speed
loop-the-loop
night-flying
vapour trail

12 control tower
crash-landing
landing strip
maiden flight
sound barrier

13 ground control
jet propulsion

14 automatic pilot
flight recorder
holding pattern

15 mid-air collision

award

Awards and prizes include:

04	Emmy		Grammy		Pulitzer	
	Tony		Orange		Stirling	
05	Bafta		Razzie	**09**	Grand Jury	
	César		Turner		Grand Prix	
	Costa	**07**	Academy		Man Booker	
	Nobel		Olivier		Templeton	
	Oscar	**08**	Audience	**10**	Golden Bear	
06	Booker		Palme d'Or		Golden Palm	

04 Emmy, Tony

05 Bafta, César, Costa, Nobel, Oscar

06 Booker

Grammy, Orange, Razzie, Turner

07 Academy, Olivier

08 Audience, Palme d'Or

Pulitzer, Stirling

09 Grand Jury, Grand Prix, Man Booker, Templeton

10 Golden Bear, Golden Palm

11 Fields Medal, Golden Globe

12 Prix Goncourt

15 Golden Raspberry

See also **literature**; **Nobel Prize**

B

Babylonian god, goddess *see* **mythology**

Bach, Johann Sebastian (1685–1750)

bacteria

Kitasato (Shibasaburo, Baron; 1852–1931, Japanese)

Leishman (Sir William; 1865–1926, Scottish)

Marshall (Barry; 1951– , Australian)

Pfeiffer (Richard; 1858–1945, German)

10 Wassermann (August von; 1866–1925, German)

11 Chamberland (Charles; 1851–1908, French)

badminton

Badminton terms include:

03 net	court	**06** racket	wood shot
set	drive	**07** doubles	**11** shuttlecock
04 bird	flick	racquet	**12** service court
kill	rally	singles	**13** underarm clear
05 clear	serve	**08** drop shot	
	smash		

See also **sport**

bag

Bags include:

03 bum	money	evening	suitcase
kit	**06** carpet	holdall	**09** briefcase
04 case	clutch	satchel	fanny pack
grip	duffel	**08** backpack	Gladstone
hand	flight	carry-all	haversack
pack	saddle	knapsack	moneybelt
sack	tucker	reticule	overnight
tote	valise	rucksack	**10** laptop case
wash	vanity	shopping	**11** attaché-case
05 ditty	**07** carrier	shoulder	

See also **container**

baking

Baked items include:

03 bun	**06** cookie	soufflé	shortcake
pie	Danish	stollen	**10** baked apple
04 cake	gateau	strudel	brandy snap
flan	muffin	tartlet	Brown Betty
loaf	parkin	tea cake	cheesecake
puff	pastry	tea loaf	Florentine
roll	quiche	**08** blackcap	shortbread
tart	sponge	en croûte	**11** baked Alaska
05 bread	square	flapjack	gingerbread
pasty	tiffin	meringue	hot cross bun
patty	waffle	tea bread	**12** bread pudding
plait	**07** bannock	traybake	Danish pastry
scone	biscuit	**09** bara brith	fruit cobbler
slice	brioche	batch loaf	fruit crumble
tarte	brownie	clafoutis	pain au raisin
torte	cobbler	clapbread	**13** sponge pudding
twist	lattice	croissant	**14** pain au chocolat
wafer	oatcake	drop scone	
	pancake		

See also **biscuit**; **bread**; **cake**; **dessert**; **food**

Balkans

Cities and notable towns in the Balkans include:

03 Niš (Serbia)

04 Iaşi (Romania)

05 Sibiu (Romania)
Sofia (Bulgaria)
Split (Croatia)
Tuzla (Bosnia and Herzegovina)
Varna (Bulgaria)
Volos (Greece)
Zadar (Croatia)

06 Athens (Greece)
Bitola (Macedonia)
Braila (Romania)
Braşov (Romania)
Burgas (Bulgaria)
Galati (Romania)
Mostar (Bosnia and Herzegovina)
Oradea (Romania)
Osijek (Croatia)
Patras (Greece)
Rijeka (Croatia)
Skopje (Macedonia)
Tirana (Albania)
Zagreb (Croatia)

07 Čakovec (Croatia)

Cetinje (Montenegro)
Craiova (Romania)
Maribor (Slovenia)
Novi Sad (Serbia)
Piraeus (Greece)
Plovdiv (Bulgaria)
Shkodër (Albania)

08 Belgrade (Serbia)
Botoşani (Romania)
Gostivar (Macedonia)
Ploieşti (Romania)
Priština (Serbia)
Sarajevo (Bosnia and Herzegovina)

09 Banja Luka (Bosnia and Herzegovina)
Bucharest (Romania)
Constanta (Romania)
Heraklion (Greece)
Ljubljana (Slovenia)
Podgorica (Montenegro)
Timişoara (Romania)

10 Cluj-Napoca (Romania)
Kragujevac (Serbia)

11 Stara Zagora (Bulgaria)

12 Thessaloniki (Greece)

ballet

Ballets, with composer, choreographer and date of first performance, include:

05 *Manon* (Massenet; MacMillan; 1974)
Rodeo (Copland; de Mille; 1942)
Rooms (Hopkins; Sokolow; 1955)

06 *Boléro* (Ravel; Bejart; 1961)
Carmen (Bizet; Petit; 1949)
Façade (Walton; Ashton; 1931)
Hamlet (Tchaikovsky; Helpmann; 1942)
Jewels (Fauré, Stravinsky, Tchaikovsky; Balanchine; 1967)
La Luna (Bach; Béjart; 1991)
Ondine (Henze; Ashton; 1958)
Onegin (Tchaikovsky, Stolze; Cranko; 1965)
Parade (Satie; Massine; 1917)

07 *Giselle* (Adam; Coralli, Perro, Petipa; 1841)
Isadora (Bennett; MacMillan; 1981)
La Valse (Ravel; Nijinska; 1929)
Orpheus (Stravinsky; Balanchine; 1948)
Requiem (Fauré; MacMillan; 1976)
Rituals (Bartók; MacMillan; 1975)

08 *Coppélia* (Delibes; St Léon; 1870)
Le Renard (Stravinsky; Nijinska; 1922)
Les Noces (Stravinsky; Nijinska; 1923)
Mathilde (Wagner; Béjart; 1965)
Nocturne (Delius; Ashton; 1936)

Raymonda (Glazunov; Petipa; 1898)
Rhapsody (Rachmaninov; Ashton; 1980)
Serenade (Tchaikovsky; Balanchine; 1934)
Swan Lake (Tchaikovsky; Petipa, Ivanov; 1895)

09 *Anastasia* (Tchaikovsky, Martinu; MacMillan; 1971)
Checkmate (Bliss; de Valois; 1937)
Fancy Free (Bernstein; Robbins; 1944)
La Ventana (Lumbye, Holm; Bournonville; 1854)
Les Biches (Poulenc; Nijinska; 1924)
Mayerling (Liszt; MacMillan; 1978)
Spartacus (Khachaturian; Grigorovich; 1968)
The Burrow (Martin; MacMillan; 1958)

10 *Cinderella* (Prokofiev; Ashton; 1948)
Don Quixote (Minkus; Petipa; 1869)
La Bayadère (Minkus; Petipa; 1877)
La Sylphide (Løvenskjold; Bournonville; 1836)
Les Saisons (Glazunov; Petipa; 1900)
Petroushka (Stravinsky; Fokine; 1911)
Prince Igor (Borodin; Fokine; 1909)
The Masques (Poulenc; Ashton; 1933)

Variations (Stravinsky; Balanchine; 1966)

11 *Billy the Kid* (Copland; Loring; 1938)
Cain and Abel (Panufnik; MacMillan; 1968)
Jeu de Cartes (Stravinsky; Balanchine; 1937)
Las Hermanas (Martin; MacMillan; 1963)
Night Shadow (Rieti; Balanchine; 1946)
Summerspace (Feldman; Cunningham; 1958)
Symphony in C (Bizet; Balanchine; 1947)
The Firebird (Stravinsky; Fokine; 1910)
Voluntaries (Poulenc; Tetley; 1973)

12 *Harlequinade* (Drigo; Balanchine; 1965)
Illumination (Britten; Ashton; 1950)
Knight Errant (Strauss; Tudor; 1968)
Les Papillons (Schumann, Tcherepnin; Fokine; 1913)
Les Patineurs (Meyerbeer, Lambert; Ashton; 1937)
Les Sylphides (Chopin; Fokine; 1909)
Night Journey (Schuman; Graham; 1947)
Schéhérazade (Rimsky-Korsakov; Fokine; 1910)
The Judas Tree (Elias; MacMillan; 1992)

13 *Duo Concertant* (Stravinsky; Balanchine; 1972)
Ebony Concerto (Stravinsky; Carter; 1957)
Lady of Shallot (Sibelius; Ashton; 1931)
Les Rendezvous (Auber, Lambert; Ashton; 1933)
Les Vainqueurs (Wagner, Indian/Tibetan music; Béjart; 1969)
Pineapple Poll (Sullivan, Mackerras; Cranko; 1951)
Stoics Quartet (Mendelssohn; Burrows; 1991)
The Invitation (Seiber; MacMillan; 1960)
The Nutcracker (Tchaikovsky; Ivanov; 1892)

14 *Daphnis et Chloé* (Ravel; Fokine; 1912)
Legend of Joseph (Strauss; Fokine; 1914)
Legend of Judith (Mordecai; Graham; 1962)
Romeo and Juliet (Prokofiev; Lavrovsky; 1940)
Russian Soldier (Prokofiev; Fokine; 1942)
Scènes de Ballet (Stravinsky; Dolin; 1944)
Scotch Symphony (Mendelssohn; Balanchine; 1952)
Song of the Earth (Mahler; MacMillan; 1965)
Tales of Hoffman (Offenbach, Lanchberg; Darrell; 1973)
The Four Seasons (Verdi; MacMillan; 1975)
The Moor's Pavane (Purcell; Limón; 1949)
The Prodigal Son (Prokofiev; Balanchine; 1929)

15 *Apollon Musagète* (Stravinsky; Bolm; 1928)
A Wedding Bouquet (Berners; Ashton; 1937)
Concerto Barocco (Bach; Balanchine; 1940)

Fall River Legend (Gould; de Mille; 1948)
Ivan the Terrible (Prokofiev, Chulaki; Grigorovich; 1975)
The Rite of Spring (Stravinsky, Roerich; Nijinsky; 1913)

16 *Enigma Variations* (Elgar; Ashton; 1968)
La Fille Mal Gardée (French songs; Dauberval; 1789)
Lament of the Waves (Masson; Ashton; 1970)
Present Histories (Schubert; Tuckett; 1991)
The Rake's Progress (Gordon; de Valois; 1935)

17 *Appalachian Spring* (Copland; Graham; 1944)
Elite Syncopations (Joplin; MacMillan; 1974)
Le Spectre de la Rose (Weber; Fokine; 1911)
The Gods Go A-Begging (Handel; Balanchine; 1928)
The Lady and the Fool (Verdi, Mackerras; Cranko; 1954)
The Sleeping Beauty (Tchaikovsky; Petipa; 1890)

18 *A Month in the Country* (Chopin, Lanchbery; Ashton; 1976)
L'Après-midi d'un Faune (Debussy; Nijinsky; 1912)
Le Chant du Rossignol (Stravinsky; Massine; 1920)
Le Malade Imaginaire (Rota; Béjart; 1976)
Le Sacré du Printemps (Stravinsky, Roerich; Nijinsky; 1913)
The Seven Deadly Sins (Weill; Balanchine; 1933)

19 *La Boutique Fantasque* (Rossini, Respighi; Massine; 1919)
Symphonic Variations (Franck; Ashton; 1946)
The Four Temperaments (Hindemith; Balanchine; 1946)
The Taming of the Shrew (Scarlatti, Stolze; Cranko; 1969)
The Three-Cornered Hat (de Falla; Massine; 1919)

20 *Le Jeune Homme et la Mort* (Bach; Petit; 1946)
Symphonie Fantastique (Berlioz; Massine; 1936)

21 *A Midsummer Night's Dream* (Mendelssohn; Balanchine; 1962)
Monumentum pro Gesualdo (Stravinsky; Balanchine; 1960)
The Prince of the Pagodas (Britten; Cranko; 1957)

24 *Symphony in Three Movements* (Stravinsky; Balanchine; 1972)

26 *The Walk to the Paradise Garden* (Delius; Ashton; 1972)

Ballet companies include:

04 Maly
West
05 Jooss
Kirov
Royal
06 Boston
07 Bolshoi
Houston
Joffrey
Rambert
08 Hong Kong
National

Scottish
09 Miami City
Stuttgart
10 Australian
Borovansky
Gulbenkian
Paris Opéra
11 New York City
Royal Danish
12 Alicia Alonso
Pennsylvania
Royal Swedish

Sadler's Wells
San Francisco
Stanislavsky
13 Dutch National
Royal Winnipeg
14 London Festival
Western Theatre
15 Birmingham Royal
English National
Royal New Zealand

Ballet dancers include:

04 Bolm (Adolph; 1884–1951, Russian)
Bull (Deborah; 1963– , English)
Dean (Laura; 1945– , US)
Edur (Thomas; 1969– , Estonian)
Feld (Eliot; 1942– , US)
Gore (Walter; 1910–79, Scottish)
Grey (Dame Beryl; 1927– , English)
Kain (Karen; 1951– , Canadian)
Kaye (Nora; 1920–87, US)
Kent (Allegra, 1938– , US)
Kidd (Michael; 1919–2007, US)
Oaks (Agnes; 1969– , Estonian)

05 Bruce (Christopher; 1945– , English)
Bruhn (Erik; 1928–86, Danish)
Clark (Michael; 1962– , Scottish)
Dolin (Anton; 1904–83, English)
Gable (Christopher; 1940–98, English)
Genée (Dame Adelin; 1878–1970, Danish)
Grahn (Lucile; 1819–1907, Danish)
Grant (Alexander; 1925– , New Zealand)
Grisi (Carlotta; 1819–99, Italian)
Jooss (Kurt; 1901–79, German)
Laban (Rudolf von; 1879–1958, Hungarian)
Legat (Nikolai; 1869–1937, Russian)
Lifar (Serge; 1905–86, Russian/French)
Manen (Hans van; 1932– , Dutch)
Marin (Maguy; 1951– , French)
Mauri (Rosita; 1849–1923, Spanish)
Neary (Patricia; 1942– , US)
Panov (Valeri; 1938– , Russian)
Petit (Roland; 1924– , French)
Sallé (Marie; 1707–56, French)
Sleep (Wayne; 1948– , English)
Somes (Michael; 1917–94, English)
Spink (Ian; 1947– , Australian)
Tudor (Antony; 1908–87, English)
Verdy (Violette; 1933– , French)

06 Alonso (Alicia; 1921– , Cuban)
Ashley (Merrill; 1950– , US)
Ashton (Sir Frederick; 1904–88, English)

Béjart (Maurice; 1927– , French)
Blasis (Carlo; 1797–1878, Italian)
Bourne (Matthew; 1960– , English)
Cooper (Adam; 1971– , English)
Dowell (Sir Anthony; 1943– , English)
Dupond (Patrick; 1959– , French)
Fokine (Michel; 1880–1942, Russian/US)
Fracci (Carla; 1936– , Italian)
Franca (Celia; 1921–2007, English)
Gilpin (John; 1930–83, English)
Haydee (Marcia; 1939– , Brazilian)
Ivanov (Lev; 1834–1901, Russian)
Kylian (Jiri; 1947– , Czech)
Lander (Harald; 1905–71, Danish/French)
Murphy (Graeme; 1950– , Australian)
Panova (Galina; 1949– , Russian)
Perrot (Jules; 1810–94, French)
Petipa (Lucien; 1815–98, French)
Petipa (Marius; 1818–1910, French)
Sibley (Dame Antoinette; 1939– , English)
St-Léon (Arthur; 1821–71, French)
Tetley (Glen; 1926–2007, US)
Valois (Dame Ninette de; 1898–2001, Irish)
Wright (Sir Peter; 1926– , English)

07 Babilée (Jean; 1923– , French)
Bintley (David; 1957– , English)
Bujones (Fernando; 1955–2005, US)
Bussell (Darcey; 1969– , English)
Camargo (Maria Anna de; 1710–70, French)
Coralli (Jean; 1779–1854, French)
Dantzig (Rudi von; 1933– , Dutch)
Didelot (Charles-Louis; 1767–1837,
Swedish/French)
Durante (Viviana; 1967– , Italian)
Edwards (Leslie; 1916–2001, English)
Elssler (Fanny; 1810–84, Austrian)
Farrell (Suzanne; 1945– , US)
Fonteyn (Dame Margot; 1919–91, English)
Gielgud (Maina; 1945– , English)
Gregory (Cynthia; 1946– , US)

Guillem (Sylvie; 1965– , French)
Hawkins (Erick; 1909–94, US)
Joffrey (Robert; 1930–88, US)
Larrieu (Daniel; 1957– , French)
Lichine (David; 1910–72, Russian/US)
Markova (Dame Alicia; 1910–2004, English)
Martins (Peter; 1946– , Danish)
Massine (Léonide; 1896–1979, Russian)
Mordkin (Mikhail; 1880–1944, Russian/US)
Nureyev (Rudolf; 1938–93, Russian)
Osipova (Natalia; 1986– , Russian)
Pavlova (Anna; 1881–1931, Russian)
Rambert (Dame Marie; 1888–1982, Polish/
  British)
Robbins (Jerome; 1918–98, US)
Seymour (Lynn; 1939– , Canadian/British)
Shearer (Moira; 1926–2006, Scottish)
Shearer (Sybil; 1918–2005, Canadian/US)
Spoerli (Heinz; 1941– , Swiss)
Ulanova (Galina; 1910–98, Russian)
Vestris (Auguste; 1760–1842, French)

08 Chauviré (Yvette; 1917– , French)
Cullberg (Birgit; 1908–99, Swedish)
d'Amboise (Jacques; 1934– , US)
Danilova (Alexandra; 1904–97, Russian/US)
Eglevsky (André; 1917–77, Russian/US)
Forsythe (William; 1949– , US)
Franklin (Frederic; 1914– , English)
Hamilton (Gordon; 1918–59, Australian)
Helpmann (Sir Robert; 1909–86, Australian)
Jasinski (Roman; 1907–91, Polish/US)
Kirkland (Gelsey; 1952– , US)
Lopukhov (Fyodor; 1886–1973, Russian)
Makarova (Natalia; 1940– , Russian)
McDonald (Elaine; 1943– , Scottish)
Messerer (Asaf; 1903–92, Russian)

Mitchell (Arthur; 1934– , US)
Moiseyev (Igor; 1906–2007, Russian)
Neumeier (John; 1942– , US)
Nijinska (Bronislava; 1891–1972, Russian)
Nijinsky (Vaslav; 1890–1950, Russian)
Stretton (Ross; 1952–2005, Australian)
Taglioni (Maria; 1804–84, Italian)
Villella (Edward; 1936– , US)
Zakharov (Rostislav; 1907–84, Russian)

09 Beauchamp (Pierre; 1636–1705, French)
Cecchetti (Enrico; 1850–1928, Italian)
Dai Ailian (1916–2006, Chinese)
Hightower (Rosella; 1920–2008, US)
Karsavina (Tamara; 1885–1978, Russian/
  British)
Lavrovsky (Leonid; 1905–67, Russian)
Macmillan (Sir Kenneth; 1929–92, Scottish)
Saint-Léon (Arthur; 1821–71, French)
Schaufuss (Peter; 1949– , Danish)
Tallchief (Maria; 1925– , US)
Trefilova (Vera; 1875–1943, Russian)
Van Praagh (Dame Peggy; 1910–90, English)

10 Borovansky (Edouard; 1902–59, Czech)
Mukhamedov (Irek; 1960– , Russian)
Nemchinova (Vera; 1899–1984, Russian)
Rubinstein (Ida; 1885–1960, Russian)
Volochkova (Anastasia; 1976– , Russian)

11 Baryshnikov (Mikhail; 1948– , Russian/US)
Grigorovich (Yuri; 1927– , Russian)
Plisetskaya (Maya; 1925– , Russian)

12 Bessmertnova (Natalia; 1941–2008, Russian)
Bournonville (August; 1805–79, Danish)
Spessivtseva (Olga; 1895–1991, Russian/US)

13 Riabouchinska (Tatiana; 1917–2000,
  Russian/US)

Ballet choreographers include:

04 Bolm (Adolph; 1884–1951, Russian)
Dean (Laura; 1945– , US)
Feld (Eliot; 1942– , US)
Kidd (Michael; 1919–2007, US)

05 Bruce (Christopher; 1945– , English)
Clark (Michael; 1962– , Scottish)
Dolin (Anton; 1904–83, English)
Gades (Antonio; 1936–2004, Spanish)
Jooss (Kurt; 1901–79, German)
Laban (Rudolf von; 1879–1958,
  Hungarian)
Legat (Nikolai; 1869–1937, Russian)
Manen (Hans van; 1932– , Dutch)
Marin (Maguy; 1951– , French)
North (Robert; 1945– , US/British)
Petit (Roland; 1924– , French)
Sleep (Wayne; 1948– , English)
Spink (Ian; 1947– , Australian)

Tudor (Antony; 1908–87, English)

06 Alonso (Alicia; 1921– , Cuban)
Ashton (Sir Frederick; 1904–88, English)
Béjart (Maurice; 1927–2007, French)
Blasis (Carlo; 1797–1878, Italian)
Bourne (Matthew; 1960– , English)
Cranko (John; 1927–73, South African)
Fokine (Michel; 1880–1942, Russian/US)
Ivanov (Lev; 1834–1901, Russian)
Kylian (Jiri; 1947– , Czech)
Lander (Harald; 1905–71, Danish/French)
Murphy (Graeme; 1950– , Australian)
Perrot (Jules; 1810–94, French)
Petipa (Marius; 1818–1910, French)
St-Léon (Arthur; 1821–71, French)
Tetley (Glen; 1926–2007, US)
Valois (Dame Ninette de; 1898–2001,
  Irish)

07 Babilée (Jean; 1923– , French)
Bintley (David; 1957– , English)
Coralli (Jean; 1779–1854, French)
Dantzig (Rudi von; 1933– , Dutch)
Darrell (Peter; 1929–87, English)
Didelot (Charles-Louis; 1767–1837, Swedish/French)
Hawkins (Erick; 1909–94, US)
Joffrey (Robert; 1930–88, US)
Larrieu (Daniel; 1957– , French)
Massine (Léonide; 1896–1979, Russian)
Noverre (Jean-Georges; 1727–1810, French)
Robbins (Jerome; 1918–98, US)
Spoerli (Heinz; 1941– , Swiss)

08 Cullberg (Birgit; 1908–99, Swedish)
d'Amboise (Jacques; 1934– , US)
Forsythe (William; 1949– , US)
Helpmann (Sir Robert; 1909–86, Australian)
Lopukhov (Fyodor; 1886–1973, Russian)
McGregor (Wayne; 1970– , English)
Messerer (Asaf; 1903–92, Russian)

Mitchell (Arthur; 1934– , US)
Moiseyev (Igor; 1906–2007, Russian)
Neumeier (John; 1942– , US)
Nijinska (Bronislava; 1891–1972, Russian)
Nijinsky (Vaslav; 1890–1950, Russian)
Wheeldon (Christopher; 1973– , English)
Zakharov (Rostislav; 1907–84, Russian)

09 Beauchamp (Pierre; 1636–1705, French)
Cecchetti (Enrico; 1850–1928, Italian)
Dai Ailian (1916–2006, Chinese)
Dauberval (Jean; 1742–1806, French)
Hightower (Rosella; 1920–2008, US)
Lavrovsky (Leonid; 1905–67, Russian)
Macmillan (Sir Kenneth; 1929–92, Scottish)
Ratmansky (Alexei; 1968– , Russian)
Saint-Léon (Arthur; 1821–71, French)

10 Balanchine (George; 1904–83, US)
Borovansky (Edouard; 1902–59, Czech)

11 Baryshnikov (Mikhail; 1948– , Russian/US)
Grigorovich (Yuri; 1927– , Russian)

12 Bournonville (August; 1805–79, Danish)

Ballet terms include:

03 bar, pas
04 jeté, plié, posé, tutu
05 adage, barre, battu, brisé, coupé, couru, fondu, gilet, passé, sauté, tendu
06 à terre, attack, ballon, chaîné, chassé, dégagé, devant, écarté, en face, en l'air, entrée, pointe, relevé, retiré

school, splits
07 allegro, à pointe, balancé, bourrée, bras bas, chaînés, ciseaux, company, coryphe, danseur, échappé, emboîté, en avant, fouetté, leotard, maillot, pas jeté, pointes, premier, sissone
08 assemblé, attitude, ballonné, ballotté, batterie, cabriole, capriole, coryphée, couronne

danseuse, demi bras, demi plié, en pointe, ensemble, figurant, fish dive, fouettés, glissade, lame duck, première, stulchak, sur place
09 arabesque, ballabile, ballabili, ballerina, battement, cou de pied, développé, élévation, en seconde, entrechat, figurante, pas de chat, pas de deux, pas de seul, pas de vals, petit jeté, pirouette, point shoe, posé coupé

promenade
régisseur
temps levé
variation
10 à la seconde
ballabiles
ballet shoe
bras croisé
changement
demi pointe
en première
en tournant
épaulement
foudroyant
grande jeté
pas de trois
pas de valse
port de bras
répétiteur
soubresaut
tour en l'air
11 changements
chassé passé
comprimario
See also **dance**

down-the-line
echaînement
en cinquième
en quatrième
en troisième
Laban system
pas ballonné
pas de basque
pas de quatre
petits tours
ports de bras
12 ballet-dancer
ballet-master
bluebird lift
choreography
danseur noble
gargouillade
labanotation
shoulder lift
13 ballet-dancing
corps de ballet
fifth position
first position
five positions

posé arabesque
sur les pointes
third position
14 ballet-mistress
divertissement
fourth position
grand battement
grand pas de deux
maître de ballet
petit battement
premier danseur
prima ballerina
second position
sur le cou-de-pied
15 attitude grecque
ballonné composé
changement battu
demi contretemps
entrechat quatre
full contretemps
posé in arabesque
principal dancer

Bartók, Béla (1881–1945)

Significant works include:

07 *Kossuth* (1903)
08 *Sonatina* (1915)
Suite No 1 (1905)
Suite No 2 (1907)
10 *Dance Suite* (1923)
Out of Doors (1926)
11 *Mikrokosmos* (1926; 1932–39)
Two Pictures (1910)
13 *Piano Rhapsody* (1904)
Romanian Dance (1911)

14 *Allegro Barbaro* (1911)
Cantata Profana (1930)
From Olden Times (1935)
15 *The Wooden Prince* (1917)
18 *Fourteen Bagatelles* (1908)
Romanian Folk Dances (1915)
20 *Duke Bluebeard's Castle* (1918)
21 *The Miraculous Mandarin* (1926)
28 *Fifteen Hungarian Peasant Songs*
(1914–18; 1933)

baseball

Major League baseball teams:

11 Chicago Cubs
New York Mets
12 Boston Red Sox
Tampa Bay Rays
Texas Rangers
13 Atlanta Braves
Detroit Tigers
Houston Astros
14 Cincinnati Reds
Florida Marlins

Minnesota Twins
New York Yankees
San Diego Padres
15 Chicago White Sox
Colorado Rockies
Seattle Mariners
Toronto Blue Jays
16 Baltimore Orioles
Cleveland Indians
Kansas City Royals

Los Angeles Angels
Milwaukee Brewers
Oakland Athletics
St Louis Cardinals
17 Los Angeles Dodgers
Pittsburgh Pirates
18 San Francisco Giants
19 Arizona Diamondbacks
Washington Nationals
20 Philadelphia Phillies

Major League baseball team nicknames include:

04 Cubs (Chicago)
Mets (New York)
Rays (Tampa Bay)
Reds (Cincinnati)

05 Twins (Minnesota)

06 Angels (Los Angeles)
Astros (Houston)
Braves (Atlanta)
Giants (San Francisco)
Padres (San Diego)

Red Sox (Boston)
Royals (Kansas City)
Tigers (Detroit)

07 Brewers (Milwaukee)
Dodgers (Los Angeles)
Indians (Cleveland)
Marlins (Florida)
Orioles (Baltimore)
Pirates (Pittsburgh)
Rangers (Texas)

Rockies (Colorado)
Yankees (New York)

08 Blue Jays (Toronto)
Mariners (Seattle)
Phillies (Philadelphia)
White Sox (Chicago)

09 Athletics (Oakland)
Cardinals (St Louis)
Nationals (Washington)

12 Diamondbacks (Arizona)

Baseball players and associated figures include:

03 Ott (Mel; 1909–58, US)

04 Cobb (Ty; 1886–1961, US)
Mack (Connie; 1862–1956, US)
Mays (Willie; 1931– , US)
Rose (Pete; 1941– , US)
Ruth (Babe; 1895–1948, US)
Ryan (Nolan; 1947– , US)
Sosa (Sammy; 1968– , Dominican)

05 Aaron (Hank; 1934– , US)
Bench (Johnny; 1947– , US)
Berra (Yogi; 1925– , US)
Boggs (Wade; 1958– , US)
Bonds (Barry; 1964– , US)
Gwynn (Tony; 1960– , US)
Paige (Satchel; 1906–82, US)
Spahn (Warren; 1921–2003, US)
Young (Cy; 1867–1955, US)

06 Gehrig (Lou; 1903–41, US)
Gibson (Bob; 1935– , US)
Gibson (Josh; 1911–47, US)
Koufax (Sandy; 1935– , US)
Mantle (Micky; 1931–95, US)
Musial (Stan; 1920– , US)
Rickey (Branch; 1881–1965, US)
Ripken (Cal, Jnr; 1960– , US)

Suzuki (Ichiro; 1973– , Japanese)
Wagner (Honus; 1874–1951, US)

07 Clemens (Roger; 1962– , US)
Gossage (Richard; 1951– , US)
Hoffman (Trevor; 1967– , US)
Hornsby (Rogers; 1896–1963, US)
Jackson (Reggie; 1946– , US)
Jackson ('Shoeless' Joe; 1888–1951, US)
Johnson (Randy; 1963– , US)
Johnson (Walter; 1887–1946, US)
McGwire (Mark; 1963– , US)
Stengel (Casey; 1890–1975, US)

08 Anderson (George 'Sparky'; 1934– , US)
Clemente (Roberto; 1932–72, Puerto Rican)
DiMaggio (Joe; 1914–99, US)
Robinson (Brooks; 1937– , US)
Robinson (Frank; 1935– , US)
Robinson (Jackie; 1919–72, US)
Sadaharo (Oh; 1940– , Japanese)
Williams (Ted; 1918–2002, US)

09 Alexander (Grover Cleveland; 1887–1950, US)
Henderson (Rickey; 1958– , US)
Mathewson (Christie; 1880–1925, US)

Baseball terms include:

03 ace
ERA
gap
hit
out
RBI
run
tag
top

04 balk
ball
base
bunt
cage

mitt
safe
save
walk

05 alley
at bat
bench
bloop
count
cycle
error
mound
pitch
plate

pop up
relay
steal

06 assist
batter
bottom
closer
cutter
double
fly out
hitter
inning
on deck
single

sinker
slider
strike
triple
wind-up

07 all-star
base hit
battery
bull pen
catcher
chopper
diamond
drive in
fly ball
home run
infield
pennant
pick off
pitcher
rundown
shutout
slugger
stretch

08 backstop
ballpark
baseline
change-up
fair ball
fastball
foul ball
foul pole
nightcap
no-hitter
outfield
pitch-out
set-up man
splitter
throw out

See also **sport**

09 curveball
cut-off man
earned run
first base
full count
gold glove
grand slam
ground out
hit-and-run
home plate
infielder
in the hole
left field
line drive
sacrifice
screwball
shortstop
strike out
third base
wild pitch

10 baserunner
batter's box
double play
first pitch
ground ball
Hall of Fame
outfielder
passed ball
right field
second base
strike zone
triple play

11 All-Star game
base on balls
basket catch
centre field
knuckleball
left fielder

major league
minor league
perfect game
pinch hitter
pinch runner
run batted in
triple crown
unearned run

12 breaking ball
complete game
double-header
extra innings
first baseman
load the bases
long reliever
on-deck circle
right fielder
switch hitter
third baseman
warning track

13 centre fielder
clean-up hitter
foul territory
lead-off hitter
relief pitcher
safety squeeze
second baseman
silver slugger

14 American League
backdoor slider
batting average
fielder's choice
middle reliever
National League
position player
suicide squeeze

15 starting pitcher

basketball

08 Utah Jazz

09 Miami Heat

11 Phoenix Suns

12 Atlanta Hawks
Chicago Bulls
Orlando Magic

13 Boston Celtics
Denver Nuggets
Indiana Pacers
New Jersey Nets

New York Knicks

14 Detroit Pistons
Houston Rockets
Milwaukee Bucks
Toronto Raptors

15 Dallas Mavericks
Sacramento Kings
San Antonio Spurs

16 Charlotte Bobcats
Los Angeles Lakers

Memphis Grizzlies

17 New Orleans Hornets
Philadelphia 76ers
Washington Wizards

18 Cleveland Cavaliers
Los Angeles Clippers

19 Golden State Warriors
Oklahoma City Thunder

20 Portland Trail Blazers

21 Minnesota Timberwolves

Basketball team nicknames include:

04 Heat (Miami)
Jazz (Utah)
Nets (New Jersey)
Suns (Phoenix)
05 Bucks (Milwaukee)
Bulls (Chicago)
Hawks (Atlanta)
Kings (Sacramento)
Magic (Orlando)
Spurs (San Antonio)

06 Knicks (New York)
Lakers (Los Angeles)
Pacers (Indiana)
07 Bobcats (Charlotte)
Celtics (Boston)
Hornets (New Orleans)
Nuggets (Denver)
Pistons (Detroit)
Raptors (Toronto)
Rockets (Houston)

Thunder (Oklahoma City)
Wizards (Washington)
08 Clippers (Los Angeles)
Warriors (Golden State)
09 Cavaliers (Cleveland)
Grizzlies (Memphis)
Mavericks (Dallas)
12 Timberwolves (Minnesota)
Trail Blazers (Portland)
13 Seventy-Sixers (Philadelphia)

Basketball players and associated figures include:

04 Bird (Larry; 1956– , US)
Nash (Stephen; 1974– , Canadian)
05 Belov (Sergei; 1944– , Russian)
Cousy (Bob; 1928– , US)
Lemon (Meadowlark; 1935– , US)
Mikan (George; 1924–2005, US)
O'Neal (Shaquille; 1972– , US)
06 Bryant (Kobe; 1978– , US)
Erving (Julius; 1950– , US)
Jordan (Michael; 1963– , US)
Malone (Karl; 1963– , US)
Miller (Cheryl; 1964– , US)
Pippen (Scottie; 1965– , US)
Rodman (Dennis; 1961– , US)

07 Barkley (Charles; 1963– , US)
Bradley (Bill; 1943– , US)
Iverson (Allen; 1975– , US)
Jackson (Phil; 1945– , US)
Johnson (Earvin 'Magic'; 1959– , US)
Russell (Bill; 1934– , US)
08 Auerbach (Arnold 'Red'; 1917–2006, US)
Nowitzki (Dirk; 1978– , German)
Olajuwon (Hakeem; 1963– , Nigerian/US)
Petrovic (Drazen; 1964–93, Croatian)
Stockton (John; 1962– , US)
09 Robertson (Oscar; 1938– , US)
11 Abdul-Jabbar (Kareem; 1947– , US)
Chamberlain (Wilt; 1936–99, US)

Basketball terms include:

03 key
NBA
04 dunk
hoop
trap
05 block
drive
guard
lay-up
pivot
steal
tap-in
06 assist
basket
box out
centre
post up
rim out
screen
tip-off
07 dribble
forward

foul out
kick out
low post
rebound
sky hook
time-out
08 alley oop
bank shot
charging
fadeaway
foul lane
foul line
hang time
high post
hook shot
inbounds
jump ball
jump hook
jump shot
sixth man
slam dunk
team foul
turnover

09 backboard
chest pass
fast break
field goal
free throw
perimeter
shot clock
violation
10 bounce pass
double pump
double team
foul circle
point guard
transition
travelling
11 goal-tending
pick and roll
zone defence
12 baseball pass
personal foul
power forward
small forward
triple double

13 double dribble
    shooting guard
See also **sport**

bat

Bats include:

03 red
05 fruit
    guano
    hoary
06 yellow
07 mastiff

    vampire
08 big brown
09 flying fox
    leaf-nosed
10 frog-eating
11 little brown

    pipistrelle
14 Kitti's hog-nosed
15 lesser horseshoe
    Mexican freetail

technical foul
14 full-court press

three-point line

battle

Battles include:

04 Jena (1806)
    Loos (1915)
    Neva (1240)
    Nile (1798)
    Zama (202 BC)
05 Alamo (1836)
    Anzio (1944)
    Boyne (1690)
    Bulge (1944)
    Crécy (1346)
    Issus (333 BC)
    Liège (1914)
    Maipó (1818)
    Maipú (1818)
    Marne (1914)
    Mylae (260 BC)
    Pavia (1525)
    Rhine (1945)
    Sedan (1870)
    Sluys (1340)
    Somme (1916)
    Spurs (1513)
    Valmy (1792)
    Varna (1828)
    Ypres (1914/1915)
06 Actium (31 BC)
    Amiens (1918)
    Arnhem (1944)
    Cannae (216 BC)
    Harlaw (1411)
    Kosovo (1389)
    Lützen (1632)
    Midway (1942)
    Mohács (1526)
    Mycale (5c BC)
    Naseby (1645)
    Pinkie (1547)

    Quebec (1759)
    Shiloh (1862)
    Tobruk (1941–42)
    Towton (1461)
    Verdun (1916)
    Wagram (1809)
07 Antwerp (1918)
    Britain (1940)
    Bull Run (1861/1862)
    Cambrai (1916)
    Cassino (1944)
    Colenso (1899)
    Corunna (1809)
    Cowpens (1781)
    Dresden (1813)
    Dunkirk (1940)
    Flodden (1513)
    Iwo Jima (1944–45)
    Jutland (1916)
    Leipzig (1813)
    Lepanto (1571)
    Leuctra (371 BC)
    Marengo (1800)
    Okinawa (1945)
    Plassey (1757)
    Salamis (5c BC)
    Salerno (1943)
    Thapsus (46 BC)
08 Atlantic (1940–43)
    Ayacucho (1824)
    Blenheim (1704)
    Carabobo (1821)
    Culloden (1746)
    Edgehill (1642)
    Fontenoy (1745)
    Formigny (1450)
    Granicus (334 BC)

    Hastings (1066)
    Mafeking (1900)
    Marathon (490 BC)
    Monmouth (1778)
    Omdurman (1898)
    Philippi (42 BC)
    Poitiers (1356)
    Pyramids (1798)
    Saratoga (1777)
    Spion Kop (1900)
    St Albans (1455)
    Waterloo (1815)
    Yorktown (1781)
09 Agincourt (1415)
    Balaclava (1854)
    Bay of Pigs (1961)
    Chaeronea (338 BC)
    Contreras (1847)
    Ebro River (1938)
    El Alamein (1943)
    Gaugamela (331 BC)
    Leyte Gulf (1944)
    Nicopolis (1396)
    Otterburn (1388)
    Pharsalus (48 BC)
    Pichincha (1822)
    Ramillies (1706)
    Sedgemoor (1685)
    Seven Days (1862)
    Solferino (1859)
    Spartacus (73–71 BC)
    Stormberg (1899)
    Trafalgar (1805)
    Vicksburg (1863)
    Worcester (1651)
10 Aboukir Bay (1798)
    Adrianople (AD 78)

Austerlitz (1805)
Brandywine (1777)
Bunker Hill (1775)
Camperdown (1797)
Charleston (1780)
Chevy Chase (1388)
Cold Harbor (1864)
Copenhagen (1801/1807)
Gettysburg (1863)
Gravelotte (1870)
Majuba Hill (1881)
Malplaquet (1709)
Oudenaarde (1708)
Paardeberg (1900)
Petersburg (1864)

River Plate (1939)
Shrewsbury (1403)
Solway Moss (1542)
Stalingrad (1942–43)
Stillwater (1777)
Tannenberg (1914)
Tel-El-Kebir (1882)
Wilderness (1864)

11 Bannockburn (1314)
Guadalcanal (1942)
Halidon Hill (1333)
Hohenlinden (1800)
Marston Moor (1644)
Modder River (1899)
Navarino Bay (1827)

Pearl Harbor (1941)
Prestonpans (1745)
Sheriffmuir (1715)
Wounded Knee (1890)

12 Mons Graupius (AD 4)
Monte Cassino (1944)
Tet offensive (1968)

13 Bosworth Field (1485)
Cape St Vincent (1797)
Killiecrankie (1689)
Little Bighorn (1876)
Magersfontein (1899)
Passchendaele (1917)
Spanish Armada (1588)

14 Fredericksburg (1862)

See also **siege**; **war**

bay

Bays include:

03 Tor (England)
04 Acre (Brazil)
Clew (Ireland)
Daya (China)
Kiel (Germany)
Luce (Scotland)
Lyme (England)
Pigs (Cuba)
Tees (England)

05 Algoa (South Africa)
Blind (Canada)
Cloud (Canada)
Enard (Scotland)
Evans (Canada)
False (South Africa)
Fundy (Canada)
Hawke (New Zealand)
Shark (Australia)
Table (South Africa)

06 Baffin (Canada)
Bantry (Ireland)
Bengal (India/Bangladesh/
   Myanmar)
Biscay (France/Spain)
Botany (Australia)
Broken (Australia)
Colwyn (Wales)
Dingle (Ireland)
Dublin (Ireland)
Galway (Ireland)

Hervey (Australia)
Hudson (Canada)
Lubeck (Germany)
Mounts (England)
Naples (Italy)
Plenty (New Zealand)
Tasman (New Zealand)
Walvis (Namibia)

07 Bustard (Australia)
Chaleur (Canada)
Donegal (Ireland)
Dundalk (Ireland)
Fortune (Canada)
Halifax (Australia)
Hudson's (Canada)
Montego (Jamaica)
Moreton (Australia)
Pegasus (New Zealand)
Prudhoe (USA)
Thunder (Canada)
Thunder (USA)
Trinity (Canada)
Volcano (Japan)

08 Campeche (Mexico)
Cardigan (Wales)
Delaware (USA)
Georgian (Canada)
Hang-Chow (China)
Portland (Australia)
Quiberon (France)

San Pablo (USA)
St Bride's (Wales)
St Magnus (Scotland)
Tremadog (Wales)
Weymouth (England)

09 Admiralty (Antarctica)
Discovery (Australia)
Discovery (USA)
Encounter (Australia)
Frobisher (Canada)
Galveston (USA)
Geographe (Australia)
Hermitage (Canada)
Mackenzie (Canada)
Morecambe (England)
Notre Dame (Canada)
Placentia (Canada)
St George's (Canada)

10 Barnstaple (England)
Bridgwater (England)
Carmarthen (Wales)
Chesapeake (USA)
Conception (Canada)
Heligoland (Germany)
Providence (Canada)
Robin Hood's (England)

11 Port Jackson (Australia)
Port Phillip (Australia)

12 San Francisco (USA)

beach

Beaches include:

04 Gold (France)
Juno (France)
Long (USA)
Utah (France)

05 Bells (Australia)
Bondi (Australia)
Cable (Australia)
Miami (USA)
Omaha (France)

Sword (France)
06 Chesil (England)
Malibu (USA)
Sunset (USA)
Tahiti (French Polynesia)
Venice (USA)

07 Daytona (USA)
Ipanema (Brazil)
Pattaya (Thailand)

Waikiki (USA)
08 St Tropez (France)
Virginia (USA)
09 Blackpool (England)
10 Copacabana (Brazil)
11 Coney Island (USA)
13 Skeleton Coast (Namibia)
15 Surfers Paradise (Australia)

bean

Beans and pulses include:

03 dal
pea
soy
wax

04 dhal
fava
gram
lima
mung
navy
okra
snap
soya

05 aduki
black
broad

carob
green
pinto
sugar
tonka

06 adzuki
Boston
butter
chilli
cowpea
French
kidney
legume
lentil
locust
runner

string
07 alfalfa
fasolia
haricot
snow pea

08 black-eye
borlotti
chickpea
garbanzo
split pea
sugar pea

09 black-eyed
black gram
flageolet
green gram
mangetout

petit pois
pigeon pea
puy lentil
red kidney
red lentil

10 beansprout
cannellini
golden gram

11 dwarf runner
garbanzo pea
green lentil

12 black-eyed pea
marrowfat pea

13 scarlet runner
water chestnut

See also **food**; **vegetable**

bear

Bears include:

03 sea
sun

04 balu
cave
Pooh
Yogi

05 baloo
black
brown

Bruin
Great
honey
koala
Nandi
polar
sloth
Sooty
teddy

water
white

06 Little
native
Rupert
woolly

07 grizzly
Malayan

08 cinnamon
09 Ursa Major
Ursa Minor
10 giant panda
Paddington
13 Iorek Byrnison
Teddy Robinson
Winnie the Pooh

bed

Beds include:

01 Z
03 box
cot

day
04 boat
bunk

camp
crib
sofa

twin
05 berth
divan

futon	sleigh	king-size	queen-size
water	07 folding	mattress	shakedown
06 cradle	hammock	platform	10 adjustable
double	trestle	put-you-up	four-poster
pallet	truckle	09 couchette	mid sleeper
Put-u-up®	trundle	king-sized	queen-sized
settee	08 bassinet	lit bateau	11 high sleeper
single	foldaway	palliasse	12 chaise longue

Bedclothes include:

05 doona	valance	pillowcase	valanced sheet
duvet	08 coverlet	pillow sham	Witney blanket
quilt	09 bed canopy	pillowslip	14 patchwork quilt
sheet	bedspread	quilt cover	15 cellular blanket
06 pillow	comforter	11 counterpane	electric blanket
07 bedroll	eiderdown	fitted sheet	
blanket	throwover	sleeping bag	
bolster	10 duvet cover	13 mattress cover	

See also **house**

beer

Beers include:

03 ale	export	microbrew
dry	gueuze	milk stout
ice	Helles	Rauchbier
IPA	Kölsch	snakebite
keg	lambic	Weissbier
04 bock	Märzen	winter ale
mild	old ale	10 barley wine
Pils	porter	black lager
rice	red ale	harvest ale
05 abbey	shandy	Hefeweizen
black	Vienna	low-alcohol
fruit	07 Altbier	malt liquor
green	bottled	sweet stout
guest	draught	Weisse Bier
heavy	Eisbock	Weizenbier
honey	pale ale	11 black-and-tan
Kriek	Pilsner	12 bière de garde
kvass	real ale	Christmas ale
lager	seventy	India Pale Ale
March	08 amber ale	oatmeal stout
plain	brown ale	13 Hefe-Weissbier
sahti	cream ale	sixty shilling
sixty	Guinness®	14 Berliner Weisse
steam	home brew	eighty shilling
stone	Irish ale	Kristall-Weizen
stout	light ale	15 cask-conditioned
wheat	Pilsener	seventy shilling
06 bitter	Trappist	
Dunkel	09 Framboise	
eighty	frambozen	

Brewing terms include:

03 fox
keg
pin
tun
04 back
bigg
butt
cask
head
hoop
hops
lees
malt
mash
stum
wort
05 draff
goods
grain
grist
middy
nappy
round
stave

yeast
06 barley
barrel
bright
browst
cooper
copper
fining
firkin
infuse
liquor
mature
multum
straik
sweets
trough
widget
07 beerage
bummock
draught
extract
ferment
flowers
gravity

hogwash
hop back
hop boil
malt tea
mashman
mash-tub
mash-tun
mash-vat
real ale
set mash
zymurgy
08 blacking
hogshead
home-brew
maltster
molasses
mucilage
pale malt
puncheon
real beer
sparging
09 amber malt
blown malt
brown malt

cleansing
isinglass
kilderkin
soft spile
under-back
10 barleycorn
black strap
brewmaster
malt-factor
malt liquor
mashing-tub
saccharine
11 attenuation
broad cooper
12 abroad cooper
attemperator
essentia bina
final gravity
microbrewery
13 brewers' pounds
carbon dioxide
saccharimeter
saccharometer

See also **drink**

Beethoven, Ludwig van (1770–1827)

Significant works include:

06 'Choral' (Symphony; 1824)
'Eroica' (Symphony; 1805)
'Spring' (Sonata; 1801)
07 *Fidelio* (1805)
'Emperor' (Concerto; 1811)
08 'Kreutzer' (Sonata; 1803)
'Pastoral' (Symphony; 1808)
09 'Les Adieux' (Sonata; 1803)
'Moonlight' (Sonata; 1801)
'Waldstein' (Sonata; 1803)
10 *Grosse Fuge* (String Quartet; 1825)

'Pathétique' (Sonata; 1798)
12 *Archduke Trio* (1811)
'Appassionata' (Sonata; 1804)
13 *Missa Solemnis* (1824)
'Hammerklavier' (Sonata; 1818)
14 *Egmont Overture* (1810)
16 *Leonora Overtures* (1805)
18 *Diabelli Variations* (1819–23)
Rasumovsky Quartets (1806)

beetle

Beetles include:

03 dor
may
oil
04 bark
dorr
dung
flea
gold

leaf
musk
pine
rose
rove
stag
05 black
click

clock
shard
snout
tiger
water
06 batler
carpet
chafer

diving
dor-fly
elater
ground
larder
may bug
museum
sacred
scarab
sexton
spider
spring
weevil
07 blister
bruchid
burying
cadelle
carabid
carrion
diamond
gold-bug
goliath
hop-flea

See also **insect**

hornbug
June bug
rose bug
08 bum-clock
cardinal
Colorado
darkling
glowworm
Hercules
Japanese
ladybird
longhorn
minotaur
skipjack
tortoise
wireworm
woodworm
09 cantharis
Christmas
clavicorn
dermestid
furniture
goldsmith

longicorn
tumblebug
whirligig
10 bloody-nose
bombardier
churchyard
cockchafer
deathwatch
pine-chafer
rhinoceros
rose chafer
scarabaean
scarabaeid
Spanish fly
tumbledung
turnip flea
11 bloody-nosed
coprophagan
grain weevil
typographer
13 argus tortoise
house longhorn

Belgium

Cities and notable towns in Belgium include:

04 Gand
Gent
Luik
Mons
05 Ghent

Ieper
Liège
Namur
Ypres
06 Anvers

Bruges
Brugge
Ostend
07 Antwerp
08 Brussels

Oostende
09 Charleroi
Zeebrugge

Administrative divisions of Belgium, with regional capitals:

05 Liège (Liège)
Namur (Namur)
07 Antwerp (Antwerp)
Hainaut (Mons)

08 Limbourg (Hasselt)
10 Luxembourg (Arlon)
12 East Flanders (Ghent)
West Flanders (Bruges)

14 Flemish Brabant (Leuven)
Walloon Brabant (Wavre)

Belgian landmarks include:

05 Meuse
Senne
07 Atomium
Belfort
Scheldt
08 Stadhuis
09 Cloth Hall
Menin Gate

See also **Low Countries**

Notre Dame
10 Grand Place
Jeaneke Pis
Market Hall
Rubenshuis
11 Gravensteen
Jeanneke Pis
Maison du Roi

Manneken Pis
Royal Palace
12 Hôtel de Ville
Rubens's House
13 Brabo Fountain
14 Ghent Cathedral
Rue des Bouchers
15 Bruges Cathedral

belief

Beliefs include:

06 holism
malism
racism
07 animism
atheism
elitism
08 demonism
feminism
hedonism
humanism
nihilism

Satanism
09 pantheism
physicism
tritheism
10 liberalism
Manicheism
monotheism
polytheism
11 agnosticism
parallelism

supremacism
tetratheism
12 Manicheanism
13 ethnocentrism
individualism
structuralism
14 fundamentalism
traditionalism
tripersonalism
15 supernaturalism

Believers include:

03 Jew
04 Babi
Jain
Sikh
Sofi
Sufi
05 Babee
Hindu
Jaina
06 holist
Muslim
07 Alawite
animist
Bahaist
Genevan
Lollard
Scotist
08 Arminian
Buddhist
Calixtin
Catholic

demonist
Erastian
Glassite
humanist
Lutheran
Nazarean
Nazarene
Pelagian
Salesian
Satanist
Wesleyan
09 animalist
Calixtine
Christian
Confucian
Eutychian
Gregorian
Methodist
Nestorian
Origenist
pantheist
Sabellian

Simeonite
Wyclifite
10 Bergsonian
Berkeleian
Cameronian
Capernaite
Holy Roller
Marcionite
polytheist
Wycliffite
11 Sandemanian
Valentinian
12 Apollinarian
Southcottian
13 Hutchinsonian
Roman Catholic
Swedenborgian
14 fundamentalist
the Oxford group
15 supernaturalist

See also **Buddhism; Christianity; Hinduism; Islam; Judaism; missionary; philosophy; politics; priest; religion; Sikhism; theology**

berry

Berries include:

05 lichi
06 lichee
litchi
lychee
07 bramble
leechee
08 bilberry
dewberry

goosegog
mulberry
tayberry
09 blaeberry
blueberry
cranberry
raspberry
shadberry

whimberry
10 blackberry
cloudberry
elderberry
gooseberry
loganberry
redcurrant
salal berry

strawberry
11 boysenberry
huckleberry
sallal berry
12 blackcurrant
serviceberry
whitecurrant
whortleberry

See also **fruit**

bet

Bets and betting systems include:

03 TAB		Yankee	**09** on the nose	
04 tote	**07** à cheval		quadrella	
06 double		each way	**10** martingale	
parlay	**08** ante-post		pari-mutuel	
roll-up		forecast	superfecta	
tierce		perfecta	**11** accumulator	
treble		quinella	daily double	
triple		trifecta	**13** double or quits	

See also **gambling**

Betjeman, Sir John (1906–84)

Significant works include:

09 *Mount Zion* (1931)	**15** *Summoned by Bells* (1960)
10 *High and Low* (1966)	**16** *Ghastly Good Taste* (1933)
12 *A Nip in the Air* (1974)	**20** *New Bats in Old Belfries* (1945)
Continual Dew (1937)	**22** *A Few Late Chrysanthemums* (1954)
14 *Collected Poems* (1958)	**23** *Old Lights For New Chancels* (1940)

Bible

Versions of the Bible include:

02 AV	Reims	Peshito	Wycliffe
RV	**06** Geneva	Tyndale	**09** Coverdale
03 NIV	Gideon	Vulgate	King James
05 Douai	Italic	**08** Breeches	**10** New English
Douay	Wyclif	Peshitta	Septuagint
Itala	**07** Matthew	Peshitto	**14** Revised Version

Old Testament books of the Bible:

03 Job (Book of)	**07** Ezekiel (Book of)
04 Amos (Book of)	Genesis (Book of)
Ezra (Book of)	Malachi (Book of)
Joel (Book of)	Numbers (Book of)
Ruth (Book of)	Obadiah (Book of)
05 Hosea (Book of)	**08** Habakkuk (Book of)
Jonah (Book of)	Jeremiah (Book of)
Kings (Books of)	Jeremiah (Letter of)
Micah (Book of)	Nehemiah (Book of)
Nahum (Book of)	Proverbs (Book of)
06 Daniel (Book of)	**09** Leviticus (Book of)
Esther (Book of)	Zechariah (Book of)
Exodus (Book of)	Zephaniah (Book of)
Haggai (Book of)	**10** Chronicles (Books of)
Isaiah (Book of)	**11** Deuteronomy (Book of)
Joshua (Book of)	**12** Ecclesiastes (Book of)
Judges (Book of)	Lamentations
Psalms (Book of)	**13** Song of Solomon
Samuel (Books of)	

New Testament books of the Bible:

04 John (Gospel according to)
John (Letters of)
Jude (Letter of)
Luke (Gospel according to)
Mark (Gospel according to)

05 James (Letter of)
Peter (Letters of)
Titus (Letter of Paul to)

06 Romans (Letter of Paul to the)

07 Hebrews (Letter of Paul to the)
Matthew (Gospel according to)
Timothy (Letters of Paul to)

08 Philemon (Letter of Paul to)

09 Ephesians (Letter of Paul to the)
Galatians (Letter of Paul to the)

10 Colossians (Letter of Paul to the)
Revelation (Book of)

11 Corinthians (Letters of Paul to the)
Philippians (Letter of Paul to the)

13 Thessalonians (Letters of Paul to the)

17 Acts of the Apostles

18 Apocalypse of St John

Apocryphal books of the Bible include:

03 Bar
Esd
Jud
Sir
Sus
Tob

04 Macc
Wisd

05 Tobit (Book of)

06 Baruch (Book of)
Ecclus

Esdras (Books of)
Judith (Book of)

07 Pr of Man
Susanna (History of)

08 Bel and Dr
Manasseh (Prayer of)

09 Maccabees

14 Ecclesiasticus (Book of)

15 Bel and the Dragon
Wisdom of Solomon (Book of)

Biblical characters include:

03 Dan	Saul	Peter	Martha
Eve	Seth	Rahab	Miriam
Gad	Shem	Rhoda	Nathan
Ham	**05** Aaron	Sarah	Nimrod
Job	Abner	Sheba	Philip
Lot	Achan	Sihon	Pilate
04 Abel	Annas	Silas	Rachel
Adam	Asher	Simon	Reuben
Ahab	Caleb	Titus	Salome
Amos	David	Tobit	Samson
Anna	Enoch	Uriah	Samuel
Baal	Hagar	**06** Andrew	Simeon
Cain	Herod	Baruch	Sisera
Esau	Hosea	Christ	Thomas
Ezra	Isaac	Daniel	Uzziah
Jehu	Jacob	Darius	Vashti
Joel	James	Elijah	**07** Abigail
John	Jesse	Elisha	Abraham
Leah	Jesus	Esther	Absalom
Levi	Jonah	Gideon	Amaziah
Luke	Judah	Hannah	Azariah
Mark	Magog	Isaiah	Cleopas
Mary	Micah	Joseph	Delilah
Noah	Moses	Joshua	Ephraim
Paul	Nahum	Josiah	Ezekiel
Ruth	Naomi	Judith	Gabriel

Goliath
Ishmael
Japheth
Jezebel
Lazarus
Malachi
Matthew
Micaiah
Michael
Obadiah
Rebecca
Rebekah
Solomon
Stephen
Susanna
Tabitha
Timothy
Zebedee
Zebulun

08 Barabbas
Barnabus
Benjamin
Caiaphas
Habbakuk
Hezekiah
Issachar
Jeremiah
Jeroboam
Jonathan
Manasseh
Matthias
Mordecai
Naphtali
Nehemiah
Rehoboam
Thaddeus
Zedekiah

09 Bathsheba
Nathanael
Nathaniel
Nicodemus
Priscilla
Zacchaeus
Zacharias
Zechariah
Zephaniah

10 Adam and Eve
Bartimaeus
Belshazzar
Methuselah
Simon Magus
Simon Peter
Theophilus

11 Bartholomew
Gog and Magog

Jehoshaphat
Jesus Christ
Melchizedek

12 Herod Agrippa
Herod Antipas
James the Less
Mephibosheth
Queen of Sheba

13 Herod the Great
Judas Iscariot
Mary Magdalene
Pontius Pilate
Simon of Cyrene

14 John the Baptist
Nebuchadnezzar
Simon the Zealot

Biblical places include:

03 Nod

04 Gaza
Rome

05 Babel
Egypt
Judah
Sodom

06 Canaan

Cyrene
Israel
Judaea
Mt Zion
Red Sea

07 Babylon
Calvary
Jericho
Mt Sinai

Nineveh

08 Bethesda
Dalmatia
Damascus
Golgotha
Gomorrah
Mt Ararat
Nazareth

09 Bethlehem
Jerusalem
Palestine

10 Alexandria
Gethsemane

11 River Jordan

12 Garden of Eden
Sea of Galilee

Biblical terms include:

02 NT
OT

03 ark
God
law

05 canon
flood

06 gospel
missal
Yahweh

07 epistle
evangel
gospels
hexapla

Jehovah
letters
Messiah
miracle
octapla
parable

08 epistles
good book
holy writ
Pharisee`
prophets
writings

09 Apocrypha
Holy Bible

Holy Ghost
leviathan
Samaritan

10 Armageddon
evangelist
Holy Spirit
Pentateuch
Philistine
revelation
Scriptures

12 New Testament
Old Testament

13 Good Samaritan

14 holy Scriptures

See also **patriarch**; **plague**; **prophet**

bicycle

Bicycles include:

03 BMX

04 push
solo

05 hobby
racer

06 safety

tandem

07 chopper
Raleigh®

touring

08 draisene
draisine

exercise	tricycle	boneshaker	stationary
kangaroo	unicycle	dandy-horse	two-wheeler
mountain	**09** recumbent	fairy-cycle	velocipede
ordinary	**10** all-terrain	fixed-wheel	**13** penny farthing

Bicycle parts include:

03 hub	hub gear	disc brake	Woods® valve
04 bell	pannier	drum brake	**11** gear shifter
fork	rim tape	gear cable	lamp bracket
gear	toe clip	gear lever	Presta® valve
lamp	tool bag	gearwheel	roller chain
pump	top tube	inner tube	speedometer
tire		kickstand	
tyre	**08** aero bars	prop stand	**12** brake caliper
	cassette	reflector	coaster brake
05 brake	chainset	seat stays	diamond frame
chain	crankset	tyre valve	spoke nipples
crank	crossbar	wheel lock	steering head
frame	down tube		steering tube
pedal	head tube	**10** brake block	stirrup guide
spoke	mudguard	brake cable	wheel bearing
wheel	rim brake	brake lever	wheel spindle
	rod brake	chain guard	
06 dynamo	seat post	chain guide	**13** bottom bracket
fender	seat tube	chain stays	clipless pedal
hanger	sprocket	chain wheel	freewheel unit
pulley	wheel nut	crank lever	handlebar stem
saddle	wheel rim	derailleur	Schrader® valve
spokes		drive train	shock absorber
		handlebars	sprocket wheel
07 bar ends	**09** brake shoe	seat pillar	
carrier	chain link	stabilizer	**14** drop handlebars
headset	chain ring		side-pull brakes

See also **cycling**

biochemistry

Biochemists include:

02 Li (Choh Hao; 1913–87, US)

03 Dam (Henrik; 1895–1976, Danish)

04 Abel (John Jacob; 1857–1938, US)
Cech (Thomas; 1947– , US)
Cori (Carl; 1896–1984, US)
Cori (Gerty; 1896–1957, US)
Doty (Paul; 1920– , US)
Duve (Christian de; 1917– , Belgian)
Endo (Akira; 1933– , Japanese)
Funk (Casimir; 1884–1967, US)
Rose (William C; 1887–1984, US)
Wald (George; 1906–97, US)

05 Bloch (Konrad; 1912–2000, US)
Boyer (Herbert; 1936– , US)
Boyer (Paul D; 1918– , US)
Brown (Rachel Fuller; 1898–1980, US)
Chain (Sir Ernst B; 1906–79, British)
Cohen (Seymour S; 1917– , US)

Cohen (Stanley; 1922– , US)
Doisy (Edward A; 1893–1986, US)
Elion (Gertrude B; 1918–99, US)
Jacob (François; 1920– , French)
Kamen (Martin; 1913–2002, US)
Krebs (Sir Edwin G; 1918– , US)
Krebs (Sir Hans; 1900–81, German/British)
Lynen (Feodor; 1911–79, German)
Monod (Jacques; 1910–76, French)
Moore (Stanford; 1913–82, US)
Smith (Lester; 1904–92, English)
Smith (Michael; 1932–2000, Canadian)
Stein (William H; 1911–80, US)
Synge (Richard L M; 1914–94, English)
Tatum (Edward; 1909–75, US)

06 Asimov (Isaac; 1920–92, US)
Beadle (George; 1903–89, US)
Chance (Britton; 1913– , US)
Collip (James 'Bert'; 1892–1965, Canadian)

de Duve (Christian; 1917–   , Belgian)
Domagk (Gerhard; 1895–1964, German)
Holley (Robert W; 1922–93, US)
Keilin (David; 1887–1963, Russian/British)
Leloir (Luis; 1906–87, Argentine)
Levene (Phoebus; 1869–1940, US)
Martin (Archer; 1910–2002, English)
Michel (Hartmut; 1948–   , German)
Mullis (Kary B; 1944–   , US)
Oparin (Aleksandr; 1894–1980, Russian)
Pardee (Arthur B; 1921–   , US)
Perutz (Max; 1914–2002, Austrian/British)
Peters (Sir Rudolf Albert; 1889–1982, English)
Porter (Rodney R; 1917–85, English)
Sanger (Frederick; 1918–   , English)
Sumner (James B; 1887–1955, US)
Walker (Sir John E; 1941–   , English)

07 Abraham (Sir Edward; 1913–99, English)
Edelman (Gerald M; 1929–   , US)
Emerson (Gladys Anderson; 1903–84, US)
Fischer (Edmond H; 1920–   , US)
Folkers (Karl; 1906–97, US)
Hopkins (Sir Frederick; 1861–1947, English)
Khorana (H Gobind; 1922–   , US)
Lipmann (Fritz; 1899–1986, US)
Needham (Joseph; 1900–95, English)
Okazaki (Reiji; 1930–75, Japanese)
Quastel (J H; 1899–1987, English)
Rodbell (Martin; 1925–98, US)
Schally (Andrew V; 1926–   , US)
Sherman (Henry C; 1875–1955, US)
Stanley (Wendell M; 1904–71, US)
Waksman (Selman; 1888–1973, US)

See also **chemistry**

Warburg (Otto; 1883–1970, German)
08 Anfinsen (Christian B; 1916–95, US)
Blumberg (Baruch S; 1925–   , US)
Chargaff (Erwin; 1905–2002, US)
Elvehjem (Conrad; 1901–62, US)
Hoagland (Mahlon; 1921–   , US)
Kornberg (Arthur; 1918–2007, US)
Kornberg (Roger D; 1947–   , US)
Kornberg (Sir Hans; 1928–   , German/British)
McCollum (Elmer; 1879–1967, US)
Meyerhof (Otto; 1884–1951, US)
Mitchell (Peter; 1920–92, English)
Northrop (John H; 1891–1987, US)
Prusiner (Stanley B; 1942–   , US)
Theorell (Hugo; 1903–82, Swedish)
Vigneaud (Vincent du; 1901–78, US)
Virtanen (Artturi; 1895–1973, Finnish)
Weinberg (Robert; 1942–   , US)

09 Bergström (Sune; 1916–2004, Swedish)
Butenandt (Adolf; 1903–95, German)
Greengard (Paul; 1925–   , US)
Hitchings (George H; 1905–98, US)
Michaelis (Leonor; 1875–1949, US)
Nirenberg (Marshall W; 1927–   , US)

10 Samuelsson (Bengt I; 1934–   , Swedish)
Sutherland (Earl W; 1915–74, US)

11 Hoppe-Seyler (Felix; 1825–95, German)

12 Euler-Chelpin (Hans von; 1873–1964, Swedish)
Schoenheimer (Rudolf; 1898–1941, US)
Szent-Györgyi (Albert von; 1893–1986, US)

14 Fraenkel-Conrat (Heinz; 1910–99, US)

biography

Biographers include:

04 Bold (Alan; 1943–98, Scottish)
Brod (Max; 1884–1968, Austrian)
Edel (Leon; 1907–97, US)

05 Croly (George; 1780–1860, Irish)
Gwynn (Stephen; 1864–1950, Irish)
Haley (Alex; 1921–92, US)
Lodge (Henry Cabot; 1850–1924, US)
Lucas (E V; 1868–1938, English)
Spark (Dame Muriel; 1918–2006, Scottish)
Weems (Mason Locke; 1759–1825, US)

06 Aubrey (John; 1626–97, English)
Martin (Sir Theodore; 1816–1909, Scottish)
Morley (John, Viscount; 1838–1923, English)
Motion (Andrew; 1952–   , English)
Sparks (Jared; 1789–1866, US)
Symons (A J A; 1900–41, English)
Symons (Julian; 1912–94, English)

Wilson (A N; 1950–   , English)
07 Ackroyd (Peter; 1949–   , English)
Barnard (Marjorie; 1897–1987, Australian)
Bedford (Sybille; 1911–2006, German/British)
Bolitho (Hector; 1898–1977, New Zealand)
Boswell (James; 1740–95, Scottish)
Debrett (John; c.1750–1822, English)
Ellmann (Richard; 1918–87, US)
Forster (John; 1812–76, English)
Granger (James; 1723–76, English)
Holroyd (Michael; 1935–   , English)
Lindsay (Philip; 1906–58, Australian)
Lubbock (Percy; 1879–1965, English)
Maurois (André; 1885–1967, French)
Pearson (Hesketh; 1887–1964, English)
Sherard (Robert; 1861–1943, English)
Sitwell (Sir Sacheverell; 1897–1988, English)

08 Berryman (John; 1914–72, US)
Chalmers (Alexander; 1759–1834, Scottish)
Lockhart (John Gibson; 1794–1854,
Scottish)
Plutarch (c.46–c.120 AD, Greek)
Quennell (Sir Peter; 1905–93, English)
Sinclair (Sir Keith; 1922–93, New Zealand)

Spurling (Hilary; 1940– , English)
Strachey (Lytton; 1880–1932, English)
Van Doren (Carl; 1885–1950, US)
09 Aldington (Richard; 1892–1962, English)
Kingsmill (Hugh; 1889–1949, English)
Suetonius (c.69–c.140 AD, Roman)
15 Sebag Montefiore (Simon; 1965– , English

biology

Biology fields include:

06 botany
07 bionics
ecology
zoology
08 biometry
cytology
genetics
genomics
mycology
taxonomy
virology
09 bionomics
Darwinism
evolution
histology
Mendelism

pathology
phycology
10 biometrics
biophysics
bioscience
embryology
enzymology
immunology
Lamarckism
morphology
physiology
proteomics
teratology
toxicology
11 aerobiology
agrobiology
biodynamics

cryobiology
cybernetics
stoichology
systematics
12 bacteriology
biochemistry
biogeography
biorhythmics
cytogenetics
human biology
hydrobiology
macroecology
microbiology
neo-Darwinism
neuroscience
organography
parasitology

pharmacology
photobiology
radiobiology
sociobiology
13 biopsychology
biotechnology
chronobiology
endocrinology
marine biology
palaeontology
14 biogeochemisty
bioinformatics
biomathematics
biometeorology
biosystematics
natural history
15 cellular biology

Biologists, marine biologists and naturalists include:

03 His (Wilhelm; 1831–1904, Swiss/German)
Ray (John; 1627–1705, English)
Say (Thomas; 1787–1834, US)
04 Axel (Richard; 1946– , US)
Baer (Karl Ernst von; 1792–1876, Estonian/
German)
Bell (Thomas; 1792–1880, English)
Berg (Paul; 1926– , US)
Cory (Charles B; 1857–1921, US)
Fell (Dame Honor; 1900–86, English)
Hume (Allan; 1829–1912, Scottish)
Hunt (Tim; 1943– , English)
Katz (Sir Bernard; 1911–2003, German/
British)
Klug (Sir Aaron; 1926– , English)
Koch (Ludwig; 1881–1974, German)
Loeb (Jacques; 1859–1924, German/US)
Lyon (Mary; 1925– , English)
Muir (John; 1838–1914, Scottish/US)
Obel (Matthias de L'; 1538–1616, Flemish)
Sars (Michael; 1805–69, Norwegian)
Savi (Paolo; 1798–1871, Italian)
Skou (Jens; 1918– , Danish)
Vogt (Peter; 1932– , German/US)
05 Arber (Werner; 1929– , Swiss)

Bacon (Francis, Viscount; 1561–1626,
English)
Baird (Spencer; 1823–87, US)
Bates (Henry; 1825–92, English)
Beebe (William; 1877–1962, US)
Belon (Pierre; 1517–64, French)
Blyth (Edward; 1810–73, English)
Brehm (Alfred Edmund; 1829–84, German)
Bruce (Sir David; 1855–1931, Australian/
British)
Cetti (Francesco; 1726–78, Italian)
Chase (Martha; 1927–2003, US)
Cohen (Stanley; 1922– , US)
Crick (Francis; 1916–2004, English)
David (Armand; 1826–1900, French)
Elton (Charles; 1900–91, English)
Evans (Alice; 1881–1975, US)
Golgi (Camillo; 1843–1926, Italian)
Gosse (Philip; 1810–88, English)
Hardy (Sir Alister; 1896–1985, English)
Huber (Robert; 1937– , German)
Lewis (Edward B; 1918–2004, US)
Lobel (Matthias de; 1538–1616, Flemish)
Luria (Salvador; 1912–91, Italian/US)
Lwoff (André; 1902–94, French)

Monod (Théodore; 1902–2000, French)
Neher (Erwin; 1944– , German)
Nurse (Sir Paul; 1949– , English)
Radde (Gustav; 1831–1903, Polish/German)
Rubin (Gerald; 1950– , US)
Sabin (Albert; 1906–93, Russian/US)
Scott (Sir Peter; 1909–89, English)
Selby (Prideaux John; 1788–1867, English)
Sharp (Phillip; 1944– , US)
Smith (Hamilton; 1931– , US)
Steno (Nicolaus; 1638–86, Danish)
Weiss (Robin; 1940– , English)
White (Gilbert; 1720–93, English)
Yalow (Rosalyn; 1921– , US)
Yonge (Charles Maurice; 1899–1986,
  English)

06 Akeley (Carl; 1864–1926, US)
Altman (Sidney; 1939– , Canadian)
Anning (Mary; 1799–1847, English)
Bishop (Michael; 1936– , US)
Blobel (Günter; 1936– , US)
Bonnet (Charles; 1720–93, Swiss)
Boveri (Theodor; 1862–1915, German)
Buffon (George-Louis, Comte de; 1707–88,
  French)
Cairns (Hugh; 1922– , English)
Carson (Rachel; 1907–64, US)
Castle (William; 1867–1962, US)
Chagas (Carlos; 1879–1934, Brazilian)
Claude (Albert; 1899–1983, Belgian)
Darwin (Charles; 1809–82, English)
Dayton (Paul K; 1941– , US)
Denton (Sir Eric; 1923–2007, English)
Finsch (Otto; 1839–1917, German)
Friend (Charlotte; 1921–87, US)
Geddes (Sir Patrick; 1854–1932, Scottish)
Gesner (Conrad; 1516–65, Swiss)
Häckel (Ernst; 1834–1919, German)
Hudson (W H; 1841–1922, Argentine/
  British)
Huxley (Hugh; 1924– , English)
Huxley (Sir Julian; 1887–1975, English)
Huxley (Thomas; 1825–95, English)
Isaacs (Alick; 1921–67, Scottish)
Kandel (Eric; 1929– , Austrian/US)
Mivart (St George; 1827–1900, English)
Morgan (Thomas Hunt; 1866–1945, US)
Müller (Otto; 1730–84, Danish)
Murray (Sir John; 1841–1914, Canadian)
Nansen (Fridtjof; 1861–1930, Norwegian)
Nocard (Edmond; 1850–1903, French)
Palade (George; 1912–2008, Romanian/US)
Pallas (Peter; 1741–1811, German)
Rathke (Martin Heinrich; 1793–1860,
  Polish/German)
Sloane (Sir Hans; 1660–1753, Northern
  Irish/British)
Turner (William; c.1510–68, English)

Ussing (Hans; 1911–2000, Danish)
Varmus (Harold; 1939– , US)
Watson (James; 1928– , US)
Wilson (Edward; 1872–1912, English)
Wilson (Edward O; 1929– , US)

07 Adamson (Joy; 1910–80, Austrian/British)
Agassiz (Elizabeth; 1822–1907, US)
Agassiz (Louis; 1807–73, US)
Andrews (Roy; 1884–1960, US)
Audouin (Jean Victor; 1797–1841, French)
Bastian (Henry; 1837–1915, English)
Beneden (Edouard; 1846–1910, Belgian)
Bombard (Alain; 1924–2005, French)
Boyd Orr (John, Lord; 1880–1971, Scottish)
Brenner (Sydney; 1927– , South African/
  British)
Britten (Roy; 1919– , US)
Davaine (Casimir; 1812–82, French)
Dawkins (Richard; 1941– , Kenyan/British)
Durrell (Gerald; 1925–95, English)
Epstein (Sir Anthony; 1921– , English)
Flavell (Richard; 1945– , British)
Flexner (Simon; 1863–1946, US)
Förster (Johann Reinhold; 1729–98,
  German)
Gilbert (Walter; 1932– , US)
Graells (Mariano de la Paz; 1809–98,
  Spanish)
Haeckel (Ernst; 1834–1919, German)
Haldane (J B S; 1892–1964, English/Indian)
Hershey (A D; 1908–97, US)
Jackson (Barbara, Baroness; 1914–81,
  English)
Kendrew (Sir John; 1917–97, English)
Lamarck (Jean; 1744–1829, French)
Lubbock (Sir John; 1834–1913, English)
McLaren (Dame Anne; 1927–2007, English)
Merriam (Clinton Hart; 1885–1942, US)
Montagu (George; 1753–1815, English)
Nathans (Daniel; 1928–99, US)
Nicolle (Charles; 1866–1936, French)
Nuttall (Thomas; 1786–1859, English/US)
Pasteur (Louis; 1822–95, French)
Ptashne (Mark; 1940– , US)
Roberts (Richard; 1943– , English)
Russell (Sir Frederick; 1897–1984, English)
Sanders (Howard; 1921–2001, US)
Sibbald (Sir Robert; 1641–1722, Scottish)
Spencer (Sir Baldwin; 1860–1929, English/
  Australian)
Stanier (Roger; 1916–82, Canadian)
Steller (Georg; 1709–46, German)
Steptoe (Patrick; 1913–88, English)
Stevens (Nettie; 1861–1912, US)
Swinhoe (Robert; 1836–77, Indian/British)
Van Niel (Cornelis; 1897–1985, Dutch)
Wallace (Alfred; 1823–1913, English)
Wyckoff (Ralph; 1897–1994, US)

08 Beverton (Raymond; 1922–95, English)
Brinster (Ralph; 1932– , US)
Brünnich (Morten Thrane; 1737–1827, Danish)
Chamisso (Adalbert von; 1781–1838, French/German)
Cousteau (Jacques; 1910–97, French)
Davidson (Eric; 1937– , US)
Delbrück (Max; 1906–01, German)
Drummond (Henry; 1851–97, Scottish)
Flemming (Walther; 1843–1905, German)
Harrison (Ross; 1870–1959, US)
Hartwell (Lee; 1939– , US)
Humboldt (Alexander, Baron von; 1769–1859, German)
Jeffreys (Sir Alec; 1950– , English)
Lacépède (Bernard de Laville, Comte de; 1756–1825, French)
Linnaeus (Carl; 1707–78, Swedish)
Li Shizen (1518–93, Chinese)
Margulis (Lynn; 1938– , US)
Meselson (Matthew; 1930– , US)
Milstein (Cesar; 1927–2002, Argentine/British)
Richmond (Sir Mark; 1931– , Australian/British)
Schimper (Karl; 1803–67, German)
Sielmann (Heinz; 1917–2006, German)
Swainson (William; 1789–1855, English)
Tonegawa (Susumu; 1939– , Japanese)
Tristram (Henry Baker; 1822–1906, English)
Weismann (August; 1834–1914, German)
Weissman (Charles; 1931– , Hungarian/Swiss)
Williams (Robley; 1908–95, US)

09 Baltimore (David; 1938– , US)
Berthelot (Sabin; 1794–1880, French)

Burroughs (John; 1837–1921, US)
Carpenter (William; 1813–85, English)
Collinson (Peter; 1694–1768, English)
Ehrenberg (Christian Gottfried; 1795–1876, German)
Lederberg (Joshua; 1925–2008, US)
MacArthur (Robert; 1930–72, US)
Schaudinn (Fritz; 1871–1906, German)
Wieschaus (Eric; 1947– , US)

10 Aldrovandi (Ulisse; 1522–1605, Italian)
Brongniart (Alexandre; 1770–1847, French)
Darlington (Cyril; 1903–81, English)
Felsenfeld (Gary; 1929– , US)
Leichhardt (Ludwig; 1813–c.1848, Prussian/Australian)
Montagnier (Luc; 1932– , French)
Richardson (Sir John; 1787–1865, Scottish)
Swammerdam (Jan; 1637–80, Dutch)
Tradescant (John, the Elder; 1570–c.1638, English)

11 Cretzschmar (Philipp Jakob; 1786–1845, German)
Deisenhofer (Johann; 1943– , US)
Goldschmidt (Richard; 1878–1958, German)
Leeuwenhoek (Antoni van; 1632–1723, Dutch)
Metchnikoff (Elie; 1845–1916, Russian)
Ramón y Cajal (Santiago; 1852–1934, Spanish)
Spallanzani (Lazaro; 1729–99, Italian)

12 Attenborough (Sir David; 1926– , English)
Maynard Smith (John; 1920–2004, English)
Wigglesworth (Sir Vincent Brian; 1899–1994, English)

14 Levi-Montalcini (Rita; 1909– , Italian)

Terms used in biology include:

02 ER	gland	globin	anatomy
GM	lysis	intron	chiasma
03 ADP	order	karyon	chimera
ATP	organ	kinase	diploid
DNA	sense	ligand	guanine
RNA	virus	mutant	habitat
04 cell	06 allele	mutate	haploid
exon	anlage	myosin	hormone
gene	chiasm	operon	kingdom
germ	cilium	phylum	linkage
05 actin	coccus	ploidy	meiosis
cilia	colony	purine	microbe
clade	embryo	stasis	mimicry
class	enzyme	tissue	mitosis
clone	family	uracil	nucleus
codon	fossil	vector	osmosis
genus	gamete	zygote	peptide
	genome	07 adenine	plasmid

protein	amino acid	symbiosis	pinocytosis
somatic	anabolism	syncytium	pluripotent
species	analogous	telophase	polypeptide
spindle	aneuploid	thymidine	replication
synapse	antisense	transfect	respiration
thymine	apoptosis	transform	transferase
tubulin	bacterium	**10** alpha helix	transfer RNA
uridine	beta sheet	beta barrel	translation
08 anaphase	biologist	catabolism	unicellular
autosome	cell cycle	centromere	**12** cell division
bacillus	chromatin	chemotaxis	conservation
bacteria	commensal	chromosome	crossing over
base pair	corpuscle	cryophilic	cytoskeleton
botanist	cytoplasm	dimorphism	glycoprotein
chimaera	Darwinism	exocytosis	growth factor
cofactor	desmosome	expression	invertebrate
cultivar	diffusion	extinction	messenger RNA
cytidine	ecosystem	haptotaxis	mitochondria
cytosine	ectoplasm	homologous	phagocytosis
ectoderm	eukaryote	interphase	phospholipid
endoderm	evolution	Lamarckism	reproduction
enhancer	excretion	metabolism	thermophilic
genetics	flagellum	nucleoside	**13** animal kingdom
globulin	food chain	nucleotide	flora and fauna
integrin	Golgi body	parasitism	micro-organism
ligation	guanosine	population	mitochondrion
lysogeny	haplotype	prokaryote	morphogenesis
membrane	karyotype	proteinase	multicellular
mesoderm	life cycle	protoplasm	proliferation
metazoan	Mendelism	pyrimidine	recombination
molecule	metaphase	speciation	sex chromosome
mutation	notochord	vertebrate	tight junction
necrosis	nutrition	**11** conjugation	tissue culture
organism	organelle	cytokinesis	transcription
parasite	oxidation	endocytosis	**14** Golgi apparatus
promoter	pollution	gap junction	photosynthesis
prophase	protozoan	genetic code	regulatory gene
receptor	reduction	Haeckel's law	**15** animal behaviour
ribosome	repressor	homeostasis	differentiation
stem cell	reticulum	kinetochore	nuclear membrane
telomere	secretion	leading edge	primitive streak
wild type	selection	living world	ribonucleic acid
09 adenosine	stop codon	phosphatase	

See also **botany**; **cell**; **enzyme**

bird

Birds include:

03 ani	owl	dodo	gull
auk	roc	dove	hawk
daw	tit	duck	huia
emu	tui	emeu	huma
hen	**04** Aves	erne	ibis
jay	chat	fowl	kagu
kea	coot	fung	kite
moa	crow	guan	kiwi

knot
lark
loom
loon
lory
myna
nene
rail
rhea
rook
ruff
shag
skua
smee
swan
taha
teal
tern
tody
wren

05 agami
ariel
avian
booby
capon
chick
colly
crane
dicky
diver
eagle
egret
eider
finch
fleet
flier
galah
goose
grebe
heron
hobby
junco
liver
lowan
macaw
mynah
noddy
ousel
pewee
piper
pipit
pitta
poaka
poker
potoo
quail
raven
reeve

robin
snipe
squab
stilt
stint
stork
swift
twite
vireo
wader

06 avocet
avoset
bantam
barbet
budgie
bulbul
canary
chough
condor
cuckoo
curlew
cushat
darter
dipper
drongo
dunlin
falcon
fulmar
gannet
godwit
grouse
hoopoe
houdan
jabiru
jaçana
kakapo
kokako
leipoa
linnet
magpie
martin
merlin
mesite
missel
motmot
oriole
osprey
ox-bird
parrot
peahen
peewee
peewit
petrel
pigeon
plover
puffin
pukeko
pullet

quelea
raptor
redcap
roller
sea-mew
shrike
simorg
simurg
siskin
takahe
thrush
tom-tit
toucan
trogon
turaco
turkey
weaver
whidah
whydah
willet
yaffle
zoozoo

07 antbird
apteryx
babbler
barn owl
bee-kite
bittern
bluecap
blue jay
blue tit
bullbat
bunting
bushtit
bustard
buzzard
catbird
chicken
coal-tit
cotinga
courlan
courser
cowbird
creeper
dottrel
dun-bird
dunnock
egg-bird
emu wren
fantail
fern-owl
fig-bird
finfoot
goshawk
grackle
halcyon
harrier
hoatzin

horn owl
jacamar
jackdaw
kamichi
kestrel
lapwing
leghorn
limpkin
mallard
manakin
manikin
manumea
marabou
may-bird
minivet
moorhen
mudlark
oilbird
ortolan
ostrich
peacock
pelican
penguin
phoenix
pintail
pochard
pockard
poe-bird
poultry
poy-bird
quetzal
redbird
redpoll
redwing
rooster
ruddock
sea dove
seagull
seriema
simurgh
sirgang
sitella
skimmer
skylark
spadger
sparrow
sunbird
swallow
tanager
tattler
tiercel
tinamou
titlark
touraco
vulture
wagtail
warbler
waxbill

waxwing
wren tit
wrybill
wryneck

08 aasvogel
accentor
adjutant
aigrette
alcatras
araponga
arapunga
bald-coot
bee-eater
bellbird
blackcap
bluebird
boatbill
bobolink
bobwhite
bushwren
cockatoo
cockerel
curassow
dabchick
dotterel
fernbird
fire-bird
fish-hawk
flamingo
great tit
grosbeak
guacharo
hawfinch
hernshaw
hoactzin
hornbill
kingbird
landrail
laverock
leafbird
lorikeet
lovebird
lyrebird
mannikin
marabout
megapode
myna bird
nightjar
notornis
nuthatch
ovenbird
oxpecker
palmchat
parakeet
percolin
pheasant
prunella
puffbird

rainbird
redshank
redstart
reed-bird
reedling
ricebird
ringtail
rock-bird
rock dove
rock lark
sand lark
screamer
sea eagle
shoebill
sittella
snowbird
starling
sungrebe
tapacolo
tapaculo
tick bird
titmouse
troopial
troupial
umbrette
water-hen
wheatear
whimbrel
whinchat
whitecap
white-eye
wire bird
woodchat
woodcock
wood duck
woodlark

09 aepyornis
albatross
ant thrush
bald eagle
baldicoot
Baltimore
beccafico
beefeater
bergander
blackbird
blackgame
blackhead
black swan
blood-bird
bowerbird
brambling
broadbill
bullfinch
campanero
cassowary
cedar-bird
chaffinch

chickadee
cockatiel
cormorant
corncrake
eider duck
fairy tern
fieldfare
fig-pecker
flute-bird
francolin
frogmouth
gallinule
gerfalcon
gnateater
goldcrest
golden eye
goldfinch
goldspink
goosander
gowdspink
grassbird
guillemot
honey-bird
horned owl
impundulu
jack-snipe
kittiwake
little owl
mallemuck
merganser
meropidan
mollymawk
mound-bird
mousebird
mynah bird
nighthawk
nutpecker
organ-bird
ossifrage
paddy-bird
partridge
peregrine
phalarope
plume-bird
porphyrio
ptarmigan
razorbill
redbreast
rifle bird
rock pipit
sandpiper
satin bird
scrub bird
seedsnipe
sheldrake
snow finch
sooty tern
spoonbill

stonechat
sugar bird
thick knee
thornbill
trumpeter
turnstone
umber-bird
wheat bird
widow bird
willow tit
wind-hover

10 aberdevine
black robin
bluebreast
bluethroat
budgerigar
bush-shrike
butter-bird
chiff-chaff
crab plover
dickcissel
fledgeling
flycatcher
goatsucker
gobemouche
greenfinch
greenshank
guinea fowl
hammerhead
harpy eagle
honeyeater
honey guide
indigo bird
junglefowl
kingfisher
kookaburra
locust bird
magpie lark
mallee-bird
missel-bird
mutton bird
night-churr
night heron
night-raven
nutcracker
parson-bird
peckerwood
pratincole
Quaker-bird
rafter-bird
rain-plover
regent-bird
sanderling
sand grouse
sand martin
shearwater
sheathbill
sicklebill

song thrush
stone snipe
sun bittern
tropicbird
turtledove
tyrant bird
wattlebird
willow wren
woodhoopoe
woodpecker
woodpigeon
zebra finch

11 black grouse
brush turkey
buffalo-bird
butcherbird
button quail
Canada goose
cock-sparrow
diamond bird
dragoon-bird
frigate bird
gobe-mouches
golden eagle
hummingbird
indigo finch
Java sparrow

king-vulture
mockingbird
nightingale
plantcutter
purple finch
reed bunting
reed-sparrow
reed warbler
sea dotterel
snow bunting
song sparrow
sparrowhawk
stone curlew
storm petrel
thunderbird
tree-creeper
tree sparrow
vanga shrike
woodcreeper
wood-swallow

12 adjutant bird
bramble-finch
cardinal-bird
cow blackbird
crested swift
cuckoo-roller
cuckoo shrike

diving petrel
false sunbird
flowerpecker
golden plover
hedge sparrow
honey buzzard
honey creeper
missel-thrush
mistle-thrush
mound-builder
painted snipe
reed-pheasant
rifleman bird
ruffed grouse
sedge warbler
standard wing
umbrella bird
yellowhammer

13 archaeopteryx
barnacle goose
boatswain-bird
coachwhip-bird
cock-of-the-rock
crocodile bird
indigo bunting
owlet-nightjar
oyster-catcher

plantain-eater
secretary bird
short-eared owl
trumpeter swan
willow warbler
zebra parakeet

14 bird of paradise
black guillemot
brain-fever bird
horned screamer
New Zealand wren
plains wanderer
rhinoceros bird
shell parrakeet
sooty albatross
St Helena plover

15 American warbler
Baltimore oriole
bearded titmouse
blue-footed booby
green woodpecker
Montagu's harrier
passenger pigeon
peregrine falcon
pied butcherbird
purple gallinule
silky flycatcher

Birds of prey include:

03 owl
04 erne
hawk
kite
pern
05 eagle
hobby
06 falcon
lanner
merlin
osprey
raptor
07 barn owl
buzzard
goshawk
harrier

hawk owl
kestrel
red kite
08 bateleur
berghaan
duck-hawk
eagle owl
fish-hawk
Scops owl
sea eagle
spar-hawk
tawny owl
09 bald eagle
black kite
eagle-hawk
fish eagle

gyrfalcon
little owl
marsh hawk
peregrine
stone hawk
10 harpy eagle
Harris hawk
hen harrier
screech owl
tawny eagle
11 booted eagle
chicken hawk
Cooper's hawk
golden eagle
sparrowhawk
stone falcon

12 great grey owl
honey buzzard
long-eared owl
marsh harrier
13 American eagle
Iceland falcon
imperial eagle
lesser kestrel
pallid harrier
secretary bird
short-eared owl
14 short-toed eagle
15 Montagu's harrier
peregrine falcon
red-footed falcon

Seabirds include:

03 auk
cob
mew
04 cobb
guga
gull
shag

skua
tern
05 solan
06 fulmar
gannet
petrel
puffin

07 pickmaw
seagull
09 black tern
cormorant
great skua
guillemot
kittiwake

little auk
mallemuck
razorbill
swart-back
10 Arctic skua
Arctic tern
common gull

common tern	**11** herring gull	**12** glaucous gull	long-tailed skua
little gull	Iceland gull	Leach's petrel	Manx shearwater
little tern	roseate tern	pomarine skua	**15** black-headed gull
saddleback	Sabine's gull	sandwich tern	
solan goose	storm petrel	**14** black guillemot	

Wading birds include:

03 ree	stilt	lapwing	turnstone
04 hern	stint	**08** dotterel	**10** greenshank
ibis	stork	flamingo	sanderling
knot	**06** avocet	redshank	**11** little stint
ruff	curlew	whimbrel	stone curlew
05 crake	dunlin	woodcock	**12** golden plover
crane	godwit	**09** dowitcher	great bustard
heron	plover	grey heron	ringed plover
reeve	**07** bittern	phalarope	**13** little bustard
snipe	bustard	sandpiper	oyster-catcher

Flightless birds include:

03 emu	rhea	takahe	notornis
04 dodo	weka	**07** ostrich	**09** cassowary
emeu	**06** kakapo	penguin	owl-parrot
kiwi	ratite	**08** great auk	solitaire

See also **falcon**; **farm**; **game: hunting**; **goose**; **mythology**; **parrot**; **poultry**; **swan**

birth symbol

Birth flowers:

04 rose (Jun)	**08** hawthorn (May)	**10** poinsettia (Dec)
05 aster (Sep)	larkspur (Jul)	**11** honeysuckle (Jun)
daisy (Apr)	primrose (Feb)	**12** morning glory (Sep)
holly (Dec)	snowdrop (Jan)	**13** chrysanthemum (Nov)
poppy (Aug)	sweet pea (Apr)	**15** lily of the valley (May)
06 cosmos (Oct)	**09** calendula (Oct)	
violet (Feb)	carnation (Jan)	
violet (Mar)	gladiolus (Aug)	
07 jonquil (Mar)	narcissus (Dec)	
	water lily (Jul)	

Birth stones:

04 opal (Oct)	**07** diamond (Apr)	**09** moonstone (Jun)
ruby (Jul)	emerald (May)	turquoise (Dec)
05 pearl (Jun)	peridot (Aug)	**10** aquamarine (Mar)
topaz (Nov)	**08** amethyst (Feb)	bloodstone (Mar)
06 garnet (Jan)	sapphire (Sep)	tourmaline (Oct)
zircon (Dec)	sardonyx (Aug)	**11** alexandrite (Jun)

See also **astrology**; **zodiac**

biscuit

Biscuits include:

03 dog
nut
sea
tea
04 kiss
Nice
puff
rice
rusk
ship
snap
tack
thin
Twix®
wine
05 Marie
ship's
wafer

water
06 cookie
HobNob
KitKat®
parkin
07 Bourbon
cracker
fig roll
Gold Bar
iced Gem®
Lincoln
oatcake
Penguin®
pretzel
ratafia
rich tea
saltine

08 biscotto
captain's
cracknel
flapjack
hardtack
macaroon
Zwieback
09 Abernethy
BreakAway®
chocolate
digestive
four-by-two
garibaldi
ginger nut
jaffa cake
party ring
petit four
shortcake

10 Bath Oliver
Blue Riband®
brandy snap
dunderfunk
florentine
gingersnap
malted milk
shortbread
Wagon Wheel®
11 brown George
fly cemetery
soda cracker
squashed fly
12 custard cream
jammie dodger
langue de chat
14 gingerbread man

See also **baking**; **cake**; **food**

bishop

Bishops include:

03 Odo (of Bayeux; c.1036–97, Bayeux)
05 Aidan (St; d.651, Lindisfarne)
Peter (St; 1c AD, Rome)
06 Blaise (St; d.c.316 AD, Sebastea)
Ninian (St; c.390–c.432 AD, Old Welsh British)
Osmund (St; d.1099, Salisbury)
07 Ambrose (St; c.339–97 AD, Milan)
Carroll (John; 1735–1815, Baltimore)

Hadrian (1100–59, Albano)
Patrick (St; 5c AD, Armagh)
08 Geoffrey (of Monmouth; c.1100–c.1154, St Asaph)
Holloway (Richard; 1933– , Edinburgh)
Nicholas (St; 4c AD, Myra)
Sheppard (David; 1929– , Liverpool)
11 Elphinstone (William; 1431–1514, Ross, Aberdeen)

See also **archbishop**; **cathedral**; **diocese**; **religion**

black

Shades of black include:

03 jet
04 blae

coal
ebon

jeat
05 dwale

ebony
sable

See also **dye**; **pigment**

Blake, William (1757–1827)

Significant works include:

06 *Tiriel* (1789/1874)
07 *The Lamb* (1789)
08 *The Tyger* (1794)
09 *Jerusalem* (1804–20)

11 *The Sick Rose* (1794)
12 *The Song of Los* (1794)
13 *The Book of Thel* (1789)
15 *Europe, a Prophecy* (1794)

The Book of Ahania (1795)
The Book of Urizen (1794)

16 *America, a Prophecy* (1793)
Poetical Sketches (1783)
Songs of Innocence (1789)

17 *An Island in the Moon* (1784–85)

Songs of Experience (1794)

18 *Valam, or The Four Zoas* (1795–1804)

19 *The French Revolution* (1791)

26 *The Marriage of Heaven and Hell* (1790–93)

29 *Visions of the Daughters of Albion* (1793)

blemish

Blemishes include:

03 zit	scar	**07** blister	blackhead
04 acne	spot	freckle	carbuncle
boil	wart	pustule	chilblain
bump	**06** bunion	verruca	whitehead
corn	callus	**08** pockmark	**13** port-wine stain
mole	naevus	**09** birthmark	**14** strawberry mark
scab	pimple		

blend *see* **coffee**

blindness

Sight impairments include:

03 AMD	**10** nyctalopia	**14** far-sightedness
06 myopia	presbyopia	night blindness
08 glaucoma	**11** astigmatism	**15** colour blindness
trachoma	hemeralopia	long-sightedness
09 amaurosis	**12** purblindness	near-sightedness
cataracts	**13** hypermetropia	

blue

Shades of blue include:

04 anil	indigo	**09** caerulean	nattier blue
aqua	**07** caerule	royal blue	peacock-blue
bice	gentian	steel-blue	ultramarine
blae	ice-blue	turquoise	**12** air-force blue
cyan	jacinth	**10** aquamarine	dumortierite
navy	sea-blue	Berlin blue	electric blue
Saxe	sky-blue	cornflower	midnight blue
teal	watchet	kingfisher	Prussian blue
05 azure	**08** baby blue	Oxford blue	Wedgwood blue
perse	cerulean	periwinkle	**13** Cambridge blue
smalt	dark blue	petrol blue	robin's-egg blue
06 cerule	mazarine	powder blue	
cobalt	Nile blue	**11** duck-egg blue	
haüyne	sapphire	lapis lazuli	

See also **dye**; **pigment**

blues *see* **jazz**

Blyton, Enid (1897–1968)

Blyton series include:

05 Noddy

10 Famous Five

11 Secret Seven

12 Malory Towers

14 The Faraway Tree

Significant characters, with appropriate gang, include:

03 Pam (Secret Seven)

04 Jack (Secret Seven)

05 Colin (Secret Seven)
Janet (Secret Seven)
Noddy
Peter (Secret Seven)
Timmy (Famous Five)

06 Amelia (Jane)
George (Secret Seven)

Kirrin (Anne; Famous Five)
Kirrin (Dick; Famous Five)
Kirrin (Georgina 'George'; Famous Five)
Kirrin (Julian; Famous Five)

07 Barbara (Secret Seven)
Big Ears
Scamper (Secret Seven)

13 The Famous Five

14 The Secret Seven

board game *see* game

boat *see* ship

bodily humour *see* humour

bomb

Bombs include:

02 V-1
V-2

03 car

04 aero
atom
buzz
dumb
mine
MOAB
nail
pipe
time

05 A-bomb
dirty
E-bomb
H-bomb

Mills
shell
smart
smoke
stink

06 binary
candle
cobalt
drogue
flying
fusion
letter
parcel
petrol
radium
rocket

07 bomblet
cluster
fission
grenade
megaton
missile
neutron
nuclear
plastic
tallboy
torpedo

08 bouncing
firebomb
hydrogen
landmine

09 doodlebug

Grand Slam

10 incendiary

11 blockbuster
daisy-cutter
depth charge
penetration
sensor fuzed
stun grenade
thermobaric

12 bunker buster
rifle grenade

13 fragmentation
thermonuclear

14 general purpose

15 Molotov cocktail

Bombers include:

03 B-10
B-17
B-19
B-52
MB-1

04 dive

05 Stuka

06 Gotha G
Harris
Sukhoi

07 Avenger

Heinkel
Junkers
stealth
suicide
Tupolev
Warthog

08 Mitchell

09 Lancaster
Liberator

13 Superfortress

14 Flying Fortress

See also **missile**; **weapon**

bone

Bones and joints include:

01 T	spine	humerus	tympanic
02 os	talus	ischium	upper jaw
03 hip	thigh	kneecap	vertebra
jaw	thumb	knuckle	**09** calcaneum
luz	tibia	malleus	calcaneus
rib	vomer	mastoid	condyloid
04 back	woven	maxilla	ellipsoid
coxa	wrist	ossicle	manubrium
knee	**06** breast	patella	navicular
rump	carpal	phalanx	occipital
shin	carpus	prootic	pterygoid
ulna	coccyx	scapula	trapezium
05 ankle	collar	shackle	turbinate
anvil	cuboid	sternum	zygomatic
blade	fibula	stirrup	**10** astragalus
cheek	hamate	**08** clavicle	cancellous
costa	hammer	cortical	innominate
facet	pecten	lamellar	metacarpal
femur	pelvis	lower jaw	metatarsal
funny	radial	mandible	premaxilla
hinge	radius	palatine	trabecular
hyoid	sacrum	parietal	**11** diarthrosis
ilium	saddle	periotic	intermedium
incus	spauld	pisiform	**12** parasphenoid
jugal	stapes	scaphoid	pelvic girdle
malar	tarsal	sesamoid	synarthrosis
nasal	tarsus	shoulder	**13** ball and socket
pivot	zygoma	sphenoid	cartilaginous
pubis	**07** cranium	splinter	shoulder-blade
share	ethmoid	synovial	zygomatic arch
skull	fibrous	temporal	**14** amphiarthrosis
spade	gliding	turbinal	

book

Books include:

03 pad	board	phrase	self-help
04 A to Z	cloth	prayer	softback
bath	comic	primer	thriller
chap	diary	sketch	**09** anthology
cook	e-book	**07** almanac	biography
copy	guide	fiction	catalogue
days	novel	Filofax®	children's
hand	pop-up	journal	detective
hymn	scrap	lexicon	directory
note	story	omnibus	gazetteer
text	**06** annual	picture	paperback
work	gradus	psalter	reference
year	hymnal	**08** exercise	thesaurus
05 album	jotter	grimoire	**10** bestseller
atlas	ledger	hardback	compendium
audio	manual	libretto	dictionary
	missal		

large print

lectionary

manuscript

11 coffee-table

concordance

instruction

travel guide

12 encyclopedia

13 penny dreadful

travel journal

15 pocket companion

Bookbinding terms include:

03 aeg

04 case

head

limp

tail

yapp

05 bolts

hinge

spine

06 boards

gather

jacket

lining

Linson®

sewing

07 binding

buckram

drawn-on

flyleaf

headcap

morocco

08 backbone

blocking

casing-in

doublure

drilling

endpaper

fore edge

hardback

headband

open-flat

shoulder

smashing

stamping

tailband

09 backboard

book block

casebound

debossing

dust cover

embossing

full bound

half bound

loose-leaf

millboard

paperback

signature

soft-cover

10 back lining

binder's die

front board

laminating

pasteboard

raised band

side-stitch

square back

stab-stitch

strawboard

varnishing

whole bound

11 comb binding

ring binding

velo binding

wire binding

wiro binding

12 all edges gilt

binder's board

binder's brass

cloth binding

flexi binding

notch binding

quarter bound

saddle-stitch

thread sewing

13 back cornering

blind blocking

spiral binding

unsewn binding

wire stitching

14 library binding

perfect binding

15 adhesive binding

cloth-lined board

hot foil stamping

See also **Bible**; **literature**; **non-fiction**; **novel**; **printing**; **publishing**; **science fiction**

boot

Boots include:

03 gum

top

04 crow

half

jack

lace

moon

snow

05 ankle

kamik

thigh

wader

welly

06 bootee

buskin

chukka

finsko

galosh

golosh

jemima

mucluc

mukluk

riding

07 blucher

bottine

Chelsea

cracowe

finnsko

galoche

Hessian

walking

08 balmoral

bootikin

climbing

finnesko

football

high shoe

larrigan

muckluck

overshoe

09 scarpetto

10 Doc Martens®

wellington

13 beetle-crusher

See also **footwear**

border

Borders and boundaries include:

07 Rubicon

09 Green Line

10 Berlin Wall

no-man's-land

11 Iron Curtain

Maginot Line

13 Bamboo Curtain

14 Mason-Dixon Line

15 cordon sanitaire

See also **wall**

borough *see* **London; New York**

Bosnia and Herzegovina *see* **Balkans**

botany

Botanists include:

03 Mee (Margaret; 1909–89, English)
Ray (John; 1627–1705, English)

04 Ball (John; 1818–89, Irish)
Bary (Anton de; 1831–88, German)
Cohn (Ferdinand; 1828–98, German)
Dahl (Anders; 1751–89, Swedish)
Gray (Asa; 1810–88, US)
Gray (Edward Whitaker; 1748–1806, English)
Gray (J E; 1800–75, English)
Gray (Samuel Frederick; 1766–1828, English)
Grew (Nehemiah; 1641–1712, English)
Mohl (Hugo von; 1805–72, German)
Ward (Nathaniel; 1791–1868, English)

05 Arber (Agnes; 1879–1960, English)
Ashby (Eric, Lord; 1904–92, Australian)
Banks (Sir Joseph; 1744–1820, English)
Blume (C L; 1796–1862, German)
Bower (Frederick; 1855–1948, English)
Braun (Lucy; 1889–1971, US)
Brown (Robert; 1773–1858, Scottish)
Davis (Peter; 1918–92, English)
Druce (G Claridge; 1850–1932, English)
Hales (Stephen; 1677–1761, English)
Sachs (Julius von; 1832–97, German)
Scott (Dukinfield Henry; 1854–1934, English)
Smith (Sir James Edward; 1759–1828, English)
Vries (Hugo de; 1848–1935, Dutch)

06 Alpino (Prospero; 1553–1616, Italian)
Aublet (Jean Baptiste Fusée; 1723–78, French)
Bailey (Liberty Hyde; 1858–1954, US)
Bauhin (Caspar; 1560–1624, Swiss)
Bauhin (Gaspard; 1560–1624, Swiss)
Biffen (Sir Rowland; 1874–1949, English)
Carver (George Washington; c.1860–1943, US)
Clarke (Charles Baron; 1832–1906, English)
Curtis (William; 1747–99, English)
Engler (Adolf; 1844–1930, German)
Farrer (Reginald; 1880–1920, English)
Gmelin (Johann Georg; 1709–55, German)
Gmelin (Samuel Gottlieb; 1745–74, German)
Godwin (Sir Harry; 1901–85, English)

Harvey (William Henry; 1811–66, Irish)
Hedwig (Johannes; 1730–99, German)
Hooker (Sir Joseph; 1817–1911, English)
Hooker (Sir William; 1785–1865, English)
Hudson (William; 1734–93, English)
Maiden (Joseph Henry; 1859–1925; Australian)
Mendel (Gregor; 1822–84, Austrian)
Müller (Sir Ferdinand von, Freiherr; 1825–96, German/Australian)
Nägeli (Karl Wilhelm von; 1817–91, Swiss)
Prance (Sir Ghillean; 1937– , English)
Spruce (Richard; 1817–93, English)
Stearn (William T; 1911–2001, English)
Torrey (John; 1796–1873, US)
Wilson (Ernest; 1876–1930, English)

07 Adanson (Michel; 1727–1806, French)
Agassiz (Louis; 1807–73, US)
Andrews (Roy Chapman; 1884–1960, US)
Bartram (John; 1699–1777, American)
Bellamy (David; 1933– , English)
Bentham (George; 1800–84, English)
Bigelow (Jacob; 1787–1879, US)
Britton (Nathaniel Lord; 1859–1934, US)
Camerer (Joachim; 1534–98, German)
Camerer (Rudolph; 1665–1721, German)
Correns (Carl; 1864–1933, German)
Douglas (David; 1799–1834, Scottish)
Forrest (George; 1873–1932, Scottish)
Gardner (George; 1812–49, Scottish)
Gilmour (John S L; 1906–86, English)
Haworth (Adrian H; 1766–1833, English)
Jackson (Benjamin Daydon; 1846–1927, English)
Jussieu (Antoine Laurent de; 1748–1836, French)
Jussieu (Bernard; c.1699–1777, French)
Lindley (John; 1799–1865, English)
Morison (Robert; 1620–83, Scottish)
Mueller (Sir Ferdinand von, Freiher; 1825–96, German/Australian)
Pfeffer (Wilhelm; 1845–1920, German)
Siebold (Philipp Franz von; 1796–1866, German)
Stewart (Ralph R; 1890–1993, US)
Tansley (Sir Arthur; 1871–1955, English)
Vavilov (Nikolai I; 1887–1943, Russian)
Wallich (Nathaniel; 1786–1854, Danish)
Warming (Eugenius; 1841–1924, Danish)

08 Airy Shaw (Kenneth; 1902–85, English)
Blackman (Frederick F; 1866–1947, English)
Boissier (Pierre-Edmond; 1810–85, Swiss)
Candolle (Alphonse de; 1806–93, Swiss)
Candolle (Augustin Pyrame de; 1778–1841, Swiss)
Falconer (Hugh; 1808–65, Scottish)
Linnaeus (Carl; 1707–78, Swedish)
Saussure (Nicolas Théodore de; 1767–1845, Swiss)
Schimper (Andreas; 1856–1901, German)
Schimper (Wilhelm Philipp; 1808–80, German)
Senebier (Jean; 1742–1809, Swiss)
Sprengel (Christian Konrad; 1750–1816, German)
Stebbins (G Ledyard; 1906–2000, US)

09 Baulcombe (David; 1952– , English)
Blakeslee (Albert; 1874–1954, US)
Boerhaave (Hermann; 1668–1738, Dutch)
Cesalpino (Andrea; 1519–1603, Italian)

Cronquist (Arthur; 1919–92, US)
Endlicher (Stephan; 1804–49, Austrian)
Grisebach (August; 1814–79, German)
Rechinger (Karl Heinz; 1906–98, Austrian)
Salisbury (Edward James; 1886–1978, English)
Salisbury (Richard Anthony; 1781–1829, English)
Schleiden (Matthias; 1804–81, German)
Takhtajan (Armen; 1910– , Armenian)

10 Aldrovandi (Ulisse; 1522–1605, Italian)
Cunningham (Allan; 1791–1839, English)
Hofmeister (Wilhelm; 1824–77, German)
Pringsheim (Nathaniel; 1823–94, German)
Tournefort (Joseph Pitton de; 1656–1708, French)
Williamson (William; 1816–95, English)

11 Strasburger (Eduard; 1844–1912, German)

12 Schweinfurth (Georg August; 1836–1925, German)

bottle

Bottles include:

03 bed	flask	pooter	demijohn
gas	gourd	siphon	hip flask
ink	Klein	stubby	hot-water
pig	phial	syphon	magnetic
04 beer	scent	Woulfe	medicine
case	snuff	**07** amphora	screwtop
codd	water	ampulla	smelling
jack	**06** carafe	costrel	weighing
junk	carboy	feeding	
mick	cutter	flacket	**09** Aristotle
milk	feeder	pilgrim	**10** apothecary
tear	fiasco	pitcher	lachrymary
vial	flacon	squeezy	Winchester
wash	flagon	sucking	
wine	hottie	torpedo	**11** vinaigrette
05 bidon	inkpot	vinegar	water bouget
cruet	lagena	washing	
cruse	magnum	**08** calabash	**12** Bologna phial
dumpy	poison	decanter	lachrymatory
			Thermos® flask

See also **container**; **wine**

boundary *see* border

boxing

Professional boxing weight divisions:

09 flyweight	**12** bantamweight
11 heavyweight	middleweight
lightweight	welterweight
strawweight	**13** cruiserweight

featherweight
mini flyweight
minimum weight
14 light flyweight
super flyweight
15 junior flyweight
16 light heavyweight
super lightweight
17 junior lightweight

light middleweight
super bantamweight
super middleweight
super welterweight
18 junior bantamweight
junior middleweight
junior welterweight
super featherweight
19 junior featherweight

Boxers and associated figures include:

03 Ali (Muhammad; 1942– , US)

04 Baer (Max; 1909–59, US)
Benn (Nigel; 1964– , English)
Bowe (Riddick; 1967– , US)
Byrd (Chris; 1970– , US)
Clay (Cassius; 1942– , US)
King (Don; 1932– , US)
Ruiz (John; 1972– , US)
Ward (Andre; 1984– , US)
Watt (Jim; 1948– , Scottish)

05 Bruno (Frank; 1961– , English)
Duran (Roberto; 1951– , Panamanian)
Hamed ('Prince' Naseem; 1974– , English)
Lewis (Lennox; 1965– , Canadian/British)
Louis (Joe; 1914–81, US)
Lynch (Benny; 1913–46, Scottish)
Moore (Archie; 1913–98, US)
Peter (Samuel; 1980– , Nigerian)
Tyson (Mike; 1966– , US)

06 Cerdan (Marcel; 1916–49, French)
Cooper (Sir Henry; 1934– , English)
Dundee (Angelo; 1923– , US)
Eubank (Chris; 1966– , English)
Hearns (Tommy; 1958– , US)
Holmes (Larry; 1949– , US)
Liston (Sonny; 1932–70, US)
Monzon (Carlos; 1942–95, Argentine)
Norton (Ken; 1943– , US)
Rahman (Hasim; 1972– , US)
Sayers (Tom; 1826–65, English)
Spinks (Leon; 1953– , US)
Tunney (Gene; 1897–78, US)
Valuev (Nikolai; 1973– , Russian)

07 Chagaev (Ruslan; 1978– , Uzbekistani)
Collins (Steve; 1964– , Irish)
Corbett ('Gentleman' Jim; 1866–1933, US)
Dempsey (Jack; 1895–1983, US)
Foreman (George; 1949– , US)
Frazier (Joe; 1944– , US)
LaMotta (Jake; 1921– , US)
Leonard (Sugar Ray; 1956– , US)
Maskaev (Oleg; 1969– , Russian)

08 Brewster (Lamon; 1973– , US)
Buchanan (Ken; 1945– , Scottish)
Calzaghe (Joe; 1972– , English/Welsh)
Graziano (Rocky; 1922–90, US)
Marciano (Rocky; 1923–69, US)
McGuigan (Barry; 1961– , Irish)
Povetkin (Aleksandr; 1979– , Russian)
Robinson (Sugar Ray; 1920–89, US)
Whitaker (Pernell 'Sweet Pea'; 1964– , US)

09 Armstrong (Henry; 1912–88, US)
Holyfield (Evander; 1962– , US)
Honeyghan (Lloyd; 1960– , Jamaican/British)
Klitschko (Vitali; 1971– , Ukrainian)
Klitschko (Vladimir; 1976– , Ukrainian)
Patterson (Floyd; 1935–2006, US)
Schmeling (Max; 1905–2005, German)
Stevenson (Teofilo; 1952– , Jamaican/Cuban)

10 Liakhovich (Sergei; 1976– , Belarussian)

11 Fitzsimmons (Bob; 1862–1917, English/New Zealand/US)
Gaydarbekov (Gaydarbek; 1976– , Russian)
Queensberry (Sir John Sholto Douglas, Marquis of; 1844–1900, Scottish)

Boxing terms include:

03 jab
04 belt
bout
down
foul
hold
hook
lead

pull
ring
spar
05 apron
count
cross
feint
guard

judge
reach
round
weave
06 canvas
clinch
corner
one-two

07 caution
counter
warning

08 blocking
knockout
passbook
pugilism
shortarm
southpaw
speed bag

See also **sport**

uppercut

09 corner man
headguard

10 eight-count
infighting
mouthpiece
outclassed
punch drunk
scoring hit

11 combination
Queensberry
rabbit punch

12 shadow boxing

13 neutral corner
split decision

14 out for the count

15 throw in the towel

boy *see* **name**

Brahms, Johannes (1833–97)

Significant works include:

12 Piano Quintet (1864)

13 *German Requiem* (1869)

14 Double Concerto (1887)
Tragic Overture (1886)
Zigeunerlieder (1888)

15 *Hungarian Dances* (1869)

16 *Four Serious Songs* (1896)

17 *Vier ernste Gesänge* (1896)

18 *Tragische Ouverture* (1881)

19 *Ein deutsches Requiem* (1869)

brain

Brain parts include:

04 pons

06 cortex

07 cinerea

08 amygdala
cerebrum
meninges
midbrain
thalamus

09 brainstem

forebrain
hindbrain
ventricle

10 Broca's area
cerebellum
grey matter
pineal body
spinal cord

11 frontal lobe
hippocampus

white matter

12 hypothalamus
limbic system
parietal lobe
Purkinje cell
temporal lobe
visual cortex

13 choroid plexus
mesencephalon
occipital lobe

olfactory bulb
optic thalamus
Wernicke's area

14 cerebral cortex
corpus callosum
left hemisphere
pituitary gland

15 right hemisphere
substantia nigra

bread

Bread and rolls include:

03 bap
cob
nan
rye
tea

04 azym
cake
corn
farl
loaf
milk
naan
pita

pone
puri
roti
soda

05 arepa
azyme
bagel
black
brown
cheat
fancy
horse
matza

matzo
pitta
plait
poori
ravel
white

06 damper
French
garlic
graham
Indian
injera
lavash

matzah
matzoh
panini
panino
simnel
stotty
wastel

07 bannock
bloomer
brioche
brownie
buttery
challah

chapati	ciabatta	burger bun	French loaf
currant	corn pone	cornbread	stotty cake
ficelle	focaccia	croissant	unleavened
granary	grissini	flatbread	vienna loaf
jannock	leavened	petit pain	wholewheat
manchet	ravelled	schnecken	**11** cottage loaf
paratha	ryebread	shewbread	French stick
pretzel	schnecke	showbread	morning roll
stottie	standard	sourdough	potato bread
wheaten	tortilla	wholemeal	potato scone
08 baguette	**09** bara brith	**10** breadstick	**12** pumpernickel
barm cake	barmbrack	bridge roll	**13** farmhouse loaf
chapatti	batch loaf	finger roll	

See also **baking**; **cake**; **food**

breakfast see **cereal**

Brecht, Bertolt (1898–1956)

Significant works include:

04 *Baal* (1922)
08 *Edward II* (1924)
10 *Coriolanus* (1959)
12 *Man Equals Man* (1926)
15 *Drums in the Night* (1922)
16 *The Life of Galileo* (1943)
  The Measures Taken (1929–30)
17 *The Duchess of Malfi* (1946)
18 *The Threepenny Opera* (1928)

The Trial of Lukullus (1940)
21 *St Joan of the Stockyards* (1929–30)
  The Good Woman of Setzuan (1938–41)
23 *Mr Puntila and His Man Matti* (1940)
  The Caucasian Chalk Circle (1944–45)
26 *He Who Says Yes and He Who Says No* (1930)
27 *Mother Courage and Her Children* (1941)
  The Resistible Rise of Arturo Ui (1941)
28 *Fear and Misery of the Third Reich* (1935)

Significant characters include:

02 Ta (Shui)
  Te (Shen)
  Ui (Arturo)
03 Gay (Gayly)
  Sun (Yang)
04 Baal
  Giri (Emanuele)
  Roma (Ernesto)
05 Azdak
  Brown (Tiger)

Eilif
Matti
06 Andrea
  Givola (Giuseppe)
07 Galileo
  Kattrin
  Kazbeki (Arsen)
  Peachum (Celia)
  Peachum (Jonathan Jeremiah)

Peachum (Polly)
Puntila
08 Fierling (Anna)
  Macheath
  Shashava (Simon)
09 Abashwili (Michael)
  Abashwili (Natella)
  Vashnadze (Grusha)

10 The Florist
11 Dogsborough
  Mac the Knife
  Swiss Cheese
12 Low-Dive Jenny
  Schweizerkas
  The Fat Prince
13 Mother Courage
  The Beggar King

breed see **cat**; **cattle**; **dog**; **horse**

brewing see **beer**

bridge

Bridge types include:

03 air	road	girder	floating
fly	rope	**07** bascule	humpback
04 arch	skew	flyover	overpass
beam	toll	lattice	**09** box girder
deck	wire	lifting	**10** cantilever
draw	**05** chain	pontoon	suspension
foot	pivot	railway	traversing
leaf	swing	through	**11** cable-stayed
over	**06** Bailey	viaduct	transporter
raft	flying	**08** aqueduct	

Bridges include:

03 Tay (Scotland)

04 Skye (Scotland)
Tyne (England)

05 Forth (Scotland)
Sighs (Italy)
Tower (England)

06 Humber (England)
Kintai (Japan)
London (England)
Rialto (Italy)
Severn (England)

07 Bifrost (Norse mythology)
Rainbow (USA)
Tsing Ma (China)
Yichang (China)

08 Bosporus (Turkey)
Brooklyn (USA)
Jiangyin (China)
Mackinac (USA)
Waterloo (England)

09 Evergreen (USA)
Forth Road (Scotland)

See also **game**

River Kwai (Thailand)

10 Bosporus II (Turkey)
Golden Gate (USA)
Höga Kusten (Sweden)
Ironbridge (England)
Kurushima-2 (Japan)
Kurushima-3 (Japan)
Millennium (England)
Pont du Gard (France)
Storebaelt (Denmark)

11 Brocade Sash (Japan)

12 Akashi-Kaikyo (Japan)
Pont d'Avignon (France)
Ponte Vecchio (Italy)

13 Great Belt East (Denmark)
Kita Bisan-Seto (Japan)
Millau Viaduct (France)
Sydney Harbour (Australia)

14 Ponte 25 de Abril (Portugal)
Quebec Railroad (Canada)

15 Minami Bisan-Seto (Japan)

bridle

Bridle parts include:

03 bit	**06** musrol	eye-flap	noseband
04 curb	pelham	snaffle	**09** headstall
05 cheek	**07** bridoon	**08** browband	**10** cheekpiece

British *see* **monarch**

Britten, Benjamin (1913–76)

Significant works include:

06 *Te Deum* (1936)
07 *Phaedra* (1976)
08 *Antiphon* (1956)
   Gloriana (1953)
   Mont Juic (1938)
   Nocturne (1958)
09 *Billy Budd* (1951)
   Lachrymae (various dates)
   Night Mail (1936)
   St Nicolas (1948)
10 *'Amo Ergo Sum'* (1949)
   Paul Bunyan (1941)
   War Requiem (1961)
   Welcome Ode (1977)
11 *A Boy Was Born* (1934)
   Curlew River (1964)
   Missa Brevis (1959)
   Noye's Fludde (1958)
   Passacaglia (1945)
   Peter Grimes (1945)
   Sinfonietta (1933)
   Winter Words (1953)
12 *On This Island* (1937)
   Owen Wingrave (1971)
13 *Albert Herring* (1947)
   Cello Symphony (1964)

Death in Venice (1973)
Hymn to St Peter (1955)
14 *Ballad of Heroes* (1939)
   Festival Te Deum (1945)
   Kinderkreuzzug (1969)
   Scottish Ballad (1941)
   Spring Symphony (1949)
   The Little Sweep (1949)
   The Prodigal Son (1968)
   Voices for Today (1965)
15 *A Simple Symphony*
   (1934)
   Five Flower Songs (1950)
   Hymn to St Cecilia (1942)
   Hymn to the Virgin (1931)
   Let's Make an Opera
   (1949)
   Prelude and Fugue (1943)
   The Beggar's Opera (1948)
   The Golden Vanity (1967)
16 *Les Illuminations* (1940)
17 *The Rape of Lucretia* (1946)
   The Turn of the Screw (1954)
21 *A Midsummer Night's Dream* (1960)
22 *The Burning Fiery Furnace* (1966)
31 *Variations on a Theme of Frank Bridge* (1937)

broadcasting

Broadcasting terms include:

02 CB	rerun	God slot	**09** announcer
OB	SECAM	hammock	cablecast
TV	video	link man	frequency
03 BSC		network	interview
DAB	**06** advert	phone-in	multicast
DBS	anchor	sponsor	multiplex
mix	Ceefax	station	off the air
PAL	filler	the pips	prime time
pan	repeat	trailer	satellite
Sky	script	webcast	simulcast
04 HDTV	serial		streaming
live	series	**08** analogue	subtitles
NTSC	studio	Freeview	syndicate
05 audio	teaser	national	watershed
bleep		newscast	
cable	**07** air play	news desk	**10** commentary
Dolby®	airtime	on the air	commercial
ident	airwave	playlist	continuity
NICAM	CB radio	producer	mixing desk
pilot	channel	regional	needle time
radio	dead air	roadshow	sportscast
	digital	schedule	telebridge
	episode	teletext	

11 aspect ratio
commentator
rolling news
telestrator

12 Citizens' Band
transmission

13 advertisement
double pumping

narrowcasting
satellite dish
telerecording

14 high definition

15 commercial break
satellite linkup

See also **journalism**; **radio**; **television**

Brontë, Anne (1820–49)

Significant works include:

09 *Agnes Grey* (1845)

23 *The Tenant of Wildfell Hall* (1848)

Significant characters include:

04 Grey (Agnes)

06 Arthur
Graham (Mrs Helen)
Murray (Rosalie)

Weston (Rev Mr Edward)

07 Markham (Gilbert)

08 Lawrence (Frederick)

10 Huntingdon (Arthur)

Brontë, Charlotte (1816–55)

Significant works include:

07 *Shirley* (1849)

08 *Jane Eyre* (1847)

Villette (1853)

12 *The Professor* (1857)

Significant characters include:

04 Beck (Madame)
Eyre (Jane)
Home (Paulina 'Polly')
Reed (Eliza)
Reed (Georgiana)
Reed (John)
Reed (Mrs)

05 Burns (Helen)
Henri (Frances)
Lloyd (Dr)
Mason (Bertha)
Moore (Louis)
Moore (Robert Gerard)
Pelet (Monsieur)
Poole (Grace)
Pryor (Mrs)

Snowe (Lucy)
Yorke (Martin)
Yorke (Mr)

06 Farren (William)
Ingram (Miss Blanche)
Miller (Miss)
Oliver (Miss Rosamond)
Reuter (Zoraide)
Rivers (Diana)
Rivers (Mary)
Rivers (St John)
Sophie
Temple (Miss Maria)

07 Bretton (Dr John)
Keeldar (Shirley)
Nasmyth (Reverend)

Nunnely (Sir Philip)

08 Emmanuel (Monsieur Paul)
Fanshawe (Ginevra)
Helstone (Caroline)
Helstone (James)
Helstone (Mr)
Helstone (Reverend
Matthewson)

09 Rochester (Adele)
Rochester (Mr Edward
Fairfax)
Scatcherd (Miss)
Walravens (Madame)

10 Crimsworth (William)

12 Brocklehurst (Mr)

Brontë, Emily (1818–48)

Significant works include:

09 'Last Lines' (1846)

10 'Plead for Me' (1846)

13 'To Imagination' (1846)

16 *Wuthering Heights* (1847)

Significant characters include:

04 Dean (Ellen 'Nelly')

05 Green (Mr)

06 Joseph

Linton (Catherine)
Linton (Edgar)
Linton (Isabella)

Linton (Mr)
Linton (Mrs)
Zillah

08	Earnshaw (Catherine 'Cathy')	Earnshaw (Hindley)	10	Heathcliff
	Earnshaw (Frances)	Earnshaw (Mr)		Heathcliff (Linton)
	Earnshaw (Hareton)	Earnshaw (Mrs)		
		Lockwood (Mr)		

brown

Shades of brown include:

03	bay	hazel	burnet	cinnamon
	dun	honey	coffee	mahogany
	tan	khaki	copper	mushroom
04	buff	mocha	ginger	nut-brown
	drab	ochre	russet	philamot
	ecru	rusty	sorrel	raw umber
	fawn	sepia	walnut	09 chocolate
	pine	taupe	07 biscuit	earth-tone
	rust	tawny	caramel	10 burnt umber
	sand	tenné	chamois	café au lait
	teak	umber	filemot	terracotta
05	beige	06 auburn	oatmeal	11 burnt sienna
	camel	bister	oxblood	orange-tawny
	cocoa	bistre	08 brunette	12 vandyke brown
	dusky	bronze	chestnut	

See also **dye**; **pigment**

buccaneer *see* **piracy**

Buddhism

Buddhist groups, schools and orders include:

03 Zen	Sakyapa	Mahayana	Theravada
06 Tendai	Shingon	Nichiren	11 Vaibhashika
	Tantric	Pure Land	13 Sarvastivadin
07 Gelugpa	Tibetan	09 Nyingmapa	
Kagyupa	08 Hinayana	Sinhalese	

See also **religion**

building

Building types include:

03 inn	cabin	museum	mansion
pub	hotel	pagoda	theatre
04 barn	house	palace	08 barracks
café	store	prison	beach hut
fort	villa	school	bungalow
mews	06 castle	stable	dovecote
mill	chapel	temple	fortress
pier	church	07 chateau	gurdwara
shed	cinema	college	high-rise
shop	garage	cottage	hospital
silo	gazebo	factory	monument
05 abbey	mandir	library	outhouse
arena	mosque	low-rise	pavilion

showroom
skilling
skillion
windmill
09 apartment
boathouse
cathedral
farmhouse

gymnasium
mausoleum
monastery
multiplex
synagogue
warehouse
10 lighthouse
maisonette

restaurant
skyscraper
sports hall
tower block
university
11 condominium
observatory
office block

public house
summerhouse
12 block of flats
power station
14 apartment house
sliver building

Building materials include:

03 MDF
04 clay
sand
tile
wood
05 brick
glass
grout
slate
steel
stone
06 ashlar
cement
girder
gravel
gypsum

lintel
lumber
marble
mastic
mortar
pavior
siding
tarmac
thatch
timber
07 asphalt
bitumen
decking
drywall
fixings
granite
lagging

plaster
plastic
plywood
sarking
shingle
08 asbestos
cast iron
cladding
concrete
hard core
roof tile
wall tile
09 aggregate
aluminium
chipboard
clapboard
flagstone

floor tile
hardboard
sandstone
steel beam
10 glass fibre
insulation
matchboard
11 breeze block
paving stone
roofing felt
12 plasterboard
13 building block
wattle and daub
14 foam insulation
stainless steel

Buildings include:

05 Duomo (Italy)
07 BT Tower (England)
CN Tower (Canada)
Kremlin (Russia)
La Scala (Italy)
St Paul's (England)
UN Plaza (USA)
08 Casa Milà (Spain)
Cenotaph (England)
Pantheon (Italy)
St Peter's (Vatican City)
Taj Mahal (India)
09 Acropolis (Greece)
Coit Tower (USA)
Colosseum (Italy)
Notre Dame (France)
Old Bailey (England)
Parthenon (Greece)
Reichstag (Germany)
Taipei 101 (Taiwan)
The Louvre (France)
US Capitol (USA)
10 Guggenheim (Spain)
Guggenheim (USA)

Sears Tower (USA)
Tate Modern (England)
The Gherkin (England)
Trump Tower (USA)
White House (USA)
11 Canary Wharf (England)
Eden Project (England)
Eiffel Tower (France)
Musée d'Orsay (France)
Space Needle (USA)
The Alhambra (Spain)
The Panthéon (France)
The Pentagon (USA)
Tower Bridge (England)
12 Globe Theatre (England)
Great Pyramid (Egypt)
Mont St Michel (France)
The Parthenon (Greece)
Winter Palace (Russia)
13 Crystal Palace (England)
Dome of the Rock (Israel)
Musée du Louvre (France)
Somerset House (England)
Tower of London (England)

14 Balmoral Castle (Scotland)
Barbican Centre (England)
Blenheim Palace (England)
Centre Pompidou (France)
Hoover Building (England)
Millennium Dome
(England)
Pompidou Centre (France)
Sagrada Familia (Spain)
Wells Cathedral (England)
15 Ashmolean Museum
(England)
Banqueting House
(England)
Brandenburg Gate
(Germany)
Capitol Building (USA)
Edinburgh Castle (Scotland)
Lincoln Memorial (USA)
Post Office Tower (England)
Royal Opera House
(England)
Statue of Liberty (USA)
Westminster Hall (England)

See also **abbey**; **accommodation**; **architecture**; **castle**; **house**; **palace**; **religion**; **tent**

bulb

Plants grown from bulbs, corms, rhizomes and tubers include:

04 iris
ixia
lily

05 tulip

06 allium
crinum
crocus
dahlia
garlic
nerine
scilla
squill

07 anemone
jonquil
muscari
peacock

08 bluebell
camassia
curtonus
cyclamen
daffodil
endymion

galtonia
gladioli
harebell
hyacinth
snowdrop
sparaxis

09 colchicum
crocosmia
galanthus
gladiolus
narcissus
snowflake
tiger lily

10 agapanthus
chionodoxa
fritillary
giant rouge
montbretia
ranunculus
snake's head
solfaterre
wand flower

11 acidanthera

African lily
erythronium
fritillaria
hippeastrum
lapeirousia
naked ladies
sternbergia
tiger flower

12 autumn crocus
ornithogalum
Solomon's seal
wild hyacinth

13 crown imperial
grape hyacinth
lily-of-the-Nile
striped squill
winter aconite

14 belladonna lily
chincherinchee
glory of the snow
Ithuriel's spear

15 dog's tooth violet
lily-of-the-valley

See also **plant**

Bulgaria *see* **Balkans**

burial ground *see* **cemetery**

Burns, Robert (1759–96)

Significant works include:

08 'To a Mouse' (1785)

10 'The Twa Dogs' (1785)

11 *Tam o'Shanter* (1791)
'Scots Wha Hae' (1793)
'The Holy Fair' (1785)

12 'Auld Lang Syne' (c.1788)

13 'The Banks o' Doon' (c.1791)

14 'Epistle to Davie' (1785)
'Where Helen Lies' (1788)

15 'Comin' Thro' the Rye' (c.1795)
'The Jolly Beggars' (1785)
'Ye Banks and Braes' (c.1791)

16 'Address to a Haggis' (1786)
'Address to the Deil' (1785)
'John Anderson My Jo' (1789)

'To a Mountain Daisy' (1776)

17 'A Man's a Man for A' That' (c.1795)
'Holy Willie's Prayer' (1785)
'Ye Jacobites by Name' (1791)

18 'Death and Dr Hornbook' (1785)

19 'Green Grow the Rashes O' (c.1784)
'The Lass o' Ballochmyle' (1786)

20 'Address to the Unco Guid' (1786)

21 'O Tibbie, I Hae Seen the Day' (c.1777)

22 'My Heart's in the Highlands' (c.1790)

23 'Man Was Made to Mourn: A Dirge' (1784)
'My Luve is Like a Red, Red Rose' (1794)
'The Cotter's Saturday Night' (1785)

24 'Ae Fond Kiss, and Then We Sever' (1791)

bushranger

04 Cash (Martin; 1808–77)
Hall (Ben; 1837–65)
Howe (Michael; 1787–1818)
Ward (Frederick 'Captain Thunderbolt';
1835–70)

05 Brady (Matthew; c.1799–1826)
Johns (Joseph Bolitho 'Moondyne Joe';
c.1827–1900)
Kelly (Edward 'Ned'; 1854–80)
Power (Harry; 1819–91)
Scott (Andrew 'Captain Moonlite'; 1842–80)

06 Caesar (John 'Black Caesar'; c.1763–96)
Morgan (Dan 'Mad Dog'; c.1830–65)

07 Donahoe (John 'Bold Jack'; c.1806–30)
Gilbert (Johnny; c.1842–65)
Pearson (Frank 'Captain Starlight'; 1837–99)

08 Charters (Daniel 'Flash Dan'; 1837–1919)
Gardiner (Francis 'Frank'; 1829–1904)
Governor (Jimmy; 1875–1901)
Melville ('Captain' Frank McCallum;
1822–57)
Westwood (William 'Jackey Jackey'; 1820–46)

business

05 sales
06 mining
07 brewing
charity
farming
fishing
joinery
storage
tanning
weaving
08 building
ceramics
cleaning
forestry
pharmacy
plumbing
printing
removals
security
spinning
teaching
09 chandlery
chemistry
chiropody
dentistry

education
mail order
mechanics
millinery
packaging
quarrying
tailoring
transport
utilities
10 coal mining
demolition
journalism
osteopathy
plastering
publishing
social work
11 accountancy
advertising
aeronautics
agriculture
bookbinding
book-keeping
engineering
oil drilling
oil refining

paper making
photography
retail trade
supermarket
viticulture
12 architecture
broadcasting
construction
dairy farming
distribution
firefighting
hairdressing
orthodontics
stone masonry
13 manufacturing
14 administration
food processing
health services
leather working
market research
office supplies
orthodentistry
slaughterhouse
wholesale trade
15 market gardening

02 3i
3M
BA
BP
03 AXA
BAA
BAT
BHS
BSB

EMI
HMV
IBM
ICI
ING
MAN
NCP
NEC
RAC

RBS
04 Asda
BASF
Dell
Esso
Fiat
HBOS
HSBC
Rank

Sony
05 Abbey
Alcan
Bayer
Boots
Canon
Corus
Exxon
Heinz
Intel
Nokia
Ricoh
Sharp
Shell
Tesco
Volvo
06 Adecco
Arriva
Boeing
Diageo
Dixons
Du Pont
Group 4
Hanson
L'Oréal
Nestlé
Pfizer
Texaco
Virgin
Wimpey
07 Arcadia
Aventis
Chevron
easyJet
Fujitsu
Harrods
Hitachi
Hyundai
Lafarge
Marconi
Matalan
Minerva
Pearson
Pepsico
Peugeot
Philips
Renault
Reuters
Safeway
Samsung
Siemens

Toshiba
Wal-Mart
W H Smith
08 Barclays
Burberry
Centrica
Chrysler
Coca-Cola
Goodyear
JP Morgan
Michelin
Olivetti
Rentokil
Rio Tinto
Unilever
Vodafone
Waitrose
09 Akzo Nobel
Carrefour
Home Depot
John Laing
Ladbrokes
Lloyds TSB
McDonald's
Microsoft
Morrisons
Schroders
Whitbread
10 BAE Systems
Bovis Homes
Electrolux
Exxon Mobil
Greene King
Honda Motor
J Sainsbury
Kingfisher
Mazda Motor
Mitsubishi
Nationwide
Pilkington
Prudential
Rolls-Royce
Sainsbury's
Somerfield
Stagecoach
Telefonica
Volkswagen
Walt Disney
11 AstraZeneca
Caterpillar
Isuzu Motors

Nippon Steel
Nissan Motor
Standard Oil
Suzuki Motor
Toyota Motor
William Hill
12 Allied Domecq
Capital Radio
DFS Furniture
Eastman Kodak
Groupe Danone
Hilton Hotels
Hyundai Motor
Merrill Lynch
Northern Rock
Philip Morris
Reed Elsevier
Sears Roebuck
Total Fina Elf
Toyota Tsusho
Union Carbide
Union Pacific
Western Union
13 Abbey National
Alcatel-Lucent
Anglo American
Balfour Beatty
Fuji Photo Film
General Motors
Harvey Nichols
J D Wetherspoon
Lever Brothers
Sanyo Electric
Taylor Woodrow
Travis Perkins
14 Akzo Nobel
Alfred McAlpine
British Airways
Credit Agricole
Hewlett-Packard
Virgin Atlantic
15 American Express
DaimlerChrysler
Deutsche Telekom
General Electric
GlaxoSmithKline
Legal and General
Marks and Spencer
National Express
News Corporation

Businesspeople, industrialists, magnates and entrepreneurs include:

03 Day (Sir Graham; 1933–   , Canadian)
Fay (Sir Michael; 1949–   , New Zealand)
Fry (Joseph; 1728–87, English)

04 Bata (Tomas; 1876–1932, Czechoslovakian)
Benz (Karl; 1844–1929, German)
Bond (Alan; 1938–   , Australian)

Boot (Sir Jesse; 1850–1931, English)
Cook (Thomas; 1808–92, English)
Coty (François; 1874–1934, French)
Dale (David; 1739–1806, Scottish)
Egan (Sir John; 1939– , English)
Ford (Henry; 1863–1947, US)
Ford (Henry II; 1917–87, US)
Jobs (Steven; 1955– , US)
King (John, Lord; 1917–2005, English)
Mond (Alfred, Lord Melchett; 1868–1930, English)
Mond (Ludwig; 1839–1909, German/British)
Shah (Eddy; 1944– , English)
Tate (Sir Henry; 1819–99, English)
Wang (An; 1920–90, US/Chinese)

05 Allan (Sir Hugh; 1810–82, Canadian)
Arden (Elizabeth; c.1880–1966, US)
Astor (John, Lord; 1886–1971, Anglo-US)
Astor (William Waldorf, Lord; 1848–1919, Anglo-US)
Bevan (Edward; 1856–1921, English)
Bezos (Jeff; 1964– , US)
Bosch (Carl; 1874–1940, German)
Brown (Sir John; 1816–96, English)
Cross (Charles; 1855–1935, English)
Dawes (Charles G; 1865–1951, US)
Elder (Sir Thomas; 1818–97, Australian)
Fayed (Mohamed al-; 1933– , Egyptian)
Firth (Mark; 1819–80, English)
Fleck (Alexander, Lord; 1889–1968, Scottish)
Forte (Charles, Lord; 1908–2007, Scottish)
Frick (Henry; 1849–1919, US)
Gates (Bill; 1955– , US)
Getty (J Paul; 1892–1976, US)
Grade (Michael; 1943– , English)
Green (Sir Philip; 1952– , English)
Guest (Sir Josiah; 1785–1852, Welsh)
Heinz (Henry John; 1844–1919, US)
Honda (Soichiro; 1906–91, Japanese)
Krupp (Alfred; 1812–87, German)
Krupp (Friedrich; 1854–1902, German)
Laker (Sir Freddie; 1922–2006, English)
Lyons (Sir Joseph; 1848–1917, English)
Marks (Simon, Lord; 1888–1964, English)
Nobel (Alfred; 1833–96, Swedish)
Rolls (Charles; 1877–1910, English)
Royce (Sir Henry; 1863–1933, English)
Sieff (Israel, Lord; 1889–1972, English)
Sugar (Alan; 1947– , English)
Trump (Donald; 1946– , US)
Zeiss (Carl; 1816–88, German)

06 Amdahl (Gene; 1922– , US)
Ansett (Sir Reg; 1909–81, Australian)
Austin (Herbert, Lord; 1866–1941, English)
Bedaux (Charles; 1886–1944, US)
Beilby (Sir George Thomas; 1850–1924, Scottish)

Boeing (William Edward; 1881–1956, US)
Butlin (Billy; 1899–1980, English)
Conran (Sir Terence; 1931– , English)
Cunard (Sir Samuel; 1787–1865, Canadian)
Davies (David; 1818–90, Welsh)
Dunlop (John Boyd; 1840–1921, Scottish)
du Pont (Eleuthère Irénée; 1771–1834, French/US)
du Pont (Pierre Samuel; 1870–1954, US)
Fairey (Sir Richard; 1887–1956, English)
Frasch (Hermann; 1851–1914, US)
Fugger (Johannes; 1348–1409, German)
Gamble (Josias; 1776–1848, Irish)
Geneen (Harold; 1910–97, US)
Girard (Stephen; 1750–1831, US)
Grange (Kenneth; 1929– , English)
Hammer (Armand; 1899–1990, US)
Hanson (James, Lord; 1922–2004, English)
Hilton (Conrad; 1887–1979, US)
Hoover (William Henry; 1849–1932, US)
Hughes (Howard; 1905–76, US)
Hulton (Sir Edward; 1906–88, English)
Mellon (Andrew; 1855–1937, US)
Mittal (Lakshmi; 1950– , Indian/British)
Morgan (J Pierpont; 1837–1913, US)
Morita (Akio; 1921–99, Japanese)
Necker (Jacques; 1732–1804, French)
Packer (Kerry; 1937–2005, Australian)
Taylor (Frederick W; 1856–1915, US)
Turner (Ted; 1938– , US)

07 Agnelli (Giovanni; 1866–1945, Italian)
Angliss (Sir William; 1865–1957, Australian)
Baldwin (Matthias; 1795–1866, US)
Barclay (Robert; 1843–1913, English)
Bourdon (Eugène; 1808–84, French)
Branson (Sir Richard; 1950– , English)
Bugatti (Ettore; 1882–1947, Italian)
Burrell (Sir William; 1861–1958, Scottish)
Cadbury (George; 1839–1922, English)
Cadbury (John; 1801–89, English)
Chandos (Oliver Lyttelton, Lord; 1893–1972, English)
Citroën (André; 1878–1935, French)
Cornell (Ezra; 1807–74, US)
De L'Isle (William Philip Sidney, Lord; 1909–91, English)
Enderby (Samuel; fl.1830–39, English)
Hackett (Deborah Vernon; 1887–1965, Australian)
Hancock (Lang; 1909–92, Australian)
Iacocca (Lee; 1924– , US)
Kennedy (Joseph P; 1888–1969, US)
Maxwell (Robert; 1923–91, English)
Murdoch (Rupert; 1931– , Australian/US)
Onassis (Aristotle; 1906–75, Greek)
Roddick (Anita; 1942–2007, English)
Seebohm (Henry; 1832–95, English)

Sotheby (John; 1740–1807, English)
Tiffany (Charles; 1812–1902, US)
Wolfson (Sir Isaac; 1897–1991, Scottish)

08 Baillieu (William Lawrence; 1859–1936, Australian)
Birchall (Derek; 1930–95, English)
Birdseye (Clarence; 1886–1956, US)
Brierley (Sir Ron; 1937– , New Zealand)
Buckland (Henry Seymour Berry, Lord; 1877–1928, Welsh)
Carnegie (Andrew; 1835–1918, Scottish/US)
Christie (James; 1730–1803, English)
Dassault (Marcel; 1892–1986, French)
Drummond (George; 1687–1766, Scottish)
Edwardes (Sir Michael; 1930– , South African/British)
Gillette (King Camp; 1855–1932, US)
Giugiaro (Giorgio; 1938– , Italian)
Guinness (Sir Benjamin Lee; 1798–1868, Irish)
McNamara (Robert; 1916– , US)
Michelin (André; 1853–1931, French)
Nuffield (William Morris, Lord; 1877–1963, English)
Olivetti (Adriano; 1901–60, Italian)
Paphitis (Theo; 1959– , Greek Cypriot)
Paterson (William; 1658–1719, Scottish)
Pulitzer (Joseph; 1847–1911, Hungarian/US)
Rathenau (Walther; 1867–1922, German)
Rowntree (Joseph; 1836–1925, English)
Sinclair (Sir Clive; 1940– , English)
Zaharoff (Sir Basil; 1850–1936, French)

09 Arkwright (Sir Richard; 1732–92, English)
Armstrong (William, Lord; 1810–1900, English)
Barr Smith (Robert; 1824–1915, Australian)
Bernstein (Sidney, Lord; 1899–1993, English)

Carothers (Wallace; 1896–1937, US)
Cockerill (John; 1790–1840, English)
Courtauld (Samuel; 1876–1947, English)
Finlayson (James; 1772–1852, Scottish)
Finniston (Monty; 1912–91, Scottish)
Firestone (Harvey S; 1868–1938, US)
Göransson (Göran; 1819–1900, Swedish)
Greenspan (Alan; 1926– , US)
Sainsbury (Alan, Lord; 1902–98, English)
Selfridge (Harry Gordon; 1858–1947, US/British)
Woolworth (Frank Winfield; 1852–1919, US)

10 Abramovich (Roman; 1966– , Russian)
Berlusconi (Silvio; 1936– , Italian)
Chardonnet (Hilaire, Comte de; 1839–1924, French)
Guggenheim (Meyer; 1828–1905, US)
Gulbenkian (Calouste; 1869–1955, British/Turkish)
Leverhulme (William Hesketh Lever, Lord; 1851–1925, English)
Pilkington (Sir Alastair; 1920–95, English)
Rothermere (Harold Harmsworth, Lord; 1868–1940, Irish)
Rothschild (Meyer; 1744–1812, German)
Vanderbilt (Cornelius; 1794–1877, US)

11 Beaverbrook (Max, Lord; 1879–1964, Canadian/British)
Haji-Ioannou (Stelios; 1967– , Greek Cypriot/British)
Harvey-Jones (Sir John; 1924–2008, English)
Rockefeller (John D; 1839–1937, US)

12 Benediktsson (Einar; 1864–1940, Icelandic)
Gyllenhammar (Pehr Gustaf; 1935– , Swedish)

Terms used in business include:

03 CBI
IPO
JIT
PLC
SKU
USP
04 FMCG
soho
05 angel
06 assets
buy-out
dot com
margin
mark-up
merger
tender
07 duopoly

synergy
08 blue chip
demerger
monopoly
oligarch
price war
takeover
trade war
unit cost
09 break even
corporate
franchise
oligopoly
10 bottom line
closed shop
dot com boom
downsizing

high street
just in time
loss leader
offshoring
sole trader
subsidiary
11 acquisition
corporation
fixed assets
golden hello
minimum wage
niche market
partnership
supply chain
white knight
12 above the line
below the line

black economy
brand loyalty
conglomerate
core business
deregulation
distribution
entrepreneur
liquid assets
productivity
profit margin
retail sector

13 acid test ratio
asset sweating
consumer goods

See also **economics**; **finance**

listed company
multinational
mutual society
organic growth
parent company
privatization
protectionism
quoted company
restructuring

14 asset stripping
capitalization
holding company
limited company
vertical market

15 barriers to entry
bricks and mortar
building society
clicks and mortar
demutualization
differentiation
diversification
golden handcuffs
golden handshake
golden parachute
nationalization
supply and demand
turnkey solution
wholesale sector

butterfly

Butterflies include:

03 map
04 blue
wall
05 argus
comma
elfin
heath
satyr
white
06 apollo
copper
hermit
morpho
pierid
psyche
07 admiral
cabbage
monarch
Papilio
peacock
ringlet
satyrid
skipper

thistle
Ulysses
vanessa
08 birdwing
cardinal
grayling
hesperid
milk-weed
09 brimstone
cleopatra
Hesperian
holly blue
nymphalid
orange-tip
wall brown
wood white
10 brown argus
common blue
fritillary
gatekeeper
hairstreak
red admiral
11 large copper

meadow-brown
painted lady
Scotch argus
small copper
swallowtail
12 cabbage-white
dingy skipper
Essex skipper
marbled-white
white admiral
13 chalkhill blue
clouded yellow
mourning cloak
purple emperor
tortoiseshell
15 black hairstreak
brown hairstreak
green hairstreak
grizzled skipper
heath fritillary
Lulworth skipper
marsh fritillary
mountain ringlet

See also **insect**; **moth**

Byron, George Gordon, Lord (1788–1824)

Significant works include:

04 *Cain* (1821)
Lara (1814)
05 *Beppo* (1818)
07 *Don Juan* (1819–24)
Manfred (1817)
Mazeppa (1819)
09 *The Giaour* (1813)

The Island (1823)
10 *Prometheus* (1816)
The Corsair (1814)
12 *Maid of Athens* (1810)
Sardanapalus (1821)
13 *Lament of Tasso* (1817)
Marino Faliero (1821)

The Two Foscari (1821)

14 *Heaven and Earth* (1823)
Hebrew Melodies (1815)
The Age of Bronze (1823)

15 *Hours of Idleness* (1807)
Prophecy of Dante (1821)

16 *The Bride of Abydos* (1813)
'She Walks in Beauty' (1814)

20 *The Prisoner of Chillon* (1816)
The Vision of Judgement (1822)

21 *So, We'll Go No More a Roving* (1817)

22 *The Deformed Transformed* (1824)

23 *Childe Harold's Pilgrimage*
(1812/1816/1818)
Poems on Various Occasions (1807)

30 *English Bards and Scotch Reviewers* (1809)

Byzantine empire

Byzantine emperors and empresses, with regnal dates:

03 Leo (II; AD 74)
Leo (III, the Isaurian; 717–41)
Leo (I, the Great; AD 57–74)
Leo (IV, the Khazar; 775–80)
Leo (VI, the Wise; 886–912)
Leo (V, the Armenian; 813–20)
Zoë (1042)

04 John (II Comnenus; 1118–43)
John (III Ducas-Vatatzes; 1222–54)
John (I Tzimisces; 969–76)
John (IV Lascaris; 1258–61)
John (VI Cantacuzene; 1347–55)
John (VIII Palaeologus; 1425–48)
John (VII Palaeologus; 1390)
John (V Palaeologus; 1341–47/1355–
76/1379–90)
Zeno (AD 76–91)

05 Basil (II; 976–1025)
Basil (I, the Macedonian; 867–86)
Irene (the Athenian; 797–802)
Isaac (I Comnenus; 1057–59)
Isaac (II Angelus; 1185–95/1203–04)

06 Jovian (AD 63–64)
Julian (the Apostate; AD 61–63)
Justin (I; 518–27)
Justin (II; 565–78)
Manuel (I Comnenus; 1143–80)
Manuel (II Palaeologus; 1391–1425)
Phocas (602–10)
Valens (AD 64–78)

07 Alexius (I Comnenus; 1081–1118)
Alexius (III Angelus-Comnenus; 1195–1203)
Alexius (IV Angelus; 1203–04)
Alexius (V; 1204)
Eudocia (1067)
Marcian (AD 50–57)
Michael (I Angelus; 1204–15)
Michael (II Comnenus-Ducas; 1237–71)
Michael (III, the Drunkard; 842–67)
Michael (II, the Amorian; 820–29)
Michael (I Rhangabe; 811–13)
Michael (IV, the Paphlagonian; 1034–41)
Michael (V Calaphates; 1041–42)

Michael (VII Ducas; 1071–78)
Michael (VIII Palaeologus; 1261–82)
Michael (VI Stratioticus; 1056–57)
Romanus (II; 959–63)
Romanus (III Argyrus; 1028–34)
Romanus (I Lecapenus; 919–44)
Romanus (IV Diogenes; 1068–71)

08 Arcadius (AD 95–408)
Constans (II; 641–68)
Leontius (695–98)
Mezezius (668–69)
Theodora (1042)
Theodore (I Comnenus-Lascaris; 1208–22)
Theodore (II Ducas-Lascaris; 1254–58)
Tiberius (II Constantine; 578–82)
Tiberius (III; 698–705)

09 Alexander (912–13)
Heraclius (610–41)
Justinian (II; 685–95/705–11)
Justinian (I, the Great; 527–65)

10 Anastasius (I; AD 91–518)
Anastasius (II; 713–15)
Andronicus (I Comnenus; 1183–85)
Andronicus (III Palaeologus; 1328–41)
Andronicus (II Palaeologus; 1282–1328)
Andronicus (IV Palaeologus; 1376–79)
Artavasdus (742–43)
Basiliscus (AD 75–76)
Nicephorus (742–43)
Nicephorus (I; 802–11)
Nicephorus (III Botaniates; 1078–81)
Nicephorus (II Phocas; 963–69)
Stauracius (811)
Theodosius (II; AD 08–50)
Theodosius (III, of Adramytium; 715–17)
Theodosius (I, the Great; AD 79–95)
Theophilus (829–42)

11 Constantine (I, the Great; AD 30–37)
Constantine (IV; 654–85)
Constantine (IX Monomachus; 1042–55)
Constantine (V Copronymus; 720–41/741–
75)
Constantine (VI; 775–97)

Constantine (VIII Porphyrogenitus; 1025–28)
Constantine (VII Porphyrogenitus; 913–59)
Constantine (X Ducas; 1059–67)
Constantine (XI Palaeologus; 1448–53)
Constantius (AD 37–61)
Heracleonas (641)
Philippicus (711–13)
12 Zeno Tarasius (AD 74–75)
13 Isaac Comnenus (1184–91)

Theophylactus (811–13)
15 Maurice Tiberius (582–602)
17 John Comnenus-Ducas (1237–42/1242–44)
Zoë Porphyrogenita (1042)
19 Manuel Comnenus-Ducas (1230–37)
20 Heraclius Constantine (641)
21 Theodore Comnenus-Ducas (1224–30)
22 Theodora Porphyrogenita (1056)

C

The Cabinet *see* government

cactus

Cacti include:

04 crab
toad

05 dildo
nopal

06 barrel
cereus
cholla
Easter
mescal
old man
orchid
peanut
peyote

07 jointed
old lady
opuntia

rainbow
saguaro

08 dumpling
gold lace
hedgehog
rat's tail
snowball
starfish
Turk's cap

09 bunny ears
Christmas
goat's horn
gold charm
Indian fig
mistletoe
sea-urchin

10 cotton-pole
sand dollar
silver ball
strawberry
zygocactus

11 grizzly bear
mammillaria
prickly pear
scarlet ball
silver torch

12 golden barrel

13 Bristol beauty
schlumbergera

14 drunkard's dream

15 queen of the night
snowball cushion

See also plant

cake

Cakes, pastries and puddings include:

03 bun
cup
fig
oat
pan
pie
tea

04 baba
flan
fool
plum
rock
seed
tart

05 angel
bombe
bride
bundt
cream
crêpe
fairy

fruit
fudge
Genoa
jelly
lardy
layer
pound
queen
scone
short
sweet
tipsy
torte
yeast

06 banana
carrot
cheese
coffee
Dundee
Eccles
éclair
gateau

ginger
girdle
junket
marble
mousse
muffin
parkin
simnel
sponge
trifle
waffle
yum-yum

07 baklava
Banbury
bannock
Bath bun
brioche
brownie
crumble
crumpet
currant
fig roll

fritter
iced bun
jam roll
jam tart
Madeira
Pavlova
plum pie
Pomfret
ratafia
rum baba
saffron
savarin
soufflé
stollen
strudel
sultana
tartlet
tea loaf
wedding
Yule log

08 apple pie
birthday
black bun
date roll
doughnut
flummery
macaroon
malt loaf
meringue
mince pie
pecan pie
sandwich
syllabub
tiramisu
turnover
whim-wham

09 angel food

banana-nut
cherry-pie
chocolate
Christmas
cranachan
cream horn
cream puff
drop scone
fruit tart
lamington
lemon tart
madeleine
panettone
Sally Lunn
sweetmeat
Swiss roll

10 banana loaf
Battenburg
Chelsea bun
key lime pie
panna cotta
Pontefract
pumpkin pie
shoofly pie
tarte tatin
toasted tea
upside-down

11 baked Alaska
banana bread
banoffee pie
choux pastry
cinnamon bun
crème brulée
custard tart
gingerbread
hot cross bun
jam roly-poly

lady's finger
Linzertorte
plum pudding
profiterole
rice pudding
Sachertorte
sago pudding
spotted dick
treacle tart

12 apfel strudel
apple fritter
Bakewell tart
chocolate log
crème caramel
custard slice
Danish pastry
figgy pudding
hasty pudding
mille-feuille
plum porridge
tarte au sucre

13 apple dumpling
apple turnover
Scotch pancake
sponge pudding
summer pudding

14 apple charlotte
charlotte russe
chocolate fudge
steamed pudding
Victoria sponge

15 black-cap pudding
chocolate éclair
queen of puddings
strawberry short

See also **baking**; **biscuit**; **dessert**; **food**

calendar

Calendars include:

05 Baha'i	solar	Julian	**09** arbitrary
Hindu	**06** Coptic	**07** Chinese	Gregorian
lunar	Hebrew	Islamic	lunisolar
Roman	Jewish	Persian	

Animals representing years in the Chinese calendar:

02 ox	cock	snake	**07** buffalo
03 dog	goat	tiger	chicken
pig	hare	**06** dragon	rooster
rat	**05** horse	monkey	serpent
04 boar	sheep	rabbit	

Months of the Hindu calendar:

04 Magh	Kartik	08 Jyaistha	Margasirsa
05 Magha	07 Ashadha	Karttika	12 Margashirsha
Pausa	Chaitra	Phalguna	13 Dvitiya Asadha
Paush	Jaystha	Vaisakha	14 Dvitiya Sravana
06 Asadha	Phalgun	Vaishakh	
Ashvin	Shravan	09 Bhadrapad	
Asvina	Sravana	10 Bhadrapada	

Months of the Islamic calendar:

05 Rabi I	06 Rabi II	Ramadan	Muharram
Rajab	Shaban	Shawwal	10 Dhu al-Qadah
Safar	07 Jumada I	08 Jumada II	11 Dhu al-Hijjah

Months of the Jewish calendar:

02 Ab	Nisan	Kislev	07 Chislev
Av	Sivan	Shebat	Heshvan
04 Abib	Tebet	Shevat	09 Adar Sheni
Adar	Tevet	Tammuz	10 Adar Rishon
Elul	Tisri	Tebeth	11 Marcheshvan
Iyar	06 Hesvan	Tishri	
05 Iyyar	Kisleu	Veadar	

See also **day**; **month**; **religion**; **season**; **time**; **year**

Cambridge University *see* college

camera

Camera parts include:

02 AF	film holder	focus control
04 lens	mirror lens	focusing hood
05 blind	object lens	focusing ring
spool	pentaprism	focus setting
06 mirror	take-up reel	frame counter
07 lens cap	viewfinder	light control
shutter		reflex viewer
08 AF lenses	11 compact lens	rewind handle
aperture	data display	13 accessory shoe
card door	film advance	exposure meter
film gate	fisheye lens	film transport
magazine	leaf shutter	iris diaphragm
zoom lens	lens release	long-focus lens
09 autofocus	program card	mirror shutter
data panel	rewind crank	release button
diaphragm	take-up spool	telephoto lens
meter cell	viewing lens	wide-angle lens
spool knob	12 cable release	14 battery chamber
10 card window	card on/off key	shutter release
	compound lens	15 autofocus sensor
	flash contact	registration pin
	flash setting	

Camera types include:

02 TV

03 APS
SLR
TLR

04 cine
disc
film
Fuji®
view

05 Canon®
Kodak®
Leica®
Nikon®
plate
press
sound
still
video

06 Konica®
Pentax®

reflex
Rollei®
stereo
Super 8®
Webcam

07 bellows
compact
digital
Minolta®
Olympus®
pinhole
Yashica®

08 dry-plate
Polaroid®
Praktica®
security
wet-plate

09 automatic
binocular
camcorder
half-plate

miniature
panoramic
Rolliflex®
single use
Steadicam®

10 box Brownie®
disposable
Instamatic®
sliding box

11 large-format

12 quarter-plate
subminiature
surveillance

13 camera obscura
daguerreotype
folding reflex
point-and-press

14 twin-lens reflex

15 cinematographic

See also **photography**

Canada

Cities and notable towns in Canada include:

06 Ottawa
Quebec
Regina

07 Calgary
Halifax
Toronto

08 Edmonton
Montreal
Victoria

Winnipeg

09 Saskatoon
Vancouver

Canadian provinces and territories, with abbreviations and regional capitals:

06 Quebec (QC; Quebec City)

07 Alberta (AB; Edmonton)
Nunavut (NU; Iqaluit)
Ontario (ON; Toronto)

08 Manitoba (MB; Winnipeg)

10 Nova Scotia (NS; Halifax)

12 New Brunswick (NB; Fredericton)

Saskatchewan (SK; Regina)

14 Yukon Territory (YT; Whitehorse)

15 British Columbia (BC; Victoria)

18 Prince Edward Island (PE; Charlottetown)

20 Northwest Territories (NT; Yellowknife)

23 Newfoundland and Labrador (NL; St John's)

Canadian landmarks include:

06 Mt Thor

07 CN Tower
Mt Logan
Niagara
Rockies
Sky Dome

08 Lake Erie

09 Hudson Bay
Lake Huron
Mt Seymour

10 Great Lakes
St Lawrence

11 Lake Ontario

12 Lake Superior
Niagara Falls

13 Algonquin Park
Parc Olympique

14 Horseshoe Falls
Rocky Mountains

See also **prime minister**

canal

Canals include:

04 Erie (US)	**06** Panama (Panama)	Welland (Canada)
Kiel (Germany)	Rideau (Canada)	**10** Caledonian (Scotland)
Suez (Egypt)	**07** Corinth (Greece)	Mittelland (Germany)
05 Grand (Italy)	Midland (Germany)	**11** Welland Ship (Canada)

canonical hour

Canonical hours include:

04 none	prime	**07** complin	evensong
sext	terce	orthros	
05 lauds	**06** matins	vespers	
nones	tierce	**08** compline	

Canterbury *see* **archbishop**

Canterbury Tales *see* **Chaucer, Geoffrey**

cape

Capes include:

03 Cod (USA)
Dra (Morocco)
Icy (USA)
Low (Canada)
Nao (Spain)
Ray (Canada)

04 Arid (Australia)
Cruz (Cuba)
East (New Zealand)
Fear (USA)
Fria (Namibia)
Frio (Brazil)
Gata (Spain)
Horn (Chile)
Howe (Australia)
Pine (Canada)
Pole (USA)
Race (Canada)
Rojo (Mexico)
Vert (Senegal)
York (Australia/Greenland)

05 Adare (Antarctica)
Beata (Dominican Republic)
Canso (Canada)
Corse (France)
Creus (Spain)
Cross (Namibia)
Falso (Dominican Republic)
Gaspé (Canada)
Jaffa (Australia)
Mount (Sierra Leone)

North (Canada/New Zealand/Norway)
Otway (Australia)
Parry (Canada)
Sable (USA/Canada)
Sandy (Australia)
South (Papua New Guinea)
St Ann (Sierra Leone)
Tappi (Japan)
Weggs (Canada)
Wrath (Scotland)

06 Arkona (Germany)
Arnhem (Australia)
Barren (Australia)
Blanca (Argentina)
Codera (Venezuela)
Comino (Italy)
Cretin (Papua New Guinea)
Egmont (New Zealand)
Engaño (Philippines)
Fartak (Yemen)
Freels (Canada)
Linaro (Italy)
Muroto (Japan)
Norman (Canada)
Orange (Brazil)
Palmas (Liberia)
Recife (South Africa)
Samana (Dominican Republic)
St John (Canada)
St Mary (The Gambia)

07 Agulhas (South Africa)

Bolinao (Philippines)
Catoche (Mexico)
Charles (USA)
Chidley (Canada)
Comorin (India)
Delgado (Mozambique)
Falaise (Vietnam)
Hallett (Antarctica)
Isabela (Dominican Republic)
Kennedy (USA)
Leeuwin (Australia)
Lévêque (Australia)
L'Eveque (New Zealand)
Lookout (USA)
Mondego (Portugal)
Negrais (Myanmar)
Ortegal (Spain)
Rachado (Malaysia)
San Blas (USA)
Timiris (Mauritania)
Tortosa (Spain)
Vincent (USA)

08 Anguille (Canada)
Bathurst (Canada)
Colville (New Zealand)
de Hornos (Chile)
des Irois (Haiti)
Espichel (Portugal)
Farewell (New Zealand/Greenland)
Farquhar (Australia)
Foulwind (New Zealand)
Fournier (New Zealand)
Gerhards (Papua New Guinea)
Good Hope (South Africa)
Hatteras (USA)
Lisburne (USA)
Lucrezia (Cuba)
Matapalo (Costa Rica)
Melville (Australia/Philippines)
Mesurado (Liberia)
Newenham (USA)
Norvegia (Antarctica)
Palliser (New Zealand)
Romanzof (USA)

Saunders (New Zealand)
Stephens (New Zealand)
St George (Canada)
Suckling (Papua New Guinea)
Vaticano (Italy)
West Howe (Australia)

09 Canaveral (USA)
Carbonara (Italy)
Dame Marie (Haiti)
de la Hague (France)
dos Bahías (Argentina)
Madeleine (Canada)
Mendocino (USA)
North West (Australia)
Nunap Isua (Greenland)
Patterson (Australia)
South East (Australia)
Southwest (New Zealand)
St Nicolas (Haiti)
St Vincent (Portugal)
Trafalgar (Spain)
Van Diemen (Australia)

10 Corrientes (Mexico/Cuba/Colombia)
de São Roque (Brazil)
Finisterre (Spain)
Kidnappers (New Zealand)
Kormakitis (Cyprus)
Providence (Canada/South Africa/New Zealand)
Tarkhankut (Ukraine)
Tormentine (Canada)

11 Londonderry (Australia)
Naturaliste (Australia)
Sierra Leone (Sierra Leone)
Spartivento (Italy)
Three Points (Ghana)
Tribulation (Australia)

12 Breton Island (Canada)
Hopes Advance (Canada)

13 Prince of Wales (USA)

14 Henrietta Maria (Canada)
Maria van Diemen (New Zealand)

capital *see* **Australia; Austria; Belgium; Canada; city; Czech Republic; Denmark; Finland; France; Germany; Greece; India; Ireland; Italy; The Netherlands; Norway; Portugal; Spain; Sweden; Switzerland; United States of America**

captain

Captains include:

04 Ahab (Captain; *Moby Dick*, 1851, Hermann Melville)
Cook (Captain James; 1728–79, English)
Hook (Captain; *Peter Pan*, 1911, J M Barrie)

Kidd (Captain William; c.1645–1701, Scottish)
Nemo (Captain; *20,000 Leagues under the Sea*, 1872, Jules Verne)

05 Bligh (Captain William; 1754–1817, English)
Flint (Captain J; *Treasure Island*, 1883, Robert Louis Stevenson)
Johns (Captain W E; 1893–1968, English)
Queeg (Captain Philip; *The Caine Mutiny*, 1951, Herman Wouk)
Smith (Captain John; 1580–1631, English)
Swing (Captain; nom de plume of Swing Rioters, 1830–31, England)

07 Corelli (Captain Antonio; *Captain Corelli's Mandolin*, 1994, Louis de Bernières)
Marryat (Captain Frederick; 1792–1848, English)

Sparrow (Captain Jack; Pirates of the Caribbean films, 2003–07)

08 Bobadill (Captain; *Every Man in His Humour*, 1598–1616, Ben Jonson)
Hastings (Captain Arthur; Poirot novels and short stories, 1920–75, Agatha Christie)
MacHeath (Captain; *The Beggar's Opera*, 1728, John Gay)

09 Singleton (Captain; *Adventures of Captain Singleton*, 1720, Daniel Defoe)

10 Hornblower (Captain Horatio; Hornblower novels, 1937–67, C S Forester)

car *see* **motoring**

cardinal

Cardinals include:

03 Sin (Jaime; 1928–2005, Philippine)

04 Gray (Gordon; 1910–93, Scottish)
Hume (Basil; 1923–99, English)
Pole (Reginald; 1500–58, English)
Retz (Jean François de; 1614–79, French)

05 Chigi (Fabio; 1599–1667, Italian)

06 Beaton (David; 1494–1546, Scottish)
Borgia (Rodrigo; 1431–1503, Spanish)
Fisher (St John; 1469–1535, English)
Heenan (John; 1905–75, English)
Medici (Giovanni de'; 1499–1565, Italian)
Newman (John Henry; 1801–90, English)
O'Brien (Keith; 1938– , Scottish)
Rovere (Francesco della; 1414–84, Italian)
Stuart (Henry, Duke of York; 1725–1807, British)
Wolsey (Thomas; c.1475–1530, English)

07 Bethune (David; 1494–1546, Scottish)
Langham (Simon; d.1376, English)
Langton (Stephen; c.1150–1228, English)
Mazarin (Jules; 1602–61, French)

Mendoza (Pedro Gonzalez de; 1428–95, Spanish)
Pandulf (d.1226, Italian)
Vaughan (Herbert; 1832–1903, English)
Winning (Thomas; 1925–2001, Scottish)
Wiseman (Nicholas; 1802–65, English)
Ximenes (1436–1517, Spanish)

08 Alberoni (Giulio; 1664–1752, Spanish/Italian)
Aubusson (Pierre d'; 1423–1503, French)
Beaufort (Henry; 1377–1447, English)
Stepinac (Aloysius; 1898–1960, Yugoslav)

09 Richelieu (Armand Jean du Plessis, Duc de; 1585–1642, French)
Wyszynski (Stefan; 1901–81, Polish)

10 Bellarmine (Robert; 1542–1621, Italian)
Breakspear (Nicolas; 1100–59, English)
Mindszenty (József; 1892–1975, Hungarian)

13 Murphy-O'Connor (Cormac; 1932– , English)

See also **archbishop**; **religion**

cards *see* **game**

Caribbean

Cities and notable towns in the Caribbean include:

06 Havana (Cuba)
Nassau (The Bahamas)

07 Holguín (Cuba)
San Juan (Puerto Rico)

08 Camagüey (Cuba)

Castries (St Lucia)
Gonaïves (Haiti)
Kingston (Jamaica)
Santiago (Dominican Republic)

10 Cap-Haïtien (Haiti)

Port-de-Paix (Haiti)
11 Port of Spain (Trinidad and Tobago)
San Fernando (Trinidad and Tobago)

12 Port-au-Prince (Haiti)
Santo Domingo (Dominican Republic)
14 Santiago de Cuba (Cuba)

carnivore

Carnivores include:

03 cat
dog
owl

04 bear
frog
hawk
kite
lion
newt
orca
puma
seal
skua
wolf

05 adder
civet
cobra
dingo
eagle
heron
hyena
mamba
otter
shark
stoat
stork
tiger
viper
whale

06 condor
coyote
falcon
ferret
hyaena
jackal
jaguar
lizard
osprey
python
taipan
walrus
weasel

07 barn owl
buzzard
cheetah
dolphin
kestrel
leopard
panther
pelican
penguin
polecat
sea lion
vulture
wildcat

08 anaconda
brown owl
eagle-owl

snowy owl
tawny owl

09 albatross
alligator
bald eagle
black bear
blue whale
brown bear
crocodile
polar bear

10 copperhead
salamander
screech owl
sperm whale
tiger shark
whale shark

11 electric eel
golden eagle
grizzly bear
killer whale
rattlesnake
sparrowhawk

14 boa constrictor

15 great white shark
hammerhead shark
peregrine falcon

See also **bear**; **bird**; **cat**; **dinosaur**; **dog**; **insectivorous plant**; **meat**; **reptile**; **shark**; **snake**

carpet

Carpets and rugs include:

03 rag
red
rya

04 kali

05 Dutch
kelim
kilim
magic

pilch
stair
throw

06 hearth
hooked
khilim
Kirman
numdah

prayer
Turkey
Wilton

07 bergama
flokati
Persian
Turkish

08 bergamot

Brussels

09 Axminster
sheepskin

10 travelling

11 Bessarabian
buffalo robe

13 Kidderminster

See also **house**

carriage

Carriages include:

03 cab	T-cart	chariot	rickshaw
gig	**06** berlin	dogcart	rockaway
04 arba	calash	droshky	sociable
baby	chaise	hackney	stanhope
drag	drosky	phaeton	victoria
dray	go-cart	pillbox	**09** britschka
ekka	hansom	ricksha	cabriolet
mail	herdic	tilbury	wagonette
pony	landau	vettura	**10** four-in hand
rath	pochay	vis-à-vis	post chaise
trap	purdah	**08** barouche	**11** family coach
05 araba	spider	britzska	hurly-hacket
aroba	spring	brougham	village cart
bandy	surrey	carriole	**13** désobligeante
buggy	**07** britska	carryall	mourning coach
coupé	britzka	clarence	spider phaeton
ratha	cariole	jump-seat	
sulky	caroche	po'chaise	

Carroll, Lewis (1832–98)

Significant works include:

14 *Phantasmagoria* (1869)
Rhyme? And Reason? (1883)
Sylvie and Bruno (1889)
20 *The Hunting of the Snark* (1876)

22 *Through the Looking-Glass* (1872)
23 *Sylvie and Bruno Concluded* (1893)
24 *Euclid and his Modern Rivals* (1879)
28 *Alice's Adventures in Wonderland* (1865)

Significant characters include:

05 Alice	Tweedledee	**13** Father William
07 The Baby	Tweedledum	The Jabberwock
The Cook	**11** The Dormouse	The Mock Turtle
08 The Snark	The Red Queen	The White Queen
09 The Walrus	**12** Humpty Dumpty	**14** The Caterpillar
10 The Duchess	The Carpenter	The Cheshire Cat
The Gryphon	The Mad Hatter	The White Knight
The Red King	The March Hare	The White Rabbit
	The White King	**15** The King of Hearts

cartography *see* geography

cartoon

Cartoon characters include:

03 Ren	Stan	Jerry
Tom	**05** Alice	Kenny
04 Bart	Bluto	Louey
Fred	Dewey	Marge
Huey	Dumbo	Mr Men
Kyle	Goofy	Robin
Lisa	Homer	Rocky

Snowy
Wally

06 Batman
Beavis
Boo Boo
Calvin
Daphne
Droopy
Hobbes
Maggie
Obelix
Popeye
Shaggy
Snoopy
Stimpy
Thelma
Tintin
Top Cat

07 Asterix
Cartman
Custard
Dilbert
Gnasher
Muttley
Old Bill
Penfold
Roobarb

08 Andy Capp
Butthead
Garfield
Krazy Kat

Olive Oyl
Super Man
Superted
Tank Girl
The Joker
Yogi Bear

09 Betty Boop
Bugs Bunny
Chip 'n' Dale
Daffy Duck
Daisy Duck
Dastardly
Dick Tracy
Elmer Fudd
Marmaduke
Oor Wullie
Pepe le Pew
Scooby Doo
Spider Man
Sylvester
The Broons
Tweety Pie

10 Bullwinkle
Donald Duck
Doonesbury
Judge Dredd
Road Runner
Scrappy Doo
The Far Side
The Riddler

11 Bart Simpson

Betty Rubble
Danger Mouse
Felix the Cat
Flash Gordon
Fred Bassett
Korky the Cat
Lisa Simpson
Mickey Mouse
Minnie Mouse
The Simpsons
Wile E Coyote

12 Barney Rubble
Charlie Brown
Desperate Dan
Homer Simpson
Little Misses
Marge Simpson
Ren and Stimpy

13 Dick Dastardly
Maggie Simpson
Modesty Blaise
Rupert the Bear
Scrooge McDuck

14 Foghorn Leghorn
Fred Flintstone
The Pink Panther

15 Calvin and Hobbes
Dennis the Menace
Penelope Pitstop
Steamboat Willie
Wilma Flintstone

Cartoonists include:

02 HB (1797–1868, Irish)

03 Low (Sir David; 1891–1963, New Zealand/British)

04 Arno (Peter; 1904–68, US)
Bell (Steve; 1951– , English)
Capp (Al; 1909–79, US)
Cohl (Emile; 1857–1938, French)
Ding (1876–1962, US)
Kane (Bob; 1915–98, US)
Matt (1964– , English)
Nast (Thomas; 1840–1902, US)
Rémi (Georges; 1907–83, Belgian)
Tidy (Bill; 1933– , English)
Trog (Walter; 1924– , Canadian/British)

05 Adams (Scott; 1957– , US)
Avery (Tex; 1908–80, US)
Block (Herbert L; 1909–2001, US)
Busch (Wilhelm; 1832–1908, German)
Dirks (Rudolph; 1877–1968, US)
Doyle (John; 1797–1868, Irish)
Emett (Rowland; 1906–90, English)
Giles (1916–95, English)

Gould (Chester; 1900–85, US)
Halas (John; 1912–95, Hungarian/British)
Hanna (William; 1910–2001, US)
Hergé (1907–83, Belgian)
Jones (Chuck; 1912–2002, US)
Kelly (Walt; 1913–73, US)
Lantz (Walter; 1900–94, US)
McCay (Winsor; 1867–1934, US)
Segar (Elzie; 1894–1938, US)
Silas (1867–1934, US)
Vicky (1913–66, German/British)
Weisz (Victor; 1913–66, German/British)
Yeats (Jack B; 1870–1957, Irish)
Young (Chic; 1901–73, US)

06 Addams (Charles; 1912–88, US)
Browne (Tom; 1870–1910, English)
Caniff (Milt; 1907–88, US)
Caplin (Alfred Gerald; 1909–79, US)
Disney (Walt; 1901–66, US)
Fisher (Bud; 1885–1954, US)
Gibson (Charles Dana; 1867–1944, US)
Graham (Alex; 1917–91, Scottish)
Iwerks (Ub; 1901–71, US)

Jaffee (Al; 1921– , US)
Larson (Gary; 1950– , US)
Miller (David Wiley; 1951– , US)
Scarfe (Gerald; 1936– , English)
Schulz (Charles M; 1922–2000, US)
Searle (Ronald; 1920– , English)
Siegel (Jerry; 1914–96, US)
Smythe (Reg; 1917–98, English)
Strube (Sidney; 1891–1956, English)
Studdy (George Edward; 1878–1948, English)
Uderzo (Albert; 1927– , French)
Wilson (Roy; 1900–65, English)

07 Barbera (Joseph; 1911–2006, US)
Bateman (H M; 1887–1970, Australian)
Courtet (Emile; 1857–1938, French)
Darling (Jay Norwood; 1876–1962, US)
Dowling (Stephen; 1904–86, English)
Godfrey (Bob; 1921– , Australian/British)
Hampson (Frank; 1918–85, English)
Hassall (John; 1868–1948, English)
Raymond (Alex; 1909–56, US)
Rushton (Willie; 1937–96, English)
Shepard (E H; 1879–1976, English)
Shuster (Joseph; 1914–92, US)
Tenniel (Sir John; 1820–1914, English)

Thurber (James; 1894–1961, US)
Trudeau (Garry; 1948– , US)
Watkins (Dudley D; 1907–69, English)
Webster (Tom; 1890–1962, English)

08 Goldberg (Rube; 1883–1970, US)
Groening (Matt; 1954– , US)
Herblock (1909–2001, US)
Herriman (George; 1880–1944, US)
Hoffnung (Gerard; 1925–59, German/British)
Kurtzman (Harvey; 1924–93, US)
Robinson (Heath; 1872–1944, English)

09 Batchelor (Joy; 1914–91, English)
Baxendale (Leo; 1930– , English)
du Maurier (George; 1834–96, French/British)
Feininger (Lyonel; 1871–1956, US)
Fleischer (Max; 1883–1972, US)
Lancaster (Sir Osbert; 1908–86, English)
Pritchett (Matthew; 1964– , English)
Sambourne (Edward Linley; 1844–1910, English)
Watterson (Bill; 1958– , US)

10 Raemaekers (Louis; 1869–1956, Dutch)

12 Bairnsfather (Bruce; 1888–1959, British)
Hanna-Barbera (US)

case *see* **grammar**

castle

Castle parts include:
---

04 berm	corbel	barbican	inner wall
keep	crenel	bartizan	**10** drawbridge
moat	donjon	brattice	murder hole
ward	merlon	buttress	portcullis
05 ditch	turret	crosslet	watchtower
fosse	**07** bastion	loophole	**11** battlements
motte	dungeon	stockade	curtain wall
mound	parados	wall walk	outer bailey
scarp	parapet	**09** arrow-slit	**12** crenellation
tower	postern	courtyard	lookout tower
06 bailey	rampart	embrasure	**13** enclosure wall
chapel	**08** approach	gatehouse	

British and Irish castles include:
---

03 Doe (Ireland)	Drum (Scotland)	Trim (Ireland)
Eye (England)	Etal (England)	Ward (Northern Ireland)
Lea (Ireland)	Hume (Scotland)	York (England)
Mey (Scotland)	Leap (Ireland)	**05** Aydon (England)
04 Birr (Ireland)	Peel (Isle of Man)	Ayton (Scotland)
Clun (England)	Piel (England)	Black (Ireland)
Coch (Wales)	Raby (England)	Blair (Scotland)
Deal (England)	Ross (Ireland)	Bowes (England)

Burgh (England)
Cabra (Ireland)
Cahir (Ireland)
Carew (Wales)
Chirk (Wales)
Clara (Ireland)
Coity (Wales)
Conna (Ireland)
Conwy (Wales)
Coole (Northern Ireland)
Corfe (England)
Cregg (Ireland)
Croft (England/Wales)
Doune (Scotland)
Dover (England)
Drogo (England)
Duart (Scotland)
Elcho (Scotland)
Ewloe (Wales)
Ferns (Ireland)
Flint (Wales)
Fyvie (Scotland)
Green (Northern Ireland)
Gylen (Scotland)
Hever (England)
Hurst (England)
Knock (Scotland)
Leeds (England)
of Mey (Scotland)
Powis (Wales)
Salem (Ireland)
Skibo (Scotland)
Slade (Ireland)
Slane (Ireland)
Sween (Scotland)
Tully (Northern Ireland)
Upnor (England)
White (Wales)
y Bere (Wales)

06 Bangor (Northern Ireland)
Belsay (England)
Bodiam (England)
Bolton (England)
Brodie (Scotland)
Brough (England)
Bungay (England)
Cadzow (Scotland)
Camber (England)
Carlow (Ireland)
Carnew (Ireland)
Cawdor (Scotland)
Conway (Ireland)
Dalkey (Ireland)
Dangan (Ireland)
Darver (Ireland)
Dublin (Ireland)
Duffus (Scotland)
Dunmoe (Ireland)

Durham (England)
Edzell (Scotland)
Floors (Scotland)
Fraser (Scotland)
Glamis (Scotland)
Glinsk (Ireland)
Grange (Ireland)
Gregan (Ireland)
Hailes (Scotland)
Howard (England)
Howard (Ireland)
Huntly (Scotland)
Hylton (England)
Kellie (Scotland)
Kilkea (Ireland)
Ludlow (England)
Lynchs (Ireland)
Maiden (England)
Mallow (Ireland)
Matrix (Ireland)
Minard (Ireland)
Morton (Scotland)
Muness (Scotland)
Nenagh (Ireland)
Newark (England/
  Scotland)
Norham (England)
Nunney (England)
Oakham (England)
Ogmore (Wales)
Orford (England)
Ormond (Ireland)
Oxwich (Wales)
Parkes (Ireland)
Raglan (Wales)
Rheban (Ireland)
Ripley (England)
Rushen (Isle of Man)
Sandal (England)
Shanid (Ireland)
Slains (Scotland)
Strome (Scotland)
Sutton (Ireland)
Swords (Ireland)
Tioram (Scotland)
Totnes (England)
Toward (Scotland)
Walmer (England)
Wiston (Wales)

07 Alnwick (England)
Appleby (England)
Arundel (England)
Ashford (Ireland)
Ashtown (Ireland)
Athenry (Ireland)
Athlone (Ireland)
Audleys (Northern Ireland)
Balfour (Northern Ireland)

Balloch (Scotland)
Barnard (England)
Beeston (England)
Belfast (Northern Ireland)
Belvoir (England)
Berwick (England)
Blarney (Ireland)
Braemar (Scotland)
Bramber (England)
Bremore (Ireland)
Brodick (Scotland)
Bullock (Ireland)
Caister (England)
Calshot (England)
Cardiff (Wales)
Chester (England)
Clifden (Ireland)
Cloghan (Ireland)
Compton (England)
Crathes (Scotland)
Culzean (Scotland)
Denbigh (Wales)
Desmond (Ireland)
Dinefwr (Wales)
Donamon (Ireland)
Donegal (Ireland)
Dundrum (Northern
  Ireland)
Dunsany (Ireland)
Dunster (England)
Eastnor (England)
Farnham (England)
Fethard (Ireland)
Granagh (Ireland)
Harlech (Wales)
Hemyock (England)
Jordan's (Northern Ireland)
Kanturk (Ireland)
Kelburn (Scotland)
Kielder (England)
Kilteel (Ireland)
Kisimul (Scotland)
Lachlan (Scotland)
Lackeen (Ireland)
Langley (England)
Leixlip (Ireland)
Lisheen (Ireland)
Lismore (Ireland)
Loughor (Wales)
Lydford (England)
Macroom (Ireland)
Markree (Ireland)
McGrath (Ireland)
Menzies (Scotland)
Mingary (Scotland)
Moydrum (Ireland)
Moygara (Ireland)
Newport (Wales)

Newtown (Ireland)
Old Wick (Scotland)
Penrhyn (Wales)
Penrith (England)
Peveril (England)
Prudhoe (England)
Redwood (Ireland)
Roscrea (Ireland)
Scotney (England)
Sizergh (England)
Skipsea (England)
Skipton (England)
Stalker (Scotland)
St Mawes (England)
Sudeley (England)
Swansea (Wales)
Threave (Scotland)
Torosay (Scotland)
Tutbury (England)
Warwick (England)
Weeting (England)
Weobley (Wales)
Wigmore (England)
Windsor (England)

08 Aberdour (Scotland)
Altidore (Ireland)
Ardvreck (Scotland)
Armadale (Scotland)
Askeaton (Ireland)
Auckland (England)
Ballybur (Ireland)
Balmoral (Scotland)
Balvaird (Scotland)
Balvenie (Scotland)
Bamburgh (England)
Barmeath (Ireland)
Bastille (France)
Berkeley (England)
Bolsover (England)
Bothwell (Scotland)
Bronllys (Wales)
Brougham (England)
Broughty (Scotland)
Bunratty (Ireland)
Burleigh (Scotland)
Campbell (Scotland)
Carlisle (England)
Chepstow (Wales)
Clonmore (Ireland)
Corgarff (Scotland)
Crichton (Scotland)
Delgatie (Scotland)
Dirleton (Scotland)
Drimnagh (Ireland)
Drishane (Ireland)
Drummond (Scotland)
Dryslwyn (Wales)
Dunashad (Ireland)

Dunollie (Scotland)
Dunottar (Scotland)
Dunrobin (Scotland)
Dunvegan (Scotland)
Dunyvaig (Scotland)
Egremont (England)
Elsinore (Denmark)
Eynsford (England)
Gallarus (Ireland)
Glenquin (Ireland)
Goodrich (England)
Grosmont (Wales)
Hadleigh (England)
Hastings (England)
Helmsley (England)
Hertford (England)
Humewood (Ireland)
Jedburgh (Scotland)
Kidwelly (Wales)
Kilcasan (Ireland)
Kilchurn (Scotland)
Kilclief (Northern Ireland)
Kilkenny (Ireland)
Killaghy (Ireland)
Killiane (Ireland)
Kisimull (Scotland)
Lawrence (England)
Leamaneh (Ireland)
Listowel (Ireland)
Loch Doon (Scotland)
Longtown (England)
Lulworth (England)
Malahide (Ireland)
Maynooth (Ireland)
Menstrie (Scotland)
Monmouth (Wales)
Neidpath (Scotland)
Noltland (Scotland)
Old Sarum (England)
Oranmore (Ireland)
Pembroke (Wales)
Pevensey (England)
Portland (England)
Portumna (Ireland)
Rhuddlan (Wales)
Richmond (England)
Rothesay (Scotland)
Shankill (Ireland)
Skipness (Scotland)
Southsea (England)
Stirling (Scotland)
Stokesay (England)
Tamworth (England)
Tintagel (England)
Tiverton (England)
Tolquhon (Scotland)
Tretower (Wales)
Urquhart (Scotland)

Wolvesey (England)
Yarmouth (England)

09 Ardgillan (Ireland)
Athlumney (Ireland)
Baldongan (Ireland)
Ballyhack (Ireland)
Ballymoon (Ireland)
Ballymote (Ireland)
Beaumaris (Wales)
Bickleigh (England)
Blackness (Scotland)
Blackrock (Ireland)
Bolebroke (England)
Cardoness (Scotland)
Carsluith (Scotland)
Caulfield (Northern Ireland)
Chipchase (England)
Cilgerran (Wales)
Claypotts (Scotland)
Criccieth (Wales)
Cromwell's (England)
Crookston (Scotland)
Culcreuch (Scotland)
Dartmouth (England)
Dolbadarn (Wales)
Dolforwyn (Wales)
Dumbarton (Scotland)
Dundonald (Scotland)
Dungarvan (Ireland)
Dunguaire (Ireland)
Dun Na Sead (Ireland)
Dunnottar (Scotland)
Dunsinane (Scotland)
Dunsoghly (Ireland)
Edinburgh (Scotland)
Edlingham (England)
Ferriters (Ireland)
Findlater (Scotland)
Garryhill (Ireland)
Gleninagh (Ireland)
Guildford (England)
Hedingham (England)
Hermitage (Scotland)
Highclere (England)
Hunginton (Ireland)
Inveraray (Scotland)
Inverness (Scotland)
Johnstown (Ireland)
Kilbolane (Ireland)
Kilcolgan (Ireland)
Kildrummy (Scotland)
Kimbolton (England)
King Johns (Ireland)
Knappogue (Ireland)
Lancaster (England)
Laugharne (Wales)
Lauriston (Scotland)
Lemaneagh (Ireland)

Llawhaden (Wales)
Lochleven (Scotland)
Lochmaben (Scotland)
Lochranza (Scotland)
Middleham (England)
Monkstown (Ireland)
Muncaster (England)
Newcastle (Wales)
O Donovans (Ireland)
Pendennis (England)
Pickering (England)
Powderham (England)
Restormel (England)
Rochester (England)
Rockfleet (Ireland)
Roscommon (Ireland)
Scalloway (Scotland)
Shankhill (Ireland)
Sherborne (England)
Skenfrith (Wales)
Spofforth (England)
St Andrews (Scotland)
Tantallon (Scotland)
Tonbridge (England)
Tynemouth (England)
Warkworth (England)

10 Auchindoun (Scotland)
Aughnanure (Ireland)
Ballinafad (Ireland)
Ballyhealy (Ireland)
Ballynahow (Ireland)
Balrothery (Ireland)
Bridgnorth (England)
Caernarfon (Wales)
Caernarvon (Wales)
Caerphilly (Wales)
Carmarthen (Wales)
Castle Acre (England)
Castlemore (Ireland)
Craigievar (Scotland)
Cubbie Row's (Scotland)
Dardistown (Ireland)
Deddington (England)
Donnington (England)
Drumlanrig (Scotland)
Foulksrath (Ireland)
Glenbuchat (Scotland)
Highcliffe (England)
Huntington (Ireland)
Inverlochy (Scotland)
Jewel Tower (England)
Kenilworth (England)
Kinnersley (England)

Kirkistown (Northern Ireland)
Launceston (England)
Liscarroll (Ireland)
Maclellan's (Scotland)
Montgomery (Wales)
Okehampton (England)
Old Wardour (England)
Pontefract (England)
Rathcoffey (Ireland)
Rockingham (England)
St Briavel's (England)
St Quentin's (Wales)
Strancally (Ireland)
Tinnahinch (Ireland)
Tullynally (Ireland)

11 Ballaghmore (Ireland)
Ballyhannan (Ireland)
Ballyragget (Ireland)
Barryscourt (Ireland)
Berkhamsted (England)
Bolingbroke (England)
Carisbrooke (England)
Carnasserie (Scotland)
Castell Coch (Wales)
Charleville (Ireland)
Chillingham (England)
Conisbrough (England)
Craigmillar (Scotland)
Craignethan (Scotland)
Dolwyddelan (Wales)
Eilean Donan (Scotland)
Enniscorthy (Ireland)
Farnham Keep (England)
Ferniehirst (Scotland)
Fotheringay (England)
Framlingham (England)
Grimsthorpe (England)
King Charles (England)
Kirby Muxloe (England)
Lindisfarne (England)
Llansteffan (Wales)
Ludgershall (England)
Narrow Water (Northern
  Ireland)
Parkavonear (Ireland)
Portchester (England)
Rathfarnham (Ireland)
Rathmacknee (Ireland)
Ravenscraig (Scotland)
Robertstown (Ireland)
Scarborough (England)
Tattershall (England)
Thirlestane (Scotland)

12 Acton Burnell (England)
Baconsthorpe (England)
Ballybrittan (Ireland)
Ballycarbery (Ireland)
Ballyloughan (Ireland)
Ballynahinch (Ireland)
Berry Pomeroy (England)
Caerlaverock (Scotland)
Carreg Cennen (Wales)
Carrigafoyle (Ireland)
Castell y Bere (Wales)
Castlemartyr (Ireland)
Castle Rising (England)
Christchurch (England)
Coulter Motte (Scotland)
Dunstaffnage (Scotland)
Dunstanburgh (England)
Huntingtower (Scotland)
King Charles's (England)
Kinnaird Head (Scotland)
Lullingstone (England)
Marmion Tower (England)
Mountfitchet (England)
New Buckenham (England)
Sherborne Old (England)
St Catherine's (England)
Tyrrellspass (Ireland)

13 Ballinacarrig (Ireland)
Ballindalloch (Scotland)
Carrickfergus (Northern
  Ireland)
Carrigaphooca (Ireland)
Chiddingstone (England)
Cloughouthter (Ireland)
Druchtag Motte (Scotland)
Knaresborough (England)
Moreton Corbet (England)
Rathnageeragh (Ireland)

14 Ashby de la Zouch
  (England)
Ballynacarriga (Ireland)
Boarstall Tower (England)
Carrigogunnell (Ireland)
Clifford's Tower (England)
Falkland Palace (Scotland)

15 Carrickabraghey (Ireland)
Kilmallock Kings (Ireland)
Longthorpe Tower (England)
St Leonard's Tower
  (England)
St Michael's Mount
  (England)
Warkworth Castle

See also **fortification; tower**

cat

Cat types include:

03 bob	**06** cougar	leopard	**12** mountain lion
04 lion	jaguar	**08** domestic	Scottish wild
lynx	kodkod	mountain	**13** little spotted
puma	margay	**09** Geoffroy's	**14** clouded leopard
05 feral	ocelot	**10** jaguarundi	
tiger	pampas	**11** snow leopard	
	07 cheetah		

Cat breeds include:

03 rex	ragdoll	Selkirk Rex
04 Manx	Siamese	Turkish Van
05 Korat	Tiffany	**11** Egyptian Mau
tabby	**08** Balinese	Foreign Blue
06 Angora	Burmilla	Russian Blue
Bengal	Devon Rex	silver tabby
Birman	Snowshoe	**12** Foreign White
Bombay	Tiffanie	Scottish Fold
Cymric	**09** Himalayan	**13** domestic tabby
Havana	Maine Coon	Tortoiseshell
LaPerm	Singapura	Turkish Angora
Ocicat	Tonkinese	**15** British longhair
Somali	**10** Abyssinian	Exotic shorthair
07 Burmese	Carthusian	Japanese Bobtail
Persian	chinchilla	Norwegian Forest
	Cornish Rex	

Cats include:

03 Gus (*Old Possum's Book of Practical Cats*, 1939, T S Eliot)
Tom (*Tom & Jerry*, 1967– , MGM cartoon)

04 Bast (Egyptian mythology)
Jess (*Postman Pat*, 1981– , children's TV animation)

05 Dinah (*Alice in Wonderland*, 1865, Lewis Carroll)
Felix (*Feline Follies*, 1919, Otto Messmer)
Korky (*The Dandy*, 1937– , D C Thomson, comic)

06 Arthur (pet food ad, UK TV)
Bastet (Egyptian mythology)
Ginger (*The Tale of Ginger and Pickles*, 1909, Beatrix Potter)
Kaspar (cat statue, The Savoy Hotel, London)
Top Cat (*Top Cat*, 1961, Hanna-Barbera animation)
Ubasti (Egyptian mythology)

07 Bagpuss (1974, UK children's TV)
Custard (*Roobarb*, 1974–2005, Grange Caveley, BBC cartoon)
Simpkin (*The Tailor of Gloucester*, 1903, Beatrix Potter)

08 Beerbohm (Globe Theatre, UK, longest serving mouser)
Garfield (*Garfield*, 1978– , Jim Davis, comic strip)
Humphrey (house cat at 10 Downing Street)
Krazy Kat (1913–44, George Herriman, comic strip)
Macavity (*Old Possum's Book of Practical Cats*, 1939, T S Eliot)

09 Mehitabel (*Archy and Mehitabel*, 1916– , Don Marquis, newspaper column)
Mrs Norris (Harry Potter series, 1997–2007, J K Rowling)
Sylvester (*Sylvester & Tweety Pie*, 1945–66, Looney Tunes & Merrie Melodies cartoons)
Thomasina (*Thomasina: The Cat who thought she was God*, 1957, Paul Gallico)
Tom Kitten (*Tale of Tom Kitten*, 1907, Beatrix Potter)

10 El Brooshna (Judao-Christian mythology)
Heathcliff (*Heathcliff*, 1973, George Gately, comic strip)

11 Cat in the Hat (1957, Dr Seuss)

Cheshire Cat (*Alice in Wonderland*, 1865, Lewis Carroll)
Crookshanks (Harry Potter series, 1997–2007, J K Rowling)
Korky the Cat (*The Dandy*, 1937– , D C Thomson, comic)
Puss in Boots (pantomime)

13 Skimbleshanks (*Old Possum's Book of Practical Cats*, 1939, T S Eliot)

14 Bustopher Jones (*Old Possum's Book of Practical Cats*, 1939, T S Eliot)
Mr Mistoffelees (*Old Possum's Book of Practical Cats*, 1939, T S Eliot)
Old Deuteronomy (*Old Possum's Book of Practical Cats*, 1939, T S Eliot)
The Cat in the Hat (1957, Dr Seuss)

Terms to do with cats include:

03 AOV
gib
mew
mog
paw
pet

04 bowl
claw
coat
comb
fawn
flea
fuff
hiss
mink
purr
puss
show
spay
spit
tail
tick
waul

05 black
breed
brush
cameo
cream
ebony
Felis
feral
groom
honey
ID tag
kitty
leash

mange
miaow
miaul
moggy
mouse
pussy
queen
ruddy
sable
smoke
tabby
white
wrawl

06 albino
basket
bronze
calico
catnep
catnip
cat toy
collar
declaw
dilute
feline
gib-cat
golden
hybrid
kitten
litter
mitted
moggie
mouser
neuter
ramcat
shaded
silver
Tib-cat

tomcat

07 allergy
Baudron
bobtail
cat-flap
catling
catmint
cattery
odd-eyed
patched
spotted

08 bi-colour
blue-eyed
brindled
cinnamon
crossing
domestic
dominant
gold-eyed
good luck
hairball
lavender
outcross
platinum
purebred
whiskers
wirehair

09 amber-eyed
blue-cream
caterwaul
cat litter
champagne
green-eyed
grimalkin
lynx point
marmalade

micro-chip
nine lives
pedigreed
purebreed
recessive
sealpoint

10 cat-carrier
cat-fancier
chinchilla
copper-eyed
flame point
flea collar
lilac point
litter tray
long-haired
smoke-white
tabby-white

11 ailurophile
ailurophobe
colourpoint
lilac-tortie
short-haired

12 ailurophilia
ailurophobia
ailurophobic
cat scratcher
silver-tipped

13 straight-eared
tortoiseshell
toxoplasmosis

14 chocolate point
scratching post

15 any other variety
seal-tortie point

cathedral

Cathedrals in the UK include:

03 Ely

05 Derby
Isles
Leeds
Ripon

Truro
Wells

06 Bangor
Brecon
Dundee

Durham
Exeter
Oxford

07 Arundel
Bristol

Cardiff
Chester
Clifton
Dornoch
Glasgow

Lincoln
Newport
Norwich
Salford
St Asaph
St John's
St Mary's
St Paul's
Swansea
Wrexham
08 Aberdeen
Bradford
Carlisle

Coventry
Hereford
Llandaff
Plymouth
St Albans
St Davids
09 Blackburn
Brentwood
Edinburgh
Guildford
Inverness
Lancaster
Leicester

Lichfield
Liverpool
Newcastle
Rochester
Salisbury
Sheffield
Southwark
St Andrews
Wakefield
Worcester
10 Birmingham
Canterbury
Chelmsford

Chichester
Gloucester
Manchester
Nottingham
Portsmouth
Shrewsbury
Winchester
11 Northampton
York Minster
12 Christ Church
Peterborough
13 Middlesbrough
St Edmundsbury

Cathedrals worldwide include:

04 Lund (Sweden)

05 Duomo (Italy)
Milan (Italy)

06 Aachen (Germany)
Rheims (France)

07 Cologne (Germany)
Córdoba (Spain)
Orvieto (Italy)
St Mark's (Italy)

08 Chartres (France)
Florence (Italy)

St Basil's (Russia)
St Peter's (Vatican City)

09 Notre-Dame (France)

10 Strasbourg (France)

11 Hagia Sophia (Turkey)

See also **church**

cattle

Cattle breeds include:

02 zo

03 dso
dzo
gir
gur
gyr
zho

04 dzho
jomo
tuli
zebu
zobo
zobu

05 Angus
black
Devon
dsobo
dsomo
Kerry
Luing
sanga

wagyu
white
zhomo
06 ankole
dexter
Durham
Jersey
Salers
Sussex
watusi
07 beefalo
brahman
brahmin
brangus
cattabu
cattalo
Latvian
red poll
08 Alderney
Ayrshire
Chianina

Friesian
Galloway
gelbvieh
Guernsey
Hereford
Highland
Holstein
illawara
Limousin
longhorn
Shetland
09 Afrikaner
braunvieh
Corriente
Romagnola
shorthorn
Simmental
Teeswater
Ukrainian
white park
10 Africander

beefmaster
Brown Swiss
Canadienne
Lincoln Red
Murray grey
Piemontese
Simmenthal
South Devon
Tarentaise
Welsh Black
11 Belgian Blue
Chillingham
Piedmontese
12 British White
Simmenthaler
13 Aberdeen Angus
droughtmaster
Texas longhorn
14 Belted Galloway
Santa Gertrudis

See also **animal; meat**

cave

Caves include:

04 Zitu (Spain)
06 Berger (France)
   Vqerdi (Spain)
08 Badalona (Spain)

09 G E S Malaga (Spain)
   Snezhnaya (Georgia)
10 Schneeloch (Austria)
11 Batmanhöhle (Austria)

Jean Bernard (France)
14 Lamprechstofen (Austria)
   Pierre-St-Martin (France)
   Sistema Huautla (Mexico)

ceilidh *see* **dance**

celebration

Celebrations include:

04 fête
   gala
05 feast
   party
06 May Day
07 banquet
   baptism
   ceilidh
   jubilee
   name-day
   reunion
   tribute

   wedding
08 birthday
   festival
   hen night
   marriage
09 centenary
   Labour Day
   reception
   stag night
10 bar mitzvah
   bat mitzvah
   graduation

   homecoming
   retirement
11 anniversary
   christening
   coming-of-age
   harvest-home
12 thanksgiving
13 commemoration
15 harvest festival
   Independence Day

See also **anniversary**; **ceremony**; **festival**; **holiday**

cell

Cells include:

01 B
   T
03 egg
   PEC
   red
   rod
   sex
   wet
04 cone
   fuel
   germ
   HeLa
   mast
   ovum
   stem
05 blood
   guard
   nerve
   plant
   solar
   sperm
   water
   white

06 animal
   cancer
   collar
   diaxon
   gamete
   goblet
   Hadley
   killer
   memory
   mother
   neuron
   oocyte
   plasma
   target
   tumour
07 cadmium
   Daniell
   gravity
   helper T
   initial
   neurone
   primary
   Schwann

   Sertoli
   somatic
   voltaic
08 akaryote
   basophil
   daughter
   galvanic
   gonidium
   gonocyte
   monocyte
   myoblast
   neoblast
   parietal
   platelet
   Purkinje
   red blood
   retinula
   sclereid
   selenium
   tracheid
   zooblast
09 acidophil
   antipodal

astrocyte	cnidoblast	erythrocyte
coenocyte	enterocyte	granulocyte
corpuscle	eosinophil	lymphoblast
fibrocyte	fibroblast	megaloblast
haemocyte	gametocyte	odontoblast
hybridoma	hepatocyte	poikilocyte
idioblast	histiocyte	thrombocyte
Leclanché	histoblast	T lymphocyte
leucocyte	leucoblast	**12** chondroblast
leukocyte	leukoblast	erythroblast
macrocyte	lymphocyte	haematoblast
microcyte	macrophage	red corpuscle
myofibril	melanocyte	reticulocyte
phagocyte	myeloblast	spermatocyte
photocell	neuroblast	spermatozoid
prokaryon	neutrophil	spermatozoon
sclereide	osteoblast	**13** chromatophore
secondary	osteoclast	natural killer
spermatid	spherocyte	photoelectric
syncytium	suppressor	spermatoblast
thymocyte	thread-cell	**14** blood corpuscle
tracheide	white blood	spermatogonium
10 choanocyte	**11** B lymphocyte	white corpuscle

See also **immune system**

Celtic god, goddess *see* mythology

cemetery

Cemeteries and burial places include:

07 Mt Holly (US)
Nunhead (England)

08 Brompton (England)
Highgate (England)
Mt Olivet (Canada/US)
Panthéon (France)

09 Abney Park (England)
Arlington (US)

10 El Escorial (Spain)
La Almudena (Spain)
Montmartre (France)

San Michele (Italy)
Weissensee (Germany)

11 Kensal Green (England)
West Norwood (England)

12 Golders Green (England)
Les Invalides (France)
Montparnasse (France)
Père Lachaise (France)
Tower Hamlets (England)

13 Mount of Olives (Israel)

15 Island of the Dead (Italy/Australia)

See also **World Heritage site**

Central and South American god, goddess *see* mythology

cereal

Cereals include:

03 oat	**04** corn	teff	spelt
rye	oats	**05** bajra	wheat
tef	rice	emmer	**06** barley
zea	sago	maize	bulgur

millet
07 bulghur
sorghum
08 amaranth

amelcorn
couscous
semolina
09 buckwheat

sweetcorn
triticale
10 Indian corn
Kaffir corn

12 common millet
13 bulrush millet
foxtail millet
Italian millet

Breakfast cereals include:

05 Alpen®
06 muesli
Weetos®
07 All Bran®
08 Cheerios®
Clusters®
Coco Pops®
Frosties®
Fruitbix®
Fruitful®
porridge
Ricicles®
Special K®

Weetabix®
09 Grape Nuts®
Just Right®
Ready Brek®
Shreddies®
10 Bran Flakes®
cornflakes
Quaker Oats®
Raisin Bran®
Sugar Puffs®
11 Common Sense®
Fruit'n'Fibre®
Oatso Simple®

Puffed Wheat®
Sultana Bran®
12 Country Crisp®
Raisin Wheats®
Rice Krispies®
13 Frosted Flakes®
Fruit and Fibre®
Golden Grahams®
Honey Nut Loops®
Shredded Wheat®
14 Nestlé Clusters®
15 Cinnamon Grahams®

See also **crop**; **food**

ceremony

Ceremonies include:

05 amrit
doseh
tangi
06 maundy
nipter
07 baptism

capping
chanoyu
chuppah
matsuri
wedding
08 marriage

nuptials
09 committal
matrimony
10 bar mitzvah
bat mitzvah
graduation

initiation
11 christening
fire-walking
12 confirmation

See also **celebration**; **Japan**

chair

Chairs include:

03 arm
lug
pew
04 Bath
camp
cane
deck
easy
form
head
high
push
wing
05 bench
elbow

king's
night
potty
sedan
stool
wheel
06 basket
carver
curule
dining
estate
jampan
Morris
pouffe
rocker

sag bag
sledge
swivel
throne
wicker
07 beanbag
Berbice
bergère
commode
guérite
kitchen
lounger
nursing
rocking
Windsor

08 captain's
electric
fauteuil
prie-dieu
recliner
wainscot
09 director's
10 boatswain's
fiddle-back
frithstool
ladder-back
11 Cromwellian
gestatorial
12 ducking-stool

See also **furniture**; **house**

channel

Channels include:

03 Kii (Japan)
04 Foxe (Canada)
05 Bashi (Taiwan/Philippines)
    Bungo (Japan)
    Kaiwi (USA)
    Kauai (USA)
    Lamma (Hong Kong)
    Minas (Canada)
    Minch (Scotland)
    North (Northern Ireland/Scotland/Canada)
06 Akashi (Japan)
    Kalohi (USA)
    Manche (France)
    Queens (Australia)
07 Babuyan (Philippines)
    Bristol (England)
    English (England/France)
    Jamaica (Haiti)
    Massawa (Ethiopia)
    Pailolo (USA)
    Sandwip (Bangladesh)
    St Lucia (St Lucia/Martinique)
    Yucatán (Cuba/Mexico)
08 Dominica (Dominica/Martinique)

La Manche (France)
Nicholas (Cuba/The Bahamas)
Santaren (Cuba/The Bahamas)
Sicilian (Italy)
St Andrew (Canada)
The Minch (Scotland)
09 Balintang (Philippines)
    Capricorn (Australia)
    East Lamma (Hong Kong)
    Geographe (Australia)
    Kaulakahi (USA)
    Northwest (Australia)
    Old Bahama (Cuba/The Bahamas)
    Skagerrak (Denmark/Norway)
    St George's (Wales/Ireland)
    West Lamma (Hong Kong)
10 Alalakeiki (USA)
    Alenuihaha (USA)
    McClintock (Canada)
    Mozambique (Mozambique)
    North Minch (Scotland)
11 Little Minch (Scotland)
12 Kealaikahiki (USA)
    Santa Barbara (USA)

See also **television**

character *see* **Austen, Jane; Bible; Blyton, Enid; Brecht, Bertolt; Brontë Anne; Brontë Charlotte; Brontë Emily; Carroll, Lewis; cartoon; Chaucer, Geoffrey; Chekhov, Anton; Christie, Dame Agatha; Defoe, Daniel; Dickens, Charles; Dostoevsky, Fyodor; Doyle, Sir Arthur Conan; Dumas, Alexandre; Eliot, George; fairy tale; Gilbert, Sir W S; Hardy, Thomas; Hemingway, Ernest; Homer; Ibsen, Henrik; James Bond; James, Henry; Joyce, James; Kipling, Rudyard; Lawrence, D H; legend; literature; Molière; Morrison, Toni; Mozart, Wolfgang Amadeus; Murdoch, Dame Iris; mythology; O'Neill, Eugene; opera; Orwell, George; pantomime; Racine, Jean-Baptiste; Rowling, J K; Scott, Sir Walter; Shakespeare, William; Stevenson, Robert Louis; Tolkien, J R R; Tolstoy, Count Leo; Trollope, Anthony; Twain, Mark; Verdi; Giuseppe; Voltaire; Wells, H G; Wilde, Oscar; Wodehouse, Sir P G; Woolf, Virginia; Zola, Émile**

charity

Charities include:

03 BHF	**05** CAFOD	Barnardo's
DEC	NSPCC	Macmillan
FOE	Oxfam	**10** Greenpeace
NCH	RSPCA	Marie Curie
RBL	Scope	**11** Comic Relief
04 PDSA	**06** Mencap	Help the Aged
RNIB	**07** Amnesty	**12** Christian Aid
RNLI	**08** Red Cross	**13** National Trust
RSPB	**09** ActionAid	Salvation Army
WRVS		

| Wellcome Trust | **14** Cancer Research | Save the Children |
| Woodland Trust | **15** Leonard Cheshire | St John Ambulance |

Charity fundraising events include:

06 fun run	swimathon	sponsored swim
raffle	**10** jumble sale	sponsored walk
08 telethon	**12** slave auction	**14** charity auction
09 radiothon	**13** coffee morning	**15** bring-and-buy sale

Chaucer, Geoffrey (c.1345–1400)

Significant works include:

14 *The House of Fame* (c.1378)	*Troilus and Criseyde* (c.1385–89)
16 *Book of the Duchess* (1369)	**20** *The Legend of Good Women* (c.1385–87)
18 *The Canterbury Tales* (c.1387–1400)	**21** *The Parliament of Fowles* (1380)

The Canterbury Tales comprise:

12 'The Cook's Tale'	'The Man of Law's Tale'
'The Monk's Tale'	'The Merchant's Tale'
13 'The Clerk's Tale'	'The Pardoner's Tale'
'The Friar's Tale'	'The Prioress's Tale'
'The Reeve's Tale'	'The Summoner's Tale'
	'The Tale of Melibee'
14 'The Knight's Tale'	
'The Miller's Tale'	**17** 'The Physician's Tale'
'The Parson's Tale'	'The Second Nun's Tale'
'The Squire's Tale'	**18** 'The General Prologue'
15 'The Shipman's Tale'	'The Nun's Priest's Tale'
	'The Tale of Sir Thopas'
16 'The Franklin's Tale'	'The Wife of Bath's Tale'
'The Manciple's Tale'	**20** 'The Canon's Yeoman's Tale'

Significant characters include:

03 May	Criseyde	**11** The Franklin
05 Emily	Griselda	The Manciple
06 Arcite	Pandarus	The Man of Law
Damien	The Canon	The Merchant
Thopas (Sir)	The Friar	The Pardoner
07 Alisoun	The Reeve	The Prioress
Bailley (Harry)	**09** Arveragus	The Summoner
Dorigen	Constance	**12** Chaunticleer
January (Old)	Eglantyne (Madame)	The Carpenter
Palamon	Pertelote	The Physician
The Cook	The Knight	The Second Nun
The Dyer	The Miller	**13** The Nun's Priest
The Host	The Parson	The Wife of Bath
The Monk	The Squire	**14** The Haberdasher
Troilus	The Weaver	
08 Aurelius	The Yeoman	
	10 The Shipman	

cheese

Cheeses include:

03 ewe
Oka

04 Brie
curd
Edam
feta
goat
skyr

05 Caboc
Carré
Derby
Gouda
quark

06 Cantal
chèvre
Dunlop
junket
Orkney
paneer
Romano
Tilsit

07 Boursin
Cheddar
crottin
crowdie
Fontina
Gruyère
kebbock
kebbuck
Limburg
Münster
ricotta

sapsago
Stilton®

08 bel paese
Cheshire
Churnton
Emmental
halloumi
Huntsman
manchego
Parmesan
pecorino
raclette
Taleggio
vacherin

09 Amsterdam
Blue Vinny
Cambozola®
Camembert
chevreton
Emmenthal
Ilchester
Jarlsberg®
Killarney
Leicester
Limburger
Lymeswold®
mouse-trap
Port Salut
processed
provolone
reblochon
Roquefort

sage Derby

10 blue cheese
Caerphilly
Danish blue
dolcelatte
Dorset Blue
Emmentaler
Gloucester
Gorgonzola
hard cheese
Lancashire
mascarpone
mozzarella
Neufchâtel
Red Windsor
soft cheese
stracchino
vegetarian

11 Coulommiers
cream cheese
Petit Suisse
Pont l'Évêque
Saint-Paulin
Wensleydale

12 Blue Cheshire
fromage frais
Monterey Jack
Philadelphia®
Red Leicester

13 Bleu d'Auvergne
cottage cheese

See also **dairy**

chef

Chefs, restaurateurs and cookery writers include:

03 Hom (Ken; 1949– , US)

04 Diat (Louis; 1885–1957, French/US)
Dods (Meg; 1781–1857, Scottish)
Kerr (Graham; 1934– , English/New Zealand)
Roux (Albert; 1935– , French)
Roux (Michel; 1941– , French)
Spry (Constance; 1886–1960, English)

05 Beard (James; 1903–85, US)
Blanc (Raymond; 1949– , French)
Brown (David; 1951– , Scottish)
Brown (Hilary; 1952– , Scottish)
Child (Julia; 1912–2004, US)
David (Elizabeth; 1913–92, English)
Floyd (Keith; 1943– , English)

Leith (Prue; 1940– , English)
Nairn (Nick; 1959– , Scottish)
Sardi (Vincent; 1885–1969, Italian/US)
Savoy (Guy; 1953– , French)
Smith (Delia; 1941– , English)
Soyer (Alexis; 1809–58, French)
Stein (Rick; 1947– , English)
White (Marco Pierre; 1961– , English)

06 Appert (Nicolas; 1749–1841, French)
Beeton (Mrs Isabella; 1836–65, English)
Bocuse (Paul; 1926– , French)
Carême (Marie Antoine; 1784–1833, French)
Farmer (Fannie; 1857–1915, US)
Fisher (M F K; 1908–92, US)

Franey (Pierre; 1921–96, French/US)
Harvey (Fred; 1835–1901, US)
Lawson (Nigella; 1960– , English)
Little (Alistair; 1950– ,English)
Oliver (Jamie; 1975– , English)
Ramsay (Gordon; 1967– , Scottish)
Rhodes (Gary; 1960– , English)
Slater (Nigel; c.1950s– , English)
Turner (Brian; 1946– , English)
Wilson (David; 1938– , Scottish)

07 Cradock (Fanny; 1909–94, English)
Eriksen (Gunn; 1956– , Norwegian/
  Scottish)
Grigson (Jane; 1928–90, English)
Grigson (Sophie; 1959– , English)
Guérard (Michel; 1933– , French)
Jaffrey (Madhur; 1933– , Indian/US)
Ladenis (Nico; 1934– , Kenyan)
Novelli (Jean-Christophe; 1961– , French)
Vickery (Philip; 1961– , English)

08 Dimbleby (Josceline; 1943– , English)

Grossman (Loyd; 1950– , US)
Harriott (Ainsley; 1957– , English)
Mosimann (Anton; 1947– , Swiss)
Paterson (Jennifer; 1928–99, English)
Robuchon (Joël; 1945– , French)
Rombauer (Irma; 1877–1962, US)

09 Carluccio (Antonio; 1937– , Italian)
Claiborne (Craig; 1920–2000, US)
Delmonico (Lorenzo, 1813–01, Swiss/US)
Escoffier (Auguste; c.1847–1935, French)
Heathcote (Paul; 1960– , English)
Johnstone (Isobel; 1781–1857, Scottish)
Locatelli (Giorgio; 1962– , Italian)
McCartney (Linda; 1941–98, US/British)
Prudhomme (Paul; 1940– , US)

10 Blumenthal (Heston; 1966– , English)

13 Dickson Wright (Clarissa; 1946– , English)

14 Brillat-Savarin (Anthelme; 1755–1826,
  French)

15 Worrall Thompson (Antony; 1952– , English)

Chekhov, Anton (1860–1904)

Significant works include:

06 *Ivanov* (1887)

07 *The Bear* (1890)

10 *The Seagull* (1896)

Uncle Vanya (1896)

11 *The Proposal* (1889)

12 *The Wood Demon* (1889)

15 *The Three Sisters* (1901)

16 *The Cherry Orchard* (1904)

Significant characters include:

04 Anna
Olga

05 Irina
Masha
Sasha
Sonya
Vanya

06 Astrov (Michael)
Helena
Ivanov (Nikolai)
Yelena

07 Lebedev (Sasha)
Treplev (Konstantin 'Kostaya' Gavrilovich)

08 Abramson (Sarah)
Arkadina (Irina Nikolayevna)
Lopakhin (Ermolai Alexeyevitch)
Ranevsky (Lubov Andreyevna 'Madame')
Trigorin (Boris Alexeyevich)

09 Voynitsky (Ivan 'Vanya')

10 Zarechnaya (Nina Mikhailovna)

11 Serebryakov (Alexander)

chemistry

Chemical elements, their symbols and atomic numbers include:

03 tin (Sn, 50)

04 gold (Au, 79)
iron (Fe, 26)
lead (Pb, 82)
neon (Ne, 10)
zinc (Zn, 30)

05 argon (Ar, 18)
boron (B, 5)
radon (Rn, 86)

xenon (Xe, 54)

06 barium (Ba, 56)
carbon (C, 6)
cerium (Ce, 58)
cobalt (Co, 27)
copper (Cu, 29)
curium (Cm, 96)
erbium (Er, 68)
helium (He, 2)

indium (In, 49)
iodine (I, 53)
nickel (Ni, 28)
osmium (Os, 76)
oxygen (O, 8)
radium (Ra, 88)
silver (Ag, 47)
sodium (Na, 11)

07 arsenic (As, 33)

bismuth (Bi, 83)
bohrium (Bh, 107)
bromine (Br, 35)
cadmium (Cd, 48)
caesium (Cs, 55)
calcium (Ca, 20)
dubnium (Db, 105)
fermium (Fm, 100)
gallium (Ga, 31)
hafnium (Hf, 72)
hahnium (Ha)
hassium (Hs, 108)
holmium (Ho, 67)
iridium (Ir, 77)
krypton (Kr, 36)
lithium (Li, 3)
mercury (Hg, 80)
niobium (Nb, 41)
rhenium (Re, 75)
rhodium (Rh, 45)
silicon (Si, 14)
sulphur (S, 16)
terbium (Tb, 65)
thorium (Th, 90)
thulium (Tm, 69)
uranium (U, 92)
yttrium (Y, 39)

08 actinium (Ac, 89)
antimony (Sb, 51)

astatine (At, 85)
chlorine (Cl, 17)
chromium (Cr, 24)
europium (Eu, 63)
fluorine (F, 9)
francium (Fr, 87)
hydrogen (H, 1)
lutetium (Lu, 71)
nitrogen (N, 7)
nobelium (No, 102)
platinum (Pt, 78)
polonium (Po, 84)
rubidium (Rb, 37)
samarium (Sm, 62)
scandium (Sc, 21)
selenium (Se, 34)
tantalum (Ta, 73)
thallium (Tl, 81)
titanium (Ti, 22)
tungsten (W, 74)
unumbium (Uub, 112)
vanadium (V, 23)

09 aluminium (Al, 13)
americium (Am, 95)
berkelium (Bk, 97)
beryllium (Be, 4)
germanium (Ge, 32)
lanthanum (La, 57)
magnesium (Mg, 12)

manganese (Mn, 25)
neodymium (Nd, 60)
neptunium (Np, 93)
palladium (Pd, 46)
plutonium (Pu, 94)
potassium (K, 19)
ruthenium (Ru, 44)
strontium (Sr, 38)
tellurium (Te, 52)
ytterbium (Yb, 70)
zirconium (Zr, 40)

10 dysprosium (Dy, 66)
gadolinium (Gd, 64)
lawrencium (Lr, 103)
meitnerium (Mt, 109)
molybdenum (Mo, 42)
phosphorus (P, 15)
promethium (Pm, 61)
rontgenium (Rg, 111)
seaborgium (Sg, 106)
technetium (Tc, 43)

11 californium (Cf, 98)
einsteinium (Es, 99)
mendelevium (Md, 101)

12 darmstadtium (Ds, 110)
praseodymium (Pr, 59)
protactinium (Pa, 91)

13 rutherfordium (Rf, 104)

Chemical compounds include:

03 PVC
04 DEET
soap
urea
06 phenol
07 ammonia
borazon
chloral
ethanol
styrene

toluene
08 atrazine
kerosene
methanol
paraffin
09 bromoform
carbazole
10 chloramine
chloroform
12 benzaldehyde

borosilicate
13 carbon dioxide
chlorhexidine
chlorobromide
14 carbon monoxide
chloral hydrate
15 organophosphate
sodium hydroxide

Chemists include:

03 Lee (Yuan T; 1936– , Taiwanese/US)
04 Abel (Sir Frederick; 1827–1902, English)
Auer (Karl, Baron von Welsbach; 1858–1929, Austrian)
Cram (Donald J; 1919–2001, US)
Curl (Robert F, Jnr; 1933– , US)
Davy (Sir Humphry; 1778–1829, English)
Dorn (Friedrich; 1848–1916, German)
Ertl (Gerhard; 1936– , German)
Fenn (John B; 1917– , US)
Gahn (Johan Gottlieb; 1745–1818, Swedish)
Hall (Charles; 1863–1914, US)

Hess (Germain Henri; 1802–50, Swiss/Russian)
Hope (Thomas Charles; 1766–1844, Scottish)
Keir (James; 1735–1820, Scottish)
Kipp (Petrus Jacobus; 1808–64, Dutch)
Kopp (Hermann; 1817–92, German)
Kuhn (Richard; 1900–67, Austrian/German)
Lehn (Jean-Marie; 1939– , French)
Levi (Primo; 1919–87, Italian)
Mond (Ludwig; 1839–1909, German/British)
Nöth (Heinrich; 1928– , German)

Olah (George A; 1927– , Hungarian/US)
Pope (Sir William Jackson; 1870–1939, English)
Swan (Sir Joseph; 1828–1914, English)
Todd (Alexander, Lord; 1907–97, Scottish)
Urey (Harold C; 1893–1981, US)

05 Abegg (Richard; 1869–1910, German)
Abney (Sir William; 1844–1920, English)
Alder (Kurt; 1902–58, German)
Allen (Sir Geoffrey; 1928– , English)
Baumé (Antoine; 1728–1804, French)
Bevan (Edward; 1856–1921, English)
Birch (Arthur; 1915–95, Australian)
Black (Joseph; 1728–99, Scottish)
Bosch (Carl; 1874–1940, German)
Boyle (Robert; 1627–91, Irish)
Brown (Herbert C; 1912–2004, English/US)
Clark (William Mansfield; 1884–1964, US)
Corey (Elias; 1928– , US)
Cross (Charles; 1855–1935, English)
Curie (Marie; 1867–1934, Polish/French)
Curie (Pierre; 1859–1906, French)
Dakin (Henry; 1880–1952, English)
Davis (Raymond, Jnr; 1914–2006, US)
Debye (Peter; 1884–1966, Dutch/US)
Dewar (Michael; 1918–97, Indian/British)
Dewar (Sir James; 1842–1923, Scottish)
Diels (Otto; 1876–1954, German)
Dufay (Charles; 1698–1739, French)
Dumas (Jean Baptiste; 1800–84, French)
Eigen (Manfred; 1917– , German)
Ernst (Richard R; 1933– , Swiss)
Ewins (A J; 1882–1957, English)
Fleck (Alexander, Lord; 1889–1968, Scottish)
Flory (Paul J; 1910–85, US)
Frémy (Edmond; 1814–94, French)
Fukui (Kenichi; 1918–98, Japanese)
Genth (Frederick A; 1820–93, German/US)
Haber (Fritz; 1868–1934, German)
Hales (Stephen; 1677–1761, English)
Henry (William; 1774–1836, English)
Hirst (Sir Edmund; 1898–1975, English)
Hooke (Robert; 1635–1703, English)
Karle (Isabella; 1921– , US)
Kolbe (Hermann; 1818–84, German)
Kroto (Sir Harold; 1939– , English)
Le Bel (Joseph Achille; 1847–1930, French)
Lewis (Gilbert N; 1875–1946, US)
Libby (Willard F; 1908–80, US)
Lowry (Martin; 1874–1936, English)
Marsh (James; 1789–1846, English)
Mayow (John; 1640–79, English)
Meyer (Lothar; 1830–95, German)
Meyer (Viktor; 1848–97, German)
Natta (Giulio; 1903–79, Italian)
Nobel (Alfred; 1833–96, Swedish)
Pope (Sir John; 1925–2004, English)
Pregl (Fritz; 1869–1930, Austrian)

Runge (Friedlieb Ferdinand; 1795–1867, German)
Soddy (Frederick; 1877–1965, English)
Stahl (Georg; 1660–1734, German)
Stock (Alfred; 1876–1946, German)
Taube (Henry; 1915–2005, Canadian/US)
Tsien (Roger Y; 1952– , US)
Vogel (Hermann Wilhelm; 1834–98, German)
Waage (Peter; 1833–1900, Norwegian)
Wiley (Harvey Washington; 1844–1930, US)
Wurtz (Adolphe; 1817–84, French)

06 Baeyer (Adolf von; 1835–1917, German)
Balard (Antoine Jérôme; 1802–76, French)
Barton (Sir Derek; 1918–98, English)
Becher (Johann Joachim; 1635–82, German)
Beilby (Sir George; 1850–1924, Scottish)
Benson (Sidney; 1918– , US)
Brandt (Georg; 1694–1768, Swedish)
Bunsen (Robert; 1811–99, German)
Calvin (Melvin; 1911–97, US)
Claude (Georges; 1870–1960, French)
Cotton (F Albert; 1930–2007, US)
Couper (Archibald Scott; 1831–92, Scottish)
Cullen (William; 1710–90, Scottish)
Dalton (John; 1766–1844, English)
Draper (John William; 1811–82, English/US)
Dulong (Pierre; 1785–1838, French)
Eyring (Henry; 1901–81, US)
Fajans (Kasimir; 1887–1975, Polish/US)
Frasch (Hermann; 1851–1914, German/US)
Gmelin (Leopold; 1788–1853, German)
Graebe (Karl; 1841–1927, German)
Graham (Thomas; 1805–69, Scottish)
Gregor (William; 1761–1817, English)
Grubbs (Robert H; 1942– , US)
Harden (Sir Arthur; 1865–1940, English)
Hassel (Odd; 1897–1981, Norwegian)
Hevesy (George de; 1885–1966, Hungarian)
Hückel (Erich; 1896–1980, German)
Ingold (Sir Christopher; 1893–1970, English)
Karrer (Paul; 1889–1971, Russian/Swiss)
Kirwan (Richard; 1733–1812, Irish)
Kossel (Albrecht; 1853–1927, German)
Lémery (Nicolas; 1645–1715, French)
Liebig (Justus von; 1803–73, German)
Marcus (Rudolph A; 1923– , Canadian/US)
Mendel (Lafayette; 1872–1935, US)
Mercer (John; 1791–1866, English)
Miller (Stanley L; 1930–2007, US)
Morley (E W; 1838–1923, US)
Müller (Franz, Baron von Reichenstein; 1740–1825, Austrian)
Müller (Paul; 1899–1965, Swiss)
Nernst (Walther; 1864–1941, German)
Niepce (Nicéphore; 1765–1833, French)
Noyori (Ryoji; 1938– , Japanese)
Odling (William; 1829–1921, English)

Orfila (Mathieu; 1787–1853, French)
Paneth (Fritz; 1887–1958, Austrian)
Parkes (Alexander; 1813–90, English)
Perkin (Sir William Henry, Snr; 1838–1907, English)
Porter (George, Lord; 1920–2002, English)
Prelog (Vladimir; 1906–98, Swiss)
Proust (Joseph Louis; 1754–1826, French)
Ramsay (Sir William; 1852–1916, Scottish)
Raoult (François Marie; 1830–1901, French)
Rideal (Sir Eric; 1890–1974, English)
Roscoe (Sir Henry; 1833–1915, English)
Solvay (Ernest; 1838–1922, Belgian)
Spence (Peter; 1806–83, Scottish)
Thorpe (Sir Edward; 1845–1925, English)
Tilden (Sir William Augustus; 1842–1926, English)
Tizard (Sir Henry; 1885–1959, English)
Traube (Moritz; 1826–94, German)
Tsvett (Mikhail S; 1872–1919, Russian)
Tswett (Mikhail S; 1872–1919, Russian)
Urbain (Georges; 1872–1938, French)
Walker (Sir James; 1863–1935, Scottish)
Werner (Alfred; 1866–1919, French/Swiss)
Wittig (Georg; 1897–1987, German)
Wöhler (Friedrich; 1800–82, German)
Zewail (Ahmed H; 1946– , Egyptian)

07 Abelson (Philip H; 1913–2004, US)
Acheson (Edward Goodrich; 1856–1931, US)
Andrews (Thomas; 1813–85, Irish)
Bergius (Friedrich; 1884–1949, German)
Bergman (Torbern; 1735–84, Swedish)
Borodin (Aleksandr; 1833–87, Russian)
Buchner (Eduard; 1860–1917, German)
Cadogan (Sir John; 1930– , Welsh)
Calvert (Frederick Crace; 1819–73, English)
Castner (Hamilton Young; 1848–99, US)
Chalfie (Martin; 1947– , US)
Chaptal (Jean, Comte de Chanteloupe; 1756–1832, French)
Charles (Jacques; 1746–1823, French)
Chauvin (Yves; 1930– , French)
Coulson (C A; 1910–74, English)
Crookes (Sir William; 1832–1919, English)
Crutzen (Paul J; 1933– , Dutch)
Curtius (Theodor; 1857–1928, German)
Dainton (Frederick, Lord; 1914–97, English)
Daniell (John; 1790–1845, English)
Ekeberg (Anders; 1767–1813, Swedish)
Faraday (Michael; 1791–1867, English)
Fischer (Emil; 1852–1919, German)
Fischer (Ernst Otto; 1918–2007, German)
Fischer (Hans; 1881–1945, German)
Friedel (Charles; 1832–99, French)
Gadolin (Johan; 1760–1852, Finnish)
Giauque (William F; 1895–1982, Canadian/US)
Gilbert (Sir Henry; 1817–1901, English)

Gomberg (Moses; 1866–1947, Russian/US)
Guthrie (Samuel; 1782–1848, US)
Hammett (Louis P; 1894–1987, US)
Haworth (Sir Norman; 1883–1950, English)
Helmont (Jan van; 1579–1644, Flemish)
Hittorf (Johann; 1824–1914, German)
Hodgkin (Dorothy; 1910–94, Egyptian/British)
Hofmann (August Wilhelm von; 1818–92, German)
Kendall (Edward C; 1886–1972, US)
Khorana (H Gobind; 1922– , Indian/US)
Kipping (Frederick Stanley; 1863–1949, English)
Knowles (William S; 1917– , US)
Laurent (Auguste; 1807–53, French)
Leblanc (Nicholas; 1724–1806, French)
Macquer (Pierre Joseph; 1718–84, French)
Moissan (Henri; 1852–1907, French)
Moscíki (Igancy; 1867–1946, Polish)
Norrish (Ronald G W; 1897–1978, English)
Ostwald (Wilhelm; 1853–1932, Latvian/German)
Pasteur (Louis; 1822–95, French)
Pauling (Linus; 1901–94, US)
Piccard (Jean Felix; 1884–1963, Swiss/US)
Polanyi (John; 1929– , German/Canadian)
Polanyi (Michael; 1891–1976, Hungarian/British)
Richter (Hieronymous; 1824–98, German)
Richter (Jeremias; 1762–1807, German)
Roberts (John D; 1918– , US)
Rowland (F Sherwood; 1927– , US)
Ruzicka (Leopold; 1887–1976, Croatian/Swiss)
Scheele (Carl; 1742–86, Swedish)
Schrock (Richard R; 1945– , US)
Seaborg (Glenn; 1912–99, US)
Semenov (Nikolai; 1896–1986, Soviet)
Sharman (Helen; 1963– , English)
Shriver (D F; 1934– , US)
Smalley (Richard E; 1943–2005, US)
Sobrero (Ascanio; 1812–88, Italian)
Tennant (Charles; 1768–1838, Scottish)
Tennant (Smithson; 1761–1815, English)
Thénard (Louis Jacques; 1777–1857, French)
Travers (Morris; 1872–1961, English)
Wallach (Otto; 1847–1931, German)
Wieland (Heinrich; 1877–1957, German)
Windaus (Adolf; 1876–1959, German)
Winkler (Clemens; 1838–1904, German)
Ziegler (Karl; 1898–1973, German)

08 Anderson (John Stuart; 1908–90, English)
Avogadro (Amedeo; 1776–1856, Italian)
Bartlett (Neil; 1932–2008, English)
Beckmann (Ernst Otto; 1853–1923, German)
Birchall (Derek; 1930–95, English)
Brønsted (Johannes; 1879–1947, Danish)

Butlerov (Aleksandr; 1828–86, Russian)
Caventou (Joseph; 1795–1877, French)
Chevreul (Michel Eugène; 1786–1889, French)
Coolidge (William D; 1873–1975, US)
Courtois (Bernard; 1777–1838, French)
Djerassi (Carl; 1923– , Austrian/US)
Fourcroy (Antoine François, Comte de; 1755–1809, French)
Gerhardt (Charles; 1816–56, French)
Grignard (Victor; 1871–1935, French)
Guldberg (Cato; 1836–1902, Norwegian)
Hadfield (Sir Robert; 1858–1940, English)
Hantzsch (Arthur; 1857–1935, German)
Harcourt (Sir William Vernon; 1789–1871, English)
Herzberg (Gerhard; 1904–99, German/Canadian)
Hoffmann (Roald; 1937– , Polish/US)
Ipatieff (Vladimir N; 1867–1952, Russian/US)
Kjeldahl (Johan; 1849–1900, Danish)
Klaproth (Martin; 1743–1817, German)
Kornberg (Roger D; 1947– , US)
Langmuir (Irving; 1881–1957, US)
Lapworth (Arthur; 1872–1941, Scottish)
Lipscomb (William; 1919– , US)
Lonsdale (Dame Kathleen; 1903–71, Irish)
Lovelock (James; 1919– , English)
Marggraf (Andreas; 1709–82, German)
Mulliken (Robert S; 1896–1986, US)
Muspratt (James; 1793–1886, Irish/British)
Newlands (John; 1837–98, English)
Pedersen (Charles; 1904–90, US)
Pimentel (George; 1922–89, US)
Regnault (Henri Victor; 1810–78, French)
Richards (Sir Rex; 1922– , English)
Richards (Theodore W; 1868–1928, US)
Robinson (Sir Robert; 1886–1975, English)
Sabatier (Paul; 1854–1941, French)
Sefström (Nils; 1765–1829, Swedish)
Sidgwick (Nevil; 1873–1951, English)
Silliman (Benjamin; 1779–1864, US)
Silliman (Benjamin; 1816–85, US)
Smithson (James; 1765–1829, English)
Sørensen (Søren; 1868–1939, Danish)
Sprengel (Hermann; 1834–1906, German/British)
Svedberg (Theo; 1884–1971, Swedish)
Takamine (Jokichi; 1834–1922, Japanese/US)
Tiselius (Arne; 1902–71, Swedish)
van't Hoff (Jacobus H; 1852–1911, Dutch)
Voelcker (Augustus; 1822–84, German)
Weizmann (Chaim; 1874–1952, Russian/Israeli)
Woodward (Robert B; 1917–79, US)
Wüthrich (Karl; 1938– , Swiss)
09 Armstrong (Henry; 1848–1937, English)

Arrhenius (Svante; 1859–1927, Swedish)
Baekeland (Leo; 1863–1944, Belgian/US)
Beilstein (Friedrich; 1838–1906, German/Russian)
Bernstein (Richard; 1923–90, US)
Berthelot (Marcellin; 1827–1907, French)
Berzelius (Jöns Jacob; 1779–1848, Swedish)
Carothers (Wallace; 1896–1937, US)
Cavendish (Henry; 1731–1810, English)
Chabaneau (François; 1754–1842, French)
Cornforth (Sir John; 1917– , Australian)
Crum Brown (Alexander; 1838–1922, Scottish)
Frankland (Sir Edward; 1825–99, English)
Fresenius (Karl Remigius; 1818–97, German)
Gay-Lussac (Joseph Louis; 1778–1850, French)
Harington (Sir Charles; 1897–1972, British)
Heyrovský (Jaroslav; 1890–1967, Czech)
Lavoisier (Antoine; 1743–94, French)
Leclanché (Georges; 1839–82, French)
Macintosh (Charles; 1766–1843, Scottish)
Nieuwland (Julius; 1878–1936, US)
Pelletier (Pierre Joseph; 1788–1842, French)
Priestley (Joseph; 1733–1804, English)
Prigogine (Ilya, Vicomte; 1917–2003, Russian/Belgian)
Roozeboom (Hendrick; 1854–1907, Dutch)
Schönbein (Christian; 1799–1868, German)
Sharpless (K Barry; 1941– , US)
Shimomura (Osamu; 1928– , Japanese)
Stromeyer (Friedrich; 1776–1835, German)
Vauquelin (Nicolas-Louis; 1763–1829, French)
Wilkinson (Sir Geoffrey; 1921–96, English)
Wollaston (William; 1766–1828, English)
Zsigmondy (Richard; 1865–1929, Austrian)
10 Berthollet (Claude Louis, Comte de; 1749–1822, French)
Bodenstein (Max; 1871–1942, German)
Brongniart (Alexandre; 1770–1847, French)
Cannizzaro (Stanislao; 1826–1910, Italian)
Chardonnet; (Hilaire, Comte de; 1839–1924, French)
Chittenden (Russell; 1856–1943, US)
Döbereiner (Johann; 1780–1849, German)
Herschbach (Dudley R; 1932– , US)
Hildebrand (Joel; 1881–1983, US)
Ingenhousz (Jan; 1730–99, Dutch)
Ingen-Housz (Jan; 1730–99, Dutch)
MacDiarmid (Alan G; 1927– , New Zealand/US)
Mendeleyev (Dmitri; 1834–1907, Russian)
Merrifield (Bruce; 1921–2006, US)
Reichstein (Tadeus; 1897–1996, Polish/Swiss)
Staudinger (Hermann; 1881–1965, German)
11 Boisbaudran (Paul Lecoq de; 1838–1912, French)

Eschenmoser (Albert; 1925– , Swiss)
Goldschmidt (Hans; 1861–1923, German)
Goldschmidt (V M; 1888–1947, Swiss/ Norwegian)
Hinshelwood (Sir Cyril; 1897–1967, English)
Hoppe-Seyler (Felix; 1825–95, German)
Le Châtelier (Henri; 1850–1936, French)
Mège Mouriés (Hippolyte; 1817–80, French)
Pettenkofer (Max von; 1818–1901, German)
Poggendorff (Johann; 1796–1877, German)
Unverdorben (Otto; 1806–73, German)
Willstätter (Richard; 1872–1942, German)

12 Boussingault (Jean Baptiste; 1802–87, French)
Christiansen (Jens Anton; 1888–1969, Danish)
Lennard-Jones (Sir John; 1894–1954, English)
Mitscherlich (Eilhard; 1794–1863, German)

14 Longuet-Higgins (H C; 1923–2004, English)
Vernon Harcourt (William; 1789–1871, English)

15 Guyton de Morveau (Louis Bernard, Baron; 1737–1816, French)

Terms used in chemistry include:

02 IR
pH

03 cis
gas
ion
sol

04 acid
atom
base
bond
mass
mole
salt
weak

05 assay
block
cycle
ester
group
IUPAC
lipid
order
phase
polar
redox
shell
trans
yield

06 alkali
alkane
alkene
buffer
chiral
Dalton
dilute
dipole
fusion
halide
isomer
ketone
ligand

liquid
matter
period
phenyl
pi bond
proton
solids
strong
symbol

07 alchemy
chelate
chemist
colloid
crystal
density
element
entropy
fission
formula
halogen
isotope
lattice
mixture
neutral
neutron
nucleus
orbital
organic
polymer
product
racemic
reagent
soluble
solvent
valency

08 analysis
aromatic
catalyst
chemurgy
compound
cracking
denature

dialysis
effusion
electron
emulsion
end point
enthalpy
fixation
half life
hydroxyl
inert gas
lone pair
meniscus
miscible
molecule
noble gas
nonpolar
physical
reactant
reaction
solution

09 aliphatic
allotrope
anhydrous
catalysis
corrosion
diffusion
electrode
empirical
homologue
hydration
hydroxide
indicator
inorganic
insoluble
ionic bond
oxidation
reduction
saturated
side chain
sigma bond
structure
substance

synthesis
titration

10 amphoteric
atomic mass
combustion
complex ion
curly arrow
double bond
enantiomer
exothermic
free energy
hydrolysis
immiscible
latent heat
litmus test
neutralize
reversible
single bond
suspension
triple bond
zwitterion

11 alkali metal
crystallize
diffraction
electrolyte
endothermic
equilibrium
evaporation
free radical
ground state
homogeneous
hydrocarbon

hygroscopic
ion exchange
ionic radius
litmus paper
phase change
precipitate
respiration
sublimation

12 atomic number
atomic radius
atomic weight
band spectrum
beta particle
biochemistry
chemical bond
chlorination
concentrated
condensation
covalent bond
deliquescent
desalination
dissociation
distillation
efflorescent
electrolysis
excited state
fermentation
fluorescence
heat capacity
heterocyclic
hydrogen bond
line spectrum

melting point
metallic bond
rate constant
reaction rate
spectroscopy
stereoisomer

13 alpha particle
chain reaction
critical point
decomposition
fractionation
freezing point
heterogeneous
hybridization
periodic table
quantum number
radioactivity
stoichiometry

14 Avogadro number
Brownian motion
buffer solution
chromatography
covalent radius
saponification

15 atomic structure
aufbau principle
chemical element
collision theory
optical activity
transition metal
transition state
van der Waals bond

See also **biochemistry**; **environment**; **Nobel Prize**; **salt**

cherry

Cherry varieties include:

04 wild

05 morel

See also **fruit**

07 morello

10 blackheart

maraschino

chess

Chess pieces include:

04 king

pawn

rook

05 queen

06 bishop

castle

knight

Chess players and computers include:

03 Tal (Mikhail; 1936–92, Soviet)

04 Euwe (Max; 1901–81, Dutch)

05 Anand (Viswanathan; 1969– , Indian)
Short (Nigel; 1965– , English)

06 Karpov (Anatoli; 1951– , Russian)

Lasker (Emanuel; 1868–1941, German)
Morphy (Paul; 1837–84, US)
Polgar (Judit; 1976– , Hungarian)
Polgar (Zsuzsa; 1969– , Hungarian)
Thomas (Sir George; 1881–1972, Turkish/
British)

Timman (Jan; 1951– , Dutch)
Xie Jun (1970– , Chinese)
07 Fischer (Bobby; 1943–2008, US)
Kramnik (Vladimir; 1975– , Russian)
Smyslov (Vasili; 1921– , Russian)
Spassky (Boris; 1937– , Russian)
Topalov (Veselin; 1975– , Bulgarian)
08 Alekhine (Alexander; 1892–1946, French)
Deep Blue
Kasparov (Garry; 1963– , Russian)

Korchnoi (Viktor; 1931– , Russian)
Philidor (François André; 1726–95, French)
Staunton (Howard; 1810–74, English)
Steinitz (Wilhelm; 1836–1900, Czech)
09 Botvinnik (Mikhail; 1911–95, Soviet)
Khalifman (Alexander; 1966– , Russian)
Petrosian (Tigran; 1929–84, Soviet)
10 Capablanca (José; 1888–1942, Cuban)
Ponomariov (Ruslan; 1983– , Ukrainian)
13 Chiburdanidze (Maya; 1961– , Russian)

Chess terms include:

03 man
pin
row
04 bind
FIDE
fork
king
move
pawn
play
rook
05 black
board
check
flank
march
piece
queen
white

06 attack
bishop
castle
centre
double
gambit
knight
master
patzer
square
07 chequer
defence
develop
endgame
en prise
j'adoube
opening
promote
retract

squeeze
08 back rank
castling
diagonal
exchange
kingside
opponent
queening
zugzwang
09 bad bishop
checkmate
Elo rating
en passant
fool's mate
miniature
promotion
queenside
stalemate

10 fianchetto
good bishop
major piece
middle game
minor piece
passed pawn
11 counterplay
grandmaster
zwischenzug
12 backward pawn
problem child
13 counter attack
fifty move rule
14 lightning chess
perpetual check
15 knight's progress

chicken

Chickens include:

06 Ancona
bantam
Cochin
houdan
sultan
07 Dorking

Hamburg
leghorn
Minorca
08 Hamburgh
Langshan
09 Orpington

Welsummer
wyandotte
10 Andalusian
Australorp
chittagong
jungle fowl

11 Spanish fowl
12 Plymouth Rock
14 Rhode Island Red

See also **bird**

chief rabbi

Chief rabbis, with dates of office:

04 Hart (Aaron; 1704–56)
Lyon (Hart; 1758–64)
05 Adler (Hermann; 1891–1911)
Adler (Nathan; 1845–91)
Hertz (J H; 1913–46)
Sacks (Jonathan; 1991–)

06 Brodie (Israel; 1948–65)
09 Hirschell (Solomon; 1802–42)
10 Jakobovits (Immanuel, Lord; 1966–91)
12 Tevele Schiff (David; 1765–91)

See also **religion**

children *see* **literature; novel**

China

Cities and notable towns in China include:

04 Xi'an	Guilin	Nanking	Victoria
05 Lhasa	Peking	Taiyuan	**09** Chongqing
Wuhan	**07** Beijing	Tianjin	Guangzhou
	Kunming	**08** Shanghai	
06 Canton	Nanjing	Shenyang	

Chinese landmarks include:

03 Han	**08** Badaling	**12** Imperial City
04 Wuyi	Gaochang	Potala Palace
05 Wei He	Shenzhen	Summer Palace
06 Harbin	**09** Great Wall	Victoria Peak
Mt Wuyi	Huangshan	**13** Forbidden City
Suzhou	Ming Tombs	Jokhang Temple
Urumqi	Mt Tai Shan	**14** Imperial Palace
07 Chengdu	Tiananmen	Maitreya Buddha
Qianmen	**10** Lama Temple	Peninsula Hotel
Tai Shan	Pearl River	Temple of Heaven
The Bund	**11** Man Mo Temple	Terracotta Army
Tiantan	Mt Huangshan	**15** Confucius Temple
Xi Jiang	Three Gorges	Tiananmen Square
Yangtze	Yellow River	

See also **Asia**

Chinese *see* **calendar**

choreography *see* **ballet**

Christianity

Christian churches and denominations include:

04 Copt	Catholic	**12** Episcopalian
05 Amish	Lutheran	Presbyterian
06 Coptic	**09** Adventist	**13** Greek Orthodox
Jesuit	Calvinist	Roman Catholic
Quaker	Methodist	Salvation Army
07 Baptist	Unitarian	**14** Society of Jesus
Gnostic	**10** Anabaptist	**15** Christadelphian
Opus Dei	Protestant	Church of England
Puritan	**11** Evangelical	Church of Ireland
08 Anglican	Pentecostal	Eastern Orthodox

See also **reformer; religion**

Christie, Dame Agatha (1890–1976)

Significant works include:

04 *N or M?* (1941)

05 *Poems* (1973)

07 *Curtain* (1975)
Nemesis (1971)
Verdict (1958)

08 *Akhnaton* (1973)

09 *Double Sin* (1961)
The Burden (1956)
The Clocks (1963)
The Hollow (1946)
Third Girl (1966)

10 *Sad Cypress* (1940)
Spider's Web (1954)
The Big Four (1927)

11 *Black Coffee* (1930)
Dumb Witness (1937)
Giant's Bread (1930)
Rule of Three (1962)
The Under Dog (1951)
Towards Zero (1944)

12 *Crooked House* (1949)
Endless Night (1967)
Murder Is Easy (1939)
The Mousetrap (1952)
The Pale Horse (1961)

13 *Dead Man's Folly* (1956)
Fiddlers Three (1972)
Postern of Fate (1973)
The ABC Murders (1936)
The Golden Ball (1971)

14 *Death on the Nile* (1937)
Five Little Pigs (1943)
Hallowe'en Party (1969)
Regatta Mystery (1939)
Sleeping Murder (1976)
Three Blind Mice (1950)

15 *After the Funeral* (1953)
An Autobiography (1977)
At Bertram's Hotel (1965)
Cards on the Table (1936)
Evil Under the Sun (1941)
Lord Edgware Dies (1933)
Mrs McGinty's Dead (1952)
Murder in the Mews (1937)
Partners in Crime (1929)
Peril at End House (1932)
Taken at the Flood (1948)
The Hound of Death (1933)
The Moving Finger (1942)
The Road of Dreams (1924)
Three-Act Tragedy (1934)

16 *A Pocket Full of Rye* (1953)

Death in the Clouds (1935)
Sparkling Cyanide (1945)

17 *4.50 from Paddington* (1957)
Absent in the Spring (1944)
A Caribbean Mystery (1964)
Ordeal by Innocence (1958)
Poirot's Early Cases (1974)
Star Over Bethlehem (1965)
They Came to Baghdad (1951)

18 *A Murder Is Announced* (1950)
Cat Among the Pigeons (1959)
Death Comes As the End (1944)
Destination Unknown (1954)
Hickory Dickory Dock (1955)
One, Two, Buckle My Shoe (1940)
Poirot Investigates (1924)
The Secret Adversary (1922)
The Unexpected Guest (1958)
Unfinished Portrait (1934)

19 *A Daughter's a Daughter* (1952)
Murder in Mesopotamia (1936)
The Body in the Library (1942)
The Murder on the Links (1923)
The Mysterious Mr Quin (1930)
The Secret of Chimneys (1925)
The Sittaford Mystery (1931)
The Thirteen Problems (1932)
They Do It with Mirrors (1952)

20 *And Then There Were None* (1939)
Appointment With Death (1938)
Come, Tell Me How You Live (1946)
Elephants Can Remember (1972)
Passenger to Frankfurt (1970)
The Labours of Hercules (1947)
The Listerdale Mystery (1934)
The Man in the Brown Suit (1924)
The Rose and the Yew Tree (1948)
The Seven Dials Mystery (1929)
Why Didn't They Ask Evans? (1934)

21 *Miss Marple's Final Cases* (1979)

22 *Parker Pyne Investigates* (1934)
The Murder at the Vicarage (1930)

23 *By the Pricking of My Thumbs* (1968)
Hercule Poirot's Christmas (1938)
The Murder of Roger Ackroyd (1926)

24 *Murder on the Orient Express* (1934)
The Mystery of the Blue Train (1928)
Witness for the Prosecution (1953)

27 *The Mysterious Affair at Styles* (1920)

29 *The Mirror Crack'd from Side to Side* (1962)

33 *The Adventure of the Christmas Pudding* (1960)

Significant characters include:

04 Japp (Chief Inspector)
Pyne (Parker)
Quin (Mr Harley)
Race (Colonel Johnny)
West (Raymond)

05 Lemon (Miss Felicity)
Slack (Inspector)

06 Bantry (Colonel Arthur)

Bantry (Mrs Dolly)
Battle (Superintendent)
Marple (Miss Jane)
Oliver (Mrs Ariadne)
Poirot (Hercule)

07 Ackroyd (Roger)
Haydock (Dr)

08 Hastings (Captain Arthur)

09 Beresford (Tommy)
Beresford (Tuppence)
Lempriere (Joan)
Protheroe (Colonel)

10 Clithering (Sir Henry)

13 Satterthwaite (Mr)

Christmas

Gifts for the Twelve Days of Christmas:

09 gold rings (5th)
10 French hens (3rd)
11 turtle doves (2nd)
12 calling birds (4th)

geese a-laying (6th)
pipers piping (11th)
13 ladies dancing (9th)
lords a-leaping (10th)

maids a-milking (8th)
14 swans a-swimming (7th)
16 drummers drumming (12th)
20 partridge in a pear tree (1st)

Santa's reindeer:

05 Comet
Cupid
Vixen

06 Dancer
Dasher
Donner

07 Blitzen
Prancer
Rudolph

Terms to do with Christmas include:

03 ivy
04 bell
card
crib
gift
king
Magi
Mary
Noël
putz
snow
star
Xmas

05 angel
carol
glogg
goose
holly
Jesus
punch
robin
waits

06 bauble
Befana
candle
donkey
Joseph
Kinara
manger

mummer
piñata
sleigh
stable
tinsel
turkey
wreath

07 chimney
cracker
glüwein
holiday
Lapland
pageant
present
Rudolph
Scrooge
snowman
stollen
wassail
wise man
Yule log

08 daft days
junkanoo
mince pie
Papa Noël
reindeer
shepherd
stocking
Yuletide

09 Bethlehem
chestnuts
John Canoe
Julinisse
level-coil
mistletoe
North Pole
panettone
pantomime

10 Babouschka
decoration
mulled wine
poinsettia
round robin
Santa Claus
St Nicholas
Twelfth Day
watch night

11 advent crown
carol singer
fairy lights
plum pudding

12 Advent candle
Midnight Mass
nativity play
Queen's Speech
Twelfth Night

13 Christmas cake
Christmas card

Christmas tree
Lord of Misrule
wrapping paper

14 advent calendar
Christmas bonus
Christmas party

white Christmas
15 Ebenezer Scrooge
Father Christmas

church

Church and cathedral parts include:

03 pew

04 apse
arch
font
nave
rood
tomb

05 aisle
altar
choir
crypt
porch
slype
spire
stall
stoup
tower
vault

06 adytum
arcade
atrium
belfry
chapel
chevet
corona
parvis

portal
pulpit
sedile
shrine
squint
vestry

07 almonry
chancel
frontal
gallery
lectern
lucarne
narthex
piscina
reredos
steeple
tambour

08 cloister
credence
crossing
keystone
parclose
pinnacle
predella
sacellum
sacristy

transept

09 antechoir
bell tower
graveyard
organ loft
sacrarium
sanctuary
sepulchre
stasidion
triforium

10 ambulatory
baptistery
bell screen
clerestory
diaconicon
fenestella
frithstool
misericord
presbytery
retrochoir
rood screen

12 chapterhouse
confessional
deambulatory

14 ringing chamber
schola cantorum

See also **cathedral**; **cemetery**; **religion**

cicada

Cicadas include:

05 Myer's
06 red-eye
09 Union Jack

10 blue prince
11 black prince
floury baker

greengrocer
green Monday
masked devil

12 floury miller
yellow Monday
13 double drummer

cigar, cigarette *see* **tobacco**

cinema

Cinema and theatre names include:

03 ABC
MGM
Rex
Rio
UCI
UGC

04 Gala
IMAX
Ritz
Roxy
05 Byron
Cameo

Forum
Grand
Kings
Metro
Odeon
Orion

Plaza
Regal
Royal
Scala
Tower

06 Albany
Apollo
Cannon
Casino
Curzon
Empire
Gaiety
Marina
Palace
Queens
Regent
Rialto
Robins
Tivoli
Virgin

07 Arcadia
Astoria
Capitol
Carlton
Central
Century
Circuit

Classic
Coronet
Embassy
Essoldo
Gaumont
Granada
La Scala
Locarno
Mayfair
Orpheum
Paragon
Phoenix
Picardy

08 Alhambra
Broadway
Charlton
Cineplex
Citizens
Colonial
Dominion
Electric
Everyman
Festival
Imperial
Landmark
Majestic
Memorial

Pavilion
The Cameo
Windmill

09 Alexandra
Cineworld
Filmhouse
Hollywood
Palladium
Paramount
Playhouse

10 Ambassador
Hippodrome
Lighthouse
Vue Cinemas

11 Her Majesty's
His Majesty's
New Victoria
Ster Century

12 Metropolitan
Picturedrome
Picturehouse
Thefilmworks

13 Picture Palace
Warner Village

14 Electric Palace

15 Screen on the Hill

See also **film**; **theatre**

circle

Circles include:

03 lap
orb

04 ball
band
belt
coil
corn
crop
curl
disc
eddy
gyre
halo
hoop
hour
loop
oval
ring
turn

See also **shape**

tyre

05 crown
cycle
dress
globe
grand
great
magic
mural
orbit
pitch
plate
polar
round
stone
upper
wheel

06 Arctic
circus

cordon
discus
girdle
rundle
saucer
sphere
spiral
tropic
vortex
wreath

07 annulet
annulus
circuit
compass
coronet
ellipse
equator
roundel
traffic

transit
turning
vicious

08 epicycle
gyration
meridian
rotation
roundure
striking
virtuous

09 Antarctic
perimeter
whirlpool
whirlwind

10 almacantar
almucantar
Circassian
revolution

13 circumference

circus

Circus terms include:

03 boo
fun
lot
wig

04 band
Bozo
cage
clap
gags
jeff
Joey
lion
mime
nose
pole
pony
rein
ring
spec
tent
whip
zany

05 antic
arena
blues
camel
cheer
clown
comic
crowd
dwarf
freak
funny
grift
horse
laugh
llama
rubes
straw
towny
Tramp
trick

See also **clown**

06 August
big top
canvas
dancer
exotic
hoop-la
houdah
howdah
humour
jester
juggle
make-up
parade
pie car
risley
squirt
stilts
tumble

07 acrobat
Auguste
balance
balloon
buffoon
butcher
caravan
costume
doniker
juggler
leotard
peanuts
Pierrot
popcorn
rigging
sawdust
speeler
spieler
trapeze
tumbler

08 Alley-Oop
Allez Oop
applause
audience

backyard
bale ring
ballyhoo
blowdown
calliope
carnival
children
chivaree
conjurer
conjuror
drum roll
elephant
guy lines
high wire
laughter
magician
mechanic
ring-side
shivaree
sideshow
tear down
unicycle

09 aerialist
bandwagon
charivari
clown suit
fire-eater
lion tamer
menagerie
rosinback
safety net
strongman
tightrope
tom-walker
Whiteface

10 acrobatics
acrobatism
Billy Smart
candy floss
circus hand
cloud swing
clown alley

custard pie
impresario
ringmaster
roustabout
somersault
spectators
trick-rider
unicyclist

11 Arabian pony
carpet clown
cotton candy
entertainer
funambulate
funambulist
greasepaint
rope dancing
straightman
tent raising

12 escape artist
funambulator
liberty horse
Ringling Bros®
roll up! roll up!
stiltwalking
trick cyclist

13 bareback rider
contortionist
entertainment
equestrian act
Neat Whiteface
sleight-of-hand
trapeze artist

14 character clown
Cirque du Soleil
Joseph Grimaldi

15 Barnum and Bailey
Comedy Whiteface
European Auguste
jerry-come-tumble
three-ring circus

CIS

Commonwealth of Independent States members:

06 Russia
07 Armenia
Belarus

Georgia
Moldova
Ukraine

10 Azerbaijan
Kazakhstan
Kyrgyzstan

Tajikistan
Uzbekistan
12 Turkmenistan

city

Capital cities include:

04 Apia (Samoa)
Baku (Azerbaijan)
Dili (East Timor)
Doha (Qatar)
Kiev (Ukraine)
Lima (Peru)
Lomé (Togo)
Malé (Maldives)
Oslo (Norway)
Riga (Latvia)
Rome (Italy)
Suva (Fiji)

05 Abuja (Nigeria)
Accra (Ghana)
Amman (Jordan)
Berne (Switzerland)
Cairo (Egypt)
Dakar (Senegal)
Dhaka (Bangladesh)
Hanoi (Vietnam)
Kabul (Afghanistan)
Koror (Palau)
La Paz (Bolivia)
Minsk (Belarus)
Paris (France)
Praia (Cape Verde)
Quito (Ecuador)
Rabat (Morocco)
Sana'a (Yemen)
Seoul (South Korea)
Sofia (Bulgaria)
Sucre (Bolivia)
Tokyo (Japan)
Tunis (Tunisia)
Vaduz (Liechtenstein)

06 Ankara (Turkey)
Asmara (Eritrea)
Astana (Kazakhstan)
Athens (Greece)
Bamako (Mali)
Bangui (Central African Republic)
Banjul (The Gambia)
Beirut (Lebanon)
Berlin (Germany)
Bissau (Guinea-Bissau)
Bogotá (Colombia)
Dodoma (Tanzania)
Dublin (Ireland)
Harare (Zimbabwe)
Havana (Cuba)
Kigali (Rwanda)
Lisbon (Portugal)
London (UK)
Luanda (Angola)

Lusaka (Zambia)
Madrid (Spain)
Majuro (Marshall Islands)
Malabo (Equatorial Guinea)
Manama (Bahrain)
Manila (Philippines)
Maputo (Mozambique)
Maseru (Lesotho)
Monaco (Monaco)
Moroni (Comoros)
Moscow (Russia)
Muscat (Oman)
Nassau (The Bahamas)
Niamey (Niger)
Ottawa (Canada)
Prague (Czech Republic)
Riyadh (Saudi Arabia)
Roseau (Dominica)
Skopje (Macedonia)
T'aipei (Taiwan)
Tarawa (Kiribati)
Tehran (Iran)
Tirana (Albania)
Vienna (Austria)
Warsaw (Poland)
Zagreb (Croatia)

07 Abidjan (Côte d'Ivoire)
Algiers (Algeria)
Baghdad (Iraq)
Bangkok (Thailand)
Beijing (China)
Bishkek (Kyrgyzstan)
Caracas (Venezuela)
Colombo (Sri Lanka)
Conakry (Guinea)
Cotonou (Benin)
El Aaiún (Western Sahara)
Honiara (Solomon Islands)
Jakarta (Indonesia)
Kampala (Uganda)
Managua (Nicaragua)
Mbabane (Swaziland)
Nairobi (Kenya)
Nicosia (Cyprus)
Palikir (Federated States of Micronesia)
San José (Costa Rica)
São Tomé (São Tomé and Príncipe)
St John's (Antigua and Barbuda)
Tallinn (Estonia)
T'bilisi (Georgia)
Thimphu (Bhutan)
Tripoli (Libya)
Vilnius (Lithuania)
Yaoundé (Cameroon)

Yerevan (Armenia)
08 Abu Dhabi (United Arab Emirates)
Ashgabat (Turkmenistan)
Asunción (Paraguay)
Belgrade (Serbia)
Belmopan (Belize)
Brasília (Brazil)
Brussels (Belgium)
Budapest (Hungary)
Canberra (Australia)
Cape Town (South Africa)
Castries (St Lucia)
Chisinau (Moldova)
Damascus (Syria)
Djibouti (Djibouti)
Dushanbe (Tajikistan)
Freetown (Sierra Leone)
Funafuti (Tuvalu)
Gaborone (Botswana)
Helsinki (Finland)
Khartoum (Sudan)
Kingston (Jamaica)
Kinshasa (Democratic Republic of the Congo)
Laayoune (Western Sahara)
Lilongwe (Malawi)
Monrovia (Liberia)
N'Djamena (Chad)
New Delhi (India)
Port-Vila (Vanuatu)
Pretoria (South Africa)
Pristina (Kosovo)
Santiago (Chile)
Sarajevo (Bosnia and Herzegovina)
Tashkent (Uzbekistan)
Valletta (Malta)
Victoria (Seychelles)
Windhoek (Namibia)
09 Ámsterdam (The Netherlands)
Bucharest (Romania)
Bujumbura (Burundi)
Islamabad (Pakistan)
Kathmandu (Nepal)
Kingstown (St Vincent and the Grenadines)
Ljubljana (Slovenia)
Mogadishu (Somalia)
Naypyidaw (Myanmar)
Nuku'alofa (Tonga)

Phnom Penh (Cambodia)
Podgorica (Montenegro)
Port Louis (Mauritius)
Porto Novo (Benin)
Pyongyang (North Korea)
Reykjavík (Iceland)
San Marino (San Marino)
Singapore (Singapore)
St George's (Grenada)
Stockholm (Sweden)
Ulan Bator (Mongolia)
Vientiane (Laos)
10 Addis Ababa (Ethiopia)
Basseterre (St Kitts and Nevis)
Bratislava (Slovakia)
Bridgetown (Barbados)
Copenhagen (Denmark)
Georgetown (Guyana)
Kuwait City (Kuwait)
Libreville (Gabon)
Luxembourg (Luxembourg)
Mexico City (Mexico)
Montevideo (Uruguay)
Nouakchott (Mauritania)
Panama City (Panama)
Paramaribo (Suriname)
Wellington (New Zealand)
11 Brazzaville (Congo)
Buenos Aires (Argentina)
Kuala Lumpur (Malaysia)
Ouagadougou (Burkina Faso)
Port Moresby (Papua New Guinea)
Port of Spain (Trinidad and Tobago)
San Salvador (El Salvador)
Tegucigalpa (Honduras)
Vatican City (Vatican City)
12 Antananarivo (Madagascar)
Bloemfontein (South Africa)
Port-au-Prince (Haiti)
Santo Domingo (Dominican Republic)
Tel Aviv-Jaffa (Israel)
Washington, DC (USA)
Yamoussoukro (Côte d'Ivoire)
13 Guatemala City (Guatemala)
Yaren District (Nauru)
14 Andorra la Vella (Andorra)

Ancient cities include:

02 Ur	Susa	Argos	Hatra
04 Acre	Troy	Bosra	Huari
Axum	Tula	Bursa	Mitla
Ebla	Tyre	Copán	Moche
Nuzi	Uruk	Cuzco	Petra
Rome	**05** Aksum	Eridu	Saida

Sidon
Tikal
Uxmal
06 Athens
Byblos
Cyrene
Jabneh
Jamnia
Napata
Nippur
Sardis
Shiloh
Sparta
Thebes
Ugarit
07 Antioch

Babylon
Bukhara
Corinth
El Tajín
Ephesus
Megiddo
Miletus
Mycenae
Nineveh
Paestum
Plataea
Pompeii
Samaria
Sybaris
Vergina
08 Carthage

Damascus
Hattusas
Hattusha
Kerkuane
Palenque
Pergamon
Pergamum
Sigiriya
Tashkent
Thysdrus
09 Byzantium
Cartagena
Epidaurus
Sukhothai
10 Alexandria
Angkor Thom

Carchemish
Heliopolis
Hierapolis
Monte Albán
Persepolis
11 Chichén Itzá
Herculaneum
Machu Picchu
Polonnaruwa
Teotihuacán
12 Anuradhapura
13 Halicarnassus
14 Constantinople

Former names of cities include:

03 Edo (Tokyo)
04 York (Toronto)
05 Gorky (Nizhniy Novgorod)
Keijo (Seoul)
Tihwa (Urumqi)
06 Angora (Ankara)
Berlin (Kitchener)
Bombay (Mumbai)
Bytown (Ottawa)
Danzig (Gdansk)
Madras (Chennai)
Mukden (Shenyang)
Peking (Beijing)
Ryojun (Lüshun)
Saigon (Ho Chi Minh City)
Siking (Xian)
Smyrna (Izmir)
07 Batavia (Jakarta)
Benares (Varanasi)
Bezmein (Abadan)
Breslau (Wroclaw)
Changan (Xian)
Hanyang (Seoul)
Kalinin (Tver)
Songjin (Kimchaek)
08 Bathurst (Banjul)
Calcutta (Kolkata)
Fengtian (Shenyang)
Fort Lamy (N'Djamena)
Kishinev (Chisinau)
Lyallpur (Faisalabad)

Titograd (Podgorica)
09 Jesselton (Kota Kinabalu)
Kingstown (Dún Laoghaire)
Leninabad (Khujand)
Leningrad (St Petersburg)
Petrograd (St Petersburg)
Salisbury (Harare)
Tsaritsyn (Volgograd)
10 Gottwaldov (Zlín)
Konigsberg (Kaliningrad)
Kristiania (Oslo)
Luluabourg (Kananga)
Nova Lisboa (Huambo)
Port Arthur (Lüshun)
Queenstown (Cobh)
Stalingrad (Volgograd)
Sverdlovsk (Yekaterinburg)
Titov Veles (Veles)
11 Christiania (Oslo)
Livingstone (Maramba)
Santa Isabel (Malabo)
Stalinogród (Katowice)
Sunda Kelapa (Jakarta)
12 Léopoldville (Kinshasa)
New Amsterdam (New York)
Stanleyville (Kisangani)
13 Aleksandropol (Gyumri)
Karl-Marx-Stadt (Chemnitz)
14 Ciudad Trujillo (Santo Domingo)
Constantinople (Istanbul)

Cities and notable towns include:

02 Bo
LA
NY

03 Åbo
Ayr
Ely

Fès
Fez
Gao

Hué
Lae
Niš

NYC	Naas	Arras	Gweru
Pau	Naha	Aspen	Hagen
Qom	Nara	Aswan	Haifa
Ufa	Nice	Ávila	Halle
Ulm	Nuuk	Baden	Hefei
Vac	Oban	Banff	Hohot
Zug	Oita	Baoji	Honan
04 Acre	Omsk	Basle	Ichun
Aden	Oran	Basra	Ieper
Agra	Oulu	Beira	Iwaki
Ajme	Pécs	Belém	Izmir
Amoy	Pegu	Benxi	Jaffa
Bari	Perm	Blida	Jedda
Bath	Pisa	Blyth	Jilin
Bonn	Pula	Boise	Jinan
Brno	Pune	Bondi	Jinja
Bury	Rand	Borga	Kaédi
Caen	Reno	Bouar	Kandy
Cali	Rhyl	Braga	Karaj
Cebu	Ruse	Breda	Kazan
Como	Ryde	Brest	Kelso
Cork	Safi	Bursa	Kirov
Dazu	Sale	Busan	Kitwe
Deal	Salt	Cádiz	Kochi
Edam	Sfax	Canea	Konya
Elat	Sian	Cavan	Köseg
Eton	Sion	Ceuta	Kursk
Faro	Soul	Chiba	Kyoto
Gand	St-Lô	Chita	Lagos
Gent	Suez	Colón	Leeds
Gifu	Sumy	Conwy	Lewes
Graz	Tema	Cowes	Lhasa
Györ	Thun	Crewe	Liège
Homs	Tula	Cuzco	Lille
Hove	Tyre	Davao	Limbe
Hull	Umeå	Davos	Luton
Iasi	Vasa	Delft	Luxor
Icel	Vigo	Delhi	Lyons
Ipoh	Waco	Derby	Mâcon
Jima	Wick	Dijon	Mainz
Jixi	Wien	Dover	Malmö
Kano	Wuhu	Duala	Masan
Kiel	Wuxi	Dubai	Mecca
Kobe	Xi'an	Dukou	Medan
Köln	York	Eilat	Miami
Kota	Zibo	Elche	Milan
Labé	Zörs	Essen	Mitla
La-sa	05 Adana	Eupen	Mopti
León	Agaña	Évora	Mosul
Linz	Ahvaz	Fiume	Namen
Lódz	Åland	Frome	Namur
Lugo	Al Ayn	Fuxin	Nancy
Luik	Aosta	Genoa	Nasik
Lund	Aqaba	Ghent	Natal
Lvov	Argos	Gijón	Ndola
Metz	Århus	Gomel	Nîmes
Mold	Arica	Gorky	Ohrid
Mons	Arles	Gouda	Omagh

Omaha	Turin	Bremen	Grozny
Omiya	Turku	Bruges	Guelph
Oryol	Tzu-po	Brugge	Guilin
Osaka	Udine	Burgos	Guimar
Otley	Ulsan	Buxton	Gujrat
Oujda	Urawa	Cairns	Guntur
Padua	Utica	Calais	Ha'apai
Parma	Vaasa	Callao	Hamina
Patan	Varna	Calmar	Handan
Patna	Vejle	Camden	Han-kou
Pavia	Vlorë	Campos	Harbin
Penza	Wells	Cancún	Harlem
Perth	Wigan	Cannes	Harlow
Plzen	Worms	Canton	Hebron
Ponce	Wuhan	Carlow	Hegang
Poole	Ypres	Casper	Himeji
Poona	Zadar	Chania	Hobart
Pusan	Zaria	Chi-nan	Howrah
Reims	Zarqa	Chonju	Huelva
Resit	06 Aachen	Cochin	Ibadan
Ripon	Aarhus	Cracow	Ichang
Ronda	Agadez	Crosby	Inchon
Rouen	Agadir	Cuenca	Indore
Rovno	Albany	Dalian	Jaffna
Rugby	Ålborg	Dallas	Jaipur
Sakai	Aleppo	Da Nang	Jarash
Salem	Amiens	Danzig	Jarrow
Salta	Annaba	Daqing	Jeddah
Sebha	Annecy	Darhan	Jiddah
Ségou	Anshan	Darwin	Jilong
Sidon	Anvers	Datong	Juneau
Siena	Anyang	Dayton	Kalmar
Skien	Arezzo	Denver	Kaluga
Sochi	Armagh	Dieppe	Kankan
Sopot	Arnhem	Douala	Kanpur
Split	Arusha	Dudley	Kaolan
Suita	Ashdod	Duluth	Kassel
Surat	Atbara	Dundee	Kaunas
Suwon	At Taif	Durban	Kendal
Taegu	Austin	Durham	Khulna
Talca	Avarua	Durrës	Kirkby
Tampa	Baguio	El Gîza	Kirkuk
Tanga	Bangor	El Paso	Kosice
Tanta	Bangui	Eugene	Kraków
Tempe	Baotou	Evreux	Kumasi
Thane	Bastia	Exeter	Kurgan
Thiès	Bengpu	Fatima	Lahore
Thule	Bergen	Fresno	Lanark
Tokyo	Bhopal	Frunze	Leiden
Tomar	Bilbao	Fu-chou	Le Mans
Tomsk	Biloxi	Fushun	Leshan
Torun	Bitola	Fuzhou	Leuven
Tours	Bochum	Galway	Leyden
Trier	Bolton	Gdansk	London
Troon	Bombay	Gdynia	Lübeck
Truro	Bootle	Geneva	Lublin
Tulsa	Boston	Gitega	Ludlow
Tunja	Brasov	Grodno	Lugano

Maceio	Raipur	Toluca	Baoding
Madras	Rajkat	Topeka	Barnaul
Makale	Rajkot	Torbay	Barossa
Málaga	Ranchi	Toulon	Bayamón
Malang	Recife	Toyama	Bedford
Manaus	Redcar	Toyota	Beeston
Mantua	Reggio	Tralee	Beijing
Matrah	Regina	Trento	Belfast
Medina	Rennes	Treves	Benares
Meerut	Rheims	Tromsø	Bendigo
Mekele	Rijeka	Troyes	Berbera
Meknès	Ryazan	Tsinan	Bergama
Meshed	Saigon	Tubruq	Bergamo
Mobile	Salala	Tucson	Bexhill
Mukden	Samara	Tyumen	Bizerta
Multan	Santos	Urumqi	Blarney
Mumbai	Schwyz	Vannes	Bologna
Muncie	Sefadu	Vargas	Bolzano
Munich	Sendai	Venice	Boulder
Murcia	Shiraz	Verona	Bourges
Mysore	Silves	Viborg	Braemar
Nablus	Sining	Weimar	Brescia
Nagano	Sintra	Whitby	Bristol
Nagoya	Skikda	Widnes	Bryansk
Nagpur	Sliema	Woking	Buffalo
Nantes	Slough	Xiamen	Burnley
Napier	Smyrna	Xining	Cáceres
Naples	Sokodé	Xuzhou	Calgary
Narvik	Sousse	Yangku	Calicut
Newark	Soweto	Yantai	Caracas
Ningbo	Sparta	Yeovil	Cardiff
Nouméa	St Ives	Yichun	Catania
Odense	St John	Yunnan	Chalcis
Odessa	St-Malo	Zabrze	Changan
Oldham	St Paul	Zigong	Cheadle
Olinda	Stroud	Zinder	Cheddar
Oporto	Stuart	Zürich	Chelsea
Örebro	Suchow	Zwolle	Chengde
Osasco	Sukkur	**07** Aberfan	Chengdu
Osijek	Suzhou	Airdrie	Cheng-tu
Ostend	Sydney	Ajaccio	Chennai
Oviedo	Szeged	Aligarh	Chester
Oxford	Tabriz	Alma-Ata	Chicago
Padang	Tacoma	Alnwick	Chifeng
Paphos	Tadmur	Antibes	Chi-lung
Pátrai	Taejon	Antioch	Chongju
Phuket	Tahoua	Antwerp	Chungho
Piatra	Tainan	Aracaju	Clonmel
Pierre	Tamale	Atlanta	Coblenz
Pilsen	Tambov	Augusta	Coimbra
Porvoo	Tarbes	Auxerre	Cologne
Potosí	Tarsus	Avignon	Concord
Poznan	Ta-t'ung	Baalbek	Córdoba
Presov	Teruel	Badajoz	Corinth
Puebla	Thurso	Bairiki	Corinto
Quebec	Tipasa	Banares	Corunna
Queluz	Tobruk	Banbury	Crawley
Quetta	Toledo	Bandung	Dandong

Detroit	Kalinin	Mombasa	Runcorn
Devizes	Kananga	Morpeth	Sagunto
Donegal	Karachi	Münster	Salamis
Donetsk	Kassala	Nanjing	Salerno
Douglas	Kayseri	Nanking	Salford
Dresden	Keelung	Nanning	Sandown
Dundalk	Kenitra	Nantong	San José
Dunedin	Keswick	Newbury	Santa Fe
Dunkirk	Kharkov	Newport	São Luis
Durango	Kherson	Newquay	Sapporo
Entebbe	Koblenz	New Ross	Saransk
Erdenet	Kolding	New York	Saratov
Esbjerg	Kolkata	Niigata	Sassari
Evesham	Kuching	Niterói	Seattle
Exmouth	Kunming	Norfolk	Segovia
Falkirk	Kutaisi	Norwich	Setúbal
Fareham	Lansing	Novi Sad	Seville
Ferrara	Lanzhou	Oakland	Shannon
Foochow	La Plata	Okayama	Shantou
Fukuoka	Larnaca	Okinawa	Shihezi
Funchal	Latakia	Olympia	Shikoku
Ganzhou	Leghorn	Orlando	Shkodër
Geelong	Le Havre	Orleans	Sialkot
Glasgow	Leipzig	Ostrava	Sinuiju
Goiânia	Lerwick	Pahsien	Songnam
Gosport	Liberia	Paisley	Spokane
Granada	Limoges	Palermo	Spoleto
Grimsby	Lincoln	Panshan	Staines
Guiyang	Lipetsk	Pattaya	Stanley
Gwalior	Liuzhou	Peebles	St Denis
Gwangju	Livorno	Penrith	St Louis
Haerbin	Logroño	Perugia	Sudbury
Halifax	Louvain	Phoenix	Sumgait
Hamburg	Lucerne	Piraeus	Swansea
Hamhumg	Lucknow	Pistoia	Swindon
Hamhung	Lugansk	Pitesti	Taiyuan
Hanover	Lumbini	Plovdiv	Tampere
Harwich	Luoyang	Poltava	Tampico
Henzada	Machida	Popayán	Tangier
Heredia	Madison	Portree	Táranto
Houston	Madurai	Potsdam	Taunton
Huaibei	Malvern	Preston	Tel Aviv
Huainan	Manzini	Prizren	Telford
Ipswich	Maracay	Qingdao	Tétouan
Iquique	Marburg	Qiqihar	Tianjin
Iquitos	Margate	Quimper	Tijuana
Irkutsk	Mashhad	Raleigh	Tilburg
Isfahan	Massawa	Randers	Tilbury
Ivanovo	Matlock	Rangoon	Tlemcen
Izhevsk	Matsudo	Ravenna	Tonghua
Jackson	Melilla	Reading	Toronto
Jericho	Memphis	Redwood	Torquay
Jiamusi	Mendoza	Reigate	Tournai
Jiaozuo	Mildura	Roanoke	Trenton
Jinzhou	Mindelo	Rosario	Trieste
Jodhpur	Miskolc	Rostock	Tucumán
Kaesong	Mitsiwa	Rotorua	Ulan-Ude
Kaifeng	Mogilev	Roubaix	Uppsala

Utrecht
Ventnor
Vicenza
Vitebsk
Vitosha
Walsall
Warwick
Watford
Weifang
Wenzhou
Wexford
Wichita
Windsor
Wrexham
Wroclaw
Wuhsien
Yakeshi
Yichang
Yingkou
Yonkers
Zermatt
Zhuzhou
Zwickau

08 Aberdeen
Acapulco
Adelaide
Akureyri
Alajuela
Albacete
Alicante
Amarillo
Amritsar
Arbroath
Arequipa
Auckland
Augsburg
Aviemore
Ayia Napa
Ballarat
Banghazi
Bareilly
Barnsley
Bathurst
Bayreuth
Beauvais
Belgorod
Benghazi
Benguela
Benidorm
Besançon
Bhadgaon
Biarritz
Bismarck
Blantyre
Bobruysk
Bordeaux
Boulogne
Bradford

Braganza
Brighton
Brindisi
Brisbane
Bulawayo
Burgundy
Cagliari
Calcutta
Campinas
Carlisle
Cebu City
Changsha
Chartres
Chemnitz
Chepstow
Cheyenne
Chiclayo
Chimbote
Chimkent
Ching-tao
Chongjin
Clevedon
Columbia
Columbus
Contagem
Coventry
Culiacán
Curitiba
Dartford
Dearborn
Debrecen
Djakarta
Dortmund
Drogheda
Duisburg
Dumfries
Dunhuang
Dunleary
Durgapur
Dzhambul
Ebbw Vale
Edmonton
El Kharga
Elsinore
Europort
Falmouth
Florence
Flushing
Freeport
Fribourg
Fujisawa
Fukuyama
Gaoxiong
Gisborne
Gorlovka
Grantham
Grasmere
Greenock

Grenoble
Guernica
Hachioji
Haiphong
Hakodate
Hamilton
Hangchow
Hangzhou
Hannover
Hartford
Hastings
Hengyang
Hereford
Hertford
Hirakata
Holyhead
Holywell
Hong Kong
Honolulu
Huangshi
Hunjiang
Ichikawa
Iowa City
Istanbul
Jabalpur
Jaboatoa
Kairouan
Kanazawa
Kandahar
Karlsbad
Katowice
Kawasaki
Keflavik
Kemerovo
Kilkenny
Kirkwall
Kismaayo
Klosters
Kolhapur
Konstanz
Koriyama
Kuei-yang
Kumamoto
Laâyoune
La Laguna
Las Vegas
Lausanne
Legoland
Leskovac
Liaoyang
Liaoyuan
Limassol
Limerick
Llanelli
Londrina
Longford
Lüderitz
Ludhiana

Lyallpur
Makassar
Mandalay
Mannheim
Marbella
Mariupal
Mariupol
Mayaguez
Mazatlán
Medellín
Mercedes
Mexicali
Mogilyov
Montreal
Montreux
Montrose
Mufulira
Mulhouse
Murmansk
Myingyan
Nagasaki
Namangan
Nanchang
Nazareth
Newhaven
New Haven
Nijmegen
Novgorod
Nuneaton
Nürnberg
Oak Ridge
Omdurman
Oostende
Orenburg
Oswestry
Pago Pago
Pamplona
Panchiao
Pasadena
Pavlodar
Penzance
Peshawar
Piacenza
Ploiesti
Plymouth
Poitiers
Portland
Portrush
Port Said
Pristina
Ramsgate
Rancagua
Randstad
Redditch
Richmond
Road Town
Rochdale
Rockford

Roskilde	Tientsin	Asahikawa	Fort Worth
Rosslare	Timbuktu	Astrakhan	Frankfort
Sabadell	Titograd	Audenarde	Frankfurt
Salonica	Tolyatti	Aylesbury	Fremantle
Salonika	Tongeren	Bakhtaran	Funabashi
Saltillo	Toulouse	Baltimore	Galveston
Salvador	Toyohasi	Bangalore	Gateshead
Salzburg	Toyonaka	Barcelona	Gaziantep
San Diego	Trujillo	Beersheba	Gippsland
Santa Ana	Tsingtao	Berbérati	Gold Coast
Santarém	Tübingen	Bethlehem	Gorakhpur
São Paulo	Uleaborg	Bhavnagar	Gravesend
Satu Mare	Ullapool	Bialystok	Greenwich
Savannah	Vadodara	Blackburn	Groningen
Schwerin	Valencia	Blackpool	Guangzhou
Semarang	Valletta	Bossangoa	Guarulhos
Shanghai	Varanasi	Botany Bay	Guayaquil
Shanklin	Veracruz	Brunswick	Guildford
Shaoguan	Vila Real	Bydgoszcz	Hallstatt
Shenyang	Vinnitsa	Cambridge	Hamamatsu
Shizuoka	Vittoria	Cartagena	Harrogate
Sholapur	Vladimir	Castlebar	Haslemere
Silk Road	Voronezh	Changchun	Helsingør
Simbirsk	Wakayama	Changzhou	Heraklion
Skegness	Wallasey	Charleroi	Hilversum
Smolensk	Wallsend	Charlotte	Hiroshima
Solihull	Warangal	Chengchow	Humpty Doo
Solingen	Weymouth	Cherbourg	Hyderabad
Sorocaba	Winnipeg	Chernobyl	Immingham
Southend	Worthing	Chiang Mai	Innsbruck
Srinagar	Würzburg	Chihuahua	Inverness
Stafford	Xiangfan	Choluteca	Ismailiya
St Albans	Xiangtan	Chongqing	Jalandhar
Stamford	Xinxiang	Chungking	Jamestown
St David's	Yangchow	Cleveland	Jerusalem
St Gallen	Yangquan	Colwyn Bay	Johnstone
St Helens	Yangzhou	Constance	Jönköping
St Helier	Yinchuan	Constanta	Kagoshima
Stirling	Yin-hsien	Davao City	Kamchatka
St Moritz	Yokohama	Des Moines	Kaohsiung
Stockton	Yokosuko	Doncaster	Karaganda
Strabane	Yorktown	Dordrecht	Karlsruhe
St-Tropez	Yukosuko	Dubrovnik	Kawaguchi
Subotica	Zakopane	Dudelange	Killarney
Suicheng	Zanzibar	Dumbarton	Kimberley
Surabaya	Zhitomir	Dungannon	King's Lynn
Swan Hill	**09** Adis Abeba	Dunstable	Kirkcaldy
Syracuse	Ahmadabad	Eastleigh	Kisangani
Szczecin	Alba Iulia	Edinburgh	Kishinyov
Taganrog	Albufeira	Eindhoven	Kitchener
Taichung	Aldershot	Eskisehir	Kitzbühel
Tamworth	Algeciras	Esztergom	Kórinthos
Tangshan	Allahabad	Fairbanks	Kozhikode
Teesside	Amagasaki	Famagusta	Krasnodar
Teresina	Ambleside	Faridabad	Krivoy Rog
Thetford	Anchorage	Fishguard	Kurashiki
Thonburi	Annapolis	Fleetwood	Kuybyshev
Tiberias	Archangel	Fortaleza	Kwang-chow

Lancaster
Las Cruces
Leicester
Lexington
Lichfield
Liverpool
Llangefni
Long Beach
Lowestoft
Lymington
Magdeburg
Mahajanga
Maidstone
Makeyevka
Mamoudzan
Manizales
Mansfield
Maracaibo
Maralinga
Marrakesh
Matsuyama
Melbourne
Middleton
Milwaukee
Monterrey
Moradabad
Morecambe
Mullingar
Nashville
Neuchâtel
Newcastle
Newmarket
Nikolayev
Nuremberg
Ogbomosho
Osnabrück
Palembang
Pamporovo
Perpignan
Peterhead
Pingxiang
Pontianak
Port Natal
Port Sudan
Pressburg
Prestwick
Princeton
Qinghai Hu
Querétaro
Riverside
Rochester
Rotherham
Rotterdam
Rovaniemi
Salisbury
Samarkand
San Miguel
Santa Cruz

Santander
Saragossa
Saskatoon
Shanchung
Sheerness
Sheffield
Sioux City
South Bend
Southport
Southwark
St Andrews
Stavanger
Stavropol
St-Étienne
Stevenage
St-Nazaire
Stockport
Stornoway
St-Quentin
Stranraer
Stuttgart
Sukhothai
Sundsvall
Surakarta
Takamatsu
Takatsuki
Tarragona
Tenkodogo
T'ien-ching
Timisoara
Toamasina
Togliatti
Toowoomba
Trondheim
Tullamore
Ulyanovsk
Vancouver
Velingrad
Vicksburg
Volgograd
Wakefield
Walvis Bay
Waterford
Wiesbaden
Wimbledon
Wolfsburg
Worcester
Wuppertal
Xiangyang
Yaroslavl
Zamboanga
Zaozhuang
Zhengzhou
Zhenjiang
Zrenjanin
10 Alexandria
Baton Rouge
Belize City

Birkenhead
Birmingham
Bridgeport
Bridgwater
Broken Hill
Caernarvon
Caerphilly
Canterbury
Carmarthen
Carnoustie
Carson City
Casablanca
Chandigarh
Charleston
Cheboksary
Chelmsford
Cheltenham
Cheng-hsien
Chichester
Chittagong
Cienfuegos
Cincinnati
Cluj-Napoca
Coatbridge
Cochabamba
Coimbatore
Colchester
Concepción
Darjeeling
Darlington
Diyarbakir
Dorchester
Düsseldorf
Dzerzhinsk
Eastbourne
El Mansoura
Faisalabad
Felixstowe
Folkestone
Fray Bentos
Galashiels
George Town
Gillingham
Glenrothes
Gloucester
Goose Green
Gothenburg
Gujranwala
Haddington
Harrisburg
Hartlepool
Heidelberg
Hermosillo
Hildesheim
Huntingdon
Huntsville
Jamshedpur
Jingdezhen

João Pessoa
Juiz de Fora
Kakopetria
Kalgoorlie
Kansas City
Kenilworth
Khabarovsk
Kilmarnock
Kitakyushu
Kompong Som
Lake Placid
Las Piedras
Launceston
Leeuwarden
Letchworth
Linlithgow
Little Rock
Liupanshui
Livingston
Llangollen
Los Angeles
Louisville
Lubumbashi
Luluabourg
Maastricht
Maidenhead
Manchester
Marseilles
Medjugorje
Miami Beach
Monte Carlo
Montego Bay
Montgomery
Montpelier
Mostaganem
Motherwell
Mudanjiang
New Orleans
Nottingham
Nouadhibou
Nova Iguacu
Oranjestad
Oudenaarde
Palmerston
Petersburg
Pittsburgh
Pontefract
Portishead
Portsmouth
Providence
Quezon City
Quinnipiac
Rawalpindi
Regensburg
Sacramento
Sagamihara
San Antonio
San Ignacio

Santa Marta
Santo André
São Gonçalo
Scunthorpe
Sebastopol
Shepparton
Shreveport
Shrewsbury
Simferapol
Simferopol
Sioux Falls
Södertälje
Strasbourg
Sunderland
Sverdlovsk
Talcahuano
Tammerfors
Tananarive
Thunder Bay
Townsville
Trivandrum
Trowbridge
Tsaochuang
Utsunomiya
Valladolid
Valparaíso
Vijayawada
Viña del Mar
Vlissingen
Wadi Medani
Wagga Wagga
Warrington
Washington
Whitehorse
Wilmington
Winchester
Windermere
Winterthur
Wittenberg
Wollongong
Workington
Yogyakarta
Yoshkar Ola
Zaporozhye

11 Aberystwyth
Albuquerque
Antofagasta
Bahía Blanca
Banjarmasin
Basingstoke
Bhilai Nagar
Bognor Regis
Bournemouth
Brandenburg
Bremerhaven
Bridlington
Broadstairs
Brownsville

Bucaramanga
Campo Grande
Carcassonne
Charlestown
Chattanooga
Chelyabinsk
Cherepovets
Cirencester
Cleethorpes
Cockermouth
Coney Island
Conisbrough
Constantine
Cumbernauld
Dar es Salaam
Differdange
Downpatrick
Dunfermline
Enniskillen
Farnborough
Fort William
Francistown
Fraserburgh
Fredericton
Glastonbury
Grangemouth
Guadalajara
Guisborough
Hälsingborg
Helsingborg
Helsingfors
High Wycombe
Johor Baharu
Juan-les-Pins
Kaliningrad
Kampong Saom
Karlovy Vary
Kompong Saom
Komsomolosk
Krasnoyarsk
Lianyungang
Londonderry
Lossiemouth
Makhachkala
Mar del Plata
Medicine Hat
Medway Towns
Minneapolis
Montpellier
Narayanganj
Newport News
New York City
Nishinomiya
Nizhny Tagil
Northampton
Novosibirsk
Palm Springs
Pointe-Noire

Polonnaruwa
Port Augusta
Porto Alegre
Prestonpans
Punta Arenas
Qinhuangdao
Resistencia
Rockhampton
Rostov-on-Don
Saarbrücken
Scarborough
Southampton
Spanish Town
Springfield
Stourbridge
Szombathely
Tallahassee
Trincomalee
Tselinograd
Vladivostok
Westminster
White Plains
Wu-lu-k'o-mu-shi
Yellowknife
Zhangjiakou

12 Alice Springs
Anuradhapura
Atlantic City
Barquisimeto
Barranquilla
Beverly Hills
Bloemfontein
Buenaventura
Caloocan City
Chesterfield
Christchurch
Ciudad Juárez
East Kilbride
Great Malvern
Higashiosaka
Hubli-Dharwar
Huddersfield
Indianapolis
Jacksonville
Johannesburg
Keetmanshoop
Kota Kinabalu
Kristianstad
Léopoldville
Lisdoonvarna
Loughborough
Luang Prabang
Ludwigshafen
Macclesfield
Magnitogorsk
Mazar-e-Sharif
Milton Keynes
New Amsterdam

Nizhniy Tagil
Novokuznetsk
Oklahoma City
Petaling Jaya
Peterborough
Philadelphia
Pingdingshan
Pointe-à-Pitre
Ponta Delgada
Port Harcourt
Puerto Cortes
Rio de Janeiro
Rostov-na-Donu
Salt Lake City
San Cristobal
San Francisco
San Pedro Sula
San Sebastian
Santa Barbara
Schaffhausen
Shijiazhuang
Shuangyashan
Sidi bel Abbès
Skelmersdale
South Shields
Speightstown
Stanleyville
St Catherines
Stoke-on-Trent
St Petersburg
Tel Aviv-Jaffa
Tennant Creek
Thessaloníki
Trichinopoly
Ujung Pandang
Villahermosa
West Bromwich
Williamsburg
Winston-Salem

13 Aix-en-Provence
Belo Horizonte
Bobo-Dioulasso
Charlottetown
Ciudad Guayana
Duque de Caxias
Ellesmere Port
Epsom and Ewell
Great Yarmouth
Ho Chi Minh City
Jefferson City
Kidderminster
Kirkcudbright
Kirkintilloch
Leamington Spa
Lytham St Anne's
Middlesbrough
Ordzhonikidze
Port Elizabeth

Portlaoighise
Quezaltenango
Ribeirão Prêto
San Bernardino
San Luis Potosí
Semipalatinsk
Sihanoukville
Veliko Turnovo
Virginia Beach
Visakhapatnam
Wolverhampton

Yekaterinburg
Zamboanga City
Zlatni Pyasaci
14 Andorra-la-Vella
Dnepropetrovsk
Elisabethville
Feira de Santana
Hemel Hempstead
Henley-on-Thames
Louangphrabang
Santiago de Cuba

Shihchiachuang
Stockton-on-Tees
Székesfehérvár
Tunbridge Wells
Ust-Kamenogorsk
Voroshilovgrad
15 Barrow-in-Furness
Burton-upon-Trent
Charlotte Amalie
Charlottesville
Chester-le-Street

Clermont-Ferrand
Colorado Springs
Frankfurt am Main
Netzahaulcoyotl
Nizhniy Novgorod
Palma de Mallorca
Palmerston North
Sekondi-Takoradi
Shoubra el-Kheima
Sutton Coldfield
Weston-super-Mare

See also **Africa; The Americas; Asia; Australasia; Australia; Austria; Balkans; Belgium; Canada; Caribbean; China; Czech Republic; Denmark; Europe; Finland; France; Germany; Greece; India; Ireland; Italy; Japan; Low Countries; Mexico; Middle East; The Netherlands; New Zealand; Norway; Portugal; Russia; South-east Asia; Spain; Sweden; Switzerland; town; United Kingdom; United States of America**

clan *see* **Scottish**

Clare, John (1793–1864)

Significant works include:

03 'I Am!' (c.1840)

05 'Decay'

11 'The Flitting' (1832)

12 *The Rural Muse* (1835)
'Remembrances' (c.1832)

18 *The Village Minstrel* (1821)
'An Invite, to Eternity'

20 *The Shepherd's Calendar* (1827)

37 *Poems Descriptive of Rural Life and Scenery* (1820)

classical *see* **musician**

classification

Classifications of living organisms include:

05 class	**06** domain	phylum	**08** division
genus	empire	**07** kingdom	
order	family	species	

Kingdoms, domains and empires include:

05 fungi	**07** animals	protista	**11** prokaryotes
06 monera	archaea	**10** eubacteria	**14** archaebacteria
plants	**08** bacteria	eukaryotes	

Classes of living organisms include:

04 Aves	**09** Arachnida	**11** Cephalopoda	
07 Insecta	Bryopsida	**12** Malacostraca	
08 Amphibia	Pinopsida	**13** Magnoliopsida	
Bivalvia	**10** Gastropoda		
Mammalia	Liliopsida		

cleaning

Cleaning products include:

04 soap	shower gel	**12** disinfectant	
06 bleach	sugar soap	**13** washing powder	
polish	**10** bubble bath	**14** scouring powder	
07 shampoo	soap powder	**15** washing-up liquid	
solvent	turpentine		
09 detergent	**11** white spirit		

clerical vestment

Clerical vestments include:

03 alb	mitre	chimere	scapular
04 cope	scarf	maniple	skullcap
cowl	stole	pallium	surplice
hood	**06** mantle	soutane	yarmulka
05 amice	rochet	tallith	**09** dog-collar
cotta	tippet	tunicle	**10** Geneva gown
ephod	wimple	**08** chasuble	**11** Geneva bands
frock	**07** biretta	dalmatic	**14** clerical collar
habit	cassock	mozzetta	

climbing *see* **mountaineering**

cloak

Cloaks include:

04 capa	jellaba	mantelet
05 amice	korowai	mantilla
grego	manteel	palliate
jelab	mantlet	**09** djellabah
manta	paenula	gabardine
pilch	pelisse	gaberdine
sagum	pluvial	gallabeah
shawl	rocklay	gallabiah
talma	rokelay	gallabieh
06 abolla	sarafan	gallabiya
capote	**08** capuchin	**10** gallabiyah
dolman	cardinal	gallabiyeh
domino	djellaba	paludament
poncho	galabeah	roquelaure
visite	galabiah	**11** buffalo robe
07 chlamys	gallabea	**12** mousquetaire
galabea	gallabia	paludamentum
galabia	himation	

clock

Clocks and watches include:

03 fob	stop	**06** atomic	quartz
Tim	**05** alarm	cuckoo	**07** bracket
04 ring	wrist	mantel	digital

pendant	carriage	**09** repeating	chronometer
sundial	longcase	**10** travelling	grandfather
08 analogue	speaking	**11** chronograph	grandmother

Clock and watch parts include:

03 bob	case screw	crutch screw
eye	clock face	entry pallet
key	cock screw	escape wheel
LCD	crown gear	fourth wheel
peg	fusee stop	hinged bezel
pin	hour wheel	lever bridge
04 case	main wheel	minute track
dial	rating nut	minute wheel
face	regulator	motion works
gear	return bar	pallet screw
hook	steady pin	pendulum rod
pawl	stop screw	ratchet pawl
stem	stud screw	wheel bridge
05 bezel	**10** balance cap	**12** balance pivot
click	banking pin	balance wheel
cover	bottom door	barrel arbour
fusee	castle gear	cannon pinion
gears	click screw	detent spring
glass	click wheel	dial foot hole
jewel	clock train	escape pinion
strap	cover plate	keyless works
wheel	crown wheel	pallet arbour
06 anchor	dial washer	pull-out piece
arbour	escapement	ratchet screw
barrel	exit pallet	ratchet wheel
bridge	front plate	safety roller
chaton	fusee chain	**13** anti-shock unit
clutch	fusee pivot	balance spring
collet	hand collet	bottom door key
crutch	hour marker	hour hand screw
pallet	mainspring	impulse roller
pillar	minute hand	lenticular bob
pinion	pallet cock	quartz crystal
screws	pallet fork	regulator boot
wheels	second hand	set lever screw
winder	third wheel	setting bridge
07 back box	train wheel	tension spring
battery	watch glass	winding pinion
ratchet	wheel train	**14** escape movement
08 dial foot	winding key	fusee stop screw
hour hand	**11** barrel pivot	quartz movement
pendulum	bottom plate	regulator index
set lever	bridge screw	**15** balance assembly
top plate	centre wheel	minute wheel cock
09 back plate	check spring	minute wheel post
	clutch lever	pallet cock screw

clothes

Clothes include:

03 aba
bra
PJs
tie
top

04 501s®
abba
belt
body
cape
gown
kilt
muff
sari
slip
sock
suit
sulu
toga
veil
vest

05 abaya
burka
cloak
cords
dhoti
dress
frock
glove
ihram
jeans
kanzu
Levis®
lungi
pants
parka
ruana
scarf
shawl
shift
shirt
shrug
skirt
smock
stole
teddy
thong
tunic

06 basque
bikini
blouse
bodice
boorka
bow tie

boxers
braces
briefs
caftan
corset
cravat
denims
dirndl
fleece
garter
girdle
jersey
jubbah
jumper
kaross
kimono
mitten
poncho
samfoo
sarong
shorts
slacks
tabard
tights
T-shirt

07 catsuit
crop top
doublet
g-string
hosiery
jimjams
leotard
muffler
necktie
nightie
overall
panties
pyjamas
singlet
sweater
tank top
twinset
uniform
vest top
wet suit
yashmak
Y-fronts

08 bathrobe
bedsocks
breeches
camisole
cardigan
culottes
earmuffs

flannels
guernsey
hipsters
hot pants
jodhpurs
jumpsuit
leggings
lingerie
negligee
pashmina
pinafore
polo neck
pullover
swimsuit
tee-shirt
trousers

09 balaclava
bed-jacket
brassière
coveralls
dress suit
dungarees
hair shirt
housecoat
jockstrap
long johns
mini skirt
outerwear
pantihose
petticoat
plus-fours
polo shirt
salopette
separates
shahtoosh
shell suit
Sloppy Joe
stockings
tracksuit
underwear
waistcoat

10 boiler suit
Capri pants
cargo pants
cummerbund
dinner-gown
drainpipes
dress shirt
flying suit
leg warmers
lounge suit
nightdress
nightshirt
romper suit

rugby shirt
string vest
suspenders
sweat-shirt
turtleneck
underpants
11 bell-bottoms
boiled shirt
boxer-shorts
leisure suit
morning suit
pencil skirt
thermal vest

trouser suit
12 body stocking
camiknickers
divided skirt
dressing-gown
evening dress
palazzo pants
pedal-pushers
shirtwaister
13 Bermuda shorts
cycling shorts
liberty bodice

pinafore skirt
shalwar-kameez
suspender belt
14 bathing costume
combat trousers
double-breasted
French knickers
jogging bottoms
single-breasted
swimming trunks
three-piece suit
15 swimming costume

See also **boot**; **clerical vestment**; **cloak**; **coat**; **dress**; **fashion**; **fur**; **hat**; **scarf**; **tie**; **underwear**

cloud

Clouds include:

06 cirrus (Ci)
07 cumulus (Cu)
stratus (St)
11 altocumulus (Ac)

altostratus (As)
12 cirrocumulus (Cc)
cirrostratus (Cs)
cumulonimbus (Cb)

nimbostratus (Ns)
13 stratocumulus (Sc)

clown

Clowns include:

04 Bozo (Bob Bell, 1922–97, US)
Coco (Nicolai Poliakoff, 1900–74, Latvian)
Hobo
Joey (Joseph Grimaldi, 1779–1837, English)
07 Pierrot (Commedia del Arté)
08 Grimaldi (Joseph; 1779–1837, English)
Owl-glass (German folklore)

Trinculo (The Tempest, 1623, William Shakespeare)
09 Owle-glass (German folklore)
10 Howleglass (German folklore)
Owlspiegle (German folklore)
11 Little Tramp (Charlie Chaplin, 1889–1977, English)

club

Club names include:

03 MCC
Ski
04 Arts
Turf
05 Buck's
Naval
06 Alpine
Cotton
Drones
Kennel
Kitcat
Pratt's
Queen's
Reform
Rotary
Savage

Savile
White's
07 Almack's
Authors'
Boodle's
Brooks's
Canning
Carlton
Country
Farmers
Garrick
Groucho
Kiwanis
Leander
Railway
Variety

08 Hell-fire
National
Oriental
Portland
09 Athenaeum
Beefsteak
East India
Green Room
Lansdowne
Wig and Pen
10 Caledonian
City Livery
Crockford's
Flyfishers'
Hurlingham
Oddfellows

Roehampton
Travellers
11 Army and Navy
Arts Theatre
Chelsea Arts
12 Anglo-Belgian

City of London
London Rowing
New Cavendish
Thames Rowing
13 Royal Air Force
14 American Women's

City University
15 National Liberal
Royal Automobile
Victory Services

Club types include:

03 fan
job
04 book
glee
golf
05 field
goose

slate
strip
yacht
youth
06 bridge
health
tennis

07 country
pudding
singles
09 Christmas
warehouse
10 investment
12 Darby and Joan

Clubs include:

03 bar
04 cosh
mace

polt
05 staff
stick

06 cudgel
07 bourdon
08 bludgeon

trunnion
09 blackjack
truncheon

See also **golf**

coat

Coats include:

03 box
car
fur
mac
04 baju
buff
cape
jack
jump
maxi
midi
over
pink
rain
sack
tail
05 acton
cimar
cymar
drape
dress
frock
gilet
great
grego
jupon
lammy
loden

parka
sayon
wamus
06 achkan
Afghan
anorak
Basque
blazer
bolero
cagoul
covert
dolman
duffel
duster
fleece
jacket
jerkin
kagool
kagoul
kirtle
lammie
reefer
riding
sacque
sports
tabard
taberd
trench

tuxedo
Zouave
07 Barbour®
blanket
blouson
cagoule
cutaway
kagoule
Mae West
matinée
morning
overall
snorkel
surtout
swagger
vareuse
zamarra
zamarro
08 Burberry®
camisole
gambeson
haqueton
mackinaw
sherwani
09 bed jacket
gabardine
gaberdine

hacqueton
macintosh
Mao-jacket
newmarket
pea-jacket
petticoat
redingote
shortgown
10 body-warmer
bumfreezer
bush jacket
carmagnole
claw-hammer
Eton jacket
flak jacket
half-kirtle
life jacket
mackintosh
mess jacket
roundabout
windjammer
11 biker jacket
puffa jacket
shell jacket
swallowtail
Windbreaker®
windcheater

12 bomber jacket
combat jacket
dinner jacket
donkey jacket

lumberjacket
monkey jacket
Prince Albert
pyjama jacket

safari jacket
sports jacket
straitjacket
13 hacking jacket

matinee jacket
Norfolk jacket
reefing-jacket
14 shooting jacket

cocktail

Cocktails include:

04 Sour
05 Bronx
06 eggnog
Gimlet
Mai tai
mojito
Rickey
Rob Roy
07 Bellini
Collins
Martini®
negroni
pink gin
Sazerac®

Sidecar
Slammer
Stinger
08 Acapulco
Brown Cow
Bullshot
Daiquiri
Pink Lady
salty dog
snowball
09 buck's fizz
Kir Royale
long vodka
Manhattan

Margarita
Rusty Nail
Sea Breeze
whisky mac
White Lady
10 Bloody Mary
blue lagoon
Caipirinha
Horse's Neck
margharita
Moscow Mule
piña colada
Tom Collins
whisky sour

11 black velvet
gin-and-tonic
gloom raiser
Screwdriver
12 Black Russian
Cosmopolitan
Old Fashioned
White Russian
13 Planter's Punch
14 American Beauty
Singapore Sling
tequila slammer
Tequila Sunrise
15 Brandy Alexander

See also **drink**

code *see* **air travel**; **country**; **United States of America**; **vehicle**

coffee

Coffee roasts and blends include:

04 Java
05 decaf
06 filter
ground

Kenyan
07 Arabica
instant
09 Colombian

dark roast
10 Costa Rican
light roast
percolated

11 French roast
12 Blue Mountain
13 decaffeinated

Coffees include:

05 black
Irish
latte
milky
Mocha
white

06 filter
Gaelic
07 Turkish
08 café noir
espresso

09 Americano
cafetière
demitasse
10 café au lait
café filtre

cappuccino
11 skinny latte

See also **drink**

coin

Coins include:

02 as
03 bit
bob
cob
dam

écu
hao
mil
moy
rap
sol

sou
zuz
04 anna
bean
cash

dime
doit
dump
fals
jane
jiao

joey
lion
mite
mule
obol
para
quid
real
rial
ryal

05 angel
baisa
bodle
brock
brown
crown
daler
daric
dinar
ducat
eagle
gerah
groat
khoum
koban
liard
livre
louis
mohur
mopus
noble
obang
paolo
piece
plack
rider
royal
sceat
scudo
scute
semis
soldo
stamp
taler

See also **currency**

tical
ticky
toman
unite

06 aureus
bawbee
bezant
boddle
copper
denier
double
escudo
florin
gilder
guinea
gulden
hansel
heller
kobang
lepton
loonie
mancus
nickel
obolus
Paduan
pagoda
sceatt
sequin
stater
stiver
talent
tanner
thaler
tickey
toonie

07 austral
cardecu
carolus
crusado
drachma
guilder
handsel
ha'penny
jacobus

millime
moidore
Pfennig
pistole
pollard
quarter
ruddock
sextant
solidus
spanker
thrimsa
thrymsa
xerafin

08 cardecue
decussis
denarius
doubloon
ducatoon
farthing
gazzetta
Groschen
half anna
half mark
imperial
johannes
louis d'or
maravedi
millième
napoleon
picayune
portague
portigue
quadrans
semuncia
sesterce
shilling
sixpence
skilling
solidare
xeraphin
zecchino

09 dandiprat
dupondius
fourpenny

gold crown
half-crown
half groat
halfpenny
luck-penny
Maple Leaf
ninepence
quadruple
rix-dollar
rose noble
sovereign
yellow-boy
zwanziger

10 broadpiece
chervonets
half-dollar
half florin
half guinea
Krugerrand
lucky-piece
sestertius
silverling
touch-piece

11 bonnet-piece
contorniate
double eagle
pocket-piece
sixpenny bit
spade guinea
sword-dollar
tetradrachm

12 antoninianus
double-header
silver dollar
unicorn-shell

13 brass farthing
half sovereign
sixpenny piece
threepenny bit

14 three-farthings
three-halfpence

15 threepenny piece

cold meat *see* **meat**

collar

Collars include:			
03 dog	ruff	shawl	**06** bertha
04 Eton	wing	steel	choker
flea	**05** horse	storm	collet
roll	ox-bow	whisk	gorget

jampot	tie-neck	polo neck	piccadillo
rabato	vandyke	rabatine	piccadilly
rebato	**08** carcanet	turn-down	**11** falling band
07 brecham	clerical	**09** holderbat	**12** mousquetaire
partlet	granddad	piccadell	
rebater	mandarin	piccadill	
stick-up	Peter Pan	**10** chevesaile	

collection

Collectors and enthusiasts include:

05 gamer (computer games)

07 gourmet (good food)

08 neophile (novelty/new things)
zoophile (animals)

09 antiquary (antiques)
cinephile (cinema)
ex-librist (bookplates)
logophile (words)
oenophile (wine)
philomath (learning)
xenophile (foreigners)

10 arctophile (teddy bears)
audiophile (broadcast sound)
cartophile (cigarette cards)
discophile (gramophone records)
ephemerist (ephemera)
gastronome (good food/wine)
hippophile (horses)
monarchist (the monarchy)

11 ailurophile (cats)
balletomane (ballet)
bibliophile (books)
canophilist (dogs)
cynophilist (dogs)
etymologist (words)
notaphilist (banknotes, cheques)
numismatist (coins/medals)
oenophilist (wine)
philatelist (stamps)

scripophile (bond/share certificates)
technophile (technology)
toxophilite (archery)

12 ailourophile (cats)
cartophilist (cigarette cards)
coleopterist (beetles)
Dantophilist (Dante)
deltiologist (postcards)
entomologist (insects)
incunabulist (early printed books)
ophiophilist (snakes)
phillumenist (matches/matchboxes)
stegophilist (climbing buildings for sport)

13 arachnologist (spiders/arachnids)
campanologist (bell-ringing)
chirographist (handwriting)
chrysophilite (gold)
documentalist (documents)
lepidopterist (butterflies)
ornithologist (birds)
scripophilist (bond/share certificates)
tegestologist (beer mats)
timbrophilist (stamps)

14 cruciverbalist (crosswords)
pteridophilist (ferns)
tegestollogist (beer mats)

15 conservationist (countryside)
paroemiographer (proverbs)
stigmatophilist (tattooing/body piercing)

collective noun *see* animal

college

Cambridge University colleges and halls:

05 Clare
Jesus
King's

06 Darwin
Girton
Queens'
Selwyn

07 Christ's

Downing
New Hall
Newnham
St John's
Trinity
Wolfson

08 Emmanuel
Homerton

Pembroke
Robinson

09 Churchill
Clare Hall
Magdalene
St Edmund's

10 Hughes Hall
Peterhouse

11 Fitzwilliam
Trinity Hall
12 Sidney Sussex

St Catharine's
13 Corpus Christi
Lucy Cavendish

16 Gonville and Caius

Oxford University colleges and private halls:

03 New
05 Green
Jesus
Keble
Oriel
06 Exeter
Merton
Queen's
Wadham
07 Balliol
Kellogg
Linacre
Lincoln
St Anne's
St Cross
St Hugh's

St John's
Trinity
Wolfson
08 All Souls
Hertford
Magdalen
Nuffield
Pembroke
St Hilda's
St Peter's
09 Brasenose
Mansfield
St Antony's
Templeton
The Queen's
Worcester

10 Somerville
University
11 Campion Hall
Regent's Park
12 Christ Church
St Benet's Hall
St Catherine's
St Edmund Hall
Wycliffe Hall
13 Corpus Christi
14 Greyfriars Hall
15 Blackfriars Hall
St Stephen's House
16 Harris Manchester
Lady Margaret Hall

See also **university**

colour

Colours include:

03 jet	black	bronze	scarlet
red	brown	canary	**08** burgundy
tan	coral	cerise	charcoal
04 anil	cream	cherry	chestnut
blue	ebony	cobalt	cinnamon
ecru	green	copper	eau de nil
fawn	khaki	indigo	lavender
gold	lemon	maroon	magnolia
grey	lilac	orange	mahogany
jade	mauve	purple	sapphire
navy	milky	salmon	**09** aubergine
pink	ochre	silver	chocolate
plum	peach	violet	tangerine
puce	sepia	yellow	turquoise
rose	slate	**07** apricot	vermilion
ruby	taupe	avocado	**10** aquamarine
rust	topaz	crimson	chartreuse
sage	umber	emerald	cobalt blue
05 amber	white	gentian	**11** burnt sienna
beige	**06** auburn	magenta	lemon yellow
	bottle	saffron	

See also **black**; **blue**; **brown**; **dye**; **green**; **grey**; **orange**; **pigment**; **pink**; **purple**; **rainbow**; **red**; **white**; **yellow**

comedy

Comedy types include:

03 gag
low
pun
wit

04 high
joke
sick

05 black
farce
Greek

06 humour
modern
satire

sitcom
visual

07 musical
stand-up

08 romantic

09 burlesque
satirical
situation
slapstick

10 comic opera
sketch show
television
theatrical

11 alternative
comedy drama
Pythonesque
restoration
tragicomedy

12 Chaplinesque
neoclassical

13 practical joke
Shakespearian

15 comedy of humours
comedy of manners
improvisational

Comedians include:

03 Dee (Jack; 1962– , English)
Fry (Stephen; 1957– , English)
Lom (Herbert; 1917– , Czech)
Loy (Myrna; 1905–93, US)
Sim (Alastair; 1900–76, Scottish)
Wax (Ruby; 1953– , US)

04 Ball (Lucille; 1910–89, US)
Carr (Alan; 1977– , English)
Cook (Peter; 1937–95, English)
Dodd (Ken; 1927– , English)
Gold (Jimmy; 1886–1967, Scottish)
Hill (Benny; 1924–92, English)
Hill (Harry; 1964 , English)
Hope (Bob; 1903–2003, English/US)
Hudd (Roy; 1936– , English)
Idle (Eric; 1943– , English)
Kaye (Danny; 1913–87, US)
Leno (Dan; 1860–1904, English)
Marx (Chico; 1891–1961, US)
Marx (Groucho; 1895–1977, US)
Marx (Harpo; 1893–1964, US)
Marx (Zeppo; 1901–79, US)
Reid (Beryl; 1919–96, English)
Sims (Joan; 1930–2001, English)
Tati (Jacques; 1908–82, French)
Wall (Max; 1908–90, English)
Wise (Ernie; 1925–99, English)
Wood (Victoria; 1953– , English)

05 Abbot (Russ; 1947– , English)
Allen (Dave; 1936–2005, Irish)
Allen (Woody; 1935– , US)
Askey (Arthur; 1900–82, English)
Benny (Jack; 1894–1974, US)
Brand (Jo; 1957– , English)
Brown (Janet; 1924– , Scottish)
Bruce (Lenny; 1925–66, US)
Burns (George; 1896–1996, US)

Cosby (Bill; 1937– , US)
Elton (Ben; 1959– , English)
Emery (Dick; 1917–83, English)
Fyffe (Will; 1885–1947, Scottish)
Hardy (Jeremy; 1961– , English)
Hardy (Oliver; 1892–1957, US)
Henry (Lenny; 1958– , English)
Hicks (Bill; 1961–94, US)
Inman (John; 1935–2007, English)
James (Sid; 1913–76, South African/British)
Jones (Terry; 1942– , Welsh)
Kempe (Will; c.1550–c.1603, English)
Large (Eddie; 1941– , Scottish)
Lewis (Jerry; 1926– , US)
Lloyd (Harold; 1893–1971, US)
Moore (Dudley; 1935–2002, English)
Oddie (Bill; 1941– , English)
Palin (Michael; 1943– , English)
Pryor (Richard; 1940–2005, US)
Robey (Sir George; 1869–1954, English)
Sayle (Alexei; 1952– , English)
Smith (Mel; 1952– , English)
Sykes (Eric; 1923– , English)

06 Abbott (Bud; 1898–1974, US)
Bailey (Bill; 1964– , English)
Barker (Ronnie; 1929–2005, English)
Baxter (Stanley; 1926– , Scottish)
Brooks (Mel; 1926– , US)
Cleese (John; 1939– , English)
Coburn (Charles; 1852–1945, English)
Coogan (Steve; 1965– , English)
Cooper (Tommy; 1922–84, Welsh)
Dawson (Les; 1934–93, English)
Fields (W C; 1880–1946, US)
French (Dawn; 1957– , English)
Fulton (Rikki; 1924–2004, Scottish)
Garden (Graeme; 1943– , Scottish)

Henson (Leslie; 1891–1957, English)
Higson (Charlie; 1958– , English)
Howerd (Frankie; 1917–92, English)
Izzard (Eddie; 1962– , Yemeni/British)
Jordan (Dorothy; 1762–1816, Irish)
Keaton (Buster; 1895–1966, US)
Lauder (Sir Harry; 1870–1950, Scottish)
Laurel (Stan; 1890–1965, English/US)
Laurie (Hugh; 1959– , English)
Little (Syd; 1942– , English)
Martin (Steve; 1945– , US)
Mayall (Rik; 1958– , English)
Merton (Paul; 1957– , English)
Midler (Bette; 1945– , US)
Miller (Max; 1895–1963, English)
Murphy (Eddie; 1961– , US)
Murray (Bill; 1950– , US)
Norton (Graham; 1963– , Irish)
O'Grady (Paul; 1955– , English)
Proops (Greg; 1959– , US)
Reeves (Vic; 1959– , English)
Rivers (Joan; 1933– , US)
Tilley (Vesta; 1864–1952, English)
Ullman (Tracey; 1959– , English)
Wilder (Gene; 1933– , US)
Wisdom (Sir Norman; 1915– , English)

07 Aykroyd (Dan; 1952– , US)
Baddiel (David; 1964– , English)
Bentine (Michael; 1921–96, English)
Bremner (Rory; 1961– , English)
Burnett (Carol; 1933– , US)
Carrott (Jasper; 1945– , English)
Chaplin (Charlie; 1889–1977, English)
Chapman (Graham; 1941–89, English)
Corbett (Ronnie; 1930– , Scottish)
Deayton (Angus; 1956– , English)
Durante (Jimmy; 1893–1980, US)
Edwards (Jimmy; 1920–88, English)
Enfield (Harry; 1961– , English)
Everett (Kenny; 1944–95, English)
Feldman (Marty; 1933–82, English)
Gervais (Ricky; 1961– , English)
Gilliam (Terry; 1940– , US)
Hancock (Tony; 1924–68, English)
Handley (Tommy; 1892–1949, English)
Jacques (Hattie; 1924–80, English)
Langdon (Harry; 1884–1944, US)
Manning (Bernard; 1930–2007, English)
Mathews (Charles; 1776–1835, English)
Mathews (Charles J; 1803–78, English)
Matthau (Walter; 1920–2000, US)
Newhart (Bob; 1929– , US)
Ó Briain (Dara; 1972– , Irish)

See also **humour**

Roscius (c.134–62 BC, Roman)
Rushton (Willie; 1937–96, English)
Secombe (Sir Harry; 1921–2001, Welsh)
Sellers (Peter; 1925–80, English)
Silvers (Phil; 1912–85, US)
Skinner (Frank; 1957– , English)
Stewart (Andy; 1933–94, Scottish)
Tarbuck (Jimmy; 1940– , English)
Tarlton (Richard; d.1588, English)
Toksvig (Sandi; 1959– , Danish/British)
Trinder (Tommy; 1909–89, English)
Ustinov (Sir Peter; 1921–2004, English)

08 Atkinson (Rowan; 1955– , English)
Coltrane (Robbie; 1950– , Scottish)
Connolly (Billy; 1942– , Scottish)
Coquelin (Benoît Constant; 1841–1909,
French)
Costello (Lou; 1908–50, US)
Grimaldi (Joseph; 1779–1837, English)
Guilbert (Yvette; c.1869–1944, French)
Marshall (Penny; 1942– , US)
Milligan (Spike; 1918–2002, Irish)
Mitchell (Warren; 1926– , English)
Mortimer (Bob; 1959– , English)
Naughton (Charles; 1887–1976, Scottish)
Robinson (Tony; 1946– , English)
Roseanne (1952– , US)
Saunders (Jennifer; 1958– , English)
Seinfeld (Jerry; 1954– , US)
Sessions (John; 1953– , Scottish)
Tarleton (Richard; d.1588, English)
The Goons
Williams (Kenneth; 1926–88, English)
Williams (Robin; 1951– , US)

09 Edmondson (Adrian; 1957– , English)
Fernandel (1903–71, French)
Grossmith (George; 1847–1912, English)
Humphries (Barry; 1934– , Australian)
Morecambe (Eric; 1926–84, English)
Rhys Jones (Griff; 1953– , Welsh)
Whitfield (June; 1925– , English)

10 The Goodies
Whitehouse (Paul; 1959– , Welsh)

11 Monty Python
Terry-Thomas (1911–90, English)

12 Brooke-Taylor (Tim; c.1940– , English)

14 Laurel and Hardy
Little and Large

15 Naughton and Gold
The Marx Brothers
The Three Stooges

comet

Comets include:

04 West	Newton	Seki-Lines
Wolf	**07** Bennett	**10** De Chéseaux
05 Cruls	Humason	Flauergues
Encke	Tebbutt	Great Comet
Kirch	**08** Daylight	**11** Arend-Roland
Mrkos	Hale-Bopp	Swift-Tuttle
Tycho	Kohoutek	**12** Pons-Winnecke
06 Donati	**09** Hyakutake	**14** Tago-Sato-Kosaka
Halley	Ikeya-Seki	**15** IRAS-Araki-Alcock
Lexell	Morehouse	

comic

Comics include:

03 Viz	Bunty	The Dandy	The Topper
04 Judy	Dandy	The Eagle	
05 Beano	**08** The Beano	**09** The Beezer	

See also **newspaper**

command

Commands include:

03 hie	whoa	huddup
hup	**05** be off	**07** give way
hye	enter	**09** stand easy
04 easy	gee up	**10** quick march
halt	**06** come by	**12** be off with you
high	entrez	**15** stand and deliver
mush	gee hup	

See also **shout**

commander

Commanders include:

03 aga	captain	risaldar	privateer
mir	general	taxiarch	seraskier
04 agha	prefect	tetrarch	trierarch
meer	warlord	**09** chieftain	**11** encomendero
06 sardar	**08** governor	chiliarch	turcopolier
sirdar	hipparch	imperator	**13** generalissimo
07 admiral	phylarch	polemarch	

See also **admiral**; **field marshal**; **general**; **governor**; **king**; **president**; **prime minister**; **queen**

commonwealth

Commonwealth members:

05 Ghana	Kenya	Nauru
India	Malta	Samoa

Tonga
06 Belize
Brunei
Canada
Cyprus
Guyana
Malawi
Tuvalu
Uganda
Zambia

07 Grenada
Jamaica
Lesotho
Namibia
Nigeria
St Lucia
Vanuatu

See also **CIS**

08 Barbados
Botswana
Cameroon
Dominica
Kiribati
Malaysia
Maldives
Pakistan
Sri Lanka
Tanzania

09 Australia
Mauritius
Singapore
Swaziland
The Gambia

10 Bangladesh
Mozambique

New Zealand
Seychelles
The Bahamas

11 Sierra Leone
South Africa

13 United Kingdom

14 Papua New Guinea
Solomon Islands

15 St Kitts and Nevis

16 Brunei Darussalam

17 Antigua and Barbuda
Trinidad and Tobago

21 St Christopher and Nevis

25 St Vincent and the
Grenadines

communication

Communications include:

02 IT
TV

03 fax
MMS
Net
PDA
SMS

04 memo
news
note
post
wire
word

05 cable
e-mail
media
pager
pay TV
press
radar
radio
telex
video

06 gossip
letter

notice
poster
report
speech
tannoy
the net

07 bleeper
Braille
cable TV
journal
leaflet
message
Prestel®,
webcast
website

08 access TV
aerogram
brochure
bulletin
circular
computer
dialogue
dispatch
Intelsat
intercom

Internet
junk mail
magazine
mailshot
pamphlet
postcard
telegram
teletext
wireless

09 broadband
catalogue
digital TV
facsimile
grapevine
mass media
megaphone
Morse code
newsflash
newspaper
publicity
satellite
semaphore
statement
telephone
voice mail

10 communiqué
dictaphone
loud-hailer
pay-per-view
television
typewriter

11 advertising
chain letter
satellite TV
Telemessage®
teleprinter
text message
the Internet

12 announcement
broadcasting
conversation
press release
sign language
walkie-talkie
World Wide Web

13 video-on-demand
word processor

14 correspondence
subscription TV

company *see* **business**; **dance**

compass

Compass points:

01 E	S by W	south by east
N	W by N	south by west
S	W by S	west by north
W	west	west by south
02 NE	**05** NE by E	**13** east-north-east
NW	NE by N	east-south-east
SE	north	west-north-west
SW	NW by N	west-south-west
03 ENE	NW by W	**14** north-north-east
ESE	SE by E	north-north-west
NNE	SE by S	south-south-east
NNW	south	south-south-west
SSE	SW by S	**15** north-east by east
SSW	SW by W	north-west by west
WNW	**09** north-east	south-east by east
WSW	north-west	south-west by west
04 east	south-east	**16** north-east by north
E by N	south-west	north-west by north
E by S	**11** east by north	south-east by south
N by E	east by south	south-west by south
N by W	north by east	
S by E	north by west	

competition *see* sport

complementary medicine *see* medicine

composer

Composers include:

03 Bax (Sir Arnold; 1883–1953, English)
Cui (César; 1835–1918, Russian)
Gál (Hans; 1890–1987, Austrian)
Puw (Guto; 1971– , Welsh)
Suk (Joseph; 1875–1935, Czech)

04 Adam (Adolphe; 1803–56, French)
Adès (Thomas; 1971– , English)
Arne (Thomas; 1710–78, English)
Bach (C P E; 1714–88, German)
Bach (Johann Christian; 1735–82, German)
Bach (Johann Christoph Friedrich; 1732–95, German)
Bach (Johann Sebastian; 1685–1750, German)
Bach (Wilhelm Friedemann; 1710–84, German)
Bart (Lionel; 1930–99, English)
Berg (Alban; 1885–1935, Austrian)
Blow (John; 1649–1708, English)
Bull (John; c.1563–1628, English)
Bush (Alan; 1900–95, English)

Byrd (William; 1543–1623, English)
Cage (John; 1912–92, US)
Cary (Tristram; 1925–2008, Australian)
Foss (Lukas; 1922– , US)
Gade (Niels; 1817–90, Danish)
Haba (Alois; 1893–1972, Czech)
Hahn (Reynaldo; 1874–1947, Venezuelan/French)
Hill (Alfred; 1870–1960, Australian)
Indy (Vincent d'; 1851–1931, French)
Ives (Charles; 1874–1954, US)
King (Carole; 1942– , US)
Lalo (Édouard; 1823–92, French)
Löwe (Karl; 1796–1869, German)
Nono (Luigi; 1924–90, Italian)
Orff (Carl; 1895–1982, German)
Pärt (Arvo; 1935– , Estonian/Austrian)
Peri (Jacopo; 1561–1633, Italian)
Raff (Joachim; 1822–82, Swiss)
Rota (Nino; 1911–79, Italian)
Shaw (Martin; 1876–1958, English)
Weir (Judith; 1954– , Scottish)

Wolf (Hugo; 1860–1903, Austrian)
Wood (Charles; 1866–1926, Irish)
Wood (Haydn; 1882–1959, English)

05 Adams (John; 1947– , US)
Alkan (1813–88, French)
Aquin (Louis Claude d'; 1694–1772, French)
Auber (Daniel-François-Esprit; 1782–1871, French)
Auric (Georges; 1899–1983, French)
Balfe (Michael William; 1808–70, English)
Banks (Don; 1923–80, Australian)
Beach (Mrs H H A; 1867–1944, US)
Berio (Luciano; 1925–2003, Italian)
Bizet (Georges; 1838–75, French)
Blake (Eubie; 1883–1983, US)
Bliss (Sir Arthur; 1891–1975, English)
Bloch (Ernest; 1880–1959, Swiss/US)
Boito (Arrigo; 1842–1918, Italian)
Boyce (William; 1711–79, English)
Brian (Havergal; 1876–1972, English)
Bruch (Max; 1838–1920, German)
Cilea (Francesco; 1866–1950, Italian)
Darke (Harold; 1888–1976, English)
Dufay (Guillaume; c.1400–74, French)
Dukas (Paul; 1865–1935, French)
Durey (Louis; 1888–1979, French)
Einem (Gottfried von; 1918–96, Austrian)
Elgar (Sir Edward; 1857–1934, English)
Falla (Manuel de; 1876–1946, Spanish)
Fasch (Johann Friedrich; 1688–1758, German)
Fauré (Gabriel; 1845–1924, French)
Field (John; 1782–1837, Irish)
Finzi (Gerald; 1901–56, English)
Friml (Rudolf; 1879–1972, US)
Glass (Philip; 1937– , US)
Gluck (Christoph; 1714–87, German)
Goehr (Alexander; 1932– , German/British)
Gould (Morton; 1913–96, US)
Grieg (Edvard; 1843–1907, Norwegian)
Grofé (Ferde; 1892–1972, US)
Harty (Sir Hamilton; 1880–1941, Northern Irish)
Haydn (Joseph; 1732–1809, Austrian)
Haydn (Michael; 1737–1806, Austrian)
Henze (Hans Werner; 1926– , German)
Holst (Gustav; 1874–1934, English)
Ibert (Jacques; 1890–1962, French)
Kagel (Mauricio; 1931–2008, Argentine)
Lawes (Henry; 1596–1662, English)
Lehár (Franz; 1870–1948, Hungarian)
Liszt (Franz; 1811–86, Hungarian)
Lloyd (George; 1913–98, English)
Locke (Matthew; c.1621–77, English)
Loewe (Karl; 1796–1869, German)
Lully (Jean Baptiste; 1632–87, French)
Meale (Richard; 1932– , Australian)
Moore (Thomas; 1779–1852, Irish)

Novák (Vitezslav; 1870–1949, Czech)
Nyman (Michael; 1944– , English)
Ogdon (John; 1937–89, English)
Parry (Sir Hubert; 1848–1918, English)
Ravel (Maurice; 1875–1937, French)
Reger (Max; 1873–1916, German)
Reich (Steve; 1936– , US)
Roman (Johan Helmich; 1694–1758, Swedish)
Rorem (Ned; 1923– , US)
Rózsa (Miklós; 1907–95, Hungarian)
Satie (Erik; 1866–1925, French)
Scott (Cyril; 1879–1970, English)
Scott (Francis George; 1880–1958, Scottish)
Smyth (Dame Ethel; 1858–1944, English)
Sousa (John Philip; 1854–1932, US)
Spohr (Ludwig; 1784–1859, German)
Still (William Grant; 1895–1978, US)
Suppé (Franz von; 1819–95, Austrian)
Swann (Donald; 1923–94, Welsh)
Tovey (Sir Donald Francis; 1873–1940, English)
Tubin (Eduard; 1905–82, Estonian/Swedish)
Verdi (Giuseppe; 1813–1901, Italian)
Weber (Carl Maria von; 1786–1826, German)
Weill (Kurt; 1900–50, German/US)
Widor (Charles Marie; 1845–1937, French)
Wirén (Dag; 1905–86, Swedish)

06 Albert (Eugen d'; 1864–1932, German)
Alford (Kenneth; 1881–1945, English)
Alfvén (Hugo; 1872–1960, Swedish)
Antill (John; 1904–86, Australian)
Arnold (Sir Malcolm; 1921–2006, English)
Avison (Charles; c.1710–70, English)
Barber (Samuel; 1910–81, US)
Bartók (Béla; 1881–1945, Hungarian)
Bishop (Sir Henry R; 1786–1855, English)
Boulez (Pierre; 1925– , French)
Brahms (Johannes; 1833–97, German)
Bridge (Frank; 1879–1941, English)
Brumby (Colin; 1933– , Australian)
Carter (Elliott, Jnr; 1908– , US)
Carver (Robert; c.1484–c.1568, Scottish)
Chávez (Carlos; 1899–1978, Mexican)
Chopin (Frédéric; 1810–49, Polish)
Clarke (Jeremiah; c.1674–1707, English)
Coates (Eric; 1886–1957, English)
Cowell (Henry; 1897–1965, US)
Czerny (Karl; 1791–1857, Austrian)
Daquin (Louis Claude; 1694–1772, French)
Davies (Sir Henry Walford; 1869–1941, Welsh)
Delius (Frederick; 1862–1934, English)
Dessau (Paul; 1894–1979, German)
Dieren (Bernard van; 1884–1936, Dutch)

Duparc (Henri; 1848–1933, French)
Dussek (Jan Ladislav; 1760–1812, Czech)
Dvořák (Antonín; 1841–1904, Czech)
Eisler (Hanns; 1898–1962, German)
Enesco (Georges; 1881–1955, Romanian)
Finger (Godfrey; fl.1685–1717, Czech)
Flotow (Friedrich, Freiherr von; 1812–83, German)
Foulds (John; 1880–1939, English)
Franck (César; 1822–90, French)
García (Manuel; 1775–1832, Spanish)
German (Sir Edward; 1862–1936, English)
Glinka (Mikhail; 1804–57, Russian)
Godard (Benjamin; 1849–95, French)
Gounod (Charles; 1818–93, French)
Grétry (André; 1741–1813, French)
Gurney (Ivor; 1890–1937, English)
Halévy (Fromental; 1799–1862, French)
Handel (George Frideric; 1685–1759, German/English)
Hanson (Howard; 1896–1981, US)
Hanson (Raymond; 1913–76, Australian)
Harper (Edward; 1941– , English)
Harris (Roy; 1898–1979, US)
Harris (Sir William; 1883–1973, English)
Hérold (Ferdinand; 1791–1833, French)
Hiller (Johann Adam; 1728–1804, German)
Hummel (Johann Nepomuk; 1778–1837, Austrian)
Jongen (Joseph; 1873–1953, Belgian)
Kodály (Zoltán; 1882–1967, Hungarian)
Koppel (Herman D; 1908–98, Danish)
Krenek (Ernst; 1900–91, Austrian/US)
Lamond (Frederic; 1868–1948, Scottish)
Lassus (Orlandus; c.1532–94, Dutch)
Lecocq (Charles; 1832–1918, French)
Liadov (Anatoli; 1855–1914, Russian)
Ligeti (Györgi; 1923–2006, Hungarian/Austrian)
Linley (Thomas; 1732–95, English)
Lyadov (Anatoli; 1855–1914, Russian)
Mahler (Gustav; 1860–1911, Czech/Austrian)
Marais (Marin; 1656–1728, French)
Martin (Frank; 1890–1974, Swiss)
Mennin (Peter; 1923–83, US)
Moeran (E J; 1894–1950, English)
Morley (Thomas; 1557–1603, English)
Mozart (Wolfgang Amadeus; 1756–91, Austrian)
Nathan (Isaac; 1790–1864, Australian)
Ó Riada (Seán; 1931–71, Irish)
Piston (Walter; 1894–1976, US)
Pleyel (Ignaz; 1757–1831, Austrian)
Previn (André; 1929– , German/US)
Quantz (Johann Joachim; 1697–1773, German)
Rameau (Jean Philippe; 1683–1764, French)

Reicha (Antonín; 1770–1836, Czech)
Rubbra (Edmund; 1901–86, English)
Schütz (Heinrich; 1585–1672, German)
Searle (Humphrey; 1915–82, English)
Seiber (Mátyás; 1905–60, Hungarian/British)
Sitsky (Larry; 1934– , Australian)
Stoker (Richard; 1938– , English)
Straus (Oscar; 1870–1954, Austrian/French)
Tallis (Thomas; c.1505–85, English)
Thomas (Ambroise; 1811–96, French)
Turina (Joaquín; 1882–1949, Spanish)
Varèse (Edgard; 1885–1965, French/US)
Vogler (Georg Joseph; 1749–1814, German)
Wagner (Richard; 1813–83, German)
Wagner (Siegfried; 1869–1930, German)
Walton (Sir William; 1902–83, English)
Webern (Anton von; 1883–1945, Austrian)
Wesley (Samuel; 1766–1837, English)
Wilson (Thomas; 1927–2001, Scottish)

07 Allegri (Gregorio; 1582–1652, Italian)
Arriaga (Juan Crisóstomo; 1806–26, Spanish)
Babbitt (Milton; 1916– , US)
Bainton (Edgar; 1880–1956, English)
Bantock (Sir Granville; 1868–1946, English)
Bellini (Vincenzo; 1801–35, Italian)
Bennett (Sir Richard Rodney; 1936– , English)
Bennett (Sir William Sterndale; 1816–75, English)
Bentzon (Niels Viggo; 1919–2000, Danish)
Berlioz (Hector; 1803–69, French)
Berners (Gerald, Lord; 1883–1950, English)
Berwald (Franz; 1796–1868, Swedish)
Borodin (Aleksandr; 1833–87, Russian)
Britten (Benjamin, Lord; 1913–76, English)
Bruneau (Alfred; 1857–1934, French)
Cabezón (Antonio de; 1500–66, Spanish)
Caccini (Giulio; c.1550–1618, Italian)
Campion (Thomas; 1567–1620, English)
Casella (Alfredo; 1883–1947, Italian)
Cavalli (Francesco; 1602–76, Italian)
Copland (Aaron; 1900–90, US)
Corelli (Arcangelo; 1653–1713, Italian)
Debussy (Claude; 1862–1918, French)
Delibes (Léo; 1836–91, French)
di Lasso (Orlando; c.1532–94, Dutch)
Dowland (John; 1563–1626, English)
Dunhill (Thomas; 1877–1946, English)
Duruflé (Maurice; 1902–86, French)
Farnaby (Giles; c.1563–1640, English)
Fricker (Peter; 1920–90, English)
Galuppi (Baldassaro; 1706–85, Italian)
Gerhard (Roberto; 1896–1970, Spanish/British)
Gibbons (Orlando; 1583–1625, English)
Górecki (Henryk; 1933– , Polish)
Herbert (Victor; 1859–1924, Irish/US)

Howells (Herbert; 1892–1983, English)
Ireland (John; 1879–1962, English)
Janácek (Leoš; 1854–1928, Czech)
Joachim (Joseph; 1831–1907, Hungarian)
Knussen (Oliver; 1952– , English)
Lambert (Constant; 1905–51, English)
Leclair (Jean Marie; 1697–1764, French)
Lilburn (Douglas; 1915–2001, New Zealand)
Lutyens (Elizabeth; 1906–83, English)
MacCunn (Hamish; 1868–1916, Scottish)
Maderna (Bruno; 1920–73, Italian)
Martinu (Bohuslav; 1890–1959, Czech)
Mathias (William; 1934–92, Welsh)
McGuire (Edward; 1948– , Scottish)
Menotti (Gian-Carlo; 1911–2007, Italian/US)
Milhaud (Darius; 1892–1974, French)
Nicolai (Otto; 1810–49, German)
Nielsen (Carl; 1865–1931, Danish)
Nikisch (Arthur; 1855–1922, Hungarian)
Nørgård (Per; 1932– , Danish)
Novello (Ivor; 1893–1951, Welsh)
Novello (Vincent; 1781–1861, English)
Okeghem (Johannes; c.1430–97, Flemish)
Pepusch (Johann Christoph; 1667–1752, German)
Poulenc (Francis; 1899–1963, French)
Puccini (Giacomo; 1858–1924, Italian)
Purcell (Henry; 1659–95, English)
Quilter (Roger; 1877–1953, English)
Riegger (Wallingford; 1885–1961, US)
Rodrigo (Joaquín; 1901–99, Spanish)
Romberg (Sigmund; 1887–1951, US)
Rossini (Gioacchino; 1792–1868, Italian)
Roussel (Albert; 1869–1937, French)
Salieri (Antonio; 1750–1825, Italian)
Schmidt (Franz; 1874–1939, Austrian)
Schuman (William; 1910–92, US)
Shankar (Ravi; 1920– , Indian)
Simpson (Robert; 1921–97, English)
Smeaton (Bruce; 1938– , Australian)
Smetana (Bedrich; 1824–84, Czech)
Sorabji (Kaikhosru; 1892–1988, English)
Sowerby (Leo; 1895–1968, US)
Stamitz (Carl; 1745–1801, German)
Stamitz (Johann; 1717–57, Bohemian)
Stanley (John; 1713–86, English)
Steiner (Max; 1888–1971, US)
Strauss (Johann, the Elder; 1804–49, Austrian)
Strauss (Johann, the Younger; 1825–99, Austrian)
Strauss (Richard; 1864–1949, German)
Taneyev (Sergei; 1856–1915, Russian)
Tartini (Giuseppe; 1692–1770, Italian)
Tavener (Sir John; 1944– , English)
Thomson (Virgil; 1896–1989, US)

Tippett (Sir Michael; 1905–98, English)
Tomkins (Thomas; 1572–1656, English)
Vivaldi (Antonio; 1678–1741, Italian)
Warlock (Peter; 1894–1930, English)
Wellesz (Egon; 1885–1974, Austrian)
Xenakis (Iannis; 1922–2001, Romanian/French)
Zwilich (Ellen Taaffe; 1939– , US)

08 Albinoni (Tomasso; 1671–1751, Italian)
Bairstow (Sir Edward; 1874 1946, English)
Barsanti (Francesco; 1690–1775, Italian)
Benedict (Sir Julius; 1804–85, German)
Berkeley (Michael; 1948– , English)
Berkeley (Sir Lennox; 1903–89, English)
Blomdahl (Karl-Birger; 1916–68, Swedish)
Boughton (Rutland; 1878–1960, English)
Bruckner (Anton; 1824–96, Austrian)
Carr-Boyd (Ann; 1938– , Australian)
Catalani (Alfredo; 1854–93, Italian)
Chabrier (Emmanuel; 1841–94, French)
Chausson (Ernest; 1855–99, French)
Chisholm (Erik; 1904–65, Scottish)
Cimarosa (Domenico; 1749–1801, Italian)
Clementi (Muzio; 1752–1832, Italian)
Cornyshe (William; c.1465–1523, English)
Couperin (François; 1668–1733, French)
Dohnanyi (Ernst von; 1877–1960, Hungarian)
Gabrieli (Andrea; c.1533–86, Italian)
Gabrieli (Giovanni; c.1555–1612, Italian)
Giordano (Umberto; 1867–1948, Italian)
Glazunov (Aleksandr; 1865–1936, Russian)
Godowsky (Leopold; 1870–1938, US)
Goldmark (Carl; 1830–1915, Hungarian)
Goossens (Sir Eugène; 1893–1962, English)
Goudimel (Claude; c.1514–72, French)
Grainger (Percy; 1882–1961, Australian/US)
Hamilton (Iain; 1922–2000, Scottish)
Henschel (Sir George; 1850–1934, Polish/British)
Herrmann (Bernard; 1911–75, US)
Hoffmann (E T A; 1776–1822, German)
Holliger (Heinz; 1939– , Swiss)
Honegger (Arthur; 1892–1955, French)
Ketèlbey (Albert William; 1875–1959, English)
Koechlin (Charles; 1867–1950, French)
Korngold (Erich Wolfgang; 1897–1957, Czech/US)
Leighton (Kenneth; 1929–88, English)
Maconchy (Dame Elizabeth; 1907–94, English)
Marcello (Benedetto; 1686–1739, Italian)
Marshall (William; 1748–1833, Scottish)
Mascagni (Pietro; 1863–1945, Italian)
Massenet (Jules; 1842–1912, French)
Messager (André; 1853–1929, French)
Messiaen (Olivier; 1908–92, French)
Monckton (Lionel; 1861–1924, English)

Musgrave (Thea; 1928– , Scottish)
Ockeghem (Johannes; c.1430–97, Flemish)
Panufnik (Sir Andrej; 1914–94, Polish/
British)
Pfitzner (Hans; 1869–1949, German)
Philidor (François André; 1726–95, French)
Pizzetti (Ildebrando; 1880–1968, Italian)
Respighi (Ottorino; 1879–1936, Italian)
Richards (Henry Brinley; 1819–85, Welsh)
Riisager (Knudäge; 1897–1975, Danish)
Sallinen (Aulis; 1935– , Finnish)
Sarasate (Pablo; 1844–1908, Spanish)
Schnabel (Artur; 1882–1951, Austrian)
Schubert (Franz; 1797–1828, Austrian)
Schumann (Clara; 1819–96, German)
Schumann (Robert; 1810–56, German)
Scriabin (Aleksandr; 1872–1915, Russian)
Sessions (Roger; 1896–1985, US)
Sibelius (Jean; 1865–1957, Finnish)
Skriabin (Aleksandr; 1872–1915, Russian)
Spontini (Gasparo; 1774–1851, Italian)
Stanford (Sir Charles Villiers; 1852–1924,
Irish)
Sullivan (Sir Arthur; 1842–1900, English)
Svendsen (Johan; 1840–1911, Norwegian)
Telemann (Georg Philipp; 1681–1767,
German)
Victoria (Tomás Luis de; 1548–1611,
Spanish)
Willaert (Adrian; c.1490–1562, Flemish)
Williams (John; 1932– , US)

09 Balakirev (Mili; 1836–1910, Russian)
Beethoven (Ludwig van; 1770–1827,
German)
Bernstein (Elmer; 1922–2004, US)
Bernstein (Leonard; 1918–90, US)
Boïeldieu (François Adrien; 1775–1834,
French)
Bononcini (Giovanni Maria; 1642–78,
Italian)
Boulanger (Lili; 1893–1918, French)
Boulanger (Nadia; 1887–1979, French)
Butterley (Nigel; 1935– , Australian)
Buxtehude (Diderik; c.1637–1707, Danish)
Carissimi (Giacomo; 1605–74, Italian)
Cavalieri (Emilio de'; c.1550–1602, Italian)
Cherubini (Luigi; 1760–1842, Italian)
Conyngham (Barry; 1944– , Australian)
Cornelius (Peter; 1824–74, German)
Donizetti (Gaetano; 1797–1848, Italian)
Dunstable (John; c.1390–1453, English)
Dutilleux (Henri; 1916– , French)
Froberger (Johann Jakob; 1616–67, German)
Goldsmith (Jerry; 1929–2004, US)
Gruenberg (Louis; 1884–1964, US)
Hindemith (Paul; 1895–1963, German)
Hoddinott (Alun; 1929–2008, Welsh)
Holbrooke (Josef; 1878–1958, English)

Järnefelt (Armas; 1869–1958, Swedish)
MacDowell (Edward; 1861–1908, US)
Mackenzie (Sir Alexander; 1847–1935,
Scottish)
Malipiero (Francesco; 1882–1973, Italian)
Merikanto (Aarre; 1893–1958, Finnish)
Meyerbeer (Giacomo; 1791–1864, German)
Morricone (Ennio; 1928– , Italian)
Musorgski (Modest; 1835–81, Russian)
Musorgsky (Modest; 1835–81, Russian)
Offenbach (Jacques; 1819–80, German)
Pachelbel (Johann; c.1653–1706, German)
Paisiello (Giovanni; 1740–1816, Italian)
Pergolesi (Giovanni Battista; 1710–36,
Italian)
Prokofiev (Sergei; 1891–1953, Russian)
Scarlatti (Alessandro; 1659–1725, Italian)
Scarlatti (Domenico; 1685–1757, Italian)
Schmelzer (Johann Heinrich; 1623–80,
Austrian)
Schnittke (Alfred; 1934–98, Russian)
Schönberg (Arnold; 1874–1951, Austrian/
US)
Shchedrin (Rodion; 1932– , Russian)
Stevenson (Ronald; 1928– , Scottish)
Stradella (Alessandro; c.1642–82, Italian)
Takemitsu (Toru; 1930–96, Japanese)
Tortelier (Paul; 1914–90, French)
Whitehead (Gillian; 1941– , New Zealand)
Zemlinsky (Alexander von; 1871–1942,
Austrian)

10 Birtwistle (Sir Harrison; 1934– , English)
Boccherini (Luigi; 1743–1805, Italian)
Buononcini (Giovanni Maria; 1642–78,
Italian)
Campenhout (François von; 1779–1849,
Belgian)
Ferrabosco (Alfonso; 1543–88, Italian)
Ferrabosco (Alfonso; c.1575–1628, English)
Ferrabosco (Domenico Maria; 1513–74,
Italian)
Kabalevsky (Dmitri; 1904–87, Russian)
Monteverdi (Claudio; 1567–1643, Italian)
Mussargsky (Modest; 1835–81, Russian)
Mussorgsky (Modest; 1835–81, Russian)
Myaskovsky (Nikolai; 1881–1950, Russian)
Paderewski (Ignacy Jan; 1860–1941, Polish)
Palestrina (Giovanni Pierluigi da; c.1525–94,
Italian)
Penderecki (Krzysztof; 1933– , Polish)
Ponchielli (Amilcare; 1834–86, Italian)
Praetorius (Michael; 1571–1621, German)
Rawsthorne (Alan; 1905–71, English)
Rubinstein (Anton; 1829–94, Russian)
Saint-Saëns (Camille; 1835–1921, French)
Schoenberg (Arnold; 1874–1951, Austrian/
US)
Sculthorpe (Peter; 1929– , Australian)

Skalkottas (Nikolaos; 1904–49, Greek)
Stravinsky (Igor; 1882–1971, Russian/US)
Sutherland (Margaret; 1897–1984, Australian)
Tcherepnin (Nikolai; 1873–1945, Russian)
Villa-Lobos (Heitor; 1887–1959, Brazilian)
Waldteufel (Emile; 1837–1915, French)
Weinberger (Jaromir; 1896–1967, Czech)
Williamson (Malcolm; 1931–2003, Australian)
Wordsworth (William Brocklesby; 1908–88, English)

11 Butterworth (George; 1885–1916, English)
Charpentier (Gustave; 1860–1956, French)
Dittersdorf (Karl Ditters von; 1739–99, Austrian)
Frescobaldi (Girolamo; 1583–1643, Italian)
Goldschmidt (Berthold; 1903–96, German/British)
Gubaydulina (Sofiya; 1931– , Russian)
Humperdinck (Engelbert; 1854–1921, German)
Leoncavallo (Ruggiero; 1858–1919, Italian)
Lutoslawski (Witold; 1913–94, Polish)
Mendelssohn (Felix; 1809–47, German)
Moussorgsky (Modest; 1835–81, Russian)
Rachmaninov (Sergei; 1873–1943, Russian)
Rakhmaninov (Sergei; 1873–1943, Russian)
Ravenscroft (Thomas; 1592–1640, English)
Reizenstein (Franz; 1911–68, German)
Stockhausen (Karlheinz; 1928–2007, German)

Tailleferre (Germaine; 1892–1983, French)
Tchaikovsky (Pyotr Ilyich; 1840–93, Russian)
Thalben-Ball (Sir George; 1896–1987, Australian/British)
Theodorakis (Mikis; 1925– , Greek)
Thorpe Davie (Cedric; 1913–83, Scottish)
Weingartner (Felix; 1863–1942, Austrian)
Wolf-Ferrari (Ermanno; 1876–1948, Italian)

12 Dallapiccola (Luigi; 1904–75, Italian)
Dargomizhsky (Aleksandr; 1813–69, Russian)
Shostakovich (Dmitri; 1906–75, Russian)

13 Khatchaturian (Aram; 1903–78, Russian)
Maxwell Davies (Sir Peter; 1934– , English)
Rouget de Lisle (Claude Joseph; 1760–1836, French)

14 Glanville-Hicks (Peggy; 1912–90, Australian)
Jaques-Dalcroze (Émile; 1865–1951, Swiss)
Josquin des Prez (c.1440–1521, Franco-Flemish)
Josquin Desprez (c.1440–1521, Franco-Flemish)
Peterson-Berger (Wilhelm; 1867–1942, Swedish)
Rimsky-Korsakov (Nikolai; 1844–1908, Russian)

15 Coleridge-Taylor (Samuel; 1875–1912, English)
Vaughan Williams (Ralph; 1872–1958, English)

See also **Bach, Johann Sebastian; Bartók, Béla; Beethoven, Ludwig van; Brahms, Johannes; Britten, Benjamin; Debussy, Claude; Dvořák, Antonín; Gilbert, Sir W S and Sullivan, Sir Arthur; Handel, George Frideric; Haydn, Joseph; libretto; Mahler, Gustav; Mozart, Wolfgang Amadeus; music; Prokofiev, Sergei; Puccini, Giacomo; Purcell, Henry; Ravel, Maurice; Rossini, Gioacchino; Schoenberg, Arnold; Schubert, Franz; Schumann, Robert; Shostakovich, Dmitri; song; Strauss, Richard; Stravinsky, Igor; Tchaikovsky, Pyotr Ilyich; Verdi, Giuseppe; Wagner, Richard**

composition *see* **music**

compound *see* **chemistry**

computer

Computers include:

03	HAL		06	UNIVAC	09	The Matrix
	IBM	**05** Eddie	08	Apple Mac®	11	Deep Thought
	Mac®	ENIAC		Colossus	12	Commodore Pet
	SAL	Holly		Deep Blue		
04	iMac®	iBook®		Spectrum		

VIKI

Computer programming languages include:

01 C++	Java	**06** Delphi	**10** Postscript
C	Perl	Pascal	
03 AWK	**05** BASIC	Python	
04 HTML	COBOL	**07** FORTRAN	

Internet suffixes include:

02 .ac	.cu	.id	.ms
.ad	.cv	.ie	.mt
.ae	.cx	.il	.mu
.af	.cy	.im	.mv
.ag	.cz	.in	.mw
.ai	.de	.io	.mx
.al	.dj	.iq	.my
.am	.dk	.ir	.mz
.an	.dm	.is	.na
.ao	.do	.it	.nc
.aq	.dz	.je	.ne
.ar	.ec	.jm	.nf
.as	.ee	.jo	.ng
.at	.eg	.jp	.ni
.au	.eh	.ke	.nl
.aw	.er	.kg	.no
.az	.es	.kh	.np
.ba	.et	.ki	.nr
.bb	.eu	.km	.nu
.bd	.fi	.kn	.nz
.be	.fj	.kp	.om
.bf	.fk	.kr	.pa
.bg	.fm	.kw	.pe
.bh	.fo	.ky	.pf
.bi	.fr	.kz	.pg
.bj	.ga	.la	.ph
.bm	.gd	.lb	.pk
.bn	.ge	.lc	.pl
.bo	.gf	.li	.pm
.br	.gg	.lk	.pn
.bs	.gh	.lr	.pr
.bt	.gi	.ls	.ps
.bv	.gl	.lt	.pt
.bw	.gm	.lu	.pw
.by	.gn	.lv	.py
.bz	.gp	.ly	.qa
.ca	.gq	.ma	.re
.cc	.gr	.mc	.ro
.cd	.gs	.md	.ru
.cf	.gt	.mg	.rw
.cg	.gu	.mh	.sa
.ch	.gw	.mk	.sb
.ci	.gy	.ml	.sc
.ck	.hk	.mm	.sd
.cl	.hm	.mn	.se
.cm	.hn	.mo	.sg
.cn	.hr	.mp	.sh
.co	.ht	.mq	.si
.cr	.hu	.mr	.sj

.sk	.tj	.us	.za
.sl	.tk	.uy	.zm
.sm	.tm	.uz	.zw
.sn	.tn	.va	**03** .biz
.so	.to	.vc	.com
.sr	.tp	.ve	.edu
.st	.tr	.vg	.gov
.sv	.tt	.vi	.int
.sy	.tv	.vn	.mil
.sz	.tw	.vu	.net
.tc	.tz	.wf	.org
.td	.ua	.ws	.pro
.tf	.ug	.ye	.sci
.tg	.uk	.yt	.soc
.th	.um	.yu	

Computer scientists and pioneers include:

04 Bell (Gordon; 1934– , US)
Brin (Sergey; 1973– , Russian/US)
Bush (Vannevar; 1890–1974, US)
Cray (Seymour; 1925–96, US)
Hoff (Ted; 1937– , US)
Hurd (Cuthbert; 1911–96, US)
Jobs (Steve; 1955– , US)
Page (Lawrence; 1973– , US)
Wang (An; 1920–90, US)
Zuse (Konrad; 1910–95, German)

05 Aiken (Howard Hathaway; 1900–73, US)
Bezos (Jeff; 1964– , US)
Burks (Arthur; 1915–2008, US)
Gates (Bill; 1955– , US)
Mazor (Stanley; 1941– , US)
Olsen (Ken; 1926– , US)
Sugar (Sir Alan; 1947– , English)

06 Amdahl (Gene; 1922– , US)
Backus (John; 1924–2007, US)
Comrie (L J; 1893–1950, New Zealand)
Eckert (J Presper; 1919–95, US)
Faggin (Federico; 1941– , Italian/US)
Hopper (Grace Murray; 1906–92, US)
Huskey (Harry; 1916– , US)
Michie (Donald; 1923–2007, Burmese/British)
Milner (Robin; 1934– , English)
Turing (Alan; 1912–54, English)

Wilkes (Sir Maurice V; 1913– , English)

07 Babbage (Charles; 1791–1871, English)
Gosling (James; 1955– , Canadian)
Hartree (Douglas; 1897–1958, English)
Kilburn (Tom; 1921–2001, English)
Mauchly (John W; 1907–80, US)
Shannon (Claude; 1916–2001, US)
Stibitz (George R; 1904–95, US)
Wheeler (David; 1927–2004, English)
Wozniak (Steve; 1950– , US)

08 Lovelace (Ada, Countess of; 1815–52, English)
Sinclair (Sir Clive; 1940– , English)
Stallman (Richard; 1953– , US)
Strachey (Christopher; 1916–75, English)
Torvalds (Linus; 1969– , Finnish)
Williams (Sir Frederic; 1911–77, English)

09 Atanasoff (John Vincent; 1903–95, US)
Engelbart (Douglas; 1925– , US)
Forrester (Jay; 1918– , US)
Goldstine (Herman H; 1913–2004, US)
Hollerith (Herman; 1860–1929, US)
Wilkinson (James H; 1919–86, English)

10 Berners-Lee (Tim; 1955– , English)
Fairclough (Sir John; 1930–2003, English)
Michaelson (Sidney; 1925–91, English)
Stroustrup (Bjarne; 1950– , Danish)
Von Neumann (John; 1903–57, Hungarian/US)

Computing terms include:

02 CD	CPU	ISP
PC	DOS	LAN
VR	DTP	Net
03 bit	DVD	P2P
bot	FAQ	PDF
bug	FTP	RAM
bus	GUI	ROM
CD-R	hit	RTF

URL
VDU
WAN
Web
WWW
04 BIOS
boot
byte
card
CD-RW
chip
data
disk
dump
file
game
hack
HTML
icon
ISDN
menu
port
SGML
Unix®
worm
05 ASCII
BASIC
cache
CD-ROM
COBOL
e-mail
forum
JANET®
Linux
login
log on
Mac OS
macro
modem
mouse
MS-DOS®
pixel
shell
virus
06 access
backup
binary
bitmap
buffer
cursor
DVD-ROM
editor
format
hacker
joypad
laptop
log off

memory
output
plug-in
reboot
screen
script
server
sprite
the Net
the Web
toggle
window
07 browser
crawler
default
desktop
FORTRAN
hacking
install
monitor
network
package
palmtop
Pentium®
pointer
printer
program
scanner
toolbar
Unicode
upgrade
Web page
Web site
Windows®
WYSIWYG
zip disk
08 autosave
bookmark
chat room
cold boot
core dump
cracking
databank
database
emoticon
firewall
freeware
function
gigabyte
graphics
handheld
hard disk
hardware
home page
Internet
joystick
keyboard

kilobyte
light pen
megabyte
metafile
mouse mat
netspeak
notebook
password
platform
protocol
software
template
terabyte
terminal
touchpad
user name
warm boot
wireless
Wordstar®
09 broadband
character
debugging
digitizer
directory
disk drive
e-commerce
hard drive
hyperlink
hypertext
interface
mainframe
newsgroup
scrolling
shareware
sound card
trackball
utilities
video card
video game
10 cable modem
domain name
floppy disk
message box
multimedia
netiquette
peer-to-peer
peripheral
rewritable
serial port
11 abandonware
application
compact disc
compression
cut and paste
floppy drive
motherboard
optical disk

screen saver
shellscript
silicon chip
spreadsheet
the Internet
Trojan horse
WordPerfect®
workstation
12 circuit board
client-server
computer game
graphics card
installation
laser printer
magnetic disk

magnetic tape
minicomputer
parallel port
search engine
spellchecker
subdirectory
user-friendly
virus checker
World Wide Web
13 character code
file extension
ink-jet printer
interoperable
microcomputer
telecommuting

user interface
14 backing storage
electronic mail
external memory
grammar checker
internal memory
microprocessor
read only memory
rich text format
virtual reality
word processing
15 operating system
read-write memory
wide area network

See also **chess**; **key**; **scanner**

concept *see* **science**

condition *see* **disease**; **psychology**

conductor

Conductors include:

04 Adès (Thomas; 1971– , English)
Böhm (Karl; 1894–1981, Austrian)
Hahn (Reynaldo; 1874–1947, Venezuelan/
  French)
Muti (Riccardo; 1941– , Italian)
Wood (Sir Henry; 1869–1944, English)

05 Boult (Sir Adrian; 1889–1983, English)
Bülow (Hans, Baron von; 1830–94,
  German)
Busch (Fritz; 1890–1951, German)
Davis (Sir Colin; 1927– , English)
Elgar (Sir Edward; 1857–1934, English)
Hallé (Sir Charles; 1819–95, Prussian/
  British)
Harty (Sir Hamilton; 1880–1941, Northern
  Irish)
Kempe (Rudolf; 1910–76, German)
Lloyd (George; 1913–98, English)
Masur (Kurt; 1927– , German)
Meale (Richard; 1932– , Australian)
Mehta (Zubin; 1936– , Indian/US)
Ozawa (Seiji; 1935– , Japanese/US)
Rizzi (Carlo; 1960– , Italian)
Solti (Sir Georg; 1912–97, Hungarian/
  British)
Sousa (John Philip; 1854–1932, US)
Spohr (Ludwig; 1784–1859, German)
Szell (George; 1897–1970, US)

06 Abbado (Claudio; 1933– , Italian)
Boulez (Pierre; 1925– , French)
Bridge (Frank; 1879–1941, English)

Casals (Pablo; 1876–1973, Spanish)
Cortot (Alfred; 1877–1962, French)
Daniel (Paul; 1958– , English)
Dessau (Paul; 1894–1979, German)
Dorati (Antal; 1906–88, US)
Galway (James; 1939– , Northern Irish)
Gibson (Sir Alexander; 1926–95, Scottish)
Glover (Jane; 1949– , English)
Groves (Sir Charles; 1915–92, English)
Heinze (Sir Bernard; 1894–1982, Australian)
Hickox (Richard; 1948–2008, English)
Jochum (Eugen; 1902–87, German)
Levine (James; 1943– , US)
Maazel (Lorin; 1930– , US)
Maazel (Lorin; 1930– , US)
Mahler (Gustav; 1860–1911, Czech/
  Austrian)
Previn (André; 1929– , German/US)
Rattle (Sir Simon; 1955– , English)
Reiner (Fritz; 1888–1963, US)
Sacher (Paul; 1906–99, Swiss)
Volkov (Ilan; 1976– , Israeli)
Wagner (Siegfried; 1869–1930, German)
Walter (Bruno; 1876–1962, German/US)

07 Bainton (Edgar; 1880–1956, English)
Beecham (Sir Thomas; 1879–1961, English)
Fiedler (Arthur; 1894–1979, US)
Gergiev (Valery; 1953– , Russian)
Giulini (Carlo Maria; 1914–2005, Italian)
Godfrey (Sir Dan; 1868–1939, English)
Haitink (Bernard; 1929– , Dutch)

Karajan (Herbert von; 1908–89, Austrian)
Kleiber (Erich; 1890–1956, Argentine)
Knussen (Oliver; 1952– , English)
Kubelik (Rafael; 1914–96, Swiss)
Lambert (Constant; 1905–51, English)
Maderna (Bruno; 1920–73, Italian)
Malcolm (George; 1917–97, English)
Monteux (Pierre; 1875–1964, US)
Nicolai (Otto; 1810–49, German)
Nikisch (Arthur; 1855–1922, Hungarian)
Ormandy (Eugene; 1899–1985, US)
Richter (Hans; 1843–1916, Hungarian)
Sargent (Sir Malcolm; 1895–1967, English)
Smetana (Bedrich; 1824–84, Czech)
Strauss (Johann, the Elder; 1804–49, Austrian)
Strauss (Johann, the Younger; 1825–99, Austrian)
Strauss (Richard; 1864–1949, German)
Swensen (Joseph; 1960– , US)

08 Atherton (David; 1944– , English)
Goossens (Eugène; 1845–1906, Belgian)
Goossens (Sir Eugène; 1893–1962, English)
Henschel (Sir George; 1850–1934, Polish/British)
Jurowski (Vladimir; 1972– , Russian)
Ketèlbey (Albert William; 1875–1959, English)
Marriner (Sir Neville; 1924– , English)
Panufnik (Sir Andrej; 1914–94, Polish/British)
Tuckwell (Barry; 1931– , Australian)
Zukerman (Pinchas; 1948– , Israeli)

09 Ashkenazy (Vladimir; 1937– , Russian/Icelandic)
Barenboim (Daniel; 1942– , Argentine/Israeli)
Bernstein (Leonard; 1918–90, US)
Boulanger (Nadia; 1887–1979, French)
Järnefelt (Armas; 1869–1958, Swedish)
Klemperer (Otto; 1885–1973, German)
Leinsdorf (Erich; 1912–93, US)
Mackerras (Sir Charles; 1925– , Australian)
Mravinsky (Yevgeni; 1903–88, Russian)
Runnicles (Donald; 1954– , Scottish)
Schönberg (Arnold; 1874–1951, Austrian/US)
Stokowski (Leopold; 1882–1977, English/US)
Tortelier (Paul; 1914–90, French)
Toscanini (Arturo; 1867–1957, Italian)
Zemlinsky (Alexander von; 1871–1942, Austrian)

10 Barbirolli (Sir John; 1899–1970, English)
Schoenberg (Arnold; 1874–1951, Austrian/US)
Villa-Lobos (Heitor; 1887–1959, Brazilian)

11 Furtwängler (Wilhelm; 1886–1954, German)
Lutoslawski (Witold; 1913–94, Polish)
Mitropoulos (Dimitri; 1896–1960, US)
Weingartner (Felix; 1863–1942, Austrian)

12 Koussevitzky (Serge; 1874–1951, Russian/US)
Rostropovich (Mstislav; 1927–2007, Russian)
Shostakovich (Maxim; 1938– , US)

See also **musician**

confectionery *see* **sweet**

constellation

Constellations include:

03 Ara	Harp	Draco
Cup	Keel	Eagle
Fly	Lion	Easel
Fox	Lynx	Hydra
Leo	Lyra	Indus
Net	Pavo	Lepus
Ram	Swan	Level
04 Apus	Vela	Libra
Bull	Wolf	Lupus
Crab	**05** Altar	Mensa
Crow	Aries	Musca
Crux	Arrow	Norma
Dove	Cetus	Orion
Grus	Clock	Pyxis
Hare	Crane	Sails

Table
Twins
Virgo
Whale

06 Antlia
Aquila
Archer
Auriga
Boötes
Caelum
Cancer
Carina
Chisel
Corvus
Crater
Cygnus
Dorado
Dragon
Fishes
Fornax
Gemini
Hydrus
Indian
Lizard
Octans
Octant
Pictor
Pisces
Puppis
Scales
Scutum
Shield
Taurus
Toucan
Tucana
Virgin
Volans

07 Air Pump
Centaur
Cepheus
Columba

Dolphin
Furnace
Giraffe
Lacerta
Peacock
Pegasus
Perseus
Phoenix
Sagltta
Sea Goat
Serpens
Serpent
Sextans
Sextant
Unicorn

08 Aquarius
Circinus
Equuleus
Eridanus
Great Dog
Hercules
Herdsman
Leo Minor
Scorpion
Scorpius
Sculptor
Triangle

09 Andromeda
Capricorn
Centaurus
Chameleon
Compasses
Delphinus
Great Bear
Little Dog
Monoceros
Ophiuchus
Reticulum
Swordfish
Telescope
Ursa Major

Ursa Minor
Vulpecula

10 Canis Major
Canis Minor
Cassiopeia
Chamaeleon
Charioteer
Flying Fish
Horologium
Little Bear
Little Lion
Microscope
Sea Serpent
Ship's Stern
Triangulum
Water Snake

11 Capricornus
Hunting Dogs
Little Horse
Sagittarius
Telescopium
Water Bearer
Winged Horse

12 Microscopium
Southern Fish

13 Berenice's Hair
Canes Venatici
Coma Berenices
Northern Crown
River Eridanus
Serpent Bearer
Southern Cross
Southern Crown

14 Bird of Paradise
Camelopardalis
Corona Borealis

15 Corona Australis
Mariner's Compass
Piscis Austrinus

See also **star**

container

Containers include:

03 bag
bin
box
can
cup
jar
jug
keg
mug
pan

pot
tin
tub
urn
vat

04 bath
bowl
case
cask
dish

drum
pack
pail
sack
tank
tube
vase
well

05 basin
chest

churn
crate
crock
glass
purse
trunk

06 barrel
basket
beaker
bottle

bucket	packet	dustbin	cylinder
carton	punnet	pannier	suitcase
casket	teapot	pitcher	tea caddy
hamper	trough	tumbler	tea chest
kettle	tureen	**08** canister	waste bin
locker	**07** cistern	cauldron	**09** water-butt

See also **bag**; **bottle**; **wine**

continent

Continents of the world:

04 Asia	**07** America	**11** Australasia
06 Africa	Oceania	**12** North America
Europe	**10** Antarctica	South America

contraceptive

Contraceptives include:

03 cap	**06** condom	the pill	**10** Lippes loop
IUD	johnny	**08** Dutch cap	protective
04 coil	rubber	minipill	**11** Depo-Provera®
IUCD	sheath	**09** birth pill	**12** female condom
loop	Vimule®	diaphragm	French letter
pill	**07** Femidom®	prolactin	prophylactic
safe	johnnie		

convent *see* **religious order**

cookery

Cooking methods include:

03 fry	grill	flambé	scramble
04 bake	poach	pan-fry	**09** casserole
boil	roast	simmer	char-grill
sear	sauté	**07** deep-fry	fricassee
stew	steam	parboil	microwave
05 broil	sweat	stir-fry	oven-roast
brown	toast	**08** barbecue	spit-roast
curry	**06** braise	pot-roast	**10** flame-grill
	coddle		

Cookery utensils include:

03 pan	bun tin	stoner
wok	grater	tureen
04 fork	juicer	zester
05 corer	karahi	**07** blender
ladle	mincer	cake tin
mouli	mortar	cleaver
sieve	peeler	cocotte
tongs	pestle	flan tin
whisk	shears	grinder
06 baster	sifter	loaf tin
	skewer	milk pan

ramekin
skillet
skimmer
spatula
steamer
terrine

08 blini pan
breadbin
colander
crêpe pan
cruet set
egg-timer
grill pan
ham stand
herb mill
mandolin
pie plate
saucepan
scissors
stockpot
tea caddy
teaspoon
wine rack

09 bain marie
blowtorch
brochette
can-opener
casserole
corkscrew
dough hook
egg slicer
fish knife
fish slice
fondue set
frying pan
gravy boat
mezzaluna
muffin tin
paella pan
pie funnel
processor
punch bowl
sharpener
soup spoon
spice rack
toast rack

10 breadboard

bread knife
butter dish
cook's knife
egg coddler
egg poacher
fish kettle
jelly mould
knife block
liquidizer
mixing bowl
nutcracker
pasta ladle
pasta maker
pepper mill
quiche dish
rice cooker
rolling pin
slow cooker
steak knife
storage jar
table knife
tablespoon
tea infuser
waffle iron
wine cooler

11 baking sheet
boning knife
butter knife
cheese board
cheese knife
chestnut pan
cooling rack
garlic press
lemon reamer
melon baller
oil drizzler
omelette pan
oyster knife
paring knife
pastry board
pastry brush
potato ricer
roasting pan
sandwich tin
soufflé dish
tea strainer
thermometer

tomato knife
wooden spoon

12 biscuit press
bottle opener
butter curler
canelle knife
carving knife
cheese slicer
deep-fat fryer
dessert spoon
egg separator
fish tweezers
flour dredger
heat diffuser
icing syringe
madeleine tin
measuring jug
nutmeg grater
palette knife
pastry cutter
potato masher
pudding basin
pudding mould
salad spinner
serving spoon
yoghurt maker

13 butcher's block
chopping-board
cocktail knife
draining spoon
food processor
ice-cream scoop
Kitchen Devils®
kitchen scales
lemon squeezer
preserving pan

14 gravy separator
measuring spoon
pressure cooker
straining spoon
vegetable brush
vegetable knife

15 asparagus cooker
grapefruit knife
meat thermometer
mortar and pestle
sharpening steel

Cookery styles include:

04 Thai

05 Greek
halal
Irish
mezze
rural
tapas

vegan
Welsh

06 French
fusion
German
Indian
kosher

Tex-Mex

07 African
British
Chinese
Eastern
English
Italian

Mexican
seafood
Spanish
Turkish

08 American
fast food
Japanese

Scottish
09 Cantonese
Caribbean
Malaysian
Provençal

10 cordon bleu
Far Eastern
gluten-free
Indonesian
Pacific Rim

vegetarian
11 home cooking
lean cuisine
12 haute cuisine

13 Mediterranean
Middle Eastern
14 cuisine minceur
15 nouvelle cuisine

Foreign cookery and food terms include:

03 jus
04 dhal
ghee
meze
miso
naan
puri
roux
sake
taco
05 balti
bhaji
blini
cajun
crêpe
gelée
halva
humus
keema
korai
korma
kulfi
mirin
murgh
penne
phall
pilaf
pilau
purée
raita
sauté
shoyu
sushi
tapas
tarka
tikka
torte
06 anelli
bargar
bhoona
bisque
blintz
bonito

byesar
canapé
coulis
dim sum
ditali
eliche
flambé
fondue
hoisin
hummus
kibbeh
Kung Po
masala
moglai
paella
pakora
paneer
panini
pullao
ragoût
samosa
tagine
tamari
wasabi
wonton
07 baklava
biriani
brinjal
buñuelo
dhansak
fusilli
gemelli
gnocchi
granite
gratiné
hoummos
lumache
merguez
nam prik
pak choi
parfait
pasanda
piccata
pierogi

polenta
ravioli
ripiene
risotto
sag aloo
sashimi
schlada
seviche
soufflé
tempura
terrine
timbale
tostada
08 au gratin
bouillon
briouate
brunoise
bucatini
chupatti
couscous
crostini
dolmades
escalope
farfalle
gazpacho
jalfrezi
julienne
kleftiko
linguini
lumaconi
macaroni
mesquite
moussaka
shashlik
sukiyaki
tandoori
tapenade
teriyaki
tonkatsu
tortilla
tzatziki
umeboshi
usukuchi
vindaloo

yaki-nori
yakitori
zarzuela
09 antipasto
bain marie
ballotine
carbonara
charmoula
cochiglie
colcannon
concassée
enchilada
entrecôte
fricassée
jambalaya
pastitsio
picadillo
rogan josh
spaghetti
10 avgolemono
cacciatore
cannelloni
fettuccine
feuilletté
jardinière
nasi goreng
parmigiana
quesadilla
salsa verde
sauerkraut
11 beurre manié
chimichanga
garam masala
hors d'oeuvre
katsuobushi
orecchiette
panch phoran
ratatouille
smorgåsbord
tagliatelli
12 taramasalata
13 cresti di gallo
14 capelli d'angelo

Cookery terms include:

03 Aga
dip

gut
hob

ice
04 chef

chop
cook

cure	grate	fillet	**08** cookbook
dice	knead	fondue	devilled
mash	mince	infuse	marinade
oven	mould	kosher	marinate
rise	press	leaven	preserve
whip	purée	recipe	**09** antipasto
05 baste	score	reduce	percolate
brown	shave	season	reduction
carve	smoke	spread	tenderize
chill	steep	**07** de-scale	**10** caramelize
chump	stuff	garnish	**11** amuse bouche
curry	whisk	nibbles	hors d'oeuvre
daube	**06** batter	proving	
devil	blanch	starter	
dress	de-bone	tandoor	
glaze	entrée	topping	

See also **chef**; **curry**; **food**

corm *see* **bulb**

cosmetics

Cosmetics include:

05 rouge	lip liner	nail polish
toner	lipstick	**11** greasepaint
07 blusher	panstick	loose powder
bronzer	**09** concealer	moisturizer
mascara	eye shadow	nail varnish
perfume	face cream	**13** eyebrow pencil
08 cleanser	**10** eyelash dye	pancake make-up
eyeliner	face powder	pressed powder
face mask	foundation	**14** false eyelashes
face pack	kohl pencil	
lip gloss	maquillage	

cotton

Cotton fabrics include:

04 aida	chintz	buckram
duck	coutil	challis
jean	dhooti	duvetyn
05 chino	diaper	fustian
denim	dimity	galatea
dhoti	humhum	gingham
drill	jersey	jaconet
jaspé	khanga	kitenge
jeans	madras	Mexican
kanga	moreen	nankeen
piqué	muslin	percale
surat	nankin	printer
toile	Oxford	silesia
06 Bengal	pongee	**08** chambray
calico	sateen	corduroy
canvas	T-cloth	coutille
	07 batiste	cretonne

drilling
frocking
lambskin
marcella
nainsook
organdie
osnaburg
shantung
thickset
09 cottonade

huckaback
longcloth
percaline
sailcloth
satin jean
swans-down
velveteen
10 Balbriggan
candlewick
monk's cloth

seersucker
winceyette
11 cheesecloth
flannelette
mutton cloth
nettle-cloth
Oxford cloth
sponge cloth
13 casement cloth

council *see* **United Kingdom**

country

Countries of the world include:

03 UAE
USA
04 Chad
Cuba
Fiji
Iran
Iraq
Laos
Mali
Oman
Peru
Togo
05 Benin
Chile
China
Congo
Egypt
Gabon
Ghana
Haiti
India
Italy
Japan
Kenya
Libya
Malta
Nauru
Nepal
Niger
Palau
Qatar
Samoa
Spain
Sudan
Syria
Tonga
Wales
Yemen
06 Angola
Belize

Bhutan
Brazil
Canada
Cyprus
France
Greece
Guinea
Guyana
Israel
Jordan
Kosovo
Kuwait
Latvia
Malawi
Mexico
Monaco
Norway
Panama
Poland
Russia
Serbia
Rwanda
Sweden
Taiwan
Turkey
Tuvalu
Uganda
Zambia
07 Albania
Algeria
Andorra
Armenia
Austria
Bahrain
Belarus
Belgium
Bolivia
Burundi
Comoros
Croatia

Denmark
Ecuador
England
Eritrea
Estonia
Finland
Georgia
Germany
Grenada
Hungary
Iceland
Ireland
Jamaica
Lebanon
Lesotho
Liberia
Moldova
Morocco
Myanmar
Namibia
Nigeria
Romania
Senegal
Somalia
St Lucia
Tunisia
Ukraine
Uruguay
Vanuatu
Vietnam
08 Barbados
Botswana
Bulgaria
Cambodia
Cameroon
Colombia
Djibouti
Dominica
Ethiopia
Honduras

Kiribati
Malaysia
Maldives
Mongolia
Pakistan
Paraguay
Portugal
Scotland
Slovakia
Slovenia
Sri Lanka
Suriname
Tanzania
Thailand
Zimbabwe

09 Argentina
Australia
Cape Verde
Costa Rica
East Timor
Guatemala
Indonesia
Lithuania
Macedonia
Mauritius
Nicaragua
San Marino
Singapore
Swaziland
The Gambia
Venezuela

10 Azerbaijan
Bangladesh
El Salvador
Kazakhstan
Kyrgyzstan
Luxembourg
Madagascar
Mauritania
Montenegro
Mozambique
New Zealand
North Korea
Seychelles
South Korea
Tajikistan
The Bahamas
Uzbekistan

11 Afghanistan
Burkina Faso
Côte d'Ivoire
Philippines
Saudi Arabia
Sierra Leone
South Africa
Switzerland
Vatican City

12 Great Britain
Guinea-Bissau
Turkmenistan
Turkmenistan

United States
13 Czech Republic
Liechtenstein
United Kingdom
Western Sahara
14 Papua New Guinea
Solomon Islands
The Netherlands
15 Marshall Islands
Northern Ireland
St Kitts and Nevis
16 Brunei Darussalam
Equatorial Guinea
17 Antigua and Barbuda
Dominican Republic
Trinidad and Tobago
18 São Tomé and Príncipe
United Arab Emirates
20 Bosnia and Herzegovina
21 United States of America
22 Central African Republic
25 St Vincent and the
Grenadines
27 Federated States of
Micronesia
28 Democratic Republic of the
Congo

Country codes include:

03 ABW (Aruba)
AFG (Afghanistan)
AGO (Angola)
AIA (Anguilla)
ALB (Albania)
AND (Andorra)
ANT (Netherlands Antilles)
ARE (United Arab Emirates)
ARG (Argentina)
ARM (Armenia)
ASM (American Samoa)
ATA (Antarctica)
ATF (French Southern and Antarctic
　Territories)
ATG (Antigua and Barbuda)
AUS (Australia)
AUT (Austria)
AZE (Azerbaijan)
BDI (Burundi)
BEL (Belgium)
BEN (Benin)
BFA (Burkina Faso)
BGD (Bangladesh)
BGR (Bulgaria)

BHR (Bahrain)
BHS (The Bahamas)
BIH (Bosnia and Herzegovina)
BLR (Belarus)
BLZ (Belize)
BMU (Bermuda)
BOL (Bolivia)
BRA (Brazil)
BRB (Barbados)
BRN (Brunei Darussalam)
BTN (Bhutan)
BVT (Bouvet Island)
BWA (Botswana)
CAF (Central African Republic)
CAN (Canada)
CCK (Cocos Islands)
CHE (Switzerland)
CHL (Chile)
CHN (China)
CIV (Côte d'Ivoire)
CMR (Cameroon)
COD (Democratic Republic of the Congo)
COG (Congo)
COK (Cook Islands)

COL (Colombia)
COM (Comoros)
CPV (Cape Verde)
CRI (Costa Rica)
CUB (Cuba)
CXR (Christmas Island)
CYM (Cayman Islands)
CYP (Cyprus)
CZE (Czech Republic)
DEU (Germany)
DJI (Djibouti)
DMA (Dominica)
DNK (Denmark)
DOM (Dominican Republic)
DZA (Algeria)
ECU (Ecuador)
EGY (Egypt)
ERI (Eritrea)
ESH (Western Sahara)
ESP (Spain)
EST (Estonia)
ETH (Ethiopia)
FIN (Finland)
FJI (Fiji)
FLK (Falkland Islands)
FRA (France)
FRO (Faroe Islands)
FSM (Federated States of Micronesia)
GAB (Gabon)
GBR (United Kingdom)
GEO (Georgia)
GHA (Ghana)
GIB (Gibraltar)
GIN (Guinea)
GLP (Guadeloupe)
GMB (The Gambia)
GNB (Guinea-Bissau)
GNQ (Equatorial Guinea)
GRC (Greece)
GRD (Grenada)
GRL (Greenland)
GTM (Guatemala)
GUF (French Guiana)
GUM (Guam)
GUY (Guyana)
HGK (Hong Kong)
HND (Honduras)
HRV (Croatia)
HTI (Haiti)
HUN (Hungary)
IDN (Indonesia)
IMN (Isle of Man)
IND (India)
IOT (British Indian Ocean Territory)
IRL (Ireland)
IRN (Iran)
IRQ (Iraq)
ISL (Iceland)

ISR (Israel)
ITA (Italy)
JAM (Jamaica)
JOR (Jordan)
JPN (Japan)
KAZ (Kazakhstan)
KEN (Kenya)
KGZ (Kyrgyzstan)
KHM (Cambodia)
KIR (Kiribati)
KNA (St Kitts and Nevis)
KOR (South Korea)
KWT (Kuwait)
LAO (Laos)
LBN (Lebanon)
LBR (Liberia)
LBY (Libya)
LCA (St Lucia)
LIE (Liechtenstein)
LKA (Sri Lanka)
LSO (Lesotho)
LTU (Lithuania)
LUX (Luxembourg)
LVA (Latvia)
MAC (Macao)
MAR (Morocco)
MCO (Monaco)
MDA (Moldova)
MDG (Madagascar)
MDV (Maldives)
MEX (Mexico)
MHL (Marshall Islands)
MKD (Macedonia)
MLI (Mali)
MLT (Malta)
MMR (Myanmar)
MNE (Montenegro)
MNG (Mongolia)
MOZ (Mozambique)
MRT (Mauritania)
MSR (Montserrat)
MTQ (Martinique)
MUS (Mauritius)
MWI (Malawi)
MYS (Malaysia)
MYT (Mayotte)
NAM (Namibia)
NCL (New Caledonia)
NER (Niger)
NFK (Norfolk Island)
NGA (Nigeria)
NIC (Nicaragua)
NIU (Niue)
NLD (The Netherlands)
NOR (Norway)
NPL (Nepal)
NRU (Nauru)
NZL (New Zealand)

OMN (Oman)
PAK (Pakistan)
PAN (Panama)
PCN (Pitcairn Island)
PER (Peru)
PHL (Philippines)
PLW (Palau)
PNG (Papua New Guinea)
POL (Poland)
PRI (Puerto Rico)
PRK (North Korea)
PRT (Portugal)
PRY (Paraguay)
PYF (French Polynesia)
QAT (Qatar)
REU (Réunion)
ROU (Romania)
RUS (Russia)
RWA (Rwanda)
SAU (Saudi Arabia)
SDN (Sudan)
SEN (Senegal)
SGP (Singapore)
SHN (St Helena)
SJM (Svalbard and Jan Mayen Islands)
SLB (Solomon Islands)
SLE (Sierra Leone)
SLV (El Salvador)
SMR (San Marino)
SOM (Somalia)
SPM (St Pierre and Miquelon)
SRB (Serbia)
STP (São Tomé and Príncipe)
SUR (Suriname)
SVK (Slovakia)
SVN (Slovenia)
SWE (Sweden)

SWZ (Swaziland)
SYC (Seychelles)
SYR (Syria)
TCA (Turks and Caicos Islands)
TCD (Chad)
TGO (Togo)
THA (Thailand)
TJK (Tajikistan)
TKL (Tokelau)
TKM (Turkmenistan)
TLS (East Timor)
TON (Tonga)
TTO (Trinidad and Tobago)
TUN (Tunisia)
TUR (Turkey)
TUV (Tuvalu)
TWN (Taiwan)
TZA (United Republic of Tanzania)
UGA (Uganda)
UKR (Ukraine)
URY (Uruguay)
USA (United States of America)
UZB (Uzbekistan)
VAT (Vatican City)
VCT (St Vincent and the Grenadines)
VEN (Venezuela)
VGB (British Virgin Islands)
VIR (United States Virgin Islands)
VNM (Vietnam)
VUT (Vanuatu)
WLF (Wallis and Futuna)
WSM (Samoa)
YEM (Yemen)
ZAF (South Africa)
ZMB (Zambia)
ZWE (Zimbabwe)

Former country names include:

04 Siam (Thailand)
USSR (Armenia/Azerbaijan/Belarus/
Estonia/Georgia/Kazakhstan/Kyrgyzstan/
Latvia/Lithuania/Moldova/Russia/
Tajikistan/Turkmenistan/Ukraine/
Uzbekistan)

05 Burma (Myanmar)
Zaire (Democratic Republic of the Congo)

06 Bengal (Bangladesh)
Ceylon (Sri Lanka)
Persia (Iran)
Urundi (Burundi)

07 Dahomey (Benin)
Formosa (Taiwan)

08 Rhodesia (Zimbabwe)

09 Abyssinia (Ethiopia)
Indochina (Cambodia/Vietnam)

Kampuchea (Cambodia)
Nyasaland (Malawi)

10 Basutoland (Lesotho)
Ivory Coast (Côte d'Ivoire)
Senegambia (The Gambia/Senegal)
Tanganyika (Tanzania)
Upper Volta (Burkina Faso)
Yugoslavia (Bosnia and Herzegovina/
Croatia/Macedonia/Montenegro/Serbia/
Slovenia)

11 Dutch Guiana (Suriname)
French Sudan (Mali)
New Hebrides (Vanuatu)
Ubangi Shari (Central African Republic)

12 Bechuanaland (Botswana)
French Guinea (Guinea)
Ruanda-Urundi (Burundi/Rwanda)

13 British Guiana (Guyana)
Ellice Islands (Tuvalu)
Khmer Republic (Cambodia)
Spanish Guinea (Equatorial Guinea)
Spanish Sahara (Western Sahara)
Trucial States (United Arab Emirates)
14 Czechoslovakia (Czech Republic/Slovakia)

French Togoland (Togo)
Gilbert Islands (Kiribati)
15 British Honduras (Belize)
British Togoland (Ghana)
Dutch East Indies (Indonesia)
South West Africa (Namibia)

Local country names include:

03 Lao (Laos)
04 Éire (Ireland)
Misr (Egypt)
'Uman (Oman)
Viti (Fiji)
05 Belau (Palau)
Eesti (Estonia)
Ellas (Greece)
Ertra (Eritrea)
Nihon (Japan)
Norge (Norway)
Suomi (Finland)
Tchad (Chad)
06 België (Belgium)
Bharat (India)
Brasil (Brazil)
Chosun (North Korea)
España (Spain)
Guinée (Guinea)
Guyane (French Guiana)
Hanguk (South Korea)
Ísland (Iceland)
Italia (Italy)
Kibris (Cyprus)
Kipros (Cyprus)
Lubnan (Lebanon)
México (Mexico)
Naoero (Nauru)
Nippon (Japan)
Polska (Poland)
Srbija (Serbia)
Suisse (Switzerland)
Svizra (Switzerland)
T'ai-wan (Taiwan)
07 Algérie (Algeria)
Al-Urdun (Jordan)
Al-Yaman (Yemen)
As-Sudan (Sudan)
Comores (Comoros)
Danmark (Denmark)
Druk Yul (Bhutan)
Føroyar (Faroe Islands)
Latvija (Latvia)
Lietuva (Lithuania)
Rossiya (Russia)
Schweiz (Switzerland)
Suriyah (Syria)

Sverige (Sweden)
Türkiye (Turkey)
Ukraïna (Ukraine)
Viêt Nam (Vietnam)
08 Al-Jaza'ir (Algeria)
Al-Kuwayt (Kuwait)
Aotearoa (New Zealand)
Belgique (Belgium)
Cameroun (Cameroon)
Crna Gora (Montenegro)
Grønland (Greenland)
Hayastan (Armenia)
Hrvatska (Croatia)
Ityop'iya (Ethiopia)
Svizzera (Switzerland)
Tunisiya (Tunisia)
Zhong Guo (China)
09 Al-Bahrayn (Bahrain)
Al Maghrib (Morocco)
Balgarija (Bulgaria)
Cabo Verde (Cape Verde)
Færøerne (Faroe Islands)
Kâmpuchéa (Cambodia)
Mongol Uls (Mongolia)
Pilipinas (Philippines)
Qazaqstan (Kazakhstan)
Shqipëria (Albania)
Slovenija (Slovenia)
Slovensko (Slovakia)
10 Azerbaycan (Azerbaijan)
Makedonija (Macedonia)
Mauritanie (Mauritania)
Moçambique (Mozambique)
Muritaniya (Mauritania)
Österreich (Austria)
Özbekiston (Uzbekistan)
Sak'art'velo (Georgia)
Soomaaliya (Somalia)
Timor-Leste (East Timor)
11 Deutschland (Germany)
Guiné-Bissau (Guinea-Bissau)
Prathet Thai (Thailand)
12 Madagasikara (Madagascar)
Magyarorszag (Hungary)
Timor Lorosa'e (East Timor)
13 Dhivehi Raajje (Maldives)

14 Ceská Republika (Czech Republic)
   Dawlat Israqa'il (Israel)
   Die Nederlanden (The Netherlands)

   Medinat Yisra'el (Israel)
15 Kalaallit Nunaat (Greenland)
   Umbuso weSwatini (Kingdom of Swaziland)

See also **Africa; The Americas; Arab League; Asia; Australasia; Australia; Austria; Belgium; Canada; China; CIS; commonwealth; Czech Republic; Denmark; dependency; Europe; Finland; France; Germany; Greece; India; Ireland; Italy; Japan; Mexico; NATO; The Netherlands; New Zealand; Norway; OPEC; Portugal; Russia; Spain; Sweden; Switzerland; United Kingdom; United Nations; United States of America**

country and western

Country and western musicians and singers include:

04 Cash (Johnny; 1932–2003, US)
   Lynn (Loretta; 1935– , US)

05 Cline (Patsy; 1932–63, US)
   Jones (George; 1931– , US)
   Pride (Charley; 1938– , US)
   Raitt (Bonnie; 1949– , US)

06 Atkins (Chet; 1924–2001, US)
   Brooks (Garth; 1962– , US)
   Denver (John; 1943–97, US)
   Harris (Emmylou; 1947– , US)
   Lovett (Lyle; 1956– , US)

Nelson (Willie; 1933– , US)
Parton (Dolly; 1946– , US)
Rogers (Kenny; 1938– , US)

07 Francis (Connie; 1938– , US)
   Haggard (Merle; 1937– , US)
   Wynette (Tammy; 1942–98, US)

08 Griffith (Nanci; 1954– , US)
   Jennings (Waylon; 1937–2002, US)
   Ronstadt (Linda; 1946– , US)
   Williams (Hank; 1923–53, US)

county *see* **town; United Kingdom**

course *see* **golf**

court

Courts include:

04 High	police	kangaroo	Common Bench
Lyon	record	Requests	Common Pleas
moot	**07** appeals	superior	High Justice
open	assizes	tribunal	magistrates'
05 burgh	borough	**09** children's	police-court
civil	circuit	Exchequer	Prerogative
Crown	Diplock	Faculties	small claims
prize	divorce	municipal	**12** court-martial
trial	federal	Old Bailey	House of Lords
World	justice	Piepowder	Privy Council
youth	Probate	the Arches	**13** first instance
06 appeal	Session	**10** Commercial	**14** Criminal Appeal
Arches	sheriff	commissary	High Commission
church	Supreme	Divisional	High Justiciary
claims	**08** coroner's	Piepowders	**15** Central Criminal
county	criminal	Protection	European Justice
family	district	**11** Arbitration	Lord Chancellor's
Honour	juvenile		

See also **law**

Coward, Sir Noël (1899–1973)

Significant works include:

08 *Hay Fever* (1925)
    Operette (1938)
    Sail Away (1961)
09 *Cavalcade* (1931)
    Quadrille (1952)
    The Vortex (1924)
10 *Easy Virtue* (1926)
    Sigh No More (1945)
11 *Bitter Sweet* (1929)

12 *Blithe Spirit* (1941)
    Fallen Angels (1925)
    Private Lives (1930)
13 *Words and Music* (1932)
14 *Brief Encounter* (1945)
    In Which We Serve (1942)
    Nude With Violin (1956)
    Peace in Our Time (1947)
    Relative Values (1951)

    This Happy Breed (1939)
15 *Design for Living* (1933)
    I'll Leave It to You (1920)
    Present Laughter (1939)
    This Year of Grace (1928)
17 *Conversation Piece* (1934)
    Waiting in the Wings (1960)

Significant characters include:

05 Bliss (David)
    Bliss (Judith)
    Bliss (Simon)
    Bliss (Sorel)
    Chase (Elyot)
    Chase (Sybil)
    Clara
06 Arcati (Madame)

Harvey (Dr Alec)
Jesson (Laura)
Prynne (Amanda)
Prynne (Victor)
Tyrell (Sandy)
07 Arundel (Myra)
    Coryton (Jackie)
    Gibbons (Ethel)

Gibbons (Frank)
Kinross (Captain)
08 Greatham (Richard)
09 Condomine (Charles)
    Condomine (Elvira)
    Condomine (Ruth)
    Lancaster (Florence)
    Lancaster (Nicky)

craft *see* **art**

cricket

Cricket teams include:

04 Kent
05 Essex
06 Durham
    Surrey
    Sussex
08 Somerset
    Victoria
09 Glamorgan

Hampshire
Middlesex
Yorkshire
10 Derbyshire
    Lancashire
    Queensland
12 Warwickshire
13 New South Wales

14 Leicestershire
    South Australia
    Worcestershire
15 Gloucestershire
    Nottinghamshire
16 Northamptonshire
    Western Australia

Cricket team nicknames include:

05 Bears (Warwickshire)
    Blues (New South Wales)
    Bulls (Queensland)
    Foxes (Leicestershire)
    Hawks (Hampshire)
06 Eagles (Essex)
    Royals (Worcestershire)
    Sabres (Somerset)
    Sharks (Sussex)
    Tigers (Tasmania)
07 Dragons (Glamorgan)
    Dynamos (Durham)

    Outlaws (Nottinghamshire)
    Phoenix (Yorkshire)
08 Phantoms (Derbyshire)
    Redbacks (South Australia)
    Warriors (Western Australia)
09 Brown Caps (Surrey)
    Crusaders (Middlesex)
    Lightning (Lancashire)
    Spitfires (Kent)
10 Gladiators (Gloucestershire)
    Steelbacks (Northamptonshire)
11 Bushrangers (Victoria)

Cricketers and associated figures include:

03 Dev (Kapil; 1959– , Indian)
Fry (C B; 1872–1956, English)

04 Ames (Les; 1905–90, English)
Bedi (Bishen; 1946– , Indian)
Bird (Harold 'Dickie'; 1933– , English)
Hall (Wes; 1937– , Barbadian)
Hick (Graeme; 1966– , Zimbabwean/
British)
Lara (Brian; 1969– , Trinidadian)
Lock (Tony; 1929–95, English)
Lord (Thomas; 1755–1832, English)

05 Allen (Sir Gubby; 1902–89, English)
Amiss (Dennis; 1943– , English)
Crowe (Martin; 1962– , New Zealand)
Evans (Godfrey; 1920–99, English)
Gibbs (Lance; 1934– , Guyanese)
Gooch (Graham; 1953– , English)
Gough (Darren; 1970– , English)
Gower (David; 1957– , English)
Grace (W G; 1848–1915, English)
Greig (Tony; 1946– , South African/British)
Healy (Ian; 1964– , Australian)
Hobbs (Sir Jack; 1882–1963, English)
Knott (Alan; 1946– , English)
Laker (Jim; 1922–86, English)
Lawry (Bill; 1937– , Australian)
Lloyd (Clive; 1944– , Guyanese/British)
Marsh (Rodney; 1947– , Australian)
Pilch (Fuller; 1804–70, English)
Walsh (Courtney; 1962– , Jamaican)
Warne (Shane; 1969– , Australian)
Waugh (Mark; 1965– , Australian)
Waugh (Steve; 1965– , Australian)

06 Arlott (John; 1914–91, English)
Bailey (Trevor; 1923– , English)
Benaud (Richie; 1930– , Australian)
Border (Allan; 1955– , Australian)
Botham (Ian; 1955– , English)
Cronje (Hansie; 1969–2002, South
African)
Dexter (Ted; 1935– , English)
Donald (Allan; 1966– , South African)
Dravid (Rahul; 1973– , Indian)
Edrich (Bill; 1916–86, English)
Garner (Joel; 1952– , Barbadian)
Hadlee (Sir Richard; 1948– , New Zealand)
Haynes (Desmond; 1956– , Barbadian)
Hutton (Sir Len; 1916–90, English)
Jessop (Gilbert; 1874–1955, English)
Lillee (Dennis; 1949– , Australian)
Miller (Keith; 1919–2004, Australian)
Rhodes (Wilfred; 1877–1973, English)
Sobers (Sir Garfield; 1936– , Barbadian)
Thorpe (Graham; 1969– , English)
Titmus (Fred; 1932– , English)

Turner (Glenn; 1947– , New Zealand)
Warner (Sir Pelham 'Plum'; 1873–1963,
Trinidadian/British)

07 Ambrose (Curtley; 1963– , Antiguan)
Boycott (Geoffrey; 1940– , English)
Bradman (Sir Don; 1908–2001, Australian)
Compton (Denis; 1918–97, English)
Cowdrey (Colin, Lord; 1932–2000,
English)
Denness (Mike; 1940– , Scottish)
De Silva (Aravinda; 1965– , Sri Lankan)
Gatting (Mike; 1957– , English)
Hammond (Wally; 1903–65, English)
Holding (Michael; 1954– , Jamaican)
Hussain (Nasser; 1968– , Indian/British)
Jardine (Douglas; 1900–58, English)
Larwood (Harold; 1904–95, English)
McGrath (Glenn; 1970– , Australian)
Pataudi (Mansur Ali, Nawab of, Jnr;
1941– , Indian)
Pollock (Graeme; 1944– , South African)
Roberts (Andy; 1951– , Antiguan)
Simpson (Bobby; 1936– , Australian)
Stewart (Alec; 1963– , English)
Thomson (Jeff; 1950– , Australian)
Trueman (Fred; 1931–2006, English)
Tufnell (Philip; 1966– , English)
Worrell (Frank; 1924–67, Barbadian)

08 Atherton (Michael; 1968– , English)
Chappell (Greg; 1948– , Australian)
Chappell (Ian; 1943– , Australian)
Flintoff (Andrew; 1977– , English)
Gavaskar (Sunil; 1949– , Indian)
Johnston (Brian; 1912–94, English)
Kapil Dev (1959– , Indian)
Lindwall (Ray; 1921–96, Australian)
Marshall (Malcolm; 1958–99, Barbadian)
Richards (Barry; 1945– , South African)
Richards (Sir Vivian; 1952– , Antiguan)

09 deFreitas (Phillip; 1966– , English)
D'Oliveira (Basil; 1931– , South African/
British)
Greenidge (Gordon; 1951– , Barbadian)
Imran Khan (1952– , Pakistani)
Pietersen (Kevin; 1980– , South African)
Ranatunga (Arjuna; 1963– , Sri Lankan)
Sutcliffe (Herbert; 1894–1978, English)
Tendulkar (Sachin; 1973– , Indian)

10 Azharuddin (Mohammad; 1963– , Indian)
Barrington (Ken; 1930–81, English)
Lillywhite (William; 1792–1854, English)
Wasim Akram (1966– , Pakistani)

11 Constantine (Sir Learie; 1901–71, West
Indian)
Heyhoe Flint (Rachael; 1939– , English)

Illingworth (Ray; 1932– , English)
Trescothick (Marcus; 1975– , English)
Zaheer Abbas (1947– , Pakistani)
12 Javed Miandad (1957– , Pakistani)

Muralitharan (Muttiah 'Murali'; 1972– , Sri Lankan)
13 Chandrasekhar (Bhagwat; 1945– , Indian)
Mohammed Hanif (1934– , Pakistani)

Cricket deliveries include:

06 doosra
googly
teesra
yorker
07 bouncer
swinger

08 bodyline
Chinaman
fastball
leg break
off break
09 inswinger

leg-cutter
off-cutter
10 outswinger
11 daisy-cutter

Cricket terms include:

01 b
c
M
w
02 by
CC
in
lb
nb
no
on
ro
03 bat
box
bye
CCC
cut
ECB
ICC
lbw
leg
MCC
net
ODI
off
pad
peg
run
six
ton
04 bail
ball
blob
bowl
deep
draw
duck
edge
four
go in
grub

hook
meat
Oval
over
pair
poke
pull
seam
slip
tail
tice
tonk
walk
wide
work
05 block
break
c and b
catch
cover
dolly
drive
extra
field
gaper
glide
guard
gully
Jaffa
knock
mid on
pitch
plumb
point
quilt
shoot
short
silly
skier
skyer
snick
spell

stand
stump
sweep
swing
throw
track
yahoo
06 appeal
beamer
bowled
bowler
bumper
carpet
caught
cherry
crease
eleven
extras
fizzer
glance
googly
ground
howzat
leg bye
length
long on
maiden
middle
mid off
no ball
not out
nurdle
onside
opener
play on
rabbit
rubber
run out
scorer
screen
seamer
seam up

single
sledge
splice
square
strike
stumps
swerve
the leg
tickle
timber
umpire
whites
wicket
willow
yorker
07 air shot
batsman
batting
bouncer
century
creeper
declare
dismiss
dot ball
fielder
fine leg
flipper
fly slip
grubber
infield
innings
inswing
knock up
last man
leg side
leg slip
leg spin
long hop
long leg
long off
offside
off spin

on drive
on the up
put down
shooter
spinner
striker
stumped
sweeper
swinger
Windies
wrong'un

08 backlift
backward
bodyline
boundary
Chinaman
delivery
fielding
flannels
follow-on
for keeps
full toss
gazunder
half-cock
hat trick
how's that
king pair
leg break
leg guard
long slip
long stop
misfield
off break
off drive
off guard
on strike

See also **sport**

outfield
over rate
pavilion
short leg
sledging
the Ashes
thigh pad
third man
throw out
uncapped

09 batswoman
big hitter
blockhole
deep field
dolly girl
fieldsman
gardening
hit wicket
inswinger
left guard
leg before
leg-cutter
leg theory
long field
mid-wicket
off-cutter
overpitch
overthrow
short slip
square cut
square leg
stonewall
test match
tip and run

10 all-rounder

cover drive
cover point
draw stumps
extra cover
fast bowler
golden duck
half-volley
inside edge
leg spinner
maiden over
off spinner
outswinger
pace bowler
right guard
scoreboard
seam bowler
silly mid-on
silly point
skittle out
spin bowler
spring line
take a guard
take strike
twelfth man

11 clean bowled
daisy-cutter
diamond duck
fast bowling
fieldswoman
grass-cutter
ground staff
half-century
limited-over
net practice
one-day match
outside edge

pace-bowling
pinch-hitter
seam bowling
sight screen
silly mid-off
spin bowling
swing bowler

12 carry your bat
middle and leg
middle and off
return crease
reverse sweep
reverse swing
scoring board
single-wicket
wicketkeeper

13 bowling crease
break one's duck
county cricket
keep your end up
maiden century
night-watchman
popping crease
pyjama cricket

14 off the back foot
sit on the splice
take out your bat

15 bodyline bowling
bowl a maiden
  over
carry out your bat
caught and bowled
leather on willow
leg before wicket
square leg umpire

crime

Crimes include:

03 ABH
GBH

04 rape

05 arson
fraud
theft

06 bigamy
hijack
murder
piracy

07 assault
battery
bribery
forgery

larceny
mugging
perjury
robbery
treason

08 banditry
burglary
homicide
poaching
sabotage
stalking

09 blackmail
extortion
hate crime
joy-riding

pilfering
terrorism
vandalism

10 corruption
cybercrime
kidnapping

11 drug dealing
hooliganism
shoplifting
trespassing

12 drink-driving
embezzlement
manslaughter

13 assassination

drug smuggling
housebreaking
identity theft

14 counterfeiting
insider dealing
insider trading

15 computer hacking

Criminal types include:

03 lag
04 hood
thug
05 crook
thief
06 bandit
forger
gunman
killer
mugger
pirate
rapist
robber
vandal

07 brigand
burglar
hoodlum
mobster
poacher
rustler
stalker
08 arsonist

assassin
batterer
bigamist
car-thief
gangster
hijacker
jailbird
joyrider
murderer
pederast
perjurer
receiver
saboteur
smuggler
swindler

09 buccaneer
cracksman
embezzler
kidnapper
larcenist
racketeer
ram-raider
strangler

terrorist
10 bootlegger
cat burglar
dope pusher
drug dealer
fire-raiser
highwayman
paedophile
pickpocket
shoplifter
trespasser
11 armed robber
blackmailer
bogus caller
drink-driver
kerb-crawler
safecracker
war criminal
12 drug smuggler
extortionist
housebreaker
sexual abuser
13 counterfeiter

Criminals and outlaws include:

03 Nym (*The Merry Wives of Windsor*, 1597,
William Shakespeare)
04 Wild (Jonathan; *The Life of Jonathan Wild
the Great*, 1743, Henry Fielding)
05 Biggs (Ronald; 1929– , English)
Blood (Thomas; c.1618–80, Irish)
Curry (Kid; 1865–1903, US)
Fagin (*Oliver Twist*, 1838, Charles Dickens)
James (Jesse; 1847–82, US)
Kelly (Ned; 1855–80, Australian)
Nancy (*Oliver Twist*, 1838, Charles Dickens)
Sikes (Bill; *Oliver Twist*, 1838, Charles
Dickens)
Tweed (William M; 1823–78, US)
06 Barrow (Clyde; 1909–34, US)
Bonney (William H; 1859–81, US)
Capone (Al; 1899–1947, US)
Dalton (Robert; 1867–92, US)
Manuel (Peter; 1931–58, Scottish)
Meehan (Patrick; 1927–94, Scottish)

See also **highwayman**; **murder**; **police**

Parker (Bonnie; 1911–34, US)
Pistol (*The Merry Wives of Windsor*, 1597,
William Shakespeare)
Rob Roy (1671–1734, Scottish)
Vidocq (Eugène; 1775–1857, French)
07 Cassidy (Butch; 1866–?1908, US)
Ireland (William Henry; 1777–1835,
English)
Luciano (Lucky; 1897–1962, Italian/US)
Raffles (*The Amateur Cracksman*, 1899, E W
Hornung)
08 Bardolph (*Henry IV Part I*, 1596/7, William
Shakespeare)
Moriarty (Professor; *The Final Problem*,
1892–93, Arthur Conan Doyle)
Sheppard (Jack; 1702–24, English)
09 Dillinger (John; 1903–34, US)
Robin Hood (c.1250–c.1350, English)
11 Billy the Kid (1859–81, US)
Sundance Kid (1870–?1908, US)

critic *see* **literature**

Croatia *see* **Balkans**

crop

Arable crops include:

03 pea
rye
yam
04 bean
corn
flax
hemp
kale
milo
oats
rice

05 colza
maize
swede
wheat
06 barley
kharif
millet
potato
turnip
07 alfalfa
cassava

linseed
lucerne
oilseed
popcorn
sorghum
soy bean
08 mung bean
soya bean
teosinte
09 milo maize
sugar beet

sugar cane
sunflower
sweetcorn
triticale
10 fodder beet
11 oilseed rape
sweet potato
12 mangel wurzel

See also **agriculture**; **cereal**; **farm**

cross

Crosses include:

01 T
03 Red
tau
04 ankh
high
Iron
ring
rood
rose
rosy
05 fiery
Greek
Latin
papal

Rouen
06 ansate
botoné
Celtic
fleury
fylfot
Geneva
George
market
moline
Norman
potent
Y-cross
07 Avelian
Calvary

capital
Cornish
Maltese
Russian
saltire
Weeping
08 Buddhist
capuchin
cardinal
crosslet
crucifix
Lorraine
military
pectoral
quadrate

Southern
St Peter's
swastika
Victoria
09 encolpion
Jerusalem
preaching
St Andrew's
St George's
10 St Anthony's
11 patriarchal
13 Constantinian
14 archiepiscopal

See also **religion**; **symbol**

crossword

Crosswords and crossword setters include:

03 Phi
04 Apex
Azed
Duck
Mass
Monk
Paul
Shed
05 Afrit

Rufus
Wynne (Arthur)
06 Aelred
Crispa
Custos
Gemini
Portia
07 Columba
Cyclops

Fidelio
Quixote
Spurius
Ximenes
08 Everyman
Giovanni
Mephisto
Pasquale
09 Araucaria

Beelzebub
Bunthorne
Cinephile
Virgilius
10 Enigmatist
Torquemada

crust

Parts of the Earth's crust include:

03 sal	sima	mantle
04 sial	**06** craton	

crustacean

Crustaceans include:

04 crab
05 krill
    prawn
    yabby
06 gilgie
    hermit
    jilgie
    marron
    partan
    scampi
    scrawl
    shrimp
    squill
    yabbie
07 camaron
    copepod
    daphnia
    dog-crab
    fiddler
    limulus
    lobster
    pagurid
    pea-crab
    pill bug
08 barnacle
    crawfish
    crayfish
    crevette
    king crab
    land crab

    ochidore
    pagurian
09 centipede
    devil-crab
    fish louse
    king prawn
    langouste
    millipede
    phyllopod
    schizopod
    sea slater
    shore crab
    soft-shell
    water flea
    woodlouse
10 acorn-shell
    edible crab
    hermit crab
    mitten-crab
    robber crab
    sandhopper
    seed shrimp
    spider crab
    stomatopod
    tiger prawn
    velvet-crab
    velvet worm
    whale louse
11 brine shrimp
    calling-crab

    coconut crab
    common prawn
    Dublin prawn
    fairy shrimp
    fiddler crab
    langoustine
    rock lobster
    soldier crab
    spectre crab
    tiger shrimp
12 common shrimp
    mantis shrimp
    mussel shrimp
    saucepan-fish
    sentinel crab
    spiny lobster
    squat lobster
13 acorn-barnacle
    common lobster
    goose barnacle
    horseshoe crab
    noble crayfish
    Norway lobster
    opossum shrimp
    spectre shrimp
    tadpole shrimp
    velvet-fiddler
14 Dublin Bay prawn
    skeleton shrimp
    woolly-hand crab

currency

Currencies, with country and smaller units, include:

03 kip (Laos: at)
    lat (Latvia: santims)
    lek (Albania: qindarka)
    leu (Moldova: bani, Romania: bani)
    lev (Bulgaria: stotinki)
    som (Kyrgyzstan: tyjyn)
    sum (Uzbekistan: tiyin)
    won (North Korea: chon, South Korea: jeon)
    yen (Japan: sen)
04 baht (Thailand: satang)
    birr (Ethiopia: cents)
    cedi (Ghana: pesewas)

dong (Vietnam: hao/xu)
dram (Armenia: lumas)
euro (Andorra/Austria/Belgium/Cyprus/
    Finland/France/Germany/Greece/Ireland/
    Italy/Luxembourg/Malta/Monaco/
    Montenegro/The Netherlands/Portugal/San
    Marino/Slovakia/Slovenia/Spain/Vatican
    City: cents)
kina (Papua New Guinea: toea)
kuna (Croatia: lipa)
kyat (Myanmar: pyas)
lari (Georgia: tetri)

lira (Turkey: kurus)
loti (Lesotho: lisente)
peso (Argentina/Chile/Colombia/Cuba/
Dominican Republic/Mexico/Philippines:
centavos)
pula (Botswana: thebe)
rand (South Africa: cents)
real (Brazil: centavos)
rial (Iran/Oman: baisas, Qatar: dirhams)
riel (Cambodia: sen)
taka (Bangladesh: poisha)
tala (Samoa: sene)
vatu (Vanuatu: centimes)
yuan (China: jiao/fen)

05 colón (Costa Rica: centimos, El Salvador:
centavos)
denar (Macedonia: deni)
dinar (Algeria: centimes, Bahrain/Iraq/
Jordan/Kuwait: fils, Libya: dirhams, Sudan:
pounds, Tunisia: millimes)
dobra (São Tomé and Príncipe: centimos)
franc (Benin/Burkina Faso/Burundi/
Cameroon/Central African Republic/
Chad/Comoros/Democratic Republic of
the Congo/Congo/Côte d'Ivoire/Djibouti/
Equatorial Guinea/Gabon/Guinea/Guinea-
Bissau/Mali/Niger/Rwanda/Senegal/Togo:
centimes, Liechtenstein/Switzerland:
centimes/rappen)
krona (Iceland: aurar, Sweden: ore)
krone (Denmark/Norway: ore)
kroon (Estonia: sents)
leone (Sierra Leone: cents)
litas (Lithuania: centas)
manat (Azerbaijan: gopik, Turkmenistan:
tenesi)
naira (Nigeria: kobo)
nakfa (Eritrea: cents)
pound (Egypt/Lebanon/Syria: piastres, UK:
pence)
riyal (Saudi Arabia: qursh/halala, Yemen: fils)
rupee (India: paise, Mauritius/Seychelles/Sri
Lanka: cents, Nepal: paise/pice, Pakistan:
paisa)
tenge (Kazakhstan: tiyn)
zloty (Poland: groszy)

06 ariary (Madagascar: iraimbilanja)
balboa (Panama: centesimos)
dalasi (The Gambia: butut)

dirham (Morocco: centimes, United Arab
Emirates: fils, West Sahara: centimes)
dollar (Antigua and Barbuda/Australia/The
Bahamas/Barbados/Belize/Brunei/Canada/
Dominica/East Timor/Ecuador/El Salvador/
Fiji/Grenada/Guyana/Jamaica/Kiribati/
Liberia/Marshall Islands/Federated States of
Micronesia/Namibia/Nauru/New Zealand/
Palau/St Kitts and Nevis/St Lucia/St Vincent/
Solomon Islands/Suriname/Trinidad and
Tobago/Tuvalu/USA/Zimbabwe: cents,
Singapore: ringgit/cents)
forint (Hungary: filler)
gourde (Haiti: centimes)
koruna (Czech Republic: haleru)
kwacha (Malawi: tambala, Zambia: ngwee)
kwanza (Angola: lwei)
maloti (Lesotho: lisente)
pa'anga (Tonga: seniti)
rouble (Belarus/Russia:kopeks)
rupiah (Indonesia: sen)
shekel (Israel: agora)
somoni (Tajikistan: dirams)
tugrik (Mongolia: mongo)
tugrug (Mongolia: mongo)

07 afghani (Afghanistan: puls)
bolivar (Venezuela: centimos)
cordoba (Nicaragua: centavos, reales)
guarani (Paraguay: centimos)
hyrvnia (Ukraine: kopiykas)
lempira (Honduras: centavos)
metical (Mozambique: centavos)
new peso (Uruguay: centimos)
ouguiya (Mauritania: khoums)
quetzal (Guatemala: centavos)
ringgit (Malaysia: cents)
rufiyaa (Maldives: laarees)

08 new dinar (Serbia: paras)
ngultrum (Bhutan: chetrum)
nuevo sol (Peru: cents)
renminbi (China: jiao/fen)
shilling (Kenya/Somalia/Tanzania/Uganda:
cents)
sterling (UK)

09 boliviano (Bolivia: centavos)
lilangeni (Swaziland: cents)
new dollar (Taiwan: cents)

10 emalangeni (Swaziland: cents)

Former currencies include:

04 lira (Italy/Malta)
mark (Germany)
punt (Ireland)

05 franc (France/Belgium/Luxembourg)
pound (Cyprus)

sucre (Ecuador)
tolar (Slovenia)
zaïre (Democratic Republic of the Congo)

06 escudo (Portugal)
Koruna (Slovakia)

markka (Finland)
peseta (Spain)
07 drachma (Greece)

guilder (The Netherlands)
09 schilling (Austria)
11 Deutschmark (Germany)

Currency abbreviations, with unit and country, include:

03 AUD (dollar; Australia)	JPY (yen; Japan)
CAD (dollar; Canada)	MXN (peso; Mexico)
CHF (franc; Switzerland)	NOK (krone; Norway)
CNY (renminbi yuan; China)	NZD (dollar; New Zealand)
DKK (krone; Denmark)	RUB (rouble; Russia)
EUR (euro; Euro member countries)	SEK (krona; Sweden)
GBP (pound; UK)	SGD (dollar; Singapore)
HKD (dollar; Hong Kong)	USD (dollar; USA)
HUF (forint; Hungary)	ZAR (rand; South Africa)
INR (rupee; India)	

See also **coin**

curry

Curries include:

05 balti	penang	pasanda	tandoori
bhuna	**07** biriani	red thai	vindaloo
korma	biryani	rendang	**09** chettinad
06 ceylon	dhansak	**08** biriyani	green thai
madras	dopiaza	jalfrezi	rogan josh
masala	hanglay	kashmiri	**10** yellow thai
pathia	malayan	massaman	**11** tikka masala

See also **herb**

cut *see* **meat**

cutlery

Cutlery items include:

04 fork	soup spoon	**11** butter knife
05 knife	**10** bread knife	carving fork
ladle	caddy spoon	cheese knife
spoon	cake server	corn holders
08 fish fork	chopsticks	**12** apostle spoon
teaspoon	pickle fork	carving knife
09 fish knife	steak knife	dessertspoon
fish slice	sugar tongs	salad servers
salt spoon	tablespoon	**14** vegetable knife

cutter

Cutters include:

03 axe	bill	mower	**06** chisel
saw	celt	plane	colter
sax	**05** blade	razor	culter
04 adze	knife	sword	dagger

ice axe
jigsaw
labrys
lopper
meat-ax
piolet
poleax
scythe
shears
sickle
sparth
07 chopper
cleaver
coulter
cutlass

fretsaw
gisarme
hacksaw
halberd
hatchet
meat-axe
poleaxe
poll-axe
sparthe
twibill
08 battle-ax
billhook
chainsaw
clippers
palstaff

palstave
partisan
scissors
shredder
stone axe
Strimmer®
tomahawk
09 battle-axe
double-axe
holing-axe
lawnmower
secateurs
10 coal-cutter
cork-cutter
guillotine

putty-knife
spokeshave
11 chaff-cutter
coup de poing
glass-cutter
grass-cutter
Lochaber axe
paper-cutter
straw-cutter
12 cookie-cutter
hedgetrimmer
Jeddart staff
marble-cutter
13 mowing machine
pinking shears

See also **dagger**; **knife**; **sword**

cycling

Cyclists include:

03 Hoy (Chris; 1976– , Scottish)
04 Gaul (Charly; 1932–2005, Luxembourg)
05 Binda (Alfredo; 1902–76, Italian)
Bobet (Louison; 1925–83, French)
Coppi (Fausto; 1919–60, Italian)
Kelly (Sean; 1956– , Irish)
Moser (Francesco; 1951– , Italian)
Zabel (Erik; 1970– , German)
06 Boonen (Thomas; 1980– , Belgian)
Burton (Beryl; 1937–96, English)
Fignon (Laurent; 1960– , French)
Harris (Reg; 1920–92, English)
LeMond (Greg; 1961– , US)
Merckx (Eddy; 1945– , Belgian)
O'Grady (Stuart; 1973– , Australian)
07 Bartali (Gino; 1914–2000, Italian)
Bettini (Paolo; 1974– , Italian)
Hinault (Bernard; 1954– , French)
Museeuw (Johan; 1965– , Belgian)
Pantani (Marco; 1970–2004, Italian)
Pereiro (Óscar; 1977– , Spanish)
Queally (Jason; 1970– , English)

Simpson (Tom; 1938–67, English)
Ullrich (Jan; 1973– , German)
Van Looy (Rik; 1933– , Belgian)
Wiggins (Bradley; 1980– , Belgian)
08 Anquetil (Jacques; 1934–87, French)
Beaumont (Mark; 1983– , Scottish)
Boardman (Chris; 1968– , English)
Contador (Alberto; 1982– , Spanish)
Indurain (Miguel; 1964– , Spanish)
Maertens (Freddy; 1953– , Belgian)
Opperman (Sir Hubert; 1904–96, Australian)
Poulidor (Raymond; 1936– , French)
Virenque (Richard; 1969– , Moroccan/French)
09 Armstrong (Lance; 1971– , US)
Zoetemelk (Joop; 1946– , Dutch)
10 Bahamontes (Federico; 1928– , Spanish)
Cancellara (Fabian; 1981– , Swiss)
van Moorsel (Leontien Ziljaard-; 1970– , Dutch)
11 De Vlaeminck (Roger; 1947– , Belgian)
Freire Gómez (Óscar; 1976– , Spanish)
13 Longo-Ciprelli (Jeannie; 1958– , French)

Cycling terms include:

02 GC
03 UCI
04 pavé
05 bidon
block
break
bunch
cleat
climb

clips
drops
field
hoods
prime
stage
06 attack
bridge
Keirin

lapped
sprint
07 banking
cadence
chasers
climber
echelon
lead-out
Madison

musette
peloton
rouleur
skid lid
08 aero bars
drafting
kermesse
paceline
pole line
road bike
road race
soigneur
sprinter
toe-clips
09 breakaway
chainring
criterium
disc wheel
freewheel
handsling

mass start
monocoque
repechage
sprockets
stage race
time trial
track bike
track race
velodrome
10 broom wagon
chainwheel
dérailleur
domestique
fixed-wheel
neutralize
points race
stand still
team sprint
11 bunch sprint
flamme rouge

green jersey
neutral zone
pursuit race
scratch race
12 bonification
voiture balai
yellow jersey
13 measuring line
slipstreaming
sprinters' lane
sprinters' line
starting block
team time trial
time-trial bike
14 clipless pedals
contre-la-montre
feeding station
neutral support
polka-dot jersey

See also **bicycle**; **sport**

Czech Republic

Cities and notable towns in the Czech Republic include:

04 Brno
Telc
05 Plzen
Praha
06 Pilsen

Prague
07 Budweis
Olomouc
Ostrava
08 Karlsbad

09 Kutná Hora
12 Ceské Krumlov
15 Ceské Budejovice

Administrative divisions of the Czech Republic, with regional capitals:

06 Prague
09 Jihocesky (Ceské Budejovice)
10 Západoesky (Plzen)
11 East Bohemia (Hradec Králové)
Severocesky (Usti nad Labem)
Stredocesky (Prague)
West Bohemia (Plzen)

12 Jihomoravsky (Brno)
North Bohemia (Usti nad Labem)
North Moravia (Ostrava)
South Bohemia (Ceské Budejovice)
South Moravia (Brno)
13 Vychodoceskya (Hradec Králové)
14 Central Bohemia (Prague)
Severomoravsky (Ostrava)

Czech landmarks include:

06 Loreta
Vltava
07 Josefov
Mihulka
08 Berounka
Hradcany
Spilberk
09 Karlstejn
Koneprusy
Vyssi Brod
10 Telc Castle

11 Petrin Tower
Powder Tower
Pražský Hrad
Tyrov Castle
Zlata Koruna
12 Cernin Palace
Prague Castle
13 Brno Cathedral
Charles Bridge
Jesuit College
Mikulov Castle

Moravian Karst
14 Cesky Sternberk
House of Two Suns
Infant of Prague
Koneprusy Caves
Litomyšl Castle
Rozmberk Castle
Tugendhat Villa
15 Bretfield Palace
Karlstejn Castle
Krivoklat Castle

D

dagger

04 dirk
kris

05 skean
skene

06 anlace
bodkin

hanjar
kirpan

07 anelace
dudgeon
handjar
jambiya

khanjar
poniard

08 baselard
jambiyah
puncheon
skean-dhu

skene-dhu
stiletto

10 misericord
skene-occle

11 misericorde

See also **knife**; **weapon**

dairy

04 ghee
milk
whey

05 cream
curds
quark

06 beurre
butter
cheese
yogurt

07 UHT milk
yoghurt

08 ice cream
yoghourt

09 butter oil
goat's milk
milk shake
sour cream
whole milk

10 buttermilk
milk powder

11 double cream
semi-skimmed
single cream
skimmed milk
soured cream

12 clotted cream
crème fraîche

fromage frais
long-life milk
powdered milk

13 condensed milk
full cream milk
low-fat yoghurt
whipping cream

14 evaporated milk
sterilized milk
unsalted butter

15 clarified butter
homogenized milk
semi-skimmed milk

See also **cheese**

Dalai Lama

11 Gedun Gyatso (1475–1542)
Gedun Truppa (1391–1475)
Sonam Gyatso (1543–88)

12 Jampel Gyatso (1758–1804)
Kezang Gyatso (1708–57)
Luntok Gyatso (1806–15)
Tenzin Gyatso (1935–   )

Trinle Gyatso (1856–75)
Yonten Gyatso (1589–17)

13 Khedrup Gyatso (1838–56)
Thupten Gyatso (1876–1933)

15 Tsang-yang Gyatso (1683–1706)
Tshultrim Gyatso (1816–37)

20 Ngawang Lobzang Gyatso (1617–82)

See also **religion**

dam

Dams include:

04 Guri (Venezuela)
Hume (Australia)
Mica (Canada)

05 Aswan (Egypt)
Ertan (China)
Nurek (Tajikistan)
Rogun (Tajikistan)

06 Bratsk (Russia)
Hoover (USA)
Inguri (Georgia)
Itaipu (Brazil/Paraguay)
Kariba (Zambia/Zimbabwe)
Vaiont (Italy)

07 Benmore (New Zealand)
Boulder (USA)
Tarbela (Pakistan)

08 Akosombo (Ghana)

Chapetón (Argentina)
Gezhouba (China)

09 Aswan High (Egypt)
Mauvoisin (Switzerland)
Owen Falls (Uganda)

10 Glen Canyon (USA)

11 Afsluitdijk (The Netherlands)
Grand Coulee (USA)
La Esmeralda (Colombia)
Three Gorges (China)

13 Alberto Lleras (Colombia)
Alvaro Obregon (Mexico)
Grande Dixence (Switzerland)
Manuel M Torres (Mexico)

14 Afsluitdijk Sea (The Netherlands)

15 Sayano-Shushensk (Russia)

dance

Dances include:

03 bop
hay
hey
jig
war

04 barn
jive
rain
reel
shag

05 conga
mambo
polka
round
rumba
salsa
samba
skank
stomp
sword
tango
twist
waltz

06 Balboa
bolero
can-can
cha-cha
hustle
minuet
morris
pavane

valeta
veleta

07 beguine
foxtrot
gavotte
hoe-down
lancers
mazurka
milonga
morrice
musette
one-step
tordion
two-step

08 boogaloo
cakewalk
excuse-me
fandango
flamenco
galliard
habanera
hay-de-guy
hey-de-guy
hornpipe
lindy hop
merengue
Playford
the twist

09 bossa nova
cha-cha-cha
clogdance

écossaise
jitterbug
paso doble
passepied
Paul Jones
quadrille
quickstep
rock 'n' roll
roundelay

10 charleston
corroboree
Gay Gordons
hokey-cokey
slow rhythm
tarantella
turkey-trot

11 black bottom
Lambeth Walk
morris dance
schottische
varsovienne

12 boogie-woogie
mashed potato
Virginia reel

13 eightsome reel
Highland fling
Viennese waltz

14 strip the willow

15 military two-step
St Bernard's waltz

Dance types include:

03 lap	disco	social	flamenco
tap	Irish	square	Highland
04 clog	Latin	street	robotics
folk	limbo	**07** bogling	skanking
jazz	salsa	ceilidh	**10** belly-dance
line	swing	country	breakdance
05 belly	**06** ballet	morrice	**11** traditional
break	hip-hop	old-time	**12** contemporary
ceroc	modern	**08** ballroom	**13** Latin-American
	morris		

Dance functions include:

03 hop	**05** disco	shindig	**10** thé dansant
04 ball	**06** social	**08** hunt ball	**11** charity ball
prom	**07** ceilidh	tea dance	dinner dance
rave	knees-up	**09** barn dance	**14** fancy dress ball

Dance steps include:

03 dig	stamp	**08** back step	**10** ball-change
dip	stomp	crab walk	chainé turn
fan	strut	flat step	change step
set	Suzi-Q	four-step	charleston
04 buck	three	hair comb	chassé turn
chop	twist	headspin	come-around
chug	whisk	heel pull	Cuban walks
clip	**06** aerial	heel turn	cucarachas
comb	breaks	hook turn	inside turn
dame	bronco	neck wrap	jackhammer
drag	chassé	pas-de-bas	rubber legs
draw	circle	push spin	spiral turn
drop	jockey	rock step	texas tommy
ocho	paddle	shedding	triple step
riff	riffle	spot turn	**11** alemana turn
spin	shimmy	swingout	impetus turn
turn	uprock	throwout	natural turn
vine	**07** box step	time step	outside turn
whip	fan kick	windmill	pas de basque
05 abajo	feather	**09** allemagne	quarter turn
brush	jig step	applejack	reverse turn
catch	locking	crazy legs	setting step
corté	lollies	cross over	**12** last shedding
cramp	popping	cross turn	shake and turn
flare	pop turn	dile que no	under-arm turn
galop	rocking	grapevine	**13** double-shuffle
glide	scuffle	lindy turn	fall off the log
grind	shuffle	pas de deux	first shedding
hitch	six-step	poussette	**14** change of places
pivot	swivels	promenade	kick-ball-change
scuff	toprock	quick stop	transition step
seven	twinkle	sugarfoot	travelling step
spike		sugarpush	

Dancers include:

03 Lee (Gypsy Rose; 1914–70, US)

04 Bird (Bonnie; 1914–95, US)
Dunn (Douglas; 1942– , US)
Holm (Hanya; 1893–1992, German/US)
Kemp (Lindsay; 1939– , Scottish)
Monk (Meredith; 1943– , Peruvian/US)
Page (Ruth; 1899–1991, US)

05 Ailey (Alvin, Jnr; 1931–89, US)
Baker (Josephine; 1906–75, French)
Cohan (Robert; 1925– , US/British)
Fagan (Garth; 1940– , Jamaican)
Falco (Louis; 1942–93, US)
Gades (Antonio; 1936–2004, Spanish)
Kelly (Gene; 1912–96, US)
Limón (José; 1908–72, Mexican/US)
North (Robert; 1945– , US/British)
Reitz (Dana; 1948– , US)
Shawn (Ted; 1891–1972, US)
Sleep (Wayne; 1948– , English)
Takei (Kei; 1939– , Japanese)
Tharp (Twyla; 1941– , US)

06 Bausch (Pina; 1940– , German)
Childs (Lucinda; 1940– , US)
Clarke (Martha; 1944– , US)
Davies (Siobhan; 1950– , English)
Duncan (Isadora; 1877–1927, US)
Dunham (Katherine; 1909– , US)
Fenley (Molissa; 1954– , US)
Fuller (Loie; 1862–1928, US)
Gordon (David; 1936– , US)
Graham (Martha; 1894–1991, US)
Horton (Lester; 1906–53, US)

See also **ballet**

Montez (Lola; 1818–61, Irish/US)
Morris (Mark; 1956– , US)
Paxton (Steve; 1939– , US)
Primus (Pearl; 1919–94, Trinidadian/US)
Rainer (Yvonne; 1934– , US)
Rogers (Ginger; 1911–95, US)
Wigman (Mary; 1886–1973, German)

07 Astaire (Adele; 1898–1981, US)
Astaire (Fred; 1899–1987, US)
Bennett (Michael; 1943–87, US)
Carlson (Carolyn; 1943– , US)
de Mille (Agnes; 1905–93, US)
Jamison (Judith; 1943– , US)
Sokolow (Anna; 1912–2000, US)
Wagoner (Dan; 1932– , US)
Weidman (Charles; 1901–75, US)

08 Armitage (Karole; 1954– , US)
Charisse (Cyd; 1921–2008, US)
Hayworth (Rita; 1918–87, US)
Humphrey (Doris; 1895–1958, US)
Nikolais (Alwin; 1910–93, US)
Petronio (Stephen; 1956– , US)

09 Argentina (La; 1890–1936, Argentine/
Spanish)
Schlemmer (Oskar; 1888–1943, German)

10 Cunningham (Merce; 1919– , US)
Saint Denis (Ruth; 1879–1968, US)

11 Mistinguett (1874–1956, French)

13 De Keersmaeker (Anne Teresa; 1960– ,
Belgian)

dandy

Dandies include:

04 Nash (Richard 'Beau'; 1674–1762, Welsh)

05 Crisp (Quentin; 1908–99, English)
Wilde (Oscar; 1854–1900, Irish)

06 Coward (Noël; 1899–1973, English)

See also **Wilde, Oscar**

08 Beerbohm (Max; 1872–1956, English)
Brummell (George 'Beau'; 1778–1840,
English)

12 Yankee Doodle (Dandy; *Little Johnny Jones*,
1904, George M Cohan)

Dante Alighieri (1265–1321)

Significant works include:

07 *Inferno* (c.1307–21)

08 *Eclogues* (c.1319)
Paradiso (c.1307–21)

10 *Il convivio* (c.1304)
On Monarchy (c.1313)

Purgatorio (c.1307–21)
The Banquet (c.1304)
The New Life (c.1292)

11 *De monarchia* (c.1313)
La vita nuova (c.1292)

14 *Divina Commedia* (c.1307–21)
15 *The Divine Comedy* (c.1307–21)
19 *De vulgari eloquentia* (1304)

25 *Concerning the Common Speech* (1304)
29 *On the Eloquence of the Vernacular* (1304)

darts

Darts players include:

04 King (Mervyn; 1966– , English)
Lowe (John; 1945– , English)
Part (John; 1966– , Canadian)

05 Adams (Martin; 1956– , English)

06 Beaton (Steve; 1964– , English)
George (Bobby; 1945– , English)
Stompe (Co; 1962– , Dutch)
Taylor (Phil; 1960– , English)
Wilson (Jocky; 1951– , Scottish)

07 Bristow (Eric; 1957– , English)

Fordham (Andy; 1962– , English)
Klaasen (Jelle; 1984– , Dutch)
Webster (Mark; 1983– , Welsh)

08 Anderson (Bob; 1947– , English)
Gulliver (Trina; 1969– , English)

09 Barneveld (Raymond van; 1967– , Dutch)
Lazarenko (Cliff; 1952– , English)
Priestley (Dennis; 1950– , English)

12 Dobromyslova (Anastasia; 1984– , Russian)

Darts terms include:

03 bed	shaft	treble	**09** bounce-out
04 bull	**06** barrel	**07** maximum	cover shot
bust	double	outshot	double top
oche	finish	**08** bull's eye	**12** hold the throw
stem	flight	checkout	with the darts
tops	game on	dartitis	**13** break the throw
05 outer	marker	game shot	**15** against the darts
	spider		

See also **sport**

daughter

Daughters include:

04 Anne (Princess; 1950– , English)
Hero (*Much Ado About Nothing*, 1598, William Shakespeare)
Kate (*The Taming of the Shrew*, 1593, William Shakespeare)
Page (Anne; *The Merry Wives of Windsor*, 1597/8, William Shakespeare)

05 Freud (Anna; 1895–1982, Austrian/British)
Lloyd (Emily; 1971– , English)
Mills (Hayley; 1946– , English)
O'Neal (Tatum; 1963– , US)
Regan (*King Lear*, 1605–6, William Shakespeare)

06 Bhutto (Benazir; 1953–2007, Pakistani)
Bianca (*The Taming of the Shrew*, 1593, William Shakespeare)
Fatima (c.605–33, Arab)
Fisher (Carrie; 1956– , US)
Forbes (Emma; 1965– , English)
Gandhi (Indira; 1917–84, Indian)

Imogen (*Cymbeline*, 1610, William Shakespeare)
Juliet (*Romeo and Juliet*, 1595, William Shakespeare)
Marina (*Pericles*, 1607, William Shakespeare)

07 Electra (Greek mythology)
Forsyte (Fleur; *The Forsyte Saga*, 1922, John Galsworthy)
Goneril (*King Lear*, 1605–6, William Shakespeare)
Jessica (*The Merchant of Venice*, 1596–7, William Shakespeare)
Lavinia (*Titus Andronicus*, 1592, William Shakespeare)
Miranda (*The Tempest*, 1611, William Shakespeare)
Ophelia (*Hamlet*, 1600–1, William Shakespeare)
Perdita (*The Winter's Tale*, 1609, William Shakespeare)
Presley (Lisa Marie; 1968– , US)

08 Cordelia (*King Lear*, 1605–6, William Shakespeare)
Lovelace (Ada; 1816–52, English)
Minnelli (Liza; 1946– , US)
Williams (Shirley; 1930– , English)

09 Cassandra (Greek mythology)
du Maurier (Daphne; 1907–89, English)
Katharina (*The Taming of the Shrew*, 1593, William Shakespeare)

McCartney (Stella; 1972– , English)
Pankhurst (Christabel; 1880–1958, English)

10 Beckinsale (Kate; 1974– , English)
Richardson (Joely; 1965– , English)
Richardson (Natasha; 1963– , English)
Rossellini (Isabella; 1952– , Italian)

13 Princess Royal (1950– , English)

day

Days of the week:

06 Friday
Monday
Sunday

07 Tuesday
08 Saturday
Thursday

09 Wednesday

French day names with English translation:

05 jeudi (Thursday)
lundi (Monday)
mardi (Tuesday)

06 samedi (Saturday)
08 dimanche (Sunday)
mercredi (Wednesday)

vendredi (Friday)

German day names with English translation:

06 Montag (Monday)
07 Freitag (Friday)
Samstag (Saturday)

Sonntag (Sunday)
08 Dienstag (Tuesday)
Mittwoch (Wednesday)

10 Donnerstag (Thursday)

Italian day names with English translation:

06 lunedì (Monday)
sabato (Saturday)
07 giovedì (Thursday)

martedì (Tuesday)
venerdì (Friday)
08 domenica (Sunday)

09 mercoledì (Wednesday)

Latin day names with English translation:

09 Jovis dies (Thursday)
Lunae dies (Monday)
Solis dies (Sunday)

10 Martis dies (Tuesday)
11 Saturni dies (Saturday)
Veneris dies (Friday)

12 Mercurii dies (Wednesday)

Spanish day names with English translation:

05 lunes (Monday)
06 jueves (Thursday)
martes (Tuesday)

sábado (Saturday)
07 domingo (Sunday)
viernes (Friday)

09 miércoles (Wednesday)

Named days include:

09 Fat Monday
Fig Sunday
Low Sunday
Red Friday
10 Care Sunday
Good Friday
Hock Monday
Holy Friday

Meal Monday
Pack Monday
Palm Sunday
Whit Monday
Whit Sunday
11 Bible Sunday
Black Friday
Black Monday

Egg Saturday
Fat Thursday
Hock Tuesday
Wakes Monday
12 Advent Sunday
Ash Wednesday
Black Tuesday
Bloody Monday

Bloody Sunday
Caring Sunday
Collop Monday
Easter Monday
Easter Sunday
Golden Friday
Holy Saturday
Holy Thursday
Plough Monday

See also **Christmas**

Stir-up Sunday
13 Black Saturday
Carling Sunday
Easter Tuesday
Handsel Monday
Mid-Lent Sunday
Passion Sunday
Shrove Tuesday
Trinity Sunday

14 Easter Saturday
Fastens Tuesday
Maundy Thursday
Pancake Tuesday
Rogation Sunday
Shrift Thursday

15 Mothering Sunday
Pulver Wednesday
Refection Sunday

death

Terms to do with death include:

03 die
DOA
end
RIP
urn
war
04 bier
cist
deid
doom
dust
hell
lily
loss
mort
obit
pall
pyre
sati
soul
toll
tomb
wake
will
05 angel
ashes
bardo
black
cairn
decay
dirge
dying
elegy
éloge
elogy
fatal
ghost
grave
Hades
haunt
inter
Lethe

mourn
shiva
shoot
skull
tangi
vigil
widow
worms
06 Azrael
bedral
behead
burial
candle
chadar
coffin
corpse
demise
die out
entomb
eulogy
exequy
finish
fossor
grieve
hearse
heaven
heroon
lament
lethal
martyr
monody
mortal
murder
obital
orphan
rosary
shibah
shivah
shroud
solemn
suttee
wreath

07 autopsy
banshee
bargest
bederal
bereave
butcher
carcass
carrion
coroner
cortège
cremate
crucify
disease
elogist
elogium
epicede
epitaph
funeral
ghostly
inquest
karoshi
keening
mastaba
mourner
obitual
passing
penalty
quietus
requiem
suicide
widower
08 bale-fire
barghest
casualty
cemetery
cenotaph
ceremony
clinical
contract
dead-fire
deathbed
death row
deceased

disinter
dispatch
eulogium
exequial
fatality
funebral
funerary
funereal
grieving
hara-kiri
homicide
hypogeum
interred
last post
lethally
long home
mortbell
mortuary
mournful
mourning
necropsy
necrosis
necrotic
obituary
paradise
post-obit
predator
sin-eater
soul-scat
soul-scot
soul-shot
suicidal
terminal
unhearse
yahrzeit
09 afterlife
anabiosis
barghaist
cataplexy
committal
cremation
damnation
dead march

dead thraw
death-bell
death duty
death mask
death rate
death-song
deathtrap
death wish
departure
disentomb
dormition
epicedium
funebrial
graveside
graveyard
headstone
homicidal
hypogaeum
interment
last enemy
last rites
mass grave
matricide
mausoleum
mortality
mortcloth
mortician
necrology
necrotize
obsequial
obsequies
passing on
patricide
plague-pit

purgatory
sacrifice
sepulchre
sepulture
taphonomy
testament
thanatoid
tombstone
transport
year's mind

10 ante mortem
apparition
catafalque
ceremonial
death knell
death squad
death-token
death-wound
defunction
euthanasia
expiration
fratricide
gravestone
grim reaper
in extremis
loss of life
month's mind
necrolatry
necrophile
necrophobe
necropolis
obituarist
pall-bearer

play possum
posthumous
post mortem
predecease
sororocide
strae death
undertaker

11 bereavement
crematorium
death-notice
death rattle
death-stroke
eternal rest
fratricidal
funeral home
grave-digger
grave robber
hic sepultus
last honours
lethiferous
mortiferous
necrophilia
necrophobia
necrophobic
passing away
passing bell
requiem mass
rest in peace
rigor mortis
sarcophagus
suicide pact
thanatology
thanatopsis

12 burial ground
commorientes
danse macabre
death warrant
debt of nature
disinterment
last farewell
mercy killing
mourning band
mourning ring
necrographer
necrophagous
necrophiliac
passage grave
pollice verso
posthumously
resting place
the other side
transmigrate

13 burial society
mourning cloak
mourning coach
mourning piece
mourning-stuff
natural causes
thanatography
thanatophobia

14 extreme unction
funeral parlour
mourning border

15 funeral director
resurrectionist

See also **execution**

Debussy, Claude (1862–1918)

Significant works include:

04 *Jeux* (1913)
05 *La Mer* (1905)
06 *Images* (1905–12)
Khamma (1912)
07 *Zuleima* (1885–86)
08 *Estampes* (1903)
Préludes (various)

09 *Nocturnes* (1899)
11 *Clair de lune* (1882)
Pour le piano (1901)
12 *L'Isle joyeuse* (1904)
13 *En blanc et noir* (1915)
15 *Etudes pour piano* (1915)
L'Enfant prodigue (1884)

Sonata for violin (1917)
16 *Mazurka pour piano*
(1890)
20 *Children's Corner Suite*
(1908)
26 *Prélude à l'après-midi d'un
faune* (1894)

decoration *see* **military**

deer

Deer include:

03 elk
hog
red

roe
04 axis
mule

musk
pudu
rusa

sika
05 moose
water

06 chital	**07** barking	carjacou	Père David's
fallow	brocket	Irish elk	**11** black-tailed
forest	caribou	reindeer	white-tailed
sambar	jumping	Virginia	**12** Chinese water
sambur	muntjac		Indian sambar
tufted	muntjak	**09** barasinga	
wapiti	**08** cariacou	**10** barasingha	**13** Indian muntjac

See also **animal**; **game: hunting**

Defoe, Daniel (1660–1731)

Significant works include:

06 *Roxana* (1724)

12 *Moll Flanders* (1722)

14 *Robinson Crusoe* (1719)

17 *Augusta Triumphans* (1728)

23 *A Journal of the Plague Year* (1722)

28 *Roxana, or The Fortunate Mistress* (1724)

31 *The Shortest Way with the Dissenters* (1702)

36 *The Farther Adventures of Robinson Crusoe* (1720)
   The Great Law of Subordination Considered (1724)

Significant characters include:

04 Jack (Colonel)
Jemy

06 Crusoe (Robinson)

Friday (Man)
Roxana

08 Flanders (Moll)

09 Singleton (Captain)

delivery *see* **cricket**

Denmark

Cities and notable towns in Denmark include:

05 Århus

06 Aarhus
Ålborg
Odense

07 Aalborg
Esbjerg
Kolding
Randers

09 København

10 Copenhagen

Administrative divisions of Denmark, with regional capitals:

03 Fyn (Odense)

04 Ribe (Ribe)

05 Århus
Vejle (Vejle)

06 Aarhus
Viborg (Viborg)

08 Bornholm (Rønne)

Roskilde (Roskilde)

09 København
Storstrøm (Nykøbing
Falster)

10 Copenhagen
Ringkøbing (Ringkøbing)

11 Nordjylland (Aalborg)

West Zealand (Sorø)

12 North Jutland (Aalborg)
South Jutland
(Aebeurace)

13 Frederiksborg (Hillerød)
Sønderjylland
(Aebeurace)
Vestsjaelland (Sorø)

Danish landmarks include:

06 Nyhavn
Tivoli

07 Jelling
Strøget

08 Legoland

09 Møns Klint

Rundetårn

10 Round Tower
Trelleborg

11 Christiansø
Egeskov Slot
Folketinget

Oresundbron
Slotsholmen

12 Ålborg Castle
Vor Frue Kirke

13 Egeskov Castle
Little Mermaid

Mermaid Statue	Ribe Cathedral	Kronborg Castle
Oresund Bridge	Rosenborg Slot	**15** Ålborg Cathedral
Radhus Pladset	**14** Århus Cathedral	Odense Cathedral

department *see* **France; government**

dependency

Dependencies include:

04 Guam (USA)
Niue (New Zealand)
05 Aruba (The Netherlands)
07 Bermuda (UK)
Mayotte (France)
Réunion (France)
Tokelau (New Zealand)
08 Anguilla (UK)
St Helena (UK)
09 Gibraltar (UK)
Greenland (Denmark)
Isle of Man (British Crown)
10 Guadeloupe (France)
Martinique (France)
Montserrat (UK)
Puerto Rico (USA)
11 Cook Islands (New Zealand)

12 Cocos Islands (Australia)
Faroe Islands (Denmark)
French Guiana (France)
New Caledonia (France)
South Georgia (UK)
13 American Samoa (USA)
Cayman Islands (UK)
Dutch Antilles (The Netherlands)
Norfolk Island (Australia)
14 Channel Islands (British Crown)
Keeling Islands (Australia)
Ross Dependency (New Zealand)
15 Christmas Island (Australia)
Falkland Islands (UK)
French Polynesia (France)
Pitcairn Islands (UK)
US Virgin Islands (USA)

desert

Deserts include:

04 Gobi (Mongolia/China)
Thar (India/Pakistan)
05 Kavir (Iran)
Namib (Namibia)
Ordos (China)
Sturt (Australia)
06 Gibson (Australia)
Mojave (USA)
Nubian (Sudan)
Sahara (Africa)

Syrian (Asia)
07 Alashan (China)
Arabian (Asia)
Atacama (Chile)
Kara Kum (Turkmenistan)
Simpson (Australia)
Sonoran (USA)
Ustyurt (Kazakhstan)
08 Kalahari (Africa)
Kyzyl-Kum (Kazakhstan)

09 Dzungaria (China)
10 Betpak-Dala (Kazakhstan)
Chihuahuan (Mexico)
Great Basin (USA)
Great Sandy (Australia)
Patagonian (Argentina)
Takla Makan (China)
13 Great Victoria (Australia)
14 Bolson de Mapimi (Mexico)

designer *see* **fashion; furniture**

despot

Despots include:

04 Amin (Idi; 1925–2003, Ugandan)
05 Timur (the Lame; 1336–1405, Turkic/Mongol)
06 Caesar (Julius; c.101–44 BC, Roman)
Führer (Der; 1889–1945, Austrian/German)
Hitler (Adolf 'Der Führer'; 1889–1945,
Austrian/German)

Stalin (Joseph; 1879–1953, Russian)
07 Papa Doc (1907–71, Haitian)
08 Duvalier (François 'Papa Doc'; 1907–71,
Haitian)
09 Ceaușescu (Nicolae; 1918–89, Romanian)
Mao Zedong (1893–1976, Chinese)

Tamerlane (1336–1405, Turkic/Mongol)
10 Mao Tse-tung (1893–1976, Chinese)
11 Robespierre (Maximilien de; 1758–94, French)

Tamburlaine (1336–1405, Turkic/ Mongol)
15 Ivan the Terrible (1530–84, Russian)

dessert

Desserts and puddings include:

03 pie
04 flan
tart
05 bombe
jelly
kulfi
salad
06 mousse
mud pie
sorbet
sundae
trifle
yogurt
07 baklava
cobbler
compote
crumble
parfait
pavlova
soufflé

tapioca
tartufo
yoghurt
08 Eton mess
ice cream
pandowdy
plum-duff
syllabub
tiramisu
vacherin
yoghourt
09 clafoutis
cranachan
10 blancmange
Brown Betty
cheesecake
egg custard
frangipane
panna cotta
peach Melba
zabaglione

11 baked Alaska
banana split
banoffee pie
crème brûlée
Eve's pudding
milk pudding
plum pudding
rice pudding
spotted dick
12 crème caramel
crêpe suzette
fruit crumble
profiteroles
13 fruit cocktail
millefeuilles
summer pudding
14 charlotte russe
15 clootie dumpling
queen of puddings
roly-poly pudding

See also **baking**; **cake**; **food**

detective

Detectives include:

03 Zen (Aurelio; *Ratking*, 1988, et seq, Michael Dibdin)
04 Bony (Napoleon Bonaparte; *The Barrakee Mystery*, 1931, et seq, Arthur Upfield)
Chan (Charlie; *The House without a Key*, 1925, et seq, Earl Derr Biggers)
Cuff (Richard; *The Moonstone*, 1868, Wilkie Collins)
Dean (Sam; *Blood Rights*, 1989, et seq, Mike Phillips)
Gray (Cordelia; *An Unsuitable Job for a Woman*, 1972, et seq, P D James)
Vane (Harriet; *Strong Poison*, 1930, et seq, Dorothy L Sayers)
05 Brown (Father; *The Innocence of Father Brown*, 1911, G K Chesterton)
Drake (Paul; *The Case of the Velvet Claws*, 1933, et seq, Erle Stanley Gardner)
Duffy (Nicholas; *Duffy*, 1980, et seq, Dan Kavanagh)

Dupin (C Auguste; 'The Mystery of Marie Roget', 1842–43, et seq, Edgar Allan Poe)
Ghote (Inspector Ganesh; *The Perfect Murder*, 1964, et seq, H R F Keating)
Grant (Alan; *A Shilling for Candles: The Story of a Crime*, 1936, et seq, Josephine Tey)
Mason (Perry; *The Case of the Velvet Claws*, 1933, et seq, Erle Stanley Gardner)
Morse (Inspector; *Last Bus To Woodstock*, 1975, et seq, Colin Dexter)
Queen (Ellery; *The Roman Hat Mystery*, 1929, et seq, Ellery Queen)
Rebus (John; *Knots and Crosses*, 1987, et seq, Ian Rankin)
Spade (Sam; *The Maltese Falcon*, 1930, et seq, Dashiell Hammett)
Vance (Philo; *The Benson Murder Case*, 1926, et seq, S S Van Dine)
Wolfe (Nero; *Fer-de-lance*, 1934, et seq, Rex Stout)

06 Alleyn (Roderick; *A Man Lay Dead*, 1934, et seq, Ngaio Marsh)
Archer (Lew; *The Moving Target*, 1949, et seq, Ross MacDonald)
Essrog (Lionel; *Motherless Brooklyn*, 1999, Jonathan Lethem)
Hanaud (Inspector; *At the Villa Rose*, 1910, et seq, A E W Mason)
Holmes (Sherlock; *A Study in Scarlet*, 1887, et seq, Arthur Conan Doyle)
Marple (Miss Jane; *Murder at the Vicarage*, 1930, et seq, Agatha Christie)
Pascoe (Peter; *A Clubbable Woman*, 1970, et seq, Reginald Hill)
Poirot (Hercule; *The Mysterious Affair at Styles*, 1920, et seq, Agatha Christie)
Silver (Miss Maude; *Pilgrim's Rest*, 1948, et seq, Patricia Wentworth)
Vidocq (Eugène François; 1775–1857, French)
Watson (Dr John; *A Study in Scarlet*, 1887, et seq, Arthur Conan Doyle)
Wimsey (Lord Peter; *Whose Body?*, 1923, et seq, Dorothy L Sayers)

07 Appleby (John; *Death at the President's Lodging*, 1936, et seq, Michael Innes)
Cadfael (Brother; *A Morbid Taste for Bones*, 1977, et seq, Ellis Peters)
Campion (Albert; *The Crime at Black Dudley*, 1929, et seq, Margery Allingham)
Charles (Nick; *The Thin Man*, 1934, Dashiell Hammett)
Dalziel (Andy; *A Clubbable Woman*, 1970, et seq, Reginald Hill)
Fansler (Kate; *Sweet Death, Kind Death*,

1984, et seq, Amanda Cross)
Laidlaw (Jack; *Laidlaw*, 1977, et seq, William McIlvanney)
Maigret (Jules; *The Death of M Gallet*, 1931, Georges Simenon)
Marlowe (Philip; *The Big Sleep*, 1939, et seq, Raymond Chandler)
Milhone (Kinsey; *A is for Alibi*, 1986, et seq, Sue Grafton)
Moseley (Hoke; *Miami Blues*, 1984, et seq, Charles Willeford)
Wexford (Reginald; *From Doon with Death*, 1964, et seq, Ruth Rendell)
Whicher (Jonathan 'Jack'; 1814–81, English)

08 Lestrade (Inspector; *A Study in Scarlet*, 1887, et seq, Arthur Conan Doyle)
Ramotswe (Precious; *The No 1 Ladies' Detective Agency*, 1998, et seq, Alexander McCall Smith)

09 Bonaparte (Napoleon; *The Barrakee Mystery*, 1931, et seq, Arthur Upfield)
Dalgliesh (Adam; *Cover Her Face*, 1962, et seq, P D James)
Hawksmoor (Nicholas; *Hawksmoor*, 1985, Peter Ackroyd)
Pinkerton (Allan; 1819–84, Scottish/US)
Scarpetta (Kay; *Postmortem*, 1990, et seq, Patricia Cornwell)

10 Van Der Valk (Piet; *Love in Amsterdam*, 1962, et seq, Nicolas Freeling)
Warshawski (V I; *Indemnity Only*, 1982, et seq, Sara Paretsky)

13 Continental Op (*Red Harvest*, 1929, Dashiell Hammett)

device

Devices include:

02 PC	lighter	hairdryer
04 iPod®	printer	hole punch
iron	stapler	magnifier
Xbox®	Walkman®	pedometer
05 clock	**08** barbecue	staple gun
phone	CD player	stopwatch
razor	computer	telephone
torch	egg timer	tin opener
watch	epilator	**10** calculator
	nail file	coin sorter
06 camera	scissors	fax machine
heater	tweezers	ice scraper
Hoover®		overlocker
juicer	**09** cafetière	percolator
scales	can opener	wine cooler
shaver	cell phone	
	corkscrew	**11** answerphone
07 foot spa	DVD player	baby monitor
Game Boy®	fan heater	electric fan

manicure set
mobile phone
patio heater
PlayStation®
thermometer
video camera
12 bottle opener
curling tongs
dehumidifier

games console
kitchen timer
nail clippers
steam cleaner
stitch ripper
13 eyelash curler
floor polisher
remote control
sewing machine

smoke detector
staple remover
vacuum cleaner
video recorder
14 eyelash curlers
needle threader
personal stereo
Swiss army knife
15 electric blanket

See also **computer**; **domestic appliance**; **electricity**; **optics**; **rhetoric**; **scanner**

diamond

Diamonds include:

04 Agra
Hope
Shah
05 Jacob
Mouna
Nepal
Nizam
Sancy
06 Gruosi
Nassak
Regent
07 Allnatt

Ashberg
Eugénie
Jubilee
Lesotho
Paragon
Tiffany
08 Cullinan
Deepdene
Idol's Eye
Kimberly
Koh-I-Noor
Nur-Ul-Ain
Red Cross

09 Amsterdam
Beau Sancy
Blue Heart
Centenary
Darya-i Nur
Earth Star
Excelsior
Graff Blue
Hortensia
10 Florentine
Ocean Dream
Portuguese
11 Premier Rose

Spoonmaker's
Wittelsbach
12 Dresden Green
Incomparable
Porter Rhodes
Taylor-Burton
13 Golden Jubilee
Star of the East
14 Archduke Joseph
Millennium Star
Star of the South
15 Heart of Eternity

diary

Diarists include:

03 Lee (Lorelei; *Gentlemen Prefer Blondes*, 1925, Anita Loos)

04 Byrd (William; 1674–1744, American)
Gide (André; 1869–1951, French)
Mole (Adrian; *The Secret Diary of Adrian Mole Aged 13¾*, 1982, et seq, Sue Townsend)
Ooka (Shohei; 1909–88, Japanese)

05 Birde (William; 1674–1744, American)
Frank (Anne; 1929–45, German)
Grant (Elizabeth; 1797–1885, Scottish)
Jones (Bridget; *Bridget Jones's Diary*, 1996, et seq, Helen Fielding)
Pasek (Jan Chryzostom; c.1636–1701, Polish)
Pepys (Samuel; 1633–1703, English)
Reyes (Alfonso; 1889–1959, Mexican)
Scott (Robert Falcon; 1868–1912, English)
Torga (Miguel; 1907–90, Portuguese)

06 Burney (Fanny; 1752–1840, English)
Evelyn (John; 1620–1706, English)

Pooter (Charles; *The Diary of a Nobody*, 1892, George and Weedon Grossmith)

07 Andrews (Pamela; *Pamela*, 1740–41, Samuel Richardson)
Carlyle (Jane Welsh; 1801–66, Scottish)
Chesnut (Mary; 1823–86, US)
Creevey (Thomas; 1768–1838, English)
Kilvert (Francis; 1840–79, English)
Shields (Rev Robert; 1918–2007, US)

08 Greville (Charles; 1794–1865, English)
Melville (James; 1556–1614, Scottish)
Robinson (Henry Crabb; 1775–1867, English)

09 Schreiber (Lady Charlotte; 1812–95, Welsh)
Slaveykov (Petko; 1827–95, Bulgarian)

11 Lichtenberg (Georg Christoph; 1742–99, German)
Thermopolis (Mia; *The Princess Diaries*, 2000, et seq, Meg Cabot)

12 Bashkirtseva (Marya; 1860–84, Russian)

Dickens, Charles (1812–70)

Significant works include:

09 *Hard Times* (1854)
The Chimes (1844)

10 *Bleak House* (1852–53)

11 *Oliver Twist* (1837–38)

12 *Barnaby Rudge* (1841)
Dombey and Son (1846–48)
Little Dorrit (1855–57)
Nobody's Fault (1855–57)

13 *American Notes* (1842)
Sketches by Boz (1833–68)
The Haunted Man (1848)

14 *Christmas Books* (1843–49)
Pickwick Papers (1836–37)

15 *A Christmas Carol* (1843)
Our Mutual Friend (1865)
The Battle of Life (1846)

16 *A Tale of Two Cities* (1859)

Christmas Stories (1859–67)
David Copperfield (1849–50)
Martin Chuzzlewit (1843–44)
Nicholas Nickleby (1838–39)

17 *Great Expectations* (1860–61)
Pictures from Italy (1846)

19 *The Old Curiosity Shop* (1840–41)

21 *The Cricket on the Hearth* (1845)
The Parish Boy's Progress (1837–38)

22 *Hard Times for These Times* (1854)
The Mystery of Edwin Drood (1870)

23 *A Child's History of England* (1851–53)

33 *Dealings with the Firm of Dombey and Son*
(1846–48)

36 *The Posthumous Papers of the Pickwick
Club* (1836–37)

Significant characters include:

02 Jo

03 Bud (Rosa)
Cly (Roger)
Gay (Walter)
Joe
Tox (Miss Lucretia)

04 Bray (Madeline)
Bray (Walter)
Cute (Alderman)
Dick (Mr)
Em'ly (Little)
Fang (Mr)
Fern (Will)
Gamp (Mrs Sarah 'Sairey')
Hawk (Sir Mulberry)
Heep (Uriah)
Hugh
Humm (Anthony)
Jupe (Signor)
Jupe (Sissy)
Omer (Mr)
Prig (Betsey)
Riah
Tigg (Montague)
Tope (Mr)
Tope (Mrs)
Veck (Margaret 'Meg')
Veck (Toby 'Trotty')
Wade (Miss)
Wegg (Silas)
Wren (Jenny)

05 Allen (Arabella)

Allen (Benjamin)
Bates (Charley)
Biddy
Brass (Sally)
Brass (Sampson)
Brown (Mrs)
Casby (Christopher)
Chick (Mrs Louisa)
Clare (Ada)
Daisy (Solomon)
Doyce (Daniel)
Drood (Edwin)
Fagin
Filer (Mr)
Flite (Miss)
Gills (Solomon)
Gowan (Henry)
Gride (Arthur)
Guppy (William)
Hexam (Charley)
Hexam (Gaffer Jesse)
Hexam (Lizzie)
Kenge (Mr)
Krook (Mr)
Lorry (Mr Jarvis)
Lupin (Mrs)
Miggs (Miss)
Molly
Nancy
Noggs (Newman)
Pinch (Ruth)
Pinch (Tom)
Pross (Miss)

Pross (Solomon)
Quilp (Betsey)
Quilp (Daniel)
Rudge (Barnaby)
Rudge (Mr)
Rudge (Mrs Mary)
Sikes (Bill)
Slyme (Chevy)
Smike
Toots (Mr)
Twist (Oliver)
Venus (Mr)
Voles (Mr)

06 Badger (Bayham)
Bagnet (Mr)
Bagnet (Mrs)
Bailey (Benjamin)
Bailey (Young)
Barkis (Mr)
Barsad (John)
Beadle (Harriet
'Tattycoram')
Bitzer
Boffin (Mr Nicodemus)
Boffin (Mrs)
Bowley (Sir Joseph)
Bucket (Mr)
Bumble (Mr)
Bunsby (Captain Jack)
Buzfuz (Serjeant)
Carker (Harriet)
Carker (James)

Carker (John)
Carton (Sydney)
Codlin (Harris 'Short')
Codlin (Thomas)
Corney (Mrs)
Cuttle (Captain Edward 'Ned')
Darnay (Charles)
Dartle (Rosa)
Dennis (Ned)
Deputy
Dombey (Edith)
Dombey (Florence)
Dombey (Mr Paul)
Dombey (Paul)
Dorrit (Amy)
Dorrit (Edward 'Tip')
Dorrit (Fanny)
Dorrit (Frederick)
Dorrit (William)
Dowler (Mr)
Endell (Martha)
Feenix (Lord)
Fizkin (Horatio)
Gordon (Lord George)
Graham (Mary)
Guster
Harmon (John)
Hawdon (Captain)
Higden (Betty)
Howler (Rev Melchisedech)
Hunter (Mrs Leo)
Hutley (Jem)
Jarley (Mrs)
Jasper (Mr John)
Jingle (Alfred)
Lammle (Alfred)
Magnus (Peter)
Maldon (Jack)
Maylie (Mrs)
Maylie (Rose)
Merdle (Mr)
Merdle (Mrs)
Nipper (Susan)
Orlick (Dolge)
Pancks (Mr)
Pegler (Mrs)
Pirrip (Philip 'Pip')
Pocket (Herbert)
Pocket (Matthew)
Puffer (Princess)
Redlaw (Mr)
Rigaud
Sapsea (Mr Thomas)
Sawyer (Bob)
Sleary (Mr)
Strong (Dr)
Strong (Mrs Annie)

Tapley (Mark)
Tartar (Mr)
Toodle (Polly)
Toodle (Robin)
Tupman (Tracy)
Varden (Dolly)
Varden (Gabriel)
Warden (Michael)
Weller (Mrs)
Weller (Mr Tony)
Weller (Sam)
Wilfer (Bella)
Wilfer (Reginald)
Willet (Joe)
Willet (John)
Winkle (Nathaniel)
Wopsle (Mr)

07 Barbara
Barbary (Miss)
Bardell (Mrs Martha)
Blimber (Doctor)
Boldwig (Captain)
Britain (Benjamin)
Browdie (John)
Chester (Edward)
Chester (Sir John, formerly Mr)
Chivery (Young John)
Chuffey (Mr)
Cleaver (Fanny)
Clennam (Arthur)
Clennam (Mrs)
Creakle (Mr)
Crewler (Sophy)
Dawkins (Jack)
Dedlock (Lady)
Dedlock (Sir Leicester)
Deedles
Defarge (Ernest)
Defarge (Madame Thérèse)
Drummle (Bentley)
Durdles
Estella
Gabelle (Theophile)
Gargery (Joe)
Gargery (Mrs Joe)
Garland (Mr Abel)
Garland (Mrs Abel)
Gaspard
General (Mrs)
Granger (Edith)
Gridley (Mr)
Jaggers (Mr)
Jeddler (Dr Anthony)
Jeddler (Grace)
Jeddler (Marion)
Jellyby (Caroline 'Caddy')
Jellyby (Mrs)

Jiniwin (Mrs)
Jobling (Tony)
Jorkins (Mr)
Kenwigs (Mr)
Kenwigs (Mrs)
Leeford (Edward 'Monks')
Lewsome (Mr)
Manette (Dr Alexandre)
Manette (Lucie)
Marwood (Alice)
Meagles (Minnie 'Pet')
Meagles (Mr)
Meagles (Mrs)
Mowcher (Miss)
Nadgett (Mr)
Neckett
Neckett (Charlotte)
Newcome (Clemency)
Nubbles (Christopher 'Kit')
Nupkins (George)
Pipchin (Mrs)
Plummer (Bertha)
Plummer (Caleb)
Plummer (Edward)
Podsnap (Mr John)
Rachael
Rachael (Mrs)
Scrooge (Ebenezer)
Skewton (The Hon Mrs)
Slammer (Doctor)
Slowboy (Tilly)
Slumkey (The Hon Samuel)
Snagsby (Mr)
Snawley (Mr)
Snubbin (Serjeant)
Sparsit (Mrs)
Spenlow (Dora)
Spenlow (Mr Francis)
Squeers (Wackford)
Stryver (Mr)
Tiny Tim
Todgers (Mrs)
Trotter (Job)
Wackles (Sophy)
Wemmick (John)

08 Bagstock (Major Joseph)
Boythorn (Lawrence)
Brownlow (Mr)
Carstone (Richard)
Chadband (Rev Mr)
Claypole (Noah)
Clickett ('The Orfling')
Cratchit (Bob)
Crummles (Mrs Vincent)
Crummles (Mr Vincent)
Cruncher (Jeremiah 'Jerry')
Datchery (Dick)
Fielding (May)

Finching (Flora)
Fledgeby (Fascination)
Gashford (Mr)
Gummidge (Mrs)
Haredale (Emma)
Haredale (Mr Geoffrey)
Havisham (Miss)
Hortense (Mademoiselle)
Jarndyce (John)
La Creevy (Miss)
Landless (Helena)
Landless (Neville)
Littimer
Magwitch (Abel)
Micawber (Mrs Emma)
Micawber (Mr Wilkins)
Montague (Tigg)
Nickleby (Kate)
Nickleby (Mrs)
Nickleby (Nicholas)
Nickleby (Ralph)
Peggotty (Clara)
Peggotty (Daniel)
Peggotty (Ham)
Petowker (Miss Henrietta)
Pickwick (Samuel)
Plornish (Mrs Thomas)
Plornish (Mr Thomas)
Skimpole (Harold)
Snitchey (Jonathan)
Sparkler (Edmund)
Stiggins (The Rev Mr)
Traddles (Thomas)
Trotwood (Miss Betsey)
Westlock (John)
Wrayburn (Eugene)

09 Billickin (Mrs)
Blackpool (Stephen)
Bounderby (Josiah)
Cheeryble (Charles)
Cheeryble (Edwin)
Compeyson
Gradgrind (Louisa)
Gradgrind (Thomas)

Gradgrind (Tom)
Grewgious (Mr Hiram)
Harthouse (James)
Headstone (Bradley)
Lightwood (Mortimer)
Lillyvick (Mr)
Mantalini (Madame)
Mantalini (Mr Alfred)
Murdstone (Jane)
Murdstone (Mr Edward)
Old Martin
Pardiggle (Mrs)
Pecksniff (Charity)
Pecksniff (Mercy)
Pecksniff (Seth)
Potterson (Abbey)
Riderhood (Roger 'Rogue')
Rokesmith (John)
Smallweed (Grandfather
  Joshua)
Smorltork (Count)
Snodgrass (Augustus)
Summerson (Esther)
Swiveller (Richard 'Dick')
Tackleton (Mr)
Tappertit (Simon 'Sim')
The Fat Boy
Trabb's boy
Veneering (Mr Hamilton)
Veneering (Mrs)
Verisopht (Lord Frederick)
Wickfield (Agnes)
Wickfield (Mr)
Woodcourt (Allan)

10 Cavalletto (John Baptist)
Chuzzlewit (Anthony)
Chuzzlewit (Jonas)
Chuzzlewit (Martin)
Chuzzlewit ('Old' Martin)
Crisparkle (Revd Septimus)
Flintwinch (Affery)
Flintwinch (Jeremiah)
Heathfield (Alfred)
Little Nell

MacStinger (Mrs)
Rouncewell (Mr)
Rouncewell (Mr George)
Rouncewell (Mrs)
Sowerberry (Mr)
Sowerberry (Mrs)
Steerforth (Mr James)
Tattycoram
The Wardles
Turveydrop (Mr)
Turveydrop (Prince)
Twinkleton (Miss)
Wititterly (Mr Henry)
Wititterly (Mrs)

11 Copperfield (David)
Copperfield (Mrs Clara)
Dismal Jemmy
Grandfather
Linkinwater (Tim)
Peerybingle (John)
Peerybingle (Mrs Mary
  'Dot')
Pumblechook (Uncle)
Slackbridge
Snevellicci (Miss)
St Evremonde (Marquis de)
Sweedlepipe (Paul 'Poll')
The Bachelor
Tulkinghorn (Mr)

12 Bailey Junior
Grip the Raven
Honeythunder (Mr Luke)
Little Dorrit
Marley's Ghost
The Barnacles
The Fezziwigs

13 M'Choakumchild (Mr)
Rob the Grinder

14 Chickenstalker (Mrs Anne)
The Marchioness

15 The Artful Dodger

diet

Diets include:

02 GI
03 FIT
  Hay
04 VLCD
  zone
05 F-plan
06 Atkins
  low fat

  Ornish
07 banting
  LA Shape
  raw food
08 beetroot
  Pritikin
  Slim-Fast
09 blood type

  body boost
  herbalife
  Hollywood
  juice fast
  low sodium
  omega zone
  Perricone
  Scarsdale
10 fit for life

grapefruit
Jenny Craig
Mayo Clinic
ready to eat
revival soy
South Beach
superfoods
vegetarian

11 cabbage soup

high protein
hip and thigh
macrobiotic
somersizing
The Hamptons
thin for life

12 Beverly Hills
protein power
sugar busters

13 food combining
radiant health
Slimming World

14 Richard Simmons
very low calorie
Weight Watchers

15 metabolic typing
nutrisystem plan
Rosemary Conley's

dinosaur

Dinosaurs include:

04 T Rex
06 raptor
08 coelurus
sauropod
theropod
09 hadrosaur
iguanodon
oviraptor
10 allosaurus
anatotitan
barosaurus
diplodocus
megalosaur
ophiacodon
torosaurus
utahraptor

11 apatosaurus
ceteosaurus
coelophysis
coelurosaur
deinonychus
dromaeosaur
polacanthus
prosauropod
saurischian
stegosaurus
triceratops
tyrannosaur
12 ankylosaurus
brontosaurus
camptosaurus
ceratosaurus
megalosaurus
ornithischia

ornithomimus
plateosaurus
titanosaurus
velociraptor
13 atlantosaurus
brachiosaurus
compsognathus
corythosaurus
dwarf allosaur
edmontosaurus
herrerasaurus
ornitholestes
styracosaurus
tyrannosaurus
14 leaellynasaura
15 cryolophosaurus
parasaurolophus

diocese

Dioceses and archdioceses of the UK, with denomination, include:

03 Ely (Anglican)
04 York (Anglican)
05 Derby (Anglican)
Derry (Catholic)
Leeds (Catholic)
Truro (Anglican)
06 Armagh (Anglican/Catholic)
Bangor (Anglican)
Connor (Anglican)
Durham (Anglican)
Exeter (Anglican)
Hallam (Catholic)
London (Anglican)
Oxford (Anglican)
07 Brechin (Anglican)
Bristol (Anglican)
Cardiff (Catholic)
Chester (Anglican)
Clifton (Catholic)
Clogher (Anglican/Catholic)

Dromore (Catholic)
Dunkeld (Catholic)
Glasgow (Catholic)
Kilmore (Catholic)
Lincoln (Anglican)
Menevia (Catholic)
Norwich (Anglican)
Paisley (Catholic)
Salford (Catholic)
St Asaph (Anglican)
Wrexham (Catholic)
08 Aberdeen (Catholic)
Bradford (Anglican)
Carlisle (Anglican)
Coventry (Anglican)
Galloway (Catholic)
Hereford (Anglican)
Llandaff (Anglican)
Monmouth (Anglican)
Plymouth (Catholic)
St Albans (Anglican)

St Davids (Anglican)
09 Blackburn (Anglican)
Brentwood (Catholic)
Edinburgh (Anglican)
Guildford (Anglican)
Lancaster (Catholic)
Leicester (Anglican)
Lichfield (Anglican)
Liverpool (Anglican/
Catholic)
Newcastle (Anglican)
Rochester (Anglican)
Salisbury (Anglican)
Sheffield (Anglican)
Southwark (Anglican/
Catholic)
Southwell (Anglican)
Wakefield (Anglican)
Worcester (Anglican)
10 Birmingham (Anglican/

Catholic)
Canterbury (Anglican)
Chelmsford (Anglican)
Chichester (Anglican)
East Anglia (Catholic)
Gloucester (Anglican)
Manchester (Anglican)
Motherwell (Catholic)
Nottingham (Catholic)

Portsmouth (Anglican/
   Catholic)
Shrewsbury (Catholic)
Winchester (Anglican)

11 Northampton (Catholic)
Sodor and Man (Anglican)
Westminster (Catholic)

12 Bath and Wells (Anglican)
Peterborough (Anglican)

13 Down and Connor
   (Catholic)
Middlesbrough (Catholic)
Ripon and Leeds (Anglican)

14 Derry and Raphoe
   (Anglican)
Down and Dromore
   (Anglican)

See also **archbishop**; **religion**

director

Film and theatre directors and producers include:

03 Cox (Brian; 1946– , Scottish)
Lee (Ang; 1954– , Taiwanese)
Lee (Spike; 1957– , US)
May (Elaine; 1932– , US)
Ozu (Yasujiro; 1903–63, Japanese)
Ray (Satyajit; 1921–92, Indian)
Wai (Wong Kar; 1956– , Chinese)
Woo (John; 1948– , Chinese)

04 Alda (Alan; 1936– , US)
Axel (Gabriel; 1918– , Danish)
Bond (Edward; 1934– , English)
Coen (Ethan; 1958– , US)
Coen (Joel; 1954– , US)
Eyre (Sir Richard; 1943– , English)
Ford (John; 1895–1973, US)
Gray (Simon; 1936–2008, English)
Hall (Sir Peter; 1930– , English)
Hare (Sir David; 1947– , English)
Hart (Moss; 1904–61, US)
Hill (George Roy; 1921–2002, US)
Lang (Fritz; 1890–1976, Austrian/US)
Lean (Sir David; 1908–91, English)
Nunn (Trevor; 1940– , English)
Papp (Joseph; 1921–91, US)
Reed (Sir Carol; 1906–76, English)
Roeg (Nicolas; 1928– , English)
Tati (Jacques; 1908–82, French)
Todd (Mike; 1909–58, US)
Weir (Peter; 1944– , Australian)
Wise (Robert; 1914–2005, US)

05 Allen (Woody; 1935– , US)
Barba (Eugenio; 1936– , Italian)
Boyle (Danny; 1956– , English)
Brook (Peter; 1925– , English)
Capra (Frank; 1897–1991, Italian/US)
Carné (Marcel; 1909–96, French)
Clair (René; 1898–1981, French)
Craig (Gordon; 1872–1966, English)
Cukor (George; 1899–1983, US)
Dante (Joe; 1946– , US)
Demme (Jonathan; 1944– , US)
Fosse (Bob; 1927–87, US)

Gance (Abel; 1889–1981, French)
Hands (Terry; 1941– , English)
Hawks (Howard; 1896–1977, US)
Ivory (James; 1928– , US)
Kazan (Elia; 1909–2003, Turkish/US)
Kelly (Gene; 1912–96, US)
Korda (Sir Alexander; 1893–1956,
   Hungarian/British)
Leigh (Mike; 1943– , English)
Leone (Sergio; 1922–89, Italian)
Lloyd (Phyllida; 1957– , English)
Losey (Joseph; 1909–84, US)
Lucas (George; 1944– , US)
Lumet (Sidney; 1924– , US)
Lynch (David; 1946– , US)
Malle (Louis; 1932–95, French)
Mamet (David; 1947– , US)
Marsh (Dame Ngaio; 1899–1982, New
   Zealand)
Mayer (Louis B; 1885–1957, US)
Miles (Bernard, Lord; 1907–91, English)
Noble (Adrian; 1950– , English)
Pabst (G W; 1895–1967, German)
Perry (Antoinette; 1888–1946, US)
Roach (Hal; 1892–1992, US)
Scott (Ridley; 1937– , English)
Stein (Peter; 1937– , German)
Stone (Oliver; 1946– , US)
Vadim (Roger; 1928–2000, French)
Varda (Agnès; 1928– , Belgian/French)
Verdy (Violette; 1933– , French)
Vidor (King; 1894–1982, US)
Wajda (Andrzej; 1926– , Polish)
Wells (John; 1936–98, English)
Wolfe (George C; 1954– , US)
Wyler (William; 1902–81, German/US)

06 Abbott (George; 1887–1995, US)
Altman (Robert; 1925–2006, US)
Ang Lee (1954– , Taiwanese)
Artaud (Antonin; 1896–1948, French)
Arzner (Dorothy; 1900–79, US)
August (Bille; 1948– , Danish)

Badham (John; 1939– , US)
Barton (John; 1928– , English)
Beatty (Warren; 1937– , US)
Besson (Luc; 1959– , French)
Brecht (Bertolt; 1898–1956, German)
Brooks (Mel; 1926– , US)
Bryden (Bill; 1942– , Scottish)
Buñuel (Luis; 1900–83, Spanish)
Burton (Tim; 1960– , US)
Callow (Simon; 1949– , English)
Cooney (Ray; 1932– , English)
Copeau (Jacques; 1879–1949, French)
Corman (Roger; 1926– , US)
Curtiz (Michael; 1888–1962, Hungarian)
Cusack (Cyril; 1910–93, Irish)
Daldry (Stephen; 1961– , English)
Davies (Howard; 1945– , English)
Davies (Terence; 1945– , English)
De Sica (Vittorio; 1902–74, Italian)
Devine (George; 1910–65, English)
Dexter (John; 1925–90, English)
Disney (Walt; 1901–66, US)
Donner (Richard; 1930– , US)
Dunlop (Frank; 1927– , English)
Dybwad (Johanne; 1867–1950, Norwegian)
Ephron (Nora; 1941– , US)
Forbes (Bryan; 1926– , English)
Forman (Miloš; 1932– , Czech/US)
Frears (Stephen; 1941– , English)
Fugard (Athol; 1932– , South African)
Gibson (Mel; 1956– , US/Australian)
Godard (Jean-Luc; 1930– , French)
Godber (John; 1956– , English)
Haydee (Marcia; 1939– , Brazilian)
Herzog (Werner; 1942– , German)
Hopper (Dennis; 1936– , US)
Howard (Ron; 1954– , US)
Hughes (Howard; 1905–76, US)
Huston (John; 1906–87, US)
Jarman (Derek; 1942–94, English)
Jordan (Neil; 1950– , Irish)
Jouvet (Louis; 1887–1951, French)
Kantor (Tadeusz; 1915–90, Polish)
Kasdan (Lawrence; 1949– , US)
Landis (John; 1950– , US)
Lupino (Ida; 1918–95, English)
Mendes (Sam; 1965– , English)
Miller (George; 1945– , Australian)
Miller (Jonathan; 1934– , English)
Moreau (Jeanne; 1928– , French)
Murnau (F W; 1888–1931, German)
Ophüls (Max; 1902–57, German/French)
Parker (Alan; 1944– , English)
Powell (Michael; 1905–90, English)
Prince (Hal; 1928– , US)
Prowse (Philip; 1937– , Scottish)
Quayle (Sir Anthony; 1913–89, English)
Reiner (Carl; 1922– , US)

Renoir (Jean; 1894–1979, French/US)
Rohmer (Eric; 1920– , French)
Siegal (Don; 1912–91, US)
Usigli (Rodolfo; 1905–79, Mexican)
Warhol (Andy; 1928–87, US)
Warner (Deborah; 1959– , English)
Warner (Jack; 1892–1978, Canadian/US)
Welles (Orson; 1915–85, US)
Wilder (Billy; 1906 2002, US)
Wilson (Robert; 1941– , US)
Zanuck (Darryl F; 1902–79, US)

07 Akerman (Chantal; 1950– , Belgian)
Aldrich (Robert; 1918–83, US)
Asquith (Anthony; 1902–68, English)
Belasco (David; 1853–1931, US)
Benigni (Roberto; 1952– , Italian)
Bennett (Alan; 1934– , English)
Bennett (Michael; 1943–87, US)
Bergman (Ingmar; 1918–2007, Swedish)
Berkoff (Steven; 1937– , English)
Bigelow (Kathryn; 1952– , US)
Boorman (John; 1933– , English)
Branagh (Kenneth; 1960– , Northern Irish)
Bresson (Robert; 1901–99, French)
Cameron (James; 1954– , Canadian)
Campion (Jane; 1954– , New Zealand)
Chabrol (Claude; 1930– , French)
Chaikin (Joseph; 1935–2003, US)
Chaplin (Charlie; 1889–1977, English)
Clavell (James; 1924–94, Australian/US)
Clurman (Harold; 1901–80, US)
Cocteau (Jean; 1889–1963, French)
Coppola (Francis Ford; 1939– , US)
Costner (Kevin; 1955– , US)
De Mille (Cecil B; 1881–1959, US)
De Palma (Brian; 1940– , US)
Douglas (Bill; 1934–91, Scottish)
Douglas (Michael; 1944– , US)
Fellini (Federico; 1920–93, Italian)
Fincher (David; 1962– , US)
Fleming (Tom; 1927– , Scottish)
Fleming (Victor; 1883–1949, US)
Forsyth (Bill; 1946– , Scottish)
Gaumont (Léon; 1864–1946, French)
Gilliam (Terry; 1940– , US)
Goldwyn (Samuel; 1882–1974, US)
Guthrie (Sir Tyrone; 1900–71, English)
Hartley (Hal; 1959– , US)
Heiberg (Gunnar; 1857–1929, Norwegian)
Holland (Agnieszka; 1948– , Polish)
Jackson (Peter; 1961– , New Zealand)
Joffrey (Robert; 1930–88, US)
Kaufman (George S; 1889–1961, US)
Kaufman (Philip; 1936– , US)
Kubrick (Stanley; 1928–99, US)
McBride (Jim; 1941– , US)
McGrath (John; 1935–2002, English)
Nichols (Mike; 1931– , German/US)

Olivier (Laurence, Lord; 1907–89, English)
Poitier (Sidney; 1924– , US)
Pollack (Sydney; 1934–2008, US)
Redford (Robert; 1937– , US)
Resnais (Alain; 1922– , French)
Robbins (Tim; 1958– , US)
Russell (Ken; 1927– , English)
Sellars (Peter; 1958– , US)
Sennett (Mack; 1880–1960, Canadian/US)
Stiller (Mauritz; 1883–1928, Finnish/
   Swedish)
Sturges (Preston; 1898–1959, US)
Sturges (Preston; 1898–1959, US)
van Sant (Gus; 1952– , US)
Wenders (Wim; 1945– , German)

08 Anderson (Lindsay; 1923–94, Indian/British)
Anderson (Paul Thomas; 1970– , US)
Barrault (Jean-Louis; 1910–94, French)
Berkeley (Busby; 1895–1976, US)
Bjørnson (Bjørnstjerne; 1832–1910,
   Norwegian)
Bogdanov (Michael; 1938– , English)
Brustein (Robert; 1927– , US)
Carrière (Jean-Claude; 1931– , French)
Clements (Sir John; 1910–88, English)
Crawford (Cheryl; 1902–86, US)
Eastwood (Clint; 1930– , US)
Friedkin (William; 1939– , US)
Griffith (D W; 1875–1948, US)
Houseman (John; 1902–88, Romanian/
   English/US)
Jarmusch (Jim; 1953– , US)
Jeffries (Lionel; 1926– , English)
Kurosawa (Akira; 1910–98, Japanese)
Levinson (Barry; 1942– , US)
Lubitsch (Ernst; 1892–1947, German)
Luhrmann (Baz; 1962– , Australian)
Lyubimov (Yuri; 1917– , Russian/Hungarian)
Marshall (Penny; 1942– , US)
Merchant (Ismail; 1936–2005, Indian)
Minnelli (Vincente; 1913–86, US)
Mitchell (Arthur; 1934– , US)
Ninagawa (Yukio; 1935– , Japanese)
Pasolini (Pier Paolo; 1922–75, Italian)
Piscator (Erwin; 1893–1966, German)
Polanski (Roman; 1933– , French/Polish)
Pudovkin (Vsevolod; 1893–1953, Russian)
Schepisi (Fred; 1939– , Australian)
Scorsese (Martin; 1942– , US)
Selznick (David O; 1902–65, US)
Sjöström (Victor; 1879–1960, Swedish)
Stroheim (Erich von; 1885–1957, Austrian)
Truffaut (François; 1932–84, French)
Visconti (Luchino; 1906–76, Italian)
von Trier (Lars; 1956– , Danish)
Zemeckis (Robert; 1952– , US)

09 Alexander (Bill; 1948– , English)

Almodóvar (Pedro; 1951– , Spanish)
Antonioni (Michelangelo; 1912–2007, Italian)
Armstrong (Gillian; 1952– , Australian)
Carpenter (John; 1948– , US)
Chen Kaige (1954– , Chinese)
Fernández (Emilio; 1904–86 , Mexican)
Greenaway (Peter; 1942– , English)
Grotowski (Jerzy; 1933–99, Polish)
Hitchcock (Sir Alfred; 1899–1980, English)
Malkovich (John; 1953– , US)
Meyerhold (Vsevolod; 1874–c.1940,
   Russian)
Minghella (Anthony; 1947–2008, English)
Mizoguchi (Kenji; 1898–1956, Japanese)
Mountford (Charles P; 1890–1976,
   Australian)
Peckinpah (Sam; 1925–84, US)
Plowright (Joan; 1929– , English)
Preminger (Otto; 1906–86, Austrian/US)
Spielberg (Steven; 1946– , US)
Stevenson (Robert; 1905–86, English)
Strasberg (Lee; 1901–82, Austrian/US)
Streisand (Barbra; 1942– , US)
Tarantino (Quentin; 1963– , US)
Tavernier (Bertrand; 1941– , French)
Von Trotta (Margarethe; 1942– , German)
Wanamaker (Sam; 1919–93, US)
Zinnemann (Fred; 1907–97, Austrian)

10 Bertolucci (Bernardo; 1941– , Italian)
Cronenberg (David; 1943– , Canadian)
Eisenstein (Sergei; 1898–1948, Russian)
Fassbinder (Rainer Werner; 1946–82,
   German)
Greengrass (Paul; 1955– , English)
Kaurismäki (Aki; 1957– , Finnish)
Kiarostami (Abbas; 1940– , Iranian)
Kieslowski (Krzysztof; 1941–96, Polish)
Littlewood (Joan; 1914–2002, English)
Makhmalbaf (Mohsen; 1957– , Iranian)
Mankiewicz (Joseph L; 1909–93, US)
Mnouchkine (Ariane; 1938– , French)
Rossellini (Roberto; 1906–77, Italian)
Saint-Denis (Michel; 1897–1971, French)
Soderbergh (Steven; 1963– , US)
Sucksdorff (Arne E; 1917–2001, Swedish)
Vakhtangov (Yevgeni; 1883–1922, Russian)
Wertmuller (Lina; 1928– , Italian)
Zeffirelli (Franco; 1923– , Italian)
Zetterling (Mai; 1925–94, Swedish)
Zhang Yimou (1951– , Chinese)

11 Bogdanovich (Peter; 1939– , US)
Dingelstedt (Franz von; 1814–81, German)
Mackendrick (Alexander; 1912–93, US)
Pressburger (Emeric; 1902–88, Hungarian)
Riefenstahl (Leni; 1902–2003, German)
Roddenberry (Gene; 1921–91, US)
Schlesinger (John; 1926–2003, English)

12 Attenborough (Richard, Lord; 1923– , English)
   Espert Romero (Nuria; 1935– , Spanish)
   Stanislavsky (1863–1938, Russian)
   Von Sternberg (Josef; 1894–1969, Austrian)

13 Aguilera Malta (Demetrio; 1909–81, Ecuadorean)
   Gutiérrez Alea (Tomás; 1928–96, Cuban)
   Stafford-Clark (Max; 1941– , English)

disease

Diseases and medical conditions include:

02 CF
ME
MS
TB

03 CFS
CJD
DVT
flu
FMS
IBS
PID
PKU
PMS
PMT
PVS
tic
TSS

04 acne
AIDS
clap
cold
coma
gout
kuru
Lyme
mono
rash
SARS

05 boils
colic
crabs
croup
favus
heart
hives
lupus
mumps
polio
rigor
ulcer
warts
Weil's
worms

06 angina
apnoea
asthma
autism
cancer

chorea
Crohn's
dropsy
eczema
emesis
goitre
Grave's
hernia
herpes
myopia
oedema
otitis
Paget's
quinsy
rabies
scurvy
sprain
squint
stroke
thrush
tumour
typhus

07 abscess
allergy
anaemia
anthrax
anxiety
aphasia
aphonia
atrophy
Batten's
bird flu
Bright's
bulimia
cholera
coeliac
kissing
leprosy
lockjaw
malaria
Marburg
measles
myalgia
mycosis
myiasis
rickets
rubella
sarcoma
scabies

tetanus
typhoid
vertigo

08 Addison's
adynamia
alopecia
aneurism
aneurysm
anorexia
avian flu
beriberi
botulism
bursitis
cachexia
club foot
cold sore
coxalgia
Cushing's
cynanche
cystitis
dementia
diabetes
dyschroa
embolism
epilepsy
exanthem
fibroids
fracture
furuncle
gangrene
glaucoma
Hodgkin's
impetigo
jaundice
kala-azar
kyphosis
listeria
lordosis
lymphoma
melanoma
Ménière's
migraine
myositis
necrosis
orchitis
pyelitis
Raynaud's
rhinitis
ringworm

sciatica
shingles
smallpox
stenosis
syphilis
tapeworm
Tay-Sachs
tinnitus
trachoma
venereal
viraemia

09 arthritis
arthrosis
Asperger's
bilharzia
black lung
brown lung
cataracts
chlamydia
chlorosis
cirrhosis
cri du chat
distemper
dysentery
dyspraxia
eclampsia
emphysema
enteritis
exanthema
halitosis
hepatitis
infection
influenza
ketonuria
king's evil
leukaemia
neoplasia
nephritis
nephrosis
neuralgia
paralysis
parotitis
pertussis
pneumonia
psoriasis
pyorrhoea
scoliosis
siderosis
silicosis
sinusitis
sunstroke
Sydenham's
toothache
Tourette's
urticaria
varicella

10 acromegaly

Alzheimer's
amoebiasis
asbestosis
Bell's palsy
Black Death
bronchitis
byssinosis
chickenpox
common cold
depression
dermatitis
diphtheria
gallstones
gingivitis
gonorrhoea
haemolysis
heat stroke
hyperaemia
laryngitis
Lassa fever
meningitis
metastasis
myasthenia
narcolepsy
ornithosis
orthopnoea
paraplegia
Parkinson's
rheumatism
salmonella
syringitis
tendonitis
thrombosis
titubation
trench foot

11 anaphylaxis
brain damage
brucellosis
cholestasis
cleft palate
consumption
dehydration
dengue fever
farmer's lung
green monkey
haemophilia
haemorrhage
heart attack
Huntington's
hydrophobia
hyperemesis
hyperplasia
hypersomnia
hypertrophy
hypotension
listeriosis
mastoiditis
motor neuron

myocarditis
peritonitis
pharyngitis
pneumonitis
proteinuria
psittacosis
rhinorrhoea
sarcoidosis
septicaemia
slipped disc
spina bifida
tennis elbow
tonsillitis
trench fever
yellow fever

12 appendicitis
athlete's foot
autoimmunity
cor pulmonale
desquamation
encephalitis
encocarditis
exophthalmia
foot-and-mouth
haematemesis
heart failure
hyperalgesia
hyperpyrexia
hypersthenia
hypertension
Legionnaires'
liver failure
lymphangitis
malnutrition
motor neurone
osteoporosis
pericarditis
quadraplegia
rhinorrhagia
scarlet fever
tuberculosis
typhoid fever

13 bronchiolitis
bubonic plague
cerebral palsy
coronary heart
Down's syndrome
dysmenorrhoea
elephantiasis
endometriosis
German measles
hyperlipaemia
hypoglycaemia
kidney failure
leishmaniasis
malabsorption
mononucleosis

osteomyelitis
poliomyelitis
Rett's syndrome
Reye's syndrome
schizophrenia
toxoplasmosis
varicose veins
West Nile virus
whooping cough
14 angina pectoris
break-bone fever
conjunctivitis

cystic fibrosis
glandular fever
housemaid's knee
hypercalcaemia
hyperglycaemia
hyperkeratosis
hypernatraemia
leukocytopenia
osteoarthritis
pneumoconiosis
rheumatic fever
river blindness
sleepy sickness

thyrotoxicosis
15 anorexia nervosa
atherosclerosis
bipolar disorder
gastro-enteritis
Gulf War syndrome
hyperadrenalism
hyperthyroidism
manic depression
Marfan's syndrome
phenylketonuria
schistosomiasis

Disease symptoms include:

04 pain
rash
05 cramp
fever
hives
06 aching
lesion
tremor
07 anxiety
fatigue
fitting
itching
08 bruising
coughing
deafness
fainting
headache
insomnia
numbness

sickness
sneezing
swelling
tingling
vomiting
weakness
09 blindness
diarrhoea
dizziness
heartburn
impotence
lassitude
nosebleed
paralysis
stiffness
twitching
10 congestion
depression
flatulence
irritation

sore throat
tenderness
11 convulsions
indigestion
loss of voice
trapped wind
12 constipation
incontinence
inflammation
irritability
loss of libido
muscle cramps
13 loss of hearing
stomach cramps
swollen glands
14 loss of appetite
pins and needles
15 high temperature
loss of sensation

Animal diseases include:

03 BSE
FMD
gid
orf
04 gape
gout
loco
roup
wind
05 bloat
braxy
farcy
frush
hoove
pearl
surra
vives
06 canker

Johne's
mad cow
Marek's
nagana
rabies
spavie
spavin
sturdy
07 anthrax
blue ear
dourine
hard pad
measles
mooneye
moorill
murrain
roaring
rubbers
scrapie

yellows
08 bovine TB
fowl-pest
glanders
pullorum
scaly-leg
seedy-toe
sheep-pox
staggers
swayback
swine-pox
wildfire
wire-heel
09 Aujeszky's
blackhead
distemper
Newcastle
scratches

sheep scab	Texas fever	cattle-plague
spauld-ill	water-brain	foot-and-mouth
St Hubert's	**11** blood-spavin	furunculosis
strangles	brucellosis	gall-sickness
10 blue tongue	mad staggers	**13** grass sickness
louping-ill	myxomatosis	grass staggers
ornithosis	parrot fever	leptospirosis
rinderpest	psittacosis	**14** sleepy staggers
sallenders		**15** Rift Valley fever
swamp fever	**12** black-quarter	stomach staggers
swine fever	bush sickness	

Plant diseases include:

04 bunt	red rot	crown rot	silver leaf
curl	**07** ferrugo	Dutch elm	sooty mould
rust	oak wilt	leaf curl	vine-mildew
smut	ring rot	loose-cut	**11** anthracnose
05 ergot	rosette	wheat eel	wheat mildew
06 blight	soft rot	**09** crown gall	**12** finger-and-toe
blotch	yellows	potato rot	peach-yellows
canker	**08** blackleg	tulip root	potato blight
mildew	black rot	**10** fire-blight	**13** powdery mildew
mosaic	clubroot	leaf mosaic	**14** psyllid yellows

See also **fever**; **inflammation**; **poison**; **skin**; **tumour**

dish see **food**; **pasta**; **potato**; **seafood**

district see **London**; **New York**; **Paris**; **United Kingdom**

diver see **swimming**

divination

Divination and fortune-telling techniques include:

04 dice

05 runes
tarot

06 I Ching
sortes (book opening)

07 dowsing (divining rod)
scrying (crystal gazing)

08 geomancy (shapes)
myomancy (mice)
taghairm (lying in a bullock's hide behind a
waterfall)
zoomancy (animals)

09 aeromancy (atmospheric phenomena)
astrology (stars and planets)
belomancy (arrows)
ceromancy (dropping melted wax in water)
gyromancy (walking in a circle and falling
from giddiness)

oenomancy (wine)
palmistry (hand)
pyromancy (fire)
sortilege (drawing lots)
tea leaves
theomancy (oracles)
tripudium (feeding birds)

10 axinomancy (an axe poised upon a stake, or
an agate upon a red-hot axe)
capnomancy (smoke)
cartomancy (playing cards)
chiromancy (reading the hand)
cleromancy (lot)
dukkeripen
hieromancy (sacrificial objects)
hydromancy (water)
lithomancy (stones)
numerology (numbers)
spodomancy (ashes)

11 bibliomancy (book opening)
botanomancy (plants)
crithomancy (strewing meal over sacrificial animals)
gastromancy (sounds from the belly, or by large-bellied glasses)
hepatoscopy (animal livers)
oneiromancy (dreams)
onychomancy (fingernails)
rhabdomancy (rod, especially divining for water or ore)
tephromancy (ashes, especially those left after a sacrifice)

12 clairvoyance
coscinomancy (sieve and shears)

lampadomancy (flame)
omphalomancy (number of future children from the knots in the navel-string)
ornithomancy (birds)
radiesthesia (various)
scapulomancy (cracks in a burning shoulder blade)

13 Book of Changes
crystal gazing
dactyliomancy (ring)
fortune cookie
omoplatoscopy (cracks in a burning shoulder blade)

14 crystallomancy (transparent bodies)

DIY

DIY terms include:

03 MDF
04 coat
glue
nail
05 joint
screw
tools
06 cement
pre-mix
router
sawing
tiling
washer
wiring
07 carving

Evo-Stik
planing
roofing
sanding
sealant
welding
08 Araldite®
concrete
drilling
flooring
fretwork
grouting
mitre box
overalls
painting

plumbing
Rawlplug®
staining
Swarfega®
woodwork
09 carpentry
hammering
lubricant
metalwork
polishing
Polyfilla®
soldering
sugar soap
superglue
wallpaper

10 decorating
multimeter
plastering
tile cutter
varnishing
wood filler
11 mains tester
masking tape
stencilling
white spirit
13 safety goggles
14 insulating tape
loft conversion
15 silicone sealant

See also **insulator**

doctor

Doctor types include:

02 GP
MO
03 vet
05 locum

06 intern
07 dentist
08 houseman
resident

09 registrar
10 consultant
12 family doctor
14 hospital doctor

medical officer

Doctors include:

04 Aziz (Dr; *A Passage to India*, 1924, E M Forster)
Cook (Frederick A; 1865–1940, US)
Davy (Edward; 1806–85, English/Australian)
Drew (Charles; 1904–50, US)
Gall (Franz Joseph; 1758–1828, German)
Gray (Edward Whitaker; 1748–1806, English)

Grew (Nehemiah; 1641–1712, English)
Hall (Marshall; 1790–1857, English)
Hill (Charles, Lord; 1904–89, English)
King (Sir Truby; 1858–1938, New Zealand)
Knox (Robert; *The Anatomist*, 1930, James Bridie)
Koch (Robert; 1843–1910, German)
Lind (James; 1716–94, Scottish)

Long (Crawford; 1815–78, US)
Razi (ar-; c.865–923/932, Persian)
Redi (Francesco; 1626–97, Italian)
Ross (Sir Ronald; 1857–1932, Indian/British)
Rush (Benjamin; 1745–1813, American)
Slop (Dr; *The Life and Opinions of Tristram Shandy*, 1759–67, Laurence Sterne)
Ward (Nathaniel; 1791–1868, English)

05 Blane (Sir Gilbert; 1749–1834, Scottish)
Borde (Andrew; c.1490–1549, English)
Brown (John; c.1735–88, Scottish)
Bruce (Sir David; 1855–1931, Scottish)
Caius (Dr; *The Merry Wives of Windsor*, 1597/8, William Shakespeare)
Caius (John; 1510–73, English)
Ellis (Havelock; 1859–1939, English)
Fanon (Frantz; 1925–61, French West Indian)
Fludd (Robert; 1574–1637, English)
Frank (Johann Peter; 1745–1821, German)
Galen (c.130–c.201 AD, Greek)
Graaf (Regnier de; 1641–73, Dutch)
Hayem (Georges; 1841–1920, French)
Hench (Philip S; 1896–1965, US)
Henry (William; 1774–1836, English)
Jones (Henry; 1831–99, English)
Kolff (Willem J; 1911– , Dutch/US)
Lange (Carl; 1834–1900, Danish)
Leete (Dr; *Looking Backward: 2000–1887*, 1888, Edward Bellamy)
Lower (Richard; 1631–91, English)
Mayer (Robert von; 1814–78, German)
Minot (George R; 1885–1950, US)
Osler (Sir William; 1849–1919, Canadian/British)
Paget (Sir James; 1814–99, English)
Pinch (Dr; *The Comedy of Errors*, 1594, William Shakespeare)
Pinel (Philippe; 1745–1826, French)
Plarr (Edouardo; *The Honorary Consul*, 1973, Graham Greene)
Prout (William; 1785–1850, English)
Remak (Robert; 1815–65, German)
Rider (Edward; *The Doctor's Family*, 1863, Margaret Oliphant)
Selye (Hans; 1907–82, Austrian/Canadian)
Skoda (Joseph; 1805–81, Austrian)
Smith (Thomas Southwood; 1788–1861, English)
Spock (Benjamin; 1903–98, US)
Steno (Nicolaus; 1638–86, Danish)
Tyson (Edward; 1651–1708, English)
Young (Thomas; 1773–1829, English)

06 Alpino (Prospero; 1553–1616, Italian)
Aselli (Gasparo; 1582–1626, Italian)
Bárány (Robert; 1876–1936, Austrian)
Bauhin (Caspar; 1560–1624, Swiss)

Bauhin (Gaspard ; 1560–1624, Swiss)
Becher (Johann Joachim; 1635–82, German)
Bichat (Marie; 1771–1802, French)
Boorde (Andrew; c.1490–1549, English)
Bowman (Sir William; 1816–92, English)
Bright (Richard; 1789–1858, English)
Bright (Timothy; c.1551–1615, English)
Browne (Sir Thomas; 1605–82, English)
Celsus (Aulus; 1 CAD, Roman)
Chagas (Carlos; 1879–1934, Brazilian)
Crofts (James; *The Small House at Allington*, 1864, Anthony Trollope)
Cullen (William; 1710–90, Scottish)
Curran (Dr; *The Ante-Room*, 1934, Kate O'Brien)
Darwin (Erasmus; 1731–1802, English)
Dawson (Bertrand, *Viscount*; 1864–1945, English)
Fernel (Jean; 1497–1558, French)
Finlay (Dr; *Country Doctor*, 1935, A J Cronin)
Finsen (Niels; 1860–1904, Danish)
Firmin (George; *A Shabby Genteel Story*, 1840, W M Thackeray)
Forman (Simon; 1552–1611, English)
Garrod (Sir Archibald; 1857–1936, English)
Gesner (Conrad; 1516–65, Swiss)
Gorgas (William; 1854–1920, US)
Graves (Robert; 1796–1853, Irish)
Halevi (Jehuda; 1075–1141, Spanish)
Hansen (Gerhard; 1841–1912, Norwegian)
Harvey (William; 1578–1657, English)
Hedwig (Johannes; 1730–99, German)
Iannis (Dr; *Captain Corelli's Mandolin*, 1994, Louis de Bernières)
Jacobi (Mary Putnam; 1842–1906, English/US)
Jacobs (Aletta; 1851–1929, Dutch)
Jekyll (Dr; *The Strange Case of Dr Jekyll and Mr Hyde*, 1886, Robert Louis Stevenson)
Jenner (Edward; 1749–1823, English)
Jenner (Sir William; 1815–98, English)
Magiot (Dr; *The Comedians*, 1966, Graham Greene)
Manson (Sir Patrick; 1844–1922, Scottish)
Mesmer (Franz; 1734–1815, Austrian)
Murphy (William P; 1892–1987, US)
Savart (Félix; 1791–1841, French)
Sloane (Sir Hans; 1660–1753, Northern Irish/British)
Thomas (E Donnall; 1920– , US)
Thorne (Thomas; *Dr Thorne*, 1858, Anthony Trollope)
Turner (William; c.1510–68, English)
Walker (Mary Edwards; 1832–1919, US)
Watson (John; *A Study in Scarlet*, 1887, Arthur Conan Doyle)
Willis (Thomas; 1621–73, English)

07 Addison (Thomas; 1793–1860, English)
Allbutt (Sir Thomas Clifford; 1836–1925, English)
Baillie (Matthew; 1761–1823, Scottish)
Beddoes (Thomas; 1760–1808, English)
Bigelow (Jacob; 1787–1879, US)
Bombard (Alain; 1924–2005, French)
Bretton (John; *Villette*, 1853, Charlotte Brontë)
Camerer (Rudolph; 1665–1721, German)
Cardano (Girolamo; 1501–76, Italian)
Carmody (Dr; *Black Jack*, 1968, Leon Garfield)
Carroll (James; 1854–1907, English/US)
Ctesias (5c BC, Greek)
Cushing (Harvey; 1869–1939, US)
Cuticle (Cadwallader; *White-Jacket*, 1850, Herman Melville)
Davaine (Casimir Joseph; 1812–82, French)
Edelman (Talbot; *Daughter Buffalo*, 1972, Janet Frame)
Eijkman (Christiaan; 1858–1930, Dutch)
Gilbert (William; 1544–1603, English)
Glauber (Johann Rudolph; 1604–70, German)
Guthrie (Samuel; 1782–1848, US)
Helmont (Jan van; 1579–1644, Flemish)
Hodgkin (Thomas; 1798–1866, English)
Imhotep (27c BC, Egyptian)
Jeddler (Anthony; *The Battle of Life*, 1846, Charles Dickens)
Laënnec (René; 1781–1826, French)
Laveran (Charles; 1845–1922, French)
Linacre (Thomas; c.1460–1524, English)
MacEwen (Sir William; 1848–1924, Scottish)
Macquer (Pierre Joseph; 1718–84, French)
Manette (Alexandre; *A Tale of Two Cities*, 1859, Charles Dickens)
Motlana (Nthato; 1925– , South African)
Nicolle (Charles; 1866–1936, French)
Pringle (Sir John; 1707–82, Scottish)
Sanchez (Francisco; c.1550–1623, Portuguese or Spanish)
Shonjen (Dr; 'The Good Anna', 1909, Gertrude Stein)
Sibbald (Sir Robert; 1641–1722, Scottish)
Siebold (Philipp von; 1796–1866, German)
Slammer (Dr; *Pickwick Papers*, 1837, Charles Dickens)
Sylvius (Franciscus; 1614–72, German)
Winston (Robert, Lord; 1940– , English)

08 Alcmaeon (fl.520 BC, Greek)
Anderson (Elizabeth Garrett; 1836–1917, English)
Aretaeus (fl.100 AD, Greek)
Avenzoar (c.1072–1162, Spanish)
Averroës (1126–98, Spanish)
Avicenna (980–1037, Persian)

Barnardo (Thomas; 1845–1905, Irish)
Billings (John Shaw; 1838–1913, US)
Birkbeck (George; 1776–1841, English)
Campbell (Jeff; 'Melanctha', 1909, Gertrude Stein)
Copeland (Benedict; *The Heart is a Lonely Hunter*, 1940, Carson McCullers)
Cournand (André F; 1895–1988, French/US)
Culpeper (Nicholas; 1616–54, English)
Duchenne (Guillaume; 1806–75, French)
Fishbein (Morris; 1889–1976, US)
Grenfell (Sir Wilfred; 1865–1940, English)
Hamilton (Alice; 1869–1970, US)
Heberden (William; 1710–1801, English)
Jeffries (John; 1744–1819, American)
Jex-Blake (Sophia; 1840–1912, English)
Linnaeus (Carl; 1707–78, Swedish)
Lombroso (Cesare; 1836–1909, Italian)
Magendie (François; 1783–1855, French)
Mitchell (Silas Weir; 1829–1914, US)
Monygham (Dr; *Nostromo*, 1904, Joseph Conrad)
Morgagni (Giovanni Battista; 1682–1771, Italian)
Mori Ogai (1862–1922, Japanese)
Prichard (James Cowles; 1786–1848, English)
Renaudot (Théophraste; 1586–1653, French)
Richards (Dickinson W; 1895–1973, US)
Sefström (Nils; 1765–1829, Swedish)
Servetus (Michael; 1511–53, Spanish)
Sherlock (Dame Sheila; 1918–2001, Irish/British)
Stoppard (Miriam; 1937– , English)
Sydenham (Thomas; 1624–89, English)
Tournier (Paul; 1898–1986, Swiss)
Villemin (Jean-Antoine; 1827–92, French)

09 Altounyan (Roger; 1922–87, Syrian/British)
Arbuthnot (John; 1667–1735, Scottish)
Armstrong (John; c.1709–79, Scottish)
Averrhoës (1126–98, Spanish)
Bartholin (Caspar, the Elder; 1585–1629, Swedish/Danish)
Bartholin (Erasmus; 1625–98, Danish)
Bartholin (Thomas, the Elder; 1616–80, Danish)
Biandrata (Giorgio; c.1515–c.1590, Italian)
Blackwell (Elizabeth; 1821–1910, English/US)
Blackwell (Emily; 1826–1910, English/US)
Blandrata (Giorgio; c.1515–c.1590, Italian)
Boerhaave (Hermann; 1668–1738, Dutch)
Cesalpino (Andrea; 1519–1603, Italian)
Dutrochet (Henri; 1776–1847, French)
Elliotson (John; 1791–1868, English)
Emin Pasha (1840–92, German)
Fabricius (Johannes; 1587–c.1615, Dutch)
Greatorex (Valentine; 1629–83, Irish)

Guillotin (Joseph; 1738–1814, French)
Hahnemann (Samuel; 1755–1843, German)
Kennicott (Will; *Main Street*, 1920, Sinclair Lewis)
Kingsford (Anna; 1846–88, English)
Long Ghost (*Omoo*, 1847, Herman Melville)
MacKenzie (Sir James; 1853–1925, Scottish)
Macnamara (Dame Jean; 1899–1968, Australian)
Parkinson (James; 1755–1824, English)
Pitcairne (Archibald; 1652–1713, Scottish)
Radcliffe (John; 1650–1714, English)
Ramazzini (Bernardini; 1633–1714, Italian)
Withering (William; 1741–99, English)

10 Arrowsmith (Martin; *Arrowsmith*, 1925, Sinclair Lewis)
Blenkinsop (Dr; *The Doctor's Dilemma*, 1906, George Bernard Shaw)
Bretonneau (Pierre; 1778–1862, French)
Camerarius (Rudolph Jacob; 1665–1721, German)
Fracastoro (Girolamo; 1483–1553, Italian)
Goldberger (Joseph; 1874–1929, Hungarian/US)
Greatrakes (Valentine; 1629–83, Irish)
Kübler-Ross (Elisabeth; 1926–2004, US)
L'Esperance (Elise; 1878–1959, US)
Mackarness (Richard; 1916–96, English)
Montessori (Maria; 1870–1952, Italian)
Paracelsus (1493–1541, German)

See also **medical**; **surgery**

Quackleben (Quentin; *St Ronan's Well*, 1823, Sir Walter Scott)
Sanctorius (1561–1636, Italian)
Wunderlich (Carl; 1815–77, German)

11 Antommarchi (Francesco; 1780–1838, French)
Asclepiades (fl.1cBC, Greek)
Auenbrugger (Leopold; 1722–1809, Austrian)
Cretzschmar (Philipp Jakob; 1786–1845, German)
Dioscorides (Pedanius; c.40–c.90AD, Greek)
Hippocrates (c.460–377/359BC, Greek)
Nostradamus (1503–66, French)
Ramón y Cajal (Santiago; 1852–1934, Spanish)
Summerskill (Edith, Baroness; 1901–80, English)

12 Kincaid-Smith (Priscilla; 1926–   , South African/Australian)

13 Prunesquallor (Alfred; *Titus Groan*, 1946, Mervyn Peake)
Turner-Warwick (Dame Margaret; 1924–   , English)

14 Doctor of Physic (the; *The Canterbury Tales*, c.1387–1400, Geoffrey Chaucer)
Paulus Aegineta (7c, Greek)

15 Kay-Shuttleworth (Sir James; 1804–77, English)
Sextus Empiricus (2cAD, Greek)

dog

Dog types include:

02 pi	**04** corn	watch	hearing
03 gun	rach	water	leading
hot	wild	zorro	mongrel
lap	**05** guard	**06** kennet	tracker
pet	guide	pariah	truffle
pie	house	police	**08** huntaway
pye	pooch	ranger	turnspit
sea	rache	ratter	**09** retriever
top	ratch	sleeve	**10** sheep-biter
toy	sheep	yellow	shin-barker
war	under	**07** harrier	**11** sleuth-hound

Dog breeds include:

03 gun	kuri	corgi
lab	Peke	dhole
Pom	tosa	dingo
pug	**05** akita	husky
04 chow	boxer	hyena

laika
spitz

06 badger
bandog
beagle
bitser
borzoi
briard
collie
poodle
saluki
Scotty
setter
vizsla
Westie

07 basenji
bouvier
bulldog
bush dog
coondog
griffon
lurcher
Maltese
mastiff
pointer
Samoyed
Scottie
Shar-Pei
sheltie
shih tzu
sloughi
spaniel
terrier
volpino
whippet

08 Airedale
Alsatian

chow-chow
coach dog
Doberman
elkhound
foxhound
keeshond
komondor
labrador
Landseer
malamute
papillon
Pekinese
Sealyham
sheepdog
warrigal

09 boar-hound
chihuahua
coonhound
dachshund
Dalmatian
Eskimo dog
Great Dane
greyhound
Kerry blue
Lhasa Apso
Pekingese
red setter
retriever
schnauzer
St Bernard
wolfhound

10 bloodhound
fox-terrier
Iceland-dog
Maltese dog
otter hound
Pomeranian
raccoon dog

Rottweiler
sausage dog
schipperke
spotted dog
St Bernard's

11 Afghan hound
basset-hound
bichon frise
bull mastiff
bull-terrier
carriage dog
Irish setter
Jack Russell
kangaroo dog
King Charles
wishtonwish

12 Border collie
cairn terrier
heelermoppet
Irish terrier
Japanese tosa
Newfoundland
West Highland

13 affenpinscher
bearded collie
Boston terrier
cocker spaniel
Dandie Dinmont
Scotch terrier

14 English terrier
German Shepherd
Irish wolfhound
pit bull terrier
Tibetan terrier

15 golden retriever
Scottish terrier
springer spaniel

Dogs include:

03 Lad (*Lad: A Dog*, 1965, A P Terhune)

04 Lucy (Blue Peter dog, 1998–)
Nana (*Peter Pan*, 1904, J M Barrie)
Odie (*Garfield*, 1978– , Jim Davis, comic strip)
Shep (Blue Peter dog, 1971–78)
Spot (Spot the Dog series, 1980– , Eric Hill)
Toby (Punch and Judy)
Toto (*The Wonderful Wizard of Oz*, 1900, L Frank Baum)

05 Balto (1919–33, Alaskan husky)
Butch (*Tom & Jerry*, 1967– , MGM cartoon)
Flush (*Flush: A Biography*, 1933, Virginia Woolf)
Goofy (1932– , Disney animation)

Laika (first dog in space, d.1957)
Petra (Blue Peter dog, 1962–77)
Pluto (1930– , Disney animation)
Pongo (*The Hundred and One Dalmatians*, 1956, Dodie Smith)
Sadie (explosives sniffer dog)
Snowy (*Tintin*, 1929–83, Herge)
Timmy (The Famous Five series, 1942–63, Enid Blyton)

06 Buster (explosives sniffer dog)
Droopy (1943–58, Tex Avery, MGM cartoon)
Gelert (Welsh mythology)
Gromit (Wallace & Gromit series, Aardman Animations)
Hector (*Hector's House*, 1960s, UK children's TV)

Lassie (*Lassie Come Home*, 1940, Eric Knight)
Missis (*The Hundred and One Dalmatians*, 1956, Dodie Smith)
Nipper (RCA 'His Master's Voice' logo)
Sirius (star)
Snoopy (*Peanuts*, 1950–2000, Charles Shulz)

07 Charley (*Travels with Charley*, 1962, John Steinbeck)
Gnasher (*The Beano*, 1938– , D C Thomson, comic)
Perdita (*The Hundred and One Dalmatians*, 1956, Dodie Smith)
Roobarb (*Roobarb*, 1974–2005, Grange Caveley, BBC cartoon)

08 Bullseye (*Oliver Twist*, 1838, Charles Dickens)

Cerberus (Greek mythology)
Dogmatix (Asterix series, 1959– , René Goscinny & Albert Uderzo)

09 Rin Tin Tin (1930–33, US radio and TV)
Scooby Doo (*Scooby Doo*, 1969– , Hanna-Barbera cartoon)

10 Deputy Dawg (1959–72, Terrytoons cartoon)
Fred Basset (1963– , Alex Graham, newspaper comic strip)

12 Real Huntsman (fl.1949–51, US greyhound)

13 Master McGrath (1866–77, Irish greyhound)
Mick the Miller (1926–39, Irish greyhound)

15 Greyfriars Bobby (d.1872)
The Littlest Hobo (1963–65/1979–85, Canadian TV series)

Terms to do with dogs include:

03 bay	yowl	ranger	huntaway
cur	**05** bitch	ratter	mahogany
paw	blaze	setter	markings
pet	brach	shaggy	mottling
pup	breed	silver	pedigree
red	brush	touser	purebred
tan	Canis	towser	ring tail
yap	cobby	toy dog	sheepdog
yip	cream	woolly	shock dog
04 bark	flews	yapper	turnspit
bite	groom	**07** apricot	watchdog
blue	growl	brindle	water dog
bone	hound	doggles	**09** button ear
bowl	leash	dogsled	cave canem
burr	liver	dropper	chocolate
claw	mange	grizzle	crop-eared
coat	pinto	harness	dog jacket
fang	pooch	lurcher	dog racing
fawn	puppy	mongrel	dog sledge
flea	rache	pastern	dogsleigh
gold	ratch	rose ear	kennelman
heel	spitz	scumber	miniature
hock	whelp	skummer	outer coat
howl	whine	sniffer	police dog
mutt	worry	starter	poop scoop
pied	**06** basket	utility	purebreed
rach	bitser	walkies	retriever
rake	bow wow	wheaten	sleeve dog
roan	canine	whiffet	steel grey
ruby	collar	wolf dog	tricolour
sick	docked	yapster	undercoat
spay	fallow	**08** brindled	**10** canophobia
tail	gun dog	curl tail	choke chain
tick	hamble	domestic	dog biscuit
tike	kennel	flecking	dog carrier
tyke	lapdog	forelegs	dog-fancier
woof	muzzle	guard dog	dog handler
yaff	neuter	guide dog	feathering

flea collar
hearing dog
long-haired
scent hound
shin-barker
sight hound

tracker dog
truffle dog
11 black-and-tan
canophilist
puppy-walker
short-haired

sleuth-hound
trendle-tail
trindle-tail
trundle-tail
12 double coated
forequarters

hindquarters
smooth-haired

13 pooper-scooper

See also **hybrid**; **spaniel**; **terrier**

doll

Dolls include:

03 kid
rag
wax
04 baby
mama
05 China
cloth
Dutch
metal
paper
Paris
Sindy®
vinyl
06 artist
Barbie®
bisque
blow-up
Daruma

ethnic
fabric
Hamble
kewpie
modern
moppet
ningyo
poppet
puppet
voodoo
wooden
07 fashion
jointed
kachina
kokeshi
nesting
rag baby
Russian

08 golliwog
gollywog
09 miniature
porcelain
tachibina
Tiny Tears®
10 matryoshka
Raggedy Ann
topsy-turvy
11 composition
gosho ningyo
Holly Hobbie®
papier-mâché
Polly Pocket®
12 reproduction
15 Cabbage Patch Kid®
frozen Charlotte

See also **toy**

dolphin *see* **whale**

domain *see* **classification**

domestic appliance

Domestic appliances include:

03 Aga®
hob
Vax®
04 iron
oven
spit
05 grill
mixer
radio
stove
06 cooker
fridge
Hoover®
juicer

kettle
washer
07 blender
fan oven
freezer
griddle
ionizer
toaster
08 barbecue
gas stove
hotplate
wireless
09 deep fryer
Dutch oven

DVD player
steam iron
10 coffee mill
deep-freeze
dishwasher
humidifier
liquidizer
percolator
rotisserie
slow cooker
steam press
television
waffle iron
11 tumble-drier
washer-drier

12 kitchen range
refrigerator
stereo system
trouser press
13 carpet sweeper
electric grill
floor polisher

food processor
fridge-freezer
ice-cream maker
microwave oven
sandwich maker
vacuum cleaner
video recorder

14 electric cooker
juice extractor
upright cleaner
washing machine
15 carpet shampooer
cylinder cleaner

See also **house**

Dostoevsky, Fyodor (1821–81)

Significant works include:

08 *Poor Folk* (1846)
The Idiot (1868)
09 *The Devils* (1871–72)
The Double (1846)
11 *The Raw Youth* (1875)
White Nights (1847)
13 *The Adolescent* (1875)
17 *The House of the Dead* (1860)
18 *Crime and Punishment* (1866)
20 *Notes from Underground* (1864)

The Brothers Karamazov (1879–80)
23 *Notes from the Underground* (1864)
24 *The Insulted and the Injured* (1861)
25 *The Village of Stepanchikovo* (1859)
26 *Notes from the House of the Dead* (1860)
30 *Winter Notes on Summer Impressions* (1863)
42 *The Village of Stepanchikovo and Its Inhabitants* (1859)

Significant characters include:

05 Rodia
Sonia
06 Dounia
Rodion
07 Myshkin (Prince Leo Nikolayevich)
Rodenka
08 Ivanovna (Katerina)
Nastasya
Petrovna (Varvara)
Rogozhin (Parfyon)
09 Karamazov (Alexei

'Alyosha' Fyodorovich)
Karamazov (Dmitri Fyodorovich)
Karamazov (Fyodor Pavlovich)
Karamazov (Ivan Fyodorovich)
Petrovich (Alexander)
Stavrogin (Nikolai)
10 Fillipnova (Nastasya)
Marmeladov (Sofya 'Sonia' Semyonovna)

11 Raskolnikov (Avdotya 'Dounia' Romanovna)
Raskolnikov (Rodion/ Rodya/Rodenka/Rodka Romanovitch)
Stepanovich (Peter)
Trofimovich (Stephan)
12 Svidrigaïlov (Arkady Ivanovitch)
13 Prince Myshkin
14 Underground Man

double agent see **spy**

Doyle, Sir Arthur Conan (1859–1930)

Significant works include:

08 *Sir Nigel* (1906)
Waterloo (1907)
11 *Micah Clarke* (1889)
Rodney Stone (1896)
12 *The Lost World* (1912)
White Company (1891)
13 *The Sign of Four* (1890)
15 *A Study in Scarlet* (1887)

19 *The War in South Africa* (1902)
24 *The History of Spiritualism* (1926)
25 *The Hound of the Baskervilles* (1901–02)
26 *The Memoirs of Sherlock Holmes* (1892–94)
28 *The Exploits of Brigadier Gerard* (1896)
29 *The Adventures of Sherlock Holmes* (1891–93)

Significant characters include:

06 Clarke (Micah)
Gerard (Brigadier Etienne)
Holmes (Sherlock)
Watson (Dr John H)

08 Lestrade (Inspector G)

Moriarty (Professor James)

10 Challenger (Professor George Edward)

11 Baskerville (Sir Charles)
Baskerville (Sir Henry)
Baskerville (Sir Hugo)

drama *see* **play**

dress

Dresses include:

03 mob

04 ball
coat
maxi
sack
sari
tent

05 shift
shirt
smock
tasar

06 caftan

dirndl
jumper
kaftan
kimono
muu-muu
sheath
tusser

07 bathing
chemise
evening
gym slip
kitenge

matinée
tussore
wedding

08 ball-gown
cocktail
gym tunic
negligée
pinafore
princess
sundress

09 cheongsam
farandine

going-away
minidress
slammakin
trollopee

10 dinner-gown
farrandine
slammerkin
wraparound

11 décolletage
Dolly Varden
riding habit

12 shirtwaister

dressing *see* **salad**

drink

Alcoholic drinks include:

03 ale
gin
kir
rum
rye

04 arak
beer
grog
hock
mead
ouzo
port
sake
vino
wine

05 cider
G and T
lager
perry
Pimm's®
plonk
stout
vodka

06 arrack
bishop
brandy
bubbly
Cognac
eggnog
grappa
porter
poteen
Scotch
shandy
sherry
whisky

07 absinth
alcopop
aquavit
Bacardi®
bourbon
Campari
Gordon's®
liqueur
Marsala
Martell®

Martini®
pink gin
red wine
retsina
sangria
sloe gin
spirits
tequila
vin rosé
whiskey

08 absinthe
advocaat
Armagnac
Calvados
cold duck
Guinness®
hot toddy
schnapps
Smirnoff®
vermouth
vin blanc
vin rouge

09 badminton

Beefeater®
champagne
cocktails
Laphroaig®
snakebite
white wine
Wincarnis®
10 ginger wine

Remy Martin®
11 black-and-tan
boilermaker
Courvoisier®
gin-and-tonic
Glenfiddich®
Irish coffee
Jack Daniel's®

12 Famous Grouse®
Glenmorangie®
malternative
13 peach schnapps
Scotch and soda
14 Bombay Sapphire®

Non-alcoholic drinks include:

03 pop
tea
04 Coke®
milk
soda
05 Assam
cocoa
float
julep
latte
mixer
Pepsi®
tonic
water
06 coffee
Indian
Irn-Bru®
Ribena®
squash
tisane
07 beef tea
cordial
limeade
Perrier®

seltzer
08 café noir
China tea
Coca-Cola®
Earl Grey
espresso
expresso
fruit tea
green tea
Horlicks®
lemonade
lemon tea
Lucozade®
Ovaltine®
root beer
smoothie
09 Aqua Libra®
ayahuasco
Canada Dry®
cherryade
cream soda
ginger ale
herbal tea
milk shake

mint-julep
orangeade
soda water
10 café au lait
café filtre
cappuccino
fizzy drink
fruit juice
ginger beer
rosehip tea
still water
tonic water
Vichy water
11 barley water
bitter lemon
camomile tea
12 hot chocolate
mineral water
sarsaparilla
13 peppermint tea
Turkish coffee
14 sparkling water
15 lapsang souchong

Drinks of the gods include:

06 amrita
nectar

08 ambrosia

Special drinks include:

03 ava
04 kava

soma
05 haoma

09 ayahuasco

See also **beer**; **cocktail**; **coffee**; **liqueur**; **spirit**; **tea**; **water**; **whisky**; **wine**

drug

Drugs include:

01 Q
03 AZT
05 Intal®
NSAID
Taxol®
Zyban®

06 opiate
Prozac®
statin
sulpha
Valium®
Viagra®

Zantac®
07 antacid
aspirin
codeine
heparin
insulin

Nurofen®
quinine
Relenza®
Ritalin®
Seroxat®
steroid

08 Antabuse®
diazepam
diuretic
hyoscine
methadon
morphine
narcotic
neomycin
orlistat
Rohypnol®
sedative
warfarin

09 aciclovir
acyclovir
analgesic
cortisone
digitalis
ibuprofen
methadone

oestrogen
stimulant
tamoxifen
temazepam

10 antibiotic
anxiolytic
chloroform
chloroquin
dimorphine
interferon
penicillin
ranitidine
salbutamol

11 allopurinol
amoxicillin
amyl nitrate
anaesthetic
beta-blocker
chloroquine
cyclosporin
haloperidol
ipecacuanha
neuroleptic
paracetamol
propranolol

vasodilator
12 ACE-inhibitor
chlorambucil
methotrexate
progesterone
sleeping pill
streptomycin
sulphonamide
tetracycline

13 antibacterial
anticoagulant
antihistamine
streptokinase
tranquillizer

14 anticonvulsant
antidepressant
azidothymidine
bronchodilator
corticosteroid
erythropoietin
hallucinogenic
hydrocortisone

15 chloramphenicol
vasoconstrictor

Illegal drugs include:

01 E
03 ice
LSD
PCP
pot
tab
04 acid
barb
blow
coke
dope
dove
gage
hash
hemp
pill
weed
05 crack

crank
dagga
jelly
opium
smack
speed
upper
06 downer
heroin
peyote
popper
07 cocaine
crystal
ecstasy
fantasy
guaraná
pep pill
roofies

08 cannabis
ketamine
laudanum
methadon
morphine
Rohypnol®
Special K
09 angel dust
dance drug
marijuana
methadone
peace pill
temazepam
11 amphetamine
barbiturate
purple heart
12 date-rape drug
13 phencyclidine

See also **analgesic**; **antibiotic**; **medicine**; **narcotic**

duck

Ducks include:

04 blue
musk
smee
smew
surf

teal
wood
05 eider
Pekin
ruddy

scaup
06 burrow
hareld
herald
magpie

Peking
runner
scoter
smeath
smeeth
spirit
tufted
velvet
wigeon
07 crested
gadwall
mallard
moulard
muscovy

See also **bird**

old wife
pintail
pochard
steamer
08 garganey
hookbill
mandarin
old squaw
shelduck
09 Cuthbert's
goldeneye
goosander
harlequin
merganser

sheldrake
shielduck
shoveller
10 bufflehead
canvasback
long-tailed
ring-necked
11 ferruginous
St Cuthbert's
white-headed
12 common scoter
Indian runner
velvet scoter
13 ruddy shelduck

Dumas, Alexandre (1802–70)

Significant works include:

07 *Anthony* (1831)
   Olympia (1851)
09 *My Memoirs* (1852–55)
11 *Queen Margot* (1845)
13 *Ten Years Later* (1848–50)
   The Black Tulip (1850)
14 *The Mouth of Hell* (1851)
15 *Isabel of Bavaria* (1835)
   The Tower of Nesle (1832)
16 *The Company of Jéhu* (1857)
   The War of the Women (1844–46)
   Twenty Years After (1845)
17 *The Queen's Necklace* (1849–50)
18 *The Lady of Monsoreau* (1845)

The Regent's Daughter (1844)
The Three Musketeers (1844)
19 *Henri III and His Court* (1829)
   Memoirs of a Physician (1846–8)
   The Bastard of Mauléon (1846–47)
   The Countess de Charny (1852–55)
20 *The Whites and the Blues* (1867–68)
21 *The Count of Monte Cristo* (1845–46)
22 *Pauline: A Tale of Normandy* (1838)
   The Knight of the Red House (1845–46)
   The Vicomte de Bragelonne (1848–50)
27 *The Memoirs of Dr Joseph Balsamo*
   (1846–48)
   The Woman with the Velvet Collar (1850)

Significant characters include:

04 Anne (Queen)
05 Faria (Abbé)
   Kitty
   Raoul
06 Busoni (The Abbé)
   Dantès (Edmond)
   Margot (Queen)
   Michon (Marie)
   Milady
07 Fouquet (Nicolas)

Grimaud
Mazarin (Cardinal)
Mondego (Fernand)
08 Danglars (Monsieur, later
   Baron)
   de Winter (Lady 'Milady')
   Louis XIV
   Mercedes
   Planchet
09 de Morcerf (Albert)

Louis XIII
Richelieu (Cardinal)
10 Bragelonne (Vicomte de)
   Buckingham (George
   Villiers, Duke of)
11 de Villefort (Monsieur
   Gérard)
   Monte Cristo (The Count of)
13 Anne of Austria (Queen)

Musketeers include:

05 Athos
06 Aramis

07 Porthos
09 D'Artagnan

Dvořák, Antonín (1841–1904)

Significant works include:

05 *Vanda* (1876)

06 *Alfred* (1938)
   Armida (1904)

07 *Jacobin* (1889)
   Rusalka (1901)

08 *Dimitrij* (1882)
   'American' (String Quartet; 1894)
   'New World' (Symphony; 1893)

09 *St Ludmila* (Oratorio; 1886)

10 *Humoresque* (1894)

11 *Requiem Mass* (1891)

14 *Dumky Piano Trio* (1891)
   Slavonic Dances (1878/1887)

15 *Josef Kajetan Tyl* (1882)
   Kate and the Devil (1899)
   'From the New World' (Symphony; 1893)

17 'The Bells of Zlonice' (Symphony; 1936)

dwarf

Snow White's seven dwarfs:

03 Doc	Happy	Sleepy	07 Bashful
05 Dopey	06 Grumpy	Sneezy	

dye

Dyes include:

04 anil	fustic	flavine	turnsole
wald	indigo	magenta	09 cochineal
weld	kamala	mauvein	nigrosine
woad	korkir	mauvine	primuline
05 chica	madder	para-red	safranine
eosin	mauvin	ponceau	Saxon blue
henna	orcein	saffron	Turkey red
mauve	orchel		Tyrian red
06 anatto	orchil	08 amaranth	
archil	07 alkanet	fuchsine	10 carthamine
corkir	annatto	mauveine	Saxony blue
flavin	azurine	orchella	tartrazine
	cudbear	orchilla	12 Tyrian purple
		safranin	

See also **pigment**

dynasty

Dynasties include:

02 Yi	Sung	Valois	Habsburg
03 Jin	Tang	Wettin	Ilkhanid
Qin	Vasa	Zangid	09 Jagiellon
Sui	Yuan	07 'Abbasid	10 Qarakhanid
04 Asen	Zhou	Ayyubid	11 Plantagenet
Avis	05 Ch'ing	Chakkri	12 Hohenstaufen
Chin	Piast	Fatimid	Hohenzollern
Lodi	Qajar	Romanov	14 Petrovic-Njegos
Ming	Shang	Safavid	
Qing	06 Chakri	Tughlaq	
Song	Sayyid	08 Capetian	

E

ear

Earth's crust *see* **crust**

eating

See also **animal**

economics

Economics types include:

10 agronomics	12 econometrics	microeconomics
11 cliometrics	14 macroeconomics	

Economics theories and schools include:

07 Marxian
09 Keynesian
Ricardian
10 Game theory
11 Physiocracy

12 Mercantilism
Neo-classical
Neo-Keynesian
Neo-Ricardian
13 Chicago school
Post-Keynesian

14 Austrian school
15 Classical school

Economists and economic historians include:

03 Say (Jean Baptiste; 1767–1832, French)
Sen (Amartya Kumar; 1933– , Indian)

04 Cole (G D H; 1889–1958, English)
Hogg (Sarah Elizabeth Mary Hogg, Baroness; 1946– , English)
Mill (James; 1773–1836, Scottish)
Nash (John F, Jnr; 1928– , US)
Webb (Beatrice; 1858–1943, English)
Webb (Sidney James, Baron Passfield; 1859–1947, English)

05 Arrow (Kenneth Joseph; 1921– , US)
Carey (Henry Charles; 1793–1879, US)
Coase (Ronald H; 1910– , English)
Hayek (Friedrich August von; 1899–1992, Austrian/British)
Hicks (Sir John Richard; 1904–89, English)
Honda (Toshiaki; 1744–1821, Japanese)
Ikeda (Hayato; 1900–65, Japanese)
Klein (Lawrence Robert; 1920– , US)
Kreps (Juanita; 1921– , US)
Lewis (Sir Arthur; 1915–91, St Lucian/British)
Lucas (Robert E, Jnr; 1937– , US)
Meade (James Edward; 1907–95, English)
North (Douglass C; 1920– , US)
Ohlin (Bertil Gotthard; 1899–1979, Swedish)
Paish (Frank Walter; 1898–1988, English)
Passy (Frédéric; 1822–1912, French)
Petty (Sir William; 1623–87, English)
Popov (Gavril Kharitonovich; 1936– , Russian)
Simon (Herbert Alexander; 1916–2001, US)
Smith (Adam; 1723–90, Scottish)
Solow (Robert Merton; 1924– , US)
Stone (Sir Richard Nicholas; 1913–91, English)
Tobin (James; 1918–2002, US)

06 Allais (Maurice; 1911– , French)

Aribau (Bonaventura Carles; 1798–1862, Spanish)
Aumann (Robert J; 1930– , Israeli/US)
Becker (Gary S; 1930– , US)
Cassel (Gustav; 1866–1945, Swedish)
Çiller (Tansu; 1946– , Turkish)
Cobden (Richard; 1804–65, English)
Coombs (H C; 1906–97, Australian)
Cripps (Sir Stafford; 1889–1952, English)
Debreu (Gerard; 1921– , French/US)
du Pont (Pierre-Samuel; 1739–1817, French/US)
Erhard (Ludwig; 1897–1977, German)
Fisher (Irving; 1867–1947, US)
Frisch (Ragnar Anton Kittil; 1895–1973, Norwegian)
George (Henry; 1839–97, US)
Giffen (Sir Robert; 1837–1910, Scottish)
Harrod (Sir Henry Roy Forbes; 1900–78, English)
Hobson (John Atkinson; 1858–1940, English)
Holmes (Sir Frank Wakefield; 1924– , New Zealand)
Horner (Francis; 1778–1817, Scottish)
Jevons (William Stanley; 1835–82, English)
Kaldor (Nicholas Kaldor, Baron; 1908–86, Hungarian/British)
Keynes (John Maynard Keynes, 1st Baron; 1883–1946, English)
Le Play (Frédéric; 1806–82, French)
Maskin (Eric S; 1950– , US)
Merton (Robert C; 1944– , US)
Miller (Merton H; 1923–2000, US)
Monnet (Jean; 1888–1979, French)
Myrdal (Gunnar; 1898–1987, Swedish)
Pareto (Vilfredo; 1848–1923, French/Italian)
Phelps (Edmund S; 1933– , US)
Rostow (Walt Whitman; 1916– , US)
Selten (Reinhard; 1930– , German/US)
Sharpe (William F; 1934– , US)

Spence (A Michael; 1943– , US)
Struve (Pyotr Berngardovich; 1870–1944, Russian)
Tawney (R H; 1880–1962, English)
Turgot (Anne Robert Jacques; 1727–81, French)
Veblen (Thorstein; 1857–1929, US)
Wilson (James; 1805–60, Scottish)

07 Abalkin (Leonid Ivanovich; 1930– , Russian)
Akerlof (George A; 1940– , US)
Bagehot (Walter; 1826–77, English)
Douglas (Sir Roger Owen; 1937– , New Zealand)
Eyskens (Gaston; 1905–88, Belgian)
Fawcett (Henry; 1833–84, English)
Heckman (James J; 1944– , US)
Hurwicz (Leonard; 1917–2008, Russian/US)
Jackson (Dame Barbara Mary Ward, Baroness; 1914–81, English)
Kalecki (Michal; 1899–1970, Polish)
Kaufman (Henry; 1927– , German/US)
Krugman (Robin; 1953– , US)
Kuznets (Simon Smith; 1901–85, Ukrainian/US)
Leacock (Stephen Butler; 1869–1944, Canadian)
Malthus (Thomas Robert; 1766–1834, English)
Mundell (Robert A; 1932– , Canadian)
Myerson (Roger; 1951– , US)
Peacock (Sir Alan Turner; 1922– , Scottish)
Quesnay (François; 1694–1774, French)
Ricardo (David; 1772–1823, English)
Robbins (Lionel Charles Robbins, Baron; 1898–1984, English)
Russell (George William; 1867–1935, Irish)
Scholes (Myron S; 1941– , US)
Schultz (Theodore William; 1902–98, US)
Stigler (George Joseph; 1911–91, US)
Toynbee (Arnold; 1852–83, English)
Vickrey (William Spencer; 1914–96, Canadian)
Volcker (Paul Adolph; 1927– , US)
Walters (Sir Alan; 1926– , English)

08 Anderson (James; 1739–1808, Scottish)
Brentano (Lujo; 1844–1931, German)
Buchanan (James McGill; 1919– , US)
Bulgakov (Sergei Nikolayevich; 1871–1944, Russian)
Crawford (Sir John Grenfell; 1910–85, Australian)

Crowther (Geoffrey Crowther, Baron; 1907–72, English)
Friedman (Milton; 1912–2006, US)
Haavelmo (Trygve Magnus; 1911–99, Norwegian)
Harsanyi (John C; 1920–2000, Hungarian/US)
Koopmans (Tjalling Charles; 1910–85, Dutch/US)
Leontief (Wassily; 1906–99, Russian/US)
Marshall (Alfred; 1842–1924, English)
McFadden (Daniel L; 1937– , US)
Mirrlees (Sir James Alexander; 1936– , Scottish)
Petrokov (Nikolai Yakovlevich; 1937– , Russian)
Primakov (Yevgeny Maksimovich; 1929– , Russian)
Robinson (Joan Violet; 1903–83, English)
Schiller (Karl; 1911–94, German)
Shatalin (Stanislav Sergeyevich; 1934–97, Soviet)
Stiglitz (Joseph E; 1943– , US)
von Mises (Ludwig; 1881–1973, Austrian)
Youngson (Alexander John; 1918– , Scottish)

09 Alexander (Sir Kenneth John Wilson; 1922–2001, Scottish)
Beveridge (William Henry Beveridge, 1st Baron; 1879–1963, Indian/British)
Bogomolov (Oleg Timofeyevich; 1927– , Russian)
Edgeworth (Francis Ysidro; 1845–1926, Irish)
Galbraith (J K; 1908–2006, Canadian/US)
Markowitz (Harry M; 1927– , US)
Rodbertus (Johann Karl; 1805–75, German)
Samuelson (Paul Anthony; 1915– , US)
Schelling (Thomas C; 1921– , US)
Tinbergen (Jan; 1903–94, Dutch)

10 Aganbegyan (Abel Gazevich; 1932– , Armenian/Russian)
Delfim Neto (Antônio; 1929– , Brazilian)
Modigliani (Franco; 1918– , Italian/US)
Schumpeter (Joseph Alois; 1883–1950, Austrian/US)

11 Balcerowicz (Leszek; 1947– , Polish)
Kantorovich (Leonid Vitalevich; 1912–86, Soviet)
Zaslavskaya (Tatyana Ivanovna; 1927– , Russian)

Terms used in economics include:

03 EMU	PEP	FTSE
GDP	WTO	GATT
GNP	**04** boom	OECD
IMF	debt	**05** asset

funds
share
slump
stock
trust
yield

06 budget
cartel
credit
mature
NASDAQ®
tariff
trader

07 annuity
autarky
buy-back
capital
deficit
embargo
futures
pension
product
savings
The City

08 cash flow
consumer
discount
dividend
e-economy
interest
leverage
monetary
monopoly
mortgage
producer
scarcity
taxation
tax haven
trade gap

09 cash ratio
commodity
deflation
excise tax
green fund
income tax

inflation
liability
liquidity
oligopoly
recession
reflation
skills gap
stamp duty
trademark
unit trust

10 bear market
bull market
capitalism
depression
excise duty
fiscal drag
fiscal year
new economy
old economy
price index
tax evasion
trade cycle
trade union
Wall Street

11 acquisition
CAT standard
Central Bank
devaluation
gold reserve
grey economy
liquid asset
money supply
open economy
overheating
reserve bank
stagflation
stakeholder
stock market
transaction

12 black economy
common market
consumer good
discount rate
economic rent
fixed capital
gold standard

human capital
marginal cost
merchant bank
mixed economy
price control
productivity
public sector
siege economy
stop-go policy
tiger economy
trade barrier
trade deficit
unemployment

13 budget deficit
business cycle
clearing-house
credit squeeze
Dow-Jones index
equity finance
financial year
free-trade area
hidden economy
liquidization
listed company
market economy
Phillips curve
private sector
protectionism
socio-economic
stock exchange
the Square Mile

14 balance of trade
command economy
commercial bank
corporation tax
disequilibrium
economy of scale
planned economy
single currency
working capital

15 Dow-Jones average
foreign exchange
marginal revenue
rationalization
reserve currency
supply and demand

See also **finance**; **Nobel Prize**

education

| *Educational establishments include:* |

03 CTC
04 poly
05 kindy
06 kinder

07 academy
college
08 seminary
10 high school

university

11 polytechnic
upper school
12 beacon school

infant school
kindergarten
middle school
public school
summer-school

Sunday school	primary school	combined school	secondary school
13 convent school	private school	**15** community school	voluntary school
grammar school	**14** boarding school	finishing school	
nursery school	business school	secondary modern	

Terms used in education include:

03 NQT	**07** diploma	final exam	scholarship
NVQ	head boy	opting out	statemented
PTA	lecture	professor	student loan
YTS	prefect	streaming	**12** exercise book
04 GCSE	proctor	test paper	literacy hour
SATs	student	timetable	student grant
05 pupil	subject	top-up fees	**13** baccalaureate
study	teacher	**10** curriculum	catchment area
06 A-level	truancy	discipline	matriculation
bursar	**08** governor	eleven-plus	modular course
campus	half-term	graduation	qualification
course	head girl	playground	Standard Grade
degree	homework	quadrangle	**14** adult education
finals	literacy	school term	common entrance
intake	numeracy	**11** certificate	parent governor
matron	playtime	coeducation	work experience
module	register	double-first	**15** course of studies
Ofsted	syllabus	examination	higher education
O-level	textbook	head teacher	refresher course
report	**09** break time	Higher Grade	teacher training
thesis	classroom	Higher Still	
	enrolment	invigilator	

See also **college**; **qualification**; **school**; **teaching**; **university**

eel

Eels and similar fish include:

03 hag	lance	gunnel	electric
sea	moray	launce	sandling
04 grig	murry	murena	**09** sand lance
lant	siren	murray	wheatworm
sand	snake	murrey	**10** spitchcock
snig	wheat	**07** hagfish	
tuna	**06** conger	muraena	
05 elver	gulper	**08** Anguilla	

Egypt

Ancient Egyptian rulers:

05 Khufu (26c BC)	Ptolemy (VIII, Euergetes II; d.116 BC)
06 Ahmose (I; 16c BC)	Ptolemy (VI, Philometor; d.145 BC)
Ahmose (II; 6c BC)	Ptolemy (XII Neos Dionysos; 1c BC)
Cheops (26c BC)	Rameses (III; 1198–1167 BC)
07 Ptolemy (III, Euergetes; c.285–222 BC)	Rameses (II, 'the Great'; 1304–1237 BC)
Ptolemy (II, Philadelphus; 308–246 BC)	**08** Berenice (I; fl.c.317–c.275 BC)
Ptolemy (I, Soter; c.367–283 BC)	Berenice (III; d.c.80 BC)
Ptolemy (IV, Philopator; d.205 BC)	Berenice (IV; d.55 BC)
Ptolemy (V, Epiphanes; c.210–180 BC)	Thutmose (I; fl.1493–1482 BC)

Thutmose (III; d.1426 BC)
Thutmose (IV; fl.1400–1390 BC)

09 Akhenaten (14c BC)
Amenhotep (II; 15c BC)
Amenhotep (III; c.1411–c.1375 BC)
Amenhotep (IV; 14c BC)
Cleopatra (69–30 BC)
Nefertiti (14c BC)

Sesostris (I; c.1980–1935 BC)
Sesostris (II; c.1906–1887 BC)
Sesostris (III; c.1887–1849 BC)
Tuthmosis (I; fl.1493–1482 BC)
Tuthmosis (III; d.1426 BC)
Tuthmosis (IV; fl.1400–1390 BC)

10 Hatshepsut (c.1540–c.1481 BC)

11 Tut'ankhamun (d.c.1340 BC)

See also **mythology**

electorate *see* **Australia; New Zealand**

electricity

Electrical components and devices include:

04 fuse

05 cable

06 socket

07 adaptor
ammeter
battery
conduit
fusebox

08 armature
neon lamp

test lamp

09 light bulb

10 lampholder
multimeter
transducer
two-pin plug

11 ceiling rose
earthed plug
fuse carrier
transformer

12 dimmer switch
three-pin plug

13 extension lead

14 bayonet fitting
circuit breaker
dry-cell battery
insulating tape
three-core cable
voltage doubler

15 copper conductor
fluorescent tube

Electricity and electronics terms include:

02 AC
DC

03 amp
ohm

04 cell
gate
volt
watt

05 anode
diode
Dolby®
farad
henry
NICAM®
valve

06 ampere
dynamo
OR gate
switch
triode
woofer

07 AND gate
battery
cathode

circuit
coulomb
EOR gate
NOR gate
siemens
tweeter
voltaic

08 galvanic
NAND gate
polarity
resistor
rheostat
solenoid

09 amplifier
capacitor
condenser
electrode
generator
impedance
logic gate
microchip
reactance
thyristor

10 alternator
commutator

grid system
inductance
oscillator
resistance
thermistor
transistor
truth table

11 capacitance
eddy current
electrolyte
Faraday cage
isoelectric
loudspeaker
silicon chip
thermionics
transformer

12 conductivity
electron tube
galvanometer
oscilloscope
power station

13 digital signal
direct current
electromagnet
isoelectronic

semiconductor
14 analogue signal
   band-pass filter
   bioelectricity

cathode-ray tube
induced current
15 Foucault current
   mutual induction

optoelectronics
turboalternator

See also **power station**

element *see* **chemistry**; **metal**

Elgar, Sir Edward (1857–1934)

Significant works include:

05 *Elegy* (1909)
07 *Polonia* (1915)
   Romance (1878, 1910)
   Sospiri (1914)
08 *Carillon* (1914)
   Falstaff (1902–13)
09 *Cockaigne* (1901)
   Froissart (1890)
   Une Idylle (1883)
10 *Caractacus* (Cantata; 1898)
   In the South (1899)
   King Arthur (1923)
   Promenades (1878)
   The Kingdom (Oratorio; 1906)
11 *Beau Brummel* (1928)

Sea Pictures (1897)
Severn Suite (1930)
The Apostles (Oratorio; 1903)
12 *Nursery Suite* (1931)
13 Cello Concerto (1919)
   Coronation Ode (1902)
   Dream Children (1902)
   Imperial March (1897)
   La Capricieuse (1891)
14 *Le Drapeau Belge* (1917)
   The Black Knight (Cantata; 1892)
   The Light of Life (Oratorio; 1896)
   The Music Makers (1912)
   The Wand of Youth (1906)
   Violin Concerto (1909)
15 *Pageant of Empire* (1924)

Eliot, George (1819–80)

Significant works include:

06 'Agatha' (1869)
   Romola (1862–3)
07 'Armgart' (1871)
08 *Adam Bede* (1859)
11 *Middlemarch* (1871–2)
   Silas Marner (1861)
12 'Brother Jacob' (1864)
13 *Daniel Deronda* (1874–6)
   'The Lifted Veil' (1859)

15 'The Spanish Gypsy' (1868)
16 *Brother and Sister* (1869)
   'The Legend of Jubal' (1870)
17 *The Mill on the Floss* (1860)
19 *Felix Holt, the Radical* (1866)
20 *Scenes of Clerical Life* (1858)
26 'O May I Join the Choir Invisible' (1867)
29 *Impressions of Theophrastus Such* (1879)

Significant characters include:

04 Bede (Adam)
   Cass (Dunstan)
   Cass (Godfrey)
   Holt (Felix)
   Kenn (Dr)
   Lyon (Esther)
05 Calvo (Baldassarre)
   Crewe (Mr)
   Deane (Lucy)
   Eppie

Garth (Caleb)
Garth (Mary)
Glegg (Mrs)
Guest (Stephen)
Jakin (Bob)
Sarti (Caterina)
Tessa
Tryan (Rev Edgar)
Vincy (Fred)
Vincy (Rosamond)

Wakem (Philip)
06 Barton (Milly)
   Barton (Rev Amos)
   Brooke (Arthur)
   Brooke (Celia)
   Brooke (Dorothea)
   Denner
   Gilfil (Maynard)
   Jermyn (Matthew)
   Marner (Silas)

Melema (Tito)
Morris (Dinah)
Poyser (Martin)
Poyser (Mrs)
Pullet (Mrs)
Romola
Sorrel (Hetty)
Wybrow (Captain Anthony)

07 Chettam (Sir James)
Deronda (Daniel)
Harleth (Gwendolen)
Klesmer (Herr)
Lydgate (Tertius)

Raffles (John)

08 Casaubon (Rev Edward)
Dempster (Janet)
Dempster (Robert)
Ladislaw (Will)
Lammeter (Nancy)
Lapidoth (Mirah)
Lapidoth (Mordecai)
Transome (Harold)
Transome (Mrs)
Tulliver (Maggie)
Tulliver (Mr Jeremy)
Tulliver (Mrs Elizabeth 'Bessy')

Tulliver (Tom)
Winthrop (Dolly)

09 Bulstrode (Harriet)
Bulstrode (Nicholas)

10 Grandcourt (Henleigh)
Savonarola (Girolamo)

11 Cadwallader (Elinor)
Charles VIII
Donnithorne (Arthur)
Machiavelli (Niccolò)

12 Featherstone (Peter)

Eliot, T S (1888–1965)

Significant works include:

05 *Poems* (1919)

07 *The Rock* (1934)

12 *Ash-Wednesday* (1930)
Four Quartets (1943)
The Hollow Men (1925)
The Waste Land (1922)

13 *The Sacred Wood* (1920)

14 *Poetry and Drama* (1951)

16 *On Poetry and Poets* (1957)
Sweeney Agonistes (1932)
The Cocktail Party (1949)
The Family Reunion (1939)

17 *Elizabethan Essays* (1934)

The Elder Statesman (1959)

19 *For Lancelot Andrewes* (1928)
The Journey of the Magi (1927)

20 *Murder in the Cathedral* (1935)
The Confidential Clerk (1954)

26 *The Idea of a Christian Society* (1939)

28 *Prufrock and Other Observations* (1917)
The Love Song of J Alfred Prufrock (1917)

29 *Old Possum's Book of Practical Cats* (1939)

32 *Notes Towards a Definition of Culture* (1948)

34 *The Use of Poetry and the Use of Criticism* (1933)

emblem

Floral and plant emblems include:

04 rose (England)

06 wattle (Australia)

07 thistle (Scotland)
waratah (New South Wales, Australia)

08 daffodil (Wales)
shamrock (Ireland)

09 maple leaf (Canada)

maple tree (Canada)

10 fleur-de-lis (France)
fleur-de-lys (France)
silver fern (New Zealand)

11 common heath (Victoria, Australia)
kangaroo paw (Western Australia)

12 golden wattle (Australia)

13 royal bluebell (Australian Capital Territory)

14 Cooktown orchid (Queensland, Australia)

15 Sturt's desert pea (South Australia)

embroidery

Embroidery stitches include:

04 back
moss
stem
tent

05 chain
cross

satin

07 blanket
bullion
chevron
feather
running

08 fishbone
straight

09 half-cross
lazy-daisy

10 French knot

longstitch

11 herringbone

12 long-and-short
Swiss darning

empire

Empires and kingdoms include:

04 Cush	Roman	Galicia	Byzantine
Inca	**06** Mughal	Ottoman	Holy Roman
Kush	Naples	Persian	**10** New Kingdom
Moab	**07** Argolis	**08** Dalriada	Old Kingdom
05 Akkad	Assyria	Japanese	**11** Northumbria
Alban	Bohemia	Lombardy	
Media	British	Sardinia	**13** Middle Kingdom
Mogul	Chinese	**09** Abyssinia	**15** Austro-Hungarian

Emperors include:

04 Otto (II; 955–83, Holy Roman)
Otto (III; 980–1002, Holy Roman)
Otto (I, the Great; 912–73, Holy Roman)
Otto (IV; c.1178–1218, Holy Roman)
Paul (1754–1801, Russian)
Pu Yi (1906–67, Chinese)

05 Akbar (the Great; 1542–1605, Mughal)
Babur (1483–1530, Mughal)
Boris (c.1551–1605, Russian)
Henry (III; 1017–56, Holy Roman)
Henry (IV; 1050–1106, Holy Roman)
Henry (V; 1081–1125, Holy Roman)
Henry (VI; 1165–97, Holy Roman)
Henry (VII; c.1274–1313, Holy Roman)
Louis (IV, the Bavarian; c.1283–1347, Holy Roman)
Murad (1612–40, Ottoman)
Peter (1672–1725, Russian)

06 Conrad (II; c.990–1039, Holy Roman)
Joseph (I; 1678–1711, Holy Roman)
Joseph (II; 1741–90, Holy Roman)
Rudolf (I; 1218–91, Holy Roman)
Rudolf (II; 1552–1612, Holy Roman)

07 Agustín (de Itúrbide; 1783–1824, Mexican)
Akihito (1933– , Japanese)
Charles (II, the Fat; 839–88, Holy Roman)
Charles (I, the Bald; 823–77, Holy Roman)
Charles (IV; 1316–78, Holy Roman)
Charles (V; 1500–58, Holy Roman)
Francis (I; 1708–65, Holy Roman)

Francis (II; 1768–1835, Holy Roman)
Leopold (I; 1640–1705, Holy Roman)
Leopold (II; 1747–92, Holy Roman)

08 Hirohito (1901–89, Japanese)
Jahangir (1569–1627, Mughal)
Matthias (1557–1619, Holy Roman)
Napoleon (1769–1821, French)
Süleyman (1494–1566, Ottoman)

09 Alexander (1777–1825, Russian)
Aurangzeb (1618–1707, Mughal)
Ferdinand (I; 1503–64, Holy Roman)
Ferdinand (II; 1578–1637, Holy Roman)
Ferdinand (III; 1608–57, Holy Roman)
Frederick (I, Barbarossa; c.1123–1190, Holy Roman)
Frederick (II; 1194–1250, Holy Roman)
Frederick (III; 1415–93, Holy Roman)
Montezuma (1466–1520, Aztec)
Mutsuhito (1852–1912, Japanese)
Shah Jahan (1592–1666, Mughal)
Sigismund (1368–1437, Holy Roman)
Yoshihito (1879–1926, Japanese)

10 Kublai Khan (1214–94, Chinese/Mongol)
Maximilian (I; 1459–1519, Holy Roman)
Maximilian (II; 1527–76, Holy Roman)
Meiji Tenno (1852–1912, Japanese)

11 Charlemagne (747–814, Frankish)

12 Chandragupta (c.350–c.250 BC, Indian)

13 Haile Selassie (1891–1975, Ethiopian)

Empresses include:

02 Lü (d.180 BC, Chinese)

03 Zoë (980–1050, Roman)

04 Anna (1693–1740, Russian)
Cixi (1835–1908, Chinese)

05 Irene (c.752–803, Byzantine)
Livia (58 BC–AD 29, Roman)

06 Helena (St; c.255–330 AD, Roman)
Tz'u Hsi (1835–1908, Chinese)

Wu Chao (625–705, Chinese)
Wu Zhao (625–705, Chinese)

07 Eugénie (1826–1920, Spanish)

08 Adelaide (St; 931–99, Holy Roman)
Cunegund (St; c.978–1033, German)
Faustina (d.140/141 AD, Roman)
Nur Jahan (d.1645, Mughal)
Theodora (c.500–548, Byzantine)
Victoria (1819–1901, British; Empress of India)

09 Agrippina (the Younger; AD 5–59, Roman)
Alexandra (1872–1918, German; Empress of Russia)
Catherine (1684–1727, Russian)
Catherine (the Great; 1729–96, Russian)
Elizabeth (1709–62, Russian)
Joséphine (1763–1814, French)
Kunigunde (St; c.978–1033, German)
Messalina (c.25–c.48 AD, Roman)

Old Buddha (1835–1908, Chinese)
Theophano (c.955–991, Byzantine/Holy Roman)

11 Marie Louise (1791–1847, French)

12 Anna Ivanovna (1693–1740, Russian)
Maria Theresa (1717–80, Holy Roman)

13 Livia Drusilla (58 BC–AD 29, Roman)

See also **Byzantine empire**; **despot**; **Inca empire**; **Rome**

engine

Engines include:

03 air	**05** steam	Wankel	**09** aerospike
gas	water	**07** orbital	turboprop
ion	**06** diesel	turbine	**10** stationary
jet	donkey	V-engine	**11** atmospheric
oil	petrol	**08** compound	sleeve-valve
04 aero	Petter	Stirling	**13** fuel-injection
beam	radial	traction	reciprocating
heat	rocket	turbojet	**15** linear aerospike
	rotary		

Engine parts include:

04 pump	**08** camshaft	crankshaft	ignition coil
sump	flywheel	inlet valve	starter motor
05 choke	radiator	petrol pump	timing pulley
06 con-rod	rotor arm	piston ring	turbocharger
gasket	**09** air filter	thermostat	**13** camshaft cover
piston	drive belt	timing belt	connecting rod
tappet	oil filter	**11** carburettor	cylinder block
07 fan belt	rocker arm	rocker cover	inlet manifold
oil pump	spark plug	**12** cylinder head	power-steering
oil seal	**10** alternator	exhaust valve	**15** exhaust manifold
push-rod	cooling fan	fuel injector	

engineering

Engineers include:

03 Cui (César Antonovich; 1835–1918, Russian)
Fox (Sir Charles; 1810–74, English)

04 Ader (Clément; 1841–1926, French)
Arup (Sir Ove Nyquist; 1895–1988, English)
Barr (Archibald; 1855–1931, Scottish)
Bell (Alexander Graham; 1847–1922, Scottish/US)
Bell (Henry; 1767–1830, Scottish)
Benz (Karl Friedrich; 1844–1929, German)
Bush (Vannevar; 1890–1974, US)
Eads (James Buchanan; 1820–87, US)
Eyde (Samuel; 1866–1940, Norwegian)
Fink (Albert; 1827–97, German/US)

Ford (Henry; 1863–1947, US)
Gibb (Sir Alexander; 1872–1958, Scottish)
Hirn (Gustave Adolphe; 1815–90, French)
Lear (William Powell; 1902–78, US)
Otto (Nikolaus August; 1832–91, German)
Page (Sir Frederick Handley; 1885–1962, English)
Shen (Gua; 1031–95, Chinese)
Shen (Kua; 1031–95, Chinese)
Thom (Alexander; 1894–1985, Scottish)
Todt (Fritz; 1891–1942, German)
Wang (Ching; d.83 AD, Chinese)
Wang (Jing; d.83 AD, Chinese)
Watt (James; 1736–1819, Scottish)

05 Adams (William Bridges; 1797–1872, English)
Arrol (Sir William; 1839–1913, Scottish)
Baird (John Logie; 1888–1946, Scottish)
Baker (Sir Benjamin; 1840–1907, English)
Benet (Juan; 1927–93, Spanish)
Bouch (Sir Thomas; 1822–80, English)
Braun (Wernher von; 1912–77, German/US)
Burns (John Elliot; 1858–1943, English)
Clark (Josiah Latimer; 1822–98, English)
Clerk (Sir Dugald; 1854–1932, Scottish)
Dalén (Nils Gustav; 1869–1937, Swedish)
Darby (Abraham; 1750–91, English)
Dodge (Grenville Mellen; 1831–1916, US)
Ellet (Charles; 1810–62, US)
Ewing (Sir Alfred; 1855–1935, Scottish)
Fowke (Francis; 1823–65, Northern Irish/British)
Gooch (Sir Daniel; 1816–89, English)
Grove (Sir George; 1820–1900, English)
Grubb (Sir Howard; 1844–1931, Irish)
Kilby (Jack S; 1923–2005, US)
Laval (Carl Gustaf Patrik de; 1845–1913, Swedish)
Leith (Emmett Norman; 1927–2005, US)
Locke (Joseph; 1805–60, English)
Maxim (Sir Hiram Stevens; 1840–1916, US/British)
Milne (John; 1850–1913, English)
Nervi (Pier Luigi; 1891–1979, Italian)
North (John Dudley; 1893–1968, English)
Noyce (Robert Norton; 1927–90, US)
Olsen (Kenneth Harry; 1926– , US)
Olson (Harry Ferdinand; 1901–82, US)
Pitot (Henri; 1695–1771, French)
Prony (Gaspard Clair François Marie Riche, Baron de; 1755–1839, French)
Reber (Grote; 1911–2002, US)
Reith (John Charles Walsham Reith, 1st Baron; 1889–1971, Scottish)
Rolls (Charles Stewart; 1877–1910, English)
Royce (Sir Henry; 1863–1933, English)
Ruska (Ernst August Friedrich; 1906–88, German)
Smith (James; 1789–1850, Scottish)
Smith (William; 1769–1839, English)
Tesla (Nikola; 1856–1943, Croatian/US)
Vicat (Louis Joseph; 1786–1861, French)
White (Canvass; 1790–1834, US)
Woolf (Arthur; 1766–1837, English)

06 Allais (Maurice; 1911– , French)
Ammann (Othmar Hermann; 1879–1965, US)
Ayrton (William Edward; 1847–1908, English)
Bailey (Sir Donald Coleman; 1901–85, English)
Besson (Jacques; c.1535–c.1575, French)

Bidder (George Parker; 1806–78, English)
Brunel (Isambard Kingdom; 1806–59, English)
Brunel (Sir Marc Isambard; 1769–1849, French)
Carnot (Sadi; 1796–1832, French)
Cayley (Sir George; 1773–1857, English)
Chappe (Claude; 1763–1805, French)
Cierva (Juan de la; 1895–1936, Spanish)
Claude (Georges; 1870–1960, French)
Coanda (Henri; 1885–1972, Romanian)
Cubitt (Sir William; 1785–1861, English)
Cugnot (Nicolas Joseph; 1725–1804, French)
Diesel (Rudolf Christian Karl; 1858–1913, German)
Donkin (Bryan; 1768–1855, English)
Eckert (J Presper; 1919–95, US)
Edison (Thomas Alva; 1847–1931, US)
Eiffel (Gustave; 1832–1923, French)
Finley (James; 1762–1828, US)
Fokker (Anthony; 1890–1939, Dutch/US)
Forbes (George; 1849–1936, Scottish)
Fowler (Sir John; 1817–98, English)
Froude (William; 1810–79, English)
Fuller (Buckminster; 1895–1983, US)
Fulton (Robert; 1765–1815, US)
Gramme (Zénobe Théophile; 1826–1901, Belgian)
Hinton (Christopher Hinton, Baron; 1901–83, English)
Hudson (Sir William; 1896–1978, New Zealand)
Jansky (Karl Guthe; 1905–50, US)
Jazari (Ibn al-Razzaz al-; fl.c.1200, Islamic)
Jessop (William; 1745–1814, English)
Kármán (Theodore von; 1881–1963, Hungarian/US)
La Hire (Philippe de; 1640–1718, French)
Lenoir (Jean Joseph Étienne; 1822–1900, French)
Le Play (Frédéric; 1806–82, French)
McAdam (John Loudon; 1756–1836, Scottish)
Murray (Matthew; 1765–1826, English)
Napier (Robert; 1791–1876, Scottish)
Navier (Claude Louis Marie Henri; 1785–1836, French)
Nipkow (Paul; 1860–1940, German)
Oatley (Sir Charles; 1904–96, English)
Pelton (Lester Allen; 1829–1918, US)
Pierce (John Robinson; 1910–2002, US)
Pisano (Nicola; c.1225–c.1284, Italian)
Preece (Sir William Henry; 1834–1913, Welsh)
Rennie (George; 1791–1866, Scottish)
Rennie (John; 1761–1821, Scottish)
Rennie (Sir John; 1794–1874, Scottish)

Rumsey (James; 1743–92, US)
Savery (Thomas; c.1650–1715, English)
Séguin (Marc; 1786–1875, French)
Slater (Samuel; 1768–1835, English/US)
Sperry (Elmer Ambrose; 1860–1930, US)
Stevin (Simon; 1548–1620, Flemish)
Taylor (Frederick W; 1856–1915, US)
Vauban (Sébastien le Prestre de; 1633–1707, French)
Wallis (Sir Barnes Neville; 1887–1979, English)
Wankel (Felix; 1902–88, German)
Wright (Benjamin; 1770–1842, US)
Wright (Orville; 1871–1948, US)
Wright (Wilbur; 1867–1912, US)

07 Baldwin (Matthias William; 1795–1866, US)
Balfour (George; 1872–1941, Scottish)
Belidor (Bernard Forest de; 1698–c.1761, French)
Blondel (Nicolas François; 1618–86, French)
Boulton (Matthew; 1728–1809, English)
Brassey (Thomas; 1805–70, English)
Brinell (Johann August; 1849–1925, Swedish)
Bulleid (Oliver Vaughan Snell; 1882–1970, New Zealand/British)
Candela (Felix; 1910–97, Spanish/Mexican)
Carlson (Chester Floyd; 1906–68, US)
Carrier (Willis Haviland; 1876–1950, US)
Citroën (André Gustave; 1878–1935, French)
Colding (Ludvig August; 1815–88, Danish)
Corliss (George Henry; 1817–88, US)
Culmann (Karl; 1821–81, German)
Daimler (Gottlieb Wilhelm; 1834–1900, German)
Daubrée (Gabriel Auguste; 1814–96, French)
Dornier (Claude; 1884–1969, German)
Duddell (William du Bois; 1872–1917, English)
Eastman (George; 1854–1932, US)
Eckener (Hugo; 1868–1954, German)
Egerton (Francis, 3rd Duke of Bridgewater; 1736–1803, English)
Everest (Sir George; 1790–1866, Welsh)
Fleming (Sir John Ambrose; 1849–1945, English)
Fleming (Sir Sandford; 1827–1915, Scottish/Canadian)
Francis (James Bicheno; 1815–92, English/US)
Freeman (Sir Ralph; 1880–1950, English)
Garstin (Sir William Edmund; 1849–1925, English)
Gautier (Hubert; 1660–1737, French)
Giffard (Henri; 1825–82, French)
Gilruth (Robert Rowe; 1913–2000, US)

Goddard (Robert Hutchings; 1882–1945, US)
Gresley (Sir Nigel; 1876–1941, English)
Grumman (Leroy Randle; 1895–1982, US)
Heinkel (Ernst Heinrich; 1888–1958, German)
Hoffman (Samuel Kurtz; 1902–95, US)
Houston (Edwin J; 1847–1914, US)
Junkers (Hugo, 1859–1935, German)
Keldysh (Mstislav Vsevolodovich; 1911–78, Russian)
Korolev (Sergei Pavlovich; 1907–66, Soviet)
Latrobe (Benjamin Henry; 1764–1820, English/US)
Lesseps (Ferdinand, Vicomte de; 1805–94, French)
Metcalf (John; 1717–1810, English)
Metford (William Ellis; 1824–99, English)
Midgley (Thomas, Jnr; 1889–1944, US)
Murdock (William; 1754–1839, Scottish)
Nasmyth (James; 1808–90, Scottish)
Neilson (James Beaumont; 1792–1865, Scottish)
Panhard (René; 1841–1908, French)
Parsons (Sir Charles Algernon; 1854–1931, Irish)
Perkins (Jacob; 1766–1849, US)
Porsche (Ferdinand; 1875–1951, German)
Poulsen (Valdemar; 1869–1942, Danish)
Ramelli (Agostino; c.1531–c.1610, Italian)
Rankine (William John MacQuorn; 1820–72, Scottish)
Ricardo (Sir Harry Ralph; 1885–1974, English)
Roberts (Richard; 1789–1864, Welsh)
Roberts (Sir Gilbert; 1899–1978, English)
Russell (John Scott; 1808–82, Scottish)
Scheutz (Edvard Georg Raphael; 1821–81, Swedish)
Schwarz (Harvey Fisher; 1905–88, US)
Scruton (Kit; 1911–90, English)
Siemens (Ernst Werner von; 1816–92, German)
Siemens (Sir William; 1823–83, German/British)
Smeaton (John; 1724–94, English)
Sopwith (Sir Thomas Octave Murdoch; 1888–1989, English)
Sprague (Frank Julian; 1857–1934, US)
Stanier (Sir William Arthur; 1876–1965, English)
Stanley (William; 1858–1916, US)
Stevens (John; 1749–1838, US)
Stevens (Robert Livingston; 1787–1856, US)
Swinton (Alan Archibald Campbell; 1863–1930, Scottish)
Telford (Thomas; 1757–1834, Scottish)
Thomson (Elihu; 1853–1937, US)

Thomson (James; 1822–92, Scottish)
Thomson (Robert William; 1822–73, Scottish)
Tupolev (Andrei Nikolayevich; 1888–1972, Soviet)
Whittle (Sir Frank; 1907–96, English)

08 Anderson (Sir Robert Rowand; 1834–1921, Scottish)
Aspinall (Sir John Audley Frederick; 1851–1937, English)
Beeching (Richard Beeching, Baron; 1913–85, English)
Bertrand (Henri Gratien, Comte; 1773–1844, French)
Bessemer (Sir Henry; 1813–98, English)
Brindley (James; 1716–72, English)
Chadwick (Roy; 1893–1947, English)
Crampton (Thomas Russell; 1816–88, English)
Crompton (Rookes Evelyn Bell; 1845–1940, English)
De Forest (Lee; 1873–1961, US)
Drummond (Dugald; 1840–1912, Scottish)
Drummond (Thomas; 1797–1840, Scottish)
Edgerton (Harold Eugene; 1903–90, US)
Ericsson (John; 1803–89, US)
Ericsson (Nils; 1802–70, Swedish)
Ferguson (Harry George; 1884–1960, Irish)
Ferranti (Sebastian Ziani de; 1864–1930, English)
Gilbreth (Frank Bunker; 1868–1924, US)
Goethals (George Washington; 1858–1928, US)
Goldmark (Peter Carl; 1906–77, Hungarian/US)
Griffith (Sir Richard John; 1784–1878, Irish)
Guericke (Otto von; 1602–86, German)
Hamilton (Sir James Arnot; 1923– , Scottish)
Hartnett (Sir Laurence John; 1898–1986, English/Australian)
Hawkshaw (Sir John; 1811–91, English)
Huntsman (Benjamin; 1704–76, English)
Ilyushin (Sergei Vladimirovich; 1894–1977, Soviet)
Kennelly (Arthur Edwin; 1861–1939, Indian/US)
Leonardo (da Vinci; 1452–1519, Italian)
Maillart (Robert; 1872–1940, Swiss)
Maudslay (Henry; 1771–1831, English)
McNaught (William; 1813–81, Scottish)
Mitchell (Reginald Joseph; 1895–1937, English)
Perronet (Jean Rodolphe; 1708–94, French)
Poncelet (Jean Victor; 1788–1867, French)
Rastrick (John Urpeth; 1780–1856, English)
Reynolds (Osborne; 1842–1912, English)
Roebling (John Augustus; 1806–69, US)
Sangallo (Antonio Giamberti da, the

Younger; 1485–1546, Italian)
Sikorsky (Igor Ivan; 1889–1972, Russian/US)
Sinclair (Sir Clive Marles; 1940– , English)
Stirling (Patrick; 1820–95, Scottish)
Terzaghi (Karl; 1883–1963, Czech/US)
Tredgold (Thomas; 1788–1829, English)
Vignoles (Charles Blacker; 1793–1875, Irish)
Williams (Sir Frederic Calland; 1911–77, English)
Zeppelin (Count Ferdinand von; 1838–1917, German)

09 Armstrong (Edwin Howard; 1890–1954, US)
Bradfield (John Job Crew; 1867–1943, Australian)
Clapeyron (Benoît Paul Émile; 1799–1864, French)
Cockerell (Sir Christopher Sydney; 1910–99, English)
Desbarres (Joseph Frederick Wallet; 1722–1824, English)
Fairbairn (Sir William; 1789–1874, Scottish)
Fessenden (Reginald Aubrey; 1866–1932, Canadian/US)
Finniston (Monty; 1912–91, Scottish)
Forrester (Jay Wright; 1918– , US)
Göransson (Göran Fredrik; 1819–1900, Swedish)
Grünewald (Matthias; c.1475–1528, German)
Hackworth (Timothy; 1786–1850, English)
Issigonis (Sir Alec; 1906–88, Turkish/British)
Kettering (Charles Franklin; 1876–1958, US)
MacCready (Paul; 1925–2007, US)
Pickering (William Hayward; 1910–2004, New Zealand/US)
Steinmetz (Charles Proteus; 1865–1923, German/US)
Stevenson (Robert; 1772–1850, Scottish)
Swinburne (Sir James Swinburne, 9th Baronet; 1858–1958, Scottish)
Symington (William; 1763–1831, Scottish)
Trésaguet (Pierre Marie Jérôme; 1716–96, French)
Vaucanson (Jacques de; 1709–82, French)
Vermuyden (Sir Cornelius; c.1595–c.1683, Dutch/English)
Waterston (John James; 1811–83, Scottish)
Whitworth (Sir Joseph; 1803–87, English)

10 Artachaies (fl.c.500 BC, Persian)
Bazalgette (Sir Joseph William; 1819–91, English)
Churchward (George Jackson; 1857–1933, English)
Dornberger (Walter Robert; 1895–1980, German/US)
Fourneyron (Benoît; 1802–67, French)
Freyssinet (Marie Eugène Léon; 1879–1962, French)

Hennebique (François; 1842–1921, French)
Hodgkinson (Eaton; 1789–1861, English)
Hornblower (Jonathan Carter; 1753–1815, English)
Hounsfield (Sir Godfrey Newbold; 1919–2004, English)
Laithwaite (Eric Roberts; 1921–97, English)
Lanchester (Frederick William; 1868–1946, English)
Leeghwater (Jan Adrianszoon; 1575–1650, Dutch)
Lilienthal (Otto; 1849–96, German)
Sanmichele (Michele; c.1484–1559, Italian)
Stephenson (George; 1781–1848, English)
Stephenson (Robert; 1803–59, English)
Timoshenko (Stepan Prokofyevich; 1878–1972, Russian/US)
Trevithick (Richard; 1771–1833, English)
van der Meer (Simon; 1925– , Dutch)

11 Biringuccio (Vannoccio Vincenzio Agustino Luca; 1480–1539, Italian)

Castigliano (Alberto; 1847–84, Italian)
De Havilland (Sir Geoffrey; 1882–1965, English)
Kouwenhoven (William Bennett; 1886–1975, US)
Montgolfier (Joseph Michel; 1740–1810, French)
Reichenbach (Georg Friedrich von; 1772–1826, German)
Walschaerts (Égide; 1820–1901, Belgian)

12 Alexanderson (Ernst Frederick Werner; 1878–1975, Swedish/US)
Bunau-Varilla (Philippe Jean; 1859–1940, French)
Grahame-White (Claude; 1879–1959, English)
Westinghouse (George; 1846–1914, US)

13 Messerschmitt (Willy; 1898–1978, German)

15 Crates of Chalkis (fl.335–325 BC, Greek)
Leonardo da Vinci (1452–1519, Italian)
Vitruvius Pollio (Marcus; 1 C AD, Roman)

Terms used in engineering include:

03 BSF
BSW
TDC

05 brace
gland
lever
O-ring
rotor
wedge
winch

06 flange
gasket
pinion
strain
thrust
torque

07 bearing
carbide
damping
density
fulcrum
galling
kinetic
pitting
S-N curve
statics
torsion
turbine

08 acoustic
dynamics
flatness
flow rate

pressure
split pin

09 axial load
corrosion
ductility
hydraulic
pneumatic
resonance
stability

10 arc welding
cantilever
compressor
deflection
efficiency
elasticity
TIG welding
turbulence
yield point

11 compression
deformation
DIN standard
laminar flow
Miner's rules
oscillation
shear stress
tensile load
Wöhler curve

12 aerodynamics
case-hardened
elastic range
electrolysis
external load

face flatness
face pressure
fatigue limit
geodesic dome
heat transfer
metal fatigue
sandblasting
spring washer

13 bearing stress
clamping force
dropping point
fluid dynamics
rack and pinion
radial bearing
sleeve bearing
tensile stress
thrust bearing
top dead centre
torque density
yield strength

14 Galvanic series

15 brake horse power
breakaway torque
compressive load
dynamic friction
low-cycle fatigue
tensile strength
tuned mass damper
tungsten carbide
Vickers hardness
Whitworth thread

English *see* **alphabet; football; monarch; town; United Kingdom**

entertainment

Entertainments include:

03 DVD
zoo

04 fête

05 dance
disco
opera
radio
revue
rodeo
video

06 casino

cinema
circus

07 airshow
cabaret
concert
karaoke
musical
pageant
recital
show biz
theatre

08 barbecue

carnival
festival
gymkhana
waxworks

09 burlesque
floor show
magic show
music hall
nightclub
pantomime
video game

10 puppet show

television

11 discothèque
variety show
wall of death

12 computer game
Punch-and-Judy
show business

13 firework party

14 laser-light show

15 greyhound racing

Entertainers include:

02 DJ

04 bard
fool
Joey

05 actor
clown
comic
mimic

06 artist
august
busker
cowboy
dancer
jester
mummer
player
singer

07 acrobat
actress
artiste
auguste
juggler

Pierrot
tumbler

08 comedian
conjuror
go-go girl
gracioso
jongleur
magician
minstrel
musician
showgirl
stripper

09 bunny girl
chanteuse
ecdysiast
fire-eater
harlequin
hypnotist
ice-skater
lap dancer
lion tamer
performer

pierrette
presenter
puppeteer
strong man

10 comedienne
disc jockey
go-go dancer
knockabout
mime artist
mind-reader
pole dancer
ringmaster
rope-walker
unicyclist
wire-dancer

11 belly dancer
chansonnier
equilibrist
funambulist
illusionist
storyteller
table-dancer

12 chat-show host
escapologist
exotic dancer
game-show host
impersonator
snake charmer
stand-up comic
street singer
trick cyclist
vaudevillean
vaudevillian

13 contortionist
impressionist
thimblerigger
trapeze artist
ventriloquist

14 pavement artist
sword-swallower

15 jerry-come-tumble
song-and-dance
act
tightrope walker

Entertainment places include:

03 pub
zoo

04 club
dogs
fair
hall

05 arena
disco

06 big top
casino

cinema
circus
museum
nitery

07 cabaret
funfair
gallery
hot spot
ice rink
marquee

niterie
stadium
theatre

08 ballroom
carnival
dog track
flesh pot

09 bandstand
bingo hall
dance hall

music hall
nightclub
strip club
10 auditorium
fairground
opera house

social club
11 boîte de nuit
concert hall
discothèque
public house
skating rink

12 amphitheatre
bowling alley
cattle market
13 leisure centre
15 amusement arcade

See also **clown**; **fair**; **fool**; **soap opera**; **television**

enthusiast *see* **collection**

entrepreneur *see* **business**

environment

Environmental problems include:

06 litter
07 drought
08 acid rain
landfill
oil slick
oil spill

09 pollution
10 extinction
fossil fuel
toxic waste
11 soil erosion
12 air pollution

nuclear waste
13 climate change
deforestation
global dimming
global warming
water shortage

14 light pollution
ozone depletion
water pollution
15 desertification
greenhouse gases

See also **chemistry**; **forest**; **fuel**; **gas**

enzyme

Enzymes include:

05 DNase
lyase
renin
RNase
06 cytase
kinase
ligase
lipase
papain
pepsin
rennin
zymase
07 amylase
emulsin
erepsin
inulase
lactase
maltase
oxidase
pepsine
plasmin
trypsin
uricase
08 bromelin
catalase
ceramide

elastase
esterase
lysozyme
nuclease
permease
protease
thrombin
09 amylopsin
bromelain
cellulase
coagulase
hydrolase
invertase
isomerase
peptidase
reductase
urokinase
10 insulinase
luciferase
peroxidase
polymerase
sulphatase
telomerase
tyrosinase
11 collagenase
glutaminase

histaminase
hydrogenase
lecithinase
nitrogenase
phosphatase
transferase
12 alpha amylase
asparaginase
chymotrypsin
endonuclease
fibrinolysin
ribonuclease
transaminase
13 decarboxylase
dehydrogenase
DNA polymerase
neuraminidase
penicillinase
phosphorylase
RNA polymerase
streptokinase
thrombokinase
transcriptase
14 cholinesterase
thromboplastin

equestrian sport

Equestrians and showjumpers include:

03 Hoy (Andrew; 1959– , Australian)
Hoy (Bettina; 1962– , German)
Law (Leslie; 1965– , English)

04 Anne (Princess; 1950– , English)
Leng (Virginia; 1955– , British)
Tait (Blyth; 1961– , New Zealand)
Todd (Mark; 1956– , New Zealand)

05 Green (Lucinda; 1953– , English)
Meade (Richard; 1938– , Welsh)
Smith (Harvey; 1938– , English)

06 Astley (Philip; 1742–1814, English)

Broome (David; 1940– , Welsh)
D'Inzeo (Raimondo; 1925– , Italian)
Klimke (Reiner; 1936–99, German)
Lennon (Dermott; 1969– , Irish)
Smythe (Pat; 1928–96, English)

07 Winkler (Hans-Günther; 1926– , German)

08 Grunsven (Anky van; 1968– , Dutch)
Phillips (Mark Anthony Peter; 1948– , English)
Phillips (Zara; 1981– , English)
Whitaker (John; 1955– , English)
Whitaker (Michael; 1960– , English)

Equestrian sport terms include:

03 aid
04 gait
gate
jump
lath
lead
rail
trot
walk
wall
whip
05 baulk
cones

fault
groom
06 canter
gallop
manège
piaffe
07 jump-off
longeur
passage
refusal
reining
routine

08 dressage
half pass
marathon
movement
obstacle
vaulting
vertical
09 grand prix
pirouette
puissance
time fault
water jump
10 clean round

lead change
natural aid
resistance
11 figure eight
showjumping
12 cross country
disobedience
steeplechase
13 half pirouette
14 roads and tracks
15 carriage driving
endurance riding

See also **horse**; **racing: horse racing**

equipment *see* **agriculture**; **laboratory**; **medical**; **office**; **photography**; **plumbing**; **sport**

espionage

Terms to do with espionage include:

03 bug
FBI
FSB
GRU
KGB
MI5
MI6
spy
04 burn
cell
code
GCHQ
mole
ring
05 agent
angel

blown
clean
cover
plant
spial
spook
06 beagle
cipher
defect
Enigma
secret
setter
shadow
target
07 apparat
Cold War

hacking
handler
mission
sleeper
08 blowback
briefing
codename
dead drop
emissary
informer
intrigue
mouchard
09 black list
blind date
informant
pseudonym

safe house
spymaster
top secret
10 cover story
dead letter
infiltrate
signal site
tradecraft
undercover
11 case officer
chicken feed
clandestine
double agent
penetration
12 brush contact
code-cracking

cold approach	interception	cryptographer	**14** cloak and dagger
cryptanalyst	surveillance	intelligencer	reconnaissance
intelligence	**13** call-out signal	Secret Service	

See also **spy**

essay

Essayists include:

04 Greg (William Rathbone; 1809–81, English)
Hunt (Leigh; 1784–1859, English)
Lamb (Charles; 1775–1834, English)
Lynd (Robert; 1879–1949, Irish)
Rodó (José Enrique; 1872–1917, Uruguayan)

05 Bacon (Francis; 1561–1626, English)
Lucas (Edward Verrall; 1868–1938, English)
Pater (Walter Horatio; 1839–94, English)
Smith (Sydney; 1771–1845, English)
White (E B; 1899–1985, US)

06 Borges (Jorge Luis; 1899–1986, Argentine)
Breton (André; 1896–1966, French)
Orwell (George; 1903–50, English)
Ruskin (John; 1819–1900, English)
Steele (Sir Richard; 1672–1729, Irish)

07 Addison (Joseph; 1672–1719, English)
Calvino (Italo; 1923–85, Italian)
Carlyle (Thomas; 1795–1881, Scottish)
Chapone (Hester; 1727–1801, English)
Emerson (Ralph Waldo; 1803–82, US)

Hayward (Abraham; 1802–84, English)
Hazlitt (William; 1778–1830, English)
Lazarus (Emma; 1849–87, US)
Meynell (Alice Christiana Gertrude; 1847–1922, English)
Montagu (Lady Mary Wortley; 1689–1762, English)
Thoreau (Henry David; 1817–62, US)

08 Beerbohm (Sir Max; 1872–1956, English)
Macaulay (Thomas Babington, Lord; 1800–59, English)

09 De Quincey (Thomas; 1785–1859, English)
Dickinson (Lowes; 1862–1932, English)
Montaigne (Michel Eyquem de; 1533–92, French)

10 Chesterton (G K; 1874–1936, English)
Crèvecoeur (Michel Guillaume Jean de; 1735–1813, US)

12 Quiller-Couch (Sir Arthur; 1863–1944, English)

Europe

Countries in Europe, with European Union membership:

02 UK (EU)

05 Italy (EU)
Malta (EU)
Spain (EU)

06 Cyprus (EU)
France (EU)
Greece (EU)
Latvia (EU)
Monaco
Norway
Poland (EU)
Russia
Serbia
Sweden (EU)
Turkey

07 Albania

Andorra
Austria (EU)
Belarus
Belgium (EU)
Croatia
Denmark (EU)
Estonia (EU)
Finland (EU)
Germany (EU)
Hungary (EU)
Iceland
Ireland (EU)
Moldova
Romania (EU)
Ukraine

08 Bulgaria (EU)

Portugal (EU)
Slovakia (EU)
Slovenia (EU)

09 Lithuania (EU)
Macedonia
San Marino

10 Luxembourg (EU)
Montenegro

11 Switzerland
Vatican City

13 Czech Republic (EU)
Liechtenstein
United Kingdom (EU)

14 The Netherlands (EU)

20 Bosnia and Herzegovina

Cities and notable towns in Northern Europe include:

04 Cork (Ireland)
Lund (Sweden)
Oslo (Norway)

Riga (Latvia)
York (England)

05 Århus (Denmark)

Derby (England)
Espoo (Finland)
Leeds (England)

Malmö (Sweden)
Narva (Estonia)
Tartu (Estonia)
Turku (Finland)
06 Ålborg (Denmark)
Bergen (Norway)
Dublin (Ireland)
Dundee (Scotland)
Kaunas (Lithuania)
London (England)
Odense (Denmark)
Örebro (Sweden)
Vantaa (Finland)
07 Belfast (Northern Ireland)
Bristol (England)
Cardiff (Wales)
Glasgow (Scotland)

Liepaja (Latvia)
Swansea (Wales)
Tallinn (Estonia)
Tampere (Finland)
Uppsala (Sweden)
Vilnius (Lithuania)
08 Aberdeen (Scotland)
Bradford (England)
Coventry (England)
Helsinki (Finland)
Klaipeda (Lithuania)
Limerick (Ireland)
Plymouth (England)
Šiauliai (Lithuania)
Västerås (Sweden)
09 Edinburgh (Scotland)
Jönköping (Sweden)

Leicester (England)
Linköping (Sweden)
Liverpool (England)
Reykjavík (Iceland)
Sheffield (England)
Stavanger (Norway)
Stockholm (Sweden)
Trondheim (Norway)
Waterford (Ireland)
10 Birmingham (England)
Copenhagen (Denmark)
Daugavpils (Latvia)
Gothenburg (Sweden)
Manchester (England)
Norrköping (Sweden)
Nottingham (England)
11 Southampton (England)

Cities and notable towns in Western Europe include:

04 Bonn (Germany)
Caen (France)
Graz (Austria)
Kiel (Germany)
Linz (Austria)
Metz (France)
Nice (France)
05 Arles (France)
Basle (Switzerland)
Berne (Switzerland)
Dijon (France)
Essen (Germany)
Lille (France)
Lyons (France)
Mainz (Germany)
Nancy (France)
Nîmes (France)
Paris (France)
Reims (France)
Tours (France)
06 Aachen (Germany)
Berlin (Germany)
Bochum (Germany)
Bremen (Germany)
Geneva (Switzerland)
Kassel (Germany)
Munich (Germany)
Nantes (France)
Rennes (France)
Toulon (France)
Vienna (Austria)
Zürich (Switzerland)
07 Avignon (France)

Cologne (Germany)
Dresden (Germany)
Hamburg (Germany)
Hanover (Germany)
Leipzig (Germany)
Limoges (France)
Lucerne (Switzerland)
Orleans (France)
Potsdam (Germany)
08 Augsburg (Germany)
Chemnitz (Germany)
Dortmund (Germany)
Duisburg (Germany)
Lausanne (Switzerland)
Mannheim (Germany)
Poitiers (France)
Salzburg (Austria)
Toulouse (France)
09 Innsbruck (Austria)
Magdeburg (Germany)
Nuremberg (Germany)
Osnabrück (Germany)
Stuttgart (Germany)
Wiesbaden (Germany)
Wuppertal (Germany)
10 Düsseldorf (Germany)
Klagenfurt (Austria)
Luxembourg (Luxembourg)
Marseilles (France)
Strasbourg (France)
11 Montpellier (France)
15 Clermont-Ferrand (France)
Frankfurt am Main (Germany)

Cities and notable towns in Eastern Europe include:

03 Ufa (Russia)

04 Brno (Czech Republic)
Györ (Hungary)
Kiev (Ukraine)
Lódz (Poland)
Lvov (Ukraine)
Omsk (Russia)
Orsk (Russia)
Pécs (Hungary)
Perm (Russia)
Tula (Russia)

05 Brest (Belarus)
Chita (Russia)
Gomel (Belarus)
Kazan (Russia)
Kursk (Russia)
Minsk (Belarus)
Penza (Russia)
Plzeň (Czech Republic)
Rovno (Ukraine)
Tomsk (Russia)

06 Gdansk (Poland)
Grozny (Russia)
Hrodna (Belarus)
Košice (Slovakia)
Kraków (Poland)
Lublin (Poland)
Moscow (Russia)
Odessa (Ukraine)
Poznan (Poland)
Prague (Czech Republic)
Samara (Russia)
Szeged (Hungary)
Warsaw (Poland)

07 Barnaul (Russia)
Donetsk (Ukraine)
Irkutsk (Russia)
Kharkov (Ukraine)
Kherson (Ukraine)
Luhansk (Ukraine)
Miskolc (Hungary)
Olomouc (Czech Republic)
Ostrava (Czech Republic)
Poltava (Ukraine)
Rybinsk (Russia)
Saratov (Russia)

Ulan-Ude (Russia)
Vitebsk (Belarus)
Wroclaw (Poland)
Yakutsk (Russia)

08 Budapest (Hungary)
Chisinau (Moldova)
Debrecen (Hungary)
Gorlovka (Ukraine)
Katowice (Poland)
Kemerovo (Russia)
Mahilyow (Belarus)
Mariupol (Ukraine)
Murmansk (Russia)
Orenburg (Russia)
Smolensk (Russia)
Szczecin (Poland)
Tiraspol (Moldova)
Vinnitsa (Ukraine)
Voronezh (Russia)

09 Archangel (Russia)
Astrakhan (Russia)
Bydgoszcz (Poland)
Krasnodar (Russia)
Krivoy Rog (Ukraine)
Makeyevka (Ukraine)
Nikolayev (Ukraine)
Volgograd (Russia)
Yaroslavl (Russia)

10 Bratislava (Slovakia)
Khabarovsk (Russia)
Simferopol (Ukraine)
Zaporozhye (Ukraine)

11 Chelyabinsk (Russia)
Kaliningrad (Russia)
Komsomolosk (Russia)
Krasnoyarsk (Russia)
Novosibirsk (Russia)
Rostov-on-Don (Russia)
Vladivostok (Russia)

12 Magnitogorsk (Russia)
Novokuznetsk (Russia)
St Petersburg (Russia)

13 Yekaterinburg (Russia)

14 Dnepropetrovsk (Ukraine)

15 Nizhniy Novgorod (Russia)

Cities and notable towns in Southern Europe include:

04 Bari (Italy)
Pisa (Italy)
Rome (Italy)

05 Genoa (Italy)
Milan (Italy)
Padua (Italy)

Palma (Majorca)
Siena (Italy)
Turin (Italy)

06 Bilbao (Spain)
Lisbon (Portugal)
Madrid (Spain)

Málaga (Spain)
Modena (Italy)
Murcia (Spain)
Naples (Italy)
Oporto (Portugal)
Venice (Italy)

Verona (Italy)
07 Bologna (Italy)
   Catania (Italy)
   Coimbra (Portugal)
   Granada (Spain)
   Messina (Italy)
   Palermo (Italy)

Ravenna (Italy)
Setúbal (Portugal)
Seville (Spain)
08 Braganza (Portugal)
   Florence (Italy)
   Valencia (Spain)
09 Barcelona (Spain)

Las Palmas (Gran Canaria)
Santander (Spain)
Saragossa (Spain)
10 Valladolid (Spain)
11 Vatican City (Vatican City)

Europeans include:

04 Balt	Briton	Andorran	Slovakian
Brit	German	Austrian	Slovenian
Dane	Nordic	Croatian	Ukrainian
Esth	Sabine	Dutchman	10 Anglo-Saxon
Finn	Salian	Estonian	Belarusian
Flem	Teuton	Irishman	Dutchwoman
Lapp	Zyrian	Moldovan	Englishman
Pict	07 Belgian	Romanian	Irishwoman
Pole	Bosnian	Scotsman	Lithuanian
Scot	Cypriot	Siberian	Macedonian
Serb	Fleming	Silurian	Monégasque
Slav	Iberian	Spaniard	Portuguese
Turk	Italian	Welshman	Welshwoman
05 Angle	Latvian	09 Britisher	11 Belarussian
Croat	Lombard	Bulgarian	Frenchwoman
Czech	Maltese	Englander	Montenegrin
Greek	Manxman	Englisher	Sammarinese
Latin	Monacan	Frenchman	12 Englishwoman
Swede	Russian	Hungarian	Luxembourger
Swiss	Samnite	Icelander	Scandinavian
Vlach	Serbian	Manxwoman	13 Herzegovinian
06 Almain	Walloon	Norwegian	15 Liechtensteiner
Basque	08 Albanian	Sardinian	

European landmarks include:

04 Alps (France/Switzerland/Italy/Austria)
05 Rhine (Switzerland/France/Germany/The
   Netherlands)
06 Danube (Germany/Austria/Slovakia/
   Hungary/Croatia/Serbia/Bulgaria/
   Romania/Moldova)
   Geysir (Iceland)
   Tatras (Poland)
08 Ardennes (France/Belgium/Luxembourg)
   Pyrenees (France/Spain/Andorra)

Strokkur (Iceland)
09 Auschwitz (Poland)
10 Bran Castle (Romania)
   Julian Alps (Slovenia)
   Lake Geneva (France/Switzerland)
11 Simplon Pass (Switzerland/Italy)
13 Lake Constance (Germany/Switzerland/
   Austria)
15 Rock of Gibraltar (Gibraltar)

See also **parliament**; **party**

evangelism *see* **missionary**

event *see* **athletics**; **gymnastics**; **Olympic Games**; **Paralympic Games**; **skiing**

execution

Execution methods include:

06 noyade
07 burning
    gassing
    hanging
    stoning

08 lynching
    shooting
09 beheading
10 garrotting
    guillotine

    the gallows
11 crucifixion
    firing squad
    stringing up
12 decapitation

13 electric chair
    electrocution
15 lethal injection

See also **death**

exercise

Exercises include:

04 yoga
05 Medau
06 qigong
    t'ai chi
07 aquafit

    chi kung
    jogging
    keep fit
    Pilates
08 aerobics
09 boxercise

    hatha yoga
10 aquarobics
    daily dozen
    dancercise
11 Callanetics
12 body-building

    calisthenics
    step aerobics
13 callisthenics
    cross-training
    physical jerks
15 circuit training

Terms to do with exercise include:

04 burn
06 warm-up
07 aerobic

    workout
08 warm down
09 anaerobic

    endurance
    low impact
10 resistance

    stretching
13 high intensity
14 cardiovascular

See also **sport**; **yoga**

exploration

Explorers and navigators include:

03 Cam (15c, Portuguese)
    Cão (15c, Portuguese)
    Rae (John; 1813–93, Scottish)

04 Anza (Juan Bautista de; 1735–88, Mexican/
    Spanish)
    Back (Sir George; 1796–1878, English)
    Beke (Charles Tilstone; 1800–74, English)
    Byrd (Richard Evelyn; 1888–1957, US)
    Cano (Juan Sebastian del; d.1526, Basque)
    Cook (Frederick Albert; 1865–1940, US)
    Cook (James; 1728–79, English)
    Dias (Bartolomeu; c.1450–1500,
    Portuguese)
    Diaz (Bartolomeu; c.1450–1500,
    Portuguese)
    Eyre (Edward John; 1815–1901, English)
    Gama (Vasco da; c.1469–1525, Portuguese)
    Gray (Robert; 1755–1806, US)
    Grey (Sir George; 1812–98, Portuguese/
    British)
    Hall (Charles Francis; 1821–71, US)
    Hume (Hamilton; 1797–1873, Australian)
    Kane (Elisha Kent; 1820–57, US)

    Park (Mungo; 1771–1806, Scottish)
    Pike (Zebulon Montgomery; 1779–1813,
    US)
    Polo (Marco; 1254–1324, Venetian)
    Ross (Sir James Clark; 1800–62, Scottish)
    Ross (Sir John; 1777–1856, Scottish)
    Soto (Fernando de; c.1500–1542, Spanish)
    Soto (Hernando de; c.1500–1542, Spanish)

05 Adams (Will; 1564–1620, English)
    Baker (Sir Samuel White; 1821–93, English)
    Barth (Heinrich; 1821–65, German)
    Beebe (William; 1877–1962, US)
    Boone (Daniel; 1735–1820, US)
    Bruce (James; 1730–94, Scottish)
    Burke (Robert O'Hara; 1820–61, Irish)
    Cabot (John; 1425–c.1500, Italian)
    Cabot (Sebastian; 1474–1557, Venetian)
    Clark (William; 1770–1838, US)
    Davis (John; c.1550–1605, English)
    Davys (John; c.1550–1605, English)
    Drake (Sir Francis; c.1540–1596, English)
    Fuchs (Sir Vivian Ernest; 1908–99, English)
    Giles (Ernest; 1835–97, English/Australian)

Gosse (William Christie; 1842–81, English/Australian)
Grant (James Augustus; 1827–92, Scottish)
Hanno (5cBC; Carthaginian)
Hayes (Isaac Israel; 1832–81, US)
Hedin (Sven Anders; 1865–1952, Swedish)
Laing (Alexander Gordon; 1793–1826, Scottish)
Laird (MacGregor; 1808–61, Scottish)
Lewis (Meriwether; 1774–1809, US)
Monod (Théodore André; 1902–2000, French)
Monts (Pierre du Gua, Sieur de; c.1560–c.1630, French)
Nares (Sir George Strong; 1831–1915, Scottish)
Newby (Eric; 1919–2006, English)
Oates (Lawrence Edward Grace; 1880–1912, English)
Parry (Sir William Edward; 1790–1855, English)
Pavie (Auguste Jean Marie; 1847–1925, French)
Peary (Robert Edwin; 1856–1920, US)
Radde (Gustav Ferdinand Richard; 1831–1903, Polish/German)
Scott (Robert Falcon; 1868–1912, English)
Smith (Jedediah Strong; 1799–1831, US)
Speke (John Hanning; 1827–64, English)
Stein (Sir Aurel; 1862–1943, Hungarian/British)
Sturt (Charles; 1795–1869, Indian/British)
Wager (Lawrence Rickard; 1904–65, English)
Wills (William John; 1834–61, English/Australian)

06 Aublet (Jean Baptiste Christophe Fusée; 1723–78, French)
Baffin (William; c.1584–1622, English)
Baikie (William Balfour; 1825–64, Scottish)
Balboa (Vasco Núñez de; 1475–1519, Spanish)
Behaim (Martin; 1440–1507, German)
Bering (Vitus Jonassen; 1681–1741, Danish)
Brazza (Pierre Savorgnan de; 1852–1905, Brazilian/French)
Burton (Sir Richard Francis; 1821–90, English)
Cabral (Pedro Álvarez; c.1467–c.1520, Portuguese)
Carson (Kit; 1809–68, US)
De Long (George Washington; 1844–81, US)
Denham (Dixon; 1786–1828, English)
Elcano (Juan Sebastian del; d.1526, Basque)
Fraser (Simon; 1776–1862, American/Canadian)
Greely (Adolphus Washington; 1844–1935, US)

Hearne (Samuel; 1745–92, English)
Hudson (Henry; c.1550–1611, English)
Joliet (Louis; 1645–1700, French)
Lander (Richard; 1803–34, English)
Mawson (Sir Douglas; 1882–1958, English/Australian)
Müller (Sir Ferdinand Jakob Heinrich von, Freiherr; 1825–96, German/Australian)
Nansen (Fridtjof; 1861–1930, Norwegian)
Philby (Harry St John Bridger; 1885–1960, Sri Lanka/British)
Pinzón (Vicente Yáñez; c.1460–c.1524, Spanish)
Quiros (Pedro Fernandez de; 1565–1615, Portuguese)
Ralegh (Sir Walter; 1552–1618, English)
Rogers (Woodes; c.1679–1732, English)
Rohlfs (Gerhard; 1831–96, German)
Sabine (Sir Edward; 1788–1883, Irish)
Selous (Frederick Courtenay; 1851–1917, English)
Stuart (John McDouall; 1815–66, Scottish/Australian)
Tasman (Abel Janszoon; 1603–c.1659, Dutch)
Torres (Luis Vaez de; fl.1605–13, Spanish)
Uemura (Naomi; 1942–84, Japanese)
Wallis (Samuel; 1728–95, English)
Wilson (Edward Adrian; 1872–1912, English)

07 Andrews (Roy Chapman; 1884–1960, US)
Balchen (Bernt; 1899–1973, Norwegian/US)
Ballard (Robert Duane; 1942– , US)
Barents (Willem; d.1597, Dutch)
Belzoni (Giovanni Battista; 1778–1823, Italian)
Borough (Steven; 1525–84, English)
Borough (William; 1536–99, English)
Cabrera (Pedro Álvarez; c.1467–c.1520, Portuguese)
Cameron (Verney Lovett; 1844–94, English)
Cartier (Jacques; 1491–1557, French)
Chesney (Francis Rawdon; 1789–1872, Irish)
Dampier (William; 1652–1715, English)
Fawcett (Percy Harrison; 1867–1925, English)
Fiennes (Sir Ranulph Twisleton-Wykeham; 1944– , English)
Fleming (Peter; 1907–71, English)
Forrest (John Forrest, 1st Baron; 1847–1918, Australian)
Frémont (John Charles; 1813–90, US)
Gardner (George; 1812–49, Scottish)
Garnier (Francis; 1839–73, French)
Gilbert (Sir Humphrey; 1537–83, English)
Gregory (Augustus Charles; 1819–1905, English/Australian)
Gregory (John Walter; 1864–1932, English)

Hawkins (Sir John; 1532–95, English)
Hawkyns (Sir John; 1532–95, English)
Herbert (Sir Wally; 1934–2007, English)
Hillary (Sir Edmund Percival; 1919–2008, New Zealand)
Jolliet (Louis; 1645–1700, French)
La Salle (René Robert Cavelier, Sieur de; 1643–87, French)
McClure (Sir Robert John Le Mesurier; 1807–73, Irish)
Moresby (John; 1830–1922, English)
Mueller (Sir Ferdinand Jakob Heinrich von, Freiherr; 1825–96, German/Australian)
Raleigh (Sir Walter; 1552–1618, English)
Rüppell (Eduard; 1794–1884, German)
Simpson (Myrtle Lillias; 1931–   , Scottish)
Simpson (Sir George; 1792–1860, Scottish/ Canadian)
Stanley (Sir Henry Morton; 1841–1904, Welsh/US/British)
Steller (Georg Wilhelm; 1709–46, German)
Thomson (Joseph; 1858–95, Scottish)
Weddell (James; 1787–1834, English)
Wilkins (Sir George Hubert; 1888–1958, Australian)
Wrangel (Ferdinand Petrovich, Baron von; 1794–1870, Russian)

08 Amundsen (Roald Engelbreth Gravning; 1872–1928, Norwegian)
Cárdenas (Garcia Lopez de; mid-16c, Spanish)
Carteret (Philip; d.1796, English)
Columbus (Christopher; 1451–1506, Genoese)
Coronado (Francisco Vázquez de; 1510–54, Spanish)
Cousteau (Jacques Yves; 1910–97, French)
Eriksson (Leif; fl.1000– , Icelandic)
Filchner (Wilhelm; 1877–1957, German)
Flaherty (Robert Joseph; 1884–1951, US)
Flinders (Matthew; 1774–1814, English)
Foucauld (Charles Eugène, Vicomte de; 1858–1916, French)
Franklin (Sir John; 1786–1847, English)
Johnston (Sir Harry H; 1858–1927, English)
Kotzebue (Otto von; 1787–1846, Russian)
Linnaeus (Carolus; 1707–78, Swedish)
Magellan (Ferdinand; c.1480–1521, Portuguese)
Malaurie (Jean; 1922– , French)
Marchand (Jean-Baptiste; 1863–1934, French)
Mitchell (Sir Thomas Livingstone; 1792–1855, Scottish)
Orellana (Francisco de; c.1500–1549, Spanish)
Ridgeway (John; 1938– , English)
Schwatka (Frederick; 1849–92, US)

Scoresby (William; 1789–1857, English)
Standish (Myles; c.1584–1656, English)
Sverdrup (Otto; 1855–1930, Norwegian)
Thesiger (Sir Wilfred Patrick; 1910– , English)
Thompson (David; 1770–1857, English/ Canadian)
Thorfinn (fl.1000, Icelandic)
Thunberg (Carl Peter; 1743–1828, Swedish)
Vespucci (Amerigo; 1451–1512, Italian/ Spanish)
Vlamingh (Willem Hesselsz de; fl.1690s, Dutch)
Williams (Roger; c.1604–1683, American)

09 Andersson (Karl Johan; 1827–67, Swedish)
Champlain (Samuel de; 1567–1635, French)
Drygalski (Erich Dagobert von; 1865–1949, German)
Eiríksson (Leif; fl.1000, Icelandic)
Ellsworth (Lincoln; 1880–1951, US)
Emin Pasha (1840–92, German)
Fernández (Juan; c.1536–c.1604, Spanish)
Frobisher (Sir Martin; c.1535–1594, English)
Heyerdahl (Thor; 1914–2002, Norwegian)
Karesefni (Thorfinn; fl.1000, Icelandic)
Lancaster (Sir James; c.1554–1618, English)
La Pérouse (Jean François de Galaup, Comte de; 1741–88, French)
Mackenzie (Sir Alexander; 1764–1820, Scottish)
MacMillan (Donald Baxter; 1874–1970, US)
Marquette (Jacques; 1637–75, French)
Rasmussen (Knud Johan Victor; 1879–1933, Danish)
Vancouver (George; 1757–98, English)
Verendrye (Pierre Gaultier de Varennes, Sieur de la; 1685–1749, French)
Verrazano (Giovanni da; c.1480–1527, Italian)
Warburton (Peter Egerton; 1813–89, English/ Australian)

10 Charlevoix (Pierre François Xavier de; 1682–1761, French)
Clapperton (Hugh; 1788–1827, Scottish)
Cunningham (Allan; 1791–1839, English)
Erik the Red (10c, Norwegian)
Huntington (Ellsworth; 1876–1943, US)
Leichhardt (Ludwig; 1813–c.1848, Prussian/ Australian)
Oglethorpe (James Edward; 1696–1785, English)
Richardson (Sir John; 1787–1865, Scottish)
Shackleton (Sir Ernest Henry; 1874–1922, Irish/British)
Stefánsson (Vilhjalmur; 1879–1962, Canadian)
van der Post (Sir Laurens Jan; 1906–96, South African)

Willoughby (Sir Hugh; d.c.1554, English)
11 Livingstone (David; 1813–73, Scottish)
Matthiessen (Peter; 1927– , US)
Ponce de León (Juan; 1460–1521, Spanish)
12 Borchgrevink (Carsten Egeberg; 1864–1934, Norwegian)
Bougainville (Louis Antoine de; 1729–1811, French)
Leif the Lucky (fl.1000, Icelandic)
Nordenskjöld (Otto; 1869–1928, Swedish)
Schweinfurth (Georg August; 1836–1925, German)

See also **sailing**

Younghusband (Sir Francis Edward; 1863–1942, Indian/British)
14 Bellingshausen (Fabian Gottlieb, von; 1778–1852, Russian)
Blashford-Snell (Colonel John; 1936– , English)
Dumont d'Urville (Jules Sébastien César; 1790–1842, French)
Hanbury-Tenison (Robin; 1936– , English)
15 Doudart de Lagrée (Ernest-Marie-Louis de Gonzague; 1823–68, French)

explosive

Explosives include:

03 RDX
TNT
04 ANFO
06 amatol
dualin
Semtex®
tonite

07 ammonal
cordite
dunnite
lyddite
08 cheddite
dynamite
melinite

roburite
xyloidin
09 cyclonite
gelignite
guncotton
gunpowder
xyloidine

11 nitrocotton
14 nitrocellulose
nitroglycerine
trinitrotoluol
15 trinitrotoluene

eye

Eye parts include:

03 rod
04 cone
iris
lens
05 fovea
pupil
white
06 areola
cornea

See also **blindness**

eyelid
macula
retina
sclera
07 choroid
eyeball
eyelash
papilla
vitreum

08 chorioid
09 blind spot
optic disc
10 optic nerve
11 ciliary body
conjunctiva
lower eyelid
upper eyelid

12 chorioid coat
lacrimal duct
ocular muscle
13 aqueous humour
sclerotic coat
14 vitreous humour
15 anterior chamber
hyaloid membrane

F

fable

'The Wolf and the Crane' (Aesop)
'The Wolf and the Stork' (La Fontaine)

19 'The Father and Jupiter' (John Gay)
'The Fawn and His Mother' (Aesop)
'The Horse and His Rider' (Aesop)
'The Old Cock and the Fox' (La Fontaine)
'The Thieves and the Ass' (La Fontaine)

20 'Against the Hard to Suit' (La Fontaine)
'By the Almshouse Window' (Hans Christian Andersen)
'The Bird of Popular Song' (Hans Christian Andersen)
'The Bitch and Her Friend' (La Fontaine)
'The Bull and the Mastiff' (John Gay)
'The Congress of the Rats' (La Fontaine)
'The Eagle and the Beetle' (La Fontaine)
'The Gardener and the Hog' (John Gay)
'The Goat Without a Beard' (John Gay)
'The Lion and Ass Hunting' (La Fontaine)
'The Princess and the Pea' (Hans Christian Andersen)
'The Wife and Her Husband' (Marie de France)
'The Wild Boar and the Ram' (John Gay)
'The Wolves and the Sheep' (La Fontaine)

21 'The Acorn and the Pumpkin' (La Fontaine)
'The Carpenter and the Ape' (Bidpai)
'The Cat Who Became a Woman' (La Fontaine)
'The Courtier and Porteus' (John Gay)
'The Emperor's New Clothes' (Hans Christian Andersen)
'The Gardener and the Bear' (Bidpai)
'The Hare and the Tortoise' (Aesop)
'The Merchant and the Iron' (Bidpai)
'The Sick Man and the Angel' (John Gay)
'The Torrent and the River' (La Fontaine)
'The Tortoise and the Hare' (Aesop)
'The Two Bulls and the Frog' (La Fontaine)

22 'Death and the Unfortunate' (La Fontaine)
'The Ass, the Fox and the Lion' (Aesop)
'The Ass, the Lion and the Fox' (Bidpai)
'The Bat and the Two Weasels' (La Fontaine)
'The Blind Man and the Snake' (Bidpai)
'The Fox, the Hen and the Drum' (Bidpai)
'The Frogs Asking for a King' (Aesop)
'The Labourer and the Snake' (Aesop)
'The Lean Cat and the Fat Cat' (Bidpai)
'The Partridge and the Crow' (Bidpai)
'The Partridge and the Hawk' (Bidpai)
'The Sparrows and the Snake' (Bidpai)
'The Tortoise and the Eagle' (Aesop)
'The Tortoise and the Geese' (Bidpai)

23 'Delaying is Not Forgetting' (Hans Christian Andersen)
'The Bird Wounded by an Arrow' (La Fontaine)

'The Conceited Apple Branch' (Hans Christian Andersen)
'The Council Held by the Rats' (La Fontaine)
'The Fox and the Piece of Meat' (Bidpai)
'The Grasshopper and the Ant' (La Fontaine)
'The Hare, the Fox and the Wolf' (Bidpai)
'The Mountain that Laboured' (La Fontaine)
'The Partridge and the Cocks' (La Fontaine)
'The Rat-Catcher and the Cats' (John Gay)
'The Stag and His Reflection' (La Fontaine)
'The Two Owls and the Sparrow' (John Gay)

24 'How the Leopard got his Spots' (Kipling)
'The Boy and the Schoolmaster' (La Fontaine)
'The Cat who Walked by Himself' (Kipling)
'The Donkey and the Little Dog' (La Fontaine)
'The Frogs Who Asked for a King' (La Fontaine)
'The Lion, the Fox and the Geese' (John Gay)

25 'About a Woman and Her Paramour' (Marie de France)
'Everything in the Right Place' (Hans Christian Andersen)
'The Camel Driver and the Adder' (Bidpai)
'The Herdsman and the Lost Bull' (Aesop)
'The Hornets and the Honey Bees' (La Fontaine)
'The Scorpion and the Tortoise' (Bidpai)
'The Spaniel and the Chameleon' (John Gay)

26 'Pythagoras and the Countryman' (John Gay)
'The Bear and the Two Travellers' (Aesop)
'The City Rat and the Country Rat' (La Fontaine)
'The Man and Wife Who Quarrelled' (Marie de France)
'The Poor Man and the Flask of Oil' (Bidpai)
'The Rustic and the Nightingale' (Bidpai)
'The Youth, the Hawk and the Raven' (Bidpai)

27 'Beauty of Form and Beauty of Mind' (Hans Christian Andersen)
'Simonides Preserved by the Gods' (La Fontaine)
'The Elephant and the Bookseller' (John Gay)
'The Farmer, the Sheep and Robbers' (Bidpai)
'The Fighting Cocks and the Eagle' (Aesop)
'The Frog, the Crab and the Serpent' (Bidpai)
'The Monkey Who Had Seen the World' (John Gay)
'The Persian, the Sun and the Cloud' (John Gay)
'The Swallow and the Little Birds' (La Fontaine)
'The Swallow and the Nightingale' (La Fontaine)

28 'The Beetle Who Went on His Travels' (Hans Christian Andersen)
'The Camel and the Floating Sticks' (La Fontaine)
'The Eagle and Assembly of Animals' (John Gay)
'The Hunter, the Fox and the Leopard' (Bidpai)
'The Rich Man and the Bundle of Wood' (Bidpai)

'The Setting-Dog and the Partridge' (John Gay)
'The Tyrant Who Became a Just Ruler' (Bidpai)

29 'The Bleacher, the Crane and the Hawk' (Bidpai)

30 'The Lion, the Tiger and the Traveller' (John Gay)

Fable writers include:

03 Ade (George; 1866–1944, US)
Fay (András; 1786–1864, Hungarian)
Gay (John; 1685–1732, English)

04 Esop (6cBC, Greek)
Ruiz (Juan; c.1283–c.1350, Spanish)

05 Aesop (6cBC, Greek)
Boner (Ulrich; 1300–49, Swiss)
Torga (Miguel; 1907–90, Portuguese)

06 Bidpai (c.4cAD, Indian)
Dryden (John; 1631–1700, English)
Halévy (Léon; 1802–83, French)
Krylov (Ivan; 1768–1844, Russian)
Ramsay (Allan; c.1685–1758, Scottish)
Tessin (Carl-Gustaf; 1695–1770, Swedish)

07 Arreola (Juan José; 1918–2001, Mexican)

Babrius (fl.c.2cAD, Greek)
Fénelon (François; 1651–1715, French)
Gellert (Christian Fürchtegott; 1715–69, German)
Iriarte (Tomás de; 1750–91, Spanish)
Kipling (Rudyard; 1865–1936, English)
Sologub (Fyodor; 1863–1927, Russian)

08 Andersen (Hans Christian; 1805–75, Danish)
de France (Marie; fl.c.1160–c.1190, French)
Phaedrus (c.15 BC–c.50 AD, Macedonian)
Saltykov (Michail; 1826–89, Russian)

09 Furetière (Antoine; 1619–88, French)

10 La Fontaine (Jean de; 1621–95, French)

15 Iriarte y Oropesa (Tomas de; 1750–91, Spanish)

fabric

Fabrics include:

03 kid
net
rep
say

04 aida
baft
ciré
cord
felt
harn
ikat
jean
lace
lamé
lawn
leno
repp
silk
tapa
wool

05 batik
beige
Binca®
camel
chino

crape
crepe
crêpe
denim
dhoti
doily
doyly
drill
duroy
gauze
gazar
gunny
linen
lisle
llama
loden
Lurex®
Lycra®
moire
ninon
nylon
Orlon®
panne
piqué
plush
rayon

satin
scrim
serge
sheer
suede
surah
tabby
tamin
tammy
tappa
terry
Tibet
toile
tulle
tweed
twill
union
voile
wigan

06 alpaca
angora
armure
barège
Bengal
bouclé

broché
burlap
calico
camlet
canvas
chintz
cloqué
coburg
cotton
coutil
crepon
cubica
cyprus
Dacron®
damask
dévoré
doyley
Dralon®
duffel
durrie
faille
fleece
gloria
harden
herden
hurden

jersey
kersey
kincob
linsey
madras
merino
mohair
moreen
muslin
Oxford
plissé
poplin
ratine
samite
sateen
shoddy
Tactel®
tamine
Thibet
tissue
tricot
tusser
velour
velvet
vicuña

07 alepine
baracan
batiste
brocade
buckram
cambric
challis
chamois
chiffon
cypress
doeskin
drabbet
droguet
drugget
duvetyn
façonné
flannel
foulard
fustian
galatea
gingham
Gore-Tex®
heather

hessian
holland
hopsack
jaconet
kidskin
leather
morocco
nacarat
nankeen
oil silk
organza
orleans
paisley
percale
rabanna
raschel
ratteen
raw silk
sagathy
satinet
schappe
spandex
tabaret
taffeta
ticking
veiling
velours
Viyella®
webbing
woolsey
worsted
zanella

08 barathea
barracan
bayadère
buckskin
cashmere
chambray
chenille
corduroy
coutille
cretonne
diamanté
duvetine
duvetyne
gossamer
jacquard
marcella

mazarine
moleskin
oilcloth
organdie
pashmina
plaiding
pleather
quilting
sarsenet
shagreen
shalloon
shantung
spun silk
suedette
swanskin
Terylene®
waxcloth
whipcord

09 Alcantara®
astrakhan
baldachin
bombasine
bombazine
calamanco
Carmelite
Chantilly
Crimplene®
crinoline
folk-weave
fur fabric
gabardine
gaberdine
georgette
grenadine
grosgrain
haircloth
horsehair
huckaback
kalamkari
matelassé
Moygashel®
organzine
paramatta
petersham
polyester
sackcloth
sailcloth
satinette

shahtoosh
sharkskin
sheepskin
stockinet
towelling
velveteen
wire gauze

10 Balbriggan
brocatelle
candlewick
florentine
hop-sacking
matellasse
mousseline
mummy-cloth
needlecord
paper-cloth
parramatta
peau de soie
polycotton
seersucker
sicilienne
Tattersall
winceyette

11 cheesecloth
flannelette
Harris tweed®
marquisette
Oxford cloth
stockinette

12 brilliantine
Brussels lace
butter-muslin
cavalry twill
crêpe-de-chine
leathercloth
Milanese silk
Shetland wool

13 casement cloth
crocodile skin
mourning-stuff
satin sheeting

14 heather mixture
terry towelling

See also **cotton**

face

Face parts include:

03 ear
eye
gum
jaw

lip
04 brow
chin
hair

iris
jowl
lips
neck

nose
skin
05 beard
cheek

mouth	temple	freckle	moustache
pupil	tongue	jawbone	**10** complexion
teeth	**07** earlobe	nostril	double chin
06 eyelid	eyeball	wrinkle	
sclera	eyebrow	**08** philtrum	
septum	eyelash	**09** cheekbone	

See also **ear**; **eye**; **hair**; **mouth**

facial hair *see* hair

fair

Fairground attractions include:

06 hoop-la	**10** bumper cars	**11** Ferris wheel	merry-go-round
07 Dodgems®	coconut shy	wall of death	tunnel of love
08 carousel	ghost train	**12** bouncy castle	**13** helter-skelter
waltzers	swing boats	chair-o-planes	rollercoaster

fairy tale

Fairy tales include:

07 *Aladdin* (Arabian Nights)
Ali Baba (Arabian Nights)
The Bell (Hans Christian Andersen)

08 *Momo Taro* (Japan)
Peter Pan (J M Barrie)
Rapunzel (Brothers Grimm)
Snowdrop (Brothers Grimm)
The Angel (Hans Christian Andersen)
The Daisy (Hans Christian Andersen)
The Raven (Brothers Grimm)
Tom Thumb (Brothers Grimm)

09 *Ashputtel* (Brothers Grimm)
Bluebeard (Charles Perrault)
Briar Rose (Brothers Grimm)
Pinocchio (Carlo Collodi)
The Shadow (Hans Christian Andersen)
The Storks (Hans Christian Andersen)

10 *Cinderella* (Charles Perrault)
Clever Hans (Brothers Grimm)
Goldilocks (traditional)
Hans in Luck (Brothers Grimm)
The Fir Tree (Hans Christian Andersen)
The Rose-Elf (Hans Christian Andersen)
Thumbelina (Hans Christian Andersen)

11 *Clever Elsie* (Brothers Grimm)
Hop o' my Thumb (Charles Perrault)
Little Thumb (Hans Christian Andersen)
Mother Elder (Hans Christian Andersen)
Mother Goose (Charles Perrault)
Puss in Boots (Charles Perrault)
The Old House (Hans Christian Andersen)
The Red Shoes (Hans Christian Andersen)

12 *Holger Danske* (Hans Christian Andersen)
Little Red-Cap (Brothers Grimm)
The Elderbush (Hans Christian Andersen)
The Goose Girl (Brothers Grimm)
The Snow Queen (Hans Christian Andersen)
The Tinderbox (Hans Christian Andersen)
The Wild Swans (Hans Christian Andersen)
Urashima Taro (Japan)

13 *Chicken Licken* (traditional)
The Frog Prince (Brothers Grimm)
The Golden Bird (Brothers Grimm)
The Neighbours (Hans Christian Andersen)
The Tin Soldier (Hans Christian Andersen)
The White Snake (Brothers Grimm)
The Wizard of Oz (L Frank Baum)

14 *Babes in the Wood* (Brothers Grimm)
Sleeping Beauty (Charles Perrault)
The Flying Trunk (Hans Christian Andersen)
The Golden Goose (Brothers Grimm)
The Juniper Tree (Brothers Grimm)
The Nightingale (Hans Christian Andersen)
The Seven Ravens (Brothers Grimm)
The Water of Life (Brothers Grimm)

15 *Dick Whittington* (traditional)
Hansel and Gretel (Brothers Grimm)
Rumpelstiltskin (Brothers Grimm)
The Elfin Hillock (Hans Christian Andersen)
The Little Lovers (Hans Christian Andersen)
The Ugly Duckling (Hans Christian Andersen)

16 *Sindbad the Sailor* (Arabian Nights)
Sweetheart Roland (Brothers Grimm)

The Little Mermaid (Hans Christian Andersen)
The Little Peasant (Brothers Grimm)
The Old Street-Lamp (Hans Christian Andersen)

17 *Beauty and the Beast* (traditional)
Little Ida's Flowers (Hans Christian Andersen)
The Miser in the Bush (Brothers Grimm)
The Twelve Huntsmen (Brothers Grimm)
The Young Swineherd (Hans Christian Andersen)

18 *Jack the Giant-Killer* (traditional)
The Brave Tin Soldier (Hans Christian Andersen)
The Little Match Girl (Hans Christian Andersen)
The Three Little Pigs (traditional)

19 *Jack and the Beanstalk* (traditional)
Little Red Riding Hood (Charles Perrault, Brothers Grimm)
Snow White and Rose Red (Brothers Grimm)
The Dog and the Sparrow (Brothers Grimm)
The Garden of Paradise (Hans Christian Andersen)
The Robber Bridegroom (Brothers Grimm)

20 *The Brave Little Tailor* (Brothers Grimm)
The Goloshes of Fortune (Hans Christian Andersen)
The Princess and the Pea (Hans Christian Andersen)
The Princess on the Bean (Hans Christian Andersen)

21 *The Emperor's New Clothes* (Hans Christian Andersen)
The Pied Piper of Hamelin (Brothers Grimm, Robert Browning)

22 *Aladdin and the Magic Lamp* (Arabian Nights)

Little Claus and Big Claus (Hans Christian Andersen)
The Fisherman and his Wife (Brothers Grimm)
The Travelling Companion (Hans Christian Andersen)
The Travelling Musicians (Brothers Grimm)
The Valiant Little Tailor (Brothers Grimm)
The Wonderful Wizard of Oz (L Frank Baum)

23 *The Elves and the Shoemaker* (Brothers Grimm)
The Three Billy Goats Gruff (traditional)

24 *Dick Whittington and his Cat* (traditional)
The Adventures of Pinocchio (Carlo Collodi)
The Town Musicians of Bremen (Brothers Grimm)

25 *Ali Baba and the Forty Thieves* (Arabian Nights)
The Shepherdess and the Sweep (Hans Christian Andersen)
The Straw, the Coal, and the Bean (Brothers Grimm)
The Three Princes of Serendip (Persian traditional)

26 *Goldilocks and the Three Bears* (traditional)
Snow White and the Seven Dwarfs (Brothers Grimm)
The King of the Golden Mountain (Brothers Grimm)
The Swineherd and the Princess (Hans Christian Andersen)
The Twelve Dancing Princesses (Brothers Grimm)

28 *The Mouse, the Bird, and the Sausage* (Brothers Grimm)

Fairy tale characters include:

03 Cat *(The Little Red Hen)*
Cat *(The Musicians of Bremen)*
Dog *(The Little Red Hen)*
Dog *(The Musicians of Bremen)*

04 Duck *(The Little Red Hen)*
Jack *(Jack and the Beanstalk)*
John *(Peter Pan)*
Liza *(Peter Pan)*
Nana *(Peter Pan)*
Nibs *(Peter Pan)*

05 Beast *(Beauty and the Beast)*
Curly *(Peter Pan)*
Wendy *(Peter Pan)*

06 Beauty *(Beauty and the Beast)*
Conrad *(The Goose Girl)*
Donkey *(The Musicians of Bremen)*

Falada *(The Goose Girl)*
Gretel *(Hansel and Gretel)*
Hansel *(Hansel and Gretel)*

07 Michael *(Peter Pan)*
Rooster *(The Musicians of Bremen)*
Rose Red *(Snow White and Rose Red)*
The King *(Puss in Boots)*
The King *(Rumpelstiltskin)*
The Ogre *(Jack and the Beanstalk)*
The Ogre *(Puss in Boots)*
The Wolf *(Little Red Riding Hood)*
Tootles *(Peter Pan)*

08 Baby Bear *(Goldilocks and the Three Bears)*
Foxy Loxy *(Chicken Licken)*
Geppetto *(Pinocchio)*
Peter Pan *(Peter Pan)*
Rapunzel *(Rapunzel)*

Slightly *(Peter Pan)*
The Elves *(The Elves and the Shoemaker)*
The Giant *(Jack and the Beanstalk)*
The Queen *(Snow White and the Seven Dwarfs)*
The Troll *(The Three Billy Goats Gruff)*
The Twins *(Peter Pan)*
Tom Thumb *(Tom Thumb)*

09 Daddy Bear *(Goldilocks and the Three Bears)*
Good Fairy *(Sleeping Beauty)*
Mummy Bear *(Goldilocks and the Three Bears)*
Pinocchio *(Pinocchio)*
Snow White *(Snow White and Rose Red)*
Snow White *(Snow White and the Seven Dwarfs)*
The Miller *(Puss in Boots)*
The Miller *(Rumpelstiltskin)*
The Mirror *(Snow White and the Seven Dwarfs)*
The Prince *(Cinderella)*
The Prince *(Rapunzel)*
The Prince *(Sleeping Beauty)*

10 Cinderella *(Cinderella)*
Ducky Lucky *(Chicken Licken)*
Goldilocks *(Goldilocks and the Three Bears)*
Henny Penny *(Chicken Licken)*
Stepmother *(Hansel and Gretel)*
The Emperor *(The Emperor's New Clothes)*
Thumbelina *(Thumbelina)*
Tinker Bell *(Peter Pan)*

11 Captain Hook *(Peter Pan)*

Grandmother *(Little Red Riding Hood)*
Pedlar Woman *(Snow White and the Seven Dwarfs)*
Puss in Boots *(Puss in Boots)*
The Huntsman *(Snow White and the Seven Dwarfs)*
The Lost Boys *(Peter Pan)*
The Princess *(Puss in Boots)*
The Princess *(The Princess and the Pea)*
Ugly Sisters *(Cinderella)*
Wicked Fairy *(Sleeping Beauty)*
Wicked Witch *(Hansel and Gretel)*

12 Goosey Loosey *(Chicken Licken)*
The Goose Girl *(The Goose Girl)*
The Shoemaker *(The Elves and the Shoemaker)*

13 Band of Robbers *(The Musicians of Bremen)*
Chicken Licken *(Chicken Licken)*
Red Riding Hood *(Little Red Riding Hood)*

14 Fairy Godmother *(Cinderella)*
The Golden Goose *(The Golden Goose)*
The Seven Dwarfs *(Snow White and the Seven Dwarfs)*

15 Alice Fitzwarren *(Dick Whittington)*
Dick Whittington *(Dick Whittington)*
Fairy Godmothers *(Sleeping Beauty)*
Mr and Mrs Darling *(Peter Pan)*
Rumpelstiltskin *(Rumpelstiltskin)*
The Little Red Hen *(The Little Red Hen)*
The Rich Merchant *(Beauty and the Beast)*
The Ugly Duckling *(The Ugly Duckling)*
Three Little Pigs *(The Three Little Pigs)*

Fairies include:

04 Moth *(A Midsummer Night's Dream*, 1595, William Shakespeare)
Ozma (Princess; *The Marvellous Land of Oz*, 1904, et seq, L Frank Baum)
Puck *(A Midsummer Night's Dream*, 1595, William Shakespeare)

05 Ariel *(The Tempest*, 1611, William Shakespeare)

06 Cobweb *(A Midsummer Night's Dream*, 1595, William Shakespeare)
Oberon *(A Midsummer Night's Dream*, 1595, William Shakespeare)

07 Titania *(A Midsummer Night's Dream*, 1595, William Shakespeare)

08 Iolanthe *(Iolanthe*, 1882, Gilbert and Sullivan)

10 Maleficent *(Sleeping Beauty* (film), 1959)
Tinkerbell *(Peter Pan*, 1904, J M Barrie)

11 Mustardseed *(A Midsummer Night's Dream*, 1595, William Shakespeare)

12 Peaseblossom *(A Midsummer Night's Dream*, 1595, William Shakespeare)
The Blue Fairy *(Pinocchio* (film), 1940)

13 Nac Mac Feegles *(The Wee Free Men*, 2003, Sir Terry Pratchett)

14 Fairy Godmother *(Cinderella/Sleeping Beauty*, fairy tales)
Sugar Plum Fairy *(The Nutcracker*, 1892, Tchaikovsky)

15 Robin Goodfellow *(A Midsummer Night's Dream*, 1595, William Shakespeare)

See also **mythology**; **pantomime**; **Shakespeare, William**

falcon

Falcons include:

05 hobby	**07** Iceland	jerfalcon	falcon-gentle
saker	kestrel	peregrine	tassel-gentle
06 gentle	**08** duck-hawk	stone hawk	tercel-gentle
lanner	**09** gerfalcon	**11** tassell-gent	tercel-jerkin
merlin	gyrfalcon	**12** falcon-gentil	

family

Family members include:

02 ex	nanna	partner	stepmother
ma	nanny	sibling	step-parent
pa	niece	stepdad	stepsister
03 dad	uncle	stepmum	twin-sister
mom	**06** cousin	stepson	**11** first cousin
mum	ex-wife	**08** daughter	foster-child
son	father	godchild	god-daughter
04 aunt	godson	grandson	grandfather
gran	grampa	**09** ex-husband	grandmother
heir	granny	godfather	grandparent
mama	mother	godmother	great nephew
nana	nephew	great aunt	half-brother
papa	parent	stepchild	stepbrother
twin	sister	**10** grandchild	twin-brother
wife	spouse	great niece	**12** foster-parent
05 daddy	**07** brother	great uncle	second cousin
mummy	grandad	half-sister	stepdaughter
	husband	stepfather	**13** grand-daughter

See also **aunt**; **daughter**; **father**; **genealogy**; **mother**; **relative**; **son**; **uncle**

fantasy see **science fiction**

farm

Farms and farming types include:

03 dry	**05** croft	salmon	intensive
ley	dairy	turkey	**10** collective
pig	mixed	**07** factory	plantation
04 deer	store	organic	**11** cattle ranch
fish	trash	ostrich	monoculture
hill	trout	poultry	subsistence
stud	**06** arable	**09** extensive	**12** sheep station
wind	estate	free-range	smallholding

Farm animals include:

02 ox	pig	calf	lamb
03 ass	ram	cock	mare
cow	sow	duck	mule
ewe	**04** boar	foal	**05** goose
hen	bull	goat	horse

llama	donkey	ostrich	wild boar
sheep	rabbit	rooster	**09** billy goat
06 alpaca	turkey	**08** cockerel	
cattle	**07** chicken	stallion	

Farming terms include:

03 CAP	shear	**08** abbatoir	pesticide
dip	straw	breeding	ploughing
hay	swill	cash crop	sharecrop
mir	**06** arable	farm cart	side-dress
pen	braird	farm hand	slaughter
sow	eat off	hacienda	**10** cereal crop
04 bale	fallow	hay-wagon	fertilizer
barn	farmer	hill farm	interplant
byre	fodder	home farm	irrigation
cart	furrow	land army	winter crop
crap	grieve	land girl	**11** agriculture
crop	manure	outfield	zero-grazing
ferm	shamba	root crop	**12** crop rotation
hind	silage	steading	foot and mouth
peon	slurry	township	tenant farmer
reap	**07** grazing	**09** after-crop	vermiculture
wick	harvest	break crop	**13** goodman's croft
05 baler	holding	catch-crop	green manuring
breer	kibbutz	cover crop	tattie howking
croft	kolkhoz	deadstock	tattie lifting
dairy	milking	farmhouse	tattie picking
field	organic	free range	**14** drip irrigation
gambo	orra man	green crop	slaughterhouse
plant	pasture	intercrop	**15** animal husbandry
ranch	tractor	livestock	

See also **agriculture**; **cattle**; **cereal**; **chicken**; **crop**; **disease**; **duck**; **horse**; **meat**; **pig**; **poultry**; **rabbit**; **sheep**

fashion

Fashion accessories include:

03 bag	stole	parasol	stockings
cap	watch	**08** hairband	victorine
fur	**06** gloves	hair clip	**10** evening bag
hat	poncho	headband	legwarmers
04 belt	tights	palatine	spectacles
boot	tippet	pashmina	sunglasses
wrap	**07** glasses	pelerine	**13** body jewellery
05 purse	handbag	umbrella	evening gloves
scarf	hosiery	**09** headscarf	leather gloves
shawl	mittens	jewellery	
shoes	muffler	scrunchie	

Fashion designers and labels include:

03 YSL	DKNY
04 Choo (Jimmy; 1952– , Malaysian/British)	fcuk
Dior (Christian; 1905–57, French)	Joop!

Joop (Wolfgang; 1944– , German)
Lang (Helmut; 1956– , Austrian)
Muir (Jean; 1928–95, English)

05 Amies (Sir Hardy; 1909–2003, English)
Chloé
D and G
Dolce (Domenico; 1958– , Italian)
Farhi (Nicole; 1946– , French/British)
Fendi
Gucci
Karan (Donna; 1948– , US)
Kenzo (1940– , Japanese)
Klein (Anne; 1923–74, US)
Klein (Calvin; 1942– , US)
Ozbek (Rifat; 1954– , Turkish)
Patou (Jean; 1880–1936, French)
Prada
Prada (Miuccia; 1949– , Italian)
Pucci (Emilio, Marchese di Barsento;
1914–92, Italian)
Quant (Mary; 1934– , English)
Ricci (Nina; 1883–1970, Italian)
Smith (Sir Paul; 1946– , English)
Worth (Charles Frederick; 1825–95, English)

06 Armani
Armani (Giorgio; 1935– , Italian)
Ashley (Laura; 1925–85, Welsh)
Cardin (Pierre; 1922– , French)
Chanel (Coco; 1883–1971, French)
Conran (Jasper; 1959– , English)
Conran (Shirley; 1932– , English)
Hermes
Jacobs (Marc; 1963– , US)
Lauren (Ralph; 1939– , US)
Miu Miu
Miyake (Issey; 1938– , Japanese)
Poiret (Paul; 1879–1944, French)
Rhodes (Zandra; 1940– , English)
Sander (Jil; 1943– , German)
Ungaro (Emanuel; 1933– , French)

07 Balmain (Pierre; 1914–82, French)
Blahnik (Manolo; 1942– , Spanish/British)
Fassett (Kaffe; 1937– , US)
Gabbana (Stefano; 1962– , Italian)
Hamnett (Katharine; 1952– , English)
Jackson (Betty; 1949– , English)
Lacoste
Lacroix (Christian; 1951– , French)
Laroche (Guy; 1923–89, French)

Max Mara
McQueen (Alexander; 1970– , English)
Missoni (Ottavio; 1921– , Italian)
Versace (Donatella; 1955– , Italian)
Versace (Gianni; 1946–97, Italian)
Vuitton (Louis; 1821–1892, French)

08 Burberry
Chalayan (Hussein; 1970– , Turkish
Cypriot)
Galliano (John; 1961– , Gibraltarian/
British)
Gaultier (Jean-Paul; 1952– , French)
Givenchy (Hubert de; 1927– , French)
Hartnell (Sir Norman; 1901–78, English)
Hilfiger (Tommy; 1951– , US)
Hugo Boss
Kawakubo (Rei; 1942– , Japanese)
Molyneux (Edward; 1891–1974, English)
Moschino
Moschino (Franco; 1950–94, Italian)
Oldfield (Bruce; 1950– , English)
Richmond (John; 1960– , English)
Ted Baker
Westwood (Vivienne; 1941– , English)
Yamamoto (Yohji; 1943– , Japanese)

09 Claiborne (Liz; 1929–2007, Belgian/US)
Courrèges (André; 1923– , French)
de la Renta (Oscar; 1932– , Dominican/
US)
Hulanicki (Barbara; 1936– , Polish/British)
Lagerfeld (Karl-Otto; 1938– , German)
McCartney (Stella; 1972– , English)
Mortensen (Erik; 1926–98, Danish)
Paul Smith
Valentino (1933– , Italian)

10 Balenciaga (Cristóbal; 1895–1972,
Spanish)
Mainbocher (c.1890–1976, US)
Vanderbilt (Gloria; 1924– , US)

11 Calvin Klein
Cath Kidston
Laura Ashley

12 Louis Vuitton
Saint Laurent (Yves; 1936–2008, French)
Schiaparelli (Elsa; 1890–1973, Italian/
French)

13 Dolce e Gabbana
Tommy Hilfiger

See also **clothes**

fast

Fast-days and fasting periods include:

04 Lent (Christian)	Friday (Christian)	**08** Moharram (Islam)
06 Ashura (Islam)	**07** Ramadan (Islam)	Muharram (Islam)

Muharrem (Islam)
Ramadhan (Islam)
Tisha Bov (Judaism)
09 Ember days (Christian)
See also **festival**

Tisha Baav (Judaism)
Tisha be'Ab (Judaism)
Tisha Be'Av (Judaism)
Tishah b'Ab (Judaism)

Tishah B'Av (Judaism)
Yom Kippur (Judaism)
10 Holy Friday (Christian)
12 Golden Friday (Christian)

fast food *see* food; restaurant

fastener

Fasteners include:

03 tie
zip
04 bond
clip
frog
hasp
hook
knot
lace
link
lock

loop
nail
stud
05 catch
clasp
hinge
latch
rivet
screw
06 button
cotter

eyelet
holder
staple
stitch
toggle
Velcro®
zipper
07 padlock
08 cufflink
shoelace
split pin

09 paperclip
press stud
10 collar stud
hook-and-eye
11 Bulldog® clip
Chelsea clip
treasury tag
13 alligator clip
crocodile clip

fate

The Greek Fates:

06 Clotho   **07** Atropos   **08** Lachesis

The Norse Fates:

03 Urd   **05** Skuld   **08** Verdande

father

Fathers include:

04 Amis (Sir Kingsley; 1922–95, English)
Bush (George; 1924– , US)
Lear (King; *King Lear*, 1605–06, William Shakespeare)
Pitt (William; 1708–78, English)
05 Dumas (Alexandre; 1802–70, French)
Ghost (*Hamlet*, 1600–01, William Shakespeare)
Isaac (Bible)
Jacob (Bible)
Mills (Sir John; 1908–2005, English)
Nehru (Jawaharlal 'Pandit'; 1889–1964, Indian)
06 Bhutto (Zulfikar Ali; 1928–79, Pakistani)
07 Abraham (Bible)
Capulet (Lord; *Romeo and Juliet*, 1595, William Shakespeare)
Chatham (William Pitt, Earl of; 1708–78, English)

Kennedy (Joseph P; 1888–1969, US)
Leontes (*The Winter's Tale*, 1609, William Shakespeare)
Shylock (*The Merchant of Venice*, 1596–97, William Shakespeare)
Simpson (Homer; *The Simpsons*, TV)
08 Campbell (Sir Malcolm; 1885–1949, English)
Dimbleby (Richard; 1913–65, English)
King Lear (*King Lear*, 1605–06, William Shakespeare)
Polonius (*Hamlet*, 1600–01, William Shakespeare)
Pontifex (Theo; *The Way of All Flesh*, 1903, Samuel Butler)
Prospero (*The Tempest*, 1611, William Shakespeare)
09 Antiochus (*Pericles*, c.1608, William Shakespeare)

Dumas père (1802–70, French)

10 Clayhanger (Darius; *Clayhanger*, 1910, Arnold Bennett)

11 Rockefeller (John D; 1839–1937, US)

12 Pitt the Elder (William; 1708–78, English)

14 Uther Pendragon (Arthurian legend)

female animal *see* animal

feminism

Feminists include:

04 Daly (Mary; 1928– , US)
Hite (Shere; 1943– , US)
Mott (Lucretia; 1793–1880, US)
Shaw (Anna Howard; 1847–1919, US)
Wolf (Naomi; 1962– , US)

05 Abzug (Bella; 1920–98, US)
Astor (Nancy; 1879–1964, US/British)
Beale (Dorothea; 1831–1906, English)
Greer (Germaine; 1939– , Australian)
Stone (Lucy; 1818–93, US)

06 Callil (Carmen; 1938– , Australian)
Cixous (Hélène; 1937– , French)
Faludi (Susan; 1960– , US)
Friday (Nancy; 1937– , US)
Fuller (Margaret; 1810–50, US)
Gilman (Charlotte Perkins; 1860–1935, US)
Grimké (Sarah; 1792–1873, US)
Orbach (Susie; 1946– , English)
Paglia (Camille; 1947– , US)
Rankin (Jeannette; 1880–1973, US)
Stopes (Marie; 1880–1958, Scottish)
Weldon (Fay; 1931– , English)

07 Anthony (Susan B; 1820–1906, US)
Davison (Emily; 1872–1913, English)
Dworkin (Andrea; 1946–2005, US)
Egerton (Sarah; 1670–1723, English)
Fawcett (Dame Millicent; 1847–1929, English)
Friedan (Betty; 1921–2006, US)
Goldman (Emma; 1869–1940, US)
Kennedy (Helena, Baroness; 1950– , Scottish)
Lenclos (Ninon de; 1620–1705, French)
Steinem (Gloria; 1934– , US)

08 Beauvoir (Simone de; 1908–86, French)
Brittain (Vera; 1893–1970, English)
MacPhail (Agnes; 1890–1954, Canadian)
Rathbone (Eleanor; 1872–1946, English)

09 Blackwell (Elizabeth; 1821–1910, US)
Pankhurst (Adela; 1885–1961, English)
Pankhurst (Christabel; 1880–1958, English)
Pankhurst (Emmeline; 1857–1928, English)
Pankhurst (Sylvia; 1882–1960, English)

11 Burgos Seguí (Carmen de; c.1870–1932, Spanish)

14 Wollstonecraft (Mary; 1759–97, Anglo-Irish)

fencing

Fencing terms include:

03 bib	piste	quinte	coquille
cut	prime	remise	plastron
hit	punto	thrust	tac-au-tac
04 bout	sabre	tierce	traverse
épée	sixte	touché	**09** disengage
foil	touch.	**07** barrage	repechage
pass	volte	counter	**10** flanconade
pink	**06** attack	en garde	imbroccata
volt	button	on guard	time-thrust
ward	come in	passado	**11** corps à corps
05 allez	doigté	reprise	punto dritto
appel	faible	riposte	**12** colichemarde
carte	flèche	seconde	counter-parry
feint	foible	septime	punto reverso
forte	octave	stop hit	punto riverso
lunge	parade	**08** back edge	**14** counter-riposte
parry	puncto	balestra	
	quarte		

See also **sport**

fern

03 lip
man
oak

04 blue
felt
fork
hard
lady
male
sago
seed
tara
tree

05 beech
brake
chain
coral
crown
glory
holly
marsh
ponga
punga
royal
scale
sword
water

06 azolla
bamboo
Boston

button
ladder
lunary
nardoo
osmund
ribbon
shield
silver
tongue

07 bladder
bracken
bristle
buckler
Byfield
cabbage
Dickie's
elkhorn
emerald
foxtail
Goldie's
leather
osmunda
ostrich
parsley
rockcap
tatting
walking
wall rue
woodsia

08 aspidium
barometz

bear's paw
ceterach
cinnamon
climbing
goldback
hairy lip
licorice
moonwort
northern
pillwort
polypody
soft tree
staghorn

09 asparagus
asplenium
bird's nest
black tree
fairy moss
flowering
hare's foot
rhizocarp
rock brake
rusty-back
sensitive
snow brake

10 Asian chain
broad beech
common rasp
golden male
hard shield
Korean rock

maidenhair
soft shield
spleenwort
woolly tree

11 hart's tongue
interrupted
nephrolepis
rabbit's foot
shuttlecock
silver balls
walking leaf

12 broad buckler
elephant's ear
golden Boston
Hawaiian tree
Japanese felt
resurrection
Wallich's wood

13 crested ribbon
European chain
hen-and-chicken
Japanese holly
narrow buckler
prickly shield
scolopendrium
squirrel's foot

14 brittle bladder
Japanese tassel

15 Japanese painted
Mrs Frizell's lady

See also **plant**

festival

03 Bon (mid-Jul)

04 Holi (Spring)
Lots (one month before Passover)
Noel (Winter)
Yule (Winter)

05 Purim (one month before Passover)
Saman (1 Nov)
Weeks (50 days after Passover)
Wesak (Apr/May)

06 Advent (four weeks before Christmas)
Diwali (Oct/Nov)
Easter (Spring)
Floria (28 Apr to 3 May)
Lammas (1 Aug)
May Day (1 May)
Oimelc (1 Feb)

Opalia (19 Dec)
Pesach (Spring)
Plebii (4–17 Nov)

07 Beltane (1 May)
Equiria (27 Feb/14 Mar/15 Oct)
Feralia (21/22 Feb)
Fugalia (24 Feb)
Imbolic (1 Feb)
Lady Day (25 Mar)
Lemuria (9–13 May)
Navrati (Sep/Oct)
Palilia (21 Apr)
Parilia (21 Apr)
Ramadan (moveable)
Samhain (1 Nov)
Sukkoth (Autumn)
Sullani (26 Oct to 1 Nov)

Theseia (Oct)
Vinalia (23 Apr)

08 Agonalia (9 Jan/17 Mar/21 May/11 Dec)
Cerealia (Apr)
Fasching (Feb)
Faunalia (13 Feb/13 Oct/5 Dec)
Floralia (28 Apr to 3 May)
Hanukkah (Winter)
Hogmanay (New Year)
Homstrom (end of Winter)
Hull Fair (Oct)
Id ul-Adha (moveable)
Id ul-Fitr (moveable)
Lucia Day (13 Dec)
Lugnasad (2 Aug)
Mahayana (mid-Jul)
Matralia (11 Jun)
Nit de foc (Mar)
Passover (Spring)
Samhuinn (1 Nov)
Setsubun (3/4 Feb)
Shabuoth (50 days after Passover)
Stow Fair (May/Oct)
Tanabata (7 Jul)
Vestalia (9 Jun)

09 Baishakhi (13/14 Apr)
Boxing Day (26 Dec)
Christmas (25 Dec)
Floralies (Summer)
Hallowe'en (31 Oct)
Hallowmas (1 Nov)
Ides of Mar (15 Mar)
Liberalia (17 Mar)
Ludi Magni (Sep)
Lugnasadh (2 Aug)
Magalesia (4–10 Apr)
Magha-puja (Feb)
Mardi Gras (Feb/Mar)
Martinmas (11 Nov)
Nemoralia (13 Aug)
Paganalia (24–26 Jan)
Pentecost (50 days after Pesach)
Puanepsia (Autumn)
Robigalia (25 Apr)
Thargelia (late May)
Ullambana (15th day of the 7th lunar
     month)
Up-Helly-Aa (Jan/Feb)
Wakes Week (Summer)
Yom Kippur (Autumn)

10 Allhallows (1 Nov)
Ambarvalia (29 May)
Barnet Fair (Sep)
Fordicidia (15 Apr)
Fornicalia (17 Feb)
Good Friday (Spring)
Larentalia (Dec)

La Tomatina (Aug)
Lee Gap Fair (24 Aug/17 Sep)
Ludi Romani (5–19 Sep)
Lupercalia (15 Feb)
Matronalia (1 Mar)
Mother's Day (Spring)
Neptunalia (23 Jul)
Palm Sunday (Sunday before Easter Day)
Pancake Day (Feb/Mar)
Parentalia (13–21 Feb)
Portunalia (17 Aug)
Quirinalia (17 Feb)
Regifugium (24 Feb)
Saturnalia (17–23 Dec)
Swan Upping (Jul)
Terminalia (23 Feb)
Volcanalia (23 Aug)

11 All Fools' Day (1 Apr)
All Souls' Day (2 Nov)
Bacchanalia (Mar)
Carmentalia (11 and 15 Jan)
Epulum Jovis (13 Nov)
Hina Matsuri (3 Mar)
Lady Luck Day (5 Apr)
Oktoberfest (Oct)
Oskhophoria (Autumn)
Panathenaea (Jul)
Quinquatrus (19–21 Mar)
Semo Sanctus (Jun)
St David's Day (1 Mar)
Tabernacles (Autumn)

12 All Saints' Day (1 Nov)
Armilustrium (19 Oct)
Ascension Day (40 days after Easter)
Ash Wednesday (Feb/Mar)
Barranquilla (Spring)
Day of the Dead (2 Nov)
Doll Festival (3 Mar)
Holy Wells Day (2 Mar)
Kanda Matsuri (mid-May)
Ludi Merceruy (15 May)
Mahashivrati (Jan/Feb)
Meditrinalia (11 Oct)
Nutters Dance (Easter Saturday)
Rosh Hashanah (Autumn)
St Andrew's Day (30 Nov)
St George's Day (23 Apr)
Thanksgiving (Nov)
Tubilustrium (23 Mar)
Twelfth Night (5 Jan)
Well-dressing (Ascension Day to Sep)

13 April Fool's Day (1 Apr)
Haxey Hood Game (5/6 Jan)
Ludi Consualia (21 Aug)
Ludi Martiales (12 May)
Midsummer's Eve (late Jun)
Raksha Bandhan (Jul/Aug)

Shrove Tuesday (Feb/Mar)
St Patrick's Day (17 Mar)
The Furry Dance (Spring)
Water Festival (13–15 Apr)
Widecombe Fair (Sep)

14 Chinese New Year (Jan/Feb)
Maundy Thursday (Mar/Apr)
St Nicholas's Day (6 Dec)
Vinalia Rustica (19 Aug)

Walpurgis Night (30 Apr–1 May)

15 Festival of Light (2 Aug)
Harvest Festival (Autumn)
Ludi Apollinares (5 Jul)
Mahavira Jayanti (Oct/Nov)
Mothering Sunday (4th Sunday of Lent)
Priddy Sheep Fair (mid-Aug)
St Valentine's Day (14 Feb)

Modern festivals and celebrations include:

05 VE Day (8 May)
VJ Day (14 Aug)
WOMAD (Jul/Aug)

08 Anzac Day (25 Apr)
Earth Day (22 Apr)
Labor Day (Sep)

09 Canada Day (1 Jul)
Labour Day (1 May)

10 Burns Night (25 Jan)

11 Bastille Day (14 Jul)
Cinco de Mayo (5 May)
Glastonbury (end Jun)

Republic Day (various)
Waitangi Day (6 Feb)

12 Armistice Day (11 Nov)
Australia Day (26 Jan)
Bonfire Night (5 Nov)
Groundhog Day (2 Feb)

13 New Zealand Day (6 Feb)

14 Guy Fawkes' Night (5 Nov)
Remembrance Day (11 Nov or nearest
Sunday)

15 Edinburgh Fringe (Aug)
Independence Day (4 Jul)

See also **celebration**; **fast**; **holiday**; **religion**

fever

Fevers include:

01 Q	dumdum	**08** childbed
03 hay	hectic	kala-azar
tap	jungle	undulant
04 ague	parrot	**09** breakbone
camp	plague	calenture
gaol	rabbit	East Coast
gold	spring	glandular
jail	trench	phrenitis
Rock	typhus	puerperal
ship	valley	relapsing
tick	yellow	remittent
worm	**07** biliary	rheumatic
05 brain	enteric	**10** blackwater
cabin	gastric	Rift Valley
dandy	malaria	scarlatina
Lassa	measles	yellow Jack
Malta	ratbite	**12** African coast
marsh	sandfly	**13** cerebrospinal
stage	scarlet	leptospirosis
swamp	splenic	Mediterranean
swine	spotted	**14** kissing disease
Texas	typhoid	**15** acute rheumatism
06 dengue	verruga	

See also **disease**

fiction

Fictional places include:

02 Ix (*Dune*, 1965, et seq, Frank Herbert)
Oz (*The Wonderful Wizard of Oz*, 1900, L Frank Baum)

04 Alph (*Kubla Khan*, 1816, Samuel Taylor Coleridge)
Rhun (*The Lord of the Rings*, 1954–55, J R R Tolkien)

05 Arnor (*The Lord of the Rings*, 1954–55, J R R Tolkien)
Holby (*Casualty/Holby City*, TV)
Moria (*The Lord of the Rings*, 1954–55, J R R Tolkien)
Rohan (*The Lord of the Rings*, 1954–55, J R R Tolkien)

06 Canley (*The Bill*, TV)
Dibley (*The Vicar of Dibley*, TV)
Gondor (*The Lord of the Rings*, 1954–55, J R R Tolkien)
Laputa (*Gulliver's Travels*, 1726, Jonathan Swift)
Lorien (*The Lord of the Rings*, 1954–55, J R R Tolkien)
Mordor (*The Lord of the Rings*, 1954–55, J R R Tolkien)
Narnia (*The Chronicles of Narnia*, 1950–56, C S Lewis)
Titipu (*The Mikado*, 1885, Gilbert and Sullivan)
Utopia (*Utopia*, 1516, Sir Thomas More)
Vulcan (*Star Trek*, TV/film)
Wessex (various novels, Thomas Hardy)
Xanadu (*Kubla Khan*, 1816, Samuel Taylor Coleridge)

07 Avonlea (*Anne of Green Gables*, 1908, L M Montgomery)
Bedrock (*The Flintstones*, TV)
Camelot (Arthurian legend)
Erewhon (*Erewhon*, 1872, Samuel Butler)
Eriador (*The Lord of the Rings*, 1954–55, J R R Tolkien)
Eurasia (*1984*, 1949, George Orwell)
Midwich (*The Midwich Cuckoos*, 1957, John Wyndham)
Mole End (*The Wind in the Willows*, 1908, Kenneth Grahame)
Sun Hill (*The Bill*, TV)
Toyland (*Noddy Goes to Toyland*, 1949, et seq, Enid Blyton)
Walford (*Eastenders*, TV)

08 Ambridge (*The Archers*, radio)
Blefuscu (*Gulliver's Travels*, 1726, Jonathan Swift)

Calormen (*The Chronicles of Narnia*, 1950–56, C S Lewis)
Earthsea (*A Wizard of Earthsea*, 1968, et seq, Ursula Le Guin)
Hobbiton (*The Lord of the Rings*, 1954–55, J R R Tolkien)
Lilliput (*Gulliver's Travels*, 1726, Jonathan Swift)
Llaregyb (*Under Milk Wood*, 1954, Dylan Thomas)
Mirkwood (*The Lord of the Rings*, 1954–55, J R R Tolkien)
Stepford (*The Stepford Wives*, 1972, Ira Levin)
Sylvania (*Duck Soup*, 1933)
Tartarus (Greek mythology)
The Shire (*The Lord of the Rings*, 1954–55, J R R Tolkien)
Toad Hall (*The Wind in the Willows*, 1908, Kenneth Grahame)

09 Barataria (*The Gondoliers*, 1889, Gilbert and Sullivan)
Brigadoon (*Brigadoon*, 1947)
Discworld (*The Colour of Magic*, 1983, et seq, Terry Pratchet)
Emmerdale (*Emmerdale*, TV)
Freedonia (*Duck Soup*, 1933)
Hollyoaks (*Hollyoaks*, TV)
Rivendell (*The Lord of the Rings*, 1954–55, J R R Tolkien)
River Alph (*Kubla Khan*, 1816, Samuel Taylor Coleridge)
Ruritania (*The Prisoner of Zenda*,1894, Anthony Hope)
Shangri-La (*Lost Horizon*, 1933, James Hilton)
Summer Bay (*Home and Away*, TV)
Venusberg (*Venusberg*, 1932, Anthony Powell)
Westworld (*Westworld*, 1973)

10 Archenland (*The Chronicles of Narnia*, 1950–56, C S Lewis)
Barchester (various novels, Anthony Trollope)
Borchester (*The Archers*, radio)
Moominland (*The Little Trolls and the Great Flood*, 1945, et seq, Tove Jansson)
Shieldinch (*River City*, TV)
Vanity Fair (*Pilgrim's Progress*, 1678/84, John Bunyan)
Wonderland (*Alice's Adventures in Wonderland*, 1865, Lewis Carroll)

11 Airstrip One (*1984*, 1949, George Orwell)

Barsetshire (various novels, Anthony Trollope)
Borsetshire (*The Archers*, radio)
Brobdingnag (*Gulliver's Travels*, 1726, Jonathan Swift)
Diagon Alley (*Harry Potter and the Philosopher's Stone*, 1997, et seq, J K Rowling)
Emerald City (*The Wonderful Wizard of Oz*, 1900, L Frank Baum)
Gormenghast (*Titus Groan*, 1946, et seq, Mervyn Peake)
Middle-Earth (*The Lord of the Rings*, 1954–55, J R R Tolkien)
Skull Island (*King Kong*, 1933)
The Wild Wood (*The Wind in the Willows*, 1908, Kenneth Grahame)

12 Albert Square (*Eastenders*, TV)
Celesteville (*The Story of Babar the Little Elephant*, 1931, et seq, Jean de Brunhoff)
Erinsborough (*Neighbours*, TV)
Glubbdubdrib (*Gulliver's Travels*, 1726, Jonathan Swift)
Jurassic Park (*Jurassic Park*, 1990, Michael Crichton)

See also **film**; **superhero**; **television**

Ramsay Street (*Neighbours*, TV)
Sleepy Hollow (*The Legend of Sleepy Hollow*, 1819, Washington Irving)
Tralfamadore (*Slaughterhouse-Five*, 1969, Kurt Vonnegut)
Weatherfield (*Coronation Street*, TV)

13 Celestial City (*Pilgrim's Progress*, 1678/84, John Bunyan)
Christminster (various novels, Thomas Hardy)
Montego Street (*River City*, TV)

14 Brookside Close (*Brookside*, TV)
Doubting-Castle (*Pilgrim's Progress*, 1678/84, John Bunyan)
Hogwarts School (*Harry Potter and the Philosopher's Stone*, 1997, et seq, J K Rowling)
Never-Never Land (*Peter Pan*, 1904, J M Barrie)
Nightmare Abbey (*Nightmare Abbey*, 1818, Thomas Love Peacock)
Treasure Island (*Treasure Island*, 1883, Robert Louis Stevenson)

15 Baskerville Hall (*The Hound of the Baskervilles*, 1902, Arthur Conan Doyle)

field marshal

Field marshals include:

04 Haig (Douglas, Earl; 1861–1928, Scottish)
05 Lucan (George Bingham, Earl of; 1800–88, English)
Monty (Bernard Viscount, Montgomery; 1887–1976, English)
06 French (Sir John; 1852–1925, English)
Raglan (Fitzroy Somerset, Lord; 1788–1855, English)
07 Allenby (Edmund Hynman, Viscount; 1861–1936, English)
Roberts (Frederick, Earl; 1832–1914, English)

08 Ironside (William, Lord; 1880–1959, Scottish)
Wolseley (Garnet Joseph, Viscount; 1833–1913, Irish/British)
09 Robertson (Sir William; 1860–1933, English)
10 Alanbrooke (Alan Francis Brooke, Viscount; 1883–1963, French/British)
Auchinleck (Sir Claude John Eyre; 1884–1981, English)
Kesselring (Albert; 1885–1960, German)
Montgomery (Bernard, Viscount 'Monty'; 1887–1976, English)

fighter

Fighters include:

05 boxer	**07** matador	wrestler	**10** rejoneador
pugil	picador	**09** gladiator	**11** bullfighter
06 fencer	sworder	kick boxer	digladiator
hitman	**08** pugilist	spadassin	**12** banderillero
knight	toreador	swordsman	prizefighter

See also **boxing**; **fencing**; **wrestling**

figure of speech *see* rhetoric

film

03 spy
war

04 blue
cult
epic
noir

05 adult
anime
buddy
crime
farce
heist
short
spoof
vogue
weepy

06 action
auteur
biopic
B-movie
comedy
Disney
erotic
family
horror
murder
police
remake
rom-com
serial
silent
weepie

07 Carry-on
cartoon
classic
fantasy
musical
neo-noir
new wave

passion
realist
robbery
slasher
tragedy
war hero
western

08 animated
disaster
escapist
film noir
gangster
newsreel
romantic
space-age
thriller

09 adventure
Bollywood
burlesque
chopsocky
detective
film à clef
flashback
Hitchcock
Hollywood
James Bond
love story
low-budget
melodrama
political
road movie
satirical
skin flick
Spielberg
whodunnit

10 avant-garde
bonkbuster
gay-lesbian
neo-realist

period epic
snuff movie
surrealist
tear-jerker
travelogue

11 black comedy
blockbuster
cliff-hanger
documentary
kitchen sink
period drama
tragicomedy
underground

12 cinéma-vérité
Ealing comedy
ethnographic
fly-on-the-wall
mockumentary
pornographic
rockumentary
social comedy

13 comic-book hero
expressionist
multiple-story
murder mystery
nouvelle vague
sexploitation
sexual fantasy
social problem

14 blaxploitation
Charlie Chaplin
comedy thriller
police thriller
rites of passage
romantic comedy
science-fiction

15 cowboy and Indian
romantic tragedy
screwball comedy

02 *If...* (1963)
03 *Big* (1988)
Cal (1984)
Hud (1963)
JFK (1991)
Kes (1970)
Ran (1985)
04 *Antz* (1998)
Babe (1995)
Bird (1988)
Diva (1981)

Dr No (1962)
Gigi (1958)
Heat (1995)
Jaws (1975)
MASH (1970)
Milk (2008)
Reds (1981)
Rope (1948)
X-Men (2000)
05 *Alfie* (1966/2004)
Alien (1973)

Angel (1982)
Bambi (1942)
Bugsy (1992)
Crash (1996/2004)
Dumbo (1941)
Fargo (1996)
Ghost (1990)
Giant (1956)
Greed (1924)
Klute (1971)
Marty (1955)
Naked (1993)
Rocky (1976)
Shane (1953)
Shrek (2001)
Texas (1941)

06 *Aliens* (1986)
Amélie (2001)
Batman (1989)
Ben-Hur (1959)
Blow-Up (1966)
Brazil (1985)
Casino (1995)
Ed Wood (1994)
Gandhi (1982)
Go West (1940)
Grease (1978)
Heimat (1984)
Kundun (1997)
Lolita (1962)
Mad Max (1979)
Marnie (1964)
Misery (1990)
Patton (1970)
Psycho (1960)
The Fly (1986)
The Kid (1921)
Top Gun (1986)
Top Hat (1935)

07 *Aladdin* (1992)
Amadeus (1984)
Big Fish (2003)
Bullitt (1968)
Cabaret (1972)
Charade (1963)
Darling (1965)
Das Boot (1981)
Dead Man (1995)
Die Hard (1988)
Dracula (1931/1958/1974/1979/1992)
Jezebel (1938)
L'Âge d'Or (1930)
Matador (1986)
Memento (2000)
Platoon (1986)
Poor Cow (1968)
Rain Man (1988)

Rebecca (1940)
Robocop (1987)
Serpico (1973)
Sunrise (1927)
The Dead (1987)
The Mask (1994)
The Omen (1976)
The Robe (1953)
Titanic (1997)
Tootsie (1982)
Traffic (2000)
Twister (1996)
Vertigo (1958)
Witness (1985)

08 *Apollo 13* (1995)
Badlands (1973)
Body Heat (1981)
Born Free (1966)
Cape Fear (1962/1991)
Cast Away (2000)
Chocolat (2000)
Clockers (1995)
Duck Soup (1933)
Election (1999)
Fantasia (1940)
Fearless (1993)
Gaslight (1944)
Gun Crazy (1950)
High Noon (1952)
Insomnia (2002)
Key Largo (1948)
Kill Bill (2003/2004)
King Kong (1933/1976/2005)
La Strada (1954)
Mamma Mia (2008)
Mona Lisa (1986)
Papillon (1973)
Rashomon (1951)
Red River (1948)
Ridicule (1996)
Riff Raff (1991)
Rio Bravo (1959)
Rushmore (1998)
Saboteur (1942)
Salvador (1986)
Scarface (1932/1983)
Showboat (1936)
Star Wars (1977)
The Birds (1963)
The Field (1990)
The Piano (1993)
The Sting (1973)
The Thing (1951)
The Tramp (1915)
Toy Story (1995)

09 *12 Monkeys* (1995)
A Bug's Life (1998)

Annie Hall (1977)
Betty Blue (1986)
Cat Ballou (1965)
Chinatown (1974)
City of God (2002)
Cleopatra (1963)
Decameron (1971)
Dick Tracy (1937/1945/1990)
Down By Law (1986)
Easy Rider (1969)
Excalibur (1981)
Funny Face (1957)
Funny Girl (1968)
Genevieve (1953)
Get Shorty (1995)
Gladiator (2000)
GoldenEye (1996)
Home Alone (1990)
Limelight (1952)
Local Hero (1983)
Love Story (1970)
Manhattan (1979)
Moonraker (1979)
Nashville (1975)
Ninotchka (1939)
Nosferatu (1922/1979)
Notorious (1946)
Octopussy (1983)
Pinocchio (1940)
Rio Grande (1950)
Robin Hood (1922/1973)
Sea of Love (1989)
Sexy Beast (2001)
Short Cuts (1993)
Spartacus (1959)
Spider-Man (2002)
Stand by Me (1986)
Straw Dogs (1971)
Talk to Her (2002)
The Damned (1969)
The Devils (1971)
The Player (1992)
The Reader (2008)
Vera Drake (2004)
Viridiana (1961)
Walkabout (1970)
White Heat (1949)
Woodstock (1970)

10 Adaptation (2002)
Bagdad Café (1987)
Barton Fink (1991)
Blue Velvet (1986)
Braveheart (1995)
Breathless (1960)
Caravaggio (1986)
Casablanca (1942)
Chicken Run (2000)
City Lights (1931)

Cry Freedom (1987)
Dirty Harry (1971)
East of Eden (1955)
Eraserhead (1977)
Fort Apache (1948)
Frost/Nixon (2008)
Goldfinger (1964)
GoodFellas (1990)
Grand Hotel (1932)
High Sierra (1941)
Jules et Jim (1962)
Men in Black (1997)
Metropolis (1927)
Moonstruck (1987)
Mrs Miniver (1942)
My Fair Lady (1964)
My Left Foot (1989)
Now, Voyager (1942)
Out of Sight (1998)
Paris, Texas (1983)
Peeping Tom (1959)
Pépé le Moko (1936)
Raging Bull (1980)
Rear Window (1954)
Rumble Fish (1983)
Run Lola Run (1998)
Safety Last (1923)
Stagecoach (1939)
Taxi Driver (1976)
The Big Easy (1987)
The Getaway (1972/1994)
The Hustler (1961)
The Insider (1999)
The Leopard (1963)
The Mission (1986)
The Postman (1994)
The Servant (1963)
The Shining (1980)
The Snapper (1993)
The Tin Drum (1979)
The Wild One (1954)
Tokyo Story (1953)
Topsy-Turvy (1999)
Unforgiven (1992)
Videodrome (1983)
Wall Street (1987)
Whale Rider (2002)

11 A Few Good Men (1992)
All About Eve (1950)
American Pie (1999)
Beetlejuice (1988)
Belle de Jour (1967)
Blade Runner (1982)
Blood Simple (1984)
Bugsy Malone (1976)
Carlito's Way (1993)
Citizen Kane (1941)
Dark Victory (1939)

Dead Ringers (1988)
Deliverance (1972)
Donnie Darko (2001)
Don't Look Now (1973)
Elmer Gantry (1960)
Finding Nemo (2003)
Forrest Gump (1994)
Gosford Park (2001)
Heaven's Gate (1981)
Intolerance (1916)
Jungle Fever (1991)
La Dolce Vita (1959)
Life is Sweet (1990)
Lost Highway (1997)
Mars Attacks! (1996)
Mary Poppins (1964/1967)
Mean Streets (1973)
Modern Times (1936)
Monsters, Inc (2001)
Moulin Rouge (2001)
My Name is Joe (1998)
Mystic River (2003)
Notting Hill (1999)
Out of Africa (1985)
Plein Soleil (1960)
Pretty Woman (1990)
Public Enemy (1931)
Pulp Fiction (1994)
The 400 Blows (1959)
The Big Chill (1983)
The Big Sleep (1946)
The Departed (2006)
The Evil Dead (1983)
The Exorcist (1973)
The Fugitive (1948/1993)
The Gold Rush (1925)
The Graduate (1967)
The Ice Storm (1997)
The King and I (1956)
The Lion King (1994)
The Music Man (1962)
The Quiet Man (1952)
The Red Shoes (1948)
The Third Man (1949)
Thunderball (1965)
Touch of Evil (1958)
Unbreakable (2000)
Wayne's World (1992)
Wild at Heart (1990)
Yellow Earth (1984)

12 *About Schmidt* (2000)
Amores Perros (2000)
Atlantic City (1980)
A View to a Kill (1985)
Bad Education (2004)
Blood and Sand (1922/1941/1989)
Brighton Rock (1947)
Casino Royale (1954/1967/2006)

Cool Hand Luke (1967)
Days of Heaven (1978)
Delicatessen (1991)
Donnie Brasco (1997)
Eyes Wide Shut (1999)
Fitzcarraldo (1982)
Frankenstein (1931)
Ghostbusters (1984)
Gregory's Girl (1980)
Groundhog Day (1993)
Hidden Agenda (1990)
Intermission (2003)
Jurassic Park (1993)
Lethal Weapon (1987)
Man on the Moon (1999)
Night on Earth (1991)
Philadelphia (1993)
Pierrot Le Fou (1965)
Prizzi's Honor (1985)
Roman Holiday (1953)
Rome, Open City (1945)
Salaam Bombay! (1988)
Seven Samurai (1954)
Sleepy Hollow (1999)
The Apartment (1960)
The Go-Between (1971)
The Godfather (1972)
The Iron Horse (1924)
The Last Waltz (1978)
The Lost World (1925)
The Naked City (1948)
The Sacrifice (1986)
The Searchers (1956)
The Two Towers (2002)
The Wicker Man (1973)
The Wild Bunch (1969)
Whisky Galore! (1949)
Withnail and I (1987)

13 *Apocalypse Now* (1979)
Babette's Feast (1987)
Basic Instinct (1992)
Batman Forever (1995)
Batman Returns (1992)
Broadcast News (1987)
Burnt by the Sun (1994)
Death in Venice (1971)
December Bride (1990)
Die Another Day (2002)
Doctor Zhivago (1965)
Dr Strangelove (1964)
Dumb and Dumber (1994)
Educating Rita (1983)
Eight and a Half (1963)
Field of Dreams (1989)
Happy Together (1997)
Hard Day's Night (1964)
His Girl Friday (1940)
Horse Feathers (1932)

Licence to Kill (1989)
Live and Let Die (1973)
Manon de Source (1986)
Mildred Pierce (1945)
Raining Stones (1993)
Reservoir Dogs (1992)
'Round Midnight (1986)
Scent of a Woman (1992)
Some Like It Hot (1959)
Sophie's Choice (1982)
The Crying Game (1992)
The Dam Busters (1955)
The Deer Hunter (1978)
The Dirty Dozen (1967)
The Fisher King (1991)
The Jazz Singer (1927)
The Jungle Book (1942)
The Longest Day (1962)
The Right Stuff (1983)
The Sixth Sense (1999)
The Terminator (1984)
To Catch a Thief (1955)
Trainspotting (1996)
Watership Down (1978)
West Side Story (1961)
Wings of Desire (1987)
Zorba the Greek (1964)

14 A Day at the Races (1937)
American Beauty (1999)
American Gigolo (1980)
American Psycho (2000)
Animal Crackers (1930)
As Good as it Gets (1997)
Black Narcissus (1947)
Blazing Saddles (1974)
Bonnie and Clyde (1967)
Brief Encounter (1946)
Bringing Up Baby (1938)
Central Station (1998)
Chariots of Fire (1981)
Cinema Paradiso (1989)
Dial M for Murder (1954)
Empire of the Sun (1987)
Enter the Dragon (1973)
Erin Brockovich (2000)
Five Easy Pieces (1970)
Fools of Fortune (1990)
Gangs of New York (2002)
Goodbye Mr Chips (1939/1969)
In a Lonely Place (1950)
In Which We Serve (1942)
Jean de Florette (1986)
LA Confidential (1997)
Land and Freedom (1995)
Les Diaboliques (1956)
Lord of the Rings (2001/2002/2003)
Michael Collins (1996)
Midnight Cowboy (1969)

Minority Report (2002)
Muriel's Wedding (1994)
Prospero's Books (1991)
Raising Arizona (1987)
Schindler's List (1993)
Secrets and Lies (1996)
The Big Lebowski (1998)
The Commitments (1991)
The Elephant Man (1980)
The Great Escape (1963)
The King of Kings (1927/1961)
The Ladykillers (1955/2004)
The Last Emperor (1987)
The Life of Brian (1979)
The Little Foxes (1941)
The Lost Weekend (1945)
The Mask of Zorro (1998)
The Music Lovers (1971)
The Night Porter (1974)
The Seventh Seal (1957)
Un Chien Andalou (1928)
Woman of the Year (1942)
Zabriskie Point (1969)

15 A Passage to India (1984)
Back to the Future (1985)
Crocodile Dundee (1986)
Dog Day Afternoon (1975)
Do the Right Thing (1989)
Double Indemnity (1944)
Fanny by Gaslight (1944)
Fatal Attraction (1987)
Forbidden Planet (1956)
For Your Eyes Only (1981)
Full Metal Jacket (1987)
Gone With the Wind (1939)
Good Will Hunting (1997)
Independence Day (1996)
Ivan the Terrible (1944)
Life Is Beautiful (1997)
Meet Me in St Louis (1944)
Midnight Express (1978)
Miller's Crossing (1990)
Mulholland Drive (2001)
Nothing Personal (1995)
On the Waterfront (1954)
Oscar and Lucinda (1997)
Quantum of Solace (2008)
Return of the Jedi (1983)
Road to Perdition (2002)
Singin' in the Rain (1952)
Sunset Boulevard (1950)
Tarzan the Ape Man (1932)
The African Queen (1951)
The Bicycle Thief (1948)
The Conversation (1974)
The House of Mirth (2000)
The King of Comedy (1983)
The Lady Vanishes (1938/1979)

Thelma and Louise (1991)
The Piano Teacher (2001)
The Sound of Music (1965)
This is Spinal Tap (1984)
Three Colours: Red (1994)

16 A Clockwork Orange (1971)
All About My Mother (1999)
American Graffiti (1973)
An Angel at my Table (1990)
A Night at the Opera (1935)
A Night to Remember (1958)
Cat on a Hot Tin Roof (1958)
Cyrano de Bergerac (1990)
Dead Poet's Society (1989)
Eat Man Drink Woman (1994)
Frankie and Johnny (1991)
How the West was Won (1962)
Husbands and Wives (1992)
Ladybird Ladybird (1994)
Last Tango in Paris (1972)
Lawrence of Arabia (1962)
Lilies of the Field (1963)
Night of the Hunter (1955)
North by Northwest (1959)
Revenge of the Sith (2005)
Strictly Ballroom (1992)
Superman: The Movie (1978)
The Cincinnati Kid (1965)
The Grapes of Wrath (1940)
The Great Dictator (1940)
The Maltese Falcon (1941)
The Phantom Menace (1999)
The Princess Bride (1987)
The Quiet American (1958/2002)
The Scarlet Letter (1926/1934/1995)
The Seven Year Itch (1955)
The Spy Who Loved Me (1977)
The Straight Story (1999)
This Sporting Life (1963)
Three Colours: Blue (1993)
To Have and Have Not (1944)
Triumph of the Will (1936)
Wild Strawberries (1957)
Wuthering Heights (1939/1970/1992)
You Only Live Twice (1967)

17 2001: A Space Odyssey (1968)
A Fistful of Dollars (1964)
A Man for all Seasons (1966)
American Splendour (2003)
An American in Paris (1951)
Arsenic and Old Lace (1944)
Attack of the Clones (2002)
Birdman of Alcatraz (1962)
Broadway Danny Rose (1984)
Dangerous Liaisons (1988)
Death and the Maiden (1994)
Dr Jekyll and Mr Hyde (1931/1941)

Fanny and Alexander (1982)
Glengarry Glen Ross (1992)
Heavenly Creatures (1995)
Hiroshima mon amour (1959)
It's a Wonderful Life (1946)
Lost in Translation (2003)
Million Dollar Baby (2004)
Mr Deeds Goes to Town (1936)
Passport to Pimlico (1949)
Pride and Prejudice (1940/2003)
Saving Private Ryan (1998)
Strangers on a Train (1951)
Terms of Endearment (1983)
The Age of Innocence (1993)
The Birth of a Nation (1915)
The Hudsucker Proxy (1994)
The Man who Never Was (1955)
The Thief of Baghdad (1924/1940)
The Wedding Banquet (1993)
Three Colours: White (1994)
Tomorrow Never Dies (1997)
When Harry Met Sally (1989)
Yankee Doodle Dandy (1942)

18 A Month in the Country (1984)
Au Revoir Les Enfants (1987)
Battleship Potemkin (1925)
Being John Malkovich (1999)
Coal Miner's Daughter (1980)
Diamonds are Forever (1971)
Edward Scissorhands (1990)
From Here to Eternity (1953)
From Russia With Love (1963)
Good Morning Vietnam (1987)
Intolerable Cruelty (2003)
It Happened One Night (1934)
McCabe and Mrs Miller (1971)
Mississippi Burning (1988)
Never Say Never Again (1983)
No Country for Old Men (2007)
Raise the Red Lantern (1991)
Rebel Without a Cause (1955)
Sleepless in Seattle (1993)
Slumdog Millionaire (2008)
The Company of Wolves (1984)
The Godfather Part II (1974)
The Last Picture Show (1971)
The Lavender Hill Mob (1951)
The Living Daylights (1987)
The Man without a Past (2002)
The Return of the King (2003)
The Royal Tenenbaums (2001)
The Thirty-Nine Steps (1935/1959/1978)
The Towering Inferno (1974)
To Kill a Mockingbird (1962)

19 All That Heaven Allows (1955)
All the President's Men (1976)
All This and Heaven Too (1940)

A Short Film about Love (1988)
Breakfast at Tiffany's (1961)
Bullets over Broadway (1994)
Farewell my Concubine (1993)
Hannah and her Sisters (1986)
How Green was my Valley (1941)
Last Year in Marienbad (1961)
Les Enfants du Paradis (1945)
My Darling Clementine (1946)
Only Angels Have Wings (1939)
Picnic at Hanging Rock (1975)
Raiders of the Lost Ark (1980)
Sense and Sensibility (1995)
sex, lies, and videotape (1989)
Shoot the Piano Player (1960)
The French Connection (1971)
The Magnificent Seven (1960)
The Man Who Wasn't There (2001)
The World is Not Enough (1999)

20 Aguirre, the Wrath of God (1972)
Angels with Dirty Faces (1938)
Children of a Lesser God (1986)
Chitty Chitty Bang Bang (1968)
My Big Fat Greek Wedding (2002)
Night of the Living Dead (1968)
O Brother, Where Art Thou (2000)
She Wore a Yellow Ribbon (1949)
Stranger than Paradise (1984)
The Empire Strikes Back (1980)
The Man who Knew Too Much (1934/1956)
The Motorcycle Diaries (2003)
The Mutiny on the Bounty (1962)
The Philadelphia Story (1940)
The Poseidon Adventure (1972)
The Pride of the Yankees (1942)
The Purple Rose of Cairo (1985)
The Silence of the Lambs (1991)
The Thomas Crown Affair (1968/1999)
The Travelling Players (1975)

21 A Matter of Life and Death (1946)
A Nightmare on Elm Street (1984)
Born on the Fourth of July (1989)
ET The Extra-Terrestrial (1982)
Gunfight at the OK Corral (1957)
Kind Hearts and Coronets (1949)
Monsieur Hulot's Holiday (1953)
My Beautiful Laundrette (1985)
The Passion of Joan of Arc (1928)

22 An Officer and a Gentleman (1982)
A Short Film about Killing (1987)
Crimes and Misdemeanours (1989)
Once upon a Time in America (1984)
The Best Years of Our Lives (1946)
The Fellowship of the Ring (2001)
The Manchurian Candidate (1962) (2004)
The Man with the Golden Gun (1974)
The Shawshank Redemption (1994)

23 Four Weddings and a Funeral (1994)
Ghost Dog: Way of the Samurai (1999)
Guess Who's Coming to Dinner (1967)
Interview with the Vampire (1994)
Mr Smith Goes to Washington (1939)
The Bridge on the River Kwai (1957)
The Draughtsman's Contract (1982)
The Enigma of Kaspar Hauser (1975)
The Good, the Bad and the Ugly (1966)
The Magnificent Ambersons (1942)
The Return of Martin Guerre (1982)

24 Pat Garrett and Billy the Kid (1973)
Robin Hood: Prince of Thieves (1991)
The Adventures of Robin Hood (1938)
The Double Life of Veronique (1991)
The Texas Chainsaw Massacre (1974/2003)

25 Fear and Loathing in Las Vegas (1998)
Leningrad Cowboys Go America (1989)
One Flew Over the Cuckoo's Nest (1975)
The Inn of the Sixth Happiness (1958)
Who's Afraid of Virginia Woolf? (1966)

26 Alice Doesn't Live Here Anymore (1974)
Crouching Tiger, Hidden Dragon (2000)
Invasion of the Body Snatchers (1956/1978)
Monty Python and the Holy Grail (1975)
On Her Majesty's Secret Service (1969)
Snow White and the Seven Dwarfs (1937)
The Postman Always Rings Twice
  (1946/1981)
What Ever Happened to Baby Jane? (1962)

27 The Man Who Shot Liberty Valance (1962)
The Nightmare Before Christmas (1993)
The Treasure of the Sierra Madre (1948)

29 Bill and Ted's Excellent Adventure (1988)
Butch Cassidy and the Sundance Kid (1969)
Close Encounters of the Third Kind (1977)
Harry Potter and the Goblet of Fire (2005)
Indiana Jones and the Last Crusade (1989)
Saturday Night and Sunday Morning (1961)
The Life and Death of Colonel Blimp (1943)

30 Indiana Jones and the Temple of Doom
  (1984)
The Curious Case of Benjamin Button
  (2008)

31 Harry Potter and the Sorcerer's Stone (2001)

32 Harry Potter and the Half-Blood Prince
  (2009)
The Discreet Charm of the Bourgeoisie
  (1972)

33 Employees Leaving the Lumière Factory
  (1895)
Harry Potter and the Chamber of Secrets
  (2002)
The Cook, the Thief, His Wife and Her Lover
  (1989)

34 *Harry Potter and the Order of the Phoenix*
(2007)
Harry Potter and the Philosopher's Stone
(2001)

Harry Potter and the Prisoner of Azkaban
(2004)
*Women on the Verge of a Nervous
Breakdown* (1988)

Film characters include:

02 ET (*ET The Extra-Terrestrial*, 1982)

03 Ash (*Alien*, 1979)
HAL (*2001: A Space Odyssey*, 1968)
Joe ('Josephine'; *Some Like It Hot*, 1959)
Neo (*The Matrix*, 1999, et seq)
Rae (Norma; *Norma Rae*, 1979)
Sam (*Casablanca*, 1942)

04 Abra (*East of Eden*, 1955)
Blue (Bubba; *Forrest Gump*, 1994)
Blue (Mr; *Reservoir Dogs*, 1991)
Bond (James; *Dr No*, 1962, et seq)
Book (John; *Witness*, 1985)
Buck (Joe; *Midnight Cowboy*, 1969)
Dory (*Finding Nemo*, 2003)
Evil (Doctor; *Austin Powers: International
Man of Mystery*, 1997, et seq)
Gale (Dorothy; *The Wizard of Oz*, 1939)
Gump (Forrest; *Forrest Gump*, 1994)
Hall (Annie; *Annie Hall*, 1977)
Hill (Henry; *Goodfellas*, 1990)
Hunt (Ethan; *Mission Impossible*, 1996, et
seq)
Iris (*Taxi Driver*, 1976)
Kane (Charles Foster; *Citizen Kane*, 1941)
Kane (Marshal Will; *High Noon*, 1952)
Kane (Sugar; *Some Like It Hot*, 1959)
Kent (Clark; *Superman*, 1978, et seq)
Kint (Roger 'Verbal'; *The Usual Suspects*,
1995)
Lane (Lois; *Superman*, 1978, et seq)
Lapp (Rachel; *Witness*, 1985)
Leia (Princess; *Star Wars*, 1977, et seq)
Léon (*Léon*, 1994)
Lime (Harry; *The Third Man*, 1949)
Lund (Isla, *Casablanca*, 1942)
Neff (Walter; *Double Indemnity*, 1944)
Nemo (*Finding Nemo*, 2003)
Pink (Mr; *Reservoir Dogs*, 1991)
Rink (Jett; *Giant*, 1956)
Ryan (Jack; *Patriot Games*, 1992, et seq)
Shaw (Raymond; *The Manchurian
Candidate*, 1962/2004)
Solo (Han; *Star Wars*, 1977, et seq)
Soze (Keyser; *The Usual Suspects*, 1995)
Spud (*Trainspotting*, 1995)
Tony (*West Side Story*, 1961)
Toto (*The Wizard of Oz*, 1939)
Vega (Vincent; *Pulp Fiction*, 1994)
Ward (Vivian; *Pretty Woman*, 1990)
Yoda (*Star Wars*, 1977, et seq)
Zorg (*Betty Blue*, 1986)

05 Baloo (*The Jungle Book*, 1967)
Barry (Father; *On the Waterfront*, 1954)
Bates (Norman; *Psycho*, 1960)
Batty (Roy; *Blade Runner*, 1982)
Betty (*Betty Blue*, 1986)
Billy (*Easy Rider*, 1969)
Boggs (Kim; *Edward Scissorhands*, 1990)
Booth (Frank; *Blue Velvet*, 1986)
Brown (Cosmo; *Singin' in the Rain*, 1952)
Brown (Doctor Emmett; *Back to the Future*,
1985)
Brown (Mr; *Reservoir Dogs*, 1992)
Brown (Oda Mae; *Ghost*, 1990)
Dobbs (Fred C; *The Treasure of the Sierra
Madre*, 1947)
Doyle (Jimmy 'Popeye'; *The French
Connection*, 1971)
Exley (Edmund 'Ed'; *LA Confidential*, 1997)
Fiona (Princess; *Shrek*, 2001, et seq)
Foley (Axel; *Beverly Hills Cop*, 1984, et seq)
Gekko (Gordon; *Wall Street*, 1987)
Hatch (Mary; *It's a Wonderful Life*, 1947)
Jerry ('Daphne'; *Some Like It Hot*, 1959)
Jones (Indiana; *Raiders of the Lost Ark*,
1980, et seq)
Klute (John; *Klute*, 1971)
Kurtz (Colonel Walter E; *Apocalypse Now*,
1979)
Lewis (Edward; *Pretty Woman*, 1990)
Marco (Bennet; *The Manchurian Candidate*,
1962/2004)
Maria (*Metropolis*, 1927)
Maria (*West Side Story*, 1961)
McFly (Marty; *Back to the Future*, 1985, et
seq)
Mills (Detective David; *Seven*, 1995)
Ocean (Danny; *Ocean's Eleven*, 2001, et
seq)
Riggs (Martin; *Lethal Weapon*, 1987, et seq)
Rizzo (Betty; *Grease*, 1978)
Rizzo (Ratso; *Midnight Cowboy*, 1969)
Rocco (Johnny; *Key Largo*, 1948)
Russo (Buddy 'Cloudy'; *The French
Connection*, 1971)
Saito (Colonel; *The Bridge on the River
Kwai*, 1957)
Sayer (Rose; *The African Queen*, 1951)
Shaft (John; *Shaft*, 1971/2000)
Shrek (*Shrek*, 2001, et seq)
Simba (*The Lion King*, 1994)
Spade (Sam; *The Maltese Falcon*, 1941)

Stark (Jim; *Rebel Without a Cause*, 1955)
Swann (Elizabeth; *Pirates of the Caribbean*, 2003, et seq)
Tibbs (Detective Virgil; *In the Heat of the Night*, 1967, et seq)
Trask (Caleb; *East of Eden*, 1955)
Vance (Susan; *Bringing Up Baby*, 1938)
Wayne (Bruce; *Batman*, 1989, et seq)
Wheat (Sam; *Ghost*, 1990)
White (Mr; *Reservoir Dogs*, 1991)
White (Wendell 'Bud'; *LA Confidential*, 1997)
Woody (*Toy Story*, 1995, et seq)
Wyatt (*Easy Rider*, 1969)
Zucco (Danny; *Grease*, 1978)

06 Allnut (Charlie; *The African Queen*, 1951)
Bailey (George; *It's a Wonderful Life*, 1947)
Balboa (Rocky; *Rocky*, 1976, et seq)
Bannon (Hud; *Hud*, 1962)
Barrow (Clyde; *Bonnie and Clyde*, 1967)
Barton (Judy; *Vertigo*, 1958)
Batman (*Batman*, 1989, et seq)
Begbie (*Trainspotting*, 1995)
Bickle (Travis; *Taxi Driver*, 1976)
Blaine (Rick; *Casablanca*, 1942)
Blonde (Mr; *Reservoir Dogs*, 1991)
Bowles (Sally; *Cabaret*, 1972)
Bowman (Mission Commander David; *2001: A Space Odyssey*, 1968)
Carter (Jack; *Get Carter*, 1971)
Casper (Billy; *Kes*, 1969)
Connor (Sarah; *The Terminator*, 1984, et seq)
Conway (Jimmy; *Goodfellas*, 1990)
Croker (Charlie; *The Italian Job*, 1969)
Curran (Jenny; *Forrest Gump*, 1994)
Cypher (*The Matrix*, 1999)
Daniel (Bree; *Klute*, 1971)
Darrow (Ann; *King Kong*, 1933/2005)
DeVito (Tommy; *Goodfellas*, 1990)
DuBois (Blanche; *A Streetcar Named Desire*, 1951)
Durden (Tyler; *Fight Club*, 1999)
Elkins (Alfie; *Alfie*, 1965/2004)
Elster (Madeleine; *Vertigo*, 1958)
Gerard (Deputy Marshal Samuel; *The Fugitive*, 1993)
Gittes (J J; *Chinatown*, 1974)
Glinda (*The Wizard of Oz*, 1939)
Harper (Willa; *The Night of the Hunter*, 1955)
Hudson (Blanche; *What Ever Happened to Baby Jane?*, 1962)
Hudson (Jane; *What Ever Happened to Baby Jane?*, 1962)
Iselin (Eleanor Shaw; *The Manchurian Candidate*, 1962/2004)
Jensen (Molly; *Ghost*, 1990)

Kambei (*Seven Samurai*, 1954)
Kenobi (Obi-Wan; *Star Wars*, 1977, et seq)
Kimble (Dr Richard; *The Fugitive*, 1993)
Lamont (Lina; *Singin' in the Rain*, 1952)
Laszlo (Victor; *Casablanca*, 1942)
Lecter (Dr Hannibal; *The Silence of the Lambs*, 1991, et seq)
Malloy (Terry; *On the Waterfront*, 1954)
Manero (Tony; *Saturday Night Fever*, 1977, et seq)
Marlin (*Finding Nemo*, 2003)
Marvel (Professor; *The Wizard of Oz*, 1939)
Mowgli (*The Jungle Book*, 1967)
Olsson (Sandy; *Grease*, 1978)
Orange (Mr; *Reservoir Dogs*, 1991)
Parker (Bonnie; *Bonnie and Clyde*, 1967)
Pierce (Mildred; *Mildred Pierce*, 1945)
Powell (Preacher Harry; *The Night of the Hunter*, 1955)
Powers (Austin; *Austin Powers: International Man of Mystery*, 1997, et seq)
Rabbit (Jessica; *Who Framed Roger Rabbit*, 1988)
Rabbit (Roger; *Who Framed Roger Rabbit*, 1988)
Renton (*Trainspotting*, 1995)
Ripley (Ellen; *Alien*, 1979, et seq)
Rubini (Marcello; *La Dolce Vita*, 1960)
Selden (Kathy; *Singin' in the Rain*, 1952)
Serizy (Séverine; *Belle de Jour*, 1967)
Shears (Commander; *The Bridge on the River Kwai*, 1957)
Singer (Alvy; *Annie Hall*, 1977)
Sylvia (*La Dolce Vita*, 1960)
Taylor (George; *Planet of the Apes*, 1967)
Taylor (Lieutenant Dan; *Forrest Gump*, 1994)
Temple (Nora; *Key Largo*, 1948)
Turner (Will; *Pirates of the Caribbean*, 2003, et seq)
Warden (Major; *The Bridge on the River Kwai*, 1957)

07 Babbitt (Charlie; *Rain Man*, 1988)
Babbitt (Raymond; *Rain Man*, 1988)
Blondie (*The Good, the Bad, and the Ugly*, 1966)
Burnham (Lester; *American Beauty*, 1999)
Clayton (Michael; *Michael Clayton*, 2007)
Daniels (Melanie; *The Birds*, 1963)
Deckard (Rick; *Blade Runner*, 1982)
DeLarge (Alex; *A Clockwork Orange*, 1971)
Desmond (Norma; *Sunset Boulevard*, 1950)
Dillard (Preston; *Jezebel*, 1938)
Edwards (Ethan; *The Searchers*, 1956)
Forrest (Alex; *Fatal Attraction*, 1987)
Higgins (Professor Henry; *My Fair Lady*, 1964)
Kendall (Eve; *North by Northwest*, 1959)

Kilgore (Lieutenant Colonel Bill; *Apocalypse Now*, 1979)

Krueger (Freddy; *A Nightmare on Elm Street*, 1984, et seq)

La Motta (Jake; *Raging Bull*, 1980)

MacGuff (Juno; *Juno*, 2007)

Marlowe (Philip; *The Big Sleep*, 1946)

Marsden (Julie; *Jezebel*, 1938)

Maximus (*Gladiator*, 2000)

McClane (John; *Die Hard*, 1988, et seq)

McCloud (Frank; *Key Largo*, 1948)

Miniver (Kay; *Mrs Miniver*, 1942)

Montana (Tony; *Scarface*, 1983)

Montoya (Inigo; *The Princess Bride*, 1987)

Poulain (Amélie; *Amélie*, 2001)

Ratched (Nurse; *One Flew Over the Cuckoo's Nest*, 1975)

Serpico (Frank; *Serpico*, 1973)

Sick Boy (*Trainspotting*, 1995)

Sparrow (Captain Jack; *Pirates of the Caribbean*, 2003, et seq)

Spicoli (Jeff; *Fast Times at Ridgemont High*, 1982)

Travers (Jerry; *Top Hat*, 1935)

Tremont (Dale; *Top Hat*, 1935)

Trinity (*The Matrix*, 1999, et seq)

Valiant (Eddie; *Who Framed Roger Rabbit*, 1988)

Vallens (Dorothy; *Blue Velvet*, 1986)

Ventura (Ace; *Ace Ventura: Pet Detective*, 1994, et seq)

Westley (*The Princess Bride*, 1987)

Willard (Captain Benjamin L; *Apocalypse Now*, 1979)

08 Barbossa (Captain; *Pirates of the Caribbean*, 2003, et seq)

Beaumont (Jeffrey; *Blue Velvet*, 1986)

Benedict (Jordan 'Bick'; *Giant*, 1956)

Benedict (Leslie Lynnton; *Giant*, 1956)

Braddock (Benjamin; *The Graduate*, 1967)

Callahan (Harry; *Dirty Harry*, 1971, et seq)

Calloway (Major; *The Third Man*, 1949)

Channing (Margo; *All About Eve*, 1950)

Clouseau (Inspector Jacques; *The Pink Panther*, 1963, et seq)

Corleone (Don Vito; *The Godfather*, 1972)

Corleone (Michael; *The Godfather*, 1972, et seq)

Corleone (Santino 'Sonny'; *The Godfather*, 1972)

Dufresne (Andy; *The Shawshank Redemption*, 1994)

Ferguson (John 'Scottie'; *Vertigo*, 1958)

Freemont (Lisa Carol; *Rear Window*, 1954)

Friendly (Johnny; *On the Waterfront*, 1954)

Greenway (Aurora; *Terms of Endearment*, 1983, et seq)

Hirayama (Shukichi; *Tokyo Story*, 1953)

King Kong (*King Kong*, 1933/2005)

Kowalski (Stanley; *A Streetcar Named Desire*, 1951)

Kowalski (Stella; *A Streetcar Named Desire*, 1951)

Lockwood (Don; *Singin' in the Rain*, 1952)

Mathilda (*Léon*, 1994)

McMurphy (Randle Patrick; *One Flew Over the Cuckoo's Nest*, 1975)

Mitchell (Pete 'Maverick'; *Top Gun*, 1986)

Morpheus (*The Matrix*, 1999, et seq)

Murtaugh (Roger; *Lethal Weapon*, 1987, et seq)

Robinson (Mrs; *The Graduate*, 1967)

Somerset (Detective-Lieutenant William; *Seven*, 1995)

Starling (Clarice; *The Silence of the Lambs*, 1991, et seq)

Superman (*Superman*, 1978, et seq)

Torrance (Jack; *The Shining*, 1980)

von Trapp (Captain Gaylord; *The Sound of Music*, 1965)

09 Breedlove (Garrett; *Terms of Endearment*, 1983, et seq)

Buttercup (*The Princess Bride*, 1987)

Chewbacca (*Star Wars*, 1977, et seq)

Cornelius (*Planet of the Apes*, 1967)

Darth Maul (*Star Wars Episode I: The Phantom Menace*, 1999)

Doolittle (Eliza; *My Fair Lady*, 1964)

Gallagher (Dan; *Fatal Attraction*, 1987)

Golightly (Holly; *Breakfast at Tiffany's*, 1961)

Gunderson (Marge; *Fargo*, 1996)

Hunsecker (J J; *Sweet Smell of Success*, 1957)

Jefferies (L B 'Jeff'; *Rear Window*, 1954)

Kutschera (Maria Augusta; *The Sound of Music*, 1965)

Nicholson (Colonel; *The Bridge on the River Kwai*, 1957)

Plainview (Daniel; *There Will Be Blood*, 2007)

Skywalker (Anakin; *Star Wars Episode I: The Phantom Menace*, 1999, et seq)

Skywalker (Luke; *Star Wars*, 1977, et seq)

Thornhill (Roger; *North by Northwest*, 1959)

Vincennes (Jack; *LA Confidential*, 1997)

Winnfield (Jules; *Pulp Fiction*, 1994)

Yakushova (Nina 'Ninotchka' Ivanova; *Ninotchka*, 1939)

10 Agent Smith (*The Matrix*, 1999, et seq)

Darth Vader (*Star Wars*, 1977, et seq)

Terminator (*The Terminator*, 1984, et seq)

11 Dietrichson (Phyllis; *Double Indemnity*, 1944)

Humperdinck (Prince; *The Princess Bride*, 1987)

McCallister (Kevin; *Home Alone*, 1990, et seq)

Rockatansky (Max; *Mad Max*, 1979, et seq)

Strangelove (Dr; *Dr Strangelove or How I Learned to Stop Worrying and Love the Bomb*, 1964)

12 O'Shaughnessy (Brigid; *The Maltese Falcon*, 1941)

Padmé Amidala (Queen; *Star Wars Episode I: The Phantom Menace*, 1999, et seq)

Scissorhands (Edward; *Edward Scissorhands*, 1990)

13 Buzz Lightyear (*Toy Story*, 1995, et seq)

de la Cheyniest (Christine; *La règle du jeu*, 1939)

Film and cinema terms include:

02 3–D
PG
VO

03 ACE
AFI
ASA
BFI
CGI
cue
cut!
dub
DVD
hit
mix
NFT
pan
POV
R18
SFX

04 16mm
35mm
70mm
BBFC
boom
cast
clip
edit
epic
grip
hero
IMAX®
porn
reel
take
tilt
wipe
wrap

05 actor
agent
anime
award
baddy
BAFTA
BECTU
blimp

cameo
crane
début
Dolby®
dolly
drama
extra
flick
focus
foley
foyer
frame
genre
goody
hammy
image
matte
mogul
morph
movie
oater
Oscar®
pitch
prize
props
sci-fi
score
set-up
short
shots
sound
stunt
tie-in
usher
video
weepy

06 action!
auteur
baddie
biopic
blow up
B-movie
camera
censor
cinema
comedy

cowboy
critic
dailys
Ealing
editor
extras
fade-in
freeze
gaffer
goodie
insert
kidult
majors
master
option
prevue
remake
retake
review
rom-com
rushes
screen
script
sequel
slow-mo
splice
studio
Super 8®
talkie
ticket
turkey
weepie
X-rated
zoom in

07 180° rule
actress
advance
backlit
backlot
best boy
billing
bit part
bootleg
cartoon
classic
close-up

costume
credits
cutaway
dailies
Dogme 95
drive-in
edit out
fade-out
fantasy
film set
footage
heroine
ingenue
jump-cut
key grip
lip sync
manager
matinée
miscast
montage
Moviola®
musical
narrate
noirish
out-take
popcorn
prequel
preview
release
reshoot
showbiz
stand-in
starlet
sunlamp
talkies
trailer
trilogy
TV movie
villain
Western
whip pan
zoom out

08 aperture
arc light
arthouse
audition

bankable
blocking
Brat Pack
cassette
ceremony
cine film
cineplex
Cinerama®
composer
contract
dialogue
director
dissolve
dramatic
emulsion
ensemble
exposure
exterior
festival
film buff
filmgoer
film noir
film star
head room
intercut
in the can
key light
lead role
location
male lead
McGuffin
morphing
on-screen
outgross
pictures
porn star
première
printing
rough cut
scenario
schedule
sequence
soundman
sprocket
stuntman
subtitle
suspense
synopsis
telefilm
thriller
timecode
to camera
wardrobe
Wild West
wrangler
zoom shot
09 angle shot
animation

archetype
auteurism
back story
billboard
blue movie
Bollywood
box office
call sheet
cameraman
cartridge
Celluloid®
chopsocky
cinematic
cinephile
colourize
copyright
crane shot
detective
directrix
docudrama
dolly grip
dolly shot
dope sheet
Dutch tilt
exhibitor
film-maker
film still
film stock
filmstrip
flashback
franchise
Hollywood
indie film
letterbox
MacGuffin
melodrama
multiplex
off-camera
off-screen
post-synch
projector
publicist
publicity
rack focus
recording
recordist
red carpet
road movie
shoot-'em-up
showbizzy
skinflick
slapstick
snuff film
soft focus
spotlight
Steadicam®
storyline
subtitled

superstar
swing gang
theme song
theme tune
time-lapse
title role
treatment
voice-over
wrap party
xenon lamp
10 action film
action hero
adaptation
blue screen
body double
buddy movie
Capraesque
cartoonist
censorship
chick flick
cinema-goer
ciné vérité
claymation
colour film
continuity
cowboy shot
crowd scene
dénouement
developing
double bill
featurette
female lead
film rights
fullscreen
head-on shot
horror film
horse opera
Kleig light
Klieg light
leading man
movie house
movie-maker
on location
pixilation
screenplay
screen test
second unit
seventh art
silent film
sleeper hit
slow-motion
snuff movie
sound mixer
soundstage
soundtrack
space opera
star system
stop-motion

storyboard
stuntwoman
tear-jerker
that's a wrap!
ultra-rapid
walk-on part
widescreen
11 art director
aspect ratio
black comedy
blockbuster
canted angle
certificate
CinemaScope®
cliffhanger
comedy drama
cutting room
cyber cinema
day-for-night
Disneyesque
distributor
documentary
dolly tracks
Europudding
fade-to-black
feature film
femme fatale
filmography
foley artist
freeze-frame
hairstylist
intertitles
lap dissolve
leading lady
martial arts
matinée idol
merchandise
mise en scène
mood montage
pixillation
pornography
protagonist
release date
reverse shot
running time
set designer
slasher film
sound effect
split screen
star-studded
synchronize
Technicolor®
title design
12 Academy Award®
Biblical epic
bird's-eye shot
bird's-eye view

boom operator
camera loader
casting couch
choreography
chromakeying
cinemathèque
cinéma vérité
clapperboard
co-production
credit titles
crosscutting
director's cut
eyeline match
film magazine
flashforward
Hitchcockian
magic lantern
make-up artist
maltese cross
method acting
movie theatre
overcranking
picture house
post-synching
quota quickie
reverse angle
rockumentary
screenwriter
script doctor

scriptwriter
shallow focus
short subject
show business
shutter speed
silver screen
slasher movie
sneak preview
splatter film
swashbuckler
tracking shot
working title

13 black and white
character part
choreographer
cinematically
ciné projector
clapper loader
continuity man
deepfocus shot
dialogue coach
diegetic sound
digital camera
disaster movie
dream sequence
Expressionism
feature-length
French New Wave

grande vedette
in development
location scout
medium close-up
merchandizing
motion picture
nouvelle Vague
preproduction
projectionist
shot selection
splatter movie
undercranking
variable focus

14 anamorphic lens
available light
back-projection
blaxploitation
cinematography
continuity girl
courtroom drama
digital editing
full-length shot
hand-held camera
knee-length shot
medium long shot
opening credits
opening weekend
post-production

production crew
property master
ripple dissolve
science-fiction
shooting script
special effects
supporting role
travelling shot

15 background noise
behind the scenes
casting director
cinematographer
cinematographic
comedy of
  manners
incidental music
location manager
non-speaking role
panoramic camera
point of view shot
screwball comedy
semidocumentary
shot composition
shot/reverse shot
stop-frame camera
supporting actor
sword and sorcery
swords and sandal

See also **cinema; director; James Bond**

finance

Terms used in finance include:

03 ATM
bid
EMU
EPS
FSA
ISA
PEP
RPI
SIB
VCT

04 OFEX
stag

05 bears
bonds
bulls
CREST
gilts
LIFFE
SERPS
SIPPS
TESSA
yield

06 bidder
bourse
broker
bubble
buy-out
listed
Nasdaq
Nikkei
quoted

07 annuity
auction
Big Bang
bullion
capital
futures
gearing
placing

08 base rate
blue chip
cash flow
churning
clawback

dawn raid
dividend
equities
Eurobond
leverage
new issue
offshore
par value
takeover
Talisman
TechMARK

09 allotment
bell curve
commodity
debenture
debit card
endowment
flotation
gazumping
hedge fund
inflation
liquidity
loan stock

ombudsman
portfolio
unit trust
10 bear market
bonus issue
bucket shop
bull market
Bundesbank
CAC 40 index
call option
charge card
credit card
day trading
grey market
kerb market
mutual fund
prospectus
redemption
remortgage
securities
settlement
11 Chinese wall
common stock
derivatives
equity bonds
fund manager
golden share
index linked
like for like
liquidation
Lloyds names

managed bond
market maker
rights issue
share option
stockbroker
tracker fund
underwriter
white knight
12 affinity card
amortization
balance sheet
banker's draft
bridging loan
concert party
contract note
depreciation
glamour stock
interest rate
offer for sale
orphan assets
share dealing
traded option
umbrella fund
13 Bank of England
best execution
corporate bond
dividend cover
equity markets
final dividend
fixed interest
listed company

mutual society
ordinary share
pension scheme
privatization
stock exchange
term insurance
14 bearer security
bid-offer spread
capitalization
deferred shares
inheritance tax
insider dealing
Lloyds of London
negative equity
offer-bid spread
unlisted shares
unquoted shares
windfall shares
15 bed and breakfast
beneficial owner
building society
capital gains tax
demutualization
golden handcuffs
guaranteed stock
interim dividend
investment trust
preference share
secondary market
with-profits bond

See also **business**; **economics**

Finland

Cities and notable towns in Finland include:

04 Oulu
Pori
05 Espoo
Lahti

Turku
Vaasa
06 Vantaa
07 Tampere

08 Helsinki
09 Rovaniemi

Administrative divisions of Finland, with regional capitals:

04 Oulu (Oulu)
05 Åland (Mariehamn)
07 Lapland (Rovaniemi)

14 Eastern Finland (Mikkeli)
Western Finland (Turku)
15 Southern Finland (Hämeenlinna)

Finnish landmarks include:

05 Manta
07 Ateneum
Lapland
10 Seurasaari
11 Havis Amanda

Korkeasaari
Lenin Museum
Suomenlinna
Turku Castle
12 Åland Islands
Lake District

Pispala Ridge
Senaatintori
Senate Square
13 Finlandia Hall
Lake Näsijärvi
Lake Pyhäjärvi

Luostarinmäki
Pyynikki Ridge
Ravadasköngäs
14 Kalevala Church
Turku Cathedral
15 Church in the Rock

fireplace

Fireplaces include:

04 kiln
  oven
05 forge
  grate
  ingle

  stove
06 boiler
  hearth
07 bonfire
  brazier

  firebox
  furnace
  gas fire
08 campfire
  open fire

10 backboiler
11 incinerator
  wood burning
12 electric fire
13 paraffin stove

firework

Fireworks include:

04 cake
  mine
  pioy
05 devil
  flare
  gerbe
  peeoy
  pioye
  shell
  squib
  wheel
06 banger

  fisgig
  fizgig
  maroon
  petard
  rocket
07 cracker
  serpent
  volcano
08 flip-flop
  fountain
  pinwheel
  slap-bang

  sparkler
  whizbang
09 firedrake
  girandola
  girandole
  sky-rocket
  throw-down
  waterfall
  whizz-bang
10 golden rain
  Indian fire
  tourbillon

11 firecracker
  firewriting
  jumping-jack
  roman candle
  tourbillion
14 Catherine wheel
  Chinese cracker
  indoor firework
15 Pharaoh's serpent
  Waterloo cracker

firth

Firths include:

03 Tay (Scotland)
04 Lorn (Scotland)
  Wide (Scotland)
05 Clyde (Scotland)
  Forth (Scotland)
  Lorne (Scotland)

  Moray (Scotland)
06 Beauly (Scotland)
  Solway (England/Scotland)
  Thames (New Zealand)
07 Dornoch (Scotland)
  Westray (Scotland)

08 Cromarty (Scotland)
  Pentland (Scotland)
  Stronsay (Scotland)
  Szczecin (Poland)
09 Inverness (Scotland)
14 North Ronaldsay (Scotland)

fish

Fish include:

02 ai
  id
03 ayu
  bar
  bib
  cod
  dab
  eel
  gar
  ide
  ray
  sar
04 barb
  bass
  blay

  bley
  brit
  carp
  cero
  chad
  char
  chub
  dace
  dare
  dart
  dory
  fugu
  gade
  goby
  hake
  hoki

  ling
  luce
  moki
  opah
  orfe
  pike
  pope
  pout
  rudd
  ruff
  scad
  scat
  scup
  seer
  seir
  shad

  sole
  tang
  tuna
05 ablet
  basse
  blain
  bleak
  bream
  brill
  charr
  cisco
  cobia
  coley
  danio
  Doras

doree
elops
grunt
guppy
lance
loach
lythe
manta
molly
perai
perch
pirai
platy
pogge
roach
ruffe
sargo
saury
shark
skate
smelt
sprat
squid
tench
tetra
torsk
trout
tunny
wahoo
whelk
whiff
zebra

06 anabas
angler
barbel
bigeye
blenny
bonito
bowfin
brassy
bumalo
burbot
callop
caplin
caribe
conger
conner
cottid
cottus
cunner
dentex
doctor
dorado
gadoid
goramy
gulper
gunnel
gurami

gurnet
inanga
jerker
kipper
launce
louvar
mahsir
maigre
marlin
meagre
medaka
minnow
mullet
murena
piraña
piraya
plaice
puffer
remora
robalo
roughy
runner
saithe
salmon
sander
sardel
sargos
sargus
sea cat
serran
shanny
shiner
skelly
sparid
sucker
tailor
tarpon
tautog
turbot
vendis
wrasse
zander
zingel

07 alewife
anchovy
azurine
batfish
bergylt
bloater
box-fish
bummalo
cabezon
capelin
catfish
cavalla
cavally
chimera
cichlid

clupeid
codfish
cowfish
crucian
crusian
dogfish
dolphin
drummer
escolar
garfish
garpike
gemfish
goldeye
gourami
grouper
growler
grunion
grunter
gudgeon
gurnard
haddock
halibut
herring
hogfish
houting
ice fish
inconnu
ink-fish
kahawai
lamprey
lampuki
mahseer
medacca
mooneye
morwong
mudfish
muraena
oar fish
octopus
old wife
panchax
pig-fish
pinfish
piranha
pollack
pollock
pomfret
pompano
pupfish
rat-tail
redfish
red moki
sandeel
sardine
sculpin
sea bass
seacock
sea pike

silurid
sleeper
snapper
sockeye
sparoid
sunfish
topknot
torpedo
vendace
vendiss
whiting

08 albacore
anableps
arapaima
atherine
bandfish
billfish
bloodfin
blowfish
bluefish
boarfish
bonefish
brisling
bullhead
carangid
characid
characin
chimaera
chimerid
clupeoid
coalfish
corkwing
cow-pilot
devil ray
dragonet
drumfish
eagle ray
fallfish
file fish
flathead
flounder
forktail
four-eyes
frogfish
gambusia
gilt-head
goat fish
goldfish
grayling
greeneye
grey-fish
hair-tail
halfbeak
hardhead
John Dory
kabeljou
kingfish
luderick

lumpfish
mackerel
manta ray
menhaden
milkfish
monkfish
moonfish
moray eel
mulloway
nannygai
pilchard
pipefish
rascasse
redbelly
rock bass
rockfish
rockling
rosefish
saibling
sailfish
sardelle
scopelid
scuppaug
sea bream
seahorse
sea perch
sea raven
sea robin
sea snail
skipjack
stingray
sturgeon
surffish
tilefish
toadfish
tuna fish
weakfish
wolffish

09 amber-fish
amberjack
angelfish
argentine
barracuda
black bass
blackfish
blindfish
carangoid
chaetodon
clingfish
conger-eel
coral-fish
coryphene
crab-eater
cramp-fish
Dover sole
globe fish

goldsinny
golomynka
goose-fish
grass carp
greenling
grenadier
hornyhead
hottentot
kabeljouw
killifish
lemon sole
mud minnow
neon tetra
pilot fish
queenfish
red mullet
red salmon
rock perch
round fish
sand smelt
scombroid
scopeloid
selachian
sheatfish
snailfish
snakehead
spadefish
spearfish
stargazer
steenbras
stone bass
stonefish
sweetfish
swine-fish
swordfish
swordtail
tiger fish
toothfish
topminnow
trumpeter
trunkfish
tunny fish
whitebait
whitebass
wreck fish

10 angler fish
archerfish
arctic char
barracouta
barramundi
bitterling
Bombay duck
bottle-fish
candlefish
cockabully
coffer-fish

craigfluke
cuttlefish
cycloidian
damselfish
demoiselle
dragon-fish
flutemouth
flying fish
golden orfe
grey mullet
groundling
hammer-fish
hammerhead
jellied eel
lancet fish
largemouth
lizardfish
lumpsucker
Maori chief
mossbunker
nettle-fish
ocean perch
paddlefish
parrot-fish
puffer fish
rabbitfish
red snapper
ribbonfish
rock salmon
rock turbot
rudderfish
sacred fish
scorpaenid
sea swallow
serrasalmo
sheathfish
sheep's-head
silverfish
smallmouth
squeteague
stone loach
suckerfish
tiger shark
torpedo ray
whale shark

11 anemone fish
bellows-fish
blue whiting
buffalo fish
cutlass fish
Dolly Varden
dolphin fish
electric eel
electric ray
Eurypharynx
lake herring

lantern fish
lophobranch
moorish idol
muskellunge
oxyrhynchus
peacock-fish
pelican-fish
salmon trout
sea hedgehog
sea scorpion
silversides
snail darter
stickleback
sucking fish
surgeon fish
triggerfish
trumpetfish
walking fish
whistle fish
whiting pout

12 basking shark
father-lasher
fighting fish
four-eyed fish
mosquito fish
orange roughy
paradise fish
parrot-wrasse
rainbow trout
scabbard fish
scorpion fish
sea porcupine
sergeant fish
skipjack tuna
smooth blenny
squirrel fish
St Peter's fish
whiptail hake

13 armed bullhead
butterfly fish
Chinook salmon
climbing perch
horse mackerel
labyrinth fish
northern porgy
porcupine fish
Sergeant Baker
sergeant-major
sockeye salmon
yellow fin tuna

14 blueback salmon

15 great white shark
hammerhead shark
Spanish mackerel

Aquarium fish include:

04 barb
05 danio
    guppy
    loach
    tetra
    zebra
06 discus
    goramy
    gurami
07 catfish
    crucian
    crusian
    fantail

    gourami
    koi carp
    piranha
08 goldfish
09 angelfish
    clownfish
    neon tetra
    tiger barb
10 clown loach
    golden barb
    zebra danio
11 Jack Dempsey

12 cardinal fish
    dwarf cichlid
    dwarf gourami
    sucking loach
13 comet goldfish
    common hatchet
    Malawi cichlid
14 common goldfish
    kissing gourami
    red-finned shark
    walking catfish
15 fantail goldfish

See also **eel**; **poison**

fishing

Fishing flies include:

03 bob
    dry
    wet
04 harl

    herl
    tail
05 sedge
06 doctor

    hackle
    palmer
    salmon
07 watchet

09 hairy Mary
    Jock Scott
10 cock-a-bondy

Fishing and angling terms include:

03 dub
    fly
    gig
    jig
    net
    rod
    set
    tag
    tie
04 bait
    barb
    bite
    boat
    bunt
    cast
    drag
    gimp
    haaf
    hook
    lead
    line
    lure
    reel
    sean
    trot
    whip
05 alder
    angle

    baker
    braid
    catch
    clean
    creel
    drail
    dress
    poach
    seine
    snell
    trace
    troll
06 angler
    antron
    bobber
    bullet
    coarse
    dibble
    dip net
    dry-fly
    fly-rod
    gentle
    gillie
    leader
    norsel
    sagene
    sinker
    tackle
    waders

    wet-fly
07 angling
    bycatch
    catworm
    chromer
    drifter
    drop-fly
    dropper
    flybook
    flyline
    fly reel
    ghillie
    gill net
    harpoon
    keepnet
    monofil
    piscary
    plummet
    pout net
    setline
    spinner
08 backcast
    buzzbait
    drift net
    give line
    hand line
    roll cast
    trotline

09 brandling
    drabbling
    egg sinker
    false cast
    halieutic
    indicator
    leger bait
    leger line
    night-line
    piscatory
    propeller
10 bait bucket
    baitrunner
    casting arc
    casting-net
    double haul
    fly casting
    fly fishing
    halieutics
    landing net
    ledger bait
    ledger line
    line grease
    multiplier
    net-fishing
    sea-fishing
    treble hook
    weigh sling

11 forward cast	spinning rod	monofilament	13 bottom-fishing
game fishing	surfcasting	night crawler	coarse fishing
haaf-fishing		night-fishery	ground-angling
line-fishing	12 black-fishing	shooting line	salmon-fishing
paternoster	drifter float	trout-fishing	14 baitcasting rod
sinking line	drift fishing	unhooking mat	15 catch-and-release
spinner bait	floating line	whale-fishing	

flag

Flag types include:

03 red	whift	signal	streamer
04 blue	06 banner	yellow	vexillum
jack	burgee	07 bunting	09 blackjack
05 black	cornet	colours	chequered
house	ensign	pennant	oriflamme
peter	fanion	08 banderol	tricolour
pilot	pennon	gonfalon	10 quarantine
whiff	prayer	standard	11 swallow tail

Flags include:

05 Union	Red Duster	11 Olympic Flag
07 Saltire	Red Ensign	Red Crescent
08 Crescent	Rising Sun	White Ensign
Old Glory	Tricolour	12 Stars and Bars
Red Cross	Union Jack	13 Royal Standard
09 Blue Peter	10 Blue Ensign	15 Cross of St George
dannebrog	Jolly Roger	Hammer and Sickle
Red Dragon	Yellow Jack	Stars and Stripes

flightless bird *see* bird

flower

Flower parts include:

05 calyx	torus	spadix	08 filament
ovary	umbel	stamen	thalamus
ovule	06 anther	stigma	09 capitulum
petal	carpel	07 corolla	dichasium
sepal	corymb	nectary	gynoecium
spike	pistil	panicle	10 receptacle
stalk	raceme	pedicel	11 monochasium
style			

Garden flowers include:

04 aloe	calla	stock	crinum
flag	camas	tulip	crocus
iris	daisy	viola	dahlia
lily	lotus	yucca	nerine
pink	lupin	06 allium	Nuphar
rose	pansy	azalea	orchid
sego	phlox	camash	salvia
05 aster	poppy	camass	Scilla

smilax
squill
violet
zinnia

07 alyssum
anemone
begonia
campion
candock
cowslip
day-lily
freesia
fuchsia
lobelia
may-lily
nemesia
peacock
petunia
primula
quamash
Tritoma
verbena

08 arum lily
asphodel
bluebell
curtonus
cyclamen
daffodil
dianthus
foxglove
galtonia
gardenia
geranium
gladioli

gloriosa
harebell
hyacinth
marigold
martagon
Nenuphar
Phormium
pond lily
primrose
snowdrop
sweet pea
trillium
Turk's cap

09 amaryllis
aubrietia
calendula
calla lily
candytuft
carnation
crocosmia
digitalis
gladiolus
grass tree
herb Paris
hollyhock
Kniphofia
narcissus
nicotiana
regal lily
Richardia
snowflake
sunflower
tiger lily
torch lily

10 agapanthus
aspidistra
busy lizzie
Canada lily
chionodoxa
coneflower
cornflower
delphinium
Easter lily
fritillary
giant rouge
nasturtium
orange-lily
poinsettia
polyanthus
ragged-lady
snake's head
snapdragon
solfaterre
sweet briar
wallflower
wand flower

11 acidanthera
African lily
antirrhinum
cabbage tree
Convallaria
erythronium
forget-me-not
gillyflower
hippeastrum
lapeirousia
love-in-a-mist
Madonna lily

naked ladies
red-hot poker
rose campion
spatterdock
sternbergia
tiger flower

12 devil-in-a-bush
flower of Jove
Hemerocallis
Ornithogalum
rose geranium
sarsaparilla
Solomon's seal
sweet william
Turk's cap lily
victoria lily
wild hyacinth
Zantedeschia

13 African violet
butcher's broom
carrion-flower
chrysanthemum
crown imperial
eglantine rose
grape hyacinth
lily of the Nile
striped squill
winter aconite

14 belladonna lily
glory of the snow
Ithuriel's spear

15 dog's tooth violet
lily of the valley
star of Bethlehem

Wild flowers include:

05 clary
daisy
poppy

06 clover
oxslip
teasel
violet
yarrow

07 ale hoof
bistort
campion
comfrey
cowslip
dog rose
goldcup
heather

08 bluebell

crowfoot
dog daisy
foxglove
harebell
lungwort
primrose
rock rose
self-heal
toadflax
wild iris

09 Aaron's rod
birth-wort
broomrape
buttercup
celandine
columbine
edelweiss
goldenrod

horsetail
moneywort
stonecrop
water lily
wild pansy

10 crane's bill
goatsbeard
heartsease
lady's smock
marguerite
masterwort
oxeye daisy
pennyroyal
wild endive
wild orchid

11 ragged robin
wild chicory

wood anemone

12 common mallow
cuckoo flower
great mullein
lady's slipper
solomon's seal
white campion
yellow rocket

13 butter-and-eggs
field cow-wheat
shepherd's club
wild gladiolus

14 black-eyed susan
bladder campion
common toadflax
multiflora rose

15 New England aster

See also **birth symbol**; **emblem**; **hybrid**; **lily**; **orchid**; **plant**

fly

Flies include:

03 bee	pium	cuckoo	Spanish
bot	sand	forest	vinegar
day	**05** alder	motuca	**08** glossina
dor	birch	muscid	ruby-tail
gad	black	mutuca	scorpion
hop	crane	pomace	sheep ked
ked	drone	robber	simulium
may	flesh	stable	tachinid
med	froth	tipula	**09** cantharis
04 beet	fruit	tsetse	ichneumon
blow	horse	turnip	screw-worm
boat	house	tzetse	**10** bluebottle
bulb	hover	tzetze	Cecidomyia
bush	march	warble	drosophila
cleg	midge	**07** blister	spittle bug
corn	onion	brommer	**11** biting midge
deer	sedge	cabbage	buffalo gnat
dung	snake	cluster	cabbage-root
fire	snipe	diptera	greenbottle
frit	water	dolphin	**12** cheesehopper
gnat	wheat	harvest	**13** cheese skipper
gout	**06** blowie	Hessian	spittle insect
kade	caddis	lantern	
lamp	carrot	sciarid	
meat		smother	

See also **fishing**; **insect**

folk

Folk music groups include:

06 Pogues	Corries	**10** The Corries	**12** Capercaillie
Runrig	**09** Dubliners	The Weavers	Steeleye Span
07 Clannad	The Pogues	**11** Lindisfarne	**13** The Chieftains

Folk musicians and singers include:

03 Gow (Niel; 1727–1807, Scottish)

04 Baez (Joan; 1941– , US)
Bain (Aly; 1946– , Scottish)
Ives (Burl; 1909–95, US)
Vega (Suzanne; 1959– , US)

05 Bragg (Billy; 1947– , English)
Dylan (Bob; 1941– , US)
Makem (Tommy; 1932–2007, Northern Irish)
Moore (Christy; 1945– , Irish)
Sharp (Cecil James; 1859–1924, English)
Simon (Paul; 1941– , US)
Waits (Tom; 1949– , US)

06 Carthy (Martin; 1941– , English)
Clancy (Tom, 1924–90, Irish)
Fisher (Archie; 1939– , Scottish)

Foster (Stephen Collins; 1826–64, US)
Fraser (Marjory Kennedy; 1857–1930, Scottish)
Imlach (Hamish; 1940–96, Indian/British)
Mackay (Charles; 1814–89, Scottish)
Martyn (John; 1948– , English)
McLean (Don; 1945– , US)
McTell (Ralph; 1944– , English)
Nairne (Carolina; 1766–1845, Scottish)
Paxton (Tom; 1937– , US)
Seeger (Pete; 1919– , US)

07 Burgess (John Davie; 1934–2005, Scottish)
Cassidy (Eva; 1963–96, US)
Collins (Judy; 1939– , US)
Dickson (Barbara; 1947– , Scottish)
Donegan (Lonnie; 1931–2002, Scottish)
Donovan (1946– , Scottish)

Elliott (Ramblin' Jack; 1931– , US)
Gaughan (Dick; 1948– , Scottish)
Guthrie (Woody; 1912–67, US)
MacColl (Ewan; 1915–89, Scottish)
Redpath (Jean; 1937– , Scottish)
Skinner (James Scott; 1843–1927, Scottish)
Thomson (George; 1757–1851)

08 Marshall (William; 1748–1833, Scottish)
Mitchell (Joni; 1943– , Canadian)
Morrison (Van; 1945– , Northern Irish)

See also **pop**

O'Donnell (Daniel; 1961– , Irish)
Rafferty (Gerry; 1947– , Scottish)
Thompson (Richard; 1949– , English)

09 Henderson (Hamish; 1919–2002, Scottish)
Leadbelly (1888–1949, US)
Robertson (Jeannie; 1908–75, Scottish)

10 Wainwright (Loudon, III; 1946– , US)
Williamson (Roy; 1936–90, Scottish)

11 Sainte-Marie (Buffy; 1941/42– , US)

food

Foods include:

03 dal
dip
pie
poi

04 cake
dhal
hash
luau
mash
mint
olio
soss
soup
stew
taco
tofu
wrap

05 apple
bacon
balti
bhaji
boxty
brose
broth
champ
chips
curry
dolma
grits
gumbo
kebab
kofta
laksa
latke
maror
pasta
pesto
pilau
pilaw
pilow
pizza

Quorn®
raita
ramen
rösti
salad
salmi
salsa
satay
sauce
sushi
tikka
toast
wafer
Wimpy®

06 bhajee
Big Mac®
borsch
burgoo
canapé
caviar
cheese
cookie
cou-cou
faggot
fajita
fondue
gratin
haggis
hot dog
hotpot
hummus
kimchi
kipper
mousse
paella
pakora
panada
panini
parkin
pilaff
quiche

ragout
salami
samosa
scampi
subgum
tahina
tamale
tsamba

07 biryani
biscuit
borscht
bourbon
burrito
chorizo
chowder
chutney
compote
corn dog
cracker
crowdie
fajitas
falafel
felafel
fritter
friture
gnocchi
goulash
gravlax
lasagne
mesclun
mustard
oatcake
polenta
ramakin
ramekin
rarebit
ratafia
risotto
sashimi
sausage
seafood

soufflé
stovies
Tabasco®
tartare
tempura
terrine
timbale
tostada

08 amaretti
barbecue
bechamel
biriyani
biscotto
brandade
calamari
chillada
chop suey
chow mein
coleslaw
consommé
coq au vin
couscous
dog's-body
dressing
empanada
feijoada
fishcake
flapjack
frittata
gado-gado
gazpacho
halloumi
kedgeree
macaroon
moussaka
nut roast
olive oil
omelette
porridge
pot-roast
raclette

ramequin
sandwich
souvlaki
tandoori
teriyaki
tortilla
tzatziki
vindaloo
yakitori
zwieback
09 casserole
cassoulet
colcannon
condiment
crab stick
cranberry
digestive
enchilada
fricassee
galantine
Garibaldi
ginger nut
gravadlax
guacamole
hamburger
howtowdie
Irish stew
jambalaya
macédoine

meatballs
nut cutlet
petit four
reistafel
rijstafel
souvlakia
succotash
tabbouleh
vol-au-vent
10 brandy snap
cannelloni
cottage pie
crispbread
enchiladas
fish-finger
Florentine
ginger snap
Greek salad
green salad
mayonnaise
minestrone
mixed grill
peperonata
quesadilla
rijstaffel
salad cream
salmagundi
salmagundy
sauerkraut

shortbread
stroganoff
white sauce
11 baba ganoush
caesar salad
cockaleekie
frankfurter
French fries
fritto misto
gefilte fish
hollandaise
horseradish
imam bayildi
potato salad
ratatouille
rumblethump
saltimbocca
sauerbraten
smorgasbord
soda cracker
vichyssoise
vinaigrette
winter salad
12 cream cracker
eggs Benedict
fish and chips
langue de chat
mulligatawny

pease pudding
pissaladière
red wine sauce
rumblethumps
Russian salad
shepherd's pie
taramasalata
Waldorf salad
water biscuit
welsh rarebit
13 aubergine roll
bouillabaisse
fisherman's pie
prawn cocktail
salade niçoise
toad-in-the-hole
tomato ketchup
14 chilli con carne
French dressing
macaroni cheese
pickled herring
Scotch woodcock
white wine sauce
Worcestershire
15 balsamic vinegar
bubble and squeak
stuffed mushroom
Wiener schnitzel

Dishes include:

03 dal
pie
04 flan
fool
hash
pâté
puff
soup
stew
tart
05 crêpe
curry
daube
grill
jelly
kebab
pasty
patty
pilau
pizza
roast
salad
tapas

06 bhajee
burger
fondue
fu yung
gratin
mousse
paella
pastry
quiche
ragout
samosa
sorbet
tamale
trifle
waffle
07 chowder
cobbler
compôte
crumble
fajitas
fritter
galette
goulash

lasagne
pancake
parfait
pavlova
platter
pudding
risotto
rissole
soufflé
stir-fry
terrine
08 barbecue
chop suey
chow mein
cocktail
consommé
dolmades
dumpling
ice cream
kedgeree
meringue
moussaka
omelette

pot-roast
syllabub
turnover
09 casserole
cassoulet
charlotte
croquette
empanadas
enchilada
fricassée
galantine
macédoine
paupiette
10 blancmange
blanquette
chaud-froid
cheesecake
spring roll
stroganoff
11 hors-d'oeuvre
ratatouille

Fast food includes:

04 taco
wrap

05 bagel
chips
donut
fries
kebab
pizza

06 Big Mac®
burger
hot dog
nachos

07 burrito
chalupa
falafel
noodles

shwarma
Whopper®

08 doughnut
sandwich

09 bacon roll
chip butty
hamburger
Happy Meal®
milkshake

10 beanburger
beefburger
doner kebab
fish 'n' chips
fish supper
onion rings
shish kebab

11 bacon burger
baked potato
French fries
sausage roll

12 cheeseburger
chicken wings
club sandwich
fish and chips
tortilla wrap
veggie burger

13 chicken burger
sausage supper

14 chicken nuggets
quarter pounder

See also **baking**; **bean**; **biscuit**; **bread**; **cake**; **cereal**; **cheese**; **cookery**; **curry**; **dairy**; **dessert**; **eating**; **fruit**; **herb**; **meal**; **meat**; **mushroom**; **nut**; **pasta**; **pastry**; **pepper**; **restaurant**; **salad**; **sauce**; **sausage**; **seafood**; **soup**; **spread**; **sugar**; **sweet**; **vegetable**

fool

Fools include:

03 ass
fon
git
nit
sot
yap

04 berk
burk
cake
clot
cony
coof
cuif
dill
dope
dork
goop
gouk
gowk
gull
lunk
nana
nerk
nong

prat
putz
shmo
soft
twit
yo-yo

05 chump
cluck
coney
divvy
droll
dweeb
eejit
galah
neddy
patch
patsy
schmo
snipe
softy
wally

06 bampot
dottle
jester

josser
madcap
motley
numpty
sawney
schmoe
turkey
wallie
wigeon

07 airhead
barmpot
bourder
buffoon
Charley
Charlie
God's ape
gubbins
jackass
jughead
lemming
muggins
saphead
schmuck
tomfool

want-wit
widgeon

08 flathead
fondling
Jack-fool
lunkhead
merryman
mooncalf
omadhaun
shlemiel
Tom-noddy

09 April fool
capocchia
chipochia
court fool
dumb-cluck
joculator
lack-brain
mumchance
schlemiel
schlemihl

13 poisson d'avril

Shakespearean fools include:

05 Feste (*Twelfth Night*)
Gobbo (Lancelot; *The Merchant of Venice*)
Speed (*The Two Gentlemen of Verona*)

06 Bottom (Nick; *A Midsummer Night's Dream*)
Yorick (*Hamlet*)

07 Costard (*Love's Labour's Lost*)

Lavache (*All's Well that Ends Well*)

08 Dogberry (*Much Ado About Nothing*)
Trinculo (*The Tempest*)

09 Autolycus (*A Winter's Tale*)
Thersites (*Troilus and Cressida*)

10 Touchstone (*As You Like It*)

football

English league football teams:

04 Bury

06 Fulham
Yeovil

07 Arsenal
Burnley
Chelsea
Everton
Reading
Walsall
Watford
Wrexham

08 Barnsley
Hull City
Millwall
Port Vale
Rochdale

09 Blackpool
Brentford
Liverpool
Luton Town
Stoke City

10 Aston Villa
Darlington
Gillingham
Portsmouth
Sunderland

11 Bournemouth
Bristol City
Cardiff City
Chester City

Derby County
Grimsby Town
Ipswich Town
Leeds United
Lincoln City
Norwich City
Notts County
Southampton
Swansea City
Swindon Town

12 Boston United
Bradford City
Chesterfield
Coventry City
Leyton Orient
Oxford United

13 Bristol Rovers
Crystal Palace
Leicester City
Mansfield Town
Middlesbrough
Torquay United
West Ham United
Wigan Athletic

14 Birmingham City
Cheltenham Town
Crewe Alexandra
Manchester City
Oldham Athletic
Plymouth Argyle
Shrewsbury Town

Southend United
Tranmere Rovers

15 Blackburn Rovers
Bolton Wanderers
Cambridge United
Doncaster Rovers
Newcastle United
Northampton Town
Preston North End
Rotherham United
Sheffield United
Stockport County

16 Charlton Athletic
Colchester United
Hartlepool United
Huddersfield Town
Macclesfield Town
Manchester United
Milton Keynes Dons
Nottingham Forest
Scunthorpe United
Tottenham Hotspur

17 Queen's Park Rangers

18 Peterborough United
Rushden and Diamonds
Sheffield Wednesday
West Bromwich Albion

21 Brighton and Hove Albion
Kidderminster Harriers

22 Wolverhampton Wanderers

Scottish league football teams:

05 Clyde

06 Celtic
Dundee
Gretna

07 Falkirk
Rangers

08 Aberdeen
Arbroath
East Fife
Montrose
St Mirren

09 Ayr United
Dumbarton
Elgin City
Hibernian

Peterhead
Stranraer

10 Kilmarnock
Livingston
Motherwell
Queen's Park
Ross County

11 Brechin City
Cowdenbeath
Raith Rovers
St Johnstone

12 Albion Rovers
Dundee United

13 Airdrie United
Alloa Athletic

Stenhousemuir

14 Berwick Rangers
Forfar Athletic
Greenock Morton
Partick Thistle
Stirling Albion

15 Queen of the South

17 East Stirlingshire
Heart of Midlothian

18 Hamilton Academical

19 Dunfermline Athletic

26 Inverness Caledonian
Thistle

European football teams include:

04 Ajax (The Netherlands)

05 Lazio (Italy)
Malmö (Sweden)
Parma (Italy)
Porto (Portugal)

06 Alavés (Spain)
AS Roma (Italy)
Bastia (France)
Monaco (France)
Napoli (Italy)
Torino (Italy)

07 AC Milan (Italy)
Antwerp (Belgium)
Benfica (Portugal)
Cologne (Germany)
Español (Spain)
FC Porto (Portugal)
Hamburg (Germany)
Schalke (Germany)

08 Bordeaux (France)
Juventus (Italy)
Mallorca (Spain)
Mechelen (Belgium)
Salzburg (Austria)
Tom Tomsk (Russia)
Valencia (Spain)

09 Barcelona (Spain)
Feyenoord (The Netherlands)
FK Austria (Austria)
Marseille (France)
Sampdoria (Italy)
St Etienne (France)
Stuttgart (Germany)
SV Hamburg (Germany)
TSV Munich (Germany)

10 Anderlecht (Belgium)
Bellinzona (Switzerland)
Club Bruges (Belgium)
Club Brugge (Belgium)

Dynamo Kiev (Ukraine)
Fiorentina (Italy)
Inter Milan (Spain)
Real Madrid (Spain)

11 Bate Borisov (Belarus)
FC Magdeburg (Germany)
Ferencvaros (Hungary)
Galatasaray (Turkey)
Hajduk Split (Croatia)
Litex Lovech (Bulgaria)
MTK Budapest (Hungary)
Rapid Vienna (Austria)
Ujpest Dozsa (Hungary)
Wisla Krakow (Poland)

12 Banik Ostrava (Czech Republic)
Bayern Munich (Germany)
Dinamo Zagreb (Croatia)
Gornik Zabrze (Poland)
Moscow Dynamo (Russia)
PSV Eindhoven (The Netherlands)
Real Zaragoza (Spain)
Stade de Reims (France)
Valenciennes (France)
Werder Bremen (Germany)

13 Carl Zeiss Jena (Germany)
Dynamo Tbilisi (Georgia)
IFK Gothenburg (Sweden)
Nordsjaelland (Denmark)
Panathinaikos (Greece)
Standard Liège (Belgium)

14 Athletic Bilbao (Spain)
Atletico Madrid (Spain)
Paris St Germain (France)
Sporting Lisbon (Portugal)
Twente Enschede (The Netherlands)

15 Bayer Leverkusen (Germany)
Red Bull Salzburg (Austria)
Red Star Belgrade (Serbia)
Shakhtar Donetsk (Ukraine)
Steaua Bucharest (Romania)

Football club nicknames include:

02 O's (Leyton Orient)
R's (Queen's Park Rangers)
U's (Cambridge United/Colchester United/
Oxford United)

03 Ton (Greenock Morton)

04 Bees (Barnsley/Brentford)
Boro (Middlesborough)
City (Brechin City/Elgin City)
Dale (Rochdale)
Dons (Aberdeen/Wimbledon)
Gers (Rangers)
Jags (Partick Thistle)

Owls (Sheffield Wednesday)
Pars (Dunfermline Athletic)
Pool (Hartlepool United)
Posh (Peterborough United)
Rams (Derby County)
Reds (Liverpool/Nottingham Forest/Stirling
Albion)
Sons (Dumbarton)
Well (Motherwell)

05 Arabs (Dundee United)
Bhoys (Celtic)
Binos (Stirling Albion)

Blues (Birmingham City/Chelsea/Stranraer/
  Wycombe Wanderers)
Foxes (Leicester City)
Gills (Gillingham)
Gulls (Torquay United)
Irons (Scunthorpe United)
Lions (Millwall)
Loons (Forfar Athletic)
Shire (East Stirlingshire)
Spurs (Tottenham Hotspur)
Stags (Mansfield Town)
Swans (Swansea City)
Wasps (Alloa Athletic)

06 Accies (Hamilton Academical)
Albion (Stirling Albion)
Bairns (Falkirk)
Blades (Sheffield United)
County (Ross County)
Eagles (Crystal Palace)
Fifers (East Fife)
Hibees (Hibernian)
Killie (Kilmarnock)
Latics (Oldham Athletic/Wigan Athletic)
Pompey (Portsmouth)
Robins (Bristol City/Cheltenham Town/
  Swindon Town/Wrexham)
Rovers (Blackburn Rovers/Doncaster Rovers/
  Raith Rovers/Tranmere Rovers)
Royals (Reading)
Saints (Southampton/St Johnstone)
Tigers (Hull City)
Whites (Leeds United)
Wolves (Wolverhampton Wanderers)

07 Addicks (Charlton Athletic)
Baggies (West Bromich Albion)
Bantams (Bradford City)
Buddies (St Mirren)
Clarets (Burnley)
Glovers (Yeovil Town)
Gunners (Arsenal)
Hammers (West Ham United)
Hatters (Luton Town/Stockport County)
Hornets (Watford)
Magpies (Newcastle United/Notts County)
Pirates (Bristol Rovers)
Potters (Stoke City)
Quakers (Darlington)
Red Imps (Lincoln City)
Shakers (Bury)
Silkmen (Macclesfield Town)
Spiders (Queen's Park)

Terrors (Dundee United)
Toffees (Everton)

08 Blue Toon (Peterhead)
Bully Wee (Clyde)
Canaries (Norwich City)
Cherries (Bournemouth)
Citizens (Manchester City)
Cobblers (Northampton Town)
Diamonds (Airdrie United/Rushden and
  Diamonds)
Harriers (Kidderminster Harriers)
Jam Tarts (Heart of Midlothian)
Mariners (Grimsby Town)
Pilgrims (Boston United/Plymouth Argyle)
Saddlers (Walsall)
Seagulls (Brighton and Hove Albion)
Sky Blues (Coventry City)
Terriers (Huddersfield Town)
Trotters (Bolton Wanderers)
Valiants (Port Vale)
Villains (Aston Villa)
Warriors (Stenhousemuir)

09 Black Cats (Sunderland)
Bluebirds (Cardiff City)
Borderers (Berwick Rangers)
Chairboys (Wycombe Wanderers)
Cottagers (Fulham)
Cumbrians (Carlisle United)
Dark Blues (Dundee)
Honest Men (Ayr United)
Red Devils (Manchester United)
Seasiders (Blackpool)
Shrimpers (Southend United)
Spireites (Chesterfield)
Throstles (West Bromich Albion)
Wee Rovers (Albion Rovers)

10 Blue Brazil (Cowdenbeath)
Doonhamers (Queen of the South)
Lilywhites (Preston North End)
Livvy Lions (Livingston)
Minstermen (York City)
Railwaymen (Crewe Alexandra)
Teddy Bears (Rangers)

11 Gable Endies (Montrose)
Red Lichties (Arbroath)
Tractor Boys (Ipswich Town)

12 Caley Thistle (Inverness Caledonian Thistle)
Merry Millers (Rotherham United)

13 Blue and Whites (Blackburn Rovers)

14 Black and Whites (Elgin City/Gretna)

Football stadia include:

03 JJB (Wigan Athletic)

04 City (Livingston)
Deva (Chester City)

05 Abbey (Cambridge United)
Ibrox (Rangers)

06 Bescot (Walsall)

Reebok (Bolton Wanderers)
07 Anfield (Liverpool)
Ballast (Hamilton Academical)
Balmoor (Peterhead)
Firhill (Partick Thistle)
Fir Park (Motherwell)
Oakwell (Barnsley)
St Mary's (Southampton)
08 Belle Vue (Doncaster Rovers)
Deepdale (Preston North End)
Emirates (Arsenal)
Dens Park (Dundee)
Firs Park (East Stirlingshire)
Gigg Lane (Bury)
Home Park (Plymouth Argyle)
Madejski (Reading)
McAlpine (Huddersfield Town)
Memorial (Bristol Rovers)
Millmoor (Rotherham United)
Molineux (Wolverhampton Wanderers)
Moss Rose (Macclesfield Town)
Nene Park (Rushden and Diamonds)
Spotland (Rochdale)
Turf Moor (Burnley)
Vale Park (Port Vale)
Withdean (Brighton and Hove Albion)
09 Britannia (Stoke City)
Broadwood (Clyde)
Cappielow (Greenock Morton)
Ewood Park (Blackburn Rovers)
Field Mill (Mansfield Town)
Forthbank (Stirling Albion)
Gay Meadow (Shrewsbury Town)
Glebe Park (Brechin City)
Huish Park (Yeovil)
Layer Road (Colchester United)
Links Park (Montrose)
Ochilview (Falkirk)
Pittodrie (Aberdeen)
Plainmoor (Torquay United)
Pride Park (Derby County)
Riverside (Middlesbrough)
Roots Hall (Southend United)
Rugby Park (Kilmarnock)
Sixfields (Northampton Town)
Stair Park (Stranraer)
St Andrews (Birmingham City)
The Kassam (Oxford United)
The New Den (Millwall)
The Valley (Charlton Athletic)
Upton Park (West Ham United)
Villa Park (Aston Villa)
10 Aggborough (Kidderminster Harriers)
Ashton Gate (Bristol City)
Caledonian (Inverness Caledonian Thistle)
Carrow Road (Norwich City)
Celtic Park (Celtic)

City Ground (Nottingham Forest)
Easter Road (Hibernian)
Elland Road (Leeds United)
Loftus Road (Queen's Park Rangers)
London Road (Peterborough United)
Meadow Lane (Notts County)
Ninian Park (Cardiff City)
Sincil Bank (Lincoln City)
Stark's Park (Raith Rovers)
The Walkers (Leicester City)
Vetch Field (Swansea City)
York Street (Boston United)
11 Bayview Park (East Fife)
Bramall Lane (Sheffield United)
Central Park (Cowdenbeath)
Cliftonhill (Albion Rovers)
East End Park (Dunfermline Athletic)
Edgeley Park (Stockport County)
Fratton Park (Portsmouth)
Griffin Park (Brentford)
Hampden Park (Queen's Park Rangers)
Old Trafford (Manchester United)
Portman Road (Ipswich Town)
Prenton Park (Tranmere Rovers)
Priestfield (Gillingham)
Raydale Park (Gretna)
Station Park (Forfar Athletic)
St James' Park (Newcastle United)
Whaddon Road (Cheltenham Town)
12 Blundell Park (Grimsby Town)
Boundary Park (Oldham Athletic)
Brisbane Road (Leyton Orient)
County Ground (Swindon Town)
Gayfield Park (Arbroath)
Glanford Park (Scunthorpe United)
Goodison Park (Everton)
Hillsborough (Sheffield Wednesday)
Selhurst Park (Crystal Palace)
Somerset Park (Ayr United)
St Mirren Park (St Mirren)
The Hawthorns (West Bromwich Albion)
Valley Parade (Bradford City)
Vicarage Road (Watford)
Victoria Park (Hartlepool United/Ross
    County)
13 Borough Briggs (Elgin City)
Craven Cottage (Fulham)
Highfield Road (Coventry City)
McDiarmid Park (St Johnstone)
New Broomfield (Airdrie United)
Ochilview Park (Stenhousemuir)
Reynolds Arena (Darlington)
Tannadice Park (Dundee United)
The Alexandria (Crewe Alexandria)
White Hart Lane (Tottenham Hotspur)
14 Bloomfield Road (Blackpool)
Kenilworth Road (Luton Town)

National Hockey (Milton Keynes Dons)
Palmerston Park (Queen of the South)
Recreation Park (Alloa Athletic)
Shielfield Park (Berwick Rangers)

Stadium of Light (Sunderland)
Stamford Bridge (Chelsea)

15 The Fitness First (Bournemouth)
Tynescastle Park (Heart of Midlothian)

Footballers and associated figures include:

03 Law (Denis; 1940– , Scottish)

04 Best (George; 1946–2005, Northern Irish)
Dean (Dixie; 1907–80, English)
Didi (1928–2001, Brazilian)
Figo (Luis; 1972– , Portuguese)
Hall (Sir John; 1933– , English)
Owen (Michael; 1979– , English)
Pelé (1940– , Brazilian)
Rush (Ian; 1961– , Welsh)
Zico (1953– , Brazilian)
Zoff (Dino; 1942– , Italian)
Zola (Gianfranco; 1966– , Italian)

05 Adams (Tony; 1966– , English)
Banks (Gordon; 1937– , English)
Busby (Sir Matt; 1909–94, Scottish)
Carey (Johnny; 1919–95, Irish)
Giggs (Ryan; 1973– , Welsh)
Greig (John; 1942– , Scottish)
Henry (Thierry; 1977– , French)
Hurst (Sir Geoff; 1941– , English)
James (Alex; 1901–53, Scottish)
Moore (Bobby; 1941–93, English)
Revie (Don; 1927–89, English)
Rimet (Jules; 1871–1956, French)
Rossi (Paulo; 1956– , Italian)
Stein (Jock; 1922–85, Scottish)

06 Baggio (Roberto; 1967– , Italian)
Baresi (Franco; 1960– , Italian)
Barnes (John; 1963– , Jamaican/British)
Baxter (Jim; 1939–2001, Scottish)
Bosman (Jean-Marc; c.1964– , Belgian)
Clough (Brian; 1935–2004, English)
Cruyff (Johan; 1947– , Dutch)
Finney (Sir Tom; 1922– , English)
Ginola (David; 1967– , French)
Graham (George; 1944– , Scottish)
Gullit (Ruud; 1962– , Dutch)
Hoddle (Glenn; 1957– , English)
Keegan (Kevin; 1951– , English)
Lawton (Tommy; 1919–96, English)
McColl (R S; 1876–1959, Scottish)
Mercer (Joe; 1914–90, English)
Müller (Gerd; 1945– , German)
Puskas (Ferenc; 1927–2006, Hungarian)
Ramsey (Sir Alf; 1920–99, English)
Robson (Bryan; 1957– , English)
Robson (Sir Bobby; 1933– , English)
Rooney (Wayne; 1985– , English)
Seaman (David; 1963– , English)
St John (Ian; 1938– , Scottish)

Wenger (Arsene; 1949– , French)
Wright (Billy; 1924–94, English)
Wright (Ian; 1963– , English)
Yashin (Lev; 1929–90, Russian)
Zidane (Zinedine; 1972– , French)

07 Ardiles (Osvaldo 'Ossie'; 1952– , Argentine)
Beckham (David; 1975– , English)
Bremner (Billy; 1942–97, Scottish)
Butcher (Terry; 1958– , English)
Cantona (Eric; 1966– , French)
Capello (Fabio; 1946– , Italian)
Charles (John; 1931–2004, Welsh)
Di Canio (Paolo; 1968– , Italian)
Edwards (Duncan; 1936–58, English)
Eusebio (1942– , Mozambican/Portuguese)
Greaves (Jimmy; 1940– , English)
Lampard (Frank; 1978– , English)
Lineker (Gary; 1960– , English)
Macleod (Ally; 1931–2004, Scottish)
Mannion (Wilf; 1918–2000, English)
McCoist (Ally; 1962– , Scottish)
McNeill (Billy; 1940– , Scottish)
Paisley (Bob; 1919–96, English)
Platini (Michel; 1955– , French)
Rivaldo (1972– , Brazilian)
Ronaldo (1976– , Brazilian)
Shankly (Bill; 1913–81, Scottish)
Shearer (Alan; 1970– , English)
Shilton (Peter; 1949– , English)
Souness (Graeme; 1953– , Scottish)
Toshack (John; 1949– , Welsh)
Walcott (Theo; 1989– , English)

08 Bergkamp (Dennis; 1969– , Dutch)
Charlton (Jack; 1935– , English)
Charlton (Sir Bobby; 1937– , English)
Dalglish (Kenny; 1951– , Scottish)
Eriksson (Sven-Göran; 1948– , Swedish)
Ferguson (Sir Alex; 1941– , Scottish)
Fontaine (Just; 1933– , French)
Jennings (Pat; 1945– , Northern Irish)
Maradona (Diego; 1960– , Argentine)
Matthaus (Lothar; 1961– , German)
Matthews (Sir Stanley; 1915–2000, English)
Mourinho (José; 1963– , Portuguese)
Rivelino (Roberto; 1946– , Brazilian)

09 Di Stefano (Alfredo; 1926– , Argentine)
Garrincha (1933–83, Brazilian)
Gascoigne (Paul; 1967– , English)
Greenwood (Ron; 1921–2006, English)
Johnstone (Jimmy; 1944–2006, Scottish)

Klinsmann (Jürgen; 1964– , German)
Lofthouse (Nat; 1925– , English)
Van Basten (Marco; 1964– , Dutch)
10 Schmeichel (Peter; 1963– , Danish)

11 Beckenbauer (Franz; 1945– , German)
12 Blanchflower (Danny; 1926–93, Northern Irish)

Football terms include:

03 box
cap
lob
net
04 back
dive
foul
goal
half
head
hole
loan
mark
pass
post
save
shot
trap
wall
05 bench
chest
pitch
06 assist
corner
double
futsal
goalie
handle
header
keeper
libero
one-two

soccer
tackle
treble
volley
winger
07 booking
caution
dribble
far post
forward
kick-off
offside
own goal
penalty
play-off
red card
referee
stopper
sweeper
throw-in
whistle
08 back heel
crossbar
dead ball
defender
free kick
friendly
full back
goal kick
goal line
half time
hand ball

hat-trick
left back
linesman
midfield
near post
outfield
play-offs
set piece
transfer
wall pass
wingback
09 extra time
five-a-side
formation
give-and-go
goalmouth
promotion
right back
touchline
10 centre back
centre half
centre spot
corner flag
corner kick
goalkeeper
golden goal
half volley
injury time
man marking
midfielder
off-the-ball
penalty box

possession
relegation
sending off
silver goal
substitute
suspension
11 bicycle kick
half-way line
keepie-uppie
obstruction
offside trap
penalty area
penalty kick
penalty spot
six-yard area
straight red
time wasting
12 back-pass rule
Bosman ruling
centre circle
overhead kick
stoppage time
13 centre forward
dangerous play
technical area
14 direct free kick
fourth official
goal difference
relegation zone
15 eighteen-yard box
two-footed tackle

See also **American football**; **Australian rules football**; **sport**

footwear

Footwear includes:

04 boot
clog
mule
pump
shoe
05 jelly
sabot
tacky
thong
wader
welly
06 bootee

brogue
casual
galosh
lace-up
loafer
Oxford
patten
sandal
slip-on
07 gumboot
slipper
sneaker

trainer
08 boat shoe
deck shoe
flip-flop
moccasin
overshoe
pantofle
plimsoll
snowshoe
snow-shoe
09 court-shoe
court shoe

rugby boot
slingback
wedge heel

10 ballet shoe
combat boot
Doc Martens®
espadrille
hiking-boot
kitten heel

kitten-heel
riding boot
riding-boot
tennis shoe

11 bowling shoe
Chelsea boot
Hush Puppies®
walking-boot

12 climbing-boot

football boot
platform heel
stiletto heel

13 beetle-crusher

14 beetle-crushers
brothel creeper
wellington boot

15 brothel-creepers

Footwear parts include:

04 heel
lace
last
lift
sole
vamp
welt

05 inlay
round
shank
upper
waist

06 buckle
button
collar
eyelet
insole
lining
middle
throat
toe box
toe cap
tongue

07 counter

midsole
outsole
quarter
top lift

08 platform

09 back-strap
back-strip
vamp wings
wedge heel

10 middle sole
shankpiece
sock lining

Footwear makes include:

03 Kit
Pod
YSL

04 Arco
Bata
DKNY
Dune
Ecco
Etro
Fila
Gola
Nike
Puma
Tod's
Vans

05 Asics
Bally
Chloe
Edina
Faith
Fendi
Gucci
Guess
Hi-Tec
Kenzo
Levi's
Loake
Marni
Prada

Sacha
Schuh
Umbro

06 Adidas
Camper
Chipie
Clarks
Diesel
Dolcis
Dunlop
Esprit
Miu Miu
Mizuno
Reebok
Rieker
Van Dal

07 Buffalo
Carvela
Church's
Dockers
Ellesse
Energie
Kickers
Lacoste
Missoni
Moshulu
Padders
Salomon
Versace

08 Burberry
Converse
Mephisto
Moschino
Skechers
Ted Baker

09 Dr Martens
Dr Scholl's
Fly London
Jil Sander
Jimmy Choo
Kangaroos
LK Bennett
Miss Sixty
Paul Smith
Red or Dead
Slazenger
Start-rite
Wranglers

10 Aquascutum
Blundstone
Bruno Magli
Helmut Lang
Kurt Geiger
Patrick Cox
Pepe London
Timberland

11 Acupuncture
Birkenstock

Caterpillar
Hush Puppies
Ralph Lauren
12 Lulu Guinness
See also **boot**

Pierre Cardin
13 Christian Dior
Dolce e Gabbana
Manolo Blahnik

14 Sergio Tacchini
15 Alberta Ferretti
Irregular Choice

force *see* police

forecast *see* ship; weather

forest

Forests and woods include:

04 bush
gapó
05 brush
igapò
monte
selva
taiga
urman
06 boreal
jungle

mallee
maquis
pinery
07 coastal
garigue
lowland
macchie
wetland
08 caatinga
garrigue
littoral

mangrove
09 chaparral
deciduous
evergreen
greenwood
10 coniferous
peat forest
rainforest
11 cloud forest
heath forest

lignum-scrub
lignum-swamp
mallee scrub
moist forest
12 vàrzea forest
13 ancient forest
gallery forest
mangrove swamp
savanna forest
14 moist evergreen

See also **environment**

Formula One *see* racing: motor racing

fortification

Fortifications include:

04 bawn
fort
gate
keep
moat
wall
05 ditch
fence
hedge
limes
tower
06 abatis
castle
glacis
laager
sconce
trench

Vauban
07 barrier
bastion
bulwark
citadel
defence
flanker
moineau
outwork
pillbox
rampart
sandbag
08 buttress
cavalier
fortress
palisade
stockade

09 barricade
earthwork
fieldwork
fortalice
gabionade
gatehouse
razor wire
10 barbed wire
bridgehead
trou de loup
11 crémaillère
13 cheval-de-frise
Martello tower
14 motte-and-bailey
15 circumvallation
contravallation

See also **castle**

fortune-telling *see* divination

fossil

04 bone
cast
05 amber
shell
06 burrow
07 bivalve
crinoid
08 ammonite

baculite
dinosaur
echinoid
nautilus
skeleton
09 belemnite
coccolith
coprolite
fish teeth

steinkern
trilobite
10 cast fossil
gastrolith
snakestone
11 ichnofossil
microfossil
mould fossil
resin fossil

sharks' teeth
trace fossil
12 Burgess shale
paleontology
stratigraphy
stromatolite
13 palaeontology
petrification

France

04 Caen
Lyon
Nice
05 Arles
Dijon
Lille
Lyons
Paris

Reims
Rouen
Tours
06 Amiens
Calais
Cannes
Le Mans
Nantes

Rennes
Rheims
07 Avignon
Dunkirk
Limoges
Orléans
08 Bordeaux

Toulouse
09 Cherbourg
10 Marseilles
Strasbourg
11 Carcassonne
Montpellier

05 Corse (Ajaccio)
06 Alsace (Strasbourg)
Centre (Orléans)
Guyane (Cayenne)
07 Corsica (Ajaccio)
Picardy (Amiens)
08 Auvergne (Clermont-Ferrand)
Bretagne (Rennes)
Brittany (Rennes)
Burgundy (Dijon)
Limousin (Limoges)
Lorraine (Nancy)
Picardie (Amiens)
09 Aquitaine (Bordeaux)
Bourgogne (Dijon)
La Réunion (Saint-Denis)

10 Guadeloupe (Basse-Terre)
Martinique (Fort-de-France)
Rhône-Alpes (Lyons)
11 Île de France (Paris)
12 Franche-Comté (Besançon)
Midi-Pyrénées (Toulouse)
13 Lower Normandy (Caen)
Pays de la Loire (Nantes)
Upper Normandy (Rouen)
14 Basse-Normandie (Caen)
Haute-Normandie (Rouen)
15 Nord-Pas-de-Calais (Lille)
Poitou-Charentes (Poitiers)
16 Champagne-Ardenne (Reims)
19 Languedoc-Roussillon (Montpellier)
22 Provence-Alpes-Côte d'Azur (Marseilles)

03 Ain (Bourg-en-Bresse)
Lot (Cahors)
Var (Toulon)
04 Aube (Troyes)
Aude (Carcassonne)
Cher (Bourges)
Eure (Évreux)
Gard (Nîmes)

Gers (Auch)
Jura (Lons-le-Saunier)
Nord (Lille)
Oise (Beauvais)
Orne (Alençon)
Tarn (Albi)
05 Aisne (Laon)
Doubs (Besançon)

Drôme (Valence)
Indre (Châteauroux)
Isère (Grenoble)
Loire (Saint-Étienne)
Marne (Châlons-en-Champagne)
Meuse (Bar-le-Duc)
Paris (Paris)
Rhône (Lyon)
Somme (Amiens)
Yonne (Auxerre)

06 Allier (Moulins)
Ariège (Foix)
Cantal (Aurillac)
Creuse (Guéret)
Guyane (Cayenne)
Landes (Mont-de-Marsan)
Loiret (Orléans)
Lozère (Mende)
Manche (Saint-Lô)
Nièvre (Nevers)
Sarthe (Le Mans)
Savoie (Chambéry)
Vendée (La Roche-sur-Yon)
Vienne (Poitiers)
Vosges (Épinal)

07 Ardèche (Privas)
Aveyron (Rodez)
Bas-Rhin (Strasbourg)
Corrèze (Tulle)
Côte-d'Or (Dijon)
Essonne (Évry)
Gironde (Bordeaux)
Hérault (Montpellier)
Mayenne (Laval)
Moselle (Metz)

08 Ardennes (Charleville-Mézières)
Calvados (Caen)
Charente (Angoulême)
Dordogne (Périgueux)
Haut-Rhin (Colmar)
Morbihan (Vannes)
Val-d'Oise (Cergy-Pontoise)
Vaucluse (Avignon)

Yvelines (Versailles)

09 Finistère (Quimper)
La Réunion (Saint-Denis)
Puy-de-Dôme (Clermont-Ferrand)

10 Corse-du-Sud (Ajaccio)
Deux-Sèvres (Niort)
Eure-et-Loir (Chartres)
Guadeloupe (Basse-Terre)
Haute-Corse (Bastia)
Haute-Loire (Le Puy-en-Velay)
Haute-Marne (Chaumont)
Haute-Saône (Vesoul)
Loir-et-Cher (Blois)
Martinique (Fort-de-France)
Val-de-Marne (Créteil)

11 Côtes-d'Armor (Saint-Brieuc)
Hautes-Alpes (Gap)
Haute-Savoie (Annecy)
Haute-Vienne (Limoges)
Pas-de-Calais (Arras)

12 Haute-Garonne (Toulouse)
Hauts-de-Seine (Nanterre)
Indre-et-Loire (Tours)
Lot-et-Garonne (Agen)
Maine-et-Loire (Angers)
Saône-et-Loire (Mâcon)
Seine-et-Marne (Melun)

13 Ille-et-Vilaine (Rennes)
Seine-Maritime (Rouen)
Tarn-et-Garonne (Montauban)

14 Alpes-Maritimes (Nice)
Bouches-du-Rhône (Marseille)
Hautes-Pyrénées (Tarbes)

15 Loire-Atlantique (Nantes)
Seine-Saint-Denis (Bobigny)

16 Charente-Maritime (La Rochelle)
Meurthe-et-Moselle (Nancy)

18 Pyrénées-Orientales (Perpignan)

19 Pyrénées-Atlantiques (Pau)
Territoire-de-Belfort (Belfort)

20 Alpes-de-Haute-Provence (Digne-les-Bains)

French landmarks include:

04 Alps
Jura

05 Loire
Meuse
Rhône
Saône
Seine
Somme

06 Carnac
Landes

Vosges

07 Garonne
Lascaux

08 Auvergne
Cévennes
Dordogne
Provence
Pyrenees

09 Mont Blanc
Notre Dame

10 Mer de Glace
Pont du Gard
Versailles

11 Canal du Midi
Chenonceaux
Eiffel Tower

12 Grand Trianon
Les Invalides
Mont St Michel
Petit Trianon

13 Arc de Triomphe
Fontainebleau
Fontenay Abbey
Lyon Cathedral
Massif Central
Millau Viaduct

14 Aiguille du Midi
Suisse Normande

15 Amiens Cathedral
Rheims Cathedral

French

03 Luc

04 Jean
 Léon
 Rémi
 Rémy
 René
 Yves

05 Alain
 André
 Denis
 Émile

Henri
Jules
Louis
Serge

06 Claude
 Didier
 Gaston
 Gérard
 Honoré
 Jérôme
 Marcel

Michel
Pascal
Pierre
Xavier

07 Antoine
 Édouard
 Étienne
 Georges
 Gustave
 Jacques
 Laurent

Olivier
Patrice
Thibaut
Thierry
Vincent

08 Frédéric
 Matthieu
 Philippe
 Stéphane
 Thibault

09 Guillaume

04 Fifi
 Gigi

05 Aimée
 Fleur
 Marie

06 Amélie
 Ariane
 Denise
 Eloise
 Evette
 Evonne
 Hélène

Janine
Jeanne
Nicole
Simone
Yvette
Yvonne

07 Blanche
 Camille
 Chantal
 Colette
 Margaux
 Monique

Racquel
Sidonie

08 Bertille
 Brigitte
 Charlize
 Danielle
 Francine
 Juliette
 Michelle
 Villette

09 Angelique
 Charmaine

Claudette
Dominique
Françoise
Gabrielle
Geneviève
Ghislaine
Madeleine
Modestine
Véronique

10 Antoinette
 Jacqueline

04 élan (flair; flamboyance)

05 à deux (for two)
 adieu (goodbye)
 blasé (dulled to enjoyment)
 coupé (two-door motor-car with sloping roof)
 doyen (most distinguished member by virtue of seniority, experience and often also excellence)
 ennui (world-weary listlessness)
 outré (beyond what is customary or proper; eccentric)

06 au fait (knowledgeable or familiar with something)
 au pair (a girl who performs domestic duties for board, lodging and pocket money)
 cliché (a hackneyed phrase or concept)
 déjà vu (an illusion of having experienced something before)
 de trop (superfluous; in the way)
 risqué (audaciously bordering on the unseemly)

07 affaire (liaison, intrigue)
 à la mode (in fashion, fashionable)

atelier (a workshop; an artist's studio)
chagrin (melancholy or vexation at disappointment)
chambré (at room temperature)
en route (let us go)
entente (a friendly agreement between nations)
faux pas (a social blunder)
peloton (main group of riders in a cycle race)
vis-à-vis (in relation to)

08 à la carte (from the menu)
 ambiance (surroundings, atmosphere, environment)
 après-ski (evening amusements after skiing)
 barrette (woman's hairclip or ornament)
 cul-de-sac (a road closed at one end)
 derrière (the buttocks)
 film noir (a movement in cinema)
 idée fixe (an obsession)
 mot juste (the word which fits the context exactly)
 prix fixe (used of a meal in a restaurant offered at a set price for a restricted choice)

09 au courant (aware of current events)
au naturel (naked)
banquette (long upholstered seat)
beau monde (fashionable society)
bel esprit (a brilliant or witty person)
bête noire (a bugbear; something one especially dislikes)
bon vivant (one who lives well, particularly enjoying good food and wine)
bon voyage (have a safe and pleasant journey)
bourgeois (a member of the middle class; conventional, conservative)
c'est la vie (denotes fatalistic resignation)
coup d'état (a violent overthrow of a government)
décolleté (with neck uncovered; low-cut dress)
de rigueur (compulsory)
grand prix (any of several international motor races; any competition of similar importance in other sports)
haut monde (high society)
n'est-ce pas? (is it not so?)
recherché (particularly choice)
sangfroid (self possession; coolness under stress)
vin du pays (a locally produced wine for everyday consumption)
volte-face (a sudden and complete change in opinion or in views expressed)

10 aide-de-camp (an officer who acts as a confidential personal assistant)
avant-garde (those in the forefront of an artistic movement)
cordon bleu (food cooked to a very high standard)
déshabillé (state of being only partially dressed, or of being casually dressed)
pied à terre (a flat kept for temporary or occasional accommodation)
table d'hôte (a set meal at a fixed price)

11 aide-mémoire (a reminder)
amuse-bouche (an appetizer)
au contraire (on the contrary)
belle époque (the time of gracious living immediately preceding World War I)
billets-doux (love letters)
chef d'oeuvre (a masterpiece)
coup de grâce (a finishing blow to end pain)
femme fatale (an irresistibly attractive

woman who brings difficulties or disasters on men; a siren)
fin de siècle (decadent)
prêt-à-porter (ready to wear)
raison d'être ('reason for existence')
savoir faire (knowing what to do and how to do it in any situation)
tour de force (feat of strength or skill)
trompe l'oeil ('an appearance of reality' in painting, architecture, etc)

12 ancien régime (an outdated political system or ruling elite)
bateau-mouche (sightseeing boat on the River Seine in Paris)
carte blanche (freedom of action)
cause célèbre (a very notable or famous trial)
c'est la guerre (denotes fatalistic resignation)
cinéma vérité (realism in films)
coup de foudre (love at first sight)
fait accompli (already done or settled, and therefore irreversible)
force majeure (an unforeseeable or uncontrollable course of events, excusing one from fulfilling a contract; a legal term)
haute couture (fashionable, expensive dress designing and tailoring)
je ne sais quoi (an indefinable something)
laissez-faire (a general principle of non-interference)
ménage à trois (a household comprising a husband and wife and the lover of one of them)
nouveau riche (one who has only lately acquired wealth, without acquiring good taste)
s'il vous plaît (please)

13 belles-lettres (literary studies or writings)
éminence grise (someone exerting power through their influence over a superior)
nouvelle vague (a movement in the French cinema)

14 crème de la crème (the very best)
double entendre (ambiguity, normally with indecent connotations)
enfant terrible (a person whose behaviour is indiscreet, embarrassing to his associates)
noblesse oblige (rank imposes obligations)

15 chargé-d'affaires (an ambassador's deputy)
nouvelle cuisine (a style of simple French cookery)

See also **day**; **month**; **number**; **shop**

Frost, Robert (1874–1963)

Significant works include:

07 'Birches' (1916)
09 *A Boy's Will* (1913)
11 'Mending Wall' (1914)
12 *A Witness Tree* (1942)
    New Hampshire (1923)

13 *In the Clearing* (1962)
    North of Boston (1914)
15 'The Road Not Taken' (1916)
16 *Mountain Interval* (1916)
21 'The Death of the Hired Man' (1914)

fruit

Fruits include:

03 bel
    fig
    haw
    hip
04 bael
    bhel
    date
    kiwi
    lime
    pear
    plum
    sloe
    Ugli®
05 apple
    carob
    grape
    guava
    lemon
    mango
    melon
    naras
    olive
    peach
06 banana
    cherry
    damson
    loquat
    lychee
    medlar

narras
orange
papaya
pawpaw
pomelo
quince
squash
tomato
wampee
07 acerola
apricot
avocado
bramble
chayote
genipap
kumquat
mineola
rhubarb
satsuma
soursop
tangelo
08 bilberry
date-plum
dewberry
goosegog
kalumpit
mandarin
minneola
mulberry

physalis
plantain
rambutan
sebesten
sunberry
tamarind
09 beach plum
blueberry
carambola
cherimoya
cranberry
greengage
Juneberry
kiwi fruit
nectarine
persimmon
pineapple
raspberry
rose apple
sapodilla
saskatoon
shadberry
star-apple
star fruit
tangerine
10 blackberry
breadfruit
clementine
elderberry

gooseberry
granadilla
grapefruit
loganberry
redcurrant
salal berry
sour cherry
spiceberry
strawberry
watermelon
11 blood orange
boysenberry
Jaffa orange
pomegranate
sallal berry
sharon fruit
sweet cherry
12 blackcurrant
buffalo-berry
custard apple
passion fruit
serviceberry
whitecurrant
winter cherry
13 kangaroo-apple
sapodilla plum
Seville orange
14 Cape gooseberry
pink grapefruit

See also **apple**; **berry**; **cherry**; **hybrid**; **melon**; **orange**; **pear**; **plum**

fuel

Fuels include:

03 gas
    LPG
    MOX
    oil
    RDF
04 coal
    coke

derv
logs
peat
slug
SURF
wood
05 argol

eldin
fagot
vraic
06 benzol
billet
borane
butane

diesel
elding
faggot
gas oil
hydyne
petrol
smudge
Sterno®

07 astatki
benzine
benzole
biofuel
Coalite®
eilding
gasahol
gasohol
mesquit
methane
propane

synfuel
08 calor gas®
charcoal
firewood
gasoline
kerosene
kerosine
kindling
mesquite
paraffin
tan balls

triptane
09 acetylene
biodiesel
Campingaz®
cane-trash
diesel oil
hydrazine
red diesel
10 anthracite
atomic fuel
fossil fuel

natural gas
Orimulsion®
11 electricity
North Sea gas
nuclear fuel
12 buffalo chips
nitromethane
nuclear power
13 smokeless fuel
14 aviation spirit

See also **environment; gas**

fungus

Fungi include:

04 rust
scab
smut
05 ergot
morel
yeast
06 blight
07 candida

08 botritis
brown rot
mushroom
09 black spot
grey mould
toadstool
10 saprophyte
slime mould

sooty mould
11 downy mildew
penicillium
slime fungus
12 brewer's yeast
potato blight
13 powdery mildew

See also **mushroom**

fur

Furs include:

03 fox
04 flix
gris
mink
vair
05 budge
civet
fitch
genet
grise
otter
sable
skunk

06 beaver
ermine
marten
nutria
ocelot
rabbit
racoon
zorino
07 blue fox
caracal
caracul
crimmer
fitchet

fitchew
genette
karakul
krimmer
minever
miniver
muskrat
opossum
raccoon
08 cony-wool
kolinsky
moleskin
musquash

ponyskin
sealskin
sea otter
zibeline
09 broadtail
silver fox
wolverene
wolverine
zibelline
10 chinchilla
11 beech marten
Persian lamb
stone marten

furnishing

Furnishings include:

03 mat
rug
04 lamp
lino
05 blind
duvet
throw

tiles
06 carpet
mirror
pelmet
pillow
07 bath mat
beanbag

blanket
curtain
cushion
doormat
picture
valance
08 bed linen

linoleum
mattress
painting
tapestry
09 bedspread
duckboard
head board

hearth rug
lampshade
panelling

wallpaper
10 bath pillow
carpet tile

Roman blind
11 roller blind
wall hanging

12 standard lamp
13 shower curtain
Venetian blind

furniture

Furniture includes:

03 bed
cot
04 bunk
desk
sofa
05 chair
chest
couch
divan
stool
suite
table
trunk
wagon
06 buffet
bureau
carver
coffer
cradle
daybed
fender
lowboy
mirror
pouffe
settee
waggon
07 armoire
beanbag
bunkbed
cabinet
camp-bed
commode
dresser
ottoman
playpen

sofa bed
tallboy
whatnot
08 armchair
bar chair
bedstead
bookcase
cupboard
end table
hatstand
recliner
toy chest
tub chair
wall unit
wardrobe
water bed
09 bed-settee
card table
coatstand
easy chair
fireplace
footstool
hallstand
high-chair
lamp table
sideboard
side table
washstand
wine table
10 blanket box
chiffonier
dumb-waiter
encoignure
escritoire
firescreen

overmantel
secretaire
truckle bed
vanity unit
11 coffee table
dining chair
dining table
mantelpiece
room-divider
studio couch
swivel chair
12 bedside table
chaise-longue
chesterfield
china cabinet
computer desk
folding table
gateleg table
kitchen chair
kitchen table
magazine rack
nest of tables
rocking chair
Welsh dresser
13 dressing table
four-poster bed
umbrella stand
14 chest of drawers
display cabinet
extending table
refectory table
15 bathroom cabinet
butcher's trolley
occasional chair
occasional table

Furniture styles include:

04 Adam
buhl
06 boulle
Empire
Gothic
rococo
Shaker
07 Art Deco
Baroque
Regency

Windsor
08 Colonial
Georgian
Sheraton
09 Charles II
Edwardian
Queen Anne
Shibayama
Victorian
William IV

10 Art Nouveau
Mackintosh
provincial
11 Anglo-Indian
Biedermeier
Chippendale
Cromwellian
Hepplewhite
Louis-Quinze
Restoration

12 Gainsborough
Transitional
Vernis Martin
13 Anglo-Colonial
Arts and Crafts
Dutch Colonial
Louis Philippe
Louis-Quatorze
14 William and Mary

Furniture makers and designers include:

04 Buhl (André Charles; 1642–1732, French)
Elfe (Thomas; 1719–75, American)
Gray (Eileen; 1878–1976, Irish)
Heal (Sir Ambrose; 1872–1959, English)

05 Aalto (Alvar; 1898–1976, Finnish)
Bevan (Charles; c.1820s–1883, English)
Eames (Charles; 1907–1978, US)
Eames (Ray; 1912–88, US)
Ednie (John; 1876–1934, Scottish)
Klint (Kaare; 1888–1954, Danish)
Logan (George; 1866–1939, Scottish)
Phyfe (Duncan; 1768–1854, US)
Scott (Mackay Hugh Baillie; 1865–1945, English)
Stead (Tim; 1952–2000, English)

06 Batley (H W; fl.1872–1910, British)
Boulle (André Charles; 1642–1732, French)
Burges (William; 1827–81, English)
Conran (Sir Terence; 1931– , English)
Gimson (Ernest William; 1864–1919, English)
Godwin (Edward; 1833–86, English)
Migeon (Pierre; 1701–58, French)
Seddon (J P; 1827–1906, English)
Starck (Philippe; 1949– , French)
Taylor (E A; 1874–1951, Scottish)
Thonet (Michael; 1796–1871, German)
Voysey (C F A; 1857–1941, English)

Walton (George; 1867–1933, Scottish)

07 Beneman (Guillaume; 1684–1764, French)
Lethaby (W R; 1857–1931, English)
Macnair (J Herbert; 1868–1955, Scottish)
Ruhlman (Jacques-Émile; 1879–1933, French)

08 Barnsley (Ernest; 1863–1926, English)
Barnsley (Sidney; 1865–1926, English)
Eastlake (Charles; 1836–1906, English)
Jacobsen (Arne; 1902–71, Danish)
Montigny (Philippe-Claude; 1734–1800, French)
Riesener (Jean Henri; 1734–1806, French)
Rietveld (Gerrit; 1888–1964, Dutch)
Saarinen (Eero; 1910–61, US)
Sheraton (Thomas; 1751–1806, English)
Tredgold (Thomas; 1788–1829, English)

09 Hitchcock (Lambert; 1795–1852, US)

10 Chermayeff (Serge; 1900–96, US)
Mackintosh (Charles Rennie; 1868–1928, Scottish)

11 Chippendale (Thomas; 1718–79, English)
Hepplewhite (George; d.1786, English)
Le Corbusier (1887–1965, Swiss/French)

12 Riemerschmid (Richard; 1868–1957, German)

Terms to do with furniture include:

03 leg
oak

04 Adam
buhl
cane
ogee
pine
toon

05 apron
beech
bombé
boule
ebony
inlay
ivory
kiaat
repro
shelf
suite

06 boulle
caster
castor
drawer
Empire

finial
ormolu
period
plinth
rococo
sapele
veneer
walnut

07 antique
bun foot
fitment
fluting
pad foot
paw foot
reeding

08 cabriole
flatpack
fretwork
harewood
mahogany
moulding
pediment
rewarewa
sabre leg

Sheraton

09 bonnet top
coachwood
Edwardian
Japanning
marquetry
panelling
Queen Anne
roundwood
saddlebag
slip cover
spade foot
Victorian
whitewood

10 block front
calamander
distressed
encoignure
oxbow front
ribbon back
rosemaling
scroll foot
shield back
upholstery

11 ball-and-claw
Biedermeier
cabriole leg
Chippendale
claw-and-ball
collapsible
haute époque
Hepplewhite

See also **antique**; **office**

marqueterie
overstuffed

12 French polish
reproduction
self-assembly
vernis martin

13 mother-of-pearl

tortoiseshell
unit furniture

14 barley-sugar leg
dental moulding
Marlborough leg

15 serpentine front
three-piece suite

fury

The Furies:

06 Alecto
Megara

09 Tisiphone

G

galaxy

gallery *see* **museum**

gambling

06 bookie
casino
chip in
fan-tan
fulham
gaming
jetton
lay off
motser
policy
punter

07 baccara
flutter
lottery
tipster

08 baccarat
levanter
long shot
outsider

See also **bet**

play-debt
roulette
teetotum

09 blackjack
bookmaker
dog racing
favourite
place a bet
vingt-et-un

10 bouillotte
punto banco
put-and-take
put money on
sweepstake

11 blind hookey
card-sharper
find the lady
go one better
horse racing

numbers game
puncto banco
rouge-et-noir
slot machine

12 break the bank
card counting
debt of honour
pitch-and-toss
scoop the pool

13 hedge one's bets
shoot the works
spread betting

14 shove-halfpenny
three-card trick
wheel of fortune

15 cash in one's chips
disorderly house
greyhound racing
make a clean sweep

game

Games include:

03 loo
nap
nim
taw

04 brag
crib
dice
faro
I-spy
ludo
mora
pool
ruff
skat
snap
tray
vint

05 bowls
chess
clubs
craps
darts
gleek
halma
jacks
Jenga®
lurch
morra
noddy
ombre
poker

rummy
whist

06 basset
boston
bridge
Cluedo®
clumps
crambo
écarté
euchre
fan-tan
hazard
niffer
piquet
quinze
squail

07 baccara
bezique
bowling
canasta
cooncan
hangman
kalooki
mah-jong
mancala
marbles
muggins
old maid
picquet
pinball
pinocle

pontoon
primero
purpose
ring taw
snooker
traybit

08 all-fives
all-fours
baccarat
card game
charades
checkers
chequers
cribbage
dominoes
draughts
forfeits
gin rummy
kalookie
Kim's game
Klondike
Klondyke
mah-jongg
Monopoly®
Napoleon
patience
penneech
penneeck
penuchle
ping pong
pinochle

reversis
roulette
sardines
Scrabble®
tredille

09 bagatelle
billiards
blackjack
board game
draw poker
floor game
Hacky Sack®
honeypots
hopscotch
jingo-ring
lanterloo
newmarket
pair-royal
Pelmanism
penny ante
quadrille
Simon says
solitaire
solo whist
spoilfive
stud poker
table game
tic-tac-toe
tredrille
twenty-one

vingt-et-un

10 backgammon
Balderdash®
Black Maria
bouillotte
criss-cross
fivestones
handy-dandy
hot-cockles
jackstraws
lansquenet
Pictionary®
spillikins
target game

11 battleships
beetle drive
bumble-puppy
catch-the-ten
chemin de fer
hide-and-seek
sancho-pedro
span-counter
speculation
table tennis
tiddlywinks
troll-my-dame

12 consequences
one-and-thirty
partner whist

pitch-and-toss
shove ha'penny
span-farthing

13 auction bridge
blindman's buff
clock patience
happy families
jingling match
musical chairs
pass the parcel
postman's knock
spin the bottle
table football
table skittles
ten-pin bowling

14 contract bridge
fives-and-threes
follow-my-leader
hunt-the-slipper
hunt-the-thimble
nine men's morris
shove-halfpenny
snip-snap-snorum
Trivial Pursuit®

15 Chinese checkers
Chinese chequers
Chinese whispers
duplicate bridge
puss in the corner

Board games include:

02 go
04 ludo
Risk®
siga

05 chess
darts
goose
halma
lurch
marls
nyout
senet
shogi
Sorry®

06 Boggle®
Cluedo®
gobang
gomuku
merels
merils
morals
morris
tables
tabula

uckers

07 Cranium®
mah-jong
mancala
marrels
merells
pachisi
petteia
reverse
reversi
Yahtzee®

08 checkers
chequers
cribbage
Dingbats®
draughts
miracles
Monopoly®
parchesi
Rummikub®
Scrabble®

09 bagatelle
Buccaneer®
Operation®

Parcheesi®
solitaire
tic-tac-toe

10 backgammon
Go for Broke®
latrunculi
Mastermind®
Pictionary®

11 battleships
fox and geese
Frustration®

12 pente grammai

13 concentration
table skittles
The Game of Life®

14 nine men's morris
Trivial Pursuit®

15 Chinese checkers
Chinese chequers
duodecim scripta
fivepenny morris
ninepenny morris
three men's morris

Card games include:

03 don
nap
pig
war

04 brag
bust
faro
fish
golf
king
loba
may I?
phat
pits
push
rook
scat
skat
snap
solo
spit
tunk
tute
ugly

05 blitz
cheat
cinch
crash
flush
knack
nerts
pairs
pedro
pitch
poker
ronda
rummy
samba
shoot
speed
tarok
tarot
whist

06 big two
boodle
bridge
casino
church
crates
cuckoo
dakota
deuces
écarté
euchre
fan tan
five up

go fish
hearts
henway
kaiser
knaves
oh hell!
palace
pepper
piquet
pounce
red dog
sevens
spades
spoons
squeal
stitch
switch
tarock
taroky
trumps
turtle
valets

07 auction
authors
bezique
bone ace
canasta
clabber
last one
old maid
pontoon
quartet
setback
spitzer
whipsaw

08 ace-deuce
all fives
all fours
anaconda
baccarat
bid whist
blackout
carousel
cribbage
drunkard
elevator
gin rummy
high five
Michigan
Napoleon
patience
pinochle
Pope Joan
sequence
shanghai
Welsh don

09 abyssinia
bid euchre
blackjack
catch five
golden ten
king pedro
king rummy
let it ride
newmarket
Pelmanism
poker bull
president
quadrille
racehorse
solitaire
solo whist
stud poker
tic-tac-toe
tile rummy
vingt-et-un

10 black maria
buck euchre
capitalism
Chinese ten
cincinnati
crazy nines
dirty clubs
German solo
parliament
preference
ride the bus
sheepshead
strip poker
three in one
Wall Street

11 cat and mouse
chase the ace
chemin de fer
chicken foot
crazy eights
English stud
find the lady
French tarot
French whist
German whist
high-low-jack
Indian poker
Mexican stud
nine-card don
Oklahoma gin
racing demon
Russian bank
six-card brag
speculation
Texas hold 'em

12 Chinese poker

devil's bridge
draw dominoes
five-card brag
five card draw
four-card brag
high card pool
kings corners
Mexican sweat
Mexican train
nine-card brag
one and thirty
pick a partner
ruff and trump
Russian poker
shoot pontoon

13 concentration
contract rummy

contract whist
happy families
knockout whist
lame-brain Pete
Michigan rummy
Romanian whist
sergeant major
seven-card brag
Shanghai rummy
three-card brag

14 Caribbean poker
contract bridge
five hundred rum
fives and threes
follow the queen
good, better, best
Jack the shifter

Liverpool rummy
Minnesota whist
rich man, poor man
ruff and honours
second hand high
spite and malice
spit in the ocean
three-card monte
trust-don't trust

15 back alley bridge
cut-throat euchre
double solitaire
nomination whist
railroad canasta
stealing bundles

Party games include:

06 bridge
Who Am I?®

07 mummies
statues
Twister®

08 charades
Kim's game
lucky dip
sardines

09 dead lions
fuzzy duck
poor pussy
Simon says

10 ducky ducky

memory game
wink murder

11 general post
hide-and-seek
truth or dare

12 consequences
musical bumps
treasure hunt

13 blindman's buff
chocolate game
musical chairs
pass the orange
pass the parcel
postman's knock

sleeping lions
spin-the-bottle
stuck in the mud
winking murder

14 British bulldog
follow-my-leader
hunt the thimble
musical statues
pass the balloon
sleeping pirate

15 Chinese whispers
egg and spoon race
murder in the dark
ring-a-ring-a-roses
three-legged race

Terms to do with games include:

02 go
03 bat
bid
die
run
set
win
04 base
beat
card
deal
dice
draw
goal

half
hand
lose
move
pass
play
shot
suit
team
tile
turn
05 board
bonus
cheat

court
field
match
piece
pitch
prize
round
rules
score
stick
table
throw
trick
trump

06 attack
gambit
player
tactic
07 counter
defence
doubles
forfeit
singles
08 opponent
role play
strategy
tie-break
10 tiebreaker

See also **chess**; **Monopoly®**

game: hunting

Game animals include:

03	elk	hyena	giraffe	squirrel
	fox	moose	leopard	wild boar
04	bear	snipe	muntjac	**09** crocodile
	boar	tiger	red deer	**10** fallow deer
	deer	zebra	roe deer	
	lion	**06** badger	**08** antelope	**12** hippopotamus
	stag	rabbit	elephant	mountain lion
	wolf	**07** buffalo	kangaroo	
05	bison	caribou	sika deer	

Game birds include:

04	coot	moorhen	waterfowl
	duck	ostrich	**10** guinea fowl
	guan	pintail	tufted duck
	teal	pochard	wild turkey
05	goose		wood grouse
	quail	**08** pheasant	woodpigeon
	scaup	shoveler	**11** black grouse
06	curlew	woodcock	Canada goose
	grouse	**09** blackcock	common snipe
	plover	blackgame	hazel grouse
	wigeon	goldeneye	**12** capercaillie
07	gadwall	jack snipe	capercailzie
	greyhen	partridge	golden plover
	greylag	ptarmigan	**15** pink-footed goose
	mallard	red grouse	
		scaup duck	

See also **poultry**

garden

Garden types include:

03	hop	water	winter	rosarium
	tea	**06** alpine	**07** botanic	**09** allotment
04	beer	arbour	cottage	arboretum
	herb	border	hanging	botanical
	knot	bottle	Italian	flower bed
	lawn	flower	kitchen	raised bed
	rest	indoor	orchard	shrubbery
	rock	market	rockery	terrarium
	roof	physic	rose bed	window box
	rose	rosary		**10** ornamental
	sink	rosery	**08** Japanese	rose arbour
		sunken	kailyard	
05	fruit	walled	pleasure	**13** vegetable plot

Gardening tools include:

03	axe	rake	gloves	**07** fan rake
	hoe	**05** Flymo®	scythe	hatchet
04	fork	spade	shears	kneeler
	pots	**06** cloche	trowel	loppers

netting
pruners
trellis
wellies

08 chainsaw
clippers
hosepipe
shredder
Strimmer®

09 cold frame
fruit cage
garden saw
lawn edger
lawnmower
lawn raker
sack truck
secateurs
sprinkler
water butt

10 compost bin
cultivator
fertilizer
garden cart
lawn roller
soil tester
weedkiller

11 brushcutter
incinerator
lawn aerator

watering can
wheelbarrow

12 drop spreader
grass trimmer
hedge trimmer
potting table

13 garden sprayer
lawn scarifier

14 rotary spreader

Gardens include:

03 Kew (England)
04 Ness (England)
05 Lawai (USA)
    Ninfa (Italy)
    Stowe (England)
06 Het Loo (The Netherlands)
    Monet's (France)
    Suzhou (China)
    Wisley (England)
07 Alnwick (England)
    Bodnant (Wales)
    Boxwood (USA)
    Byodoin (Japan)
    Giverny (France)
    Heligan (England)
    Kane'ohe (USA)
    Motsuji (Japan)
    Mt Usher (Ireland)
    Nemours (USA)
    Rousham (England)
    Ryoanji (Japan)
    Urakuen (Japan)
08 Aalsmeer (The Netherlands)
    Alhambra (Spain)
    Bagh-e Fin (Iran)
    Bartram's (USA)
    Biltmore (USA)
    Blenheim (England)
    Butchart (Canada)
    Charbagh (India)
    Claymont (USA)
    Ermitage (Germany)
    Hopewood (Australia)
    Hyde Hall (England)
    Korakuen (Japan)
    La Granja (Spain)
    Longwood (USA)
    Mt Vernon (USA)
    Nanzenji (Japan)
    Pleasure (China)
    Rikugien (Japan)
    Rosedown (USA)
    Rosemoor (England)

    Sankeien (Japan)
    Vaucluse (Australia)
09 Arley Hall (England)
    Ascog Hall (Scotland)
    Bagatelle (France)
    Claremont (England)
    Kenrokuen (Japan)
    Keukenhof (The Netherlands)
    Landriana (Italy)
    Lingering (China)
    Lion Grove (China)
    Lodge Park (Ireland)
    Majorelle (Morocco)
    Maplelawn (Canada)
    Mirabelle (Austria)
    Newby Hall (England)
    Sanssouci (Germany)
    Stourhead (England)
    Tuileries (France)
    Upton Grey (England)
10 Afton Villa (USA)
    Buen Retiro (Spain)
    Chatsworth (England)
    El Escorial (Spain)
    Generalife (Spain)
    Harlow Carr (England)
    Hatley Park (Canada)
    Holker Hall (England)
    Isola Bella (Italy)
    Kensington (England)
    La Mortella (Italy)
    Levens Hall (England)
    Monticello (USA)
    Schönbrunn (Austria)
    Sen No Rikyu (Japan)
    Versailles (France)
    Villa d'Este (Italy)
    Villa Lante (Italy)
    Winterthur (USA)
11 Chanticleer (USA)
    Eden Project (England)
    Great Dixter (England)
    Ji Chang Yuan (China)
    Leonardslee (England)

Naranjestan (Iran)
Old Westbury (USA)
Parc Monceau (France)
Powerscourt (Ireland)
Villa Madama (Italy)
Wallenstein (Germany)

12 Castle Howard (England)
Chiddingfold (New Zealand)
Hampton Court (England)
Hidcote Manor (England)
Jingshan Park (China)
Katsura Rikyu (Japan)
Orto Botanico (Italy)
Ritsurin Koen (Japan)
Royal Botanic (Australia/England/Scotland)
Sissinghurst (England)

Studley Royal (England)
Villa Adriana (Italy)

13 Dumbarton Oaks (USA)
Harewood House (England)
Orange Botanic (Australia)
Vaux le Vicomte (France)

14 Benmore Botanic (Scotland)
Biddulph Grange (England)
Drummond Castle (Scotland)
Hua Ching Palace (China)
Middleton Place (USA)
Stone Lion Grove (China)
Wakehurst Place (England)
Younger Botanic (Scotland)

15 Arnold Arboretum (USA)

Gardeners include:

03 Don (Monty; 1955– , English)

04 Cane (Percy; 1881–1976, English)
Emes (William; 1730–1803, English)
Kent (William; 1684–1748, English)
Page (Russell; 1906–85, English)
Peto (Harold Ainsworth; 1854–1933, English)
Wise (Henry; 1653–1738, English)

05 Banks (Sir Joseph; 1744–1820, English)
Brown (Lancelot 'Capability'; 1715–83, English)
Enshu (Kobori; 1579–1647, Japanese)
Gavin (Diarmuid; 1964– , Irish)
Klein (Carol; 1945– , English)
Marot (Daniel; 1661–1752, French)
Monet (Claude; 1840–1926, French)
Roper (Lanning; 1912–83, US)
Swift (Joe; 1965– , English)
Wilde (Kim; 1960– , English)

06 Copijn (Hendrik; 1842–1923, Dutch)
Evelyn (John; 1620–1706, English)
Farrer (Reginald; 1880–1920, English)
Gerard (John; 1545–1612, English)
Gilpin (William Sawrey;1762–1845, English)
Hanmer (Sir Thomas; fl.1659; English)
Hooker (Sir William Jackson; 1785–1865, English)
Ingram (Collingwood 'Cherry'; 1880–1981, English)
Jekyll (Gertrude; 1843–1932, English)
London (George; d.1714, English)
Loudon (John Claudius; 1783–1843, Scottish)
Mawson (Thomas; 1861–1933, English)
Miller (Philip; 1691–1771, Scottish)
Mollet (André; d.c.1665, French)
Paxton (Sir Joseph; 1801–65, English)
Repton (Humphrey; 1752–1818, English)

Soseki (Muso; 1275–1351, Japanese)

07 Bartram (John; 1699–1777, American)
Blaikie (Thomas; 1751–1838, Scottish)
Clusius (Carolus; 1526–1609, Flemish)
Compton (Edward; d.1977, English)
de Thame (Rachel; 1961– , English)
Duchêne (Achille; 1866–1947, French)
Farrand (Beatrix; 1872–1959, US)
Forsyth (William; 1737–1804, Scottish)
Hanbury (Sir Thomas; 1832–1907; English)
L'Ecluse (Charles de; 1526–1609, Flemish)
Le Nôtre (André; 1613–1700, French)
Thrower (Percy; 1913–88, English)
Walling (Edna Margaret; 1896–1973, English/Australian)

08 Aislabie (John; d.1742, English)
Beaumont (Guillaume; fl.1680s/90s, French)
Buczacki (Stefan; 1945– , British)
Hamilton (Geoff; 1936–96 , English)
Hessayon (David G; 1928– , English)
Jellicoe (Sir Geoffrey; 1900–96, English)
Johnston (Lawrence; 1871–1958, US)
Nesfield (William Andrews; 1793–1881, English)
Robinson (William; 1838–1935, Irish)

09 Backhouse (James; 1794–1869, English)
Blomfield (Sir Reginald; 1856–1942, English)
Bridgeman (Charles; d.1738, English)
Forestier (Jean-Claude Nicolas; 1861–1930, French)

10 Aberconway (Henry Duncan, Lord; 1879–1953, English)
Blackburne (John; 1694–1786, English)
Titchmarsh (Alan; 1949– , English)

Tradescant (John, the Elder; 1570–c.1638, English)
Tradescant (John, the Younger; 1608–62, English)

11 Abercrombie (John; 1726–1806, English)

13 Sackville-West (Vita; 1892–1962, English)

Gardening terms include:

03 bed
04 bulb
clay
loam
plot
roji
seed
soil
tree
weed
05 bower
graft
hardy
hedge
mulch
plant
shrub
06 annual
arbour
hoeing
hybrid
manure
raking
07 climber
compost
cutting
digging

growing
herbary
olitory
organic
potager
produce
pruning
staking
topiary
topsoil
weeding
08 chinampa
dividing
gardener
layering
planting
thinning
watering
09 deciduous
evergreen
germinate
leaf-mould
perennial
pesticide
plantsman
pleasance
10 composture
coniferous

fertilizer
greenhouse
hardy plant
sharawadgi
sharawaggi
11 crazy paving
cultivation
green manure
ground cover
hydroponics
landscaping
plantswoman
potting shed
propagation
tender plant
tree surgeon
tree surgery
12 bedding plant
conservatory
horticulture
hybrid vigour
13 double digging
growing season
horticultural
plantie-cruive
transplanting
15 window gardening

See also **flower**; **insecticide**; **park**

gas

Gases include:

02 CS
04 neon
tear
town
05 ether
marsh
nerve
niton
ozone

radon
xenon
06 butane
helium
ketene
07 ammonia
krypton
methane
mustard

natural
propane
08 cyanogen
ethylene
firedamp
laughing
09 acetylene
black damp
chokedamp

10 chloroform
12 nitrous oxide
13 carbon dioxide
dimethylamine
14 carbon monoxide

See also **fuel**

gate

Gates include:

03 New (Israel)

04 Dung (Israel)
Iron (Spain)
Land (Croatia)
Lion (Greece)
Nola (Italy)
Zion (Israel)

05 Black (England)
Black (*The Lord of the Rings*, J R R Tolkien)
Delhi (Pakistan)
Green (Poland)
Jaffa (Israel)
Lion's (Israel)
Menin (Belgium)
Roman (Croatia)
Sarno (Italy)
Sheep (ancient world/ Bible)
Water (Belgium)

06 Alcalá (Spain)
Appian (ancient world)
Bhatti (Pakistan)
Bridge (Croatia)
Double (Israel)
Golden (Israel)
Golden (Russia)
Golden (Ukraine)
Hebron (Israel)
Herod's (Israel)
Ishtar (ancient world)
Marine (Italy)
Nocera (Italy)
Sanmon (Japan)
Sather (USA)
Scaean (*The Iliad*)
Single (Israel)

Sunset (Japan)
Toledo (Spain)
Triple (Israel)
Upland (Poland)

07 Balawat (ancient world)
Colline (ancient world)
Gennath (ancient world/ Bible)
Harbour (Croatia)
Karamon (Japan)
Kashmir (India)
Monk Bar (England)
Nicanor (ancient world/ Bible)
Paisley (England)
Shankly (England)
Stabian (Italy)
St Rocco (Croatia)
Swedish (Latvia)
Tallinn (Estonia)
Thunder (Japan)
Victory (Egypt)
Zuwayla (Egypt)

08 Asinaria (Italy)
Conquest (Egypt)
Damascus (Israel)
Hadrian's (Greece)
Kashmiri (Pakistan)
Landport (England)
Maggiore (Italy)
Memorial (Gates; England)
Pinciana (Italy)
Rashomon (Japan)
Raushnai (Pakistan)
San Paolo (Italy)
Traitors' (England)
Vesuvius (Italy)

09 Bab Agnaou (Morocco)
Beautiful (ancient world/ Bible)
Bukdaemun (South Korea)
Great East (South Korea)
Namdaemun (South Korea)
Ostiensis (ancient world)

10 Bootham Bar (England)
Dongdaemun (South Korea)
Gate of Dawn (Lithuania)
gate of horn (Greek mythology)
Grand Torii (Japan)
Great North (South Korea)
Great South (South Korea)
Porta Nigra (Germany)
St Vincent's (Spain)
Sungnyemun (South Korea)
Waterpoort (Belgium)

11 Brandenburg (Germany)
Gate of China (China)
gate of ivory (Greek mythology)
Gate of Light (Pakistan)
Herculaneum (Italy)
Kaminarimon (Japan)
Walmgate Bar (England)

12 Heunginjimun (South Korea)
St John's Abbey (England)

13 Micklegate Bar (England)
San Sebastiano (Italy)

14 Gateway of India (India)
The Gates of Hell (sculpture, Rodin)

See also **Germany; London; sculpture**

gauge

Gauges include:

03 oil

04 plug
rain
ring
slip
snap
tide
tyre
wind

wire

05 block
broad
drill
limit
paper
steam
taper
water

06 feeler
radius
strain
vacuum

07 Bourdon
counter
cutting
loading
marking

mortise

08 gauge rod
pressure

10 gauge glass
gauge wheel
micrometer

See also **measurement**

gem

Gemstones include:

03 jet

04 jade
onyx
opal
ruby

05 agate
amber
beryl
coral
pearl
topaz

06 garnet
jasper

zircon

07 cat's eye
citrine
crystal
diamond
emerald
peridot

08 amethyst
fire opal
sapphire
sunstone

09 cairngorm
carbuncle

carnelian
cornelian
demantoid
malachite
marcasite
moonstone
morganite
soapstone
tiger's eye
turquoise
uvarovite

10 aquamarine
bloodstone
chalcedony

chrysolite
rhinestone
rose quartz
serpentine
spinel ruby
tourmaline

11 alexandrite
chrysoberyl
chrysoprase
lapis lazuli
spessartite

13 cubic zirconia
mother-of-pearl
white sapphire

See also **diamond**

genealogy

Terms to do with genealogy include:

03 DSP
IGI
née

04 AGRA
clan
deed
heir
late
race
will

05 issue
trace
widow

06 census
degree
estate
legacy
relict

07 archive
bastard
bequest
consort
descent
divorce
epitaph
kinship
lineage
peerage
probate
progeny
removed

soundex
surname
testate
trustee
widower
witness

08 ancestor
ancestry
bachelor
base-born
bequeath
cadastra
canon law
deceased
decedent
emigrant
forebear
maternal
paternal
pedigree
relation
spinster
theogony

09 ascendant
given name
immigrant
indenture
intestate
necrology
offspring
sine prole
testament

10 ahnentafel
descendant
family name
family tree
forefather
generation
maiden name
onomastics
progenitor
succession

11 beneficiary
genealogist
record agent

12 burial record
census record
cousin-german
Domesday Book
illegitimate
primogenitor
vital records

13 Christian name
consanguinity
died sine prole
pedigree chart
primary record
primogeniture

14 cemetery record
common ancestor
marriage record

15 secondary record
vital statistics

See also **family**

general

Generals include:

03 Dix (John A; 1798–1879, US)
Doe (Samuel K; 1951–90, Liberian)
Lee (Robert E; 1807–70, US)
Ney (Michel; 1769–1815, French)

04 Alba (Ferdinand Alvarez de Toledo, Duke of; 1508–82, Spanish)
Alva (Ferdinand Alvarez de Toledo, Duke of; 1508–82, Spanish)
Asad (Hafez al-; 1928–2000, Syrian)
Dyer (Reginald; 1864–1927, British)
Haig (Alexander; 1924– , US)
Jehu (842–815 BC, Hebrew)
Jodl (Alfred; 1890–1946, German)
Juin (Alphonse; 1888–1967, French)
Pope (John; 1822–92, US)
Prem (Tinsulanonda; 1920– , Thai)

05 Assad (Hafez al-; 1928–2000, Syrian)
Booth (William; 1829–1912, English)
Bragg (Braxton; 1817–76, US)
Clive (Robert, Lord; 1725–74, English)
Davis (Benjamin Oliver; 1877–1970, US)
Deane (Richard; 1610–53, English)
Eanes (António Ramalho; 1935– , Portuguese)
Gates (Horatio; 1728–1806, American)
Gough (Sir Hubert; 1870–1963, Irish)
Grant (Ulysses S; 1822–85, US)
Ramos (Fidel; 1928– , Philippine)
Salan (Raoul; 1899–1984, French)
Scott (Winfield; 1786–1866, US)
Soult (Nicolas Jean de Dieu; 1769–1851, French)
Wolfe (James; 1727–59, English)

06 Aëtius (Flavius; c.390–454 AD, Roman)
Anders (Wladyslaw; 1892–1970, Polish)
Aranda (Pedro Pablo Abarca y Bolea, Conde de; 1718–99, Spanish)
Arnold (Benedict; 1741–1801, American)
Buller (Sir Redvers; 1839–1908, English)
Butler (Benjamin Franklin; 1818–93, US)
Caesar (Julius; 100/102–44 BC, Roman)
Church (Sir Richard; 1785–1873, Irish)
Custer (George Armstrong; 1839–76, US)
Davout (Louis Nicolas; 1770–1823, French)
De Bono (Emilio; 1866–1944, Italian)
Douhet (Giulio; 1869–1930, Italian)
Dunois (Jean d'Orléans, Comte de; 1403–68, French)
Fabius (Caius Fabius; fl.304 BC, Roman)
Fabius (Quintus Fabius Rullianus; 4c BC, Roman)
Franco (Francisco; 1892–1975, Spanish)
Geisel (Ernesto; 1908–96, Brazilian)

Gordon (Charles; 1833–85, English)
Joffre (Joseph; 1852–1931, French)
Jomini (Henri, Baron de; 1779–1869, French)
Kearny (Philip; 1814–62, US)
Kearny (Stephen Watts; 1794–1848, US)
Kléber (Jean Baptiste; 1753–1800, French)
Leslie (Alexander, Earl of Leven; c.1580–1661, Scottish)
Marion (Francis; c.1732–95, American)
Marius (Gaius; 157–86 BC, Roman)
Moreau (Jean Victor; 1761–1813, French)
Morgan (John Hunt; 1825–64, US)
Napier (Sir Charles; 1782–1853, English)
Narses (c.478–573 AD, Byzantine)
Outram (James; 1803–63, English)
Patton (George S; 1885–1945, US)
Putnam (Rufus; 1738–1824, American)
Rommel (Erwin; 1891–1944, German)
Scipio (the Younger; 185–129 BC, Roman)
Sharon (Ariel; 1928– , Israeli)
Spaatz (Carl A; 1891–1974, US)
Suchet (Louis Gabriel, Duc d'Albufera da Valencia; 1770–1826, French)
Thomas (George Henry; 1816–70, US)
Zhukov (Georgi; 1896–1974, Soviet)

07 Agrippa (Marcus Vipsanius; c.63–12 BC, Roman)
Atatürk (Mustapha Kemal; 1881–1938, Turkish)
Berwick (James Fitzjames, Duke of; 1670–1734, French)
Bouillé (François Claude Amour, Marquis de; 1739–1800, French)
Bradley (Omar N; 1893–1981, US)
Carmona (Antonio; 1869–1951, Portuguese)
Delgado (Humberto; 1906–65, Portuguese)
Duilius (Gaius; fl.260 BC, Roman)
Eyadéma (Gnassingbé; 1937–2005, Togolese)
Fairfax (Thomas, Lord; 1612–71, English)
Hampton (Wade; c.1751–1835, American)
Katsura (Taro; 1847–1913, Japanese)
Lambert (John; 1619–84, English)
Lincoln (Benjamin; 1733–1810, American)
Masséna (André; 1758–1817, French)
Obregón (Alvaro; 1880–1928, Mexican)
Paullus (Lucius Aemilius; d.216 BC, Roman)
Pickett (George E; 1825–75, US)
Regulus (Marcus Atilius; d.c.250 BC, Roman)
Ridgway (Matthew B; 1895–1993, US)
Sherman (William T; 1820–91, US)
Spínola (António de; 1910–96, Portuguese)

08 Agricola (Gnaeus Julius; 40–93 AD, Roman)
Anderson (Sir Kenneth; 1891–1959, Indian/British)

Badoglio (Pietro; 1871–1956, Italian)
Billiere (Sir Peter de la; 1934–   , English)
Bourmont (Louis de Ghaisnes, Comte de; 1773–1846, French)
Brisbane (Sir Thomas Makdougall; 1773–1860, Scottish)
Camillus (Marcus Furius; 447–365 BC, Roman)
Cárdenas (Lázaro; 1895–1970, Mexican)
Cardigan (James Thomas Brudenell, Earl of; 1797–1868, English)
de Gaulle (Charles; 1890–1970, French)
Guderian (Heinz; 1888–1953, German)
Hamilton (Sir Ian Standish Monteith; 1853–1947, English)
Hannibal (247–182 BC, Carthaginian)
Johnston (Albert Sidney; 1803–62, US)
Johnston (Joseph E; 1807–91, US)
Josephus (Flavius; 37–c.100 AD, Jewish)
Kolingba (André; 1936–   , Central African Republic)
Kornilov (Lavr Georgiyevich; 1870–1918, Russian)
Marshall (George C; 1880–1959, US)
Montrose (James Graham, Marquis of; 1612–50, Scottish)
Nearchus (4c BC, Macedonian)
Pershing (John J; 1860–1948, US)
Samsonov (Aleksandr Vasilevich; 1859–1914, Russian)
Schuyler (Philip John; 1733–1804, American)
Seleucus (I Nicator; c.358–281 BC, Macedonian)
Timoleon (d.c.337 BC, Greek)

09 Alekseyev (Mikhail Vasilevich; 1857–1918, Russian)
Alexander (Sir Harold, Earl; 1891–1969, Irish)
Antigonus (d.301 BC, Macedonian)
Antonescu (Ion; 1882–1946, Romanian)
Aristides (c.550–c.467 BC, Athenian)
Boulanger (Georges; 1837–91, French)
Brownrigg (Sir Robert; 1759–1833, English)
Doubleday (Abner; 1819–93, US)
Dumouriez (Charles François; 1739–1823, French)
Faidherbe (Louis; 1818–89, French)
Flaminius (Gaius; d.217 BC, Roman)
Hasdrubal (d.207 BC, Carthaginian)
Lemnitzer (Lyman L; 1899–1988, US)
MacArthur (Douglas; 1880–1964, US)

Marcellus (Marcus Claudius; c.268–208 BC, Roman)
McClellan (George Brinton; 1826–85, US)
Menshikov (Aleksandr Sergeyevich; 1789–1869, Russian)
Miltiades (the Younger; c.550–489 BC, Athenian)
Montholon (Charles Tristan, Marquis de; 1783–1853, French)
Musharraf (Pervaiz; 1943–   , Pakistani)
Omar Pasha (1806–71, Ottoman)
Santander (Francisco de Paula; 1792–1840, Colombian)
Townshend (George, Viscount and Marquess; 1724–1807, English)
Townshend (Sir Charles Vere Ferrers; 1861–1924, English)

10 Abercromby (Sir Ralph; 1734–1801, Scottish)
Beauregard (P G T; 1818–93, US)
Belisarius (505–65, Byzantine)
Christison (Sir Philip; 1893–1993, Scottish)
Cunningham (Sir Alan Gordon; 1887–1983, Irish/British)
Eisenhower (Dwight D; 1890–1969, US)
Empecinado (El; 1775–1825, Spanish)
Hardie Boys (Sir Michael; 1931–   , New Zealand)
Lysimachus (d.281 BC, Macedonian)
Oglethorpe (James Edward; 1696–1785, English)
Peng Dehuai (1899–1974, Chinese)
Schlieffen (Alfred, Count von; 1833–1913, Prussian)
Timoshenko (Semyon; 1895–1970, Russian)

11 Baden-Powell (Robert, Lord; 1857–1941, English)
Beauharnais (Eugène de; 1781–1824, French)
Epaminondas (c.418–362 BC, Theban)
Jiang Jieshi (1887–1975, Chinese)
Schwarzkopf (H Norman; 1934–   , US)

12 Smith-Dorrian (Sir Horace; 1858–1930, English)

13 Chiang Kai-shek (1887–1975, Chinese)
Primo de Rivera (Miguel, Marqués de Estella; 1870–1930, Spanish)
Schwarzenberg (Karl Philipp, Prince of; 1771–1820, Austrian)

14 Osman Nuri Pasha (1832–1900, Turkish)

genetics

Geneticists include:

04 Ford (Edmund Brisco; 1901–88, English)

05 Brown (Michael S; 1941–   , US)

Crick (Francis Harry Compton; 1916–2004, English)

Jones (Steve; 1944– , Welsh)
Leder (Philip; 1934– , US)
Ochoa (Severo; 1905–93, US)
Sager (Ruth; 1918–97, US)
Snell (George Davis; 1903–96, US)
Vries (Hugo de; 1848–1935, Dutch)

06 Beadle (George Wells; 1903–89, US)
Benzer (Seymour; 1921–2007, US)
Biffen (Sir Rowland; 1874–1949, English)
Bodmer (Sir Walter; 1936– , English)
Boveri (Theodor; 1862–1915, German)
Cantor (Charles; 1942– , US)
Clarke (Bryan; 1932– , English)
Fisher (Sir Ronald Aylmer; 1890–1962, English)
Galton (Sir Francis; 1822–1911, English)
Gurdon (Sir John; 1933– , English)
Harris (Sir Henry; 1925– , Australian/British)
Mendel (Gregor; 1822–84, Austrian)
Morgan (Thomas Hunt; 1866–1945, US)
Müller (Hermann Joseph; 1890–1967, US)
Venter (Craig; 1946– , US)
Watson (James Dewey; 1928– , US)
Wright (Sewall; 1889–1988, US)
Zinder (Norton; 1928– , US)

07 Bateson (William; 1861–1926, English)
Borlaug (Norman; 1914– , US)
Collins (Francis S; 1950– , US)
Correns (Carl; 1864–1933, German)

Gehring (Walter; 1939– , Swiss)
Hopwood (Sir David; 1933– , English)
Lysenko (Trofim Denisovich; 1898–1976, Soviet)
McLaren (Dame Anne; 1927–2007, English)
Penrose (Lionel Sharples; 1898–1972, English)
Vavilov (Nikolai Ivanovich; 1887–1943, Russian)

08 Auerbach (Charlotte; 1899–1994, German)
Franklin (Rosalind; 1920–58, English)
Lewontin (Richard; 1929– , US)
Palmiter (Richard; 1942– , US)
Sheppard (Philip MacDonald; 1921–76, English)
Yanofsky (Charles; 1925– , US)

09 Ashburner (Michael; 1942– , English)
Baltimore (David; 1938– , US)
Goldstein (Joseph Leonard; 1940– , US)
Johanssen (Wilhelm; 1857–1927, Danish)
Lederberg (Joshua; 1925–2008, US)

10 Darlington (Cyril Dean; 1903–81, English)
Dobzhansky (Theodosius; 1900–75, US)
Kettlewell (Bernard; 1907–79, English)
McClintock (Barbara; 1902–92, US)
Pontecorvo (Guido; 1907–99, Italian/British)
Sturtevant (Alfred Henry; 1891–1970, US)
Waddington (C H; 1905–75, English)
Weatherall (Sir David; 1933– , English)

12 Maynard Smith (John; 1920–2004, English)

Terms used in genetics include:

02 GM
03 DNA
egg
RNA
04 base
gene
mRNA
tRNA
05 clone
codon
helix
sperm
06 allele
gamete
genome
hybrid
intron
parent

uracil
vector
zygote
07 adenine
diploid
guanine
meiosis
mitosis
thymine
08 autosome
cytosine
dominant
genetics
heredity
mutation
promoter
sequence
09 amino acid
behaviour

homologue
inversion
karyotype
offspring
recessive
repressor
variation
10 adaptation
chromosome
generation
geneticist
homozygous
nucleosome
nucleotide
polymerase
speciation
11 double helix
epigenetics
genetic code

inheritance
nucleic acid
polypeptide
X-chromosome
Y-chromosome
12 cell division
F1 generation
F2 generation
heterozygous
mitochondria
reproduction
13 DNA sequencing
fertilization
mitochondrion
recombination
transcription
translocation
15 self-replication

geography

Geographical regions include:

04 veld
05 basin
coast
heath
plain
06 Arctic
desert
forest
jungle
orient

pampas
steppe
tundra
07 outback
prairie
riviera
seaside
tropics
08 lowlands
midlands

occident
savannah
woodland
09 Antarctic
grassland
green belt
marshland
scrubland
wasteland
10 Third World

wilderness
11 countryside
13 rural district
urban district
14 developed world
15 developing world

Geographical features include:

03 alp
bar
bay
bog
cay
col
cwm
fen
key
ria
sea
04 arch
bank
bush
cape
cave
core
cove
dike
dune
dyke
gulf
hill
lake
loch
mesa
moor
mull
pass
pole
pond
reef
rock
spit
veld
wadi
wady
05 abyss
atoll
basin
beach

brook
butte
canal
chasm
cliff
coast
creek
crust
delta
esker
fault
fiard
fiord
fjard
fjord
gorge
heath
horst
inlet
karst
kopje
levée
lough
marsh
nappe
oasis
ocean
plate
point
river
scree
shore
sound
stack
swamp
veldt
06 arroyo
barrow
canyon
cirque
corrie

crater
desert
forest
graben
ice cap
island
lagoon
mantle
pampas
rapids
ravine
riegel
steppe
strait
stream
trench
tundra
valley
07 caldera
channel
estuary
fissure
glacier
hillock
iceberg
ice fall
ice floe
isthmus
moraine
mud flat
plateau
pothole
prairie
savanna
sea arch
terrace
volcano
wetland
08 blowhole
crevasse
headland

ice field
ice sheet
ice shelf
moorland
mountain
ocean bed
sand dune
savannah
seamount
sea stack
09 chaparral
continent
coral reef
grassland
hot desert
ice stream
island arc
ox-bow lake
peninsula
quicksand
salt marsh
stream bed
string bog

tidal flat
waterfall
10 barrier bar
blanket bog
block field
cold desert
escarpment
fault plane
fault scarp
finger lake
floodplain
ocean basin
ocean floor
promontory
rainforest
rift valley
11 archipelago
barrier reef
block stream
coastal dune
glacial lake
ocean trench
rock glacier

swallow hole
12 abyssal plain
barrier beach
fold mountain
oceanic crust
oceanic plate
oceanic ridge
subcontinent
13 barrier island
block mountain
glacial trough
glacial valley
hanging valley
mangrove swamp
monsoon forest
mountain range
shore platform
tectonic plate
U-shaped valley
valley glacier
14 tropical forest
15 paternoster lake

Geographers and cartographers include:

03 Dee (John; 1527–1608, English)

04 Cary (John; c.1754–1835, English)
Mela (Pomponius; fl.40 AD, Latin)

05 Adair (John; c.1655–c.1722, Scottish)
Barth (Heinrich; 1821–65, German)
Cabot (Sebastian; 1474–1557, Venetian)
Darby (Sir Clifford; 1909–92, Welsh)
Guyot (Arnold; 1807–84, US)
Hedin (Sven; 1865–1952, Swedish)
Imhof (Eduard; 1895–1986, Swiss)
Penck (Albrecht; 1858–1945, German)
Sauer (Carl; 1889–1975, US)
Speed (John; 1542–1629, English)
Stamp (Sir Dudley; 1898–1966, English)

06 Batuta (1304–68, Arab)
Behaim (Martin; 1440–1507, German)
Bowman (Isaiah; 1878–1950, US)
Clüver (Phillip; 1580–1622, German)
Edrisi (c.1100–64, Arab)
Gmelin (Johann Georg; 1709–55, German)
Harvey (David; 1935– , English)
Idrisi (c.1100–64, Arab)
Ritter (Karl; 1779–1859, German)
Saxton (Christopher; 1542/44–c.1611, English)
Strabo (c.60 BC–c.21 AD, Greek)

07 Gilbert (G K; 1843–1918, US)
Haggett (Peter; 1933– , English)
Hakluyt (Richard; c.1552–1616, English)
Hondius (Jodocus; 1563–1612, Flemish)

Markham (Sir Clements; 1830–1916, English)
Ogilvie (Alan; 1887–1954, Scottish)
Ptolemy (c.90–168 AD, Egyptian)
Wallace (Alfred Russel; 1823–1913, English)

08 Büsching (Anton Friedrich; 1724–93, German)
Filchner (Wilhelm; 1877–1957, German)
Humboldt (Alexander, Baron von; 1769–1859, German)
Mercator (Gerardus; 1512–94, Flemish)
Ortelius (Abraham Ortel; 1527–98, Flemish)
Robinson (Arthur; 1915–2004, US)

09 Cluverius (Phillip; 1580–1622, German)
Grisebach (A H R; 1814–79, German)
Kropotkin (Prince Peter; 1842–1921, Russian)
Mackinder (Sir Halford John; 1861–1947, English)
Muqaddasi (945–88, Arab)
Pausanias (2c AD, Greek)

10 Arrowsmith (Aaron; 1750–1823, English)
Hartshorne (Richard; 1899–1992, US)
Huntington (Ellsworth; 1876–1943, US)
Richthofen (Ferdinand, Baron von; 1833–1905, German)
Wooldridge (Sydney; 1900–63, English)

11 Bartholomew (John George; 1860–1920, Scottish)
Christaller (Walter; 1893–1969, German)

Hägerstrand (Torsten; 1916–2004, Swedish)
Ibn Battutah (1304–68, Arab)
Kingdon-Ward (Frank; 1885–1958, English)

12 Eratosthenes (c.276–194 BC, Greek)
Leo Africanus (c.1494–c.1552, Arab)

13 Waldseemüller (Martin; c.1480–c.1521, German)

15 Eudoxus of Cnidus (408–353 BC, Greek)
Vidal de la Blache (Paul; 1845–1918, French)

Terms used in geography include:

04 arid
crag
tail
05 shott
taiga
07 aggrade
equator
glacial
hachure
08 alluvium
altitude
landmass
landslip
latitude

meridian
prograde
09 accretion
antipodes
base level
billabong
deviation
ethnology
landslide
longitude
metroplex
relief map
10 coordinate
demography

glaciation
landlocked
topography
11 cartography
chorography
conurbation
demographic
hydrography
triangulate
vulcanology
13 Ordnance Datum
shield volcano
14 plate tectonics
roche moutonnée

See also **bay**; **beach**; **cape**; **cave**; **channel**; **compass**; **desert**; **firth**; **gulf**; **island**; **lake**; **mountain**; **ocean**; **passage**; **peninsula**; **plain**; **river**; **sea**; **sound**; **strait**; **volcano**; **waterfall**

geology

Geological time periods include:

04 Lias (Epoch/Series)
Malm (Epoch/Series)

06 Albian (Stage)
Antian (Stage)
Aptian (Stage)
Arenig (Epoch/Series)
Danian (Stage)
Dogger (Epoch/Series)
Emsian (Stage)
Eocene (Epoch/Series)
Ludlow (Epoch/Series)
Recent (Epoch/Series)
Viséan (Epoch/Series)

07 Anglian (Stage)
Ashgill (Epoch/Series)
Caradoc (Epoch/Series)
Hoxnian (Stage)
Miocene (Epoch/Series)
Neogene (Period)
Permian (Period)
Riphean (Era)
Vendian (Era)
Wenlock (Epoch/Series)

08 Aalenian (Stage)
Aphebian (Era)

Archaean (Eon)
Bajocian (Stage)
Cambrian (Period)
Cenozoic (Era)
Chattian (Stage)
Devonian (Period)
Eifelian (Stage)
Frasnian (Stage)
Givetian (Stage)
Holocene (Epoch/Series)
Jurassic (Period)
Langhian (Stage)
Llanvirn (Epoch/Series)
Lutetian (Stage)
Mesozoic (Era)
Namurian (Epoch/Series)
Pliocene (Epoch/Series)
Rhaetian (Stage)
Rupelian (Stage)
Silesian (Period)
Silurian (Period)
Tertiary (Sub-era)
Thurnian (Stage)
Toarcian (Stage)
Tremadoc (Epoch/Series)
Triassic (Period)

Turonian (Stage)
Ypresian (Stage)
Zanclian (Stage)

09 Barremian (Stage)
Bartonian (Stage)
Bathonian (Stage)
Baventian (Stage)
Callovian (Stage)
Campanian (Stage)
Coniacian (Stage)
Cromerian (Stage)
Devensian (Stage)
Dinantian (Period)
Flandrian (Stage)
Gedinnian (Stage)
Llandeilo (Epoch/Series)
Ludhamian (Stage)
Messinian (Stage)
Oligocene (Epoch/Series)
Oxfordian (Stage)
Pastonian (Stage)
Ryazanian (Stage)
Santonian (Stage)
Siegenian (Stage)
Thanetian (Stage)
Tortonian (Stage)
Waltonian (Stage)
Zechstein (Epoch/Series)

10 Aquitanian (Stage)
Beestonian (Stage)
Cenomanian (Stage)
Cretaceous (Period)
Hettangian (Stage)
Ipswichian (Stage)
Llandovery (Epoch/Series)
Ordovician (Period)
Palaeocene (Epoch/Series)
Palaeogene (Period)
Palaeozoic (Era)

Placenzian (Stage)
Priabonian (Stage)
Quaternary (Period)
Sinemurian (Stage)
Stephanian (Epoch/Series)
Wolstonian (Stage)

11 Burdigalian (Stage)
Famerianian (Stage)
Hauterivian (Stage)
Phanerozoic (Eon)
Pleistocene (Epoch/Series)
Portlandian (Stage)
Precambrian (Eon)
Proterozoic (Eon)
Tournaisian (Epoch/Series)
Valanginian (Stage)
Westphalian (Epoch/Series)

12 Kimmeridgian (Stage)
Rotliegendes (Epoch/Series)
Serravallian (Stage)

13 Carboniferous (Period)
Lower Cambrian (Epoch/Series)
Lower Devonian (Epoch/Series)
Lower Jurassic (Epoch/Series)
Lower Triassic (Epoch/Series)
Maastrichtian (Stage)
Mississippian (Period)
Pennsylvanian (Period)
Pliensbachian (Stage)
Upper Cambrian (Epoch/Series)
Upper Devonian (Epoch/Series)
Upper Jurassic (Epoch/Series)
Upper Triassic (Epoch/Series)

14 Middle Cambrian (Epoch/Series)
Middle Devonian (Epoch/Series)
Middle Jurassic (Epoch/Series)
Middle Triassic (Epoch/Series)

15 Lower Cretaceous (Epoch/Series)
Upper Cretaceous (Epoch/Series)

Terms used in geology include:

02 aa
03 bar
cwm
mya
ore
04 clay
dome
dune
fold
lava
limb
lode
Moho
till

trap
tuff
vein
wadi
05 agate
atoll
basin
butte
chert
delta
epoch
esker
fault
fiord

fjord
focus
gorge
gully
guyot
horst
joint
Karst
lahar
levee
magma
plain
P-wave
ridge
S-wave

talus
06 albite
arkose
arroyo
basalt
bolson
canyon
cirque
corrie
debris
gabbro
geyser
gneiss
graben
mantle
oolite
quartz
runoff
schist
scoria
stress
tephra
trench
uplift

07 aquifer
barchan
bauxite
bed-load
blowout
breccia
caldera
drumlin
glacier
granite
hogback
igneous
isograd
lapilli
meander
mineral
moraine
orogeny
outwash
plateau
pothole
vesicle
volcano

08 A-horizon
alluvium
backwash
basement

See also **crust**; **rock**

B-horizon
C-horizon
feldspar
fumarole
isostasy
leaching
lopolith
monolith
mountain
obsidian
oilfield
oil shale
pahoehoe
pediment
regolith
rhyolite
syncline
xenolith

09 alabaster
batholith
carbonate
deflation
epicentre
flood tide
hot spring
intrusion
laccolith
landslide
limestone
Mohs scale
monadnock
monocline
oxidation
peneplain
rock cycle
rockslide
sandstone
slip fault
striation
tableland
viscosity
volcanism

10 anthracite
astrobleme
block fault
cinder cone
deposition
depression
earthquake
flood plain
kettle hole
mineralogy

rift valley
subsidence
topography
travertine
water table
weathering

11 alluvial fan
central vent
exfoliation
geosyncline
groundwater
maar volcano
metamorphic
normal fault
sublimation
swallow hole
thrust fault
volcanic ash

12 artesian well
coastal plain
fringing reef
magma chamber
pyroclastics
stratigraphy
unconformity
volcanic bomb
volcanic cone
volcanic dome
volcanic pipe

13 angle of repose
barrier island
drainage basin
geomorphology
hanging valley
recumbent fold
shield volcano
stratovolcano
U-shaped valley
V-shaped valley

14 bituminous coal
eustatic change
lateral moraine
longshore drift
stratification
subduction zone
transform fault
wave-cut terrace

15 million years ago
sedimentary rock
strike-slip fault
terminal moraine

German

German boys' names include:

03 Jan
Max
Uwe
04 Dirk
Eric
Erik
Jens
Jörg
Ralf

Sven
Swen
05 Bernd
Erich
Fritz
Jonas
Klaus
Lukas
Ralph

06 Dieter
Jürgen
Markus
Niklas
Stefan
Tobias
Ulrich
07 Andreas
Dominik

Mathias
Steffen
Stephan
Torsten
08 Kristian
Matthias
Thorsten
Wolfgang

German girls' names include:

04 Elke
Irma
Lili
05 Berta
Erika
Gerda
Heidi
Helga
Hilde
Lotti

Petra
Trudi
06 Angela
Astrid
Birgit
Dagmar
Frieda
Ingrid
Liesel
Monika

Sigrun
Steffi
Ulrika
Ursula
07 Bettina
Jolanda
Kristin
08 Adelheid
Angelika

Birgitta
Brunhild
Christin
Gretchen
09 Brunhilde
Elisabeth
Franziska
Hildegard
10 Wilhelmina

German words and expressions include:

04 echt (denotes authenticity, typicality)
Flak (abuse, criticism)
über (prefix used to mean ultimate, above all)

05 Angst (anxiety; anguish)
Blitz (lightning; also short for Blitzkrieg)
Geist (spirit)
kaput (broken; destroyed)
Reich (empire)
Stasi (former East German secret police)
U-Boot (submarine)

06 abseil (to descend a vertical face using rope)
ersatz (fake; substitute)
Führer (leader; dictator)
Kaiser (emperor)
Kitsch (something trashy)
Landau (type of carriage)
Panzer (military tank)
Umlaut (two dots indicating change in vowel sound)

07 Achtung (Attention!)
Bauhaus (architectural school and style)
Gestalt (original whole or unit)
Gestapo (former Nazi secret state police)
Pilsner (beer from Pilsen in Czech Republic)
Pretzel (hard, salted biscuit)
Strudel (type of pastry/dessert)

08 Autobahn (motorway)

Dummkopf (blockhead; idiot)
Hausfrau (housewife)
Kohlrabi (vegetable)
Pinscher (breed of dog)
Schnapps (distilled alcoholic drink)
spritzer (drink of wine and soda water)
Zugzwang (compulsion to make bad move, especially in chess)

09 Alpenhorn (musical instrument)
Anschluss (annexation of Austria in WWII)
Bratwurst (type of sausage)
Bundestag (German parliament)
Dachshund (breed of dog)
Edelweiss (type of flowering plant)
gemütlich (amiable; comfortable; cosy)
Hamburger (meat patty said to have originated in Hamburg)
Leitmotiv (recurrent theme in a literary or musical work)
Luftwaffe (air force)
nicht wahr? (isn't that so?)
Reichstag (German parliament)
Schnauzer (breed of dog)
Schnitzel (meat cutlet)
Wehrmacht (former German armed forces)
zeitgeist (spirit of the age)

10 Alpenstock (walking stick)
Blitzkrieg (a sudden overwhelming attack by ground and air forces)

Bundesbank (German Federal bank)
Gesundheit (your health, said to someone who has just sneezed)
Hinterland (remote area beyond coast)
Jugendstil ('youth style'; the German term for art nouveau)
Lebensraum ('room to live', ie justification for expansionism)
Lederhosen (leather trousers)
Meerschaum (tobacco pipe made from mineral of the same name)
Ostpolitik (former political stance of Western Germany towards the Communist bloc)
Rottweiler (breed of dog)
Sauerkraut (cabbage preserved in salt)
Übermensch (superman)
Volkswagen (people's car)
Wanderlust (desire to wander)
wunderkind (child prodigy)

11 Frankfurter (type of sausage originally from Frankfurt)
Kulturkampf (cultural battle, ie Church vs State)
Poltergeist (ghost that makes noises and moves objects)

See also **day**; **month**; **number**

Realpolitik (politics based on practical considerations)
und so weiter (and so forth)
Weltschmerz (sympathy with universal misery; utter pessimism)

12 Doppelgänger (double; look-alike)
eile mit Weile ('make speed with leisure')
Gastarbeiter (an immigrant worker, especially one who does menial work)
Glockenspiel (musical instrument)
Kindergarten (children's nursery)
Machtpolitik (power politics)
Pumpernickel (dark rye bread)

13 Bildungsroman (novel dealing with a character's formative years)
Kristallnacht (anti-Jewish pogrom of 9–10 Nov 1938)
Schadenfreude (enjoyment of another's misfortune)
Sturm und Drang (literary movement)

14 Weltanschauung (way of looking at the world)

15 Götterdämmerung (the downfall of any once powerful system)

Germany

Cities and notable towns in Germany include:

04 Bonn	Munich	Leipzig	Stuttgart
05 Essen	Weimar	**08** Würzburg	**10** Düsseldorf
Trier	**07** Cologne	**09** Frankfurt	**15** Frankfurt am Main
06 Berlin	Hamburg	Nuremberg	

Administrative divisions of Germany, with regional capitals:

06 Berlin (Berlin)	**11** Brandenburg (Potsdam)	**18** Nordrhein-Westfalen (Düsseldorf)
Bremen (Bremen)	**13** Niedersachsen (Hannover)	
Hessen (Wiesbaden)	Sachsen-Anhalt (Magdeburg)	**21** Mecklenburg-Vorpommern (Schwerin)
07 Bavaria (Munich)	**14** Rheinland-Pfalz (Mainz)	
Hamburg (Hamburg)	**16** Baden-Württemberg (Stuttgart)	
Sachsen (Dresden)	**17** Schleswig-Holstein (Kiel)	
08 Saarland (Saarbrücken)		
09 Thüringen (Erfurt)		

German landmarks include:

04 Elba	Danube	**09** Helgoland
Elbe	**07** Brocken	Linderhof
Main	Moselle	Reichenau
Oder	Rathaus	Reichstag
05 Rhine	**08** Residenz	Starnberg
06 Dachau		**10** Buchenwald

Heidelberg
Tiergarten
Wies Church
11 Berliner Dom
Black Forest
Fernsehturm
Königsplatz
Mariensäule
Rhine valley
Trostbrücke
12 Bavarian Alps

Frauenkirche
Museumsinsel
13 Bonn Cathedral
Colditz Castle
Festspielhaus
Harz Mountains
Moselle valley
14 Alexanderplatz
Essen Cathedral
Gemäldegalerie
Herrenchiemsee

Neuschwanstein
Potsdamer Platz
Trier Cathedral
Unter den Linden
Wartburg Castle
15 Aachen Cathedral
Auerbach's Keller
Brandenburg Gate
East Side Gallery
Munich Cathedral
Speyer Cathedral

giant

Giants include:

03 Gog
Oni
04 Bali
Bana
Bres
Caca
Corb
Ériu
Gaia
Gerd
Gorm
Grid
Hrod
Kari
Loki
Otus
Rhea
Ymir
05 Aegir
Arges
Argus
Atlas
Balor
Banba
Baugi
Cacus
Fodla
Gjalp
Greip
Gymir
Hymir
Jotun
Magog
Orion
Pan Gu
Skadi
Talos
Theia
Thrym
06 Albion
Anakim

Bestla
Cronus
Echion
Elatha
Fachan
Fafnir
Fasolt
Geryon
Hagrid
Phoebe
Tethra
Tethys
Themis
Thiazi
Titans
Tityus
Typhon
07 Antaeus
Ashuras
Brontes
Cyclops
Daityas
Ethlinn
Geirrod
Gilling
Goliath
Iapetus
Klytius
Oceanus
Olvaldi
Purusha
Suttung
Telemos
Telemus
Windigo
Zipacna
08 Angrboda
Bolthorn
Briareus
Cethlenn
Cyclopes
Eurytion

Firbolgs
Gigantes
Gogmagog
Hrungnir
Hyperion
Jarnsaxa
Morgante
Nephilim
Panoptes
Steropes
Upelluri
09 Angerboda
Aurgelmir
Bergelmir
Enceladus
Fomorians
Gandareva
Gargantua
Grantorto
Menoetius
Mnemosyne
Olentzero
10 Angerbotha
Buarainech
Epimetheus
Pantagruel
Paul Bunyan
Polyphemus
Prometheus
Ysbaddaden
11 Finn MacCool
Galligantus
Gog and Magog
Hiranyaksha
Thrudgelmir
Utgardaloki
12 Vafthruthnir
14 Hiranyakashipu
15 Cerne Abbas Giant
Fionn MacCumhail

gift *see* **Christmas**

Gilbert, Sir W S (1836–1911) and Sullivan, Sir Arthur (1842–1900)

Significant works include:

07 *Thespis* (1871)

08 *Iolanthe* (1882)
Patience (1881)

09 *Ruddigore* (1887)
The Mikado (1885)

11 *HMS Pinafore* (1878)
Princess Ida (1884)

The Sorcerer (1877)
Trial by Jury (1875)

12 *The Grand Duke* (1896)

13 *The Gondoliers* (1889)
Utopia, Limited (1893)

19 *The Yeomen of the Guard* (1888)

20 *The Pirates of Penzance* (1879)

Significant characters include:

03 Ada
Ida (Princess)

04 Arac
Daly (Dr)
Gama (King)
Hebe
Inez
Jane (Lady)
Kate
Ko-Ko
Lisa
Luiz
Ruth
Zara (Princess)

05 Cyril
Mabel
Point (Jack)
Sophy (Lady)
Tessa
Wells (John Wellington)

06 Angela
Apollo
Becket (Bob)
Bolero (Don Alhambra del)
Giulia
Ludwig
Maybud (Rose)
Meryll (Leonard)
Meryll (Sergeant)

Notary
Peep-Bo
Porter (Rt Hon Sir Joseph)
Psyche (Lady)
Willis (Private)
Yum-Yum

07 Antonio
Blanche (Lady)
Bobstay (Bill)
Casilda
Deadeye (Dick)
Fairfax (Colonel)
Florian
Giorgio
Katisha
Pooh-Bah

08 Annibale
Corcoran (Captain Sir Edward)
Dummkopf (Ernest)
Fiametta
Frederic
Gianetta
Hilarion
Iolanthe
Jellicoe (Julia)
Nanki-Poo
Oakapple (Richard)
Oakapple (Robin)
Palmieri (Giuseppe)

Palmieri (Marco)
Patience
Pish-Tush
Shadbolt (Wilfred)
Strephon
Vittoria

09 Bunthorne (Reginald)
Francesco
Grosvenor (Archibald)
Plaza-Toro (Duke of)
Rackstraw (Ralph)
Sangazure (Aline)
Sangazure (Lady)

10 Ben Hashbaz
Carruthers (Dame)
Hildebrand (King)
Monte Carlo (Prince of)
Murgatroyd (Sir Despard)
Murgatroyd (Sir Ruthven)
Pirate King
Tannhäuser (Dr)

11 Mad Margaret
Pointdextre (Alexis)
Pointdextre (Sir Marmaduke)

12 Cholmondeley (Sir Richard)

14 Von Krakenfeldt (Baroness)

15 Little Buttercup

girl *see* **name**

gland

Glands include:

05 lymph
ovary
06 cortex

pineal
thymus
07 adrenal

eccrine
mammary
medulla

parotid
thyroid
08 apocrine

exocrine	testicle	lachrymal	pituitary
pancreas	**09** endocrine	lymph node	sebaceous
prostate	holocrine	merocrine	**11** parathyroid

glass

Glass sizes include:

03 pot	**05** bobby	**07** butcher
six	middy	sleever
ten	seven	**08** half pint
04 pint	**06** handle	schooner

gods *see* **drink; Hinduism; mythology**

Goethe, Johann Wolfgang von (1749–1832)

Significant works include:

05 *Faust* (1808/1832)

06 'Autumn' (1775)
Egmont (1788)
Stella (1776)

07 *Clavigo* (1774)
'May Song' (1775)
Novelle (1828)
Pandora (1810)
Satyros (1817)

09 'Achilleis' (1808)
'To the Moon' (1778)

10 *Prometheus* (1830)
'The Erl-King' (1782)

11 *The Agitated* (1817)
'Tour in Italy' (1816–17)

12 'Reineke Fuchs' (1794)
Roman Elegies (1795)
Siege of Mainz (1820–21)

13 'Alexis and Dora' (1797)
'Reynard the Fox' (1794)
The Lover's Whim (1779)
Torquato Tasso (1790)

14 *Erwin and Elmire* (1775)
'French Campaign' (1820–21)
'New Love, New Life' (1775–76)
Poetry and Truth (1811–33)
The Accomplices (1776)

The Gross-Cophta (1791)

16 'To Coachman Kronos' (1789)
Trilogy of Passion (1827)
West-Eastern Divan (1819)

17 *Iphigenia in Tauris* (1787)
'The Bride of Corinth' (1798)
The Burgher-General (1793)

18 'Hermann and Dorothea' (1797)
The Natural Daughter (1803)
'Welcome and Farewell' (1775)

19 *Götz von Berlichingen* (1773)

21 *Claudine von Villa Bella* (1788)
'Only He Who Knows Longing' (1795–96)
The Elective Affinities (1809)
'The Wanderer's Night Song' (1776)
'The Wanderer's Storm Song' (1772)

22 'The Sorcerer's Apprentice' (1798)

23 'Spirit Song over the Waters' (1779)

24 *The Metamorphosis of Plants* (1790)
The Sorrows of Young Werther (1774)

25 *Wilhelm Meister's Wanderings* (1821)

29 *Wilhelm Meister's Apprenticeship* (1795)

32 *Wilhelm Meister's Theatrical Mission* (1795–96)

34 'Winter Journey over the Hartz Mountains' (1777)

golf

Golf clubs include:

04 iron	cleek	bulger
wood	spoon	driver
05 baffy	wedge	jigger
blade	**06** brassy	mashie

putter
07 blaster
 brassie
 midiron
 niblick
08 long iron
09 midmashie

sand wedge
short iron
10 mashie iron
11 belly putter
 driving iron
 fairway wood
 spade mashie

12 putting-cleek
13 mashie niblick
 pitching wedge
 two-ball putter
15 pitching niblick

Golf courses include:

04 Deal (England)
 Eden (England)
05 Troon (Scotland)
06 Manito (USA)
 Merion (USA)
 Skokie (USA)
07 Balgove (Scotland)
 Buffalo (USA)
 Hoylake (England)
 Jubilee (Scotland)
 Medinah (USA)
 Newport (USA)
 Oak Hill (USA)
 Oakmont (USA)
 Oak Tree (USA)
 Prince's (Scotland)
 Sahalee (USA)
08 Bethesda (USA)
 Birkdale (England)
 Blue Hill (USA)
 Glen View (USA)
 Portland (USA)
 Sandwich (England)
 Valhalla (USA)

09 Aronimink (USA)
 Baltimore (USA)
 Baltusrol (USA)
 Bellerive (USA)
 Brookline (USA)
 Englewood (USA)
 Hazeltine (USA)
 Inverness (USA)
 Minikahda (USA)
 Muirfield (Scotland)
 New Course (Scotland)
 Old Course (Scotland)
 Onwentsia (USA)
 Pinehurst (USA)
 Prestwick (Scotland)
 St Andrews (Scotland)
 The Belfry (Scotland)
 Turnberry (Scotland)
10 Canterbury (USA)
 Carnoustie (Scotland)
 Garden City (USA)
 Royal Troon (Scotland)
 Shoal Creek (USA)
 Tanglewood (USA)
 Winged Foot (USA)

11 Cherry Hills (USA)
 Kemper Lakes (USA)
 Miami Valley (USA)
 Musselburgh (Scotland)
 Olympic Club (USA)
 Pebble Beach (USA)
 Strathtyrum (Scotland)
12 Crooked Stick (USA)
 Laurel Valley (USA)
 Oakland Hills (USA)
13 Northwood Club (USA)
 Olympia Fields (USA)
 Royal Birkdale (England)
 Royal Portrush (Northern
  Ireland)
 Southern Hills (USA)
14 Keller Golf Club (USA)
 Myopia Hunt Club (USA)
 NCR Country Club (USA)
 Pelham Golf Club (USA)
15 Augusta National (USA)
 Chicago Golf Club (USA)
 Shinnecock Hills (USA)

Golfers include:

03 Els (Ernie; 1969– , South African)
 Wie (Michelle; 1989– , US)
04 Berg (Patty; 1918–2006, US)
 Daly (John; 1966– , US)
 Love (Davis, III; 1964– , US)
 Lyle (Sandy; 1958– , Scottish)
 Park (Willie, Jnr; 1864–1925, Scottish)
 Park (Willie, Snr; 1834–1903, Scottish)
 Webb (Karrie; 1974– , Australian)
05 Braid (James; 1870–1950, Scottish)
 Faldo (Nick; 1957– , English)
 Furyk (James 'Jim'; 1970– , US)
 Hagen (Walter; 1892–1969, US)
 Hogan (Ben; 1912–97, US)
 Jones (Bobby; 1902–71, US)
 Locke (Bobby; 1917–87, South African)
 Lopez (Nancy; 1957– , US)
 Singh (Vijay; 1963– , Fijian)
 Snead (Sam; 1912–2002, US)

 Woods (Tiger; 1976– , US)
06 Alliss (Peter; 1931– , English)
 Cotton (Sir Henry; 1907–87, English)
 Curtis (Ben; 1977– , US)
 Davies (Laura; 1963– , English)
 Garcia (Sergio; 1980– , Spanish)
 Goosen (Retief; 1969– , South African)
 Langer (Bernhard; 1957– , German)
 Morris (Old Tom; 1821–1908, Scottish)
 Morris (Young Tom; 1851–75, Scottish)
 Nelson (Byron, Jnr; 1912–2006, US)
 Norman (Greg; 1955– , Australian)
 Ogilvy (Geoff; 1977– , Australian)
 O'Meara (Mark; 1957– , US)
 Palmer (Arnold; 1929– , US)
 Player (Gary; 1936– , South African)
 Taylor (J H; 1871–1963, English)
 Vardon (Harry; 1870–1937, British)
 Watson (Tom; 1949– , US)

07 Cabrera (Angel; 1969– , Argentine)
 Charles (Bob; 1936– , New Zealand)
 Couples (Fred; 1959– , US)
 Creamer (Paula; 1986– , US)
 Jacklin (Tony; 1944– , English)
 Johnson (Zack; 1976– , US)
 Sarazen (Gene; 1902–99, US)
 Strange (Curtis; 1955– , US)
 Thomson (Peter; 1929– , Australian)
 Trevino (Lee; 1939– , US)
 Woosnam (Ian; 1958– , Welsh)
 Zoeller (Fuzzy; 1951– , US)

08 Campbell (Michael; 1969– , New Zealand)

 Hamilton (Todd; 1965– , US)
 Immelman (Trevor; 1979– , South
  African)
 Nicklaus (Jack; 1940– , US)
 Olazábal (José-María; 1966– , Spanish)
 Torrance (Sam; 1953– , Scottish)
 Westwood (Lee; 1973– , English)
 Zaharias (Babe; 1914–56, US)

09 Mickelson (Phil; 1970– , US)
 Sorenstam (Annika; 1970– , Swedish)

10 Harrington (Padraig; 1971– , Irish)

11 Ballesteros (Seve; 1957– , Spanish)
 Montgomerie (Colin; 1963– , Scottish)

Golf terms include:

03 cup
 cut
 fat
 lie
 par
 pin
 tee
 toe
 top

04 away
 card
 chip
 club
 draw
 drop
 fade
 flag
 fore
 heel
 hook
 iron
 loft
 plug
 pull
 push
 putt
 sole
 thin
 trap
 turn
 wood
 yips

05 apron
 baffy
 bogey
 break
 carry
 divot
 drive
 eagle
 flier

 green
 gutty
 hosel
 lay up
 links
 Major
 pitch
 punch
 rough
 shaft
 shank
 skins
 skull
 slice
 spoon
 swing
 tap-in
 wedge

06 balata
 birdie
 blades
 borrow
 bounce
 bunker
 caddie
 chip-in
 dimple
 dog leg
 dormie
 driver
 fringe
 gimmie
 hazard
 honour
 jigger
 mashie
 Nassau
 putter
 relief
 socket
 stance

 stymie
 tee box
 tee off

07 address
 air shot
 blaster
 brassie
 fairway
 gallery
 get down
 Haskell
 hole out
 low side
 midiron
 niblick
 pin high
 putt out
 scratch
 tee shot
 twosome

08 approach
 back nine
 bestball
 club face
 clubhead
 duck hook
 first cut
 flop shot
 fourball
 foursome
 free drop
 handicap
 high side
 lob wedge
 long iron
 mulligan
 overclub
 Road Hole
 Ryder Cup
 sand save
 sand trap

whipping

09 albatross
backswing
Crow's Nest
downswing
featherie
flagstick
front nine
grand slam
hole in one
matchplay
medalplay
overshoot
pitch mark
Rae's Creek
sand wedge
short game
short iron
sink a putt
stone dead
sweet spot

See also **sport**

tee marker
the Maiden
underclub
up-and-down

10 Amen Corner
betterball
bump and run
cavity back
fore caddie
greensomes
hanging lie
Hell Bunker
Stableford
stimpmeter
strokeplay
unplayable
Vardon grip

11 belly putter
casual water
compression
driving iron

fairway wood
gutta-percha
leaderboard
out of bounds
pin position
pitch and run
provisional
stroke index
Valley of Sin

12 approach shot

13 Challenge Tour
explosion shot
mashie niblick
pitching wedge
preferred lies
Texas scramble
two-ball putter

14 Eisenhower Tree

15 cross-handed grip
overlapping grip

goose

Geese include:

04 bean	Ross's	greylag	**10** blue-winged
kelp		Orinoco	pink-footed
nene	**06** Andean		spur-winged
snow	Canada	**08** barnacle	
swan	Embden	Egyptian	**11** red-breasted
	upland	Hawaiian	ruddy-headed
05 Brent		Toulouse	
pygmy	**07** Chinese		**12** white-fronted
	emperor	**09** bar-headed	

government

Government systems include:

05 junta	communism	plutocracy
06 empire	democracy	**11** triumvirate
07 kingdom	despotism	**12** commonwealth
08 monarchy	theocracy	dictatorship
republic	**10** absolutism	
09 autocracy	federation	
	hierocracy	

UK government departments include:

02 DH	MoD	DECC
03 CPS	NIO	DFID
CSA	PCO	DIUS
DCA	SEU	HMRC
DfT	**04** BERR	**05** Defra
DWP	DCLG	**08** Treasury
FCO	DCMS	**09** Exchequer
FSA	DCSF	

Met Office	**11** Film Council	Law Commission
10 HM Treasury	Wales Office	**14** Scotland Office
Home Office	**13** Cabinet Office	**15** Audit Commission

UK government Cabinet positions:

13 Lord Privy Seal
   Prime Minister

22 First Lord of the Treasury

24 Chancellor of the Exchequer
   Secretary of State for Wales

25 Leader of the House of Commons
   Secretary of State for Health

26 Minister for the Civil Service
   Secretary of State for Defence

27 Chief Secretary to the Treasury
   Secretary of State for Scotland

28 Secretary of State for Transport

29 Minister for Women and Equalities

34 Secretary of State for Northern Ireland
   Secretary of State for Work and Pensions

36 Secretary of State for the Home
   Department

39 Secretary of State for Culture, Media and
   Sport

41 Secretary of State for Energy and Climate
   Change

43 Secretary of State for International
   Development
   Secretary of State for Justice and Lord
   Chancellor

45 Secretary of State for Children, Schools and
   Families

48 Secretary of State for Communities and
   Local Government
   Secretary of State for Foreign and
   Commonwealth Affairs

49 Secretary of State for Environment, Food and
   Rural Affairs

50 Secretary of State for Innovation,
   Universities and Skills

51 Leader of the House of Lords and Lord
   President of the Council

56 Secretary of State for Business, Enterprise
   and Regulatory Reform

US government departments include:

02	ED	DOC	FPA	**04** ONAP
	OA	DOD	FBI	OSTP
	VA	DOE	FDA	USDA
03	BEA	DOI	FSA	USTR
	BIA	DOJ	HHS	WHMO
	CEA	DOL	HUD	**05** USCIS
	CEQ	DOS	IRS	**06** Senate
	CIA	DOT	NSA	**08** Congress
	DHS	DPC	NSC	**10** White House
	DIA	EOP	OMB	

See also **legislation**; **office**; **parliament**; **politics**; **republic**

governor

Types of governor include:

03 Ban	**06** eparch	nomarch	**09** beglerbeg
bey	exarch	podestà	castellan
dey	legate	voivode	proconsul
04 khan	satrap	**08** burgrave	**10** adelantado
naik	tuchun	ethnarch	proveditor
vali	**07** alcaide	hospodar	**11** stadtholder
05 hakim	catapan	pentarch	
mudir	harmost	subahdar	

Colonial governors of New South Wales:

04 King (Captain Philip Gidley; 1758–1808)

05 Bligh (Captain William; 1754–1817)
Gipps (Sir George; 1791–1847)

06 Bourke (Major-General Richard; 1777–1855)
Hunter (Captain John; 1737–1821)

07 Darling (Lieutenant-General Ralph; 1772–1858)
Denison (Sir William; 1804–71)
FitzRoy (Sir Charles; 1796–1858)
Phillip (Captain Arthur; 1738–1814)

08 Brisbane (Sir Thomas; 1777–1855)

09 Macquarie (Colonel Lachlan; 1762–1824)

Governors-general of Australia:

04 Kerr (Sir John; 1974–77)
Slim (Field-Marshal Sir William; 1953–60)

05 Bryce (Ms Quentin; 2008–)
Casey (Richard Gardiner, Baron; 1961–65)
Cowen (Sir Zelman; 1977–82)
Deane (Sir William; 1996–2001)

06 Denman (Thomas, Baron; 1911–14)
Dudley (William Humble Ward, Earl of; 1908–11)
Gowrie (Alexander Hore-Ruthven, Baron, 1936–45)
Hayden (William; 1989–96)
Isaacs (Sir Isaac; 1931–36)
McKell (Sir William; 1947–53)

07 De L'Isle (William, Viscount; 1961–65)

Forster (Henry William, Baron; 1920–25)
Hasluck (Sir Paul; 1969–74)
Jeffery (Major-General Michael; 2003–08)
Stephen (Sir Ninian; 1982–89)

08 Hopetoun (John Adrian Louis Hope, Earl of)
Tennyson (Hallam, Baron; 1902–03)

09 Dunrossil (William, Viscount; 1960–61)
Northcote (Henry, Baron; 1904–08)

10 Gloucester (Prince Henry, Duke of; 1945–47)
Stonehaven (Sir John Lawrence Baird, Baron; 1925–31)

12 Hollingworth (Dr Peter; 2001–03)

13 Munro-Ferguson (Sir Ronald; 1914–20)

Governors of New Zealand:

04 Grey (Sir George, 1848–53, 1861–68)

05 Bowen (Sir George Ferguson, 1868–73)

06 Browne (Colonel Thomas Robert Gore, 1855–61)
Gordon (Sir Arthur Hamilton, 1880–82)
Hobson (Sir William, 1841–42)
Onslow (Earl of, 1889–92)

07 FitzRoy (Sir Robert, 1843–45)
Glasgow (Earl of, 1892–97)

Jervois (William Francis Drummond, 1883–89)
Plunket (Lord, 1904–10)

08 Normanby (Marquess of, 1875–79)
Ranfurly (Earl of, 1897–1904)
Robinson (Sir Hercules George Robert, 1879–80)

09 Fergusson (Sir James, 1873–74)
Islington (Lord; 1910–12)
Liverpool (Earl of, 1912–17)

Governors-general of New Zealand:

06 Cobham (Charles George Lyttleton; 1957–62)
Galway (Earl of; 1935–41)
Newall (Cyril Louis Norton; 1941–46)
Norrie (Lord; 1952–57)
Reeves (Paul Alfred; 1985–90)
Tizard (Catherine; 1990–96)

07 Beattie (David Stuart; 1980–85)
Porritt (Arthur Espie; 1967–72)

08 Blundell (Edward Denis; 1972–77)

Freyberg (Bernard Cyril; 1946–52)
Holyoake (Keith Jacka; 1977–80)
Jellicoe (John Henry Rushworth; 1920–24)

09 Bledisloe (Charles Bathurst; 1930–35)
Fergusson (Bernard; 1962–67)
Fergusson (Charles; 1924–30)
Liverpool (Earl of; 1917–20)

10 Cartwright (Silvia, 2001–06)
Hardie Boys (Michael; 1996–2001)

grace

The Three Graces:

06 Aglaia
   Thalia

10 Euphrosyne

grade *see* nurse

grammar

Parts of speech include:

01 a	prep	08 singular	preposition
n	verb	09 adjective	12 abbreviation
v	06 adnoun	gerundive	interjection
02 vb	adverb	10 common noun	13 auxiliary verb
vi	gerund	connective	14 transitive verb
vt	plural	copulative	15 definite article
03 adj	prefix	participle	relative pronoun
adv	suffix	proper noun	
art	07 article	11 conjunction	
04 noun	pronoun	phrasal verb	

Grammatical cases include:

06 dative	ablative	inessive	comitative
essive	adessive	locative	nominative
	allative	vocative	possessive
07 elative	genitive	09 objective	subjective
08 abessive	illative	10 accusative	11 translative

Grammatical tenses include:

02 pt	present	past perfect	present simple
03 pat	08 preterit	12 future simple	simple present
04 past	09 imperfect	gnomic aorist	14 past continuous
06 aorist	preterite	past historic	present perfect
future	10 pluperfect	simple future	15 paragogic future
07 perfect	11 conditional	13 future perfect	

Grand Prix *see* racing: motor racing

grape *see* wine

grass

Grasses include:

03 rye	oats	couch
04 bent	reed	maize
cane	rice	paddy
corn	05 arrow	wheat
knot	beard	06 bamboo
moor	brome	barley

fescue
marram
meadow
melick
millet
pampas
rattan
switch
twitch
07 esparto
papyrus

See also **plant**

quaking
sacaton
sorghum
timothy
wild oat
08 cat's-tail
dog's-tail
kangaroo
ryegrass
09 buckwheat
cocksfoot

marijuana
sugar cane
10 Italian rye
11 vernal grass
12 Kentucky blue
squirrel-tail
13 meadow foxtail
15 English ryegrass
Italian ryegrass

Great Lakes *see* **lake**

Greece

Cities and notable towns in Greece include:

05 Volos
06 Athens
Lárisa

Patras
07 Corinth
Knossos

Larissa
Piraeus
08 Iráklion

09 Heraklion
11 Peristérion
12 Thessaloníki

Administrative divisions of Greece, with regional capitals:

05 Crete (Heraklion)
Kríti (Heraklion)
06 Attica (Athens)
Attikí (Athens)
Epirus (Ioannina)
Ípiros (Ioannina)
08 Thessaly (Larissa)
09 Thessalía (Larissa)
10 West Greece (Patras)
11 Iónioi Nísoi (Corfu)
North Aegean (Mytilene)
Peleponnese (Tripolis)
South Aegean (Hermoupolis)

Stereá Ellás (Lamia)
12 Dhytikí Ellás (Patras)
Pelopónnisos (Tripolis)
13 Central Greece (Lamia)
Ionian Islands (Corfu)
Nótion Aiyaíon (Hermoupolis)
West Macedonia (Kozani)
14 Vóreion Aiyaíon (Mytilene)
16 Central Macedonia (Thessaloníki)
17 Dhytikí Makedhonía (Kozani)
Kedrikí Makedhonía (Thessaloníki)
22 East Macedonia and Thrace (Comotini)
28 Anatolikí Makedhonía kaí Thráki (Comotini)

Greek landmarks include:

05 Agora
Delos
Thera
Thíra
06 Delphi
Rhodes

07 Heraion
Metéora
Mt Athos
Mystras
Olympia
Theseum

09 Acropolis
Epidaurus
Mt Olympus
Parthenon
Santoríni
11 Mt Parnassus

12 Samaria Gorge
Tower of Winds
13 Palace of Minos

Greeks include:

04 Esop (6c BC, author)
05 Aesop (6c BC, author)
Galen (c.130–c.201 AD, physician)
Homer (c.8c BC, poet)

Plato (c.428–c.348 BC, philosopher)
06 Euclid (fl.300 BC, mathematician)
Lucian (c.117–c.180 AD, satirist)
Pindar (c.518–c.438 BC, poet)

Sappho (c.610–c.580 BC, poet)
Thales (c.620–c.555 BC, philosopher)

07 Hypatia (c.370–415 AD, philosopher)
Pytheas (of Marseilles; 4c BC, navigator)

08 Damocles (4c BC, courtier)
Epicurus (c.341–270 BC, philosopher)
Plotinus (c.205–270 AD, philosopher)
Plutarch (c.46–c.120 AD, historian)
Polybius (c.205–c.123 BC, historian)
Socrates (469–399 BC, philosopher)
Xenophon (c.435–c.354 BC, historian)

09 Aeschylus (c.525–c.456 BC, playwright)
Aristotle (384–322 BC, philosopher and scientist)
Euripides (484/480–406 BC, playwright)
Herodotus (c.485–425 BC, historian)
Sophocles (c.496–405 BC, playwright)

10 Archimedes (c.287–212 BC, mathematician)
Democritus (c.460–c.370 BC, philosopher)
Empedocles (fl.c.450 BC, philosopher and poet)
Heraclitus (d.460 BC, philosopher)
Hipparchos (c.180–125 BC, astronomer and mathematician)
Hipparchus (c.180–125 BC, astronomer and mathematician)
Praxiteles (4c BC, sculptor)
Protagoras (c.490–c.420 BC, philosopher)
Pythagoras (c.580–500 BC, philosopher)
Theocritus (c.310–250 BC, poet)
Thucydides (c.460–c.400 BC, historian)
Xenophanes (c.570–c.480 BC, philosopher)

11 Hippocrates (c.460–377/359 BC, physician)

12 Aristophanes (c.448–c.385 BC, playwright)
Theophrastus (c.372–c.286 BC, philosopher)

See also **Balkans**; **fable**; **history**; **Homer**; **mathematics**; **philosophy**; **play**; **poetry**

Greek *see* **alphabet**; **fate**; **Greece**; **muse**; **mythology**

green

Shades of green include:

04 jade	sludge	sea green	chartreuse
lime	**07** avocado	viridian	rifle green
sage	celadon	**09** moss green	terre verte
teal	corbeau	Nile green	**11** bottle green
vert	emerald	pistachio	forest green
05 lovat	**08** eau de Nil	turquoise	**12** Lincoln green
olive	pea-green	**10** apple-green	
06 reseda	sap-green	aquamarine	**14** turquoise-green

See also **party**; **pigment**

grey

Shades of grey include:

03 ash	slate	**07** grizzle	platinum
04 drab	steel	**08** blue-grey	**09** field grey
05 liard	stone	charcoal	
liart	taupe	dove grey	**10** dapple-grey
lyart	**06** isabel	feldgrau	dove-colour
pearl	pewter	graphite	Payne's grey
perse	silver	gridelin	pigeon grey

gulf

Gulfs include:

04 Aden (Yemen)
Huon (Papua New Guinea)
Lion (France)
Moro (Philippines)

Oman (Oman)
Riga (Latvia/Estonia)
Siam (Thailand/Cambodia)
Suez (Egypt)

05 Ancud (Chile)
Aqaba (Jordan)
Cádiz (Spain)
Davao (Philippines)
Dulce (Costa Rica)
Gabes (Tunisia)
Gaeta (Italy)
Genoa (Italy)
Kutch (India)
Lions (France)
Maine (USA/Canada)
Panay (Philippines)
Papua (Papua New Guinea)
Penas (Chile)
Ragay (Philippines)
Saros (Turkey)
Sidra (Libya)
Sirte (Libya)
Tunis (Tunisia)

06 Aegina (Greece)
Alaska (USA)
Cambay (India)
Chania (Crete, Greece)
Darien (Panama)
Gdansk (Poland)
Guinea (Africa)
Kavala (Greece)
Mannar (India/Sri Lanka)
Mexico (Mexico)
Naples (Italy)
Nicoya (Costa Rica)
Orosei (Italy)
Panama (Panama)
Parita (Panama)
Patras (Greece)
St Malo (France)
Tonkin (China/Vietnam)
Triste (Venezuela)
Venice (Italy)

07 Almeria (Spain)
Arabian (Middle East)
Asinara (Italy)
Boothia (Canada)
Bothnia (Sweden/Finland)
Cazones (Cuba)
Corinth (Greece)
Edremit (Turkey)
Exmouth (Australia)
Finland (Finland/Estonia)
Fonseca (Honduras)
Hauraki (New Zealand)
Kachchh (India)
Lepanto (Greece)
Obskaya (Russia)
Persian (Middle East)
Salerno (Italy)

San Blas (Panama)
Saronic (Greece)
Spencer (Australia)
Taranto (Italy)
The Gulf (Middle East)
Trieste (Italy)
Udskaya (Russia)

08 Amundsen (Canada)
Batabano (Cuba)
Cagliari (Italy)
Campeche (Mexico)
Chiriqui (Panama)
Honduras (Honduras)
Khambhat (India)
Liaotung (China)
Lingayen (Philippines)
Martaban (Myanmar)
Mosquito (Panama)
Oristano (Italy)
Papagayo (Costa Rica)
San Jorge (Argentina)
Taganrog (Russia/Ukraine)
Thailand (Thailand/Cambodia)
Valencia (Spain)

09 Buor-Khaya (Russia)
Corcovado (Chile)
Dvinskaya (Russia)
Guayaquil (Ecuador)
Queen Maud (Canada)
San Matias (Argentina)
San Miguel (Panama)
St Florent (Corsica, France)
St Vincent (Australia)
Van Diemen (Australia)
Venezuela (Venezuela)

10 California (Mexico)
Chaunskaya (Russia)
Cheshskaya (Russia)
Coronation (Canada)
Kyparissia (Greece)
Policastro (Italy)
St Lawrence (Canada)
Tazovskaya (Russia)
Thermaikos (Greece)

11 Carpentaria (Australia)
Guacanayabo (Cuba)
Manfredonia (Italy)
Pechorskaya (Russia)
Strymonikos (Greece)
Tehuantepec (Mexico)

12 los Mosquitos (Panama)
Penzhinskaya (Russia)

13 Baydaratskaya (Russia)
Santa Catalina (USA)

15 Joseph Bonaparte (Australia)

gun

Guns include:

02 MG
03 air
gas
gat
ray
six
Uzi
04 AK-47
Bren
burp
Colt®
hand
pump
punt
shot
sten
stun
05 baton
field

fusil
Lewis
Maxim
rifle
siege
spear
tommy
06 airgun
Archie
Bofors
cannon
mortar
musket
needle
pistol
pom-pom
Purdey®
Quaker
turret

07 bazooka
carbine
chopper
gatling
Long Tom
machine
pounder
scatter
08 air rifle
amusette
arquebus
elephant
falconet
firelock
howitzer
magazine
pederero
petronel
revolver

starting
Sterling
09 Archibald
Big Bertha
flintlock
harquebus
10 black Maria
demi-cannon
six shooter
submachine
Winchester®
11 blunderbuss
four-pounder
half-pounder
Kalashnikov
12 fowling-piece
mitrailleuse
three-pounder

See also **weapon**

gymnastics

Gymnastics events include:

04 ball
beam
05 clubs
floor
rings

vault
07 high bar
08 tumbling
10 horse vault

uneven bars
11 balance beam
pommel horse
12 parallel bars
trampolining

13 horizontal bar
14 asymmetric bars
floor exercises
side horse vault
sports aerobics

Gymnasts include:

03 Kim (Nellie; 1957– , Russian)
Ono (Takashi; 1931– , Japanese)
06 Korbut (Olga Valentinovna; 1956– ,
Belarussian)
Liukin (Nastia; 1989– , Russian/US)
Miller (Shannon; 1977– , US)
Retton (Mary Lou; 1968– , US)
07 Johnson (Shawn; 1992– , US)
Scherbo (Vitaly; 1972– , Belarussian)
Yang Wei (1980– , Chinese)

08 Comaneci (Nadia; 1961– , Romanian)
Ditiatin (Aleksandr; 1957– , Russian)
Kanayeva (Yevgeniya; 1990– , Russian)
Latynina (Larissa; 1935– , Ukrainian)
Shakhlin (Boris; 1932–2008, Ukrainian)
09 Andrianov (Nikolai; 1952– , Russian)
Cáslavská (Vera; 1942– , Czech)
10 Boginskaya (Svetlana; 1973– , Belarussian)
Turischeva (Lyudmila; 1952– , Russian)

Gymnastics terms include:

04 beam
Endo
nail
pike
rudi
tuck

05 cross
flair
floor
giant
rings
salto
stick

twist
vault
06 aerial
bridge
Cuervo
Kovacs

layout

07 element
flyaway
Gaylord
Gienger
Stalder

08 dismount
flic-flac
rotation
round-off
straddle
whip back

09 all-around
apparatus

See also **sport**

cartwheel
execution
handstand
hip circle
leg circle
pirouette
Tsukahara
Yurchenko

10 double back
handspring
somersault
uneven bars

11 balance beam
double twist

pommel horse
Swedish fall

12 back walkover
compulsories
parallel bars

13 back-in, full-out
front walkover
full-in, back-out
half-in, half-out
horizontal bar
inverted cross

14 asymmetric bars
back handspring

15 front handspring

H

hair

Hairstyles include:

02 DA

03 bob
bun
wig

04 Afro
crop
perm
shed

05 bangs
braid
plait
quiff

weave

06 curled
fringe
mullet
pouffe
toupee

07 beehive
bunches
chignon
cowlick
crewcut
crimped
Mohican

pageboy
pigtail
shingle
tonsure
topknot

08 bouffant
combover
corn rows
Eton crop
frisette
ponytail
ringlets
skinhead

undercut

09 duck's arse
hair-piece
Hoxton fin
pompadour
sideburns

10 backcombed
dreadlocks
Marcel wave
sideboards

11 French pleat

13 hair extension

Terms to do with hair include:

03 bob
cue
cut
dod
dye
gel
jel
not
pow
wax
wig

04 bald
body
clip
coif
comb
crop
curl
down
fine
friz
grey
grip
hank
kesh
lank
lice
lock
mane
must
nott
perm

pouf
tête
tint
tips
tong
trim
tuft
wavy
wiry

05 baldy
bangs
black
blond
bluey
braid
brown
brush
crimp
curly
foils
frizz
hairy
heare
henna
layer
meche
moult
moust
mousy
muist
queue
quiff

rinse
roots
sandy
serum
shade
shaft
shine
short
slick
slide
snood
tease
thick
toner
toque
tress

06 auburn
bagwig
baldie
barber
barnet
blonde
bobble
bodkin
brunet
coarse
colour
crease
crinal
fillet
flaxen
fringe

frizzy
ginger
greasy
haffet
haffit
hairdo
hearie
kangha
lacker
mousey
mousse
peruke
pomade
pompom
pompon
pouffe
ribbon
roller
silver
tangle
tettix
tie-wig
titian
toorie
tourie
wigged

07 balding
bandeau
blow-dry
bristle
carroty
cowlick
crinate
crinite
crinose
flaught
flyaway
foretop
frizzle
frizzly
greying
haircut
hair gel
hair net
hair oil
hennaed
hirsute
keratin
lacquer
melanin
parting
periwig
peruked
pileous
pin curl
pompoon
rat-tail
redhead

ringlet
shampoo
streaks
stylist
texture
tonsure
topknot
tow-head
tressed
undight
upstare
upswept
weaving
wet-look
xerasia

08 alopecia
ash-blond
back-comb
back-hair
baldpate
barrette
bar slide
bleached
bouffant
brunette
canities
chestnut
clippers
coiffeur
coiffure
combover
cordless
cow's lick
crinated
dandruff
demi-wave
diffuser
elflocks
fixature
follicle
forelock
full-head
grizzled
hair band
hairless
hairline
hair-wave
half-head
headring
lovelock
peroxide
rat's-tail
receding
roulette
scissors
scrunchy
side comb
sidelock

split end
straight
strammel
strummel
volumize
wig block
wig-maker

09 accessory
Alice band
ash-blonde
bandoline
bleaching
blue rinse
Brylcreem®
capillary
chevelure
coiffeuse
colourant
curlpaper
finger-dry
fright wig
hairbrush
hairdryer
hairpiece
hair slide
hairspray
hairstyle
hair-waver
headdress
hirsutism
Kirbigrip®
lowlights
madarosis
mop-headed
papillote
redheaded
scalp lock
scrunchie
tow-headed
trichosis
water wave

10 bad hair day
bald-headed
bathing cap
cockernony
curled-pate
detangling
extensions
fair-haired
fair-headed
finger wave
hair-powder
hairsetter
highlights
leiotrichy
long-haired
manageable

perruquier
piliferous
pocket-comb
scrunch-dry
transplant
trichology
widow's peak

11 banana slide
bottle-blond
conditioner
crinigerous
flame-haired
hairdresser
hairstylist
redding-comb
redding-kame

side-parting
tow-coloured
white-haired
white-headed

12 bottle-blonde
brilliantine
Cain-coloured
close-cropped
crimping-iron
curling tongs
cymotrichous
feather razor
hair restorer
leiotrichous
straightener
trichologist

13 centre-parting
corkscrew curl
deep condition
Judas-coloured
lissotrichous
pepper-and-salt
permanent wave
platinum-blond
straighteners

14 shoulder-length

15 deep conditioner
full-bottomed wig
permanent colour
strawberry blond
styling products

Terms to do with facial hair include:

05 beard
pluck
razor

06 goatee
tweeze
waxing

07 epilate
goateed
shaving
stubble

08 bumfluff

depilate
stubbled
sugaring
tweezers

09 depilator
moustache
sideburns

10 aftershave
depilation
depilatory
face-fungus
pogonotomy

shaving gel

11 clean-shaven
shaving foam
shaving-soap

12 electrolysis
shaving-brush
shaving-stick
side whiskers

13 eyebrow pencil
eyelash curler

15 designer stubble

hall *see* **college**

Handel, George Frideric (1685–1759)

Significant works include:

04 *Nero* (1705)
Saul (1739)

05 *Serse* (1738)
Silla (1713)
Teseo (1713)

06 *Admeto* (1726)
Alcina (1735)
Almira (1705)
Daphne (1708)
Esther (1718)
Samson (1743)
Semele (1744)
Xerxes (1738)

07 *Amadigi* (1715)
Athalia (1733)
Deborah (1733)
Jephtha (1752)

Messiah (1742)
Orlando (1733)
Rinaldo (1711)
Rodrigo (1707)
Solomon (1749)

08 *Deidamia* (1741)
Florindo (1706)
Hercules (1745)
Theodora (1750)

09 *Agrippina* (1709)
Ariodante (1735)
Radamisto (1720)
Tamerlano (1724)

10 *Alessandro* (1726)
Floridante (1721)
Water Music (1717)

11 *Pastoral Ode* (1740)

12 *Giulio Cesare* (1724)
Il Pastor Fido (1712/1734)

13 *Israel in Egypt* (1739)

14 *Acis and Galatea*
(1718/1732)
Concerti Grossi (1739)
Grand Concertos (1739)
La Resurrezione (1708)
Zadok the Priest (1727)

15 *Alexander's Feast* (1736)
Judas Maccabaeus (1747)

16 *The Power of Musick*
(1736)

17 *Il Trionfo del Tempo* (1707)
Tolomeo re di Egitto (1728)

Hardy, Thomas (1840–1928)

Significant works include:

10 *A Laodicean* (1881)
Human Shows (1925)

11 *Two on a Tower* (1882)
Wessex Poems (1898)
Wessex Tales (1888)
Winter Words (1928)

14 *Jude the Obscure* (1895)
The Well-Beloved (1897)
The Woodlanders (1887)

15 *A Pair of Blue Eyes* (1873)
Moments of Vision (1917)
The Trumpet-Major (1880)

17 *Desperate Remedies* (1871)

18 *A Group of Noble Dames* (1890)

Life's Little Ironies (1894)

19 *The Hand of Ethelberta* (1876)
Time's Laughingstocks (1909)

20 *Late Lyrics and Earlier* (1922)
The Poor Man and the Lady (unpublished)
The Return of the Native (1878)

21 *Satires of Circumstance* (1914)
Tess of the D'Urbervilles (1891)
Under the Greenwood Tree (1872)

22 *Far from the Madding Crowd* (1874)
The Mayor of Casterbridge (1886)

24 *Poems of the Past and Present* (1901)

36 *The Famous Tragedy of the Queen of Cornwall* (1923)

Significant characters include:

03 Day (Fancy)
Day (Geoffrey)
Oak (Gabriel)
Vye (Eustacia)

04 Caro (Avice)
Donn (Arabella)
Troy (Sergeant Francis 'Frank')
Venn (Diggory)

05 Brook (Rhoda)
Clare (Angel)
Dewey (Reuben)
Dewey (Richard 'Dick')
Graye (Cytherea)
Grebe (Barbara)
Power (Paula)
Robin (Fanny)
Smith (Stephen)
South (Marty)
Trewe (Robert)

06 Fawley (Jude)

Knight (Henry)
Newson (Elizabeth-Jane)

07 Farfrae (Donald)
Garland (Anne)
Le Sueur (Lucetta)
Loveday (John)
Loveday (Robert 'Bob')
Manston (Aeneas)
Maybold (Parson)
Melbury (George)
Melbury (Grace)
Wildeve (Damon)

08 Boldwood (William)
Charmond (Felice)
Derriman (Festus)
Everdene (Bathsheba)
Henchard (Michael)
Newberry (Lizzy)
Ollamoor (Wat 'Mop')
Pierston (Jocelyn)
St Cleeve (Swithin)

Willowes (Edmond)

09 Aldclyffe (Miss)
Bridehead (Susanna Florence Mary 'Sue')
Chickerel (Ethelberta)
Fitzpiers (Edred)
Marchmill (Ella)
Stockdale (Richard)
Swancourt (Elfride)
Yeobright (Clement 'Clym')
Yeobright (Mrs)
Yeobright (Thomasin 'Tamsin')

10 Father Time
Phillotson (Richard)
Springrove (Edward)

11 Constantine (Lady Viviette)
D'Urberville (Alec)
Durbeyfield (Tess)
Winterborne (Giles)

12 Uplandtowers (Earl of)

hare *see* **rabbit**

hat

Hats, headdresses and helmets include:

03 cap
fez
lum
pot
red
sun
taj

tin
top

04 chip
doek
hard
hive

hood
kell
kepi
plug
silk
sola
tall

tête
tile
tire
topi

05 armet
beret

Bronx
busby
crush
derby
gibus
mitre
mutch
pixie
salet
shako
straw
tammy
terai
tiara
topee
toque
tower
tuque

06 basher
basnet
beanie
beaver
bicorn
big-gin
boater
bobble
bonnet
bowler
Breton
casque
castor
chapka
cloche
cocked
cockle
coolie
cornet
fedora
heaume
helmet
hennin
kalpak
mob cap

modius
morion
panama
pileus
pinner
sailor
sallet
shovel
slouch
toorie
topper
trilby
turban
witch's

07 basinet
bicorne
biretta
bycoket
Christy
commode
coronet
Cossack
flat cap
Homburg
kufiyeh
leghorn
montero
morrion
murrion
petasus
picture
pillbox
plateau
pork-pie
Ramilie
scarlet
skid lid
steeple
Stetson®
sundown
tarbush
tricorn

08 balmoral
bearskin
bongrace
burganet
burgonet
chaperon
Christie
coiffure
fontange
fool's cap
gimme cap
head tire
kaffiyeh
keffiyeh
knapscal
mushroom
nightcap
Ramilies
Ramillie
ship tire
skullcap
sombrero
stephane
tarboosh
tarboush
thrummed
tricorne
yarmulka

09 Balaclava
billycock
broad-brim
cock's-comb
dunce's cap
Dunstable
forage cap
glengarry
headpiece
jockey cap
knapscull
knapskull
muffin-cap
peaked cap
porringer

Ramillies
school cap
sou'wester
stovepipe
sun bonnet
tarpaulin
ten-gallon
war bonnet

10 balibuntal
blue-bonnet
chimney pot
cockernony
college cap
hunting-cap
Kilmarnock
pith helmet
poke bonnet
sola helmet

11 baseball cap
cabbage-tree
chapeau-bras
crash helmet
deerstalker
Dolly Varden
kamelaukion
mortarboard
pickelhaube
smoke helmet
stocking cap
Tam o' Shanter
trencher cap

12 cheesecutter
fore-and-after
hummle bonnet
Scotch bonnet
steeple-crown
toorie bonnet

13 feather bonnet

14 Kilmarnock cowl
pressure helmet

15 Balaclava helmet

See also **clothes**

Haydn, Joseph (1732–1809)

Significant works include:

03 'Hen' (Symphony; 1785)

04 'Bear' (Symphony; 1786)
'Bird' (String Quartet; 1781)
'Fire' (Symphony; c.1778)
'Hunt' (Symphony; 1781)
'Joke' (String Quartet; 1781)
'Lark' (String Quartet; 1790)

05 'Clock' (Symphony; 1794)

'Feuer' (Symphony; c.1778)
'Queen' (Symphony; 1785)
'Razor' (String Quartet; 1788)
'Rider' (String Quartet; 1793)

06 'Laudon' (Symphony; c.1778)
'Le Midi' (Symphony; c.1761)
'Le Soir' (Symphony; c.1761)
'London' (Symphony; 1795)

'Midday' (Symphony; c.1761)
'Oxford' (Symphony; 1791)
'Trauer' (Symphony; c.1771)

07 'Emperor' (String Quartet; 1797)
'Evening' (Symphony; c.1761)
'La Reine' (Symphony; 1785)
'Le Matin' (Symphony; c.1761)
'Mercury' (Symphony; c.1771)
'Miracle' (Symphony; 1792)
'Morning' (Symphony; c.1761)
'Passion' (Symphony; 1768)
'Sunrise' (String Quartet; 1797)

08 'Alleluia' (Symphony; 1765)
'Drum Roll' (Symphony; 1795)
'Farewell' (Symphony; 1772)
'Imperial' (Symphony; c.1780)
'La Chasse' (Symphony; 1781)
'Military' (Symphony; 1794)
'Mourning' (Symphony; c.1771)
'Surprise' (Symphony; 1791)

10 'Horn Signal' (Symphony; 1765)
'La Passione' (Symphony; 1768)

'La Roxelane' (Symphony; c.1780)
'L'Imperiale' (Symphony; c.1780)
'Palindrome' (Symphony; 1772)
The Seasons (1801)

11 'Il distratto' (Symphony; 1774)
'Philosopher' (Symphony; 1764)
Stabat Mater (1767)
The Creation (1798)

12 *Die Schöpfung* (1798)
Emperor's Hymn (1797)
'Lamentations' (Symphony; c.1770)
'Lamentazione' (Symphony; c.1770)
'Maria Theresa' (Symphony; c.1768)
'Maria Therese' (Symphony; c.1768)
'Schoolmaster' (Symphony; 1774)

14 'In Nomine Domini' (Symphony; 1786)

15 *Die Jahreszeiten* (1801)
'Tempora Mutantur' (Symphony; 1775)

17 *The Seven Last Words* (1796)

21 *Die sieben letzten Worte* (1796)

head cloth *see* **scarf**

headdress *see* **hat**

Heaney, Seamus (1939–)

Significant works include:

05 *North* (1975)
07 *Beowulf* (1999)
09 *Field Work* (1979)

11 *Eleven Poems* (1965)
12 *Wintering Out* (1972)
14 *Preoccupations* (1980)

15 *Door into the Dark* (1969)
18 *Death of a Naturalist* (1966)

heart

Heart parts include:

04 vein
05 aorta
   valve
06 artery
   atrium
   AV node
   muscle
   SA node
07 auricle
08 vena cava

09 sinus node
   ventricle
10 epicardium
   left atrium
   myocardium
11 aortic valve
   endocardium
   mitral valve
   pericardium
   right atrium
13 bicuspid valve

   carotid artery
   left ventricle
14 ascending aorta
   pulmonary valve
   Purkinje fibres
   Purkinje system
   right ventricle
   sino-atrial node
   tricuspid valve
15 papillary muscle

Hebrew *see* **alphabet**

helmet *see* **hat**

Hemingway, Ernest (1899–1961)

Significant works include:

09 *In Our Time* (1925)
14 *A Moveable Feast* (1964)
15 *A Farewell to Arms* (1929)
Men without Women (1927)
Selected Letters (1981)
The Sun Also Rises (1926)
17 *Winner Take Nothing* (1933)

18 *The Old Man and the Sea* (1952)
19 *Death in the Afternoon* (1932)
For Whom the Bell Tolls (1940)
The Torrents of Spring (1926)
21 *The Green Hills of Africa* (1935)
23 *Three Stories and Ten Poems* (1923)
29 *Across the River and into the Trees* (1950)

Significant characters include:

05 Adams (Nick)
Harry
Henry (Frederic)
Maria
Pablo

Pilar
06 Ashley (Lady Brett)
Barnes (Jake)
Jordan (Robert)
Morgan (Harry)

07 Barkley (Catherine)
Manolin
08 Macomber (Francis)
Macomber (Margot)
Santiago

heraldry

Terms to do with heraldry include:

02 or
04 arms
lion
orle
pall
pile
semé
urdé
vert
05 azure
badge
crest
eagle
eisen
field
gules
motto
sable
tawny
tenné

undee
06 argent
bezant
blazon
canton
centre
charge
dexter
emblem
ensign
helmet
impale
mullet
murrey
sejant
shield
volant
wivern
07 annulet
bordure

cendrée
chevron
dormant
griffin
gyronny
lozenge
martlet
passant
phoenix
quarter
rampant
regalia
roundel
saltire
statant
tierced
unicorn
urinant
08 addorsed
antelope
caboched

couchant
insignia
mantling
sanguine
sinister
tincture
09 carnation
displayed
hatchment
10 camelopard
cinquefoil
coat of arms
cockatrice
emblazonry
escutcheon
fleur-de-lis
quatrefoil
supporters
11 bleu celeste
compartment

herb

Herbs and spices include:

03 bay
04 balm
dill
mace
mint
sage
05 anise

basil
caper
clove
cumin
curry
thyme
06 borage
cassia

chilli
chives
cloves
fennel
garlic
ginger
hyssop
lovage

nutmeg	saffron	tarragon
pepper	vanilla	turmeric
savory	**08** allspice	**09** chamomile
sesame	angelica	coriander
sorrel	bergamot	fenugreek
07 catmint	camomile	hypericum
chervil	cardamom	lemon balm
comfrey	cardamon	**10** gaillardia
mustard	cardamum	**11** St John's wort
oregano	cinnamon	**12** caraway seeds
paprika	lavender	**13** cayenne pepper
parsley	marjoram	
pimento	rosemary	

herbal tea *see* **tea**

heroism

Heroes and heroines include:

04 Bond (James; *Casino Royale*, 1953, et seq, Ian Fleming)
Dare (Dan; comic/film)
Hood (Robin; English legend)

05 Bruce (Robert; 1274–1329, Scottish)
Croft (Lara; video game/film)
Jason (Greek mythology)
Jones (Indiana; *Raiders of the Lost Ark*, 1981, et seq)
Kelly (Ned; 1855–80, Australian)
Zorro (TV/film)

06 Arthur (c.6c; Arthurian legend)
Barton (Dick; radio)
Batman (comic/TV/film)
Lassie (film/TV)
Ripley (Ellen; *Alien*, 1979, et seq)
Rogers (Buck; comic/film)
Sharpe (Richard; *Sharpe's Eagle*, 1981, et seq, Bernard Cornwell)
Tarzan (TV/film)

07 Beowulf (Scandinavian legend)
Biggles (*The Camels Are Coming*, 1932, et seq, Captain W E Johns)
Darling (Grace; 1815–42, English)
Deirdre (Irish legend)
Glyn Dwr (Owain; c.1350–c.1416, Welsh)
Ivanhoe (*Ivanhoe*, 1820, Sir Walter Scott)
Wallace (William; 1272–1305, Scottish)

08 Boadicea (d.61 AD, British)
Boudicca (d.61 AD, British)
Lancelot (English legend)

See also **legend**; **mythology**

Superman (comic/film)

09 Churchill (Sir Winston; 1874–1965, English)
D'Artagnan (*The Three Musketeers*, 1844, Alexandre Dumas)
Glendower (Owain; c.1350–c.1416, Welsh)
Joan of Arc (1412–31, French)
Macdonald (Flora; 1722–90, Scottish)
MacGregor (Rob Roy; 1671–1734, Scottish)
Rin Tin Tin (film/TV)
Schindler (Oskar; 1908–74, German)
Snow White (Grimm Brothers fairytale)
Spiderman (comic/film)

10 Cinderella (European folklore)
Cú Chulainn (Irish legend)
Hornblower (Horatio; *The Happy Return*, 1937, et seq, C S Forester)
Little John (English legend)
Lone Ranger (TV/film)
Richthofen (Manfred von, 'the Red Baron'; 1892–1918, German)

11 Finn MacCool (Irish legend)
Nightingale (Florence; 1820–1910, Italian/British)
Wilberforce (William; 1759–1833; English)
Wonderwoman (comic/film)

14 Finn MacCumhail (Irish legend)

15 Three Musketeers (*The Three Musketeers*, 1844, Alexandre Dumas)

highwayman

Highwaymen include:

04 King (Tom; 18c, English)

05 Duval (Claude; 1643–70, English)

06 Turpin (Dick; 1706–39, English)

07 Brennan (Willie; d.1804, Irish)
Nevison (John/William; 1648–84, English)

08 MacHeath (*The Beggar's Opera*, 1728, John Gay/*The Threepenny Opera*, 1958, Kurt Weill/Bertolt Brecht)

09 Abershawe (Jerry; 1773–95, English)
Swift Nick (1648–84, English)

12 Mack the Knife (*The Beggar's Opera*, 1728, John Gay/*The Threepenny Opera*, 1958, Kurt Weill/Bertolt Brecht)

hill *see* **mountain; Rome**

Hinduism

Hindu groups, movements and denominations include:

06 Aghori

07 Saivism
Saktism
Smartha

08 Lingayat
Shaivism

Shaktism
Tantrism

09 Vedantism

10 Bhakti Yoga
Radha Soami
Siddha Yoga

11 Hare Krishna
Vaishnavism

12 Swaminarayan

15 Kashmir Shaivism
Shaiva Siddhanta

Hindu gods include:

04 Agni (fire)
Kama (lust/desire)
Rama (incarnation of Vishnu)
Siva (creation/destruction)
Soma (speech)
Yama (death)

05 Indra (storms/war)
Kurma (incarnation of Vishnu)
Rudra (destructive aspect of Shiva)
Shani (bringer of bad luck)
Shiva (creation/destruction)
Surya (sun)

06 Brahma (creation)
Ganesa (elephant-headed son of Shiva)
Ganesh (elephant-headed son of Shiva)
Garuda (bird that carries Shiva)
Iswara (nature/soul)

Narada (incarnation of Vishnu)
Pushan (enlightenment)
Ravana (demon king)
Skanda (war/son of Shiva)
Varuna (sea)
Vishnu (creation)

07 Ganesha (elephant-headed son of Shiva)
Hanuman (monkey)
Krishna (incarnation of Vishnu)

08 Ganapati (elephant-headed son of Shiva)
Nataraja (aspect of Shiva as the Lord of Dance)

09 Kartikeya (war)
Lakshmana (half-brother of Rama)
Narasimha (incarnation of Vishnu)

10 Jagannatha (incarnation of Vishnu)

Hindu goddesses include:

03 Uma (destruction/wife of Shiva)

04 Kali (destruction; wife of Shiva)
Sita (Rama's wife)

05 Aditi (all existence)
Durga (Shiva's wife)
Gauri (purity)
Radha (love; consort of Krishna)

Sakti (female principle of power and energy)

06 Shakti (female principle of power and energy)

07 Lakshmi (wealth/good luck)
Parvati (Shiva's wife)

09 Sarasvati (mother/art/learning/music)

See also **calendar; religion**

history

Historical periods include:

05 Bruce	Dark Ages	Lancastrian
Tudor	Medieval	Plantagenet
06 Norman	**09** Edwardian	Reformation
Stuart	Mediaeval	Renaissance
07 Angevin	Modern Age	Restoration
Cold War	Victorian	Roman Empire
post-war	**10** Anglo-Saxon	Romanticism
Regency	Hanoverian	**13** British Empire
Stewart	Middle Ages	Enlightenment
Yorkist	**11** Interbellum	Ottoman Empire
08 Civil War	Interregnum	**15** Byzantine Empire

Historians include:

04 Bede (St, 'the Venerable'; c.673–735, Anglo-Saxon)
Livy (59 BC–17 AD, Roman)
Read (Sir Herbert; 1893–1968, English)
Webb (Sidney, Lord Passfield; 1859–1947, English)

05 Barth (Heinrich; 1821–65, German)
Blunt (Anthony; 1907–83, English)
Clark (Kenneth, Lord; 1903–83, English)
Ensor (Sir Robert; 1877–1958, English)
Gates (Henry Louis, Jnr; 1950–   , US)
Henry (of Huntingdon; c.1084–1155, English)
Lodge (Henry Cabot; 1850–1924, US)
Nepos (Cornelius; c.99–c.24 BC, Roman)
Paris (Matthew; c.1200–59, English)
Ranke (Leopold von; 1795–1886, German)
Renan (Ernest; 1823–92, French)
Stone (Norman; 1941–   , Scottish)

06 Arrian (c.95–180 AD, Greek)
Berlin (Sir Isaiah; 1907–97, British)
Bolton (Geoffrey; 1931–   , Australian)
Du Bois (W E B; 1868–1963, US)
Eliade (Mircea; 1907–86, Romanian)
Froude (James; 1818–94, English)
Gibbon (Edward; 1737–94, English)
Guizot (François; 1787–1874, French)
Hollis (Patricia, Baroness; 1941–   , English)
Holmes (Richard; 1946–   , English)
Namier (Sir Lewis; 1888–1960, British)
O'Brien (Conor Cruise;1917–2008, Irish)
Schama (Simon; 1945–   , English)
Strabo (c.60 BC–c.21 AD, Greek)
Strong (Sir Roy; 1935–   , English)
Tabari (Abu Jafar Mohammed Ben Jarir al-; 839–923, Arab)
Tawney (R H; 1880–1962, English)
Taylor (A J P; 1906–90, English)
Terkel (Studs; 1912–2008, US)

Thiers (Adolphe; 1797–1877, French)
Vasari (Giorgio; 1511–74, Italian)

07 Bullock (Alan, Lord; 1914–2004, English)
Carlyle (Thomas; 1795–1881, Scottish)
Mommsen (Theodor; 1817–1903, German)
Pevsner (Sir Nikolaus; 1902–83, British)
Sallust (86–34 BC, Roman)
Severin (Tim; 1940–   , English)
Starkey (David; 1945–   , English)
Tacitus (c.55–120 AD, Roman)
Toynbee (Arnold; 1852–83, English)
William (of Malmesbury; c.1090–c.1143, English)
William (of Tyre; c.1130–85, Syrian)

08 Commines (Philippe de; 1445–1509, French)
Foucault (Michel; 1926–84, French)
Geoffrey (of Monmouth; c.1100–c.1154, Welsh)
Gombrich (Sir Ernst; 1909–2001, Austrian/British)
Josephus (Flavius; 37–c.100 AD, Jewish)
Macaulay (Thomas, Lord; 1800–59, English)
Michelet (Jules; 1798–1874, French)
Palgrave (Sir Francis; 1824–97, English)
Panofsky (Erwin; 1892–1968, US)
Plutarch (c.46–c.120 AD, Greek)
Polybius (c.205–c.123 BC, Greek)
Wedgwood (Dame Veronica; 1910–97, English)
Xenophon (c.435–c.354 BC, Greek)

09 Dionysius (of Halicarnassus; 1c BC, Greek)
Froissart (Jean; c.1333–c.1404, French)
Herodotus (c.485–425 BC, Greek)
Holinshed (Raphael; d.c.1580, English)
Pausanias (2 CAD, Greek)
Plekhanov (Georgi; 1856–1918, Russian)
Procopius (c.499–565 AD, Byzantine)
Rowbotham (Sheila; 1943–   , English)
Suetonius (c.69–c.140 AD, Roman)

Trevelyan (G M; 1876–1962, English)
10 Baldinucci (Filippo; 1624–96, Italian)
Burckhardt (Jacob; 1818–97, Swiss)
Dio Cassius (c.150–c.235 AD, Roman)
Thucydides (c.460–c.400 BC, Greek)
11 Schlesinger (Arthur M; 1888–1965, US)

Tocqueville (Alexis de; 1805–59, French)
Trevor-Roper (Hugh, Lord Dacre; 1914–2003, English)
12 Guicciardini (Francesco; 1483–1540, Italian)
15 Diodorus Siculus (1c BC, Greek)

Terms used in history include:

02 AD
BC
03 age
AUC
war
05 reign
siege
06 battle

empire
period
source
treaty
07 dynasty
08 evidence
monarchy
10 chronology

11 anachronism
Eurocentric
oral history
13 modern history
primary source
14 ancient history
15 secondary source

See also **archaeology**; **Rome**

hobby

Hobbies and pastimes include:

05 batik
chess
06 acting
am-dram
baking
bonsai
hiking
poetry
raffia
07 camping
CB radio
collage
cookery
crochet
dancing
drawing
macramé
mosaics
origami
pottery
quizzes
reading
singing
tatting
topiary
weaving
writing
08 antiques
basketry
cat shows
dog shows
draughts
feng shui

knitting
knotting
lacework
lapidary
marbling
painting
quilling
quilting
spinning
tapestry
09 astrology
astronomy
decoupage
gardening
genealogy
marquetry
millinery
model cars
philately
rug-making
sketching
strawwork
toy-making
train sets
10 beekeeping
board games
crosswords
doll-making
embroidery
kite-flying
lace-making
phillumeny
pub quizzes

pyrography
renovating
upholstery
wine-making
11 archaeology
beadworking
bell-ringing
book-binding
calligraphy
card playing
cat breeding
cross-stitch
dog breeding
dressmaking
home brewing
model-making
model trains
needlepoint
numismatics
ornithology
paper crafts
papier-mâché
photography
wine-tasting
woodcarving
woodworking
12 amateur radio
basketmaking
candle-making
games playing
phillumenism
13 bungee jumping
egg decorating

toy collecting
14 book collecting
coin collecting
cruciverbalism
doll collecting

flower pressing
herpetoculture
metal detecting
15 aquarium keeping
ballroom dancing

flower arranging
jewellery making
model aeroplanes
stamp collecting

See also **collection**; **crossword**

hockey

Hockey terms include:

01 D	red card	right back	inside right
03 hit	striker	right half	obstruction
04 ball	sweeper	right wing	short corner
feet	**08** back line	**10** centre half	**12** penalty flick
push	bully-off	centre pass	reverse stick
05 flick	left back	goal circle	**13** centre forward
scoop	left half	goalkeeper	penalty corner
06 aerial	left wing	inside left	penalty stroke
tackle	**09** corner hit	long corner	**14** shooting circle
07 dribble	drag flick	yellow card	striking circle
free hit	field goal	**11** field player	
	green card	hockey stick	

holiday

National holidays include:

07 Flag Day	Martyrs' Day	Australia Day	**14** Armed Forces Day
08 Anzac Day	Mothers' Day	Children's Day	Queen's Birthday
Unity Day	Victory Day	Discovery Day	Remembrance Day
09 Labour Day	**11** Bastille Day	Thanksgiving	Unification Day
Women's Day	National Day	**13** King's Birthday	**15** Constitution Day
10 Culture Day	Republic Day	Liberation Day	Emancipation Day
Freedom Day	**12** Armistice Day	Revolution Day	Independence Day

See also **religion**

Homer (c.8c BC)

Significant characters include:

04 Aias *(Iliad)*	**06** Aeneas *(Iliad)*	Atrides *(Odyssey)*
Ajax *(Iliad)*	Aeolus *(Odyssey)*	Briseis *(Iliad)*
Ares *(Iliad)*	Apollo *(Iliad)*	Calchas *(Iliad)*
Hera *(Iliad)*	Athena *(Iliad)*	Chryses *(Iliad)*
Iris *(Iliad)*	Hector *(Iliad)*	Danaans *(Iliad)*
Zeus *(Iliad)*	Hecuba *(Iliad)*	Eumaeus *(Odyssey)*
	Hektor *(Iliad)*	Glaucos *(Iliad)*
05 Arete *(Odyssey)*	Hekuba *(Iliad)*	Glaucus *(Iliad)*
Argos *(Odyssey)*	Hermes *(Iliad)*	Glaukos *(Iliad)*
Circe *(Odyssey)*	Nestor *(Iliad)*	Helenos *(Iliad)*
Dione *(Iliad)*	Thetis *(Iliad)*	Kalchas *(Iliad)*
Dolon *(Iliad)*	Tydeus *(Iliad)*	Laertes *(Odyssey)*
Hades *(Iliad)*		Machaon *(Iliad)*
Helen *(Iliad)*	**07** Antenor *(Iliad)*	Phoenix *(Iliad)*
Paris *(Iliad)*	Argives *(Iliad)*	Telamon *(Iliad)*
Priam *(Iliad)*	Artemis *(Iliad)*	

Trojans *(Iliad)*
Tydides *(Iliad)*
Xanthos *(Iliad)*

08 Achaeans *(Iliad)*
Achilles *(Iliad)*
Alcinous *(Odyssey)*
Antinous *(Odyssey)*
Astyanax *(Iliad)*
Chryseis *(Iliad)*
Diomedes *(Iliad)*
Eupithes *(Odyssey)*
Melantho *(Odyssey)*
Menelaos *(Iliad)*
Menelaus *(Iliad)*
Nausicaa *(Odyssey)*

Odysseus *(Iliad/Odyssey)*
Pandarus *(Iliad)*
Penelope *(Odyssey)*
Poseidon *(Iliad)*
Sarpedon *(Iliad)*
Tiresias *(Odyssey)*

09 Agamemnon *(Iliad)*
Anticleia *(Odyssey)*
Aphrodite *(Iliad)*
Automedon *(Iliad)*
Cassandra *(Iliad)*
Euphorbus *(Iliad)*
Eurycleia *(Odyssey)*
Eurypylus *(Iliad)*
Idomeneus *(Iliad)*

Myrmidons *(Iliad)*
Patroclus *(Iliad)*
Patroklos *(Iliad)*

10 Alexandros *(Iliad)*
Andromache *(Iliad)*
Antilochos *(Iliad)*
Eurymachus *(Odyssey)*
Hephaestus *(Iliad)*
Melanthius *(Odyssey)*
Philoetius *(Odyssey)*
Polyphemus *(Odyssey)*
Poulydamas *(Iliad)*
Telemachus *(Odyssey)*

12 Clytemnestra *(Iliad)*
13 Aias the Lesser *(Iliad)*

honour

Honours include:

02 GC
KG
VC

03 CBE
DBE
DSC
DSO
GBE

KBE
MBE
OBE

09 Iron Cross

10 Bronze Star
Grand Cross
knighthood

Silver Star

11 George Cross
Purple Heart

12 Order of Lenin
Order of Merit

13 Croix de Guerre
Legion of Merit

Medal for Merit
Medal of Honour
Victoria Cross
Victoria Medal

14 Légion d'Honneur

See also **military**

hormone

Hormones include:

05 kinin

07 gastrin
insulin
relaxin

08 abscisin
androgen
autacoid
estrogen

florigen
glucagon
oxytocin
secretin
thyroxin

09 adrenalin
cortisone
melatonin
oestrogen

pituitrin
prolactin
thyroxine

10 adrenaline
calcitonin

11 thyrotropin
vasopressin

12 androsterone

melanotropin
noradrenalin
progesterone
somatostatin
somatotropin
testosterone
thyrotrophin

14 erythropoietin
glucocorticoid

horse

Horse and pony breeds include:

03 Don

04 Arab
Barb
Fell

05 Dales
Iomud
Lokai
Pinto
Shire

Toric
Waler
Welsh

06 Auxois
Breton
Brumby
Exmoor
Morgan
Nonius

Tersky

07 Comtois
Criollo
Finnish
Furioso
Hackney
Hispano
Jutland
Masuren

Muraköz
Murgese
Mustang
Salerno

08 Budyonny
Danubian
Dartmoor
Friesian
Highland
Holstein
Kabardin
Karabair
Karabakh
Lusitano
Palomino
Paso Fino
Poitevin
Shetland
Welsh Cob

09 Akhal-Teké
Alter-Réal
Anglo-Arab
Appaloosa
Ardennias
Brabançon
Calabrese

Connemara
Falabella
Groningen
Kladruber
Knabstrup
Kustanair
Maremmana
New Forest
New Kirgiz
Oldenburg
Percheron
Sardinian
Tchenaran
Trakehner

10 Andalusian
Boulonnais
Clydesdale
Einsiedler
Freiberger
Gelderland
Hanoverian
Lipizzaner
Mangalarga
Shagya Arab

11 Anglo-Norman
Døle Trotter

Irish Hunter
Mecklenburg
Przewalski's
Trait du Nord
Württemberg

12 Cleveland Bay
Dutch Draught
East Friesian
French Saddle
Irish Draught
Metis Trotter
North Swedish
Orlov Trotter
Suffolk Punch
Thoroughbred

13 East Bulgarian
Frederiksborg
French Trotter
German Trotter
Welsh Mountain

14 American Saddle
Latvian Harness
Plateau Persian

15 American Quarter
American Trotter
Swedish Halfbred

Points of a horse include:

03 ear
eye
hip

04 back
chin
dock
face
head
heel
hock
hoof
knee
lips
mane
neck
nose
poll
ribs
rump
shin
tail

05 atlas

belly
canon
cheek
chest
crest
croup
elbow
ergot
flank
girth
loins
mouth
thigh

06 breast
cannon
gaskin
haunch
muzzle
sheath
stifle
temple
throat

07 abdomen
brisket
buttock
coronet
crupper
fetlock
forearm
hind leg
pastern
quarter
shannon
tendons
withers

08 chestnut
forefoot
forehead
forelock
lower jaw
lower lip
nostrils
shoulder
under lip
upper lip

windpipe

09 hamstring
hock joint
nasal peak

10 chin groove
point of hip
wall of foot

11 back tendons
point of hock
stifle joint

12 fetlock joint
hindquarters
hollow of heel
point of elbow

13 dock of the tail
flexor tendons
jugular groove
root of the tail

14 Achilles tendon
crest of the neck

15 point of shoulder

A horse's tack includes:

03 bit
05 arson

cinch
girth

hames
reins

06 bridle
cantle

collar	housing	breeching	shabracque
halter	stirrup	hackamore	throatlash
numnah	**08** backband	headstall	**11** bearing rein
pommel	blinders	saddlebag	saddlecloth
saddle	blinkers	saddlebow	saddle-girth
traces	noseband	saddlepad	throatlatch
07 alforja	shabrack	surcingle	
bridoon		**10** martingale	**13** saddle blanket
crupper	**09** bellyband	saddletree	

Horses include:

03 Pie (The; *National Velvet*, 1935, Enid Bagnold)

04 Bree (*The Horse and His Boy*, 1954, C S Lewis)
Hwin (*The Horse and His Boy*, 1954, C S Lewis)

05 Arion (Greek mythology)
Arkle (racehorse; b.1957)
Binky (*The Colour of Magic*, 1985, et seq, Terry Pratchett)
Boxer (*Animal Farm*, 1945, George Orwell)
Misty (*Misty of Chincoteague*, 1947, et seq, Marguerite Henry)
Scout (*The Lone Ranger*, 1949–57, TV series)

06 Balius (Greek mythology)
Bayard (French folklore)
Diablo (*The Cisco Kid*, 1950–56, TV series)
Flicka (*My Friend Flicka*, 1941, Mary O'Hara)
Red Rum (racehorse; b.1965)
Silver (*The Lone Ranger*, 1949–57, TV series)
Stormy (*Stormy, Misty's Foal*, 1965, Marguerite Henry)

07 Burmese (Queen Elizabeth II's horse)
Capulet (*Twelfth Night*, 1601, William Shakespeare)
Eclipse (racehorse; 18c)
Galathe (*Troilus and Cressida*, 1602, William Shakespeare)
Lisette (Baron de Marbot's horse)
Llamrai (Arthurian legend)
Llamrei (Arthurian legend)
Marengo (Napoleon Bonaparte's horse)

Pegasus (Greek mythology)
Phantom (*Zorro*, 1957–59, TV series)
Roheryn (*The Lord of the Rings*, 1954–55, J R R Tolkien)
Shergar (racehorse; b.1978)
Tornado (*Zorro*, 1957–59, TV series)
Trigger (Roy Rogers's horse)
Xanthus (Greek mythology)

08 Champion (*Champion the Wonder Horse*, 1955–6, TV series)
Comanche (Captain Myles Keogh's horse)
Hengroen (Arthurian legend)
Mister Ed (*Mister Ed*, 1961–66, TV series)
Sleipnir (Scandinavian mythology)
Snowmane (*The Lord of the Rings*, 1954–55, J R R Tolkien)

09 Black Bess (Dick Turpin's horse)
Gringolet (Arthurian legend)
Incitatus (Emperor Caligula's horse)
Rosinante (Don Quixote's horse)
Rozinante (Don Quixote's horse)
Shadowfax (*The Lord of the Rings*, 1954–55, J R R Tolkien)
Traveller (General Robert E Lee's horse)

10 Bucephalus (Alexander the Great's horse; d.326 BC)
Copenhagen (Duke of Wellington's horse)
Seabiscuit (racehorse; b.1934)

11 Black Beauty (*Black Beauty*, 1877, Anna Sewell)
White Surrey (King Richard III's horse)

12 Desert Orchid (racehorse; b.1979)
Little Sorrel (General Jackson's horse)

Terms to do with horses include:

03 bay	buck	walk	nappy
cob	colt	**05** break	pinto
dun	foal	forge	steed
hie	gait	gee up	**06** bronco
hup	grey	groom	brumby
nag	mare	hands	canter
shy	roan	lunge	equine
04 bolt	stud	mount	gallop
	trot		

hippic	hacking	stallion	**11** riding habit
livery	nosebag	**09** horseshoe	**12** broken-winded
manège	paddock	roughshod	draught horse
riding	passade	**10** blood horse	pony-trekking
stable	piebald	draft horse	thoroughbred
07 astride	**08** chestnut	en cavalier	**13** champ at the bit
blanket	dismount	equestrian	mounting block
gelding	horse box	heavy horse	put out to grass
giddy-up	skewbald	side-saddle	**14** strawberry roan

See also **animal**; **bridle**; **equestrian sport**; **racing: horse racing**

horse racing *see* **racing: horse racing**

host *see* **quiz**

hotel

Hotels and hotel chains include:

03 Dom (Germany)
04 Ibis
05 Adlon (Germany)
Grand (Austria/England)
Hyatt
Lotti (France)
Peace (China)
Savoy (England)
06 Alcron (Czech Republic)
Brown's (England)
Gritti (Italy)
Hilton
Pierre (USA)
Sacher (Austria)
07 Astoria (Russia)
Cadogan (England)
Carlton
Chelsea (USA)
Crillon (France)
De Paris (Monaco)
Empress (Canada)
George V (France)
Hassler (Italy)
Le Royal (Cambodia)
Meikles (Zimbabwe)
Norfolk (Kenya)
Peabody (USA)
Pujiang (China)
Raffles (Singapore)
Sofitel
St James (England)
The Ritz (England)
Thistle
Windsor (Australia)
08 Cipriani (Italy)

Du Palais (France)
Elephant (Germany)
El Minzah (Morocco)
Fairmont
Imperial (Austria/Japan)
Landmark
Marriott
Metropol (Russia)
New Grand (Japan)
Palliser (Canada)
Radisson
Sheraton
The Plaza (USA)
09 Algonquin (USA)
Claridge's (England)
Copthorne
Esplanade (Croatia)
Kingsgate
Lancaster (France)
Le Bristol (France)
Le Meurice (France)
Metropole (Belgium)
Old Course (Scotland)
Park Hyatt (Japan)
Royal York (Canada)
Splendido (Italy)
Taft Hotel (*The Graduate*, 1967)
10 Astor House (China)
Bates Motel (*Psycho*, 1960)
Gleneagles (Scotland)
Holiday Inn
Hotel du Lac (*Hotel du Lac*, 1984, Anita Brookner)
Lake Palace (India)
La Mamounia (Morocco)
Millennium

Pera Palace (Turkey)
Rocco Forte
The Langham (England)
Villa D'Este (Italy)

11 Ambos Mundos (Cuba)
Best Western
Del Coronado (USA)
Dolder Grand (Switzerland)
Four Seasons
Mount Nelson (South Africa)
Old Cataract (Egypt)
Palace Praha (Czech Republic)
The Balmoral (Scotland)
The Berkeley (England)
The Park Lane (England)
The Scotsman (Scotland)

12 Alvear Palace (Argentina)
Fawlty Towers (TV series)
Le Beauvallon (France)
Nevsky Palace (Russia)
Strand Palace (England)
The Connaught (England)
The Peninsula (Hong Kong)

13 Ashford Castle (Ireland)

See also **London**; **New York**; **Paris**

Knickerbocker (USA)
Overlook Hotel (*The Shining*, 1980)
Rambagh Palace (India)
The Ambassador (USA)
The Dorchester (England)
The Shelbourne (Ireland)
Trianon Palace (France)
Victoria Falls (Zimbabwe)
Waldorf Hilton (England)

14 Bayerischer Hof (Germany)
Chateau Laurier (Canada)
Frankfurter Hof (Germany)
Grand Hotel Pupp (Czech Republic)
Grosvenor House (England)
Hotel Splendide (*Casino Royale*, 2006)
Landmark London (England)
Moana Surfrider (USA)
Nacional de Cuba (Cuba)
Prince de Galles (France)
The Shakespeare (England)
Waldorf Astoria (USA)

15 Beverly Wilshire (USA)
Heartbreak Hotel (song, Elvis Presley)
Hotel California (song, The Eagles)
The Lanesborough (England)

hour

Hours include:

04 rush	**06** dinner	working	visiting
05 flexi	golden	**08** business	witching
happy	office	eleventh	
lunch	waking	midnight	
small	**07** trading	unsocial	

See also **canonical hour**; **time**

house

House types include:

03 hut	chalet	detached	villa home
04 flat	duplex	hacienda	villa unit
hall	grange	log cabin	**10** granny flat
semi	mia-mia	terraced	maisonette
weem	pondok	vicarage	pied-à-terre
05 croft	prefab	**09** apartment	ranch house
igloo	shanty	but and ben	state house
lodge	studio	farmhouse	
manor	wurley	homestead	**11** condominium
manse	**07** cottage	parsonage	**12** council house
shack	mansion	penthouse	semi-detached
villa	rectory	single-end	
06 bedsit	**08** bungalow	town house	**14** chalet bungalow
		treehouse	**15** thatched cottage

House parts include:

04 dado
door
hall
loft
roof

05 attic
beams
grate
ingle
joist
newel
porch
slate
study
walls

06 alcove
boiler
cellar
coving
hallan

hearth
larder
lounge
pantry
socket
stairs
switch
thatch
window
wiring

07 balcony
bedroom
ceiling
chimney
cornice
en-suite
kitchen
landing
laundry
parlour

parquet
rafters
transom

08 baluster
banister
bathroom
dado rail
doorbell
radiator
skylight

09 bay window
cloakroom
fireplace
water tank

10 balustrade
chambranle
dining room
family room
floorboard

insulation
living room

11 ceiling rose
curtain rail
drawing room
mantelpiece
sitting room
utility room
window ledge

12 chimney piece
dormer window
light fitting

13 chimneybreast
double glazing
skirting board

14 central heating

15 air conditioning
built-in wardrobe
immersion heater

Household items include:

03 bin
mop

04 comb
hook
pram
vase

05 broom
brush
diary
match
potty
range
towel

06 basket
candle
duster
pet bed
sponge

07 ashtray
coaster
dustpan
flannel
key rack

key ring
wash bag

08 aquarium
bassinet
birdcage
calendar
coat hook
dish rack
fish tank
hat stand
hip flask
ornament
place mat
shoe rack
soap dish
suitcase
tea towel
waste bin
wine rack

09 cat basket
dishcloth
dog basket
door wedge
fireguard

hairbrush
hearth rug
highchair
memo board
phone book
pushchair
sponge bag
stair gate
stepstool
towel rail
washboard
washcloth

10 baby bottle
baby walker
coathanger
laundry bag
letter rack
oven gloves
photo album
photo frame
stepladder
storage box
toothbrush

11 address book

candlestick
changing mat
first aid kit
paperweight
toilet brush

12 clothes airer
clothes-brush
clothes horse
ironing board
magazine rack
perambulator
picnic basket
Thermos® flask

13 feather duster
laundry basket
satellite dish
soap dispenser
umbrella stand
washing-up bowl

14 hot water bottle

15 draught excluder
photograph album
photograph frame

See also **accommodation**; **opera**; **tent**

Hughes, Ted (1930–98)

Significant works include:

04 *Crow* (1970)
05 *River* (1983)

Wodwo (1967)
07 *Orghast* (1971)

08 *Lupercal* (1960)
   Moortown (1979)
09 *Cave Birds* (1975)
11 *Season Songs* (1974)

14 *Remains of Elmet* (1979)
15 *Birthday Letters* (1998)
16 *The Hawk in the Rain* (1957)

Hugo, Victor (1802–85)

Significant works include:

04 *Odes* (1822)
07 *Hernani* (1830)
   Ruy Blas (1838)
08 *Cromwell* (1827)
13 *Les Châtiments* (1853)
   Les Misérables (1862)
   Les Orientales (1829)
14 *Odes et Ballades* (1826)
16 *Notre-Dame de Paris* (1831)

17 *Les Contemplations* (1856)
   Quatrevingt-treize (1874)
18 *Les Voix intérieures* (1837)
19 *La Légende des siècles* (1859–83)
   Les Feuilles d'automne (1831)
20 *Les Rayons et les ombres* (1840)
21 *Les Chants du crépuscule* (1835)
22 *Les Travailleurs de la mer* (1866)
23 *The Hunchback of Notre Dame* (1831)

humour

Humour includes:

03 dry	**07** gallows	**09** satirical	**11** barrack-room
04 sick	surreal	slapstick	Pythonesque
05 black	**08** farcical	**10** lavatorial	**12** Chaplinesque

Bodily humours include:

05 blood	phlegm	**10** melancholy
06 choler	**09** black bile	yellow bile

See also **comedy**

hybrid

Hybrids include:

02 zo	oxlip	tangelo	**10** clementine
03 dso	tigon	tea rose	loganberry
dzo	topaz	**08** citrange	polyanthus
zho	**06** oxslip	limequat	**11** boysenberry
04 dzho	**07** beefalo	noisette	bull-mastiff
mule	Bourbon	sunberry	Jacqueminot
OEIC	cattabu	tayberry	Lonicera fly
Ugli®	cattalo	**09** perpetual	marionberry
05 hinny	Jersian	tiger tail	miracle rice
liger	lurcher	triticale	**13** polecat-ferret
	plumcot		

See also **dog**; **fruit**; **mythology**

hydrocarbon

Hydrocarbons include:

03 wax

05 halon

06 aldrin
alkane
alkene
alkyne
butane
cetane
decane

ethane
hexane
indene
nonane
octane
olefin
picene
pyrene
retene

07 benzene

heptane
methane
olefine
pentane
propane
styrene
terpene

08 camphane
camphene
diphenyl

isoprene
pristane
stilbene

09 butadiene

10 benzpyrene
mesitylene

11 hatchettite
naphthalene

12 cyclopropane

I

Ian Fleming *see* **James Bond**

Ibsen, Henrik (1828–1906)

Significant works include:

05 *Brand* (1866)
06 *Ghosts* (1881)
08 *Catiline* (1850)
Peer Gynt (1867)
11 *A Doll's House* (1879)
Hedda Gabler (1890)
Little Eyolf (1894)
Love's Comedy (1862)
Rosmersholm (1886)
The Wild Duck (1884)

13 *The Pretenders* (1863)
14 *The Burial Mound* (1850)
16 *The Master Builder* (1892)
When We Dead Awaken (1899)
17 *The Lady from the Sea* (1888)
18 *An Enemy of the People* (1882)
Emperor and Galilean (1873)
John Gabriel Borkman (1896)
19 *The Pillars of Society* (1877)

Significant characters include:

04 Aase
Gynt (Peer)
Rank (Dr)
05 Brack (Judge)
Ekdal (Hedvig)
Ekdal (Hjalmar)
Werle (Gregers)
Werle (Haakon)

06 Alving (Mrs Helene)
Alving (Oswald)
Gabler (Hedda)
Helmer (Nora)
Helmer (Torvald)
Tesman (Jörgen)
Tesman (Miss Juliane)
Tesman (Mrs Hedda)

07 Elvsted (Mrs)
Lövborg (Ejlert)
Manders (Pastor)
Solveig
08 Krogstad (Nils)
09 Engstrand (Regine)
12 the Troll King

ice

Ice includes:

03 dry
pan
sea
04 floe
grew
grue
hail
pack

rime
slob
snow
05 black
brash
crust
drift
field

shelf
shell
sleet
virga
06 anchor
frazil
ground
icicle

stream
07 glacier
hummock
pancake
verglas
10 silver thaw
13 tickly-benders

See also **snow**

ice hockey

Ice hockey players and associated figures include:

03 Orr (Bobby; 1948–   , Canadian)
04 Hand (Tony; 1967–   , Scottish)
Howe (Gordie; 1928–   , Canadian)
Hull (Bobby; 1939–   , Canadian)
Hull (Brett; 1964–   , Canadian)

Jagr (Jaromir; 1972–   , Czech)
05 Hasek (Dominik; 1965–   , Czech)
Shore (Eddie; 1902–85, Canadian)
06 Bowman (Scotty; 1933–   , Canadian)
Iginla (Jarome; 1977–   , Canadian)

Malkin (Evgeni; 1986– , Russian)
Mikita (Stan; 1940– , Czech/Canadian)
Plante (Jacques; 1929–86, Canadian)
07 Gretzky (Wayne; 1961– , Canadian)
Lafleur (Guy; 1951– , Canadian)
Lemieux (Mario; 1965– , Canadian)
Richard (Maurice; 1921–2000, Canadian)
Sawchuk (Terry; 1929–70, Canadian/US)

Tretiak (Vladislav; 1952– , Russian)
08 Beliveau (Jean; 1931– , Canadian)
Esposito (Phil; 1942– , Canadian)
Forsberg (Peter; 1973– , Swedish)
Ovechkin (Alexander; 1985– , Russian)
09 Kharlamov (Valery; 1948–81, Russian)
Kovalchuk (Ilya; 1983– , Russian)

Ice hockey terms include:

04 cage	shut-out	centreman
puck	Zamboni	netminder
05 check	**08** blue line	power play
icing	boarding	**10** centre line
stick	defender	cross-check
zones	five-hole	defenceman
06 boards	linesman	goaltender
period	one-timer	penalty box
sin-bin	overtime	**11** penalty shot
07 face-off	slap shot	short-handed
forward	slashing	sudden-death
offside	spearing	**12** icing the puck
penalty	**09** blueliner	penalty bench
red line	bodycheck	**13** defending zone

See also **sport**

ice skating

Ice skaters include:

04 Dean (Christopher; 1958– , English)
Koss (Johann Olav; 1968– , Norwegian)
Kwan (Michelle; 1980– , US)
Meng (Wang; 1985– , Chinese)
Witt (Katarina; 1965– , German)
Yang (Yang 'A'; 1975– , Chinese)

05 Baiul (Oksana; 1977– , Ukrainian)
Blair (Bonnie; 1964– , US)
Curry (John; 1949–94, English)
Heiss (Carol; 1940– , US)
Henie (Sonja; 1912–69, Norwegian/US)
Kania (Karin; 1961– , German)
Syers (Madge; 1882–1917, English)

06 Button (Dick; 1929– , US)
Hamill (Dorothy; 1956– , US)

07 Arakawa (Shizuka; 1981– , Japan)
Boitano (Brian; 1963– , US)
Cousins (Robin; 1957– , English)
Fleming (Peggy; 1948– , US)
Grinkov (Sergei; 1967–95, Russian)

Harding (Tonya; 1971– , US)
Marinin (Maxim; 1977– , Russian)
Rodnina (Irina; 1949– , Russian)
Salchow (Ulrich; 1877–1949, Swedish)
Torvill (Jayne; 1957– , English)
Yagudin (Alexei; 1980– , Russian)

08 Browning (Kurt; 1966– , Canadian)
Dijkstra (Sjoukje; 1942– , Dutch)
Dmitriev (Artur; 1968– , Russian)
Eldredge (Todd; 1971– , US)
Gordeeva (Ekaterina; 1971– , Russian)
Hamilton (Scott; 1958– , US)
Kazakova (Oksana; 1975– , Russian)
Kerrigan (Nancy; 1969– , US)
Lipinski (Tara; 1982– , US)
Petrenko (Viktor; 1969– , Ukrainian)

09 Plushenko (Evgeny; 1982– , Russian)
Yamaguchi (Kristi; 1971– , US)

10 Ahn Hyun-Soo (1985– , Korean)
Ballangrud (Ivar; 1904–69, Norwegian)
Totmianina (Tatiana; 1981– , Russian)

Ice skating terms include:

04 Axel
edge
flip
loop
Lutz
05 blade
pairs
skate
waltz
06 figure
Mohawk
rocker
walley
07 bracket

See also **sport**

Choctaw
Salchow
sit spin
toe jump
toe loop
toe pick
08 ice dance
Ina Bauer
stag leap
09 camel spin
crossover
free dance
10 inside edge
11 death spiral

flying camel
layback spin
outside edge
spread eagle
upright spin
12 headless spin
speed skating
13 Biellmann spin
figure skating
flying sit spin
free programme
14 short programme
15 compulsory dance
set pattern dance

ideology *see* politics

illegal drug *see* drug

immune system

Immune system components include:

05 T-cell
06 NK cell
spleen
07 antigen
08 antibody
lysosome
lysozyme
09 commensal
histamine
leucocyte

leukocyte
lymph node
phagocyte
white pulp
10 interferon
lymphocyte
memory cell
plasma cell
11 B-lymphocyte
helper T-cell

killer T-cell
T-lymphocyte
12 receptor site
13 cytotoxic cell
dendritic cell
immune complex
14 germinal centre
immunoglobulin
15 lymphatic system

imprint *see* publishing

Inca empire

Inca emperors, with regnal dates:

07 Huascar (1525–32)
08 Inca Roca (dates unknown)
09 Atahualpa (1532–33)
Inca Urcon (dates unknown)
10 Manco Capac (dates unknown)
Mayta Capac (dates unknown)
Sayri Tupac (1545–60)
Sinchi Roca (dates unknown)
Tupac Amaru (1571–72)
11 Huayna Capac (1493–1525)

Topa Huallpa (1533)
12 Yahuar Huacac (dates unknown)
13 Capac Yupanqui (dates unknown)
Viracocha Inca (dates unknown)
14 Lloque Yupanqui (dates unknown)
16 Titu Cusi Yupanqui (1560–71)
Topa Inca Yupanqui (1471–93)
17 Manco Inca Yupanqui (1533–45)
21 Pachacuti Inca Yupanqui (1438–71)

incarnation

04 Rama
05 Kurma
06 Narada

07 Krishna
09 Jugannath
Narasimha

10 Jagannatha
Juggernaut

See also **Hinduism; mythology; religion**

India

Cities and notable towns in India include:

04 Agra	Jaipur	Nagpur	**08** Calcutta
05 Delhi	Kanpur	Shimla	New Delhi
Poona	Madras	**07** Chennai	**09** Ahmadabad
Simla	Mumbai	Kolkata	Bangalore
06 Bombay	Mysore	Lucknow	Hyderabad

Indian states and union territories:

03 Goa
05 Assam
Behar
Bihar
Delhi
06 Kerala
Orissa
Punjab
Sikkim
07 Gujarat
Haryana
Manipur
Mizoram

Tripura
08 Nagaland
09 Jharkhand
Karnataka
Meghalaya
Rajasthan
Tamil Nadu
10 Chandigarh
West Bengal
11 Daman and Diu
Lakshadweep
Maharashtra

Pondicherry
Punducherry
Uttaranchal
12 Chhattisgarh
Uttar Pradesh
13 Andhra Pradesh
Madhya Pradesh
15 Himachal Pradesh
Jammu and Kashmir
16 Arunachal Pradesh
17 Andaman and Nicobar
19 Dadra and Nagar Haveli

Indian landmarks include:

06 Ganges
07 Raj Ghat
Red Fort

08 Taj Mahal
09 India Gate
10 Thar Desert

11 Brahmaputra
12 Golden Temple
14 Imperial Palace

15 Parliament House

See also **Asia**

industrialist *see* business

inflammation

Inflammations include:

03 RSI (tendons and joints of the hands and lower arms)
sty (eye)

04 acne (sebaceous follicles)
boil
bubo (lymph nodes)
stye (eye)

05 croup (larynx and trachea)
felon (sore)
mange (animal skin)

06 ancome (finger or toe)
angina (throat)
bunion (big toe)
canker (horse's feet)

garget (throat or udder in cows or swine)
grease (horse's heels)
iritis (iris of the eye)
otitis (ear)
quinsy (tonsils)
thrush (frog of a horse's foot)
ulitis (gum)

07 abscess
cecitis (caecum)
colitis (colon)
ileitis (ileum)
pink-eye (conjunctiva)
sycosis (hair follicles)
tylosis (eyelids)
uveitis (iris, ciliary body and choroid)
whitlow (finger or toe)

08 adenitis (glands)
aortitis (aorta)
bursitis (bursa)
caecitis (caecum)
carditis (heart)
cynanche (tonsils)
cystitis (inner lining of the bladder)
mastitis (breast or udder)
metritis (uterus)
myelitis (bone marrow)
neuritis (nerves)
orchitis (testicle)
ovaritis (ovary)
prunella (tonsils)
pyelitis (pelvis of the kidney)
rectitis (rectum)
rhinitis (mucous membrane of the nose)
uteritis (womb)
uvulitis (uvula)
vulvitis (vulva)
windburn (skin)

09 arteritis (artery)
arthritis (joint)
balanitis (glans penis in mammals)
barotitis (ear)
carbuncle (skin and subcutaneous tissues)
ceratitis (cornea)
cheilitis (lips/corners of the mouth)
conchitis (concha)
enteritis (intestines)
fasciitis (plantar fascia of the foot)
frostbite
gastritis (stomach lining)
glossitis (tongue)
hepatitis (liver)
keratitis (cornea)
laminitis (horse's lamina)
nephritis (kidneys)
onychitis (soft parts about the nail)
phlebitis (wall of a vein)
phrenitis (brain)

proctitis (rectum)
retinitis (retina)
sinusitis (sinus)
splenitis (spleen)
squinancy (tonsils)
strumitis (thyroid gland)
synovitis (synovial membrane)
typhlitis (blind-gut)
vaginitis (vagina)

10 alveolitis (alveoli in the lungs)
antiaditis (tonsils)
bronchitis (lining of the bronchial tubes)
cellulitis (subcutaneous body tissue)
cephalitis (brain)
cerebritis (cerebrum)
cervicitis (neck of the womb)
chondritis (cartilage)
dermatitis (skin)
duodenitis (duodenum)
erysipelas (skin)
fibrositis (fibrous tissue)
gingivitis (gums)
hysteritis (uterus)
intertrigo (skin)
laryngitis (larynx)
meningitis (meninges)
myringitis (eardrum)
oophoritis (ovary)
papillitis (head of the optic nerve)
paronychia (finger or toe)
sore throat (throat)
stomatitis (mucous membrane of the mouth)
syringitis (Eustachian tube)
tendinitis (tendon)
tonsilitis (tonsil)
tracheitis (trachea)
tympanitis (membrane of the ear)
ureteritis (ureter)
urethritis (urethra)
valvulitis (valve of the heart)
vasculitis (blood vessel)

11 blepharitis (eyelid)
choroiditis (choroid)
mad staggers (animal brain)
mastoiditis (air cells of the mastoid
   processes)
myocarditis (myocardium)
parotiditis (parotid gland)
periostitis (periosteum)
peritonitis (peritoneum)
pharyngitis (mucous membrane of the
   pharynx)
pneumonitis (alveoli)
prickly heat (sweat glands)
prostatitis (prostate gland)
salpingitis (tube, especially a Fallopian tube)
shin splints (muscles around the shinbone)

   spondylitis (synovial joints of the backbone)
   staphylitis (uvula)
   tennis elbow (elbow)
   thoroughpin (horse's hock joint)
   thyroiditis (thyroid gland)
   tonsillitis (tonsil)

12 appendicitis (appendix)
   crystallitis (crystalline lens)
   encephalitis (brain)
   endocarditis (endocardium)
   endometritis (endometrium)
   lymphangitis (lymphatic vessel)
   panarthritis (all the structures of a joint)
   pancreatitis (pancreas)
   pericarditis (pericardium)
   perineuritis (perineurium)
   polymyositis (several muscles at the same time)
   polyneuritis (several nerves)
   sacroiliitis (sacroiliac joint)
   vestibulitis (labyrinth and cochlea of the inner ear)

13 arachnoiditis (arachnoid membrane)

See also **disease; skin**

cholecystitis (gall bladder)
epicondylitis (tissues beside the epicondyle of the humerus)
jogger's nipple (nipple)
labyrinthitis (inner ear)
perigastritis (outer surface of the stomach)
perihepatitis (peritoneum covering the liver)
perinephritis (perinephrium)
periodontitis (tissues surrounding the teeth)
perityphlitis (caecum or blind-gut)
tenosynovitis (tendon)
tenovaginitis (fibrous wall of the sheath surrounding a tendon)

14 conjunctivitis (conjunctiva)
   diverticulitis (one or more diverticula)
   housemaid's knee (knee)
   lobar pneumonia (lung lobe)
   sleepy staggers (animal brain)

15 diaphragmatitis (diaphragm)
   gastroenteritis (lining of the stomach and intestines)
   panophthalmitis (whole eye)

ingredient *see* **salad**

insect

Insects include:

03 ant	sedge	locust
bee	vespa	maggot
bug	**06** bedbug	mantis
fly	bee fly	may bug
ked	beetle	mayfly
nit	bembex	medfly
04 cleg	bembix	motuca
flea	bum-bee	muscid
frit	capsid	mutuca
gnat	chigoe	nasute
kade	chigre	psylla
moth	chinch	red ant
pium	cicada	sawfly
wasp	cicala	sow bug
zimb	coccid	thrips
05 aphid	cootie	tipula
aphis	day-fly	tsetse
cimex	dor-fly	tzetse
culex	drongo	tzetze
emmet	earwig	weevil
louse	gadfly	**07** antlion
midge	gru-gru	army ant
ox-bot	hop-fly	beet-fly
roach	hornet	blowfly
sauba	jigger	boat-fly

brommer
bulb fly
bull ant
bush-fly
buzzard
chalcid
chigger
cornfly
cricket
deer fly
diptera
duck-ant
dung-fly
fig wasp
fire ant
fritfly
gallfly
gold-bug
goutfly
grayfly
hive bee
June bug
katydid
lace bug
ladybug
lamp fly
meat-fly
pill bug
pismire
rose bug
sciarid
soldier
termite
vedalia
wood ant

08 alder-fly
berry bug
birch fly
black fly
bombycid
bookworm
cercopid
cornworm
crane fly
drone fly
ephemera
firebrat
flesh-fly
froth-fly
fruit fly
gall wasp
glossina
glow-worm
greenfly
groo-groo
honey ant
honey bee
horntail

horsefly
housefly
hoverfly
lacewing
ladybird
Maori bug
mason bee
mealy bug
mosquito
onion fly
ox-warble
reduviid
ruby-tail
ruby-wasp
sand wasp
sauba ant
sedge fly
sheep ked
simulium
snake fly
snipe fly
stink bug
stonefly
tachinid
water fly
wheat fly
white ant
whitefly
wood wasp
woodworm

09 amazon ant
ambush bug
ant weaver
bark-louse
bird-louse
booklouse
bumblebee
butterfly
caddis fly
campodeid
cantharis
capsid bug
carpet bug
carrot fly
chinch bug
cochineal
cockroach
coffee bug
Croton bug
cuckoo bee
cuckoo fly
damselfly
doodlebug
dragonfly
driver ant
ephemerid
forest-fly
golden-eye

humble-bee
ichneumon
leaf miner
mason wasp
may beetle
mining bee
mud dauber
nut-weevil
paper wasp
pomace-fly
robber fly
shield bug
squash bug
stable fly
strawworm
tsetse fly
turnip fly
tzetse fly
tzetze fly
velvet ant
warble fly
wax insect
wood-borer
woodlouse

10 blister fly
bluebottle
boll weevil
bulldog ant
cabbage-fly
cicadellid
cluster fly
cockchafer
corn thrips
corn weevil
digger-wasp
dolphin-fly
drosophila
frog-hopper
grapelouse
harvest bug
harvest-fly
Hessian fly
kissing bug
lantern fly
leaf-cutter
leaf insect
Pharaoh ant
phylloxera
pond skater
potter wasp
silverfish
smother-fly
spittlebug
springtail
vinegar-fly
web spinner
wheat midge

11 backswimmer
biting louse
biting midge
bristletail
buffalo gnat
bush cricket
caterpillar
chalcid wasp
coleopteran
coleopteron
froth-hopper
grasshopper
greenbottle
honeypot ant
mole cricket
neuropteran
Pharaoh's ant
scale insect
scorpion fly
snout beetle
stick insect

trombiculid
umbrella-ant
vine-fretter
walking leaf
walking twig

12 buzzard-clock
carpenter-ant
carpenter-bee
cheesehopper
desert locust
European flea
groundhopper
harvest louse
house cricket
ichneumon fly
lightning bug
San Jose scale
screw-worm fly
sucking louse
trichopteran
walking stick

walking straw
water boatman
water strider
yellow jacket

13 blister beetle
cheese skipper
daddy longlegs
diamond-beetle
green lacewing
leatherjacket
praying insect
praying mantis
spectre insect
spittle insect
water measurer
water scorpion

14 cabbage-root fly
European hornet

15 cochineal insect
migratory locust

Insect parts include:

03 eye
jaw
leg
rib

04 coxa
gula
head
horn
legs
palp
rasp
vein
wing

05 chela
colon
costa
femur
media
nerve
notum
scape
sting
tibia

06 air-sac
antlia
arista
cercus
feeler

glossa
labium
ligula
median
mentum
palpus
proleg
radius
scapus
scutum
sheath
somite
squama
stilet
stylet
tarsus
tegmen
tegula
tergum
thorax
unguis
venule

07 abdomen
aculeus
antenna
clypeus
cuticle
elytron
elytrum

maxilla
nervure
ocellus
pedicel
phalanx
pleuron
segment
sternum
strigil
terebra
torulus

08 antennae
cheliped
false leg
forewing
frenulum
gnathite
hindwing
labellum
mandible
onychium
ovariole
peduncle
pronotum
pygidium
spiracle
sternite
subcosta
tympanum

wing case

09 mouthpart
prescutum
proboscis
propodeon
prothorax
pulvillus
scutellum
sectorial
sensillum
subcostal
submentum
tentorium
underwing

10 acetabulum
epicuticle
haustellum
integument
mesothorax
metathorax
ovipositor
paraglossa
trochanter

11 compound eye
retinaculum

13 sclerodermite

14 proventriculus

See also **ant**; **beetle**; **butterfly**; **cicada**; **fly**; **moth**; **poison**

insecticide

Insecticides include:

02 Bt	safrole	rotenone	dimethoate
03 BHC	08 camphene	09 chlordane	Paris green
DDT	carbaryl	Gammexane®	piperazine
05 timbó	chlordan	Malathion®	15 organophosphate
zineb	chromene	parathion	
06 aldrin	diazinon	pyrethrum	
derris	dieldrin	toxaphene	
07 cinerin	flyspray	10 carbofuran	
	nicotine		

See also **poison**

insectivorous plant

Insectivorous plants include:

06 sundew	09 cobra lily	sun pitcher	Venus flytrap
07 pitcher	corkscrew	waterwheel	13 Albany pitcher
rainbow	monkey cup	11 bladderwort	Venus's flytrap
08 dewy pine	10 butterwort	12 marsh pitcher	15 tropical pitcher

institute

Institutes include:

02 IA (Institute of Aging)
IM (Institute of Management)
WI (Women's Institute)

03 BFI (British Film Institute)
CGI (City and Guilds of London Institute)
CIB (Chartered Institute of Bankers)
CMI (Chartered Management Institute)
EMI (European Monetary Institute)
ICA (Institute of Chartered Accountants;
Institute of Contemporary Art)
MIT (Massachusetts Institute of Technology)

04 NICE (National Institute of Clinical Excellence)

RIBA (Royal Institute of British Architects)
RNIB (Royal National Institute of Blind
People)
RNID (Royal National Institute for Deaf
People)
RTPI (Royal Town Planning Institute)

05 C and G (City and Guilds of London Institute)
UMIST (University of Manchester Institute of
Science and Technology)
UWIST (University of Wales Institute of
Science and Technology)

07 Caltech (California Institute of Technology)

See also **charity**; **university**

instrument *see* **laboratory**; **measurement**; **music**; **musician**; **optics**; **science**; **torture**

insulator

Insulators include:

03 lag	tea cosy	10 dielectric	14 insulating tape
04 mica	08 rock wool	11 vermiculite	Willesden paper
07 bushing	09 Pink Batts®	12 friction tape	

International Vehicle Registration code *see* **vehicle**

Internet suffix *see* **computer**

invention

01 I (Hsing; 682–727, Chinese)

02 Su (Song; 1020–1101, Chinese)
Su (Sung; 1020–1101, Chinese)
Yi (Xing; 682–727, Chinese)

03 Hoe (Richard; 1812–86, US)
Kay (John; 1704–c.1780, English)
Lee (James; 1831–1904, Scottish/US)
Sax (Adolphe; 1814–94, Belgian)
Zai (Lun; c.50–118 AD, Chinese)

04 Abel (Sir Frederick; 1827–1902, English)
Bell (Alexander Graham; 1847–1922, Scottish/US)
Bell (Patrick; 1799–1869, Scottish)
Benz (Karl; 1844–1929, German)
Biró (Laszlo; 1899–1985, Hungarian/Argentine)
Böhm (Theobald; 1794–1881, German)
Bush (Vannevar; 1890–1974, US)
Cohl (Emile; 1857–1938, French)
Colt (Samuel; 1814–62, US)
Davy (Sir Humphry; 1778–1829, English)
Eads (James; 1820–87, US)
Gray (Elisha; 1835–1901, US)
Gray (Gustave Le; 1820–82, French)
Hein (Piet; 1905–96, Danish)
Hood (Thomas; 1799–1845, English)
Howe (Elias; 1819–67, US)
Ives (Frederick; 1856–1937, US)
Jobs (Steve; 1955– , US)
Kyan (John; 1774–1850, Irish)
Land (Edwin; 1909–91, US)
Lear (William; 1902–78, US)
Lyot (Bernard; 1897–1952, French)
Moon (William; 1818–94, English)
Otis (Elisha; 1811–61, US)
Paul (Lewis; d.1759, English)
Swan (Sir Joseph; 1828–1914, English)
Tiro (Marcus Tullius; 1c AD, Roman)
Tsai (Lun; c.50–118 AD, Chinese)
Tull (Jethro; 1674–1741, English)
Very (Edward; 1847–1910, US)
Watt (James; 1736–1819, Scottish)
Yale (Linus; 1821–68, US)

05 Adams (William Bridges; 1797–1872, English)
Baird (John Logie; 1888–1946, Scottish)
Basov (Nikolai; 1922–2001, Russian)
Beach (Moses; 1800–68, US)
Boehm (Theobald; 1794–1881, German)
Boyle (Robert; 1627–91, Irish)
Chang (Heng; 78–139 AD, Chinese)
Clegg (Samuel; 1781–1861, English)
Cooke (Sir William Fothergill; 1806–79, English)
Creed (Frederick; 1871–1957, Scottish)
Cyril (St; 827–69, Greek)
Deere (John; 1804–86, US)
Dunne (John William; 1875–1949, English)
Dyson (James; 1947– , English)
Evans (Oliver; 1755–1819, US)
Gregg (John Robert; 1867–1948, US)
Hertz (Heinrich; 1857–94, German)
Hyatt (John Wesley; 1837–1920, US)
Kelly (William; 1811–88, US)
Kilby (Jack S; 1923–2005, US)
König (Friedrich; 1774–1833, German)
Manby (George William; 1765–1854, English)
Maxim (Sir Hiram; 1840–1916, US/British)
Monge (Gaspard; 1746–1818, French)
Morey (Samuel; 1762–1843, US)
Morse (Samuel; 1791–1872, US)
Nobel (Alfred; 1833–96, Swedish)
Olson (Harry F; 1901–82, US)
Peale (Charles Willson; 1741–1827, US)
Pupin (Michael; 1858–1935, US)
Rubik (Ernö; 1944– , Hungarian)
Smith (Sir Francis Pettit; 1808–74, English)
Sousa (John Philip; 1854–1932, US)
Tesla (Nikola; 1856–1943, US)
Volta (Alessandro, Count; 1745–1827, Italian)
Wynne (Arthur; 1862–1945, English)
Zeiss (Carl; 1816–88, German)

06 Ampère (André Marie; 1775–1836, French)
Appert (Nicolas; 1749–1841, French)
Aspdin (Joseph; 1779–1855, English)
Ayrton (William; 1847–1908, English)
Baylis, (Trevor; 1937– , English)
Berger (Hans; 1873–1941, German)
Besson (Jacques; c.1535–c.1575, French)
Bodmer (Johann Georg; 1786–1864, Swiss)
Bramah (Joseph; 1748–1814, English)
Bright (Timothy; c.1551–1615, English)
Brunel (Isambard Kingdom; 1806–59, English)
Brunel (Sir Marc; 1769–1849, French)
Bunsen (Robert; 1811–99, German)
Chappe (Claude; 1763–1805, French)
Church (William; c.1778–1863, US)
Cooper (Peter; 1791–1883, US)
Curtis (Charles; 1860–1953, US)
Diesel (Rudolf; 1858–1913, German)
Donald (Ian; 1910–87, Scottish)
Donkin (Bryan; 1768–1855, English)
Dunlop (John Boyd; 1840–1921, Scottish)
Eckert (J Presper; 1919–95, US)

Edison (Thomas Alva; 1847–1931, US)
Fairey (Sir Richard; 1887–1956, English)
Frisch (Otto; 1904–79, Austrian/British)
Fuller (Richard Buckminster; 1895–1983, US)
Gurney (Sir Goldsworthy; 1793–1875, English)
Hansom (Joseph; 1803–82, English)
Haynes (Elwood; 1857–1925, US)
Hedley (William; 1779–1843, English)
Hornby (Frank; 1863–1936, English)
Hubble (Edwin; 1889–1953, US)
Hughes (D E; 1831–1900, English/US)
Hussey (Obed; 1792–1860, US)
Kaplan (Viktor; 1876–1934, Austrian)
Lenoir (Jean Joseph Étienne; 1822–1900, French)
Lister (Samuel, Lord; 1815–1906, English)
Mauser (P P von; 1838–1914, German)
McAdam (John; 1756–1836, Scottish)
Meikle (Andrew; 1719–1811, Scottish)
Murray (Matthew; 1765–1826, English)
Napier (John; 1550–1617, Scottish)
Newton (Sir Isaac; 1642–1727, English)
Oatley (Sir Charles; 1904–96, English)
Parkes (Alexander; 1813–90, English)
Pascal (Blaise; 1623–62, French)
Pelton (Lester; 1829–1918, US)
Pitman (Sir Isaac; 1813–97, English)
Rumsey (James; 1743–92, US)
Savery (Thomas; c.1650–1715, English)
Schick (Jacob; 1878–1937, US)
Singer (Isaac; 1811–75, US)
Sperry (Elmer; 1860–1930, US)
Stroud (William; 1860–1938, English)
Talbot (William Fox; 1800–77, English)
Walker (John; c.1781–1859, English)
Wallis (Sir Barnes; 1887–1979, English)
Wright (Orville; 1871–1948, US)
Wright (Wilbur; 1867–1912, US)

07 Acheson (Edward; 1856–1931, US)
Babbage (Charles; 1791–1871, English)
Babbitt (Isaac; 1799–1862, US)
Bednorz (J Georg; 1950–   , German)
Bentham (Sir Samuel; 1757–1831, English)
Bigelow (Erastus; 1814–79, US)
Bourdon (Eugène; 1808–84, French)
Byrgius (Justus; 1552–1633, Swiss)
Carlson (Chester; 1906–68, US)
Carrier (Willis H; 1876–1950, US)
Corliss (George H; 1817–88, US)
Curtiss (Glenn; 1878–1930, US)
Daimler (Gottlieb; 1834–1900, German)
Drebbel (Cornelis; c.1572–1633, Dutch/British)
Eastman (George; 1854–1932, US)
Faraday (Michael; 1791–1867, English)
Forsyth (Alexander John; 1769–1843, Scottish)

Francis (James Bicheno; 1815–92, English/US)
Gatling (Richard; 1818–1903, US)
Gaumont (Léon; 1864–1946, French)
Giffard (Henri; 1825–82, French)
Goddard (Robert; 1882–1945, US)
Hancock (Thomas; 1786–1865, English)
Hartley (David; 1732–1813, English)
Holland (John; 1840–1914, Irish/US)
Huygens (Christiaan; 1629–93, Dutch)
Jacuzzi (Candido; 1903–86, Italian/US)
Janssen (Zacharias; 1580–1638, Dutch)
Laënnec (René; 1781–1826, French)
Lanston (Tolbert; 1844–1913, US)
Lumière (Auguste; 1862–1954, French)
Lumière (Louis; 1865–1948, French)
Marconi (Guglielmo, Marchese; 1874–1937, Italian)
Mauchly (John W; 1907–80, US)
Maxwell (James Clerk; 1831–79, Scottish)
Maybach (Wilhelm; 1846–1929, German)
Metford (William; 1824–99, English)
Midgley (Thomas, Jnr; 1889–1944, US)
Panhard (René; 1841–1908, French)
Pasteur (Louis; 1822–95, French)
Perkins (Jacob; 1766–1849, US)
Pullman (George; 1831–97, US)
Roberts (Richard; 1789–1864, Welsh)
Roebuck (John; 1718–94, English)
Ronalds (Sir Francis; 1788–1873, English)
Scheutz (Georg; 1785–1873, Swedish)
Sprague (Frank; 1857–1934, US)
Stanley (Francis; 1849–1918, US)
Starley (James; 1831–81, English)
Stevens (John; 1749–1838, US)
Stevens (Robert L; 1787–1856, US)
Swinton (Alan Campbell; 1863–1930, Scottish)
Swinton (Sir Ernest; 1868–1951, Indian/British)
Thomson (Elihu; 1853–1937, US)
Thomson (Robert; 1822–73, Scottish)
Whitney (Eli; 1765–1825, US)
Whittle (Sir Frank; 1907–96, English)

08 Berliner (Émile; 1851–1929, US)
Berthoud (Ferdinand; 1727–1807, Swiss)
Bessemer (Sir Henry; 1813–98, English)
Bickford (William; 1774–1834, English)
Birdseye (Clarence; 1886–1956, US)
Bogardus (James; 1800–74, US)
Browning (John M; 1855–1926, US)
Chalmers (James; 1782–1853, Scottish)
Coolidge (William D; 1873–1975, US)
Crompton (Samuel; 1753–1827, English)
Daguerre (Louis; 1789–1851, French)
De Forest (Lee; 1873–1961, US)
Ericsson (John; 1803–89, Swedish/US)
Ferguson (Harry; 1884–1960, Irish)

Ferguson (Patrick; 1744–80, Scottish)
Ferranti (Sebastian Ziani de; 1864–1930, English)
Franklin (Benjamin; 1706–90, US)
Geissler (Heinrich; 1814–79, German)
Gillette (King Camp; 1855–1932, US)
Goldmark (Peter; 1906–77, Hungarian/US)
Goodyear (Charles; 1800–60, US)
Harrison (John; 1693–1776, English)
Huntsman (Benjamin; 1704–76, English)
Janszoon (Laurens; c.1370–1440, Dutch)
Maudslay (Henry; 1771–1831, English)
McNaught (William; 1813–81, Scottish)
Newcomen (Thomas; 1663–1729, English)
Sandwich (John Montagu, Earl of; 1718–92, English)
Schawlow (Arthur L; 1921–99, US)
Sinclair (Sir Clive; 1940– , English)
Sprengel (Hermann; 1834–1906, German/British)
Stirling (Robert; 1790–1878, Scottish)
Thompson (John T; 1860–1940, US)
Zamenhof (Ludwig; 1859–1917, Polish)
Zeppelin (Count Ferdinand von; 1838–1917, German)

09 Applegath (Augustus; 1788–1871, English)
Arkwright (Sir Richard; 1732–92, English)
Armstrong (Edwin H; 1890–1954, US)
Armstrong (William, Lord; 1810–1900, English)
Blanchard (Jean Pierre; 1753–1809, French)
Burroughs (William Seward; 1855–98, US)
Butterick (Ebenezer; 1826–1903, US)
Carothers (Wallace; 1896–1937, US)
Cockerell (Sir Christopher; 1910–99, English)
Ctesibius (2c BC, Greek)
de Mestral (George; 1907–90, Swiss)
Elkington (George; 1801–65, English)
Fessenden (Reginald; 1866–1932, Canadian/US)
Fleischer (Max; 1883–1972, Austrian/US)
Greathead (James Henry; 1844–96, South African/British)
Gutenberg (Johannes; 1400–68, German)
Heathcoat (John; 1783–1861, English)
Hollerith (Herman; 1860–1929, US)
Hotchkiss (Benjamin B; 1826–85, US)
MacCready (Paul; 1925–2007, US)

Macintosh (Charles; 1766–1843, Scottish)
Macmillan (Kirkpatrick; 1813–78, Scottish)
McCormick (Cyrus; 1809–84, US)
Muybridge (Eadweard; 1830–1904, English/US)
Nicholson (William; 1753–1815, English)
Pinchbeck (Christopher; c.1710–1783, English)
Remington (Philo; 1816–89, US)
Schickard (Wilhelm; 1592–1635, German)
Symington (William; 1763–1831, Scottish)
Vaucanson (Jacques de; 1709–82, French)
Whitehead (Robert; 1823–1905, English)
Whitworth (Sir Joseph; 1803–87, English)
Wilkinson (John; 1728–1808, English)
Worcester (Edward Somerset, Earl of; 1601–67, English)

10 Archimedes (c.287–212 BC, Greek)
Berners-Lee (Tim; 1955– , English)
Cartwright (Edmund; 1743–1823, English)
Cristofori (Bartolommeo; 1655–1731, Italian)
Fahrenheit (Gabriel; 1686–1736, German)
Fourneyron (Benoît; 1802–67, French)
Hargreaves (James; c.1720–1778, English)
Laithwaite (Eric; 1921–97, English)
Lanchester (Frederick; 1868–1946, English)
Lilienthal (Otto; 1849–96, German)
Pilkington (Sir Alastair; 1920–95, English)
Senefelder (Aloys; 1771–1834, German)
Stephenson (George; 1781–1848, English)
Torricelli (Evangelista; 1608–47, Italian)
Trevithick (Richard; 1771–1833, English)

11 Cristofaloi (Bartolommeo; 1655–1731, Italian)
Desaguliers (J T; 1683–1744, French/British)
Mège Mouriés (Hippolyte; 1817–80, French)
Montgolfier (Jacques; 1745–99, French)
Montgolfier (Joseph; 1740–1810, French)
Reichenbach (Georg von; 1772–1826, German)

12 Alexanderson (Ernst; 1878–1975, Swedish/US)
Friese-Greene (William; 1855–1921, English)
Mergenthaler (Ottmar; 1854–99, German/US)
Stringfellow (John; 1799–1883, English)

invertebrate

Invertebrates include:

05	**06**	**07**
coral	chiton	bivalve
fluke	insect	crinoid
hydra	spider	mollusc
leech	sponge	sea lily

sea wasp

08 arachnid
flatworm
nematode
sea pansy
starfish
tapeworm

09 arthropod
centipede
earthworm
gastropod
jellyfish
millipede

planarian
roundworm
sea spider
sea urchin
spoonworm
trilobite
water bear

10 cephalopod
crustacean
echinoderm
sand dollar
sea anemone
tardigrade

11 annelid worm
brittle star
chaetognath
feather star
globigerina
sea cucumber

12 box jellyfish
coelenterate
Venus's girdle

13 crown-of-thorns
horseshoe crab
sea gooseberry

15 dead-men's fingers

See also **ant**; **beetle**; **butterfly**; **crustacean**; **insect**; **jellyfish**; **mollusc**; **moth**; **spider**; **worm**

Ireland

Cities and notable towns in Ireland include:

04 Cork
05 Sligo

06 Dublin
Galway

07 Dundalk
08 Drogheda

Limerick
09 Waterford

Administrative divisions of Ireland, with regional capitals:

04 Cork
Leix (Portlaoise)
Mayo (Castlebar)
05 Cavan
Clare (Ennis)
Kerry (Tralee)
Louth (Dundalk)
Meath (Trim)
Sligo

06 Carlow
Dublin
Galway
Offaly (Tullamore)
07 Donegal (Lifford)
Kildare (Naas)
Leitrim (Carrick)
Wexford
Wicklow

08 Kilkenny
Laoighis (Portlaoise)
Limerick
Longford
Monaghan
09 Roscommon
Tipperary (Clonmel)
Waterford
Westmeath (Mullingar)

Ancient Irish provinces:

06 Ulster
07 Munster

08 Connacht
Leinster

Irish landmarks include:

03 Lee
05 Boyne
06 Liffey
07 Shannon
09 Bantry Bay
Connemara

Dublin Bay
Temple Bar
10 Sligo Abbey
11 Ferns Castle
12 Abbey Theatre
Blarney Stone

Dublin Castle
13 Ha'penny Bridge
14 O'Connell Street
Trinity College
15 Dingle Peninsula

See also **mythology**; **United Kingdom**

Irish

Irish boys' names include:

03 Kit
Pat

04 Colm
Edel

Elva
Eoin

Euan
Ewan

Ewen
Finn
Liam
Neal
Neil
Owen
Rory
Ryan
Sean

05 Aidan
Aiden
Barry
Cahal
Colum
Conor

Duane
Dwane
Elvis
Kelly
Kerry
Kevan
Kevin
Neale
Niall
Oscar
Paddy
Ronan
Shane
Shaun
Shawn

Ultan
06 Arthur
Cathal
Ciaran
Connor
Declan
Eamonn
Eamunn
Finbar
Fingal
Fintan
Kieran
Kieron
Kilian
Lorcan

Seamas
Seamus
Shamus
Tyrone
07 Brendan
Christy
Desmond
Feargal
Finbarr
Killian
Padraic
Padraig
Patrick
Shannon
08 Ruaidhri

Irish girls' names include:

03 Ena
Una
04 Aine
Cait
Erin
Kath
Kyra
Maev
Maud
Mona
Nola
Nora
Sine
Tara
05 Brona
Ciara

Ethna
Ethne
Fionn
Kelly
Kiera
Maeve
Maire
Maude
Maura
Moira
Moyra
Niamh
Norah
Nuala
Rowan
06 Aileen

Ailish
Dervla
Dympna
Eileen
Eithna
Eithne
Finola
Garret
Grania
Granya
Noreen
Roisin
Sheila
Sinead
Sorcha
07 Aisling

Bronach
Bronagh
Caitlin
Clodagh
Colleen
Deirdre
Dymphna
Grainne
Mairead
Maureen
Shannon
Shelagh
Siobhan
08 Kathleen
09 Fionnuala

Islam

Muslim groups and denominations include:

04 Shia
05 Ibadi
Shiah
Sunni
06 Senusi
Shiite

07 Alawite
dervish
Mevlevi
Senussi
Sonnite
Sunnite

08 Senoussi
10 Karmathian
11 Black Muslim
15 whirling dervish

See also **calendar**; **religion**

island

Islands and island groups include:

03 Cos (Aegean Sea)
Fyn (Baltic Sea)
Ios (Aegean Sea)
Man (Irish Sea)
Rab (Mediterranean Sea)
Rum (Sea of the Hebrides)

04 Aran (Atlantic Ocean)
Bali (Indian Ocean)
Coll (Atlantic Ocean)
Cook (Pacific Ocean)
Corn (Caribbean Sea)
Cuba (Caribbean Sea)

Eigg (Sea of the Hebrides)
Elba (Tyrrhenian Sea/Mediterranean Sea)
Fiji (Pacific Ocean)
Gozo (Mediterranean Sea)
Guam (Pacific Ocean)
Herm (English Channel)
Holy (North Sea)
Iona (Atlantic Ocean)
Java (Java Sea/Indian Ocean)
Jura (Atlantic Ocean)
Line (Pacific Ocean)
Long (Atlantic Ocean)
Mahe (Indian Ocean)
Maui (Pacific Ocean)
Muck (Sea of the Hebrides)
Mull (Sea of the Hebrides/Atlantic Ocean)
Nias (Indian Ocean)
Niue (Pacific Ocean)
Oahu (Pacific Ocean)
Rota (Pacific Ocean)
Sado (Sea of Japan)
Sark (English Channel)
Skye (Sea of the Hebrides/Atlantic Ocean)
Wake (Pacific Ocean)

05 Arran (Atlantic Ocean)
Barra (Atlantic Ocean)
Bioko (Atlantic Ocean)
Bonin (Pacific Ocean)
Capri (Tyrrhenian Sea/Mediterranean Sea)
Chios (Aegean Sea)
Cocos (Indian Ocean)
Coney (Atlantic Ocean)
Corfu (Ionian Sea)
Crete (Aegean Sea/Mediterranean Sea)
Éfaté (Coral Sea/Pacific Ocean)
Ellis (Atlantic Ocean)
Faroe (Atlantic Ocean/Arctic Ocean)
Handa (Atlantic Ocean)
Hondo (East China Sea)
Hydra (Aegean Sea)
Ibiza (Mediterranean Sea)
Islay (Atlantic Ocean)
Kauai (Pacific Ocean)
Kuril (Pacific Ocean)
Lanai (Pacific Ocean)
Lundy (Celtic Sea/Atlantic Ocean)
Luzon (South China Sea/Pacific Ocean)
Malta (Mediterranean Sea)
Melos (Aegean Sea)
Nauru (Pacific Ocean)
Naxos (Aegean Sea)
North (Tasman Sea/Pacific Ocean)
Öland (Baltic Sea)
Orust (North Sea)
Palau (Pacific Ocean)
Paros (Aegean Sea)
Pearl (Indian Ocean)
Pemba (Indian Ocean)

Samoa (Pacific Ocean)
Samos (Aegean Sea)
South (Tasman Sea/Pacific Ocean)
Sunda (Celebes Sea/South China Sea)
Timor (Timor Sea/Indian Ocean)
Tiree (Sea of the Hebrides/Atlantic Ocean)
Tonga (Pacific Ocean)
Wight (English Channel)

06 Aegean (Aegean Sea)
Aegina (Aegean Sea)
Andros (Atlantic Ocean)
Azores (Atlantic Ocean)
Baffin (Labrador Sea/Arctic Ocean)
Bikini (Pacific Ocean)
Borneo (South China Sea/Celebes Sea)
Caicos (Atlantic Ocean)
Canary (Atlantic Ocean)
Chagos (Indian Ocean)
Comino (Mediterranean Sea)
Cyprus (Mediterranean Sea)
Devil's (Atlantic Ocean)
Easter (Pacific Ocean)
Euboea (Aegean Sea)
Flores (Pacific Ocean)
Flotta (Atlantic Ocean)
Hainan (South China Sea)
Harris (Atlantic Ocean)
Hawaii (Pacific Ocean)
Honshu (Pacific Ocean/East China Sea/Sea
   of Japan)
Icaria (Aegean Sea)
Ionian (Ionian Sea)
Jersey (English Channel)
Kodiak (Pacific Ocean)
Komodo (Flores Sea/Indian Ocean)
Kosrae (Pacific Ocean)
Kyushu (East China Sea/Pacific Ocean)
Lesbos (Aegean Sea)
Limnos (Aegean Sea/Mediterranean Sea)
Midway (Pacific Ocean)
Orkney (North Sea/Atlantic Ocean)
Patmos (Aegean Sea)
Penghu (South China Sea)
Rhodes (Aegean Sea/Mediterranean Sea)
Scilly (Atlantic Ocean)
Sicily (Mediterranean Sea)
Skiros (Aegean Sea)
Staffa (Sea of the Hebrides/Atlantic Ocean)
Staten (Atlantic Ocean)
Tahiti (Pacific Ocean)
Taiwan (China Sea/Pacific Ocean)
Tinian (Philippine Sea/Pacific Ocean)
Tobago (Caribbean Sea/Atlantic Ocean)
Tubuai (Pacific Ocean)
Tuvalu (Pacific Ocean)
Virgin (Caribbean Sea/Atlantic Ocean)

07 Anjouan (Indian Ocean)

Antigua (Caribbean Sea/Atlantic Ocean)
Bahrain (Persian Gulf)
Barbuda (Caribbean Sea/Atlantic Ocean)
Bermuda (Atlantic Ocean)
Bonaire (Caribbean Sea)
Cabrera (South China Sea)
Celebes (Celebes Sea/Molucca Sea/Java Sea/
  Banda Sea)
Channel (English Channel)
Chatham (Pacific Ocean)
Comoros (Indian Ocean)
Corsica (Mediterranean Sea)
Curaçao (Caribbean Sea)
Frisian (North Sea)
Gilbert (Pacific Ocean)
Gotland (Baltic Sea)
Grenada (Atlantic Ocean)
Iceland (Greenland Sea/Atlantic Ocean)
Ireland (Irish Sea/Atlantic Ocean)
Iwo Jima (Pacific Ocean)
Jamaica (Caribbean Sea)
La Digue (Indian Ocean)
Leeward (Caribbean Sea/Atlantic Ocean)
Lofoten (Arctic Ocean)
Loyalty (Coral Sea/Pacific Ocean)
Madeira (Atlantic Ocean)
Majorca (Mediterranean Sea)
Mayotte (Indian Ocean)
Menorca (Mediterranean Sea)
Mikonos (Aegean Sea)
Mindoro (South China Sea/Sulu Sea)
Minorca (Mediterranean Sea)
Molokai (Pacific Ocean)
Nicobar (Indian Ocean)
Norfolk (Pacific Ocean)
Okinawa (East China Sea)
Palawan (South China Sea/Sulu Sea)
Phoenix (Pacific Ocean)
Praslin (Indian Ocean)
Rathlin (Atlantic Ocean)
Réunion (Indian Ocean)
Salamis (Aegean Sea/Mediterranean Sea)
Siberut (Indian Ocean)
Society (Pacific Ocean)
Solomon (Solomon Sea/Pacific Ocean)
Stewart (Tasman Sea/Pacific Ocean)
St Kilda (Atlantic Ocean)
St Lucia (Caribbean Sea/Atlantic Ocean)
Sumatra (Indian Ocean)
Surtsey (Atlantic Ocean)
Tokelau (Pacific Ocean)
Vanuatu (Coral Sea/Pacific Ocean)
Visayan (Pacific Ocean)
Wrangel (Chukchi Sea/East Siberian Sea/
  Arctic Ocean)
Zealand (Baltic Sea)

08 Alderney (English Channel)
Aleutian (Bering Sea)

Anglesey (Irish Sea)
Anguilla (Caribbean Sea)
Balearic (Mediterranean Sea)
Barbados (Caribbean Sea/Atlantic Ocean)
Bornholm (Baltic Sea)
Colonsay (Atlantic Ocean)
Coral Sea (Coral Sea/Pacific Ocean)
Cyclades (Aegean Sea)
Dominica (Caribbean Sea/Atlantic Ocean)
Falkland (Atlantic Ocean)
Guernsey (English Channel)
Hawaiian (Pacific Ocean)
Hebrides (Atlantic Ocean)
Hokkaido (Sea of Japan/Sea of Okhotsk/
  Pacific Ocean)
Hong Kong (South China Sea)
Jan Mayen (Arctic Ocean)
Johnston (Pacific Ocean)
Kiribati (Pacific Ocean)
Lord Howe (Pacific Ocean)
Maldives (Indian Ocean)
Mallorca (Mediterranean Sea)
Marshall (Pacific Ocean)
Mindanao (Philippine Sea/Sulu Sea/Pacific
  Ocean)
Moluccas (Pacific Ocean)
Pitcairn (Pacific Ocean)
Sakhalin (Sea of Okhotsk/Pacific Ocean)
Sandwich (Pacific Ocean)
São Tiago (Atlantic Ocean)
Sardinia (Mediterranean Sea)
Shetland (Atlantic Ocean)
Skiathos (Aegean Sea)
Sri Lanka (Indian Ocean)
St Helena (Atlantic Ocean)
Sulawesi (Banda Sea/Java Sea/Molucca Sea)
Svalbard (Arctic Ocean)
Tasmania (Indian Ocean/Pacific Ocean)
Tenerife (Atlantic Ocean)
Trinidad (Caribbean Sea/Atlantic Ocean)
Victoria (Atlantic Ocean; Arctic Ocean)
Viti Levu (Pacific Ocean)
Westmann (Atlantic Ocean)
Windward (Caribbean Sea/Atlantic Ocean)
Zanzibar (Indian Ocean)

09 Admiralty (Bismarck Sea)
Ascension (Atlantic Ocean)
Australia (Tasman Sea/Coral Sea/Pacific
  Ocean/Indian Ocean)
Benbecula (Atlantic Ocean)
Cape Verde (Atlantic Ocean)
Christmas (Indian Ocean)
Ellesmere (Arctic Ocean)
Galápagos (Pacific Ocean)
Greenland (Atlantic Ocean/Arctic Ocean)
Halmahera (Pacific Ocean)
Indonesia (Indian Ocean/Pacific Ocean)
Irian Jaya (Indian Ocean/Pacific Ocean)

Isle of Man (Irish Sea)
Kárpathos (Aegean Sea/Mediterranean Sea)
Lanzarote (Atlantic Ocean)
Las Palmas (Atlantic Ocean)
Macquarie (Pacific Ocean)
Manhattan (Atlantic Ocean)
Marquesas (Pacific Ocean)
Mascarene (Indian Ocean)
Mauritius (Indian Ocean)
Melanesia (Pacific Ocean)
Nantucket (Atlantic Ocean)
New Guinea (Coral Sea/Solomon Sea/Pacific Ocean)
North Uist (Sea of the Hebrides/Atlantic Ocean)
Rodrigues (Indian Ocean)
Santorini (Aegean Sea)
Singapore (South China Sea)
South Uist (Sea of the Hebrides/Atlantic Ocean)
Stromboli (Tyrrhenian Sea)
Vanua Levu (Pacific Ocean)
Zacynthus (Ionian Sea/Mediterranean Sea)

10 Ahvenanmaa (Baltic Sea)
Basse-Terre (Caribbean Sea/Atlantic Ocean)
Cape Breton (Atlantic Ocean)
Cephalonia (Ionian Sea/Mediterranean Sea)
Dodecanese (Aegean Sea)
Formentera (Mediterranean Sea)
Heligoland (North Sea)
Hispaniola (Caribbean Sea/Atlantic Ocean)
Ile d'Oléron (Atlantic Ocean)
Kalimantan (Celebes Sea)
Kiritimati (Pacific Ocean)
Madagascar (Indian Ocean)
Martinique (Caribbean Sea/Atlantic Ocean)
Micronesia (Pacific Ocean)
Montserrat (Caribbean Sea)
New Britain (Solomon Sea/Bismarck Sea/Pacific Ocean)
New Ireland (Solomon Sea/Bismarck Sea/Pacific Ocean)
Puerto Rico (Caribbean Sea/Atlantic Ocean)
Samothrace (Aegean Sea)

See also **archipelago**

Seychelles (Indian Ocean)
The Bahamas (Caribbean Sea)
Vesterålen (Norwegian Sea/Arctic Ocean)
West Indies (Caribbean Sea)

11 Gran Canaria (Atlantic Ocean)
Grand Bahama (Atlantic Ocean)
Grand Cayman (Caribbean Sea)
Grande-Terre (Indian Ocean)
Guadalcanal (Pacific Ocean)
Iles d'Hyères (Mediterranean Sea)
Iles du Salut (Atlantic Ocean)
Isla Cozumel (Caribbean Sea)
Isle of Wight (English Channel)
Scilly Isles (Atlantic Ocean)
South Orkney (North Sea/Atlantic Ocean)

12 Bougainville (Pacific Ocean)
Grande Comore (Indian Ocean)
Great Britain (North Sea/Irish Sea/Atlantic Ocean)
Isla de Pascua (Pacific Ocean)
Newfoundland (Atlantic Ocean)
Novaya Zemlya (Kara Sea/Arctic Ocean)
Prince Edward (Atlantic Ocean)
South Georgia (Atlantic Ocean)

13 American Samoa (Pacific Ocean)
British Virgin (Caribbean Sea)
Inner Hebrides (Atlantic Ocean)
Isla Contadora (Pacific Ocean)
Isles of Scilly (Atlantic Ocean)
New Providence (Atlantic Ocean)
Outer Hebrides (Atlantic Ocean)
South Shetland (Atlantic Ocean)

14 Oki Archipelago (Sea of Japan)
Papua New Guinea (Pacific Ocean)
Tierra del Fuego (Atlantic Ocean/Pacific Ocean/Southern Ocean)
Tristan da Cunha (Atlantic Ocean)
Turks and Caicos (Atlantic Ocean)

15 French Polynesia (Pacific Ocean)
Lewis with Harris (Atlantic Ocean)
Martha's Vineyard (Atlantic Ocean)
Wallis and Futuna (Pacific Ocean)

Italian

Italian words and expressions include:

04 ciao (hello; bye)

05 prego (you're welcome)
salve (hello)

06 grazie (thanks)
stucco (ornamental plasterwork)

07 al dente (culinary term denoting cooked but firm)

barista (espresso coffee machine operator)

08 al fresco (in the open air)
intaglio (engraving)
seraglio (a harem or place of confinement)

09 a cappella (sung without instrumental accompaniment)
antipasto (appetizer)

paparazzo (photographer who pursues celebrities)
sgraffito (decoration achieved by scratching through to subsurface)
sotto voce (in an undertone; aside)

10 buongiorno (good morning)
Cosa Nostra (the Mafia)
prima donna (leading female singer in an opera)

11 arrivederci (good-bye)

See also **day**; **month**; **number**

che sarà sarà (what will be will be)
chiaroscuro (painting in which only light and shade are represented)
gran turismo (a car designed for high speed touring in luxury)
la dolce vita (a life of wealth, pleasure and self-indulgence)

12 così fan tutte (all women are like that)
lingua franca (a language chosen as a medium of communication among speakers of different languages)

Italy

Cities and notable towns in Italy include:

04 Pisa
Rome
05 Genoa
Milan
Turin
06 Naples
Venice
07 Bologna
Palermo
08 Florence

Administrative divisions of Italy, with regional capitals:

05 Lazio (Rome)
06 Marche (Ancona)
Molise (Campobasso)
Puglia (Bari)
Sicily (Palermo)
Umbria (Perugia)
Veneto (Venice)
07 Abruzzi (L'Aquila)
Liguria (Genoa)
Sicilia (Palermo)
Toscana (Florence)
Tuscany (Florence)
08 Calabria (Catanzaro)
Campania (Naples)
Lombardy (Milan)
Piedmont (Turin)
Piemonte (Turin)
Sardegna (Cagliari)
Sardinia (Cagliari)
09 Lombardia (Milan)
10 Basilicata (Potenza)
11 Valle d'Aosta (Aosta)
13 Emilia-Romagna (Bologna)
17 Trentino-Alto Adige (Bozen/Trient)
19 Friuli-Venezia Giulia (Trieste)

Italian landmarks include:

02 Po
04 Arno
Como
Etna
Lido
05 David
Forum
Garda
Tiber
06 Mt Etna
07 La Scala
Pompeii
08 Lake Como
Maggiore
Pantheon
St Peter's
Vesuvius
09 Appian Way
Campanile
Colosseum
Dolomites
Lake Garda
10 Grand Canal
Mt Vesuvius
11 Doge's Palace
Herculaneum
Vatican City
12 Lake Maggiore
Leaning Tower
Ponte Vecchio
Rialto Bridge
13 Bridge of Sighs
Sistine Chapel
St Mark's Square
Uffizi Gallery
Vatican Palace
14 Palazzo Vecchio
Piazza San Marco
St Peter's Square
Via Appia Antica

IVR code *see* **vehicle**

Ivy League *see* **university**

J

James Bond

Characters in James Bond films include:

01 M
Q
03 Aki
Zao
04 Bibi
Jaws
Jinx
05 Irina
Mr Big
Naomi
06 Bianca
Fields
Mathis
May Day
Oddjob
Renard
TeeHee
Wai Lin
07 Blofeld
Camille
Columbo
Mr White
Sanchez
Stamper

08 Hugo Drax
Max Zorin
Nick Nack
Red Grant
Whitaker
09 Kristatos
Le Chiffre
Octopussy
Rosa Klebb
Solitaire
Stromberg
10 Fiona Volpe
Goldfinger
Honey Ryder
Kara Milovy
Lupe Lamora
Pam Bouvier
Scaramanga
Vesper Lynd
11 Anya Amasova
Elektra King
Emilio Largo
Felix Leiter
Helga Brandt
Kissy Suzuki

Paris Carver
Pola Ivanova
Pussy Galore
Rosie Carver
Tiffany Case
Tiger Tanaka
12 Andrea Anders
Domino Derval
Ernst Blofeld
Plenty O'Toole
Stacey Sutton
Xenia Onatopp
13 Corinne Dufour
Dominic Greene
Holly Goodhead
Mary Goodnight
14 Christmas Jones
Melina Havelock
Miss Moneypenny
Tracy Di Vicenzo
15 Auric Goldfinger
Natalya Simonova
Patricia Fearing
Tatiana Romanova

James, Henry (1843–1916)

Significant works include:

09 *In the Cage* (1898)
11 *Daisy Miller* (1879)
The American (1877)
12 *Terminations* (1895)
The Two Magics (1898)
Watch and Ward (1871)
13 *The Awkward Age* (1899)
The Bostonians (1886)
The Golden Bowl (1904)
The Other House (1896)
The Tragic Muse (1890)
14 *Roderick Hudson* (1875)
The Ambassadors (1903)

What Maisie Knew (1897)
15 *Portrait of a Lady* (1881)
The Aspern Papers (1888)
The Reverberator (1888)
16 *The American Scene* (1907)
Washington Square (1881)
17 *The Turn of the Screw* (1898)
The Wings of the Dove (1902)
18 *A Small Boy and Others* (1913)
The Spoils of Poynton (1897)
21 *Notes of a Son and Brother* (1914)
22 *The Princess Casamassima* (1886)

Significant characters include:

03 Wix (Mrs)
04 Croy (Kate)
Erme (Gwendolen)
Mark (Lord)
05 Acton (Robert)
Brand (Mr)
Deane (Drayton)
Flora
Merle (Madame Serena)

Miles
Pupin (Monsieur)
Quint (Peter)
Stant (Charlotte)
Vetch (Anastasius)
Vetch (Fleda)
Young (Felix)
06 Archer (Isabel)
Aspern (Jeffrey)

Brydon (Spencer)
Claude (Sir)
Gereth (Mrs)
Gereth (Owen)
Hudson (Roderick)
Jessel (Miss)
Lowder (Mrs Maud)
Miller (Daisy, properly
Annie P)

Newman (Christopher)
Nioche (Noémie)
Osmond (Gilbert)
Osmond (Pansy)
Pocock (Sarah)
Ransom (Basil)
Sloper (Catherine)
Sloper (Dr Austin)
Theale (Milly)
Verver (Adam)
Verver (Maggie)

07 Amerigo (Prince)
Corvick
Densher (Merton)
Eugenia (Baroness Münster)
Farange (Beale)
Farange (Ida)
Farange (Maisie)
Gostrey (Maria)

Marcher (John)
Newsome (Chadwick 'Chad')
Newsome (Mrs)
Pynsent (Miss 'Pinnie')
Tarrant (Verena)
Vereker (Hugh)

08 Birdseye (Miss)
De Cintré (Claire)
Goodwood (Caspar)
Muniment (Paul)
Overmore (Miss)
Robinson (Hyacinth)
Strether (Lewis Lambert)
Touchett (Ralph)
Townsend (Morris)
Waymarsh
Wingrave (Owen)

09 Bordereau (Miss Juliana)
Bordereau (Miss Tina)
Brigstock (Mona)
De Vionnet (Madame)
Stackpole (Henrietta)
Stringham (Mrs Susan)
the editor
Warburton (Lord)
Wentworth (Charlotte)
Wentworth (Clifford)
Wentworth (Gertrude)

10 Brookenham (Nanda)
Chancellor (Olive)
Giovanelli (Mr)

11 Casamassima (Princess)
the narrator

12 the governess
Winterbourne (Frederick)

Japan

Cities and notable towns in Japan include:

04 Kobe	Osaka	**07** Sapporo	Yokohama
Nara	Tokyo	**08** Kawasaki	**09** Hiroshima
05 Kyoto	**06** Nagoya	Nagasaki	

Japanese landmarks include:

03 Ise	Horyu-ji	**10** Sea of Japan
05 Kokyo	Todaiji	**11** Genbaku Dome
Nikko	Tosho-gu	Itsukushima
06 Mt Fuji	**08** Miyajima	Shirakawa-go
Mt Koya	**09** Inland Sea	**12** Southern Alps
Ryukyu	Japan Alps	**14** Imperial Palace
07 Asakusa	Yakushima	**15** Shirakami-Sanchi

Japanese art forms include:

02 no	Imari	ukiyo-e	**08** kakemono
03 noh	kendo	**07** bunraku	kakiemon
04 raku	**06** gagaku	chanoyu	tsutsumu
05 haiku	kabuki	ikebana	**11** linked verse
Hizen	nogaku	nihonga	tea ceremony
	saikei	origami	

See also **Asia**

jazz

Jazz includes:

03 bop	jive	funky	**06** fusion
hot	soul	kwela	groove
04 acid	trad	modal	modern
Afro	**05** bebop	spiel	**07** classic
cool	blues	swing	hard bop

New Wave	**09** Afro-Cuban	**10** avant-garde	**11** barrelhouse
post-bop	bossa nova	improvised	third stream
ragtime	Dixieland	mainstream	traditional
08 free-form	gutbucket	neo-classic	**12** boogie-woogie
high life	West Coast	New Orleans	

Jazz and blues musicians and singers include:

03 Guy (Buddy; 1936– , US)
Ory (Kid; 1886–1973, US)

04 Bley (Carla; 1938– , US)
Byrd (Charlie; 1925–99, US)
Cole (Nat 'King'; 1919–65, US)
Cray (Robert; 1953– , US)
Getz (Stan; 1927–91, US)
Kidd (Carol; 1944– , Scottish)
King (B B; 1925– , US)
Kirk (Roland; 1936–77, US)
Lacy (Steve; 1934–2004, US)
Monk (Thelonious; 1917–82, US)
Pass (Joe; 1929–94, US)
Pine (Courtney; 1964– , English)
Shaw (Artie; 1910–2004, US)

05 Ayler (Albert; 1936–70, US)
Baker (Chet; 1929–88, US)
Basie (Count; 1904–84, US)
Brown (Sandy; 1929–75, Indian/Scottish)
Cooke (Sam; 1931–64, US)
Corea (Chick; 1941– , US)
Davis (Miles; 1926–91, US)
Dodds (Johnny; 1892–1940, US)
Ellis (Don; 1934–78, US)
Evans (Bill; 1929–80, US)
Evans (Gil; 1912–88, Canadian)
Handy (W C; 1873–1958, US)
Hines (Earl; 1903–83, US)
James (Elmore; 1918–63, US)
Jones (Elvin; 1927–2004, US)
Jones (Norah; 1979– , US)
Jones (Quincy; 1933– , US)
Krupa (Gene; 1909–73, US)
Laine (Dame Cleo; 1927– , English)
Lewis (John; 1920–2001, US)
Melly (George; 1926–2007, English)
Roach (Max; 1924–2007, US)
Scott (Ronnie; 1927–96, English)
Shepp (Archie; 1937– , US)
Smith (Bessie; 1894–1937, US)
Smith (Tommy; 1967– , Scottish)
Solal (Martial; 1927– , Algerian/French)
Sun Ra (1914–93, US)
Tatum (Art; 1910–56, US)
Tormé (Mel; 1925–99, US)
Tyner (McCoy; 1938– , US)
Weber (Eberhard; 1940– , German)
Young (Lester; 1909–59, US)

06 Barber (Chris; 1930– , English)

Bechet (Sidney; 1897–1959, US)
Blakey (Art; 1919–90, US)
Burton (Gary; 1943– , US)
Carter (Betty; 1929–98, US)
Cherry (Don; 1936–95, US)
Clarke (Kenny; 1914–85, US)
Dolphy (Eric; 1928–64, US)
Domino (Fats; 1928– , US)
Dorsey (Tommy; 1905–56, US)
Garner (Errol; 1921–77, US)
Gordon (Dexter; 1923–90, US)
Herman (Woody; 1913–87, US)
Hodges (Johnny; 1906–70, US)
Hooker (John Lee; 1920–2001, US)
Joplin (Janis; 1943–70, US)
Joplin (Scott; 1868–1917, US)
Kenton (Stan; 1912–79, US)
Miller (Glenn; 1904–44, US)
Mingus (Charles; 1922–79, US)
Morton (Jelly Roll; 1890–1941, US)
Oliver (King; 1885–1938, US)
Parker (Charlie; 1920–55, US)
Portal (Michel; 1935– , US)
Powell (Bud; 1924–66, US)
Rainey ('Ma'; 1886–1939, US)
Silver (Horace; 1928– , US)
Simone (Nina; 1933–2003, US)
Surman (John; 1944– , English)
Taylor (Cecil; 1933– , US)
Tharpe (Sister Rosetta; 1915–73, US)
Tracey (Stan; 1926– , English)
Walker (T-Bone; 1910–75, US)
Waller (Fats; 1904–43, US)
Waters (Ethel; 1896–1977, US)
Waters (Muddy; 1915–83, US)

07 Bennett (Tony; 1926– , US)
Broonzy (Big Bill; 1893–1958, US)
Brubeck (Dave; 1920– , US)
Charles (Ray; 1930–2004, US)
Clapton (Eric; 1945– , English)
Coleman (Ornette; 1930– , US)
Collins (Albert; 1932–93, US)
Goodman (Benny; 1909–86, US)
Hampton (Lionel; 1909–2002, US)
Hancock (Herbie; 1940– , US)
Hawkins (Coleman; 1904–69, US)
Holiday (Billie; 1915–59, US)
Hopkins (Lightnin'; 1912–82, US)
Ibrahim (Abdullah; 1934– , South African)
Jackson (Milt; 1923–99, US)

Jarrett (Keith; 1945– , US)
Johnson (James P; 1894–1955, US)
Johnson (J J; 1924–2001, US)
Johnson (Robert; 1911–38, US)
Metheny (Pat; 1954– , US)
Mezzrow (Mezz; 1899–1972, US)
Peyroux (Madeleine; 1974– , US)
Rollins (Sonny; 1930– , US)
Shorter (Wayne; 1933– , US)
Vaughan (Sarah; 1924–90, US)
Webster (Ben; 1909–73, US)
Winding (Kai; 1922–83, Danish/US)

08 Adderley (Cannonball; 1928–75, US)
Barbieri (Gato; 1934– , Argentine)
Calloway (Cab; 1907–94, US)
Coltrane (John; 1926–67, US)
Eldridge (Roy; 1911–89, US)
Franklin (Aretha; 1942– , US)
Garbarek (Jan; 1947– , Norwegian)
Gershwin (George; 1898–1937, US)
Gorelick (Kenneth 'Kenny G'; 1956– , US)
Johnston (Lonny; 1889–1970, US)
Marsalis (Wynton; 1961– , US)
Mulligan (Gerry; 1927–96, US)
Peterson (Oscar; 1925–2007, Canadian)
Tristano (Lennie; 1919–78, US)
Williams (Mary Lou; 1910–81, US)

See also **pianist**

Williams (Tony; 1945–97, US)

09 Armstrong (Louis; 1901–71, US)
Christian (Charlie; 1916–42, US)
Dankworth (John; 1927– , English)
Ellington (Duke; 1899–1974, US)
Gillespie (Dizzy; 1917–93, US)
Grappelli (Stéphane; 1908–97, French)
Henderson (Fletcher; 1897–1952, US)
Henderson (Joe; 1937–2001, US)
Jefferson (Blind Lemon; 1897–1929, US)
Leadbelly (1888–1949, US)
Lunceford (Jimmie; 1902–47, US)
Lyttelton (Humphrey; 1921–2008, English)
Reinhardt (Django; 1910–53, Belgian)
Teagarden (Jack; 1905–64, US)
Westbrook (Mike; 1936– , English)

10 Fitzgerald (Ella; 1917–96, US)
Howlin' Wolf (1910–76, US)
McLaughlin (John; 1942– , English)
Montgomery (Wes; 1923–68, US)
Thielemans (Toots; 1922– , Belgian)
Washington (Dinah; 1924–63, US)

11 Beiderbecke (Bix; 1903–31, US)

14 Ørsted Pedersen (Niels-Henning; 1946–2005, Danish)

jellyfish

Jellyfish include:

03 box

04 bell
blue
moon
pink

05 brown
crown
warty

06 barrel
common
helmet
jimble
purple
saucer
Tamoya

07 acaleph
aurelia
blubber

compass
Nomura's
sea wasp
snottie
stalked
thimble

08 acalephe
Black Sea
blue fire
clinging
football
fried egg

09 Arctic red
fire jelly
flower hat
hair jelly
irukandji
lion's mane
root-mouth

sea nettle

10 blue button
cannonball
cassiopeia
dustbin-lid
freshwater
sea blubber
upside-down

11 blue blubber
mushroom cap
sea mushroom

12 jelly blubber
mauve stinger
white-spotted

13 Mediterranean
purple stinger

15 Arctic lion's mane

Jew *see* **Judaism**

jewellery

Jewellery includes:

04 prop
ring
stud

05 beads
bindi
cameo
chain
tiara

06 amulet
anklet
bangle
brooch
choker
corals
diadem

hatpin
locket
pearls
tiepin
torque

07 armilla
coronet
earring
necklet
pendant
rivière
sautoir
toe ring

08 bracelet
cufflink

necklace
negligee
nose ring
wristlet

09 medallion
navel ring

10 signet ring

11 mangalsutra
wedding ring

12 eternity ring

13 charm bracelet
solitaire ring

14 engagement ring

15 belly-button ring

jockey *see* **racing: horse racing**

joint *see* **bone; meat**

journalism

Journalists, broadcast journalists, editors and newsreaders include:

03 Day (Sir Robin; 1923–2000, English)
Mee (Arthur; 1875–1943, English)

04 Adie (Kate; 1945– , English)
Bell (Martin; 1938– , English)
Birt (John, Lord; 1944– , English)
Coty (François; 1874–1934, French)
Foot (Michael; 1913– , English)
Ford (Anna; 1943– , English)
Gall (Sandy; 1927– , Scottish)
Hogg (Sarah, Baroness; 1946– , English)
Jane (Fred T; 1865–1916, English)
Mair (Eddie; 1965– , Scottish)
Marr (Andrew; 1959– , Scottish)
Neil (Andrew; 1949– , Scottish)
Rook (Jean; 1931–91, English)
Self (Will; 1961– , English)
Snow (Jon; 1947– , English)
Snow (Peter; 1938– , Irish)
Wade (Rebekah; 1968– , English)
Wark (Kirsty; 1955– , Scottish)

05 Astor (William, Viscount; 1848–1919, US/
British)
Brown (Helen Gurley; 1922– , US)
Buerk (Michael; 1946– , English)
Cooke (Alistair; 1908–2004, English/US)
Dacre (Paul; 1948– , English)
Ensor (Sir Robert; 1877–1958, English)
Evans (Sir Harold; 1928– , English)

Frost (Sir David; 1939– , English)
Green (Charlotte; 1956– ; English)
James (Clive; 1939– , Australian)
Junor (Sir John; 1919–98, English)
Laski (Marghanita; 1915–88, English)
Levin (Bernard; 1928–2004, English)
Lewis (Martyn; 1945– , Northern Irish)
Reith (John, Lord; 1889–1971, Scottish)
Scott (C P; 1846–1932, English)
Twain (Mark; 1835–1910, US)
Tynan (Kenneth; 1927–80, English)
Waugh (Auberon; 1939–2001, English)
Wolfe (Tom; 1931– , US)
Woods (Donald; 1933–2001, South African)
Young (Toby; 1963– , English)

06 Baring (Maurice; 1874–1946, English)
Barron (Brian; 1940– , English)
Bierce (Ambrose; 1842–1914, US)
Burnet (Sir Alastair; 1928– , English)
Craven (John; 1941– , English)
Deedes (Bill, Lord; 1913–2007, English)
Gallup (George; 1901–84, US)
Gordon (John; 1890–1974, Scottish)
Greene (Sir Hugh; 1910–87, English)
Hislop (Ian; 1960– , English)
Hulton (Sir Edward; 1906–88, English)
Hutton (Will; 1950– , English)
Isaacs (Sir Jeremy; 1932– , Scottish)

Martin (Kingsley; 1897–1969, English)
Massie (Allan; 1938– , Scottish)
Morgan (Charles; 1894–1958, English)
Morgan (Piers; 1965– , English)
Morris (Jan; 1926– , English)
Murrow (Edward R; 1908–65, US)
O'Brien (Conor Cruise; 1917–2008, Irish)
Packer (Sir Frank; 1906–74, Australian)
Parker (Dorothy; 1893–1967, US)
Paxman (Jeremy; 1950– , English)
Pilger (John; 1939– , Australian)
Rayner (Claire; 1931– , English)
Reuter (Paul, Baron von; 1816–99, German/
British)
Rippon (Angela; 1944– , English)
Stuart (Moira; c.1950– , English)
Suchet (John; 1944– , English)
Wilkes (John; 1727–97, English)

07 Alagiah (George; 1955– , Sri Lankan/British)
Barclay (Sir David; 1934– , English)
Barclay (Sir Frederick; 1934– , English)
Barclay (William; 1907–78, Scottish)
Boycott (Rosie; 1951– , English)
Bradlee (Ben; 1921– , US)
Brunson (Michael; 1940– , English)
Buckley (William F, Jnr; 1925–2008, US)
Bushell (Garry; 1955– , English)
Cameron (James; 1911–85, Scottish)
Cobbett (William; 1763–1835, English)
Dunnett (Sir Alastair; 1908–98, Scottish)
Edwards (Huw; 1961– , Welsh)
Fairfax (John; 1804–77, Australian)
Fleming (Peter; 1907–71, English)
Goodman (Elinor; 1946– , English)
Hellyer (A G L; 1902–93, English)
Ingrams (Richard; 1937– , English)
Jackson (Dame Barbara, Baroness; 1914–81,
English)
Johnson (Boris; 1964– , English)
Kennedy (Helena, Baroness; 1950– ,
Scottish)
Kennedy (Sir Ludovic; 1919– , Scottish)
Leeming (Jan; 1942– , English)
Malcolm (Derek; 1932– , English)
Mencken (H L; 1880–1956, US)
Perkins (Brian; 1943– , New Zealand/British)
Rowland (Tiny; 1917–98, British)
Simpson (John; 1944– , English)
Sissons (Peter; 1942– , English)
Stanley (Sir Henry; 1841–1904, Welsh/US/
British)

08 Burchill (Julie; 1959– , English)
Cronkite (Walter, Jnr; 1916– , US)
Dimbleby (David; 1938– , English)
Dimbleby (Jonathan; 1944– , English)
Dimbleby (Richard; 1913–65, English)
Douglass (Frederick; 1817–95, US)
Drawbell (James; 1899–1979, Scottish)
Gellhorn (Martha; 1908–98, US)
Hanrahan (Brian; 1949– , English)
Hobhouse (Leonard; 1864–1929, English)
Horrocks (Sir Brian; 1895–1985, English)
Humphrys (John; 1943– , Welsh)
Lippmann (Walter; 1889–1974, US)
McCarthy (John; 1957– , English)
McDonald (Sir Trevor; 1939– , Trinidadian)
Naughtie (James; 1951– , Scottish)
Nevinson (Henry; 1856–1941, English)
Rees-Mogg (William, Lord; 1928– , English)
Robinson (Henry Crabb; 1775–1867,
English)
Thompson (Hunter S; 1937–2005, US)
Woodward (Bob; 1943– , US)

09 Bernstein (Carl; 1944– , US)
Bosanquet (Reginald; 1932–84, English)
Hopkinson (Sir Tom; 1905–90, English)
Macdonald (Gus, Lord; 1940– , Scottish)
MacGregor (Sue; 1941– , English)
Mackenzie (Kelvin; 1946– , English)
Magnusson (Magnus; 1929–2007, Icelandic/
Scottish)
Magnusson (Sally; 1955– , Scottish)
Plekhanov (Georgi; 1856–1918, Russian)
Streicher (Julius; 1885–1946, German)
Trethowan (Sir Ian; 1922–90, English)

10 Delescluze (Charles; 1809–71, French)
Desmoulins (Camille; 1760–94, French)
Greenslade (Roy; 1946– , English)
Guru-Murthy (Krishnan; 1970– , English)
Harmsworth (Alfred, Viscount Northcliffe;
1865–1922, Irish/British)
McIlvanney (Hugh; 1933– , Scottish)
Muggeridge (Malcolm; 1903–90, English)
Rothermere (Harold Harmsworth, Viscount;
1868–1940, English)
Rusbridger (Alan; 1953– , English)
Waterhouse (Keith; 1929– , English)
Worsthorne (Sir Peregrine; 1923– , English)

11 Northcliffe (Alfred Harmsworth, Viscount;
1865–1922, Irish/British)

12 Street-Porter (Janet; 1944– , English)

Terms used in journalism include:

03 cub	tip	deck
cut	**04** blat	desk
NPA	bump	kill
run	copy	leak

news
op-ed
05 angle
blatt
blurb
break
extra
gonzo
local
media
pitch
quote
radio
scoop
squib
story
tie in
06 anchor
Balaam
byline
column
editor
hourly
impact
kicker
leader
leg-man
rookie
source
07 advance
article
caption
compact
editing
feature
journal

kill fee
spoiler
subhead
tabloid
topical
writing
08 causerie
follow-up
headline
magazine
masthead
national
newshawk
news item
reporter
revision
stringer
09 broadcast
columnist
editorial
exclusive
freelance
freesheet
front-page
interview
newshound
newspaper
paragraph
pull quote
redletter
reportage
scare-head
scare-line
soundbite
statement
stop-press
strapline

10 background
broadsheet
centrefold
credit line
daily paper
journalese
journalist
leaderette
multimedia
newsreader
periodical
publishing
retraction
standfirst
television
11 city article
Fleet Street
Sunday paper
12 breaking news
centre spread
extra-special
gossip-writer
press council
press release
scare-heading
13 correspondent
human interest
middle article
14 banner headline
blind interview
current affairs
leading article
15 cyber-journalist
photojournalism
press conference

See also **news**; **newspaper**

Joyce, James (1882–1941)

Significant works include:

07 *The Dead* (1914)
Ulysses (1922)
09 *Dubliners* (1914)
11 *Stephen Hero* (1944)
12 *Chamber Music* (1907)

13 *Finnegans Wake* (1939)
Pomes Penyeach (1927)
31 *A Portrait of the Artist as a Young Man* (1916)

Significant characters include:

04 Issy
05 Bloom (Leopold)
Bloom (Molly 'Marion Tweed')
Duffy (James)

Maria
06 Conroy (Gabriel)
Conroy (Gretta)
07 Dedalus (Stephen 'Kinch')
08 Mulligan (Malachi 'Buck')

09 Earwicker (Humphrey Chimpden)
10 Plurabelle (Anna Livia)
12 Shaun the Post
13 Shem the Penman

Judaism

Jewish groups, movements and denominations include:

06 Reform	**08** Chasidim	Sephardim	**12** Conservative
07 Haredim	Hasidism	**10** Ashkenazim	**13** Jewish Renewal
Hasidim	Masortes	Humanistic	**14** Modern Orthodox
Karaism	Orthodox	**11** Progressive	
Liberal	**09** Massortes		

See also **calendar**; **religion**

judge

Judges include:

04 Coke (Sir Edward; 1552–1634, English)

05 Allen (Florence E; 1884–1966, US)
Burgh (Hubert de; d.1243, English)
Minos (Greek mythology)

06 Aeacus (Greek mythology)
Burger (Warren; 1907–95, US)
Cullen (William, Lord; 1935– , Scottish)
Gideon (biblical Israelite)
Irvine (Alexander, Lord; 1940– , Scottish)
Mackay (James, Lord; 1927– , Scottish)
Taylor (Peter, Lord; 1930–97, English)
Warren (Earl; 1891–1974, US)

07 Brennan (William J; 1906–97, US)
Denning (Alfred, Lord; 1899–1999, English)
Erskine (Thomas, Lord; 1750–1823, Scottish)
O'Connor (Sandra Day; 1930– , US)
Scarman (Leslie, Lord; 1911–2004, English)

08 Gardiner (Gerald, Lord; 1900–90, English)

Ginsburg (Ruth Bader; 1933– , US)
Hailsham (Quintin Hogg, Viscount;
1907–2001, English)
Jeffreys (George, Lord; 1648–89, English)
Marshall (John; 1755–1835, US)
Marshall (Thurgood; 1908–93, US)

09 Rehnquist (William; 1924–2005, US)
Vyshinsky (Andrei; 1883–1954, Soviet)

10 Elwyn-Jones (Frederick, Lord; 1909–89,
Welsh)
Odio Benito (Elizabeth; 1939– , Costa
Rican)

11 Butler-Sloss (Dame Elizabeth; 1933– ,
English)
Montesquieu (Charles-Louis de Secondat,
Baron de; 1689–1755, French)

12 Rhadamanthus (Greek mythology)

K

karate

Keats, John (1795–1821)

key

Keys on a computer keyboard include:

03 alt	**04** ctrl		shift	**07** control
del	home	**06** delete	num lock
end	pg dn	escape	
esc	pg up	insert	**08** caps lock
ins	**05** alt gr	page up	page down
tab	enter	return	**09** backspace

See also **lock**; **music**

king

Common kings' names include:

04 Erik	Peter	Rudolf	Kristian
Ivan		**07** Alfonso	
John	**06** Albert	Charles	**09** Alexander
Karl	Conrad	Francis	Antiochus
Olaf	Darius	Kenneth	Christian
	Edmund	Leopold	Ferdinand
05 David	Edward	Ptolemy	Frederick
Henri	George	Richard	Theodoric
Henry	Harald	William	
James	Harold		**10** Artaxerxes
Louis	Philip	**08** Frederik	**11** Constantine

Kings include:

03 Aed (d.878, Scotland)
Ban (Arthurian legend, Benwick)
Ida (d.559, Bernicia)
Ine (d.c.726, West Saxon)
Lot (Arthurian legend, Orkney)
Lud (British legend, Britain)
Zog (I; 1895–1961, Albania)

04 Agis (IV; c.263–241 BC, Sparta)
Ahab (9c BC, Israel)
Cnut ('the Great'; c.995–1035, England/
   Denmark/Norway)
Dubh (d.966, Scotland)
Duff (d.966, Scotland)
Edwy (c.941–959, England)
Fahd (1923–2005, Saudi Arabia)
Ivan (III, 'the Great'; 1440–1505, Russia)
Ivan (IV, 'the Terrible'; 1530–84, Russia)
Jehu (842–815 BC, Israel)
John (Lackland; 1167–1216, England)
John (*King John*, 1590/1, William Shakespeare)
Lear (British legend, Britain)
Lear (*King Lear*, c.1605–06, William
   Shakespeare)
Lear (*Lear*, 1973, Edward Bond)
Mark (Celtic mythology, Cornwall)
Offa (d.796, Mercia)
Olav (V; 1903–91, Norway)
Otto (I, 'the Great'; 912–73, Germany)
Paul (I; 1901–64, Greece)
Quin (Auberon; *The Napoleon of Notting
   Hill*, 1904, G K Chesterton)

Saud (1902–69, Saudi Arabia)

05 Brian (c.926–1014, Ireland)
Bruce (Robert; 1274–1329, Scotland)
Capet (Hugo; c.938–996, France)
Carol (I; 1839–1914, Romania)
Carol (II; 1893–1953, Romania)
Creon (Greek mythology, Thebes)
Culen (d.971, Scotland)
David (11c BC, Israel)
David (I; c.1080–1153, Scotland)
David (II; 1324–71, Scotland)
Edgar (944–75, England)
Edgar (1074–1107, Scotland)
Edred (c.923–55, England)
Edwin (St; c.585–633, Northumbria)
Giric (d.889, Scotland)
Gyges (d.c.648 BC, Lydia)
Henry (I; 1068–1135, England)
Henry (II; 1133–89, England)
Henry (III; 1207–72, England)
Henry (IV; c.1366–1413, England)
Henry (V; 1387–1422, England)
Henry (V; *Henry V*, 1599, William
   Shakespeare)
Henry (VI; 1421–71, England)
Henry (VI; *Henry VI, Parts I, II, III*, early
   1590s, William Shakespeare)
Henry (VII; 1457–1509, England)
Henry (VII; *Henry VI Part III*, early 1590s,
   William Shakespeare)
Henry (VIII; 1491–1547, England)

Henry (VIII; *Henry VIII*, c.1613, William Shakespeare/John Fletcher)
Herod ('the Great'; c.74–4 BC, Judea)
Hiero (I; d.467/466 BC, Syracuse)
Ixion (Greek mythology, Thessaly)
James (I, of England; *The Fortunes of Nigel*, 1822, Sir Walter Scott)
James (I; 1394–1437, Scotland)
James (I; 1566–1625, England)
James (II; 1430–60, Scotland)
James (II; 1633–1701, England/Ireland)
James (III; 1452–88, Scotland)
James (IV; 1473–1513, Scotland)
James (V; 1512–42, Scotland)
James (VI/I; 1566–1625, Scotland/England)
James (VII/II; 1633–1701, Scotland, England/Ireland)
Laius (Greek mythology, Thebes)
Louis (XIV, 'the Sun King'; 1638–1715, France)
Louis (XV; 1710–74, France)
Louis (XVI; 1754–93, France)
Media (*Mardi*, 1849, Herman Melville)
Midas (Greek mythology, Phrygia)
Minos (Greek mythology, Crete)
Pepin (III, 'the Short'; c.715–768, Franks)
Peter (*The Lion, the Witch and the Wardrobe*, 1950, C S Lewis)
Priam (Greek mythology, Troy)
Priam (*Troilus and Cressida*, 1601/2, William Shakespeare)
Svein (I Haraldsson, 'Fork-Beard'; d.1014, Denmark/England)

06 Aeetes (Greek mythology, Colchis)
Agenor (Greek mythology, Tyre)
Ahmose (I; 16c BC, Egypt)
Ahmose (II; 6c BC, Egypt)
Alaric (I; c.370–410 AD, Visigoths)
Alaric (II; 450–507 AD, Visigoths)
Albert (I; 1875–1934, Belgians)
Albert (II; 1934–   , Belgians)
Alfred ('the Great'; 849–99, Wessex)
Alonso (*The Tempest*, 1611, William Shakespeare)
Arthur (Arthurian legend, Britain)
Arthur ('Morte d'Arthur', 1842, Alfred, Lord Tennyson)
Attila (c.406–453 AD, Huns)
Atreus (Greek mythology, Argos)
Baliol (Edward de; c.1283–1364, Scotland)
Baliol (John de; c.1250–1315, Scotland)
Bladud (British legend, Britain)
Canute (c.995–1035, England/Denmark/Norway)
Cheops (26c BC, Memphis)
Clovis (465–511 AD, Franks)
Donald (I; d.862, Scotland)
Donald (II; d.900, Scotland)
Donald (III, 'Bane'; 1033–1100, Scotland)

Duncan (*Macbeth*, c.1606, William Shakespeare)
Duncan (I; c.1010–40, Scotland)
Duncan (II; c.1060–94, Scotland)
Eadgar (944–75, England)
Edmund (*The Lion, the Witch and the Wardrobe*, 1950, C S Lewis)
Edmund (I; 921–46, English)
Edmund (II, 'Ironside'; c.990–1016, England)
Edmund (St; c.841–870, East Anglia)
Edward (c.870–c.924, Wessex)
Edward (I; 1239–1307, England)
Edward (II; 1284–1327, England)
Edward (II, St, 'the Martyr'; c.963–978, England)
Edward (II; *Edward II*, 1594, Christopher Marlowe)
Edward (III; 1312–77, England)
Edward (III, 'the Confessor'; c.1003–66, England)
Edward (IV; 1442–83, England)
Edward ('the Elder'; d.924, England)
Edward (V; 1470–83, England)
Edward (VI; 1537–53, England/Ireland)
Edward (VII; 1841–1910, Great Britain/Ireland)
Edward (VIII; 1894–1972, Great Britain/Northern Ireland)
Egbert (d.839, Britain)
Faisal (1905–75, Saudi Arabia)
Faisal (I; 1885–1933, Iraq)
Faisal (II; 1935–58, Iraq)
Farouk (I; 1920–65, Egypt)
George (I; 1660–1727, Great Britain/Ireland)
George (II; 1683–1760, Great Britain/Ireland)
George (III; 1738–1820, Great Britain/Ireland/Hanover)
George (III; *The Madness of George III*, 1991, Alan Bennett)
George (IV; 1762–1830, Great Britain/Ireland/Hanover)
George (V; 1819–78, Hanover)
George (V; 1865–1936, Great Britain/Northern Ireland)
George (VI; 1895–1952, Great Britain/Northern Ireland)
Gustav (V; 1858–1950, Sweden)
Gustav (VI; 1882–1973, Sweden)
Haakon (VII; 1872–1957, Norway)
Harald (V; 1937–   , Norway)
Harold (I Knutsson, 'Harefoot'; d.1040, England)
Harold (II; c.1022–66, England)
Hassan (II; 1929–99, Morocco)
Indulf (d.962, Scotland)
Josiah (649–609 BC, Judah)
Khalid (1913–82, Saudi Arabia)
Letsie (III; 1963–   , Lesotho)

Lulach (1032–58, Scotland)
Magnus (*The Apple Cart*, 1929, George Bernard Shaw)
Oberon (*A Midsummer Night's Dream*, c.1594, William Shakespeare)
Oberon (European mythology, fairies)
Oileus (Greek mythology, Locris)
Oswald (St; c.605–642, Northumbria)
Peleus (Greek mythology, Phythia)
Philip (*King John*, 1590/1, William Shakespeare)
Philip (I, 'the Handsome'; 1478–1506, Castile)
Philip (III, 'the Bold'; 1245–85, France)
Philip (IV; 'the Fair'; 1268–1314, France)
Robert (II; 1316–90, Scotland)
Robert (III; c.1340–1406, Scotland)
Robert (III; *The Fair Maid of Perth*, 1828, Sir Walter Scott)
Sargon (II; d.705 BC, Assyria)
Tereus (Greek mythology, Thrace)
Xerxes (I; c.520–465 BC, Persia)

07 Aragorn (*The Lord of the Rings*, 1954–55, J R R Tolkien)
Arbaces (*A King and No King*, 1611, Francis Beaumont/John Fletcher)
Baldwin (II; d.1131, Jerusalem)
Baldwin (III; c.1130–62, Jerusalem)
Balliol (Edward de; c.1283–1364, Scotland)
Balliol (John de; c.1250–1315, Scotland)
Boabdil (d.c.1493, Granada)
Cecrops (Greek mythology, Athenians)
Cepheus (Greek mythology, Ethiopians)
Charles (I; 1600–49, Great Britain/Ireland)
Charles (II; 1630–85, Great Britain/Ireland)
Charles (II; *Peveril of the Peak*, 1823, Sir Walter Scott)
Charles (II; *Woodstock, or The Cavalier*, 1826, Sir Walter Scott)
Charles (VI; *Henry V*, 1599, William Shakespeare)
Croesus (6c BC, Lydia)
Dingaan (d.1843, Zululand)
Eumenes (II; d.159 BC, Pergamon)
Guthorm (d.890, East Anglia)
Hussein (1935–99, Jordan)
Ibn Saud (1880–1953, Saudi Arabia)
Kenneth (I; d.858, Scots)
Kenneth (II; d.995, Scotland)
Kenneth (III; d.1005, Scotland)
Latinus (Roman mythology, Latins)
Leontes (*The Winter's Tale*, 1611, William Shakespeare)
Leopold (I; 1790–1865, Belgium)
Leopold (II; 1835–1909, Belgium)
Leopold (III; 1901–83, Belgium)
Macbeth (c.1005–57, Scotland)
Macbeth (*Macbeth*, c.1606, William Shakespeare)

Malcolm (I; d.954, Scotland)
Malcolm (II; c.954–1034, Scotland)
Malcolm (III, 'Canmore'; c.1031–93, Scotland)
Malcolm (IV, 'the Maiden'; c.1141–65, Scotland)
Michael (1921– , Romania)
Pandion (Greek mythology, Athens)
Perseus (c.213–c.165 BC, Macedonia)
Polybus (Greek mythology, Corinth)
Ptolemy (I, Soter; c.367–283 BC, Egypt)
Ptolemy (II, Philadelphus; 308–246 BC, Egypt)
Ptolemy (VI, Philometor; d.145 BC, Egypt)
Ptolemy (VIII, Euergetes II; d.116 BC, Egypt)
Ptolemy (XII, Neos Dionysos; 1c BC, Egypt)
Pyrrhus (c.319–272 BC, Epirus)
Rameses (II; 1304–1237 BC, Egypt)
Richard (*Ivanhoe*, 1819, Sir Walter Scott)
Richard (I, 'the Lion Heart'; 1157–99, England)
Richard (II; *Richard II*, c.1595, William Shakespeare)
Richard (II; 1367–1400, England)
Richard (III; 1452–85, England)
Romulus (d.c.715 BC, Rome)
Solomon (c.962–922 BC, Israel)
Stephen (c.1097–1154, England)
Stephen (I; c.977–1038, Hungary)
Telamon (Greek mythology, Salamis)
Theoden (*The Lord of the Rings*, 1954–55, J R R Tolkien)
Umberto (I; 1844–1900, Italy)
Umberto (II; 1904–83, Italy)
Wilhelm (I; 1797–1888, Prussia)
Wilhelm (II; 1859–1941, Prussia)
William (I, 'the Conqueror'; 1027–87, England)
William (I; 1143–1214, Scotland)
William (II, 'Rufus'; c.1056–1100, England)
William (II/III, of Orange; 1650–1702, Great Britain/Ireland)
William (IV; 1765–1837, Great Britain)

08 Acrisius (Greek mythology, Argos)
Baudouin (I; 1930–93, Belgians)
Birendra (1945–2001, Nepal)
Cambyses (II; d.522 BC, Medes/Persians)
Cetewayo (c.1826–1884, Zululand)
Chosroes (d.579, Persia)
Chosroes (d.628, Persia)
Claudius (*Hamlet*, 1601/2, William Shakespeare)
Clotaire (II; 584–629, Franks)
Eteocles (Greek mythology, Thebes)
Ethelred (I; d.871, Wessex)
Ethelred (II, 'the Unready'; c.968–1016, England)
Gaiseric (c.390–477 AD, Vandals/Alans)
Genseric (c.390–477 AD, Vandals/Alans)
Gorboduc (British legend, Britain)

Jeroboam (I; 10c BC, Israel)
Jeroboam (II; 8c BC, Israel)
Jugurtha (d.104 BC, Numidia)
Leonidas (d.c.480 BC, Sparta)
Lycurgus (Greek mythology, Thrace)
Manasseh (7c BC, Judah)
Menelaus (Greek mythology, Sparta)
Mohammed (VI; 1963– , Morocco)
Napoleon (II; 1811–32, Rome)
Pentheus (Greek mythology, Thebes)
Sihamoni (Norodom; 1953– , Cambodia)
Sihanouk (Norodom; 1922– , Cambodia)
Sisyphus (Greek mythology, Corinth)
Tantalus (Greek mythology, Sipylus)
Thutmose (I; fl.1493–1482 BC, Egypt)

09 Agamemnon (Greek mythology, Argos)
Agesilaus (444–360 BC, Sparta)
Akhenaten (14c BC, Egypt)
Alexander (I; 1888–1934, Serbs, Croats/
  Slovenes/Yugoslavia)
Alexander (I; c.1077–1124, Scotland)
Alexander (II; 1198–1249, Scotland)
Alexander (III; 1241–86, Scotland)
Amenhotep (II; 15c BC, Egypt)
Amenhotep (III; c.1411–c.1375 BC, Egypt)
Antiochus (*Pericles*, c.1608, William
  Shakespeare)
Archelaus (d.399 BC, Macedonia)
Athelstan (c.895–939, Anglo-Saxon)
Bonaparte (Jérôme; 1784–1860,
  Westphalia)
Bonaparte (Joseph; 1768–1844, Naples/
  Sicily/Spain)
Bonaparte (Louis; 1778–1846, Holland)
Cadwallon (d.634, Gwynedd)
Cassander (c.358–297 BC, Macedonia)
Cetshwayo (c.1826–1884, Zululand)
Cleomenes (I; d.490 BC, Sparta)
Cleomenes (III; c.260–219 BC, Sparta)
Cuchulain ('Cuchulain's Fight with the Sea',
  1893, W B Yeats)
Cymbeline (*Cymbeline*, 1609/10, William
  Shakespeare)
Ermanaric (fl.c.375 AD, Ostrogoths)
Ethelbald (d.860, England)
Ethelbert (d.616/618, Kent)
Ethelbert (d.866, England)
Ethelwulf (d.c.858, Wessex)
Ferdinand (*Love's Labour's Lost*, c.1594,
  William Shakespeare)
Frederick (I, Barbarossa; c.1123–90,
  Germany/Italy)
Gilgamesh (Sumerian mythology, Uruk)
Gyanendra (1947– , Nepal)
Hammurabi (d.c.1750 BC, Babylon)
Humanitas (Rex; *Ane Pleasant Satyre of the
  Thrie Estaitis*, 1540, Sir David Lindsay)
Masinissa (238–149 BC, Numidia)

Nadir Shah (1688–1747, Persia)
Perithous (Greek mythology, Lapiths)
Polixenes (*The Winter's Tale*, 1611, William
  Shakespeare)
Pygmalion (Greek mythology, Cyprus)
Rajasinha (II; 1629–87, Kandy)
Sesostris (Egyptian mythology, Egypt)
Simonides (*Pericles*, c.1608, William
  Shakespeare)
Taufa'ahau (Tupou IV; 1918–2006, Tonga)
Theoderic ('the Great'; c.455–526 AD,
  Ostrogoths)
Theodoric (I; d.451 AD, Visigoths)
Theodoric (II; d.466 AD, Visigoths)
Tuthmosis (I; fl.1493–1482 BC, Egypt)
Vortigern (fl.425–c.450 AD, Britain)
Wenceslas (St; c.907–929, Bohemia)
Zahir Shah (Mohammed; 1914–2007,
  Afghanistan)

10 Aethelstan (c.895–939, Anglo-Saxon)
Conchobhar (Celtic mythology, Ulster)
Erechtheus (Greek mythology, Athens)
Esarhaddon (d.669 BC, Assyria)
Fisher King (Arthurian legend)
Juan Carlos (I; 1938– , Spain)
Lysimachus (d.281 BC, Thrace)
Moshoeshoe (II; 1938–96, Lesotho)
Ozymandias ('Ozymandias', 1820, Percy
  Bysshe Shelley)
Wenceslaus (St; c.907–929, Bohemia)

11 Charlemagne (747–814, Franks)
Constantine (I; d.877, Scotland)
Constantine (II; d.952, Scotland)
Constantine (II; d.997, Scotland)
Constantine (II; 1940– , Greece)
Franz Joseph (1830–1916, Hungary)
Hardacanute (1018–42, Denmark/England)
Hardicanute (1018–42, Denmark/England)
Mithridates (VI; c.132–63 BC, Pontus)
Sennacherib (d.681 BC, Assyria)
Tut'ankhamun (d.c.1340 BC, Egypt)

12 Ancus Marcius (640–616 BC, Rome)
Ashurbanipal (7c BC, Assyria)
Boris Godunov (c.1551–1605, Russia)
Herod Agrippa (I; 10 BC–44 AD, Judea)
Sardanapalus (*Sardanapalus: A Tragedy*,
  1821, Lord Byron)

13 Carl XVI Gustaf (1946– , Sweden)
Chulalongkorn (Phra Paramindr Maha;
  1853–1910, Siam)
Edgar Atheling (c.1060–c.1125, England)
Hussein ibn 'Ali (1856–1931, Hejaz)
Knut Sveinsson (c.995–1035, England/
  Denmark/Norway)
Louis Philippe (1773–1850, French)
Numa Pompilius (8c–7c BC; Rome)

14 Cassivellaunus (1c BC, Catuvellauni)
Harald Gormsson ('Blue-Tooth'; c.910–985, Denmark)
Nebuchadnezzar (II; d.562 BC, Babylon)
Servius Tullius (fl.578–535 BC, Rome)

See also **legend**; **Rome**

Uther Pendragon (Arthurian legend, Britain)
Victor Emmanuel (III; 1869–1947, Italy)

15 Ptolemy Dionysus (*Caesar and Cleopatra*, 1898, George Bernard Shaw)
Tullus Hostilius (d.642 BC; Rome)

kingdom *see* **classification**; **empire**

Kipling, Rudyard (1865–1936)

Significant works include:

02 *If* (1910)

03 *Kim* (1901)

06 'Red Dog' (1895)

08 'Quiquern' (1895)

10 'Tiger! Tiger!' (1894)

11 'How Fear Came' (1895)
'Kaa's Hunting' (1894)
Stalky and Co (1899)
The Day's Work (1898)
The Naulahka (1891–92)

12 *The Seven Seas* (1896)
'The White Seal' (1894)

13 *Life's Handicap* (1891)
Soldiers Three (1888)
The Jungle Book (1894)
'The King's Ankus' (1895)

14 *Many Inventions* (1893)
'Rikki-Tikki-Tavi' (1894)
Songs from Books (1912)
The Five Nations (1903)
'The Undertakers' (1895)

15 'Mowgli's Brothers' (1894)
Puck of Pook's Hill (1906)
Schoolboy Lyrics (1881)
The Years Between (1919)
Wee Willie Winkie (1888)

16 *Debits and Credits* (1926)
'The Spring Running' (1895)

17 *Limits and Renewals* (1932)
Rewards and Fairies (1910)
Something of Myself (1937)
'The Elephant's Child' (1902)

18 *Barrack Room Ballads* (1890)
Captains Courageous (1897)

'Letting in the Jungle' (1895)
The Light That Failed (1890)

19 *Actions and Reactions* (1909)
Departmental Ditties (1886)
'Her Majesty's Servants' (1894)
The Second Jungle Book (1895)

20 'The Recall Recessional' (1894)
'Toomai of the Elephants' (1894)

21 *A Diversity of Creatures* (1917)
'How the Alphabet Was Made' (1902)
'How the Camel Got His Hump' (1902)

22 *Plain Tales from the Hills* (1888)
Traffics and Discoveries (1904)

23 'How the Whale Got His Throat' (1902)
'The Butterfly That Stamped' (1902)
'The Miracle of Purun Bhagat' (1902)

24 'How the Leopard Got His Spots' (1902)

25 'The Cat That Walked by Himself' (1902)

26 'How the Rhinoceros Got His Skin' (1902)

27 'How the First Letter Was Written' (1902)
'The Beginning of the Armadillos' (1902)
'The Crab That Played with the Sea' (1902)
'The Sing-Song of Old Man Kangaroo' (1902)

28 *Soldiers Three: In Black and White* (1888)

30 *Just So stories for Little Children* (1902)
Wee Willie Winkie: Under the Deodars (1888)

32 *Thy Servant a Dog and Other Dog Stories* (1930)

33 *Land and Sea Tales for Scouts and Guides* (1923)
Soldiers Three: The Story of the Gadsbys (1888)
Wee Willie Winkie: The Phantom Rickshaw (1888)

Significant characters include:

03 Dan	**04** Puck	Jukes (Morrowbie)	'Kim')
Kaa	**05** Akela	M'Turk ('Turkey')	**06** Beetle
Una	Baloo	O'Hara (Kimball	Cheyne (Harvey)

Deever (Danny)
Lungri
Mowgli
Stalky
Toomai
07 Learoyd (Private)

08 Bagheera
Gunga Din
Hauksbee (Mrs)
Mulvaney (Private)
Ortheris (Private)
09 Gunga Dass

Shere Khan
10 Strickland
14 Rikki-Tikki-Tavi
15 Hobden the Hedger

kitchen

Kitchen parts include:

03 Aga®
bin
gas
hob
04 lino
oven
ring
sink
taps
unit
05 grill
pipes
range
shelf
stove
table

tiles
U-bend
06 boiler
box-bed
chairs
cooker
drawer
fridge
gas hob
larder
pantry
stools
trivet
07 freezer
griddle
trammel

twin tub
worktop
08 cupboard
hotplate
wine rack
09 sideboard
spin dryer
10 ceramic hob
deep-freeze
dishwasher
halogen hob
rotisserie
slow cooker
splashback
white goods

11 tumble dryer
water filter
12 breakfast bar
butcher block
chest freezer
extractor fan
refrigerator
service hatch
13 draining board
fridge-freezer
microwave oven
14 ice compartment
peninsular unit
pressure cooker
washing machine
waste compactor

knife

Knives include:

02 da
03 dah
hay
pen
04 bolo
case
chiv
dirk
fish
jack
moon
simi
05 bowie
bread
clasp
craft
cutto
flick

fruit
gully
kukri
panga
paper
putty
skean
skene
spade
steak
table
06 barong
butter
carver
chakra
cradle
cuttle
cuttoe

dagger
gulley
oyster
parang
pocket
sheath
trench
07 bayonet
carving
catling
drawing
dudgeon
hunting
leather
machete
palette
pruning
scalpel

Stanley®
whittle
08 bistoury
chopping
scalping
skean-dhu
skene-dhu
tranchet
09 butterfly
jockteleg
Swiss army
toothpick
10 skene-occle
11 snickersnee
switchblade
13 Kitchen Devils®
pusser's dagger

See also **dagger**; **sword**

knight

Knights include:

04 grey
05 black
    white
06 Bayard
    carpet
    errant

See also **legend**

    kemper
    ritter
07 paladin
08 bachelor
    banneret
    cavalier

    douzeper
    vavasour
09 chevalier
    doucepere
    valvassor
10 kempery-man

11 hospitaller
14 knight-bachelor
    Knights Templar
    preux chevalier

knitting

Knitting terms include:

03 rib
    row
04 Aran
    purl
    wire
    wool
05 chart
    pearl
    plain
06 cast on
    chunky
    intake
    marker
    narrow
    needle
    stitch
    two-ply

07 cast off
    chevron
    four-ply
    layette
    tension
    twin rib
08 ball band
    Fair Isle
    intarsia
    pavilion
    three-ply
09 box stitch
    double rib
    fingering
    garter rib
    honeycomb
    single rib

10 chain cable
    double knit
    French heel
    mistake rib
    moss panels
    moss stitch
    rice stitch
    row counter
    seed stitch
    slip stitch
    Swiss check
    tricoteuse
11 basketweave
    cable needle
    cable stitch
    chain stitch
    diagonal rib

    drop a stitch
    plain stitch
    Roman stripe
    thumb method
12 basket stitch
    braided cable
    garter stitch
    lattice cable
    stitch holder
13 fisherman's rib
    stocking frame
14 circular needle
    double knitting
    knitting needle
    stocking stitch
15 knitting machine
    knitting pattern

knot

Knots include:

03 bow
    tie
04 bend
    flat
    loop
    love
    reef
    wale
    wall
05 blood
    chain
    hitch
    plait
    thief
    thumb
    turle
06 Domhof

    granny
    lover's
    prusik
    square
07 bowline
    Gordian
    running
    seizing
    weaver's
    Windsor
08 overhand
    slipknot
    spade-end
    surgeon's
    true-love
09 half hitch
    lark's head

    sheet bend
    swab hitch
    Turk's head
10 clove hitch
    common bend
    fisherman's
    Flemish eye
    sheepshank
    true-lover's
11 carrick bend
    donkey hitch
    double blood
    Englishman's
    Hunter's bend
    timber hitch
12 marling hitch
    rolling hitch

    simple sennit
    weaver's hitch
13 drummer's chain
    figure of eight
    slippery hitch
14 Blackwall hitch
    common whipping
    double Cairnton
    double-overhand
    double-overhang
    Englishman's tie
    fisherman's bend
    Matthew Walker's
    running bowline

L

label *see* **fashion**

laboratory

lace

lair *see* **animal**

lake

Lakes, lochs and loughs include:

03 Awe (Scotland)
Van (Turkey)

04 Abbé (Djibouti/Ethiopia)
Biwa (Japan)
Bled (Switzerland)
Chad (Chad/Niger/Nigeria)
Como (Italy)
Derg (Ireland)
Earn (Scotland)
Erie (USA/Canada)
Eyre (Australia)
Kivu (Democratic Republic
of the Congo/Rwanda)
Ness (Scotland)
Tana (Ethiopia)

05 Foyle (Ireland)
Garda (Italy)
Great (Australia)
Huron (USA/Canada)
Kyoga (Uganda)
Leven (Scotland)
Mjøsa (Norway)
Morar (Scotland)
Neagh (Ireland)
Nyasa (Mozambique/
Malawi/Tanzania)
Ohrid (Albania/FYR
Macedonia)
Onega (Russia)
Patos (Brazil)
Poopó (Bolivia)
Tahoe (Canada)
Taupo (New Zealand)
Traun (Austria)
Volta (Ghana)

06 Albert (Democratic
Republic of the Congo/
Uganda)
Baikal (Russia)
Corrib (Ireland)
Crater (USA)
Edward (Democratic
Republic of the Congo/
Uganda)

Finger (USA)
Geneva (France/
Switzerland)
Izabal (Guatemala)
Ladoga (Russia)
Lomond (Scotland)
Malawi (Mozambique/
Malawi/Tanzania)
Müritz (Germany)
Nasser (Egypt/Sudan)
Nelson (USA)
Peipsi (Estonia/Russia)
Peipus (Estonia/Russia)
Rudolf (Kenya/Ethiopia)
Saimaa (Finland)
Skadar (Montenegro/
Albania)
Taimyr (Russia)
Taymyr (Russia)
Te Anau (New Zealand)
Vänern (Sweden)
Zurich (USA)

07 Aral Sea (Kazakhstan/
Uzbekistan)
Balaton (Hungary)
Bourget (France)
Chapala (Mexico)
Dead Sea (Israel/Jordan)
Katrine (Scotland)
Lucerne (Switzerland; USA)
Ontario (USA/Canada)
Rannoch (Scotland)
Scutari (Montenegro/
Albania)
Torrens (Australia)
Turkana (Kenya/Ethiopia)
Vättern (Sweden)

08 Attersee (Austria)
Balkhash (Kazakhstan)
Bodensee (Austria/
Germany/Switzerland)
Chiemsee (Germany)
Issyk Kul (Kyrgyzstan)
Lac Léman (France/

Switzerland)
Maggiore (Italy/Switzerland)
Manitoba (Canada)
Michigan (USA)
Päijänne (Finland)
Poyang Hu (China)
Sniardwy (Poland)
Superior (USA/Canada)
Tiberias (Israel)
Titicaca (Bolivia/Peru)
Tonlé Sap (Cambodia)
Victoria (Tanzania/Uganda/
Kenya)
Winnipeg (Canada)

09 Athabasca (Canada)
Constance (Austria/
Germany/Switzerland)
Great Bear (Canada)
Great Salt (USA)
Kammersee (Austria)
Maracaibo (Venezuela)
Neuchâtel (Switzerland)
Nicaragua (Nicaragua)
Trikhonís (Greece)
Ullswater (England)
Willandra (Australia)
Zeller See (Germany)

10 Caspian Sea (Russia/
Azerbaijan/Iran/
Turkmenistan/Kazakhstan)
Great Slave (Canada)
Okeechobee (USA)
Tanganyika (Burundi/
Democratic Republic
of the Congo/Tanzania/
Zambia)
Windermere (England)
Wörther See (Austria)

11 Great Bitter (Egypt)

12 Derwent Water (England)
Kielder Water (England)
Winnipegosis (Canada)

13 Bassenthwaite (England)
Coniston Water (England)

landmark *see* **Africa; Asia; Australia; Austria; Belgium; Canada; China; Czech Republic; Denmark; Europe; Finland; France; Germany; Greece; India; Ireland; Italy; Japan; London; Mexico; Middle East; The Netherlands; New York; New Zealand; Norway; Paris; Portugal; Russia; Spain; Sweden; Switzerland; United Kingdom; United States of America**

language

02 Wu

03 ASL
BSL
Edo
Gan
Giz
Ibo
Kru
Lao
Mam
Mon
Yue

04 Ainu
Chad
Cham
Crow
Dari
Efik
Erse
Fang
Fula
Gaul
Ge'ez
Hopi
Igbo
Inca
Krio
Kroo
Lapp
Manx
Maya
Motu
Nupe
Pali
Shan
Sulu
Thai
Urdu
Xosa
Zend
Zulu

05 Attic
Azeri
Aztec
Bantu
Cajun
Carib
Creek
Croat
Czech
Doric
Dutch
Fanti
Farsi

Greek
Hakka
Hausa
Hindi
husky
Inuit
Ionic
Iraqi
Irish
Karen
Kazak
Khmer
Ladin
Latin
Malay
Maori
Masai
Mayan
Mende
Norse
Oriya
Osage
Oscan
Osean
Punic
Sango
Saxon
Scots
Shona
Sioux
Sotho
Suomi
Swiss
Taino
Tajik
Tamil
Temne
Tetum
Uzbek
Vedic
Welch
Welsh
Wolof
Xhosa
Xiang
Yakut
Yupik

06 Afghan
Arabic
Aymara
Bahasa
Baluch
Bangla
Basque

Berber
Bihari
Bokmål
Burman
Canuck
Celtic
Chadic
Coptic
Creole
Cymric
Dakota
Danish
Danisk
Djerma
Eskimo
Fantee
Fijian
French
Gaelic
German
Gothic
Gullah
Hattic
Hebrew
Herero
Innuit
Kalmyk
Kanaka
Kazakh
Kikuyu
Korean
Kyrgyz
Ladino
Lakota
Lydian
Magyar
Manchu
Micmac
Minbei
Minnan
Minoan
Mixtec
Mohawk
Mongol
Navaho
Navajo
Nepali
Ojibwa
Ostiak
Ostyak
Palaic
Pashto
Polish
Romani

Romany
Samoan
Sepedi
Shelta
Sherpa
Slovak
Somali
Tartar
Telugu
Temnel
Tongan
Wendic
Yoruba

07 Amharic
Aramaic
Arapaho
Armoric
Ashanti
Avestan
Avestic
Ayamará
Baluchi
Bambara
Barotse
Basotho
Bengali
Bislama
Bosnian
British
Burmese
Calmuck
Catalan
Chaldee
Chechen
Chinese
Chinook
Comoran
Cornish
Crioulo
Dhivehi
Ebonics
English
Euskara
Euskera
Finnish
Flemish
Frisian
Gallego
Guaraní
Haitian
Hittite
Iranian
isiXosa
isiZulu
Italian
Kalmuck
Kannada
Kikongo

Kirghiz
Kirundi
Kurdish
Laotian
Lappish
Latvian
Lingala
Malinke
Maltese
Manchoo
Marathi
Mexican
Miskito
Mohegan
Mohican
Mordvin
Morisco
Nahuatl
Nauruan
Nynorsk
Palauan
Persian
Punjabi
Quechua
Quichua
Riksmål
Russian
Semitic
Serbian
Sesotho
Siamese
Sinhala
SiSwati
Slovene
Sorbian
Sosetho
Spanish
Swahili
Swedish
Tagálog
Tibetan
Turkish
Turkmen
Umbrian
Walloon
Wendish
Yiddish
Zapotec

08 Akkadian
Albanian
Armenian
Assamese
Assyrian
Balinese
Bohemian
Canarese
Chaldaic
Cherkess

Cherokee
Cheyenne
Chichewa
Croatian
Demotiki
Dzongkha
Egyptian
Estonian
Etruscan
Fanagalo
Galician
Georgian
Gujarati
Gujerati
Hawaiian
Illyrian
isiXhosa
Japanese
Javanese
Kanarese
Kashmiri
Khoikhoi
Kwakiutl
Lusatian
Malagash
Malagasy
Mandarin
Mandinka
Menomini
Moldovan
Phrygian
Pilipino
Polabian
Romanian
Romansch
Rumanian
Sanskrit
Scottish
Scythian
Setswana
Slavonic
Sumerian
Tahitian
Tigrinya
Tuvaluan
Volscian
Xitsonga
Yanomami

09 Aborigine
Afrikaans
Algonquin
Bulgarian
Cantonese
Castilian
Dalmatian
Ethiopian
Hottentot
Hungarian

Icelandic
I-Kiribati
Inuktitut
Kiswahili
Malayalam
Maldivian
Marquesan
Menominee
Norwegian
Nostratic
Old French
Provençal
Putonghua
Sardinian
Shikomoro
Sindebele
Sinhalese
Slovenian
Tamazight
Tshivenda
Ukrainian

Varangian
10 Aethiopian
Anglo-Irish
Anglo-Saxon
Babylonian
beach-la-mar
Belarusian
Circassian
High German
Hindustani
Indonesian
isiNdebele
Lithuanian
Macedonian
Malayalaam
Old English
Phoenician
Portuguese
Serbo-Croat
Vietnamese

11 Anglo-French
Anglo-Indian
Anglo-Romani
Azerbaijani
Belarussian
Belorussian
Celtiberian
Kazakhstani
Kinyarwanda
Marshallese
12 ancient Greek
Byelorussian
Katharevousa
Sranang Tongo
13 Middle English
14 Bahasa Malaysia
Church Slavonic
Lëtzebuergesch
15 Bahasa Indonesia

Invented languages include:

03 Ido
Neo
06 Novial
07 Volapük
08 Newspeak
09 Esperanto
10 Occidental
11 Interglossa
Interlingua
12 Idiom Neutral

Terms used in linguistics include:

03 ASR
NLP
04 cant
05 argot
idiom
lingo
slang
usage
06 accent
brogue
creole
jargon
patois
pidgin
syntax
tongue
07 dialect
grammar
08 idiolect
localism
standard
09 etymology
phonetics
semantics
10 journalese
vernacular
vocabulary
11 doublespeak
linguistics
non-standard
orthography
post-lingual
regionalism
12 lexicography
lingua franca
13 colloquialism

See also **alphabet**; **The Americas**; **French**; **German**; **grammar**; **Italian**; **Latin**; **punctuation**; **rhetoric**; **rhyme**; **Spanish**; **word**

Latin

Latin words and expressions include:

03 sic (used in printed matter to show that the original is faithfully reproduced even if incorrect)
04 idem (the same)
pace (indicating polite disagreement)
stet ('let it stand' – an instruction used in printed matter to restore after marking for deletion)
05 ad hoc (for this special purpose)
circa (approximately)

id est (that is, that is to say)
per se (by itself, in itself)
06 gratis (free of charge)
ibidem (used in footnotes to indicate that the same book has been cited previously)
passim (dispersed through a book)
07 alumnus (a former pupil or student)
a priori (deductive reasoning)
de facto (in fact, actually)

erratum (an error in writing or printing)

floruit (denotes a period during which a person lived)

in vitro (in the test tube)

sub rosa (in secret, privately)

08 ab initio (from the beginning)

addendum (supplementary material for a book)

emeritus (holding a position on an honorary basis only)

et cetera (and the rest)

ex gratia (of a payment, one that is made as a favour, without any legal obligation)

gravitas (seriousness)

infra dig (below one's dignity)

mea culpa (an admission of fault and an expression of repentance)

nota bene (observe well, note well)

subpoena (a writ commanding attendance in court)

09 ad nauseam (disgustingly endless or repetitive)

alma mater (one's former school, college, or university)

carpe diem (seize the day)

et tu, Brute ('you too, Brutus' – Caesar's alleged exclamation when he saw Brutus amongst his assassins)

ex officio (by virtue of office or position)

inter alia (among other things)

ipso facto (thereby)

per capita (per head of the population)

status quo (the existing condition)

sub judice (under consideration by a judge or a court of law)

vox populi (public or popular opinion)

10 anno Domini (in the year of the Lord)

ante-bellum (denotes a period before a specific war, especially the American Civil War)

ex cathedra (from the chair of office)

in absentia (in absence, used for occasions when the recipient would normally be present)

in extremis (at the point of death; in desperate circumstances)

magnum opus (a person's greatest achievement, especially a literary work)

post mortem (an examination of a body in order to determine the cause of death)

prima facie (a legal term for evidence that is assumed to be true unless disproved by other evidence)

quid pro quo (something given or taken as equivalent to another, often as retaliation)

sine qua non (an indispensable condition)

tabula rasa (a mind not yet influenced by outside impressions and experience)

11 ad infinitum (denotes endless repetition)

memento mori (an object, such as a skull, or anything to remind one of mortality)

non sequitur (a remark that has no relation to what has gone before)

tempus fugit (time flies)

12 ante meridiem (between midnight and noon)

caveat emptor (let the buyer beware)

compos mentis (being sane)

habeas corpus (maintains the right of the subject to protection from unlawful imprisonment)

post meridiem (between noon and midnight)

13 camera obscura (a light-free chamber in which an image of outside objects is thrown upon a screen)

deus ex machina (a contrived solution to a difficulty in a plot)

exempli gratia (by way of example)

modus operandi (the characteristic methods employed by a particular criminal)

14 annus mirabilis (a remarkably successful or auspicious year)

in loco parentis (in place of a parent)

pro bono publico (something done for no fee)

terra incognita (an unknown land)

15 annus horribilis (a dreadful year)

curriculum vitae (a summary of someone's educational qualifications and work experience)

delirium tremens (a condition caused by alcoholism)

persona non grata (one who is not welcome or favoured)

See also **day**; **month**; **number**

law

Scientific and other laws include:

04 Ohm's	**05** lemon	**06** Boyle's
Oral	Roman	Hooke's
Sod's	Salic	Mosaic

Snell's
Stoke's
07 Dalton's
Hubble's

Kepler's
Murphy's
natural
08 Charles's

09 Avogadro's
10 Parkinson's
13 inverse square

Laws and Acts include:

04 DORA (1914)
07 Riot Act (1714)
Test Act (1673)
08 Corn Laws (1815)
Poor Laws (1562–1601)
Stamp Act (1765)
Sugar Act (1764)
10 Act of Union (1707, 1800)
Magna Carta (1215)
Patriot Act (2001)
Reform Acts (various)

11 Abortion Act (1967)
Equal Pay Act (1970)
Scotland Act (1998)
12 Bill of Rights (1689)
Homestead Act (1862)
Terrorism Act (2000)
13 Act of Congress (various)
Enclosure Acts (various)
Parliament Act (1911/1949)
14 Act of Supremacy (1534)
Cat and Mouse Act (1913)

Civil Rights Act (1964)
Corporation Act (1661)
Declaratory Act (1766)
Human Rights Act (1998)
Native Title Act (1993)
Taft-Hartley Act (1947)
15 Act of Parliament (various)
Act of Settlement (1701)
Act of Succession (1534)
Habeas Corpus Act (1679)

Lawyer types include:

02 QC
05 avoué
brief
judge
06 avocat
jurist
07 bencher
coroner
counsel
justice
mukhtar
sheriff
shyster
08 advocate

attorney
green-bag
Law Lords
man of law
Recorder
09 barrister
lawmonger
solicitor
10 legal eagle
11 conveyancer
crown lawyer
pettifogger
12 circuit judge
jurisconsult

Lord Advocate
13 attorney at law
Crown attorney
district judge
Queen's Counsel
sheriff depute
14 criminal lawyer
deputy recorder
High Court judge
Lord Chancellor
public defender
Vice-Chancellor
15 ambulance-chaser
Attorney-General

Lawyers include:

04 Hill (Anita; 1956– , US)
John (Otto; 1909–97, German)
Reno (Janet; 1938– , US)

05 Baird (Vera; 1951– , English)
Booth (Cherie; 1954– , English)
Finch (Atticus; *To Kill a Mockingbird*, 1960,
Harper Lee)
Judge (Lord Igor; 1941– , Maltese/British)
Mason (Perry; *The Case of the Velvet Claws*,
1933, et seq, Erle Stanley Gardner)
Mills (Dame Barbara; 1940– , English)
Nader (Ralph; 1934– , US)
Obama (Barack; 1961– , US)
Obama (Michelle; 1964– , US)
Slovo (Joe; 1926–95, South African)
Stark (Willie; *All the King's Men*, 1946,
Robert Penn Warren)
Vance (Cyrus R; 1917–2002, US)

06 Bailey (F Lee; 1933– , US)
Butler (Benjamin F; 1818–93, US)
Carton (Sydney; *A Tale of Two Cities*, 1859,
Charles Dickens)
Darrow (Clarence; 1857–1938, US)
Devlin (Patrick, Lord; 1905–92, English)
Harker (Jonathan; *Dracula*, 1897, Bram Stoker)
Harman (Harriet; 1950– , English)
Holmes (Oliver Wendell; 1841–1935, US)
Martin (Richard; 1754–1834, Irish)
07 Acheson (Dean; 1893–1971, US)
Clinton (Bill; 1946– , US)
Clinton (Hillary; 1947– , US)
Haldane (Richard, Viscount; 1856–1928,
Scottish)
Kennedy (Helena, Baroness; 1950– ,
Scottish)
Mondale (Walter F; 1928– , US)

O'Connor (Sandra Day; 1930–   , US)

Peachum (Thomas; *The Beggar's Opera*, 1728, John Gay)

08 Gonzales (Alberto; 1955–   , US)
Marshall (Thurgood; 1908–93, US)
Mortimer (Sir John; 1923–   , English)
Scotland (Baroness Patricia; 1955–   , British)

09 La Guardia (Fiorello H; 1882–1947, US)

Shawcross (Hartley, Lord; 1902–2003, English)

10 Birkenhead (Frederick Edwin Smith, Earl of; 1872–1930, English)

11 Hore-Belisha (Leslie, Lord; 1893–1957, English)

12 Guicciardini (Francesco; 1483–1540, Italian)

14 Brillat-Savarin (Anthelme; 1755–1826, French)

Legal terms include:

02 JP
QC

03 bar
DPP
sue

04 bail
deed
dock
fine
jury
oath
plea
will
writ

05 alibi
asset
bench
brief
by-law
claim
felon
grant
judge
juror
lease
party
proof
proxy
title
trial

06 appeal
arrest
bigamy
charge
client
demand
equity
estate
guilty
lawyer
legacy
pardon
parole

patent
remand
repeal
the bar
waiver

07 accused
alimony
amnesty
caution
charter
codicil
convict
coroner
custody
damages
defence
divorce
hearing
inquest
inquiry
Law Lord
lawsuit
mandate
penalty
perjury
probate
pursuer
sheriff
statute
summons
tenancy
verdict
warrant
witness

08 act of God
adultery
advocate
civil law
claimant
contract
covenant
criminal
defender
easement

eviction
evidence
executor
freehold
hung jury
innocent
judgment
juvenile
legal aid
mortgage
offender
prisoner
receiver
reprieve
sanction
sentence
subpoena
tribunal

09 accessory
acquittal
affidavit
agreement
annulment
barrister
common law
copyright
court case
defendant
endowment
fee simple
indemnity
intestacy
judgement
judiciary
leasehold
liability
not guilty
not proven
plaintiff
precedent
probation
solicitor
testimony
trademark

10 accomplice
allegation
confession
conveyance
decree nisi
indictment
injunction
liquidator
magistrate
settlement

11 adjournment
arbitration
extradition
foreclosure
inheritance
local search
maintenance
plea bargain
plead guilty
proceedings
prosecution
ward of court

12 age of consent
Bill of Rights
constitution
court martial
cross-examine
Lord Advocate
misadventure
notary public

13 King's evidence
public inquiry
Queen's Counsel
young offender

14 decree absolute
Lord Chancellor
plead not guilty
Queen's evidence

15 Act of Parliament
Attorney-General
clerk of the court
contempt of court
power of attorney

See also **astronomy**; **chemistry**; **judge**; **legislation**; **physics**

Lawrence, D H (1885–1930)

Significant works include:

06 *Amores* (1916)

07 *Pansies* (1929)

08 *Kangaroo* (1923)

09 *Aaron's Rod* (1922)

10 *Apocalypse* (1931)
The Rainbow (1915)

11 *The Lost Girl* (1920)
Women in Love (1920)

12 *Boy in the Bush* (1924)

13 *Sons and Lovers* (1913)
The Trespasser (1912)

14 *Etruscan Places* (1932)
Sea and Sardinia (1921)

15 *The White Peacock* (1911)
Twilight in Italy (1916)

16 *England, My England* (1922)
Mornings in Mexico (1927)
The Plumed Serpent (1926)

18 *Love Poems and Others* (1913)
The Prussian Officer (1914)

19 *The Woman Who Rode Away* (1928)

20 *Lady Chatterley's Lover* (1928)

21 *Birds, Beasts and Flowers* (1923)
Look! We Have Come Through! (1917)

24 *Fantasia of the Unconscious* (1922)

26 *Movements in European History* (1921)

31 *Psychoanalysis and the Unconscious* (1921)

Significant characters include:

05 Cicio
Crich (Gerald)
Dawes (Baxter)
Dawes (Clara)
Lilly (Rawdon)
March (Ellen)
Morel (Gertrude)
Morel (Paul)
Morel (Walter)

06 Birkin (Rupert)
Colley (Ben 'Kangaroo')
Egbert
Lensky (Anna)
Lensky (Lydia)

Leslie (Kate)
McNair (Siegmund)
Saxton (George)
Sisson (Aaron)
Somers (Harriet)
Somers (Richard)
St Mawr

07 Banford (Jill)
Grenfel (Henry)
Leivers (Miriam)
Mellors (Oliver)
Roddice (Hermione)

08 Brangwen (Gudrun)

Brangwen (Tom)
Brangwen (Ursula)
Brangwen (Will)
Callcott (Jack)
Cipriano (Don)
Houghton (Alvina)

09 Beardsall (Lettie)

10 Carrington (Lou)
Chatterley (Lady Constance 'Connie')
Chatterley (Sir Clifford)
Skrebensky (Anton)

15 Prussian Officer (the)

lawyer *see* **law**

layer *see* **atmosphere**

leaf

Leaf parts include:

03 tip	midrib	stomata	leaf-stalk
04 vein	sheath	**08** leaf axil	**11** axillary bud
05 blade	stipel	leaf cell	chloroplast
sinus	**07** lacinia	phyllode	
stoma	petiole	**09** epidermis	
06 margin	stipule	footstalk	

Leaf shapes include:

04 oval	lobed	**06** cusped
05 acute	ovate	entire

linear
lyrate
oblong
07 acerose
ciliate
cordate
crenate
dentate
falcate
hastate

obovate
palmate
peltate
pinnate
ternate
08 digitate
elliptic
reniform
subulate
09 acuminate

mucronate
orbicular
runcinate
sagittate
10 lanceolate
pinnatifid
spathulate
trifoliate
13 doubly dentate
15 abruptly pinnate

See also **disease**

leather

Leathers include:

03 kid
taw
04 buff
butt
calf
fair
fell
napa
pelt
roan
shoe
wash
yuft
05 grain
Mocha
nappa
neat's
plate

split
suede
waxed
white
06 chammy
chrome
Nubuck®
patent
Rexine®
Russia
shammy
skiver
spruce
07 chamois
cowhide
dogskin
hog-skin
kidskin

kipskin
morocco
pigskin
saffian
08 buckskin
cabretta
calfskin
capeskin
cheverel
cheveril
cordovan
cordwain
deerskin
goatskin
japanned
lambskin
maroquin
shagreen

09 crocodile
lacquered
sheepskin
slinkskin
snakeskin
10 artificial
checklaton
shecklaton
11 aqualeather
cuir-bouilli
cuir-bouilly
schecklaton
whitleather
13 French morocco
Levant morocco
14 Persian morocco

legal *see* **law**

legend

Legends include:

05 El Cid (Spain)
Faust (Germany)
06 Roland (France)
07 Aladdin (Arabia/Europe)
Ali Baba (Arabia)
Beowulf (Scandinavia)
Don Juan (Spain)
08 El Dorado (Spain/South America)
Kalevala (Finland)
St George (Britain)
The Eddas (Scandinavia/Iceland)
09 Bluebeard (France)
Elder Edda (Scandinavia/Iceland)
Prose Edda (Scandinavia/Iceland)

Robin Hood (Britain)
St Brendan (Ireland)
The Fianna (Ireland)
10 Blackbeard (Britain/USA)
Cúchulainn (Ireland)
Kalevipoeg (Estonia)
Lady Godiva (Britain)
Paul Bunyan (USA)
Poetic Edda (Scandinavia/Iceland)
11 Captain Kidd (Britain/USA)
Esplanadian (Spain)
Magic Carpet (Asia)
Puss in Boots (France)
William Tell (Switzerland)
Younger Edda (Scandinavia/Iceland)

12 Blarney Stone (Ireland)
Song of Roland (France)
The Holy Grail (Middle East/Europe)
The Three Sons (Ireland)
Völsunga Saga (Iceland)

13 Arabian Nights (Middle East)

Conán the Brave (Ireland)
Niebelunglied (Germany)

14 Flying Dutchman (The Netherlands)
Vlad the Impaler (Transylvania)

15 Johnny Appleseed (USA)

Characters in the Robin Hood legend include:

07 Sheriff

08 Merry Men

09 Alan A Dale

Friar Tuck

Robin Hood

10 Little John

Maid Marian

Prince John

11 King Richard

Will Scarlet

13 Guy of Gisborne

Much the Miller

Knights of the Round Table in Arthurian legend:

06 Sir Cai
Sir Kay

07 Sir Bors

08 Sir Lucan
Sir Owain
Sir Safer
Sir Yvain

09 Sir Bedwyr
Sir Degore
Sir Gareth
Sir Gawain
Sir Safere

10 King Arthur
Sir Alymere
Sir Dagonet
Sir Gaheris

Sir Galahad
Sir Gawaine
Sir Geraint
Sir Lamorak
Sir Lionell
Sir Mordred
Sir Pelleas
Sir Tristam
Sir Tristan

11 Sir Aglovale
Sir Agravain
Sir Aristant
Sir Bedivere
Sir Florence
Sir Lancelot
Sir Perceval

Sir Percival
Sir Tristram

12 Sir Agravaine
Sir Bleoberis
Sir Palomedes
Sir Percivale

14 Sir Bors de Ganis
Sir Constantine

15 La Cote Male Taile
Sir Brunor le Noir
Sir Ector de Maris

16 Sir Lancelot Du Lac

17 Sir Launcelot Du Lac
Sir Le Bel Desconneu

22 Sir Palamedes the Saracen

Other characters in Arthurian legend include:

03 Ban
Lot

04 Elen
Mark
Urre

05 Alice
Amant
Balan
Balin
Balyn
Belin
Brine
Cador
David
Dinas
Eliot
Gayus
Harry
Hebes
Howel
Isoud
Labor

Lovel
Mador
Nimue
Nymue
Pinel
Tirre
Torre
Ulfin
Uther

06 Andred
Blamor
Bliant
Brisen
Bromel
Castor
Clegis
Elaine
Elamet
Elayne
Fergus
Iseult
Isolde

Lucius
Melias
Melion
Meliot
Melwas
Merlin
Modred
Nacien
Ozanna
Pellam
Pelles
Phelot
Ulfius
Uriens

07 Accolon
Aliduke
Anguish
Annowre
Argante
Baudwin
Bernard
Caradoc

Carados
Clarrus
Claudas
Dinadan
Dodinas
Eliazar
Evelake
Faramon
Gaheret
Galihud
Griflet
Hurlame
Igraine
Jacound
Jordans
Ladinas
Lanceor
Launfal
Lavaine
Lynette
Marhaus
Myrddyn
Nentres
Nimiane
Patrise
Peredur
Persant
Ragnell
Rivalin
Selises
Tarquin
Tolleme
Turquin
Walwain
Ygaerne

08 Anfortas
Angharad
Anglides
Astamore
Bersules
Brastias

Childric
Galahaut
Gingalin
Guenever
Hellawes
Ironside
Kehydius
Lambegus
Lyonesse
Margawse
Meliodas
Menaduke
Morgawse
Nerovens
Ontzlake
Palmerin
Parsifal
Pecchere
Pellinor
Petipase
Selivant
Tryamour
Villiars

09 Achefleur
Alisander
Arondight
Bragwaine
Brandiles
Elizabeth
Epinogrus
Estorause
Galihodin
Grail King
Guinevere
Pellinore
Sagramore
Tramtrist

10 Bagdemagus
Curselaine
Dame Brisen

Fisher King
Gouvernail
Guanhamara
Maimed King
Meliagaunt
Plenorious
Segwarides
Sentraille

11 Bellengerus
Brandegoris
Constantine
Galahantine
Leodegrance
Meliagrance
Morgan le Fay
Wounded King

12 Colgrevaunce
La Beale Isoud
Suppinabiles

13 Accolon of Gaul
Blamor de Ganis
Dame Bragwaine
Elaine le Blank
Elayne the Fair
Lady of Shalott
Lady of the Lake
Melias de Lisle
Persant of Inde
Pinel le Savage
Urre of Hungary

14 Duke of Tintagel
Elayne Sans Pere
Mador de la Porte
Meliot de Logris
Uther Pendragon

15 Cador of Cornwall
Damsel of the Lake
Dodinas le Savage
Hebes le Renoumes

Terms to do with Arthurian legend include:

03 Usk

04 Bath
Gaul
York

05 Arroy
Badon

06 Albion
Avalon
Camlan
Eildon
Logres
Meliot
Orkney

Thanet

07 Avelion
brachet
Camelot
Camlann
Carleon
Chester
Tarabel

08 Brittany
Caerleon
Caliburn
Camelerd
Camelide

Cornwall
Lyonesse
Tintagel

09 Badon Hill
Boscastle
Camelford
Cameliard
Excalibur
Holy Grail
Llyn Dinas
loadstone
Red Dragon
Roche Rock
Seat Royal

white hart
white stag

10 Black Cross
Cader Idris
Caledfwlch
Grail Table
Llyn Barfog
North Umber
Round Table
Stonehenge
Tintagalon
Winchester

11 Arthur's Seat
Cadbury Hill
Castle Taruc
Chalice Well
Craig y Dinas
Glastonbury

See also **mythology**

Grantmesnle
Merlin's Cave

12 Alderley Edge
Arthur's Cross
Dozemary Pool
Fescamp Abbey
Isle of Avalon
Perilous Seat
Seat Perilous
Vale of Avalon

13 Bleeding Lance
Cadbury Castle
City of Legions
Questing Beast
Ship of Damsels
Ship of Fairies
Siège Perilous
The Waste Lands

14 Bamburgh Castle
Caerleon Castle
Dolorous Stroke
enchanted rings
Glastonbury Tor
Island of Avalon
Northumberland
St Govan's Chapel
Tintagel Castle

15 Caerleon upon Usk
Slaughterbridge
St Michael's Mount
Sword in the Stone
The Giant's castle
The Tristan Stone
Valley of Delight

legislation

Terms to do with legislation include:

02 Cm
03 Act
aye
law
04 Bill
06 repeal
Treaty
08 Decision
Division
09 Amendment
directive
Public Act

See also **law**; **politics**

10 Commission
devolution
Green Paper
guillotine
Public Bill
referendum
regulation
White Paper
11 legislation
Report Stage
Royal Assent
12 First Reading
House of Lords

Personal Bill
Third Reading
13 Command Papers
European Union
Letters Patent
Second Reading
14 Committee Stage
Government Bill
House of Commons
15 Act of Parliament
Pre-Budget Report
Programme Motion

letter *see* **alphabet**

lettuce

Lettuce varieties include:

03 cos
04 flat
05 lamb's
round

See also **salad**

06 frisée
07 cabbage
Chinese
iceberg

romaine

08 Batavian
09 little gem
10 butterhead

lollo rosso

lexicography

Lexicographers and associated figures include:

04 Bopp (Franz; 1791–1867, German)
Fick (August; 1833–1916, German)

05 Aasen (Ivar; 1813–96, Norwegian)
Grant (William; 1863–1946, Scottish)
Kimhi (David; c.1160–1235, French)
March (Francis Andrew; 1825–1911, US)
Pliny (Gaius 'the Elder'; 23–79 AD, Roman)
Sapir (Edward; 1884–1939, US)
Skeat (Walter William; 1835–1912, English)
Smith (Benjamin Eli; 1857–1912, US)
Smith (Sir William; 1813–93, English)

06 Bailey (Nathan; d.1742, English)
Benfey (Theodor; 1809–81, German)
Bierce (Ambrose; 1842–1914, US)
Blount (Thomas; 1618–79, English)
Brewer (E Cobham; 1810–97, English)
Cooper (Thomas; c.1517–94, English)
Couper (Thomas; c.1517–94, English)
Florio (John; c.1533–1625, English)
Fowler (H W; 1858–1933, English)
Freund (Wilhelm; 1806–94, German)
Hornby (A S; 1898–1978, English)
Kimchi (David; c.1160–1235, French)
Littré (Émile; 1801–81, French)
Murray (Sir James; 1837–1915, Scottish)
Onions (C T; 1873–1965, English)
Robert (Paul; 1910–80, French)
Trench (Richard Chenevix; 1807–86, Irish)
Walker (John; 1732–1807, English)
Wright (Joseph; 1855–1930, English)

07 Adelung (Johann Christoph; 1732–1806, German)
Bradley (Henry; 1845–1923, English)

Chomsky (Noam; 1928– ; US)
Craigie (Sir William; 1867–1957, Scottish)
Curtius (Georg; 1820–85, German)
Diderot (Denis; 1713–84, French)
Johnson (Samuel; 1709–84, English)
Lönnrot (Elias; 1802–84, Finnish)
Mencken (H L; 1880 1956, US)
Simpson (John; 1953– , English)
Vámbéry (Arminius; 1832–1913, Hungarian)
Ventris (Michael; 1922–56, English)
Webster (Noah; 1758–1843, US)
Whitney (William Dwight; 1827–94, US)

08 Bosworth (Joseph; 1789–1876, English)
Calepino (Ambrogio; 1440–1510, Italian)
Chambers (Ephraim; c.1680–1740, English)
Chambers (Robert; 1802–71, Scottish)
Chambers (William; 1800–83, Scottish)
Jamieson (John; 1759–1838, Scottish)
Larousse (Pierre; 1817–75, French)
Saussure (Ferdinand de; 1857–1913, Swiss)

09 Ainsworth (Robert; 1660–1743, English)
Furetière (Antoine; 1619–88, French)
Furnivall (Frederick James; 1825–1910, English)
Jespersen (Otto; 1860–1943, Danish)
Partridge (Eric; 1894–1979, New Zealand/British)
Worcester (Joseph E; 1784–1865, US)

10 Amarasimha (probably 6c; Sanskrit)
Burchfield (Robert; 1923–2004, English)

13 Aguilo i Fuster (Marian; 1825–97, Spanish)

libertine *see* **womanizer**

libretto

Librettists and lyricists include:

04 Bart (Lionel; 1930–99, English)
Hart (Lorenz; 1895–1943, US)
Jouy (Étienne; 1764–1846, French)
Rice (Sir Tim; 1944– , English)
Stow (Randolph; 1935– , Australian)
Vega (Ventura de la; 1807–65, Argentine/Spanish)

05 Boito (Arrigo; 1842–1918, Italian)
Piave (Francesco; 1810–76; Italian)
Rolli (Paolo; 1687–1765, Italian)
Swann (Donald; 1923–94, Welsh)

06 Berlin (Irving; 1888–1989, US)
Fields (Dorothy; 1904–74, US)

Lerner (Alan Jay; 1918–86, US)
Malouf (David; 1934– , Australian)
Porter (Cole; 1891–1964, US)
Scribe (Eugène; 1791–1861, French)

07 Crozier (Eric; 1914–94, English)
Da Ponte (Lorenzo; 1749–1838, Italian)
Elmslie (Kenward; 1929– , US)
Gilbert (Sir W S; 1836–1911, English)
Harwood (Gwen; 1920–95, Australian)
Ryskind (Morrie; 1895–1985, US)
Sedaine (Michel-Jean; 1719–97, French)

08 Ferretti (Jacopo; 1784–1852, Italian)
Gershwin (Ira; 1896–1983, US)

Meredith (William Morris; 1919–2007, US)
Sondheim (Stephen; 1930– , US)
09 Benserade (Isaac de; 1613–91, French)
See also **composer**; **opera**; **song**

Delavigne (Casimir; 1793–1843, French)
11 Hammerstein (Oscar, II; 1895–1960, US)

lichen *see* algae

lie

Lies include:

03 fib	story	untruth	**10** concoction
04 cram	**06** unfact	whopper	fairy story
flam	**07** cretism	**08** white lie	taradiddle
whid	fiction	**09** fairy tale	**11** fabrication
05 fable	leasing	falsehood	pseudologia
porky	romance	mendacity	tarradiddle

lily

Lilies include:

03 day	scilla	kniphofia
may	smilax	of the Nile
04 aloe	**07** candock	Richardia
arum	Madonna	**10** agapanthus
pond	quamash	aspidistra
sego	Tritoma	belladonna
05 calla	**08** asphodel	fritillary
camas	galtonia	**11** cabbage-tree
lotus	gloriosa	Convallaria
regal	hyacinth	of the valley
tiger	martagon	red-hot poker
torch	nenuphar	spatterdock
yucca	Phormium	**12** Annunciation
06 camash	trillium	Hemerocallis
camass	Turk's cap	Solomon's seal
Canada	victoria	zantedeschia
crinum	**09** amaryllis	**13** butcher's broom
Easter	grass tree	**15** star of Bethlehem
Nuphar	herb-Paris	

liqueur

Liqueurs include:

04 ouzo (aniseed/liquorice)
05 Aurum® (brandy/orange/saffron)
noyau (fruit kernels/almond)
06 Averna (herbs/roots)
Glayva® (heather honey/orange peel)
Izarra® (armagnac/herbs)
Kahlúa® (coffee)
kirsch (cherry)
kümmel (cumin/caraway seeds)
Malibu® (white rum/coconut)

Midori® (melon)
Nocino (green walnuts)
pastis (aniseed/liquorice)
Pernod® (aniseed/liquorice)
Ponche (brandy/fruit/spices)
Ricard® (aniseed/liquorice)
Strega® (saffron/herbs)
07 Amarula® (marula fruit/cream)
Baileys® (whiskey/cream)
curaçao (bitter orange peel)

ratafia (fruit kernels)
sambuca (aniseed/elderberry)

08 absinthe (aniseed/herbs)
advocaat (egg)
amaretto (almond/apricot)
anisette (anise)
Drambuie® (whisky/heather honey)
Galliano® (anise/liquorice/vanilla)
prunelle (sloe/wild plum)
rum shrub (rum/sugar/citrus)
Tia Maria® (cask-aged rum/coffee bean/
  spices)

09 Cointreau® (bitter orange peel)
Irish Mist® (cognac/honey/herbs)
mirabelle (plum)
Triple sec (grape brandy/ bitter orange peel)
Van der Hum (brandy/tangerine/spices)

10 Chartreuse® (orange/herbs/spices)
Frangelico® (hazelnut)

See also **spirit**

limoncello (lemon)
maraschino (cherry)

11 Benedictine (orange/herb/spices)
Vana Tallinn (rum/vanilla)

12 cherry brandy (cherry)
crème de cacao (chocolate)
Goldschlager® (Scotch whisky/aniseed)
Grand Marnier® (orange)
Jägermeister (Irish whiskey/herbs/roots/fruit)
kirschwasser (wild cherry)
Parfait Amour (rose petal/vanilla/almond)

13 Cherry Heering (cherry)
crème de cassis (blackcurrant)
crème de menthe (peppermint)
Cuarenta y Tres (vanilla/citrus)
eau des creoles (mammee-apple flowers)

15 Southern Comfort® (American whiskey/
  peaches/orange)

literature

Literature and story types include:

03 spy

04 epic
love
myth
saga
tale
yarn

05 crime
drama
essay
fable
fairy
farce
ghost
novel
prose
sci-fi
short
spiel
squib
triad
verse

06 comedy
horror
legend
masque
parody
poetry
postil
satire
thesis

07 Aga saga
bedtime
epistle
faction
fantasy
fiction
lampoon
mystery
novella
parable
polemic
romance
tragedy
trilogy
western

08 allegory
anecdote
chick lit
folk tale
libretto
pastiche
tall tale
thriller
treatise

09 adventure
anti-novel
biography
children's
criticism
detective
dime novel

fairytale
interlude
melodrama
novelette
saga novel
shaggy-dog
whodunnit

10 bonkbuster
magnum opus
non-fiction
photonovel
river novel
roman à clef
short story
travelogue
yellowback

11 black comedy
blockbuster
Gothic novel
interactive
pulp fiction
roman à thèse
roman fleuve
terror novel
thesis novel
three-decker

12 bodice-ripper
classic novel
crime fiction
double-decker
graphic novel

Mills and Boon®
nouveau roman
novelization
outside novel
problem novel
spine-chiller
swashbuckler

13 autobiography
belles-lettres
Bildungsroman
penny dreadful
roman à tiroirs
travel writing

14 science fiction

sex-and-shopping

15 epistolary novel
historical novel
non-fiction novel
picaresque novel
shilling shocker

10 Nobel Prize (worldwide)
11 Booker Prize (UK)
Orange Prize (UK)

12 Prix Goncourt (France)
13 Carnegie Medal (UK)
Pulitzer Prize (US)

14 Man Booker Prize (UK)
15 Costa Book Awards (UK)

Literary critics include:

04 Beer (John; 1926– , English)
Bell (Clive; 1881–1964, English)
Blum (Léon; 1872–1950, French)
Frye (Northrop; 1912–91, Canadian)

05 Carey (John; 1934– , English)
Hicks (Granville; 1901–82, US)
Kazin (Alfred; 1915–88, US)
Lodge (David; 1935– , English)
Stead (C K; 1932– , New Zealand)

06 Arnold (Matthew; 1822–88, English)
Empson (Sir William; 1906–84, English)
Leavis (F R; 1895–1978, English)
Leavis (Q D; 1906–81, English)
Lukacs (Georg; 1885–1971, Hungarian)
Ransom (John; 1888–1974, US)
Sontag (Susan; 1933–2005; US)
Wilson (Edmund; 1895–1972, US)

07 Ackroyd (Peter; 1949– , English)

Alvarez (A; 1929– , English)
Barthes (Roland; 1915–80, French)
Daiches (David; 1912–2005, Scottish)
Derrida (Jacques; 1930–2004, French)
Hoggart (Richard; 1918– , English)
Kermode (Sir Frank; 1919– , Manx)
Wimsatt (William, Jnr; 1907–75, US)

08 Bradbury (Sir Malcolm; 1932–2000, English)
Eagleton (Terry; 1943– , British)
Longinus (c.1CAD, Greek)
Nicolson (Sir Harold; 1886–1968, English)
Richards (I A; 1893–1979, English)
Trilling (Lionel; 1905–75, US)
Williams (Raymond; 1921–88, Welsh)

10 Saintsbury (George; 1845–1933, English)

11 Matthiessen (F O; 1902–50, US)
Sainte-Beuve (Charles Augustin; 1804–69, French)

Literary characters include:

02 Pi (*Life of Pi*, 2002, Yann Martel)

03 Jim (Lord; *Lord Jim*, 1900, Joseph Conrad)
Kim (*Kim*, 1901, Rudyard Kipling)
Lee (Lorelei; *Gentlemen Prefer Blondes*, 1925, Anita Loos)
Pip (*Great Expectations*, 1861, Charles Dickens)
Una (*The Faerie Queene*, 1590–96, Sir Edmund Spenser)

04 Ahab (Captain; *Moby-Dick*, 1851, Herman Melville)
Bede (Adam; *Adam Bede*, 1859, George Eliot)
Bond (James; *Casino Royale*, 1954, et seq, Ian Fleming)
Budd (Billy; *Billy Budd, Foretopman*, 1924, Herman Melville)
Dent (Arthur; *The Hitch-Hiker's Guide to the Galaxy*, 1979, et seq, Douglas Adams)
Eyre (Jane; *Jane Eyre*, 1847, Charlotte Brontë)

Finn (Phineas; *Phineas Finn: The Irish Member*, 1869, Anthony Trollope)
Fogg (Phileas; *Around the World in Eighty Days*, 1873, Jules Verne)
Gamp (Sarah; *Martin Chuzzlewit*, 1844, Charles Dickens)
Gray (Charlotte; *Charlotte Gray*, 1998, Sebastian Faulks)
Gray (Dorian; *The Picture of Dorian Gray*, 1891, Oscar Wilde)
Haze (Dolores; *Lolita*, 1955, Vladimir Nabokov)
Heep (Uriah; *David Copperfield*, 1850, Charles Dickens)
Hood (Robin; *Ivanhoe*, 1819, Sir Walter Scott)
Hyde (Mr; *The Strange Case of Dr Jekyll and Mr Hyde*, 1886, Robert Louis Stevenson)
Mole (Adrian; *The Secret Diary of Adrian*

Mole, aged 13¾, 1982, et seq, Sue Townsend)
Ridd (John; *Lorna Doone*, 1869, R D Blackmore)
Slop (Doctor; *The Life and Opinions of Tristram Shandy*, 1759–67, Laurence Sterne)
Tigg (Montague; *Martin Chuzzlewit*, 1844, Charles Dickens)
Trim (Corporal; *The Life and Opinions of Tristram Shandy*, 1759–67, Laurence Sterne)
Troy (Sergeant Francis; *Far from the Madding Crowd*, 1874, Thomas Hardy)
Tuck (Friar; *Ivanhoe*, 1819, Sir Walter Scott)
Wilt (Henry; *Wilt*, 1976, et seq, Tom Sharpe)

05 Athos (*The Three Musketeers*, 1844, Alexandre Dumas père)
Avery (Shug; *The Color Purple*, 1983, Alice Walker)
Bates (Miss; *Emma*, 1816, Jane Austen)
Bloom (Leopold; *Ulysses*, 1922, James Joyce)
Bloom (Molly; *Ulysses*, 1922, James Joyce)
Boxer (*Animal Farm*, 1945, George Orwell)
Brown (Father; *The Innocence of Father Brown*, 1911, G K Chesterton)
Celie (*The Color Purple*, 1983, Alice Walker)
Chips (Mr; *Goodbye, Mr Chips*, 1934, James Hilton)
Clare (Angel; *Tess of the D'Urbervilles*, 1891, Thomas Hardy)
Darcy (Fitzwilliam; *Pride and Prejudice*, 1813, Jane Austen)
Darcy (Mark; *Bridget Jones's Diary*, 1996, *Bridget Jones: The Edge of Reason*, 1999, Helen Fielding)
Doone (Lorna; *Lorna Doone*, 1869, R D Blackmore)
Drood (Edwin; *The Mystery of Edwin Drood*, 1870, Charles Dickens)
Geste (Beau; *Beau Geste*, 1924, P C Wren)
Jones (Bridget; *Bridget Jones's Diary*, 1996, *Bridget Jones: The Edge of Reason*, 1999, Helen Fielding)
Jones (Tom; *The History of Tom Jones*, 1749, Henry Fielding)
Kipps (Arthur; *Kipps*, 1904, H G Wells)
Kurtz (*Heart of Darkness*, 1902, Joseph Conrad)
Loman (Willy; *Death of a Salesman*, 1949, Arthur Miller)
Lucky (*Waiting for Godot*, 1955, Samuel Beckett)
Mitty (Walter; *The Secret Life of Walter Mitty*, 1939, James Thurber)
Moore (Mrs; *A Passage to India*, 1924, E M Forster)

Mosca (*Volpone, or The Fox*, 1606, Ben Jonson)
Nancy (*Oliver Twist*, 1838, Charles Dickens)
O'Hara (Kimball; *Kim*, 1901, Rudyard Kipling)
O'Hara (Scarlett; *Gone with the Wind*, 1936, Margaret Mitchell)
Polly (Alfred; *The History of Mr Polly*, 1910, H G Wells)
Porgy (*Porgy*, 1925, DuBose Heyward)
Pozzo (*Waiting for Godot*, 1955, Samuel Beckett)
Price (Fanny; *Mansfield Park*, 1814, Jane Austen)
Quilp (Daniel; *The Old Curiosity Shop*, 1841, Charles Dickens)
Rebus (Inspector John; *Knots and Crosses*, 1987, et seq, Ian Rankin)
Rudge (Barnaby; *Barnaby Rudge*, 1841, Charles Dickens)
Satan (*Paradise Lost*, 1667, *Paradise Regained*, 1671, John Milton)
Sharp (Becky; *Vanity Fair*, 1848, W M Thackeray)
Sikes (Bill; *Oliver Twist*, 1838, Charles Dickens)
Slope (Reverend Obadiah; *Barchester Towers*, 1857, Anthony Trollope)
Smike (*Nicholas Nickleby*, 1839, Charles Dickens)
Smith (Winston; *1984*, 1949, George Orwell)
Spade (Sam; *The Maltese Falcon*, 1930, et seq, Dashiell Hammett)
Stubb (*Moby-Dick*, 1851, Herman Melville)
Tarka (the Otter; *Tarka the Otter*, 1927, Henry Williamson)
Trent (Little Nell; *The Old Curiosity Shop*, 1841, Charles Dickens)
Twist (Oliver; *Oliver Twist*, 1838, Charles Dickens)

06 Aramis (*The Three Musketeers*, 1844, Alexandre Dumas père)
Archer (Isabel; *The Portrait of a Lady*, 1881, Henry James)
Archer (Newland; *The Age of Innocence*, 1920, Edith Wharton)
Arthur (King; 'Morte d'Arthur', 1842, Alfred, Lord Tennyson)
Barkis (Mr; *David Copperfield*, 1850, Charles Dickens)
Belial (*Paradise Lost*, 1667, John Milton)
Bennet (Elizabeth; *Pride and Prejudice*, 1813, Jane Austen)
Bourgh (Lady Catherine de; *Pride and Prejudice*, 1813, Jane Austen)
Bovary (Emma; *Madame Bovary*, 1857, Gustave Flaubert)

Brodie (Miss Jean; *The Prime of Miss Jean Brodie*, 1961, Muriel Spark)

Brooke (Dorothea; *Middlemarch*, 1871–72, George Eliot)

Bumble (Mr; *Oliver Twist*, 1838, Charles Dickens)

Bumppo (Natty; *The Pioneers*, 1823, et seq, James Fenimore Cooper)

Butler (Rhett; *Gone with the Wind*, 1936, Margaret Mitchell)

Carton (Sydney; *A Tale of Two Cities*, 1859, Charles Dickens)

Dombey (Paul; *Dombey and Son*, 1848, Charles Dickens)

Dorrit (Amy; *Little Dorrit*, 1857, Charles Dickens)

Dorrit (William; *Little Dorrit*, 1857, Charles Dickens)

DuBois (Blanche; *A Streetcar Named Desire*, 1947, Tennessee Williams)

Gamgee (Sam; *The Lord of the Rings*, 1954–55, J R R Tolkien)

Gatsby (Jay; *The Great Gatsby*, 1925, F Scott Fitzgerald)

Gawain (Sir; 'Sir Gawain and the Green Knight', 14c, anon)

Gollum (*The Hobbit*, 1937, *The Lord of the Rings*, 1954–55, J R R Tolkien)

Hannay (Richard; *The Thirty-Nine Steps*, 1915, et seq, John Buchan)

Holmes (Sherlock; *A Study in Scarlet*, 1887, et seq, Arthur Conan Doyle)

Jeeves (Reginald; *The Inimitable Jeeves*, 1924, et seq, P G Wodehouse)

Jekyll (Doctor Henry; *The Strange Case of Dr Jekyll and Mr Hyde*, 1886, Robert Louis Stevenson)

Little (Vernon Gregory; *Vernon God Little*, 2003, D B C Pierre)

Lolita (*Lolita*, 1955, Vladimir Nabokov)

Marley (Jacob; *A Christmas Carol*, 1843, Charles Dickens)

Marner (Silas; *Silas Marner*, 1861, George Eliot)

Marple (Jane; *Murder at the Vicarage*, 1930, et seq, Agatha Christie)

Moreau (Doctor; *The Island of Doctor Moreau*, 1896, H G Wells)

Omnium (Duke of; *Can You Forgive Her?*, 1864–65, et seq, Anthony Trollope)

Pickle (Peregrine; *The Adventures of Peregrine Pickle*, 1751, Tobias Smollett)

Pinkie (*Brighton Rock*, 1938, Graham Greene)

Pliant (Dame; *The Alchemist*, 1610, Ben Jonson)

Poirot (Hercule; *The Mysterious Affair at Styles*, 1920, et seq, Agatha Christie)

Rabbit (*Rabbit, Run*, 1960, et seq, John Updike)

Random (Roderick; *The Adventures of Roderick Random*, 1748, Tobias Smollett)

Rob Roy (*Rob Roy*, 1817, Sir Walter Scott)

Salmon (Susie; *The Lovely Bones*, 2002, Alice Sebold)

Sawyer (Bob; *Pickwick Papers*, 1837, Charles Dickens)

Shandy (Tristram; *The Life and Opinions of Tristram Shandy*, 1759–67, Laurence Sterne)

Subtle (*The Alchemist*, 1610, Ben Jonson)

Tarzan (*Tarzan of the Apes*, 1914, et seq, Edgar Rice Burroughs)

Tyrone (James; *Long Day's Journey into Night*, 1956, Eugene O'Neill)

Varden (Dolly; *Barnaby Rudge*, 1841, Charles Dickens)

Wadman (Widow; *The Life and Opinions of Tristram Shandy*, 1759–67, Laurence Sterne)

Watson (Doctor John; *A Study in Scarlet*, 1887, et seq, Arthur Conan Doyle)

Weller (Samuel; *Pickwick Papers*, 1837, Charles Dickens)

Wimsey (Lord Peter; *Whose Body?*, 1923, et seq, Dorothy L Sayers)

Wopsle (Mr; *Great Expectations*, 1861, Charles Dickens)

Yahoos (*Gulliver's Travels*, 1726, Jonathan Swift)

07 Andrews (Pamela; *Pamela*, 1740–41, Samuel Richardson)

Baggins (Bilbo; *The Hobbit*, 1937, *The Lord of the Rings*, 1954–55, J R R Tolkien)

Baggins (Frodo; *The Lord of the Rings*, 1954–55, J R R Tolkien)

Beowulf (*Beowulf*, 7c/8c, anon)

Biggles (*The Camels Are Coming*, 1932, et seq, Captain W E Johns)

Bramble (Matthew; *The Expedition of Humphry Clinker*, 1771, Tobias Smollett)

Bromden (Chief; *One Flew over the Cuckoo's Nest*, 1962, Ken Kesey)

Clinker (Humphry; *The Expedition of Humphry Clinker*, 1771, Tobias Smollett)

Corelli (Captain Antonio; *Captain Corelli's Mandolin*, 1994, Louis de Bernières)

Crackit (Toby; *Oliver Twist*, 1838, Charles Dickens)

Danvers (Mrs; *Rebecca*, 1938, Daphne Du Maurier)

Dawkins (Jack; *Oliver Twist*, 1838, Charles Dickens)

Dedalus (Stephen; *A Portrait of the Artist as a Young Man*, 1916, et seq, James Joyce)

Deronda (Daniel; *Daniel Deronda*, 1876, George Eliot)

Despair (Giant; *The Pilgrim's Progress*, Part I 1678, Part II 1684, John Bunyan)

Don Juan (*Don Juan*, 1819–24, George Gordon Byron, 6th Lord Byron)

Dorigen ('The Franklin's Tale' in *The Canterbury Tales*, c.1387–1400, Geoffrey Chaucer)

Dracula (Count; *Dracula*, 1897, Bram Stoker)

Estella (*Great Expectations*, 1861, Charles Dickens)

Fairfax (Jane; *Emma*, 1816, Jane Austen)

Gandalf (*The Hobbit*, 1937, *The Lord of the Rings*, 1954–55, J R R Tolkien)

Gargery (Joe; *Great Expectations*, 1861, Charles Dickens)

Grendel (*Beowulf*, 7c/8c, anon)

Harding (Reverend Septimus; *The Warden*, 1855, et seq, Anthony Trollope)

Harlowe (Clarissa; *Clarissa*, 1748, Samuel Richardson)

Higgins (Professor Henry; *Pygmalion*, 1913, George Bernard Shaw)

Hopeful (*The Pilgrim's Progress*, Part I 1678, Part II 1684, John Bunyan)

Humbert (Humbert; *Lolita*, 1955, Vladimir Nabokov)

Ishmael (*Moby-Dick*, 1851, Herman Melville)

Jaggers (Mr; *Great Expectations*, 1861, Charles Dickens)

Jellyby (Mrs; *Bleak House*, 1853, Charles Dickens)

Jenkins (Nicholas; *A Question of Upbringing*, 1921, et seq, Anthony Powell)

Le Fever (Lieutenant; *The Life and Opinions of Tristram Shandy*, 1759–67, Laurence Sterne)

Maigret (Jules; *The Death of Monsieur Gallet*, 1931, et seq, Georges Simenon)

Marlowe (Philip; *The Big Sleep*, 1939, et seq, Raymond Chandler)

Mellors (Oliver; *Lady Chatterley's Lover*, 1928, D H Lawrence)

Newsome (Chad; *The Ambassadors*, 1903, Henry James)

Obadiah (*The Life and Opinions of Tristram Shandy*, 1759–67, Laurence Sterne)

Olenska (Countess Ellen; *The Age of Innocence*, 1920, Edith Wharton)

Orlando (*Orlando*, 1928, Virginia Woolf)

Peachum (Thomas; *The Beggar's Opera*, 1728, John Gay)

Porthos (*The Three Musketeers*, 1844, Alexandre Dumas père)

Prefect (Ford; *The Hitch-Hiker's Guide to the Galaxy*, 1979, et seq, Douglas Adams)

Proudie (Doctor; *Barchester Towers*, 1857, et seq, Anthony Trollope)

Raffles (*The Amateur Cracksman*, 1899, *The Black Mask*, 1901, *The Thief in the Night*, 1905, E W Hornung)

Rebecca (*Ivanhoe*, 1819, Sir Walter Scott)

Scrooge (Ebenezer; *A Christmas Carol*, 1843, Charles Dickens)

Shalott (Lady of; 'The Lady of Shalott', 1833, Alfred, Lord Tennyson)

Slumkey (Samuel; *Pickwick Papers*, 1837, Charles Dickens)

Squeers (Wackford; *Nicholas Nickleby*, 1839, Charles Dickens)

Surface (Charles; *The School for Scandal*, 1777, Richard Brinsley Sheridan)

Surface (Joseph; *The School for Scandal*, 1777, Richard Brinsley Sheridan)

Tiny Tim (*A Christmas Carol*, 1843, Charles Dickens)

Wemmick (Mr; *Great Expectations*, 1861, Charles Dickens)

Wickham (George; *Pride and Prejudice*, 1813, Jane Austen)

Witches (The Three; *Macbeth*, c.1606, William Shakespeare)

Wooster (Bertie; *The Inimitable Jeeves*, 1924, et seq, P G Wodehouse)

Would-be (Sir Politic; *Volpone, or The Fox*, 1606, Ben Jonson)

08 Absolute (Captain; *The Rivals*, 1775, Richard Brinsley Sheridan)

Anderson (Pastor Anthony; *The Devil's Disciple*, 1897, George Bernard Shaw)

Backbite (Sir Benjamin; *The School for Scandal*, 1777, Richard Brinsley Sheridan)

Bedivere (Sir; 'Morte d'Arthur', 1842, Alfred, Lord Tennyson)

Casaubon (Reverend Edward; *Middlemarch*, 1871–72, George Eliot)

Cratchit (Bob; *A Christmas Carol*, 1843, Charles Dickens)

Criseyde (*Troilus and Criseyde*, c.1385–89, Geoffrey Chaucer)

Dalloway (Mrs Clarissa; *The Voyage Out*, 1915, *Mrs Dalloway*, 1925, Virginia Woolf)

Dashwood (Elinor; *Sense and Sensibility*, 1811, Jane Austen)

Dashwood (Marianne; *Sense and Sensibility*, 1811, Jane Austen)

de Winter (Max; *Rebecca*, 1938, Daphne Du Maurier)

de Winter (Rebecca; *Rebecca*, 1938, Daphne Du Maurier)

Estragon (*Waiting for Godot*, 1955, Samuel Beckett)

Everdene (Bathsheba; *Far from the Madding Crowd*, 1874, Thomas Hardy)

Faithful (*The Pilgrim's Progress*, Part I 1678, Part II 1684, John Bunyan)

Fezziwig (Mr; *A Christmas Carol*, 1843, Charles Dickens)

Flanders (Moll; *Moll Flanders*, 1722, Daniel Defoe)

Flashman (*Tom Brown's Schooldays*, 1857, et seq, Thomas Hughes)

Gloriana (*The Faerie Queene*, 1590–96, Sir Edmund Spenser)

Griselda (Patient; 'The Clerk's Tale' in *The Canterbury Tales*, c.1387–1400, Geoffrey Chaucer)

Gulliver (Lemuel; *Gulliver's Travels*, 1726, Jonathan Swift)

Havisham (Miss; *Great Expectations*, 1861, Charles Dickens)

Hiawatha (*The Song of Hiawatha*, 1855, Henry Wadsworth Longfellow)

Hrothgar (*Beowulf*, 7c/8c, anon)

Jarndyce (John; *Bleak House*, 1853, Charles Dickens)

Kowalski (Stanley; *A Streetcar Named Desire*, 1947, Tennessee Williams)

Kowalski (Stella; *A Streetcar Named Desire*, 1947, Tennessee Williams)

Ladislaw (Will; *Middlemarch*, 1871–72, George Eliot)

Lancelot (Sir; 'The Lady of Shalott', 1833, Alfred, Lord Tennyson)

Lestrade (Inspector; *A Study in Scarlet*, 1887, et seq, Arthur Conan Doyle)

MacHeath (Captain; *The Beggar's Opera*, 1728, John Gay)

Magwitch (Abel; *Great Expectations*, 1861, Charles Dickens)

Malaprop (Mrs; *The Rivals*, 1775, Richard Brinsley Sheridan)

McMurphy (Randle Patrick; *One Flew over the Cuckoo's Nest*, 1962, Ken Kesey)

Micawber (Wilkins; *David Copperfield*, 1850, Charles Dickens)

Moriarty (Dean; *On the Road*, 1957, Jack Kerouac)

Moriarty (Professor James; *The Memoirs of Sherlock Holmes*, 1892–93, Arthur Conan Doyle)

Napoleon (*Animal Farm*, 1945, George Orwell)

Nickleby (Nicholas; *Nicholas Nickleby*, 1839, Charles Dickens)

Nostromo (*Nostromo*, 1904, Joseph Conrad)

Paradise (Sal; *On the Road*, 1957, Jack Kerouac)

Peggotty (Clara; *David Copperfield*, 1850, Charles Dickens)

Pickwick (Samuel; *Pickwick Papers*, 1837, Charles Dickens)

Queequeg (*Moby-Dick*, 1851, Herman Melville)

Ramotswe (Precious; *The No 1 Ladies' Detective Agency*, 1998, et seq, Alexander McCall Smith)

Snowball (*Animal Farm*, 1945, George Orwell)

Starbuck (*Moby-Dick*, 1851, Herman Melville)

Svengali (*Trilby*, 1894, George Du Maurier)

Tashtego (*Moby-Dick*, 1851, Herman Melville)

The Clerk (*The Canterbury Tales*, c.1387–1400, Geoffrey Chaucer)

The Friar (*The Canterbury Tales*, c.1387–1400, Geoffrey Chaucer)

The Reeve (*The Canterbury Tales*, c.1387–1400, Geoffrey Chaucer)

Trotwood (Betsey; *David Copperfield*, 1850, Charles Dickens)

Tulliver (Maggie; *The Mill on the Floss*, 1860, George Eliot)

Twitcher (Jemmy; *The Beggar's Opera*, 1728, John Gay)

Vladimir (*Waiting for Godot*, 1955, Samuel Beckett)

09 Archimago (*The Faerie Queene*, 1590–96, Sir Edmund Spenser)

Bounderby (Josiah; *Hard Times*, 1854, Charles Dickens)

Britomart (*The Faerie Queene*, 1590–96, Sir Edmund Spenser)

Bulstrode (Nicholas; *Middlemarch*, 1871–72, George Eliot)

Caulfield (Holden; *The Catcher in the Rye*, 1951, J D Salinger)

Cheeryble (Charles; *Nicholas Nickleby*, 1839, Charles Dickens)

Christian (*The Pilgrim's Progress*, Part I 1678, Part II 1684, John Bunyan)

Churchill (Frank; *Emma*, 1816, Jane Austen)

Constance ('The Man of Law's Tale' in *The Canterbury Tales*, c.1387–1400, Geoffrey Chaucer)

D'Artagnan (*The Three Musketeers*, 1844, Alexandre Dumas père)

Doolittle (Eliza; *Pygmalion*, 1913, George Bernard Shaw)

Golightly (Holly; *Breakfast at Tiffany's*, 1958, Truman Capote)

Gradgrind (Thomas; *Hard Times*, 1854, Charles Dickens)

Grandison (Sir Charles; *Sir Charles Grandison*, 1754, Samuel Richardson)

Knightley (George; *Emma*, 1816, Jane Austen)

Lismahago (Obadiah; *The Expedition of Humphry Clinker*, 1771, Tobias Smollett)

Lochinvar (*Marmion*, 1808, Sir Walter Scott)

Minnehaha (*The Song of Hiawatha*, 1855, Henry Wadsworth Longfellow)

Pecksniff (Seth; *Martin Chuzzlewit*, 1844, Charles Dickens)

Pendennis (Arthur; *The History of Pendennis*, 1848–50, *The Newcomes*, 1853–55, W M Thackeray)

Pollyanna (*Pollyanna*, 1913, *Pollyanna Grows Up*, 1915, Eleanor H Porter)

Rochester (Edward Fairfax; *Jane Eyre*, 1847, Charlotte Brontë)

Scudamour (Sir; *The Faerie Queene*, 1590–96, Sir Edmund Spenser)

The Knight (*The Canterbury Tales*, c.1387–1400, Geoffrey Chaucer)

The Miller (*The Canterbury Tales*, c.1387–1400, Geoffrey Chaucer)

The Squire (*The Canterbury Tales*, c.1387–1400, Geoffrey Chaucer)

Van Winkle (Rip; 'Rip Van Winkle', 1819, Washington Irving)

Woodhouse (Emma; *Emma*, 1816, Jane Austen)

Yossarian (Captain John; *Catch-22*, 1961, Joseph Heller)

Zenocrate (*Tamburlaine the Great: Parts I and II*, 1587–90, Christopher Marlowe)

10 Big Brother (*1984*, 1949, George Orwell)

Challenger (Professor; *The Lost World*, 1912, et seq, Arthur Conan Doyle)

Chatterley (Lady Constance; *Lady Chatterley's Lover*, 1928, D H Lawrence)

Chuzzlewit (Martin; *Martin Chuzzlewit*, 1844, Charles Dickens)

Evangelist (*The Pilgrim's Progress*, Part I 1678, Part II 1684, John Bunyan)

Great-heart (Mr; *The Pilgrim's Progress*, Part I 1678, Part II 1684, John Bunyan)

Heathcliff (*Wuthering Heights*, 1848, Emily Brontë)

Hornblower (Horatio; *The Happy Return*, 1937, et seq, C S Forester)

Houyhnhnms (*Gulliver's Travels*, 1726, Jonathan Swift)

Little Nell (*The Old Curiosity Shop*, 1841, Charles Dickens)

The Tar Baby (*Tar Baby*, 1981, Toni Morrison)

11 Copperfield (David; *David Copperfield*, 1850, Charles Dickens)

D'Urberville (Alec; *Tess of the D'Urbervilles*, 1891, Thomas Hardy)

Durbeyfield (Tess; *Tess of the D'Urbervilles*, 1891, Thomas Hardy)

Mutabilitie (*The Faerie Queene*, 1590–96, Sir Edmund Spenser)

Pumblechook (Mr; *Great Expectations*, 1861, Charles Dickens)

The Franklin (*The Canterbury Tales*, c.1387–1400, Geoffrey Chaucer)

The Man of Law (*The Canterbury Tales*, c.1387–1400, Geoffrey Chaucer)

The Merchant (*The Canterbury Tales*, c.1387–1400, Geoffrey Chaucer)

The Pardoner (*The Canterbury Tales*, c.1387–1400, Geoffrey Chaucer)

The Prioress (*The Canterbury Tales*, c.1387–1400, Geoffrey Chaucer)

The Summoner (*The Canterbury Tales*, c.1387–1400, Geoffrey Chaucer)

12 Blatant Beast (*The Faerie Queene*, 1590–96, Sir Edmund Spenser)

Chaunticleer ('The Nun's Priest's Tale' in *The Canterbury Tales*, c.1387–1400, Geoffrey Chaucer)

Frankenstein (Victor; *Frankenstein, or, The Modern Prometheus*, 1818, Mary Shelley)

Lilliputians (*Gulliver's Travels*, 1726, Jonathan Swift)

Osbaldistone (Francis; *Rob Roy*, 1817, Sir Walter Scott)

Rip Van Winkle ('Rip Van Winkle', 1819, Washington Irving)

The Pied Piper (of Hamelin; 'The Pied Piper of Hamelin', in *Dramatic Romances*, 1845, Robert Browning)

13 The Wife of Bath (*The Canterbury Tales*, c.1387–1400, Geoffrey Chaucer)

14 Worldly Wiseman (Mr; *The Pilgrim's Progress*, Part I 1678, Part II 1684, John Bunyan)

15 The Artful Dodger (*Oliver Twist*, 1838, Charles Dickens)

Valiant-for-Truth (*The Pilgrim's Progress*, Part I 1678, Part II 1684, John Bunyan)

Characters from children's literature include:

03 BFG (*The BFG*, 1982, Roald Dahl)

Eva (Little; *Uncle Tom's Cabin, or, Life Among the Lowly*, 1851–52, Harriet Beecher Stowe)

Fox (Brer; *Uncle Remus*, 1880, Joel Chandler Harris)

Kaa (*The Jungle Book*, 1894, Rudyard Kipling)

Pan (Peter; *Peter Pan*, 1904, J M Barrie)

Roo (*Winnie-the-Pooh*, 1926, et seq, A A Milne)

Tom (Uncle; *Uncle Tom's Cabin, or, Life*

Among the Lowly, 1851–52, Harriet
Beecher Stowe)

04 Carr (Katy; *What Katy Did*, 1872, et seq,
Susan Coolidge)
Finn (Huckleberry; *The Adventures of Tom
Sawyer*, 1876, et seq, Mark Twain)
Gunn (Ben; *Treasure Island*, 1883, Robert
Louis Stevenson)
Hook (Captain; *Peter Pan*, 1904, J M Barrie)
Long (Tom; *Tom's Midnight Garden*, 1958,
Philippa Pearce)
Lucy (*The Lion, the Witch and the
Wardrobe*, 1950, et seq, C S Lewis)
Mole (*The Wind in the Willows*, 1908,
Kenneth Grahame)
Pooh (*Winnie-the-Pooh*, 1926, et seq, A A
Milne)
Toad (Mr; *The Wind in the Willows*, 1908,
Kenneth Grahame)
Wart (*The Sword in the Stone*, 1958, et seq,
T H White)

05 Akela (*The Jungle Book*, 1894, Rudyard
Kipling)
Alice (*Alice's Adventures in Wonderland*,
1865, Lewis Carroll)
Aslan (*The Lion, the Witch and the
Wardrobe*, 1950, et seq, C S Lewis)
Baloo (*The Jungle Book*, 1894, Rudyard
Kipling)
Fiver (*Watership Down*, 1972, Richard
Adams)
Flint (Captain; *Swallows and Amazons*,
1930, et seq, Arthur Ransome)
Hatty (*Tom's Midnight Garden*, 1958,
Philippa Pearce)
Hazel (*Watership Down*, 1972, Richard
Adams)
Heidi (*Heidi*, 1880, Johanna Spyri)
Kanga (*Winnie-the-Pooh*, 1926, et seq, A A
Milne)
March (Amy; *Little Women*, 1868, et seq,
Louisa M Alcott)
March (Beth; *Little Women*, 1868, et seq,
Louisa M Alcott)
March (Jo; *Little Women*, 1868, et seq,
Louisa M Alcott)
March (Meg; *Little Women*, 1868, et seq,
Louisa M Alcott)
Parry (Will; *The Subtle Knife*, 1997, *The
Amber Spyglass*, 2000, Philip Pullman)
Peter (*Heidi*, 1880, Johanna Spyri)
Peter (*The Lion, the Witch and the
Wardrobe*, 1950, et seq, C S Lewis)
Peter (*The Railway Children*, 1906, E
Nesbit)
Ratty (*The Wind in the Willows*, 1908,
Kenneth Grahame)

Remus (Uncle; *Uncle Remus*, 1880, Joel
Chandler Harris)
Susan (*The Lion, the Witch and the
Wardrobe*, 1950, et seq, C S Lewis)
Topsy (*Uncle Tom's Cabin, or, Life Among the
Lowly*, 1851–52, Harriet Beecher Stowe)
Wendy (*Peter Pan*, 1904, J M Barrie)
Wonka (Willy; *Charlie and the Chocolate
Factory*, 1964, *Charlie and the Great Glass
Elevator*, 1973, Roald Dahl)

06 Arable (Fern; *Charlotte's Web*, 1952, E B
White)
Badger (*The Wind in the Willows*, 1908,
Kenneth Grahame)
Beaker (Tracey; *The Story of Tracey Beaker*,
1991, Jacqueline Wilson)
Bucket (Charlie; *Charlie and the Chocolate
Factory*, 1964, *Charlie and the Great Glass
Elevator*, 1973, Roald Dahl)
Bunter (Billy; *Billy Bunter of Greyfriars
School*, 1949, et seq, Frank Richards)
Craven (Colin; *The Secret Garden*, 1911,
Frances Hodgson Burnett)
Crusoe (Robinson; *Robinson Crusoe*, 1719,
*The Farther Adventures of Robinson
Crusoe*, 1720, *The Serious Reflections … of
Robinson Crusoe*, 1720, Daniel Defoe)
Dickon (*The Secret Garden*, 1911, Frances
Hodgson Burnett)
Edmund (*The Lion, the Witch and the
Wardrobe*, 1950, et seq, C S Lewis)
Eeyore (*Winnie-the-Pooh*, 1926, et seq, A A
Milne)
Friday (Man; *Robinson Crusoe*, 1719, *The
Farther Adventures of Robinson Crusoe*,
1720, *The Serious Reflections … of
Robinson Crusoe*, 1720, Daniel Defoe)
Gollum (*The Hobbit*, 1937, *The Lord of the
Rings*, 1954–55, J R R Tolkien)
Hagrid (Rubeus; *Harry Potter and the
Philosopher's Stone*, 1997, et seq, J K
Rowling)
Legree (Simon; *Uncle Tom's Cabin, or,
Life Among the Lowly*, 1851–52, Harriet
Beecher Stowe)
Lennox (Mary; *The Secret Garden*, 1911,
Frances Hodgson Burnett)
Little (Stuart; *Stuart Little*, 1945, E B White)
Malfoy (Draco; *Harry Potter and the
Philosopher's Stone*, 1997, et seq, J K
Rowling)
Mowgli (*The Jungle Book*, 1894, Rudyard
Kipling)
Piglet (*Winnie-the-Pooh*, 1926, et seq, A A
Milne)
Potter (Harry; *Harry Potter and the
Philosopher's Stone*, 1997, et seq, J K
Rowling)

Rabbit (Brer; *Uncle Remus*, 1880, Joel Chandler Harris)

Thatcher (Becky; *The Adventures of Tom Sawyer*, 1876, et seq, Mark Twain)

Sawyer (Tom; *The Adventures of Tom Sawyer*, 1876, et seq, Mark Twain)

Silver (Long John; *Treasure Island*, 1883, Robert Louis Stevenson)

Sophie (*The BFG*, 1982, Roald Dahl)

Tigger (*The House at Pooh Corner*, 1928, A A Milne)

Walker (John; *Swallows and Amazons*, 1930, et seq, Arthur Ransome)

Walker (Roger; *Swallows and Amazons*, 1930, et seq, Arthur Ransome)

Walker (Susan; *Swallows and Amazons*, 1930, et seq, Arthur Ransome)

Walker (Titty; *Swallows and Amazons*, 1930, et seq, Arthur Ransome)

07 Baggins (Bilbo; *The Hobbit*, 1937, *The Lord of the Rings*, 1954–55, J R R Tolkien)

Biggles (*The Camels are Coming*, 1932, et seq, Captain W E Johns)

Brer Fox (*Uncle Remus*, 1880, Joel Chandler Harris)

Diamond (*At the Back of the North Wind*, 1871, George Macdonald)

Dorothy (*The Wonderful Wizard of Oz*, 1900, L Frank Baum)

Gandalf (*The Hobbit*, 1937, *The Lord of the Rings*, 1954–55, J R R Tolkien)

Granger (Hermione; *Harry Potter and the Philosopher's Stone*, 1997, et seq, J K Rowling)

Hawkins (Jim; *Treasure Island*, 1883, Robert Louis Stevenson)

Phyllis (*The Railway Children*, 1906, E Nesbit)

Poppins (Mary; *Mary Poppins*, 1934, P L Travers)

Roberta (*The Railway Children*, 1906, E Nesbit)

Shirley (Anne; *Anne of Green Gables*, 1908, et seq, L M Montgomery)

Weasley (Ron; *Harry Potter and the Philosopher's Stone*, 1997, et seq, J K Rowling)

William (*Just William*, 1922, et seq, Richmal Crompton)

08 Bagheera (*The Jungle Book*, 1894, Rudyard Kipling)

Belacqua (Lyra; *Northern Lights*, 1995, *The Subtle Knife*, 1997, *The Amber Spyglass*, 2000, Philip Pullman)

Blackett (Nancy; *Swallows and Amazons*, 1930, et seq, Arthur Ransome)

Blackett (Peggy; *Swallows and Amazons*, 1930, et seq, Arthur Ransome)

Jennings (*Jennings Goes to School*, 1950, et seq, Anthony Buckeridge)

Peterkin (*The Coral Island*, 1857, R M Ballantyne)

Peter Pan (*Peter Pan*, 1904, J M Barrie)

09 Charlotte (*Charlotte's Web*, 1952, E B White)

Mad Hatter (*Alice's Adventures in Wonderland*, 1865, Lewis Carroll)

Shere Khan (*The Jungle Book*, 1894, Rudyard Kipling)

The Pauper (*The Prince and the Pauper*, 1882, Mark Twain)

The Prince (*The Prince and the Pauper*, 1882, Mark Twain)

The Walrus (*Through the Looking-Glass, and What Alice Found There*, 1872, Lewis Carroll)

Tiger Lily (*Through the Looking-Glass, and What Alice Found There*, 1872, Lewis Carroll)

Voldemort (Lord; *Harry Potter and the Philosopher's Stone*, 1997, et seq, J K Rowling)

10 Brer Rabbit (*Uncle Remus*, 1880, Joel Chandler Harris)

Dumbledore (Albus; *Harry Potter and the Philosopher's Stone*, 1997, et seq, J K Rowling)

Fauntleroy (Little Lord; *Little Lord Fauntleroy*, 1885, Frances Hodgson Burnett)

The Red King (*Through the Looking-Glass, and What Alice Found There*, 1872, Lewis Carroll)

Tinkerbell (*Peter Pan*, 1904, J M Barrie)

Tweedledee (*Through the Looking-Glass, and What Alice Found There*, 1872, Lewis Carroll)

Tweedledum (*Through the Looking-Glass, and What Alice Found There*, 1872, Lewis Carroll)

11 The Dormouse (*Alice's Adventures in Wonderland*, 1865, Lewis Carroll)

The Red Queen (*Through the Looking-Glass, and What Alice Found There*, 1872, Lewis Carroll)

White Rabbit (*Alice's Adventures in Wonderland*, 1865, Lewis Carroll)

12 Humpty-Dumpty (*Through the Looking-Glass, and What Alice Found There*, 1872, Lewis Carroll)

Longstocking (Pippi; *Pippi Longstocking*, 1945, Astrid Lindgren)

Silvertongue (Lyra; *Northern Lights*, 1995, *The Subtle Knife*, 1997, *The Amber Spyglass*, 2000, Philip Pullman)

The Carpenter (*Through the Looking-Glass, and What Alice Found There*, 1872, Lewis Carroll)

The Mad Hatter (*Alice's Adventures in Wonderland*, 1865, Lewis Carroll)

The March Hare (*Alice's Adventures in Wonderland*, 1865, Lewis Carroll)

The Red Knight (*Through the Looking-Glass, and What Alice Found There*, 1872, Lewis Carroll)

The Scarecrow (*The Wonderful Wizard of Oz*, 1900, L Frank Baum)

Wilbur the Pig (*Charlotte's Web*, 1952, E B White)

13 The Jabberwock (*Through the Looking-Glass, and What Alice Found There*, 1872, Lewis Carroll)

The Mock Turtle (*Alice's Adventures in Wonderland*, 1865, Lewis Carroll)

The Tin Woodman (*The Wonderful Wizard of Oz*, 1900, L Frank Baum)

Winnie-the-Pooh (*Winnie-the-Pooh*, 1926, et seq, A A Milne)

14 Rikki-Tikki-Tavi (*The Jungle Book*, 1894, Rudyard Kipling)

The White Rabbit (*Alice's Adventures in Wonderland*, 1865, Lewis Carroll)

15 The Cowardly Lion (*The Wonderful Wizard of Oz*, 1900, L Frank Baum)

Literary terms include:

03 act
lay
ode

04 acto
bard
Edda
epic
foil
foot
iamb
mood
myth
plot
saga
tone

05 aside
canon
canto
elegy
essay
fable
farce
frame
genre
haiku
idyll
irony
meter
motif
motiv
muses
novel
paean
story
style
tanka
theme
voice

06 accent

ballad
bathos
chorus
climax
comedy
dactyl
legend
masque
oeuvre
parody
pathos
rococo
satire
sequel
sestet
simile
sonnet
stanza

07 analogy
ballade
baroque
cadence
caesura
canzone
conceit
couplet
Dadaism
diction
eclogue
epigram
episode
epistle
epithet
euphony
fabliau
fantasy
georgic
imagery
imagism
lampoon

memoirs
novella
parable
paradox
persona
polemic
preface
prosody
realism
romance
rondeau
setting
spondee
subplot
tragedy
trilogy
trochee

08 abstract
acrostic
allegory
allusion
analogue
anapaest
anecdote
anti-hero
aphorism
apologue
bestiary
chick lit
conflict
dialogue
didactic
dystopia
epigraph
epilogue
epiphany
epitasis
euphuism
exemplum
foreword

futurism
Gruppe 47
hamartia
humanism
lapidary
limerick
metaphor
metonymy
mock epic
narrator
oxymoron
pastoral
prologue
protasis
quatrain
samizdat
scansion
sub-genre
suspense
The Group
thriller
travesty
trouvère

09 absurdism
Agrarians
ambiguity
anthology
anti-novel
apocrypha
archetype
assonance
Beat Poets
biography
burlesque
cacophony
character
chronicle
complaint
Decadents
Dionysian
euphemism
fairytale
flashback
folk tales
free verse
Gilded Age
grotesque
hyperbole
inference
Lake Poets
La Pléiade
leitmotiv
lyric poem
mannerism
melodrama
modernism
monologue
narrative

pantheism
Platonism
soliloquy
symbolism
terza rima
vers libre
Zeitgeist

10 antagonist
antimasque
antithesis
Apollonian
apostrophe
avant-garde
blank verse
bonkbuster
classicism
conclusion
consonance
dénouement
dissonance
enjambment
epistolary
exposition
incunabula
in media res
Lake School
manuscript
naturalism
nom de plume
pure poetry
raisonneur
resolution
rhyme-royal
roman à clef
short story
stereotype
synecdoche
tetrameter
tragic flaw
troubadour
utopianism

11 Age of Reason
black comedy
catastrophe
comic relief
courtly love
dream vision
epic theatre
Festschrift
fin de siècle
generation X
gothic novel
Greek chorus
hagiography
Jacobean Age
lyric poetry
Minnesinger

mise en scène
noble savage
poète maudit
primitivism
protagonist
pulp fiction
rhyme-scheme
romanticism
The Apostles
The Movement
thesis novel
tragicomedy
Weltschmerz

12 aestheticism
Age of Johnson
alliteration
Beat Movement
bodice-ripper
concrete poem
Doppelgänger
epithalamion
epithalamium
Jindyworobak
magic realism
nouveau roman
novel of ideas
nursery rhyme
onomatopoeia
Poet Laureate
rising action
synaesthesia
three unities
urban realism
utopian novel

13 Angry Young Men
autobiography
belles-lettres
Bildungsroman
carpe diem poem
Cavalier Poets
deus ex machina
dream allegory
expressionism
falling action
foreshadowing
Georgian Poets
heroic couplet
Kunstlerroman
narrative poem
neoclassicism
new journalism
nonsense verse
Parnassianism
poetic justice
poetic licence
postmodernism
social realism

structuralism
Sturm und Drang
vers de société
versification
14 Art for Art's Sake
Celtic Twilight
concrete poetry
deconstruction
dramatic poetry
dystopian novel
existentialism
figure of speech

Horatian satire
hypertext novel
Lost Generation
novel of manners
Pre-Raphaelites
Restoration Age
revenge tragedy
science fiction
tragedy of blood
understatement
verisimilitude
Weltanschauung

15 Bloomsbury Group
chansons de geste
comedy of manners
Erziehungsroman
Graveyard School
historical novel
occasional verse
pathetic fallacy
personification
picaresque novel
teatro grottesco

See also **Austen, Jane; Blyton, Enid; Brontë, Anne; Brontë, Charlotte; Brontë, Emily; Carroll, Lewis; Chaucer, Geoffrey; Christie, Dame Agatha; Defoe, Daniel; Dickens, Charles; Dostoevsky, Fyodor; Doyle, Sir Arthur Conan; Dumas, Alexandre; Eliot, George; fable; Hardy, Thomas; Hemingway, Ernest; James, Henry; Joyce, James; Kipling, Rudyard; Lawrence, D H; legend; miser; Morrison, Toni; Murdoch, Dame Iris; mythology; Nobel Prize; non-fiction; novel; Orwell, George; play; poetry; Potter, Beatrix; prosody; Proust, Marcel; Rowling, J K; science fiction; Scott, Sir Walter; Shakespeare, William; Stevenson, Robert Louis; Tolkien, J R R; Tolstoy, Count Leo; Trollope, Anthony; Twain, Mark; Voltaire; Wells, H G; Wodehouse, Sir P G; Woolf, Virginia; writing; Zola, Émile**

lizard

Lizards include:

03 eft
04 gila
sand
seps
wall
worm
05 anole
blind
Draco
fence
gecko
guana
night
skink

snake
varan
06 agamid
beaded
dragon
flying
goanna
horned
iguana
Komodo
Moloch
worral
worrel
zonure

07 bearded
frilled
monitor
perenty
serpent
stellio
08 basilisk
perentie
slowworm
stellion
sungazer
teguexin
wall newt
09 chameleon

galliwasp
10 blue-tongue
chamaeleon
glass snake
horned toad
11 chisel-tooth
gila monster
12 flying dragon
girdle-tailed
Komodo dragon
13 bearded dragon
14 Bornean earless

loch see **lake**

lock

Locks include:

03 pad
rim
04 dead
Yale®
05 child

Chubb®
wagon
06 safety
spring
07 mortice

mortise
08 cylinder
10 night latch
11 combination

Lock parts include:

03 bit
key
pin
04 bolt
hasp
knob
rose
sash
05 latch
06 barrel

keyway
spring
staple
07 key card
keyhole
spindle
08 cylinder
dead bolt
sash bolt
09 face-plate

latch bolt
10 escutcheon
latch lever
push-button
11 mortise bolt
spindle hole
strike plate
12 cylinder hole
13 latch follower

London

London boroughs:

05 Brent
06 Barnet
Bexley
Camden
Ealing
Harrow
Merton
Newham
Sutton
07 Bromley
Croydon

Enfield
Hackney
Lambeth
08 Haringey
Havering
Hounslow
Lewisham
09 Greenwich
Islington
Redbridge
Southwark

10 Hillingdon
Wandsworth
12 Tower Hamlets
13 Waltham Forest
17 City of Westminster
18 Barking and Dagenham
Kingston upon Thames
Richmond upon Thames
20 Hammersmith and Fulham
Kensington and Chelsea

Other districts of London include:

03 Bow
Kew
Lee
04 Bank
Oval
Soho
05 Acton
Angel
Erith
Hayes
Penge
06 Arkley
Balham
Barnes
Debden
Eltham
Epping
Euston
Fulham
Hendon
Heston
Hoxton
Ilford
Kenton
Leyton

Malden
Morden
Pinner
Poplar
Purley
Putney
Temple
Waddon
07 Aldgate
Archway
Barking
Beckton
Belmont
Borough
Brixton
Catford
Chelsea
Clapham
Cranham
Dalston
Dulwich
East End
East Ham
Edgware
Elm Park
Feltham

Hampton
Hanwell
Holborn
Hornsey
Kilburn
Mayfair
Mile End
Mitcham
Neasden
Norwood
Old Ford
Olympia
Peckham
Pimlico
Selsdon
Stepney
The City
Tooting
Wapping
Welling
Wembley
West End
West Ham
Yeading
08 Alperton
Bankside

Barbican
Brockley
Brompton
Chiswick
Coulsdon
Crayford
Dagenham
Deptford
Edmonton
Elmstead
Finchley
Finsbury
Grays Inn
Hanworth
Hatch End
Heathrow
Highbury
Highgate
Holloway
Homerton
Hyde Park
Ickenham
Kingston
Mill Hill
Mortlake
New Cross
Nine Elms
Northolt
Osterley
Perivale
Plaistow
Richmond
Shadwell
Southall
Stanmore
Surbiton
Sydenham
Tolworth
Uxbridge
Vauxhall
Victoria
Walworth
Wanstead
Waterloo
Woodford
Woolwich

09 Abbey Wood
Addington
Barnsbury
Battersea
Bayswater
Beckenham
Becontree
Belgravia
Blackwall
Brentford
Brimsdown
Canonbury

Chalk Farm
Chingford
Colindale
Crouch End
Docklands
Fitzrovia
Foots Cray
Gant's Hill
Gidea Park
Gipsy Hill
Goodmayes
Gospel Oak
Greenford
Green Park
Hampstead
Harefield
Harlesden
Harringay
Herne Hill
Isleworth
Kidbrooke
Kingsbury
Kingsland
Limehouse
Maida Vale
Mark's Gate
Newington
Northwood
Orpington
Park Royal
Petts Wood
Plumstead
South Bank
Southgate
Stockwell
St Pancras
Stratford
Streatham
Tottenham
Tower Hill
Tulse Hill
Upminster
Whetstone
White City
Whitehall
Willesden
Wimbledon
Wood Green

10 Addiscombe
Albany Park
Arnos Grove
Beddington
Bellingham
Bermondsey
Blackheath
Bloomsbury
Brent Cross
Camberwell

Chase Cross
Collier Row
Creekmouth
Dollis Hill
Earls Court
Earlsfield
Embankment
Farringdon
Forest Gate
Forest Hill
Goddington
Green Lanes
Haggerston
Harlington
Harold Hill
Harold Wood
Horse Ferry
Isle of Dogs
Kennington
Kensington
King's Cross
Manor House
Marylebone
Mottingham
Paddington
Piccadilly
Queensbury
Raynes Park
Seven Dials
Seven Kings
Shad Thames
Shoreditch
Silvertown
Smithfield
Teddington
Thamesmead
Totteridge
Twickenham
Wallington
Wealdstone

11 Bedford Park
Belsize Park
Bexleyheath
Blackfriars
Bounds Green
Brondesbury
Canada Water
Canary Wharf
Canning Town
Chessington
Clerkenwell
Cockfosters
Cricklewood
East Dulwich
Fortis Green
Gunnersbury
Hammersmith
Highams Park

Holland Park
Kensal Green
Kentish Town
Leytonstone
Lincoln's Inn
Little Italy
Ludgate Hill
Muswell Hill
Notting Hill
Pentonville
Regent's Park
Rotherhithe
Snaresbrook
St John's Wood
Surrey Quays
Tufnell Park
Walthamstow
Westminster
Whitechapel

12 Bethnal Green
Billingsgate
Bromley-by-Bow

Charing Cross
City of London
Colliers Wood
Covent Garden
Crossharbour
Epping Forest
Finsbury Park
Golders Green
Hatton Garden
Havering Park
London Bridge
London Fields
Palmers Green
Parsons Green
Pool of London
Primrose Hill
Seven Sisters
Sloane Square
Stamford Hill
Swiss Cottage

13 Ardleigh Green
Chadwell Heath

Crystal Palace
Harmondsworth
Knightsbridge
Ladbroke Grove
Lancaster Gate
North Woolwich
Petticoat Lane
Shepherd's Bush
Thornton Heath
Tottenham Hale
Wanstead Flats
Winchmore Hill

14 Angel Islington
Becontree Heath
Hackney Marshes
Stoke Newington
Tottenham Green
Wormwood Scrubs

15 Alexandra Palace
Leicester Square
Westbourne Green

London streets include:

06 Strand

07 Aldgate
Aldwych
The Mall
Westway

08 Kingsway
Long Acre
Millbank
Minories
Pall Mall
Park Lane
York Road

09 Bow Street
Cheapside
Drury Lane
Haymarket
King's Road
Maida Vale
Queensway
Tower Hill
Whitehall

10 Bond Street
Dean Street
Eaton Place
Euston Road
Fetter Lane
Fulham Road
London Wall
Onslow Road
Piccadilly
Queen's Gate
Soho Square

Vine Street

11 Baker Street
Eaton Square
Edgware Road
Fleet Street
Goswell Road
Gower Street
High Holborn
Lambeth Road
Leather Lane
Ludgate Hill
Old Kent Road
Pimlico Road
Savoy Street
Warwick Road

12 Albany Street
Belgrave Road
Birdcage Walk
Brompton Road
Cannon Street
Chancery Lane
Cromwell Road
Gray's Inn Road
Hatton Garden
Jermyn Street
Oxford Street
Regent Street
Sloane Square
Sloane Street
Tooley Street

13 Bayswater Road
Bedford Square

Berwick Street
Carnaby Street
Downing Street
Garrick Street
Gerrard Street
Grosvenor Road
Knightsbridge
Lombard Street
Ludgate Circus
New Bond Street
New Fetter Lane
Newgate Street
Old Bond Street
Petticoat Lane
Portland Place
Portman Square
Russell Square
Wardour Street

14 Belgrave Square
Berkeley Square
Coventry Street
Earl's Court Road
Earnshaw Street
Exhibition Road
Gloucester Road
Holborn Viaduct
Horseferry Road
Hyde Park Square
Kensington Road
Marylebone Road
Mayfair Gardens
Portobello Road
Stamford Street

15 Albemarle Street
Blackfriars Road
Clerkenwell Road
Grosvenor Square
Horse Guards Road

Leicester Square
Liverpool Street
New Bridge Street
Pentonville Road
Southwark Street

St John's Wood Road
Trafalgar Square
Whitechapel Road

London landmarks include:

03 ICA
Kew

04 City
Eros
Oval
Soho

05 Lord's
V and A

06 Big Ben
Lloyds
Temple
Thames

07 Harrods
Mayfair
St Paul's
The City
The Mall

08 Bow bells
Cenotaph
Gray's Inn
Hyde Park
Liberty's
Monument
St Bride's

09 Chinatown
Cutty Sark
George Inn
Green Park
Guildhall
London Eye
London Zoo
Old Bailey
Rotten Row
Royal Mews
South Bank
Staple Inn
The Temple
Trocadero

10 Albert Hall
Camden Lock

Cock Tavern
Earl's Court
HMS Belfast
Jewel Tower
Kew Gardens
Marble Arch
Selfridge's
Serpentine
Tate Modern
the Gherkin

11 Apsley House
Canary Wharf
Golden Hinde
Lincoln's Inn
OXO building
Queen's House
Regent's Park
River Thames
St John's Gate
St Margaret's
St Mary-Le-Bow
Tate Britain
Tower Bridge

12 Charterhouse
Covent Garden
Design Museum
Dickens House
Guards Museum
Hatton Garden
Hay's Galleria
London Bridge
Mansion House
Spencer House
statue of Eros
St James's Park
Telecom Tower
Temple Church
Traitors' Gate

13 Admiralty Arch
Bank of England
British Museum
Carnaby Street

Clarence House
Gabriel's Wharf
Geffrye Museum
Greenwich Park
Lambeth Palace
London Dungeon
Nelson's Column
Petticoat Lane
Queen's Gallery
Royal Exchange
Science Museum
Somerset House
Tower of London
Wesley's Chapel

14 Albert Memorial
Barbican Centre
British Library
Hayward Gallery
Hermitage Rooms
Lancaster House
London Aquarium
Madame Tussaud's
Millennium Dome
Museum of London
Portobello Road
Speakers' Corner
St Clement Danes
St James's Palace
Waterloo Bridge
Wellington Arch

15 Bankside Gallery
Banqueting House
Brompton Oratory
Burlington House
Cabinet War Rooms
Dr Johnson's House
National Gallery
Royal Albert Hall
Royal Opera House
Temple of Mithras
Trafalgar Square
Westminster Hall

London Underground lines:

06 Circle (yellow)

07 Central (red)
Jubilee (grey)

08 Bakerloo (brown)

District (green)
Northern (black)
Victoria (sky blue)

10 East London (orange)

Piccadilly (navy blue)

12 Metropolitan (maroon)

15 Waterloo and City (jade green)

18 Hammersmith and City (pink)

21 Docklands Light Railway (sea green and white)

London Underground stations:

04 Bank (Central/Docklands Light Railway/ Northern/Waterloo and City)
Oval (Northern)

05 Angel (Northern)

06 Balham (Northern)
Cyprus (Docklands Light Railway)
Epping (Central)
Euston (Northern/Victoria)
Leyton (Central)
Morden (Northern)
Pinner (Metropolitan)
Poplar (Docklands Light Railway)
Temple (Circle/District)

07 Aldgate (Circle/Metropolitan)
Archway (Northern)
Arsenal (Piccadilly)
Barking (District/Hammersmith and City)
Beckton (Docklands Light Railway)
Borough (Northern)
Bow Road (District/Hammersmith and City)
Brixton (Victoria)
Chesham (Metropolitan)
East Ham (District/Hammersmith and City)
Edgware (Northern)
Holborn (Central/Piccadilly)
Kilburn (Jubilee)
Mile End (Hammersmith and City/Central/ District)
Neasden (Jubilee)
Pimlico (Victoria)
Ruislip (Piccadilly/Metropolitan)
St Paul's (Central)
Wapping (East London)
Watford (Metropolitan)
West Ham (Hammersmith and City/District/ Jubilee)

08 Amersham (Metropolitan)
Barbican (Circle/Hammersmith and City/ Metropolitan)
Chigwell (Central)
Hainault (Central)
Heathrow (Piccadilly)
Highgate (Northern)
Lewisham (Docklands Light Railway)
Monument (Circle/District)
Moorgate (Northern/Circle/Metropolitan/ Hammersmith and City)
Mudchute (Docklands Light Railway)
New Cross (East London)
Northolt (Central)

Perivale (Central)
Plaistow (Hammersmith and City/District)
Richmond (District)
Royal Oak (Hammersmith and City)
Shadwell (East London/Docklands Light Railway)
Stanmore (Jubilee)
Uxbridge (Piccadilly/Metropolitan)
Vauxhall (Victoria)
Victoria (Victoria/Circle/District)
Wanstead (Central)
Waterloo (Waterloo and City/Bakerloo/ Northern/Jubilee)

09 Acton Town (District/Piccadilly)
All Saints (Docklands Light Railway)
Bayswater (Circle/District)
Blackwall (Docklands Light Railway)
Bow Church (Docklands Light Railway)
Chalk Farm (Northern)
Cutty Sark (Docklands Light Railway)
East Acton (Central)
East India (Docklands Light Railway)
Greenford (Central)
Green Park (Jubilee/Piccadilly/Victoria)
Greenwich (Docklands Light Railway)
Hampstead (Northern)
Harlesden (Bakerloo)
Kingsbury (Jubilee)
Limehouse (Docklands Light Railway)
Maida Vale (Bakerloo)
Old Street (Northern)
Park Royal (Piccadilly)
Queensway (Central)
South Quay (Docklands Light Railway)
Southwark (Jubilee)
Stockwell (Victoria/Northern)
Stratford (Jubilee/Central/Docklands Light Railway)
Tower Hill (Circle/District)
Upton Park (District/Hammersmith and City)
West Acton (Central)
Westferry (Docklands Light Railway)
White City (Central)
Wimbledon (District)
Wood Green (Piccadilly)

10 Bermondsey (Jubilee)
Bond Street (Central/Jubilee)
Brent Cross (Northern)
Camden Town (Northern)
Canons Park (Jubilee)
Devons Road (Docklands Light Railway)

Dollis Hill (Jubilee)
Earl's Court (District/Piccadilly)
East Putney (District)
Embankment (Bakerloo/Circle/District/
Northern)
Farringdon (Circle/Metropolitan/
Hammersmith and City)
Grange Hill (Central)
Hanger Lane (Central)
Heron Quays (Docklands Light Railway)
Hillingdon (Metropolitan/Piccadilly)
Hornchurch (District)
Kennington (Northern)
Kew Gardens (District)
Manor House (Piccadilly)
Marble Arch (Central)
Marylebone (Bakerloo)
North Acton (Central)
Paddington (Circle/District/Hammersmith
and City/Bakerloo)
Queensbury (Jubilee)
Queen's Park (Bakerloo)
Shoreditch (East London)
Tooting Bec (Northern)

11 Aldgate East (District/Hammersmith and
City)
Baker Street (Bakerloo/Circle/Hammersmith
and City/Jubilee/Metropolitan)
Barons Court (District/Piccadilly)
Beckton Park (Docklands Light Railway)
Belsize Park (Northern)
Blackfriars (Circle/District)
Bounds Green (Piccadilly)
Canada Water (East London/Jubilee)
Canary Wharf (Docklands Light Railway/
Jubilee)
Canning Town (Docklands Light Railway/
Jubilee)
Chorleywood (Metropolitan)
Cockfosters (Piccadilly)
Custom House (Docklands Light Railway)
Edgware Road (Bakerloo/Circle/District/
Hammersmith and City)
Gunnersbury (District)
Hammersmith (District/Hammersmith and
City/Piccadilly)
Holland Park (Central)
Kensal Green (Bakerloo)
Kentish Town (Northern)
Kilburn Park (Bakerloo)
Latimer Road (Hammersmith and City)
Leytonstone (Central)
North Ealing (Piccadilly)
Northfields (Piccadilly)
Regent's Park (Bakerloo)
Rotherhithe (East London)
Royal Albert (Docklands Light Railway)
South Ealing (Piccadilly)

Southfields (District)
St John's Wood (Jubilee)
Surrey Quays (East London)
Tufnell Park (Northern)
Wembley Park (Jubilee/Metropolitan)
Westminster (Jubilee/Circle/District)
Whitechapel (East London/Hammersmith
and City/District)

12 Bethnal Green (Circle)
Bromley-by-Bow (District/Hammersmith
and City)
Cannon Street (Circle/District)
Chancery Lane (Central)
Charing Cross (Bakerloo/Northern)
Chiswick Park (District)
Clapham North (Northern)
Clapham South (Northern)
Colliers Wood (Northern)
Covent Garden (Piccadilly)
Dagenham East (District)
Ealing Common (District/Piccadilly)
East Finchley (Northern)
Elverson Road (Docklands Light Railway)
Euston Square (Circle/Hammersmith and
City/Metropolitan)
Finchley Road (Jubilee/Metropolitan)
Finsbury Park (Piccadilly/Victoria)
Golders Green (Northern)
Goldhawk Road (Hammersmith and City)
Goodge Street (Northern)
Holloway Road (Piccadilly)
Lambeth North (Bakerloo)
London Bridge (Northern/Jubilee)
Mansion House (Circle/District)
New Cross Gate (East London)
Oxford Circus (Victoria/Bakerloo/Central)
Parsons Green (District)
Prince Regent (Docklands Light Railway)
Putney Bridge (District)
Seven Sisters (Victoria)
Sloane Square (Circle/District)
Stepney Green (Hammersmith and City/
District)
St James's Park (Circle/District)
Swiss Cottage (Jubilee)
Tower Gateway (Docklands Light Railway)
Turnham Green (Piccadilly/District)
Turnpike Lane (Piccadilly)
Warren Street (Northern/Victoria)
West Brompton (District)

13 Clapham Common (Northern)
Gallions Reach (Docklands Light Railway)
Hendon Central (Northern)
Island Gardens (Docklands Light Railway)
Knightsbridge (Piccadilly)
Ladbroke Grove (Hammersmith and City)
Lancaster Gate (Central)

Rickmansworth (Metropolitan)
Royal Victoria (Docklands Light Railway)
Russell Square (Piccadilly)
Shepherd's Bush (Central/Hammersmith and
   City)
Stamford Brook (District)
Tottenham Hale (Victoria)
Warwick Avenue (Bakerloo)
West Hampstead (Jubilee)
West India Quay (Docklands Light Railway)
Wimbledon Park (District)

14 Blackhorse Road (Victoria)
Caledonian Road (Piccadilly)
Deptford Bridge (Docklands Light Railway)
Ealing Broadway (Central/District)
Fulham Broadway (District)
Gloucester Road (Circle/District/Piccadilly)
Hyde Park Corner (Piccadilly)
North Greenwich (Jubilee)
South Wimbledon (Northern)
Westbourne Park (Hammersmith and City)
West Kensington (District)
Willesden Green (Jubilee)

15 Finchley Central (Northern)
Harrow-on-the-Hill (Metropolitan)
Hounslow Central (Piccadilly)

See also **bridge**; **museum**; **palace**

lough *see* **lake**

lover

Leicester Square (Piccadilly/Northern)
Liverpool Street (Central/Hammersmith and
   City/Circle/Metropolitan)
Notting Hill Gate (Circle/Central/District)
Pudding Mill Lane (Docklands Light
   Railway)
Ravenscourt Park (District)
South Kensington (Piccadilly/Circle/District)
Stonebridge Park (Bakerloo)
Tooting Broadway (Northern)

16 Piccadilly Circus (Piccadilly/Bakerloo)

17 Elephant and Castle (Bakerloo/Northern)
Kensington Olympia (District)
Willesden Junction (Bakerloo)

18 Chalfont and Latimer (Metropolitan)
Mornington Crescent (Northern)
Tottenham Court Road (Northern/Central)
Walthamstow Central (Victoria)

19 Great Portland Street (Circle/Hammersmith
   and City/Metropolitan)
King's Cross St Pancras (Circle/Hammersmith
   and City/Metropolitan/Northern/Piccadilly/
   Victoria)

20 Highbury and Islington (Victoria)
High Street Kensington (Circle/District)

Lovers include:

04 Juan (Don; *Don Juan*, 1819–24, Lord Byron)
08 Casanova (Giacomo Girolamo; 1725–98,
   Italian)

Lothario (*The Fair Penitent*, 1703, Nicholas
   Rowe)
09 Valentino (Rudolph; 1895–1926, Italian/US)

Pairs of lovers include:

11 Rick and Ilsa (*Casablanca*, 1942)
Zeus and Hera (Greek mythology)

12 Darby and Joan (possibly from an 18c song)
Porgy and Bess (*Porgy*, 1925, DuBose
   Heyward)

13 Dido and Aeneas (Greek mythology)
Harry and Sally (*When Harry met Sally*,
   1989)
Paris and Helen (Greek mythology)
Psyche and Eros (Greek mythology)

14 Bonnie and Clyde (Clyde Barrow; 1909–34,
   US/Bonnie Parker; 1911–34, US)
Hero and Leander (Greek mythology)
Romeo and Juliet (*Romeo and Juliet*,
   1591–96, William Shakespeare)

16 Dante and Beatrice (Dante Alighieri; 1265–
   1321, Italian/Beatrice Portinari; c.1265–90,
   Italian)
Petrarch and Laura (Francesco Petrarca;
   1304–74, Italian/possibly Laure de Noves,
   d.1348, Italian)
Pyramus and Thisbe (Greek mythology)
Rhiannon and Pwyll (Celtic mythology)
Samson and Delilah (Bible: Judges 16)
Tristan and Isolde (Celtic mythology)

17 Abelard and Héloïse (Peter Abelard;
   1079–1142, French/Héloïse; c.1098–1164,
   French)

18 Antony and Cleopatra (Mark Antony;
   c.83–30 BC, Roman/Cleopatra; 69–30 BC,
   Egyptian)

Caesar and Cleopatra (Julius Caesar; 100 or 102–44 BC, Roman/Cleopatra; 69–30 BC, Egyptian)

Cathy and Heathcliff (*Wuthering Heights*, 1848, Emily Brontë)

Orpheus and Eurydice (Greek mythology)

Rosalind and Orlando (*As You Like It*, c.1600, William Shakespeare)

Troilus and Cressida (Greek mythology/ medieval fiction)

19 Beatrice and Benedick (*Much Ado About Nothing*, 1598/1600, William Shakespeare)

Chopin and George Sand (Frédéric Chopin; 1810–49, Polish/George Sand; 1804–76, French)

Odysseus and Penelope (Greek mythology)

20 Charles II and Nell Gwyn (Charles II; 1630–85, English/Nell Gwyn; c.1650–1687, English)

Napoleon and Joséphine (Napoleon I; 1769–1821, French/Joséphine de Beauharnais; 1763–1814, French)

22 Adolf Hitler and Eva Braun (Adolf Hitler; 1889–1945; German/Eva Braun; 1912–45, German)

Jane Eyre and Mr Rochester (*Jane Eyre*, 1847, Charlotte Brontë)

Robin Hood and Maid Marian (English legend)

23 Edward VIII and Mrs Simpson (Edward VIII; 1894–1972, English/Wallis Simpson, Duchess of Windsor; 1896–1986, US)

Sir Lancelot and Guinevere (Arthurian legend)

24 Lady Chatterley and Mellors (*Lady Chatterley's Lover*, 1928, D H Lawrence)

25 Sid Vicious and Nancy Spungen (Sid Vicious; 1957–79, English/Nancy Spungen; 1958–78, US)

26 Elizabeth Bennett and Mr Darcy (*Pride and Prejudice*, 1813, Jane Austen)

Launcelot du Lac and Guinevere (Arthurian legend)

27 Anna Karenina and Count Vronsky (*Anna Karenina*, 1874–76, Leo Tolstoy)

Louis XV and Madame de Pompadour (Louis XV; 1710–74 , French/Madame de Pompadour; 1721–64, French)

Rhett Butler and Scarlett O'Hara (*Gone With the Wind*, 1939)

28 Arthur Rimbaud and Paul Verlaine (Arthur Rimbaud; 1854–91, French/Paul Verlaine; 1844–96, French)

Lord Byron and Lady Caroline Lamb (Lord Byron; 1788–1824, English/Lady Caroline Lamb; 1795–1828, English)

29 Humphrey Bogart and Lauren Bacall (Humphrey Bogart; 1899–1957, US/Lauren Bacall; 1924– , US)

Lord Nelson and Lady Emma Hamilton (Lord Horatio Nelson; 1758–1805, English/ Lady Emma Hamilton; c.1761–1815, English)

31 Katharine Hepburn and Spencer Tracy (Katharine Hepburn; 1907–2003, US/ Spencer Tracy; 1900–67, US)

Richard Burton and Elizabeth Taylor (Richard Burton; 1925–84, Welsh/Dame Elizabeth Taylor; 1932– , English/US)

33 Elizabeth Barrett and Robert Browning (Elizabeth Barrett; 1806–61, English/Robert Browning; 1812–89, English)

Low Countries

Cities and notable towns in the Low Countries include:

05 Breda (The Netherlands)
Delft (The Netherlands)
Ghent (Belgium)
Liège (Belgium)
Namur (Belgium)

06 Arnhem (The Netherlands)
Bruges (Belgium)
Leiden (The Netherlands)

07 Antwerp (Belgium)
Haarlem (The Netherlands)
Tilburg (The Netherlands)

Utrecht (The Netherlands)

08 Brussels (Belgium)
The Hague (The Netherlands)

09 Amsterdam (The Netherlands)
Charleroi (Belgium)
Eindhoven (The Netherlands)
Groningen (The Netherlands)
Rotterdam (The Netherlands)

10 Luxembourg (Luxembourg)
Maastricht (The Netherlands)

luggage

Luggage includes:

03 bag
     box
04 case
     grip
05 chest
     trunk
06 basket

hamper
kitbag
valise
07 holdall
     satchel
08 backpack
     knapsack

rucksack
suitcase
09 briefcase
     flight bag
     haversack
     portfolio
     travel bag

10 vanity case
11 attaché case
     hand-luggage
     portmanteau
12 Gladstone bag
     overnight bag

lunar sea *see* **moon**

Luxembourg *see* **Low Countries**

lyricist *see* **libretto**

M

Macedonia *see* **Balkans**

machinery

Machinery includes:

03 Cat®
    JCB®
05 crane
    dozer
06 digger
    dumper
    grader
    jigger
07 dredger
    grapple
    gritter
    skidder
    tractor
08 dragline
    dustcart
    jib crane
See also **agriculture**

09 bulldozer
    calfdozer
    dump truck
    excavator
10 angledozer
    earthmover
    pile-driver
    road roller
    snowplough
    tower crane
    tracklayer
    truck crane
    water crane
11 Caterpillar®
    dumper truck
    gantry crane
    road-sweeper

    wheel loader
12 cherry picker
    crawler crane
    luffing crane
    pick-up loader
13 concrete mixer
    floating crane
    fork-lift truck
    grabbing crane
    platform hoist
14 container crane
    crawler tractor
    tractor-scraper
15 hydraulic shovel
    luffing-jib crane
    walking dragline

magazine *see* **newspaper**

magnate *see* **business**; **newspaper**

Mahler, Gustav (1860–1911)

Significant works include:

05 'Titan' (Symphony; 1885–88)
06 'Tragic' (Symphony; 1903–05)
12 'Resurrection' (Symphony; 1888–94)
15 *Das klagende Lied* (1880)
16 *Five Rückert Songs* (1905)
    Songs of a Wayfarer (1884–85)
    The Boy's Magic Horn (1888–99)
17 *Das Lied von der Erde* (1907–09)

    Kindertotenlieder (1901–04)
    The Song of the Earth (1907–09)
19 *Des Knaben Wunderhorn* (1888–99)
21 *Funf Lieder nach Rückert* (1905)
26 *Songs on the Deaths of Children* (1901–04)
28 *Lieder eines fahrenden Gesellen* (1884–85)
31 *Drei Lieder for tenor and pianoforte* (1880)

Major League *see* baseball

maker

05 baker (bread)
roper (rope)
tawer (white leather)
tiler (tiles)
tyler (tiles)

06 bowyer (bows for archery)
coiner (coins)
cutler (cutlery)
fencer (fences)
framer (picture frames)
glover (gloves)
hatter (hats)
hosier (hosiery)
joiner (wooden components for buildings)
nailer (nails)
pinner (pins)
potter (pottery)
roofer (roofs)
tailor (clothes)

07 clogger (clogs)
dialist (dials)
girdler (girdles)
hurdler (hurdles)
lorimer (metal parts of a horse-harness)
loriner (metal parts of a horse-harness)
luthier (lutes, guitars, stringed instruments)
saddler (saddles)
wheeler (wheels)

08 armourer (arms and armour)
ceramist (ceramics)
chandler (candles)
clothier (clothes)
costumer (costumes)
fletcher (arrows)
glassman (glass)
gunsmith (guns)
jeweller (jewellery)
medalist (medals)
milliner (headgear)
optician (spectacles)
perfumer (perfumes)
spurrier (spurs)
wig-maker (wigs)

09 carpenter (wooden objects)
casemaker (book covers)

corsetier (corsets)
costumier (costumes)
horologer (clocks)
jacksmith (roasting jacks)
locksmith (locks)
medallist (medals)
outfitter (outfits)
pottinger (pottage)
robe maker (official robes)
shoemaker (shoes)
staymaker (corsets)
toolmaker (tools)
whittawer (saddles, harnesses, white leather)

10 blacksmith (iron objects)
butter-wife (butter)
cartwright (carts)
ceramicist (ceramics)
corsetière (corsets)
dressmaker (clothes)
file-cutter (metal files)
frame-maker (picture frames)
habit-maker (riding habits)
horseshoer (horseshoes)
mixologist (cocktails)
pastrycook (pastry)
perruquier (wigs)
shipwright (ships)
stockinger (stockings)
trunk maker (travelling trunks)
unguentary (unguents)
wainwright (wagons)
watchmaker (watches)
woodcutter (woodcuts)

11 butter-woman (butter)
chocolatier (chocolate sweets)
glass-blower (glassware)
mechanician (machines)
vitraillist (glass, stained glass)
wagonwright (wagons)
wax-chandler (wax candles)
wheelwright (wheels, wheeled carriages)

12 cabinet-maker (furniture)
confectioner (confectionery)
ploughwright (ploughs)
wood engraver (wood engravings)

See also **art**; **chef**; **footwear**; **furniture**; **motoring**; **occupation**; **pottery**; **sculpture**

male animal *see* animal

mammal

Mammals include:

03 ape
ass
bat
cat
cow
dog
elk
fox
gnu
pig
rat
yak

04 bear
boar
cavy
deer
goat
hare
ibex
kudu
lion
lynx
mink
mole
paca
puma
seal
soor
tahr
vole
wolf
zebu

05 aguti
bison
camel
civet
coney
coypu
dingo
eland
genet
horse
human
hyena
hyrax
koala
lemur
llama
loris
moose
mouse
okapi
otter
ounce

panda
potto
rhino
sheep
shrew
skunk
sloth
stoat
takin
tapir
tiger
whale
zebra

06 aye-aye
baboon
badger
beaver
beluga
bobcat
cattle
colugo
cougar
coyote
cuscus
dassie
dugong
duiker
ermine
ferret
galago
gerbil
gibbon
gopher
hacker
impala
jackal
jaguar
jerboa
langur
marmot
marten
monkey
numbat
ocelot
possum
rabbit
racoon
rhebok
sea cow
serval
tenrec
vicuña
walrus
wapiti

weasel
wombat

07 ant-bear
bosvark
buffalo
caracal
caribou
chamois
cheetah
dolphin
echidna
fur seal
gazelle
gerenuk
giraffe
gorilla
grampus
grizzly
guanaco
guereza
gymnura
hamster
lemming
leopard
macaque
manatee
meercat
meerkat
mole rat
muntjac
muskrat
narwhal
opossum
pack rat
panther
peccary
polecat
primate
raccoon
red deer
roe deer
sea lion
sun bear
tamarin
tarsier
wallaby
warthog
wild ass
wildcat

08 aardvark
aardwolf
anteater
antelope
bushbaby

bushbuck
capybara
chipmunk
dormouse
duckbill
elephant
fruit bat
grey wolf
harp seal
hedgehog
house bat
kangaroo
mandrill
mangabey
marmoset
mongoose
musk deer
oppossum
pacarana
pangolin
platypus
porpoise
reedbuck
reindeer
sea otter
sewer rat
squirrel
steenbok
steinbok
talapoin
wild goat

09 Arctic fox
armadillo
bamboo rat
bandicoot

black bear
blue sheep
blue whale
brown bear
dromedary
flying fox
grey whale
grindhval
guinea pig
jungle cat
mouse-deer
orang-utan
palm civet
phalanger
polar bear
porcupine
springbok
steinbuck
waterbuck
wolverine

10 Barbary ape
chevrotain
chimpanzee
chinchilla
coatimundi
common seal
fallow deer
field mouse
giant panda
hartebeest
house mouse
human being
jack rabbit
kodiak bear
pilot whale

pine marten
prairie dog
rhinoceros
sperm whale
springbuck
springhare
vampire bat
white whale
wildebeest

11 beaked whale
flying lemur
green monkey
grizzly bear
honey badger
killer whale
muntjac deer
pipistrelle
rat kangaroo
red squirrel
snow leopard

12 Arabian camel
barbary sheep
elephant seal
grey squirrel
harvest mouse
hippopotamus
leaf-nosed bat
mountain goat
mountain lion
rhesus monkey
river dolphin
spider monkey
two-toed sloth
vervet monkey
water buffalo

13 American bison
Bactrian camel
colobus monkey
dwarf antelope
elephant shrew
European bison
hanuman monkey
howling monkey
humpback whale
marsupial mole
mouse-eared bat
spiny anteater
Tasmanian wolf
thylacine wolf

14 capuchin monkey
edible dormouse
flying squirrel
Indian elephant
marsupial mouse
mountain beaver
Patagonian hare
squirrel monkey
Tasmanian devil
three-toed sloth

15 African elephant
black rhinoceros
brushtail possum
hamadryas baboon
humpbacked
  whale
proboscis monkey
ring-tailed lemur
Thomson's gazelle
white rhinoceros

See also **ape**; **bat**; **bear**; **carnivore**; **cat**; **cattle**; **deer**; **dog**; **horse**; **marsupial**; **monkey**; **pig**; **primate**; **rabbit**; **rodent**; **seal**; **sheep**; **whale**

mania

Manias include:

08 egomania (oneself)
09 cynomania (dogs)
demomania (crowds)
ergomania (work)
infomania (gathering information)
logomania (talking)
melomania (music)
monomania (single thought, idea or activity)
oenomania (alcohol)
opsomania (special kind of food)
pyromania (fire-raising)
theomania (God, religion)
tomomania (surgery)
xenomania (foreign things)
10 anthomania (flowers)

dipsomania (alcohol)
erotomania (sexual passion)
hippomania (horses)
hydromania (water)
methomania (alcohol)
metromania (writing verse)
mythomania (lying or exaggerating)
narcomania (drugs)
necromania (dead bodies)
nostomania (returning to familiar places)

11 ablutomania (personal cleanliness)
acronymania (forming acronyms)
ailuromania (cats)
bibliomania (books)
cleptomania (stealing)

demonomania (being possessed by devils)
etheromania (taking ether)
graphomania (writing)
hedonomania (pleasure)
kleptomania (stealing)
megalomania (power)
nymphomania (sexual desire)
technomania (technology)
toxicomania (poison)
tulipomania (tulip-growing)

12 arithmomania (numbers)
balletomania (ballet)
orchidomania (orchids)
potichomania (imitating Oriental porcelain)
pteridomania (ferns)
thanatomania (death)
theatromania (play-going)

13 flagellomania (beating and flogging)
morphinomania (morphine)

14 eleutheromania (freedom)

Maori

Maori leaders include:

05 Ngata (Sir Apirana Turupa; 1874–1950)

06 Cooper (Dame Whina; 1895–1994)
Mahuta (Sir Robert; 1897–1947)
O'Regan (Sir Tipene; 1939–   )
Pomare (Sir Maui; 1876–1930)
Ratana (Tuhupotiki Wiremu; 1873–1939)

07 Te Kooti (Arikirangi Te Turuki; date

See also **mythology**

unknown–1893)

09 Heke Potai (Hone Wiremu; date
unknown–1850)
Hongi Hika (1772–1828)
Rua Kenana (Hepetipa; 1869–1937)

11 Te Rauparaha (date unknown–1849)

14 Te Heuheu Tukino (Sir Hepi; 1919–97)

marine biologist *see* biology

marketing

Terms used in marketing include:

03 ASA
B2B
CRM
CSI
dog
PLC
USP

04 AIDA
MVCs
star

05 ACORN
BOGOF
churn
FMCGs
R and D

06 BOGOFF
DAGMAR
four p's
jingle
launch
mock-up
sell-in
slogan

07 adopter
canvass

cash cow
generic
gimmick
hit rate

08 call rate
campaign
cold call
coverage
footfall
free gift
giveaway
hard sell
mailshot
own-brand
own-label
sales aid
up-market
wildcats

09 flash pack
frequency
heavy user

10 brand image
commercial
data mining
direct mail
door-to-door

face-to-face
free sample
Gallup poll
Giffen good
halo effect
loss-leader
media buyer
normal good
sales drive
visualizer

11 aided recall
cannibalism
dealer brand
demarketing
demographic
family brand
gap analysis
late adopter
loyalty card
market share
observation
point-of-sale
recognition
retail audit
sell-through
three-for-two

word of mouth
12 area sampling
brand loyalty
buyers' market
early adopter
field selling
house-to-house
key prospects
market demand
marketing mix
market leader
media planner
Nielsen index
party selling
response rate
solus mailing
static market
SWOT analysis
target market
13 buying motives
captive market
consumer panel
corner a market
impulse buying
island display

market profile
matched sample
merchandizing
necessity good
perceptual map
rolling launch
sales campaign
solus position
tachistoscope
test marketing
unaided recall
14 brand awareness
concept testing
corporate image
credibility gap
email marketing
filter question
inertia selling
lead generation
macro marketing
marketing audit
marketing board
market research
micro marketing
opinion leaders

prompted recall
pyramid selling
random sampling
reference group
target audience
viral marketing
15 blanket coverage
brand management
captive audience
cluster sampling
core positioning
customer profile
diversification
family life cycle
group discussion
journey planning
leading question
market potential
personal selling
problem children
public relations
saturation point
skimming pricing
social marketing
supply and demand

marriage

Terms to do with marriage and weddings include:

03 dot
vow
wed
04 ring
veil
wife
05 aisle
altar
banns
bride
dowry
elope
groom
in-law
jugal
piper
tiara
toast
usher
vicar
06 affair
affine
beenah
bigamy
digamy
favour
fiancé

garter
genial
huppah
pre-nup
priest
speech
spouse
the Mrs
07 best man
betroth
bouquet
chuppah
consort
divorce
espouse
exogamy
fiancée
flowers
husband
Ketubah
kirking
marital
merchet
Mr Right
nuptial
page boy
propose

punalua
trigamy
wedding
08 affiance
bedright
best maid
confetti
conjugal
endogamy
hen night
jointure
levirate
maritage
minister
monogamy
monogyny
polygamy
shidduch
09 annulment
best woman
coemption
common-law
communion
connubial
honeymoon
hope chest
horseshoe

hypergamy
love match
matrimony
other half
reception
registrar
stag night
threshold
trousseau

10 bridesmaid
buttonhole
consortium
consummate
engagement
first dance
first night
flower girl
her indoors
him indoors
honeymonth
intermarry
invitation
Lucy Stoner
maiden name
matrilocal

morganatic
patrilocal
separation
settlement
unfaithful
uxorilocal
wedding day

11 deuterogamy
dissolution
Gretna Green
handfasting
misalliance
morning gift
mother in-law
outmarriage
wedding cake
wedding list

12 bottom drawer
bridal shower
concubitancy
give one's hand
mariage blanc
open marriage
photographer

prothalamion
something new
something old
wedding dress
wedding march
wedding night

13 church service
civil marriage
fortune-hunter
hedge-marriage
holy matrimony
marriage-lines
seven-year itch
something blue
the better half

14 matron of honour
pop the question
special licence
steal a marriage

15 chief bridesmaid
decree of nullity
going-away outfit
marriage-licence
plight one's troth

See also **anniversary**

marshal

Marshals include:

03 Ney (Michel; 1769–1815, French)

04 Earp (Wyatt; 1848–1929, US)
Foch (Ferdinand; 1851–1929, French)
Saxe (Maurice, Comte de; 1696–1750, French)
Tito (Josip Broz; 1892–1980, Yugoslavian)

06 Hickok (Wild Bill; 1837–76, US)
Pétain (Philippe; 1856–1951, French)
Tedder (Arthur, Lord; 1890–1967, Scottish)
Zhukov (Georgi; 1896–1974, Russian)

08 MacMahon (Patrice de; 1808–93, French)

marsupial

Marsupials include:

04 euro
tuan

05 koala
quoll

06 boodie
cuscus
glider
numbat
possum
quokka
tammar
wombat

07 bettong
dasyure
dibbler
dunnart

opossum
potoroo
wallaby

08 kangaroo
macropod
tarsiped
wallaroo

09 bandicoot
boodie-rat
koala bear
native cat
pademelon
petaurist
phalanger
wambenger

10 native bear

Notoryctes

11 diprotodont
honey possum
rat kangaroo
rock wallaby

12 marsupial rat
pouched mouse
tree kangaroo

13 brush kangaroo
marsupial mole
Tasmanian wolf

14 marsupial mouse
Tasmanian devil
vulpine opossum

15 flying phalanger

martial art

Martial arts and forms of self-defence include:

04 judo
05 lai-do
sambo
wushu
06 aikido

karate
kung fu
t'ai chi
07 capuera
ju-jitsu

08 capoeira
jiu-jitsu
ninjitsu
ninjutsu
Shotokan

09 tae kwon do
10 kick boxing
11 self-defence
t'ai chi ch'uan

See also **karate**

massacre

Massacres include:

04 Hama (1982, Syria)
Lari (1953, Kenya)
05 Ambon (1623, Dutch East Indies)
Katyn (1940, Russia)
My Lai (1968, Vietnam)
Paris (1871, France)
Sabra (1982, Lebanon)
06 Bezier (1209, France)
Boston (1770, America)
Catavi (1941, Bolivia)
Herrin (1922, USA)
Kanpur (1857, India)
Lidice (1942, Czechoslovakia)
Rishon (1991, Israel)
07 Amboyna (1623, Dutch East Indies)
Babi Yar (1941, Ukraine)
Badajoz (1936, Spain)
Baghdad (1258, now Iraq)
Chatila (1982, Lebanon)
Glencoe (1695, Scotland)
Halabja (1988, Iraq)
Nanking (1937–38, China)
Tianjin (1870, China)
08 Amritsar (1919, India)
Cawnpore (1857, India)
Drogheda (1649, Ireland)
El Mozote (1981, El Salvador)

Kishinev (1903, now Moldova)
Novgorod (1570, Russia)
Peterloo (1819, England)
Tientsin (1870, China)
09 Fetterman (1866, USA)
Innocents (c.1 AD, Bethlehem)
Jerusalem (1099)
Sand Creek (1864, USA)
September (1792, France)
Trebizond (1915, Turkey)
10 Addis Ababa (1937, Ethiopia)
Fort Pillow (1864, USA)
Myall Creek (1838, Australia)
Paxton Boys (1763, America)
Sack of Rome (1527, Italy)
Srebrenica (1995, Bosnia)
Tlatelolco (1968, Mexico)
11 Janissaries (1826, Turkey)
Sharpeville (1960, South Africa)
Wounded Knee (1890, USA)
12 Bloody Sunday (1905, Russia)
Sabra/Chatila (1982, Lebanon)
15 Oradour-sur-Glane (1944, France)
Sicilian Vespers (1282, Italy)
St Valentine's Day (1929, Chicago, USA)
Tiananmen Square (1989, Beijing, China)

material *see* **art**; **building**; **fabric**

mathematics

Branches of mathematics include:

06 conics
07 algebra
applied
fluxion
08 calculus
geometry

09 set theory
10 arithmetic
game theory
statistics
11 games theory
group theory

12 number theory
trigonometry
13 combinatorics
14 biomathematics
15 metamathematics
pure mathematics

Mathematicians include:

03 Dee (John; 1527–1608, English)
Lie (Sophus; 1842–99, Norwegian)

04 Abel (Niels Henrik; 1802–29, Norwegian)
Hopf (Heinz; 1894–1971, German)
Kerr (Roy; 1934– , New Zealand)
Pell (John; 1610–85, English)
Tait (Peter Guthrie; 1831–1901, Scottish)
Thom (René; 1923–2002, French)
Venn (John; 1834–1923, English)
Weil (André; 1906–98, French)
Weyl (Hermann; 1885–1955, German)

05 Aiken (Howard; 1900–73, US)
Artin (Emil; 1898–1962, Austrian)
Bayes (Thomas; 1702–61, English)
Blaeu (Willem; 1571–1638, Dutch)
Boole (George; 1815–64, English)
Borda (Jean Charles de; 1733–99, French)
Borel (Émile; 1871–1956, French)
Cotes (Roger; 1682–1716, English)
Craig (John; d.1731, Scottish)
Dirac (Paul; 1902–84, English)
Euler (Leonhard; 1707–83, Swiss)
Frege (Gottlob; 1848–1925, German)
Gauss (Carl Friedrich; 1777–1855, German)
Gödel (Kurt; 1906–78, US)
Green (Ben; 1977– , English)
Green (George; 1793–1841, English)
Hardy (Godfrey; 1877–1947, English)
Hoyle (Sir Fred; 1915–2001, English)
Klein (Felix; 1849–1925, German)
Mises (Richard von; 1883–1953, Austrian/US)
Monge (Gaspard; 1746–1818, French)
North (John Dudley; 1893–1968, English)
Peano (Giuseppe; 1858–1932, Italian)
Pratt (John Henry; 1809–71, English)
Riesz (Frigyes; 1880–1956, Hungarian)
Schur (Issai; 1875–1941, Russian)
Serre (Jean-Pierre; 1926– , French)
Smith (Henry; 1826–83, Irish)
Snell (Willebrod; 1580–1626, Dutch)
Sturm (Charles François; 1803–55, French)
Vieta (Franciscus; 1540–1603, French)
Wiles (Sir Andrew John; 1953– , English)

06 Agnesi (Maria; 1718–99, Italian)
Ampère (André; 1775–1836, French)
Argand (Jean-Robert; 1768–1822, Swiss)
Atiyah (Sir Michael; 1929– , English)
Banach (Stefan; 1892–1945, Polish)
Barrow (Isaac; 1630–77, English)
Bessel (Friedrich; 1784–1846, German)
Besson (Jacques; c.1535–c.1575, French)
Bidder (George Parker; 1806–78, English)
Bolyai (János; 1802–60, Hungarian)
Briggs (Henry; 1561–1630, English)

Bullen (Keith; 1906–76, New Zealand)
Cantor (Georg; 1845–1918, Russian/German)
Cartan (Élie Joseph; 1869–1951, French)
Cauchy (Augustin Louis, Lord; 1789–1857, French)
Cayley (Arthur; 1821–95, English)
Ceulen (Ludolph van; 1540–1610, Dutch)
Digges (Leonard; 1520–c.1559, English)
Euclid (fl.300 BC, Greek)
Feller (William; 1906–70, Croatian/US)
Fermat (Pierre de; 1601–65, French)
Ferrel (William; 1817–91, US)
Fields (J C; 1863–1932, Canadian)
Fisher (Sir Ronald; 1890–1962, English)
Froude (William; 1810–79, English)
Galois (Évariste; 1811–32, French)
Goedel (Kurt; 1906–78, US)
Gunter (Edmund; 1581–1626, English)
Hadley (John; 1682–1744, English)
Halley (Edmond; 1656–1742, English)
Hariot (Thomas; c.1560–1621, English)
Jacobi (Carl; 1804–51, German)
Jordan (Camille; 1838–1922, French)
Kelvin (William Thomson, Lord; 1824–1907, Scottish)
Keulen (Ludolph van; 1540–1610, Dutch)
Kummer (Ernst; 1810–93, German)
La Hire (Philippe de; 1640–1718, French)
Lorenz (Edward; 1917–2008, US)
Markov (Andrei; 1856–1922, Russian)
McCrea (Sir William; 1904–99, Irish)
Milnor (John; 1931– , US)
Möbius (August Ferdinand; 1790–1868, German)
Moivre (Abraham de; 1667–1754, French)
Napier (John; 1550–1617, Scottish)
Newton (Sir Isaac; 1642–1727, English)
Pascal (Blaise; 1623–62, French)
Peirce (Benjamin; 1809–80, US)
Peirce (Charles; 1839–1914, US)
Picard (Émile; 1856–1941, French)
Ramsey (Frank Plumpton; 1903–30, English)
Robins (Benjamin; 1707–51, English)
Stevin (Simon; 1548–1620, Flemish)
Stokes (Sir George; 1819–1903, Irish)
Tarski (Alfred; 1902–83, US)
Taylor (Brook; 1685–1731, English)
Taylor (Sir Geoffrey; 1886–1975, English)
Turing (Alan; 1912–54, English)
Wallis (John; 1616–1703, English)
Werner (Wendelin; 1968– , German/French)
Wiener (Norbert; 1894–1964, US)
Zeeman (Sir Christopher; 1925– , English)

07 Alhazen (c.965–c.1040, Arab)
Arnauld (Antoine; 1612–94, French)
Babbage (Charles; 1791–1871, English)

Bolzano (Bernard; 1781–1848, Czech)
Borelli (Giovanni; 1608–79, Italian)
Brouwer (Luitzen; 1881–1966, Dutch)
Byrgius (Justus; 1552–1633, Swiss)
Cardano (Girolamo; 1501–76, Italian)
Carroll (Lewis; 1832–98, English)
Charney (Jule; 1917–81, US)
Courant (Richard; 1888–1972, German/US)
Dickson (Leonard; 1874–1954, US)
Fourier (Joseph, Baron de; 1768–1830, French)
Galileo (1564–1642, Italian)
Gelfand (Izrail; 1913– , Russian)
Germain (Sophie; 1776–1831, French)
Gregory (James; 1638–75, Scottish)
Guarini (Guarino; 1624–83, Italian)
Harriot (Thomas; c.1560–1621, English)
Hartree (Douglas; 1897–1958, English)
Hermite (Charles; 1822–1901, French)
Hilbert (David; 1862–1943, German)
Khazini (al-; fl.c.1115–30, Arab)
Lambert (Johann; 1728–77, Swiss)
Laplace (Pierre, Marquis de; 1749–1827, French)
Leibniz (Gottfried; 1646–1716, German)
Noether (Emmy; 1882–1935, German)
Pearson (Karl; 1857–1936, English)
Penrose (Sir Roger; 1931– , English)
Plücker (Julius; 1801–68, German)
Poisson (Siméon; 1781–1840, French)
Purbach (Georg von; 1423–61, Austrian)
Recorde (Robert; c.1510–58, English)
Riemann (Bernhard; 1826–66, German)
Russell (Bertrand, Earl; 1872–1970, English)
Shannon (Claude; 1916–2001, US)
Stibitz (George; 1904–95, US)
Størmer (Carl; 1874–1957, Norwegian)
Waerden (Bartel van der; 1903–96, Dutch)
Whiston (William; 1667–1752, English)
Zermelo (Ernst; 1871–1953, German)

08 Alembert (Jean le Rond d'; 1717–83, French)
Banneker (Benjamin; 1731–1806, US)
Birkhoff (George David; 1884–1944, US)
Bjerknes (Vilhelm; 1862–1951, Norwegian)
Bourbaki (Nicolas; 1930s pseudonym of several French mathematicians)
Burnside (William; 1852–1927, English)
Clairaut (Alexis Claude; 1713–65, French)
Clifford (William; 1845–79, English)
Dedekind (Julius; 1831–1916, German)
De Morgan (Augustus; 1806–71, English)
Guldberg (Cato; 1836–1902, Norwegian)
Hadamard (Jacques; 1865–1963, French)
Hamilton (Sir William Rowan; 1805–65, Irish)
Jeffreys (Sir Harold; 1891–1989, English)
Khinchin (Aleksandr; 1894–1959, Soviet)
Lagrange (Joseph de, Comte; 1736–1813, French)

Lebesgue (Henri; 1875–1941, French)
Legendre (Adrien-Marie; 1752–1833, French)
Lovelace (Ada, Countess of; 1815–52, English)
Lyapunov (Aleksandr; 1857–1918, Russian)
Margulis (Gregori; 1946– , Russian)
Mercator (Nicolaus; c.1620–1687, German)
Mersenne (Marin; 1588–1648, French)
Okounkov (Andrei Yuryevich; 1969– , Russian)
Oughtred (William; 1575–1660, English)
Perelman (Grigori; 1966– , Russian)
Playfair (John; 1748–1819, Scottish)
Poincaré (Jules; 1854–1912, French)
Poncelet (Jean Victor; 1788–1867, French)
Rheticus (1514–74, German)
Stirling (James; 1692–1770, Scottish)
Subbotin (Mikhail Fyodorovich; 1893–1966, Russian)
Volterra (Vito; 1860–1940, Italian)

09 Bartholin (Erasmus; 1625–98, Danish)
Bartholin (Thomas, the Elder; 1616–80, Danish)
Bernoulli (Daniel; 1700–82, Swiss)
Bernoulli (Jacques; 1654–1705, Swiss)
Bernoulli (Jakob; 1654–1705, Swiss)
Bernoulli (Jean; 1667–1748, Swiss)
Bernoulli (Johann; 1667–1748, Swiss)
Boscovich (Roger Joseph; 1711–87, Croatian)
Bronowski (Jacob; 1908–74, Polish)
Brouncker (William Brouncker, 2nd Viscount; 1620–84, Irish)
Cavalieri (Bonaventura; 1598–1647, Italian)
Chebyshev (Pafnutii; 1821–94, Russian)
Condorcet (Marie Jean Antoine Nicolas de Caritat, Marquis de; 1743–94, French)
Desargues (Gérard; 1591–1661, French)
Descartes (René; 1596–1650, French)
Dieudonné (Jean; 1906–92, French)
Dirichlet (Lejeune; 1805–59, German)
Fibonacci (Leonardo; c.1170–c.1250, Italian)
Frobenius (Georg; 1849–1917, German)
Grassmann (Hermann; 1809–77, German)
Hausdorff (Felix; 1868–1942, German)
Khwarizmi (Muhammad ibn Musa al; c.800–c.850, Arab)
Kronecker (Leopold; 1823–91, German)
Lefschetz (Solomon; 1884–1972, Russian/US)
Liouville (Joseph; 1809–82, French)
Maclaurin (Colin; 1698–1746, Scottish)
MacLaurin (Richard Cockburn; 1870–1920, Scottish/New Zealand)
Minkowski (Hermann; 1864–1909, Russian/German)
Peuerbach (Georg von; 1423–61, Austrian)

Ramanujan (Srinivasa; 1887–1920, Indian)
Silvester (James; 1814–97, English)
Sylvester (James; 1814–97, English)
Tartaglia (Niccolò; c.1500–57, Italian)
Whitehead (Alfred; 1861–1947, English)
Wilkinson (James; 1919–86, English)

10 Archimedes (c.287–212 BC, Greek)
Chi-Shen Tao (Terence; 1975– , Australian)
Diophantus (fl.3 C AD, Greek)
Hipparchos (c.180–125 BC, Greek)
Hipparchus (c.180–125 BC, Greek)
Kolmogorov (Andrei; 1903–87, Soviet)
Levi-Civita (Tullio; 1873–1941, Italian)
Littlewood (John; 1885–1977, English)
Maupertuis (Pierre Louis de; 1698–1759, French)
Menaechmus (fl.4 C BC, Greek)
Pontryagin (Lev Semyonovich; 1908–88, Russian)
Pythagoras (c.580–c.500 BC, Greek)
Sacrobosco (Johannes de; fl.mid-13c, English)
Sierpinski (Wactaw; 1882–1969, Polish)
Somerville (Mary; 1780–1872, Scottish)
Theaetetus (c.414–c.369 BC, Greek)
Torricelli (Evangelista; 1608–47, Italian)
Von Neumann (John; 1903–57, Hungarian/US)

Wedderburn (Joseph; 1882–1948, Scottish/US)
Zeno of Elea (c.490–c.420 BC, Greek)

11 Aleksandrov (Pavel; 1896–1982, Russian)
Kantorovich (Leonid; 1912–86, Soviet)
Lacondamine (Charles Marie de; 1701–74, French)
Lobachevski (Nikolai; 1792–1856, Russian)
Omar Khayyám (c.1048–c.1122, Persian)
Shcharansky (Natan; 1948– , Ukrainian)
Weierstrass (Karl; 1815–97, German)

12 Bougainville (Louis Antoine de; 1729–1811, French)
Carathéodory (Constantin; 1873–1950, Greek)
Eratosthenes (c.276–194 BC, Greek)
Grothendieck (Alexandre; 1928– , German/French)
Kovalevskaya (Sofya; 1850–91, Russian)
Spottiswoode (William; 1825–83, English)

13 Regiomontanus (1436–76, German)

14 Châtelet-Lomont (Émilie, Marquise du; 1706–49, French)
Klingenstierna (Samuel; 1698–1765, Swedish)

15 Eudoxus of Cnidus (408–353 BC, Greek)

Terms used in mathematics include:

02 pi	equal	radian
03 arc	graph	radius
set	group	sample
04 apex	helix	secant
area	locus	sector
axes	minus	spiral
axis	ogive	square
base	point	subset
cube	ratio	vector
edge	solid	vertex
face	speed	volume
line	total	**07** algebra
mean	width	average
mode	**06** binary	bearing
plus	chance	bounded
root	convex	breadth
side	cosine	chaotic
sine	degree	concave
skew	factor	decimal
unit	height	divisor
zero	length	formula
05 angle	linear	fractal
chaos	matrix	integer
chord	median	mapping
curve	number	maximum
depth	origin	measure

minimum
modulus
oblique
product
segment
tangent

08 addition
analysis
antipode
argument
bar chart
bar graph
binomial
calculus
capacity
constant
converse
cube root
diagonal
diameter
discrete
dividend
division
equation
exponent
fraction
function
geometry
gradient
identity
infinity
latitude
less than
multiple
parabola
pie chart
quadrant
quartile
quotient
rotation
symmetry
variable
variance
velocity
vertical

09 algorithm
Cartesian
congruent
factorial

See also **measurement**

frequency
histogram
hyperbola
iteration
logarithm
longitude
numerator
odd number
operation
parameter
perimeter
remainder

10 acute angle
arithmetic
complement
continuous
coordinate
covariance
derivative
even number
horizontal
hypotenuse
percentage
percentile
place value
proportion
protractor
Pythagoras
real number
reciprocal
reflection
regression
right-angle
square root
statistics
subtractor

11 approximate
coefficient
combination
coordinates
correlation
denominator
determinant
enlargement
equidistant
exponential
greater than
integration
magic square

mirror image
Möbius strip
obtuse angle
permutation
plane figure
prime number
probability
Pythagorean
real numbers
reflex angle
translation
Venn diagram
whole number

12 asymmetrical
cross section
distribution
random sample
straight line
trigonometry
universal set

13 circumference
complex number
Mandelbrot set
mixed fraction
natural number
ordinal number
parallel lines
perpendicular
quadrilateral
scalar segment
triangulation

14 axis of symmetry
cardinal number
common fraction
directed number
mirror symmetry
multiplication
negative number
parallel planes
positive number
rational number
transformation
vulgar fraction

15 conjugate angles
differentiation
imaginary number
scalene triangle

meal

Meals include:

03 BBQ
tea

04 bite

05 feast
lunch
snack

06 barbie
brunch
buffet
dinner

nosh-up
picnic
repast
spread
supper
tiffin

07 banquet
blow-out
high tea

08 barbecue

cream tea
luncheon
takeaway
tea break
tea party
TV dinner

09 breakfast
cold table
elevenses

10 fork supper

midday meal
slap-up meal

11 dinner party
evening meal

12 afternoon tea
safari supper

13 harvest supper

measurement

Measuring instruments include:

04 rule

05 gauge
meter

06 octant

07 ammeter
balance
burette
pipette
sextant

08 luxmeter
odometer
ohmmeter
quadrant

09 altimeter
barometer
callipers
cryometer
dosimeter
flowmeter
focimeter
hodometer
hourglass
manometer
milometer
optometer
pedometer
plumb line
pyrometer
rheometer
steelyard
stopwatch
vinometer

voltmeter
volumeter
wattmeter
wavemeter

10 anemometer
audiometer
bathometer
clinometer
cyclometer
gravimeter
hydrometer
hyetometer
hygrometer
hypsometer
micrometer
mileometer
multimeter
ombrometer
photometer
planimeter
protractor
pulsimeter
radiosonde
tachometer
tachymeter
theodolite
vibrograph
vibrometer
viscometer

11 calorimeter
chronometer
colorimeter
dynamometer

pluviometer
pyranometer
salinometer
seismograph
seismometer
speedometer
spherometer
tape measure
tensiometer
thermometer
vaporimeter
velocimeter
weighbridge

12 Breathalyser®
densitometer
evaporimeter
evaporometer
galvanometer
inclinometer
magnetometer
psychrometer
respirometer
spectrometer
sphygmometer
viscosimeter

13 accelerometer
decelerometer
Geiger counter
saccharometer

14 geothermometer
interferometer

SI units include:

04 mole (mol)

05 metre (m)

06 ampere (A)
kelvin (K)

second (s)

07 candela (cd)

08 kilogram (kg)

10 kilogramme (kg)

SI-derived units include:

03 lux (lx)
    ohm (Ω)

04 gray (Gy)
    volt (V)
    watt (W)

05 farad (F)
    henry (H)
    hertz (Hz)
    joule (J)
    katal (kat)
    lumen (lm)

    tesla (T)
    weber (Wb)

06 newton (N)
    pascal (Pa)
    radian (rad)

07 coulomb (C)
    siemens (S)
    sievert (Sv)
    volt amp (VA)

09 becquerel (Bq)
    steradian (sr)

10 cubic metre (m^3)

11 newton metre (N m)
    square metre (m^2)

13 degree Celsius (°C)
    volts per metre (V m^{-1})

14 farads per metre (F m^{-1})
    henrys per metre (H m^{-1})

15 metres per second (m s^{-1})
    newtons per metre (N m^{-1})
    volt amp reactive (VAr)

Metric units include:

03 are (a)

04 gram (g)

05 litre (l)
    metre (m)
    tonne (t)

06 gramme (g)

07 hectare (ha)

08 decigram (dg)
    kilogram (kg)

09 centigram (cg)
    decilitre (dl)

    decimetre (dm)
    hectogram (hg)
    kilolitre (kl)
    kilometre (km)
    metric ton (t)
    milligram (mg)

10 centilitre (cl)
    centimetre (cm)
    cubic metre (cu m)
    decigramme (dg)
    hectolitre (hl)
    hectometre (hm)

    kilogramme (kg)
    millilitre (ml)
    millimetre (mm)

11 centigramme (cg)
    milligramme (mg)
    square metre (sq m)

14 cubic decimetre (cu dm)

15 cubic centimetre (cu cm or cc)
    square decimetre (sq dm)
    square kilometre (sq km)

Other units of measurement include:

02 as
    em
    en
    li

03 bar
    bel
    cab
    cor
    cup
    ell
    erg
    hin
    kat
    kin
    kip
    kos
    lay
    lea
    ley
    log
    mil
    mna
    nit
    oke
    pin
    rad

    rod
    tod
    ton
    tun
    wey

04 acre (a)
    aune
    bath
    baud
    boll
    bolt
    butt
    coss
    cran
    dram
    dyne
    epha
    foot (ft)
    gill
    hand
    inch (in)
    kati
    khat
    mile (mi)
    mina
    muid

    nail
    obol
    omer
    peck (pk)
    pica
    pint (pt)
    pipe
    pole
    pood
    ream
    rood
    rope
    rotl
    seer
    sone
    span
    thou
    tola
    torr
    vara
    yard (yd)

05 barye
    cable
    candy
    caneh
    carat

    catty
    chain
    cubit
    ephah
    grain
    kandy
    kaneh
    katti
    maund
    ounce (oz)
    perch
    picul
    pikul
    point
    pound (lb)
    quart (qt)
    stere
    stone (st)
    therm
    tical
    todde

06 barrel
    bushel (bu)
    candie
    cantar
    carrat

degree	decibel	short ton	square foot (sq ft)
denier	fresnel	**09** board foot	square inch (sq in)
drachm	furlong	cubic foot (cu ft)	square mile (sq mi)
fathom	lispund	cubic inch (cu in)	square yard (sq yd)
firkin	long ton	cubic yard (cu yd)	**12** cable's length
fother	megabar	decastere	nautical mile
gallon (gal)	quarter	decistere	**13** hundredweight
kantar	scruple	light year	(cwt)
league	**08** angstrom	**10** atmosphere	
parsec	cord foot	barleycorn	
shekel	hogshead	fluid ounce (fl oz)	
talent	lispound	hoppus foot	
07 calorie	microbar	millistere	
centner	millibar		

See also **angle**; **gauge**; **glass**; **paper**; **time**

meat

Cuts and joints of meat include:

03 leg	shin	fillet	noisette
rib	**05** chine	saddle	popeseye
04 chop	chuck	**07** best end	shoulder
clod	flank	brisket	spare rib
hand	round	buttock	**09** aitchbone
hock	scrag	knuckle	médaillon
loin	shank	sirloin	**10** silverside
neck	**06** breast	topside	**11** filet mignon
rack	collar	**08** escalope	porterhouse
rump	cutlet	forehock	

Meats and meat products include:

03 ham	quail	turkey	scrapple
MRM	speck	**07** biltong	trotters
red	steak	chicken	**09** forcemeat
04 beef	tripe	fatback	frikkadel
duck	vivda	griskin	hamburger
fowl	white	harslet	partridge
hare	**06** brains	long pig	rillettes
lamb	burger	pemican	**10** beefburger
pâté	faggot	poultry	horseflesh
pork	gammon	rissole	minced beef
Spam®	grouse	sausage	sweetbread
spek	haggis	variety	Weisswurst
veal	haslet	venison	**11** pig's knuckle
05 bacon	kidney	**08** bushmeat	sausage meat
brawn	mutton	escalope	**12** black pudding
goose	oxtail	foie gras	luncheon meat
heart	pigeon	fricadel	**13** shield of brawn
liver	polony	meat loaf	**14** mousse de canard
mince	rabbit	pemmican	
offal	tongue	pheasant	

Cold meats include:

03 ham

04 beef
game
pâté
pork
Spam®

06 salami
tongue
turkey

07 biltong
chicken
chorizo
game pie
kabanos
pork pie
sausage
terrine
venison

08 bresaola
Cervelat
cold cuts

cured ham
meat loaf
ox tongue
parma ham
pastrami
salt beef

09 Bierwurst
glazed ham
liver paté
Mettwurst
pepperoni
rillettes
roast beef
saucisson
scotch egg

10 breaded ham
corned beef
crispy duck
crumbed ham
liverwurst
mortadella
prosciutto

Serrano ham

11 crispy bacon
roast turkey
sausage roll

12 Ardennes pâté
Brunswick ham
Brussels pâté
Cajun chicken
jamón serrano
liver sausage
luncheon meat
peppered beef
roast chicken
Wiltshire ham

13 chicken breast
garlic sausage
honey roast ham
Schinkenwurst
smoked sausage

14 Chinese chicken

15 luncheon sausage

medical

Medical and surgical equipment includes:

03 ECG
MRI

05 clamp
swabs

06 canula
scales

07 cannula
curette
dilator
forceps
inhaler
scalpel
scanner
syringe

08 catheter
iron lung
speculum
tweezers
X-ray unit

09 aspirator

auriscope
autoclave
CT scanner
endoscope
incubator
inhalator
nebulizer
retractor

10 audiometer
CAT scanner
ear syringe
hypodermic
kidney dish
microscope
MRI scanner
oxygen mask
rectoscope
respirator
rhinoscope
sterilizer
ultrasound

11 body scanner
first aid kit
laparoscope
stethoscope
stomach pump
thermometer

12 bronchoscope
isolator tent
laryngoscope
resuscitator
surgical mask
urethroscope

13 aural speculum
defibrillator
specimen glass

14 oesophagoscope
operating table
ophthalmoscope
oxygen cylinder

15 instrument table
vaginal speculum

Medical specialists include:

07 dentist

08 optician

09 dietician
homeopath

10 homoeopath
oncologist
orthoptist
pharmacist

11 audiologist
chiropodist
neurologist
optometrist

pathologist
radiologist
12 anaesthetist
cardiologist
chiropractor
embryologist
geriatrician
immunologist
obstetrician

orthodontist
orthopaedist
psychiatrist
psychologist
toxicologist
13 dermatologist
gerontologist
gynaecologist
haematologist

paediatrician
vaccinologist
14 bacteriologist
microbiologist
pharmacologist
rheumatologist
15 endocrinologist
ophthalmologist
physiotherapist

Medical terms include:

03 CPR
HRT
IVF
MRI
04 cure
gene
scan
X-ray
05 donor
enema
nurse
pulse
sling
virus
06 biopsy
clinic
CT scan
doctor
injury
labour
splint
stitch
suture
trauma
tumour
07 allergy
bandage
CAT scan
check-up
hospice
placebo
relapse
surgery
symptom
therapy
vaccine
08 abortion

casualty
compress
C-section
dialysis
hospital
recovery
specimen
syndrome
09 blood bank
blood test
Caesarean
diagnosis
dislocate
dressings
home visit
infection
injection
operation
pregnancy
prognosis
remission
smear test
treatment
10 amputation
barium meal
blood count
blood donor
blood group
childbirth
consultant
convulsion
dissection
incubation
paraplegia
post-mortem
prosthesis
quarantine

side effect
tourniquet
transplant
11 case history
circulation
examination
inoculation
miscarriage
respiration
temperature
transfusion
vaccination
12 chemotherapy
circumcision
complication
consultation
immunization
implantation
inflammation
microsurgery
mouth-to-mouth
prescription
radiotherapy
13 amniocentesis
blood pressure
cauterization
cervical smear
contraception
intensive care
psychosomatic
resuscitation
sterilization
14 defibrillation
keyhole surgery
laser treatment
rehabilitation
15 health screening

See also **doctor**; **nurse**; **surgery**

medicine

Medicines include:

04 pill	inhaler	ointment	gripe-water
05 tonic	linctus	pastille	nasal spray
06 arnica	lozenge	sedative	painkiller
emetic	pessary	Ventolin®	penicillin
gargle	steroid	09 analgesic	11 suppository
tablet	08 ear drops	paregoric	13 anti-histamine
07 antacid	eye drops	10 antibiotic	cough medicine
capsule	laxative	antiseptic	tranquillizer

Branches of medicine include:

05 ob-gyn	pathology	diagnostics	radiotherapy
07 otology	radiology	gerontology	rheumatology
urology	10 cardiology	gynaecology	13 cytopathology
08 nosology	embryology	haematology	endocrinology
obs/gynae	geriatrics	paediatrics	ophthalmology
oncology	immunology	physiatrics	physiotherapy
pharmacy	obstetrics	12 anaesthetics	psychotherapy
09 andrology	osteopathy	bacteriology	14 electrotherapy
audiology	pediatrics	kinesiatrics	neuropathology
chiropody	psychiatry	microbiology	neuroradiology
dentistry	psychology	orthodontics	sports medicine
neurology	toxicology	orthopaedics	15 neuropsychiatry
optometry	11 dermatology	perinatology	
		pharmacology	

Branches of complementary medicine include:

04 yoga	iridology	aura therapy	hydrotherapy
05 reiki	10 art therapy	kinesiology	hypnotherapy
07 massage	autogenics	moxibustion	macrobiotics
Pilates	homeopathy	naturopathy	14 autosuggestion
Rolfing	meditation	reflexology	crystal healing
shiatsu	osteopathy	t'ai chi ch'uan	herbal medicine
08 Ayurveda	11 acupressure	12 aromatherapy	15 Chinese medicine
09 herbalism	acupuncture	Bach remedies	thalassotherapy
		chiropractic	

See also **anaesthetic**; **analgesic**; **antibiotic**; **antiseptic**; **drug**; **Nobel Prize**

melon

Melon varieties include:

04 musk	sweet	07 cassaba	10 cantaloupe
Ogen	water	08 honeydew	Charentais
rock	06 casaba	09 cantaloup	
05 galia	winter		

memorial *see* **monument**

metal

Metallic elements and their symbols:

03 tin (Sn)

04 gold (Au)
   iron (Fe)
   lead (Pb)
   zinc (Zn)

06 barium (Ba)
   cerium (Ce)
   cobalt (Co)
   copper (Cu)
   curium (Cm)
   erbium (Er)
   indium (In)
   nickel (Ni)
   osmium (Os)
   radium (Ra)
   silver (Ag)
   sodium (Na)

07 bismuth (Bi)
   cadmium (Cd)
   caesium (Cs)
   calcium (Ca)
   fermium (Fm)
   gallium (Ga)
   hafnium (Hf)
   holmium (Ho)
   iridium (Ir)
   lithium (Li)

   mercury (Hg)
   niobium (Nb)
   rhenium (Re)
   rhodium (Rh)
   terbium (Tb)
   thorium (Th)
   thulium (Tm)
   uranium (U)
   wolfram (W)
   yttrium (Y)

08 actinium (Ac)
   antimony (Sb)
   chromium (Cr)
   europium (Eu)
   francium (Fr)
   lutetium (Lu)
   nobelium (No)
   platinum (Pt)
   polonium (Po)
   rubidium (Rb)
   samarium (Sm)
   scandium (Sc)
   tantalum (Ta)
   thallium (Tl)
   titanium (Ti)
   tungsten (W)
   vanadium (V)

09 aluminium (Al)

   americium (Am)
   berkelium (Bk)
   beryllium (Be)
   germanium (Ge)
   lanthanum (La)
   magnesium (Mg)
   manganese (Mn)
   neodymium (Nd)
   neptunium (Np)
   palladium (Pd)
   plutonium (Pu)
   potassium (K)
   ruthenium (Ru)
   strontium (Sr)
   ytterbium (Yb)
   zirconium (Zr)

10 dysprosium (Dy)
   gadolinium (Gd)
   lawrencium (Lr)
   molybdenum (Mo)
   promethium (Pm)
   technetium (Tc)

11 californium (Cf)
   einsteinium (Es)
   mendelevium (Md)

12 praseodymium (Pr)
   protactinium (Pa)

Metal alloys include:

03 pot

04 type

05 brass
   Dutch
   Invar®
   Muntz
   potin
   steel
   terne
   white

06 Alnico®
   billon
   bronze
   latten
   occamy
   ormolu
   oroide

   pewter
   solder
   tambac
   tombac
   tombak
   Y-alloy

07 amalgam
   Babbit's
   chromel
   Nitinol
   prince's
   shakudo
   similor
   tutania
   tutenag

08 Babbitt's
   cast iron

   gunmetal
   Manganin®
   Nichrome®
   orichalc
   speculum
   zircaloy
   Zircoloy®

09 Britannia
   Duralumin®
   Dutch gold
   Dutch leaf
   magnalium
   pinchbeck
   shibuichi
   white gold

10 constantan
   ferro-alloy

   iridosmine
   iridosmium
   mischmetal
   Monel metal®
   mosaic gold
   osmiridium
   white brass

11 chrome steel
   cupro-nickel
   nicrosilial
   white copper

12 German silver
   nickel silver

14 high-speed steel
   phosphor-bronze
   stainless steel

meteor

Meteor showers include:

06 Lyrids (19–25 Apr)
Ursids (19–24 Dec)

07 Leonids (14–20 Nov)
Taurids (25 Oct-25 Nov)

08 Geminids (8–14 Dec)
Orionids (15–25 Oct)

Perseids (27 Jul-17 Aug)

11 Quadrantids (1–6 Jan)

12 Eta Aquariids (1–8 May)

14 Alpha-Scorpiids (20 Apr-19 May)
Delta Aquariids (15 Jul-10 Aug)

meteorology

Terms used in meteorology include:

04 calm
eddy
flux
haar
haze
ITCZ
rime

05 flood
front
frost
lidar
polar
Q-code
radar
ridge
SIGWX
solar
taiga
virga

06 albedo
arctic
el Niño
flurry
haboob
ice fog
isobar
Kelvin
la Niña
oxygen
parcel
steppe
trough
zephyr

07 adiabat
air mass
ceiling
Celsius
chinook
climate
cyclone
density
drizzle

drought
graupel
isotach
mistral
monsoon
rainbow
thunder
tornado
typhoon
weather

08 acid rain
anabatic
blizzard
dewpoint
diabatic
doldrums
emission
föhn wind
forecast
humidity
isotherm
maritime
millibar
nitrogen
rainfall
sastrugi
semi-arid
wind rose
windsock
wind vane

09 accretion
adiabatic
advection
aerograph
altimeter
barograph
barometer
cold front
cut-off low
diffusion
exosphere
frequency
gust front

harmattan
heat index
hurricane
hyetology
ice nuclei
isotropic
jet stream
lapse rate
lightning
mesopause
mesoscale
Met Office
nephology
omega high
orography
radiation
rain gauge
reflected
satellite
scattered
stable air
sub-arctic
tephigram
trade wind
turbulent
upwelling
viscosity
vorticity
warm front
wind chill
wind field
wind shear
wind speed
zonal flow

10 absorption
aerography
air quality
anemometer
atmosphere
baroclinic
barotropic
cloud cover
conduction

convection
dart leader
depression
Fahrenheit
frost point
Hadley Cell
hemisphere
homosphere
hyetograph
hyetometer
hygrometer
ice pellets
insolation
ionosphere
isallobars
isothermal
Kelvin wave
latent heat
macroburst
macroscale
meridional
mesosphere
microburst
microscale
nephograph
nephoscope
nowcasting
ozone layer
radiosonde
rain shadow
rain shower
Rossby wave
saturation
squall line
storm track
streamline
subsidence
tropopause
valley wind
visibility
waterspout
wavelength
weather man

11 aggregation
air pressure
Aleutian Low
anticyclone
chemosphere
circulation
climatology
coalescence
continental

dissipation
Ekman spiral
entrainment
evaporation
frontolysis
global scale
gravity wave
ground frost
hectapascal
hyetography
instability
mixing ratio
pollen count
pyranometer
satellitize
steady state
stratopause
supercooled
temperature
thermal belt
thermal wind
thermocline
thermograph
thermometer
thermopause
troposphere
ultra violet
unstable air
water vapour
wave cyclone
weather girl

12 advection fog
anabatic wind
cloud seeding
condensation
coupled model
cyclogenesis
heat capacity
heterosphere
meteorograph
microclimate
mountain wind
optical depth
pilot balloon
psychrometer
radiation fog
return stroke
seeder-feeder
sensible heat
Siberian High
station model
stratosphere

thermosphere
thunderstorm
transmission
water balance
weather chart
weather watch

13 ball lightning
Beaufort scale
boundary layer
carbon dioxide
climate change
cyclostrophic
fork lightning
freezing level
friction layer
frontogenesis
katabatic wind
magnetosphere
occluded front
onshore breeze
precipitation
radiant energy
remote sensing
stepped leader
synoptic chart
synoptic scale
thermodynamic
wind direction

14 air temperature
continentality
geostropic wind
horse latitudes
multicell storm
offshore breeze
orographic rain
prevailing wind
sheet lightning
supercell storm
transmissivity
twenty-foot wind
vapour pressure
weather station

15 contact freezing
hyetometrograph
polar easterlies
prognostic chart
stationary front
supersaturation
synoptic weather
water equivalent
weather forecast
wind-chill factor

See also **cloud**; **ice**; **precipitation**; **snow**; **storm**; **weather**; **wind**

metric unit *see* **measurement**

metro *see* **Underground**

Mexico

Cities and notable towns in Mexico include:

04 Léon
06 Mérida
    Oaxaca
    Puebla

07 Tijuana
    Torréon
08 Mazatlán
    Veracruz

09 Chihuahua
    Monterrey
10 Mexico City
11 Guadalajara

12 Ciudad Juárez
    Villahermosa
13 San Luis Potosí
14 Ciudad de México

Mexican landmarks include:

06 Cancún
    Zócalo
08 Acapulco
    Palenque
    Río Bravo
09 Ciudadela
    Rio Grande

10 El Castillo
    Monte Albán
11 Chichén Itzá
    La Ciudadela
    Sierra Madre
    Teotihuacán
12 Citlaltépetl
    Ixtaccihuatl

    Jaguar Palace
    Popocatépetl
14 Alameda Central
15 Avenue of the Dead
    Cerro del Tepeyac
    Palacio National
    Puebla Cathedral
    Pyramid of the Sun

Middle East

Cities and notable towns in the Middle East include:

03 Qom (Iran)
    Sur (Lebanon)
04 Abha (Saudi Arabia)
    Acre (Israel)
    Aden (Yemen)
    Arak (Iran)
    Doha (Qatar)
    Gïza (Egypt)
    Hama (Syria)
    Hims (Syria)
    Homs (Syria)
    Ilam (Iran)
    Khoy (Iran)
    Kufa (Iraq)
    Qena (Egypt)
    Ruwi (Oman)
    Sari (Iran)
    Suez (Egypt)
    Taif (Saudi Arabia)
    Ta'iz (Yemen)
    Tyre (Lebanon)
    Yazd (Iran)
05 Ahvaz (Iran)
    Amman (Jordan)
    Aqaba (Jordan)
    Arbil (Iraq)
    Aswan (Egypt)
    Asyut (Egypt)
    Basra (Iraq)
    Cairo (Egypt)

    Dubai (United Arab Emirates)
    Haifa (Israel)
    Halab (Syria)
    Hilla (Iraq)
    Irbid (Jordan)
    Jedda (Saudi Arabia)
    Karaj (Iran)
    Karak (Jordan)
    Luxor (Egypt)
    Mecca (Saudi Arabia)
    Mosul (Iraq)
    Najaf (Iraq)
    Nazwa (Oman)
    Petra (Jordan)
    Rasht (Iran)
    Sana'a (Yemen)
    Sayda (Lebanon)
    Sidon (Lebanon)
    Tanta (Egypt)
    Zahle (Lebanon)
    Zarqa (Jordan)
06 Abadan (Iran)
    Aleppo (Syria)
    Ashdod (Israel)
    Beirut (Lebanon)
    Dammam (Saudi Arabia)
    Dezful (Iran)
    Gorgan (Iran)
    Hebron (Palestinian Autonomous Areas/West Bank)
    Jahrah (Kuwait)

Kerman (Iran)
Kirkuk (Iraq)
Manama (Bahrain)
Matrah (Oman)
Medina (Saudi Arabia)
Muscat (Oman)
Qazvin (Iran)
Ramadi (Iraq)
Riyadh (Saudi Arabia)
Semnan (Iran)
Shiraz (Iran)
Tabriz (Iran)
Tehran (Iran)
Zanjan (Iran)

07 Ardabil (Iran)
Baghdad (Iraq)
Baqubah (Iraq)
Bushehr (Iran)
El Minya (Egypt)
Esfahan (Iran)
Hamadan (Iran)
Hodeida (Yemen)
Isfahan (Iran)
Jericho (Palestinian Autonomous Areas/West Bank)
Karbala (Iraq)
Latakia (Syria)
Mashhad (Iran)
Netanya (Israel)
Salalah (Oman)
Samarra (Iraq)
Sharjah (United Arab Emirates)
Tel Aviv (Israel)
Tripoli (Lebanon)
Unayzah (Saudi Arabia)
Zagazig (Egypt)
Zahedan (Iran)

08 Abu Dhabi (United Arab Emirates)

Al Wafrah (Kuwait)
Ashqelon (Israel)
Beni Suef (Egypt)
Buraydah (Saudi Arabia)
Damanhur (Egypt)
Damascus (Syria)
El Faiyum (Egypt)
Fujairah (United Arab Emirates)
Gaza City (Palestinian Autonomous Areas/ Gaza Strip)
Ismailia (Egypt)
Kazimayn (Iraq)
Orumiyeh (Iran)
Port Said (Egypt)
Ramallah (Palestinian Autonomous Areas/ West Bank)
Sabzevar (Iran)
Sanandaj (Iran)
Tiberias (Israel)

09 Bakhtaran (Iran)
Beersheba (Israel)
El Mansura (Egypt)
Jerusalem (Israel)
Nahariyya (Israel)
Najafabad (Iran)
Nasiriyah (Iraq)
Neyshabur (Iran)
Tarabulus (Lebanon)

10 Alexandria (Egypt)
Al Muharraq (Bahrain)
Kuwait City (Kuwait)

11 Bandar Abbas (Iran)
Khorramabad (Iran)

12 Ras al-Khaimah (United Arab Emirates)
Sulaymaniyah (Iraq)

14 Rishon Le Ziyyon (Israel)

15 Shubra al-Khaymah (Egypt)

Middle Eastern landmarks include:

05 Kabaa
Petra
06 Masada
Qumran
Red Sea
Tigris
07 Baalbek

Dead Sea
Palmyra
09 Euphrates
The Sphinx
10 Persepolis
11 Grand Mosque
River Jordan

The Pyramids
Via Dolorosa
Wailing Wall
Western Wall
12 Sea of Galilee
13 Dome of the Rock
15 Elburz Mountains

military

Military ranks in the UK and US armies:

05 major
07 captain
colonel

general
private
08 corporal

sergeant
09 brigadier
10 lieutenant

12 field marshal
major-general
13 lance-corporal
staff sergeant
14 warrant officer

15 first lieutenant
16 brigadier general
general of the army
second lieutenant
17 lieutenant-colonel

lieutenant-general
private first class
20 company sergeant major
23 regimental sergeant major

Military ranks in the UK and US navies:

06 ensign
rating
seaman
07 admiral
captain
09 captain RN
commander

commodore
10 able seaman
lieutenant
midshipman
11 rear-admiral
vice-admiral
12 fleet admiral

petty officer
13 sub-lieutenant
14 warrant officer
17 admiral of the fleet
chief petty officer
19 lieutenant-commander
21 lieutenant junior grade

Military ranks in the UK and US air forces:

05 major
06 airman
07 captain
colonel
general
08 corporal
sergeant
10 air marshal
12 air commodore
group captain

major general
pilot officer
13 flying officer
staff sergeant
wing commander
14 air vice-marshal
flight sergeant
master sergeant
squadron leader
warrant officer

15 air chief marshal
first lieutenant
16 brigadier general
flight lieutenant
second lieutenant
17 lieutenant colonel
lieutenant general
20 general of the air force
25 marshal of the Royal Air
Force

Military decorations and honours include:

02 GC
GM
MC
MM
VC
03 AFC
AFM
BEM

CGM
CMH
DCM
DFC
DFM
DSC
DSM
DSO

09 Iron Cross
10 Bronze Star
Silver Star
11 George Cross
George Medal
Purple Heart
13 Air Force Cross

Air Force Medal
Croix de Guerre
Legion of Merit
Military Cross
Military Medal
Victoria Cross
14 Oak-leaf Cluster

Military units include:

04 file
post
wing
05 corps
flank
fleet
group
squad
troop
06 cohort

convoy
flight
legion
patrol
picket
07 battery
brigade
company
militia
phalanx

platoon
section
08 commando
division
flotilla
garrison
regiment
squadron
09 battalion
effective

task force
10 detachment
flying camp
rifle corps
11 battle group
flying party
12 flying column
Royal Marines
13 guard of honour

Military terms include:

03 ADC
arm
foe
POW
van
WMD

04 army
AWOL
base
bomb
camp
duty
mess
navy
rank
rear
rout
tank
unit
wing

05 AWACS
corps
demob
depot
draft
drill
enemy
flank
fleet
foray
force
front
guard
leave
lines
march
NAAFI
padre
radar
range
recce
shell
sonar
squad
troop
truce

06 action
allies
ambush
attack
battle
billet
brevet
call up
charge

combat
decamp
defeat
detail
disarm
enlist
ensign
flight
kit bag
muster
mutiny
orders
parade
parley
parole
patrol
ration
salute
sentry
signal
sniper
sortie
stores
target
tattoo
trench

07 air-drop
arsenal
bivouac
brigade
canteen
colours
command
company
defence
fall out
landing
latrine
liaison
mission
outpost
platoon
posting
recruit
retreat
tactics
victory

08 adjutant
air cover
air force
barracks
blockade
briefing
campaign
citation
conquest

demotion
division
fatigues
flotilla
garrison
infantry
insignia
invasion
last post
martinet
mobilize
ordnance
quarters
regiment
reveille
roll-call
skirmish
squadron
standard
strategy
supplies
the front
training
vanguard

09 about turn
armistice
artillery
attention
beachhead
bugle call
ceasefire
conscript
crossfire
desertion
discharge
epaulette
excursion
first post
front line
fusillade
incursion
left wheel
logistics
march past
minefield
munitions
offensive
rearguard
slow march
surrender
task force
white flag

10 aide-de-camp
bridgehead
camouflage
close ranks

commission
debriefing
decoration
demobilize
detachment
dispatches
encampment
evacuation
expedition
firing line
inspection
manoeuvres
operations
quick march
rifle range
route march
shell-shock

11 armed forces
bombardment
disarmament
forced march
requisition

12 conscription
court-martial
demilitarize
friendly fire
installation
intelligence
mission creep
parade ground
peacekeeping

13 assault course
atomic warfare

battle fatigue
counter-attack
prisoner of war
quartermaster
square-bashing
trench warfare

14 action stations
marching orders
nuclear warfare
pincer movement
reconnaissance
reinforcements

15 chemical warfare
insubordination
married quarters
national service
observation post

See also **admiral**; **army**; **field marshal**; **general**; **missile**; **regiment**; **soldier**

Milton, John (1608–74)

Significant works include:

05 *Poems* (1645)
07 'Arcades' (c.1634)
     Lycidas (1637)
08 'L'Allegro' (c.1631)
10 'The Passion' (1645)
11 'Il Penseroso' (c.1631)
     Of Education (1644)
12 *Areopagitica* (1644)
     Comus: A Masque (1634)
     Paradise Lost (1667)
13 *Eikonoklastes* (1649)

15 *Defensio Secunda* (1654)
     Samson Agonistes (1671)
16 *Paradise Regained* (1671)
17 *Epitaphium Damonis* (1639)
19 *The History of Britain* (1670)
20 *De Doctrina Christiana* (unfinished)
26 *Pro Populo Anglicano Defensio* (1651)
30 *The Tenure of Kings and Magistrates* (1649)
33 *The Doctrine and Discipline of Divorce* (1643)

mineral

Main trace minerals include:

04 iron (liver, kidney, green leafy vegetables, egg yolk, dried fruit, potatoes, molasses)
zinc (meat, whole grains, legumes, oysters, milk)

06 copper (green vegetables, fish, oysters, liver)
iodine (seafood, saltwater fish, seaweed, iodized salt, table salt)
sodium (table salt)

07 calcium (milk, butter, cheese, sardines, green leafy vegetables, citrus fruits)

08 chromium (brewer's yeast, black pepper, liver, wholemeal bread, beer)

fluorine (fluoridated drinking water, seafood, tea)
selenium (seafood, cereals, meat, egg yolk, garlic)

09 magnesium (green leafy vegetables (eaten raw), nuts, whole grains)
manganese (legumes, cereal grains, green leafy vegetables, tea)
potassium (fresh vegetables, meat, orange juice, bananas, bran)

10 molybdenum (legumes, cereal grains, liver, kidney, some dark green vegetables)
phosphorus (meat, poultry, fish, eggs, dried beans and peas, milk products)

Minerals include:

03 jet

04 alum
mica
ruby
salt
spar
talc

05 beryl
borax
emery
flint
fluor
topaz
umber

06 albite
blende
cerite
galena
gangue
garnet
glance
gypsum
halite
haüyne
humite
illite
jasper
kermes
lithia
maltha
natron
nosean
pyrite
quartz
rutile
silica
sphene
spinel
talcum
zircon

07 anatase
apatite
axinite
azurite
barytes
biotite
bornite
brucite
calcite
cassite
crystal
cuprite
desmine
diamond

dysodil
epidote
jacinth
jadeite
jargoon
kandite
kyanite
leucite
nacrite
olivine
pennine
peridot
pyrites
realgar
syenite
thorite
uralite
uranite
zeolite
zincite
zoisite

08 allanite
ankerite
asbestos
autunite
blue john
boracite
brookite
calamine
calcspar
chlorite
chromite
cinnabar
corundum
crocoite
cryolite
diallage
diaspore
dolomite
dysodile
dysodyle
epsomite
erionite
euxenite
feldspar
fluorite
goethite
graphite
gyrolite
hematite
hyacinth
idocrase
ilmenite
iodyrite
lazulite

lazurite
lewisite
melilite
mimetite
nephrite
orpiment
plumbago
prehnite
pyroxene
rock salt
sanidine
sapphire
siderite
smaltite
sodalite
stannite
stibnite
stilbite
titanite
wurtzite

09 alabaster
amphibole
anhydrite
aragonite
atacamite
bentonite
blacklead
cairngorm
carnotite
celestite
chabazite
cheralite
cobaltite
columbite
covellite
dichroite
elaterite
enstatite
evaporite
fibrolite
fluorspar
fool's gold
goslarite
grossular
haematite
kaolinite
kermesite
kieserite
lodestone
magnesite
magnetite
malachite
marcasite
margarite
microlite

mispickel
muscovite
nepheline
niccolite
olivenite
ottrelite
pearl spar
phenacite
polianite
powellite
quartzite
rhodolite
rhodonite
rubellite
saltpetre
scheelite
scolecite
soapstone
sylvanite
tantalite
tremolite
turquoise
uraninite
variscite
vulpinite
wavellite
zinkenite

10 alabandite
andalusite
antimonite
aquamarine
argyrodite
aventurine
bastnäsite

See also **ore**

bloodstone
chalcedony
chalcocite
chrysolite
cordierite
cylindrite
dyscrasite
erubescite
glauberite
glauconite
halloysite
hornblende
Jamesonite
meerschaum
microcline
orthoclase
perovskite
polyhalite
pyrolusite
redruthite
samarskite
sapphirine
serpentine
smaragdite
sperrylite
sphalerite
tennantite
thaumasite
tourmaline
vanadinite

11 alexandrite
amblygonite
amphibolite
annabergite

apophyllite
baddeleyite
cassiterite
cerargyrite
chrysoberyl
clinochlore
crocidolite
franklinite
French chalk
greenockite
josephinite
lapis lazuli
molybdenite
piedmontite
pitchblende
sal ammoniac
sillimanite
smithsonite
tetradymite
vesuvianite
yttrocerite

12 chalcanthite
chalcopyrite
copper-nickel
hemimorphite
skutterudite

13 arsenopyrites
cummingtonite

14 hydroxyapatite
sodium chloride
yttro-columbite

15 gooseberry-stone
montmorillonite

mineral water *see* water

miser

Misers include:

05 Burns (Montgomery; *The Simpsons*, 1989– , Matt Groening)

06 Mammon (Bible)
Marner (Silas; *Silas Marner*, 1861, George Eliot)

07 Scrooge (Ebenezer; *A Christmas Carol*, 1843, Charles Dickens)

08 Nickleby (Ralph; *Nicholas Nickeby*,

See also **Eliot, George**; **Molière**

1838–39, Charles Dickens)
Trapbois (*The Fortunes of Nigel*, 1822, Sir Walter Scott)

10 Fardorough (*Fardorough the Miser*, 1939, William Carleton)
Van Swieten (Ghysbrecht; *The Cloister and the Hearth*, 1861, Charles Reade)

11 Earlforward (Henry; *Riceyman Steps*, 1923, Arnold Bennett)

missile

Missiles include:

02 MX	**04** ALCM	**05** smart	Tomahawk
V-2	ASBM	**06** AMRAAM	**09** ballistic
03 AAM	ICBM	cruise	Minuteman
ABM	IRBM	Exocet®	
AGM	MIRV	guided	**10** Sidewinder
ASM	MRBM	**07** Polaris	wire-guided
ATM	Scud	Trident	**11** heat-seeking
SAM	SLBM		
SSM	TASM	**08** Maverick	**12** surface-to-air

missionary

Missionaries and evangelists include:

03 Fox (George; 1624–91, English)
Huc (Evariste Régis; 1813–60, French)

04 Luke (St; 1 c AD)
Mark (St; 1 c AD)
Paul (St; d.c.64/68 AD)

05 Bliss (Philip; 1838–76, US)
Bruno (St; 970–1009, German)
Carey (William; 1761–1834, English)
David (Père Armand; 1826–1900, French)
Egede (Hans; 1686–1758, Norwegian)
Eliot (John; 1604–90, English)
Ellis (William; 1794–1872, English)
Grubb (Sir Kenneth; 1900–80, English)
Jones (Bob; 1883–1968, US)
Jones (Eli Stanley; 1884–1973, US)
Laval (François, de Montmorency; 1622–1708, French)
Legge (James; 1815–97, Scottish)
Moody (Dwight L; 1837–99, US)
Neill (Stephen; 1900–84, Scottish)
Niles (Daniel Thambyrajah; 1908–70, Tamil)
Paton (William; 1886–1943, Scottish)
Ricci (Matteo; 1552–1610, Italian)
Scott (Michael; 1907–83, English)
Serra (Junípero; 1713–84, Spanish)
Smith (Eli; 1801–57, US)
Smith (Rodney; 1860–1947, English)
Soong (Charlie; d.1927, Chinese)

06 Damien (Father Joseph; 1840–89, Belgian)
Graham (Billy; 1918– , US)
Judson (Adoniram; 1788–1850, US)
Kagawa (Toyohiko; 1888–1960, Japanese)
Martyn (Henry; 1781–1812, English)
Moffat (Robert; 1795–1883, Scottish)
Schall (Johann von; 1591–1669, German)
Teresa (Mother; 1910–97, Albanian)
Vieira (Antonio de; 1608–97, Portuguese)

Wesley (Charles; 1707–88, English)
Wesley (John; 1703–91, English)
Zwemer (Samuel; 1867–1952, US)

07 Andrews (Charles Freer; 1871–1940, English)
Aylward (Gladys; 1902–70, English)
Buchman (Frank; 1878–1961, US)
Columba (St; 521–97, Irish)
Falwell (Jerry; 1933–2007, US)
Laubach (Frank; 1884–1970, US)
Liddell (Eric; 1902–45, Scottish)
Roberts (Oral; 1918– , US)
Slessor (Mary; 1848–1915, Scottish)
ten Boom (Corrie; 1892–1983, Dutch)
Timothy (St; fl.c.50 AD)

08 Adalbert (St; d.981, German)
Boniface (St; c.680–c.754, Anglo-Saxon)
Brainerd (David; 1718–47, American)
Buchanan (Claudius; 1766–1815, Scottish)
Columban (St; 543–615, Irish)
Crowther (Samuel; 1809–91, African)
Cuthbert (St; c.635–87, Anglo-Saxon)
Duchesne (St Rose Philippine; 1769–1852, French)
Falconer (Ion Keith; 1856–87, Irish)
Grenfell (Sir Wilfred; 1865–1940, English)
Las Casas (Bartolomé de; 1474–1566, Spanish)
Morrison (Robert; 1782–1834, Scottish)
Newbigin (Lesslie; 1909–98, English)
Williams (John; 1796–1839, English)

09 Marquette (Jacques; 1637–75, French)
McPherson (Aimee Semple; 1890–1944, US)
Southwell (Robert; 1561–95, English)
Stapleton (Ruth; 1929–83, US)
Willibald (St; 700–86, Anglo-Saxon)

10 Columbanus (St; 543–615, Irish)
Hannington (James; 1847–85, English)

Huddleston (Trevor; 1913–98, English)
Macpherson (Annie; fl.1860s, Scottish)
Schweitzer (Albert; 1875–1965, Alsatian)
Whitefield (George; 1714–70, English)

11 Livingstone (David; 1813–73, Scottish)
Vivekananda (1863–1902, Indian)
13 Francis Xavier (St; 1506–52, Spanish)
Keith-Falconer (Ion; 1856–87, Irish)

Molière (1622–73)

Significant works include:

06 *L'Avare* (1668)
08 *L'Étourdi* (1658)
Tartuffe (1664/1667)
The Miser (1668)
09 *The Quacks* (1665)
10 *Amphitryon* (1668)
Les Fâcheux (1662)
Sganarelle (1660)
The Picture (1660)
11 *The Dumb Lady* (1666)
12 *George Dandin* (1668)
13 *L'Amour médecin* (1665)
Le Misanthrope (1665)
The Blunderers (1658)
14 *L'Ecole des maris* (1662)
Le Mariage forcé (1664)
The Misanthrope (1665)
15 *L'Ecole des femmes* (1662)
Le Dépit amoureux (1658)
The Impertinents (1662)
16 *The Learned Ladies* (1672)
17 *La Princesse d'Élide* (1664)
Les Femmes savantes (1672)
The Amorous Quarrel (1658)

The Cheats of Scapin (1671)
The Forced Marriage (1664)
The School for Wives (1662)
18 *Don Garcia of Navarre* (1661)
Don Garcie de Navarre (1661)
Le Malade imaginaire (1673)
Le Médecin malgré lui (1666)
The Female Virtuosos (1672)
19 *The Imaginary Cuckold* (1660)
The Imaginary Invalid (1673)
The Universal Passion (1664)
20 *The School for Husbands* (1662)
21 *Impromptu de Versailles* (1663)
Les Fourberies de Scapin (1671)
The Bourgeois Gentleman (1671)
22 *Don Juan or the Stone Guest* (1665)
Le Bourgeois gentilhomme (1671)
Les Précieuses ridicules (1659)
Monsieur de Pourceaugnac (1669)
23 *The Conceited Young Ladies* (1659)
24 *School for Wives Criticised* (1663)
The Impromptu of Versailles (1663)
25 *The Citizen turned Gentleman* (1671)
27 *La Critique de l'école des femmes* (1663)

Significant characters include:

05 Agnès
Argan
Célie
Elise
Lélie
Orgon
06 Ariste
Bélise
Cathos
Dorine
Elmire
Elvire
Horace
L'Avare

Léonor
Purgon
 (Monsieur)
Vadius
Valère
07 Alceste
Anselme
Armande
Arsinoé
Cléante
Cléonte
Dom Juan
Don Juan
Dorante

Eliante
Mariane
08 Arnolphe
Célimène
Chrysale
Dimanche
 (Monsieur)
Gorgibus
Harpagon
Isabelle
Jourdain (Madame)
Jourdain
 (Monsieur)
Magdelon

Philinte
Tartuffe
Toinette
09 Angélique
Clitandre
Diafoirus
 (Monsieur)
Henriette
Trissotin
10 Philaminte
Sganarelle
13 Le Misanthrope

mollusc

Molluscs include:

04 clam
slug

05 conch
cowry
snail
spoot
squid
whelk

06 chiton
cockle
cowrie
cuttle
dodman
limpet

loligo
mussel
nerite
oyster
winkle

07 abalone
octopus
piddock
scallop
sea slug

08 escargot
nautilus
sea snail
shipworm

wallfish

09 cone shell
hodmandod
land snail
pond snail
razorclam
razorfish
tusk shell
wing shell
wing snail

10 cuttlefish
giant squid
nudibranch
periwinkle

razor shell
Roman snail

11 horse mussel
marine snail

12 sea butterfly

13 common octopus
great grey slug
keyhole limpet
ramshorn snail
slipper limpet

15 freshwater snail

monarch

Anglo-Saxon and English monarchs, with regnal dates:

04 Cnut ('the Great'; 1016–35)
Edwy (955–59)
Grey (Lady Jane; 1553)
John (Lackland; 1199–1216)
Mary (I, Tudor; 1553–58)
Offa (757–96)

05 Edgar (959–75)
Edred (946–55)
Henry (I; 1100–35)
Henry (II; 1154–89)
Henry (III; 1216–72)
Henry (IV; 1399–1413)
Henry (V; 1413–22)
Henry (VI; 1422–61/1470–71)
Henry (VII; 1485–1509)
Henry (VIII; 1509–47)
Svein (I Haraldsson, 'Fork-Beard'; 1013–14)

06 Alfred ('the Great'; 871–99)
Canute (1016–35)
Edmund (I; 939–46)
Edmund (II, 'Ironside'; 1016)
Edward (I; 1272–1307)
Edward (II; 1307–27)
Edward (III; 1327–77)
Edward (III, 'the Confessor'; 1042–66)

Edward (II, 'the Martyr'; 975–979)
Edward (IV; 1461–70/1471–83)
Edward ('the Elder'; 899–924)
Edward (V; 1483)
Edward (VI; 1547–53)
Egbert (802–39)
Harold (II; 1066)
Harold (I Knutsson, 'Harefoot'; 1035–40)

07 Richard (II; 1377–99)
Richard (III; 1483–85)
Richard (I, 'the Lion Heart'; 1189–99)
Stephen (1135–54)
William (II, 'Rufus'; 1087–1100)
William (I, 'the Conqueror'; 1066–87)

08 Ethelred (866–71)
Ethelred (II, 'the Unready'; 979–1013/1014–16)

09 Athelstan (924–39)
Elizabeth (I; 1558–1603)
Ethelbald (856–60)
Ethelbert (860–66)
Ethelwulf (839–56)

11 Hardicanute (1035–42)

13 Edgar Atheling (1066)
Knut Sveinsson (1016–35)

Scottish monarchs, with regnal dates:

03 Aed (877–78)

04 Dubh (962–66)
Duff (962–66)
Mary (Queen of Scots; 1542–67)

05 Bruce (Robert; 1306–29)

Culen (966–71)
David (I; 1124–53)
David (II; 1329–71)
Edgar (1097–1107)
Giric (878–89)
James (I; 1406–37)

James (II; 1437–60)
James (III; 1460–88)
James (IV; 1488–1513)
James (V; 1513–42)
James (VI; 1567–1625)

06 Baliol (Edward de; 1332)
Baliol (John de; 1292–96)
Donald (I; 858–62)
Donald (II; 889–900)
Donald (III, 'Bane'; 1093–94/1094–97)
Duncan (I; 1034–40)
Duncan (II; 1094)
Indulf (954–62)
Lulach (1057–58)
Robert (II; 1371–90)
Robert (III; 1390–1406)
Robert (I, 'the Bruce'; 1306–29)

07 Balliol (Edward de; 1332)

Balliol (John de; 1292–96)
Kenneth (I; 843–58)
Kenneth (II; 971–95)
Kenneth (III; 997–1005)
Macbeth (1040–57)
Malcolm (I; 943–54)
Malcolm (II; 1005–34)
Malcolm (III, 'Canmore'; 1058–93)
Malcolm (IV, 'the Maiden'; 1153–65)
William (I; 1165–1214)

08 Margaret ('Maid of Norway'; 1286–90)

09 Alexander (I; 1107–24)
Alexander (II; 1214–49)
Alexander (III; 1249–86)

11 Constantine (I; 862–77)
Constantine (II; 900–43)
Constantine (III; 995–97)

16 Mary, Queen of Scots (1542–67)

British monarchs, with regnal dates:

04 Anne (1702–14)
Mary (II; 1689–94)

05 James (VI and I; 1603–25)
James (VII and II; 1685–88)

06 Edward (VII; 1901–10)
Edward (VIII; 1936)
George (I; 1714–27)

George (II; 1727–60)
George (III; 1760–1820)
George (IV; 1820–30)
George (V; 1910–36)
George (VI; 1936–52)

07 Charles (I; 1625–49)
Charles (II; 1660–85)
William (II and III, of

Orange; 1689–1702)
William (IV; 1830–37)

08 Victoria (1837–1901)

09 Elizabeth (II; 1952–   )

14 William and Mary (William
II and III and Mary II;
1689–94)

monastery, monk *see* **religious order**

money *see* **coin**; **currency**

monkey

Monkeys include:

03 ape
pug
sai

04 douc
leaf
mico
mona
saki
titi
zati

05 Diana
drill
green
magot
night

sajou
Satan
toque

06 baboon
bandar
bonnet
coaita
grivet
guenon
howler
langur
malmag
rhesus
sagoin
saguin
spider

tee-tee
uakari
vervet
woolly

07 cacajou
colobus
guereza
hanuman
macaque
sagouin
saimiri
sapajou
tamarin
tarsier

08 Capuchin

durukuli
entellus
mandrill
mangabey
marmoset
squirrel
talapoin
wanderoo

09 proboscis

10 Barbary ape
moustached

11 douroucouli
platyrrhine
white-eyelid

13 platyrrhinian

Monopoly®

Monopoly® properties:

06 Strand (red; £220)

07 Mayfair (dark blue; £400)

08 Pall Mall (pink; £140)
Park Lane (dark blue; £350)

09 Bow Street (orange; £180)
Whitehall (pink; £140)

10 Bond Street (green; £320)
Euston Road (light blue; £100)
Piccadilly (yellow; £280)
Vine Street (orange; £200)
Water Works (£150)

11 Fleet Street (red; £220)
Old Kent Road (brown; £60)
Whitechapel (brown; £60)

12 Oxford Street (green; £300)
Regent Street (green; £300)

14 Coventry Street (yellow; £260)

15 Electric Company (£150)
Leicester Square (yellow; £260)
Pentonville Road (light blue; £120)
Trafalgar Square (red; £240)

17 King's Cross Station (£200)
Marlborough Street (orange; £180)
Marylebone Station (£200)
The Angel Islington (light blue; £100)

20 Northumberland Avenue (pink; £160)

22 Fenchurch Street Station (£200)
Liverpool Street Station (£200)

Monopoly® terms include:

02 Go

03 buy
own
tax

04 bank
boot
cash
deal
debt
dice
fine
iron
jail
loan
rent
sell
ship

turn

05 asset
board
bonus
hotel
house
money
price
rules
token

06 banker
bidder
borrow
Chance
pewter
salary
top hat

07 auction
circuit
doubles
low-rent
race car
repairs
rewards

08 bankrupt
birthday
high-rent
interest
mortgage
opponent
property
Super Tax
windfall

09 Income Tax

mortgaged
penalties
play money
racing car
tax return
throw dice
title deed
utilities

10 de-mortgage
raise money
Scottie dog

11 Advance to Go
collect rent
colour group
Free Parking

12 'Just Visiting'

14 Community Chest

monster

Monster types include:

03 orc
roc

04 cete
ogre

05 gulon
harpy
lamia
phoca
yowie
zombi

06 ajatar

bunyip
gorgon
kraken
nicker
ogress
sphinx
wyvern
zombie

07 cyclops
Grendel
griffin

griffon
gryphon
prodigy
satyral
taniwha
wendigo
windigo
ziffius

08 basilisk
behemoth
bogeyman

dinosaur
lindworm
mooncalf
mushussu
seahorse

09 leviathan
manticore
marakihau
rosmarine
sea satyre
wasserman

whirlpool	cockatrice	sea monster	hippocampus
10 Black Annis	crio-sphinx	sea serpent	
chupacabra	salamander	**11** amphisbaena	

Monsters include:

03 orc (*The Lord of the Rings*, 1954–55, J R R Tolkien)

04 uruk (*The Lord of the Rings*, 1954–55, J R R Tolkien)

05 Alien (*Alien*, 1979, et seq)
Beast ('Beauty and the Beast' fairy tale)
Hydra (Greek mythology)
Smaug (*The Lord of the Rings*, 1954–55, J R R Tolkien)
snark (*The Hunting of the Snark*, 1876, Lewis Carroll)

06 Balrog (*The Lord of the Rings*, 1954–55, J R R Tolkien)
Duessa (*The Faerie Queene*, 1590–96, Sir Edmund Spenser)
Empusa (Greek mythology)
Fafnir (Norse mythology)
Geryon (Greek mythology)
Medusa (Greek mythology)
Nazgul (*The Lord of the Rings*, 1954–55, J R R Tolkien)
Python (Greek mythology)
Scylla (Greek mythology)
Shelob (*The Lord of the Rings*, 1954–55, J R R Tolkien)
Sphinx (Greek mythology)
Stheno (Greek mythology)
Typhon (Greek mythology)

07 Bathies (*The Kraken Wakes*, 1953, John Wyndham)
Caliban (*The Tempest*, 1611, William Shakespeare)
Cecrops (Greek mythology)
Chimera (Greek mythology)
Cyclops (Greek mythology)
Dracula (*Dracula*, 1897, Bram Stoker)

Echidna (Greek mythology)
Euryale (Greek mythology)
Grendel (*Beowulf*, 7c/8c, anon)
triffid (*The Day of the Triffids*, 1951, John Wyndham)

08 Cerberus (Greek mythology)
Chimaera (Greek mythology)
Godzilla (*Gojira*, 1954)
King Kong (*King Kong*, 1933/2005)
Minotaur (Greek mythology)
the Beast ('Beauty and the Beast' fairy tale)
Typhoeus (Greek mythology)

09 Charybdis (Greek mythology)

10 jabberwock (*Through the Looking-Glass*, 1872, Lewis Carroll)
Jormangund (Norse mythology)
jubjub bird (*Through the Looking-Glass*, 1872, Lewis Carroll)
Polyphemus (Greek mythology)

12 bandersnatch (*Through the Looking-Glass*, 1872, Lewis Carroll)
Blatant Beast (*The Faerie Queene*, 1590–96, Sir Edmund Spenser)
Count Dracula (*Dracula*, 1897, Bram Stoker)

13 Cookie Monster (*Sesame Street*, TV show)
Hecatonchires (Greek mythology)
Questing Beast (*Le Morte d'Arthur*, c.1469/70, Sir Thomas Malory)

14 Incredible Hulk (*The Incredible Hulk*, TV show)
Midgard serpent (Norse mythology)

15 Glatysaunt Beast (*Le Morte d'Arthur*, c.1469/70, Sir Thomas Malory)
Loch Ness monster (legend)

See also **mythology**

Montenegro *see* Balkans

month

Months:

03 May	**05** April	**07** January	February
04 July	March	October	November
June	**06** August	**08** December	**09** September

French month names with English translation:

03 mai (May)
04 août (August)
juin (June)
mars (March)

05 avril (April)
07 février (February)
janvier (January)
juillet (July)

octobre (October)
08 décembre (December)
novembre (November)
09 septembre (September)

German month names with English translation:

03 Mai (May)
04 Juli (July)
Juni (June)
März (March)

05 April (April)
06 August (August)
Januar (January)
07 Februar (February)

Oktober (October)
08 Dezember (December)
November (November)
09 September (September)

Italian month names with English translation:

05 marzo (March)
06 agosto (August)
aprile (April)
giugno (June)

luglio (July)
maggio (May)
07 gennaio (January)
ottobre (October)

08 dicembre (December)
febbraio (February)
novembre (November)
09 settembre (September)

Latin month names with English translation:

05 Maius (May)
06 Julius (July)
Junius (June)
07 Aprilis (April)
Martius (March)

October (October)
08 Augustus (August)
December (December)
November (November)
Sextilis (August)

09 Januarius (January)
Quintilis (July)
September (September)
10 Februarius (February)

Spanish month names with English translation:

04 mayo (May)
05 abril (April)
enero (January)
julio (July)

junio (June)
marzo (March)
06 agosto (August)
07 febrero (February)

octubre (October)
09 diciembre (December)
noviembre (November)
10 septiembre (September)

French Revolutionary calendar month names with English translation:

06 Nivôse (snow)
07 Floréal (blossom)
Ventôse (wind)
08 Brumaire (mist)

Frimaire (frost)
Germinal (seed)
Messidor (harvest)
Pluviôse (rain)

Prairial (meadow)
09 Fructidor (fruits)
Thermidor (heat)
11 Vendémiaire (vintage)

See also **calendar**

monument

Monuments and memorials include:

04 Eros (England)
Homo (The Netherlands)
05 Grant (USA)
Scott (Scotland)
06 Albert (England)
07 Lincoln (USA)
Martyr's (Iraq)

08 Boadicea (England)
Cenotaph (England)
Taj Mahal (India)
Victoria (England)
09 Charminar (India)
Menin Gate (Belgium)
10 Broken Ring (Russia)

Marble Arch (England)
Mt Rushmore (USA)
Navigators' (Portugal)
Washington (USA)
11 Civil Rights (USA)
Voortrekker (South Africa)
12 Great Pyramid (Egypt)

Statue of Zeus (Greece)
13 Admiralty Arch (England)
Arc de Triomphe (France)
Nelson's Column (England)
People's Heroes (China)

See also **cemetery**

Trajan's Column (Italy)
14 Eleanor Crosses (England)
Gateway of India (India)
Hands of Victory (Iraq)
Hiroshima Peace (Japan)

Lenin Mausoleum (Russia)
Wright Brothers (USA)
15 Brandenburg Gate
(Germany)

moon

Lunar seas:

08 Bay of Dew (Sinus Roris)
09 Moscow Sea (Mare Moscoviense)
Sea of Cold (Mare Frigoris)
Smyth's Sea (Mare Smythii)
10 Bay of Heats (Sinus Aestuum)
Central Bay (Sinus Medii)
Eastern Sea (Mare Orientale)
Foaming Sea (Mare Spumans)
Mare Nubium (Sea of Clouds)
Sea of Waves (Mare Undarum)
Sinus Medii (Central Bay)
Sinus Roris (Bay of Dew)
11 Lacus Mortis (Lake of Death)
Lake of Death (Lacus Mortis)
Mare Crisium (Sea of Crises)
Mare Humorum (Sea of Moisture)
Mare Imbrium (Sea of Showers)
Mare Ingenii (Sea of Geniuses)
Mare Smythii (Smyth's Sea)
Mare Spumans (Foaming Sea)
Mare Undarum (Sea of Waves)
Mare Vaporum (Sea of Vapours)
Marginal Sea (Mare Marginis)
Palus Somnii (Marsh of Sleep)
Sea of Clouds (Mare Nubium)
Sea of Crises (Mare Crisium)
Sea of Nectar (Mare Nectaris)
Sinus Iridum (Bay of Rainbows)
Southern Sea (Mare Australe)
12 Humboldt's Sea (Mare Humboldtianum)
Lake of Dreams (Lacus Somniorum)

Mare Australe (Southern Sea)
Mare Frigoris (Sea of Cold)
Mare Marginis (Marginal Sea)
Mare Nectaris (Sea of Nectar)
Marsh of Decay (Palus Putredinis)
Marsh of Mists (Palus Nebularum)
Marsh of Sleep (Palus Somnii)
Sea of Showers (Mare Imbrium)
Sea of Vapours (Mare Vaporum)
Sinus Aestuum (Bay of Heats)
13 Bay of Rainbows (Sinus Iridum)
Mare Orientale (Eastern Sea)
Ocean of Storms (Oceanus Procellarum)
Sea of Geniuses (Mare Ingenii)
Sea of Moisture (Mare Humorum)
Sea of Serenity (Mare Serenitatis)
14 Lacus Somniorum (Lake of Dreams)
Palus Nebularum (Marsh of Mists)
Sea of Fertility (Mare Fecunditatis)
15 Mare Moscoviense (Moscow Sea)
Mare Serenitatis (Sea of Serenity)
Palus Putredinis (Marsh of Decay)
16 Mare Fecunditatis (Sea of Fertility)
Marsh of Epidemics (Palus Epidemiarum)
Palus Epidemiarum (Marsh of Epidemics)
17 Mare Humboldtianum (Humboldt's Sea)
Sea of Tranquillity (Mare Tranquillitatis)
18 Oceanus Procellarum (Ocean of Storms)
19 Mare Tranquillitatis (Sea of Tranquillity)

Moons include:

02 Io (Jupiter)
04 Moon (Earth)
Rhea (Saturn)
05 Ariel (Uranus)
Dione (Saturn)
Mimas (Saturn)
Titan (Saturn)
06 Charon (Pluto)

Deimos (Mars)
Europa (Jupiter)
Nereid (Neptune)
Oberon (Uranus)
Phobos (Mars)
Tethys (Saturn)
Triton (Neptune)
07 Iapetus (Saturn)
Miranda (Uranus)

Proteus (Neptune)
Titania (Uranus)
Umbriel (Uranus)
08 Callisto (Jupiter)
Cruithne (Earth)
Ganymede (Jupiter)
Hyperion (Saturn)
09 Enceladus (Saturn)

Terms to do with the moon include:

05 lunar	new moon	near side	hunter's moon
phase	**08** blue moon	**09** blood moon	last quarter
06 waning	crescent	moonlight	quarter moon
waxing	dark side	moonscape	**12** first quarter
	full moon	moonshine	man in the moon
07 far side	half-moon		synodic month
gibbous	lunation	**11** harvest moon	third quarter

Morrison, Toni (1931–)

Significant works include:

04 *Jazz* (1992)	**07** *Beloved* (1987)	**12** *The Bluest Eye* (1970)
Love (2003)	*Tar Baby* (1981)	**13** *Song of Solomon* (1977)
Sula (1973)	**08** *Paradise* (1998)	

Significant characters include:

01 L	Gigi	Peace (Sula)	Wright (Nel)
03 Son	Heed	Sethe	**07** Beloved
04 Dead (Macon	Sosa (Consolata)	Trace (Joe)	Manfred (Dorcas)
'Jake')	**05** Bains (Guitar)	Trace (Violet)	**08** Albright (Mavis)
Dead (Macon	Belle (True)	**06** Childs (Jadine)	Truelove (Pallas)
'Milkman')	Cosey (Bill)	Connie	**09** Breedlove (Pecola)
Dead (Pilate)	Grace	Junior	Consolata
Dear (Rose)	Hagar	Seneca	

moss

Mosses include:

03 bog	long	**06** hypnum	staghorn
bur	peat	**07** acrogen	**09** wolf's claw
cup	tree	foggage	wolf's foot
fog		lycopod	**10** fontinalis
04 burr	**05** fairy	**08** sphagnum	ground pine
club	usnea		

moth

Moths include:

01 Y	tiger	winter	peppered
02 Io	**06** bogong	**07** buff-tip	silkworm
03 pug	bugong	clothes	**10** death's-head
wax	burnet	emerald	**11** garden tiger
04 goat	carpet	emperor	pale tussock
hawk	kitten	hook-tip	swallowtail
luna	lackey	silver-Y	**12** Kentish glory
puss	lappet	six-spot	peach blossom
05 ghost	magpie	tussock	red underwing
gypsy	sphinx	**08** cinnabar	**13** processionary
	turnip		

See also **butterfly**

mother

Mothers include:

04 Joad (Ma; *The Grapes of Wrath*, 1939, John Steinbeck)
Mary (Bible)
Page (Mistress Margaret/Meg; *The Merry Wives of Windsor*, 1597–98, William Shakespeare)

05 Morel (Mrs; *Sons and Lovers*, 1913, D H Lawrence)
Niobe (Greek mythology)

06 Thaisa (*Pericles*, 1607, William Shakespeare)

07 Capulet (Lady; *Romeo and Juliet*, 1595, William Shakespeare)
Courage (Mother; *Mother Courage and her Children*, 1941, Bertolt Brecht)

Hubbard (nursery rhyme)

08 Gertrude (*Hamlet*, 1600–01, William Shakespeare)
Hermione (*The Winter's Tale*, 1609, William Shakespeare)

09 Agrippina (the Elder; c.14 BC–33 AD, Roman)
Elizabeth (Bible)
Pankhurst (Emmeline; 1857–1928, English)

10 Virgin Mary (Bible)

11 Queen Mother (1900–2002)
Worthington (Mrs; *Mrs Worthington*, 1935, Noël Coward)

15 Whistler's Mother (painting)

motor racing, motorcyclist *see* racing: motor racing

motoring

Motor vehicle parts include:

03 ABS

04 axle
boot
door
gear
hood
horn
jack
sill
tyre
vent
wing

05 bezel
brake
clock
grill
shaft
trunk
wheel

06 airbag
bonnet
bumper
clutch
dimmer
engine
fender
heater
hub-cap
towbar

07 ashtray
battery
chassis
fog lamp
gas tank
gearbox
kingpin
spoiler
sunroof

08 air brake
air inlet
bodywork
brake pad
car phone
car radio
door-lock
fog light
headrest
ignition
jump lead
lift gate
oil gauge
roof rack
seat belt
silencer
solenoid
sun visor
track rod

09 bench seat
brake drum

brake shoe
crankcase
dashboard
disc brake
drum brake
filler cap
fuel gauge
gear-lever
gearshift
gear-stick
handbrake
headlight
indicator
monocoque
overrider
prop shaft
rear light
reflector
sidelight
spare tyre
stoplight
wheel arch

10 brake light
drive shaft
petrol tank
power brake
rev counter
side mirror
stick shift
suspension

windscreen
windshield
wing mirror

11 accelerator
anti-roll bar
backup light
exhaust pipe
folding seat
ignition key
number plate
parcel shelf
speedometer

12 license plate
parking-light
quarterlight
transmission

13 centre console
courtesy light
cruise control
flasher switch
pneumatic tyre
rack and pinion
radial-ply tyre
reclining seat
shock absorber
side-impact bar
steering-wheel

14 air-conditioner
central locking

electric window hydraulic brake steering-column child-safety seat
emergency light rear-view mirror **15** antiglare switch instrument panel
four-wheel drive reversing light antitheft device windscreen-wiper

Motor manufacturers include:

02 MG (UK)

03 BMW (Germany)
Kia (South Korea)

04 Audi (Germany)
Fiat (Italy)
Ford (USA)
Jeep (USA)
Lada (Russia)
Mini (UK)
Saab (Sweden)
Seat (Spain)
Yugo (Yugoslavia)

05 Buick (USA)
Dodge (USA)
Honda (Japan)
Isuzu (Japan)
Lexus (Japan)
Lotus (UK)
Mazda (Japan)
Riley (UK)
Rover (UK)
Skoda (Czech Republic)
Smart (USA)

Volvo (Sweden)

06 Austin (UK)
Daewoo (South Korea)
Datsun (Japan)
Jaguar (UK)
Lancia (Italy)
Morgan (UK)
Morris (UK)
Nissan (Japan)
Proton (Malaysia)
Subaru (Japan)
Talbot (France)
Toyota (Japan)

07 Bentley (UK)
Bugatti (Italy)
Citroen (France)
Daimler (Germany)
Ferrari (Italy)
Hillman (UK)
Hyundai (South Korea)
Peugeot (France)
Pontiac (US)
Porsche (Germany)
Reliant (UK)

Renault (France)
Trabant (East Germany)
Triumph (UK)

08 Cadillac (USA)
Chrysler (USA)
Daihatsu (Japan)
De Lorean (US)
Maserati (Italy)
Mercedes (Germany)
Standard (UK)
Vauxhall (UK)
Wolseley (UK)

09 Alfa Romeo (Italy)
Chevrolet (USA)
Land Rover (UK)

10 Mitsubishi (Japan)
Oldsmobile (US)
Rolls Royce (UK)
Vanden Plas (UK)
Volkswagen (Germany)

11 Aston Martin (UK)
Lamborghini (Italy)

12 Mercedes-Benz (Germany)

Motor car types include:

03 cab
MPV
SUV

04 auto
jeep
limo
Mini®
taxi

05 buggy
coupé
sedan

06 banger
Beetle®
estate
hearse
hybrid
jalopy
kit-car
saloon

07 minivan

08 fastback
panda car
roadster

runabout
Smart car®
stock car

09 all-roader
automatic
bubble-car
cabriolet
hatchback
Land Rover®
limousine
off-roader
patrol car

sports car

10 Model T Ford®
Range Rover®
Sinclair C5
veteran car
vintage car

11 convertible

12 station wagon

13 people carrier
shooting brake

14 four-wheel drive

Motor cars include:

04 FAB1 (*Thunderbirds, TV series*)

06 Herbie (*The Love Bug*, 1969)

08 Blue Bird (Malcolm Campbell/land speed record)
De Lorean (*Back to the Future*, 1985, et seq)

09 Batmobile (*Batman* comic)
Christine (*Christine*, 1983, Stephen King)
Genevieve (*Genevieve*, 1953)

11 Flintmobile (*The Flintstones*, TV series)

Road signs include:

04 ford
stop
06 cattle
one-way
07 give way
08 clearway
keep left
no U-turns
red route
turn left
09 ahead only
keep right
no waiting
risk of ice
road works

side winds
T-junction
trams only
turn right
10 bend to left
crossroads
double bend
hump bridge
no left turn
roundabout
speed limit
11 no right turn
tunnel ahead
12 falling rocks
no overtaking

passing place
slippery road
13 end of clearway
end of motorway
level crossing
no through road
one-way traffic
14 mini-roundabout
road works ahead
stop and give way
traffic signals
turn right ahead
15 no motor vehicles
single-track road
start of motorway

Motoring terms include:

02 AA
03 ABS
dip
GPS
LRP
map
MOT
RAC
tow
04 exit
park
skid
SORN
stop
05 amber
brake
crash
cut up
flash
layby
on tow
prang
shunt
06 diesel
fill up
filter
garage
hold-up
L-plate
octane
petrol
pile-up
pull in
07 blowout
bollard
bus lane

car park
car wash
cat's-eye
give way
logbook
MOT test
neutral
pull out
reverse
road map
snarl-up
tax disc
traffic
08 accident
change up
coasting
declutch
fast lane
flat tyre
gridlock
indicate
junction
main beam
overtake
puncture
red light
road rage
services
slip road
slow lane
speeding
tailback
taxi rank
turn left
unleaded
09 blind spot
breakdown

collision
cycle lane
fifth gear
first gear
green card
hit-and-run
radar trap
road atlas
road studs
roadworks
sixth gear
third gear
T junction
turn right
wheelspin
white line
10 accelerate
amber light
arm signals
bottleneck
change down
change gear
change lane
contraflow
crossroads
fourth gear
green light
inside lane
middle lane
pedestrian
petrol pump
roundabout
second gear
speed limit
stay in lane
straight on
tailgating

traffic jam
yellow line

11 box junction
crawler lane
drink-driver
driving test
hand signals
highway code
outside lane
speed camera
traffic cone
traffic cops
traffic news
zigzag lines

12 drink-driving
hard shoulder
left-hand lane
motorway toll
one-way system
parking meter
passing place
road junction

See also **vehicle**

speeding fine
tyre pressure

13 Belisha beacon
drink and drive
driving lesson
driving school
flashing amber
handbrake turn
jump the lights
left-hand drive
level crossing
no-claims bonus
parking ticket
pay and display
penalty points
petrol station
power steering
right-hand lane
super unleaded
traffic lights
traffic police
zebra crossing

14 cadence braking
double declutch
driver's license
driving licence
four-wheel drive
mini-roundabout
MOT certificate
motorway pile-up
overtaking lane
poor visibility
puffin crossing
right-hand drive
service station
speeding ticket
unleaded petrol

15 pelican crossing
put your foot down
road fund licence
test certificate
traction control
warning triangle

mountain

Mountains, mountain ranges and hills include:

02 K2 (Kashmir-Jammu/China)

03 Apo (Philippines)
Dom (Switzerland)
Tai (China)

04 Alai (Kyrgyzstan)
Alps (Switzerland/France/Germany/Austria/
Liechtenstein/Italy/Slovenia/Croatia)
Blue (Australia)
Cook (New Zealand)
Etna (Italy)
Fuji (Japan)
Jura (France/Switzerland)
Meru (Hinduism/Buddhism)
Ossa (Australia)
Rila (Bulgaria)
Ural (Russia/Kazakhstan)

05 Altai (Russia/China/Mongolia)
Andes (Argentina/Chile/Bolivia/Peru/
Ecuador/Colombia/Venezuela)
Atlas (Morocco/Algeria/Tunisia)
Coast (Canada/USA/Mexico)
Downs (England)
Eiger (Switzerland)
Ghats (India)
Halti (Finland)
Huang (China)
Kamet (India)
Kékes (Hungary)

Kenya (Kenya)
Logan (Canada)
Matra (Hungary)
Ozark (USA)
Qogir (Kashmir-Jammu/China)
Rocky (Mexico/USA/Canada)
Sinai (Egypt)
Snowy (Australia)
Table (South Africa)
Tatra (Poland/Slovakia)

06 Ararat (Turkey)
Cho Oyu (China/Nepal)
Denali (USA)
Egmont (New Zealand)
Elbert (USA)
Elbrus (Russia)
Haltia (Finland)
Hoggar (Algeria)
Lhotse (China/Nepal)
Makalu (China/Nepal)
Mendip (England)
Mourne (Northern Ireland)
Musala (Bulgaria)
Pindus (Greece)
Taurus (Turkey)
Vosges (France)
Zagros (Iran)

07 Ahaggar (Algeria)
Belukha (Russia/Kazakhstan)

Beskids (Poland/Slovakia)
Cascade (Canada/USA)
Cheviot (England/Scotland)
Darling (Australia)
Everest (China/Nepal)
Fuji-san (Japan)
Hua Shan (China)
Manaslu (Nepal)
Nilgiri (India)
Olympus (Cyprus)
Rainier (USA)
Rhodope (Bulgaria/Greece)
Rockies (Mexico/USA/Canada)
Roraima (Brazil/Guyana/Venezuela)
Ruapehu (New Zealand)
Skiddaw (England)
Snowdon (Wales)
Stanley (Democratic Republic of the Congo/
    Uganda)
Tai Shan (China)
Troödos (Cyprus)

08 Ben Nevis (Scotland)
Cameroon (Cameroon)
Catskill (USA)
Caucasus (Russia/Georgia/Armenia/
    Azerbaijan/Turkey/Iran)
Cévennes (France)
Chiltern (England)
Damavand (Iran)
Five Holy (China)
Flinders (Australia)
Fujiyama (Japan)
Heng Shan (China)
Jungfrau (Switzerland)
Kinabalu (Malaysia)
Mauna Kea (USA)
Mauna Loa (USA)
McKinley (USA)
Musgrave (Australia)
Pennines (England)
Pyrenees (France/Spain/Andorra)
Rushmore (USA)
Song Shan (China)
St Helens (USA)
Stirling (Australia)
Taranaki (New Zealand)

09 Aconcagua (Argentina)
Allegheny (USA)
Altai Shan (Russia/China/Mongolia)
Annapurna (Nepal)
Apennines (Italy)
Blue Ridge (USA)
Broad Peak (Kashmir-Jammu)
Cotswolds (England)
Dolomites (Italy)
Grampians (Australia/Scotland)
Hamersley (Australia)

Helvellyn (England)
Himalayas (central Asia)
Hindu Kush (central Asia)
Inyangani (Zimbabwe)
Karakoram (Kashmir-Jammu)
Kosciusko (Australia)
Lenin Peak (Tajikistan/Kyrgyzstan)
Mackenzie (Canada)
Mont Blanc (France/Italy)
Muz Tag Ata (China)
Nanda Devi (India)
Rakaposhi (Kashmir-Jammu)
Tirichmir (Pakistan)
Tirol Alps (Germany/Austria)
Zugspitze (Germany)

10 Adirondack (USA)
Cader Idris (Wales)
Cairngorms (Scotland)
Cantabrian (Spain)
Carpathian (Slovakia/Poland/Ukraine/
    Romania)
Chimborazo (Ecuador)
Dhaulagiri (Nepal)
Gasherbrum (Kashmir-Jammu)
Gosainthan (China)
Great Smoky (USA)
MacDonnell (Australia)
Matterhorn (Switzerland)
Pobedy Peak (China/Kyrgyzstan)
Puncak Jaya (Indonesia)
Sagarmatha (China/Nepal)

11 Appalachian (Canada/USA)
Chomolungma (China/Nepal)
Drakensberg (South Africa)
Kilimanjaro (Tanzania)
Mongo-Ma-Loba (Cameroon)
Nanga Parbat (Kashmir-Jammu)
Pico Bolívar (Venezuela)
Scafell Pike (England)
Siula Grande (Peru)

12 Bavarian Alps (Germany/Austria)
Dufourspitze (Switzerland/Italy)
Kanchenjunga (India/Nepal)
Popocatepetl (Mexico)
Sierra Nevada (USA)
Southern Alps (New Zealand)
Tibet Plateau (China)
Ulugh Muztagh (China)
Vinson Massif (Antarctica)

13 Carrantuohill (Ireland)
Communism Peak (Tajikistan)
Great Dividing (Australia)
Haltiatunturi (Finland)
Kangchenjunga (India/Nepal)
Ojos del Salado (Argentina/Chile)

14 Australian Alps (Australia)

Bohemian Forest (Germany/Czech Republic)
Fichtelgebirge (Germany)
Qomolangma Feng (China/Nepal)
Thadentsonyane (Lesotho)

Trans-Antarctic (Antarctica)

15 Guiana Highlands (Venezuela/Brazil/
Guyana)
Nevado de Illampu (Bolivia)

Mountain passes include:

04 Ofen (Italy/Switzerland)

05 Haast (New Zealand)
Lewis (New Zealand)
South (USA)

06 Khyber (Pakistan/Afghanistan)
Lindis (New Zealand)
Shipka (Bulgaria)

07 Arthur's (New Zealand)
Brenner (Italy/Austria)
Oberalp (Switzerland)
Plöcken (Italy/Austria)
Simplon (Italy/Switzerland)

See also **pike**; **volcano**

Wrynose (England)

08 Hongshan (China)
Yangguan (China)

09 Khunjerab (China/Pakistan)
St Bernard (Italy/France/Switzerland)

10 St Gotthard (Switzerland)

12 Roncesvalles (Spain/France)

13 Cilician Gates (Turkey)
San Bernardino (Switzerland)

14 Grand St Bernard (Italy/Switzerland)

15 Little St Bernard (France/Italy)

mountaineering

Mountaineers include:

04 Hunt (John, Lord; 1910–98, English)

05 Brown (Joe; 1930– , English)
Bruce (C G; 1866–1939, English)
Meyer (Hans; 1858–1929, German)
Munro (Sir Hugh; 1856–1919, Scottish)
Scott (Doug; 1941– , English)
Tabei (Junko; 1939– , Japanese)
Wills (Sir Alfred; 1828–1912, English)

06 Haston (Dougal; 1940–77, Scottish)
Herzog (Maurice; 1919– , French)
Irvine (Andrew; 1902–24, English)
Smythe (Frank; 1900–49, English)
Tilman (Bill; 1898–1977, English)
Uemura (Naomi; 1942–84, Japanese)

07 Hillary (Sir Edmund; 1919–2008, New
Zealand)

Mallory (George; 1886–1924, English)
Messner (Reinhold; 1944– , Austrian)
Shipton (Eric; 1907–77, English)
Simpson (Myrtle; 1931– , Scottish)
Tazieff (Haroun; 1914–98, Polish/French)
Tenzing (Sherpa; 1914–86, Nepalese)
Whymper (Edward; 1840–1911, English)

08 Coolidge (W A B; 1850–1926, US/British)
MacInnes (Hamish; 1930– , Scottish)
Whillans (Don; 1933–85, English)

09 Bonington (Sir Chris; 1934– , English)

10 Eckenstein (Oscar; 1859–1921, English)
Freshfield (Douglas; 1845–1934, English)
Hargreaves (Alison; 1962–95, English)

12 Purtscheller (Ludwig; 1849–1900, Austrian)

13 Tenzing Norgay (1914–86, Nepalese)

Mountaineering and climbing terms include:

02 ax	rock	ridge	ice axe
03 adz	rope	scree	piolet
axe	spur	sérac	saddle
cam	**05** arête	shunt	Sherpa
col	belay	sling	summit
hut	chock	spike	top out
nut	cleft	stack	unrope
04 adze	gully	**06** ascent	**07** belayer
crag	Munro	corrie	bivouac
pick	pitch	étrier	bolting
	piton	helmet	chimney

cornice
crampon
descent
fissure
glacier
harness
ice step
tying in
wallnut

08 Alpinism
ascender
base camp
chalk bag
climbing
crevasse
hand hold
ice piton

ice ridge
ice screw
ice slope
overhang
rock face
rock wall
sea stack
traverse

09 abseiling
avalanche
carabiner
debolting
descender
hammer axe
karabiner
on the rope
rapelling

rock spike
rope sling
sling seat
trad route

10 bouldering
chalk cliff
chockstone
Dülfer seat
helmet lamp
non-belayer
prusik knot
prusik loop
sit harness
snow bridge
solo ascent
wrist sling

11 abseil piton

abseil sling
dynamic rope
ice climbing
ringed piton
snow cornice
snow gaiters
snow goggles

12 climbing wall
self-belaying
standing rope

13 abseil station
sport climbing

14 corkscrew piton
kernmantel rope

15 climbing harness
drive-in ice piton

mouth

Mouth parts include:

03 gum	**05** uvula	**08** lower lip	**11** cleft palate
jaw	**06** tongue	upper lip	**13** alveolar ridge
lip	tonsil	**10** hard palate	**15** isthmus of fauces
04 lips	**07** hare lip	soft palate	

See also **teeth**

movement see **art**; **poetry**

Mozart, Wolfgang Amadeus (1756–91)

Significant works include:

04 'Hunt' (String Quartet; 1784)
'Linz' (Symphony; 1783)

05 'Paris' (Symphony; 1778)

06 'Lutzow' (Concerto; 1776)
'Prague' (Symphony; 1786)

07 Don Juan (1787)
'Haffner' (Symphony; 1782)
'Jupiter' (Symphony; 1788)

08 Idomeneo (1781)

10 'Coronation' (Concerto; 1788)
'Jeunehomme' (Concerto; 1777)
Lucio Silla (1772)

11 Don Giovanni (1787)
'Great G minor' (Symphony; 1788)

12 Così fan tutte (1790)
Little G minor' (Symphony; 1773)
Scipio's Dream (1772)

13 Ascanio in Alba (1771)
Missa in C minor (1783)

The Impresario (1786)
The Magic Flute (1791)

14 Die Zauberflöte (1791)

15 La finta semplice (1769)
Le nozze di Figaro (1786)
Requiem in D minor (1791)

16 La Clemenza di Tito (1791)

17 Il dissoluto punito (1787)
Il sogno di Scipione (1772)

18 Apollo et Hyacinthus (1767)
La finta giardiniera (1775)
Mitridate, Rè di Ponto (1770)
The School for Lovers (1790)

19 Bastien und Bastienne (1768)
La Scuola degli Amanti (1790)
The Marriage of Figaro (1786)

20 Eine Kleine Nachtmusik (1787)
The Dissolute Punished (1787)
The Pretended Gardener (1775)

21 *Der Schauspieldirektor* (1786)
    The Pretended Simpleton (1769)
23 *Mithridates, King of Pontus* (1770)

25 *Die Entführung aus dem Serail* (1782)
27 *The Abduction from the Seraglio* (1782)

Significant characters include:

04 Tito
06 Apollo
    Figaro
    Pamina
    Rosina
    Tamino
07 Bastien
    Susanna
08 Almaviva

Belmonte
Ferrando
Papagena
Papageno
Sarastro
Scipione
09 Bastienne
    Cherubino
    Constanze

Dorabella
Guglielmo
10 Flordiligi
    Hyacinthus
    Monostatos
11 Don Giovanni
    Donna Elvira
15 Queen of the Night

murder

Murderers, alleged murderers and assassins include:

03 Ray (James Earl; 1928–98, US)

04 Aram (Eugene; 1704–59, English)
    Bell (Mary; 1957–   , English)
    Edny (Clithero; *Edgar Huntly*, 1799, Charles
      Brockden Brown)
    Gacy (John Wayne; 1942–94, US)
    Gein (Edward; 1906–84, US)
    Hare (William; 1790–1860, Irish)
    Kray (Reggie; 1933–2000, English)
    Kray (Ronnie; 1933–95, English)
    Retz (Gilles de Laval, Baron; 1404–40, French)
    Ruby (Jack; 1911–67, US)
    Todd (Sweeney; late 18c, English)
    West (Fred; 1942–95, English)
    West (Rosemary; 1953–   , English)

05 Beane (Sawney; fl.c.1600, Scottish)
    Booth (John Wilkes; 1839–65, US)
    Brady (Ian; 1938–   , Scottish)
    Bundy (Ted; 1946–89, US)
    Burke (William; 1792–1829, Irish)
    Craig (Christopher; c.1936–   , English)
    Ellis (Ruth; 1926–55, Welsh)
    Haigh (John; 1909–49, English)
    Havoc (Jack; *The Tiger in the Smoke*, 1952,
      Margery Allingham)
    Rudge (*Barnaby Rudge*, 1841, Charles
      Dickens)

06 Barrow (Clyde; 1909–34, US)
    Borden (Lizzie; 1860–1927, US)
    Corday (Charlotte; 1768–93, French)
    Dahmer (Jeffrey; 1960–94, US)
    Lecter (Dr Hannibal; *Red Dragon*, 1981, et
      seq, Thomas Harris)
    Manson (Charles; 1934–   , US)
    Misfit (the; *A Good Man is Hard to Find*,
      1948, Flannery O'Connor)

Nilsen (Dennis; 1945–   , Scottish)
Oswald (Lee Harvey; 1939–63, US)
Parker (Bonnie; 1911–34, US)
Sirhan (Sirhan; c.1943–   , Palestinian/US)

07 Bathori (Elizabeth; d.1614, Polish)
    Bentley (Derek; c.1933–1953, English)
    Bianchi (Kenneth; 1950–   , US)
    Chapman (Mark; c.1955–   , US)
    Crippen (Hawley Harvey; 1862–1910, US)
    DeSalvo (Albert; 1931–73, US)
    Hindley (Myra; 1942–2002, English)
    Macbeth (*Macbeth*, c.1606, William
      Shakespeare)
    Manston (Aeneas; *Desperate Remedies*,
      1871, Thomas Hardy)
    Neilson (Donald; 1936–   , English)
    Shipman (Harold; 1946–2004, English)

08 Barabbas (1c AD, Bible)
    Christie (John Reginald Halliday; 1898–
      1953, English)
    Claudius (*Hamlet*, 1601/2, William
      Shakespeare)
    Dominici (Gaston; 1877–1965, French)
    Hanratty (James; c.1936–1962, English)
    Son of Sam (David Berkowitz; c.1953–   , US)
    Thompson (Edith; d.1923, English)

09 Berkowitz (David; c.1953–   , US)
    Harmodius (d.514 BC, Athenian)
    McNaghten (Daniel; 19c, English)
    Sutcliffe (Peter; 1946–   , English)

10 McNaughten (Daniel; 19c, English)
    Nirdlinger (Phyllis; *Double Indemnity*, 1944,
      James M Cain)

11 Anckarström (Johan Jakob; 1762–92, Swedish)
    Quare Fellow (the; *The Quare Fellow*, 1954,
      Brendan Behan)

12 Starkweather (Charles; 1938–59, US)

13 Jack the Ripper (19c, unknown)

14 Moors Murderers (Ian Brady; 1938– ,

Scottish/Myra Hindley; 1942–2002, English)

15 Yorkshire Ripper (Peter Sutcliffe; 1946– ,
English)

Murdoch, Dame Iris (1919–99)

Significant works include:

07 *The Bell* (1958)

10 *A Word Child* (1975)

11 *Bruno's Dream* (1969)
Under the Net (1954)

12 *A Severed Head* (1961)
The Sea, The Sea (1978)

14 *The Black Prince* (1973)
The Green Knight (1993)

17 *The Good Apprentice* (1985)

The Red and the Green (1965)

18 *The Time of the Angels* (1966)

20 *The Philosopher's Pupil* (1983)
The Sovereignty of Good (1970)

21 *The Message to the Planet* (1989)

24 *The Book and the Brotherhood* (1987)

25 *Sartre: Romantic Rationalist* (1953)

27 *Metaphysics as a Guide to Morals* (1992)

Significant characters include:

03 Fox (Mischa)
Mor (William)

04 Duno (Stuart)
Finn (Peter O'Finney)
King (Julius)
Mead (Michael)

05 Blick (Calvin)
Burde (Hilary)
Gashe (Toby)
Keepe (Hunter)
Keepe (Rosa)
Klein (Honor)
Odell (Danby)
Sands (Emma)

06 Baffin (Arnold)
Browne (Morgan)
Browne (Tallis)
Carter (Rain)
Ducane (John)
Fawley (Catherine)
Fawley (Nick)
Forbes (Cato)

Foster (Hilda)
Foster (Rupert)
Foster (Simon)
Ludens (Alfred)
Saward (Peter)
Vallar (Marcus)
Watkin (Lisa)

07 Arrowby (Charles)
Baltram (Edward)
Baltram (Jesse)
Cavidge (Anne)
Crimond (David)
Fischer (Carel)
Fischer (Elizabeth)
Fischer (Marcus)
Fischer (Muriel)
Nilsson (Axel)
Pearson (Bradley)
Peshkov (Eugene)
Peshkov (Leo)
Rozanov (John Robert)

08 Cockeyne (Annette)

Donaghue (Jake James)
Openshaw (Gertrude)
Peronett (Hugh)
Tinckham (Mrs)

09 Lusiewicz (Jan)
Lusiewicz (Stefan)
McCaffrey (George)
O'Driscoll (Pattie)

10 Belfounder (Hugo)
Gibson Grey (Austin)
Greenfield (Dora)
Greenfield (Paul)
Marshalson (Henry)
Tayper Pace (James)

11 Greensleave (Bruno)
Greensleave (Diana)
Greensleave (Miles)
Lynch-Gibbon (Martin)
Magistretti (Maria 'Maggie')
Szczepanski (Wojciech
'Peter', the Count)

muscle

Muscles include:

05 psoas

06 biceps
rectus
soleus

07 cardiac
deltoid
gluteus
iliacus
omohyid

triceps

08 detrusor
masseter
platysma
pronator
risorius
scalenus
splenius

09 abdominal

complexus
eye-string
perforans
sartorius
stapedius
supinator
trapezius

10 buccinator
quadriceps

11 ciliary body
rhomboideus

13 gastrocnemius

14 xiphihumeralis

15 latissimus dorsi
pectoralis major
pectoralis minor
peroneal muscles

muse

The Nine Muses of Greek mythology:

04 Clio (history and lyre-playing)

05 Erato (lyric poetry and hymns)

06 Thalia (comedy and idyllic poetry)
Urania (astronomy)

07 Euterpe (flute-playing)

08 Calliope (epic poetry)

09 Melpomene (tragedy)

10 Polyhymnia (dance, mime and acting)

11 Terpsichore (dance and lyric poetry)

museum

Museums and galleries include:

02 RA (England)

03 ICA (England)

04 MoMA (USA)
Tate (England)

05 Prado (Spain)
Terme (Italy)
V and A (England)

06 Correr (Italy)
London (England)
Louvre (France)
The Met (USA)
Uffizi (Italy)

07 British (England)
Fogg Art (USA)
Hayward (England)
Hofburg (Austria)
Mankind (England)
Pushkin (Russia)
Russian (Russia)
Science (England)
Vatican (Vatican City)
Whitney (USA)

08 Bargello (Italy)
Borghese (Italy)
National (various)
Pergamon (Germany)

09 Accademia (Italy)
Albertina (Austria)
Arnolfini (England)
Ashmolean (England)
Belvedere (Austria)
Deutsches (Germany)
Hermitage (Russia)
Holocaust (various)
Modern Art (various)
Sans Souci (Germany)
Tretyakov (Russia)
Whitworth (England)

10 Guggenheim (various)
Jeu de Paume (France)
Pinakothek (Germany)
Pitt-Rivers (England)
Serpentine (England)
Tate Modern (England)

11 Fitzwilliam (England)
Imperial War (England)
Mauritshuis (The Netherlands)
Musée d'Orsay (France)
Pitti Palace (Italy)
Rijksmuseum (The Netherlands)
Smithsonian (USA)
Tate Britain (England)

12 Royal Academy (England)
The Cloisters (USA)

13 Jean Paul Getty (USA)
Peace Memorial (Japan)
Royal Pavilion (England)

14 Barbican Centre (England)
Natural History (England)
Pompidou Centre (France)
State Hermitage (Russia)

15 Centre Beaubourg (France)
Frick Collection (USA)

mushroom

Mushrooms and toadstools include:

03 cep

04 base
ugly
wood

05 brain
field

gypsy
horse
magic
march
morel
naked

06 blewit
button
edible
elf cup

ink cap
meadow
mower's
oyster
satan's
winter

07 amanita
blewits
blusher
boletus
Caesar's
griping
parasol
porcini
truffle

08 chestnut
death cap
deceiver
hedgehog
inedible
penny bun
shiitake
sickener

09 cramp ball
earth ball
fairy ring
fly agaric
poisonous
St George's
stinkhorn

10 champignon

See also **fungus**

cultivated
false morel
lawyer's wig
liberty cap
panther cap
sweetbread
wood agaric

11 chanterelle
clean mycena
common morel
dingy agaric
honey fungus
stout agaric
sulphur tuft
the goat's lip
velvet shank

12 common ink cap
dryad's saddle
false blusher
horn of plenty
larch boletus
lurid boletus
purple blewit
shaggy ink cap
slippery jack
white truffle
winter fungus
wood hedgehog

13 buckler agaric
clouded agaric
copper trumpet

devil's boletus
emetic russula
firwood agaric
Jew's ear fungus
purple boletus
satan's boletus
shaggy milk cap
shaggy parasol
summer truffle
trumpet agaric
woolly milk cap
yellow stainer

14 common grisette
common laccaria
common puffball
fairies' bonnets
man on horseback
penny-bun fungus
saffron milk cap
yellow-staining

15 beefsteak fungus
chestnut boletus
common earthball
common stinkhorn
destroying angel
garlic marosmius
périgord truffle
Piedmont truffle
stinking parasol
stinking russula
verdigris agaric

music

02 do (first)
fa (fourth)
la (sixth)
me (third)
mi (third)

re (second)
si (seventh)
so (fifth)
te (seventh)
ti (seventh)

ut (first)
03 doh (first)
fah (fourth)
lah (sixth)
ray (second)

soh (fifth)
sol (fifth)

Music types include:

03 AOR
MOR
pop
rap
ska

04 folk
funk
jazz
jive
mood
rock

soul
05 bebop
blues
cajun
dance
disco
house
indie
muzak
R and B
salsa

samba
swing
world
06 atonal
ballet
choral
doo-wop
fusion
garage
gospel
grunge

hip-hop
jungle
lounge
reggae
sacred
techno
trance

07 ambient
baroque
bhangra
Big Beat
calypso
chamber
country
gamelan
gangsta
jazz-pop
karaoke
nu-metal

ragtime
skiffle
trip-hop

08 acid jazz
ballroom
folk rock
glam rock
hardcore
hard rock
jazz-funk
jazz-rock
operatic
oratorio
punk rock
romantic
soft rock

09 acid house
bluegrass

classical
Dixieland
honky-tonk

10 electronic
heavy metal
incidental
orchestral
twelve-tone

11 country rock
drum and bass
rock and roll
thrash metal

12 boogie-woogie
instrumental

13 easy listening

14 rhythm and blues

15 middle-of-the-road

Music compositions include:

03 jig
lay
rag

04 aria
hymn
lied
mass
opus
raga
reel
song
tune

05 canon
carol
étude
fugue
gigue
march
motet
opera
piece
polka
rondo
round
suite
tango
track

waltz

06 anthem
aubade
ballad
bolero
chorus
lament
lieder
masque
minuet
number
pavane
shanty
sonata

07 ballade
bourrée
cantata
chorale
fanfare
gavotte
mazurka
partita
prelude
requiem
scherzo
toccata

08 berceuse
cavatina
chaconne
concerto
fandango
fantasia
galliard
hornpipe
madrigal
nocturne
operetta
overture
rhapsody
saraband
serenade
sonatina
symphony
zarzuela

09 allemande
arabesque
bagatelle
cabaletta
capriccio
écossaise
farandole
impromptu
invention

pastorale
polonaise
sarabande
spiritual
voluntary

10 barcarolle
bergamasca
concertino
humoresque
intermezzo
opera buffa
strathspey
tarantella

11 bacchanalia
ballad opera
composition
pastourelle
sinfonietta

12 divertimento
extravaganza
nursery rhyme

13 Missa solemnis

14 chorale fantasy
chorale prelude
concerto grosso

Pieces of music include:

04 *Saul* (Handel, 1739)

05 *Rodeo* (Copland, 1942)

06 *Boléro* (Ravel, 1928)
Elijah (Mendelssohn, 1846)
Façade (Walton, 1920–21)

Images (Debussy, 1905–12)

07 *Epitaph* (Mingus, 1989)
Jephtha (Handel, 1751)
Mazeppa (Liszt, 1851)

08 *Creation* (Haydn, 1796–98)

Drum Mass (Haydn, 1796)
'Ode to Joy' (Beethoven, 1822–24)
Peer Gynt (Grieg, 1876)
09 Finlandia (Sibelius, 1899)
'Jerusalem' (Elgar, 1922)
10 'Nelson Mass' (Haydn, 1798)
Prozession (Stockhausen, 1967)
The Messiah (Handel, 1742)
The Planets (Holst, 1914–16)
The Seasons (Haydn, 1799–1801)
Water Music (Handel, c.1717)
11 Curlew River (Britten, 1964)
Gymnopédies (Satie, 1888)
'Minute Waltz' (Chopin, 1846–47)
Stabat Mater (unknown)
The Creation (Haydn, 1796–98)
Winterreise (Schubert, 1827)
12 A Sea Symphony (Vaughan Williams, 1910)
Danse Macabre (Saint-Saëns, 1874)
'Golden Sonata' (Purcell, 1697)
Karelia Suite (Sibelius, 1893)
Kinderscenen (Schumann, 1838)
'Linz Symphony' (Mozart, 1783)
Scheherazade (Rimsky-Korsakov, 1888)
'Trout Quintet' (Schubert, 1819)
13 Alpensinfonie (Richard Strauss, 1911–15)
Carmina Burana (Orff, 1937)

Ebony Concerto (Stravinsky, 1946)
'Faust Symphony' (Liszt, 1854–57)
Fêtes Galantes (Debussy, 1891–1904)
German Requiem (Brahms, 1857–68)
Israel in Egypt (Handel, 1739)
Metamorphosen (Richard Strauss, 1945)
On Wenlock Edge (Vaughan Williams, 1909)
The Art of Fugue (Bach, 1740s)
14 Canticum Sacrum (Stravinsky, 1956)
'Choral Symphony' (Beethoven, 1823–24)
Colour Symphony (Bliss, 1932)
'Eroica Symphony' (Beethoven, 1803–04)
Glagolitic Mass (Janácek, 1926)
'Prague Symphony' (Mozart, 1786)
Rhapsody in Blue (Gershwin, 1924)
Slavonic Dances (Dvořák, 1878–86)
The Four Seasons (Vivaldi, 1725)
15 A Child of our Time (Tippett, 1941)
Alexander's Feast (Handel, 1736)
Children's Corner (Debussy, 1908)
'Emperor Concerto' (Beethoven, 1809)
'Haffner Symphony' (Mozart, 1782)
Italian Concerto (Bach, 1735)
Judas Maccabaeus (Handel, 1747)
'Jupiter Symphony' (Mozart, 1788)
Manfred Symphony (Tchaikovsky, 1885)
Peter and the Wolf (Prokofiev, 1936)
Sicilian Vespers (Verdi, 1855)

Musical instruments include:

03	sax	flute	guitar
04	bass	gusla	rattle
	bell	gusle	spinet
	drum	gusli	tabour
	erhu	hi-hat	tom-tom
	fife	kazoo	violin
	gong	mbira	zither
	harp	organ	07 alphorn
	horn	piano	bagpipe
	kora	pipes	baryton
	koto	rebec	bassoon
	lute	shalm	bodhran
	lyre	shawm	buccina
	Moog®	sitar	celeste
	oboe	tabla	cembalo
	pipe	tabor	cithara
	tuba	vibes	cithern
	viol	viola	cittern
	zeze	zanze	clarion
05	Amati	zirna	clavier
	banjo	zurna	cowbell
	bells	06 cither	hautboy
	bongo	cornet	lyricon
	bugle	cymbal	maracas
	cello	Fender	marimba
	chime	fiddle	ocarina

pandora
Pianola®
piccolo
sackbut
sambuca
saxhorn
serpent
sistrum
tambura
theorbo
timpani
trumpet
ukulele
vihuela
whistle

08 angklung
bagpipes
barytone
bass drum
bouzouki
Calliope
carillon
cimbalom
clappers
clarinet
clarsach
cornpipe
crumhorn
dulcimer
handbell
hornpipe
humstrum
jew's harp
keyboard
mandolin
manzello
melodeon
Pan-pipes
polyphon
recorder
side-drum

spinette
Steinway
theramin
theremin
timbales
triangle
trombone
virginal
vocalion
zambomba

09 accordion
alpenhorn
balalaika
banjolele
bugle-horn
castanets
chime bars
decachord
euphonium
flageolet
harmonica
harmonium
Mellotron®
polyphone
saxophone
snare-drum
tenor-drum
wood block
Wurlitzer®
xylophone

10 bass guitar
bird-scarer
bongo-drums
bullroarer
clavichord
concertina
cor anglais
didgeridoo
double bass
eolian harp
flugelhorn

French horn
grand piano
hurdy-gurdy
kettle-drum
mouth organ
oboe d'amore
pentachord
pianoforte
sousaphone
squeeze-box
tambourine
thumb piano
tin whistle
vibraphone

11 aeolian harp
barrel organ
harpsichord
phonofiddle
player-piano
sleigh bells
synthesizer
violoncello

12 glockenspiel
harmonichord
penny whistle
stock and horn
Stradivarius
tubular bells
viola da gamba

13 contra-bassoon
Ondes Martenot
panharmonicon
slide trombone
Swanee whistle

14 acoustic guitar
electric guitar
jingling Johnny

15 Moog synthesizer®
wind synthesizer

Musical instrument parts include:

03 bag
bow
key
lug
rib

04 bell
butt
capo
foot
fret
frog
jack
mute

neck
pipe
reed
rose
skin
stop

05 belly
brace
crook
crown
drone
pedal
snare

spike
waist

06 beater
bridge
damper
end-pin
hammer
keybed
key rod
pegbox
pick-up
pillar
scroll

string
tom-tom

07 cup mute
peg hole
tail-pin

08 bass drum
blow hole
chin rest
drumhead
floor tom
hitch pin
keylever
ligature
lip plate
pedestal
pin block
plectrum
purfling
shoulder
tonehole
truss rod
water key

09 bass joint
bell joint
body joint
finger key
fretboard
head joint

headstock
pedal stop
resonator
scroll eye
snare drum
soft pedal
sound-hole
swell stop
tailpiece
tenor drum
tenor mute
thumb hook
toe piston
tuning peg
tuning pin

10 bass bridge
double reed
finger hole
finger ring
hammer rail
long bridge
mouthpiece
pedal board
ride cymbal
slide brace
soundboard
swell pedal
tenor joint
tension rod

touchpiece
tremolo bar
upper joint
valve slide
vibrato arm
wrest plank

11 choir manual
crash cymbal
damper pedal
fingerboard
great manual
hi-hat cymbal
keyboard lid
machine head
middle joint
piston valve
pressure bar
swell manual
tuning slide

12 scratchplate
treble bridge

13 right-hand rest
una corda pedal

14 lower octave key
sostenuto pedal
upper octave key

15 sustaining pedal

Terms used in music include:

03 bar
bis
cue
key
tie

04 a due
alto
arco
bass
beat
clef
coda
fine
flat
fret
hold
mode
mute
note
part
rest
root
slur
solo
tone
tune

turn

05 ad lib
breve
buffo
chord
dolce
drone
forte
grave
largo
lento
lyric
major
metre
minim
minor
molto
pause
piano
piece
pitch
scale
score
senza
shake
sharp

staff
stave
swell
tacet
tanto
tempo
tenor
theme
triad
trill
tutti

06 adagio
al fine
a tempo
da capo
duplet
encore
finale
legato
manual
medley
melody
octave
phrase
presto
quaver

rhythm
sempre
subito
tenuto
timbre
treble
tuning
unison
upbeat
vivace

07 agitato
allegro
al segno
amoroso
andante
animato
attacca
bar line
cadence
con brio
concert
con moto
descant
harmony
langsam
marcato
mediant
middle C
mordent
natural
recital
refrain
soprano
tremolo
triplet
vibrato

08 acoustic
alto clef
arpeggio
baritone
bass clef
col canto
con fuoco
crotchet
diatonic
doloroso
dominant
downbeat
ensemble
interval
maestoso
moderato
movement

ostinato
perdendo
ritenuto
semitone
semplice
sequence
staccato
vigoroso
virtuoso

09 alla breve
altissimo
cantabile
cantilena
chromatic
contralto
crescendo
glissando
harmonics
imitation
larghetto
mezza voce
microtone
non troppo
obbligato
orchestra
pizzicato
semibreve
sextuplet
sforzando
smorzando
sostenuto
sotto voce
spiritoso
tablature
tenor clef

10 accidental
affettuoso
allargando
allegretto
consonance
diminuendo
dissonance
dotted note
dotted rest
double flat
expression
fortissimo
intonation
ledger line
mezzo forte
modulation
pedal point
pentatonic

pianissimo
quadruplet
quintuplet
resolution
semiquaver
simple time
submediant
supertonic
tonic sol-fa
treble clef
two-two time

11 accelerando
arrangement
capriccioso
decrescendo
double sharp
double trill
fingerboard
leading note
quarter tone
rallentando
rinforzando
subdominant
syncopation

12 acciaccatura
alla cappella
appoggiatura
compound time
counterpoint
four-four time
key signature
six-eight time

13 accompaniment
double bar line
fifth interval
improvisation
major interval
minor interval
orchestration
sixth interval
sul ponticello
third interval
three-four time
time signature
transposition

14 cross-fingering
demisemiquaver
fourth interval
second interval

15 perfect interval
seventh interval

See also **Bach, Johann Sebastian; Bartók, Béla; Beethoven, Ludwig van; Brahms, Johannes; Britten, Benjamin; composer; conductor; country and western; Debussy, Claude; Dvořák, Antonín; Elgar, Sir Edward; folk; Gilbert, Sir W S and Sullivan, Sir Arthur; Handel, George Frideric; Haydn, Joseph; jazz; key; Mahler, Gustav;**

Mozart, Wolfgang Amadeus; opera; organ stop; overture; pop; Prokofiev, Sergei; Puccini, Giacomo; Purcell, Henry; Ravel, Maurice; Rossini, Gioacchino; Schoenberg, Arnold; Schubert, Franz; Schumann, Robert; Shostakovich, Dmitri; song; Strauss, Richard; Stravinsky, Igor; Tchaikovsky, Pyotr Ilyich; Verdi, Giuseppe; Wagner, Richard

musical

Musicals include:

04 Cats
Fame
Gigi
Hair
Rent
05 Annie
Blitz
Chess
Evita
Queen
Zorba
06 Grease
Joseph
Kismet
Oliver!
The Wiz
Wicked
07 Avenue Q
Cabaret
Camelot
Chicago
Company
Follies
08 Carnival
Carousel
Fiorello!
Godspell
Mamma Mia!
Oklahoma!
Peter Pan

Show Boat
09 Brigadoon
Funny Girl
Girl Crazy
Hairspray
On the Town
10 42nd Street
Hello Dolly!
Jersey Boys
Kiss Me Kate
Miss Saigon
My Fair Lady
11 A Chorus Line
Babes in Arms
Bitter Sweet
Carmen Jones
Mary Poppins
Me and My Girl
Sweeney Todd
The King and I
The Lion King
The Music Man
12 Anything Goes
Bombay Dreams
Bye Bye Birdie
Calamity Jane
Guys and Dolls
Martin Guerre
South Pacific
The Boy Friend

13 Aspects of Love
Blood Brothers
Les Misérables
Man of La Mancha
The Pajama Game
West Side Story
14 Babes in Toyland
Victor/Victoria
15 Annie Get Your Gun
La Cage aux Folles
Mister Wonderful
Singin' in the Rain
Sunset Boulevard
The Sound of Music
The Woman in White
16 Fiddler on the Roof
Starlight Express
18 Saturday Night Fever
Whistle Down the Wind
19 Little Shop of Horrors
20 Jesus Christ Superstar
The Phantom of the Opera
21 Jerry Springer: The Opera
27 Seven Brides for Seven Brothers
39 Joseph and the Amazing Technicolor Dreamcoat

Songs from musicals include:

03 'One' (A Chorus Line)
04 'Fame' (Fame)
'Kids' (Bye Bye Birdie)
05 'Heart' (Damn Yankees)
'Hoops' (The Band Wagon)
'Maria' (Sound of Music)
'Maybe' (Annie)
06 'Anthem' (Chess)
'Do-Re-Mi' (The Sound of Music)
'Memory' (Cats)
'People' (Funny Girl)
07 'America' (West Side Story)
'Bali Ha'i' (South Pacific)
'Cabaret' (Cabaret)

'Camelot' (Camelot)
'Tonight' (West Side Story)
08 'All I Know' (Martin Guerre)
'Aquarius' (Hair)
'By My Side' (Godspell)
'Day by Day' (Godspell)
'Oklahoma!' (Oklahoma!)
'Time Warp' (The Rocky Horror Picture Show)
'Tomorrow' (Annie)
09 'Easy Terms' (Blood Brothers)
'Edelweiss' (Sound of Music)
'Evergreen' (A Star is Born)
'Footloose' (Footloose)
'Hymn to Him' (My Fair Lady)

'Somewhere' (West Side Story)
'Superstar' (Jesus Christ Superstar)
'Tradition' (Fiddler on the Roof)
'Windy City' (Calamity Jane)

10 '42nd Street' (42nd Street)
'Be Our Guest' (Beauty and the Beast)
'Big Spender' (Sweet Charity)
'Friendship' (DuBarry Was a Lady)
'Gimme, Gimme' (Thoroughly Modern Millie)
'Hello, Dolly' (Hello, Dolly)
'I Am What I Am' (La Cage Aux Folles)
'I Got Rhythm' (Girl Crazy)
'Matchmaker' (Fiddler on the Roof)
'Night Fever' (Saturday Night Fever)
'Ol' Man River' (Show Boat)
'Secret Love' (Calamity Jane)
'Small World' (Gypsy)
'Too Darn Hot' (Kiss Me Kate)
'Toot Sweets' (Chitty Chitty Bang Bang)
'Willkommen' (Cabaret)

11 '2 Good 2 Be Bad' (The Goodbye Girl)
'76 Trombones' (The Music Man)
'All That Jazz' (Chicago)
'Good Morning' (Singin' in the Rain)
'If I Loved You' (Carousel)
'I Love Louisa' (The Band Wagon)
'Luck, Be a Lady' (Guys and Dolls)
'Night and Day' (Gay Divorce)
'Old Man River' (Show Boat)
'Summer Lovin'' (Grease)
'Where is Love?' (Oliver!)
'You're the Top' (Anything Goes)

12 'All I Ask of You' (The Phantom of the Opera)
'Bosom Buddies' (Mame)
'Broadway Baby' (Follies)
'Circle of Life' (The Lion King)
'Dancing Queen' (Mamma Mia!)
'Easter Parade' (As Thousands Cheer)
'Endless Night' (The Lion King)
'Hakuna Matata' (The Lion King)
'I'd Do Anything' (Oliver!)
'It's a Fine Life' (Oliver!)
'Losing My Mind' (Follies)
'Mack the Knife' (The Threepenny Opera)
'Makin' Whoopee' (Whoopee!)
'No Matter What' (Whistle Down the Wind)
'Rich Man's Frug' (Sweet Charity)
'Shall We Dance?' (The King and I)
'Sound of Music' (The Sound of Music)
'Staying Alive' (Saturday Night Fever)
'Summer Nights' (Grease)
'There She Goes' (Fame)
'We Go Together' (Grease)

13 'All I Care About' (Chicago)
'American Dream' (Miss Saigon)

'Comedy Tonight' (A Funny Thing Happened on the Way to the Forum)
'Skimbleshanks' (Cats)
'Song of the King' (Joseph and the Amazing Technicolour Dreamcoat)
'Sunrise, Sunset' (Fiddler on the Roof)

14 'Ain't Misbehavin'' (Ain't Misbehavin')
'A Man Doesn't Know' (Damn Yankees)
'Any Dream Will Do' (Joseph and the Amazing Technicolour Dreamcoat)
'Change Partners' (Carefree)
'Chim Chim Cher-ee' (Mary Poppins)
'Close Every Door' (Joseph and the Amazing Technicolour Dreamcoat)
'I Dreamed a Dream' (Les Misérables)
'I Know Him So Well' (Chess)
'Lonely Goatherd' (Sound of Music)
'Mr Mistoffelees' (Cats)
'New York, New York' (It's a Wonderful Town)
'So Long, Farewell' (The Sound of Music)
'The Trolley Song' (Meet Me in St Louis)
'They All Laughed' (Shall We Dance)
'This Can't Be Love' (The Boys From Syracuse)
'We're In the Money' (42nd Street)

15 'A Boy From Nowhere' (Matador)
'A Bushel and a Peck' (Guys and Dolls)
'A Lot of Livin' to Do' (Bye Bye Birdie)
'Bells Are Ringing' (Bells Are Ringing)
'Bring On Tomorrow' (Fame)
'Greased Lightnin'' (Grease!)
'Honeysuckle Rose' (Ain't Misbehavin')
'I Am the Starlight' (Starlight Express)
'If I Were a Rich Man' (Fiddler on the Roof)
'Impossible Dream' (Man of La Mancha)
'Music of the Night' (The Phantom of the Opera)
'Put On a Happy Face' (Bye Bye Birdie)
'Send in the Clowns' (A Little Night Music)
'Singin' in the Rain' (Singin' in the Rain)
'Sunset Boulevard' (Sunset Boulevard)
'Tell Me on A Sunday' (Song and Dance)
'The Lady is a Tramp' (Babes in Arms)
'Till There Was You' (The Music Man)
'What I Did For Love' (A Chorus Line)

16 'A Heart Full of Love' (Les Misérables)
'Anything You Can Do' (Annie Get Your Gun)
'Consider Yourself' (Oliver!)
'Five Guys Named Moe' (Five Guys Named Moe)
'Food, Glorious Food' (Oliver!)
'Gee, Officer Krupke' (West Side Story)
'Getting to Know You' (The King and I)
'High Flying Adored' (Evita)
'My Funny Valentine' (Babes in Arms)

'Starlight Express' *(Starlight Express)*
'Tell Me It's Not True' *(Blood Brothers)*
'The Deadwood Stage *(Whip-Crack-Away)'*
  (Calamity Jane)
'Those Good Old Days' *(Damn Yankees)*
'Truly Scrumptious' *(Chitty Chitty Bang Bang)*
'Winner Takes It All' *(Mamma Mia!)*

17 'A Little Fall of Rain' *(Les Misérables)*
'Anything But Lonely' *(Aspects of Love)*
'As Long as He Needs Me' *(Oliver!)*
'Beauty and the Beast' *(Beauty and the Beast)*
'Ease on Down the Road' *(The Wiz)*
'Forget About the Boy' *(Thoroughly Modern Millie)*
'Hernando's Hideaway' *(The Pajama Game)*
'How Deep is Your Love' *(Saturday Night Fever)*
'I Get a Kick Out of You' *(Anything Goes)*
'Let Me Entertain You' *(Gypsy)*
'Lullaby of Broadway' *(42nd Street)*
'Miracle of Miracles' *(Fiddler on the Roof)*
'My Favourite Things' *(The Sound of Music)*
'My Heart Stood Still' *(A Connecticut Yankee)*
'One Night in Bangkok' *(Chess)*
'Someone Else's Story' *(Chess)*
'To Keep My Love Alive' *(A Connecticut Yankee)*
'Whatever Lola Wants' *(Damn Yankees)*
'What Kind of Fool Am I?' *(Stop The World I Want to Get Off)*
'Yankee Doodle Dandy' *(George M!)*

18 'Children Will Listen' *(Into the Woods)*
'Climb Every Mountain' *(The Sound of Music)*
'Don't Rain on My Parade' *(Funny Girl)*
'Holding Out For a Hero' *(Footloose)*
'Something Wonderful' *(The King and I)*
'Spring, Spring, Spring' *(Seven Brides for Seven Brothers)*
'Wouldn't It be Loverly?' *(My Fair Lady)*
'You Do Something to Me' *(Can-Can)*

19 'Beauty School Dropout' *(Grease)*
'It's the Hard-Knock Life' *(Annie)*
'Last Night of the World' *(Miss Saigon)*
'Let's Hear it For the Boy' *(Footloose)*
'Little Shop of Horrors' *(Little Shop of Horrors)*
'Look at Me, I'm Sandra Dee' *(Grease)*
'Springtime for Hitler' *(The Producers)*
'Thank You For the Music' *(Mamma Mia!)*
'Time Heals Everything' *(Mack and Mabel)*
'Tomorrow Belongs to Me' *(Cabaret)*
'Too Much In Love to Care' *(Sunset Boulevard)*

'You'll Never Walk Alone' *(Carousel)*

20 'Good Morning Starshine' *(Hair)*
'If Ever I Would Leave You' *(Camelot)*
'I've Got You Under My Skin' *(Born to Dance)*
'Kiss of the Spider Woman' *(Kiss of the Spider Woman)*
'Shuffle Off the Buffalo' *(42nd Street)*
'Some Enchanted Evening' *(South Pacific)*
'Someone to Watch Over Me' *(Crazy For You)*
'The Age of Not Believing' *(Bedknobs and Broomsticks)*
'The Music and the Mirror' *(A Chorus Line)*

21 'Almost Like Being in Love' *(Brigadoon)*
'Don't Cry For Me, Argentina' *(Evita)*
'Falling in Love With Love' *(The Boys From Syracuse)*
'Got to Pick a Pocket or Two' *(Oliver!)*
'I Don't Know How to Love Him' *(Jesus Christ Superstar)*
'Love Changes Everything' *(Aspects of Love)*
'The Black Hills of Dakota' *(Calamity Jane)*
'What's the Use of Wonderin'' *(Carousel)*
'Younger Than Springtime' *(South Pacific)*

22 'As If We Never Said Goodbye' *(Sunset Boulevard)*
'Brush Up Your Shakespeare' *(Kiss Me Kate)*
'Hopelessly Devoted to You' *(Grease)*
'I Loved You Once in Silence' *(Camelot)*
'June is Bustin' Out All Over' *(Carousel)*
'The First Man You Remember' *(Aspects of Love)*

23 'Another Op'nin', Another Show' *(Kiss Me Kate)*
'Bless Your Beautiful Bride' *(Seven Brides for Seven Brothers)*
'Give My Regards to Broadway' *(George M!)*
'Oh What a Beautiful Morning' *(Oklahoma!)*
'On The Street Where You Live' *(My Fair Lady)*
'People Will Say We're in Love' *(Oklahoma!)*
'Sixteen, Going on Seventeen' *(The Sound of Music)*
'Substitutiary Locomotion' *(Bedknobs and Broomsticks)*
'Take That Look Off Your Face' *(Song and Dance)*
'There is Nothing Like A Dame' *(South Pacific)*
'You'll Never Get Away from Me' *(Gypsy)*

24 'Can You Feel the Love Tonight?' *(The Lion King)*

'Everything's Coming Up Roses' *(Gypsy)*
'I Could Have Danced all Night' *(My Fair Lady)*
'Is You Is or Is You Ain't My Baby?' *(Five Guys Named Moe)*
'It's a Grand Night for Singing' *(State Fair)*
'Let's Call the Whole Thing Off' *(Shall We Dance)*

25 'How are Things in Glocca Morra?' *(Finian's Rainbow)*
'It's Harry I'm Planning To Marry' *(Calamity Jane)*
'Life is Just a Bowl of Cherries' *(Fosse)*
'Thank Heaven For Little Girls' *(Gigi)*

26 'Just Blew In From the Windy City' *(Calamity Jane)*
'They Can't Take That Away From Me' *(Shall We Dance)*

27 'Diamonds Are a Girl's Best Friend' *(Gentlemen Prefer Blondes)*
'On a Clear Day, You Can See Forever' *(On a Clear Day, You Can See Forever)*
'There are Worse Things I Could Do' *(Grease)*

28 'Another Suitcase in Another Hall' *(Evita)*
'Jellicle Songs for Jellicle Cats' *(Cats)*

30 'Bewitched, Bothered and Bewildered' *(Pal Joey)*

32 'There's No Business Like Show Business' *(Annie Get Your Gun)*

34 'I'm Gonna Wash That Man Right Outta My Hair' *(South Pacific)*
'Supercalifragilisticexpialidocious' *(Mary Poppins)*

36 'There's Gotta Be Something Better Than This' *(Sweet Charity)*

People associated with musicals include:

04 Ball (Michael; 1962– , English)
Bart (Lionel; 1930–99, English)
Cahn (Sammy; 1913–93, US)
Eddy (Nelson; 1901–67, US)
Grey (Joel; 1932– , US)
Hart (Lorenz; 1895–1943, US)
Hart (Moss; 1904–61, US)
Kaye (Danny; 1913–87, US)
Keel (Howard; 1917–2004, US)
Kern (Jerome; 1885–1945, US)
Lahr (Bert; 1895–1967, US)
Lane (Nathan; 1956– , US)
Nunn (Trevor; 1940– , English)
Rice (Tim; 1944– , English)

05 Black (Don; 1936– , English)
Brice (Fanny; 1891–1951, US)
Caird (John; 1948–, English)
Cohan (George; 1878–1942, US)
Donen (Stanley; 1924– , US)
Fosse (Bob; 1927–87, US)
Kelly (Gene; 1912–96, US)
Lenya (Lotte; 1898–1981, Austrian)
Loewe (Frederick; 1904–88, Austrian/US)
Paige (Elaine; 1948– , English)
Styne (Jule; 1905–94, US)

06 Berlin (Irving; 1888–1989, Russian/US)
Castle (Irene; 1893–1969, US)
Castle (Vernon; 1887–1918, English/US)
Coward (Sir Noel; 1899–1973, English)
Gaynor (Mitzi; 1931– , US)
Herman (Jerry; 1932– , US)
Jolson (Al; 1886–1950, US)
Lerner (Alan Jay; 1918–86, US)
MacRae (Gordon; 1921–86, US)
Martin (Mary; 1913–90, US)

Martin (Millicent; 1934– , English)
Merman (Ethel; 1909–84, US)
Miller (Ann; 1919–2004, US)
Newley (Anthony; 1931–99, English)
Peters (Bernadette; 1948– , US)
Porter (Cole; 1891–1964, US)
Prince (Hal; 1928– , US)
Rogers (Ginger; 1911–95, US)
Steele (Tommy; 1936– , English)
Tucker (Sophie; 1884–1966, Russian/US)

07 Astaire (Fred; 1899–1987, US)
Boublil (Alain; 1941– , Tunisian)
Burnett (Carol; 1933– , US)
Garland (Judy; 1922–69, US)
Grayson (Kathryn; 1922– , US)
Novello (Ivor; 1893–1951, Welsh)
O'Connor (Donald; 1925–2003, US)
Robbins (Jerome; 1918–98, US)
Rodgers (Richard; 1902–79, US)
Sharaff (Irene; 1910–93, US)
Sherman (Richard M; 1928– , US)
Sherman (Robert B; 1925– , US)
Ulvaeus (Björn; 1945– , Swedish)

08 Berkeley (Busby; 1895–1976, US)
Bricusse (Leslie; 1931– , English)
Buchanan (Jack; 1891–1957, Scottish)
Channing (Carol; 1921– , US)
Crawford (Michael; 1942– , English)
Gershwin (George; 1898–1937, US)
Gershwin (Ira; 1896–1983, US)
Lawrence (Gertrude; 1898–1952, English)
Matthews (Jessie; 1907–81, English)
McKenzie (Julia; 1941– , English)
Minnelli (Liza; 1946– , US)
Reynolds (Debbie; 1932– , US)

Robinson (Bill 'Bojangles'; 1878–1949, US)
Sondheim (Stephen; 1930– , US)
Ziegfeld (Florenz, Jnr; 1867–1932, US)
09 Andersson (Benny; 1946– , Swedish)
Bernstein (Leonard; 1918–90, US)
MacDonald (Jeanette; 1901–65, US)

Macintosh (Cameron; 1946– , Scottish)
Schönberg (Claude-Michel; 1944– , French)
Streisand (Barbra; 1942– , US)
11 Hammerstein (Oscar, II; 1895–1960, US)
Lloyd Webber (Andrew; 1948– , English)

musician

Musicians and musical groups include:

03 duo
04 band
bard
diva
duet
trio
05 choir
griot
group
nonet
octet
piper
06 bugler
busker
folkie
jazzer
oboist
player
sextet

singer
07 cellist
drummer
fiddler
harpist
maestro
Orphean
pianist
quartet
quintet
soloist
08 clarsair
composer
ensemble
flautist
lutenist
minstrel
organist
virtuoso
vocalist

09 balladeer
conductor
guitarist
itinerant
orchestra
performer
trumpeter
violinist
10 one-man band
prima donna
trombonist
11 accompanist
saxophonist
12 backing group
clarinettist
13 percussionist
session singer
15 instrumentalist
session musician

Classical musicians, musicologists and instrument makers include:

02 Ma (Yo-Yo; 1955– , French/US)
03 Fou (Ts'ong; 1934– , Chinese)
Sax (Adolphe; 1814–94, Belgian)
Suk (Joseph; 1875–1935, Czech)
Tye (Christopher; c.1505–c.1572, English)
04 Adès (Thomas; 1971– , English)
Böhm (Theobald; 1794–1881, German)
Bush (Alan; 1900–95, English)
Hess (Dame Myra; 1890–1966, English)
Rosa (Carl, 1842–89, German)
Wood (Haydn; 1882–1959, English)
05 Alkan (1813–88, French)
Arrau (Claudio; 1903–91, Chilean)
Beach (Mrs H H A; 1867–1944, US)
Benda (Georg; 1722–95, Bohemian)
Boehm (Theobald; 1794–1881, German)
Bolet (Jorge; 1914–90, US)
Borge (Victor; 1909–2000, Danish/US)
Bream (Julian; 1933– , English)
Bülow (Hans, Baron von; 1830–94, German)
Busch (Adolf; 1891–1952, German/Swiss)
Chung (Kyung-Wha; 1948– , South Korean/US)

du Pré (Jacqueline; 1945–87, English)
Dupré (Marcel; 1886–1971, French)
Elman (Mischa; 1891–1967, Russian/US)
Field (John; 1782–1837, Irish)
Friml (Rudolf; 1879–1972, Czech/US)
Gould (Glenn; 1932–82, Canadian)
Grove (Sir George; 1820–1900, English)
Hallé (Sir Charles; 1819–95, German/British)
Harty (Sir Hamilton; 1880–1941, Northern Irish)
Joyce (Eileen; 1912–91, Australian)
Liszt (Franz; 1811–86, Hungarian)
Manns (Sir August; 1825–1907, German)
Nyman (Michael; 1944– , English)
Ogdon (John; 1937–89, English)
Sharp (Cecil; 1859–1924, English)
Spohr (Ludwig; 1784–1859, German)
Stern (Isaac; 1920–2001, Russian/US)
Szell (George; 1897–1970, Hungarian/US)
Tovey (Sir Donald Francis; 1873–1940, English)
Weber (Carl Maria von; 1786–1826, German)
Ysaye (Eugène; 1858–1931, Belgian)

06 Albert (Eugen d'; 1864–1932, German)
Alfvén (Hugo; 1872–1960, Swedish)
Busoni (Ferruccio; 1866–1924, Italian)
Casals (Pablo; 1876–1973, Spanish)
Chopin (Frédéric; 1810–49, Polish)
Cortot (Alfred; 1877–1962, French)
Cramer (Johann Baptist; 1771–1858, German/British)
Curzon (Sir Clifford; 1907–82, English)
Czerny (Karl; 1791–1857, Austrian)
Dussek (Jan Ladislav; 1760–1812, Czech)
Galway (Sir James; 1939– , Northern Irish)
Godard (Benjamin; 1849–95, French)
Hummel (Johann; 1778–1837, Austrian)
Köchel (Ludwig von; 1800–77, Austrian)
Koppel (Herman D; 1908–98, Danish)
Lamond (Frederic; 1868–1948, Scottish)
Lassus (Orlandus; c.1532–94, Netherlandish)
Levine (James; 1943– , US)
Maazel (Lorin; 1930– , French/US)
Martin (Frank; 1890–1974, Swiss)
Mutter (Anne-Sophie; 1963– , German)
Quantz (Johann Joachim; 1697–1773, German)
Riccio (David; c.1533–66, Italian)
Rizzio (David; c.1533–66, Italian)
Serkin (Rudolf; 1903–91, Hungarian/US)
Sitsky (Larry; 1934– , Chinese/Australian)
Stoker (Richard; 1938– , English)
Suggia (Guilhermina; 1888–1950, Portuguese)
Turina (Joaquín; 1882–1949, Spanish)
Viotti (Giovanni Battista; 1753–1824, Italian)
Wagner (Siegfried; 1869–1930, German)

07 Albéniz (Isaac; 1860–1909, Spanish)
Attwood (Thomas; 1765–1838, English)
Bennett (Sir William Sterndale; 1816–75, English)
Bentzon (Niels Viggo; 1919–2000, Danish)
Blondel (fl.12c, French)
Brendel (Alfred; 1931– , Austrian)
Campoli (Alfredo; 1906–91, Italian)
Casella (Alfredo; 1883–1947, Italian)
Glennie (Evelyn; 1965– , Scottish)
Goodman (Isador; 1909–82, South African/Australian)
Heifetz (Jascha; 1901–87, Russian/US)
Joachim (Joseph; 1831–1907, Hungarian)
Kennedy (Nigel; 1956– , English)
Kentner (Louis; 1905–87, Hungarian/British)
Leclair (Jean Marie; 1697–1764, French)
Lipatti (Dinu; 1917–50, Romanian)
Malcolm (George; 1917–97, English)
Marbeck (John; d.c.1585, English)
Mathias (William; 1934–92, Welsh)
Matthay (Tobias; 1858–1945, English)
McClary (Susan; 1946– , US)

McGuire (Edward; 1948– , Scottish)
Medtner (Nikolai; 1880–1951, Russian)
Menuhin (Yehudi, Lord; 1916–99, US/British)
Perahia (Murray; 1947– , US)
Perlman (Itzhak; 1945– , Israeli)
Richter (Sviatoslav; 1915–97, Russian)
Segovia (Andrés; 1893–1987, Spanish)
Shankar (Ravi; 1920– , Indian)
Solomon (1902–88, English)
Sorabji (Kaikhosru Shapurji; 1892–1988, English)
Stamitz (Carl; 1745–1801, German)
Stamitz (Johann; 1717–57, Bohemian)
Strauss (Johann, the Elder; 1804–49, Austrian)
Strauss (Johann, the Younger; 1825–99, Austrian)
Szeryng (Henryk; 1918–88, Polish/Mexican)
Taneyev (Sergei; 1856–1915, Russian)
Tartini (Giuseppe; 1692–1770, Italian)
Thibaud (Jacques; 1880–1953, French)
Vivaldi (Antonio; 1678–1741, Italian)
Zwilich (Ellen; 1939– , US) ·

08 Clementi (Muzio; 1752–1832, Italian)
Dohnanyi (Ernst von; 1877–1960, Hungarian)
Fournier (Pierre; 1906–86, French)
Godowsky (Leopold; 1870–1938, Russian/US)
Goossens (Eugène; 1867–1958, French/Belgian)
Goossens (Léon; 1897–1988, English)
Grainger (Percy; 1882–1961, Australian/US)
Guarneri (fl.16–17c; Italian)
Henschel (Sir George; 1850–1934, Polish/British)
Holliger (Heinz; 1939– , Swiss)
Horowitz (Vladimir; 1904–89, Russian/US)
Kreisler (Fritz; 1875–1962, Austrian/US)
Leighton (Kenneth; 1929–88, English)
Lhévinne (Josef; 1874–1944, Russian/US)
Lortzing (Albert; 1801–51, German)
Marriner (Sir Neville; 1924– , English)
Merbecke (John; d.c.1585, English)
Milstein (Nathan; 1904–92, Russian/US)
Oistrakh (David; 1908–74, Russian)
Pachmann (Vladimir de; 1848–1933, Russian)
Paganini (Niccolò; 1782–1840, Italian)
Pfitzner (Hans; 1869–1949, German)
Richards (Henry Brinley; 1819–85, Welsh)
Sarasate (Pablo; 1844–1908, Spanish)
Schnabel (Artur; 1882–1951, Austrian)
Schumann (Clara; 1819–96, German)
Scriabin (Aleksandr; 1872–1915, Russian)
Skriabin (Aleksandr; 1872–1915, Russian)
Steinway (Henry; 1797–1871, German/US)

Thalberg (Sigismond; 1812–71, German or Austrian)
Williams (John; 1941– , Australian)
Zukerman (Pinchas; 1948– , Israeli)

09 Ashkenazy (Vladimir; 1937– , Russian/Icelandic)
Barenboim (Daniel; 1942– , Argentine/Israeli)
Bernstein (Leonard; 1918–90, US)
Bottesini (Giovanni; 1823–89, Italian)
Boulanger (Nadia; 1887–1979, French)
Broadwood (John; 1732–1812, Scottish)
Butterley (Nigel; 1935– , Australian)
Dolmetsch (Arnold; 1858–1940, French/British)
Gieseking (Walter; 1895–1956, German)
Guarnieri (fl.16–17c; Italian)
Landowska (Wanda; 1879–1959, Polish)
MacDowell (Edward; 1861–1908, US)
Moscheles (Ignaz; 1794–1870, Bohemian)
Stevenson (Ronald; 1928– , Scottish)
Tortelier (Paul; 1914–90, French)
Zimbalist (Efrem; 1889–1985, Russian/US)

10 Barbirolli (Sir John; 1899–1970, English)
Campenhout (François von; 1779–1849, Belgian)
Cristofori (Bartolommeo; 1655–1731, Italian)
Gottschalk (Louis Moreau; 1829–69, US)
Moszkowski (Moritz; 1854–1925, Polish)
Paderewski (Ignacy; 1860–1941, Polish)

Rubinstein (Anton; 1829–94, Russian)
Rubinstein (Artur; 1887–1982, Polish/US)
Scharwenka (Xaver; 1850–1924, Polish)
Stradivari (Antonio; c.1644–1737, Italian)
Vieuxtemps (Henri; 1820–81, Belgian)
Villa-Lobos (Heitor; 1887–1959, Brazilian)
Williamson (Malcolm; 1931–2003, Australian)

11 Cristofaloi (Bartolommeo; 1655–1731, Italian)
Dittersdorf (Karl Ditters von; 1739–99, Austrian)
Farren-Price (Ronald; 1930– , Australian)
Mitropoulos (Dimitri; 1896–1960, Greek/US)
Piatigorsky (Gregor; 1903–76, Russian/US)
Rachmaninov (Sergei; 1873–1943, Russian)
Rakhmaninov (Sergei; 1873–1943, Russian)
Reizenstein (Franz; 1911–68, German)
Theodorakis (Mikis; 1925– , Greek)

12 Guido d'Arezzo (c.990–1050, Italian)
Michelangeli (Arturo Benedetti; 1920–95, Italian)
Moiseiwitsch (Benno; 1890–1963, Russian/British)
Rostropovich (Mstislav; 1927–2007, Russian)
Shostakovich (Maxim Dmitriyevich; 1938– , Russian/US)
Stradivarius (Antonio; c.1644–1737, Italian)

14 Jaques-Dalcroze (Émile; 1865–1951, Swiss)
Orlando di Lasso (c.1532–94, Netherlandish)

See also **Bach, Johann Sebastian**; **Bartók, Béla**; **Beethoven, Ludwig van**; **Brahms, Johannes**; **Britten, Benjamin**; **composer**; **conductor**; **Debussy, Claude**; **Dvořák, Antonín**; **Elgar, Sir Edward**; **Gilbert, Sir W S and Sullivan, Sir Arthur**; **Handel, George Frideric**; **Haydn, Joseph**; **jazz**; **Mahler, Gustav**; **Mozart, Wolfgang Amadeus**; **pianist**; **pop**; **Prokofiev, Sergei**; **Puccini, Giacomo**; **Purcell, Henry**; **Ravel, Maurice**; **Rossini, Gioacchino**; **Schoenberg, Arnold**; **Schubert, Franz**; **Schumann, Robert**; **Shostakovich, Dmitri**; **song**; **Strauss, Richard**; **Stravinsky, Igor**; **Tchaikovsky, Pyotr Ilyich**; **Verdi, Giuseppe**; **Wagner, Richard**

musketeer *see* **Dumas, Alexandre**

muslim *see* **Islam**

mythology

Mythical animals and spirits include:

03		**04**		**05**	
elf		faun		afrit	
fay		fung		demon	
fée		huma		devil	
fum		jinn		djinn	
hob		peri		dobby	
imp		pixy		dryad	
Mab		puck		dwarf	
nis		yale		fairy	
nix		yeti		genie	

ghost
ghoul
giant
gnome
golem
jinni
kelpy
kylin
naiad
nisse
nixie
nymph
oread
pisky
pixie
pooka
pouke
satyr
shade
silky
Siren
sylph
troll
wight

06 afreet
dobbie
dragon
dybbuk
goblin

jinnee
kelpie
kobold
maelid
merman
nereid
Oberon
selkie
silkie
sprite
wyvern

07 banshee
Bigfoot
brownie
centaur
gremlin
griffin
incubus
Lorelei
mermaid
oceanid
Pegasus
phoenix
rusalka
rye wolf
sandman
unicorn
vampire

08 antelope

basilisk
Nibelung
succubus
werewolf
whistler

09 hamadryad
hobgoblin
impundulu
Julunggul
mermaiden
sasquatch
tokoloshe
tragelaph
water bull

10 hippogriff
hippogryph
leprechaun
salamander
sea serpent
tooth fairy

11 hircocervus
lubber fiend
scolopendra
thunderbird

12 little people
Rainbow Snake

15 Lob-lie-by-the-fire
Robin Goodfellow

Mythical birds include:

03 fum
roc
rok

ruc
04 fung
huma

rukh
07 phoenix
08 whistler

09 impundulu
11 Thunderbird
12 bird of wonder

Mythical places include:

03 Dis
Hel
04 Hell
Styx
05 Argos
Babel
Hades
Lethe
Limbo
Pluto
Thule
06 Albion
Anghar
Asgard
Avalon
Heaven
Heorot

Nedyet
Utgard
Xanadu
07 Agartha
Alfheim
Alpheus
Arcadia
Bifrost
Boeotia
Camelot
Elysium
Lemuria
Nirvana
Pohjola
Tuonela
08 Amazonia
Archeron
Atlantis

El Dorado
Lyonesse
Niflheim
Paradise
Tlalocan
Valhalla
Vanaheim

09 Cockaigne
Fairyland
Purgatory
River Styx
Shangri-la
Yggdrasil

10 River Lethe
Stymphalos

11 Ultima Thule

12 River Alpheus

13 Jewel Mountain   **14** Lake Stymphalos   The Isle of Avalon
River Archeron   **15** Cloudcuckooland   The Tower of Babel
The Underworld   The Garden of Eden

Mythological rivers include:

04 Styx   Oceanus
05 Lethe   **10** Phlegethon
07 Acheron

Babylonian gods include:

02 Ea (water/wisdom/spells/writing/building)

03 Anu (heavens/father of the gods)
Bel (king of the gods/thunderstorms/light/life)
Sin (Moon)

04 Adad (wind/storm/flood)
Apsu (primordial sweet-water ocean)
Baal (king of the gods/thunderstorms/light/life)
Enki (water/wisdom/spells/writing/building)
Nabu (scribe/herald of the gods)

05 Ellil (air/land/earth/men's fates)

Enlil (air/land/earth/men's fates)
Hadad (fertility/thunder)
Mummu (mists)

06 Anshar (heaven/sky)
Dumuzi (animal/plant fertility)
Marduk (king of the gods/thunderstorms/light/life)
Nergal (death/underworld)
Tammuz (fertility/vegetation)

07 Ninurta (warrior)
Shamash (sun/justice)
Thammuz (fertility/vegetation)

Babylonian goddesses include:

03 Aja (the dawn)

04 Antu (consort of Anu)

05 Antum (mother of Ishtar)
Belit (wife of Bel/Baal/Marduk)
Nintu (motherhood)

06 Ishtar (love/fertility/war)
Kishar (consort of Anshar)

Ningal (consort of Sin)
Ninlil (consort of Enlil)
Nintur (motherhood)
Tiamat (chaos/salt-water ocean/sky)

07 Anunitu (Moon)
Damkina (Earth mother)

10 Ereshkigal (underworld)

Celtic gods include:

03 Bel (sun/light/fire)
Don (chief/lord of the Otherworld)
Lug (sun/arts/healing)

04 Beli (sun/light/fire)
Lleu (hero/crafts/commerce/youth/games)
Llyr (sea/water)
Ogma (eloquency/physical strength)

05 Balor (death)
Dylan (sea)
Mabon (youth/healing/music/hunting)
Nuada (harpers/healing/learning/warfare)
Nuadu (harpers/healing/learning/warfare)
Ogmia (strength/eloquence)
Pwyll (underworld)
Taran (thunder/war)

06 Merlin (guardian of the land)
Ogmios (strength/eloquence)

07 Belinus (sun/light/fire)

Goibniu (smithcraft)
Grannos (healing)
Gwydion (enchantment/illusion)
Pryderi (underworld)

08 Gofannon (smiths/strength)
Silvanus (underworld)
Sucellus (underworld)
the Dagda (earth/fertility/prosperity)

09 Cernunnos (fertility/plenty/underworld/animals/lord of the Underworld)
Manawydan (wisdom/patience)

10 Manawyddan (wisdom/patience)

11 Aengus Mac Og (youth/love/beauty)
Gwynn ap Nudd (underworld)

14 Bran the Blessed (prophecy/arts/war)
Manannan Mac Lir (sea-god/regeneration)

15 Manawydan ap Llyr (sea/regeneration)

Celtic goddesses include:

03 Don (mother of the gods/rivers/wisdom/
magic)

04 Aine (love/fertility)
Anna (mother/fecundity/plenty)
Danu (mother/rivers/wisdom/magic)
Eriu (Ireland)

05 Badhb (battle/enlightenment)
Boann (river/water/fertility)
Édain (Otherworld)
Epona (horses/prosperity)
Étain (Otherworld)
Macha (warrior/horses/death/cunning)

06 Badhbh (battle/enlightenment)
Brigid (agriculture/smithcraft/inspiration)
Brigit (agriculture/smithcraft/inspiration)
Matres (Earth/fecundity/motherhood)
Medhbh (warrior/sexuality)

Modron (mother)

07 Branwen (love/beauty)
Brighid (midwifery/poetry/crafts)
Cliodna (peace/beauty)
Nemhain (war)

08 Cliodhna (peace/beauty)
Flidhais (wild animals)
Matronae (Earth/fecundity/motherhood)
Morrigan (war/lust/revenge/magic)
Rhiannon (horses/birds/the moon/wit)

09 Arianrhod (Earth)
Brigantia (livestock/agriculture)
Cerridwen (underworld)
Morríghan (war/lust/revenge/magic)

10 Blodeuwedd (love/generosity)

11 Dea Arduinna (wild animals)

Celtic mythological and legendary characters include:

03 Anu
Lug

04 Badb
Bran
Danu
Lugh
Medb
Ogma

05 Balor
Boann
Dagda
Macha
Maeve
Neman
Nuada
Oisin
Pwyll

06 Arthur
Brigit
Danaan
Deidre
Imbolc
Isolde
Ogmios
Ossian

07 banshee
Beltane
Branwen
Brighid
Deirdre
Samhain
Tristan

08 Manannan
Morrigan
Rhiannon
The Dagda
Tir nan-Og

09 Bean Sidhé
Cernunnos
Conchobar

10 Cú Chulainn
Lughnasadh

11 Finn mac Cool

13 Bendigeidfran
Finn mac Cumhal

14 Bran the Blessed
Finn mac Cumhail
Tuatha dé Danaan

Central and South American gods include:

04 Chac (Mayan; rain)
Inti (Inca; sun)

06 Tlaloc (Aztec; rain/mountains/springs)

07 Huang-ti (Aztec; war/protector of the
city)
Hunab Ku (Mayan; supreme creator)

Itzamma (Mayan; founder of culture/heaven/
maize/fertility/moon)

08 Catequil (Inca; thunder/lightning)
Kukulkan (Mayan; elements/creator)

09 the Bacabs (Mayan; wind)
Viracocha (Inca; supreme creator)

Xipe Totec (Aztec; springtime/renewal/
nocturnal rain).

10 Apu Punchau (Inca; sun)
Manco Capac (Inca; sun/father of Incans)
Pachacamac (Inca; earth/creator)
Xochipilli (Aztec; flowers/love/song/dance)

12 Quetzalcoatl (Aztec; creator/vegetation/
wind)
Tezcatlipoca (Aztec; trickster/sun)
Xiuhtecuhtli (Aztec; hearth/fire/sun/
volcanoes)

15 Huitzilopochtil (Aztec; war/sun)

Central and South American goddesses include:

05 Aknah (Mayan; birth)

06 Ixchel (Mayan; storm)

09 Coatlicue (Aztec; earth)
Ixazaluoh (Mayan; water/inventor of
weaving)
Mama Oella (Inca; inventor of spinning)

Pachamama (Inca; earth)

10 Mama Quilla (Inca; moon)

11 Tlazolteotl (Aztec; lust)

12 Xochiquetzal (Aztec; flowers/love/childbirth)

15 Chalchiuhtlicue (Aztec; water)

Egyptian gods include:

02 Ra (Sun)
Re (Sun)

03 Bes (home/childbirth/family)
Geb (earth)
Nut (sky)

04 Apis (fecundity/fertility/strength)
Aten (unique god)
Atum (ancestor of human race)
Ptah (creation/protector of artists)

Seth (evil)

05 Horus (light/sun)
Thoth (moon/learning/supreme scribe)

06 Amun-Re (universal)
Anubis (funerals)
Osiris (vegetation/death)

07 Khonsou (son of Amun-Re)
Sarapis (compound of Osiris and Apis)
Serapis (compound of Osiris and Apis)

Egyptian goddesses include:

04 Isis (magic/fertility/mother)

Maat (order/law/justice)

05 Khnum (creation)

06 Hathor (love/fertility)
Sakmet (might)
Sekmet (might)

07 Nepthys (funerals)

Sakhmet (might)

Sekhmet (might)

08 Nephthys (funerals)

Greek gods include:

03 Pan (male sexuality/woods/
shepherds)

04 Ares (war)
Atys (vegetation)
Eros (love)
Zeus (king of the gods/sky/
light/weather)

05 Atlas (Titan who bears
Earth)
Attis (vegetation)
Hades (underworld)

06 Adonis (vegetation/rebirth)
Aeolus (winds)
Apollo (prophecy/music/
youth/archery/healing)
Boreas (north wind)
Cronus (father of Zeus)
Helios (sun)
Hermes (messenger of the
gods)
Hypnos (sleep)
Nereus (sea)

Plutus (wealth)

07 Oceanus (river Oceanus)

08 Dionysus (wine/vine)
Ganymede (rain)
Morpheus (dreams)
Poseidon (sea)
Thanatos (death)

09 Asclepius (healing)

10 Hephaestus (fire)

11 Aesculapius (healing)

Greek goddesses include:

03 Eos (dawn)
Nyx (night)

04 Gaea (Earth)
Gaia (Earth)
Hebe (youth)

Hera (marriage/childbirth/
queen of the gods)
Iris (rainbow)
Nike (victory)
Rhea (mother of Zeus)

05 Tyche (chance/luck)

06 Athene (prudence/wisdom/
protectress of Athens)
Cybele (earth)
Hecate (moon)

Hestia (hearth/home)
Hygeia
Selene (moon)
Themis (established law/
    justice)
Thetis

07 Alphito (barley/goddess of
    Argos)

Artemis (fertility/chastity/
    hunting)
Demeter (corn/harvest)
Erinyes (vengeance)
Nemesis (destiny/
    moderation/vengeance)

08 Arethusa (springs/fountains)
the Fates (destiny)

the Horae (seasons)
the Muses (the liberal arts)

09 Aphrodite (love/beauty)
the Furies (vengeance)
the Graces (charm/beauty)

10 Persephone (underworld)

Greek mythological and legendary characters include:

02 Io

04 Ajax
Dido
Echo
Eris
Hero
Leda
Leto
Rhea

05 Atlas
Chloe
Circe
Creon
Danae
Helen
Horae
Hydra
Irene
Ixion
Jason
Kreon
Laius
Lamia
Medea
Midas
Minos
Niobe
Orion
Paris
Priam
Rheia

06 Aeneas
Aeolus
Alecto
Amazon
Atreus
Cadmus
Castor
Charon
Chiron
Cronus
Danaoi
Daphne
Dryads
Europa
Europe

Furies
Graiae
Hecabe
Hector
Hecuba
Hellen
Icarus
Iolaus
Kronos
Latona
Medusa
Megara
Memnon
Naiads
Nessus
Nestor
nymphs
Oreads
Peleus
Pelops
Phoebe
Pollux
Python
satyrs
Scylla
Semele
Sileni
Sirens
Stheno
Syrinx
Titans
Triton
Typhon

07 Actaeon
Alcyone
Arachne
Ariadne
Calchas
Calypso
Cecrops
Cepheus
Chimera
Cyclops
Danaans
Daphnis
Diomede
Echidna

Electra
Epigoni
Erinyes
Euryale
Galatea
Gorgons
Griffin
Gryphon
Harpies
Iapetus
Jocasta
Kekrops
Laocoon
Lapiths
Leander
Maenads
Marsyas
Nereids
Oceanus
Oedipus
Orestes
Orpheus
Pandora
Pegasus
Perseus
Phaedra
Silenus
Theseus
Titania
Troilus
Ulysses

08 Achilles
Alcestis
Alcmaeon
Anchises
Antigone
Arethusa
Atalanta
Basilisk
Centaurs
Cerberus
Chimaera
Cressida
Cyclopes
Daedalus
Diomedes
Endymion

Eteocles
Eurydice
Ganymede
Gigantes
Halcyone
Heracles
Hyperion
Iphicles
Lycurgus
Meleager
Menelaus
Minotaur
Nausicaa
Oceanids
Odysseus
Pasiphae
Penelope
Pentheus
Phaethon
Pleiades
Sarpedon
Sisyphus
Tantalus
Thyestes
Tiresias
Typhoeus

09 Aegisthus
Agamemnon
Andromeda
Argonauts
Autolycus
Cassandra
Charybdis
Deucalion
Idomeneus
Lotophagi
Mnemosyne
Myrmidons
Narcissus
Patroclus
Polynices
Pygmalion
Semiramis
Tisiphone

10 Amphitryon
Andromache

Cassiopeia
Cockatrice
Erechtheus
Hamadryads
Hesperides

Hippolytus
Iphigeneia
Polyneices
Polyphemus
Procrustes

Prometheus
Telemachus
11 Bellerophon
Lotus-eaters
Neoptolemus

Philoctetes
12 Clytemnestra
Hyperboreans
Rhadamanthus
Rhadamanthys

Maori gods include:

02 Tu
03 Uru
04 Maui
Tane

05 Rangi
Rongo
06 Haumia
07 Tawhiri

08 Ranginui
Ruaumoko
Tangaroa
10 Tane Mahuta

11 Rongomatane
Tumatauenga
12 Tawhiri Matea

Maori goddesses include:

04 Papa
10 Hinetitama

11 Hinenuitepo
Papatuanuku

Maori mythological and legendary characters include:

04 Kupe
Maui
Rona

05 Pania
07 Hinemoa
Mahuika

09 Tutanekai

Norse gods include:

03 Bor (father of Odin)
Otr (otter god)
Tyr (battle/sky)
Ull (stepson of Thor/enchanter)
04 Frey (fertility/sunshine/growth)
Logi (fire)
Loki (mischief)
Odin (father/war/death/magic/law/poetic inspiration)
Thor (thunder/war/good crops)
05 Aegir (sea)
Aesir (warlike gods)
Alcis (sky)
Bragi (poetry)
Donar (thunder/war/good crops)
Freyr (fertility/fecundity)

Hoder (blind god who killed Balder)
Mimir (wisdom)
Njord (ships/the sea)
Vanir (benevolent gods)
Vidar (slayer of the wolf Fenrir)
Woden (father/war/death/magic/law/poetic inspiration)
Wotan (father/war/death/magic/law/poetic inspiration)
06 Balder (son of Odin/light/sovereignty/power)
Fafnir (dragon)
Hermod (son of Odin)
Hoenir (companion to Odin and Loki)
Kvasir (wise utterances)
07 Volundr (craftsman)
08 Heimdall (sentinel/dawn)

Norse goddesses include:

03 Hel (death; Queen of Niflheim/underworld)
Ran (sea)
Sif (wife of Thor)
04 Hela (death; Queen of Niflheim/underworld)
05 Frigg (fertility/wife of Odin)
Idunn (guardian of golden apples of youth)
Nanna (wife of Balder)
Norns (destiny)
Sigyn (wife of Loki)

06 Freyja (love/fertility/fecundity/victory/peace)
Gefion (received virgins after death)
07 Nerthus (earth)
08 Fjorgynn (mother of Thor)
09 Valkyries (warrior women/helpers of gods of war)
10 Nehallenia (plenty)

Norse mythological and legendary characters include:

03 Lif

06 Gudrun
Kraken
Sigurd
Weland

07 Beowulf
Grendel

Wayland
Weiland
Weyland

08 Brunhild

09 berserker

10 Lifthrasir

Roman gods include:

04 Mars (war)

05 Cupid (love)
Fides (honesty)
Janus (entrances/travel/dawn)
Lares (house)
Orcus (death)
Picus (woods)
Pluto (underworld)

06 Apollo (sun)
Consus (nature/agriculture)
Faunus (crops and herbs)
Genius (protector of individuals and the state)

Mithra (sun/regeneration)
Saturn (fertility/agriculture)
Vulcan (fire)

07 Bacchus (wine and ecstasy)
Jupiter (sky/sun/moon/thunder)
Mercury (messenger/merchants)
Mithras (sun/regeneration)
Neptune (sea)
Penates (food/drink)

08 Portunus (husbands)
Silvanus (trees/forests)

09 Vertumnus (fertility)

10 Liber Pater (fertility)

Roman goddesses include:

03 Ops (harvest)

04 Juno (marriage/childbirth/light)
Luna (moon)
Maia (fertility)

05 Ceres (corn/agriculture)
Diana (fertility/hunting/moon)
Fauna (fertility)
Flora (fruitfulness/flowers)
Pales (protectress of flocks)
Venus (spring/gardens/love)
Vesta (hearth)

06 Aurora (dawn)
Pomona (fruits)
Rumina (nursing mothers)

07 Bellona (war)
Egreria (fountains/childbirth)
Feronia
Fortuna (chance)
Minerva (war/craftsmen/education/arts)

08 Libitina
Victoria (victory)

10 Proserpina (underworld)

Roman mythological and legendary characters include:

05 Lamia
Lares
Manes
Remus
Sibyl

07 Latinus
Lemures
Lucrece
Penates
Romulus
Sibylla

Tarpeia

08 Anchises
Callisto
Hercules
Lucretia

Verginia

09 Androcles

10 Coriolanus
Rhea Silvia
Rhea Sylvia

Gods and goddesses of other regions and cultures include:

03 Anu (Sumerian)
Rod (Slavic)
Sin (Sumerian)
Wak (Ethiopian)

04 Adad (Mesopotamian)

Amma (Dogon)
Baal (Phoenician)
Enki (Sumerian)
Kane (Pacific islands)
Tane (Pacific islands)

05 Enlil (Sumerian)
   Epona (Gallic)
   Hadad (Assyrian)
   Pan Gu (Chinese)
   Perun (Slavic)
06 Adonis (Phoenician)
   Cybele (Phrygian)
   Guan Di (Chinese)
   Inanna (Sumerian)
   Ishtar (Mesopotamian)
   Kuan Ti (Chinese)
   Mithra (Indo-European)
   Modimo (African)
   Moloch (Canaanite)

Shango (African)
Svarog (Slavic)
Tengri (Mongol)
Teshub (Hurrian)
Tiamat (Akkadian)
Vahagn (Armenian)
07 Anahita (Persian)
   Astarte (Mesopotamian)
   Kumarbi (Hurrian)
   Ninurta (Sumerian)
   Taranis (Gallic)
   Triglav (Slavic)
   Zanhary (Madagascan)
08 Rosmerta (Gallo-Roman)

Skyamsen (Native
   American)
Sucellus (Gallic)
Teutates (Gallic)
09 Amaterasu (Japanese)
   Sventovit (Slavic)
10 Ahura Mazda (Indo-Iranian)
11 Thunderbird (Native
   American)
15 Izanagi no Mikoto
   (Japanese)
   Izanami no Mikoto
   (Japanese)

Mythological and legendary characters of other regions and cultures include:

03 Qat (Oceania)
04 Tell (William; Swiss)
05 Adapa (Akkadian)
   El Cid (Spanish)
   Faust (German)
   Frost (Jack; Scandinavian)
06 Anansi (African)
   Bunyan (Paul; American)
   Enkidu (Sumerian)
   George (St; English)
   Godiva (Lady; English)
   Merlin (British)
   Roland (French)
07 Aladdin (Chinese)
   Ali Baba (Arabian)
08 Baba Yaga (Russian/Slavic)

Hang Tuah (Malay)
Hiawatha (American)
Parsifal (European)
09 Appleseed (Johnny; American)
   Bluebeard (French)
   Lohengrin (Germanic)
   Robin Hood (English)
10 King Arthur (British)
   Yu the Great (Chinese)
11 Old King Cole (English)
12 Lemminkäinen (Finnish)
   Rip Van Winkle (American)
   Scheherazade (Middle Eastern)
   Will-o'-the-Wisp (European)
14 Flying Dutchman (Dutch)
15 Father Christmas (universal)

See also **fairy tale**; **fate**; **Homer**; **horse**; **king**; **legend**; **lover**; **monster**; **muse**; **opera**;
pantomime; **play**; **Shakespeare, William**

N

name

Ivor	Abd-al	Denis	Jared
Jack	Abdul	Denny	Jason
Jake	Abram	Denys	Jerry
Jeff	Adeel	Derek	Jesse
Jock	Adnan	Dicky	Jimmy
Joel	Ahmad	Dilip	Jools
Joey	Ahmed	Dipak	Kamal
John	Aidan	Donal	Kasim
Josh	Aiden	Duane	Keith
Joss	Alfie	Dwane	Kelly
Jude	Allan	Dylan	Kenny
Jule	Allen	Eddie	Kerry
Karl	Alwin	Edgar	Kevan
Kirk	Alwyn	Edwin	Kevin
Kurt	Amrit	Elroy	Kiran
Liam	Andie	Elton	Kumar
Luke	Angel	Elvis	Lance
Mark	Angus	Elwyn	Larry
Matt	Anwar	Emlyn	Leigh
Mick	Archy	Emrys	Lenny
Mike	Arran	Enoch	Leroy
Neal	Avril	Ernie	Lewie
Neil	Barry	Errol	Lewis
Nick	Basil	Farid	Linus
Noah	Bazza	Faruq	Lloyd
Noel	Benny	Felix	Logan
Omar	Billy	Fionn	Lorne
Owen	Bobby	Floyd	Louie
Ozzy	Boris	Frank	Louis
Paul	Brent	Gabby	Lucas
Pete	Brett	Gamal	Madoc
Phil	Brian	Garry	Manny
Rana	Bruce	Gavin	Micky
Ravi	Bruno	Geoff	Miles
Raza	Bryan	Gerry	Moray
René	Bunny	Giles	Moses
Reza	Cahal	Glenn	Moshe
Rhys	Calum	Gopal	Mungo
Rick	Cecil	Hamza	Murdo
Riza	Chaim	Harry	Myles
Rolf	Chris	Harun	Neale
Rory	Chuck	Hasan	Neddy
Ross	Claud	Haydn	Niall
Ryan	Clint	Henry	Nicky
Saul	Clive	Homer	Nicol
Sean	Clyde	Howel	Nigel
Seth	Colin	Humph	Ollie
Siôn	Colum	Husni	Orson
Theo	Conor	Hywel	Oscar
Toby	Corin	Idris	Ozzie
Tony	Cosmo	Ieuan	Paddy
Umar	Craig	Inigo	Percy
Walt	Cyril	Isaac	Perry
Will	Cyrus	Jacob	Peter
Yves	Damon	Jamal	Piers
Zach	Danny	James	Qasim
Zack	David	Jamie	Rajiv
05 Aaron	Davie	Jamil	Ralph

Randy
Ricky
Roald
Robin
Roddy
Roger
Rowan
Rufus
Sacha
Salim
Samir
Sammy
Sandy
Sasha
Scott
Shane
Shaun
Shawn
Silas
Simon
Solly
Steve
Sunil
Taffy
Tariq
Teddy
Terry
Tommy
Tudor
Ulric
Ultan
Vijay
Vinay
Waldo
Walid
Wally
Wasim
Watty
Wayne
Willy
Wynne
Zahir

06 Adrian
Albert
Alexei
Alexej
Alexis
Alfred
Andrew
Antony
Archie
Arnold
Arthur
Ashley
Ashraf
Aubrey
Austin
Averil

Barney
Benjie
Bernie
Bertie
Bharat
Billie
Blaise
Bobbie
Bunnie
Callum
Calvin
Caspar
Cathal
Cedric
Ciaran
Clancy
Claude
Clovis
Colley
Connor
Conrad
Dafydd
Damian
Damien
Daniel
Darren
Debdan
Declan
Deepak
Delroy
Dennis
Denzil
Dermot
Deryck
Devdan
Dicken
Dickie
Dickon
Dilwyn
Dobbin
Donald
Donnie
Dougal
Dudley
Dugald
Duggie
Duncan
Dustin
Eamonn
Eamunn
Edmund
Edward
Elijah
Ernest
Esmond
Eugene
Faisal
Fareed

Faysal
Fergus
Finbar
Fingal
Finlay
Finley
Fintan
Freddy
Gareth
Garret
George
Georgy
Gerald
Gerard
Gerrie
Gideon
Gobind
Gordon
Govind
Graeme
Graham
Gussie
Gwilym
Hamish
Hamzah
Harold
Haroun
Harvey
Hassan
Hayden
Haydon
Hector
Herbie
Hervey
Hilary
Horace
Howard
Howell
Hubert
Hughie
Husain
Husayn
Isaiah
Iseult
Ismail
Israel
Jarvis
Jasper
Jemmie
Jeremy
Jerome
Jervis
Jethro
Jimmie
Jockie
Jolyon
Jordan
Joseph

Joshua
Julian
Julius
Justin
Kelvin
Kennie
Kieran
Kieron
Kilian
Lachie
Laurie
Lawrie
Lennie
Leslie
Lester
Lionel
Lorcan
Lucius
Luther
Lynsey
Magnus
Mahmud
Marcel
Marcus
Marlon
Martin
Martyn
Marvin
Melvin
Melvyn
Mervyn
Milton
Morgan
Morris
Murray
Nathan
Neddie
Nichol
Ninian
Norman
Oliver
Osbert
Oswald
Pascal
Pearce
Philip
Pierce
Rabbie
Rajesh
Ramesh
Ranald
Randal
Ranulf
Reggie
Reuben
Richie
Robbie
Robert

Rodney
Roland
Ronald
Ruairi
Rudolf
Rupert
Rushdi
Saleem
Samuel
Sanjay
Seamas
Seamus
Seumas
Shamus
Sharif
Sidney
Sorley
Steven
Stevie
St John
Stuart
Suhayl
Sydney
Teddie
Thomas
Timmie
Tobias
Trevor
Tyrone
Vernon
Victor
Vikram
Virgil
Vivian
Vyvian
Vyvyan
Walter
Willie
Xavier
Zaheer

07 Abraham
Alister
Ambrose
Aneirin
Aneurin
Anthony
Auberon
Barnaby
Bernard
Bertram
Brendan
Brynmor
Chander
Chandra

Charles
Charley
Charlie
Christy
Clement
Crispin
Derrick
Desmond
Dominic
Douglas
Eustace
Feargal
Finbarr
Francie
Francis
Frankie
Freddie
Gabriel
Geordie
Georgie
Geraint
Gervase
Gilbert
Godfrey
Grahame
Gwillym
Herbert
Humphry
Hussain
Hussein
Ibrahim
Isadore
Isidore
Isodore
Jeffrey
Jocelin
Jocelyn
Johnnie
Kenneth
Killian
Krishna
Lachlan
Leonard
Leopold
Lindsay
Lindsey
Ludovic
Malcolm
Matthew
Maurice
Michael
Murdoch
Mustafa
Myrddin

Neville
Nicolas
Orlando
Patrick
Peredur
Phillip
Quentin
Quintin
Quinton
Randall
Randolf
Ranulph
Raymond
Reynold
Richard
Rowland
Rudolph
Russell
Shankar
Shelley
Solomon
Stanley
Stephen
Steuart
Stewart
Terence
Timothy
Torquil
Tristan
Vaughan
Vincent
Wilfred
Wilfrid
William
Winston
Zachary

08 Alasdair
Alastair
Algernon
Alistair
Ashleigh
Augustus
Barnabas
Benedick
Benedict
Benjamin
Beverley
Christie
Clarence
Clifford
Courtney
Crispian
Cuthbert
Dominick

Emmanuel
Frederic
Geoffrey
Humphrey
Jonathan
Jonathon
Joscelin
Kimberly
Kingsley
Lancelot
Laurence
Lawrence
Leontine
Leontyne
Llewelyn
Ludovick
Matthias
Meredith
Mordecai
Muhammad
Nicholas
Perceval
Percival
Randolph
Reginald
Roderick
Ruaidhri
Ruairidh
Ruaraidh
Rupinder
Terrance
Theodore
Tristram

09 Alexander
Archibald
Augustine
Christian
Ferdinand
Frederick
Gillespie
Kimberley
Launcelot
Nathaniel
Peregrine
Sebastian
Siegfried
Silvester
Somhairle
Sylvester
Valentine

10 Maximilian
11 Bartholomew
Christopher

Girls' names include:

02
Di
Do
Ib
Jo
Mo

03 Ada
Ali
Amy
Ann
Bab
Bea
Bee
Bel
Bet
Cis
Con
Deb
Dee
Die
Dot
Edy
Emm
Ena
Eva
Eve
Fay
Flo
Gay
Ida
Ina
Isa
Ivy
Jan
Jay
Jen
Joe
Joy
Kay
Kim
Kit
Lea
Lee
Liv
Liz
Lou
Mae
Mag
Mat
May
Meg
Mia
Nan
Pat
Peg
Pen

Pia
Rae
Ray
Ria
Ros
Roz
Sal
Sue
Tib
Una
Val
Viv
Win
Zoë

04 Abby
Abir
Addy
Afra
Aggy
Alex
Ally
Alma
Angy
Anna
Anne
Asma
Babs
Bell
Bess
Beth
Cara
Caro
Cass
Ceri
Cher
Cleo
Cora
Dana
Dawn
Dian
Dora
Edel
Edie
Edna
Ella
Elma
Elva
Emma
Emmy
Enid
Erin
Evie
Faye
Floy
Fred
Gabi

Gaea
Gaia
Gail
Gale
Gaye
Gene
Gert
Gill
Gina
Gita
Gwen
Hope
Ibby
Ines
Inez
Inga
Inge
Iona
Iris
Irma
Isla
Jade
Jane
Jean
Jess
Jill
Joan
Jodi
Jody
Joey
Joni
Joss
Jozy
Jude
Judy
June
Kate
Kath
Katy
Kaye
Kyra
Lala
Lara
Leah
Lena
Lian
Lily
Lina
Lisa
Lise
Livy
Liza
Lois
Lola
Lucy
Lynn

Maev
Mary
Maud
Meta
Mina
Moll
Mona
Myra
Nell
Nina
Nita
Noel
Nola
Nona
Nora
Olga
Page
Phyl
Poll
Prue
Rana
Rene
Rita
Romy
Rona
Rosa
Rose
Ruby
Ruth
Sara
Sian
Sìne
Siri
Sita
Suke
Suky
Susy
Suzy
Tess
Thea
Tina
Toni
Trix
Vera
Vita
Zara
Zena
Zola

05 Addie
Adela
Adèle
Aggie
Agnes
Ailie
Ailsa
Aisha

Alexa	Doris	Jessy	Mercy
Alice	Edith	Jinny	Meryl
Allie	Effie	Jodie	Moira
Amber	Eliza	Joely	Molly
Amina	Ellen	Josie	Morag
Anaïs	Ellie	Joyce	Morna
Angel	Elsie	Judie	Moyra
Angie	Emily	Julia	Myrna
Anila	Emmie	Julie	Nabby
Anita	Erica	Kanta	Nadia
Annie	Essie	Karen	Nance
Annis	Ethel	Karin	Nancy
Annot	Ethna	Karla	Nelly
Aphra	Ethne	Kathy	Nerys
April	Faith	Katie	Nessa
Areta	Fanny	Katya	Nesta
Aruna	Farah	Kelly	Netta
Avril	Ffion	Kenna	Netty
Aysha	Fiona	Kerry	Ngaio
Becky	Fleur	Kiera	Niamh
Bella	Flora	Kitty	Nicky
Belle	Freda	Kylie	Noele
Beryl	Freya	Lalla	Norah
Bessy	Gabby	Lally	Norma
Betsy	Gauri	Laura	Nuala
Betty	Gayle	Leigh	Olive
Biddy	Geeta	Leila	Olwen
Bride	Gemma	Leona	Olwin
Brona	Gerda	Letty	Olwyn
Bunny	Ginny	Liana	Onora
Bunty	Golda	Libby	Oprah
Candy	Golde	Linda	Paddy
Carla	Grace	Lindy	Padma
Carly	Greta	Lorna	Paige
Carol	Haley	Lorne	Pansy
Carys	Hatty	Louie	Patsy
Cathy	Hazel	Lubna	Patty
Celia	Heidi	Lucia	Paula
Chère	Helen	Lydia	Pearl
Chloe	Helga	Lynda	Peggy
Chris	Hetty	Lynne	Penny
Ciara	Hilda	Mabel	Petra
Cindy	Holly	Madge	Pippa
Cissy	Honor	Maeve	Polly
Clara	Ilana	Magda	Priya
Clare	Ilona	Máire	Raine
Coral	Irena	Màiri	Rajni
Daisy	Irene	Mamie	Renée
Debby	Isbel	Mandy	Rhian
Debra	Isold	Margo	Rhoda
Delia	Ivana	Maria	Rhona
Della	Jaime	Marie	Robin
Diana	Jamie	Matty	Robyn
Diane	Janet	Maude	Rosie
Dilys	Janis	Maura	Sacha
Dinah	Jemma	Mavis	Sadie
Dolly	Jenna	Meena	Sally
Donna	Jenny	Megan	Sarah

Sasha
Senga
Shona
Shula
Sibyl
Sindy
Sonia
Sonya
Sophy
Stacy
Sukie
Susan
Susie
Sybil
Tamar
Tammy
Tania
Tanya
Terry
Tessa
Thora
Tibby
Tilda
Tilly
Tracy
Trina
Trish
Trixy
Trudy
Unity
Viola
Wanda
Wendy
Wilma
Zahra
Zelda
Zowie

06 Adella
Agatha
Aileen
Alexia
Alexis
Alicia
Alison
Althea
Amabel
Amanda
Amelia
Andrea
Angela
Anneka
Annika
Anthea
Aphrah
Aretha
Ashley
Astrid

Audrey
Auriel
Auriol
Aurora
Aurore
Averil
Ayesha
Babbie
Barbie
Beatty
Bertha
Bertie
Bessie
Bianca
Biddie
Blanch
Bonnie
Brenda
Bridie
Brigid
Brigit
Briony
Bryony
Bunnie
Caddie
Candia
Carina
Carlie
Carmel
Carmen
Carola
Carole
Carrie
Cassie
Cathie
Cecily
Celina
Cherie
Cherry
Cheryl
Cicely
Cissie
Claire
Connie
Daphne
Davina
Deanna
Deanne
Debbie
Delyth
Denise
Dervla
Dianne
Dionne
Dolina
Doreen
Dorrie
Dottie

Dulcie
Dympna
Eartha
Edwina
Eileen
Eilidh
Eirian
Eirlys
Eithna
Eithne
Elaine
Elinor
Eloisa
Eloise
Elspet
Eluned
Elvira
Esther
Eunice
Evadne
Evelyn
Evonne
Fatima
Fedora
Felice
Finola
Flavia
Freddy
Frieda
Gaynor
Gertie
Gladys
Glenda
Glenys
Gloria
Glynis
Goldie
Gracie
Grania
Granya
Gudrun
Gwenda
Hannah
Hattie
Hayley
Helena
Hermia
Hester
Hilary
Honora
Honour
Imelda
Imogen
Indira
Ingrid
Isabel
Iseult
Ishbel

Isobel
Isolda
Isolde
Jamila
Jancis
Janice
Janina
Janine
Jeanie
Jemima
Jennie
Jessie
Joanie
Joanna
Joanne
Joelle
Joleen
Jolene
Judith
Juliet
Kamala
Karena
Karina
Kathie
Kirsty
Kittie
Kumari
Lalage
Lalita
Lallie
Laurel
Lauren
Laurie
Leanne
Leonie
Lesley
Lettie
Lianna
Lianne
Lilian
Lilias
Linnet
Lisbet
Lizzie
Lolita
Lottie
Louisa
Louise
Lynsey
Madhur
Maggie
Maisie
Marcia
Marian
Marina
Marion
Marsha
Martha

Mattie
Maxine
Melody
Meriel
Millie
Minnie
Miriam
Monica
Morven
Muriel
Myriam
Myrtle
Nabila
Nadine
Nellie
Nessie
Nettie
Nicola
Nicole
Noelle
Noreen
Odette
Olivia
Olwyne
Paloma
Pamela
Pattie
Petula
Phemie
Phoebe
Rachel
Rajani
Raquel
Regina
Renata
Rhonda
Robina
Rodney
Roisin
Roshan
Rosina
Rowena
Roxana
Roxane
Rubina
Sabina
Sabine
Salome
Sandra
Saskia
Selina
Seonag
Serena
Sharon
Shashi
Sheela
Sheena
Sheila

Sherry
Sheryl
Sidney
Sidony
Silvia
Simone
Sinéad
Sophia
Sophie
Sorcha
Stacey
Stella
Suhair
Sydney
Sylvia
Tamara
Tammie
Tamsin
Teenie
Teresa
Thelma
Tibbie
Tracey
Tricia
Trisha
Trixie
Ulrica
Ursula
Vanora
Verity
Vijaya
Vinaya
Violet
Vivian
Vivien
Vyvian
Vyvyan
Winnie
Winona
Wynona
Xanthe
Yasmin
Yvette
Yvonne
Zainab
Zaynab

07 Abigail
Aisling
Allegra
Allison
Andrina
Annabel
Annette
Antonia
Anushka
Ariadne
Augusta

Barbara
Beatrix
Belinda
Bernice
Bethany
Bettina
Bharati
Blanche
Bridget
Bronach
Bronagh
Bronwen
Caitlín
Camilla
Candace
Candice
Candida
Carleen
Carlene
Carolyn
Cecilia
Chandra
Chantal
Charity
Charley
Chelsea
Chelsey
Christy
Clarice
Claudia
Clodagh
Colette
Colleen
Corinna
Corinne
Crystal
Cynthia
Daniela
Deborah
Deepika
Deirdre
Demelza
Désirée
Dolores
Dorothy
Dymphna
Eiluned
Eleanor
Elspeth
Emerald
Estella
Estelle
Eugenia
Eugénie
Felicia
Fenella
Floella
Florrie

Flossie
Frances
Francie
Frankie
Freddie
Georgia
Georgie
Gillian
Giselle
Gráinne
Gwennie
Gwenyth
Gwyneth
Haniyya
Harriet
Heather
Heloise
Isadora
Iseabal
Isidora
Jacinta
Jacinth
Janetta
Janette
Jasmine
Jeannie
Jenifer
Jessica
Jillian
Jocasta
Jocelin
Jocelyn
Johanna
Jonquil
Josepha
Josette
Juliana
Justina
Justine
Kathryn
Katrina
Katrine
Khadija
Kirstie
Kirstin
Krystal
Krystle
Lakshmi
Laraine
Lavinia
Leonora
Letitia
Lettice
Lillian
Lillias
Lindsay
Lindsey
Linette

Lisbeth
Lisette
Lizbeth
Loretta
Lucilla
Lucille
Lucinda
Lynette
Madonna
Margery
Marilyn
Marjory
Marlene
Martina
Martine
Matilda
Maureen
Melanie
Melissa
Merriel
Mildred
Miranda
Myfanwy
Nanette
Natalia
Natalie
Natasha
Nichola
Nigella
Ninette
Ophelia
Ottilie
Pandora
Parvati
Pascale
Paulina
Pauline
Phyllis
Queenie
Rachael
Raelene
Rebecca
Roberta
Rosabel
Rosalie
Rosanna
Rosetta
Roxanne
Sabrina
Saffron
Seonaid
Sharifa
Shelagh
Shelley
Shirley
Sidonie
Silvana
Siobhán

Surayya
Susanna
Sybilla
Tabitha
Theresa
Tiffany
Valerie
Vanessa
Venetia
Wasimah
Wenonah
Yolanda
Zubaida
Zuleika

08 Adelaide
Adrianne
Adrienne
Angelica
Angelina
Angharad
Arabella
Ashleigh
Beatrice
Berenice
Beverley
Caroline
Catriona
Charlene
Charmian
Chrissie
Christie
Chrystal
Clarinda
Clarissa
Claudine
Cordelia
Cornelia
Courtney
Cressida
Daniella
Danielle
Dominica
Dorothea
Eleanore
Emmeline
Euphemia
Eustacia
Felicity
Florence
Francine
Georgina
Germaine
Gertrude
Gervaise
Griselda
Grizelda
Hermione

Isabella
Iseabail
Jacintha
Jacinthe
Jannetta
Jeanette
Jennifer
Joceline
Joscelin
Katerina
Kathleen
Kimberly
Kirsteen
Larraine
Lauretta
Leontine
Leontyne
Linnette
Lorraine
Madeline
Magdalen
Marcella
Marcelle
Margaret
Marianne
Marigold
Marjorie
Mathilda
Meredith
Michaela
Michelle
Morwenna
Ottoline
Patience
Patricia
Paulette
Penelope
Philippa
Primrose
Prudence
Prunella
Rhiannon
Rosalind
Rosamond
Rosamund
Roseanna
Roseanne
Rosemary
Samantha
Scarlett
Shakirah
Susannah
Theodora
Theresia
Tomasina
Veronica
Victoria
Virginia

Winifred
09 Albertina
Albertine
Alexandra
Anastasia
Annabella
Annabelle
Cassandra
Catharine
Catherina
Catherine
Charlotte
Charmaine
Christian
Christina
Christine
Claudette
Cleopatra
Constance
Elisabeth
Elizabeth
Fionnuala
Frederica
Gabrielle
Genevieve
Georgette
Georgiana
Geraldine
Ghislaine
Guinevere
Gwendolen
Gwenllian
Henrietta
Jackeline
Jacquelyn
Jacquetta
Jaqueline
Jeannette
Josephine
Katharine
Katherine
Kimberley
Madeleine
Magdalene
Mélisande
Millicent
Nicolette
Priscilla
Rosemarie
Serenella
Sharmaine
Sigourney
Silvestra
Stephanie
Sylvestra
Thomasina
Valentine

10	Antoinette	Christiana	Jacqueline	11	Constantine
	Bernadette	Clementina	Shakuntala		
	Christabel	Clementine	Wilhelmina		

See also **cinema**; **city**; **club**; **country**; **French**; **German**; **Irish**; **king**; **pseudonym**; **public house**; **queen**; **Scottish**; **Welsh**

narcotic

Narcotics include:

03 ava
04 bang
   coca
   dope
   kava
05 bhang
   dagga
06 charas
   datura

   pituri
07 churrus
   narceen
08 narceine
10 belladonna
11 Indian berry
   laurel-water
15 cocculus indicus

See also **drug**

National Football League *see* **American football**

national holiday *see* **holiday**

national park *see* **park**

nationality

Nationalities include:

03 Lao (Laos)
04 Kiwi (New Zealand)
   Thai (Thailand)
05 Bajan (Barbados)
   Congo (Congo/Democratic Republic of the Congo)
   Cuban (Cuba)
   Czech (Czech Republic)
   Dutch (The Netherlands)
   Greek (Greece)
   Iraqi (Iraq)
   Irish (Ireland)
   Omani (Oman)
   Saudi (Saudi Arabia)
   Swazi (Swaziland)
   Swiss (Switzerland)
   Tajik (Tajikistan)
   Uzbek (Uzbekistan)
   Welsh (Wales)
06 Afghan (Afghanistan)
   Danish (Denmark)
   Fijian (Fiji)
   French (France)

   German (Germany)
   Indian (India)
   Kenyan (Kenya)
   Korean (North Korea/South Korea)
   Kyrgyz (Kyrgyzstan)
   Libyan (Libya)
   Malian (Mali)
   Polish (Poland)
   Qatari (Qatar)
   Samoan (Samoa)
   Somali (Somalia)
   Syrian (Syria)
   Tongan (Tonga)
   Yapese (Federated States of Micronesia)
   Yemeni (Yemen)
07 Angolan (Angola)
   Basotho (Lesotho)
   Belgian (Belgium)
   Bosnian (Bosnia and Herzegovina)
   British (United Kingdom)
   Burmese (Myanmar)
   Chadian (Chad)
   Chilean (Chile)

Chinese (China)
Comoran (Comoros)
Cypriot (Cyprus)
Emirati (United Arab Emirates)
English (England)
Finnish (Finland)
Gambian (The Gambia)
Guinean (Guinea)
Haitian (Haiti)
Iranian (Iran)
Israeli (Israel)
Italian (Italy)
Ivorian (Côte d'Ivoire)
Kosraen (Federated States of Micronesia)
Kuwaiti (Kuwait)
Laotian (Laos)
Latvian (Latvia)
Maltese (Malta)
Mexican (Mexico)
Monacan (Monaco)
Mosotho (Lesotho)
Nauruan (Nauru)
Palauan (Palau)
Russian (Russia)
Rwandan (Rwanda)
Sahrawi (Western Sahara)
Serbian (Serbia)
Spanish (Spain)
Swedish (Sweden)
Tadzhik (Tajikistan)
Turkish (Turkey)
Turkmen (Turkmenistan)
Ugandan (Uganda)
Zambian (Zambia)

08 Albanian (Albania)
Algerian (Algeria)
American (United States of America)
Andorran (Andorra)
Antiguan (Antigua and Barbuda)
Armenian (Armenia)
Austrian (Austria)
Bahamian (The Bahamas)
Bahraini (Bahrain)
Barbudan (Antigua and Barbuda)
Batswana (Botswana)
Belizean (Belize)
Beninese (Benin)
Bolivian (Bolivia)
Bruneian (Brunei Darussalam)
Canadian (Canada)
Chuukese (Federated States of Micronesia)
Croatian (Croatia)
Egyptian (Egypt)
Eritrean (Eritrea)
Estonian (Estonia)
Filipina (Philippines)
Filipino (Philippines)
Gabonese (Gabon)

Georgian (Georgia)
Ghanaian (Ghana)
Grenadan (Grenada)
Guyanese (Guyana)
Honduran (Honduras)
Jamaican (Jamaica)
Japanese (Japan)
Lebanese (Lebanon)
Liberian (Liberia)
Malagasy (Madagascar)
Malawian (Malawi)
Moldovan (Moldova)
Moroccan (Morocco)
Motswana (Botswana)
Namibian (Namibia)
Nepalese (Nepal)
Nevisian (St Kitts and Nevis)
Nigerian (Nigeria)
Nigerien (Niger)
Peruvian (Peru)
Romanian (Romania)
Sahraoui (Western Sahara)
Scottish (Scotland)
St Lucian (St Lucia)
Sudanese (Sudan)
Timorese (East Timor)
Togolese (Togo)
Tunisian (Tunisia)
Tuvaluan (Tuvalu)

09 Argentine (Argentina)
Barbadian (Barbados)
Bhutanese (Bhutan)
Brazilian (Brazil)
Bulgarian (Bulgaria)
Burkinabé (Burkina Faso)
Burundian (Burundi)
Cambodian (Cambodia)
Colombian (Colombia)
Congolese (Congo/Democratic Republic of the Congo)
Dominican (Dominica/Dominican Republic)
Ethiopian (Ethiopia)
Grenadian (Grenada)
Hungarian (Hungary)
Icelandic (Iceland)
I-Kiribati (Kiribati)
Jordanian (Jordan)
Kittitian (St Kitts and Nevis)
Malaysian (Malaysia)
Maldivian (Maldives)
Mauritian (Mauritius)
Mongolian (Mongolia)
Ni-Vanuatu (Vanuatu)
Norwegian (Norway)
Pakistani (Pakistan)
Pohnpeian (Federated States of Micronesia)
Sahrawian (Western Sahara)
Santoméan (São Tomé and Príncipe)

São Toméan (São Tomé and Príncipe)
Singapore (Singapore)
Slovakian (Slovakia)
Slovenian (Slovenia)
Sri Lankan (Sri Lanka)
Taiwanese (Taiwan)
Tanzanian (Tanzania)
Ukrainian (Ukraine)
Uruguayan (Uruguay)

10 Australian (Australia)
Belarusian (Belarus)
Costa Rican (Costa Rica)
Djiboutian (Djibouti)
Ecuadorean (Ecuador)
Ecuadorian (Ecuador)
Guatemalan (Guatemala)
Indonesian (Indonesia)
Lithuanian (Lithuania)
Luxembourg (Luxembourg)
Macedonian (Macedonia)
Monégasque (Monaco)
Mozambican (Mozambique)
Myanmarese (Myanmar)
New Zealand (New Zealand)
Nicaraguan (Nicaragua)
Panamanian (Panama)
Paraguayan (Paraguay)
Philippine (Philippines)
Portuguese (Portugal)
Sahraouian (Western Sahara)
Salvadoran (El Salvador)
Senegalese (Senegal)
Surinamese (Suriname)
Tobagonian (Trinidad and Tobago)
Venezuelan (Venezuela)

Vietnamese (Vietnam)
Vincentian (St Vincent and the Grenadines)
Zimbabwean (Zimbabwe)

11 Argentinian (Argentina)
Azerbaijani (Azerbaijan)
Bangladeshi (Bangladesh)
Cameroonian (Cameroon)
Cape Verdean (Cape Verde)
Kazakhstani (Kazakhstan)
Marshallese (Marshall Islands)
Mauritanian (Mauritania)
Micronesian (Federated States of Micronesia)
Montenegrin (Montenegro)
North Korean (North Korea)
Sammarinese (San Marino)
Seychellois (Seychelles)
Singaporean (Singapore)
South Korean (South Korea)
Tajikistani (Tajikistan)
Trinidadian (Trinidad and Tobago)

12 Luxembourger (Luxembourg)
Saudi Arabian (Saudi Arabia)
South African (South Africa)
St Vincentian (St Vincent and the Grenadines)

13 Equatoguinean (Equatorial Guinea)
Herzegovinian (Bosnia and Herzegovina)
Liechtenstein (Liechtenstein)
Sierra Leonean (Sierra Leone)

14 Central African (Central African Republic)
Guinea-Bissauan (Guinea-Bissau)

15 Liechtensteiner (Liechtenstein)
Papua New Guinean (Papua New Guinea)
Solomon Islander (Solomon Islands)

See also **Africa**; **Asia**; **Europe**; **Scandinavia**

Native American *see* **The Americas**

NATO

North Atlantic Treaty Organization (NATO) members:

02	UK		Latvia		Hungary	
03	USA		Norway		Iceland	
			Poland		Romania	
05	Italy		Turkey			
	Spain	**07**	Belgium	**08**	Bulgaria	
06	Canada		Denmark		Portugal	
	France		Estonia		Slovakia	
	Greece		Germany		Slovenia	

09	Lithuania
10	Luxembourg
13	Czech Republic
	United Kingdom
14	The Netherlands
21	United States of America

See also **alphabet**

NATO phonetic alphabet *see* **alphabet**

natural history

Terms used in natural history include:

03 era
sea
04 bird
bush
cell
dune
fish
life
moor
park
reef
rock
soil
tree
05 algae
atoll
biome
coast
Earth
epoch
fungi
grass
ocean
plant
river
swamp
virus

06 animal
botany
desert
energy
famine
flower
forest
fossil
fungus
garden
growth
insect
jungle
mammal
nature
period
phylum
planet
07 biology
climate
drought
ecology
estuary
geology
habitat
mineral
peat bog

prairie
reserve
savanna
species
wetland
zoology
08 acid rain
bacteria
dinosaur
genetics
hedgerow
heredity
mountain
savannah
skeleton
wildlife
woodland
09 bacterium
behaviour
breathing
digestion
evolution
geography
grassland
pollution
10 ecotourism
entomology

extinction
mineralogy
naturalist
population
rainforest
vertebrate
11 archaeology
circulation
environment
groundwater
living world
ornithology
pollination
reclamation
respiration
12 anthropology
biodiversity
conservation
invertebrate
national park
paleontology
reproduction
13 fertilization
global warming
palaeontology
14 photosynthesis

See also **biology**; **zoology**

naturalist *see* **biology**

nature reserve *see* **park**

nautical

Nautical terms include:

03 aft
jib
lee
row
run
yaw
04 beam
beat
dock
fore
gybe
heel
helm
knot
list

moor
quay
reef
roll
sink
tack
tide
trim
wake
wash
wave
05 cargo
ferry
fleet
float

haven
jetty
lay up
plane
put in
reach
refit
watch
wharf
wreck
06 afloat
broach
convoy
course
cruise

embark
jetsam
launch
marina
marine
maroon
mayday
mutiny
voyage
07 ballast
bow-wave
capsize
cast off
current
dry dock

ebb tide
flotsam
foghorn
go about
harbour
heave to
leeward
low tide
mooring
on board
ride out
riptide
salvage
sea lane
sea legs
seasick
set sail
sheet in

slipway
weather

08 bear away
becalmed
chandler
dockyard
flotilla
high tide
lee shore
life buoy
life-raft
make fast
neap tide
put to sea
shipping
shipyard
stowaway

windward

09 amidships
disembark
foreshore
seafaring
seaworthy
ship water
shipwreck
stevedore

10 coastguard
deadweight
harbour-bar
head to wind
heavy swell
lay a course
life-jacket
life-rocket

navigation
run aground
seamanship
shore leave
slip anchor

11 harbour dues
weigh anchor

12 air-sea rescue
breeches-buoy
pitch and toss
shipping lane
ship's company

13 dead reckoning
harbour-master

14 circumnavigate
compass bearing

See also **navigation**; **sailing**

navigation

Navigational aids and systems include:

03 gee
GPS
INS
log
Vor

05 chart
loran
pilot

radar

07 compass
navarho
sextant

08 bell buoy
dividers
VHF radio

09 lightship
omnirange

10 depth gauge
lighthouse
marker buoy

11 chronometer
conical buoy

echo-sounder
gyrocompass

13 nautical table
parallel ruler

15 astronavigation
flux-gate compass
magnetic compass

See also **signal**

navigator *see* **exploration**; **sailing**

navy *see* **military**

nerve

Nerves include:

05 optic
sural
ulnar
vagus

06 facial
lumbar
median
radial
sacral
tibial

07 femoral

phrenic
plantar
sciatic

08 abducens
axillary
peroneal
thoracic

09 coccygeal
obturator
olfactory
saphenous

trochlear

10 oculomotor
splanchnic
trigeminal

11 hypoglossal
intercostal

12 ilioinguinal
long thoracic
suboccipital

13 genitofemoral
suprascapular

thoracodorsal

14 dorsal scapular
medial pectoral

15 iliohypogastric
inferior gluteal
lateral pectoral
lesser auricular
lesser occipital
spinal accessory
superior gluteal

nest *see* **animal**

The Netherlands

Cities and notable towns in The Netherlands include:

05 Delft	Haarlem	**09** Amsterdam	**10** Leeuwarden
06 Arnhem	Utrecht	Eindhoven	Maastricht
	08 Nijmegen	Groningen	Middelburg
07 Den Haag	The Hague	Rotterdam	**11** 's-Gravenhage

Administrative divisions of The Netherlands, with regional capitals:

07 Drenthe (Assen)
Limburg (Maastricht)
Utrecht (Utrecht)
Zeeland (Middelburg)
09 Flevoland (Lelijstad)
Friesland (Leeuwarden)
Groningen (Groningen)
10 Gelderland (Arnhem)

Overijssel (Zwolle)
11 Zuid-Holland (The Hague)
12 Noord-Brabant ('s-Hertogenbosch)
Noord-Holland (Haarlem)
North Brabant ('s-Hertogenbosch)
North Holland (Haarlem)
South Holland (The Hague)

Dutch landmarks include:

04 Maas	**08** Oude Kerk	**10** IJsselmeer	**13** Anne Frank Huis
06 Amstel	**09** Keukenhof	Nieuwe Kerk	**15** Ann Frank's house
07 Scheldt	Zuider Zee	**11** Afsluitdijk	Stedelijk Museum
		Rijksmuseum	

See also **Low Countries**

New York

New York boroughs:

05 Bronx	**08** Brooklyn	**12** Staten Island
06 Queens	**09** Manhattan	

Other districts of New York include:

04 Noho
Soho
06 Corona
Harlem
Hollis
Inwood
Nolita
Queens
07 Astoria
Chelsea
Clifton
Kips Bay
Midtown
Midwood
Tribeca
08 Brooklyn
Canarsie
East Side

El Barrio
Elmhurst
Flatbush
Flatiron
Flushing
Gramercy
Rego Park
Steinway
The Bronx
West Side
09 Briarwood
Chinatown
Flatlands
Manhattan
Ozone Park
Park Slope
Princeton
Ridgewood

The Bowery
Turtle Bay
Woodhaven
Yorkville
10 Cobble Hill
Douglaston
Greenpoint
Ground Zero
Kew Gardens
Marble Hill
Sunset Park
11 Borough Park
Central Park
Coney Island
East Village
Ellis Island
Forest Hills
Howard Beach

Little Italy
Little Korea
New Brighton
West Village
12 Alphabet City
Crown Heights
Cypress Hills
Hell's Kitchen

South Jamaica
Staten Island
Williamsburg
13 Brighton Beach
Lower East Side
Spanish Harlem
Upper East Side
Upper West Side

14 Jackson Heights
Long Island City
Lower Manhattan
Manhattan Beach
Stuyvesant Town
15 Brooklyn Heights
Garment District
Roosevelt Island

New York streets include:

06 Bowery
07 Park Row
08 Broadway
FDR Drive
10 14th Street
21st Avenue
23rd Street
34th Street
36th Avenue
42nd Street
57th Street
79th Street
96th Street
Park Avenue
Wall Street
11 Canal Street
Fifth Avenue

First Avenue
Grand Street
Sixth Avenue
Third Avenue
Union Square
Vesey Street
12 Broome Street
Eighth Avenue
Fourth Avenue
Fulton Street
Hudson Street
Second Avenue
Spring Street
Varick Street
13 Houston Street
Jackson Avenue
JFK Expressway
Madison Square

Seventh Avenue
14 Bleecker Street
Columbus Circle
Delancey Street
East 42nd Street
Flatbush Avenue
Harrison Street
Riverside Drive
Sheridan Square
Sunrise Highway
West 42nd Street
15 Central Park West
Cortlandt Street
Greenwich Street
Lexington Avenue
Queens Boulevard
West Side Highway

New York landmarks include:

03 EWR
JFK
NYU
04 CBGB
MoMA
05 Macy's
06 The Met
07 Barneys
Factory
Whitney
08 Broadway
Bronx Zoo
Studio 54
09 East River
The Dakota
10 Bronx River
Cotton Club
FAO Schwarz
Ground Zero

Guggenheim
Rose Center
Wall Street
11 Battery Park
Central Park
Coney Island
Ellis Island
Federal Hall
Harlem River
Hudson River
Penn Station
Shea Stadium
Times Square
Union Square
12 Carnegie Hall
Chelsea Hotel
Hotel Chelsea
Prospect Park
Staten Island
The Cloisters

13 Apollo Theater
Bloomingdale's
Gracie Mansion
Lincoln Center
Lincoln Tunnel
Pan Am Building
St Paul's Church
Yankee Stadium
14 Brooklyn Bridge
Fraunces Tavern
Grand Army Plaza
Waldorf Astoria
Washington Arch
15 Flushing Meadows
Frick Collection
Manhattan Bridge
Metlife Building
Saks Fifth Avenue
Seagram Building
Statue of Liberty
Trump World Tower

New Zealand

Cities and notable towns in New Zealand include:

06 Napier
Nelson
Timaru

07 Dunedin
Manukau
Rotorua

08 Auckland
Gisborne
Hamilton
Hastings
Tauranga
Wanganui

09 Whangarei

10 Wellington

11 New Plymouth

12 Christchurch
Invercargill

15 Palmerston North

Regions and territories of New Zealand, with regional capitals:

04 Niue (Alofi)
05 Otago (Dunedin)
06 Nelson (Nelson)
Tasman (Richmond)
07 Tokelau
Waikato (Hamilton)
08 Auckland (Auckland)
Gisborne (Gisborne)
Taranaki (New Plymouth)
09 Hawke's Bay (Napier)

Northland (Whangarei)
Southland (Invercargill)
West Coast (Greymouth)
10 Canterbury (Christchurch)
Wellington (Wellington)
11 Bay of Plenty (Tauranga)
Cook Islands (Avarua)
Marlborough (Blenheim)
14 Chatham Islands
16 Manawatu-Wanganui (Palmerston North)

New Zealand electorates:

04 Ilam
Mana
05 Epsom
Otago
Otaki
Piako
Taupo
06 Aoraki
Napier
Nelson
Rakaia
Rodney
Tainui
Tamaki
Wigram
07 Mangere
New Lynn
Rotorua
Te Atatu
08 Clevedon
Manurewa
Mt Albert
Rimutaka

Rongotai
Tauranga
Tukituki
Waiariki
09 East Coast
Hutt South
Mt Roskill
Northcote
Northland
Pakuranga
Wairarapa
Waitakere
Whanganui
Whangarei
10 Coromandel
North Shore
Rangitikei
Te Tai Tonga
11 Bay of Plenty
Helensville
Manukau East
New Plymouth
Port Waikato

Waimakariri
12 Dunedin North
Dunedin South
Hamilton East
Hamilton West
Invercargill
Maungakiekie
Te Tai Hauauru
Te Tai Tokerau
13 East Coast Bays
Ikaora-Rawhiti
Ohariu-Belmont
14 Banks Peninsula
Tamaki Makaurau
15 Auckland Central
Clutha-Southland
Palmerston North
West Coast-Tasman
16 Christchurch East
17 Wellington Central
19 Christchurch Central
Taranaki-King Country

New Zealand landmarks include:

05 Hawea
06 Mt Cook
Te Anau

Wanaka
07 Aorangi
Rotorua

Ruapehu
Waikato
08 Mt Egmont

Wakatipu	**11** Rakaia Gorge	**15** Mangere Mountain
Wanganui	**12** Milford Sound	Ninety Mile Beach
09 Fiordland	Southern Alps	Whangaparaoa Bay
Lake Taupo	**13** Stewart Island	
10 Mt Victoria	**14** Otago Peninsula	

See also **Australasia**; **governor**; **mythology**; **prime minister**

news

News agencies include:

02 AP (Associated Press)
PA (Press Association)

03 AAP (Australian Associated Press)
AFP (Agence France-Presse)
UPI (United Press International)

04 NZPA (New Zealand Press Association)

Tass (Telegraph Agency of the Soviet Union)

07 Reuters

08 ITAR-Tass (Information Telegraph Agency of
Russia)

15 Associated Press

newspaper

Newspapers and magazines include:

02 *GQ*
Ms
OK!
XL
Ya

03 *FHM*
NME
Red
She
TES
TLS
Viz

04 *Best*
Bild
Chat
Chic
Elle
Heat
Judy
Life
Lion
Look
Mind
Mizz
Mojo
More!
Puck
Time
Trud
TV21
Zest

05 *Arena*
Bella
Bliss

Bunty
Chips
Ebony
Globe
Hello!
Honey
Iskra
Jinty
Judge
Mandy
Maxim
Metro
Prima
Punch
Shoot
Stern
Tammy
Tiger
Vogue
Which?
Wired
Woman
World

06 *Avanti*
Buster
Cheeky
Closer
El Pais
Forbes
Granta
Herald
Hornet
Jackie
Lancet

Le Soir
Loaded
Nature
Pippin
Pravda
Scraps
Sparky
Tatler
The Sun
Topper
War Cry
Wonder

07 *Annabel*
Company
Die Welt
Esquire
Film Fun
Fortune
Glamour
Hotspur
Hustler
Jackpot
Journal
Kerrang!
La Libre
Le Monde
L'Equipe
Mayfair
Men Only
Newsday
Options
Playboy
Rainbow
Science

The Face
The Lady
The List
The Star
The Week
Time Out
Titbits
Tribune
TV Times
Twinkle
Valiant
Whizzer
Whoopee

08 Campaign
Decanter
Die Woche
European
Gay Times
Izvestia
Knockout
La Presse
La Stampa
Le Figaro
My Weekly
Newsweek
New Woman
Prospect
Scotsman
Smart Set
Sparkler
The Beano
The Dandy
The Eagle
The Field
The Idler
The Month
The Oldie
The Queen
The Times
USA Today

09 Adventure
Comic Cuts
Daily Mail
Daily News
Daily Star
Good Words
Home Notes
Ideal Home
Mirabelle
New Yorker
Penthouse
Petticoat
Q Magazine
Red Pepper
Smash Hits
The Beezer
The Friend

The Grocer
The Herald
The Lancet
The Mirror
The People
The Tablet
The Tatler
The Victor
Woman's Day
Woman's Own

10 Asian Times
Daily Sport
Der Spiegel
Eve's Weekly
Irish Times
Men's Health
New Society
Paris-Match
Private Eye
Racing Post
Radio Times
Sunday Post
The Courier
The Express
Vanity Fair
Weekly News

11 Church Times
Country Life
Daily Herald
Daily Mirror
Daily Record
Daily Sketch
Jack and Jill
Marie Claire
Melody Maker
Morning Star
New Republic
New York Post
Picture Post
Sunday Press
Sunday Sport
Sunday World
The Big Issue
The European
The Guardian
The Listener
The Observer
The Universe
Western Mail
Woman's Realm

12 Angling Times
Asahi Shimbun
Cosmopolitan
Daily Courant
Family Circle
Fortean Times
History Today

La Repubblica
Look and Learn
Mail on Sunday
New Scientist
New Statesman
New York Times
Nursing Times
Poetry Review
Rolling Stone
Sunday Mirror
Tagesspiegel
The Economist
The Pink Paper
The Spectator
Time Magazine
Woman and Home
Woman's Weekly

13 Catholic Times
Country Living
Daltons Weekly
Farmers Weekly
Financial News
Glasgow Herald
Harper's Bazaar
Harper's Weekly
Homes and Ideas
Horse and Hound
Just Seventeen
London Gazette
Mother and Baby
Penny Magazine
People's Friend
Reader's Digest
The Bookseller
The Sunday Post
The Watchtower
Wales on Sunday
Woman's Journal

14 Caribbean Times
Catholic Herald
Financial Times
House and Garden
House Beautiful
Literary Review
News of the World
Roy of the Rovers
Simplicissimus
The Boston Globe
The Gentlewoman
The Independent
The New York Post
The Suffragette
The Sunday Times
Washington Post

15 Evening Standard
Exchange and Mart
Express on Sunday

Harpers and Queen
Homes and Gardens
Los Angeles Times
Picture Politics
Press and Journal

Socialist Worker
Sunday Telegraph
The Boston Herald
The Boy's Own Paper
The Mail on Sunday

The National Post
The New York Times
The Times of India
Whizzer and Chips

Newspaper proprietors and magnates include:

04 King (Cecil Harmsworth; 1901–87, English)
Ochs (Adolph Simon; 1858–1935, US)
Shah (Eddy; 1944– , English)

05 Astor (John Jacob, Lord; 1886–1971, US/British)
Astor (William Waldorf, Viscount; 1848–1919, US/British)
Black (Conrad, Lord; 1944– , Canadian/British)

06 Aitken (Sir Max; 1910–85, Canadian/British)
Graham (Katherine Meyer; 1917–2001, US)
Hearst (William Randolph; 1863–1951, US)
Packer (Sir Frank; 1906–74, Australian)
Ridder (Bernard H, Jnr; 1916–2002, US)
Walter (John; 1739–1812, English)
Walter (John; 1819–94, English)

07 Barclay (Sir David; 1934– , English)
Barclay (Sir Frederick; 1934– , English)
Camrose (William Ewert Berry, Viscount; 1879–1954, Welsh)

See also **journalism**

Kemsley (James Gomer Berry, Viscount; 1883–1968, Welsh)
Maxwell (Robert; 1923–91, Czech/British)
Murdoch (Rupert; 1931– , Australian/US)
Pearson (Sir Cyril Arthur; 1866–1921, English)
Riddell (George, Lord; 1865–1934, Scottish)
Scripps (Edward Wyllis; 1854–1926, US)
Thomson (D C; 1861–1954, Scottish)
Thomson (Roy, Lord; 1894–1976, Canadian/British)

08 Pulitzer (Joseph; 1847–1911, US)

10 Berlusconi (Silvio; 1936– , Italian)
Rothermere (Harold Harmsworth, Viscount; 1868–1940, English)

11 Beaverbrook (Max Aitken, Lord; 1879–1964, Canadian/British)
Northcliffe (Alfred Harmsworth, Viscount; 1865–1922, Irish/British)

nickname *see* **American football**; **Australia**; **Australian rules football**; **baseball**; **basketball**; **cricket**; **football**; **Rugby League**; **Rugby Union**; **United States of America**

Nine Muses *see* muse

Nobel Prize

Nobel Prize for Chemistry winners:

03 Lee (Yuan T; 1986)

04 Agre (Peter; 2003)
Berg (Paul; 1980)
Cech (Thomas R; 1989)
Cram (Donald J; 1987)
Curl (Robert F, Jnr; 1996)
Ertl (Gerhard; 2007)
Fenn (John B; 2002)
Hahn (Otto; 1944)
Klug (Sir Aaron; 1982)
Kohn (Walter; 1998)
Kuhn (Richard; 1938)
Lehn (Jean-Marie; 1987)
Olah (George A; 1994)
Rose (Irwin; 2004)

Skou (Jens C; 1997)
Todd (Lord; 1957)
Urey (Harold C; 1934)

05 Alder (Kurt; 1950)
Aston (Francis W; 1922)
Bosch (Carl; 1931)
Boyer (Paul D; 1997)
Brown (Herbert C; 1979)
Corey (Elias James; 1990)
Curie (Marie; 1911)
Debye (Peter; 1936)
Diels (Otto; 1950)
Eigen (Manfred; 1967)
Ernst (Richard R; 1991)
Flory (Paul J; 1974)

Fukui (Kenichi; 1981)
Haber (Fritz; 1918)
Huber (Robert; 1988)
Karle (Jerome; 1985)
Kroto (Sir Harold; 1996)
Libby (Willard F; 1960)
Moore (Stanford; 1972)
Natta (Giulio; 1963)
Pople (John; 1998)
Pregl (Fritz; 1923)
Smith (Michael; 1993)
Soddy (Frederick; 1921)
Stein (William H; 1972)
Synge (Richard LM; 1952)
Taube (Henry; 1983)
Tsien (Roger Y; 2008)

06 Altman (Sidney; 1989)
Baeyer (Adolf von; 1905)
Barton (Sir Derek; 1969)
Calvin (Melvin; 1961)
Grubbs (Robert H; 2005)
Harden (Arthur; 1929)
Hassel (Odd; 1969)
Heeger (Alan; 2000)
Hevesy (George de; 1943)
Joliot (Frédéric; 1935)
Karrer (Paul; 1937)
Leloir (Luis; 1970)
Marcus (Rudolph A; 1992)
Martin (Archer JP; 1952)
Michel (Hartmut; 1988)
Molina (Mario J; 1995)
Mullis (Kary B; 1993)
Nernst (Walther; 1920)
Noyori (Ryoji; 2001)
Perutz (Max F; 1962)
Porter (George, Lord; 1967)
Prelog (Vladimir; 1975)
Ramsay (Sir William; 1904)
Sanger (Frederick; 1958, 1980)
Sumner (James B; 1946)
Tanaka (Koichi; 2002)
Walker (John E; 1997)
Werner (Alfred; 1913)
Wittig (Georg; 1979)
Zewail (Ahmed; 1999)

07 Bergius (Friedrich; 1931)
Buchner (Eduard; 1907)
Chalfie (Martin; 2008)
Chauvin (Yves; 2005)
Crutzen (Paul J; 1995)
Fischer (Emil; 1902)
Fischer (Ernst Otto; 1973)
Fischer (Hans; 1930)
Giauque (William F; 1949)
Gilbert (Walter; 1980)
Haworth (Sir Norman; 1937)

Hershko (Avram; 2004)
Hodgkin (Dorothy C; 1964)
Kendrew (Sir John C; 1962)
Knowles (William S; 2001)
Moissan (Henri; 1906)
Norrish (Ronald GW; 1967)
Onsager (Lars; 1968)
Ostwald (Wilhelm; 1909)
Pauling (Linus; 1954)
Polanyi (John C; 1986)
Rowland (F Sherwood; 1995)
Ruzicka (Leopold; 1939)
Schrock (Richard R; 2005)
Seaborg (Glenn T; 1951)
Semenov (Nikolay; 1956)
Smalley (Richard E; 1996)
Stanley (Wendell M; 1946)
Wallach (Otto; 1910)
Wieland (Heinrich; 1927)
Windaus (Adolf; 1928)
Ziegler (Karl; 1963)

08 Anfinsen (Christian; 1972)
Grignard (Victor; 1912)
Hauptman (Herbert A; 1985)
Herzberg (Gerhard; 1971)
Hoffmann (Roald; 1981)
Kornberg (Roger D; 2006)
Langmuir (Irving; 1932)
Lipscomb (William; 1976)
McMillan (Edwin M; 1951)
Mitchell (Peter; 1978)
Mulliken (Robert S; 1966)
Northrop (John H; 1946)
Pedersen (Charles J; 1987)
Richards (Theodore W; 1914)
Robinson (Sir Robert; 1947)
Sabatier (Paul; 1912)
Svedberg (Theodor; 1926)
Tiselius (Arne; 1948)
van 't Hoff (Jacobus H; 1901)
Vigneaud (Vincent du; 1955)
Virtanen (Artturi; 1945)
Woodward (Robert B; 1965)
Wüthrich (Kurt; 2002)

09 Arrhenius (Svante; 1903)
Butenandt (Adolf; 1939)
Cornforth (Sir John; 1975)
Heyrovsky (Jaroslav; 1959)
MacKinnon (Roderick; 2003)
Prigogine (Ilya; 1977)
Sharpless (K Barry; 2001)
Shimomura (Osamu; 2008)
Shirakawa (Hideki; 2000)
Wilkinson (Sir Geoffrey; 1973)
Zsigmondy (Richard; 1925)

10 Herschbach (Dudley R; 1986)
MacDiarmid (Alan G; 2000)

Merrifield (Bruce; 1984)
Rutherford (Ernest, Lord; 1908)
Staudinger (Hermann; 1953)
11 Ciechanover (Aaron; 2004)
Deisenhofer (Johann; 1988)

Hinshelwood (Sir Cyril; 1956)
Joliot-Curie (Irène; 1935)
Willstätter (Richard; 1915)
12 Euler-Chelpin (Hans von; 1929)

Nobel Prize for Economics winners:

03 Sen (Amartya; 1998)
04 Nash (John F, Jnr; 1994)
05 Arrow (Kenneth J; 1972)
Coase (Ronald H; 1991)
Engle (Robert F, III; 2003)
Fogel (Robert W; 1993)
Hayek (Friedrich August von; 1974)
Hicks (Sir John R; 1972)
Klein (Lawrence R; 1980)
Lewis (Sir Arthur; 1979)
Lucas (Robert E, Jnr; 1995)
Meade (James E; 1977)
North (Douglass C; 1993)
Ohlin (Bertil; 1977)
Simon (Herbert A; 1978)
Smith (Vernon L; 2002)
Solow (Robert M; 1987)
Stone (Sir Richard; 1984)
Tobin (James; 1982)
06 Allais (Maurice; 1988)
Aumann (Robert J; 2005)
Becker (Gary S; 1992)
Debreu (Gerard; 1984)
Frisch (Ragnar; 1969)
Maskin (Eric S; 2007)
Merton (Robert C; 1997)
Miller (Merton H; 1990)
Myrdal (Gunnar; 1974)
Phelps (Edmund S; 2006)
Selten (Reinhard; 1994)
Sharpe (William F; 1990)

Spence (A Michael; 2001)
07 Akerlof (George A; 2001)
Granger (Clive WJ; 2003)
Heckman (James J; 2000)
Hurwicz (Leonid; 2007)
Krugman (Paul; 2008)
Kuznets (Simon; 1971)
Kydland (Finn E; 2004)
Mundell (Robert A; 1999)
Myerson (Roger B; 2007)
Scholes (Myron S; 1997)
Schultz (Theodore W; 1979)
Stigler (George J; 1982)
Vickrey (William; 1996)
08 Buchanan (James M, Jnr; 1986)
Friedman (Milton; 1976)
Haavelmo (Trygve; 1989)
Harsanyi (John C; 1994)
Kahneman (Daniel; 2002)
Koopmans (Tjalling C; 1975)
Leontief (Wassily; 1973)
McFadden (Daniel L; 2000)
Mirrlees (James A; 1996)
Prescott (Edward C; 2004)
Stiglitz (Joseph E; 2001)
09 Markowitz (Harry M; 1990)
Samuelson (Paul A; 1970)
Schelling (Thomas C; 2005)
Tinbergen (Jan; 1969)
10 Modigliani (Franco; 1985)
11 Kantorovich (Leonid Vitaliyevich; 1975)

Nobel Prize for Literature winners:

02 Fo (Dario; 1997)
Oe (Kenzaburo; 1994)
03 Paz (Octavio; 1990)
04 Böll (Heinrich; 1972)
Buck (Pearl; 1938)
Cela (Camilo José; 1989)
Gard (Roger Martin du; 1937)
Gide (André; 1947)
Mann (Thomas; 1929)
Shaw (George Bernard; 1925)
05 Agnon (Samuel; 1966)
Bunin (Ivan; 1933)
Camus (Albert; 1957)
Eliot (TS; 1948)

Grass (Günter; 1999)
Hesse (Hermann; 1946)
Heyse (Paul; 1910)
Lewis (Sinclair; 1930)
Pamuk (Orhan; 2006)
Perse (Saint-John; 1960)
Sachs (Nelly; 1966)
Simon (Claude; 1985)
White (Patrick; 1973)
Yeats (W B; 1923)
06 Andric (Ivo; 1961)
Bellow (Saul; 1976)
Elytis (Odysseus; 1979)
Eucken (Rudolf; 1908)

France (Anatole; 1921)
Hamsun (Knut; 1920)
Heaney (Seamus; 1995)
Jensen (Johannes V; 1944)
Milosz (Czeslaw; 1980)
Neruda (Pablo; 1971)
O'Neill (Eugene; 1936)
Pinter (Harold; 2005)
Sartre (Jean-Paul; 1964)
Singer (Isaac Bashevis; 1978)
Tagore (Rabindranath; 1913)
Undset (Sigrid; 1928)

07 Beckett (Samuel; 1969)
Bergson (Henri; 1927)
Brodsky (Joseph; 1987)
Canetti (Elias; 1981)
Coetzee (JM; 2003)
Deledda (Grazia; 1926)
Golding (William; 1983)
Jelinek (Elfriede; 2004)
Jiménez (Juan Ramón; 1956)
Johnson (Eyvind; 1974)
Kertész (Imre; 2002)
Kipling (Rudyard; 1907)
Laxness (Halldór; 1955)
Lessing (Doris; 2007)
Mahfouz (Naguib; 1988)
Márquez (Gabriel García; 1982)
Mauriac (François; 1952)
Mistral (Frédéric; 1904)
Mistral (Gabriela; 1945)
Mommsen (Theodor; 1902)
Montale (Eugenio; 1975)
Naipaul (VS; 2001)
Reymont (Wladyslaw; 1924)
Rolland (Romain; 1915)
Russell (Bertrand; 1950)
Seferis (Giorgos; 1963)
Seifert (Jaroslav; 1984)

Soyinka (Wole; 1986)
Walcott (Derek; 1992)

08 Asturias (Miguel Angel; 1967)
Bjørnson (Bjørnstjerne; 1903)
Carducci (Giosuè; 1906)
Faulkner (William; 1949)
Gordimer (Nadine; 1991)
Kawabata (Yasunari; 1968)
Lagerlöf (Selma; 1909)
Le Clézio (Jean-Marie Gustave; 2008)
Morrison (Toni; 1993)
Saramago (José; 1998)
Xingjian (Gao; 2000)

09 Benavente (Jacinto; 1922)
Churchill (Sir Winston; 1953)
Echegaray (José; 1904)
Gjellerup (Karl; 1917)
Hauptmann (Gerhart; 1912)
Hemingway (Ernest; 1954)
Karlfeldt (Erik Axel; 1931)
Martinson (Harry; 1974)
Pasternak (Boris; 1958)
Prudhomme (Sully; 1901)
Quasimodo (Salvatore; 1959)
Sholokhov (Mikhail; 1965)
Sillanpää (Frans Eemil; 1939)
Spitteler (Carl; 1919)
Steinbeck (John; 1962)

10 Aleixandre (Vicente; 1977)
Galsworthy (John; 1932)
Heidenstam (Verner von; 1916)
Lagerkvist (Pär; 1951)
Pirandello (Luigi; 1934)
Szymborska (Wislawa; 1996)

11 Maeterlinck (Maurice; 1911)
Pontoppidan (Henrik; 1917)
Sienkiewicz (Henryk; 1905)

12 Solzhenitsyn (Alexander; 1970)

Nobel Peace Prize winners:

04 Belo (Carlos Filipe Ximenes; 1996)
Gore (Albert 'Al', Jnr; 2007)
Hull (Cordell; 1945)
Hume (John; 1998)
King (Martin Luther, Jnr, 1964)
Mott (John R; 1946)
Pire (Georges; 1958)
Root (Elihu; 1912)
Sato (Eisaku; 1974)
Tutu (Desmond; 1984)

05 Annan (Kofi; 2001)
Asser (Tobias; 1911)
Bajer (Fredrik; 1908)
Balch (Emily; 1946)
Begin (Menachem; 1978)

Cecil (Robert, Viscount; 1937)
Dawes (Charles G; 1925)
Ebadi (Shirin; 2003)
Fried (Alfred; 1911)
Gobat (Albert; 1902)
Lamas (Carlos Saavedra; 1936)
Lange (Christian; 1921)
Passy (Frédéric; 1901)
Peres (Shimon; 1994)
Rabin (Yitzhak; 1994)
Yunus (Muhammad; 2006)

06 Addams (Jane; 1931)
Angell (Sir Norman; 1933)
Arafat (Yasser; 1994)
Brandt (Willy; 1971)

Briand (Aristide; 1926)
Bunche (Ralph; 1950)
Butler (Nicholas; 1931)
Carter (Jimmy; 2002)
Cassin (René; 1968)
Cremer (Randal; 1903)
Dunant (Henry; 1901)
Lutuli (Albert; 1960)
Moneta (Ernesto Teodoro; 1907)
Myrdal (Alva; 1982)
Nansen (Fridtjof; 1922)
Quidde (Ludwig; 1927)
Walesa (Lech; 1983)
Wiesel (Elie; 1986)
Wilson (Woodrow; 1919)

07 al-Sadat (Anwar; 1978)
Borlaug (Norman; 1970)
Boyd Orr (Lord; 1949)
Buisson (Ferdinand; 1927)
Dae-jung (Kim; 2000)
de Klerk (FW; 1993)
Jouhaux (Léon; 1951)
Kellogg (Frank B; 1929)
Maathai (Wangari; 2004)
Mandela (Nelson; 1993)
Pauling (Linus; 1962)
Pearson (Lester B; 1957)
Renault (Louis; 1907)
Rotblat (Joseph; 1995)
Suttner (Bertha von; 1905)
Trimble (David; 1998)

08 Branting (Hjalmar; 1921)
Constant (Paul Henri d'Estournelles de; 1909)
Corrigan (Mairead; 1976)
Ducommun (Élie; 1902)
Le Duc Tho (1973)
MacBride (Seán; 1974)
Marshall (George C; 1953)
Sakharov (Andrei; 1975)
Williams (Betty; 1976)
Williams (Jody; 1997)

09 Ahtisaari (Martti; 2008)
Arnoldson (Klas; 1908)
Beernaert (Auguste; 1909)
Bourgeois (Léon; 1920)
Dalai Lama (14th; 1989)
ElBaradei (Mohamed; 2005)
Gorbachev (Mikhail; 1990)
Henderson (Arthur; 1934)

Kissinger (Henry; 1973)
Menchú Tum (Rigoberta; 1992)
Noel-Baker (Lord; 1959)
Ossietzky (Carl von; 1935)
Roosevelt (Theodore; 1906)
Söderblom (Nathan; 1930)

10 La Fontaine (Henri; 1913)
Ramos-Horta (José; 1996)
Schweitzer (Albert; 1952)
Stresemann (Gustav; 1926)

11 Chamberlain (Sir Austen; 1925)
Grameen Bank (2006)

12 Arias Sánchez (Oscar; 1987)
García Robles (Alfonso; 1982)
Hammarskjöld (Dag; 1961)
Mother Teresa (1979)

13 Aung San Suu Kyi (1991)
Pérez Esquivel (Adolfo; 1980)
United Nations (2001)

20 Amnesty International (1977)

21 Friends Service Council (1947)

22 Médecins Sans Frontières (1999)

25 League of Red Cross Societies (1963)

26 United Nations Children's Fund (1965)

27 Institute of International Law (1904)

31 American Friends Service Committee (1947)
International Atomic Energy Agency (2005)
International Labour Organization (1969)
United Nations Peacekeeping Forces (1988)

33 Permanent International Peace Bureau (1910)

35 International Campaign to Ban Landmines (1997)
International Committee of the Red Cross (1917, 1944, 1963)

36 Nansen International Office for Refugees (1938)

37 Intergovernmental Panel on Climate Change (2007)

42 Pugwash Conferences on Science and World Affairs (1995)

51 International Physicians for the Prevention of Nuclear War (1985)
Office of the United Nations High Commissioner for Refugees (1954, 1981)

Nobel Prize for Physics winners:

03 Chu (Steven; 1997)
Lee (David M; 1996)

04 Bohr (Aage N; 1975)
Bohr (Niels; 1922)

Born (Max; 1954)
Fert (Albert; 2007)
Hall (John L; 2005)
Hess (Victor F; 1936)

Lamb (Willis E; 1955)
Laue (Max von; 1914)
Mott (Sir Nevill; 1977)
Néel (Louis; 1970)
Paul (Wolfgang; 1989)
Perl (Martin L; 1995)
Rabi (Isidor Isaac; 1944)
Ryle (Sir Martin; 1974)
Tamm (Igor Y; 1958)
Ting (Samuel CC; 1976)
Tsui (Daniel C; 1998)
Wien (Wilhelm; 1911)

05 Basov (Nicolay G; 1964)
Bethe (Hans; 1967)
Bloch (Felix; 1952)
Bothe (Walther; 1954)
Bragg (Lawrence; 1915)
Bragg (William; 1915)
Braun (Ferdinand; 1909)
Curie (Marie; 1903)
Curie (Pierre; 1903)
Dalén (Gustaf; 1912)
Davis (Raymond, Jnr; 2002)
Dirac (Paul AM; 1933)
Esaki (Leo; 1973)
Fermi (Enrico; 1938)
Fitch (Val; 1980)
Frank (Ilja M; 1958)
Gabor (Dennis; 1971)
Gross (David J; 2004)
Hertz (Gustav; 1925)
Hulse (Russell A; 1993)
Kilby (Jack S; 2000)
Kusch (Polykarp; 1955)
Nambu (Yoichiro; 2008)
Onnes (Heike Kamerlingh; 1913)
Pauli (Wolfgang; 1945)
Raman (Venkata; 1930)
Ruska (Ernst; 1986)
Salam (Abdus; 1979)
Segrè (Emilio; 1959)
Shull (Clifford G; 1994)
Smoot (George F; 2006)
Stark (Johannes; 1919)
Stern (Otto; 1943)
Vleck (John H van; 1977)

06 Alfvén (Hannes; 1970)
Barkla (Charles G; 1917)
Binnig (Gerd; 1986)
Cooper (Leon N; 1972)
Cronin (James; 1980)
Fowler (William A; 1983)
Franck (James; 1925)
Glaser (Donald A; 1960)
Hänsch (Theodor W; 2005)
Hewish (Antony; 1974)
Jensen (J Hans D; 1963)

Landau (Lev; 1962)
Lenard (Philipp; 1905)
Mather (John C; 2006)
Müller (K Alex; 1987)
Perrin (Jean Baptiste; 1926)
Planck (Max; 1918)
Powell (Cecil; 1950)
Ramsey (Norman F; 1989)
Reines (Frederick; 1995)
Rohrer (Heinrich; 1986)
Rubbia (Carlo; 1984)
Taylor (Joseph H, Jnr; 1993)
Taylor (Richard E; 1990)
't Hooft (Gerardus; 1999)
Townes (Charles H; 1964)
Walton (Ernest TS; 1951)
Wieman (Carl E; 2001)
Wigner (Eugene; 1963)
Wilson (CTR; 1927)
Wilson (Kenneth G; 1982)
Wilson (Robert Woodrow; 1978)
Yukawa (Hideki; 1949)
Zeeman (Pieter; 1902)

07 Alferov (Zhores I; 2000)
Alvarez (Luis; 1968)
Bardeen (John; 1956, 1972)
Bednorz (J Georg; 1987)
Broglie (Louis de; 1929)
Charpak (Georges; 1992)
Compton (Arthur H; 1927)
Cornell (Eric A; 2001)
Dehmelt (Hans G; 1989)
Feynman (Richard P; 1965)
Giaever (Ivar; 1973)
Glashow (Sheldon; 1979)
Glauber (Roy J; 2005)
Kapitsa (Pyotr; 1978)
Kastler (Alfred; 1966)
Kendall (Henry W; 1990)
Koshiba (Masatoshi; 2002)
Kroemer (Herbert; 2000)
Leggett (Anthony J; 2003)
Lorentz (Hendrik A; 1902)
Marconi (Guglielmo; 1909)
Maskawa (Toshihide; 2008)
Penzias (Arno; 1978)
Purcell (E M; 1952)
Richter (Burton; 1976)
Röntgen (Wilhelm Conrad von; 1901)
Störmer (Horst L; 1998)
Thomson (Sir George; 1937)
Thomson (JJ; 1906)
Veltman (Martinus JG; 1999)
Wilczek (Frank; 2004)
Zernike (Frits; 1953)

08 Anderson (Carl D; 1936)
Anderson (Philip W; 1977)

Appleton (Sir Edward; 1947)
Blackett (Patrick, Lord; 1948)
Brattain (Walter H; 1956)
Bridgman (Percy W; 1946)
Chadwick (Sir James; 1935)
Davisson (Clinton; 1937)
de Gennes (Pierre-Gilles; 1991)
Einstein (Albert; 1921)
Friedman (Jerome I; 1990)
Gell-Mann (Murray; 1969)
Giacconi (Riccardo; 2002)
Ginzburg (Vitaly L; 2003)
Grünberg (Peter; 2007)
Ketterle (Wolfgang; 2001)
Klitzing (Klaus von; 1985)
Laughlin (Robert B; 1998)
Lawrence (Ernest; 1939)
Lederman (Leon M; 1988)
Lippmann (Gabriel; 1908)
Millikan (Robert A; 1923)
Osheroff (Douglas D; 1996)
Phillips (William D; 1997)
Politzer (H David; 2004)
Rayleigh (Lord; 1904)
Schawlow (Arthur L; 1981)
Schwartz (Melvin; 1988)
Shockley (William B; 1956)
Siegbahn (Kai M; 1981)
Siegbahn (Manne; 1924)
Tomonaga (Sin-Itiro; 1965)
Weinberg (Steven; 1979)

09 Abrikosov (Alexei A; 2003)
Becquerel (Henri; 1903)
Cherenkov (Pavel A; 1958)
Cockcroft (Sir John; 1951)
Guillaume (Charles Edouard; 1920)
Josephson (Brian D; 1973)
Kobayashi (Makoto; 2008)
Michelson (Albert A; 1907)
Mössbauer (Rudolf; 1961)
Mottelson (Ben R; 1975)
Prokhorov (Aleksandr M; 1964)
Rainwater (James; 1975)
Schwinger (Julian; 1965)

10 Brockhouse (Bertram N; 1994)
Heisenberg (Werner; 1932)
Hofstadter (Robert; 1961)
Richardson (Owen Willans; 1928)
Richardson (Robert C; 1996)
Schrieffer (Robert; 1972)
van der Meer (Simon; 1984)

11 Bloembergen (Nicolaas; 1981)
Chamberlain (Owen; 1959)
Schrödinger (Erwin; 1933)
Steinberger (Jack; 1988)
Tsung-Dao Lee (1957)
van der Waals (Johannes Diderik; 1910)

12 Chen Ning Yang (1957)

13 Chandrasekhar (Subramanyan; 1983)
Goeppert-Mayer (Maria; 1963)

14 Cohen-Tannoudji (Claude; 1997)

Nobel Prize for Physiology or Medicine winners:

03 Dam (Henrik; 1943)

04 Axel (Richard; 2004)
Buck (Linda B; 2004)
Cori (Carl; 1947)
Cori (Gerty; 1947)
Dale (Sir Henry; 1936)
Duve (Christian de; 1974)
Fire (Andrew Z; 2006)
Hess (Walter; 1949)
Hill (Archibald V; 1922)
Hunt (Tim; 2001)
Katz (Sir Bernard; 1970)
Koch (Robert; 1905)
Ross (Ronald; 1902)
Rous (Peyton; 1966)
Vane (Sir John; 1982)
Wald (George; 1967)

05 Arber (Werner; 1978)
Black (Sir James; 1988)
Bloch (Konrad; 1964)
Bovet (Daniel; 1957)
Brown (Michael S; 1985)
Chain (Sir Ernst; 1945)

Cohen (Stanley; 1986)
Crick (Francis; 1962)
Doisy (Edward A; 1943)
Elion (Gertrude B; 1988)
Euler (Ulf von; 1970)
Evans (Sir Martin; 2007)
Golgi (Camillo; 1906)
Hench (Philip S; 1950)
Hubel (David H; 1981)
Jacob (François; 1965)
Jerne (Niels K; 1984)
Krebs (Edwin G; 1992)
Krebs (Sir Hans; 1953)
Krogh (August; 1920)
Lewis (Edward B; 1995)
Loewi (Otto; 1936)
Luria (Salvador E; 1969)
Lwoff (André; 1965)
Lynen (Feodor; 1964)
Mello (Craig C; 2006)
Minot (George R; 1934)
Moniz (Egas; 1949)
Monod (Jacques; 1965)

Murad (Ferid; 1998)
Neher (Erwin; 1991)
Nurse (Sir Paul; 2001)
Ochoa (Severo; 1959)
Sharp (Phillip A; 1993)
Smith (Hamilton O; 1978)
Snell (George D; 1980)
Tatum (Edward; 1958)
Temin (Howard M; 1975)
Yalow (Rosalyn; 1977)

06 Adrian (Edgar; 1932)
Bárány (Robert; 1914)
Beadle (George; 1958)
Békésy (Georg von; 1961)
Bishop (J Michael; 1989)
Blobel (Günter; 1999)
Bordet (Jules; 1919)
Burnet (Sir F Macfarlane; 1960)
Carrel (Alexis; 1912)
Claude (Albert; 1974)
Domagk (Gerhard; 1939)
Eccles (Sir John; 1963)
Enders (John F; 1954)
Finsen (Niels Ryberg; 1903)
Florey (Howard, Lord; 1945)
Frisch (Karl von; 1973)
Gasser (Herbert S; 1944)
Gilman (Alfred G; 1994)
Granit (Ragnar; 1967)
Hausen (Harald zur; 2008)
Holley (Robert W; 1968)
Huxley (Sir Andrew; 1963)
Kandel (Eric R; 2000)
Kocher (Theodor; 1909)
Köhler (Georges JF; 1984)
Kossel (Albrecht; 1910)
Lorenz (Konrad; 1973)
Morgan (Thomas H; 1933)
Muller (Hermann J; 1946)
Müller (Paul; 1948)
Murphy (William P; 1934)
Murray (Joseph E; 1990)
Palade (George E; 1974)
Pavlov (Ivan; 1904)
Porter (Rodney R; 1972)
Richet (Charles; 1913)
Sperry (Roger W; 1981)
Thomas (E Donnall; 1990)
Varmus (Harold E; 1989)
Warren (J Robin; 2005)
Watson (James; 1962)
Weller (Thomas H; 1954)
Wiesel (Torsten N; 1981)

07 Axelrod (Julius; 1970)
Banting (Frederick G; 1923)
Behring (Emil von; 1901)
Brenner (Sydney; 2002)

Cormack (Allan M; 1979)
Dausset (Jean; 1980)
Doherty (Peter C; 1996)
Edelman (Gerald M; 1972)
Ehrlich (Paul; 1908)
Eijkman (Christiaan; 1929)
Fibiger (Johannes; 1926)
Fischer (Edmond H; 1992)
Fleming (Sir Alexander; 1945)
Hershey (Alfred D; 1969)
Heymans (Corneille; 1938)
Hodgkin (Sir Alan; 1963)
Hopkins (Sir Frederick; 1929)
Horvitz (H Robert; 2002)
Houssay (Bernardo; 1947)
Huggins (Charles B; 1966)
Ignarro (Louis J; 1998)
Kendall (Edward C; 1950)
Khorana (H Gobind; 1968)
Laveran (Alphonse; 1907)
Lipmann (Fritz; 1953)
Macleod (John; 1923)
Medawar (Sir Peter; 1960)
Nathans (Daniel; 1978)
Nicolle (Charles; 1928)
Robbins (Frederick C; 1954)
Roberts (Richard J; 1993)
Rodbell (Martin; 1994)
Sakmann (Bert; 1991)
Schally (Andrew V; 1977)
Spemann (Hans; 1935)
Sulston (John E; 2002)
Theiler (Max; 1951)
Waksman (Selman A; 1952)
Warburg (Otto; 1931)
Whipple (George H; 1934)
Wilkins (Maurice; 1962)

08 Blumberg (Baruch S; 1976)
Capecchi (Mario R; 2007)
Carlsson (Arvid; 2000)
Cournand (André F; 1956)
Delbrück (Max; 1969)
Dulbecco (Renato; 1975)
Erlanger (Joseph; 1944)
Gajdusek (D Carleton; 1976)
Hartline (Haldan K; 1967)
Hartwell (Leland H; 2001)
Kornberg (Arthur; 1959)
Marshall (Barry J; 2005)
Meyerhof (Otto; 1922)
Milstein (César; 1984)
Prusiner (Stanley B; 1997)
Richards (Dickinson W; 1956)
Smithies (Oliver; 2007)
Theorell (Hugo; 1955)
Tonegawa (Susumu; 1987)

09 Baltimore (David; 1975)

Bergström (Sune K; 1982)
Einthoven (Willem; 1924)
Forssmann (Werner; 1956)
Furchgott (Robert F; 1998)
Goldstein (Joseph L; 1985)
Greengard (Paul; 2000)
Guillemin (Roger; 1977)
Hitchings (George H; 1988)
Lauterbur (Paul C; 2003)
Lederberg (Joshua; 1958)
Mansfield (Sir Peter; 2003)
Mechnikov (Ilya; 1908)
Nirenberg (Marshall W; 1968)
Tinbergen (Nikolaas; 1973)
Wieschaus (Eric F; 1995)
10 Benacerraf (Baruj; 1980)
Gullstrand (Allvar; 1911)

Hounsfield (Godfrey N; 1979)
McClintock (Barbara; 1983)
Montagnier (Luc; 2008)
Reichstein (Tadeus; 1950)
Samuelsson (Bengt I; 1982)
Sutherland (Earl W, Jnr; 1971)
11 Landsteiner (Karl; 1930)
Ramón y Cajal (Santiago; 1906)
Sherrington (Sir Charles; 1932)
Zinkernagel (Rolf M; 1996)
12 Szent-Györgyi (Albert; 1937)
13 Barré-Sinoussi (Françoise; 2008)
Wagner-Jauregg (Julius; 1927)
14 Levi-Montalcini (Rita; 1986)
15 Nüsslein-Volhard (Christiane; 1995)

nobility

Ranks of the nobility include:

02 Bt	05 baron	duchess	09 grand duke
Kt	count	marquis	liege lord
03 Dom	laird	peeress	magnifico
Don	liege	vicomte	patrician
Duc	nawab	08 baroness	10 aristocrat
Sir	noble	countess	baronetess
04 Bart	thane	life peer	noblewoman
dame	06 daimio	margrave	11 marchioness
duke	Junker	marquess	viscountess
earl	knight	nobleman	12 grand duchess
jarl	squire	seigneur	13 grand seigneur
lady	vidame	starosta	14 knight bachelor
lord	07 baronet	vavasour	
peer	dowager	viscount	

See also **title**

non-alcoholic drink *see* drink

non-fiction

Non-fiction works include:

03 *OED* (1st edn, 1884–1928)
06 *Walden* (1854, Henry David Thoreau)
07 *Capital* (1867–94, Karl Marx)
Who's Who (annual; 1st edn, 1849)
08 *Self-Help* (1859, Samuel Smiles)
09 *Kama Sutra* (undated, Vatsyayana)
Leviathan (1651, Thomas Hobbes)
Mein Kampf (1925, Adolf Hitler)
On Liberty (1859, John Stuart Mill)
Table Talk (1821, William Hazlitt)
The Phaedo (4c BC, Plato)
10 *Das Kapital* (1867–94, Karl Marx)

The Annales (3c-2c BC, Quintus Ennius)
The Gorgias (4c BC, Plato)
The Poetics (4c BC, Aristotle)
The Timaeus (4c BC, Plato)
11 *Down the Mine* (1937, George Orwell)
Mythologies (1957, Roland Barthes)
The Agricola (1c–2c AD, Tacitus)
The Analects (5c BC, Confucius)
The Germania (1c–2c AD, Tacitus)
The Phaedrus (4c BC, Plato)
The Republic (4c BC, Plato)
12 *Novum Organum* (1620, Francis Bacon)
Silent Spring (1962, Rachel Carson)

The City of God (413–26 AD, St Augustine of Hippo)
The Second Sex (1949, Simone de Beauvoir)
The Symposium (4c BC, Plato)

13 The Story of Art (1950, Ernst Gombrich)

14 A Room of One's Own (1929, Virginia Woolf)
Birds of America (1827–38, John James Audubon)
Eudemian Ethics (4c BC, Aristotle)
Inside the Whale (1940, George Orwell)
Modern Painters (1843–60, John Ruskin)
Sartor Resartus (1833–34, Thomas Carlyle)
The Age of Reason (1794–96, Tom Paine)
The Golden Bough (1890–1915, Sir James Frazer)
The Life of Jesus (1926, John Middleton Murry)
The Rights of Man (1791–92, Tom Paine)
The Selfish Gene (1976, Richard Dawkins)

15 Lives of the Poets (1779–81, Samuel Johnson)
The Essays of Elia (1823–33, Charles Lamb)
The Female Eunuch (1970, Germaine Greer)
The Sleepwalkers (1931–32, Hermann Broch)

16 Pears Cyclopaedia (annual; 1st edn, 1897)

17 Whitaker's Almanack (annual; 1st edn, 1868)

18 The Origin of Species (1859, Charles Darwin)

19 A Brief History of Time (1988, Stephen Hawking)
Eats, Shoots and Leaves (2003, Lynne Truss)

23 Encyclopaedia Britannica (1st edn, 1768)
Oxford English Dictionary (1st edn, 1884–1928)

25 Schott's Original Miscellany (2002, Ben Schott)

28 Debrett's Peerage and Baronetage (1st edn, 1769)

29 National Dictionary of Biography (1st edn, 1885–1900)

30 Chambers Biographical Dictionary (1st edn, 1897)
Dictionary of the English Language (1755, Samuel Johnson)

33 Brewer's Dictionary of Phrase and Fable (1st edn, 1870)

39 Ecclesiastical History of the English People (c.731, St Bede)

Non-fiction writers include:

04 Bede (St, 'the Venerable'; c.673–735, Anglo-Saxon)

05 Newby (Eric; 1919–2006, English)
Paine (Tom; 1737–1809, English)
Pliny (Gaius, the Younger; c.62–c.113 AD, Roman)

06 Beevor (Antony; 1946– , English)
Binyon (T J; 1936–2004, English)
Bryson (Bill; 1951– , US)
Carson (Rachel; 1907–64, US)
Fraser (Antonia; 1932– , English)
Gibbon (Edward; 1737–94, English)
Leavis (F R; 1895–1978, English)

Schama (Simon; 1945– , English)
Walton (Izaak; 1593–1683, English)

07 Boswell (James; 1740–95, Scottish)
Carlyle (Thomas; 1795–1881, Scottish)
Hazlitt (William; 1778–1830, English)

08 Plutarch (c.46–c.120 AD, Greek)
Strachey (Lytton; 1880–1932, English)

09 De Quincey (Thomas; 1785–1859, English)
Suetonius (c.69–c.140 AD, Roman)

10 Washington (Booker T; 1856–1915, US)

14 Chandrasekaran (Rajiv; 1969– , Indian/US)

Norse *see* fate; mythology

North Atlantic Treaty Organization *see* NATO

Northern Ireland *see* town; United Kingdom

Norway

Cities and notable towns in Norway include:

04 Oslo

06 Bergen
Drøbak
Tromsø

07 Drammen
Ølesund

09 Stavanger
Trondheim

10 Hammerfest

11 Lillehammer

12 Kristiansand

Administrative divisions of Norway, with regional capitals:

04 Oslo (Oslo)

05 Troms (Tromsø)

07 Hedmark (Hamar)
Oppland (Lillehammer)
Østfold (Moss)

08 Akershus
Buskerud (Drammen)

Finnmark (Vadsø)
Nordland (Bodø)
Rogaland (Stavanger)
Telemark (Skien)
Vestfold (Tønsberg)

09 Aust-Agder (Arendal)
Hordaland (Bergen)

Vest-Agder (Kristiansand)

12 Sør-Trøndelag (Trondheim)

13 Møre og Romsdal (Molde)
Nord-Trøndelag (Steinkjer)

14 Sogn og Fjordane
(Leikanger)

Norwegian landmarks include:

05 fjord

07 Bryggen

08 Snøhetta
Svalbard

09 Hardanger

10 Sognefjord

11 Jotunheimen
Royal Palace
Trollveggen

12 Galdhøpiggen
Gaustatoppen
Jiehkkevarri
Trollfjorden
Vigeland Park

13 Oslo Cathedral

14 Geirangerfjord
Jostedalsbreen

15 Svinesund Bridge

note *see* **music**

novel

Novels include:

01 *V* (1963, Thomas Pynchon)

03 *Kim* (1901, Rudyard Kipling)
She (1887, Sir H Rider Haggard)

04 *1984* (1949, George Orwell)
Emma (1816, Jane Austen)
Jazz (1992, Toni Morrison)

05 *Kipps* (1904, H G Wells)
Porgy (1925, DuBose Heyward)
Scoop (1938, Evelyn Waugh)

06 *Ben Hur* (1880, Lew Wallace)
Carrie (1974, Stephen King)
Herzog (1964, Saul Bellow)
Lanark (1981, Alasdair Gray)
Lolita (1955, Vladimir Nabokov)
Pamela (1740–41, Samuel Richardson)
Rob Roy (1817, Sir Walter Scott)
The Sea (1973, Edward Bond)
The Sea (2005, John Banville)
Trilby (1894, George Du Maurier)

07 *Babbitt* (1922, Sinclair Lewis)
Beloved (1988, Toni Morrison)
Catch-22 (1961, Joseph Heller)
Cat's Eye (1988, Margaret Atwood)
Dracula (1897, Bram Stoker)
Erewhon (1872, Samuel Butler)
Ivanhoe (1819, Sir Walter Scott)
Lord Jim (1900, Joseph Conrad)
Orlando (1928, Virginia Woolf)
Rebecca (1938, Daphne Du Maurier)
Shirley (1849, Charlotte Brontë)
The Bell (1958, Iris Murdoch)

Ulysses (1914, James Joyce)

08 *Adam Bede* (1859, George Eliot)
Birdsong (1993, Sebastian Faulks)
Clarissa (1748, Samuel Richardson)
Cranford (1853, Elizabeth Gaskell)
Disgrace (1999, J M Coetzee)
Germinal (1885, Émile Zola)
Jane Eyre (1847, Charlotte Brontë)
Lucky Jim (1954, Kingsley Amis)
Moby-Dick (1851, Herman Melville)
Nostromo (1904, Joseph Conrad)
Oroonoko (c.1688, Aphra Behn)
The Waves (1931, Virginia Woolf)
The Years (1937, Virginia Woolf)
Villette (1853, Charlotte Brontë)
Vineland (1990, Thomas Pynchon)
Waverley (1814, Sir Walter Scott)

09 *About a Boy* (1998, Nick Hornby)
Amsterdam (1998, Ian McEwan)
Billy Budd (1924, Herman Melville)
Billy Liar (1959, Keith Waterhouse)
Brick Lane (2003, Monica Ali)
Hard Times (1854, Charles Dickens)
Kidnapped (1886, Robert Louis Stevenson)
On The Road (1957, Jack Kerouac)
The Egoist (1879, George Meredith)
The Hobbit (1937, J R R Tolkien)
The Warden (1855, Anthony Trollope)
White Fang (1906, Jack London)

10 *A Man in Full* (1998, Tom Wolfe)
Animal Farm (1945, George Orwell)
Bleak House (1853, Charles Dickens)

Cannery Row (1945, John Steinbeck)
Clayhanger (1910, Arnold Bennett)
East of Eden (1952, John Steinbeck)
Ethan Frome (1911, Edith Wharton)
Hotel du Lac (1984, Anita Brookner)
Howards End (1910, E M Forster)
Jamaica Inn (1936, Daphne du Maurier)
Kenilworth (1821, Sir Walter Scott)
Lorna Doone (1869, R D Blackmore)
Naked Lunch (1959, William Burroughs)
Parade's End (1924–28, Ford Madox Ford)
Persuasion (1818, Jane Austen)
Possession (1990, A S Byatt)
The Bell Jar (1963, Sylvia Plath)
The Leopard (1960, Giuseppe di Lampedusa)
The Rainbow (1915, D H Lawrence)
Titus Alone (1959, Mervyn Peake)
Uncle Remus (1880, Joel Chandler Harris)
Vanity Fair (1848, W M Thackeray)
Westward Ho! (1855, Charles Kingsley)
White Teeth (2000, Zadie Smith)

11 *A Perfect Spy* (1986, John Le Carré)
A Scots Quair (1946, Lewis Grassic Gibbon)
Black Beauty (1877, Anna Sewell)
Cakes and Ale (1930, W Somerset Maugham)
Daisy Miller (1878, Henry James)
Gormenghast (1950, Mervyn Peake)
Greenmantle (1916, John Buchan)
Heat and Dust (1975, Ruth Prawer Jhabvala)
Little Women (1868, Louisa M Alcott)
Mary Poppins (1934, P L Travers)
Middlemarch (1871–72, George Eliot)
Mrs Dalloway (1925, Virginia Woolf)
Night and Day (1919, Virginia Woolf)
Oliver Twist (1838, Charles Dickens)
Silas Marner (1861, George Eliot)
Small Island (2004, Andrea Levy)
Steppenwolf (1927, Hermann Hesse)
The Big Sleep (1939, Raymond Chandler)
The Crow Road (1992, Iain Banks)
The Hireling (1957, L P Hartley)
The Third Man (1950, Graham Greene)
War and Peace (1863–69, Count Leo Tolstoy)
Women in Love (1920, D H Lawrence)

12 *Anna Karenina* (1874–76, Count Leo Tolstoy)
A Severed Head (1961, Iris Murdoch)
A Suitable Boy (1993, Vikram Seth)
Barnaby Rudge (1841, Charles Dickens)
Brighton Rock (1938, Graham Greene)
Casino Royale (1954, Ian Fleming)
Cover Her Face (1962, P D James)
Dombey and Son (1848, Charles Dickens)
Enduring Love (1997, Ian McEwan)
Invisible Man (1952, Ralph Ellison)

Le Père Goriot (1835, Honoré de Balzac)
Little Dorrit (1857, Charles Dickens)
Madame Bovary (1857, Gustave Flaubert)
Manon Lescaut (1738, Abbé Prévost)
Moll Flanders (1722, Daniel Defoe)
Of Mice and Men (1937, John Steinbeck)
Rip Van Winkle (1819, Washington Irving)
The Dubliners (1914, James Joyce)
The Europeans (1878, Henry James)
The Ghost Road (1995, Pat Barker)
The Go-Between (1953, L P Hartley)
The Lost World (1912, Arthur Conan Doyle)
The Moonstone (1868, Wilkie Collins)
The Old Devils (1986, Kingsley Amis)
The Sea, The Sea (1978, Iris Murdoch)
Tortilla Flat (1935, John Steinbeck)
Whisky Galore (1947, Compton Mackenzie)

13 *A Kind of Loving* (1960, Stan Barstow)
Brave New World (1932, Aldous Huxley)
Carry On, Jeeves (1925, P G Wodehouse)
Charlotte Gray (1998, Sebastian Faulks)
Cousin Phillis (1864, Elizabeth Gaskell)
Daniel Deronda (1876, George Eliot)
Eyeless in Gaza (1936, Aldous Huxley)
Fahrenheit 451 (1953, Ray Bradbury)
Finnegans Wake (1939, James Joyce)
Les Misérables (1862, Victor Hugo)
Mansfield Park (1814, Jane Austen)
North and South (1854, Elizabeth Gaskell)
Right Ho, Jeeves (1934, P G Wodehouse)
Schindler's Ark (1982, Thomas Keneally)
Smiley's People (1980, John Le Carré)
Song of Solomon (1978, Toni Morrison)
Sons and Lovers (1913, D H Lawrence)
Tarka the Otter (1927, Henry Williamson)
The Awkward Age (1899, Henry James)
The Bone People (1985, Keri Hulme)
The Bostonians (1886, Henry James)
The Cancer Ward (1968–69, Aleksandr Solzhenitsyn)
The Golden Bowl (1904, Henry James)
The Jungle Book (1894, Rudyard Kipling)
Thérèse Raquin (1867, Émile Zola)
The Virginians (1857–59, W M Thackeray)
The White Tiger (2008, Aravind Adiga)
Watership Down (1972, Richard Adams)
Zuleika Dobson (1911, Max Beerbohm)

14 *A Handful Of Dust* (1934, Evelyn Waugh)
All the King's Men (1946, Robert Penn Warren)
American Psycho (1991, Bret Easton Ellis)
Another Country (1962, James Baldwin)
A Room With a View (1908, E M Forster)
A Town Like Alice (1950, Nevil Shute)
Between the Acts (1941, Virginia Woolf)
Cider With Rosie (1959, Laurie Lee)

Death on the Nile (1937, Dame Agatha Christie)
Decline and Fall (1928, Evelyn Waugh)
Goodbye, Mr Chips (1934, James Hilton)
Jude the Obscure (1895, Thomas Hardy)
Lord of the Flies (1954, William Golding)
My Cousin Rachel (1951, Daphne du Maurier)
Our Man in Havana (1958, Graham Greene)
Robinson Crusoe (1719, Daniel Defoe)
Tales of the City (1978, Armistead Maupin)
The Ambassadors (1903, Henry James)
The Caine Mutiny (1951, Herman Wouk)
The Color Purple (1983, Alice Walker)
The Corrections (2001, Jonathan Franzen)
The Forsyte Saga (1922, John Galsworthy)
The Good Soldier (1915, Ford Madox Ford)
The Great Gatsby (1925, F Scott Fitzgerald)
The Kraken Wakes (1953, John Wyndham)
The Lovely Bones (2002, Alice Sebold)
The L-Shaped Room (1960, Lynne Reid Banks)
The Secret Agent (1907, Joseph Conrad)
The Time Machine (1895, H G Wells)
The Wasp Factory (1984, Iain Banks)
The Woodlanders (1887, Thomas Hardy)
Treasure Island (1883, Robert Louis Stevenson)
Tristram Shandy (1759–67, Laurence Sterne)
Tropic of Cancer (1934, Henry Miller)
Uncle Tom's Cabin (1852, Harriet Beecher Stowe)
What Maisie Knew (1897, Henry James)

15 *A Christmas Carol* (1843, Charles Dickens)
A Farewell to Arms (1929, Ernest Hemingway)
A Passage to India (1924, E M Forster)
A Study in Scarlet (1887, Arthur Conan Doyle)
Bulldog Drummond (1920, 'Sapper')
Cold Comfort Farm (1932, Stella Gibbons)
Flaubert's Parrot (1984, Julian Barnes)
Frenchman's Creek (1942, Daphne Du Maurier)
Gone with the Wind (1936, Margaret Mitchell)
Gravity's Rainbow (1973, Thomas Pynchon)
Heart of Darkness (1902, Joseph Conrad)
Le Rouge et le noir (1830, Stendhal)
Northanger Abbey (1818, Jane Austen)
Oscar and Lucinda (1988, Peter Carey)
Our Mutual Friend (1865, Charles Dickens)
Slaughterhouse 5 (1969, Kurt Vonnegut)
Tarzan of the Apes (1914, Edgar Rice Burroughs)
The African Queen (1935, C S Forester)
The Famished Road (1991, Ben Okri)
The House of Mirth (1905, Edith Wharton)

The Invisible Man (1897, H G Wells)
The Old Wives' Tale (1908, Arnold Bennett)
The Shipping News (1993, Annie Proulx)
The Sun Also Rises (1926, Ernest Hemingway)
The Trumpet Major (1880, Thomas Hardy)
The Woman in White (1860, Wilkie Collins)
Things Fall Apart (1958, Chinua Achebe)
Three Men in a Boat (1889, Jerome K Jerome)
To the Lighthouse (1927, Virginia Woolf)
Vernon God Little (2003, D B C Pierre)
Where Eagles Dare (1967, Alistair MacLean)
Wide Sargasso Sea (1966, Jean Rhys)

16 *A Clockwork Orange* (1962, Anthony Burgess)
A Tale of Two Cities (1859, Charles Dickens)
Barchester Towers (1857, Anthony Trollope)
Bonjour tristesse (1954, Françoise Sagan)
David Copperfield (1850, Charles Dickens)
England, My England (1922, D H Lawrence)
Gulliver's Travels (1726, Jonathan Swift)
Martin Chuzzlewit (1844, Charles Dickens)
Memoirs of a Geisha (1997, Arthur Golden)
Mr Midshipman Easy (1836, Captain Frederick Marryat)
Nicholas Nickleby (1839, Charles Dickens)
Tender is the Night (1934, F Scott Fitzgerald)
The Blind Assassin (2000, Margaret Atwood)
The Call of the Wild (1903, Jack London)
The Crying of Lot 49 (1966, Thomas Pynchon)
The Grapes of Wrath (1939, John Steinbeck)
The Handmaid's Tale (1986, Margaret Atwood)
The Maltese Falcon (1930, Dashiell Hammett)
The Quiet American (1955, Graham Greene)
The Satanic Verses (1988, Salman Rushdie)
The Scarlet Letter (1850, Nathaniel Hawthorne)
To Have and Have Not (1937, Ernest Hemingway)
Wuthering Heights (1848, Emily Brontë)

17 *A Kestrel for a Knave* (1968, Barry Hines)
Anne of Green Gables (1925, L M Montgomery)
Fire on the Mountain (1977, Anita Desai)
Great Expectations (1861, Charles Dickens)
King Solomon's Mines (1885, Sir H Rider Haggard)
Midnight's Children (1981, Salman Rushdie)
Portnoy's Complaint (1969, Philip Roth)
Pride and Prejudice (1813, Jane Austen)
The Age of Innocence (1920, Edith Wharton)
The Day of the Jackal (1971, Frederick Forsyth)

The Diary of a Nobody (1892, George and Weedon Grossmith)
The End of the Affair (1951, Graham Greene)
The English Patient (1992, Michael Ondaatje)
The Lord of the Rings (1954–55, J R R Tolkien)
The Mill on the Floss (1860, George Eliot)
The Pickwick Papers (1837, Charles Dickens)
The Turn of the Screw (1898, Henry James)
The Wings of the Dove (1902, Henry James)
Travels With My Aunt (1969, Graham Greene)
Tropic of Capricorn (1938, Henry Miller)
Wives and Daughters (1866, Elizabeth Gaskell)

18 *A High Wind in Jamaica* (1929, Richard Hughes)
Bridget Jones's Diary (1996, Helen Fielding)
The Catcher in the Rye (1951, J D Salinger)
The Cider House Rules (1985, John Irving)
The Last Picture Show (1966, Larry McMurtry)
The Naked and the Dead (1949, Norman Mailer)
The Old Man and the Sea (1952, Ernest Hemingway)
The Portrait of a Lady (1881, Henry James)
The Prisoner of Zenda (1894, Anthony Hope)
The Sound and the Fury (1929, William Faulkner)
The Thirty-Nine Steps (1915, John Buchan)
The Three Musketeers (1844, Alexandre Dumas)
The Trials of Rumpole (1979, John Mortimer)
To Kill A Mockingbird (1960, Harper Lee)

19 *Breakfast at Tiffany's* 1958, Truman Capote)
Brideshead Revisited (1945, Evelyn Waugh)
For Whom the Bell Tolls (1940, Ernest Hemingway)
How Late It Was, How Late (1994, James Kelman)
Murder at the Vicarage (1930, Dame Agatha Christie)
Sense and Sensibility (1811, Jane Austen)
The Buddha of Suburbia (1995, Hanif Kureishi)
The Darling Buds of May (1958, H E Bates)
The Day of the Triffids (1951, John Wyndham)
The God of Small Things (1997, Arundhati Roy)
The Old Curiosity Shop (1841, Charles Dickens)

The Robber Bridegroom (1942, Eudora Welty)
The Scarlet Pimpernel (1905, Baroness Orczy)
The Talented Mr Ripley (1956, Patricia Highsmith)
The Well of Loneliness (1928, Radclyffe Hall)
Tom Brown's Schooldays (1857, Thomas Hughes)

20 *Anthills of the Savanna* (1987, Chinua Achebe)
Cry, the Beloved Country (1948, Alan Paton)
Lady Chatterley's Lover (1928, D H Lawrence)
Lark Rise to Candleford (1945, Flora Thompson)
Little Lord Fauntleroy (1885, Frances Hodgson Burnett)
The History of Tom Jones (1749, Henry Fielding)
The Last of the Mohicans (1826, James Fenimore Cooper)
The Optimist's Daughter (1972, Eudora Welty)
The Return of the Native (1878, Thomas Hardy)
The Silence of the Lambs (1988, Thomas Harris)
The Witches of Eastwick (1984, John Updike)

21 *Girl With a Pearl Earring* (1999, Tracy Chevalier)
Tess of the d'Urbervilles (1891, Thomas Hardy)
The Count of Monte Cristo (1844–45, Alexandre Dumas)
The Mysteries of Udolpho (1794, Ann Radcliffe)
The Snows of Kilimanjaro (1936, Ernest Hemingway)
The Tenderness of Wolves (2006, Stef Penney)
Under the Greenwood Tree (1872, Thomas Hardy)

22 *A Dance to the Music of Time* (12 volumes, 1951–75, Anthony Powell)
Far from the Madding Crowd (1874, Thomas Hardy)
Gentlemen Prefer Blondes (1925, Anita Loos)
Les Liaisons dangereuses (1782, Choderlos de Laclos)
Life and Times of Michael K (1983, J M Coetzee)
The Man with the Golden Arm (1949, Nelson Algren)

The Mayor of Casterbridge (1886, Thomas Hardy)

The Mystery of Edwin Drood (1870, Charles Dickens)

The Picture of Dorian Gray (1891, Oscar Wilde)

Tinker, Tailor, Soldier, Spy (1974, John Le Carré)

Where Angels Fear to Tread (1905, E M Forster)

23 *Captain Corelli's Mandolin* (1994, Louis de Bernières)

Keep the Aspidistra Flying (1936, George Orwell)

The Bonfire of the Vanities (1987, Tom Wolfe)

The Heart is a Lonely Hunter (1940, Carson McCullers)

The Island of Doctor Moreau (1896, H G Wells)

The Magnificent Ambersons (1918, Booth Tarkington)

The Murder of Roger Ackroyd (1926, Dame Agatha Christie)

The Tenant of Wildfell Hall (1848, Anne Brontë)

The World According to Garp (1976, John Irving)

24 *Á la recherche du temps perdu* 1913–27, Marcel Proust

Murder on the Orient Express (1934, Dame Agatha Christie)

The Adventures of Tom Sawyer (1876, Mark Twain)

The Fall of the House of Usher (1839, Edgar Allan Poe)

Their Eyes Were Watching God (1937, Zora Neale Hurston)

The Prime of Miss Jean Brodie (1961, Muriel Spark)

25 *One Flew Over the Cuckoo's Nest* (1962, Ken Kesey)

Oranges are Not the Only Fruit (1985, Jeanette Winterson)

The French Lieutenant's Woman (1969, John Fowles)

26 *Around the World in Eighty Days* (1873, Jules Verne)

The Life and Loves of a She-Devil (1983, Fay Weldon)

The Postman Always Rings Twice (1934, James M Cain)

The Secret Life of Walter Mitty (1939, James Thurber)

The Spy Who Came in from the Cold (1963, John Le Carré)

27 *The Mysterious Affair at Styles* (1920, Dame Agatha Christie)

29 *A Journey to the Centre of the Earth* (1864, Jules Verne)

Saturday Night and Sunday Morning (1958, Alan Sillitoe)

30 *The Adventures of Huckleberry Finn* (1884, Mark Twain)

The Hitch-Hiker's Guide to the Galaxy (1979, Douglas Adams)

31 *One Day in the Life of Ivan Denisovich* (1963, Aleksandr Solzhenitsyn)

32 *The Beastly Beatitudes of Balthazar B* (1968, J P Donleavy)

Twenty Thousand Leagues Under the Sea (1869, Jules Verne)

33 *Frankenstein, or, The Modern Prometheus* (1818, Mary Shelley)

The Strange Case of Dr Jekyll and Mr Hyde (1886, Robert Louis Stevenson)

34 *The Life and Opinions of Tristram Shandy* (1759–67, Laurence Sterne)

36 *The Loneliness of the Long Distance Runner* (1959, Alan Sillitoe)

40 *The Curious Incident of the Dog in the Night-Time* (2003, Mark Haddon)

41 *The Infernal Desire Machines of Doctor Hoffmann* (1972, Angela Carter)

Novels and books for children include:

04 *Junk* (1996, Melvin Burgess)

05 *Heidi* (1880, Johanna Spyri)

Noddy (series from 1949, Enid Blyton)

Smith (1967, Leon Garfield)

06 *Tehanu* (1972, Ursula Le Guin)

The BFG (1982, Roald Dahl)

07 *Forever* (1975, Judy Blume)

Matilda (1988, Roald Dahl)

Skellig (1998, David Almond)

08 *Peter Pan* (1904, J M Barrie)

The Twits (1980, Roald Dahl)

09 *Kidnapped* (1886, Robert Louis Stevenson)

Pollyanna (1913, Eleanor H Porter)

The Hobbit (1937, J R R Tolkien)

10 *Dr Dolittle* (series from 1920, Hugh Lofting)

Goggle-Eyes (1989, Anne Fine)

The Witches (1983, Roald Dahl)

Uncle Remus (series from 1880–1906, Joel Chandler Harris)

11 *Artemis Fowl* (2001, Eoin Colfer)
Ballet Shoes (1936, Noel Streatfeild)
Just William (1922, Richmal Crompton)
Little Women (1868, Louisa May Alcott)
Mary Poppins (1934, P L Travers)
Now We Are Six (1927, A A Milne)
Tennis Shoes (1937, Noel Streatfeild)
The Sheep-Pig (1983, Dick King-Smith)
What Katy Did (1872, Susan Coolidge)

12 *The Borrowers* (1952, Mary Norton)

13 *Charlotte's Web* (1952, E B White)
Just So Stories (1902, Rudyard Kipling)
Stig of the Dump (1963, Clive King)
Struwwelpeter (1848, Heinrich Hoffman)
The Famous Five (series from 1942, Enid
Blyton)
The Jungle Book (1894, Rudyard Kipling)
The Owl Service (1967, Alan Garner)
Watership Down (1972, Richard Adams)
Winnie-the-Pooh (1926, A A Milne)

14 *Lord of the Flies* (1954, William Golding)
Masterman Ready (1841–42, Captain
Frederick Marryat)
National Velvet (1935, Enid Bagnold)
Northern Lights (1995, Philip Pullman)
Paddington Bear (series from 1958, Michael
Bond)
Robinson Crusoe (1719, Daniel Defoe)
The Cat in the Hat (1957, Dr Seuss)
The Coral Island (1858, R M Ballantyne)
The Secret Seven (series from 1949, Enid
Blyton)
The Subtle Knife (1997, Philip Pullman)
The Water-Babies (1863, Charles Kingsley)
Treasure Island (1883, Robert Louis
Stevenson)
Uncle Tom's Cabin (1851–52, Harriet
Beecher Stowe)

15 *A Gathering Light* (2003, Jennifer Donnelly)
A Little Princess (1905, Frances Hodgson
Burnett)
Eagle of the Ninth (1954, Rosemary
Sutcliff)
Madame Doubtfire (1987, Anne Fine)
The Chocolate War (1974, Robert Cormier)
The Secret Garden (1911, Frances Hodgson
Burnett)
Tuck Everlasting (1975, Natalie Babbit)

16 *His Dark Materials* (1995–2000, Philip
Pullman)
I Hate My Teddy Bear (1982, David
McKee)
Outside Over There (1981, Maurice Sendak)
The Amber Spyglass (2000, Philip Pullman)
The Call of the Wild (1903, Jack London)
The Secret Passage (1963, Nina Bawden)

17 *Anne of Green Gables* (1908, L M
Montgomery)
A Wizard of Earthsea (1967, Ursula Le
Guin)
Diary of a Young Girl (1952, Anne Frank)
Pippi Longstocking (1945, Astrid Lindgren)
The Machine-Gunners (1975, Robert
Westall)

18 *Goodnight Mister Tom* (1980, Michelle
Magorian)
Swallows and Amazons (series from
1930–1947, Arthur Ransome)
The Railway Children (1906, Edith Nesbit)
The Tale of Tom Kitten (1907, Beatrix Potter)
Tom's Midnight Garden (1958, Philippa
Pearce)

19 *Swiss Family Robinson* (1812, Johann Rudolf
Wyss)
The Wind in the Willows (1908, Kenneth
Grahame)
Tom Brown's Schooldays (1857, Thomas
Hughes)
When We Were Very Young (1924, A A Milne)

20 *Little Lord Fauntleroy* (1886, Frances
Hodgson Burnett)
The Great Gilly Hopkins (1978, Kathleen
Paterson)
The House at Pooh Corner (1928, A A
Milne)
The Tale of Peter Rabbit (1900, Beatrix
Potter)

21 *James and the Giant Peach* (1961, Roald
Dahl)
The Prince and the Pauper (1882, Mark
Twain)
The Tailor of Gloucester (1902, Beatrix
Potter)
Where the Wild Things Are (1963, Maurice
Sendak)

22 *Seven Little Australians* (1894, Ethel Turner)
The Phoenix and the Carpet (1904, Edith
Nesbit)
The Story of Tracey Beaker (1991,
Jacqueline Wilson)
The Wonderful Wizard of Oz (1900, L Frank
Baum)
Through the Looking-Glass (1871, Lewis
Carroll)

24 *Little House in the Big Woods* (1932, Laura
Ingalls Wilder)
The Adventures of Pinocchio (1883, Carlo
Collodi)
The Adventures of Tom Sawyer (1876, Mark
Twain)
The Very Hungry Caterpillar (1969, Eric
Carle)

25 *The Children of the New Forest* (1847, Captain Frederick Marryat)

26 *Danny the Champion of the World* (1975, Roald Dahl)
How the Grinch Stole Christmas (1957, Dr Seuss)
The Weirdstone of Brisingamen (1960, Alan Garner)
The Wolves of Willoughby Chase (1963, Joan Aiken)

28 *Alice's Adventures in Wonderland* (1865, Lewis Carroll)
The Story of the Treasure Seekers (1899, Edith Nesbit)

29 *Charlie and the Chocolate Factory* (1964, Roald Dahl)
Harry Potter and the Goblet of Fire (2000, J K Rowling)

The Lion, the Witch and the Wardrobe (1950, C S Lewis)

30 *The Adventures of Huckleberry Finn* (1884, Mark Twain)

31 *Harry Potter and the Deathly Hallows* (2007, J K Rowling)

32 *Harry Potter and the Half-Blood Prince* (2005, J K Rowling)

33 *Harry Potter and the Chamber of Secrets* (1998, J K Rowling)

34 *Harry Potter and the Order of the Phoenix* (2003, J K Rowling)
Harry Potter and the Philosopher's Stone (1997, J K Rowling)
Harry Potter and the Prisoner of Azkaban (1999, J K Rowling)

Novelists and short-story writers include:

02 Mo (Timothy; 1950– , English)
Oë (Kenzaburo; 1935– , Japanese)

03 Abe (Kobo; 1924–93, Japanese)
Ali (Monica; 1967– , Bangladeshi/British)
Eco (Umberto; 1932– , Italian)
Eri (Vincent Serei; 1936–93, Papua New Guinean)
Fay (András; 1786–1864, Hungarian)
Gyp (1849–1932, French)
Han (Suyin; 1917– , Chinese/British)
Hay (Ian; 1876–1952, Scottish)
Kay (Jackie; 1961– , Scottish)
Kee (Robert; 1919– , English)
Lee (Harper; 1926– , US)
Lee (Laurie; 1914–97, English)
Lie (Jonas; 1833–1908, Norwegian)
Poe (Edgar Allan; 1809–49, US)
Pym (Barbara; 1913–80, English)
Rao (Raja; 1908– , Indian)
Roe (Edward Payson; 1838–88, US)
Roy (Arundhati; 1961– , Indian)
Sue (Eugène; 1804–57, French)
Tey (Josephine; 1897–1952, Scottish)

04 Adam (Paul; 1862–1920, French)
Agee (James; 1909–55, US)
Amis (Martin; 1949– , English)
Amis (Sir Kingsley; 1922–95, English)
Arlt (Roberto; 1900–42, Argentine)
Bage (Robert; 1728–1801, English)
Bahr (Hermann; 1863–1934, Austrian)
Baum (Vicki; 1888–1960, Austrian/US)
Behn (Aphra; 1640–89, English)
Bely (Andrei; 1880–1934, Russian)
Böll (Heinrich; 1917–85, German)
Boyd (Martin; 1893–1972, Australian)
Boyd (William; 1952– , Ghanaian/British)

Boye (Karin; 1900–41, Swedish)
Brod (Max; 1884–1968, Austrian)
Buck (Pearl S; 1892–1973, US)
Bury (Lady Charlotte; 1775–1861, Scottish)
Cain (James M; 1892–1977, US)
Cary (Joyce; 1888–1957, English)
Cela (Camilo José; 1916–2002, Spanish)
Dahl (Roald; 1916–90, Welsh/British)
Dane (Clemence; 1888–1965, English)
Dark (Eleanor; 1901–85, Australian)
Dell (Ethel M; 1881–1939, English)
Droz (Antoine Gustave; 1832–95, French)
Duun (Olav; 1876–1939, Norwegian)
Egge (Peter; 1869–1959, Norwegian)
Endo (Shusako; 1923–96, Japanese)
Fast (Howard; 1914–92, US)
Fine (Anne; 1947– , English)
Ford (Ford Madox; 1873–1939, English)
Ford (Richard; 1944– , US)
Gale (Zona; 1874–1938, US)
Galt (John; 1779–1839, Scottish)
Gass (William H; 1924– , US)
Gide (André; 1869–1951, French)
Glyn (Elinor; 1864–1943, British)
Gore (Catherine; 1799–1861, English)
Gray (Alasdair; 1934– , Scottish)
Grey (Zane; 1875–1939, US)
Gunn (Neil M; 1891–1973, Scottish)
Head (Bessie; 1937–86, South African)
Heym (Stefan; 1913–2001, German)
Hill (Reginald; 1936– , English)
Hill (Susan; 1942– , English)
Hogg (James; 1770–1835, Scottish)
Hope (Anthony; 1863–1933, English)
Huch (Ricarda; 1864–1947, German)
Hugo (Victor; 1802–85, French)
Hunt (E Howard; 1918–90, US)

Jane (Frederick Thomas; 1870–1916, English)
Karr (Alphonse; 1808–90, French)
King (Stephen; 1947– , US)
Kivi (Aleksis; 1834–72, Finnish)
Koch (C J; 1932– , Australian)
Kock (Charles Paul de; 1794–1871, French)
Laye (Camera; 1928–80, French Guinea)
Levi (Primo; 1919–87, Italian)
Levy (Andrea; 1956– , English)
Lily (John; c.1554–1606, English)
Loos (Anita; 1893–1981, US)
Lyly (John; c.1554–1606, English)
Mack (Louise; 1874–1935, Australian)
Mais (Roger; 1905–55, Jamaican)
Mann (Heinrich; 1871–1950, German)
Mann (Thomas; 1875–1955, German)
Muir (Willa; 1890–1970, Scottish)
Neal (John; 1793–1876, US)
Nexö (Martin Andersen; 1869–1954, Danish)
Okri (Ben; 1959– , Nigerian)
Page (Thomas Nelson; 1853–1922, US)
Prus (Boleslaw; 1847–1912, Polish)
Puig (Manuel; 1932–90, Argentine)
Puzo (Mario; 1920–99, US)
Reed (Ishmael; 1938– , US)
Renn (Ludwig; 1889–1979, German)
Rhys (Jean; 1894–1979, West Indian/British)
Rice (James; 1843–82, English)
Roth (Henry; 1906–95, Austrian/US)
Roth (Joseph; 1894–1939, Austrian)
Roth (Philip; 1933– , US)
Sade (Marquis de; 1740–1814, French)
Saki (Hector Hugh Munro; 1870–1916, British)
Sala (George; 1828–95, English)
Sand (George; 1804–76, French)
Seth (Vikram; 1952– , Indian)
Snow (C P, Lord; 1905–80, English)
Stow (Randolph; 1935– , Australian)
Vian (Boris; 1920–59, French)
Wain (John; 1925–94, English)
Wang (Meng; 1934– , Chinese)
Ward (Mary Augusta; 1851–1920, English)
Ward (Mrs Humphry; 1851–1920, English)
Webb (Mary; 1881–1927, English)
West (Dame Rebecca; 1892–1983, Irish)
West (Morris; 1916–99, Australian)
West (Nathanael; 1903–40, US)
Wolf (Christa; 1929– , German)
Wood (Mrs Henry; 1814–87, English)
Wouk (Herman; 1915– , US)
Wren (P C; 1885–1941, English)
Zola (Émile; 1840–1902, French)
05 About (Edmond; 1828–85, French)
Acker (Kathy; 1944–97, US)
Adams (Douglas; 1952–2001, English)

Adams (Richard; 1920– , English)
Adiga (Aravind; 1974– , Indian/Australian)
Agnon (S Y; 1888–1970, Israeli)
Aiken (Conrad; 1889–1973, US)
Akins (Zoë; 1886–1958, US)
Allen (Walter; 1911–95, English)
Amado (Jorge; 1912–2001, Brazilian)
Anand (Mulk Raj; 1905–2004, Indian)
Arlen (Michael; 1895–1956, Bulgarian/British)
Banks (Iain; 1954– , Scottish)
Banks (Lynne Reid; 1929– , English)
Barke (James; 1905–58, Scottish)
Barth (John; 1930– , US)
Bates (H E; 1905–74, English)
Bazin (René; 1853–1932, French)
Behan (Brendan; 1923–64, Irish)
Behan (Dominic; 1928–89, Irish)
Benet (Juan; 1927–93, Spanish)
Benét (Stephen Vincent; 1898–1943, US)
Berry (Wendell; 1934– , US)
Bloch (Jean-Richard; 1884–1947, French)
Bowen (Elizabeth; 1899–1973, Irish)
Boyle (Kay; 1902–92, US)
Bragg (Melvyn, Lord; 1939– , English)
Brand (Max; 1892–1944, US)
Brink (André; 1935– , South African)
Broch (Hermann; 1886–1951, Austrian)
Brown (Charles Brockden; 1771–1810, US)
Brown (George Mackay; 1921–96, Scottish)
Bruce (Mary Grant; 1878–1958, Australian)
Buber (Martin; 1878–1965, Austrian)
Bunin (Ivan; 1870–1953, Russian)
Byatt (Dame A S; 1936– , English)
Cahan (Abraham; 1860–1951, US)
Caine (Sir Hall; 1853–1931, English)
Camus (Albert; 1913–60, French)
Cantú (Cesare; 1804–95, Italian)
Capek (Karel; 1890–1938, Czech)
Carey (Peter; 1943– , Australian)
Chase (James Hadley; 1906–85, English)
Clift (Charmian; 1923–69, Australian)
Crace (Jim; 1946– , English)
Craik (Dinah Maria; 1826–87, English)
Crane (Stephen; 1871–1900, US)
Cross (Amanda; 1926–2003, US)
Davie (Elspeth; 1919–95, Scottish)
Davis (Richard Harding; 1863–1916, US)
Defoe (Daniel; 1660–1731, English)
Desai (Anita; 1937– , Indian)
Doyle (Sir Arthur Conan; 1859–1930, Scottish)
Doyle (Roddy; 1958– , Irish)
Dumas (Alexandre, père; 1802–70, French)
Duras (Marguerite; 1914–96, French)
Ebers (Georg Moritz; 1837–98, German)
Eliot (George; 1819–80, English)
Elkin (Stanley; 1930–95, US)

Ellis (Alice Thomas; 1932–2005, British)
Ellis (Bret Easton; 1964–   , US)
Elton (Ben; 1959–   , English)
Evans (Caradoc; 1878–1945, Welsh)
Faure (Edgar; 1908–88, French)
Féval (Paul; 1817–87, French)
Foote (Shelby; 1916–2005, US)
Frame (Janet; 1924–2004, New Zealand)
Frank (Leonhard; 1882–1961, German)
Frank (Waldo David; 1889–1967, US)
Frayn (Michael; 1933–   , English)
Friel (George; 1910–75, Scottish)
Genet (Jean; 1910–86, French)
Gogol (Nikolai; 1809–52, Russian)
Gorky (Maxim; 1868–1936, Russian)
Grand (Sarah; 1854–1943, British)
Grass (Günter; 1927–   , German)
Green (Henry; 1905–73, English)
Green (Julien; 1900–98, French)
Haley (Alex; 1921–92, US)
Hardy (Thomas; 1840–1928, English)
Harte (Bret; 1836–1902, US)
Hašek (Jaroslav; 1883–1923, Czech)
Hauff (Wilhelm; 1802–27, German)
Hearn (Lafcadio; 1850–1904, Greek)
Henry (O; 1862–1910, US)
Henty (G A; 1832–1902, English)
Hesse (Hermann; 1877–1962, German/
   Swiss)
Heyer (Georgette; 1902–74, English)
Himes (Chester; 1909–84, US)
Hines (Barry; 1939–   , English)
Hulme (Keri; 1947–   , New Zealand)
Innes (Hammond; 1913–98, English)
Jacob (Violet; 1863–1946, Scottish)
James (George Payne Rainsford; 1799–1860,
   English)
James (Henry; 1843–1916, US)
James (P D, Baroness; 1920–   , English)
Jesse (F Tennyson; 1888–1958, English)
Johns (Captain W E; 1893–1968, English)
Jókai (Maurus; 1825–1904, Hungarian)
Jókai (Mór; 1825–1904, Hungarian)
Jones (James; 1921–77, US)
Joyce (James; 1882–1941, Irish)
Kafka (Franz; 1883–1924, Austrian)
Keane (Molly; 1904–96, Irish)
Kesey (Ken; 1935–2001, US)
Kinck (Hans E; 1865–1926, Norwegian)
Laski (Marghanita; 1915–88, English)
Lavin (Mary; 1912–96, Irish)
Lever (Charles; 1806–72, Irish)
Lewis (C S; 1898–1963, British)
Lewis (M G; 1775–1818, English)
Lewis (Sinclair; 1885–1951, US)
Lewis (Wyndham; 1882–1957, English)
Linna (Väinö; 1920–92, Finnish)
Locke (William John; 1863–1930, English)

Lodge (David; 1935–   , English)
Louÿs (Pierre; 1870–1925, Belgian/French)
Lowry (Malcolm; 1909–57, English)
Lurie (Alison; 1926–   , US)
Marsé (Juan; 1933–   , Spanish)
Marsh (Dame Ngaio; 1899–1982, New
   Zealand)
Mason (A E W; 1865–1948, English)
Mayor (F M; 1872–1931, English)
Meyer (Conrad; 1825–98, Swiss)
Milne (A A; 1882–1956, English)
Moore (Brian; 1921–99, Northern Irish/
   Canadian)
Moore (George; 1852–1933, Irish)
Moore (Thomas; 1779–1852, Irish)
Munro (Alice; 1931–   , Canadian)
Munro (Hector Hugh; 1870–1916, British)
Munro (Neil; 1864–1930, Scottish)
Musil (Robert; 1880–1942, Austrian)
Niven (Frederick; 1878–1944, Scottish)
Oates (Joyce Carol; 1938–   , US)
O'Hara (John; 1905–70, US)
Orczy (Baroness; 1865–1947, Hungarian/
   British)
Ouida (1839–1908, English)
Ozick (Cynthia; 1928–   , US)
Paton (Alan; 1903–88, South African)
Peake (Mervyn; 1911–68, English)
Pears (Tim; 1956–   , English)
Percy (Walker; 1916–90, US)
Plath (Sylvia; 1932–63, US)
Potok (Chaim; 1929–2002, US)
Powys (John Cowper; 1872–1963, English)
Powys (T F; 1875–1953, English)
Praed (Rosa; 1851–1935, Australian)
Preda (Marin; 1922–80, Romanian)
Queen (Ellery; Frederick Dannay, 1905–82,
   US and Manfred B Lee, 1905–71, US)
Ramos (Graciliano; 1892–1953, Brazilian)
Reade (Charles; 1814–84, English)
Reeve (Clara; 1729–1807, English)
Rojas (Fernando de; c.1465–1541, Spanish)
Rolfe (Frederick William; 1860–1913,
   English)
Rulfo (Juan; 1918–86, Mexican)
Sagan (Françoise; 1935–2004, French)
Scott (Paul; 1920–78, English)
Scott (Sir Walter; 1771–1832, Scottish)
Selby (Hubert, Jnr; 1928–2004, US)
Serao (Matilde; 1856–1927, Greek/Italian)
Shute (Nevil; 1899–1960, English)
Silko (Leslie Marmon; 1948–   , US)
Simms (William Gilmore; 1806–70, US)
Simon (Claude; 1913–2005, French)
Skram (Amalie; 1847–1905, Norwegian)
Smith (Alexander McCall; 1948–   ,
   Scottish)
Smith (Dodie; 1896–1990, English)

Smith (Iain Crichton; 1928–98, Scottish)
Smith (Stevie; 1902–71, English)
Smith (Wilbur; 1933– , Rhodesian/South
 African)
Smith (Zadie; 1975– , English)
Souza (Madame de; 1761–1836, French)
Spark (Dame Muriel; 1918–2006, Scottish)
Staël (Madame de; 1766–1817, French)
Stead (Christina; 1902–83, Australian)
Stone (Irving; 1903–89, US)
Stout (Rex; 1886–1975, US)
Stowe (Harriet Beecher; 1811–96, US)
Svevo (Italo; 1861–1928, Italian)
Swift (Graham; 1949– , English)
Swift (Jonathan; 1667–1745, Irish)
Tam'si (Tchicaya U; 1931–88, Congolese)
Tartt (Donna; 1963– , US)
Toole (John Kennedy; 1937–69, US)
Torga (Miguel; 1907–90, Portuguese)
Turow (Scott; 1949– , US)
Twain (Mark; 1835–1910, US)
Tyler (Anne; 1941– , US)
Tynan (Katharine; 1861–1931, Irish)
Unruh (Fritz von; 1885–1970, German)
Verga (Giovanni; 1840–1922, Italian)
Verne (Jules; 1828–1905, French)
Viaud (Louis Marie Julien; 1850–1923,
 French)
Vidal (Gore; 1925– , US)
Waugh (Alec; 1898–1981, English)
Waugh (Auberon; 1939–2001, English)
Waugh (Evelyn; 1903–66, English)
Wells (H G; 1866–1946, English)
Welsh (Irvine; 1961– , Scottish)
Welty (Eudora; 1909–2001, US)
White (Antonia; 1899–1979, English)
White (E B; 1899–1985, US)
White (Patrick; 1912–90, English/Australian)
White (T H; 1906–64, English)
White (William Hale; 1831–1913, English)
Wilde (Oscar; 1854–1900, Irish)
Wolfe (Thomas; 1900–38, US)
Wolfe (Tom; 1931– , US)
Woolf (Virginia; 1882–1941, English)
Yates (Dornford; 1885–1960, English)
Yonge (Charlotte M; 1823–1901, English)
Young (Francis Brett; 1884–1954, English)
Zweig (Arnold; 1887–1968, German)

06 Achebe (Chinua; 1930– , Nigerian)
Alcott (Louisa M; 1832–88, US)
Aldiss (Brian W; 1925– , English)
Alemán (Mateo; 1547–1610 or 1620,
 Spanish)
Algren (Nelson; 1909–81, US)
Alvaro (Corrado; 1895–1956, Italian)
Ambler (Eric; 1909–98, English)
Amicis (Edmondo de; 1846–1908, Italian)
Aragon (Louis; 1897–1983, French)

Archer (Jeffrey, Lord; 1940– , English)
Arenas (Reinaldo; 1943–90, Cuban)
Asimov (Isaac; 1920–92, Russian/US)
Atwood (Margaret; 1939– , Canadian)
Austen (Jane; 1775–1817, English)
Auster (Paul; 1947– , US)
Azorín (1873–1967, Spanish)
Balzac (Honoré de; 1799–1850, French)
Barham (R H; 1788–1845, English)
Barker (George Granville; 1913 91, English)
Barker (Pat; 1943– , English)
Barnes (Djuna; 1892–1982, US)
Barnes (Julian; 1946– , English)
Barrès (Maurice; 1862–1923, French)
Barrie (J M; 1860–1937, Scottish)
Bellow (Saul; 1915–2005, Canadian/US)
Berger (John; 1926– , English)
Besant (Sir Walter; 1836–1901, English)
Binchy (Maeve; 1940– , Irish)
Blixen (Karen; 1885–1962, Danish)
Blunck (Hans Friedrich; 1888–1961,
 German)
Blyton (Enid; 1897–1968, English)
Borges (Jorge Luis; 1899–1986, Argentine)
Bowles (Paul; 1910–99, US)
Braine (John; 1922–86, English)
Bratby (John; 1928–92, English)
Brazil (Angela; 1868–1947, English)
Bremer (Fredrika; 1801–65, Swedish)
Brenan (Gerald; 1894–1987, English)
Brontë (Anne; 1820–49, English)
Brontë (Charlotte; 1816–55, English)
Brontë (Emily; 1818–48, English)
Brooks (Gwendolyn; 1917–2000, US)
Brophy (Brigid; 1929–95, English)
Buchan (John; 1875–1940, Scottish)
Bunyan (John; 1628–88, English)
Burney (Fanny; 1752–1840, English)
Butler (Samuel; 1835–1902, English)
Cabell (James Branch; 1879–1958, US)
Capote (Truman; 1924–84, US)
Carter (Angela; 1940–92, English)
Castro (Rosalía de; 1837–85, Spanish)
Cather (Willa; 1873–1947, US)
Céline (Louis-Ferdinand; 1894–1961,
 French)
Chabon (Michael; 1963– , US)
Chopin (Katherine; 1851–1904, US)
Church (Richard Thomas; 1893–1972,
 English)
Clancy (Tom; 1947– , US)
Clarke (Arthur C; 1917–2008, English)
Clarke (Marcus; 1846–81, Australian)
Cleary (Jon; 1917– , Australian)
Conrad (Joseph; 1857–1924, Polish/British)
Conway (Hugh; 1847–85, English)
Cooper (James Fenimore; 1789–1851, US)
Cooper (Jilly; 1937– , English)

Cronin (A J; 1896–1981, Scottish)
Davies (Robertson; 1913–95, Canadian)
Dekker (Eduard Douwes; 1820–87, Dutch)
Desani (G V; 1909–2000, Kenyan/US)
Dexter (Colin; 1930– , English)
Dibdin (Michael; 1947–2007, English)
Dickey (James; 1923–97, US)
Didion (Joan; 1934– , US)
Döblin (Alfred; 1878–1957, German/French)
Donoso (José; 1928–96, Chilean)
Drezen (Youenn; 1899–1972, Breton)
Dutton (Geoffrey; 1922–98, Australian)
Faulks (Sebastian; 1953– , English)
Fowles (John; 1926–2005, English)
France (Anatole; 1844–1924, French)
Fraser (George MacDonald; 1925–2008, English)
French (Marilyn; 1929– , US)
Frisch (Max; 1911–91, Swiss)
Fuller (Margaret; 1810–50, US)
Fuller (Roy; 1912–91, English)
Gaddis (William; 1922–98, US)
Garner (Alan; 1934– , English)
Gibbon (Lewis Grassic; 1901–35, Scottish)
Godden (Rumer; 1907–98, English)
Godwin (William; 1756–1836, English)
Goethe (Johann Wolfgang von; 1749–1832, German)
Golden (Arthur; 1957– , US)
Goudge (Elizabeth; 1900–84, English)
Graham (Winston; 1910–2003, English)
Graves (Robert; 1895–1985, English)
Greene (Graham; 1904–91, English)
Guzman (Martín Luis; 1887–1976, Mexican)
Haddon (Mark; 1962– , English)
Hailey (Arthur; 1920–2004, English/Canadian)
Halévy (Ludovic; 1834–1908, French)
Hamsun (Knut; 1859–1952, Norwegian)
Hansen (Martin Alfred; 1909–55, Danish)
Harris (Thomas; 1940– , US)
Harris (Wilson; 1921– , British)
Heller (Joseph; 1923–99, US)
Heller (Zoë; 1965– , English)
Hilton (James; 1900–54, English)
Holtby (Winifred; 1898–1935, English)
Hornby (Nick; 1957– , English)
Hughes (Richard; 1900–76, English)
Hughes (Thomas; 1822–96, English)
Hunter (Evan; 1926–2005, US)
Huxley (Aldous; 1894–1963, English)
Huxley (Elspeth; 1907–97, English)
Ibáñez (Vicente Blasco; 1867–1928, Spanish)
Irving (John; 1942– , US)
Irving (Washington; 1783–1859, US)
Jensen (Johannes V; 1873–1950, Danish)

Jerome (Jerome K; 1859–1927, English)
Jewett (Sarah Orne; 1849–1909, US)
Jósika (Miklós, Baron von; 1794–1865, Hungarian)
Jünger (Ernst; 1895–1998, German)
Keller (Gottfried; 1819–90, Swiss)
Kelman (James; 1946– , Scottish)
Laclos (Pierre Choderlos de; 1741–1803, French)
La Guma (Alex; 1925–85, South African)
L'Amour (Louis; 1908–88, US)
Larkin (Philip; 1922–85, English)
Le Fanu (Sheridan; 1814–73, Irish)
Le Guin (Ursula; 1929– , US)
L'Engle (Madeleine; 1918–2007, US)
Lennox (Charlotte; c.1729–1804, American/British)
Lesage (Alain René; 1668–1747, French)
Lethem (Jonathan; 1964– , US)
Lewald (Fanny; 1811–89, German)
Lively (Penelope; 1933– , English)
London (Jack; 1876–1916, US)
Lytton (Edward Bulwer-Lytton, Lord; 1803–73, English)
Machen (Arthur; 1863–1947, British)
Mahfuz (Naguib; 1911–2006, Egyptian)
Mailer (Norman; 1923–2007, US)
Mallea (Eduardo; 1903–82, Argentine)
Malouf (David; 1934– , Australian)
Martel (Yann; 1963– , Canadian)
Massie (Allan; 1938– , Scottish)
McCabe (Patrick; 1955– , Irish)
McEwan (Ian; 1948– , English)
Miller (Henry; 1891–1980, US)
Milosz (Czeslaw; 1911–2004, Russian/US)
Mistry (Rohinton; 1952– , Indian/Canadian)
Molnár (Ferenc; 1878–1952, Hungarian)
Moodie (Susanna; 1803–85, English)
Morgan (Charles Langbridge; 1894–1958, English)
Morgan (Lady Sydney; 1783–1859, Irish)
Moricz (Zsigmond; 1879–1942, Hungarian)
Mörike (Eduard; 1804–75, German)
Morley (Christopher; 1890–1957, US)
Nesbit (E; 1858–1924, English)
Niland (D'Arcy; 1919–67, Australian)
Norris (Frank; 1870–1902, US)
Norton (Mary; 1903–92, English)
O'Brian (Patrick; 1914–2000, English)
O'Brien (Edna; 1932– , Irish)
O'Brien (Flann; 1911–66, Irish)
O'Brien (Kate; 1897–1974, Irish)
O'Duffy (Eimar; 1893–1935, Irish)
Onetti (Juan Carlos; 1909–94, Uruguayan)
Orwell (George; 1903–50, English)
Palmer (Vance; 1885–1959, Australian)
Pavese (Cesare; 1908–50, Italian)

Penney (Stef; 1969– , Scottish)
Pereda (José Maria de; 1833–1906, Spanish)
Peters (Ellis; 1913–95, English)
Piercy (Marge; 1936– , US)
Pierre (D B C; 1961– , Australian)
Porter (Eleanor; 1868–1920, US)
Porter (Katherine Anne; 1890–1980, US)
Powell (Anthony; 1905–2000, English)
Proulx (Annie; 1935– , US)
Proust (Marcel; 1871–1922, French)
Rankin (Ian; 1960– , Scottish)
Riding (Laura; 1901–91, US)
Rubens (Bernice; 1928–2004, Welsh)
Sábato (Ernesto; 1911– , Argentine)
Salten (Felix; 1869–1945, Austrian)
Sapper (1888–1937, English)
Sartre (Jean-Paul; 1905–80, French)
Sayers (Dorothy L; 1893–1957, English)
Sayles (John; 1950– , US)
Schlaf (Johannes; 1862–1941, German)
Sebold (Alice; 1963– , US)
Sewell (Anna; 1820–78, English)
Sharpe (Tom; 1928– , English)
Singer (Isaac Bashevis; 1904–91, Polish/US)
Spring (Howard; 1889–1965, Welsh)
Steele (Danielle; 1947– , US)
Sterne (Laurence; 1713–68, Irish)
Stoker (Bram; 1847–1912, Irish)
Storey (David; 1933– , English)
Strong (L A G; 1896–1958, English)
Styron (William; 1925–2006, US)
Susann (Jacqueline; c.1926–74, US)
Tagore (Rabindranath; 1861–1941, Indian)
Taylor (Elizabeth; 1912–75, English)
Taylor (Peter; 1917–94, US)
Thomas (D M; 1935– , English)
Thomas (Leslie; 1931– , Welsh)
Traven (B; c.1890–1969, German)
Trevor (William; 1928– , Irish)
Turner (Ethel S; 1872–1958, English/
Australian)
Undset (Sigrid; 1882–1949, Danish/
Norwegian)
Updike (John; 1932– , US)
Valera (Don Juan; 1824–1905, Spanish)
Vesaas (Tarjei; 1897–1970, Norwegian)
Viebig (Clara; 1860–1952, German)
Walker (Alice; 1944– , US)
Warner (Alan; 1964– , Scottish)
Warner (Marina; 1946– , English)
Warner (Susan Bogert; 1819–85, US)
Warner (Sylvia Townsend; 1893–1978,
English)
Warren (Robert Penn; 1905–89, US)
Waters (Sarah; 1966– , Welsh)
Weldon (Fay; 1931– , English)
Wesley (Mary; 1912–2002, English)
Weyman (Stanley John; 1855–1928, English)

Wiggin (Kate Douglas; 1856–1953, US)
Wilder (Thornton; 1897–1975, US)
Wilson (A N; 1950– , English)
Wilson (Jacqueline; 1945– , English)
Wilson (Sir Angus; 1913–91, English)
Wister (Owen; 1860–1938, US)
Wright (Richard; 1908–60, US)

07 Ackroyd (Peter; 1949– , English)
Aksakov (Sergei; 1791–1859, Russian)
Allende (Isabel; 1942– , Chilean)
Angelou (Maya; 1928– , US)
Arrabal (Fernando; 1932– , Spanish)
Ashford (Daisy; 1881–1972, English)
Bagnold (Enid; 1889–1981, English)
Baldwin (James; 1924–87, US)
Ballard (J G; 1930– , British)
Barnard (Marjorie; 1897–1987, Australian)
Barrios (Eduardo; 1884–1963, Chilean)
Barstow (Stan; 1928– , English)
Bassani (Giorgio; 1916–2000, Italian)
Beckett (Samuel; 1906–89, Irish)
Bellamy (Edward; 1850–98, US)
Bennett (Arnold; 1867–1931, English)
Bentine (Michael; 1921–96, English)
Bentley (Edmund Clerihew; 1875–1956,
English)
Bergman (Hjalmar; 1883–1931, Swedish)
Bernard (Tristan; 1866–1947, French)
Biggers (Earl Derr; 1884–1933, US)
Blicher (Steen Steensen; 1782–1848,
Danish)
Bogarde (Sir Dirk; 1921–99, English)
Bonnard (Abel; 1883–1968, French)
Bourget (Paul; 1852–1935, French)
Braddon (Mary Elizabeth; 1835–1915,
English)
Branner (H C; 1903–66, Danish)
Burgess (Anthony; 1917–93, English)
Burnett (Frances Hodgson; 1849–1924,
English/US)
Calvino (Italo; 1923–85, Italian)
Canetti (Elias; 1905–94, Bulgarian/British)
Carroll (Lewis; 1832–98, English)
Chatwin (Bruce; 1940–89, English)
Cheever (John; 1912–82, US)
Chekhov (Anton; 1860–1904, Russian)
Clavell (James; 1924–94, Australian/US)
Cleland (John; 1709–89, English)
Cocteau (Jean; 1889–1963, French)
Coetzee (J M; 1940– , South African)
Colette (1873–1954, French)
Collett (Camilla; 1813–95, Norwegian)
Collins (Wilkie; 1824–89, English)
Cookson (Dame Catherine; 1906–98,
English)
Corelli (Marie; 1855–1924, English)
Cozzens (James Gould; 1903–78, US)
Deeping (Warwick; 1877–1950, English)

Deledda (Grazia; 1875–1936, Italian)
DeLillo (Don; 1936– , US)
Deutsch (Babette; 1895–1982, US)
De Vries (Peter; 1910–93, US)
Dickens (Charles; 1812–70, English)
Diderot (Denis; 1713–84, French)
Dinesen (Isak; 1885–1962, Danish)
Dorfman (Ariel; 1942– , Argentine/
  Chilean/US)
Douglas (Norman; 1868–1952, Scottish)
Drabble (Margaret; 1939– , English)
Dreiser (Theodore; 1871–1945, US)
Duhamel (Georges; 1884–1966, French)
Dunnett (Dorothy; 1923–2001, Scottish)
Dunsany (Edward Plunkett, Lord; 1878–
  1957, Irish)
Durrell (Gerald; 1925–95, English)
Durrell (Lawrence; 1912–90, English)
Edwards (Amelia; 1831–92, English)
Elliott (Sumner Locke; 1917–91, Australian/
  US)
Ellison (Ralph Waldo; 1914–94, US)
Enquist (Per Olov; 1934– , Swedish)
Enright (Anne; 1962– , Irish)
Fadeyev (Aleksandr; 1901–56, Russian)
Farrell (James T; 1904–79, US)
Farrell (J G; 1935–79, British)
Ferrier (Susan Edmonstone; 1782–1854,
  Scottish)
Feydeau (Ernest; 1821–73, French)
Firbank (Ronald; 1886–1926, English)
Fleming (Ian; 1908–64, English)
Fontane (Theodor; 1819–98, German)
Forster (E M; 1879–1970, English)
Forster (Margaret; 1938– , English)
Forsyth (Frederick; 1938– , English)
Francis (Dick; 1920– , English)
Frankau (Gilbert; 1884–1953, English)
Frankau (Pamela; 1908–67, English)
Franzen (Jonathan; 1959– , US)
Franzos (Karl Emil; 1848–1904, Austrian)
Frazier (Charles; 1950– , US)
Freytag (Gustav; 1816–95, German)
Fuentes (Carlos; 1928– , Mexican)
Gallant (Mavis; 1922– , Canadian)
Gallico (Paul; 1897–1976, US)
Ganivet (Angel; 1865–98, Spanish)
Gardner (Erle Stanley; 1889–1970, US)
Garnett (David; 1892–1981, English)
Gaskell (Mrs Elizabeth; 1810–65, English)
Gautier (Théophile; 1811–72, French)
Gibbons (Stella; 1902–89, English)
Gilbert (William; 1804–89, English)
Gippius (Zinaida; 1869–1945, Russian)
Gissing (George; 1857–1903, English)
Glasgow (Ellen; 1874–1945, US)
Golding (Sir William; 1911–93, English)
Grafton (Sue; 1940– , US)

Grahame (Kenneth; 1859–1932, Scottish)
Griffin (Gerald; 1803–40, Irish)
Grisham (John; 1955– , US)
Haggard (Sir H Rider; 1856–1925, English)
Hammett (Dashiell; 1894–1961, US)
Hansson (Ola; 1860–1925, Swedish)
Harland (Henry; 1861–1905, US)
Hartley (L P; 1895–1972, English)
Haywood (Eliza; c.1693–1756, English)
Hazzard (Shirley; 1931– , Australian/US)
Herbert (Xavier; 1901–84, Australian)
Herriot (James; 1916–95, English)
Hervieu (Paul; 1857–1915, French)
Hewlett (Maurice; 1861–1923, English)
Heyward (DuBose; 1885–1940, US)
Hiaasen (Carl; 1953– , US)
Hichens (Robert Smythe; 1864–1950, English)
Higgins (George V; 1939–99, US)
Hippius (Zinaida; 1869–1945, Russian)
Holland (Josiah Gilbert; 1819–81, US)
Hornung (E W; 1866–1921, English)
Housman (Laurence; 1865–1959, English)
Howells (William Dean; 1837–1920, US)
Hurston (Zora Neale; c.1901–1960, US)
Jameson (Storm; 1891–1986, English)
Jenkins (Robin; 1912–2005, Scottish)
Johnson (Dorothy M; 1905–84, US)
Johnson (Eyvind; 1900–76, Swedish)
Johnson (Pamela Hansford; 1912–81,
  English)
Keating (H R F; 1926– , English)
Kennedy (A L; 1965– , Scottish)
Kennedy (William; 1928– , US)
Kerouac (Jack; 1922–69, US)
Kincaid (Jamaica; 1949– , Antiguan/US)
Kipling (Rudyard; 1865–1936, English)
Klinger (Friedrich Maximilian von; 1752–
  1831, German)
Kretzer (Max; 1854–1941, German)
Kundera (Milan; 1929– , Czech/French)
La Farge (Oliver; 1901–63, US)
Lamming (George; 1927– , Barbadian)
Lardner (Ring; 1885–1933, US)
Laxness (Halldór; 1902–98, Icelandic)
Le Carré (John; 1931– , English)
Lehmann (Rosamond; 1901–90, English)
Leonard (Elmore; 1925– , US)
Lessing (Doris; 1919– , Rhodesian/
  British)
Lindsay (Jack; 1900–90, Australian)
Lindsay (Philip; 1906–58, Australian)
Lofting (Hugh; 1886–1947, English)
MacBeth (George; 1932–92, Scottish)
MacGill (Patrick; 1890–1963, Irish)
MacLean (Alistair; 1922–87, Scottish)
Mahfouz (Naguib; 1911– , Egyptian)
Maistre (Xavier, Comte de; 1763–1852,
  French)

Malamud (Bernard; 1914–86, US)
Malraux (André; 1901–76, French)
Manning (Olivia; 1908–80, English)
Manzoni (Alessandro; 1785–1873, Italian)
Márquez (Gabriel García; 1928– ,
  Colombian)
Marquis (Don; 1878–1937, US)
Marryat (Captain Frederick; 1792–1848,
  English)
Maturin (Charles Robert; 1782–1824, Irish)
Maugham (W Somerset; 1874–1965, British)
Mauriac (François; 1885–1970, French)
Maurois (André; 1885–1967, French)
Mérimée (Prosper; 1803–70, French)
Mirbeau (Octave; 1850–1917, French)
Mishima (Yukio; 1925–70, Japanese)
Mitford (Mary Russell; 1786–1855, English)
Mitford (Nancy; 1904–73, English)
Moravia (Alberto; 1907–90, Italian)
Murdoch (Dame Iris; 1919–99, Irish)
Nabokov (Vladimir; 1899–1977, Russian/
  US)
Naipaul (Sir V S; 1932– , Trinidadian)
Narayan (R K; 1906–2001, Indian)
Nemerov (Howard; 1920–91, US)
Novalis (1772–1801, German)
O'Connor (Flannery; 1925–64, US)
Ostenso (Martha; 1900–63, Norwegian/
  Canadian)
Parsons (Tony; 1955– , English)
Peacock (Thomas Love; 1785–1866,
  English)
Prévost (Abbé; 1697–1763, French)
Pullman (Philip; 1946– , English)
Pushkin (Alexander; 1799–1837, Russian)
Pynchon (Thomas; 1937– , US)
Queneau (Raymond; 1903–76, French)
Ransome (Arthur; 1884–1967, English)
Raphael (Frederic; 1931– , US/British)
Régnier (Henri de; 1864–1936, French)
Renault (Mary; 1905–83, English/South
  African)
Rendell (Ruth, Baroness; 1932– , English)
Reymont (Wladyslaw Stanislaw; 1867–1925,
  Polish)
Richler (Mordecai; 1931–2001, Canadian)
Richter (Conrad; 1890–1968, US)
Richter (Johann Paul Friedrich; 1763–1825,
  German)
Robbins (Harold; 1916–97, US)
Roberts (Kate; 1891–1985, Welsh)
Roberts (Kenneth; 1885–1957, US)
Rolland (Romain; 1866–1944, French)
Rowling (J K; 1965– , English)
Rushdie (Salman; 1947– , Indian/British)
Saroyan (William; 1908–81, US)
Sassoon (Siegfried; 1886–1967, English)
Scudéry (Madeleine de; 1608–1701, French)

Shelley (Mary Wollstonecraft; 1797–1851,
  English)
Shields (Carol; 1935–2003, Canadian)
Shvarts (Yevgeni; 1896–1958, Russian)
Simenon (Georges; 1903–89, Belgian/
  French)
Sitwell (Sir Osbert; 1892–1969, English)
Sologub (Fyodor; 1863–1927, Russian)
Soyinka (Wole; 1934– , Nigerian)
Spender (Sir Stephen; 1909–95, English)
Stewart (J I M; 1906–94, Scottish)
Stifter (Adalbert; 1805–68, Austrian)
Surtees (Robert Smith; 1803–64, English)
Suttner (Bertha von; 1843–1914, Czech)
Tennant (Emma; 1937– , English)
Tennant (Kylie; 1912–88, Australian)
Theroux (Paul; 1941– , US)
Thubron (Colin; 1939– , English)
Thurber (James; 1894–1961, US)
Tolkien (J R R; 1892–1973, South African/
  British)
Tolstoy (Count Aleksei; 1817–75, Russian)
Tolstoy (Count Leo; 1828–1910, Russian)
Tranter (Nigel; 1909–99, Scottish)
Tremain (Rose; 1943– , English)
Tutuola (Amos; 1920–97, Nigerian)
Upfield (Arthur; 1888–1964, Australian)
Vallejo (César; 1892–1938, Peruvian)
Van Dine (S S; 1887–1939, US)
Wallace (Lew; 1827–1905, US)
Walpole (Horace; 1717–97, English)
Walpole (Sir Hugh; 1884–1941, New
  Zealand/English)
Waltari (Mika Toimi; 1908–79, Finnish)
Wescott (Glenway; 1901–87, US)
Wharton (Edith; c.1861–1937, US)
Wyndham (John; 1903–69, English)

08 Andersen (Hans Christian; 1805–75, Danish)
Apuleius (Lucius; 2 CAD, Roman)
Asturias (Miguel Angel; 1899–1974,
  Guatemalan)
Atherton (Gertrude; 1857–1948, US)
Auerbach (Berthold; 1812–82, German)
Banville (John; 1945– , Irish)
Barbusse (Henri; 1873–1935, French)
Beauvoir (Simone de; 1908–86, French)
Beckford (William; 1759–1844, English)
Beerbohm (Sir Max; 1872–1956, English)
Berryman (John; 1914–72, US)
Björnson (Björnstjerne; 1832–1910,
  Norwegian)
Bradbury (Ray; 1920– , US)
Bradbury (Sir Malcolm; 1932–2000, English)
Bradford (Barbara Taylor; 1933– , English)
Brentano (Clemens von; 1778–1842,
  German)
Brittain (Vera; 1893–1970, English)
Brookner (Anita; 1928– , English)

Buchanan (Robert Williams; 1841–1901, English)
Bukowski (Charles; 1920–94, US)
Bulgakov (Mikhail; 1891–1940, Russian)
Caldwell (Erskine; 1903–87, US)
Calisher (Hortense; 1911– , US)
Carleton (William; 1794–1869, Irish)
Cartland (Dame Barbara; 1901–2000, English)
Chandler (Raymond; 1888–1959, US)
Christie (Dame Agatha; 1890–1976, English)
Claretie (Jules; 1840–1913, French)
Cornwell (Bernard; 1944– , English)
Cornwell (Patricia; 1956– , US)
Couperus (Louis; 1863–1923, Dutch)
Crawford (F Marion; 1854–1909, Italian/US)
Crichton (Michael; 1942–2008, US)
Crockett (Samuel Rutherford; 1860–1914, Scottish)
Crompton (Richmal; 1890–1969, English)
Davidson (John; 1857–1909, Scottish)
Day-Lewis (Cecil; 1904–72, Irish)
Deighton (Len; 1929– , English)
de la Mare (Sir Walter; 1873–1956, English)
Disraeli (Benjamin, Earl of Beaconsfield; 1804–81, English)
Doctorow (E L; 1931– , US)
Donleavy (J P; 1926– , Irish)
Emecheta (Buchi; 1944– , Nigerian/British)
Erenburg (Ilya; 1891–1967, Soviet)
Faulkner (William; 1897–1962, US)
Fielding (Helen; 1958– , English)
Fielding (Henry; 1707–54, English)
Flaubert (Gustave; 1821–80, French)
Forester (C S; 1899–1966, British)
Francome (John; 1952– , English)
Franklin (Miles; 1879–1954, Australian)
Frederic (Harold; 1856–98, US)
Freeling (Nicolas; 1927–2003, English)
Frenssen (Gustav; 1863–1945, German)
Gallegos (Rómulo; 1884–1969, Venezuelan)
Garfield (Leon; 1921–96, English)
Gerhardi (William; 1895–1977, English)
Gilliatt (Penelope; 1932–93, English)
Goncourt (Edmond de; 1822–96, French)
Goncourt (Jules de; 1830–70, French)
Gordimer (Nadine; 1923– , South African)
Gourmont (Rémy de; 1858–1915, French)
Gréville (Henry; 1842–1902, French)
Hahn-Hahn (Ida Gräfin; 1805–80, German)
Hamilton (Patrick; 1904–62, English)
Hochhuth (Rolf; 1931– , German)
Holcroft (Thomas; 1745–1809, English)
Huysmans (J K; 1848–1907, French)
Inchbald (Elizabeth; 1753–1821, English)
Ingemann (Bernhard Severin; 1789–1862, Danish)
Ishiguro (Kazuo; 1954– , Japanese/British)

Jacobsen (Jens Peter; 1847–85, Danish)
Jewsbury (Geraldine; 1812–80, English)
Jhabvala (Ruth Prawer; 1927– , German/British)
Karamzin (Nikolai; 1766–1826, Russian)
Kavanagh (Patrick; 1905–67, Irish)
Kawabata (Yasunari; 1899–1972, Japanese)
Keneally (Thomas; 1935– , Australian)
Kennaway (James; 1928–68, Scottish)
Kielland (Alexander L; 1849–1906, Norwegian)
Kingsley (Charles; 1819–75, English)
Kingsley (Henry; 1830–76, English)
Kingsley (Mary St Leger; 1852–1931, English)
Koestler (Arthur; 1905–83, Hungarian/British)
Kosinski (Jerzy; 1933–91, Polish/US)
Kureishi (Hanif; 1954– , English)
Lagerlöf (Selma; 1858–1940, Swedish)
Laurence (Margaret; 1926–87, Canadian)
Lawrence (D H; 1885–1930, English)
Leverson (Ada; 1865–1936, English)
Lindgren (Astrid; 1907–2002, Swedish)
Lockhart (John Gibson; 1794–1854, Scottish)
Macaulay (Dame Rose; 1881–1958, English)
Magorian (Michelle; 1948– , English)
Marquand (John P; 1893–1960, US)
McCarthy (Cormac, 1933– , US)
McCarthy (Mary; 1912–89, US)
McGahern (John; 1934–2006, Irish)
McMurtry (Larry; 1936– , US)
McNickle (D'Arcy; 1904–77, US)
Melville (Herman; 1819–91, US)
Meredith (George; 1828–1909, English)
Michener (James A; 1907–97, US)
Milligan (Spike; 1918–2002, Irish)
Mitchell (Margaret; 1900–49, US)
Mitchell (W O; 1914–98, Canadian)
Montague (Charles E; 1867–1928, English)
Moorcock (Michael; 1939– , English)
Morrison (Arthur; 1863–1945, English)
Morrison (Toni; 1931– , US)
Mortimer (Penelope; 1918–99, English)
Mortimer (Sir John; 1923– , English)
Murakami (Haruki; 1949– , Japanese)
Murasaki (Shikibu; c.970–c.1015, Japanese)
Naughton (Bill; 1910–92, English)
Nedreaas (Torborg; 1906–87, Norwegian)
Ó Cadhain (Máirtín; 1906–70, Irish)
Oliphant (Margaret; 1828–97, Scottish)
Ondaatje (Michael; 1943– , Ceylonese/Canadian)
Paretsky (Sara; 1947– , US)
Pasolini (Pier Paolo; 1922–75, Italian)
Petersen (Nis; 1897–1943, Danish)

Phillips (David Graham; 1867–1911, US)
Radiguet (Raymond; 1903–23, French)
Rawlings (Marjorie; 1896–1953, US)
Remarque (Erich Maria; 1898–1970,
   German/US)
Richards (Alun; 1929–2004, Welsh)
Richepin (Jean; 1849–1926, French)
Robinson (Marilynne; 1943– , US)
Robinson (Mary; 1758–1800, English)
Rosegger (Peter; 1843–1918, Austrian)
Rousseau (Jean Jacques; 1712–78, French)
Sabatini (Rafael; 1875–1950, Italian/British)
Salinger (J D; 1919– , US)
Sargeson (Frank; 1903–82, New Zealand)
Schaefer (Jack; 1907–91, US)
Scheffel (Joseph Victor von; 1826–86,
   German)
Sciascia (Leonardo; 1921–89, Sicilian)
Sedgwick (Catharine Maria; 1789–1867, US)
Sherriff (R C; 1896–1975, English)
Sillitoe (Alan; 1928– , English)
Sinclair (May; 1863–1946, English)
Sinclair (Upton; 1878–1968, US)
Smollett (Tobias; 1721–71, Scottish)
Spillane (Mickey; 1918–2006, US)
Stafford (Jean; 1915–79, US)
Stendhal (1783–1842, French)
Tanizaki (Junichiro; 1886–1965, Japanese)
Thirkell (Angela; 1891–1961, English)
Topelius (Zacharias; 1818–98, Finnish)
Townsend (Sue; 1945– , English)
Tressell (Robert; 1870–1911, Irish)
Trollope (Anthony; 1815–82, English)
Trollope (Frances; 1780–1863, English)
Trollope (Joanna; 1943– , English)
Turgenev (Ivan; 1818–83, Russian)
Unsworth (Barry; 1930– , English)
Urquhart (Fred; 1912–95, Scottish)
Voltaire (1694–1778, French)
Vonnegut (Kurt; 1922–2007, US)
Williams (Raymond; 1921–88, Welsh)
Williams (William Carlos; 1883–1963, US)
Zeromski (Stefan; 1864–1925, Polish)

09 Ainsworth (William Harrison; 1805–82,
   English)
Aldington (Richard; 1892–1962, English)
Allingham (Margery; 1904–66, English)
Andersson (Dan; 1888–1920, Swedish)
Bacchelli (Riccardo; 1891–1985, Italian)
Barthelme (Donald; 1931–89, US)
Benedetti (Mario; 1920– , Uruguayan)
Bergelson (David; 1884–1952, Russian)
Blackmore (Richard Doddridge; 1825–1900,
   English)
Blackwood (Algernon; 1869–1951, English)
Bromfield (Louis; 1896–1956, US)
Burroughs (Edgar Rice; 1875–1950, US)
Burroughs (William S; 1914–97, US)

Caballero (Fernán; 1797–1877, Swiss/
   Spanish)
Callaghan (Morley Edward; 1903–90,
   Canadian)
Cambridge (Ada; 1844–1926, Australian)
Cervantes (Miguel de; 1547–1616, Spanish)
Charteris (Leslie; 1907–93, US)
Chevalier (Tracy; 1962– , US)
Churchill (Winston; 1871–1947, US)
Crébillon (Claude Prosper Jolyot de;
   1707–77, French)
Crnjanski (Milos; 1893–1977, Serbian)
d'Annunzio (Gabriele; 1863–1938, Italian)
Delafield (E M; 1890–1943, English)
de la Roche (Mazo; 1885–1961, Canadian)
De Quincey (Thomas; 1785–1859, English)
Dos Passos (John; 1896–1970, US)
du Maurier (Dame Daphne; 1907–89,
   English)
du Maurier (George; 1834–96, French/
   British)
Edgeworth (Maria; 1767–1849, Irish)
Ehrenburg (Ilya; 1891–1967, Soviet)
Findlater (Jane; 1866–1946, Scottish)
Findlater (Mary; 1865–1963, Scottish)
Fromentin (Eugène; 1820–76, French)
Futabatei (Shimei; 1864–1909, Japanese)
Gerhardie (William; 1895–1977, English)
Goldsmith (Oliver; 1730–74, Irish)
Goncharov (Ivan; 1812–91, Russian)
Goytisolo (Juan; 1931– , Spanish)
Greenwood (Walter; 1903–74, English)
Grossmith (George; 1847–1912, English)
Grossmith (Weedon; 1854–1919, English)
Guareschi (Giovanni; 1908–68, Italian)
Güiraldes (Ricardo; 1886–1927, Argentine)
Gütersloh (Albert Paris; 1887–1973,
   Austrian)
Hauptmann (Gerhart; 1862–1946, German)
Hawthorne (Nathaniel; 1804–64, US)
Hemingway (Ernest; 1899–1961, US)
Highsmith (Patricia; 1921–95, US)
Hölderlin (Friedrich; 1770–1843, German)
Hopkinson (Sir Tom; 1905–90, English)
Humphreys (Emyr; 1919– , Welsh)
Immermann (Karl Leberecht; 1796–1840,
   German)
Isherwood (Christopher; 1904–86, US)
Jefferies (Richard; 1848–87, English)
Johnstone (Isobel; 1781–1857, Scottish)
Jörgensen (Johannes; 1866–1956, Danish)
Kaye-Smith (Sheila; 1887–1956, English)
King-Smith (Dick; 1922– , English)
Korolenko (Vladimir; 1853–1921, Russian)
La Fayette (Madame de; 1634–93, French)
Lampedusa (Giuseppe di; 1896–1957,
   Italian)
Lermontov (Mikhail; 1814–41, Russian)

Linklater (Eric; 1899–1974, Scottish)
Llewellyn (Richard; 1907–83, Welsh)
MacDonald (George; 1824–1905, Scottish)
Mackenzie (Sir Compton; 1883–1972, English)
Maclennan (Hugh; 1907–90, Canadian)
Mankowitz (Wolf; 1924–98, English)
Mansfield (Katherine; 1888–1923, New Zealand)
Marinetti (Filippo Tommaso; 1876–1944, Italian)
Martinson (Harry; 1904–78, Swedish)
Masefield (John; 1878–1967, English)
McCullers (Carson; 1917–67, US)
Middleton (Stanley; 1919– , English)
Mitchison (Naomi; 1897–1999, Scottish)
Monsarrat (Nicholas; 1910–79, English)
Mukherjee (Bharati; 1940– , Indian/US)
Oppenheim (E Phillips; 1866–1946, English)
Palahniuk (Chuck; 1961– , US)
Pasternak (Boris; 1890–1960, Russian)
Pratchett (Sir Terry; 1948– , English)
Priestley (J B; 1894–1984, English)
Radcliffe (Ann; 1764–1823, English)
Roa Bastos (Augusto; 1917–2005, Paraguayan)
Schreiner (Olive; 1855–1920, South African)
Sholokhov (Mikhail; 1905–84, Russian)
Sillanpää (Frans Eemil; 1888–1964, Finnish)
Söderberg (Hjalmar; 1869–1941, Swedish)
Spitteler (Carl; 1845–1924, Swiss)
Steinbeck (John; 1902–68, US)
Stevenson (Robert Louis; 1850–94, Scottish)
Strcuvels (Stijn; 1871–1969, Flemish)
Sudermann (Hermann; 1857–1928, German)
Thackeray (William Makepeace; 1811–63, English)
Vittorini (Elio; 1908–66, Italian)
Wentworth (Patricia; 1878–1961, English)
Whitehead (Charles; 1804–62, English)
Willeford (Charles; 1919–88, US)
Winterson (Jeanette; 1959– , English)
Wodehouse (Sir P G; 1881–1975, English)
Yourcenar (Marguerite; 1903–87, Belgian/US/French)

10 Bainbridge (Dame Beryl; 1934– , English)
Ballantyne (Robert Michael; 1825–94, Scottish)
Boldrewood (Rolf; 1826–1915, English/Australian)
Carpentier (Alejo; 1904–80, Cuban)
Chatterjee (Bankim Chandra; 1838–94, Indian)
Cherbuliez (Joel; 1806–70, Swiss)
Cherbuliez (Victor; 1829–99, Swiss/French)
Chesterton (G K; 1874–1936, English)
Chevallier (Gabriel; 1895–1969, French)
Conscience (Hendrik; 1812–83, Flemish)

Cunningham (Michael; 1952– , US)
Dostoevsky (Fyodor; 1821–81, Russian)
Fairbairns (Zoë; 1948– , English)
Falkberget (Johann; 1879–1967, Norwegian)
Fitzgerald (F Scott; 1896–1940, US)
Fitzgerald (Penelope; 1916–2000, English)
Galsworthy (John; 1867–1933, English)
Gombrowicz (Witold; 1904–69, Polish)
Gunnarsson (Gunnar; 1889–1975, Icelandic)
Kraszewski (Józef Ignacy; 1812–87, Polish)
Lagerkvist (Pär; 1891–1974, Swedish)
Lezama Lima (José; 1910–76, Cuban)
MacLaverty (Bernard; 1942– , Irish)
Manchester (William; 1922–2004, US)
Maupassant (Guy de; 1850–93, French)
McCullough (Colleen; 1937– , Australian)
McIlvanney (William; 1936– , Scottish)
Millhauser (Steven; 1943– , US)
Montemayor (Jorge de; c.1515–61, Portuguese)
Montgomery (L M; 1874–1942, Canadian)
Phillpotts (Eden; 1862–1960, English)
Pirandello (Luigi; 1867–1936, Italian)
Richardson (Dorothy M; 1873–1957, English)
Richardson (H H; 1870–1946, Australian)
Richardson (Samuel; 1689–1761, English)
Schnitzler (Arthur; 1862–1931, Austrian)
Somerville (Edith; 1858–1949, Irish)
Strindberg (August; 1849–1912, Swedish)
Tarkington (Booth; 1869–1946, US)
Thoroddsen (Jón; 1818–68, Icelandic)
van der Post (Sir Laurens; 1906–96, South African)
Wassermann (Jakob; 1873–1934, German)
Waterhouse (Keith; 1929– , English)
Williamson (Henry; 1895–1977, English)

11 Anzengruber (Ludwig; 1839–89, Austrian)
Auchincloss (Louis; 1917– , US)
Blessington (Marguerite Gardiner, Countess of; 1789–1849, Irish)
Bontempelli (Massimo; 1878–1960, Italian)
de Bernières (Louis; 1954– , English)
Dostoyevsky (Fyodor; 1821–81, Russian)
Eichendorff (Joseph, Freiherr von; 1788–1857, German)
Goldschmidt (Meïr; 1819–87, Danish)
Kazantzakis (Nikos; 1883–1957, Greek)
Matthiessen (Peter; 1927– , US)
Montherlant (Henri Millon de; 1896–1972, French)
Pérez Galdós (Benito; 1843–1920, Spanish)
Pontoppidan (Henrik; 1857–1944, Danish)
Sienkiewicz (Henryk; 1846–1916, Polish)
Valle-Inclán (Ramón del; 1869–1936, Spanish)
Vargas Llosa (Mario; 1936– , Peruvian)

Wildenbruch (Ernst von; 1845–1909, German)

12 Andrzejewski (Jerzy; 1909–83, Polish)
Ashton-Warner (Sylvia; 1908–84, New Zealand)
Eça de Queiros (José Maria de; 1845–1900, Portuguese)
Kovalevskaya (Sofya; 1850–91, Russian)
Martin du Gard (Roger; 1881–1958, French)
Martín-Santos (Luis; 1924–64, Spanish)
Merezhkovsky (Dmitri; 1865–1941, Russian)
Pérez de Ayala (Ramón; 1881–1962, Spanish)
Quiller-Couch (Sir Arthur; 1863–1944, English)
Robbe-Grillet (Alain; 1922–2008, French)
Saint-Exupéry (Antoine de; 1900–44, French)
Solzhenitsyn (Aleksandr; 1918–2008, Russian)

13 Aguilera Malta (Demetrio; 1909–81, Ecuadorean)

Alain-Fournier (Henri; 1886–1914, French)
Beresford-Howe (Constance; 1922– , Canadian)
Castelo Branco (Camilo; 1825–90, Portuguese)
Guimarães Rosa (João; 1908–69, Brazilian)
Przybyszewski (Stanislaw; 1868–1927, Polish)
Sackville-West (Vita; 1892–1962, English)
Whyte-Melville (George; 1821–78, Scottish)

14 Cabrera Infante (Guillermo; 1929–2005, Cuban)
Compton-Burnett (Dame Ivy; 1884–1969, English)
Grimmelshausen (Hans Jacob Christoffel von; c.1622–1676, German)
Machado de Assis (Joaquim Maria; 1839–1908, Brazilian)

15 Hansford Johnson (Pamela; 1912–81, English)
Sergeyev-Tsensky (Sergei; 1875–1958, Russian)

See also **biography**; **essay**; **fable**; **history**; **literature**; **play**; **poetry**; **science fiction**

number

Numbers include:

03 nil	**06** eighty	fourteen
one	eleven	nineteen
six	googol	thirteen
ten	nought	thousand
two	ninety	trillion
04 five	thirty	**09** decillion
four	twelve	nonillion
half	twenty	octillion
nine		seventeen
zero	**07** billion	
	chiliad	**10** centillion
05 eight	fifteen	googolplex
fifty	hundred	one hundred
forty	million	septillion
seven	seventy	sextillion
sixty	sixteen	
three		**11** quadrillion
	08 eighteen	quintillion

French numbers include:

02 un (1)	sept (7)	treize (13)
03 dix (10)	zéro (0)	trente (30)
six (6)	**05** douze (12)	**07** dix-huit (18)
04 cent (100)	mille (1,000)	dix-neuf (19)
cinq (5)	seize (16)	dix-sept (17)
deux (2)	trois (3)	million (1,000,000)
huit (8)	vingt (20)	**08** milliard (1,000,000,000)
neuf (9)	**06** quatre (4)	quarante (40)
onze (11)	quinze (15)	quatorze (14)

soixante (60)
09 cinquante (50)
deux mille (2,000)

un million (1,000,000)
10 un milliard (1,000,000,000)
11 soixante-dix (70)

12 quatre-vingts (80)

German numbers include:

03 elf (11)
04 acht (8)
drei (3)
eins (1)
fünf (5)
neun (9)
null (0)
vier (4)
zehn (10)
zwei (2)
05 sechs (6)
zwölf (12)

06 sieben (7)
07 achtzig (80)
Billion
fünfzig (50)
hundert (100)
Million (1,000,000)
neunzig (90)
sechzig (60)
siebzig (70)
tausend (1,000)
vierzig (40)
zwanzig (20)

08 achtzehn (18)
dreissig (30)
dreizehn (13)
fünfzehn (15)
neunzehn (19)
sechzehn (16)
siebzehn (17)
vierzehn (14)
09 Milliarde (1,000,000,000)
10 einhundert (100)
eintausend (1,000)

Italian numbers include:

03 due (2)
sei (6)
tre (3)
uno (1)
04 nove (9)
otto (8)
zero (0)
05 cento (100)
dieci (10)
sette (7)

venti (20)
06 cinque (5)
dodici (12)
sedici (16)
trenta (30)
undici (11)
07 novanta (90)
ottanta (80)
quattro (4)
tredici (13)

08 diciotto (18)
quaranta (40)
quindici (15)
sessanta (60)
settanta (70)
09 cinquanta (50)
10 diciannove (19)
11 diciassette (17)
quattordici (14)

Latin numbers include:

03 duo (2)
nil (0)
sex (6)
04 octo (8)
tres (3)
unus (1)
05 decem (10)
mille (1,000)
novem (9)
06 centum (100)

septem (7)
07 quinque (5)
sedecim (16)
undecim (11)
viginti (20)
08 duodecim (12)
quattuor (4)
tredecim (13)
trigenta (30)
09 nonaginta (90)

octoginta (80)
quindecim (15)
sexaginta (60)
11 quadraginta (40)
septendecim (17)
septuaginta (70)
undeviginti (19)
12 duodeviginti (18)
quinquaginta (50)
13 quattuordecim (14)

Spanish numbers include:

03 dos (2)
mil (1,000)
uno (1)
04 cero (0)
diez (10)
doce (12)
ocho (8)
once (11)
seis (6)

tres (3)
05 cinco (5)
nueve (9)
siete (7)
trece (13)
06 ciento (100)
cuatro (4)
millón (1,000,000)
quince (15)

veinte (20)
07 catorce (14)
noventa (90)
ochenta (80)
sesenta (60)
setenta (70)
treinta (30)
08 cuarenta (40)
un millón

09 cincuenta (50)
dieciocho (18)
dieciséis (16)

10 diecinueve (19)
diecisiete (17)
quinientos (500)

11 mil millones
(1,000,000,000)

See also **numeral**

numeral

Roman numerals include:

01 C (100)
D (500)
I (1)
L (50)
M (1,000)
V (5)

X (10)
02 II (2)
IV (4)
IX (9)
VI (6)
XI (11)

XV (15)
XX (20)
03 III (3)
VII (7)
XII (12)
XIV (14)

XIX (19)
XVI (16)
04 VIII (8)
XIII (13)
XVII (17)
05 XVIII (18)

nun *see* **religious order**

nurse

Nurse types include:

03 dry
wet
04 home
maid
sick
05 nanny
night
staff
tutor

06 charge
dental
matron
school
sister
07 midwife
nursery
08 district

09 auxiliary
children's
community
Macmillan
10 consultant
Iain Rennie
Marie Curie
ward sister
11 night sister

psychiatric
12 practitioner
13 health visitor
State Enrolled
theatre sister
15 locality manager
State Registered

Nurse grades include:

06 Grade A (Auxiliary/Assistant)
Grade B (Auxiliary/Assistant)
Grade C (Enrolled/Auxiliary)
Grade D (Newly Qualified Nurse)
Grade E (Experienced Staff Nurse)
Grade F (Senior Nurse)

Grade G (Senior/Charge Nurse)
Grade H (Modern Matron)
Grade H (Nurse Specialist)
Grade I (Modern Matron)
Grade I (Nurse Specialist)

Nurses include:

04 Gamp (Mrs Sarah; *Martin Chuzzlewit*, 1844,
Charles Dickens)
Hana (*The English Patient*, 1992, Michael
Ondaatje)
Nana (*Peter Pan*, 1904, J M Barrie)
Prig (Betsey; *Martin Chuzzlewit*, 1844,
Charles Dickens)

05 Kenny (Elizabeth; 1886–1952, Australian)
Nurse (*Romeo and Juliet*, 1591–96, William
Shakespeare)
Nurse (the; *Too True to be Good*, 1932,
George Bernard Shaw)

06 Cavell (Edith; 1865–1915, English)
Glaucé (*The Faerie Queene*, 1590–96,

Sir Edmund Spenser)
Purfoy (Sarah; *For the Term of His Natural
Life*, 1874, Marcus Clarke)
Rayner (Claire; 1931– , English)
Sanger (Margaret; 1883–1966, US)
Toodle (Polly; *Dombey and Son*, 1848,
Charles Dickens)
Wright (Vera; *Cabin Fever*, 1990, Elizabeth
Jolley)

07 McMahon (Phyllis Jean/Fay; *Loot*, 1966, Joe
Orton)
Rachael (Mrs; *Bleak House*, 1853, Charles
Dickens)
Ratched (Nurse Mildred; *One Flew Over the*

    Cuckoo's Nest, 1962, Ken Kesey)
    Seacole (Mary; 1805–81, Jamaican)
08 Espinosa (Carla; *Scrubs*, TV sitcom,
    2001–)
    Fairhead (Charlie; *Casualty*, TV series,
    1986–)
    Houlihan (Margaret 'Hot Lips'; *MASH*,
    1968, Richard Hooker)
    Pattison (Dorothy; 1832–78, English)
    Saunders (Cicely; 1918–2005, English)

Saunders (Daisy; *The Gate of Angels*, 1990,
    Penelope Fitzgerald)
10 Cunningham (Nurse; *The Ante-Room*, 1934,
    Kate O'Brien)
    Flintwinch (Affery; *Little Dorrit*, 1857,
    Charles Dickens)
    Ftatateeta (*Caesar and Cleopatra*, 1898,
    George Bernard Shaw)
    Stephenson (Elsie; 1916–67, English)
11 Nightingale (Florence; 1820–1910, English)

nut

Nuts include:

04 pine	brazil	walnut	hazelnut
05 beech	cashew	**07** coconut	**09** groundnut
pecan	cobnut	filbert	macadamia
	monkey		
06 almond	peanut	**08** chestnut	pistachio

nutrition

Terms to do with nutrition include:

02 GI	glucose	**10** blood sugar
03 BMI	mineral	calciferol
fat	organic	catabolism
HDL	portion	deficiency
LDL	protein	low-calorie
RDA	retinol	metabolism
RDI	serving	nut allergy
TPN	vitamin	overweight
04 diet	**08** additive	provitamin
iron	anorexic	riboflavin
SACN	appetite	supplement
salt	carotene	tocopherol
05 fibre	coenzyme	trophology
lipid	diabetic	vegetarian
obese	eutrophy	weight gain
sugar	holozoic	weight loss
vegan	lycopene	**11** antioxidant
06 biotin	nutrient	axerophthol
citrin	roughage	bone density
energy	thiamine	cholesterol
enzyme	trophesy	dehydration
folate	**09** amino acid	electrolyte
gluten	anabolism	food allergy
iodine	anorectic	growth chart
low-fat	dietician	innutrition
niacin	diet sheet	kilocalorie
sodium	digestion	macrobiotic
07 allergy	dystrophy	mixotrophic
anaemic	fatty acid	trigger food
bulimic	folic acid	underweight
calorie	food group	**12** ascorbic acid
coeliac	kilojoule	balanced diet
	probiotic	bioflavonoid

carbohydrate
food aversion
lean body mass
malnutrition
multi-vitamin
nicotinamide
nutritionist
phytonadione
saturated fat

See also **diet**; **food**

13 body mass index
macronutrient
malabsorption
micronutrient
nicotinic acid
phylloquinone

14 bad cholesterol
eating disorder
glycaemic index

HDL cholesterol
LDL cholesterol
monounsaturate
polyunsaturate
trophoneurosis

15 cholecalciferol
good cholesterol
malassimilation
obsessive eating

O

observatory

occult

See also **witch**

occupation

hack
maid
monk
page
poet

05 abbot
actor
agent
baker
boxer
buyer
caddy
clerk
coach
diver
envoy
friar
guide
judge
juror
mason
mayor
medic
miner
model
nanny
nurse
pilot
slave
smith
tawer
tutor
usher
valet
vicar

06 abbess
artist
au pair
author
banker
barber
barman
bishop
bookie
bowyer
brewer
broker
butler
cabbie
cleric
cooper
copper
coster
cowboy
critic
curate
dancer
dealer

doctor
draper
driver
editor
eggler
factor
farmer
fitter
forger
gaffer
glazer
grocer
herald
hermit
hosier
hunter
jailer
jester
jockey
joiner
lawyer
mercer
miller
nannie
oilman
ostler
packer
parson
pastor
pig-man
pirate
player
porter
potter
priest
ragman
ranger
roofer
sailor
salter
server
singer
skater
skivvy
sniper
sparks
spicer
tailor
tanner
teller
tinner
trader
tycoon
typist
vendor
verger
waiter
warden

warder
weaver
welder
whaler
writer

07 acrobat
actress
actuary
admiral
adviser
almoner
analyst
artisan
artiste
athlete
attaché
auditor
aviator
bailiff
barista
barmaid
bellboy
bellhop
bottle-o
breeder
builder
butcher
cashier
chemist
cleaner
climber
coalman
cobbler
collier
coroner
courier
cowherd
crofter
curator
cyclist
dentist
doorman
dresser
drummer
equerry
farrier
fiddler
fighter
fireman
florist
footman
foreman
frogman
general
glazier
gymnast
hangman
haulier

hostess
janitor
junkman
lace-man
lineman
lorimer
luthier
magnate
manager
marshal
midwife
milkman
oculist
officer
orderly
painter
partner
pianist
planner
plumber
poacher
popstar
postman
prefect
printer
rancher
referee
saddler
scholar
senator
servant
shearer
sheriff
showman
soldier
spinner
stapler
steward
student
surgeon
teacher
trainee
trainer
trapper
vintner
warrior
woolman
workman

08 advocate
animator
armourer
attorney
banksman
botanist
bottle-oh
brakeman
callgirl
cardinal

chairman
chandler
chaplain
comedian
compiler
composer
conjurer
conjuror
corporal
costumer
coxswain
croupier
dairyman
deckhand
diplomat
director
druggist
educator
embalmer
engineer
engraver
essayist
executor
factotum
farmhand
ferryman
film star
fishwife
forester
gangster
gardener
goatherd
governor
gunsmith
handyman
henchman
herdsman
hireling
home help
hotelier
huntsman
inventor
jeweller
labourer
landlady
landlord
lecturer
linguist
lyricist
magician
maltster
mapmaker
masseuse
mechanic
merchant
milkmaid
milliner
minister

minstrel
muleteer
musician
novelist
operator
optician
organist
pardoner
perfumer
pig-woman
polisher
preacher
producer
promoter
publican
quarrier
recorder
reporter
retailer
reviewer
salesman
satirist
scrap-man
sculptor
seedsman
sergeant
shepherd
showgirl
smuggler
sorcerer
spaceman
spurrier
stockman
stripper
stuntman
supplier
surveyor
thatcher
upholder
waitress
watchman
wet nurse
wig-maker
woodsman
wrangler

09 alchemist
anatomist
announcer
antiquary
architect
archivist
art critic
art dealer
assistant
associate
astronaut
attendant
barperson

barrister
biologist
bodyguard
bookmaker
buccaneer
bus driver
cab driver
caretaker
carpenter
charwoman
chauffeur
clergyman
coal miner
collector
columnist
commander
concierge
conductor
constable
cosmonaut
costumier
couturier
cricketer
decorator
detective
dietician
dramatist
ecologist
economist
executive
financier
fisherman
fruiterer
gas fitter
geologist
goldsmith
governess
guitarist
gutter-man
harvester
herbalist
historian
homeopath
horologer
housemaid
hypnotist
innkeeper
inspector
ironsmith
jacksmith
landowner
launderer
laundress
librarian
lifeguard
locksmith
machinist
messenger

musketeer
navigator
newsagent
nursemaid
osteopath
outfitter
paralegal
paramedic
performer
physician
physicist
plasterer
ploughman
policeman
pop singer
poulterer
professor
publicist
publisher
puppeteer
registrar
robe maker
sailmaker
secretary
shoemaker
signaller
signalman
songsmith
spokesman
stagehand
stationer
staymaker
stevedore
subeditor
swineherd
therapist
towncrier
tradesman
traveller
trumpeter
usherette
van driver
violinist
volunteer
whittawer
yachtsman
zookeeper
zoologist

10 accountant
advertiser
air hostess
air steward
amanuensis
apothecary
apprentice
archbishop
astrologer
astronomer

auctioneer
baby sitter
bank teller
beautician
bellringer
bill-broker
biochemist
biographer
blacksmith
bookbinder
bookkeeper
bookseller
bricklayer
bureaucrat
campaigner
cartoonist
cartwright
chairmaker
clockmaker
coastguard
compositor
consultant
controller
copywriter
corn-dealer
corn-factor
councillor
counsellor
disc jockey
dishwasher
dramaturge
dressmaker
dry cleaner
equestrian
fellmonger
fishmonger
footballer
forecaster
frame-maker
fundraiser
gamekeeper
game warden
gatekeeper
geneticist
geochemist
geographer
glassmaker
handmaiden
headhunter
headmaster
highwayman
horologist
instructor
ironmonger
journalist
junk-dealer
keyboarder
legislator

librettist
lumberjack
magistrate
manageress
manicurist
manservant
midshipman
millwright
missionary
naturalist
negotiator
newscaster
newsmonger
nurseryman
obituarist
pallbearer
park ranger
pawnbroker
peltmonger
perruquier
pharmacist
piano tuner
playwright
podiatrist
politician
postmaster
private eye
programmer
proprietor
prospector
railwayman
removal man
researcher
ringmaster
roadmender
sales clerk
saleswoman
sempstress
shipbroker
shipwright
shopfitter
shopkeeper
signwriter
songstress
stewardess
stock agent
stockinger
stonemason
supervisor
taxi driver
technician
translator
typesetter
undertaker
unguentary
wainwright
wharfinger
whitesmith

wholesaler
woodcarver
woodcutter

11 accompanist
antiquarian
art director
astrologist
audio typist
bank manager
bingo caller
broadcaster
bullfighter
burn-the-wind
businessman
candlemaker
car salesman
chambermaid
cheerleader
chiropodist
clergywoman
commentator
coppersmith
delivery man
distributor
draughtsman
electrician
entertainer
estate agent
etymologist
executioner
firefighter
foot soldier
fund manager
glass blower
grave digger
greengrocer
haberdasher
hairdresser
hair stylist
head teacher
horse-dealer
illustrator
interpreter
interviewer
lifeboatman
linen-draper
lollipop man
lorry driver
metalworker
money broker
mountaineer
music-seller
neurologist
optometrist
panel beater
parlourmaid
pathologist
philatelist

philologist
philosopher
policewoman
proofreader
radiologist
relic-monger
secret agent
set designer
sharebroker
ship builder
silversmith
sociologist
steelworker
stockbroker
taxidermist
telephonist
ticket agent
tobacconist
travel agent
tree surgeon
truck driver
upholsterer
wagonwright
wax-chandler
web designer
wheelwright
wool-stapler
youth worker

12 anaesthetist
broker-dealer
cabinet maker
calligrapher
cartographer
cheesemonger
chimney sweep
chiropractor
churchwarden
civil servant
coal merchant
corn-merchant
costermonger
demonstrator
dramaturgist
entomologist
entrepreneur
event manager
fent-merchant
film director
garret-master
hotel manager
immunologist
IT consultant
longshoreman
maitre d'hotel
make-up artist
media planner
metallurgist
mineralogist

nutritionist
obstetrician
orthodontist
photographer
physiologist
ploughwright
postal worker
practitioner
PR consultant
press officer
prison warder
psychologist
radiographer
receptionist
sales manager
schoolmaster
screenwriter
scriptwriter
ship chandler
slink butcher
social worker
spokesperson
stage manager
statistician
stenographer
toxicologist
urban planner
veterinarian
wine merchant
wood engraver

13 administrator
antique dealer
archaeologist
charity worker
choreographer
civil engineer

See also **maker**

crane operator
criminologist
dental surgeon
food scientist
groundskeeper
gynaecologist
harbour master
health visitor
home economist
Industrialist
lexicographer
lollipop woman
mathematician
meteorologist
nightwatchman
oceanographer
old-clothesman
police officer
prison officer
rag-and-bone-man
rent collector
retail manager
scrap merchant
security guard
ship's chandler
shop assistant
sound engineer
streetcleaner
streetsweeper
traffic warden
window cleaner
woollen-draper

14 anthropologist
camera operator
claims assessor
draughtsperson

gutter-merchant
market gardener
marriage-broker
merchant tailor
microbiologist
military member
music therapist
naval architect
pharmacologist
pharmacopolist
store detective
superintendent
systems analyst
tallow chandler

15 biotechnologist
business analyst
commission agent
computer analyst
conservationist
costume designer
dental hygienist
fashion designer
flight attendant
funeral director
graphic designer
marine biologist
military officer
ophthalmologist
personal trainer
physiotherapist
police constable
refuse collector
speech therapist
stock controller
ticket collector

ocean

Oceans include:

06 Arctic
Indian
07 Pacific

08 Atlantic
Southern
12 North Pacific

South Pacific
13 North Atlantic
South Atlantic

Ocean trenches include:

03 Yap (Pacific)
04 Java (Indian)
05 Japan (Pacific)
Kuril (Pacific)
Palau (Pacific)
Tonga (Pacific)
06 Cayman (Atlantic)
Ryukyu (Pacific)

07 Atacama (Pacific)
Mariana (Pacific)
08 Aleutian (Pacific)
Izu Bonin (Pacific)
Kermadec (Pacific)
Marianas (Pacific)
Mindanao (Pacific)
Romanche (Atlantic)

09 Peru-Chile (Pacific)
10 Philippine (Pacific)
Puerto Rico
(Atlantic)
11 Nansei Shoto
(Pacific)
12 Bougainville
(Pacific)

West Caroline
(Pacific)
13 Middle America
(Pacific)
South Sandwich
(Southern)

See also **sea**

Oceania *see* **Australasia**

office

Offices include:

02 CO
FO
PO
TO
WO

03 box
COI
CRO
DLO
EPO
FCO
GAO
GPO
IIP
IRO
Met
NAO
OFT
OME
ONS
OPW
ORR
OSS
OST
pay
PRO
RLO
SFO
War

04 back

BFPO
fire
HMSO
Holy
Home
land
loan
Pipe
Post

05 Assay
Crown
front
Ofcom
Offer
Ofgas
Ofgem
Oflot
Oftel
Ofwat
paper
press
stamp

06 Ofsted
Patent
Pat Off
police
Record
ticket

07 booking
Foreign

sorting

08 Chancery
Colonial
Eurostat
incident
printing
register
registry
Scottish

09 personnel
receiving
telegraph

10 dead-letter
employment
Quai d'Orsay
registered
Stationery

11 general post
left-luggage
victualling

12 Commonwealth
Serious Fraud

13 Inland Revenue
National Audit

14 European Patent
Meteorological
returned letter

15 Criminal Records

Office furniture includes:

04 desk
safe

07 lectern

08 desk lamp
fire safe

09 partition
plan chest
stepstool
work table

11 storage unit
swivel chair
workstation

12 computer desk
drawing-board
fire cupboard
printer stand
typist's chair

13 executive desk

filing cabinet
filing trolley

14 boardroom table
display cabinet
executive chair
filing cupboard
reception chair

15 conference table
secretarial desk

Office equipment includes:

03 fax
OHP
VDU

05 mouse

06 inkpad

screen
tacker

07 cash box
monitor
planner

printer
scanner
stapler
trimmer

08 computer

intercom
keyboard
mouse mat
plan file
shredder

09 date-stamp
dust cover
laminator
telephone
textphone
time clock
wages book

10 calculator
comb binder
copy holder
Dictaphone®
duplicator
fax machine
guillotine

letter tray
monitor arm
paper punch
printwheel
ring binder
typewriter

11 comb binding
hole puncher
noticeboard
photocopier
switchboard

12 acoustic hood
letter opener
letter scales
message board
parcel scales
screen filter
telex machine
visitors' book

wire bindings

13 data cartridge
desk organizer
lever arch file
microcassette
planning board
reference book
staple-remover
thermal binder
waste-paper bin
word processor

14 adhesive binder
diskette mailer
flip-chart easel
laptop computer
slide projector
telephone index

15 terminal trolley

See also **government; stationery**

official

Officials include:

02 JP
MP
03 MEP
05 agent
chief
clerk
elder
envoy
hakim
mayor
usher
06 consul
Euro-MP
notary
07 bailiff
captain

coroner
equerry
manager
marshal
monitor
prefect
proctor
senator
sheriff
steward
08 alderman
chairman
delegate
diplomat
director
Eurocrat

executor
governor
mandarin
mayoress
minister
overseer
09 commander
commissar
executive
Gauleiter
inspector
ombudsman
president
principal
registrar
10 ambassador

bureaucrat
chairwoman
chancellor
councillor
magistrate
proprietor
supervisor
11 chairperson
congressman
12 civil servant
commissioner
13 administrator
congresswoman
14 representative
superintendent

oil

Oils include:

03 ben
gas
nim
nut
til
04 baby
bone
cade
coal
corn
crab

derv
dika
fish
fuel
hair
palm
poon
rape
rock
rose
rusa

seed
tall
tung
wood
wool
yolk
zest
05 attar
beech
benne
carap

crude
fusel
grass
heavy
joint
macaw
niger
olive
poppy
pulza
rosin
salad
savin
shale
shark
snake
sperm
spike
stand
sweet
thyme
train
whale

06 ajowan
almond
banana
butter
canola
carron
castor
chrism
cloves
cohune
croton
diesel
garlic

illipe
jojoba
macoya
neroli
peanut
savine
Seneca
sesame

07 arachis
cajuput
camphor
coconut
gingili
jinjili
linseed
lumbang
mineral
mirbane
mustard
myrrhol
retinol
rhodium
spindle
verbena
vitriol

08 ambrosia
bergamot
camphine
cinnamon
cod-liver
creosote
gingelly
kerosene
kerosine
lavender

macahuba
macassar
North Sea
paraffin
pristane
rapeseed
rosewood

09 black gold
candlenut
grapeseed
neat's-foot
patchouli
patchouly
safflower
sassafras
spikenard
sunflower
vanaspati
vegetable

10 citronella
eucalyptus
peppermint
petit grain
turpentine
ylang-ylang

11 camphorated
chaulmoogra
wintergreen

12 benzaldehyde
brilliantine

13 bitter almonds

14 glutaraldehyde

15 evening primrose

See also **refining**

Olympic Games

Summer Olympic venues:

04 Rome (Italy; 1960)

05 Paris (France; 1900/1924)
Seoul (South Korea; 1988)
Tokyo (Japan; 1964)

06 Athens (Greece; 1896/1906/2004)
Berlin (Germany; 1936)
London (UK; 1908/1948)
Moscow (USSR; 1980)
Munich (West Germany; 1972)
Sydney (Australia; 2000)

07 Antwerp (Belgium; 1920)

Atlanta (USA; 1996)
Beijing (China; 2008)
St Louis (USA; 1904)

08 Helsinki (Finland; 1952)
Montréal (Canada; 1976)

09 Amsterdam (The Netherlands; 1928)
Barcelona (Spain; 1992)
Melbourne (Australia; 1956)
Stockholm (Sweden; 1912)

10 Los Angeles (USA; 1932/1984)
Mexico City (Mexico; 1968)

Summer Olympic events include:

03 BMX

04 beam
judo
trap

05 rings
skeet
vault

06 boxing
dinghy
discus
diving
hammer
hockey
rowing
sprint
tennis

07 archery
cycling
fencing
javelin
jumping
sailing
shot put

08 20km walk
50km walk
50m rifle
baseball
canoeing
dressage
eventing
football
handball
high jump

keelboat
long jump
marathon
shooting
softball
swimming

09 100 metres
200 metres
25m pistol
400 metres
50m pistol
800 metres
athletics
badminton
decathlon
multihull
pole vault
tae kwon do
triathlon
water polo
wrestling

10 1,500 metres
5,000 metres
basketball
double trap
equestrian
gymnastics
heptathlon
points race
team sprint
trampoline
triple jump
uneven bars
volleyball

11 10,000 metres
100m hurdles
10m air rifle
10m platform
110m hurdles
4×100m relay
4×400m relay
400m hurdles
discus throw
hammer throw
pommel horse
table tennis
team pursuit
windsurfing

12 10m air pistol
1km time trial
50m freestyle
cross-country
javelin throw
parallel bars

13 100m butterfly
100m freestyle
200m butterfly
200m freestyle
3m springboard
400m freestyle
500m time trial
50m rifle prone
800m freestyle
horizontal bar

14 100m backstroke
1,500m freestyle
200m backstroke
floor exercises

Winter Olympic venues:

04 Oslo (Norway; 1952)

05 Turin (Italy; 2006)

06 Nagano (Japan; 1998)

07 Calgary (Canada; 1988)
Cortina (Italy; 1956)
Sapporo (Japan; 1972)

08 Chamonix (France; 1924)
Grenoble (France; 1968)
Sarajevo (Yugoslavia; 1984)

St Moritz (Switzerland; 1928/1948)

09 Innsbruck (Austria; 1964/1976)

10 Lake Placid (USA; 1932/1980)

11 Albertville (France; 1992)
Lillehammer (Norway; 1994)
Squaw Valley (USA; 1960)

12 Salt Lake City (USA; 2002)

21 Garmisch-Partenkirchen (Germany; 1936)

Winter Olympic events include:

04 luge

05 pairs

06 moguls
skiing
slalom

super-G
two-man

07 aerials
curling
four-man

skating

08 biathlon
downhill
halfpipe
skeleton

09 500 metres
bobsleigh
ice hockey
snowboard

10 1,000 metres
1,500 metres
1.5km sprint
3,000 metres
3,000m relay
4×5km relay
5,000 metres
5,000m relay

ice dancing
individual
ski jumping

11 10,000 metres
4×10km relay
giant slalom

12 alpine skiing
speed skating

13 10km classical
15km classical
15km freestyle

30km classical
30km freestyle
50km classical
figure skating
relay biathlon

14 alpine combined
Nordic combined
snowboard cross

15 combined pursuit
freestyle skiing
pursuit biathlon

Olympians include:

03 Coe (Sebastian, Lord; 1956– ; English, athletics)
Hoy (Sir Chris; 1976– , Scottish, cycling)

04 Bolt (Usain; 1986– , Jamaican, athletics)
Clay (Cassius; 1942– ; US, boxing)
Dean (Christopher; 1958– ; English, figure skating)
Ewry (Ray; 1873–1937; US, athletics)
Otto (Kristin; 1966– ; German, swimming)
Papp (Laszlo; 1926–2003; Hungarian, boxing)
Todd (Mark; 1956– ; New Zealand, equestrianism)
Witt (Katarina; 1965– ; German, figure skating)

05 Blair (Bonnie; 1964– ; US, speed skating)
Bubka (Sergei; 1963– ; Soviet/Ukrainian, athletics)
Chand (Dhyan; 1905–79; Indian, hockey)
Cranz (Christl; 1914–2004; German, alpine skiing)
Curry (John; 1949–94; English, figure skating)
Henie (Sonja; 1912–69; Norwegian, figure skating)
Killy (Jean-Claude; 1943– ; French, alpine skiing)
Lewis (Carl; 1961– ; US, athletics)
Lewis (Denise; 1972– ; English, athletics)
Longo (Jeannie; 1958– ; French, cycling)
Meade (Richard; 1938– ; English, equestrianism)
Nurmi (Paavo; 1897–1973; Finnish, athletics)
Ottey (Merlene; 1960– ; Jamaican/Slovenian, athletics)
Owens (Jesse; 1913–80; US, athletics)
Popov (Aleksandr; 1971– ; Russian, swimming)
Savon (Felix; 1967– ; Cuban, boxing)
Spitz (Mark; 1950– ; US, swimming)
Tomba (Alberto; 1966– ; Italian, alpine skiing)

06 Aamodt (Kjetil; 1971– ; Norwegian, alpine skiing)
Beamon (Bob; 1946– ; US, athletics)
Bikila (Abebe; 1932–73; Ethiopian, athletics)
Biondi (Matt; 1965– ; US, swimming)
Button (Dick; 1929– ; US, figure skating)
D'Inzeo (Raimondo; 1925– ; Italian, equestrianism)
Fraser (Dawn; 1937– ; Australian, swimming)
Heiden (Eric; 1958– ; US, speed skating)
Holmes (Dame Kelly; 1970– ; English, athletics)
Korbut (Olga; 1955– ; Belarussian, gymnastics)
Oerter (Al; 1936–2007; US, athletics)
Phelps (Michael; 1985– ; US, swimming)
Ritola (Ville; 1896–1982; Finnish, athletics)
Sailer (Toni; 1936– ; Austrian, alpine skiing)
Thorpe (Ian; 1982– ; Australian, swimming)
Thorpe (Jim; c.1888–1953; US, athletics)

07 Ainslie (Ben; 1977– , English, sailing)
Boitano (Brian; 1963– ; US, figure skating)
Cousins (Robin; 1957– ; English, figure skating)
Daehlie (Bjorn; 1967– ; Norwegian, Nordic skiing)
Edwards (Jonathan; 1966– , English, triple jump)
Fischer (Birgit; 1962– ; German; canoeing)
Johnson (Michael; 1967– ; US, athletics)
Klammer (Franz; 1953– ; Austrian, alpine skiing)
Mathias (Bob; 1930–2006; US, athletics)
Nykänen (Matti; 1963– ; Finnish, ski-jumping)
Pinsent (Sir Matthew; 1970– ; English, rowing)
Rodnina (Irina; 1949– ; Soviet, pairs skating)

Scherbo (Vitaly; 1972–   ; Soviet/
Belarussian, gymnastics)
Schmidt (Birgit; 1962–   ; German,
canoeing)
Torvill (Jayne; 1957–   ; English, figure
skating)
Voronin (Mikhail; 1945–2004; Soviet,
gymnastics)
Zatopek (Emil; 1922–2000; Czech, athletics)
Zelezny (Jan; 1966–   ; Czech, athletics)

08 Christie (Linford; 1960–   , English, athletics)
Comaneci (Nadia; 1961–   ; Romanian,
gymnastics)
Cuthbert (Betty; 1938–   ; Australian,
athletics)
de Bruijn (Inge; 1973–   ; Dutch, swimming)
Dityatin (Aleksandr; 1957–   ; Russian,
gymnastics)
Elvstrøm (Paul; 1928–   ; Danish, sailing)
Gerevich (Aladár; 1910–91; Hungarian,
fencing)
Jernberg (Sixten; 1929–   ; Swedish, Nordic
skiing)
Latynina (Larissa; 1934–   ; Ukrainian,
gymnastics)
Louganis (Greg; 1960–   ; US, diving)
Ohuruogu (Christine; 1984–   , British,
400m)
Redgrave (Sir Steve; 1962–   ; English,
rowing)
Stenmark (Ingemar; 1956–   ; Swedish,
alpine skiing)
Thompson (Daley; 1958–   ; English,
athletics)
Zijlaard (Leontien; 1970–   ; Dutch, cycling)

09 Adlington (Rebecca; 1989–   , English,
swimming)
Andrianov (Nikolay; 1952–   ; Russian,
gymnastics)

Babashoff (Shirley; 1957–   ; US, swimming)
Cáslavská (Vera; 1942–   ; Czech,
gymnastics)
Egerszegi (Krisztina; 1974–   ; Hungarian,
swimming)
Gräfström (Gillis; 1893–1938; Swedish,
figure skating)
Pendleton (Victoria; 1980–   , English,
cycling)
Schneider (Vreni; 1964–   ; Swiss, alpine
skiing)
Seizinger (Katja; 1972–   ; German, alpine
skiing)
Stevenson (Teófilo; 1952–   ; Cuban, boxing)

10 Linsenhoff (Liselott; 1927–99; German,
equestrianism)
Moser-Proll (Annemarie; 1953–   ; Austrian,
alpine skiing)
van Moorsel (Leontien; 1970–   ; Dutch,
cycling)

11 Mangiarotti (Edouardo; 1919–   ; Italian,
fencing)
Weissmuller (Johnny; 1904–84; US,
swimming)

12 Blankers-Koen (Fanny; 1918–2004; Dutch,
athletics)
Gebrselassie (Haile; 1973–   ; Ethiopian,
athletics)
Germeshausen (Bernhard; 1951–   ;
German, bobsledding)
Joyner-Kersee (Jackie; 1962–   ; US,
athletics)
Suleymanoglu (Naim; 1967–   ; Bulgarian/
Turkish, weightlifting)

13 Longo-Ciprelli (Jeannie; 1958–   ; French,
cycling)

14 Griffith-Joyner (Florence; 1959–98; US,
athletics)

O'Neill, Eugene (1888–1953)

Significant works include:

11 *The Fountain* (1925)
The Hairy Ape (1922)

12 *Ah, Wilderness* (1933)
Anna Christie (1921)

13 *Marco Millions* (1928)

14 *Days Without End* (1934)
Lazarus Laughed (1928)

15 *The Emperor Jones* (1920)
The Iceman Cometh (1946)

16 *Beyond the Horizon* (1920)

Strange Interlude (1928)
The Great God Brown (1926)

18 *Desire Under the Elms* (1924)
Moon of the Caribbees (1918)

19 *Bound East for Cardiff* (1916)

21 *Moon for the Misbegotten* (1947)

22 *All God's Chillun Got Wings* (1924)
Mourning Becomes Electra (1931)

24 *Long Day's Journey Into Night* (1956)

Significant characters include:

03 Lem

04 Mayo (Andrew)
Mayo (Robert)
Yank

05 Brant (Captain Adam)
Brown (William A)
Burke (Mat)
Cabot (Eben)
Cabot (Ephraim)

Jones (Brutus)
Leeds (Nina)

06 Downey (Ella)
Mannon (Brigadier-General Ezra)
Mannon (Christine)
Mannon (Lavinia)
Mannon (Orin)
Putnam (Abbie)

Tyrone (Edmund)
Tyrone (James)
Tyrone (Jamie)
Tyrone (Mary)

07 Anthony (Dion)
Douglas (Mildred)

08 Smithers (Henry)

14 Christopherson (Anna)
Christopherson (Chris)

OPEC

Organization of Petroleum Exporting Countries (OPEC) members:

04 Iran
Iraq

05 Libya
Qatar

06 Angola
Kuwait

07 Algeria
Ecuador

Nigeria

09 Venezuela

11 Saudi Arabia

18 United Arab Emirates

opera

Operas and operettas include:

04 *Aïda* (Verdi, 1871)
Lulu (Berg, 1937)

05 *Faust* (Gounod, 1859)
Manon (Massenet, 1884)
Norma (Bellini, 1831)
Tosca (Puccini, 1900)

06 *Carmen* (Bizet, 1875)
Jenufa (Janácek, 1904)
Otello (Verdi, 1887)
Salome (Richard Strauss, 1911)

07 *Elektra* (Richard Strauss, 1909)
Fidelio (Beethoven, 1814)
Macbeth (Verdi, 1847)
Nabucco (Verdi, 1842)
The Ring (Wagner, 1876)
Thespis (Gilbert & Sullivan, 1871)
Werther (Massenet, 1892)
Wozzeck (Berg, 1925)

08 *Falstaff* (Verdi, 1893)
Idomeneo (Mozart, 1781)
La bohème (Puccini, 1896)
Parsifal (Wagner, 1882)
Patience (Gilbert & Sullivan, 1881)
Turandot (Puccini, 1926)

09 *Billy Budd* (Britten, 1951)
Capriccio (Richard Strauss, 1942)
Don Carlos (Verdi, 1867)
King Priam (Tippett, 1962)
Lohengrin (Wagner, 1850)
Pagliacci (Leoncavallo, 1892)
Rigoletto (Verdi, 1851)
Ruddigore (Gilbert & Sullivan, 1887)

Siegfried (Wagner, 1876)
The Mikado (Gilbert & Sullivan, 1885)
Véronique (Andre Messager, 1898)

10 *Cendrillon* (Massenet, 1899)
Cinderella (Rossini, 1817; Massenet, 1899)
Die Walküre (Wagner, 1870)
I Pagliacci (Leoncavallo, 1892)
La traviata (Verdi, 1853)
Oedipus Rex (Stravinsky, 1928)
Tannhäuser (Wagner, 1845)

11 *Don Giovanni* (Mozart, 1787)
Don Pasquale (Donizetti, 1843)
HMS Pinafore (Gilbert & Sullivan, 1878)
Il trovatore (Verdi, 1853)
La Périchole (Offenbach, 1868)
Peter Grimes (Britten, 1945)
Princess Ida (Gilbert & Sullivan, 1884)
The Sorceror (Gilbert & Sullivan, 1877)
Trial by Jury (Gilbert & Sullivan, 1875)
William Tell (Rossini, 1829)

12 *Boris Godunov* (Mussorgsky, 1874)
Così fan tutte (Mozart, 1790)
Das Rheingold (Wagner, 1869)
Eugene Onegin (Tchaikovsky, 1879)
La sonnambula (Bellini, 1831)
Manon Lescaut (Puccini, 1893)
Moses und Aron (Schönberg, 1954)
Nixon in China (John Adams, 1990)
Porgy and Bess (Gershwin, 1935)
The Grand Duke (Gilbert & Sullivan, 1896)
The Huguenots (Meyerbeer, 1836)
The Rhinegold (Wagner, 1869)

The Valkyries (Wagner, 1870)

13 *Albert Herring* (Britten, 1947)
Andrea Chénier (Umberto Giordano, 1896)
Der Freischütz (Carl Maria von Weber, 1821)
Dido and Aeneas (Purcell, 1689)
Die Fledermaus (Johann Strauss, 1874)
La Belle Hélène (Offenbach, 1864)
La Cenerentola (Rossini, 1819)
Moses and Aaron (Schönberg, 1954)
Powder Her Face (Ades, 1995)
The Fairy Queen (Purcell, 1692)
The Gondoliers (Gilbert & Sullivan, 1889)
The Gypsy Baron (Johann Strauss, 1885)
The Knot Garden (Tippett, 1970)
The Magic Flute (Mozart, 1791)
Utopia Limited (Gilbert & Sullivan, 1893)

14 *Die Zauberflöte* (Mozart, 1791)
Le Grand Macabre (Ligeti, 1978)
Samson et Dalila (Saint-Saëns, 1877)

15 *Ariadne auf Naxos* (Richard Strauss, 1916)
Götterdämmerung (Wagner, 1876)
Hansel and Gretel (Humperdinck, 1893)
Le nozze di Figaro (Mozart, 1786)
Madama Butterfly (Puccini, 1904)
Madame Butterfly (Puccini, 1904)
Orfeo ed Euridice (Gluck, 1762)
Simon Boccanegra (Verdi, 1857)
The Beggar's Opera (Gay, 1728)
The Pearl Fishers (Bizet, 1863)

16 *Der Rosenkavalier* (Richard Strauss, 1911)
Der Zigeunerbaron (Johann Strauss, 1885)
The Bartered Bride (Smetana, 1866)

The Rake's Progress (Stravinsky, 1951)
Tristan und Isolde (Wagner, 1865)

17 *La Fille du régiment* (Donizetti, 1840)
Lucia di Lammermoor (Donizetti, 1835)
The Flying Dutchman (Wagner, 1843)
The Tales of Hoffman (Offenbach, 1881)
The Turn of the Screw (Britten, 1954)
Un ballo in maschera (Verdi, 1859)

18 *Einstein on the Beach* (Philip Glass, 1976)
La Damnation de Faust (Berlioz, 1846)
Pelléas et Mélisande (Debussy, 1902)
The Barber of Seville (Rossini, 1816)
The Threepenny Opera (Weill, 1928)

19 *Cavalleria rusticana* (Mascagni, 1890)
The Marriage of Figaro (Mozart, 1786)
The Yeoman of the Guard (Gilbert & Sullivan, 1888)

20 *Der Ring des Nibelungen* (Wagner, 1876)
Duke Bluebeard's Castle (Bartók, 1918)
Il barbiere di Siviglia (Rossini, 1816)
Lady Macbeth of Mtsensk (Shostakovich, 1934)
The Midsummer Marriage (Tippett, 1955)
The Pirates of Penzance (Gilbert & Sullivan, 1879)
The Twilight of the Gods (Wagner, 1876)

21 *The Cunning Little Vixen* (Janácek, 1924)

22 *Orpheus in the Underworld* (Offenbach, 1858)
The Love for Three Oranges (Prokofiev, 1920)
The Merry Wives of Windsor (Otto Nicolai, 1849)

Opera characters include:

03 Cis *(Albert Herring)*
Eva *(The Mastersingers of Nuremberg)*
Ida *(Die Fledermaus)*
Jim *(Porgy and Bess)*
Liu *(Turandot)*
Sid *(Albert Herring)*

04 Aïda *(Aïda)*
Bess *(Porgy and Bess)*
Budd (Billy; *Billy Budd)*
Budd (Superintendent; *Albert Herring)*
Doxy (Betty; *The Beggar's Opera)*
Erda *(Der Ring des Nibelungen)*
Erik *(The Flying Dutchman)*
Ford (Alice; *Falstaff)*
Ford (Frank; *Falstaff)*
Froh *(Der Ring des Nibelungen)*
Goro *(Madame Butterfly)*
Gzak *(Prince Igor)*
Iago *(Otello)*
Ines *(Il Trovatore)*
Jake *(Porgy and Bess)*

John *(Peter Grimes)*
Lily *(Porgy and Bess)*
Loge *(Der Ring des Nibelungen)*
Lola *(Cavalleria rusticana)*
Luna (The Count/Il Conte de; *Il Trovatore)*
Mary *(The Flying Dutchman)*
Mime *(Der Ring des Nibelungen)*
Mimì *(La bohème)*
Ochs (Baron; *Der Rosenkavalier)*
Olga *(Eugene Onegin)*
Page (Meg; *Falstaff)*
Pang *(Turandot)*
Pike (Florence; *Albert Herring)*
Ping *(Turandot)*
Pong *(Turandot)*
Ruiz *(Il trovatore)*
Vere (Captain; *Billy Budd)*
Zorn (Balthasar; *The Mastersingers of Nuremberg)*

05 Adele *(Die Fledermaus)*
Alfio *(Cavalleria rusticana)*

Alice *(Lucia di Lammermoor)*
Alisa *(Lucia di Lammermoor)*
Annie *(Porgy and Bess)*
Berta *(The Barber of Seville)*
Blind (Doctor; *Die Fledermaus)*
Boles (Bob; *Peter Grimes)*
Borsa (Matteo; *Rigoletto)*
Budge (Ben; *The Beggar's Opera)*
Caius (Doctor; *Falstaff)*
Calaf *(Turandot)*
Canio *(I Pagliacci)*
Clara *(Porgy and Bess)*
Colas *(Bastien und Bastienne)*
Creon *(Oedipus Rex)*
Crown *(Porgy and Bess)*
David *(The Mastersingers of Nuremberg)*
Diver (Jenny; *The Beggar's Opera)*
Emmie *(Albert Herring)*
Falke (Doctor; *Die Fledermaus)*
Faust *(Faust/La Damnation de Faust)*
Filch *(The Beggar's Opera)*
Flora (Bervoix; *La traviata)*
Foltz (Hans; *The Mastersingers of Nuremberg)*
Frank *(Die Fledermaus)*
Freia *(Der Ring des Nibelungen)*
Gedge (Mr; *Albert Herring)*
Gilda *(Rigoletto)*
Harry *(Albert Herring)*
Herod *(Salome)*
Jeník *(The Bartered Bride)*
Jones (Arthur; *Billy Budd)*
Kecal *(The Bartered Bride)*
Keene (Ned; *Peter Grimes)*
Lucia (Mama; *Cavalleria rusticana)*
Lucia *(The Rape of Lucretia)*
Maria *(Porgy and Bess)*
Marie *(Wozzeck)*
Marke (King; *Tristan und Isolde)*
Melot *(Tristan und Isolde)*
Mícha (Tobia; *The Bartered Bride)*
Mingo *(Porgy and Bess)*
Moser (Augustin; *The Mastersingers of Nuremberg)*
Nancy *(Albert Herring)*
Nedda *(I Pagliacci)*
Ortel (Hermann; *The Mastersingers of Nuremberg)*
Peppe *(I Pagliacci)*
Peter *(Hansel and Gretel)*
Peter *(Porgy and Bess)*
Pimen *(Boris Godunov)*
Porgy *(Porgy and Bess)*
Rocco *(Fidelio)*
Sachs (Hans; *The Mastersingers of Nuremberg)*
Senta *(The Flying Dutchman)*
Timur *(Turandot)*

Titus *(La clemenza di Tito)*
Tonio *(I Pagliacci)*
Tosca (Floria; *Tosca)*
Trull (Dolly; *The Beggar's Opera)*
Vasek *(The Bartered Bride)*
Venus *(Tannhäuser)*
Vixen (Miss; *The Beggar's Opera)*
Wotan *(Der Ring des Nibelungen)*
Xenia *(Boris Godunov)*

06 Alcina *(Alcina)*
Altoum (Emperor; *Turandot)*
Alvaro *(Alzira)*
Alzira *(Alzira)*
Annina *(Der Rosenkavalier)*
Annina *(La traviata)*
Annius *(La clemenza di Tito)*
Ashton (Lucy/Lucia; *Lucia di Lammermoor)*
Ashton (Sir Henry/Enrico; *Lucia di Lammermoor)*
Benoît *(La bohème)*
Bianca *(The Rape of Lucretia)*
Brazen (Molly; *The Beggar's Opera)*
Carmen *(Carmen)*
Cassio *(Otello)*
Coaxer (Mrs; *The Beggar's Opera)*
Daland *(The Flying Dutchman)*
Donald *(Billy Budd)*
Donner *(Der Ring des Nibelungen)*
Emilia *(Otello)*
Fafner *(Der Ring des Nibelungen)*
Fasolt *(Der Ring des Nibelungen)*
Fenton *(Falstaff)*
Feodor *(Boris Godunov)*
Figaro *(The Barber of Seville/The Marriage of Figaro)*
Frantz *(The Tales of Hoffmann)*
Fricka *(Der Ring des Nibelungen)*
Frosch *(Die Fledermaus)*
Fyodor *(Boris Godunov)*
Golaud *(Pelléas et Mélisande)*
Gremin (Prince; *Eugene Onegin)*
Gretel *(Hansel and Gretel)*
Grimes (Peter; *Peter Grimes)*
Hänsel *(Hansel and Gretel)*
Isolde *(Tristan und Isolde)*
Junius *(The Rape of Lucretia)*
Kundry *(Parsifal)*
Larina (Marina; *Eugene Onegin)*
Lensky *(Eugene Onegin)*
Lockit (Lucy; *The Beggar's Opera)*
Lockit (Lucy; *The Beggar's Opera)*
Lockit *(The Beggar's Opera)*
Luther *(The Tales of Hoffmann)*
Mantua (Duke of; *Rigoletto)*
Nelson *(Porgy and Bess)*
Norman *(Lucia di Lammermoor)*
Oberto *(Alcina)*
Onegin (Eugene; *Eugene Onegin)*

Orford (Ellen; *Peter Grimes*)
Oronte (*Alcina*)
Ortrud (*Lohengrin*)
Otello (*Otello*)
Otumbo (*Alzira*)
Ovando (*Alzira*)
Ovlour (*Prince Igor*)
Pamina (*The Magic Flute*)
Pastia (Lillas; *Carmen*)
Pogner (Veit; *The Mastersingers of Nuremberg*)
Ramfis (*Aïda*)
Rosina (*The Barber of Seville*)
Salome (*Salome*)
Serena (*Porgy and Bess*)
Sextus (*La clemenza di Tito*)
Siebel (*Faust*)
Silvio (*I Pagliacci*)
Sophie (*Der Rosenkavalier*)
Squeak (*Billy Budd*)
Stella (*The Tales of Hoffmann*)
Suzuki (*Madame Butterfly*)
Tamino (*The Magic Flute*)
Tawdry (Suky; *The Beggar's Opera*)
Trapes (Mrs; *The Beggar's Opera*)
Upfold (Mr; *Albert Herring*)
Valery (Violetta; *La traviata*)
Wagner (*Faust*)
Yniold (*Pelléas et Mélisande*)
Zamoro (*Alzira*)
Zuniga (*Carmen*)

07 Alfredo (Germont; *La traviata*)
Amneris (*Aïda*)
Antonio (*The Marriage of Figaro*)
Ataliba (*Alzira*)
Azucena (*Il trovatore*)
Bartolo (*The Barber of Seville/The Marriage of Figaro*)
Basilio (*The Barber of Seville*)
Bastien (*Bastien und Bastienne*)
Bervoix (Flora; *La traviata*)
Billows (Lady; *Albert Herring*)
Bucklow (Lord Arturo/Arthur; *Lucia di Lammermoor*)
Colline (*La bohème*)
Crab Man (*Porgy and Bess*)
Dansker (*Billy Budd*)
Despina (*Cosí fan tutte*)
Don José (*Carmen*)
Douphol (Baron; *La traviata*)
Eroshka (*Prince Igor*)
Faninal (*Der Rosenkavalier*)
Frazier (*Porgy and Bess*)
Gastone (*La traviata*)
Germont (Alfredo; *La traviata*)
Germont (Giorgio; *La traviata*)
Godfrey (*Lohengrin*)
Godunov (Boris; *Boris Godunov*)

Gunther (*Der Ring des Nibelungen*)
Gusmano (*Alzira*)
Gutrune (*Der Ring des Nibelungen*)
Heraldo (*Lohengrin*)
Hermann (*Tannhäuser*)
Hermann (*The Tales of Hoffmann*)
Herring (Albert; *Albert Herring*)
Herring (Mrs; *Albert Herring*)
Hunding (*Der Ring des Nibelungen*)
Jaquino (*Fidelio*)
Jocasta (*Oedipus Rex*)
Kothner (Fritz; *The Mastersingers of Nuremberg*)
Leonora (*Fidelio*)
Leonora (*Il trovatore*)
Lindorf (*The Tales of Hoffmann*)
Mahomet (*Der Rosenkavalier*)
Manrico (*Il trovatore*)
Marenka (*The Bartered Bride*)
Marullo (Cavaliere; *Rigoletto*)
Masetto (*Don Giovanni*)
Melisso (*Alcina*)
Micaëla (*Carmen*)
Miracle (Doctor; *The Tales of Hoffmann*)
Missail (*Boris Godunov*)
Mnishek (Marina; *Boris Godunov*)
Montano (*Otello*)
Morales (*Carmen*)
Morgana (*Alcina*)
Musetta (*La bohème*)
Oedipus (*Oedipus Rex*)
Olympis (*The Tales of Hoffmann*)
Peachum (Polly; *The Beggar's Opera*)
Peachum (*The Beggar's Opera*)
Pelléas (*Pelléas et Mélisande*)
Pistola (*Falstaff*)
Publius (*La clemenza di Tito*)
Quickly (Mistress; *Falstaff*)
Radamès (*Aïda*)
Rangoni (*Boris Godunov*)
Redburn (Mr; *Billy Budd*)
Robbins (*Porgy and Bess*)
Rodolfo (*La bohème*)
Rofrano (Octavian; *Der Rosenkavalier*)
Scarpia (Baron; *Tosca*)
Schwarz (Hans; *The Mastersingers of Nuremberg*)
Susanna (*The Marriage of Figaro*)
Tatiana (*Eugene Onegin*)
Titurel (King; *Parsifal*)
Triquet (Monsieur; *Eugene Onegin*)
Tristan (*Tristan und Isolde*)
Trouble (*Madame Butterfly*)
Turiddu (*Cavalleria rusticana*)
Varlaam (*Boris Godunov*)
Walther (von Stolzing; *The Mastersingers of Nuremberg*)
Wozzeck (*Wozzeck*)

Zerlina *(Don Giovanni)*

08 Alberich *(Der Ring des Nibelungen)*
Almaviva *(Count/Il Conte d'; The Barber of Seville/The Marriage of Figaro)*
Almaviva *(Countess/Il Contessa di; The Marriage of Figaro)*
Ambrogio *(The Barber of Seville)*
Amfortas *(Parsifal)*
Amonasro *(Aïda)*
Archdale *(Mr; Porgy and Bess)*
Bardolfo *(Falstaff)*
Bidebent *(Raymond/Raimondo; Lucia di Lammermoor)*
Biterolf *(Tannhäuser)*
Brangäne *(Tristan und Isolde)*
Claggart *(Billy Budd)*
Falstaff *(Sir John; Falstaff)*
Fernando *(Fidelio)*
Ferrando *(Cosí fan tutte)*
Ferrando *(Il trovatore)*
Fiorello *(The Barber of Seville)*
Galitsky *(Prince; Prince Igor)*
Gerhilde *(Der Ring des Nibelungen)*
Gertrude *(Hansel and Gretel)*
Giovanna *(Rigoletto)*
Giuseppe *(La traviata)*
Grigorij *(Boris Godunov)*
Grigoriy *(Boris Godunov)*
Helmwige *(Der Ring des Nibelungen)*
Herodias *(Salome)*
Hoffmann *(The Tales of Hoffmann)*
Jacquino *(Fidelio)*
Klingsor *(Parsifal)*
Kontchak *(Prince Igor)*
Kurvenal *(Tristan und Isolde)*
Kurwenal *(Tristan und Isolde)*
Lodovico *(Otello)*
Lucretia *(The Rape of Lucretia)*
Macheath *(Captain; The Beggar's Opera)*
Marcello *(La bohème)*
Mercédès *(Carmen)*
Nannetta *(Falstaff)*
Nicklaus *(The Tales of Hoffmann)*
Nikitich *(Boris Godunov)*
Normando *(Lucia di Lammermoor)*
Octavian *(Rofrano; Der Rosenkavalier)*
Orlofsky *(Prince; Die Fledermaus)*
Orlovsky *(Prince; Die Fledermaus)*
Ortlinde *(Der Ring des Nibelungen)*
Papagena *(The Magic Flute)*
Papageno *(The Magic Flute)*
Parsifal *(Parsifal)*
Rhadames *(Aïda)*
Roderigo *(Otello)*
Ruggiero *(Alcina)*
Santuzza *(Cavalleria rusticana)*
Sarastro *(The Magic Flute)*
Servilia *(La clemenza di Tito)*

Siegmund *(Der Ring des Nibelungen)*
Spoletta *(Tosca)*
Stolzing *(Walter von; The Mastersingers of Nuremberg)*
The Bonze *(Madame Butterfly)*
The Witch *(Hansel and Gretel)*
Tiresias *(Oedipus Rex)*
Turandot *(Princess; Turandot)*
Twitcher *(Jemmy; The Beggar's Opera)*
Valentin *(Faust)*
Violetta *(Valery; La traviata)*
Vitellia *(La clemenza di Tito)*
Woglinde *(Der Ring des Nibelungen)*
Yamadori *(Prince; Madame Butterfly)*
Zaretski *(Eugene Onegin)*

09 Alcindoro *(La bohème)*
Angelotti *(Cesare; Tosca)*
Barbarina *(The Marriage of Figaro)*
Bastienne *(Bastien und Bastienne)*
Butterfly *(Madame; Madame Butterfly)*
Chelkalov *(Andrey/Andrei; Boris Godunov)*
Cherubino *(The Marriage of Figaro)*
Cio-Cio-San *(Madame Butterfly)*
Coppelius *(The Tales of Hoffmann)*
Desdemona *(Otello)*
Don Curzio *(The Marriage of Figaro)*
Donna Anna *(Don Giovanni)*
Dorabella *(Cosí fan tutte)*
Elisabeth *(Tannhäuser)*
Escamillo *(Carmen)*
Esmerelda *(The Bartered Bride)*
Florestan *(Fidelio)*
Frasquita *(Carmen)*
Genevieve *(Pelléas et Mélisande)*
Grimgerde *(Der Ring des Nibelungen)*
Guglielmo *(Cosí fan tutte)*
Gurnemanz *(Parsifal)*
Leporello *(Don Giovanni)*
Lohengrin *(Lohengrin)*
Maddalena *(Rigoletto)*
Magdalena *(The Mastersingers of Nuremberg)*
Magdalene *(The Mastersingers of Nuremberg)*
Mélisande *(Pelléas et Mélisande)*
Narraboth *(Salome)*
Nathanael *(The Tales of Hoffmann)*
Parpignol *(La bohème)*
Pinkerton *(Kate; Madame Butterfly)*
Pinkerton *(Lieutenant Benjamin; Madame Butterfly)*
Red Indian *(The Bartered Bride)*
Rigoletto *(Rigoletto)*
Rosalinda *(Die Fledermaus)*
Sacristan *(Tosca)*
Schaunard *(La bohème)*
Sciarrone *(Tosca)*
Sharpless *(Madame Butterfly)*

Siegfried (Der Ring des Nibelungen)
Sieglunde (Der Ring des Nibelungen)
Telramund (Frederick/Frederico; Lohengrin)
The Dewman (Hansel and Gretel)
Valzacchi (Der Rosenkavalier)
Vogelsang (Kunz; The Mastersingers of Nuremberg)
Von Zweter (Reinmar; Tannhäuser)
Waltraute (Der Ring des Nibelungen)
Wellgunde (Der Ring des Nibelungen)

10 Beckmesser (Sixtus; The Mastersingers of Nuremberg)
Bradamante (Alcina)
Brünnhilde (Der Ring des Nibelungen)
Collatinus (The Rape of Lucretia)
Dapertutto (The Tales of Hoffmann)
Don Alfonso (Cosí fan tutte)
Don Basilio (The Marriage of Figaro)
Don Ottavio (Don Giovanni)
Don Pizarro (Fidelio)
Eisenstein (Gabriel von; Die Fledermaus)
Eisslinger (Ulrich; The Mastersingers of Nuremberg)
El Dancairo (Carmen)
Filipievna (Eugene Onegin)
Fiordiligi (Cosí fan tutte)
Flosshilde (Der Ring des Nibelungen)
Igorevitch (Vladimir; Prince Igor)
Jaroslavna (Prince Igor)
La Contessa (Rigoletto)
Marcellina (Fidelio)
Marcellina (The Marriage of Figaro)
Marguérite (Faust/La Damnation de Faust)
Marzelline (Fidelio)
Monostatos (The Magic Flute)
Nachtigall (Konrad; The Mastersingers of Nuremberg)
Nimming Ned (The Beggar's Opera)
Paddington (Harry; The Beggar's Opera)
Prince Igor (Prince Igor)
Ravenswood (Sir Edgar/Edgardo; Lucia di Lammermoor)

Rey Enrique (Lohengrin)
Rossweisse (Der Ring des Nibelungen)
Schwerlein (Marthe; Faust)
Spalanzani (The Tales of Hoffmann)
Tannhäuser (Heinrich; Tannhäuser)
The Sandman (Hansel and Gretel)
The Speaker (The Magic Flute)
Wordsworth (Miss; Albert Herring)
Yaroslavna (Prince Igor)

11 Cavaradossi (Mario; Tosca)
Chochenille (The Tales of Hoffmann)
Don Giovanni (Don Giovanni)
Donna Elvira (Don Giovanni)
El Remendado (Carmen)
King of Egypt (Aïda)
Marschallin (Der Rosenkavalier)
Red Whiskers (Billy Budd)
Sparafucile (Rigoletto)
Sportin' Life (Porgy and Bess)
Taumännchen (Hansel and Gretel)
The Dutchman (The Flying Dutchman)
Vogelgesang (Kunz; The Mastersingers of Nuremberg)

12 Der Schreiber (Heinrich; Tannhäuser)
Kontchakovna (Prince Igor)
Leitmetzerin (Marianne; Der Rosenkavalier)
Mat of the Mint (The Beggar's Opera)
Sandmännchen (Hansel and Gretel)
The Steersman (The Flying Dutchman)

13 Elsa of Brabant (Lohengrin)
Von Eschenbach (Wolfram; Tannhäuser)

14 Customs Officer (La Bohème)
Henry the Fowler (Lohengrin)
John the Baptist (Salome)
Mephistopheles (Faust/La Damnation de Faust)
Pittichinaccio (The Tales of Hoffmann)
Usciere di Corte (Rigoletto)
Yaroslavovitch (Vladimir; Prince Igor)

15 Il duca di Mantova (Rigoletto)
Ochs von Lercheau (Baron; Der Rosenkavalier)

Opera houses include:

04 Lyon (France)

05 Cairo (Egypt)
Lyric (USA)
Royal (England)
State (Czech Republic)

06 De Munt (Belgium)
Semper (Germany)
Sydney (Australia)
Zurich (Switzerland)

07 La Scala (Italy)

Leipzig (Germany)

08 Bastille (France)
La Fenice (Italy)
San Carlo (Italy)

09 La Monnaie (Belgium)

10 Gothenburg (Sweden)
Monte-Carlo (Monaco)
Mussorgsky (Russia)

11 Teatro Liceo (Spain)

Verona Arena (Italy)
Vienna State (Austria)

12 Glyndebourne (England)
Hamburg State (Germany)
Komische Oper (Germany)
Metropolitan (USA)
Opéra-Comique (France)

13 Kennedy Center (USA)
Lincoln Center (USA)

Muziektheater (The Netherlands)
Palais Garnier (France)
Teatro Massimo (Italy)
14 Bolshoi Theatre (Russia)

Estates Theatre (Czech Republic)
Hungarian State (Hungary)
Kungliga Operan (Sweden)
London Coliseum (England)

Unter den Linden (Germany)
15 Royal Opera House (England)
Teatro alla Scala (Italy)

Opera singers include:

03 Mei (Lanfang; 1894–1961, Chinese)
04 Butt (Dame Clara; 1872–1936, English, contralto)
Lind (Jenny; 1820–87, Swedish, soprano)
Nash (Heddle; 1896–1961, English, tenor)
Pons (Lily; 1898–1976, French/US, soprano)
Popp (Lucia; 1939–93, Czech, soprano)
Prey (Hermann; 1929–98, German, baritone)
Tear (Robert; 1939– , Welsh, tenor)
Ward (David; 1922–83, Scottish, bass)
05 Allen (Sir Thomas; 1944– , English, baritone)
Baker (Dame Janet; 1933– , English, mezzo-soprano)
Bonci (Alessandro; 1870–1940, Italian, tenor)
Craig (Charles; 1922–97, English, tenor)
Evans (Sir Geraint; 1922–92, Welsh, baritone)
Ewing (Maria; 1950– , US, mezzo-soprano)
Field (Helen; 1951– , Welsh, soprano)
Freni (Mirella; 1936– , Italian, soprano)
Gedda (Nicolai; 1925– , Swedish, tenor)
Gigli (Beniamino; 1890–1957, Italian, tenor)
Gobbi (Tito; 1913–84, Italian, baritone)
Grisi (Giuditta; 1805–40, Italian, mezzo-soprano)
Grisi (Giulia; 1811–69, Italian, soprano)
Horne (Marilyn; 1934– , US, mezzo-soprano)
Jones (Dame Gwyneth; 1936– , Welsh, soprano)
Kollo (René; 1937– , German, tenor)
Kraus (Alfredo; 1927–99, Spanish, tenor)
Lanza (Mario; 1921–59, US, tenor)
Luxon (Benjamin; 1937– , English, baritone)
Major (Dame Malvina; 1943– , New Zealand, soprano)
Meier (Johanna; 1938– , US, soprano)
Melba (Dame Nellie; 1861–1931, Australian, soprano)
Patti (Adelina; 1843–1919, Italian, soprano)
Pears (Sir Peter; 1910–86, English, tenor)
Pinza (Ezio; 1892–1957, Italian, bass)
Price (Leontyne; 1927– , US, soprano)
Siepi (Cesare; 1923– , Italian, bass)
Sills (Beverly; 1929–2007, US, soprano)
Teyte (Dame Maggie; 1888–1976, English, soprano)
06 Bowman (James; 1941– , English, counter-tenor)

Braham (John; 1774–1856, English, tenor)
Callas (Maria; 1923–77, US/Greek, soprano)
Carden (Joan; 1937– , Australian, soprano)
Caruso (Enrico; 1873–1921, Italian, tenor)
Davies (Arthur; 1950– , Welsh, tenor)
Davies (Ryland; 1943– , Welsh, tenor)
Dawson (Peter; 1882–1961, Australian, bass-baritone)
Deller (Alfred; 1912–79, English, counter-tenor)
de Luca (Giuseppe; 1876–1950, Italian, baritone)
Farrar (Geraldine; 1882–1967, US, soprano)
García (Manuel; 1775–1832, Spanish, tenor)
Garden (Mary; 1874–1967, Scottish, soprano)
Harper (Heather; 1930– , Northern Irish, soprano)
Hislop (Joseph; 1884–1977, Scottish, tenor)
Hotter (Hans; 1909–2003, German, bass-baritone)
Ludwig (Christa; 1928– , German, mezzo-soprano)
Mangin (Noel; 1931–95, New Zealand, bass)
Minton (Yvonne; 1938– , Australian, mezzo-soprano)
Norman (Jessye; 1945– , US, soprano)
Reszke (Edouard de; 1856–1917, Polish, bass)
Reszke (Jean de; 1850–1925, Polish, tenor)
Reszke (Joséphine de; 1855–91, Polish, soprano)
Scotto (Renata; 1934– , Italian, soprano)
Studer (Cheryl; 1955– , US, soprano)
Tauber (Richard; 1892–1948, Austrian/British, tenor)
Terfel (Bryn; 1965– , Welsh, bass-baritone)
Turner (Dame Eva; 1892–1990, English, soprano)
Upshaw (Dawn; 1960– , US, soprano)
van Dam (José; 1940– , Belgian, bass-baritone)
Wiener (Otto; 1911–2000, Austrian, baritone)
07 Austral (Florence; 1894–1968, Australian, soprano)
Baillie (Dame Isobel; 1895–1983, Scottish, soprano)
Barstow (Dame Josephine; 1940– , English, soprano)

Bartoli (Cecilia; 1966– , Italian, mezzo-soprano)
Bocelli (Andrea; 1958– , Italian, tenor)
Caballé (Montserrat; 1933– , Spanish, soprano)
Collier (Maria; 1926–71, Australian, soprano)
Corelli (Franco; 1921–2003, Italian, tenor)
De Lucia (Fernando; 1860–1925, Italian, tenor)
Domingo (Placido; 1941– , Spanish, tenor)
Farrell (Eileen; 1920–2002, US, soprano)
Ferrier (Kathleen; 1912–53, English, contralto)
Garrett (Lesley; 1955– , English, soprano)
Hammond (Dame Joan; 1912–96, New Zealand/Australian, soprano)
Jurinac (Sena; 1921– , Yugoslav/Bosnian, soprano)
Lehmann (Lilli; 1848–1929, German, soprano)
Lehmann (Lotte; 1888–1976, US, soprano)
Migenes (Julia; 1945– , US, soprano)
Milanov (Zinka; 1906–89, Croatian, soprano)
Nilsson (Birgit; 1918–2006, Swedish, soprano)
Santley (Sir Charles; 1834–1922, English, baritone)
Smirnov (Dimitri; 1882–1944, Russian, tenor)
Stratas (Teresa; 1938– , Canadian, soprano)
Tebaldi (Renata; 1922–2004, Italian, soprano)
Tibbett (Lawrence; 1896–1960, US, baritone)
Tinsley (Pauline; 1928– , English, soprano)
Traubel (Helen; 1899–1972, US, soprano)
Vickers (Jon; 1926– , Canadian, tenor)

08 Anderson (Marian; 1902–93, US, contralto)
Berganza (Teresa; 1935– , Spanish, mezzo-soprano)
Bergonzi (Carlo; 1924– , Italian, tenor)
Björling (Jussi; 1911–60, Swedish, tenor)
Borgatti (Giuseppe; 1871–1950, Italian, tenor)
Borgioli (Dino; 1891–1960, Italian, tenor)
Bronhill (June; 1929–2005, Australian, soprano)
Brownlee (John; 1900–69, Australian, baritone)
Carreras (José; 1946– , Spanish, tenor)
Crossley (Ada; 1871–1929, Australian, contralto)
Dernesch (Helga; 1939– , Austrian, soprano)
Flagstad (Kirsten; 1895–1962, Norwegian, soprano)

Fremstad (Olive; 1871–1951, US, soprano)
Ghiaurov (Nicolai; 1929–2004, Bulgarian, bass)
Lablache (Luigi; 1794–1858, Italian, bass)
Lawrence (Marjorie; 1908–79, Australian, soprano)
Malibran (Marie; 1808–36, Spanish, mezzo-soprano)
Melchior (Lauritz; 1890–1973, Danish/US, tenor)
Piccaver (Alfred; 1884–1958, English, tenor)
Ponselle (Rosa; 1897–1981, US, soprano)
Schumann (Elisabeth; 1889–1952, US, soprano)
Seefried (Irmgard; 1919–88, Austrian, soprano)
Te Kanawa (Dame Kiri; 1944– , New Zealand, soprano)
Williams (Harold; 1893–1976, Australian, baritone)

09 Berberian (Cathy; 1925–83, US, soprano)
Brannigan (Owen; 1908–73, English, bass-baritone)
Chaliapin (Feodor; 1873–1938, Russian, bass)
Christoff (Boris; 1914–93, Bulgarian, bass-baritone)
della Casa (Lisa; 1919– , Swiss, soprano)
Del Monaco (Mario; 1915–82, Italian, tenor)
Forrester (Maureen; 1930– , Canadian, contralto)
Hendricks (Barbara; 1948– , US, soprano)
McCormack (John; 1884–1945, Irish/US, tenor)
McCracken (James; 1927–88, US, tenor)
Pavarotti (Luciano; 1935–2007, Italian, tenor)
Tomlinson (Sir John; 1946– , English, bass)

10 Battistini (Mattia; 1856–1928, Italian, baritone)
Galli-Curci (Amelita; 1882–1963, Italian, soprano)
Galli-Marie (Celestine; 1840–1905, French, mezzo-soprano)
Los Angeles (Victoria de; 1923–2005, Spanish, soprano)
Martinelli (Giovanni; 1885–1969, Italian, tenor)
Söderström (Elisabeth; 1927– , Swedish, soprano)
Sutherland (Dame Joan; 1926– , Australian, soprano)
Tetrazzini (Luisa; 1871–1940, Italian, soprano)

11 Schwarzkopf (Dame Elisabeth; 1915–2006, Austrian/British, soprano)

12 de los Angeles (Victoria; 1923–2005, Spanish, soprano)

Shirley-Quirk (John; 1931– , English, bass-baritone)

13 Viardot-García (Pauline; 1821–1910, Spanish, mezzo-soprano)

14 Fischer-Dieskau (Dietrich; 1925– , German, baritone)

See also **Bartók, Béla; Beethoven, Ludwig van; Britten, Benjamin; Gilbert, Sir W S and Sullivan, Sir Arthur; Handel, George Frideric; libretto; Mozart, Wolfgang Amadeus; overture; Prokofiev, Sergei; Puccini, Giacomo; Purcell, Henry; Ravel, Maurice; Rossini, Gioacchino; Schubert, Franz; Shostakovich, Dmitri; Strauss, Richard; Stravinsky, Igor; Tchaikovsky, Pyotr Ilyich; Verdi, Giuseppe; Wagner, Richard**

optics

Optical instruments and devices include:

05 laser	telescope	stereocamera
06 camera	**10** binoculars	**13** film projector
07 sextant	microscope	**14** slide projector
08 spyglass	opera-glass	**15** magnifying glass
09 endoscope	theodolite	photomicroscope
periscope	**12** field-glasses	telescopic sight

See also **observatory**

orange

Orange varieties include:

04 mock	sweet	naartje	mandarin
Ruta	topaz	nartjie	**09** Clockwork
sour	**06** bitter	satsuma	mandarine
05 blood		Seville	tangerine
Jaffa	**07** cumquat	**08** bergamot	**10** clementine
navel	kumquat	bigarade	

Shades of orange include:

04 gold	**06** anatta	tawney	**08** croceate
05 amber	anatto	**07** annatta	croceous
chica	aurora	annatto	mandarin
chico	chicha	apricot	**09** bilirubin
coral	kamala	arnotto	tangerine
henna	kamela	jacinth	**13** cadmium yellow
tawny	kamila	nacarat	canthaxanthin
tenné	roucou	paprika	
tenny	salmon	saffron	

See also **fruit**

oratorio

Oratorios include:

04 *Saul* (1739, Handel)

06 *Elijah* (1846, Mendelssohn)
Esther (1732, Handel)
Joshua (1747, Handel)
Samson (1743, Handel)

Semele (1743, Handel)
St Paul (1836, Mendelssohn)

07 *Athalia* (1733, Handel)
Deborah (1733, Handel)
Jephtha (1751, Handel)

Messiah (1742, Handel)	*The Seasons* (1801, Haydn)
Solomon (1749, Handel)	**11** *The Creation* (1798, Haydn)
Susanna (1748, Handel)	
08 *Christus* (1866, Liszt)	**13** *Israel in Egypt* (1739, Handel)
Hercules (1744, Handel)	**14** *Alexander Balus* (1747, Handel)
Theodora (1749, Handel)	*La Resurrezione* (1708, Handel)
09 *Christmas* (1734, J S Bach)	**15** *Judas Maccabaeus* (1747, Handel)
10 *Belshazzar* (1744, Handel)	**16** *Belshazzar's Feast* (1931, Walton)
Oedipus Rex (1927, Stravinsky)	*L'enfance du Christ* (1854, Berlioz)

See also **music**; **musician**

orchestra

Common orchestra names include:

07 Chamber	Sinfonia	**12** Philharmonic
08 National	Symphony	

orchid

Orchids include:

03 bee	queen	small white
bog	tiger	**11** cockleshell
bug	tulip	dancing lady
fen	**06** lizard	early purple
fly	monkey	early spider
man	spider	green-winged
sun	**07** leopard	**12** black vanilla
04 blue	slipper	heath spotted
frog	vanilla	Lapland marsh
king	**08** crucifix	narrow-leaved
kite	fragrant	one-leaved bog
lady	military	western marsh
moth	**09** birds-nest	**13** Chinese ground
musk	chocolate	common spotted
wasp	Christmas	dense-flowered
05 burnt	coralroot	elder-flowered
clown	false musk	loose-flowered
comet	pyramidal	orange blossom
ghost	**10** early marsh	southern marsh
giant	late spider	**15** lesser butterfly
pansy		violet birds-nest

order *see* **religious order**

orders of angel *see* **angel**

ore

Ores include:

03 wad (manganese)	**06** bog ore (iron)	rutile (titanium)
04 wadd (manganese)	coltan (tantalum)	**07** bauxite (aluminium)
wadt (manganese)	galena (lead)	bog iron (iron)

bornite (copper)
cuprite (copper)
iron ore (iron)
oligist (iron)
wood tin (tin)

08 beauxite (aluminium)
braunite (manganese)
calamine (zinc)
enargite (copper)
hematite (iron)
limonite (iron)
siderite (iron)
sinopite (iron)
taconite (iron)
tenorite (copper)

See also **mineral**

09 anglesite (lead)
blackband (iron)
coffinite (uranium)
haematite (iron)
hedyphane (lead)
ironstone (iron)
kidney ore (iron)
lodestone (iron)
magnetite (iron)
manganite (manganese)
morass ore (iron)
proustite (silver)
tantalite (tantalum)

10 erubescite (copper)
melaconite (copper)

peacock ore (copper)
sphalerite (zinc)
stephanite (silver)

11 cassiterite (tin)
chloanthite (nickel)
pyrargyrite (silver)
tetradymite (tellurium)

12 babingtonite (iron)
chalcopyrite (copper)
pyromorphite (lead)
tetrahedrite (copper)

13 copper pyrites (copper)
horseflesh ore (copper)
ruby silver ore (silver)

15 stilpnosiderite (iron)

organ

Organs include:

03 ear
eye

04 nose
skin

05 bowel
brain
colon
liver
lungs
lymph
penis
vulva

06 cervix
rectum
spleen
testes
throat
thymus
ureter

See also **anatomy**

uterus
vagina

07 bladder
kidneys
ovaries
oviduct
pharynx
scrotum
stomach
tonsils
trachea
urethra

08 adenoids
appendix
bronchus
clitoris
pancreas
prostate
windpipe

09 diaphragm
pituitary
taste buds

10 epididymis
intestines
lymph nodes
oesophagus
spinal cord

11 gall bladder
vas deferens

12 hypothalamus
thymus glands
thyroid gland

13 adrenal glands

14 fallopian tubes
large intestine
small intestine

15 ejaculatory duct
seminal vesicles

organ stop

Organ stops include:

04 echo
oboe
sext
tuba

05 dolce
gamba
quint

06 cornet
nasard

octave
tierce

07 bombard
bourdon
clarino
clarion
fagotto
mixture
piccolo

salicet
trumpet

08 carillon
crumhorn
diapason
diaphone
dulciana
gemshorn
krumhorn

register	pyramidon	**11** superoctave
waldhorn	vox humana	voix céleste
09 fifteenth	waldflute	**12** sesquialtera
furniture	**10** clarabella	**15** corno di bassetto
krummhorn	fourniture	
principal	salicional	

organism *see* **classification**

Organization of Petroleum Exporting Countries *see* OPEC

Orwell, George (1903–50)

Significant works include:

10 *Animal Farm* (1945)
11 *Burmese Days* (1934)
14 *Coming up for Air* (1939)
   Critical Essays (1946)
   Inside the Whale (1940)
17 *Homage to Catalonia* (1938)
18 *Nineteen Eighty-Four* (1949)

Shooting an Elephant (1936)
The Road to Wigan Pier (1937)
19 *A Clergyman's Daughter* (1935)
   Such, Such Were The Joys (1953)
20 *The Lion and the Unicorn* (1941)
23 *Keep the Aspidistra Flying* (1936)
26 *Down and Out in Paris and London* (1933)

Significant characters include:

04 Hare (Dorothy)
05 Boxer
   Jones (Farmer)
   Julia
   Moses
   Smith (Winston)
06 Clover

Mollie
O'Brien
07 Bowling (George)
   Whymper
08 Benjamin
   Comstock (Gordon)
   Napoleon

Old Major
Snowball
Squealer
09 Frederick (Mr)
10 Big Brother
   Pilkington (Mr)
11 Charrington (Mr)

outlaw *see* **crime**

overture

Overtures include:

05 *Cuban* (Gershwin)
   Herod (Hadley)
06 *Choral* (Beethoven)
   Comedy (Harty)
   Esther (d'Albert)
   French (Lully)
   Heroic (Panufnik)
   Solemn (Sallinen)
   Spring (Sibelius)
   Thalia (Chadwick)
   Tragic (Brahms)
07 *Adonais* (Chadwick)
   Aladdin (Nielsen)
   Euterpe (Chadwick)
   Festive (Shostakovich)

Holiday (Carter)
Idyllic (Reznicek)
Jubilee (von Weber)
Leonora (Beethoven)
Maytime (Phillips)
Othello (Dvorak)
08 *Carnival* (Dvorak)
   Columbus (Wagner)
   Coriolan (Beethoven)
   Hebrides (Mendelssohn)
   Hyperion (Schubert)
   In Autumn (Sibelius)
   King Lear (Berlioz)
   Romantic (Bruckner)
   The Wasps (Vaughan Williams)
   Waverley (Berlioz)

09 *Britannia* (Wagner)
Children's (Quilter)
Fairy Land (Mendelssohn)
In Bohemia (Balakirev)
Pinocchio (Toch)
The Naiads (Schumann)

10 *Amid Nature* (Dvorak)
In the South (Elgar)
Salutatory (Myaskovsky)

11 *East and West* (Bach)
'Fingal's Cave' (Mendelssohn)
Pickwickian (Gal)
Shéhérazade (Ravel)
William Tell (Rossini)

12 *Fair Melusina* (Mendelssohn)

In London Town (Elgar)
Rip van Winkle (Chadwick)
Street Corner (Rawsthorne)

13 *Shadowy Waters* (Seeger)
The Wood-Nymphs (Sterndale Bennett)

14 *Eighteen Twelve* (Tchaikovsky)
Eighteen-Twelve (Tchaikovsky)
In Nature's Realm (Dvorak)
In the Highlands (Loewe)
In the Mountains (Berlioz)
Romeo and Juliet (Tchaikovsky)
Venus and Adonis (Blow)

15 *Comes Autumn Time* (Sowerby)
Portsmouth Point (Walton)
The Fair Melusina (Mendelssohn)

Oxford University *see* **college**

P

paint

View on the Stour (1819; John Constable)

15 Absinthe Drinker (1859; Édouard Manet)
Commodore Keppel (1753; Sir Joshua
Reynolds)
Flight into Egypt (1753; Giandomenico
Tiepolo)
Madonna del Prato (c.1505; Raphael)
Marriage à la Mode (1743–45; William
Hogarth)
The Annunciation (1333; Simone
Martini/1423–24; Antonio Pisanello)
The Birth of Venus (c.1482–84; Sandro
Botticelli)
The Charnel House (1945; Pablo Picasso)
The Death of Marat (1793; Jacques Louis
David)
The Flagellation (c.1456–57; Piero della
Francesca)
The Potato Eaters (1885; Vincent Van Gogh)
Triumph of Caesar (c.1486; Andrea
Mantegna)

16 Agony in the Garden (c.1450; Andrea
Mantegna/c.1465; Giovanni Bellini)
At the Moulin Rouge (1895; Henri de
Toulouse-Lautrec)
Monarch of the Glen (1851; Sir Edwin
Landseer)
The Artist's Mother (1871–72; James Abbott
McNeill Whistler)
The Harvest Waggon (1767; Thomas
Gainsborough)
The Last Judgement (1536–41;
Michelangelo)
The Toilet of Venus (1647–51; Diego
Velázquez)
The Watering Place (1777; Thomas
Gainsborough)
Women in the Garden (1866–67; Claude
Monet)

17 Bacchus and Ariadne (c.1523; Titian)
Campbell's Soup Cans (1962; Andy Warhol)
Child Holding a Dove (1902–04; Pablo
Picasso)
Family of Charles IV (1800; Goya)
Grande Odalisque, La (1814; Jean Auguste
Dominique Ingres)
Rain, Steam and Speed (1844; J M W Turner)
The Human Condition (1934/35; René
Magritte)
The Jewish Cemetery (17c; Jacob van
Ruisdael)
The School of Athens (1509–11; Raphael)
The Windmill at Wijk (c.1665; Jacob van
Ruïsdael)

18 36 Views of Mount Fuji (c.1826–33;
Hokusai)
Adoration of the Magi (1481–c.1482;

Leonardo da Vinci/1573; Paolo
Veronese/1619; Diego Velázquez)
Salisbury Cathedral (1823; John Constable)
The Football Players (1908; Henri Rousseau)
The Light of the World (1854; William
Holman Hunt)
The Menaced Assassin (1926; René
Magritte)
The Mills of Gardanne (1885–86; Paul
Cézanne)
The Raft of the Medusa (1819; Théodore
Géricault)
The Seven Sacraments (1640s; Nicolas
Poussin)
The Triumph of Venice (c.1535; Paolo
Veronese)
White on White square (1915; Kazimir
Malevich)
Woman with a Water Jug (c.1658–60; Jan
Vermeer)

19 Dancer Lacing Her Shoe (c.1878; Edgar
Degas)
Impression: Rising Sun (1872; Claude Monet)
Le Déjeuner sur l'herbe (1863; Édouard
Manet)
Peasant Wedding Dance (1566; Pieter
Breughel)
The Blinding of Samson (1636; Rembrandt)
The Boyhood of Raleigh (1870; Sir John
Everett Millais)
The Fate of the Animals (1913; Franz Marc)
The Judgement of Paris (c.1914; Pierre
Auguste Renoir)
The Laughing Cavalier (1624; Frans Hals)
Une Baignade, Asnières (1883–84; Georges
Seurat)

20 Broadway Boogie-Woogie (1942–43; Piet
Mondrian)
Crucifixion of St Peter (1542–50;
Michelangelo)
Madonna of the Long Neck (c.1535;
Parmigiano)
Sacred and Profane Love (c.1515; Titian)
St George and the Dragon (c.1460; Paolo
Uccello)
The Fighting Téméraire (1839; J M W Turner)

21 Assumption of the Virgin (1577; El Greco)
Feast in the House of Levi (1573; Paolo
Veronese)
Girl with a Pearl Earring (17c; Jan Vermeer)
Madonna of the Goldfinch (c.1505;
Raphael)
Temptation of St Anthony (c.15–16c;
Hieronymus Bosch)
The Burial of Count Orgaz (1586; El Greco)
Un Bar aux Folies-Bergère (1881–82;
Édouard Manet)

22 *Impression: soleil levant* (1872; Claude Monet)
  Les Demoiselles d'Avignon, (1906–07; Pablo Picasso)
  The Marriage Feast at Cana (1562–63; Paolo Veronese)
  The Old Woman Cooking Eggs (1618; Diego Velázquez)
  The Persistence of Memory (1931; Salvador Dalí)
  The Resurrection: Cookham (1922–27; Sir Stanley Spencer)

23 *On the Threshold of Liberty* (1930; René Magritte)
  The Avenue at Middelharnis (1689; Meindert Hobbema)
  The Girlhood of Mary Virgin (1849; Dante Gabriel Rossetti)
  The Legend of the Holy Cross (c.1452–c.1466; Piero della Francesca)

24 *Between the Clock and the Bed* (1940; Edvard Munch)
  Christ in the House of Martha (c.1618; Diego Velázquez)
  Christ of St John of the Cross (1951; Salvador Dalí)
  Courtyard of a House in Delft (1658; Pieter de Hooch)
  Experiment with the Air Pump (1768; Joseph Wright)
  The Anatomy Lesson of Dr Tulp (1632; Rembrandt)
  Virgin and Child with St Anne (c.1501–12; Leonardo da Vinci)

25 *Madonna of Burgomaster Meyer* (1526; Hans Holbein the Younger)

  The Return of the Prodigal Son (1669; Rembrandt)
  The Rev Robert Walker Skating (1784; Henry Raeburn)

26 *Christ Reproved by His Parents* (1342; Simone Martini)
  The Garden of Earthly Delights (c.15–16c; Hieronymus Bosch)
  The Resurrection: Port Glasgow (1950; Sir Stanley Spencer)

27 *Sarah Siddons as the Tragic Muse* (1784; Sir Joshua Reynolds)
  The Adoration of the Golden Calf (c.1560; Tintoretto/c.1635; Nicolas Poussin)

28 *Christ in the House of His Parents* (1850; Sir John Everett Millais)
  King Cophetua and the Beggar Maid (1884; Sir Edward Burne-Jones)
  Regents of the Old Men's Alms House (1664; Frans Hals)

30 *L'Embarquement pour l'île de Cythère* (1717; Jean-Antoine Watteau)

32 *The Battle of the Lapiths and Centaurs* (1486; Piero de Cosimo)

34 *Joshua Commanding the Sun to Stand Still* (1816; John Martin)

41 *Arrangement in Grey and Black: the Artist's Mother* (1871–72; James Abbott McNeill Whistler)

44 *Reverend Robert Walker Skating on Duddingston Loch* (1784; Henry Raeburn)

50 *The Banquet of the Officers of the St George Militia Company* (Frans Hals)

Painters, printmakers and other artists include:

03 Arp (Jean; 1887–1966, Alsatian)
  Dix (Otto; 1891–1969, German)
  Ray (Man; 1890–1976, US)

04 Bell (Vanessa; 1879–1961, English)
  Dalí (Salvador; 1904–89, Spanish)
  Doré (Gustave; 1832–83, French)
  Dufy (Raoul; 1877–1953, French)
  Emin (Tracey; 1963– , English)
  Eyck (Jan van; c.1389–1441, Flemish)
  Goya (Francisco de; 1746–1828, Spanish)
  Gris (Juan; 1887–1927, Spanish)
  Hals (Frans; c.1580–1666, Dutch)
  Hunt (Holman; 1827–1910, English)
  John (Augustus; 1878–1961, Welsh)
  John (Gwen; 1876–1939, Welsh)
  Kent (William; 1684–1748, English)
  Klee (Paul; 1879–1940, Swiss)
  Lely (Sir Peter; 1618–1680, British)

  Long (Richard; 1945– , English)
  Marc (Franz; 1880–1916, German)
  Miró (Joán; 1893–1983, Spanish)
  Nash (Paul; 1889–1946, English)
  Watt (Alison; 1965– , Scottish)

05 Bacon (Francis; 1909–92, British)
  Bakst (Léon; 1866–1924, Russian)
  Blake (Peter; 1932– , English)
  Blake (William; 1757–1827, English)
  Bosch (Hieronymus; c.1450–1516, Dutch)
  Brown (Ford Madox; 1821–93, British)
  Burra (Edward; 1905–76, English)
  Clark (Kenneth, Lord; 1903–83, English)
  Corot (Camille; 1796–1875, French)
  David (Jacques Louis; 1748–1825, French)
  Degas (Edgar; 1834–1917, French)
  Dürer (Albrecht; 1471–1528, German)
  Ernst (Max; 1891–1976, German)

Freud (Lucian; 1922– , British)
Gorky (Arshile; 1905–48, US)
Greco (El; 1541–1614, Spanish)
Grosz (George; 1893–1959, US)
Hirst (Damien; 1965– , English)
Homer (Winslow; 1836–1910, US)
Hooch (Pieter de; c.1629–1684, Dutch)
Johns (Jasper; 1930– , US)
Kahlo (Frida; 1907–54, Mexican)
Kitaj (R B; 1932–2007, US)
Klimt (Gustav; 1862–1918, Austrian)
Kline (Franz; 1910–62, US)
Léger (Fernand; 1881–1955, French)
Lewis (Wyndham; 1882–1957, English)
Lippi (Filippino; c.1458–1504, Italian)
Lippi (Fra Filippo; c.1406–69, Italian)
Lowry (L S; 1887–1976, English)
Lucas (Sarah; 1962– , English)
Manet (Édouard; 1832–83, French)
Monet (Claude; 1840–1926, French)
Mucha (Alphonse; 1860–1939, Czech)
Munch (Edvard; 1863–1944, Norwegian)
Nolan (Sir Sidney; 1917–92, Australian)
Peake (Mervyn; 1911–68, English)
Piper (John; 1903–92, English)
Riley (Bridget; 1931– , English)
Sarto (Andrea del; 1486–1531, Italian)

06 Braque (Georges; 1882–1963, French)
Bratby (John; 1928–92, English)
Cadell (Francis C B; 1883–1937, Scottish)
Claude (Claude Le Lorrain; 1600–82, French)
Derain (André; 1880–1954, French)
Escher (Maurits Cornelis; 1898–1972, Dutch)
Fuseli (Henry; 1741–1825, British)
Giotto (di Bondone; c.1267–1337, Italian)
Gordon (Douglas; 1967– , Scottish)
Hunter (Leslie; 1879–1931, Scottish)
Ingres (Jean; 1780–1867, French)
Jarman (Derek; 1942–94, English)
Knight (Dame Laura; 1877–1970, English)
Lavery (Sir John; 1856–1941, British)
Mabuse (Jan; c.1470–1532, Flemish)
Marini (Marino; 1901–80, Italian)
Martin (John; 1789–1854, English)
Massys (Quentin; c.1466–c.1531, Flemish)
Millet (Jean François; 1814–75, French)
Morley (Malcolm; 1931– , English)
Moroni (Giovanni Battista; 1525–78, Italian)
Morris (William; 1834–96, English)
Newman (Barnett; 1905–70, US)
Orozco (José; 1883–1949, Mexican)
Palmer (Samuel; 1805–81, English)
Peploe (Samuel John; 1871–1935, Scottish)
Pisano (Nicola; c.1225–c.1284, Italian)
Ramsay (Allan; 1713–84, Scottish)
Renoir (Pierre Auguste; 1841–1919, French)

Rivera (Diego; 1886–1957, Mexican)
Rothko (Mark; 1903–70, US)
Rubens (Peter Paul; 1577–1640, Flemish)
Scarfe (Gerald; 1936– , English)
Searle (Ronald; 1920– , English)
Seurat (Georges; 1859–91, French)
Sisley (Alfred; 1839–99, French)
Strong (Sir Roy; 1935– , English)
Stubbs (George; 1724–1806, English)
Tanguy (Yves; 1900–55, US)
Tissot (James; 1836–1902, French)
Titian (c.1488–1576, Venetian)
Turner (J M W; 1775–1851, English)
Warhol (Andy; 1928–87, US)
Wilkie (Sir David; 1785–1841, Scottish)
Wright (Joseph; 1734–97, English)

07 Attwell (Mabel Lucie; 1879–1964, English)
Bellini (Giovanni; c.1430–1516, Venetian)
Bonnard (Pierre; 1867–1947, French)
Boucher (François; 1703–70, French)
Cassatt (Mary; 1844–1926, US)
Cézanne (Paul; 1839–1906, French)
Chagall (Marc; 1887–1985, French)
Chapman (Dinos; 1962– , English)
Chapman (Jake; 1966– , English)
Chirico (Giorgio de; 1888–1978, Italian)
Christo (1935– , US)
Cimabué (Giovanni; c.1240–c.1302, Italian)
Courbet (Gustave; 1819–77, French)
Cranach (Lucas, the Elder; 1472–1553, German)
Daumier (Honoré; 1808–78, French)
Delvaux (Paul; 1897–1994, Belgian)
Duchamp (Marcel; 1887–1968, US)
El Greco (1541–1614, Spanish)
Gauguin (Paul; 1848–1903, French)
Guthrie (Sir James; 1859–1930, Scottish)
Hobbema (Meindert; 1638–1709, Dutch)
Hockney (David; 1937– , English)
Hodgkin (Sir Howard; 1932– , English)
Hogarth (William; 1697–1764, English)
Hokusai (Katsushika; 1760–1849, Japanese)
Holbein (Hans, the Younger; 1497–1543, German)
Howison (Peter; 1958– , Scottish)
Keating (Tom; 1917–84, English)
Martini (Simone; c.1284–1344, Italian)
Matisse (Henri; 1869–1954, French)
Millais (Sir John Everett; 1829–96, English)
Morisot (Berthe; 1841–95, French)
O'Keeffe (Georgia; 1887–1986, US)
Pevsner (Antoine; 1886–1962, French)
Picabia (Francis; 1879–1953, French)
Picasso (Pablo; 1881–1973, Spanish)
Pollock (Jackson; 1912–56, US)
Poussin (Nicolas; 1594–1665, French)
Rackham (Arthur; 1867–1939, English)
Raeburn (Sir Henry; 1756–1823, Scottish)

Raphael (Raffaello Sanzio; 1483–1520, Italian)
Sargent (John Singer; 1856–1925, US)
Saville (Jenny; 1970– , English)
Schiele (Egon; 1890–1918, Austrian)
Sickert (Walter; 1860–1942, British)
Spencer (Sir Stanley; 1891–1959, English)
Tenniel (Sir John; 1820–1914, English)
Thurber (James; 1894–1961, US)
Tiepolo (Giovanni; 1696–1770, Italian)
Uccello (Paolo; c.1396–1475, Florentine)
Utrillo (Maurice; 1883–1955, French)
Van Dyck (Sir Anthony; 1599–1641, Flemish)
Vandyke (Sir Anthony; 1599–1641, Flemish)
van Eyck (Jan; c.1389–1441, Flemish)
Van Gogh (Vincent; 1853–90, Dutch)
Vermeer (Jan; 1632–75, Dutch)
Watteau (Antoine; 1684–1721, French)
Wearing (Gillian; 1963– , English)

08 Angelico (Fra; c.1387–1455, Italian)
Annigoni (Pietro; 1910–88, Italian)
Auerbach (Frank; 1931– , British)
Breughel (Jan, the Elder; 1568–1625, Flemish)
Breughel (Pieter, the Younger; c.1564–1638, Flemish)
Brueghel (Jan, the Elder; 1568–1625, Flemish)
Brueghel (Pieter, the Younger; c.1564–1638, Flemish)
Campbell (Steven; 1953–2007, Scottish)
cummings (e e; 1894–1962, US)
Delaunay (Robert; 1885–1941, French)
Dubuffet (Jean; 1901–85, French)
Goncourt (Edmond de; 1822–96, French)
Gossaert (Jan; c.1470–1532, Flemish)
Hamilton (Richard; 1922– , English)
Hilliard (Nicholas; c.1547–1619, English)
Landseer (Sir Edwin; 1802–73, English)
Magritte (René; 1898–1967, Belgian)
Malevich (Kasimir; 1878–1935, Russian)
Mantegna (Andrea; 1431–1506, Italian)
Masaccio (1401–c.1428, Italian)
Mondrian (Piet; 1872–1944, Dutch)
Munnings (Sir Alfred; 1878–1959, English)
Perugino (Pietro; c.1450–1523, Italian)
Piranesi (Giambattista; 1720–78, Italian)
Pissarro (Camille; 1830–1903, French)
Reynolds (Sir Joshua; 1723–92, English)
Rossetti (Dante Gabriel; 1828–82, English)
Rousseau (Henri, 'Le Douanier'; 1844–1910, French)
Rousseau (Théodore; 1812–67, French)
Ruïsdael (Jacob van; c.1628–1682, Dutch)
Ruysdael (Jacob van; c.1628–1682, Dutch)
Topolski (Feliks; 1907–89, British)
Vasarely (Viktor; 1908–97, French)

Veronese (Paolo Caliari; c.1528–88, Venetian)
Vlaminck (Maurice de; 1876–1958, French)
Whistler (James McNeill; 1834–1903, US)

09 Beardsley (Aubrey; 1872–98, English)
Canaletto (1697–1768, Italian)
Carpaccio (Vittore; c.1455–1522, Italian)
Constable (John; 1776–1837, English)
Correggio (Antonio Allegri da; c.1494–1534, Italian)
De Kooning (Willem; 1904–97, US)
Delacroix (Eugène; 1798–1863, French)
Fergusson (John Duncan; 1874–1961, Scottish)
Fragonard (Jean; 1732–1806, French)
Friedrich (Caspar David; 1774–1840, German)
Géricault (Théodore; 1791–1824, French)
Giorgione (c.1478–1511, Italian)
Greenaway (Kate; 1846–1901, English)
Greenaway (Peter; 1942– , English)
Grünewald (Matthias; c.1475–1528, German)
Hiroshige (Ando; 1797–1858, Japanese)
Kandinsky (Wassily; 1866–1944, French)
Kokoschka (Oskar; 1886–1980, British)
Lancaster (Sir Osbert; 1908–86, English)
Nicholson (Ben; 1894–1982, English)
Nollekens (Joseph; 1737–1823, English)
Pisanello (Antonio; 1395–1455, Italian)
Rembrandt (van Rijn; 1606–69, Dutch)
Rodchenko (Aleksandr; 1891–1956, Russian)
Velázquez (Diego; 1599–1660, Spanish)
Vettriano (Jack; 1951– , Scottish)

10 Alma-Tadema (Sir Lawrence; 1836–1912, British)
Botticelli (Sandro; 1445–1510, Florentine)
Burne-Jones (Sir Edward; 1833–98, English)
Caravaggio (Michelangelo Merisi da; 1573–1610, Italian)
Caravaggio (Polidoro da; c.1492–1543, Italian)
Giacometti (Alberto; 1901–66, Swiss)
Modigliani (Amedeo; 1884–1920, Italian)
Motherwell (Robert; 1915–91, US)
Parmigiano (Girolamo Mazzola; 1503–40, Italian)
Sutherland (Graham; 1903–80, English)
Tintoretto (1518–94, Italian)

11 Domenichino (1581–1641, Italian)
Ghirlandaio (Domenico; 1449–94, Italian)

12 Bairnsfather (Bruce; 1888–1959, British)
Fantin-Latour (Henri; 1836–1904, French)
Gainsborough (Thomas; 1727–88, English)
Lichtenstein (Roy; 1923–97, US)

Michelangelo (1475–1564, Italian)
13 Piero di Cosimo (c.1462–c.1521, Italian)
14 Andrea del Sarto (1486–1531, Italian)
Claude Lorraine (1600–82, French)

Lucas Van Leyden (1494–1533, Dutch)
15 Leonardo da Vinci (1452–1519, Italian)
Toulouse-Lautrec (Henri de; 1864–1901, French)

Painting terms include:

04 icon
tint
tone
wash
05 bloom
brush
easel
gesso
mural
paint
pietà
secco
tondo
06 canvas
fresco
frieze
primer
sketch
07 atelier
aureola
aureole
cartoon
collage
diptych
drawing
facture
gallery
gouache

impasto
limning
montage
palette
pastels
paysage
picture
pigment
scumble
sfumato
stipple
tempera
08 abstract
aquatint
bleeding
charcoal
esquisse
fixative
frottage
hard edge
hatching
oil paint
paintbox
pastoral
portrait
seascape
skyscape
thinners
triptych

vignette
09 alla prima
aquarelle
brushwork
capriccio
encaustic
flat brush
grisaille
grotesque
landscape
lay figure
mahlstick
maulstick
miniature
oil colour
polyptych
scumbling
sgraffito
still life
10 art gallery
craquelure
dead colour
figurative
hair-pencil
monochrome
paintbrush
pentimento
pochade box

round brush
sable brush
silhouette
turpentine
11 canvas board
chiaroscuro
composition
fête galante
foreshorten
found object
illusionism
objet trouvé
oil painting
perspective
pointillism
trompe l'oeil
watercolour
12 anamorphosis
brush strokes
camera lucida
filbert brush
illustration
palette knife
pencil sketch
13 fête champêtre
genre painting
underpainting
14 foreshortening

See also **art**; **picture**

palace

Palaces include:

05 Pitti (Italy)
Royal (The Netherlands)
Savoy (England)
06 Louvre (France)
Mirror (Iran)
Potala (Tibet)
Winter (Russia)
07 Bishop's (England)
Crystal (England)
People's (Scotland)
Vatican (Vatican City)
08 Alhambra (Spain)
Blenheim (England)
Borghese (Italy)

Imperial (Japan)
National (Portugal)
St James's (England)
09 Episcopal (Portugal)
Maharaja's (India)
Sans Souci (Germany)
Tuileries (France)
Whitehall (England)
10 Buckingham (England)
El Escorial (Spain)
Fishbourne (England)
Generalife (Spain)
Kensington (England)
Linlithgow (Scotland)
President's (Poland)

Qusayr Amra (Jordan)
Quseir Amra (Jordan)
Schönbrunn (Austria)
Versailles (France)
11 Archbishop's (Portugal)
Umaid Bhawan (India)
Westminster (England)

13 Forbidden City (China)
Holyrood House (Scotland)
Royal Pavilion (England)
Tower of London (England)
Windsor Castle (England)
14 Charlottenburg (Germany)
15 Palais de l'Elysée (France)

palaeontology

Palaeontologists include:

04 Cope (Edward Drinker; 1840–97, US)
Hall (James; 1811–98, US)
Owen (Sir Richard; 1804–92, English)

05 Boule (Marcellin; 1861–1942, French)
Broom (Robert; 1866–1951, South African)
Dollo (Louis; 1857–1931, Belgian)
Foote (Michael J; 1963– , US)
Gould (Stephen Jay; 1941–2002, US)
Leidy (Joseph; 1823–91, US)
Marsh (O C; 1831–99, US)
Romer (Alfred Sherwood; 1894–1973, US)

06 Dubois (Eugène; 1858–1940, Dutch)
Forbes (Edward; 1815–54, British)
Foulke (William Parker; 1816–65, US)
Hallam (Tony; 1933– , English)
Kurtén (Björn; 1924–88, Finnish)
Lartet (Édouard; 1801–71, French)
Leakey (Louis; 1903–72, British)

Leakey (Mary; 1913–96, English)
Leakey (Richard; 1944– , Kenyan)
Osborn (Henry Fairfield; 1857–1935, US)
Zittel (Karl von; 1839–1904, German)

07 Colbert (Edwin 'Ned'; 1905–2001, US)
Mantell (Gideon; 1790–1852, English)
Simpson (George Gaylord; 1902–84, US)

08 Eldredge (Niles; 1943– , US)
Falconer (Hugh; 1808–65, Scottish)
Guettard (Jean Étienne; 1715–86, French)
Johanson (Donald; 1943– , US)
Sepkoski (J John; 1948–99, US)

09 Parkinson (James; 1755–1824, English)
Seilacher (Adolf 'Dolf'; 1925– , German)

10 Williamson (William Crawford; 1816–95, English)

11 Schindewolf (Otto Heinrich; 1896–1971, German)

Terms used in palaeontology include:

03 eon
era
04 Lucy
06 Eocene
Eryops
fossil
ice age
period
tar pit
07 Baltica
bivalve
carpoid
crinoid
hominid
ichnite
Java man
mammoth
Miocene
mollusc
Neogene
Pangaea
Permian
protist

remains
saurian
Vendian
08 agnathan
ammonite
ammonoid
bacteria
Cambrian
Cenozoic
conodont
cromlech
cruziana
Devonian
dinosaur
echinoid
Eoraptor
Gondwana
Jurassic
mastodon
Mesozoic
nautilus
Pliocene
Ponginae

primeval
sauropod
Silurian
skeleton
Tertiary
theropod
Triassic
09 acritarch
arthropod
belemnite
bryophyte
chondrite
coccolith
coprolite
Cro-Magnon
cubichnia
Ediacaran
eukaryote
eumetazoa
fodichnia
homalozoa
ichnolite
ichnology

Iguanodon
Lepidotes
marsupial
Oligocene
ostraderm
Oviraptor
Peking man
placoderm
pterosaur
reliquiae
repichnia
Rhabdodon
sea urchin
subfossil
taphonomy
thecodont
therapsid
trilobite

10 Allosaurus
Archeozoic
Barosaurus
bilaterian
bipedalism
brachiopod
Cretaceous
Diplodocus
echinoderm
graptolite
nanofossil
Nodosaurus
Ordovician
ornithopod
Palaeocene
Palaeogene

Palaeozoic
pascichnia
prokaryote
protohuman
Pteranodon
Quaternary
saurischia
Utahraptor
vertebrate

11 acanthodian
Apatosaurus
Archaeozoic
Archosaurus
asteriacite
ceratopsian
chlorophyte
guide fossil
Hadrosaurus
Homo erectus
Homo habilis
Homo sapiens
ichnofossil
index fossil
macrofossil
microfossil
Microraptor
Neanderthal
Phanerozoic
Precambrian
Protocardia
Stegosaurus
titanothere
trace fossil
Triceratops

12 Ankylosaurus
Burgess shale
chalicothere
Gondwanaland
Homo ergaster
invertebrate
Megalosaurus
palaeobotany
Palaeolithic
Plesiosaurus
stromatolite
type locality
Velociraptor

13 Archaeopteryx
Brachiosaurus
Carboniferous
ornithischian
palaeobiology
palaeoecology
palaeontology
palaeozoology
phytoplankton
Pterodactylus
sedimentology
Thalassinoide
Tyrannosaurus
Zephyrosaurus

14 Giganotosaurus

15 Argentinosaurus
biostratigraphy
Homo rudolfensis
lophotrochozoan
palaeomagnetism

See also **fossil**; **geology**

palm

Palms include:

03 dum
ita
oil
wax

04 atap
coco
date
doom
doum
hemp
nipa
sago

05 areca
assai
bussu

macaw
nikau
peach
royal
Sabal
sugar
toddy

06 buriti
cohune
corozo
Elaeis
gomuti
gru-gru
jupati
kentia

kittul
miriti
raffia
Raphia
rattan
troely

07 babassu
cabbage
calamus
coconut
coquito
Corypha
Euterpe
moriche
palmyra

paxiuba
pupunha
talipat
talipot
troelie
troolie

08 carnauba
coco-tree
date-tree
groo-groo
palmetto

10 Chamaerops

12 chiquichiqui
Washingtonia

15 cabbage-palmetto

pantomime

Pantomimes include:

07 *Aladdin*
Cinders
08 *Peter Pan*
Rapunzel
09 *Pinocchio*
Robin Hood
10 *Cinderella*
11 *Mother Goose*
Old King Cole
Puss in Boots
12 *The Snow Queen*
14 *Babes in the Wood*
Robinson Crusoe
Sleeping Beauty
Treasure Island
15 *Hansel and Gretel*
Rumpelstiltskin

Sinbad the Sailor
The Swan Princess
17 *Alice in Wonderland*
Beauty and the Beast
18 *Jack the Giant Killer*
The Three Musketeers
19 *Jack and the Beanstalk*
Little Red Riding Hood
21 *The Pied Piper of Hamelin*
24 *Dick Whittington and His Cat*
Stromboli the Puppet Master
25 *Ali Baba and the Forty Thieves*
Robin Hood and the Singing Nun
26 *Goldilocks and the Three Bears*
Snow White and the Seven Dwarfs
28 *Alice's Adventures in Wonderland*

Pantomime characters include:

04 Jack *(Babes in the Wood)*
Jack *(Jack and the Beanstalk)*
Jill *(Babes in the Wood)*
05 Giant *(Jack and the Beanstalk)*
Wendy *(Peter Pan)*
06 Beauty *(Beauty and the Beast)*
Gretel *(Hansel and Gretel)*
Hansel *(Hansel and Gretel)*
07 Buttons *(Cinderella)*
Dandini *(Cinderella)*
Emperor *(Aladdin)*
King Rat *(Dick Whittington)*
08 Abanazer *(Aladdin)*
Idle Jack *(Dick Whittington)*
Peter Pan *(Peter Pan)*
The Beast *(Beauty and the Beast)*
09 Alan-a-Dale *(Babes in the Wood/Robin Hood)*
Friar Tuck *(Babes in the Wood/Robin Hood)*
Robin Hood *(Babes in the Wood/Robin Hood)*
10 Billy Goose *(Mother Goose)*
Cinderella *(Cinderella)*
Little John *(Babes in the Wood/Robin Hood)*
Maid Marian *(Babes in the Wood/Robin Hood)*
Maid Marion *(Babes in the Wood/Robin Hood)*
Prince John *(Babes in the Wood/Robin Hood)*

Tinkerbell *(Peter Pan)*
11 Baron Hardup *(Cinderella)*
Captain Hook *(Peter Pan)*
Daisy the Cow *(Jack and the Beanstalk)*
Jack's Mother *(Jack and the Beanstalk)*
King Richard *(Babes in the Wood/Robin Hood)*
Mother Goose *(Mother Goose)*
Simple Simon *(Jack and the Beanstalk)*
Will Scarlet *(Babes in the Wood/Robin Hood)*
12 Pantomime Cow
Principal Boy
Sarah the Cook *(Dick Whittington)*
Widow Twankey *(Aladdin)*
Will Scarlett *(Babes in the Wood/Robin Hood)*
Wishee Washee *(Aladdin)*
13 Principal Girl
14 Baroness Hardup *(Cinderella)*
Fairy Godmother *(Cinderella/Sleeping Beauty)*
Pantomime Horse
Prince Charming *(Cinderella/Sleeping Beauty)*
Princess Aurora *(Sleeping Beauty)*
Slave of the Ring *(Aladdin)*
The Ugly Sisters *(Cinderella)*
15 Alice Fitzwarren *(Dick Whittington)*
Princess Jasmine *(Aladdin)*
Rumpelstiltskin *(Rumpelstiltskin)*

See also **mythology**

paper

Papers include:

03 art	**05** crêpe	vellum	recycled
rag	graph	**07** manilla	wrapping
04 bank	sugar	papyrus	**09** cardboard
bond	**06** carbon	tracing	cartridge
card	manila	writing	parchment
note	silver	**08** acid-free	**10** pasteboard
rice	tissue	blotting	**11** greaseproof
wall	toilet	handmade	

Paper sizes include:

02 A0	**04** demy	legal	**08** elephant
A1	post	royal	foolscap
A2	pott	**06** letter	imperial
A3	**05** atlas	medium	**09** antiquary
A4	crown	quarto	music-demy
A5	folio	**07** emperor	**10** super-royal
03 pot	jésus		

See also **Japan**

Paralympic Games

Summer Paralympic venues:

04 Rome (Italy; 1960)
05 Seoul (South Korea; 1988)
Tokyo (Japan; 1964)
06 Arnhem (The Netherlands; 1980)
Athens (Greece; 2004)
Sydney (Australia; 2000)
07 Atlanta (USA; 1996)

Beijing (China; 2008)
New York (USA; 1984)
Tel Aviv (Israel; 1968)
Toronto (Canada; 1976)
09 Barcelona (Spain; 1992)
10 Heidelberg (West Germany; 1972)
15 Stoke Mandeville (UK; 1952/1984)

Summer Paralympic events include:

04 epée	marathon	4×100m relay
foil	road race	4×400m relay
judo	shooting	table tennis
05 sabre	swimming	**12** 10m air pistol
06 boccia	**09** 100 metres	1km time trial
discus	200 metres	50m butterfly
rowing	400 metres	50m free rifle
07 archery	800 metres	50m freestyle
cycling	athletics	double sculls
javelin	coxed four	powerlifting
sailing	**10** 1500 metres	single sculls
shot put	3000 metres	tandem sprint
08 dressage	5000 metres	**13** 100m butterfly
goalball	equestrian	100m freestyle
high jump	pentathlon	200m freestyle
keelboat	triple jump	400m freestyle
long jump	volleyball	50m backstroke
	11 10,000 metres	50m free pistol

50m sport rifle
14 100m backstroke
25m sport pistol

football 5-a-side
football 7-a-side
tandem road race

15 50m breaststroke
wheelchair rugby

Winter Paralympic venues:

05 Geilo (Norway; 1980)
Turin (Italy; 2006)

06 Nagano (Japan; 1998)

09 Innsbruck (Austria; 1984/1988)

11 Albertville (France; 1992)
Lillehammer (Norway; 1994)

12 Örnsköldsvik (Sweden; 1976)
Salt Lake City (USA; 2002)

Winter Paralympic events include:

05 relay

06 slalom
super-G

08 biathlon
downhill

10 sled hockey

11 giant slalom

12 alpine skiing
cross-country
long distance

Nordic skiing
sledge hockey

13 short distance

14 middle distance

15 ice sledge hockey

Paralympic athletes include:

04 Toit (Natalie du; 1984– , South African)
Weir (David; 1979– , English)

05 Innes (Caroline; 1974– , Scottish)

06 Holmes (Chris; 1971– , English)

07 Jackson (Simon; 1972– , English)
McEleny (Maggi; 1965– , Scottish)
Sauvage (Louise; 1973– , Australian)

08 Anderson (James 'Jim the Swim'; 1963– , Scottish)
Simmonds (Eleanor; 1994– , English)
Thatcher (Noel; 1966– , English)

09 Tesoriero (Paula; 1975– , New Zealand)

12 Grey-Thompson (Dame Tanni; 1969– , Welsh)

parasite

Parasites include:

03 bot
ked
nit

04 bott
chat
crab
flea
kade
mite
tick

05 fluke

06 chigoe
chigre
cootie
jigger

07 argulus
ascarid
ascaris
Babesia
bonamia
cestode
chalcid
chigger
Giardia
pinworm

08 hookworm
itch-mite
lungworm
nematode
sheep ked

strongyl
tapeworm
toxocara
whipworm

09 Bilharzia
bird louse
crab louse
fish louse
fluke-worm
head louse
pediculus
roundworm
sheep tick
sporozoan
strongyle

trematode

10 Guinea worm
Plasmodium
threadworm

11 biting louse
sarcocystis
scabies mite
trichomonad
trypanosome

12 echinococcus
ectoparasite
endoparasite
semiparasite

13 hyperparasite

parasol *see* umbrella

Paris

Paris districts include:

05 Bercy
   Opéra
06 Étoile
   Louvre
   Marais
07 Pigalle
08 Bastille
   Chaillot
   Left Bank
   Sorbonne

09 Chinatown
   La Défense
   Les Halles
   Right Bank
   Trocadero
   Tuileries
10 Belleville
   La Villette
   Montmartre
   Rive Droite
   Rive Gauche

   Tour Eiffel
11 Batignolles
12 Latin Quarter
   Les Invalides
   Montparnasse
   Place d'Italie
13 Champs Élysées
   Quartier Latin
15 Butte-aux-cailles
   Neuilly-sur-Seine

Paris streets include:

07 Pigalle
09 Port Royal
   Rue de Buci
   Rue de Rome
10 Avenue Foch
   Quai d'Orsay
   Rue d'Alésia
11 Rue Dauphine
   Rue de Clichy
   Rue de Rennes
   Rue de Rivoli

   Rue de Sèvres
   Rue des Levis
   Rue Mazarine
   Rue St-Honoré
12 périphérique
   Place d'Italie
   Place Vendôme
   Quai de la Gare
   Quai du Louvre
   Quai Voltaire
   Rue de Paradis

   Rue François I
   Rue St-Antoine
13 Avenue George V
   Place du Tertre
   Rue des Rosiers
   Rue Mouffetard
14 Place des Vosges
   Rue de Chevalier
   Rue de Richelieu
15 Avenue Montaigne
   Quai d'Austerlitz

Paris landmarks include:

04 Dôme
05 Géode
   Seine
06 Bourse
   Louvre
07 Pyramid
08 Bastille
   Panthéon
   Pont Neuf
   Sorbonne
09 Beaubourg
   Bon Marché
   Invalides
   Madeleine
   Notre-Dame
   Orangerie
   St-Severin
   St-Sulpice
   Trocadero
   Tuileries
10 Carnavalet
   Gare du Nord

   Île St-Louis
   Longchamps
   Montmartre
   Musée Rodin
   Sacré Coeur
11 Champ de Mars
   Eiffel Tower
   Grande Arche
   Grand Palais
   Île de la Cité
   Moulin Rouge
   Musée d'Orsay
   Palais Royal
   Parc Monceau
   Petit Palais
   Pont des Arts
12 Conciergerie
   Église du Dôme
   Hôtel de Rohan
   Hôtel de Ville
   Musée de Cluny
   Musée Picasso
   Opéra Garnier
   Porte Maillot

13 Arc de Triomphe
   Champs-Élysées
   Les Catacombes
   Napoleon's tomb
   Opéra Bastille
   Pont Alexandre
14 Arènes de Lutèce
   Bois de Boulogne
   École Militaire
   Forum des Halles
   Hôtel de Soubise
   Maison de Balzac
   Palais du Louvre
   Parc des Princes
   Parc Montsouris
   Place de l'Étoile
   Pompidou Centre
   Sainte Chapelle
15 Bois de Vincennes
   Cité des Sciences
   Le Stade de France
   Musée Carnavalet
   Palais de Justice

park

Park types include:

03 car
fun

04 ball
deer
wind

05 coach
theme
water

06 oyster
pocket
public
retail
safari

07 caravan
country
holiday

hunting
science
terrain
trailer

08 business
national
research
wildlife

09 adventure
amusement

10 industrial
skateboard
technology
vest-pocket
zoological

14 multistorey car

Parks include:

04 Hyde (England/Australia)
West (South Africa)

05 Green (England)
Güell (Spain)
Kings (Australia)

06 Albert (Australia)
Domain (Australia)

07 Battery (USA)

Central (USA)
Phoenix (Ireland)
Regent's (England)
Stanley (Canada)

08 Gramercy (USA)
Richmond (England)
St James's (England)
Victoria (Australia)

09 Battersea (England)

Tuileries (France)

10 Tiergarten (Germany)

11 Champ de Mars (France)
Vienna Woods (Austria)

13 Madison Square (USA)
Tivoli Gardens (Denmark)

14 Bois de Boulogne (France)

15 Bois de Vincennes (France)

National parks in the UK include:

06 Exmoor (1954; moorland/coastline)

08 Dartmoor (1951; moorland)

09 New Forest (2005; woodland)
Snowdonia (1951; mountains/valleys)
The Broads (1989; waterways/fens)

10 Cairngorms (2003; mountains/moorland/
forest)
Loch Lomond (2002; lochs/mountains)

12 Lake District (1951; mountains/valleys/
glaciated lakes)
Peak District (1951; moorland/dales)

13 Brecon Beacons (1957; mountains/valleys)

14 Northumberland (1956; hills)
North York Moors (1952; woodland/
moorland)
Yorkshire Dales (1954; dales)

National parks and nature reserves worldwide include:

03 Gir (India)

04 Manu (Peru)
Waza (Cameroon)
Yoho (Canada)
Zion (USA)

05 Banff (Canada)
Chaco (Argentina)
El Rey (Argentina)
Fundy (Canada)
Kafue (Zambia)
Mt Apo (Philippines)
Royal (Australia)
Sarek (Sweden)
Swiss (Switzerland)
Tatra (Czech Republic/Poland)
Tikal (Guatemala)
Tsavo (Kenya)
Uluru (Australia)

06 Abisko (Sweden)
Acadia (USA)
Angkor (Cambodia)
Arches (USA)
Burren (Ireland)
Denali (USA)
Doñana (Spain)
Egmont (New Zealand)
Etosha (Namibia)
Iguaçu (Brazil/Argentina)
Iguazú (Brazil/Argentina)
Jasper (Canada)
Kakadu (Australia)
Katmai (USA)
Kruger (South Africa)
Mt Cook (New Zealand)
Muddus (Sweden)
Phu Rua (Thailand)
Wolong (China)

07 Bicayne (USA)
Big Bend (USA)
Canaima (Venezuela)
Chitwan (Nepal)
Corbett (India)
Gemsbok (Botswana)
Glacier (USA)
Khao Yai (Thailand)
Nairobi (Kenya)
Olympic (USA)
Paparoa (New Zealand)
Rakiura (New Zealand)
Redwood (USA)
Saguaro (USA)
Sequoia (USA)
Toubkal (Morocco)
Urewera (New Zealand)
Virunga (Democratic Republic of the Congo)

08 Amazonia (Brazil)
Badlands (USA)
Camargue (France)
Kinabalu (Malaysia)
Kootenay (Canada)
Rwenzori (Uganda)
Taranaki (New Zealand)
Westland (New Zealand)
Wind Cave (USA)
Yosemite (USA)

09 Carnarvon (Australia)
Connemara (Ireland)
Fiordland (New Zealand)
Galápagos (Ecuador)
Glenveagh (Ireland)
Kahurangi (New Zealand)
Kaziranga (India)
Killarney (Ireland)
Kosciusko (Australia)
Lake Clark (USA)
Mesa Verde (USA)
Mt Olympus (Greece)
Mt Rainier (USA)
Ruwenzori (Uganda)
Serengeti (Tanzania)
The Burren (Ireland)
Tongariro (New Zealand)
Voyageurs (USA)
Whanganui (New Zealand)

10 Abel Tasman (New Zealand)
Crater Lake (USA)
Everglades (USA)
Glacier Bay (USA)
Hoge Veluwe (The Netherlands)

See also **World Heritage site**

Hot Springs (USA)
Joshua Tree (USA)
Mercantour (France)
Mt Aspiring (New Zealand)
Ngorongoro (Tanzania)
Sagarmatha (Nepal)
Shenandoah (USA)
Tai Poutini (New Zealand)
Ujung-Kulon (Indonesia)

11 Arthur's Pass (New Zealand)
Bialowieski (Poland)
Bryce Canyon (USA)
Canyonlands (USA)
Daisetsuzan (Japan)
Death Valley (USA)
Grand Canyon (USA)
Heron Island (Australia)
Kenai Fjords (USA)
Kilimanjaro (Tanzania)
Kobuk Valley (USA)
Mammoth Cave (USA)
Nelson Lakes (New Zealand)
Pfälzerwald (Germany)
Tumucumaque (Brazil)
Wood Buffalo (Canada)
Yellowstone (USA)

12 Gammon Ranges (Australia)
Gran Paradiso (Italy)
Komodo Island (Indonesia)
Los Glaciares (Argentina/Chile)
Popocatépetl (Mexico)
Warrumbungle (Australia)
Wooroonooran (Australia)

13 Blue Mountains (Australia)
Fuji-Hakone-Izu (Japan)
Namib-Naukluft (Namibia)
North Cascades (USA)
Rocky Mountain (USA)
Royal National (Australia)
Victoria Falls (Zimbabwe/Zambia)
Virgin Islands (USA)
Waterton Lakes (Canada)

14 Altos de Campana (Panama)
Great Sand Dunes (USA)
Hardangervidda (Norway)
Lassen Volcanic (USA)
Tierra del Fuego (Argentina)
Uluru-Kata Tjuta (Australia)

15 Carlsbad Caverns (USA)
Hawaii Volcanoes (USA)
Petrified Forest (USA)
Wrangell-St Elias (USA)

parliament

Parliament types include:

04 diet
duma
moot

05 boule
douma
gemot
jirga

06 majlis
senate

07 commons

08 assembly
congress

09 volksraad

10 consistory
lower house
upper house

12 lower chamber
upper chamber

14 Council of State

15 House of Assembly

Parliaments, political assemblies and venues include:

02 EP
HK
HP

04 Dáil (Ireland)
Diet (Japan)
Duma (Russia)
Keys (Isle of Man)
Long (England)
Pnyx (Ancient Athens)
Rump (England)
Sejm (Poland)

05 boule (Greece)
gemot (Anglo-Saxons)
Lords (UK)
Porte (Turkey)

06 Cortes (Portugal/Spain)
kgotla (Botswana)
Majlis (Iran)
Mejlis (Iran)
Seanad (Ireland)
Senate (Australia/Canada/France/USA)
Senato (Italy)

07 Althing (Iceland)
comitia (Ancient Rome)
Commons (UK)
Knesset (Israel)
Lagting (Norway/Faroe Islands)
Landtag (Germany)
Rigsdag (Denmark)
Riksdag (Sweden)
Tynwald (Isle of Man)
zemstvo (Russia)

08 Congress (USA)
ecclesia (Ancient Athens)
European (European Union)
folkmoot (Anglo-Saxons)
Imperial (UK)
Lagthing (Norway/Faroe Islands)
Lok Sabha (India)
Scottish (Scotland)
Sobranje (Bulgaria)

Sobranye (Bulgaria)
Stannary (Cornish tinners)
Storting (Norway)

09 Bundesrat (Austria/Germany/Switzerland)
Bundestag (Germany)
Eduskunta (Finland)
Folketing (Denmark)
Landsting (Denmark)
Loya Jirga (Afghanistan)
Odelsting (Norway)
Reichsrat (Germany)
Reichstag (Germany)
Skupstina (Serbia/Montenegro/Yugoslavia)
Ständerat (Switzerland)
State Duma (Russia)

10 Bundesrath (Austria/Germany/Switzerland)
Landsthing (Denmark)
Odelsthing (Norway)
Oireachtas (Ireland)
Rajya Sabha (India)
Reichsrath (Germany)
Skupshtina (Serbia/Montenegro/Yugoslavia)
St Stephen's (UK)

11 Dáil Eireann (Ireland)
House of Keys (Isle of Man)
Nationalrat (Austria/Switzerland)
Volkskammer (German Democratic
Republic)
Westminster (UK)

12 House of Lords (UK)

13 House of States (India)
Seanad Eireann (Ireland)
States General (The Netherlands)
Supreme Soviet (USSR)
Welsh Assembly (Wales)

14 House of Commons (UK/Canada)
Staten-Generaal (The Netherlands)

15 Council of States
House of Assembly (South Africa)
People's Assembly (Egypt)

See also **politics**

parrot

Parrots include:

03 fig	conure	paroquet	Psittacus
kea	kakapo	Pesquet's	Stringops
04 grey	Nestor	Strigops	**10** budgerigar
kaka	**07** corella	**09** cockateel	ring-necked
lory	hanging	cockatiel	**11** African grey
05 galah	rosella	green leek	night-parrot
macaw	**08** cockatoo	owl-parrot	shell parrot
pygmy	lorikeet	paraquito	**13** Major Mitchell
06 Amazon	lovebird	parrakeet	shell parakeet
budgie	parakeet	parroquet	zebra parakeet
		parrotlet	

particle *see* **atom**

parts of speech *see* **grammar**

party

Parties include:

02 do	hangi	New Year	reception
03 hen	**06** dinner	potluck	sleepover
key	drinks	slumber	stag night
tea	garden	**08** barbecue	welcoming
04 bash	grog-on	birthday	**10** baby shower
foam	hooley	bunfight	fancy dress
orgy	picnic	cocktail	hootenanny
rave	pyjama	farewell	**11** discotheque
stag	social	surprise	flat-warming
toga	soirée	**09** acid-house	**12** bridal shower
wrap	supper	beanfeast	house-warming
05 beano	**07** ceilidh	Christmas	**13** cheese and wine
disco	knees-up	Hallowe'en	
	leaving	hootnanny	

Political parties in the UK include:

03 BNP	**05** Green	**09** Communist	**13** National Front
DUP	**06** Labour	**10** Democratic	Parliamentary
PLP	Lib Dem	Plaid Cymru	Scottish Green
PUP	**07** Liberal	Republican	**14** Militant Labour
SNP	Veritas	UK Unionist	UK Independence
SSP	**08** Alliance	**11** Co-operative	Ulster Unionist
SWP	Sinn Féin	**12** Conservative	**15** British National
04 SDLP			Popular Alliance

Political parties worldwide include:

02 AN (Italy)	NDP (Canada)	Green (USA)
FN (France)	NPD (Canada)	**06** Labour (Ireland)
PP (Spain)	UMP (France)	**08** Batasuna (Spain)
03 ALP (Australia)	**04** PSOE (Spain)	Democrat (USA)
CDU (Germany)	**05** Green (Ireland)	Fine Gael (Ireland)

Sinn Féin (Ireland)
09 One Nation (Australia)
Socialist (Ireland)
10 Fianna Fáil (Ireland)
See also **game**; **politics**

Republican (USA)
12 Workers' Party (Ireland)
13 Bloc Québécois (Canada)
Front National (France)

National Front (France)
14 Partido Popular (Spain)

party game *see* **game**

pass *see* **mountain**

passage

Passages include:

04 Mona (Puerto Rico/Dominican Republic)
05 Drake (Antarctica)
Gaspé (Canada)
Umnak (Aleutian Islands, USA)
06 Akutan (Aleutian Islands, USA)
Amukta (Aleutian Islands, USA)
Burias (Philippines)
Caicos (The Bahamas)
Colvos (USA)
Mompog (Philippines)
Seguam (Aleutian Islands, USA)
Unimak (Aleutian Islands, USA)
07 Oronsay (Scotland)
Palawan (Philippines)
08 Amchitka (Aleutian Islands, USA)
Dominica (Dominica/Martinique)

Fenimore (Aleutian Islands, USA)
Mouchoir (The Bahamas)
Saratoga (USA)
Windward (Cuba/Haiti)
09 Deception (USA)
Mayaguana (The Bahamas)
St Vincent (St Vincent/St Lucia)
10 Backstairs (Australia)
Guadeloupe (Guadeloupe/Montserrat)
Martinique (Martinique/Dominica)
Mira Por Vos (The Bahamas)
Silver Bank (The Bahamas)
11 Turks Island (The Bahamas)
Verde Island (Philippines)
13 Crooked Island (The Bahamas)
14 Jacques Cartier (Canada)

pasta

Pasta includes:

04 orza
zite
ziti
05 penne
ruoti
06 anelli
ditali
noodle
trofie
07 fusilli
gnocchi
lasagna
lasagne
lumache
mafalde
maruzze
mezzani
noodles

pennine
ravioli
08 bucatini
farfalle
fedelini
linguine
linguini
macaroni
rigatoni
stelline
09 agnolotti
angel hair
casarecci
crescioni
fettucine
fettucini
fiochetti
manicotti

spaghetti
10 angel's hair
bombolotti
cannelloni
conchiglie
farfalline
fettuccine
strangozzi
tagliarini
taglierini
tortellini
vermicelli
11 cappelletti
pappardelle
tagliatelle
12 lasagne verde
noodle farfel
13 elbow macaroni

Pasta dishes include:

07 lasagna	**08** marinara	manicotti	puttanesca
lasagne	tortelli	spaghetti	**14** macaroni cheese
ravioli	**09** arrabiata	**10** cannelloni	
spag bol	carbonara	minestrone	

pastime *see* **hobby**

pastry

Pastry includes:

04 filo	sweet	suetcrust	**12** biscuit-crumb
flan	**06** cheese	**10** pâte brisée	pâte à savarin
puff	Danish	pâte frolle	**13** American crust
05 choux	**07** pork-pie	pâte sablée	hot-water crust
flaky	**08** one-stage	pâte sucrée	**14** rich shortcrust
plain	**09** rough-puff	shortcrust	
short		wholewheat	

See also **cake**

patriarch

Patriarchs include:

04 Levi	Abram	Jacob	Ishmael
Noah	Enoch	**06** Joseph	**10** Methuselah
05 Aaron	Isaac	**07** Abraham	Theophilus

patron saint *see* **saint**

peace *see* **Nobel Prize**

pear

Pear varieties include:

04 musk	poprin	blanquet	poppering
05 nelis	seckel	muscadel	**10** conference
06 beurré	seckle	muscatel	jargonelle
Colmar	warden	Williams	**11** bon chrétien
comice	**07** poperin	**09** Catherine	queez-maddam
nelies	**08** bergamot	muscadine	**12** cuisse-madame

peninsula

Peninsulas include:

04 Ards (Northern Ireland)	Gower (Wales)
Cape (South Africa)	Italy (Italy)
Eyre (Australia)	Lleyn (Wales)
Gyda (Russia)	Malay (Malaysia)
Huon (Papua New Guinea)	Otago (New Zealand)
Kola (Russia)	Qatar (Qatar)
05 Gaspé (Canada)	Sinai (Egypt)

06 Alaska (USA)
Avalon (Canada)
Azuero (Panama)
Balkan (Eastern Europe)
Carnac (France)
Crimea (Ukraine)
Iberia (Portugal/Spain)
Istria (Croatia/Slovenia)
Jaffna (Sri Lanka)
Korean (North Korea/South Korea)
Recife (Brazil)
Seward (USA)
Taymyr (Russia)
Wirral (England)

07 Alaskan (USA)
Arabian (Middle East)
Cape Cod (USA)
Chukchi (Russia)
Florida (USA)
Furness (England)
Iberian (Portugal/Spain)
Jiulong (Hong Kong)
Jutland (Denmark)
Kintyre (Scotland)
Kowloon (Hong Kong)

See also **cape**

Olympic (USA)
Yucatán (Mexico)

08 Apsheron (Azerbaijan)
Cape York (Australia)
Cotentin (Normandy)
Musandam (Oman)
Pinellas (USA)
Sorrento (Italy)
Yorktown (USA)

09 Cape Verde (Senegal)
Gallipoli (Turkey)
Kamchatka (Russia)
Paraguana (Venezuela)
Peary Land (Greenland)

10 Arnhem Land (Australia)
Graham Land (Antarctica)
Isle of Dogs (England)
Nova Scotia (Canada)

11 Peloponnese (Greece)

12 Scandinavian (Scandinavia)

14 Baja California (Mexico)
Isle of Portland (England)

15 Rinns of Galloway (Scotland)

people

Peoples include:

03 Han (China)
Ibo (Nigeria)
Jat (India/Pakistan)
Kru (Liberia)
Mam (Guatemala)
Mon (Myanmar/Thailand)
San (South Africa)
Tiv (Nigeria)
Twi (Ghana)

04 Ainu (Japan)
Cham (Vietnam/Cambodia)
Efik (Nigeria)
Goth (Germanic)
Hutu (Rwanda/Burundi)
Igbo (Nigeria)
Jute (Germanic)
Kroo (Liberia)
Lett (Latvia)
Moor (North Africa)
Motu (Papua New Guinea)
Nair (India)
Nupe (Nigeria)
Roma (Europe)
Saba (Yemen)
Shan (Asia)
Sulu (Philippines)

Susu (West Africa)
Tshi (Ghana)
Zulu (South Africa)

05 Bajau (Malaysia)
Bantu (Africa)
Hausa (Nigeria)
Iceni (Britain)
Inuit (Arctic)
Karen (Myanmar)
Khmer (Cambodia)
Maori (New Zealand)
Masai (Africa)
Nayar (India)
Nguni (South/East Africa)
Oriya (India)
Saxon (German)
Swazi (Swaziland)
Taino (West Indies)
Tamil (India/Sri Lanka)
Temne (Sierra Leone)
Tonga (Africa)
Tutsi (Rwanda/Burundi)
Vedda (Sri Lanka)
Wolof (West Africa)
Yakut (Russia)
Yupik (Arctic)

06 Angles (Germanic)
   Aymara (South America)
   Griqua (South Africa)
   Gurkha (Nepal)
   Herero (Namibia)
   Innuit (Arctic)
   Kabyle (North Africa)
   Kalmyk (China/Russia)
   Kikuyu (Kenya)
   Manchu (China)
   Nyanja (Malawi)
   Ostiak (Russia)
   Ostyak (Russia)
   Sherpa (Nepal)
   Tswana (Botswana)
   Tungus (Russia)
   Yoruba (West Africa)
   Zyrian (Russia)
07 Barotse (Zambia)
   Basotho (Lesotho)
   Calmuck (China/Russia)
   Cossack (Russia)

   Goorkha (Nepal)
   Hittite (Syria)
   Kalmuck (China/Russia)
   Manchoo (China)
   Maratha (India)
   Pashtun (Afghanistan)
   Quechua (Peru)
   Quichua (Peru)
   Samoyed (Russia)
   Swahili (Africa)
   Tagálog (Philippines)
   Walloon (Belgium)
08 Khoikhoi (South Africa)
   Mahratta (India)
   Polabian (Slavonic)
   Yanomami (Brazil/Venezuela)
09 Himyarite (Yemen)
   Ostrogoth (Germanic)
   Ruthenian (Ukraine)
   Sinhalese (Sri Lanka)
   Tocharian (Asia)
   Tokharian (Asia)

See also **aborigine**; **Africa**; **The Americas**; **Asia**

pepper

Pepper and peppercorns include:

03 red	green	07 cayenne	habañero
04 bird	sweet	Jamaica	jalapeño
pink	white	paprika	pimiento
05 black	06 cherry	pimento	piquillo
chile	chilli	08 allspice	
chili	yellow	capsicum	12 Scotch bonnet

period *see* **geology**; **history**; **time**

pet

Pets include:

03 cat	05 goose	jerboa	parakeet
cow	horse	lizard	terrapin
dog	llama	parrot	tortoise
pig	mouse	rabbit	09 guinea pig
rat	sheep	turtle	tarantula
04 bird	06 alpaca	07 chicken	10 budgerigar
fish	canary	hamster	chinchilla
goat	donkey	08 chipmunk	salamander
newt	ferret	cyberpet	virtual pet
pony	gerbil	goldfish	11 stick insect

See also **cat**; **dog**; **fish**; **horse**; **parrot**; **rabbit**

Petrarch (1304–74)

Significant works include:

06 *Africa* (1338–42)
08 *Secretum* (c.1343–58)
10 *Canzoniere* (1327–74)

15 *De vita solitaria* (c.1346–56)
27 *De remediis utriusque fortunae* (c.1354–60)

philately

Famous and rare stamps include:

08 Bull's eye
    Penny Red
09 Basel dove
    Penny Blue
10 Mount Athos

    Penny Black
    Red Mercury
    Scinde Dawk
    VR official
11 Jenny invert

    St Louis bear
12 Inverted swan
13 Black Honduras
    Inverted Jenny
    Uganda Cowries

Philately terms include:

02 NH
    OC
    OG
03 gum
    NVI
04 coil
    pair
    pane
    used
05 block
    cover
    flown
    grill
    hinge
    mount
    stamp
06 cachet
    cancel
    cliché
    crease
    entire
    gutter
    invert

    matrix
    unused
07 Machins
    perfins
    selvage
    Smilers
    tagging
08 centring
    line pair
    multiple
    postmark
    selvedge
    se-tenant
    stamp pen
    thematic
09 approvals
    backstamp
    catalogue
    face value
    handstamp
    regionals
    watermark
10 gutter pair

    rouletting
    semipostal
    stamp album
    stamp tongs
    stocksheet
11 imperforate
    maximaphily
    never hinged
    original gum
12 cancellation
    denomination
13 commemorative
    first day cover
    generic stamps
    mint condition
    original cover
    souvenir sheet
14 controlled mail
    miniature sheet
15 greetings stamps
    magnifying glass
    stamp collecting

philosophy

Branches of philosophy include:

03 law
04 mind
05 logic
    moral
06 ethics
07 biology
    eastern

    history
    science
08 axiology
    language
    medicine
    ontology
    politics
    religion

09 bioethics
    economics
    education
    semiotics
10 aesthetics
    literature
    psychology

11 informatics
    mathematics
    metaphysics
12 epistemology
13 applied ethics
    jurisprudence
    phenomenology

Philosophical schools, doctrines and theories include:

05 deism

06 egoism
monism
Taoism
theism

07 atheism
atomism
dualism
fideism
Marxism
realism
Thomism

08 altruism
ascetism
cynicism
fatalism
feminism
hedonism
humanism
idealism
nihilism
Stoicism

09 dogmatism
pantheism
Platonism
pluralism

solipsism

10 absolutism
Eleaticism
empiricism
gnosticism
Kantianism
naturalism
nominalism
positivism
pragmatism
Pyrrhonism
relativism
scepticism

11 agnosticism
determinism
Hegelianism
historicism
materialism
objectivism
rationalism
Sankhya-Yoga

12 behaviourism
Cartesianism
Confucianism
Epicureanism
essentialism

Neoplatonism
reductionism
subjectivism

13 antinomianism
conceptualism
descriptivism
immaterialism
Neo-Kantianism
occasionalism
phenomenalism
scholasticism
structuralism

14 existentialism
interactionism
intuitionalism
libertarianism
Nyaya-Vaisesika
prescriptivism
Pythagoreanism
sensationalism
utilitarianism
Vedanta-Mimamsa

15 Aristotelianism
experimentalism
Frankfurt School
instrumentalism

Philosophers include:

04 Ayer (Sir A J; 1910–89, English)
Bain (Alexander; 1818–1903, Scottish)
Hick (John; 1922–   , English)
Hook (Sidney; 1902–89, US)
Hume (David; 1711–76, Scottish)
Joad (C E M; 1891–1953, English)
Kant (Immanuel; 1724–1804, German)
Kuhn (Thomas; 1922–96, US)
Marx (Karl; 1818–83, German)
Mill (Harriet Taylor; 1807–58, English)
Mill (James; 1773–1836, Scottish)
Mill (John Stuart; 1806–73, English)
More (Henry; 1614–87, English)
Otto (Rudolf; 1869–1937, German)
Reid (Thomas; 1710–96, Scottish)
Ryle (Gilbert; 1900–76, English)
Vico (Giambattista; 1668–1744, Italian)
Weil (Simone; 1909–43, French)
Wolf (Christian von; 1679–1754, German)

05 Amiel (Henri Frédéric; 1821–81, Swiss)
Bacon (Francis, Lord; 1561–1626, English)
Bacon (Roger; c.1214–92, English)
Bayle (Pierre; 1647–1706, French)
Benda (Julien; 1867–1956, French)
Bodin (Jean; c.1530–96, French)
Broad (Charlie Dunbar; 1887–1971, English)

Bruno (Giordano; 1548–1600, Italian)
Buber (Martin; 1878–1965, Austrian)
Burke (Edmund; 1729–97, Irish)
Burke (Kenneth; 1897–1992, US)
Burks (Arthur; 1915–2008, US)
Cohen (Hermann; 1842–1912, German)
Comte (Auguste; 1798–1857, French)
Croce (Benedetto; 1866–1952, Italian)
Dewey (John; 1859–1952, US)
Duhem (Pierre; 1861–1916, French)
Dunne (John William; 1875–1949, English)
Frege (Gottlob; 1848–1925, German)
Gödel (Kurt; 1906–78, Czech/US)
Hegel (Georg Wilhelm Friedrich; 1770–1831, German)
Hulme (T E; 1883–1917, English)
Iqbal (Sir Muhammad; 1875–1938, Indian)
James (William; 1842–1910, US)
Kames (Henry Home, Lord; 1696–1782, Scottish)
Kindi (al-; c.800–c.870, Arab)
Laozi (6c BC, Chinese)
Lewis (Hywel; 1910–92, Welsh)
Locke (John; 1632–1704, English)
Lotze (Rudolf; 1817–81, German)
Moore (G E; 1873–1958, English)

Nagel (Ernest; 1901–85, Czech/US)
Nagel (Thomas; 1937– , Yugoslav/US)
Occam (William of; c.1285–c.1349, English)
Plato (c.428–c.348 BC, Greek)
Price (H H; 1899–1985, Welsh)
Price (Richard; 1723–91, Welsh)
Quine (William Van Orman; 1908–2000, US)
Rawls (John; 1921–2002, US)
Rhees (Rush; 1905–89, US)
Rorty (Richard McKay; 1931–2007, US)
Royce (Josiah; 1855–1916, US)
Smith (Adam; 1723–90, Scottish)
Sorel (Georges; 1847–1922, French)
Stein (Edith; 1891–1942, German)
Stout (George Frederick; 1860–1944,
 English)
Taine (Hippolyte Adolphe; 1828–93, French)
Vives (Juan Luis; 1492–1540, Spanish)
Wolff (Christian von; 1679–1754, German)

06 Adorno (Theodor; 1903–69, German)
Anselm (St; 1033–1109, Italian)
Arendt (Hannah; 1906–75, German/US)
Austin (J L; 1911–60, English)
Baader (Franz von; 1765–1841, German)
Berlin (Sir Isaiah; 1907–97, Latvian/British)
Bonnet (Charles; 1720–93, Swiss)
Butler (Joseph; 1692–1752, English)
Carnap (Rudolf; 1891–1970, German/US)
Celsus (2 CAD, Roman)
Clarke (Samuel; 1675–1729, English)
Cousin (Victor; 1792–1867, French)
Eliade (Mircea; 1907–86, Romanian)
Engels (Friedrich; 1820–95, German)
Eucken (Rudolf; 1846–1926, German)
Farabi (Abu Nasr al-; 878–c.950, Islamic)
Fichte (Johann Gottlieb; 1762–1814,
 German)
Ficino (Marsilio; 1433–99, Italian)
Gehlen (Arnold; 1904–76, German)
Gilson (Étienne; 1884–1978, French)
Goedel (Kurt; 1906–78, Czech/US)
Halevi (Jehuda; 1075–1141, Spanish)
Hamann (Johann; 1730–88, German)
Herder (Johann; 1744–1803, German)
Hobbes (Thomas; 1588–1679, English)
Kaplan (Mordecai; 1881–1983, Lithuanian/
 US)
Kripke (Saul; 1940– , US)
Langer (Susanne K; 1895–1985, US)
Lao Tzu (6c BC, Chinese)
Littré (Émile; 1801–81, French)
Lukacs (Georg; Hungarian)
Madhva (14c, Indian)
Marcel (Gabriel; 1889–1973, French)
Ockham (William of; c.1285–c.1349,
 English)
Peirce (Charles; 1839–1914, US)
Popper (Sir Karl; 1902–94, Austrian/British)

Putnam (Hilary; 1926– , US)
Pyrrho (c.365–270 BC, Greek)
Ramsey (Frank; 1903–30, English)
Ramsey (Ian; 1915–72, English)
Sa'adia (ben Joseph; 882–942, Egyptian-
 Babylonian)
Sartre (Jean-Paul; 1905–80, French)
Schutz (Alfred; 1899–1959, Austrian/US)
Searle (John; 1932– , US)
Seneca (Lucius Annaeus; c.4 BC–c.65 AD,
 Roman)
Simmel (Georg; 1858–1918, German)
Suárez (Francisco; 1548–1617, Spanish)
Tagore (Rabindranath; 1861–1941, Indian)
Tarski (Alfred; 1902–83, Polish)
Thales (c.620–c.555 BC, Greek)
Vanini (Lucilio; 1584–1619, Italian)
Wright (Georg Henrik von; 1916–2003,
 Finnish)

07 Abelard (Peter; 1079–1142, French)
Adelard (12c, English)
Aquinas (St Thomas; 1225–74, Italian)
Arnauld (Antoine; 1612–94, French)
Bentham (Jeremy; 1748–1832, English)
Bergson (Henri; 1859–1941, French)
Bolzano (Bernard; 1781–1848, Czech)
Bradley (Francis Herbert; 1846–1924,
 Welsh)
Buridan (Jean; c.1300–c.1358, French)
Collier (Arthur; 1680–1732, English)
Deleuze (Gilles; 1925–95, French)
Dennett (Daniel; 1942– , US)
Derrida (Jacques; 1930–2004, French)
Diderot (Denis; 1713–84, French)
Dilthey (Wilhelm; 1833–1911, German)
Driesch (Hans; 1867–1941, German)
Dummett (Sir Michael; 1925– , English)
Edwards (Jonathan; 1703–58, American)
Erasmus (Desiderius; c.1466–1536, Dutch)
Erigena (John Scotus; c.810–c.877, Irish)
Ferrier (James Frederick; 1808–64, Scottish)
Gadamer (Hans-Georg; 1900–2002,
 German)
Gassend (Pierre; 1592–1655, French)
Gautama (1 CAD, Indian)
Gentile (Giovanni; 1875–1944, Italian)
Ghazali (al-; 1058–1111, Persian)
Gorgias (c.490–c.385 BC, Greek)
Gracian (Baltasar; 1601–58, Spanish)
Haldane (Richard, Viscount; 1856–1928,
 Scottish)
Hartley (David; 1705–57, English)
Herbart (Johann; 1776–1841, German)
Herbert (Edward, Lord; 1583–1648, English)
Holberg (Ludvig, Baron; 1684–1754,
 Norwegian)
Husserl (Edmund; 1859–1938, German)
Hypatia (c.370–415 AD, Greek)

Ibn Daud (Abraham; c.1100–c.1180, . Spanish)
Jaspers (Karl; 1883–1969, German)
Johnson (Alexander Bryan; 1786–1867, English/US)
Lakatos (Imre; 1922–74, Hungarian)
Lambert (Johann Heinrich; 1728–77, Swiss)
Leibniz (Gottfried Wilhelm; 1646–1716, German)
Lovejoy (Arthur O; 1873–1963, German/US)
Maistre (Joseph Marie, Comte de; 1753–1821, French)
Marcuse (Herbert; 1898–1979, German/US)
Meinong (Alexius von; 1853–1920, Austrian)
Mencius (c.372–c.289 BC, Chinese)
Murdoch (Dame Iris; 1919–99, Irish)
Neurath (Otto; 1882–1945, Austrian)
Polanyi (Michael; 1891–1976, Hungarian/ British)
Proclus (c.410–485 AD, Greek)
Pyrrhon (c.365–270 BC, Greek)
Rickert (Heinrich; 1863–1936, German)
Ricoeur (Paul; 1913–2005, French)
Russell (Bertrand, Earl; 1872–1970, English)
Sanchez (Francisco; c.1550–1623, Portuguese or Spanish)
Sankara (c.700–750, Indian)
Scheler (Max; 1874–1928, German)
Schlick (Moritz; 1882–1936, German)
Scruton (Roger; 1944– , British)
Spencer (Herbert; 1820–1903, English)
Spinoza (Benedict de; 1632–77, Dutch)
Steiner (Rudolf; 1861–1925, Austrian)
Stewart (Dugald; 1753–1828, Scottish)
Tillich (Paul; 1886–1965, German/US)
Tolstoy (Count Leo; 1828–1910, Russian)
Unamuno (Miguel de; 1864–1936, Spanish)
Warnock (Mary, Baroness; 1924– , English)

08 Alembert (Jean le Rond d'; 1717–83, French)
Ammonius (c.160–242 AD, Greek)
Anderson (John; 1893–1962, Scottish/ Australian)
Anscombe (Elizabeth; 1919–2001, Irish)
Antiphon (5c BC, Greek)
Averroës (1126–98, Spanish)
Avicenna (980–1037, Persian)
Beauvoir (Simone de; 1908–86, French)
Beccaria (Cesare, Marchese de; 1738–94, Italian)
Berdyaev (Nikolai; 1874–1948, Russian)
Berkeley (George; 1685–1753, Irish)
Boethius (Anicius Manlius Severinus; c.475–524 AD, Roman)
Brentano (Franz; 1838–1917, German)
Buchanan (George; c.1506–82, Scottish)
Bulgakov (Sergei; 1871–1944, Russian)
Campbell (Charles; 1897–1974, Scottish)

Cassirer (Ernst; 1874–1945, Polish/German)
Cudworth (Ralph; 1617–88, English)
Davidson (Donald; 1917–2003, US)
Epicurus (c.341–270 BC, Greek)
Ferguson (Adam; 1723–1816, Scottish)
Foucault (Michel; 1926–84, French)
Gassendi (Pierre; 1592–1655, French)
Geulincx (Arnold; 1624–69, Belgian)
Glanvill (Joseph; 1636–80, English)
Habermas (Jürgen; 1929– , German)
Hamilton (Sir William; 1788–1856, Scottish)
Harrison (Frederic; 1831–1923, English)
Hintikka (Jaakko; 1929– , Finnish)
Hobhouse (Leonard Trelawney; 1864–1929, English)
Lonergan (Bernard; 1904–85, Canadian)
Longinus (1c AD, Greek)
Maritain (Jacques; 1882–1973, French)
Melissus (5c BC, Greek)
M'Taggart (John M'Taggart Ellis; 1866–1925, English)
Passmore (John; 1914–2004, Australian)
Plessner (Helmuth; 1892–1985, German)
Plotinus (c.205–270 AD, Greek)
Plutarch (c.46–c.120 AD, Greek)
Porphyry (c.232–c.305 AD, Greek)
Ramanuja (11c–12c, Tamil)
Ram Singh (1816–85, Indian)
Rousseau (Jean Jacques; 1712–78, French)
Sidgwick (Henry; 1838–1900, English)
Socrates (469–399 BC, Greek)
Soloviev (Vladimir; 1853–1900, Russian)
Spengler (Oswald; 1880–1936, German)
Strawson (Sir Peter Frederick; 1919–2006, English)
Waismann (Friedrich; 1896–1959, Austrian)
Williams (Sir Bernard; 1929–2003, English)

09 Alexander (Samuel; 1859–1938, Australian)
Althusser (Louis; 1918–90, French)
Arcesilas (c.316–c.241 BC, Greek)
Aristotle (384–322 BC, Greek)
Aurobindo (Sri; 1872–1950, Indian)
Averrhoës (1126–98, Spanish)
Avicebrón (c.1020–c.1070,Spanish)
Bachelard (Gaston; 1884–1962, French)
Basilides (fl.c.125 AD, Syrian)
Bosanquet (Bernard; 1848–1923, English)
Carneades (c.214–129 BC, Greek)
Cleänthes (c.331–232 BC, Greek)
Condillac (Étienne Bonnot de; 1715–80, French)
Condorcet (Marie Jean Antoine Nicolas de Caritat, Marquis de; 1743–94, French)
Confucius (551–479 BC, Chinese)
Copleston (Frederick; 1907–93, English)
Cratippus (1c BC, Greek)
Descartes (René; 1596–1650, French)
Epictetus (1c AD, Greek)

Euhemerus (fl.c.300 BC, Greek)
Feuerbach (Ludwig; 1804–72, German)
Heidegger (Martin; 1889–1976, German)
Helvétius (Claude-Adrien; 1715–71, French)
Hutcheson (Francis; 1694–1746, British)
La Mettrie (Julien de; 1709–51, French)
Leucippus (5c BC, Greek)
Lévy-Bruhl (Lucien; 1857–1939, French)
Lucretius (c.99–55 BC, Roman)
MacIntyre (Alasdair Chalmers; 1929– , Scottish)
Mackinnon (Donald; 1913–94, Scottish)
Nagarjuna (c.150–c.250 AD, Indian)
Nietzsche (Friedrich; 1844–1900, German)
Oakeshott (Michael; 1901–90, English)
Ouspensky (Peter; 1878–1947, Russian)
Panaetius (c.185–c.110 BC, Greek)
Plantinga (Alvin; 1932– , US)
Plekhanov (Georgi; 1856–1918, Russian)
Rothacker (Erich; 1888–1965, German)
Santayana (George; 1863–1952, Spanish/US)
Schelling (Friedrich; 1775–1854, German)
Whichcote (Benjamin; 1609–83, English)

10 Anaxagoras (500–428 BC, Ionian)
Anaximenes (d.c.500 BC, Greek)
Arcesilaus (c.316–c.241 BC, Greek)
Aristippus (410–350 BC, Greek)
Baumgarten (Alexander; 1714–62, German)
Campanella (Tommaso; 1568–1639, Italian)
Chrysippus (c.280–c.206 BC, Greek)
Cumberland (Richard; 1631–1718, English)
Democritus (c.460–c.370 BC, Greek)
Duns Scotus (John; c.1265–1308, Scottish)
Empedocles (fl.c.450 BC, Greek)
Heraclitus (d.460 BC, Greek)
Horkheimer (Max; 1895–1973, German)
Ibn Khaldun (1332–1406; Arab)
Maimonides (Moses; 1135–1204, Spanish)
Pashukanis (Yevgeni; 1894–c.1937, Russian)
Posidonius (c.135–c.51 BC, Greek)
Protagoras (c.490–c.420 BC, Greek)
Pythagoras (c.580–c.500 BC, Greek)
Schweitzer (Albert; 1875–1965, Alsatian)
Windelband (Wilhelm; 1848–1915, German)
Xenocrates (c.395–314 BC, Greek)

Xenophanes (c.570–c.480 BC, Greek)
Zeno of Elea (c.490–c.420 BC, Greek)

11 Aenesidemus (1c BC, Greek)
Anaximander (611–547 BC, Ionian)
Antisthenes (c.455–c.360 BC, Greek)
Collingwood (R G; 1889–1943, English)
Kierkegaard (Søren; 1813–55, Danish)
Lévi-Strauss (Claude; 1908– , French)
Machiavelli (Niccolò; 1469–1527, Italian)
Malebranche (Nicolas; 1638–1715, French)
Mendelssohn (Moses; 1729–86, German)
Montesquieu (Charles-Louis de Secondat, Baron de; 1689–1755, French)
Reichenbach (Hans; 1891–1953, German/US)
Shaftesbury (Anthony Ashley Cooper, 3rd Earl of; 1671–1713, English)

12 Frohschammer (Jakob; 1821–93, German)
Merleau-Ponty (Maurice; 1908–61, French)
Philo Judaeus (c.20 BC–c.40 AD, Hellenistic)
Royer-Collard (Pierre Paul; 1763–1845, French)
Schopenhauer (Arthur; 1788–1860, German)
Theophrastus (c.372–c.286 BC, Greek)
Wittgenstein (Ludwig; 1889–1951, Austrian/British)
Zeno of Citium (c.334–c.265 BC, Greek)

13 Arete of Cyrene (5c–4c BC, Greek)
Dio Chrysostom (c.40–c.112 AD, Greek)
Ortega y Gasset (José; 1883–1955, Spanish)
Radhakrishnan (Sir Sarvepalli; 1888–1975, Indian)
Timon of Phlius (c.325–c.235 BC, Greek)

14 Albertus Magnus (St, Graf von Bollstädt; c.1200–80, German)
Crates of Athens (early 3c BC, Greek)
Dion Chrysostom (c.40–c.112 AD, Greek)
Marcus Aurelius (AD121–80, Roman)
Nicholas of Cusa (1401–64, German)
Rosmini-Serbati (Antonio; 1797–1855, Italian)
Schleiermacher (Friedrich Ernst Daniel; 1768–1834, German)

15 Sextus Empiricus (2c AD, Greek)

Terms used in philosophy include:

07 a priori	**09** deduction	substance	entailment
falsafa	induction	syllogism	**11** a posteriori
08 identity	intuition	teleology	**13** jurisprudence
ontology	sense data	**10** deontology	phenomenology
See also **belief**			

phobia

Phobias include:

08 euphobia (good news)

09 apiphobia (bees)
atephobia (ruin)
ecophobia (one's home surroundings)
neophobia (newness/novelty)
panphobia (everything)
zoophobia (animals)

10 acrophobia (heights)
aerophobia (draughts/air)
algophobia (pain)
aquaphobia (water)
aulophobia (flutes)
autophobia (being by oneself)
barophobia (gravity)
basophobia (walking)
canophobia (dogs)
cynophobia (dogs)
demophobia (crowds)
dikephobia (injustice)
doraphobia (fur)
eosophobia (dawn)
ergophobia (work)
genophobia (sex)
gynophobia (women)
hadephobia (hell)
hodophobia (travel)
ideophobia (ideas)
kenophobia (empty spaces/voids)
kopophobia (fatigue)
logophobia (words)
misophobia (contamination)
monophobia (one thing/being alone)
musophobia (mice)
mysophobia (contamination)
nelophobia (glass)
nosophobia (disease)
ochophobia (vehicles)
oikophobia (home)
polyphobia (many things)
potophobia (alcoholic drink)
pyrophobia (fire)
rypophobia (soiling)
selaphobia (flashes)
sitophobia (food)
theophobia (God)
toxiphobia (poison)
xenophobia (strangers/foreigners)
zelophobia (jealousy)

11 acerophobia (sourness)
agoraphobia (open spaces)
amakaphobia (carriages)
androphobia (men)
anemophobia (wind/draughts)
antlophobia (flood)
astraphobia (lightning)
bathophobia (falling from a high place)
cnidophobia (stings)
cyberphobia (computers)
dromophobia (crossing streets)
emctophobia (vomiting)
eremophobia (solitude)
eretephobia (pins)
erotophobia (sexual involvement)
geumaphobia (taste)
gymnophobia (nudity)
haphephobia (touch)
hierophobia (sacred objects)
hippophobia (horses)
hormephobia (shock)
hydrophobia (water)
hypnophobia (sleep)
laliophobia (stuttering)
lyssophobia (insanity)
maniaphobia (insanity)
necrophobia (corpses)
nephophobia (clouds)
nyctophobia (night/darkness)
ochlophobia (crowds)
ophiophobia (snakes)
pantophobia (everything)
pathophobia (disease)
peniaphobia (poverty)
phagophobia (eating)
phobophobia (fears)
phonophobia (noise/speaking aloud)
photophobia (light)
poinephobia (punishment)
scopophobia (being looked at)
scotophobia (darkness)
sitiophobia (food)
stasiphobia (standing)
tachophobia (speed)
taphephobia (being buried alive)
taphophobia (being buried alive)
tremophobia (trembling)

12 achluophobia (darkness)
aichmophobia (sharp/pointed objects)
ailurophobia (cats)
amathophobia (dust)
anginophobia (narrowness)
apeirophobia (infinity)
auroraphobia (Northern Lights)
belonephobia (needles)
bibliophobia (books)
brontophobia (thunder)
cancerphobia (cancer)
cheimaphobia (cold)

chionophobia (snow)
chromophobia (colour)
chronophobia (duration)
cometophobia (comets)
demonophobia (demons)
entomophobia (insects)
graphophobia (writing)
hedonophobia (pleasure)
kinesophobia (motion)
kleptophobia (stealing)
linonophobia (string)
musicophobia (music)
odontophobia (teeth)
ommatophobia (eyes)
oneirophobia (dreams)
ouranophobia (heaven)
phasmophobia (ghosts)
phengophobia (daylight)
satanophobia (the Devil)
scoptophobia (being looked at)
siderophobia (stars)
spermaphobia (germs)
stygiophobia (hell)
technophobia (technology)
thaasophobia (sitting)
thermophobia (heat)
toxicophobia (poison)

13 aichurophobia (points)
arachnophobia (spiders)
arithmophobia (numbers)
asthenophobia (weakness)
astrapophobia (lightning)
bacilliphobia (microbes)
cancerophobia (cancer)
dermatophobia (skin)
electrophobia (electricity)
ergasiophobia (work)
erythrophobia (blushing)

haematophobia (blood)
harpaxophobia (robbers)
herpetophobia (reptiles)
hypegiaphobia (responsibility)
keraunophobia (thunder)
mastigophobia (flogging)
mechanophobia (machinery)
metallophobia (metals)
meteorophobia (meteors)
olfactophobia (smell)
ophidiophobia (snakes)
ornithophobia (birds)
patroiophobia (heredity)
pnigerophobia (smothering)
pteronophobia (feathers)
syphilophobia (syphilis)
thanatophobia (death)
tonitrophobia (thunder)

14 anthropophobia (people/society)
batrachophobia (frogs/toads/newts)
chrometophobia (money)
claustrophobia (closed spaces)
eisoptrophobia (mirrors)
ereuthrophobia (blushing)
hamartiophobia (sin)
homichlophobia (fog)
katagelophobia (ridicule)
parthenophobia (girls)
spermatophobia (germs)
symmetrophobia (symmetry)
thalassophobia (sea)

15 akousticophobia (sound)
dysmorphophobia (personal physical deformity)
eleutherophobia (freedom)
helminthophobia (worms)
kristallophobia (ice)
ophthalmophobia (being stared at)

photography

Photographic equipment includes:

05 easel	stop bath	enlarger timer
stand	**09** camcorder	film projector
06 camera	safelight	flash umbrella
screen	**10** fixing bath	**14** contact printer
tripod	paper drier	developing tank
viewer	Vertoscope®	focus magnifier
07 boom arm	**11** print washer	slide projector
08 enlarger	slide viewer	**15** negative carrier
light-box	**13** developer bath	print-drying rack

Photographic accessories include:

04 film	**05** snoot	filter
lens	**06** eye-cup	**07** battery

hot shoe
lens cap

08 diffuser
disc film
film pack
flashgun
lens hood
zoom lens

09 barn doors
camera bag
flashbulb
flash card
flashcube
flash unit
macro lens

polarizer
spot meter

10 afocal lens
heat filter
lens shield
light meter
memory card
slide mount
video light
video mixer
viewfinder

11 close-up lens
fish-eye lens
sepia filter
video editor

12 cable release
cassette film
colour filter
memory reader

13 auxiliary lens
cartridge film
exposure meter
remote control
teleconverter
telephoto lens
wide-angle lens

14 skylight filter

15 cassette adaptor

Photographers include:

03 Ray (Man; 1890–1976, US)

04 Bing (Ilse; 1899–1998, German)
Capa (Robert; 1913–54, US)
Chim (US; 1911–56, US)
Gill (Sir David; 1843–1914, Scottish)
Gray (Gustave Le; 1820–82, French)
Haas (Ernst; 1921–86, Austrian)
Hill (David Octavius; 1802–70, Scottish)
Hine (Lewis W; 1874–1940, US)
Hiro (1930– , Japanese)
Penn (Irving; 1917– , US)

05 Adams (Ansel; 1902–84, US)
Adams (Eddie; 1933–2004, US)
Adams (Marcus Algernon; 1875–1959, English)
Annan (James Craig; 1864–1946, Scottish)
Annan (Thomas; 1829–87, Scottish)
Arbus (Diane; 1923–71, US)
Atget (Eugène; 1857–1927, French)
Beals (Jessie Tarbox; 1870–1942, US)
Brady (Mathew B; 1823–96, US)
Evans (Frederick; 1853–1943, English)
Evans (Walker; 1903–75, US)
Firth (Francis; 1822–98, English)
Frank (Robert; 1924– , Swiss)
Frith (Francis; 1822–98, English)
Hardy (Bert; 1913–95, English)
Henri (Florence; 1893–1982, US)
Karsh (Yousuf; 1908–2002, Canadian)
Keith (Thomas; 1827–95, Scottish)
Lange (Dorothea; 1895–1965, US)
Marey (Étienne Jules; 1830–1903, French)
Maude (Clementina, Lady Hawarden; 1822–65, Scottish)
Model (Lisette; 1901–83, US)
Nadar (1820–1910, French)
Parer (Damien; 1912–44, Australian)
Parks (Gordon; 1912–2006, US)
Ritts (Herb; 1952– , US)

Smith (W Eugene; 1918–78, US)
White (Minor; 1908–76, US)

06 Abbott (Berenice; 1898–1991, US)
Arnold (Eve; 1913– , US)
Atkins (Anna; 1799–1871, English)
Avedon (Richard; 1923–2004, US)
Bailey (David; 1938– , English)
Beaton (Sir Cecil; 1904–80, English)
Boubat (Édouard; 1923–99, French)
Brandt (Bill; 1904–83, English)
Burgin (Victor; 1941– , English)
Coburn (Alvin Langdon; 1882–1966, British)
Curtis (Edward; 1868–1952, US)
Draper (Henry; 1837–82, US)
Du Camp (Maxime; 1822–94, French)
Eakins (Thomas; 1844–1916, US)
Erwitt (Elliott; 1928– , US)
Fenton (Roger; 1819–69, English)
Genthe (Arnold; 1869–1942, US)
Gilpin (Laura; 1891–1979, US)
Godwin (Fay; 1931–2005, English)
Halász (Gyula; 1899–1984, French)
Jacobi (Lotte; 1896–1990, US)
Levitt (Helen; 1913– , US)
Martin (Paul; 1864–1942, Anglo-French)
McBean (Angus Rowland; 1904–90, Welsh)
Miller (Lee; 1907–77, US)
Morgan (Barbara Brooks; 1900–92, US)
Newman (Arnold; 1918–2006, US)
Newton (Helmut; 1920–2004, Australian)
Niepce (Joseph; 1765–1833, French)
Notman (William; 1826–91, Canadian)
Porter (Eliot; 1901–90, US)
Rankin (1966– , Scottish)
Rodger (George; 1908–95, English)
Sander (August; 1876–1964, German)
Sawada (Kyoichi; 1936–70, Japanese)
Smythe (Frank; 1900–49, English)
Strand (Paul; 1890–1976, US)

Szymin (David; 1911–56, US)
Talbot (William Henry Fox; 1800–77, English)
Warhol (Andy; 1926–87, US)
Weston (Edward; 1886–1958, US)
Wilson (George Washington; 1823–93, Scottish)

07 Adamson (Robert; 1821–48, Scottish)
Akiyama (Shotaro; 1920–2003, Japanese)
Bischof (Werner; 1916–54, Swiss)
Brassaï (1899–1984, French)
Bullock (Wynn; 1902–75, US)
Cameron (Julia Margaret; 1815–79, British)
Carroll (Lewis; 1832–98, English)
Clergue (Lucien; 1934– , French)
Dodgson (Charles Lutwidge; 1832–98, English)
Donovan (Terence; 1936–96, English)
Eastman (George; 1854–1932, US)
Gardner (Alexander; 1821–82, US)
Halsman (Philippe; 1906–79, US)
Jackson (William Henry; 1843–1942, US)
Kertész (André; 1894–1985, Hungarian/US)
Lumière (Auguste; 1862–1954, French)
Lumière (Louis; 1865–1948, French)
McCurry (Steve; 1950– , US)
Modotti (Tina; 1896–1942, Mexican)
Nilsson (Lennart; 1922– , Swedish)
Plummer (Edith; 1893–1975, English)
Salgado (Sebastião; 1944– , Brazilian)
Salomon (Erich; 1886–1944, German)
Seymour (David; 1911–56, US)
Sheeler (Charles; 1883–1965, US)
Siskind (Aaron; 1903–91, US)
Snowdon (Antony Armstrong-Jones, Lord; 1930– , English)
Thomson (John; 1837–1921, Scottish)
Waddell (Rankin; 1966– , Scottish)
Watkins (Carleton E; 1829–1916, US)
Watkins (Margaret; 1884–1969, Canadian)
Yevonde (Madame/Philonie; 1893–1975, English)

08 Anschütz (Ottomar; 1846–1907, German)
Biermann (Aenne; 1898–1933, German)
Chadwick (Helen; 1953–96, English)
Cosindas (Marie; 1925– , US)
Crawford (Osbert Guy Stanhope; 1886–1957, British)
Daguerre (Louis; 1787–1851, French)
Davidson (Bruce; 1933– , US)
DeCarava (Roy; 1919– , US)
Doisneau (Robert; 1912–94, French)
Edgerton (Harold; 1903–90, US)

See also **camera**

Johnston (Frances Benjamin; 1864–1952, US)
Käsebier (Gertrude; 1852–1934, US)
Lartigue (Jacques-Henri; 1894–1986, French)
Lavenson (Alma; 1897–1989, US)
McCullin (Don; 1935– , English)
Robinson (Henry Peach; 1830–1901, English)
Sielmann (Heinz; 1917–2006, German)
Steichen (Edward; 1879–1973, US)

09 Feininger (Andreas; 1906–99, US)
Friedmann (Andrei; 1913–54, US)
Leibovitz (Annie; 1949– , US)
Lichfield (Patrick, 5th Earl of; 1939– , English)
Mountford (Charles Percy; 1890–1976, Australian)
Muybridge (Eadweard; 1830–1904, Anglo-US)
O'Sullivan (Timothy H; 1840–82, US)
Parkinson (Norman; 1913–90, English)
Rodchenko (Alexander; 1891–1956, Russian)
Rosenblum (Walter; 1919–2006, US)
Rothstein (Arthur; 1915–85, US)
Stieglitz (Alfred; 1864–1946, US)
Sutcliffe (Frank Meadow; 1853–1941, English)
Winogrand (Garry; 1928–84, US)

10 Blumenfeld (Erwin; 1897–1969, US)
Cunningham (Imogen; 1883–1976, US)
Macpherson (Robert; d.1872, Scottish)
Moholy-Nagy (László; 1895–1946, US)
Muggeridge (Edward James; 1830–1904, Anglo-US)
Rabinovich (Emanuel; 1890–1976, US)
Tournachon (Gaspard-Felix; 1820–1910, French)

11 Bourke-White (Margaret; 1904–71, US)
Eisenstaedt (Alfred; 1898–1995, US)
Saint Joseph (John Kenneth Sinclair; 1912–94, English)
Wakabayashi (Yasuhiro; 1930– , Japanese)

12 Friese-Greene (William; 1855–1921, English)
Mapplethorpe (Robert; 1946–1989, US)
Van der Elsken (Ed; 1925–90, Dutch)

13 Ducos du Hauron (Louis; 1837–1920, French)

14 Armstrong-Jones (Antony; 1930– , English)
Cartier-Bresson (Henri; 1908–2004, French)

physics

Physicists include:

03 Lee (David; 1931– , US)
Ohm (Georg; 1787–1854, German)

04 Abbe (Ernst; 1840–1905, German)
Bohr (Niels; 1885–1962, Danish)
Born (Max; 1882–1970, German)
Bose (Satyendra Nath; 1894–1974, Indian)
Bose (Sir Jagadis Chandra; 1858–1937, Indian)
Fert (Albert; 1938– , French)
Hall (John L; 1934– , US)
Hess (Victor; 1883–1964, Austrian/US)
Katz (Sir Bernard; 1911–2003, German/British)
Kerr (John; 1824–1907, Scottish)
Kohn (Walter; 1923– , Austrian/US)
Lamb (Willis; 1913–2008, US)
Laue (Max von; 1879–1960, German)
Mach (Ernst; 1838–1916, Austrian)
Mott (Sir Nevill; 1905–96, English)
Néel (Louis; 1904–2000, French)
Paul (Wolfgang; 1913–93, German)
Rabi (Isidor Isaac; 1898–1988, Austrian/US)
Snow (C P, Lord; 1905–80, English)
Ting (Samuel C C; 1936– , US)
Wien (Wilhelm; 1864–1928, German)
Yang (Chen Ning; 1922– , Chinese/US)

05 Adams (Sir John; 1920–84, English)
Allen (Sir Geoffrey; 1928– , English)
Aston (Francis; 1877–1945, English)
Auger (Pierre; 1899–1993, French)
Basov (Nikolai; 1922–2001, Russian)
Bethe (Hans; 1906–2005, German/US)
Bloch (Felix; 1905–83, Swiss/US)
Bondi (Sir Hermann; 1919–2005, Austrian/British)
Bothe (Walther; 1891–1957, German)
Boyle (Robert; 1627–91, Irish)
Bragg (Sir Lawrence; 1890–1971, Australian/British)
Bragg (Sir William; 1862–1942, English)
Braun (Ferdinand; 1850–1918, German)
Curie (Marie; 1867–1934, Polish/French)
Curie (Pierre; 1859–1906, French)
Debye (Peter; 1884–1966, Dutch/US)
Dewar (Sir James; 1842–1923, Scottish)
Dirac (Paul; 1902–84, English)
Dyson (Freeman; 1923– , English/US)
Esaki (Leo; 1925– , Japanese)
Ewing (Sir Alfred; 1855–1935, Scottish)
Fabry (Charles; 1867–1945, French)
Fermi (Enrico; 1901–54, Italian/US)
Fuchs (Klaus; 1912–88, German/British)
Gauss (Carl Friedrich; 1777–1855, German)
Gibbs (J Willard; 1839–1903, US)

Grove (Sir William; 1811–96, Welsh)
Henry (Joseph; 1797–1878, US)
Hertz (Gustav; 1887–1975, German)
Hertz (Heinrich; 1857–94, German)
Higgs (Peter; 1929– , English)
Hooke (Robert; 1635–1703, English)
Jeans (Sir James; 1877–1946, English)
Joule (James Prescott; 1818–89, English)
Kusch (Polykarp; 1911–93, German/US)
Lodge (Sir Oliver; 1851–1940, English)
Nambu (Yoichiro; 1921– , Japanese/US)
Pauli (Wolfgang; 1900–58, Austrian/Swiss/US)
Popov (Aleksandr; 1859–1905, Russian)
Porta (Giovanni; 1535–1615, Italian)
Segrè (Emilio; 1905–89, Italian/US)
Smoot (George F; 1946– , US)
Stark (Johannes; 1874–1957, German)
Stern (Otto; 1888–1969, German/US)
Tesla (Nikola; 1856–1943, Austro-Hungarian/US)
Volta (Alessandro, Count; 1745–1827, Italian)
Waals (Johannes van der; 1837–1923, Dutch)
Young (Thomas; 1773–1829, English)

06 Alfvén (Hannes; 1908–96, Swedish)
Ampère (André Marie; 1775–1836, French)
Barkla (Charles Glover; 1877–1944, English)
Barlow (Peter; 1776–1862, English)
Binnig (Gerd; 1947– , German)
Bunsen (Robert; 1811–99, German)
Carnot (Sadi; 1796–1832, French)
Cooper (Leon N; 1930– , US)
Cronin (James; 1931– , US)
Dalton (John; 1766–1844, English)
Edison (Thomas Alva; 1847–1931, US)
Franck (James; 1882–1964, German/US)
Frisch (Otto; 1904–79, Austrian/British)
Geiger (Hans; 1882–1945, German)
Glaser (Donald; 1926– , US)
Hänsch (Theodor W; 1941– , German)
Jensen (Hans; 1907–73, German)
Kelvin (William Thomson, Lord; 1824–1907, Scottish)
Landau (Lev; 1908–68, Soviet)
Leslie (Sir John; 1766–1832, Scottish)
Lorenz (Ludwig Valentin; 1829–91, Danish)
Mather (John C; 1945– , US)
Newton (Sir Isaac; 1642–1727, English)
Pascal (Blaise; 1623–62, French)
Perrin (Jean Baptiste; 1870–1942, French)
Planck (Max; 1858–1947, German)
Powell (Cecil; 1903–69, English)
Stroud (William; 1860–1938, English)

Talbot (William Fox; 1800–77, English)
Townes (Charles; 1915– , US)
Walton (Ernest; 1903–95, Irish)
Wigner (Eugene; 1902–95, Hungarian/US)
Wilson (Charles Thomson Rees; 1869–1959, Scottish)
Wilson (Robert Woodrow; 1936– , US)
Yukawa (Hideki; 1907–81, Japanese)
Zwicky (Fritz; 1898–1974, Swiss/US)

07 Alferov (Zhores; 1930– , Russian)
Alvarez (Luis; 1911–88, US)
Babinet (Jacques; 1794–1872, French)
Bardeen (John; 1908–91, US)
Bednorz (Georg; 1950– , German)
Broglie (Louis, Duc de; 1892–1987, French)
Charles (Jacques; 1746–1823, French)
Compton (Arthur; 1892–1962, US)
Coulomb (Charles Augustin de; 1736–1806, French)
Crookes (Sir William; 1832–1919, English)
Doppler (Christian; 1803–53, Austrian)
Faraday (Michael; 1791–1867, English)
Fechner (Gustav; 1801–87, German)
Feynman (Richard; 1918–88, US)
Fresnel (Augustin; 1788–1827, French)
Galileo (1564–1642, Italian)
Gilbert (William; 1544–1603, English)
Glauber (Roy J; 1925– , US)
Goddard (Robert; 1882–1945, US)
Hawking (Stephen; 1942– , English)
Huygens (Christiaan; 1629–93, Dutch)
Kapitza (Peter; 1894–1984, Soviet)
Langley (Samuel; 1834–1906, US)
Lebedev (P N; 1866–1912, Russian)
Leggett (Anthony J; 1938– , English)
Lorentz (Hendrik; 1853–1928, Dutch)
Marconi (Guglielmo, Marchese; 1874–1937, Italian)
Maskawa (Toshihide; 1940– , Japanese)
Mauchly (John W; 1907–80, US)
Maxwell (James Clerk; 1831–79, Scottish)
Meitner (Lise; 1878–1968, Austrian)
Moseley (Harry; 1887–1915, English)
Oersted (Hans Christian; 1777–1851, Danish)
Peierls (Sir Rudolf; 1907–95, German/British)
Piccard (Auguste; 1884–1962, Swiss)
Purcell (Edward Mills; 1912–97, US)
Réaumur (René; 1683–1757, French)
Richter (Burton; 1931– , US)
Röntgen (Wilhelm; 1845–1923, German)
Rotblat (Sir Joseph; 1908–2005, Polish/British)
Seaborg (Glenn; 1912–99, US)
Szilard (Leo; 1898–1964, Hungarian/US)
Thomson (Sir George Paget; 1892–1975, English)

Thomson (Sir J J; 1856–1940, English)
Tyndall (John; 1820–93, Irish)
Wheeler (John; 1911–2008, US)
Wilkins (Maurice; 1916–2004, New Zealand/British)

08 Anderson (Carl; 1905–91, US)
Anderson (Philip W; 1923– , US)
Ångström (Anders Jonas; 1814–74, Swedish)
Appleton (Sir Edward; 1892–1965, English)
Avogadro (Amedeo; 1776–1856, Italian)
Beaufort (Sir Francis; 1774–1857, British)
Blackett (Patrick Stuart, Lord; 1897–1974, English)
Brattain (Walter; 1902–87, US)
Brewster (Sir David; 1781–1868, Scottish)
Bridgman (P W; 1882–1961, US)
Chadwick (Sir James; 1891–1974, English)
Cherwell (Frederick Lindemann, Viscount; 1886–1957, English)
Clausius (Rudolf; 1822–88, German)
Davisson (Clinton; 1881–1958, US)
Einstein (Albert; 1879–1955, German/Swiss/US)
Foucault (Léon; 1819–68, French)
Gell-Mann (Murray; 1929– , US)
Ginzburg (Vitaly L; 1916– , Russian)
Grünberg (Peter; 1939– , German)
Ketterle (Wolfgang; 1957– , German)
Lawrence (Ernest; 1901–58, US)
Mulliken (Robert S; 1896–1986, US)
Oliphant (Sir Mark; 1901–2000, Australian)
Rayleigh (John William Strutt, Lord; 1842–1919, English)
Roentgen (Wilhelm; 1845–1923, German)
Sakharov (Andrei; 1921–89, Soviet)
Shockley (William; 1910–89, US)
Siegbahn (Kai M; 1918–2007, Swedish)
Van Allen (James; 1914–2006, US)
Weinberg (Steven; 1933– , US)
Zworykin (Vladimir; 1889–1982, Russian/US)

09 Abrikosov (Alexei A; 1928– , Russian)
Atanasoff (John; 1903–95, US)
Bartholin (Erasmus; 1625–98, Danish)
Becquerel (Henri; 1852–1908, French)
Boltzmann (Ludwig; 1844–1906, Austrian)
Cavendish (Henry; 1731–1810, English)
Cherenkov (Pavel; 1904–90, Soviet)
Cockcroft (Sir John; 1897–1967, English)
Gay-Lussac (Joseph; 1778–1850, French)
Heaviside (Oliver; 1850–1925, English)
Helmholtz (Hermann von; 1821–94, German)
Josephson (Brian; 1940– , Welsh)
Kirchhoff (Gustav; 1824–87, German)
Kobayashi (Makoto; 1944– , Japanese)

Kurchatov (Igor; 1903–60, Soviet)
Michelson (Albert; 1852–1931, Polish/US)
Mössbauer (Rudolf; 1929–   , German)
Uhlenbeck (George; 1900–88, Dutch/US)
Waterston (John James; 1811–83, Scottish)

10 Barkhausen (Heinrich; 1881–1956, German)
Fahrenheit (Daniel; 1686–1736, German)
Fraunhofer (Joseph von; 1787–1826, German)
Glazebrook (Sir Richard; 1854–1935, English)
Heisenberg (Werner; 1901–76, German)
Richardson (Sir Owen Willans; 1879–1959, English)
Rutherford (Ernest, Lord; 1871–1937, New Zealand)
Torricelli (Evangelista; 1608–47, Italian)
Watson-Watt (Sir Robert; 1892–1973, Scottish)

Weizsäcker (Carl, Freiherr von; 1912–2007, German)
Wheatstone (Sir Charles; 1802–75, English)

11 Chamberlain (Owen; 1920–2006, US)
Joliot-Curie (Frédéric; 1900–58, French)
Joliot-Curie (Irène; 1897–1956, French)
Leeuwenhoek (Antoni van; 1632–1723, Dutch)
Oppenheimer (Robert; 1904–67, US)
Schrödinger (Erwin; 1887–1961, Austrian)
Van de Graaff (Robert J; 1901–67, US)

12 Lennard-Jones (Sir John; 1894–1954, English)
Spottiswoode (William; 1825–83, English)

13 Chandrasekhar (Subrahmanyan; 1910–95, Indian/US)
Goeppert-Mayer (Maria; 1906–72, German/US)

Terms used in physics include:

03 gal
gas
GeV
GUT
ion
law
QCD
QED
SHM
TOE

04 area
atom
barn
flux
heat
lens
mass
node
rule
spin
torr
wave
WIMP
work
X-ray

05 chaos
crith
fermi
field
focus
force
henry
laser
lever
light
phase

power
quark
ratio
sabin
sound
speed
SQUID
state

06 albedo
atomic
charge
couple
dipole
energy
engine
exergy
Kelvin
liquid
mirror
moment
motion
optics
phonon
photon
plasma
proton
quench
scalar
SI unit
string
theory
vacuum
volume
weight

07 astatic
capture

carrier
chronon
density
digital
dynamic
entropy
formula
gravity
inertia
isotope
kinetic
lambert
maxwell
neutron
nuclear
nucleus
oersted
orbital
poundal
process
singlet
speckle
statics
tension

08 absorber
adhesion
adynamic
alpha ray
antinode
critical
electron
ensemble
enthalpy
equation
friction
gamma ray

graviton
half-life
harmonic
infrared
molecule
momentum
monopole
neutrino
nutation
particle
periodic
polarity
pressure
rest mass
spectrum
velocity
vibronic
wormhole

09 abundance
acoustics
amplitude
aperiodic
atmolysis
black body
collision
conductor
cosmology
deviation
dimension
elastance
frequency
hyperfine
incidence
induction
insulator
isenergic
magnetism
mechanics
Mohs scale
multiplet
potential
principle
radiation
radio wave
resonance
schlieren
sound wave
subatomic
substance
transient
vibration
viscosity
weak force
white heat
world line

10 anharmonic
annihilate

athermancy
attraction
Cooper pair
cryogenics
degenerate
diacaustic
efficiency
elasticity
flash point
force field
gauge boson
heavy water
Higgs boson
hydraulics
isentropic
Kerr effect
latent heat
Mach number
microwaves
multiplier
pulsatance
quadrupole
reflection
refraction
relativity
relaxation
resistance
resolution
scattering
separation
shear force
spallation
straggling
ultrasound
wavelength
world sheet

11 Auger effect
backscatter
catacaustic
diffraction
electricity
equilibrium
evaporation
homocentric
illuminance
light source
mode-locking
ordinary ray
oscillation
periodic law
sensitivity
spintronics
steady state
strong force
temperature
ultraviolet

12 absolute zero

acceleration
apochromatic
Balmer series
beta particle
boiling point
caustic curve
centre of mass
critical mass
Fresnel zones
hydrostatics
impenetrable
interference
Kelvin effect
laws of motion
Lorentz force
luminescence
pyro-electric
radioisotope
recalescence
spectroscopy
speed of light
standing wave
string theory
time dilation
wave equation
wave property
work function
Zeeman effect

13 alpha particle
Appleton layer
Big Bang theory
binding energy
chain reaction
change of state
freezing point
hydrodynamics
incandescence
kinetic energy
kinetic theory
light emission
magnetic field
nuclear fusion
optical centre
photonegative
photopositive
Poisson's ratio
potential well
quantum theory
radioactivity
self-shielding
semiconductor
stopping power
strange matter
supersymmetry
Thomson effect
transmittance
transmutation
twistor theory

wave mechanics
14 analogue signal
applied physics
bremsstrahlung
caustic surface
Coriolis effect
Dirac's constant
interferometry
internal energy
light intensity
Meissner effect
nuclear fission
nuclear physics
parallel motion
Schottky defect

states of matter
superconductor
surface tension
thermodynamics
transverse wave
viscous damping
15 angular momentum
capillary action
centre of gravity
charged particle
conservation law
degree of freedom
electric current
electrodynamics
Fourier analysis

impact parameter
moment of inertia
Mössbauer effect
optical activity
optical spectrum
perpetual motion
Planck's constant
potential energy
renormalization
specific gravity
thermal capacity
visible spectrum
weak interaction
zero-point energy

See also **Nobel Prize**

physiology

Physiologists include:

04 Bert (Paul; 1833–86, French)
Best (Charles; 1899–1978, Canadian)
Dale (Sir Henry; 1875–1968, English)
Fick (Adolph; 1829–1901, German)
Hall (Marshall; 1790–1857, English)
Hess (Walter; 1881–1973, Swiss)
Hill (A V; 1886–1977, English)
Hyde (Ida; 1857–1945, US)
Loeb (Jacques; 1859–1924, German/US)
Roux (Wilhelm; 1850–1924, German)

05 Beale (Lionel; 1828–1906, English)
Crile (George; 1864–1943, US)
Hubel (David; 1926– , US)
Krogh (August; 1874–1949, Danish)
Kühne (Wilhelm; 1837–1900, German)
Lower (Richard; 1631–91, English)
Marey (Etienne-Jules; 1830–1904, French)
Mayow (John; 1640–79, English)
Weber (Ernst Heinrich; 1795–1878, German)
Wundt (Wilhelm; 1832–1920, German)

06 Adrian (Edgar, Lord; 1889–1977, English)
Békésy (Georg von; 1899–1972, Hungarian/US)
Bordet (Jules; 1870–1961, Belgian)
Cannon (Walter B; 1871–1945, US)
Foster (Sir Michael; 1836–1907, English)
Gasser (Herbert; 1888–1963, US)
Gmelin (Leopold; 1788–1853, German)
Granit (Ragnar; 1900–91, Swedish)
Haller (Albrecht von; 1708–77, Swiss)
Harvey (William; 1578–1657, English)
Hensen (Viktor; 1835–1924, German)
Hogben (Lancelot; 1895–1975, English)
Hunter (John; 1728–93, Scottish)
Huxley (Sir Andrew; 1917– , English)

Ludwig (Karl; 1816–95, German)
Müller (Johannes; 1801–58, German)
Pavlov (Ivan; 1849–1936, Russian)
Pincus (Gregory; 1903–67, US)
Richet (Charles; 1850–1935, French)
Waller (Augustus; 1816–70, English)

07 Banting (Sir Frederick; 1891–1941, Canadian)
Bayliss (Sir William; 1860–1924, English)
Beddoes (Thomas Lovell; 1803–49, English)
Bernard (Claude; 1813–78, French)
Borelli (Giovanni; 1608–79, Italian)
Diamond (Jared; 1937– , US)
Driesch (Hans; 1867–1941, German)
Edwards (Robert; 1925– , British)
Galvani (Luigi; 1737–98, Italian)
Gaskell (Walter; 1847–1914, English)
Guthrie (Charles; 1880–1963, US)
Haldane (John Scott; 1860–1936, Scottish)
Helmont (Jan Baptista van; 1579–1644, Flemish)
Heymans (Corneille; 1892–1968, Belgian)
Hodgkin (Sir Alan; 1914–98, English)
Horsley (Sir Victor; 1857–1916, English)
Houssay (Bernardo; 1887–1971, Argentine)
Langley (John; 1852–1925, English)
Macleod (John; 1876–1935, Scottish)
Purkyne (Jan; 1787–1869, Czech)
Robbins (Frederick; 1916–2003, US)
Rudbeck (Olof; 1630–1702, Swedish)
Schwann (Theodor; 1810–82, German)

08 Barcroft (Sir Joseph; 1872–1947, Irish)
Bowditch (Henry; 1840–1911, US)
Erlanger (Joseph; 1874–1965, US)
Flourens (Pierre; 1794–1867, French)
Hartline (Haldan K; 1903–83, US)

Magendie (François; 1783–1855, French)
Mariotte (Edmé; c.1620–1684, French)
Purkinje (Jan; 1787–1869, Czech)
Senebier (Jean; 1742–1809, Swiss)
Starling (Ernest Henry; 1866–1927, English)
Voronoff (Serge; 1866–1951, Russian)

09 Blakemore (Colin; 1944– , British)
Cesalpino (Andrea; 1519–1603, Italian)
Dutrochet (Henri; 1776–1847, French)
Einthoven (Willem; 1860–1927, Dutch)
Guillemin (Roger; 1924– , French/US)
Helmholtz (Hermann von; 1821–94, German)

11 Bois-Reymond (Emil du; 1818–96, German)
Sherrington (Sir Charles; 1857–1952, English)

12 Brown-Séquard (Édouard; 1817–94, French)
Papanicolaou (George; 1883–1962, Greek/US)

13 Du Bois-Reymond (Emil; 1818–96, German)

14 Schmidt-Nielsen (Knut; 1915–2007, Norwegian)
Sharpey-Schäfer (Sir Edward; 1850–1935, English)

Terms used in physiology include:

04 bone
cell
skin

05 blood
brain
gland
nerve
organ
sleep

06 enzyme
growth
muscle
tissue
torpor

07 anatomy
fatigue
hormone
ketosis

vitamin

08 dormancy
genetics
reflexes
skeleton

09 digestion
endocrine
lymphatic
pathology
secretion
urination

10 estivation
excitation
immunology
metabolism
motor nerve
psychology
salivation

11 blood typing
circulation
contraction
hibernation
homeostasis
respiration

12 homoeostasis
immune system
reproduction
sensory nerve

13 fertilization

14 cardiovascular
photosynthesis

15 circadian rhythm
neurophysiology
plant physiology

See also **anatomy**; **doctor**; **Nobel Prize**; **surgery**

pianist

Pianists include:

02 Ax (Emmanuel; 1949– , US)

03 Fou (Ts'ong; 1934– , Chinese)

04 Bush (Alan; 1900–95, English)
Cole (Nat 'King'; 1919–65, US)
Hess (Dame Myra; 1890–1966, English)
John (Sir Elton; 1947– , English)
Lupu (Radu; 1945– , Romanian)
Monk (Thelonious; 1917–82, US)
Wild (Earl; 1915– , US)

05 Alkan (Valentin; 1813–88, French)
Arrau (Claudio; 1903–91, Chilean)
Basie (Count; 1904–84, US)
Beach (Amy 'Mrs H H A'; 1867–1944, US)
Blake (James Hubert 'Eubie'; 1887–1983, US)
Bolet (Jorge; 1914–90, Cuban)

Borge (Victor; 1909–2000, Danish/US)
Bülow (Hans von; 1830–94, German)
Corea (Chick; 1941– , US)
Evans (Bill; 1929–80, US)
Evans (Gil; 1912–88, Canadian)
Field (John; 1782–1837, Irish)
Friml (Rudolf; 1879–1972, Czech/US)
Gould (Glenn; 1932–82, Canadian)
Hallé (Sir Charles; 1819–95, German/British)
Harty (Sir Hamilton; 1880–1941, Northern Irish)
Hines (Earl; 1903–83, US)
Joyce (Eileen; 1912–91, Australian)
Lewis (Jerry Lee; 1935– , US)
Liszt (Franz; 1811–86, Hungarian)
Nyman (Michael; 1944– , English)
Ogdon (John; 1937–89, English)

Szell (George; 1897–1970, Hungarian/US)
Tatum (Art; 1910–56, US)
Tovey (Sir Donald Francis; 1873–1940, English)
Weber (Carl Maria von; 1786–1826, German)

06 Albert (Eugen d'; 1864–1932, German)
Arnaud (Yvonne; 1892–1958, French)
Atwell (Winifred; 1914–83, Trinidadian)
Busoni (Ferruccio; 1866–1924, Italian)
Chopin (Frédéric; 1810–49, Polish)
Cortot (Alfred; 1877–1962, French)
Cramer (Johann Baptist; 1771–1858, German/British)
Curzon (Sir Clifford; 1907–82, English)
Czerny (Karl; 1791–1857, Austrian)
Domino (Fats; 1928– , US)
Dussek (Jan Ladislav; 1760–1812, Czech)
Garner (Errol; 1921–77, US)
Hummel (Johann; 1778–1837, Austrian)
Joplin (Scott; 1868–1917, US)
Kenton (Stan; 1912–79, US)
Kissin (Evgeny; 1971– , Russian)
Koppel (Herman D; 1908–98, Danish)
Lamond (Frederic; 1868–1948, Scottish)
Levine (James; 1943– , US)
Martin (Frank; 1890–1974, Swiss)
Morton (Jelly Roll; 1890–1941, US)
Powell (Bud; 1924–66, US)
Schiff (András; 1953– , Hungarian/British)
Serkin (Rudolf; 1903–91, Hungarian/US)
Sitsky (Larry; 1934– , Chinese/Australian)
Stoker (Richard; 1938– , English)
Taylor (Cecil; 1933– , US)
Tracey (Stan; 1926– , English)
Turina (Joaquín; 1882–1949, Spanish)
Waller (Fats; 1904–43, US)
Wilson (Teddy; 1912–86, US)

07 Albéniz (Isaac; 1860–1909, Spanish)
Bennett (Sir William Sterndale; 1816–75, English)
Bentzon (Niels; 1919–2000; Danish)
Brendel (Alfred; 1931– , Czech)
Brubeck (Dave; 1920– , US)
Charles (Ray; 1930–2004, US)
Goodman (Isador; 1909–82, South African/Australian)
Hancock (Herbie; 1940– , US)
Ibrahim (Abdullah; 1934– , South African)
Johnson (James P; 1894–1955, US)
Kentner (Louis; 1905–87, Hungarian/British)
Malcolm (George; 1917–97, English)
Mathias (William; 1934–92, Welsh)
Matthay (Tobias; 1858–1945, English)
Medtner (Nikolai; 1880–1951, Russian)
Perahia (Murray; 1947– , US)

Richter (Sviatoslav; 1915–97, Russian)
Solomon (1902–88, English)
Sorabji (Kaikhosru Shapurji; 1892–1988, English)
Taneyev (Sergei; 1856–1915, Russian)
Vaughan (Sarah; 1924–90, US)

08 Argerich (Martha; 1941– , Argentine)
Bronfman (Yefim; 1958– , Russian/US)
Browning (John; 1933–2003, US)
Clementi (Muzio; 1752–1832, Italian)
Dohnányi (Ernst von; 1877–1960, Hungarian)
Franklin (Aretha; 1942– , US)
Godowsky (Leopold; 1870–1938, Russian/US)
Grainger (Percy; 1882–1961, Australian/US)
Henschel (Sir George; 1850–1934, Polish/British)
Horowitz (Vladimir; 1904–89, Russian/US)
Leighton (Kenneth; 1929–88, English)
Lhévinne (Josef; 1874–1944, Russian/US)
Pachmann (Vladimir de; 1848–1933, Russian)
Peterson (Oscar; 1925– , Canadian)
Richards (Henry Brinley; 1819–85, Welsh)
Schnabel (Artur; 1882–1951, Austrian)
Schumann (Clara; 1819–96, German)
Scriabin (Aleksandr; 1872–1915, Russian)
Skriabin (Aleksandr; 1872–1915, Russian)
Thalberg (Sigismond; 1812–71, German or Austrian)
Williams (Mary Lou; 1910–81, US)

09 Ashkenazy (Vladimir; 1937– , Icelandic)
Barenboim (Daniel; 1942– , Israeli)
Bernstein (Leonard; 1918–90; US)
Butterley (Nigel; 1935– , Australian)
Ellington (Duke; 1899–1974, US)
Gieseking (Walter; 1895–1956, German)
Henderson (Fletcher; 1897–1952, US)
Landowska (Wanda; 1879–1959, Polish)
MacDowell (Edward; 1861–1908, US)
Moscheles (Ignaz; 1794–1870, Bohemian)
Stevenson (Ronald; 1928– , Scottish)
Westbrook (Mike; 1936– , English)

10 de Larrocha (Alicia; 1923– , Spanish)
Gottschalk (Louis Moreau; 1829–69, US)
Moszkowski (Moritz; 1854–1925, Polish)
Paderewski (Ignacy; 1860–1941, Polish)
Rubinstein (Anton; 1829–94, Russian)
Rubinstein (Artur; 1887–1982, Polish/US)
Scharwenka (Xaver; 1850–1924, Polish)

11 Farren-Price (Ronald; 1930– , Australian)
Mitropoulos (Dimitri; 1896–1960, Greek/US)
Reizenstein (Franz; 1911–68, German)

12 Michelangeli (Arturo Benedetti; 1920–95, Italian)

Moiseiwitsch (Benno; 1890–1963, Russian/British)

Shostakovich (Maxim Dmitriyevich; 1938– , Russian/US)

13 Little Richard (Penniman; 1932– , US)

See also **jazz**; **pop**

picture

Pictures include:		

04 icon
snap

05 cameo
image
mural
pin-up
plate
print
slide
still
study

06 bitmap
canvas
design
doodle
effigy
fresco
Kit-Cat
mosaic
sketch
veduta

07 cartoon
collage
diptych
drawing

etching
modello
montage
mugshot
tableau
tracing
vanitas

08 abstract
anaglyph
graffiti
graphics
kakemono
likeness
monotype
negative
painting
Photofit®
portrait
snapshot
tapestry
transfer
triptych
vignette

09 bricolage
engraving

identikit
landscape
miniature
old master
oleograph
still life

10 altarpiece
caricature
photograph
silhouette

11 oil painting
trompe l'oeil
watercolour

12 illustration
photogravure
reproduction
self-portrait
transparency

13 passport photo

14 action painting
cabinet picture
representation

15 acrylic painting

See also **art**; **paint**; **photography**

pig

Pigs include:		

05 Duroc
07 Old Spot
warthog
08 landrace
Pietrain

Tamworth
wild boar
09 Berkshire
Hampshire
Yorkshire

10 Large White
potbellied
saddleback
11 Middle White
14 Chinese Meishan

pigment

Pigments include:		

03 hem
04 haem
heme
05 henna
ochre
sepia

smalt
umber
06 bister
bistre
cobalt
cyanin

lutein
madder
sienna
zaffer
zaffre
07 carmine

etiolin
gamboge
melanin
sinopia
turacin
08 cinnabar
luteolin
orpiment
rose-pink
verditer
viridian
09 anthocyan
bilirubin
colcothar
Indian red
lamp-black
lithopone
phycocyan
quercetin
vermilion
See also **dye**

zinc white
10 Berlin blue
biliverdin
Chinese red
chlorophyl
green earth
lipochrome
madder-lake
Paris-green
pearl white
rhodophane
terre verte
11 anthochlore
anthocyanin
chlorophyll
King's-yellow
phycocyanin
phycophaein
phytochrome
ultramarine

Venetian red
12 anthoxanthin
Cappagh-brown
Chinese white
chrome yellow
Naples-yellow
phaeomelanin
phycoxanthin
Prussian blue
turacoverdin
Tyrian purple
xanthopterin
13 cadmium yellow
phycoerythrin
Scheele's green
titanium white
xanthopterine
15 purple of Cassius

pike

Pikes include:

03 Esk
Red
04 Cold
High
05 Heron
Rispa

06 Causey
Kidsty
Ullock
07 Rossett
Scafell
08 Kentmere

Langdale
09 Angletarn
Grisedale
Sheffield
10 Dollywagon
Nethermost

pine

Pine trees include:

03 nut
red
04 blue
Huon
jack
pond
05 beach
black
Chile
kauri
piñon
Scots
shore
slash
stone
sugar
swamp
Swiss
white

06 Aleppo
arolla
Bhutan
bishop
celery
cembra
cowdie
cowrie
Jersey
Korean
limber
Norway
Paraná
pinyon
Scotch
spruce
Yunnan
07 Amboina
ancient
Armand's

Bosnian
Chilean
cluster
hickory
Jeffrey
Mexican
prickly
radiata
Turkish
08 Austrian
Corsican
Holford's
Japanese
Jeffrey's
knobcone
lacebark
loblolly
longleaf
maritime
Monterey

mountain
Pandanus
pinaster
Scots fir
Sumatran
umbrella
Virginia
Weymouth

09 Jerusalem
Korean nut
lodgepole
ponderosa
Scotch fir
shortleaf

whitebark

10 Macedonian
Swiss stone

11 bristlecone
Canadian red
Japanese red
Siberian nut

12 Canary island
Chinese white
eastern white
frankincense
Mexican white
monkey puzzle

Western white

13 dwarf mountain
European black
Japanese black
Japanese white
Norfolk Island
northern pitch
Siberian cedar
Siberian dwarf
Table Mountain
western yellow

14 Mexican weeping
three-leaved nut

pink

Shades of pink include:

04 puce
rose

05 coral
peach

06 oyster
salmon
shrimp

07 old rose

08 cyclamen

09 carnation
pompadour
shell pink

12 mushroom pink
shocking pink

pipe *see* **tobacco**

piracy

Pirates, privateers and buccaneers include:

03 Tew (Thomas; d.1695, American)

04 Bart (Jean; 1651–1702, French)
Gunn (Ben; *Treasure Island*, 1883, Robert
Louis Stevenson)
Hook (Captain; *Peter Pan*, 1904, J M Barrie)
Kidd (Captain William; c.1645–1701,
Scottish)
Otto (*A High Wind in Jamaica*, 1929,
Richard Hughes)
Read (Mary; b.c.1675, English)
Smee (*Peter Pan*, 1904, J M Barrie)

05 Barth (Jean; 1651–1702, French)
Bones (Billy; *Treasure Island*, 1883, Robert
Louis Stevenson)
Bonny (Anne; b.c.1697, Irish)
Bunce (Jack; *The Pirate*, 1821, Sir Walter
Scott)
Drake (Sir Francis; c.1540–96, English)
Every (Henry; b.c.1653, English)
Ewart (Nanty; *Redgauntlet*, 1824, Sir Walter
Scott)
Flint (Captain; *Swallows and Amazons*,
1930, Arthur Ransome)
Selim (*The Bride of Abydos: A Turkish Tale*,
1813, Lord Byron)
Tache (Edward; d.1718, English)
Teach (Edward; d.1718, English)

06 Aubery (Jean-Benoit; *Frenchman's Creek*,
1942, Daphne Du Maurier)
Butler (Nathaniel; c.1577–date unknown,
English)
Conrad (*The Corsair: A Tale*, 1814, Lord
Byron)
Fleury (Jean; d.1527, French)
Jonsen (Captain; *A High Wind in Jamaica*,
1929, Richard Hughes)
Morgan (Sir Henry; c.1635–88, Welsh)
Silver (Long John; *Treasure Island*, 1883,
Robert Louis Stevenson)
Thatch (Edward; d.1718, English)
Walker (William; 1824–60, US)

07 Bellamy (Samuel 'Black Sam'; c.1689–1717,
English)
Dampier (William; 1652–1715, English)
Lafitte (Jean; c.1780–c.1826, French)
O'Malley (Grace; c.1530–1603, Irish)
Rackham (John; d.1720)
Roberts (Bartholomew; c.1682–1722, Welsh)
Sparrow (Captain Jack; *Pirates of the
Caribbean*, 2003)
Surcouf (Robert; 1773–1827, French)
Trumpet (Solomon; *Jack Holborn*, 1964,
Leon Garfield)
Zheng Yi (d.1807; Chinese)

08 Altamont (Frederick; *The Pirate*, 1821, Sir Walter Scott)
Black Dog (*Treasure Island*, 1883, Robert Louis Stevenson)
Blackett (Nancy; *Swallows and Amazons*, 1930, Arthur Ransome)
Blackett (Peggy; *Swallows and Amazons*, 1930, Arthur Ransome)
Blind Pew (*Treasure Island*, 1883, Robert Louis Stevenson)

Redbeard (Khair-ed-din Barbarossa; d.1546, Barbary)
Ringrose (Basil; c.1653–86, English)
09 Black Bart (Bartholomew Roberts; c.1682–1722, Welsh)
Cleveland (Clement; *The Pirate*, 1821, Sir Walter Scott)
10 Barbarossa (Khair-ed-din; d.1546, Barbary)
Blackbeard (Edward Teach; d.1718, English)
Calico Jack (John Rackham; d.1720)

plague

The ten Biblical plagues:

04 lice	**07** locusts	**18** disease of livestock
05 boils	**08** darkness	**19** death of the firstborn
flies	**09** hailstorm	**21** Nile waters turn to blood
frogs		

plain

Plains include:

04 vega	**06** maidan	tundra	sabkhat
05 carse	pampas	**07** lowland	**08** savannah
lande	sabkha	prairie	
llano	steppe	sabkhah	

planet

Planets of the solar system:

04 Mars	Venus	**07** Jupiter
05 Earth	**06** Saturn	Mercury
Pluto	Uranus	Neptune

Terms to do with planets include:

04 axis	Jovian	gas giant	perihelion
body	Saturn	prograde	retrograde
Mars	Uranus	rotation	revolution
moon	**07** gravity	**09** axial tilt	**11** Jovian winds
05 Earth	Jupiter	celestial	morning star
orbit	Martian	magnitude	planetology
Pluto	Mercury	red planet	sidereal day
rings	Neptune	satellite	solar system
Venus	red spot	**10** atmosphere	**12** Great Red Spot
06 crater	**08** aphelion	blue planet	perturbation

See also **satellite**

plant

Plants include:

04 bulb	herb	vine	grass
bush	moss	weed	shrub
fern	tree	**05** algae	**06** annual

cactus
cereal
flower
fungus
hybrid
lichen

07 climber
sapling

08 air-plant
biennial
cultivar

pot plant
seedling

09 evergreen
perennial
succulent

vegetable

10 house plant
water plant
wild flower

15 herbaceous plant

Terms to do with plants include:

03 bud
ear
set

04 bark
base
bast
bine
bulb
corm
curl
gall
germ
leaf
node
root
rust
seed
shaw
soma
stem
twig
wart

05 arrow
crown
floss
frond
fruit
gemma
graft
kinin
scion
shoot
stalk
stele
stoma
thorn
trunk
tuber

06 blotch
branch
bulbel
bulbil
caulis
collar
collet

cortex
cyanin
embryo
enarch
flower
inarch
phloem
phyton
runner
stolon
succus
sucker

07 clasper
crenate
crosier
crozier
cutting
foliage
pot-sick
prickle
rhizome
sapling
soft rot
tendril
thallus

08 abscisin
blastema
brown rot
crenated
domatium
endogamy
epicotyl
etiolate
leaf curl
leaf spot
plantule
pot-bound
root ball
seedling
tegument
trichome

09 acropetal
chlorosis
cotyledon
cytokinin

diandrous
emergence
epidermis
hypocotyl
internode
pericycle
porphyrin
propagule
rootstock
subentire

10 abscission
calmodulin
distichous
fungus-gall
monoecious
perfoliate
phytotoxin
propagulum
protoplast
root nodule
starveling

11 allelopathy
chlorophyll
downy mildew
inoculation
phytochrome
pollination
sinistrorse
xeromorphic
xerophilous
xerothermic

12 monadelphous
phytohormone
sclerenchyma
xeromorphous

13 hermaphrodite
inflorescence
phytoestrogen
powdery mildew

14 gynomonoecious
photosynthesis

15 andromonoecious

See also **algae**; **bulb**; **cactus**; **crop**; **disease**; **emblem**; **fern**; **flower**; **fruit**; **fungus**; **garden**; **grass**; **hybrid**; **insectivorous plant**; **leaf**; **lily**; **moss**; **mushroom**; **nut**; **orchid**; **palm**; **pine**; **poison**; **seaweed**; **sedge**; **shrub**; **tree**; **vegetable**; **weed**; **wood**

plastic

Plastics include:

03 PVC	Teflon®	Plexiglas®	**12** polyethylene
04 PTFE	**07** Perspex®	polyester	polyurethane
UPVC	**08** Bakelite®	polythene	**13** phenolic resin
05 vinyl	silicone	**10** epoxy resin	polypropylene
06 Biopol®	**09** Celluloid®	plexiglass	**14** polynorbornene
		11 polystyrene	

play

Plays include:

04 *Loot* (1966; Joe Orton)
Not I (1972; Samuel Beckett)

05 *Eh Joe* (1965; Samuel Beckett)
Equus (1973; Peter Schaffer)
Faust (c.1775–1832; Johann Wolfgang von Goethe)
Le Cid (1637; Pierre Corneille)
Medea (2000; Liz Lochhead)
Medea (431 BC; Euripides)
Médée (1946; Jean Anouilh)
Roots (1959; Arthur Wesker)
Yerma (1934; Federico García Lorca)

06 *Becket* (1959; Jean Anouilh)
Luther (1961; John Osborne)
Phèdre (1677; Jean Racine)
St Joan (1923; George Bernard Shaw)

07 *Amadeus* (1979; Peter Schaffer)
Candida (1897; George Bernard Shaw)
Electra (c.418–410 BC; Sophocles)
Endgame (1958; Samuel Beckett)
Galileo (1938; Bertolt Brecht)
La Ronde (1900; Arthur Schnitzler)
Oedipus (c.429 BC; Sophocles)
Oleanna (1992; David Mamet)
Orestes (408 BC; Euripides)
Our Town (1938; Thornton Wilder)
Volpone (1606; Ben Jonson)
Woyzeck (1837; Georg Büchner)

08 *Antigone* (1946; Jean Anouilh)
Antigone (441 BC; Sophocles)
Betrayal (1978; Harold Pinter)
Edward II (1594; Christopher Marlowe)
Everyman (15c)
Hay Fever (1925; Noël Coward)
Huis Clos (1944; Jean-Paul Sartre)
Oresteia (c.458 BC; Aeschylus)
Peer Gynt (1867; Henrik Ibsen)
Tartuffe (1667; Molière)
The Birds (c.414 BC; Aristophanes)
The Flies (1943; Jean-Paul Sartre)
The Frogs (405 BC; Aristophanes)
The Miser (1668; Molière)

The Price (1968; Arthur Miller)
The Visit (1958; Friedrich Dürrenmatt)
The Wasps (422 BC; Aristophanes)
War Horse (2007; Nick Stafford/Michael Morpurgo)

09 *All My Sons* (1947; Arthur Miller)
Come and Go (1965; Samuel Beckett)
Happy Days (1961; Samuel Beckett)
L'Alouette (1953; Jean Anouilh)
Miss Julie (1888; August Strindberg)
Party Time (1991; Harold Pinter)
Pygmalion (1913; George Bernard Shaw)
The Chairs (1952; Eugène Ionesco)
The Clouds (423 BC; Aristophanes)
The Father (1887; August Strindberg)
The Rivals (1775; Richard Brinsley Sheridan)
The Vortex (1924; Noël Coward)

10 *A Dream Play* (1902; August Strindberg)
All for Love (1677; John Dryden)
Andromache (425 BC; Euripides)
Andromaque (1667; Jean Racine)
Lysistrata (411 BC; Aristophanes)
Misery Guts (2002; Liz Lochhead)
No Man's Land (1975; Harold Pinter)
The Bacchae (405 BC; Euripides)
The Robbers (1781; Friedrich von Schiller)
The Seagull (1912; Anton Chekhov)
Uncle Vanya (1896; Anton Chekhov)

11 *A Doll's House* (1879; Henrik Ibsen)
Blood and Ice (1982; Liz Lochhead)
Hedda Gabler (1890; Henrik Ibsen)
Love for Love (1695; William Congreve)
Maria Stuart (1800; Friedrich von Schiller)
Restoration (1981; Edward Bond)
The Blue Bird (1908; Maurice Maeterlinck)
The Crucible (1953; Arthur Miller)
The Hairy Ape (1922; Eugene O'Neill)
The Wild Duck (1884; Henrik Ibsen)
Trojan Women (415 BC; Euripides)

12 *Anna Christie* (1922; Eugene O'Neill)
Blithe Spirit (1941; Noël Coward)
Blood Wedding (1933; Federico García Lorca)

Boris Godunov (1825; Alexander Pushkin)
Cabal and Love (1783; Friedrich von
   Schiller)
Major Barbara (1905; George Bernard Shaw)
Private Lives (1930; Noël Coward)
Punch and Judy (traditional)
Speed-the-Plow (1988; David Mamet)
The Alchemist (1610; Ben Jonson)
The Apple Cart (1929; George Bernard
   Shaw)
The Caretaker (1958; Harold Pinter)
The Litigants (1715; Jean Racine)
The Mousetrap (1952; Agatha Christie)
Translations (1980; Brian Friel)

13 A Patriot for Me (1965; John Osborne)
Arms and the Man (1898; George Bernard
   Shaw)
A Taste of Honey (1958; Shelagh Delaney)
Bailegangaire (1986; Tom Murphy)
Doctor Faustus (1594–1601; Christopher
   Marlowe)
Educating Rita (1979; Willy Russell)
The Cryptogram (1994; David Mamet)
The Homecoming (1965; Harold Pinter)
The Jew of Malta (c.1592–94; Christopher
   Marlowe)
The Physicists (1962; Friedrich Dürrenmatt)
The Shaughraun (1876; Dion Boucicault)
The White Devil (1612; John Webster)
The Winslow Boy (1946; Terence Rattigan)

14 Can't Pay? Won't Pay! (1974; Dario Fo)
Krapp's Last Tape (1958; Samuel Beckett)
Man and Superman (1902; George Bernard
   Shaw)
Orlando Furioso (1594; Robert Greene)
Riders to the Sea (1904; J M Synge)
Separate Tables (1954; Terence Rattigan)
The Country Wife (1675; William
   Wycherley)
The Entertainer (1957; John Osborne)
The Misanthrope (1666; Molière)
The Plain Dealer (1676/7; William
   Wycherley)
The Silent Woman (1609; Ben Jonson)
Venice Preserv'd (1682; Thomas Otway)

15 American Buffalo (1975; David Mamet)
Angels in America (1991–92; Tony Kushner)
Bartholomew Fair (1614; Ben Jonson)
Heartbreak House (1919; George Bernard
   Shaw)
Look Back in Anger (1956; John Osborne)
Prometheus Bound (c.430 BC; Aeschylus)
Spring Awakening (1909; Frank Wedekind)
The Beggar's Opera (1728; John Gay)
The Emperor Jones (1920; Eugene O'Neill)
The Gigli Concert (1984; Tom Murphy)
The Iceman Cometh (1946; Eugene O'Neill)

The Three Sisters (1901; Anton Chekhov)
Too Late for Logic (1990; Tom Murphy)
Waiting for Godot (1955; Samuel Beckett)

16 Back to Methuselah (1921; George Bernard
   Shaw)
Beyond the Horizon (1920; Eugene O'Neill)
Cat on a Hot Tin Roof (1955; Tennessee
   Williams)
Death of a Salesman (1949; Arthur Miller)
Lettice and Lovage (1987; Peter Schaffer)
Shirley Valentine (1986; Willy Russell)
Strange Interlude (1928; Eugene O'Neill)
Sweet Bird of Youth (1959; Tennessee
   Williams)
The Birthday Party (1959; Harold Pinter)
The Cherry Orchard (1904; Anton Chekhov)
The Great God Brown (1926; Eugene
   O'Neill)
The Sanctuary Lamp (1976; Tom Murphy)
The Way of the World (1700; William
   Congreve)
When We Dead Awaken (1899; Henrik
   Ibsen)

17 Dancing at Lughnasa (1990; Brian Friel)
Glengarry Glen Ross (1983; David Mamet)
Juno and the Paycock (1924; Sean O'Casey)
Orpheus Descending (1958; Tennessee
   Williams)
The Beaux Stratagem (1707; George
   Farquhar)
The Duchess of Malfi (1623; John Webster)
The Glass Menagerie (1945; Tennessee
   Williams)
'Tis Pity She's a Whore (c.1631; John Ford)

18 An Enemy of the People (1882; Henrik Ibsen)
A View from the Bridge (1955; Arthur Miller)
Desire under the Elms (1924; Eugene
   O'Neill)
Suddenly Last Summer (1958; Tennessee
   Williams)
The Threepenny Opera (1928; Bertolt
   Brecht)

19 Androcles and the Lion (1912; George
   Bernard Shaw)
The Night of the Iguana (1961; Tennessee
   Williams)
The School for Scandal (1777; Richard
   Brinsley Sheridan)

20 Inadmissible Evidence (1964; John Osborne)
In the Shadow of the Glen (1903; J M Synge)
John Bull's Other Island (1904; George
   Bernard Shaw)
Mrs Warren's Profession (1898; George
   Bernard Shaw)
The Plough and the Stars (1926; Sean
   O'Casey)

The School for Husbands (1662; Molière)
21 Chicken Soup with Barley (1957; Arthur Wesker)
Philadelphia, Here I Come! (1964; Brian Friel)
The Cripple of Inishmaan (1996; Martin McDonagh)
The Lady's Not for Burning (1949; Christopher Fry)
22 Mourning Becomes Electra (1931; Eugene O'Neill)
The Good Person of Setzuan (1943; Bertolt Brecht)
The Government Inspector (1836; Nikolai Gogol)
23 I'm Talking About Jerusalem (1958–59; Arthur Wesker)
Someone Who'll Watch Over Me (1992; Frank McGuinness)

Tales from the Vienna Woods (1931; Ödön von Horváth)
The Beauty Queen of Leenane (1996; Martin McDonagh)
The Caucasian Chalk Circle (1947; Bertolt Brecht)
24 Long Day's Journey Into Night (1956; Eugene O'Neill)
The Lieutenant of Inishmore (2001; Martin McDonagh)
25 Sexual Perversity in Chicago (1977; David Mamet)
26 Conversations on a Homecoming (1985; Tom Murphy)
27 Mother Courage and her Children (1941; Bertolt Brecht)
The Playboy of the Western World (1907; J M Synge)

Playwrights, dramatists and screenwriters include:

02 Fo (Dario; 1926– , Italian)
03 Ade (George; 1866–1944, US)
Box (Muriel; 1905–91, English)
Day (John; 1574–1640, English)
Fry (Christopher; 1907–2005, English)
Gay (John; 1685–1732, English)
Hay (Ian; 1876–1952, Scottish)
Kyd (Thomas; 1558–94, English)
Lee (Nathaniel; c.1649/53–1692, English)
May (Elaine; 1932– , US)
04 Bahr (Hermann; 1863–1934, Austrian)
Bale (John; 1495–1563, English)
Behn (Aphra; 1640–89, English)
Bolt (Robert; 1924–95, English)
Bond (Edward; 1934– , English)
Coen (Ethan; 1957– , US)
Coen (Joel; 1954– , US)
Cruz (Ramón de la; 1731–94, Spanish)
Dahl (Roald; 1916–90, British)
Daly (Augustin; 1838–99, US)
Dane (Clemence; 1888–1965, English)
Fast (Howard; 1914–2003, US)
Ford (John; c.1586–c.1640, English)
Gale (Zona; 1874–1938, US)
Gems (Pam; 1925– , English)
Gray (Simon; 1936–2008, English)
Hall (Willis; 1929–2005, English)
Hare (Sir David; 1947– , English)
Hart (Moss; 1904–61, US)
Hill (Aaron; 1685–1750, English)
Home (John; 1722–1808, Scottish)
Inge (William; 1913–73, US)
Jouy (Étienne; 1764–1846; French)
Kivi (Aleksis; 1834–72, Finnish)
Lily (John; c.1554–1606, English)

Lyly (John; c.1554–1606, English)
More (Hannah; 1745–1833, English)
Munk (Kaj; 1898–1944, Danish)
Rice (Elmer; 1892–1967, US)
Rowe (Nicholas; 1674–1718, English)
Shaw (George Bernard; 1856–1950, Irish)
Tate (Nahum; 1652–1715, Irish)
Ts'ao (Yü; 1910–96, Chinese)
Vega (Lope de; 1562–1635, Spanish)
Vian (Boris; 1920–59, French)
West (Morris; 1916–99, Australian)
05 Abell (Kjeld; 1901–61, Danish)
Akins (Zoë; 1886–1958, US)
Albee (Edward, III; 1928– , US)
Allen (Woody; 1935– , US)
Arden (John; 1930– , English)
Ayrer (Jacob; 1543–1605, German)
Barry (Philip; 1896–1949, US)
Behan (Brendan; 1923–64, Irish)
Betti (Ugo; 1892–1953, Italian)
Bhasa (fl.3CAD, Sanskrit)
Boker (George Henry; 1823–90, US)
Brome (Richard; c.1590–1652, English)
Byrne (John; 1940– , Scottish)
Canth (Minna; 1844–97, Finnish)
Cao Yu (1910–96, Chinese)
Čapek (Karel; 1890–1938, Czech)
Colum (Pádraic; 1881–1972, Irish)
Csiky (Gregor; 1842–91, Hungarian)
Cueva (Juan de la; c.1550–1610, Spanish)
Dumas (Alexandre; 1802–70, French)
Edgar (David; 1948– , English)
Eliot (T S; 1888–1965, US/British)
Esson (Louis; 1879–1943, Scottish/Australian)

Ewald (Johannes; 1743–81, Danish)
Field (Nathan; 1587–c.1620, English)
Foote (Horton; 1916– , US)
Frayn (Michael; 1933– , English)
Friel (Brian; 1929– , Northern Irish)
Genet (Jean; 1910–86, French)
Gogol (Nikolai; 1809–52, Russian)
Gozzi (Count Carlo; 1720–1806, Italian)
Greif (Andreas; 1616–64, German)
Grieg (Nordahl; 1902–43, Norwegian)
Guare (John; 1938– , US)
Hardy (Alexandre; c.1570–c.1631, French)
Havel (Václav; 1936– , Czech)
Hayes (Alfred; 1911–85, English/US)
Ibsen (Henrik; 1828–1906, Norwegian)
Jesse (F Tennyson; 1888–1958, English)
Jones (Henry Arthur; 1851–1929, English)
Kinck (Hans E; 1865–1926, Norwegian)
Laube (Heinrich; 1806–84, German)
Lewis (Saunders; 1893–1985, Welsh)
Lillo (George; 1693–1739, English)
Lodge (Thomas; c.1558–1625, English)
Mamet (David; 1947– , US)
Moody (William Vaughn; 1869–1910, US)
Moore (Edward; 1712–57, English)
Nashe (Thomas; 1567–1601, English)
Odets (Clifford; 1906–63, US)
Orton (Joe; 1933–67, English)
Otway (Thomas; 1652–85, English)
Payne (John Howard; 1791–1852, US)
Peele (George; c.1558–96, English)
Piron (Alexis; 1689–1773, French)
Reade (Charles; 1814–84, English)
Rueda (Lope de; c.1510–65, Spanish)
Sachs (Hans; 1494–1576, German)
Sachs (Nelly; 1891–1970, German/Swedish)
Sheil (Richard Lalor; 1791–1851, Irish)
Simon (Neil; 1927– , US)
Smith (Dodie; 1896–1990, English)
Stone (Oliver; 1946– , US)
Sutro (Alfred; 1863–1933, English)
Synge (J M; 1871–1909, Irish)
Udall (Nicholas; 1504–56, English)
Unruh (Fritz von; 1885–1970, German)
Weiss (Peter; 1916–82, German)
Wells (John; 1936–98, English)
Wilde (Oscar; 1854–1900, Irish)
Wills (William Gorman; 1828–91, Irish)
Wolfe (George C; 1954– , US)
Yeats (W B; 1865–1939, Irish)
Young (Douglas; 1913–73, Scottish)

06 Abbott (George; 1887–1995, US)
Adamov (Arthur; 1908–70, Russian/French)
Artaud (Antonin; 1896–1948, French)
Augier (Émile; 1820–89, French)
Baraka (Amiri; 1934– , US)
Barker (Howard; 1946– , English)
Barnes (Peter; 1931–2004, English)

Barrie (J M; 1860–1937, Scottish)
Baxter (James K; 1926–72, New Zealand)
Becque (Henry; 1837–99, French)
Belloy (Dormont de; 1727–75, French)
Binchy (Maeve; 1940– , Irish)
Bowles (Jane; 1918–73, US)
Brecht (Bertolt; 1898–1956, German)
Bridie (James; 1888–1951, Scottish)
Brieux (Eugène; 1858–1932, French)
Bryden (Bill; 1942– , Scottish)
Casona (Alejandro; 1903–65, Spanish)
Cibber (Colley; 1671–1757, English)
Clarke (Austin; 1896–1974, Irish)
Colman (George, the Elder; 1732–94,
English)
Colman (George, the Younger; 1762–1836,
English)
Cooney (Ray; 1932– , English)
Cooper (Giles; 1918–66, Irish)
Coward (Sir Noël; 1899–1973, English)
Cowley (Hannah; 1743–1809, English)
Dantas (Julio; 1876–1962, Portuguese)
Davies (Terence; 1945– , English)
Dekker (Thomas; c.1570–1632, English)
Donnay (Maurice; 1859–1945, French)
Drezen (Youenn; 1899–1972, Breton)
Druten (John van; 1901–57, US)
Dryden (John; 1631–1700, English)
D'Urfey (Tom; 1653–1723, English)
Encina (Juan del; c.1469–c.1530, Spanish)
Enzina (Juan del; c.1469–c.1530, Spanish)
Ephron (Nora; 1941– , US)
Ervine (St John; 1883–1971, Irish)
Favart (Charles Simon; 1710–92, French)
Frisch (Max; 1911–91, Swiss)
Fugard (Athol; 1932– , South African)
Fuller (Charles H, Jnr; 1939– , US)
Gibson (Wilfrid; 1878–1962, English)
Godber (John; 1956– , English)
Goethe (Johann Wolfgang von; 1749–1832,
German)
Grabbe (Christian; 1801–36, German)
Greene (Robert; 1558–92, English)
Guerra (Tonino; 1920– , Italian)
Guitry (Sacha; 1885–1957, Russian/French)
Halévy (Ludovic; 1834–1908, French)
Handke (Peter; 1942– , Austrian)
Hebbel (Friedrich; 1813–63, German)
Herzog (Werner; 1942– , German)
Hewett (Dorothy; 1923–2002, Australian)
Hilton (James; 1900–54, English)
Howard (Sidney; 1891–1939, US)
Huston (John; 1906–87, US)
Jonson (Ben; 1572–1637, English)
Kaiser (Georg; 1878–1945, German)
Kelman (James; 1946– , Scottish)
Kleist (Heinrich von; 1777–1811, German)
Kneale (Nigel; 1922–2006, Manx)

Lawler (Ray; 1921– , Australian)
Lerner (Alan Jay; 1918–86, US)
Lesage (Alain René; 1668–1747, French)
Linney (Romulus; 1930– , US)
Lytton (Bulwer; 1803–73, English)
Maffei (Francesco Scipione, Marchese di; 1675–1755, Italian)
Marcel (Gabriel; 1889–1973, French)
Marion (Frances; 1887–1973, US)
Mercer (David; 1928–80, English)
Miller (Arthur; 1915–2005, US)
Miller (Henry; 1891–1980, US)
Molnár (Ferenč; 1878–1952, Hungarian)
Morton (John Maddison; 1811–91, English)
Morton (Thomas; 1764–1838, English)
Murphy (Arthur; 1727–1805, Irish)
Musset (Alfred de; 1810–57, French)
Oakley (Barry; 1931– , Australian)
O'Brien (Kate; 1897–1974, Irish)
O'Casey (Sean; 1884–1964, Irish)
O'Duffy (Eimar; 1893–1935, Irish)
O'Neill (Eugene; 1888–1953, US)
Pagnol (Marcel; 1895–1974, French)
Patten (Brian; 1946– , English)
Pinero (Sir Arthur Wing; 1855–1934, English)
Pinter (Harold; 1930–2008, English)
Plater (Alan; 1935– , English)
Porter (Hal; 1911–84, Australian)
Potter (Dennis; 1935–94, English)
Powell (Michael; 1905–90, English)
Racine (Jean; 1639–99, French)
Riskin (Robert; 1897–1955, US)
Rotrou (Jean de; 1609–50, French)
Rowley (William; c.1585–c.1626, English)
Sardou (Victorien; 1831–1908, French)
Sartre (Jean-Paul; 1905–80, French)
Sayles (John; 1950– , US)
Scribe (Eugène; 1791–1861, French)
Seneca (Lucius Annaeus; c.4 BC–AD65, Roman)
Settle (Elkanah; 1648–1724, English)
Storey (David; 1933– , English)
Tagore (Rabindranath; 1861–1941, Indian)
Taylor (Tom; 1817–80, Scottish)
Thomas (Brandon; 1849/56–1914, English)
Trevor (William; 1928– , Irish)
Ts'ao Yü (1910–96, Chinese)
Usigli (Rodolfo; 1905–79, Mexican)
Vitrac (Roger; 1899–1952, French)
Vondel (Joost van den; 1587–1679, Dutch)
Werner (Zacharias; 1768–1823, German)
Wesker (Arnold; 1932– , English)
Wilder (Thornton; 1897–1975, US)
Wilson (August; 1945–2005, US)

07 Akerman (Chantal; 1950– , Belgian)
Alarcón (Juan Ruiz de; c.1580–1639, Spanish)

Alfieri (Vittorio, Count; 1749–1803, Italian)
Anouilh (Jean; 1910–87, French)
Arbuzov (Aleksei; 1908–86, Soviet)
Arrabal (Fernando; 1932– , Spanish)
Barbier (Jules; 1825–1901, French)
Barlach (Ernst; 1870–1938, German)
Beckett (Samuel; 1906–89, Irish)
Behrman (S N; 1893–1973, US)
Belasco (David; 1853–1931, US)
Benelli (Sem; 1877–1949, Italian)
Bennett (Alan; 1934– , English)
Bergman (Hjalmar; 1883–1931, Swedish)
Berkoff (Steven; 1937– , English)
Bernard (Tristan; 1866–1947, French)
Branner (H C; 1903–66, Danish)
Brenton (Howard; 1942– , English)
Büchner (Georg; 1813–37, German)
Burnand (Sir Francis; 1836–1917, English)
Césaire (Aimé; 1913–2008, West Indian)
Chapman (George; c.1559–1634, English)
Chekhov (Anton; 1860–1904, Russian)
Chettle (Henry; c.1560–c.1607, English)
Claudel (Paul; 1868–1955, French)
Cocteau (Jean; 1889–1963, French)
Coppola (Francis Ford; 1939– , US)
Delaney (Shelagh; 1939– , English)
Dennery (Adolphe; 1811–99, French)
D'Errico (Ezio; 1892–1973, Italian)
Diamond (I A L; 1920–88, Romanian/US)
Diderot (Denis; 1713–84, French)
Dodsley (Robert; 1704–64, English)
Dorfman (Ariel; 1942– , Argentine/ Chilean)
Dunsany (Edward Plunkett, Lord; 1878–1957, Irish)
Elliott (Sumner Locke; 1917–91, Australian/ US)
Enquist (Per Olov; 1934– , Swedish)
Ferrari (Paolo; 1822–89, Italian)
Feydeau (Georges; 1862–1921, French)
Freytag (Gustav; 1816–95, German)
Garnier (Robert; 1534–90, French)
Giacosa (Giuseppe; 1847–1906, Italian)
Goldoni (Carlo; 1707–93, Italian)
Gregory (Augusta, Lady; 1852–1932, Irish)
Guevara (Luis Vélez de; 1570–1644, Spanish)
Guimerá (Ángel; 1849–1924, Catalan)
Hampton (Christopher; 1946– , English)
Harwood (Harold Marsh; 1874–1959, English)
Heiberg (Gunnar; 1857–1929, Norwegian)
Heiberg (Johan; 1791–1860, Danish)
Hellman (Lillian; 1907–84, US)
Hervieu (Paul; 1857–1915, French)
Heywood (John; c.1497–c.1580, English)
Heywood (Thomas; c.1574–1641, English)
Hibberd (Jack; 1940– , Australian)

Holberg (Ludvig, Baron; 1684–1754, Norwegian)
Horváth (Ödön von; 1901–38, Austro-Hungarian)
Housman (Laurence; 1865–1959, English)
Ionesco (Eugène; 1912–94, Romanian/French)
Jerrold (Douglas; 1803–57, English)
Jodelle (Étienne, Sieur de Lymodin; 1532–73, French)
Kaufman (George S; 1889–1961, US)
Klinger (Friedrich M von; 1752–1831, German)
Knowles (Sheridan; 1784–1862, Irish)
Kubrick (Stanley; 1928–99, US)
Kushner (Tony; 1956– , US)
Labiche (Eugène; 1815–88, French)
La Motte (Antoine Houdar de; 1672–1731, French)
Lardner (Ring; 1885–1933, US)
Larivey (Pierre; c.1550–1612, French)
Marlowe (Christopher; 1564–93, English)
Marquis (Don; 1878–1937, US)
Marston (John; 1576–1634, English)
Maturin (Charles; 1782–1824, Irish)
McGough (Roger; 1937– , English)
Medwall (Henry; 1462–c.1505, English)
Meilhac (Henri; 1831–97, French)
Mirbeau (Octave; 1850–1917, French)
Mishima (Yukio; 1925–70, Japanese)
Molière (1622–73, French)
Moratin (Leandro de; 1760–1828, Spanish)
Naevius (Gnaeus; c.264–c.201 BC, Roman)
Nestroy (Johann; 1801–62, Austrian)
Osborne (John; 1929–94, English)
Patrick (John; 1905–95, US)
Planché (James Robinson; 1795–1880, English)
Plautus (Titus Maccius; c.250–184 BC, Roman)
Prévert (Jacques; 1900–77, French)
Rastell (John; 1475–1536, English)
Regnard (Jean François; 1655–1709, French)
Richler (Mordecai; 1931–2001, Canadian)
Romeril (John; 1945– , Australian)
Rostand (Edmond; 1868–1918, French)
Russell (Willy; 1947– , English)
Saroyan (William; 1908–81, US)
Serling (Rod; 1924–75, US)
Seymour (Alan; 1927– , Australian)
Shaffer (Peter Levin; 1926– , English)
Shepard (Sam; 1943– , US)
Shirley (James; 1596–1666, English)
Shvarts (Yevgeni; 1896–1958, Russian)
Soyinka (Wole; 1934– , Nigerian)
Speight (Johnny; 1920–98, English)
Sturges (Preston; 1898–1959, US)
Terence (c.195–159 BC, Roman)

Tolstoy (Count Aleksei Konstantinovich; 1817–75, Russian)
Travers (Ben; 1886–1980, English)
Ustinov (Sir Peter; 1921–2004, English)
Uvedale (Nicholas; 1504–56, English)
Vicente (Gil; c.1470–c.1537, Portuguese)
Walcott (Derek; 1930– ; West Indian)
Webster (John; c.1580–c.1625, English)
Welland (Colin; 1934– , English)
Whiting (John; 1917–63, English)

08 Andersen (Hans Christian; 1805–75, Danish)
Anderson (Maxwell; 1888–1959, US)
Banville (Théodore de; 1823–91, French)
Beaumont (Francis; c.1584–1616, English)
Bjørnson (Bjørnstjerne; 1832–1910, Norwegian)
Brentano (Clemens von; 1778–1842, German)
Bulgakov (Mikhail; 1891–1940, Russian)
Burgoyne (John; 1722–92, English)
Congreve (William; 1670–1729, English)
Connelly (Marc; 1890–1980, US)
Dancourt (Florent; 1661–1725, French)
D'Avenant (Sir William; 1606–68, English)
Etherege (Sir George; c.1635–1691, English)
Farquhar (George; c.1677–1707, Irish)
Fielding (Henry; 1707–54, English)
Fitzball (Edward; 1792–1873, English)
Fletcher (John; 1579–1625, English)
Gilliatt (Penelope; 1932–93, English)
Gryphius (Andreas; 1616–64, German)
Hochhuth (Rolf; 1931– , German)
Holcroft (Thomas; 1745–1809, English)
Houghton (Stanley; 1881–1913, English)
Inchbald (Elizabeth; 1753–1821, English)
Johnston (Denis; 1901–84, Irish)
Kálidása (fl.450 BC, Indian)
Kotzebue (August von; 1761–1819, German)
Lemaître (Jules; 1853–1914, French)
Lissauer (Ernst; 1882–1937, German)
Lochhead (Liz; 1947– , Scottish)
Lonsdale (Frederick; 1881–1954, British)
Marivaux (Pierre de; 1688–1763, French)
Menander (c.343–c.291 BC, Greek)
Mortimer (Sir John; 1923– , English)
Pasolini (Pier Paolo; 1922–75, Italian)
Polanski (Roman; 1933– , French/Polish)
Randolph (Thomas; 1605–35, English)
Rattigan (Sir Terence; 1911–77, English)
Richards (Alun; 1929–2004, Welsh)
Robinson (Lennox; 1886–1958, Irish)
Ruzzante (1502–42, Italian)
Salacrou (Armand; 1899–1990, French)
Schiller (Friedrich von; 1759–1805, German)
Schröder (Friedrich; 1744–1816, German)
Shadwell (Thomas; c.1642–1692, English)
Sheridan (Richard Brinsley; 1751–1816, Irish)

Sherriff (R C; 1896–1975, English)
Sherwood (Robert E; 1896–1955, US)
Stoppard (Sir Tom; 1937– , Czech/British)
Suckling (Sir John; 1609–42, English)
Tourneur (Cyril; c.1575–1626, English)
Vanbrugh (Sir John; 1664–1726, English)
von Trier (Lars; 1956– , Danish)
Wedekind (Frank; 1864–1918, German)
Wildgans (Anton; 1881–1932, Austrian)
Williams (Emlyn; 1905–87, Welsh)
Williams (Tennessee; 1911–83, US)

09 Aeschylus (c.525–c.456 BC, Greek)
Ayckbourn (Sir Alan; 1939– , English)
Bleasdale (Alan; 1946– , English)
Bottomley (Gordon; 1874–1948, English)
Brighouse (Harold; 1882–1958, English)
Centlivre (Susannah; c.1667–c.1723, English)
Charteris (Leslie; 1907–93, US)
Chayefsky (Paddy; 1923–81, US)
Chiarelli (Luigi; 1884–1947, Italian)
Churchill (Caryl; 1938– , English)
Corneille (Pierre; 1606–84, French)
Corneille (Thomas; 1625–1709, French)
Crébillon (Prosper Jolyot de; 1674–1762, French)
d'Annunzio (Gabriele; 1863–1938, Italian)
Delavigne (Casimir; 1793–1843, French)
Euripides (484/480–406 BC, Greek)
Fierstein (Harvey; 1954– , US)
Giraudoux (Jean; 1882–1944, French)
Goldsmith (Oliver; 1730–74, Irish)
Griffiths (Trevor; 1935– , English)
Hansberry (Lorraine; 1930–65, US)
Hauptmann (Gerhart; 1862–1946, German)
Immermann (Karl; 1796–1840, German)
Isherwood (Christopher; 1904–86, US)
Killigrew (Thomas; 1612–83, English)
Kisfaludy (Karoly; 1788–1830, Hungarian)
Lenormand (Henri-René; 1882–1951, French)
MacArthur (Charles; 1895–1956, US)
MacDonagh (Donagh; 1912–68, Irish)
Mankowitz (Wolf; 1924–98, English)
Marinetti (Tommaso; 1876–1944, Italian)
Massinger (Philip; 1583–1640, English)
Middleton (Thomas; c.1580–1627, English)
Minghella (Anthony; 1954–2008, English)
Ostrovsky (Aleksandr; 1823–86, Russian)
Poliakoff (Stephen; 1952– , English)
Priestley (J B; 1894–1984, English)
Robertson (T W; 1829–71, English)
Rosenthal (Jack; 1931–2004, English)
Sackville (Thomas; 1553–1608, English)
Söderberg (Hjalmar; 1869–1941, Swedish)
Sophocles (c.496–405 BC, Greek)
Southerne (Thomas; 1660–1746, Irish)
Sudermann (Hermann; 1857–1928, German)

Tarantino (Quentin; 1963– , US)
Wergeland (Hendrik; 1808–45, Norwegian)
Whitehead (William; 1715–85, English)
Wycherley (William; c.1640–1716, English)
Zavattini (Cesare; 1902–89, Italian)
Zuckmayer (Carl; 1896–1977, German)

10 Bhavabhûti (fl.8c, Indian)
Boucicault (Dion; 1820–90, Irish)
Cartwright (William; 1611–43, English)
Courteline (Georges; 1860–1929, French)
Cumberland (Richard; 1732–1811, English)
Destouches (Philippe; 1680–1754, French)
Drinkwater (John; 1882–1937, English)
Galsworthy (John; 1867–1933, English)
La Chaussée (Pierre Claude Nivelle de; 1692–1754, French)
Lagerkvist (Pär; 1891–1974, Swedish)
Mankiewicz (Herman; 1897–1953, US)
Mayakovsky (Vladimir; 1894–1930, Russian)
Mnouchkine (Ariane; 1938– , French)
Phillpotts (Eden; 1862–1960, English)
Pirandello (Luigi; 1867–1936, Italian)
Porto-Riche (Georges de; 1849–1930, French)
Schnitzler (Arthur; 1862–1931, Austrian)
Strindberg (August; 1849–1912, Swedish)
Vörösmarty (Michael; 1800–55, Hungarian)
Waterhouse (Keith; 1929– , English)
Williamson (David; 1942– , Australian)

11 Anzengruber (Ludwig; 1839–89, Austrian)
Bontempelli (Massimo; 1878–1960, Italian)
Douglas-Home (William; 1912–92, Scottish)
García Lorca (Federico; 1898–1936, Spanish)
Hasenclever (Walter; 1890–1940, German)
Maeterlinck (Maurice, Count; 1862–1949, Belgian)
Montherlant (Henri de; 1896–1972, French)
Núñez de Arce (Gaspar; 1834–1903, Spanish)
Pérez Galdós (Benito; 1843–1920, Spanish)
Pixérécourt (Guilbert de; 1773–1844, French)
Pressburger (Emeric; 1902–88, Hungarian)
Shakespeare (William; 1564–1616, English)
Valle-Inclán (Ramón del; 1869–1936, Spanish)
Wildenbruch (Ernst von; 1845–1909, German)

12 Aristophanes (c.448–c.385 BC, Greek)
Beaumarchais (Pierre de; 1732–99, French)
Bickerstaffe (Isaac; c.1735–c.1812, Irish)
Campton, David (1924–2006, English)
Cecchi D'Amico (Suso; 1914– , Italian)
Hofmannsthal (Hugo von; 1874–1929, Austrian)

Sigurjónsson (Jóhann; 1880–1919, Icelandic)

13 Gonçalves Dias (António; 1823–64, Brazilian)

Przybyszewski (Stanisław; 1868–1927, Polish)

Tirso de Molina (c.1571–1648, Spanish)

14 Castro y Bellvis (Guillén de; 1569–1631, Spanish)

Oehlenschläger (Adam; 1779–1850, Danish)

Zorrilla y Moral (José; 1817–93, Spanish)

15 Fabre d'Églantine (Philippe; 1750–94, French)

García Gutiérrez (Antonio; 1813–84, Spanish)

Granville-Barker (Harley; 1877–1946, English)

See also **Brecht, Bertolt; Chekhov, Anton; Coward, Noël; Ibsen, Henrik; Molière; O'Neill, Eugene; Racine, Jean; Shakespeare, William; theatre; Wilde, Oscar**

player *see* **baseball; basketball; chess; darts; football; ice hockey; Rugby League; Rugby Union; snooker; tennis**

plum

Plum varieties include:

03 egg

04 gage
musk

05 prune

06 cherry
damask
damson
French
mussel

07 quetsch

08 victoria

09 greengage
mirabelle

plumbing

Plumbing fittings and equipment include:

02 WC

03 pan
tap
tee

04 bath
bend
bowl
flux
hose
pipe
plug
pump
sink
tank
trap

05 auger
basin
bidet
float
joint
P-trap
U-bend
union
valve

06 boiler
faucet
gasket

geyser
hopper
nipple
shower
solder
toilet
urinal
washer

07 cistern
coupler
plunger
reducer
stop end
Y-branch

08 ballcock
cylinder
drain rod
lavatory
lever tap
mixer tap
pedestal
pipe clip
radiator
soil vent
stopcock
sump pump
valve key

09 ball valve
blowtorch
draincock
gate valve
mains pipe
nipple key
waste pipe

10 back boiler
bottle trap
check valve
copper pipe
copper tube
elbow joint
flare joint
header tank
pipe bender
pipe cutter
pipe wrench
programmer
septic tank
shower head
Teflon® tape
thermostat
tube cutter

11 water closet

12 basin spanner
monkey wrench

overflow bend
pipe coupling
siphon washer
13 deburring tool

expansion tank
lavatory chain
14 gas water heater
Stillson® wrench

15 immersion heater
lockshield valve
tube flaring tool

Poe, Edgar Allan (1809–49)

Significant works include:

05 *Poems* (1831)

08 *Al Aaraaf* (1829)
'The Raven' (1845)

10 'Annabel Lee' (1849)
'The Gold Bug' (1843)

13 'William Wilson' (1839)

14 'The Balloon-Hoax' (1844)

18 'The Purloined Letter' (1844)

20 'The Cask of Amontillado' (1847)

'The Pit and the Pendulum' (1842)

22 *Tamerlane and Other Poems* (1827)
'The Masque of the Red Death' (1842)

24 'The Fall of the House of Usher' (1839)
'The Murders in the Rue Morgue' (1841)

26 *The Philosophy of Composition* (1846)

28 'The Facts in the Case of M Valdemar' (1845)

31 *Tales of the Grotesque and Arabesque* (1840)

poetry

Poetry includes:

03 lay
ode

04 epic
song

05 ditty
elegy
epode
haiku
idyll
lyric
rhyme

tanka
verse

06 ballad
epopee
monody
sonnet

07 bucolic
couplet
eclogue
epigram
georgic

pantoum
rondeau
sestina
triolet
virelay

08 cinquain
clerihew
limerick
lipogram
madrigal
palinode

pastoral
thin poem
verselet
versicle

09 roundelay
shape poem

10 villanelle

12 concrete poem
epithalamium
nursery rhyme
prothalamion

Poems and poetry collections include:

02 'If' (1910, Rudyard Kipling)

04 *Crow* (1970, Ted Hughes)
'Days' (1964, Philip Larkin)
Edda (c.1000–1300, anon)
'Hope' (1815, John Keats)
'Howl' (1956, Allen Ginsberg)
'Maud' (1855, Alfred, Lord Tennyson)
Odes (23 BC, Horace)

05 *Comus* (1637, John Milton)
'Lamia' (1819, John Keats)

06 *Façade* (1923, Dame Edith Sitwell)
'Heaven' (1915, Rupert Brooke)
Hellas (1822, Percy Bysshe Shelley)
'The Fly' (1732, William Oldys)

07 'A Vision' (1881, Oscar Wilde)
Beowulf (c.1000, anon)
Don Juan (1819, Lord Byron)
Lycidas (1637, John Milton)

'Mariana' (1830, Alfred, Lord Tennyson)
Marmion (1808, Sir Walter Scott)
'Requiem' (1887, Robert Louis Stevenson)
'Rondeau' (1838, Leigh Hunt)
'The Quip' (1633, George Herbert)

08 'Bermudas' (1686–87, Andrew Marvell)
Endymion (1818, John Keats)
Georgics (c.29 BC, Virgil)
'Gunga Din' (1892, Rudyard Kipling)
Hiawatha (1855, Henry Wadsworth
Longfellow)
Hudibras (1663–78, Samuel Butler)
'Insomnia' (1881, Dante Gabriel Rossetti)
Kalevala (1835, Elias Lönnrot)
Lupercal (1960, Ted Hughes)
Queen Mab (1813, Percy Bysshe Shelley)
Ramayana (c.250 BC, Valmiki)
The Iliad (c.8c BC, Homer)
The Pearl (c.1400, anon)

'The Tyger' (1794, William Blake)
'Tithonus' (1833–59, Alfred, Lord Tennyson)
'To Autumn' (1819, John Keats)

09 *Decameron* (1358, Giovanni Boccaccio)
Human Life (1815, Samuel Taylor Coleridge)
Jerusalem (1804–20, William Blake)
'Kubla Khan' (1816, Samuel Taylor Coleridge)
The Aeneid (c.19 BC, Virgil)
The Cantos (1917, Ezra Pound)

10 'Cherry Ripe' (Thomas Campion)
'Christabel' (1816, Samuel Taylor Coleridge)
Dream Songs (1955–68, John Berryman)
In Memoriam (1850, Alfred, Lord Tennyson)
Lalla Rookh (1817, Thomas Moore)
The Dunciad (1728, Alexander Pope)
The Odyssey (c.8c BC, Homer)
The Poetics (c.330 BC, Aristotle)
The Prelude (1805, William Wordsworth)
The Village (1783, George Crabbe)
'View of a Pig' (1960, Ted Hughes)

11 'A Red, Red Rose' (1787–1803, Robert Burns)
Ars Amatoria (c.1 BC, Ovid)
'Empty Vessel' (1926, Hugh MacDiarmid)
High Windows (1974, Philip Larkin)
Holy Sonnets (17c, John Donne)
'Jabberwocky' (1872, Lewis Carroll)
Mahabharata (c.350 AD, Vyasa)
'Memorabilia' (1855, Robert Browning)
'Remembrance' (1845, Emily Brontë)
Song of My Cid (12c, Juan Ruiz)
'Sudden Light' (1863, Dante Gabriel Rossetti)
'Tam O'Shanter' (1790, Robert Burns)
The Eclogues (37 BC, Virgil)
'The Exstasie' (1896, John Donne)
'The Retreate' (1650, Henry Vaughan)
'The Sick Rose' (1794, William Blake)
'The Sluggard' (c.1700, Isaac Watts)

12 *A Glass of Beer* (17c, Dáibhidh Ó Bruadair)
'Ash Wednesday' (1930, T S Eliot)
'A Song to Celia' (1616, Ben Jonson)
A Song to David (1763, Christopher Smart)
'Auld Lang Syne' (1787–1803, Robert Burns)
Bhagavad Gita (c.400 BC)
Eugene Onegin (1828, Alexander Pushkin)
'Faith Healing' (1960, Philip Larkin)
Four Quartets (1935, T S Eliot)
Goblin Market (1862, Christina Rossetti)
'Hawk Roosting' (1957, Ted Hughes)
Homage to Clio (1960, W H Auden)
Jubilate Agno (1939, Christopher Smart)
Mercian Hymns (1971, Geoffrey Hill)
Morte d'Arthur (1469–70, Sir Thomas Malory)
'Ode to Evening' (1747, William Collins)

Paradise Lost (1667, John Milton)
Piers Plowman (14c, William Langland)
The Lucy Poems (1801, William Wordsworth)
The Visionary (1870, Jonas Lie)
The Waste Land (1922, T S Eliot)
'The Windhover' (1877, Gerard Manley Hopkins)

13 'Arms and the Boy' (1918, Wilfred Owen)
Gilgamesh Epic (1942–53, Willi Baumeister)
Leaves of Grass (1855, Walt Whitman)
Metamorphoses (8 CAD, Ovid)
'Missing the Sea' (1965, Derek Walcott)
'Naming of Parts' (1942, Henry Reed)
Roman de la Rose (13c, Guillaume de Lorris and Jean de Meung)
'September Song' (1968, Geoffrey Hill)
'Song by Isbrand' (1825–50, Thomas Lovell Beddoes)
The Book of Thel (1789, William Blake)

14 *A Shropshire Lad* (1896, A E Housman)
Divina Commedia (c.1307, Dante Alighieri)
Elegiac Sonnets (1784, Charlotte Smith)
'Leda and the Swan' (1928, W B Yeats)
Les Fleurs du mal (1857, Charles Baudelaire)
'Love Songs in Age' (1964, Philip Larkin)
Lyrical Ballads (1798, Samuel Taylor Coleridge and William Wordsworth)
Orlando Furioso (1516, Ludovico Ariosto)
Song of Hiawatha (1855, Henry Wadsworth Longfellow)
'Strange Meeting' (1918, Wilfred Owen)
'The Divine Image' (1789, William Blake)
'The Feel of Hands' (1973, Thom Gunn)
'The Lotus-Eaters' (1833, Alfred, Lord Tennyson)
'The Ship of Death' (1929–30, D H Lawrence)

15 *Canterbury Tales* (c.1387–1400, Geoffrey Chaucer)
Cautionary Tales (1907, Hilaire Belloc)
'Love without Hope' (1925, Robert Graves)
'Magna Est Veritas' (1975, Stevie Smith)
'Ode on Melancholy' (1820, John Keats)
Summoned by Bells (1960, Sir John Betjeman)
The Age of Anxiety (1948, W H Auden)
The Divine Comedy (c.1307, Dante Alighieri)
'The Eve of St Agnes' (1819, John Keats)
The Faerie Queene (1590/1596, Edmund Spenser)
'The Garden of Love' (1794, William Blake)
'The Grauballe Man' (1975, Seamus Heaney)
'The Second Coming' (1920, W B Yeats)
'The Sorrow of Love' (1893, W B Yeats)

Poetry movements include:

04 Beat

07 Acmeism
digital
epitaph
imagism

08 concrete
medieval
pastoral
Trouvère

09 modernism

symbolism
Troubador
Victorian

10 Parnassian

11 found poetry
Minnesinger
objectivist
Romanticism
sound poetry
The Movement

traditional

12 metaphysical

13 Black Mountain
erasure poetry
New York School
non-conformism
post-modernism

14 chanson de geste

15 automatic poetry

Poets include:

03 Gay (John; 1685–1732, English)
Key (Francis Scott; 1780–1843, US)
Paz (Octavio; 1914–98, Mexican)
Poe (Edgar Allan; 1809–49, US)
Pye (Henry; 1745–1813, English)

04 Agee (James; 1909–55, US)
Amis (Sir Kingsley; 1922–95, English)
Benn (Gottfried; 1886–1956, German)
Blok (Aleksandr; 1880–1921, Russian)
Bold (Alan; 1943– , Scottish)
Cope (Wendy; 1945– , English)
Cory (William Johnson; 1823–92, English)
Cruz (Sor Juana Inés de la; 1648–95,
Mexican)
Dunn (Douglas; 1942– , Scottish)
Dyer (Sir Edward; c.1545–1607, English)
Gray (Thomas; 1716–71, English)
Gunn (Thom; 1929–2004, English)
Hill (Geoffrey; 1932– , English)
Hogg (James; 1770–1835, Scottish)
Hood (Thomas; 1799–1845, English)
Hugo (Victor; 1802–85, French)
Hunt (Leigh; 1784–1859, English)
Muir (Edwin; 1887–1959, Scottish)
Okri (Ben; 1959– , Nigerian)
Ovid (43 BC–AD17, Roman)
Owen (Wilfred; 1893–1918, English)
Pope (Alexander; 1688–1744, English)
Read (Sir Herbert; 1893–1968, English)
Rich (Adrienne; 1929– , US)
Rowe (Nicholas; 1674–1718, English)
Sádi (c.1184–c.1292, Persian)
Tate (Allen; 1899–1979, US)
Tate (Nahum; 1652–1715, Irish)
Vega (Lope de; 1562–1635, Spanish)

05 Aiken (Conrad; 1889–1973, US)
Arany (János; 1817–82, Hungarian)
Auden (W H ; 1907–73, English/US)
Basho (Matsuo; 1644–94, Japanese)
Benét (Stephen Vincent; 1898–1943, US)
Blair (Robert; 1699–1746, Scottish)
Blake (William; 1757–1827, English)

Brant (Sebastian; 1458–1521, German)
Burns (Robert; 1759–96, Scottish)
Byron (George Gordon, Lord; 1788–1824,
English)
Carew (Thomas; 1595–1639, English)
Clare (John; 1793–1864, English)
Colum (Pádraic; 1881–1972, Irish)
Crane (Hart; 1899–1932, US)
Darío (Rubén; 1867–1916, Nicaraguan)
Donne (John; c.1572–1631, English)
Duffy (Carol Ann; 1955– , Scottish)
Ewald (Johannes; 1743–81, Danish)
Eliot (T S; 1888–1965, US/British)
Frost (Robert; 1874–1963, US)
Gower (John; c.1325–1408, English)
Hafiz (c.1326–90, Persian)
Hardy (Thomas; 1840–1928, English)
Harry (Blind; fl.1470–92, Scottish)
Heine (Heinrich; 1797–1856, German)
Henri (Adrian; 1932–2000, English)
Hesse (Hermann; 1877–1962, German/
Swiss)
Homer (c.8c BC; Greek)
Hulme (T E; 1883–1917, English)
Iqbal (Sir Muhammad; 1875–1938, Indian)
Joyce (James; 1882–1941, Irish)
Keats (John; 1795–1821, English)
Keble (John; 1792–1866, English)
Keyes (Sidney; 1922–43, English)
Lodge (Thomas; c.1558–1625, English)
Lucan (AD39–65, Roman)
Marot (Clément; c.1497–1544, French)
Meyer (Conrad; 1825–98, Swiss)
Moore (Marianne; 1887–1972, US)
Moore (Thomas; 1779–1852, Irish)
Myers (Frederic; 1843–1901, English)
Noyes (Alfred; 1880–1958, English)
Péguy (Charles; 1873–1914, French)
Plath (Sylvia; 1932–63, US)
Pound (Ezra; 1885–1972, US)
Prior (Matthew; 1664–1721, English)
Pulci (Luigi; 1432–84, Italian)
Reyes (Alfonso; 1889–1959, Mexican)

Rilke (Rainer Maria; 1875–1926, Austrian)
Sachs (Hans; 1494–1576, German)
Sachs (Nelly; 1891–1970, German/Swedish)
Scott (Sir Walter; 1771–1832, Scottish)
Smart (Christopher; 1722–71, English)
Smith (Charlotte; 1749–1806, English)
Smith (Stevie; 1902–71, English)
Tasso (Torquato; 1544–95, Italian)
Tynan (Katharine; 1861–1931, Irish)
Wilde (Oscar; 1854–1900, Irish)
Wolfe (Charles; 1791–1823, Irish)
Wyatt (Sir Thomas; 1503–42, English)
Yeats (W B; 1865–1939, Irish)
Young (Edward; 1683–1765, English)

06 Achebe (Chinua; 1930– , Nigerian)
Adcock (Fleur; 1934– , New Zealand)
Arnold (Matthew; 1822–88, English)
Austin (Alfred; 1835–1913, English)
Barnes (William; 1801–86, English)
Belloc (Hilaire; 1870–1953, French/British)
Bishop (Elizabeth; 1911–79, US)
Brooke (Rupert; 1887–1915, English)
Camões (Luís de; 1524–80, Portuguese)
Brooks (Gwendolyn; 1917–2000, US)
Carver (Raymond; 1939–88, US)
Cibber (Colley; 1671–1757, English)
Clough (Arthur Hugh; 1819–61, English)
Cowper (William; 1731–1800, English)
Crabbe (George; 1754–1832, English)
Dowson (Ernest; 1867–1900, English)
Dryden (John; 1631–1700, English)
Dunbar (William; c.1460–c.1520, Scottish)
Dutton (Geoffrey; 1922–98, Australian)
Éluard (Paul; 1895–1952, French)
Empson (Sir William; 1906–84, English)
Ennius (Quintus; c.239–169 BC; Roman)
Eusden (Laurence; 1688–1730, English)
George (Stefan; 1868–1933, German)
Goethe (Johann Wolfgang von; 1749–1832,
    German)
Graves (Robert; 1895–1985, English)
Heaney (Seamus; 1939– , Northern Irish)
Hegley (John; 1953– , English)
Hesiod (c.8c BC; Greek)
Horace (65–8 BC; Roman)
Hughes (Langston; 1902–67, US)
Hughes (Ted; 1930–98, English)
Jonson (Ben; 1572–1637, English)
Larkin (Philip; 1922–85, English)
Lowell (Amy; 1874–1925, US)
Lowell (Robert, Jnr; 1917–77, US)
Millay (Edna St Vincent; 1892–1950, US)
Milosz (Czeslaw; 1911–2004, Lithuanian/
    US)
Milton (John; 1608–74, English)
Morgan (Edwin; 1920– , Scottish)
Morris (Sir Lewis; 1833–1907, Welsh)
Motion (Andrew; 1952– , English)

Neruda (Pablo; 1904–73, Chilean)
O'Brien (Sean; 1952– , English)
Ossian (c.3c AD, Irish)
Patten (Brian; 1946– , English)
Pindar (c.518–c.438 BC; Greek)
Porter (Peter; 1929– , Australian)
Racine (Jean; 1639–99, French)
Riding (Laura; 1901–91, US)
Sappho (c.610–c.580 BC; Greek)
Sidney (Sir Philip; 1554–86, English)
Snyder (Gary; 1930– , US)
Soutar (William; 1898–1943, Scottish)
Tagore (Rabindranath; 1861–1941, Indian)
Thomas (Dylan; 1914–53, Welsh)
Thomas (Edward; 1878–1917, British)
Thomas (R S; 1913–2000, Welsh)
Trench (Richard Chenevix; 1807–86, Irish)
Vergil (70–19 BC; Roman)
Villon (François; 1431–after 1463, French)
Virgil (70–19 BC; Roman)
Waller (Edmund; 1606–87, English)
Warton (Thomas; 1728–90, English)
Wright (Judith; 1915–2000, Australian)

07 Alcaeus (c.620–after 580 BC; Greek)
Aneirin (fl.6c–7c; British)
Aneurin (fl.6c–7c; British)
Angelou (Maya; 1928– , US)
Aretino (Pietro; 1492–1556, Italian)
Ariosto (Ludovico; 1474–1533, Italian)
Beddoes (Thomas Lovell; 1803–49, English)
Belleau (Rémy; 1528–77, French)
Bennett (Louise; 1919–2006, Jamaican)
Blunden (Edmund; 1896–1974, English)
Bridges (Robert; 1844–1930, English)
Brodsky (Iosif; 1940–96, Russian/US)
Caedmon (7c; Anglo-Saxon)
Camoëns (Luis de; 1524–80, Portuguese)
Campion (Thomas; 1567–1620, English)
Causley (Charles; 1917–2003, English)
Chaucer (Geoffrey; c.1345–1400, English)
Collins (William; 1721–59, English)
Emerson (Ralph Waldo; 1803–82, US)
Flecker (James Elroy; 1884–1915, English)
Herbert (George; 1593–1633, English)
Heredia (José María; 1803–39, Cuban)
Herrick (Robert; 1591–1674, English)
Hodgson (Ralph; 1871–1962, English)
Hopkins (Gerard Manley; 1844–89, English)
Housman (A E; 1859–1936, English)
Johnson (Linton Kwesi; 1952– , Jamaican)
Layamon (fl. early 13c; English)
Lazarus (Emma; 1849–87, US)
Leonard (Tom; 1944– , Scottish)
MacCaig (Norman; 1910–96, Scottish)
MacLean (Sorley; 1911–96, Scottish)
Martial (c.40–c.104 AD; Roman)
Marvell (Andrew; 1621–78, English)
McGough (Roger; 1937– , English)

Mistral (Frédéric; 1830–1914, French)
Newbolt (Sir Henry; 1862–1938, English)
Peacock (Thomas Love; 1785–1866, English)
Pushkin (Alexander; 1799–1837, Russian)
Rexroth (Kenneth; 1905–82, US)
Rimbaud (Arthur; 1854–91, French)
Roethke (Theodore; 1908–63, US)
Ronsard (Pierre de; 1524–85, French)
Russell (George; 1867–1935, Irish)
Sassoon (Siegfried; 1886–1967, English)
Seifert (Jaroslav; 1901–86, Czech)
Service (Robert; 1874–1958, English/
   Canadian)
Shelley (Percy Bysshe; 1792–1822, English)
Sitwell (Dame Edith; 1887–1964, English)
Skelton (John; c.1460–1529, English)
Southey (Robert; 1774–1843, English)
Soyinka (Wole; 1934– , Nigerian)
Spender (Sir Stephen; 1909–95, English)
Spenser (Edmund; c.1552–99, English)
Statius (Publius Papinius; c.45–96 AD;
   Roman)
Stevens (Wallace; 1879–1955, US)
Szirtes (George; 1948– , Hungarian)
Vaughan (Henry; 1622–95, Welsh)
Walcott (Derek; 1930– , West Indian)
Whitman (Walt; 1819–92, US)

08 Anacreon (c.570–c.475 BC; Greek)
Berryman (John; 1914–72, US)
Betjeman (Sir John; 1906–84, English)
Browning (Elizabeth Barrett; 1806–61,
   English)
Browning (Robert; 1812–89, English)
Bukowski (Charles; 1920–94, German/US)
Campbell (Thomas; 1777–1844, Scottish)
Catullus (Gaius Valerius; c.84–c.54 BC;
   Roman)
Congreve (William; 1670–1729, English)
Cynewulf (c.700–c.800, Anglo-Saxon)
D'Avenant (Sir William; 1606–68, English)
Day-Lewis (Cecil; 1904–72, Irish)
de la Mare (Walter; 1873–1956, English)
Fanshawe (Richard; 1608–66, English)
Ginsberg (Allen; 1926–97, US)
Hamilton (William; 1704–54, Scottish)
Hatfield (Jen; 1958– , English)
Henryson (Robert; c.1425–c.1508, Scottish)
Jennings (Elizabeth; 1926–2001, English)
Kavanagh (Patrick; 1905–67, Irish)
Langland (William; c.1332–c.1400, English)
Lawrence (D H; 1885–1930, English)
Leopardi (Giacomo; 1798–1837, Italian)
Lochhead (Liz; 1947– , Scottish)
Lovelace (Richard; 1618–57, English)
MacNeice (Louis; 1907–63, Northern Irish)
Mallarmé (Stéphane; 1842–98, French)
Menander (c.343–c.291 BC; Greek)
Petrarch (Francesco; 1304–74, Italian)

Rossetti (Christina; 1830–94, English)
Rossetti (Dante Gabriel; 1828–82, English)
Schiller (Friedrich; 1759–1805, German)
Shadwell (Thomas; c.1642–1692, English)
Stephens (James; 1882–1950, Irish)
Suckling (Sir John; 1609–42, English)
Tennyson (Alfred, Lord; 1809–92, English)
Thompson (Francis; 1859–1907, English)
Traherne (Thomas; c.1636–1674, English)
Tyrtaeus (fl.c.685–668 BC; Greek)
Verlaine (Paul; 1844–96, French)
Whittier (John Greenleaf; 1807–92, US)
Williams (William Carlos; 1883–1963, US)

09 Coleridge (Samuel Taylor; 1772–1834,
   English)
Dickinson (Emily; 1830–86, US)
Doolittle (Hilda; 1886–1961, US)
Fanthorpe (U A ; 1929– , English)
Goldsmith (Oliver; 1730–74, Irish)
Lamartine (Alphonse de; 1790–1869,
   French)
Lovecraft (H P; 1890–1937, US)
Lucretius (c.99–55 BC; Roman)
Masefield (John; 1878–1967, English)
Quasimodo (Salvatore; 1901–68, Italian)
Rochester (John Wilmot, 2nd Earl of;
   1647–80, English)
Rosenberg (Isaac; 1890–1918, English)
Shenstone (William; 1714–63, English)
Swinburne (Algernon; 1837–1909, English)
Whitehead (William; 1715–85, English)
Zephaniah (Benjamin; 1958– , British)

10 Baudelaire (Charles; 1821–67, French)
Chatterton (Thomas; 1752–70, English)
Drinkwater (John; 1882–1937, English)
Fitzgerald (Edward; 1809–83, English)
Gawain Poet (The; fl.c.1370, English)
Longfellow (Henry Wadsworth; 1807–82,
   US)
MacDiarmid (Hugh; 1892–1978, Scottish)
McGonagall (William; 1830–1902, Scottish)
Propertius (Sextus; c.48–c.15 BC; Roman)
Szymborska (Wislawa; 1923– , Polish)
Tannhäuser (Der; c.1210–c.1270, German)
Theocritus (c.310–250 BC; Greek)
Wordsworth (William; 1770–1850, English)

11 Apollinaire (Guillaume; 1880–1918, Italian/
   French)
Callimachus (c.305–c.240 BC; Hellenistic)
Omar Khayyám (c.1048–c.1122, Persian)
Shakespeare (William; 1564–1616, English)

12 Ferlinghetti (Lawrence; 1919– , US)

14 Dafydd ap Gwilym (c.1315–c.1370, Welsh)
Dante Alighieri (1265–1321, Italian)

15 Thomas the Rhymer (c.1220–c.1297,
   Scottish)

Poets Laureate, with date of appointment:

03 Pye (Henry; 1745–1813, English; 1790)

04 Rowe (Nicholas; 1674–1718, English; 1715)
Tate (Nahum; 1652–1715, Irish; 1692)

06 Austin (Alfred; 1835–1913, English; 1896)
Cibber (Colley; 1671–1757, English; 1730)
Dryden (John; 1631–1700, English; 1668)
Eusden (Laurence; 1688–1730; English)
Hughes (Ted; 1930–98, English; 1984)
Jonson (Ben; 1572–1637, English; 1617)
Motion (Andrew; 1952– , English; 1999)
Warton (Thomas; 1728–90, English; 1785)

07 Bridges (Robert Seymour; 1844–1930, English; 1913)
Southey (Robert; 1774–1843, English; 1813)

08 Betjeman (Sir John; 1906–84, English; 1972)
D'Avenant (Sir William; 1606–68, English; 1638)
Day-Lewis (Cecil; 1904–72, Irish; 1968)
Shadwell (Thomas; c.1642–1692, English; 1689)
Tennyson (Alfred, Lord; 1809–92, English; 1850)

09 Masefield (John; 1878–1967, English; 1930)
Whitehead (William; 1715–85, English; 1757)

10 Wordsworth (William; 1770–1850, English; 1843)

Poetry terms include:

03 bob	**07** sapphic	**09** free verse	short metre
05 rubai	sestina	terza rima	**12** ballad stanza
06 sonnet	**08** bobwheel	**10** blank verse	**13** Italian sonnet
stanza	cinquain	end-stopped	**14** Miltonic sonnet
tercet	quatrain	ottava rima	Sicilian octave

See also **Betjeman, Sir John**; **Blake, William**; **Burns, Robert**; **Byron, George Gordon, Lord**; **Clare, John**; **Dante Alighieri**; **Eliot, T S**; **Frost, Robert**; **Goethe, Johann Wolfgang von**; **Heaney, Seamus**; **Homer**; **Hughes, Ted**; **Keats, John**; **Milton, John**; **Petrarch**; **Poe, Edgar Allan**; **prosody**; **rhyme**; **Shakespeare, William**; **Tennyson, Alfred, Lord**; **Virgil**; **Whitman, Walt**; **Wordsworth, William**; **Yeats, W B**

points of a horse *see* horse

poison

Poisoning types include:

04 food	sausage	lead colic	stibialism
lead	**08** botulism	mephitism	strychnism
05 algae	ergotism	sapraemia	**11** phosphorism
blood	plumbism	saturnism	septicaemia
06 iodism	ptomaine	zinc colic	**12** hydrargyrism
07 bromism	toxaemia	**10** alcoholism	intoxication
gassing	**09** brominism	molybdosis	strychninism
pyaemia	crotalism	salicylism	**13** mycotoxicosis
	fluorosis	salmonella	

Poisons and toxic substances include:

03 BHC	ricin	curare
04 bane	sarin	dioxin
lead	toxin	G-agent
05 abrin	venin	iodine
conin	venom	ketene
lysol	VX gas	V-agent
ozone	**06** arsine	wabain

war gas
07 arsenic
bromine
cacodyl
coniine
cyanide
digoxin
dioxane
mercury
mineral
neurine
ouabain
stibine
tanghin
08 antimony
atropine
chlordan
chlorine
cyanogen
cytisine
fluorine
gossypol
lobeline

melittin
nerve gas
Paraquat®
phosgene
ptomaine
ratsbane
rotenone
thebaine
urushiol
09 aflatoxin
amygdalin
chaconine
chlordane
muscarine
mycotoxin
nux vomica
saxitoxin
white damp
10 acrylamide
aqua Tofana
bufotenine
domoic acid
heptachlor

mustard gas
neurotoxin
oxalic acid
phosphorus
phytotoxin
picrotoxin
strychnine
tetrotoxin
11 enterotoxin
hyoscyamine
nitric oxide
prussic acid
sugar of lead
12 strophanthin
tetrodotoxin
13 Scheele's green
silver nitrate
14 carbon monoxide
glutaraldehyde
15 alpha-chloralose
hydrogen cyanide
nitrogen dioxide

Poisonous plants include:

05 dwale
07 aconite
amanita
anemone
cowbane
hemlock
lantana
08 banewort
foxglove
laburnum
mandrake

oleander
wild arum
09 digitalis
monkshood
naked boys
naked lady
poison ivy
stinkweed
wake-robin
wolfsbane
10 belladonna
cuckoo pint

jimson weed
nightshade
stramonium
thorn apple
windflower
12 giant hogweed
helmet flower
13 meadow saffron
14 castor oil plant
lords-and-ladies
15 black nightshade

Poisonous creatures include:

03 asp
04 fugu
gila
seps
weta
05 adder
cobra
viper
06 dugite
katipo
taipan
07 redback

sea wasp
08 blowfish
cerastes
jararaca
jararaka
mocassin
moccasin
ringhals
rinkhals
scorpion
sea snake
09 berg-adder
boomslang

funnel-web
globe fish
hamadryad
king cobra
puff adder
stonefish
tarantula
10 bandy-bandy
black snake
black widow
bushmaster
copperhead
coral snake

death adder
puffer fish
11 cottonmouth
gaboon viper
gila monster
rattlesnake
12 box jellyfish
scorpion fish
sea porcupine
violin spider
13 water moccasin
15 funnel-web spider

See also **insect**; **insecticide**; **narcotic**; **snake**

poker

Poker terms include:

03 pat
shy

04 ante
call
flop
pair
stay

stud

05 blind
bluff
check
flush

06 kicker

suited

08 hole card
showdown
stand pat
straight

09 four-flush

full house

10 royal flush

11 busted flush
pass the buck

13 community card
straight flush

police

Police ranks in the UK:

08 Sergeant

09 Commander
Constable
Inspector

12 Commissioner

14 Chief Constable
Chief Inspector
Superintendent

18 Deputy Commissioner

19 Chief Superintendent

20 Deputy Chief Constable

21 Assistant Commissioner

23 Assistant Chief Constable

27 Deputy Assistant Commissioner

Police forces and branches include:

02 AP
KP
MP
PD
SS

03 CIB
CID
KGB
Met
MGB
RMP

04 Ogpu
PSNI
RCMP
SWAT

05 cheka
Garda

Stasi

07 Europol
Gestapo
sweeney
the Yard

08 Interpol
Mounties

09 Air Police
bomb squad
drug squad
porn squad
riot squad
task force
vice squad

10 riot police
Securitate
water guard

11 flying squad
gendarmerie
strike force
sweeney todd
Yardie squad

12 mobile police
Scotland Yard
secret police
Texas Rangers

13 Garda Siochana
mounted police
Schutzstaffel
Special Branch
traffic police

14 military police

15 New Scotland Yard

Terms to do with the police include:

02 PC
PD
PS

03 cop
WPC

04 ACPO
beat
book
bust
cell

fuzz
nark
nick
plod
raid
rank
shop
tana
tank

05 ACPOS

baton
beast
bobby
cheka
cuffs
filth
fit-up
force
frame
garda

go off
grass
jawan
manor
plant
polis
pound
set-up
snout
squad
sting
tanna
thana
tunic

06 arrest
batoon
charge
copper
cordon
curfew
fisgig
fizgig
helmet
line-up
patrol
peeler
Q-train
rozzer
rumble
sbirro
search
tannah
thanah
thanna
wanted

07 captain
caution
copshop
custody
dragnet
epaulet
Europol
jemadar
manhunt
marshal
mugshot
officer
Old Bill
pentito

See also **detective**

round-up
station
stinger
stoolie
sweeney
thannah
the Bill
the Yard
trooper
uniform
warrant

08 evidence
gendarme
Interpol
mouchard
panda car
precinct
prowl car
sergeant
serjeant
speed gun
squad car

09 blue light
bomb squad
centenier
commander
constable
detective
drug squad
handcuffs
identikit
inspector
meat wagon
on the beat
police dog
policeman
porn squad
radar trap
riot squad
shakedown
speed trap
task force
truncheon
vice squad

10 body armour
boys in blue
carabinero
gangbuster

lieutenant
police cell
police trap
supergrass
tenderloin
tracker dog
watch house

11 carabiniere
fingerprint
flying squad
jam sandwich
Judges' Rules
police force
policewoman
stool pigeon
strike force
sweeney todd
utility belt
warrant card
Yardie squad

12 bertillonage
constabulary
incident room
mobile police
peace officer
police escort
police-manure
Scotland Yard
secret police
surveillance
walkie-talkie

13 branch officer
mounted police
police station
rogues' gallery
search warrant
Special Branch
stop-and-search
traffic police

14 catch red-handed
Chief Constable
chief inspector
criminal record
police sergeant

15 bullet-proof vest
long arm of the law
New Scotland Yard
scene of the crime

political party *see* **party**

politics

06 holism
Maoism
Nazism
07 fascism
Marxism
08 third way
Whiggism
09 anarchism
communism
democracy
neo-Nazism

pluralism
socialism
theocracy
10 absolutism
Bolshevism
federalism
liberalism
neo-fascism
Trotskyism
11 imperialism
nationalism

syndicalism
Thatcherism
12 collectivism
conservatism
13 individualism
republicanism
unilateralism
14 egalitarianism
neocolonialism
15 social democracy
totalitarianism

02 Nu (U; 1907–95, Burmese)

03 Coe (Sebastian, Lord; 1956– , English)
Doe (Samuel; 1951–90, Liberian)
Lie (Trygve; 1896–1968, Norwegian)
Moi (Daniel arap; 1924– , Kenyan)
Rao (P V Narasimha; 1921–2004, Indian)
Rau (Johannes; 1931–2006, German)
Sun (Yat-sen; 1866–1925, Chinese)
Zia (Khaleda; 1945– , Bangladeshi)

04 Amin (Idi; 1925–2003, Ugandan)
Benn (Tony; 1925– , English)
Bird (Vere Cornwall; 1910–99, Antiguan)
Blum (Léon; 1872–1950, French)
Bush (George Herbert Walker; 1924– , US)
Bush (George W; 1946– , US)
Coty (René; 1882–1962, French)
Deng (Xiaoping; 1904–97, Chinese)
Dole (Bob; 1923– , US)
Eden (Sir Anthony, 1st Earl of Avon; 1897–1977, English)
Foot (Michael; 1913– , English)
Ford (Gerald R; 1913–2006, US)
Gore (Al, Jnr; 1948– , US)
Hays (Will; 1879–1954, US)
Hess (Rudolf; 1894–1987, German)
Home (Alec Douglas-Home, Lord; 1903–95, English)
Hoon (Geoff; 1953– , English)
Howe (Geoffrey, Lord; 1926– , British)
Hume (John; 1937– , Northern Irish)
Hurd (Douglas, Lord; 1930– , English)
King (Mackenzie; 1874–1950, Canadian)
King (William; 1786–1853, US)
Kohl (Helmut; 1930– , German)
Meir (Golda; 1898–1978, Russian/US/Israeli)
More (Sir Thomas, St; 1478–1535, English)
Nagy (Imre; 1895–1958, Hungarian)
Owen (David, Lord; 1938– , English)
Peel (Sir Robert; 1788–1850, English)

Pitt (William; 1759–1806, English)
Polk (James K; 1795–1849, US)
Reid (John; 1947– , Scottish)
Reno (Janet; 1938– , US)
Rice (Condoleezza; 1954– , US)
Röhm (Ernst; 1887–1934, German)
Taft (William; 1857–1930, US)
Tito (1892–1980, Yugoslav)

05 Adams (Gerry; 1948– , Northern Ireland)
Adams (John; 1735–1826, US)
Adams (John Quincy; 1767–1848, US)
Agnew (Spiro T; 1918–96, US)
Ahern (Bertie; 1951– , Irish)
Amory (Derick Heathcoat Amory, 1st Viscount; 1899–1981, English)
Arens (Moshe; 1925– , Lithuanian/Israeli)
Astor (Nancy, Viscountess; 1879–1964, US/ British)
Astor (Waldorf, Viscount; 1879–1952, US/ British)
Bacon (Francis, Lord; 1561–1626, English)
Baker (James, III; 1930– , US)
Baker (Kenneth, Lord; 1934– , English)
Banda (Hastings; 1898–1997, Malawian)
Barak (Ehud; 1942– , Israeli)
Barre (Mohamed Siad; 1919–95, Somali)
Begin (Menachem; 1913–92, Polish/Israeli)
Bevan (Aneurin; 1897–1960, Welsh)
Biden (Joe; 1942– , US)
Blair (Tony; 1953– , British)
Botha (Louis; 1862–1919, South African)
Botha (P W; 1916–2006, South African)
Brown (Gordon; 1951– , Scottish)
Burke (Edmund; 1729–97, Irish)
Byers (Stephen; 1953– , English)
Cecil (Robert, Marquis of Salisbury; 1830–1903, English)
Clark (Alan; 1928–99, English)
Clark (Helen; 1950– , New Zealand)

Cowen (Brian; 1960–   , Irish)
Craxi (Bettino; 1934–2000, Italian)
Dacko (David; 1930–2003, Central African
   Republic)
Dayan (Moshe; 1915–81, Israeli)
Dewar (Donald; 1937–2000, Scottish)
Ewing (Winnie; 1929–   , Scottish)
Grant (Bernie; 1944–2000, British)
Grant (Ulysses S; 1822–85, US)
Hácha (Emil; 1872–1945, Czechoslovak)
Hague (William; 1961–   , English)
Havel (Václav; 1936–   , Czech)
Hawke (Bob; 1929–   , Australian)
Hayes (Rutherford B; 1822–93, US)
Heath (Sir Edward; 1916–2005, English)
Hoxha (Enver; 1908–85, Albanian)
Juppé (Alain; 1945–   , French)
Khama (Sir Seretse; 1921–80, African)
Klima (Viktor; 1947–   , Austrian)
Krenz (Egon; 1937–   , German)
Lenin (Vladimir Ilyich; 1870–1924, Russian)
Le Pen (Jean-Marie; 1928–   , French)
Major (John; 1943–   , English)
Mbeki (Thabo; 1942–   , South African)
Menem (Carlos; 1935–   , Argentine)
Mogae (Festus; 1939–   , Botswana)
Nehru (Jawaharlal; 1889–1964, Indian)
Ne Win (U; 1911–2002, Burmese)
Nixon (Richard; 1913–94, US)
Obama (Barack; 1961–   , US)
Obote (Milton; 1924–2005, Ugandan)
Palme (Olof; 1927–86, Swedish)
Peres (Shimon; 1923–   , Polish/Israeli)
Perón (Isabelita; 1931–   , Argentine)
Perón (Juan; 1895–1974, Argentine)
Perot (Ross; 1930–   , US)
Prodi (Romano; 1939–   , Italian)
Putin (Vladimir; 1952–   , Russian)
Rabin (Yitzhak; 1922–95, Israeli)
Roehm (Ernst; 1887–1934, German)
Sadat (Anwar el-; 1918–81, Egyptian)
Short (Clare; 1946–   , English)
Smith (Ian; 1919–2007, Rhodesian)
Smuts (Jan; 1870–1950, South African)
Steel (David, Lord; 1938–   , Scottish)
Straw (Jack; 1946–   , English)
Tambo (Oliver; 1917–93, South African)
Vance (Cyrus R; 1917–2002, US)

06 Abacha (Sani; 1943–98, Nigerian)
Abbott (Diane; 1953–   , English)
Ancram (Michael; 1945–   , English)
Antony (Mark; c.83–30 BC, Roman)
Aquino (Benigno; 1932–83, Philippine)
Aquino (Cory; 1933–   , Philippine)
Archer (Jeffrey, Lord; 1940–   , English)
Attlee (Clement, Earl; 1883–1967, English)
Bhutto (Benazir; 1953–2007, Pakistani)
Bhutto (Zulfikar; 1928–79, Pakistani)

Brandt (Willy; 1913–92, German)
Briand (Aristide; 1862–1932, French)
Caesar (Julius; 100/102–44 BC, Roman)
Carter (Jimmy; 1924–   , US)
Castle (Barbara, Baroness; 1910–2002,
   English)
Castro (Fidel; 1926–   , Cuban)
Cheney (Dick; 1941–   , US)
Chirac (Jacques; 1932–   , French)
Cicero (Marcus Tullius; 106–43 BC, Roman)
Clarke (Kenneth; 1940–   , English)
Delors (Jacques; 1925–   , French)
Dönitz (Karl; 1891–1980, German)
Dubček (Alexander; 1921–92,
   Czechoslovak)
Dulles (John Foster; 1888–1959, US)
Ecevit (Bülent; 1925–2006, Turkish)
Engels (Friedrich; 1820–95, German)
Fillon (François, 1955–   , French)
Franco (Francisco; 1892–1975, Spanish)
Gandhi (Indira; 1917–84, Indian)
Gandhi (Rajiv; 1944–91, Indian)
Giroud (Françoise; 1916–2003, French)
Göring (Hermann Wilhelm; 1893–1946,
   German)
Gummer (John; 1939–   , English)
Hardie (Keir; 1856–1915, Scottish)
Harman (Harriet; 1950–   , English)
Healey (Denis, Lord; 1917–   , English)
Hitler (Adolf; 1889–1945, German)
Hoover (Herbert; 1874–1964, US)
Howard (John; 1939–   , Australian)
Howard (Michael; 1941–   , British)
Hun Sen (1952–   , Cambodian)
Jospin (Lionel; 1937–   , French)
Kabila (Joseph; 1970–   , Congolese)
Kabila (Laurent-Désiré; 1939–2001,
   Congolese)
Kaunda (Kenneth; 1924–   , Zambian)
Kruger (Paul; 1825–1904, South African)
Lamont (Norman, Lord; 1942–   , Scottish)
Lawson (Nigel, Lord; 1932–   , English)
Lilley (Peter; 1943–   , English)
Machel (Samora; 1933–86, Mozambique)
Marcos (Ferdinand; 1917–89, Philippine)
Marcos (Imelda; c.1930–   , Philippine)
Merkel (Angela; 1954–   , Germany)
Mobutu (Sese Seko; 1930–97, Zairean)
Mowlam (Mo; 1949–2005, English)
Mugabe (Robert; 1924–   , Zimbabwean)
Nasser (Gamal Abd al-; 1918–70, Egyptian)
Norris (Steven; 1945–   , English)
Patten (Chris; 1944–   , English)
Pétain (Philippe; 1856–1951, French)
Pol Pot (1925–98, Cambodian)
Powell (Colin; 1937–   , US)
Powell (Enoch; 1912–98, English)
Prasad (Rajendra; 1884–1963, Indian)

Quayle (Dan; 1947– , US)
Reagan (Ronald; 1911–2004, US)
Rhodes (Cecil; 1853–1902, South African)
Seneca (Lucius Annaeus; c.4 BC–c.65 AD,
  Roman)
Sharon (Ariel; 1928– , Israeli)
Stalin (Joseph; 1879–1953, Soviet)
Tebbit (Norman, Lord; 1931– , English)
Truman (Harry S; 1884–1972, US)
Walesa (Lech; 1943– , Polish)
Wilson (Harold, Lord; 1916–95, English)
Wilson (Woodrow; 1856–1924, US)
Wolsey (Thomas; c.1475–1530, English)

07 Acheson (Dean; 1893–1971, US)
Akihito (1933– , Japanese)
Allende (Salvador; 1908–73, Chilean)
Ashdown (Paddy, Lord; 1941– , English)
Asquith (H H, 1st Earl of Oxford and
  Asquith; 1852–1928, English)
Atatürk (Mustapha Kemal; 1881–1938,
  Turkish)
Baldwin (Stanley Baldwin, 1st Earl; 1867–
  1947, English)
Balfour (Arthur James Balfour, 1st Earl of;
  1848–1930, Scottish)
Beckett (Margaret; 1943– , English)
Bingham (Hiram; 1875–1956, US)
Boateng (Paul; 1951– , British)
Bokassa (Jean Bédel; 1921–96, Central
  African Republic)
Chalker (Lynda, Baroness; 1942– , English)
Chatham (William Pitt, Earl of; 1708–78,
  English)
Clinton (Bill; 1946– , US)
Clinton (Hillary; 1947– , US)
Collins (Michael; 1890–1922, Irish)
Cresson (Edith; 1934– , French)
Dalyell (Tam; 1932– , Scottish)
Darling (Alistair; 1953– , Scottish)
de Klerk (F W; 1936– , South African)
Dukakis (Michael; 1933– , US)
Göbbels (Joseph; 1897–1945, German)
Goering (Hermann; 1893–1946, German)
Halonen (Tarja; 1943– , Finnish)
Harding (Warren G; 1865–1923, US)
Haughey (Charles; 1925–2006, Irish)
Hussein (Saddam; 1937–2006, Iraqi)
Iliescu (Ion; 1930– , Romanian)
Jackson (Andrew; 1767–1845, US)
Jackson (Glenda; 1936– , English)
Jenkins (Roy, Lord; 1920–2003, Welsh)
Johnson (Lyndon B; 1908–73, US)
Keating (Paul; 1944– , Australian)
Kennedy (Edward; 1932– , US)
Kennedy (John F; 1917–63, US)
Kennedy (Robert F; 1925–68, US)
Khatami (Mohammad; 1943– , Iranian)
Kinnock (Neil; 1942– , Welsh)

Klestil (Thomas; 1932–2004, Austrian)
Koizumi (Junichiro; 1942– , Japanese)
Kosygin (Aleksei; 1904–80, Soviet)
Liddell (Helen; 1950– , Scottish)
Lincoln (Abraham; 1809–65, US)
Mandela (Nelson; 1918– , South African)
Mazarin (Jules; 1602–61, Italian/French)
McLeish (Henry; 1948– , Scottish)
Mondale (Walter F; 1928– , US)
Mubarak (Hosni; 1928– , Egyptian)
Nkrumah (Kwame; 1909–72, Ghanaian)
Noriega (General Manuel; 1940– ,
  Panamanian)
Nyerere (Julius; 1922–99, Tanzanian)
Paisley (Ian; 1926– , Northern Irish)
Parnell (Charles Stewart; 1846–91, Irish)
Pearson (Lester; 1897–1972, Canadian)
Profumo (John Dennis; 1915–2006, English)
Rifkind (Sir Malcolm; 1946– , Scottish)
Salazar (Antonio; 1889–1970, Portuguese)
Salmond (Alex; 1955– , Scottish)
Sarkozy (Nicolas; 1955– , French)
Shipley (Jenny; 1952– , New Zealand)
Suharto (Thojib N J; 1921–2008, Indonesian)
Sukarno (Ahmed; 1902–70, Indonesian)
Swinney (John; 1964– , Scottish)
Trimble (David; 1944– , Northern Irish)
Trudeau (Pierre; 1919–2000, Canadian)
Tudjman (Franjo; 1922–99, Croatian)
Walpole (Sir Robert, 1st Earl of Orford;
  1676–1745, English)
Whitlam (Gough; 1916– , Australian)
Wilhelm (II, Kaiser; 1859–1941, Prusso-
  German)
Yeltsin (Boris; 1931–2007, Russian)

08 Adenauer (Konrad; 1876–1967, German)
Andropov (Yuri; 1914–84, Soviet)
Ashcroft (John; 1942– , US)
Balladur (Edouard; 1929– , Turkish/French)
Banerjea (Sir Surendranath; 1848–1925,
  Indian)
Ben Bella (Ahmed; 1916– , Algerian)
Bismarck (Prince Otto von; 1815–98,
  Prusso-German)
Blunkett (David; 1947– , English)
Brezhnev (Leonid; 1906–82, Soviet)
Campbell (Kim; 1947– , Canadian)
Chamorro (Violetta; 1919– , Nicaraguan)
Chrétien (Jean; 1934– , Canadian)
Coolidge (Calvin; 1872–1933, US)
Cromwell (Oliver; 1599–1658, English)
de Gaulle (Charles; 1890–1970, French)
de Valera (Éamon; 1882–1975, Irish)
Disraeli (Benjamin, 1st Earl of Beaconsfield;
  1804–81, English)
Franklin (Benjamin; 1706–90, US)
Fujimori (Alberto; 1939– , Peruvian)
Galtieri (Leopoldo; 1926–2003, Argentine)

Garfield (James A; 1831–81, US)
Gingrich (Newt; 1943–   , US)
Giuliani (Rudolph 'Rudy'; 1944–   , US)
Goebbels (Joseph; 1897–1945, German)
Hailsham (Quintin Hogg, 2nd Viscount;
    1907–2001, English)
Harrison (Benjamin; 1833–1901, US)
Harrison (William Henry; 1773–1841, US)
Hirohito (1901–89, Japanese)
Honecker (Erich; 1912–94, German)
Iturbide (Agustín de; 1783–1824, Mexican)
Karadjic (Radovan; 1945–   , Bosnian-Serb)
Karadžić (Radovan; 1945–   , Bosnian-Serb)
Kenyatta (Jomo; c.1889–1978, Kenyan)
Le Duc Tho (1911–90, Vietnamese)
McAleese (Mary; 1951–   , Irish)
McCarthy (Joseph; 1909–57, US)
McKinley (William; 1843–1901, US)
Medvedev (Dmitry Anatolyevich; 1965–   ,
    Russian)
Mengistu (Haile Mariam; 1941–   ,
    Ethiopian)
Mulroney (Brian; 1939–   , Canadian)
Napoleon (I, Bonaparte; 1769–1821,
    French)
Nicholas (I, Tsar; 1868–1918, Russian)
Obasanjo (Olusegun; 1937–   , Nigerian)
Pericles (c.490–429 BC, Athenian)
Pinochet (Augusto; 1915–2006, Chilean)
Pompidou (Georges; 1911–74, French)
Portillo (Michael; 1953–   , English)
Prescott (John; 1938–   , English)
Robinson (Mary; 1944–   , Irish)
Rumsfeld (Donald; 1932–   , US)
Schröder (Gerhard; 1944–   , German)
Schüssel (Wolfgang; 1945–   , Austrian)
Sihanouk (King Norodom; 1922–   ,
    Cambodian)
Thatcher (Margaret, Baroness; 1925–   ,
    English)
Van Buren (Martin; 1782–1862, US)
Verwoerd (Hendrik; 1901–66, Dutch/South
    African)
Waldheim (Kurt; 1918–2007, Austrian)
Whitelaw (Willie Whitelaw, 1st Viscount;
    1918–99, Scottish)
Williams (Shirley, Baroness; 1930–   ,
    English)
Zia ul-Haq (Mohammed; 1924–88,
    Pakistani)

09 Aristides (c.550–c.467 BC, Athenian)
Ben-Gurion (David; 1886–1973, Polish/
    Israeli)
Boothroyd (Betty, Baroness; 1929–   ,
    English)
Bottomley (Virginia; 1948–   , British)
Buthelezi (Chief Mangosuthu; 1928–   ,
    South African)

Callaghan (James, Lord; 1912–2005, English)
Ceauşescu (Nicolae; 1918–89, Romanian)
Churchill (Lord Randolph; 1849–95, English)
Churchill (Sir Winston; 1874–1965, English)
Clarendon (Edward Hyde, 1st Earl of;
    1609–74, English)
Clarendon (George William Frederick
    Villiers, 4th Earl of; 1800–70, English)
Cleveland (Grover; 1837–1908, US)
Garibaldi (Giuseppe; 1807–82, Italian)
Gladstone (William; 1809–98, English)
Gorbachev (Mikhail; 1931–   , Russian)
Heseltine (Michael; 1933–   , English)
Ho Chi Minh (1890–1969, Vietnamese)
Jefferson (Thomas; 1743–1826, US)
Kim-Il Sung (1912–94, North Korean)
Kim Jong Il (1942–   , North Korean)
La Guardia (Fiorello H; 1882–1947, US)
Mao Zedong (1893–1976, Chinese)
Mawhinney (Sir Brian; 1940–   , British)
McConnell (Jack; 1960–   , Scottish)
Melbourne (William Lamb, 2nd Viscount;
    1779–1848, English)
Milošević (Slobodan; 1941–2006, Serbian)
Musharraf (Pervaiz; 1943–   , Pakistani)
Mussolini (Benito; 1883–1945, Italian)
Netanyahu (Binyamin; 1949–   , Israeli)
Parkinson (Cecil, Lord; 1932–   , English)
Pretorius (Marthinus; 1819–1901, Afrikaner)
Richelieu (Armand Jean Duplessis, Duc de;
    1585–1642, French)
Roosevelt (Franklin D; 1882–1945, US)
Roosevelt (Theodore; 1858–1919, US)
Sun Yat-Sen (1866–1925, Chinese)

10 Berlusconi (Silvio; 1936–   , Italian)
Clemenceau (Georges; 1841–1929, French)
Eisenhower (Dwight D; 1890–1969, US)
Enver Pasha (1881–1922, Turkish)
Fox Quesada (Vicente; 1942–   , Mexican)
Hattersley (Roy, Lord); 1932–   , English)
Jiang Zemin (1926–   , Chinese)
Khrushchev (Nikita; 1894–1971, Soviet)
Kim Dae-Jung (1925–   , South Korean)
Mitterrand (François; 1916–96, French)
Palmerston (Henry John Temple, 3rd
    Viscount; 1784–1865, English)
Rafsanjani (Hojatoleslam Ali Akbar
    Hashemi; 1934–   , Iranian)
Talleyrand (Charles Maurice de, Prince of
    Benevento; 1754–1838, French)
Tsvangirai (Morgan; 1952–   , Zimbabwean)
Waldegrave (William, Lord; 1946–   ,
    English)
Walsingham (Sir Francis; c.1530–90,
    English)
Washington (George; 1732–99, US)
Wellington (Arthur, Duke of; 1769–1852,
    Irish)

Widdecombe (Ann; 1947– , English)

11 Chamberlain (Neville; 1869–1940, English)
Duncan Smith (Iain; 1954– , English)
Kumaratunga (Chandrika; 1945– , Sri Lankan)
Livingstone (Ken; 1945– , English)
Lloyd-George (David Lloyd George, 1st Earl; 1863–1945, Welsh)
Machiavelli (Niccolò; 1469–1527, Italian)
Mountbatten (Louis, Earl; 1900–79, English)
Robespierre (Maximilien; 1758–94, French)
Rockefeller (Nelson; 1908–79, US)
Verhofstadt (Guy; 1953– , Belgian)

12 Bandaranaike (Sirimavo; 1916–2000, Sri Lankan)
Bandaranaike (S W R D; 1899–1959, Ceylonese)
Boutros-Ghali (Boutros; 1922– , Egyptian)

Chernomyrdin (Viktor; 1938– , Russian)
Hammarskjöld (Dag; 1905–61, Swedish)
Shevardnadze (Eduard; 1928– , Georgian/Soviet)

13 Belaúnde Terry (Fernando; 1913–2002, Peruvian)
Chateaubriand (René, Vicomte de; 1768–1848, French)
Chiang Kai-shek (1887–1975, Chinese)

14 Bjelke-Petersen (Sir Joh; 1911–2005, New Zealand/Australian)
Finnbogadóttir (Vígdis; 1930– , Icelandic)
Pinochet Ugarte (Augusto; 1915–2006, Chilean)

15 Giscard d'Estaing (Valéry; 1926– , French)
Macapagal-Arroyo (Gloria; 1948– , Philippine)

Terms used in politics include:

04 bill
FPTP
veto
vote
whip

05 lobby
party
state

06 ballot
summit

07 cabinet
council
détente
Hansard
mandate

08 alliance
blockade
campaign

election
left wing
majority
sanction

09 apartheid
coalition
coup d'état
judiciary
manifesto
party line
right wing

10 devolution
filibuster
focus group
government
green paper
parliament
propaganda
referendum

trade union
white paper

11 ginger group
sovereignty

12 civil service
constitution
term of office
welfare state

13 electoral roll
privatization
shadow cabinet
three-line whip

14 go to the country
hung parliament

15 general election
local government
nationalization

See also **economics**; **parliament**; **party**; **president**; **prime minister**; **republic**

pony *see* **horse**

pop

Pop and rock music groups include:

02 U2

03 ABC
REM
Yes

04 ABBA
AC/DC
Blur
Free

INXS
Pulp
T-Rex
Wham!

05 Bread
Cream
Oasis
Queen

Slade
Texas
ZZ Top

06 Boney M
The Jam
The Who
Travis

07 Bee Gees

Blondie
Bon Jovi
Boyzone
Genesis
Madness
Nirvana
Rainbow
Santana
Strawbs
The Band
The Cure
The Move
Traffic
Wizzard

08 Coldplay
Hawkwind
Ink Spots
New Order
Platters
Take That
The Byrds
The Clash
The Doors
The Faces
The Kinks

09 Aerosmith
Buzzcocks
Catatonia
Marillion
Motorhead
Pink Floyd
Roxy Music
Status Quo
Steely Dan
The Damned
The Eagles
The Pogues
The Police

The Smiths
The Troggs
Thin Lizzy
Uriah Heep
Wet Wet Wet
Yardbirds

10 Bad Company
Deep Purple
Def Leppard
Duran Duran
Eurythmics
Iron Maiden
Jamiroquai
Jethro Tull
Moody Blues
New Seekers
Sex Pistols
Small Faces
Spice Girls
The Animals
The Beatles
The Hollies
The Monkees
The Osmonds
The Ramones
The Seekers
The Shadows

11 Culture Club
Depeche Mode
Dire Straits
Four Seasons
Jackson Five
Judas Priest
Led Zeppelin
Manfred Mann
Procol Harum
Simple Minds
The Drifters

The Four Tops
The Scaffold
The Supremes
Wishbone Ash

12 Black Sabbath
Boomtown Rats
Fleetwood Mac
Talking Heads
The Bachelors
The Beach Boys
The Searchers
The Tremeloes
Three Degrees

13 Dave Clark Five
Isley Brothers
Lynyrd Skynyrd
Mott the Hoople
Rolling Stones
Spandau Ballet
The Carpenters
The Chieftains
The Commodores
The Communards
The Stone Roses
The Stranglers

14 Adam and the Ants
Bay City Rollers
Everly Brothers
Herman's Hermits
Tangerine Dream
The Foundations
The Temptations
Walker Brothers

15 Neville Brothers
The Grateful Dead
The Style Council
The White Stripes

Pop and rock musicians and singers include:

03 Eno (Brian; 1948– , English)
Lee (Peggy; 1920–2002, US)
Pop (Iggy; 1947– , US)
Ray (Johnnie; 1927–90, US)

04 Bush (Kate; 1958– , English)
Cher (1946– , US)
Crow (Sheryl; 1962– , US)
Dion (Céline; 1968– , Canadian)
Dury (Ian; 1942–2000, English)
Gaye (Marvin; 1939–84, US)
Gray (David; 1970– , English)
Joel (Billy; 1949– , US)
John (Sir Elton; 1947– , English)
Khan (Chaka; 1953– , US)
King (B B; 1925– , US)
King (Ben E; 1938– , US)

King (Carole; 1942– , US)
Lulu (1948– , Scottish)
Page (Jimmy; 1944– , English)
Reed (Lou; 1944– , US)
Ross (Diana; 1944– , US)
Sade (1959– , Nigerian/British)
Shaw (Sandie; 1947– , English)
Vega (Suzanne; 1959– , US)

05 Adams (Bryan; 1959– , Canadian)
Berry (Chuck; 1926– , US)
Black (Cilla; 1943– , English)
Blunt (James; 1974– , English)
Bowie (David; 1947– , English)
Brown (James; 1928–2006, US)
Byrne (David; 1952– , Scottish/US)
Carey (Mariah; 1969– , US)

Cohen (Leonard; 1934– , Canadian)
Cooke (Sam; 1935–64, US)
Davis (Sammy, Jnr; 1925–90, US)
Dylan (Bob; 1941– , US)
Ferry (Bryan; 1945– , English)
Flack (Roberta; 1939– , US)
Green (Al; 1946– , US)
Haley (Bill; 1925–81, US)
Harry (Deborah; 1945– , US)
Holly (Buddy; 1936–59, US)
Jarre (Jean-Michel; 1948– , French)
Jones (Grace; 1952– , Jamaican)
Jones (Tom; 1940– , Welsh)
Lewis (Jerry Lee; 1935– , US)
Moyet (Alison; 1961– , English)
Plant (Robert; 1948– , English)
Simon (Carly; 1945– , US)
Simon (Paul; 1941– , US)
Smith (Patti; 1946– , US)
Sting (1951– , English)
Tormé (Mel; 1925–99, US)
Twain (Shania; 1965– , Canadian)
Waits (Tom; 1949– , US)
White (Barry; 1944–2003, US)
Wills (Bob; 1905–75, US)
Young (Neil; 1945– , Canadian)
Young (Will; 1979– , English)
Zappa (Frank; 1940–93, US)

06 Cocker (Joe; 1944– , English)
Cooper (Alice; 1948– , US)
Domino (Fats; 1928– , US)
Easton (Sheena; 1959– , Scottish)
Joplin (Janis; 1943–70, US)
Knight (Gladys; 1944– , US)
Lauper (Cyndi; 1953– , US)
Lennon (John; 1940–80, English)
Lennox (Annie; 1954– , Scottish)
Marley (Bob; 1945–81, Jamaican)
Mayall (John; 1933– , English)
Midler (Bette; 1945– , US)
Miller (Steve; 1943– , US)
Nelson (Ricky; 1940–85, US)
Newman (Randy; 1944– , US)
Palmer (Robert; 1949–2003, English)
Pitney (Gene; 1941–2006, US)
Prince (1958– , US)
Richie (Lionel; 1949– , US)
Sedaka (Neil; 1939– , US)
Simone (Nina; 1933–2003, US)
Spears (Britney; 1981– , US)
Summer (Donna; 1948– , US)
Taylor (James; 1948– , US)
Turner (Tina; 1938– , US)
Valens (Ritchie; 1941–59, US)
Watson (Doc; 1923– , US)
Weller (Paul; 1958– , English)
Wilson (Brian; 1942– , US)

Wonder (Stevie; 1950– , US)
Yoakam (Dwight; 1956– , US)

07 Bennett (Tony; 1926– , US)
Charles (Ray; 1930–2004, US)
Clapton (Eric; 1945– , English)
Cochran (Eddie; 1938–60, US)
Collins (Phil; 1951– , English)
Diamond (Neil; 1941– , US)
Diddley (Bo; 1928–2008, US)
Gabriel (Peter; 1950– , English)
Hendrix (Jimi; 1942–70, US)
Holland (Jools; 1958– , English)
Houston (Whitney; 1963– , US)
Jackson (Janet; 1966– , US)
Jackson (Michael; 1958– , US)
Madonna (1958– , US)
Manilow (Barry; 1946– , US)
Michael (George; 1963– , English)
Minogue (Kylie; 1968– , Australian)
O'Connor (Sinéad; 1966– , Irish)
Orbison (Roy; 1936–88, US)
Pickett (Wilson; 1941–2006, US)
Presley (Elvis; 1935–77, US)
Redding (Otis; 1941–67, US)
Richard (Sir Cliff; 1940– , English)
Rodgers (Jimmie; 1897–1933, US)
Santana (Carlos ; 1947– , Mexican)
Shannon (Del; 1939–90, US)
Stevens (Cat; 1947– , English)
Stewart (Rod; 1945– , English)
Vincent (Gene; 1935–71, US)
Warwick (Dionne; 1940– , US)

08 Costello (Elvis; 1955– , English)
Franklin (Aretha; 1942– , US)
Harrison (George; 1943–2001, English)
Knopfler (Mark; 1949– , British)
Morrison (Van; 1945– , Northern Irish)
Oldfield (Mike; 1953– , English)
Robinson (Smokey; 1940– , US)
Thompson (Richard; 1949– , English)
Vandross (Luther; 1951–2005, US)
Williams (Robbie; 1974– , English)

09 Boy George (1961– , English)
Etheridge (Melissa; 1962– , US)
Faithfull (Marianne; 1946– , English)
McCartney (Sir Paul; 1942– , English)
Morrissey (Steven; 1959– , English)
Streisand (Barbra; 1942– , US)
Winehouse (Amy; 1983– , English)

10 Fitzgerald (Ella; 1917–96, US)
Morissette (Alanis; 1974– , Canadian)

11 Armatrading (Joan; 1950– , West Indian/
British)
Springfield (Dusty; 1939–99, English)
Springsteen (Bruce; 1949– , US)

13 Little Richard (1935– , US)

Pop songs include:

03 'Bad' (Michael Jackson)

04 '1999' (Prince)
'Gold' (Spandau Ballet)
'Help!' (The Beatles)
'Sing' (Travis)
'True' (Spandau Ballet)

05 'Clair' (Gilbert O'Sullivan)
'Crazy' (Patsy Cline)
'Diana' (Paul Anka)
'Ernie' (Benny Hill)
'Faith' (George Michael)
'Fever' (Peggy Lee)
'Layla' (Derek & the Dominoes)
'My Way' (Elvis Presley/Frank Sinatra)
'Relax' (Frankie Goes to Hollywood)
'Shout' (Lulu)
'Smile' (Lily Allen)

06 'Apache' (Shadows)
'Atomic' (Blondie)
'Exodus' (Bob Marley & the Wailers)
'Rock DJ' (Robbie Williams)
'The End' (The Doors)
'Vienna' (Ultravox)
'Volare' (Dean Martin)
'Yellow' (Coldplay)

07 'Delilah' (Tom Jones)
'D.I.V.O.R.C.E.' (Tammy Wynette)
'Grandad' (St Winifred's School Choir)
'Hey Jude' (The Beatles)
'Holiday' (Madonna)
'I Like it' (Gerry & the Pacemakers)
'Imagine' (John Lennon)
'Jamming' (Bob Marley & the Wailers)
'La Bamba' (Richie Valens)
'Let It Be' (The Beatles)
'Rat Trap' (Boomtown Rats)
'Respect' (Aretha Franklin)
'Sailing' (Rod Stewart)
'Starman' (David Bowie)

08 'Answer Me' (Frankie Laine)
'Antmusic' (Adam & the Ants)
'At the Hop' (Danny & the Juniors)
'Baby Love' (Supremes)
'Downtown' (Petula Clark)
'I Want You' (Bob Dylan)
'Love Me Do' (The Beatles)
'Mamma Mia' (Abba)
'Mony Mony' (Tommy James & the Shondells)
'Our House' (Madness)
'Paranoid' (Black Sabbath)
'Parklife' (Blur)
'Peggy Sue' (Buddy Holly)
'The Boxer' (Simon & Garfunkel)
'The Model' (Kraftwerk)

'Thriller' (Michael Jackson)
'Wannabee' (Spice Girls)
'Waterloo' (Abba)

09 'Albatross' (Fleetwood Mac)
'Born to Run' (Bruce Springsteen)
'Dance Away' (Roxy Music)
'Glory Days' (Bruce Springsteen)
'I Feel Love' (Donna Summer)
'Jean Genie' (David Bowie)
'Maggie May' (Rod Stewart)
'Metal Guru' (T Rex)
'Penny Lane' (The Beatles)
'Praise You' (Fatboy Slim)
'Release Me' (Engelbert Humperdinck)
'Something' (The Beatles)
'Stand by Me' (Ben E King)
'Two Tribes' (Frankie Goes to Hollywood)
'Wild Thing' (The Troggs)
'Yesterday' (The Beatles)

10 'All Shook Up' (Elvis Presley)
'Annie's Song' (John Denver)
'Band of Gold' (Freda Payne)
'Billie Jean' (Michael Jackson)
'Blue Monday' (New Order)
'Bye Bye Baby' (Bay City Rollers)
'Close to You' (Carpenters)
'House of Fun' (Madness)
'Jealous Guy' (John Lennon)
'King Creole' (Elvis Presley)
'Lay, Lady, Lay' (Bob Dylan)
'Lazy Sunday' (Small Faces)
'Living Doll' (Cliff Richard)
'Millennium' (Robbie Williams)
'Moving On Up' (Primal Scream)
'Night Fever' (Bee Gees)
'Perfect Day' (Lou Reed)
'Purple Haze' (Jimi Hendrix)
'Purple Rain' (Prince)
'Reet Petite' (Jackie Wilson)
'Ring of Fire' (Johnny Cash)
'Sex Machine' (James Brown)
'Sugar Sugar' (The Archies)
'Wonderwall' (Oasis)

11 'All Right Now' (Free)
'American Pie' (Don McLean)
'Back for Good' (Take That)
'Baker Street' (Gerry Rafferty)
'Cathy's Clown' (Everly Brothers)
'Firestarter' (Prodigy)
'From Me to You' (The Beatles)
'Glad All Over' (Dave Clark Five)
'Golden Brown' (The Stranglers)
'Greatest Day' (Take That)
'I Got You Babe' (Sonny & Cher)
'I Have a Dream' (Abba)

'I'm Not in Love' (10CC)
'Light My Fire' (The Doors)
'Like a Prayer' (Madonna)
'Like a Virgin' (Madonna)
'Lily the Pink' (The Scaffold)
'Mrs Robinson' (Simon and Garfunkel)
'Oliver's Army' (Elvis Costello & The Attractions)
'She Loves You' (The Beatles)
'Space Oddity' (David Bowie)
'Tainted Love' (Soft Cell)
'Venus as a Boy' (Bjork)
'Voodoo Chile' (Jimi Hendrix)

12 'A Boy Named Sue' (Johnny Cash)
'All Or Nothing' (Small Faces)
'Ashes to Ashes' (David Bowie)
'Bat out of Hell' (Meatloaf)
'Born in the USA' (Bruce Springsteen)
'Born to Be Wild' (Steppenwolf)
'Come on Eileen' (Dexys Midnight Runners)
'Common People' (Pulp)
'Dancing Queen' (Abba)
'Eleanor Rigby' (The Beatles)
'God Only Knows' (The Beach Boys)
'Heart of Glass' (Blondie)
'How Do You Do It?' (Gerry & the Pacemakers)
'It Ain't Me, Babe' (Bob Dylan)
'I Walk the Line' (Johnny Cash)
'Johnny B Goode' (Chuck Berry)
'Material Girl' (Madonna)
'No Woman No Cry' (Bob Marley & the Wailers)
'Paint It Black' (Rolling Stones)
'Pretty Vacant' (Sex Pistols)
'The Birdy Song' (The Tweets)
'The Passenger' (Iggy Pop)
'West End Girls' (Pet Shop Boys)

13 'Blueberry Hill' (Fats Domino)
'Brass in Pocket' (The Pretenders)
'Can't Buy Me Love' (The Beatles)
'Chantilly Lace' (The Big Bopper)
'Club Tropicana' (Wham)
'Design for Life' (Manic Street Preachers)
'Don't You Want Me' (Human League)
'Get off My Cloud' (Rolling Stones)
'Into the Groove' (Madonna)
'It's Not Unusual' (Tom Jones)
'It's Now Or Never' (Elvis Presley)
'Jailhouse Rock' (Elvis Presley)
'Last Christmas' (Wham!)
'London Calling' (The Clash)
'Long Tall Sally' (Little Richard)
'Mary's Boy Child' (Boney M)
'Mull of Kintyre' (Wings)
'Oh, Pretty Woman' (Roy Orbison)
'Only the Lonely' (Roy Orbison)

'Pinball Wizard' (The Who)
'Road to Nowhere' (Talking Heads)
'Rock the Casbah' (The Clash)
'Summer Holiday' (Cliff Richard)
'Tears in Heaven' (Eric Clapton)
'Urban Spaceman' (Bonzo Dog Doodah Band)

14 '20th Century Boy' (T Rex)
'A Hard Day's Night' (The Beatles)
'Always on My Mind' (Elvis Presley)
'Blue Suede Shoes' (Elvis Presley/Carl Perkins)
'Good Vibrations' (Beach Boys)
'Just Like a Woman' (Bob Dylan)
'Karma Chameleon' (Culture Club)
'Spirit in the Sky' (Norman Greenbaum)
'Stand by Your Man' (Tammy Wynette)
'Sunny Afternoon' (Kinks)
'That'll Be the Day' (Buddy Holly & the Crickets)
'The Mighty Quinn' (Bob Dylan)
'The Power of Love' (Huey Lewis & the News)
'Waterloo Sunset' (Kinks)
'White Christmas' (Bing Crosby)
'Wonderful World' (Louis Armstrong)
'You're Beautiful' (James Blunt)

15 'Baby One More Time' (Britney Spears)
'Begin the Beguine' (Julio Iglesias)
'Blowin' in the Wind' (Bob Dylan)
'Candle in the Wind' (Elton John)
'Careless Whisper' (George Michael)
'Congratulations' (Cliff Richard)
'God Save the Queen' (Sex Pistols)
'Heartbreak Hotel' (Elvis Presley)
'Hotel California' (Eagles)
'In the Name of Love' (U2)
'I Shot the Sheriff' (Bob Marley & the Wailers)
'Jumpin' Jack Flash' (Rolling Stones)
'Killing Me Softly' (Roberta Flack)
'Living on a Prayer' (Bon Jovi)
'Love Is All Around' (Troggs/Wet Wet Wet)
'Me and Bobby McGee' (Kris Kristofferson)
'Money for Nothing' (Dire Straits)
'Money, Money, Money' (Abba)
'Mr Tambourine Man' (Bob Dylan)
'Paperback Writer' (The Beatles)
'Puppet on a String' (Sandie Shaw)
'Rivers of Babylon' (Boney M)
'Silence Is Golden' (The Tremeloes)
'Smoke on the Water' (Deep Purple)
'This Charming Man' (The Smiths)
'Unchained Melody' (Righteous Brothers)
'When I Fall in Love' (Nat King Cole)
'Yellow Submarine' (The Beatles)

16 '24 Hours from Tulsa' (Gene Pitney)

'All You Need Is Love' (The Beatles)
'Bohemian Rhapsody' (Queen)
'Dancing in the Dark' (Bruce Springsteen)
'Going Underground' (Jam)
'Great Balls of Fire' (Jerry Lee Lewis)
'I Don't Like Mondays' (Boomtown Rats)
'I Should Be So Lucky' (Kylie Minogue)
'The Real Slim Shady' (Eminem)
'The Tears of a Clown' (Smokey Robinson & the Miracles)
'With Or Without You' (U2)
'Wuthering Heights' (Kate Bush)

17 'California Dreamin'' (Mamas & the Papas)
'Folsom Prison Blues' (Johnny Cash)
'Here Comes the Night' (Them)
'Like a Rolling Stone' (Bob Dylan)
'Nothing Compares 2 U' (Sinead O'Connor)
'Walk on the Wild Side' (Lou Reed)
'We Are the Champions' (Queen)
'Your Cheating Heart' (Hank Williams)

18 'Anyone Who Had a Heart' (Cilla Black)
'Dancing in the Street' (Martha & the Vandellas)
'Good Golly Miss Molly' (Little Richard)
'Merry Xmas Everybody' (Slade)
'Nights in White Satin' (Moody Blues)
'Rock around the Clock' (Bill Haley & the Comets)
'Stranger in Paradise' (Tony Bennett)
'The Air That I Breathe' (Hollies)
'Three Steps to Heaven' (Eddie Cochran)

19 'All I Have to Do Is Dream' (Everly Brothers)
'Don't Look Back in Anger' (Oasis)
'Ferry Cross the Mersey' (Gerry & the Pacemakers)
'House of the Rising Sun' (Animals)
'I Want to Hold Your Hand' (The Beatles)
'Knowing Me Knowing You' (Abba)
'Stop in the Name of Love' (Supremes)
'Strangers in the Night' (Frank Sinatra)
'What a Wonderful World' (Louis Armstrong)
'When a Man Loves a Woman' (Percy Sledge)
'You'll Never Walk Alone' (Gerry & the Pacemakers)

20 'Don't Stand So Close to Me' (Police)
'I Only Want to Be with You' (Dusty Springfield)
'Knockin' on Heaven's Door' (Bob Dylan)
'Make It Easy on Yourself' (Walker Brothers)
'My Baby Just Cares for Me' (Nina Simone)
'Smells Like Teen Spirit' (Nirvana)
'Why Do Fools Fall in Love' (Frankie Lymon & the Teenagers)

21 'All along the Watchtower' (Bob Dylan)
'Another Brick in the Wall' (Pink Floyd)

'Are You Lonesome Tonight?' (Elvis Presley)
'Can't Get You out of My Head' (Kylie Minogue)
'Can't Help Falling in Love' (Andy Williams)
'Don't Go Breaking My Heart' (Elton John & Kiki Dee)
'Green Green Grass of Home' (Tom Jones)
'It's All Over Now, Baby Blue' (Bob Dylan)
'River Deep Mountain High' (Ike & Tina Turner)
'The Wind beneath My Wings' (Lee Greenwood/Bette Midler)
'Wake Me Up before You Go-Go' (Wham)

22 'All Day and All of the Night' (Kinks)
'Do They Know It's Christmas' (Band Aid)
'(I Can't Get No) Satisfaction' (Rolling Stones)
'Should I Stay Or Should I Go' (The Clash)

23 'Bridge over Troubled Water' (Simon & Garfunkel)
'Donald Where's Yer Troosers' (Andy Stewart)
'Do You Really Want to Hurt Me' (Culture Club)
'He Ain't Heavy, He's My Brother' (Hollies)
'I Wanna Dance with Somebody' (Whitney Houston)
'(Sittin' on) The Dock of the Bay' (Otis Redding)
'The Times They Are A-Changin'' (Bob Dylan)

24 'Ain't No Mountain High Enough' (Diana Ross)
'(Everything I Do) I Do It for You' (Bryan Adams)
'Hit Me with Your Rhythm Stick' (Ian Dury & the Blockheads)
'You've Lost That Lovin' Feelin'' (Righteous Brothers)

25 'Heaven Knows I'm Miserable Now' (The Smiths)
'Subterranean Homesick Blues' (Bob Dylan)
'You Don't Have to Say You Love Me' (Dusty Springfield)

26 'I Left My Heart in San Francisco' (Tony Bennett)
'These Boots Are Made for Walkin'' (Nancy Sinatra)

27 'I Heard It through the Grapevine' (Marvin Gaye)
'The Sun Ain't Gonna Shine Any More' (Walker Brothers)

28 'With a Little Help from My Friends' (The Beatles)

See also **jazz**

pope

03 Leo (I; 440–61)
Leo (II; 682–83)
Leo (III; 795–816)
Leo (IV; 847–55)
Leo (IX; 1048–54)
Leo (V; 903)
Leo (VI; 928)
Leo (VII; 936–39)
Leo (X; 1513–21)
Leo (XI; 1605)
Leo (XII; 1823–29)
Leo (XIII; 1878–1903)

04 Cono (686–87)
John (I; 523–26)
John (II; 533–35)
John (III; 561–74)
John (IV; 640–42)
John (IX; 898–900)
John (V; 685–86)
John (VI; 701–05)
John (VII; 705–07)
John (VIII; 872–82)
John (X; 914–28)
John (XI; 931–35)
John (XII; 955–64)
John (XIII; 965–72)
John (XIV; 983–84)
John (XIX; 1024–32)
John (XV; 985–96)
John (XVII; 1003)
John (XVIII; 1004–09)
John (XXI; 1276–77)
John (XXII; 1316–34)
John (XXIII; 1958–63)
Mark (336)
Paul (I; 757–67)
Paul (II; 1464–71)
Paul (III; 1534–49)
Paul (IV; 1555–59)
Paul (V; 1605–21)
Paul (VI; 1963–78)
Pius (I; c.140–c.154)
Pius (II; 1458–64)
Pius (III; 1503)
Pius (IV; 1559–65)
Pius (IX; 1846–78)
Pius (V; 1566–72)
Pius (VI; 1775–99)
Pius (VII; 1800–23)
Pius (VIII; 1829–30)
Pius (X; 1903–14)
Pius (XI; 1922–39)
Pius (XII; 1939–58)

05 Caius (283–96)

Donus (676–78)
Felix (I; 269–74)
Felix (III; 483–92)
Felix (IV; 526–30)
Lando (913–14)
Linus (c.64–c.76)
Peter (until c.64)
Soter (c.166–c.175)
Urban (I; 222–30)
Urban (II; 1088–99)
Urban (III; 1185–87)
Urban (IV; 1261–64)
Urban (V; 1362–70)
Urban (VI; 1378–89)
Urban (VII; 1590)
Urban (VIII; 1623–44)

06 Agatho (678–81)
Fabian (236–50)
Julius (I; 337–52)
Julius (II; 1503–13)
Julius (III; 1550–55)
Lucius (I; 253–54)
Lucius (II; 1144–45)
Lucius (III; 1181–85)
Martin (I; 649–55)
Martin (IV; 1281–85)
Martin (V; 1417–31)
Sixtus (I; c.117–c.127)
Sixtus (II; 257–58)
Sixtus (III; 432–40)
Sixtus (IV; 1471–84)
Sixtus (V; 1585–90)
Victor (I; 189–98)
Victor (II; 1055–57)
Victor (III; 1086–87)

07 Anterus (235–36)
Clement (I; c.90–c.99)
Clement (II; 1046–47)
Clement (III; 1187–91)
Clement (IV; 1265–68)
Clement (IX; 1667–69)
Clement (V; 1305–14)
Clement (VI; 1342–52)
Clement (VII; 1523–34)
Clement (VIII; 1592–1605)
Clement (X; 1670–76)
Clement (XI; 1700–21)
Clement (XII; 1730–40)
Clement (XIII; 1758–69)
Clement (XIV; 1769–74)
Damasus (I; 366–84)
Damasus (II; 1048)
Gregory (I; 590–604)
Gregory (II; 715–31)

Gregory (III; 731–41)
Gregory (IV; 827–44)
Gregory (IX; 1227–41)
Gregory (V; 996–99)
Gregory (VI; 1045–46)
Gregory (VII; 1073–85)
Gregory (VIII; 1187)
Gregory (X; 1271–76)
Gregory (XI; 1370–78)
Gregory (XII; 1406–15)
Gregory (XIII; 1572–85)
Gregory (XIV; 1590–91)
Gregory (XV; 1621–23)
Gregory (XVI; 1831–46)
Hadrian (I; 772–95)
Hadrian (II; 867–72)
Hadrian (III; 884–85)
Hadrian (IV; 1154–59)
Hadrian (V; 1276)
Hadrian (VI; 1522–23)
Hilarus (461–68)
Hyginus (c.137–c.140)
Marinus (I; 882–84)
Marinus (II; 942–46)
Paschal (I; 817–24)
Paschal (II; 1099–1118)
Pontian (230–35)
Romanus (897)
Sergius (I; 687–701)
Sergius (II; 844–47)
Sergius (III; 904–11)
Sergius (IV; 1009–12)
Stephen (I; 254–57)
Stephen (II; 752)
Stephen (II; III; 752–57)
Stephen (III; IV; 768–72)
Stephen (IV; V; 816–17)
Stephen (V; VI; 885–91)
Stephen (VI; VII; 896–97)
Stephen (VII; VIII; 928–31)
Stephen (VIII; IX; 939–42)
Stephen (IX; X; 1057–58)
Zosimus (417–18)

08 Agapetus (I; 535–36)
Agapetus (II; 946–55)
Anicetus (c.154–c.166)
Benedict (I; 575–79)
Benedict (II; 684–85)
Benedict (III; 855–58)
Benedict (IV; 900–03)
Benedict (IX; 1032–44/1045/1047–48)
Benedict (V; 964)
Benedict (VI; 973–74)
Benedict (VII; 974–83)
Benedict (VIII; 1012–24)
Benedict (XI; 1303–04)
Benedict (XII; 1334–42)
Benedict (XIII; 1724–30)

Benedict (XIV; 1740–58)
Benedict (XV; 1914–22)
Benedict (XVI; 2005–   )
Boniface (I; 418–22)
Boniface (II; 530–32)
Boniface (III; 607)
Boniface (IV; 608–15)
Boniface (IX; 1389–1404)
Boniface (V; 619–25)
Boniface (VI; 896)
Boniface (VIII; 1294–1303)
Eugenius (I; 654–57)
Eugenius (II; 824–27)
Eugenius (III; 1145–53)
Eugenius (IV; 1431–47)
Eusebius (310)
Formosus (891–96)
Gelasius (I; 492–96)
Gelasius (II; 1118–19)
Honorius (I; 625–38)
Honorius (II; 1124–30)
Honorius (III; 1216–27)
Honorius (IV; 1285–87)
Innocent (I; 402–17)
Innocent (II; 1130–43)
Innocent (III; 1198–1216)
Innocent (IV; 1243–54)
Innocent (IX; 1591)
Innocent (V; 1276)
Innocent (VI; 1352–62)
Innocent (VII; 1404–06)
Innocent (VIII; 1484–92)
Innocent (X; 1644–55)
Innocent (XI; 1676–89)
Innocent (XII; 1691–1700)
Innocent (XIII; 1721–24)
John Paul (I; 1978)
John Paul (II; 1978–2005)
Liberius (352–66)
Nicholas (I; 858–67)
Nicholas (II; 1059–61)
Nicholas (III; 1277–80)
Nicholas (IV; 1288–92)
Nicholas (V; 1447–55)
Pelagius (I; 556–61)
Pelagius (II; 579–90)
Siricius (384–99)
Theodore (I; 642–49)
Theodore (II; 897)
Vigilius (537–55)
Vitalian (657–72)

09 Adeodatus (I; 615–18)
Adeodatus (II; 672–76)
Alexander (I; c.105–c.117)
Alexander (II; 1061–73)
Alexander (III; 1159–81)
Alexander (IV; 1254–61)
Alexander (VI; 1492–1503)

Alexander (VII; 1655–67)
Alexander (VIII; 1689–91)
Anacletus (c.76–c.90)
Callistus (I; 217–22)
Callistus (II; 1119–24)
Callistus (III; 1455–58)
Celestine (I; 422–32)
Celestine (II; 1143–44)
Celestine (III; 1191–98)
Celestine (IV; 1241)
Celestine (V; 1294)
Cornelius (251–53)
Deusdedit (615–18)
Dionysius (259–68)
Evaristus (c.99–c.105)
Hormisdas (514–23)
Marcellus (I; 308–09)
Marcellus (II; 1555)
Miltiades (311–14)
Severinus (640)

Silverius (536–37)
Sisinnius (708)
Sylvester (I; 314–35)
Sylvester (II; 999–1003)
Sylvester (III; 1045)
Symmachus (498–514)
Valentine (827)
Zacharias (741–52)

10 Anastasius (I; 399–401)
Anastasius (II; 496–98)
Anastasius (III; 911–13)
Anastasius (IV; 1153–54)
Sabinianus (604–06)
Simplicius (468–83)
Zephyrinus (198–217)

11 Constantine (708–15)
Eleutherius (175–89)
Eutychianus (275–83)
Marcellinus (296–304)
Telesphorus (c.127–c.137)

Antipopes, with regnal dates (all AD) include:

03 Leo (VIII; 963–65)

04 John (844)
John (XVI; 997–98)
John (XXIII; 1410–15)

05 Felix (II; 355–65)
Felix (V; 1439–49)

06 Albert (1102)
Philip (768)
Victor (IV; 1138)
Victor (IV; 1159–64)

07 Clement (III; 1080/1084–1100)
Clement (VII; 1378–94)
Clement (VIII; 1423–29)
Gregory (1012)
Gregory (VIII; 1118–21)
Paschal (687–92)
Paschal (III; 1164–68)
Ursinus (366–67)

08 Benedict (X; 1058–59)

Benedict (XIII; 1394–1423)
Benedict (XIV; 1425–30)
Boniface (VII; 974/984–85)
Eulalius (418–19)
Honorius (II; 1061–72)
Innocent (III; 1179–80)
Nicholas (V; 1328–30)
Novatian (251–c.258)
Theodore (687)

09 Alexander (V; 1409–10)
Anacletus (II; 1130–38)
Callistus (III; 1168–78)
Celestine (II; 1124)
Dioscorus (530)
Sylvester (IV; 1105–11)
Theodoric (1100–02)

10 Hippolytus (217–c.235)
Laurentius (498/501–05)

11 Christopher (903–04)
Constantine (II; 767–69)

porcelain

Porcelain includes:

05 Imari
Kraak

06 bisque
Canton
Parian

07 biscuit

faience
nankeen

08 eggshell
kakiemon
Yingqing

09 bone china

copper red
hard paste
soft paste

10 salt-glazed

11 Capodimonte
chinoiserie

famille-rose

12 blue and white
famille-verte

14 soapstone paste

Porcelain makes include:

03 Bow	**06** Minton	Meissen	Davenport
04 Ming	Sèvres	Nanking	Worcester
Noke	Vienna	Satsuma	**10** Cookworthy
Wade	**07** Belleek	**08** Caughley	Crown Derby
05 Arita	Bristol	Coalport	Rockingham
Delft	Chelsea	Copeland	
Derby	Dresden	Wedgwood	**12** Royal Doulton
Spode	Limoges	**09** Chantilly	**14** Royal Worcester

Porcelain makers include:

04 Noke (Charles John; 1858–1941, English)

05 Spode (Josiah; 1754–1827, English)

06 Lladró (Juan/José/Vicente; Spanish)
Minton (Thomas; 1765–1836, English)

See also **pottery**

07 Böttger (Johann Friedrich; 1682–1719, German)

08 Copeland (William Taylor; 1797–1868, English)
Wedgwood (Josiah; 1730–95, English)

10 Cookworthy (William; 1705–80, English)

port

Ports include:

04 Aden (Yemen)
Apia (Samoa)
Baku (Azerbaijan)
Bari (Italy)
Caen (France)
Cebu (Philippines)
Cork (Ireland)
Doha (Qatar)
Elat (Israel)
Faro (Portugal)
Hull (England)
Kiel (Germany)
Kobe (Japan)
Lomé (Togo)
Lüda (China)
Nice (France)
Oran (Algeria)
Oslo (Norway)
Oulu (Finland)
Pula (Croatia)
Riga (Latvia)
Safi (Morocco)
Sfax (Tunisia)
Suez (Egypt)
Suva (Fiji)
Tyre (Lebanon)
Vigo (Spain)

05 Accra (Ghana)
Aqaba (Jordan)
Arica (Chile)
Beira (Mozambique)
Belem (Brazil)
Brest (France)
Busan (South Korea)

Cadiz (Spain)
Chiba (Japan)
Colón (Panama)
Dakar (Senegal)
Davao (Philippines)
Dover (England)
Dubai (United Arab Emirates)
Emden (Germany)
Gavle (Sweden)
Genoa (Italy)
Ghent (Belgium)
Gijon (Spain)
Goole (England)
Haifa (Israel)
Ibiza (Ibiza)
Izmir (Turkey)
Koper (Slovenia)
Lagos (Nigeria)
Larne (Northern Ireland)
Leith (Scotland)
Liège (Belgium)
Macao (China)
Malmö (Sweden)
Masan (South Korea)
Miami (USA)
Nampo (North Korea)
Natal (Brazil)
Osaka (Japan)
Palma (Majorca)
Paris (France)
Poole (England)
Pusan (South Korea)
Rouen (France)
Sakai (Japan)

Sitra (Bahrain)
Split (Croatia)
Tampa (USA)
Tanga (Tanzania)
Tokyo (Japan)
Tunis (Tunisia)
Turku (Finland)
Ulsan (South Korea)
Vaasa (Finland)
Varna (Bulgaria)

06 Aarhus (Denmark)
Abadan (Iran)
Agadir (Morocco)
Ancona (Italy)
Annaba (Algeria)
Ashdod (Israel)
Aveiro (Portugal)
Aviles (Spain)
Balboa (Panama)
Banjul (The Gambia)
Basrah (Iraq)
Batumi (Georgia)
Beirut (Lebanon)
Bergen (Norway)
Bilbao (Spain)
Bissau (Guinea-Bissau)
Boston (USA)
Bremen (Germany)
Calais (France)
Callao (Peru)
Cannes (France)
Cochin (India)
Dalian (China)
Dammam (Saudi Arabia)
Darwin (Australia)
Dieppe (France)
Douala (Cameroon)
Dublin (Ireland)
Duluth (USA)
Dundee (Scotland)
Durban (South Africa)
Durres (Albania)
Galway (Ireland)
Gdánsk (Poland)
Gdynia (Poland)
Havana (Cuba)
Hobart (Australia)
Inchon (South Korea)
Jarrow (England)
Jeddah (Saudi Arabia)
Juneau (USA)
Kalmar (Sweden)
Kandla (India)
Khulna (Bangladesh)
Kuwait (Kuwait)
Lisbon (Portugal)
Lobito (Angola)
London (England)

Luanda (Angola)
Lübeck (Germany)
Malaga (Spain)
Manama (Bahrain)
Manaus (Brazil)
Manila (Philippines)
Maputo (Mozambique)
Mersin (Turkey)
Mobile (USA)
Mumbai (India)
Muscat (Oman)
Nacala (Mozambique)
Nagoya (Japan)
Nantes (France)
Napier (New Zealand)
Naples (Italy)
Narvik (Norway)
Nassau (The Bahamas)
Nelson (New Zealand)
Noumea (New Caledonia)
Nyborg (Denmark)
Odense (Denmark)
Odessa (Ukraine)
Oporto (Portugal)
Ostend (Belgium)
Penang (Malaysia)
Quebec (Canada)
Recife (Brazil)
Rijeka (Croatia)
Rimini (Italy)
Samsun (Turkey)
Santos (Brazil)
Sasebo (Japan)
Savona (Italy)
Sittwe (Myanmar)
Sousse (Tunisia)
St John (Canada)
St Malo (France)
Sydney (Australia)
Sydney (Canada)
Tacoma (USA)
Timaru (New Zealand)
Toledo (USA)
Toulon (France)
Toyama (Japan)
Velsen (The Netherlands)
Venice (Italy)
Yangon (Myanmar)

07 Aalborg (Denmark)
Abidjan (Côte d'Ivoire)
Ajaccio (Corsica)
Alcudia (Majorca)
Algiers (Algeria)
Almeria (Spain)
Antwerp (Belgium)
Bangkok (Thailand)
Belfast (Northern Ireland)
Bizerta (Tunisia)

Bourgas (Bulgaria)
Bristol (England)
Buffalo (USA)
Cabinda (Angola)
Calabar (Nigeria)
Caldera (Costa Rica)
Calicut (India)
Cardiff (Wales)
Catania (Sicily)
Cayenne (French Guiana)
Chennai (India)
Chicago (USA)
Cologne (Germany)
Colombo (Sri Lanka)
Conakry (Guinea)
Corinth (Greece)
Corinto (Nicaragua)
Cotonou (Benin)
Dampier (Australia)
Detroit (USA)
Douglas (Isle of Man)
Dunedin (New Zealand)
Dunkirk (France)
Esbjerg (Denmark)
Funchal (Madeira)
Geelong (Australia)
Glasgow (Scotland)
Grimsby (England)
Halifax (Canada)
Hamburg (Germany)
Harstad (Norway)
Harwich (England)
Hodeida (Yemen)
Honiari (Solomon Islands)
Houston (USA)
Jakarta (Indonesia)
Karachi (Pakistan)
Kolkata (India)
Kowloon (Hong Kong)
Kuching (Malaysia)
Kushiro (Japan)
La Plata (Argentina)
Larnaca (Cyprus)
La Union (El Salvador)
Le Havre (France)
Livorno (Italy)
Marsala (Sicily)
Messina (Sicily)
Mindelo (Cape Verde)
Mombasa (Kenya)
Newport (Wales)
New York (USA)
Oakland (USA)
Palermo (Sicily)
Papeete (Tahiti)
Paradip (India)
Pasajes (Spain)
Piraeus (Greece)

Rangoon (Myanmar)
Ravenna (Italy)
Rosaria (Argentina)
Rostock (Germany)
Salerno (Italy)
San José (Guatemala)
San Juan (Puerto Rico)
San Remo (Italy)
Santa Fé (Argentina)
São Tomé (São Tomé and Príncipe)
Seattle (USA)
Seville (Spain)
Shimizu (Japan)
St John's (Antigua)
St John's (Canada)
Swansea (Wales)
Tallinn (Estonia)
Tampico (Mexico)
Tangier (Morocco)
Taranto (Italy)
Tianjin (China)
Toronto (Canada)
Trieste (Italy)
Tripoli (Lebanon)
Tripoli (Libya)
Valetta (Malta)
Vitoria (Brazil)
Xingang (China)
Zhdanov (Ukraine)

08 Aberdeen (Scotland)
Abu Dhabi (United Arab Emirates)
Acajutla (El Salvador)
Acapulco (Mexico)
Adelaide (Australia)
Alicante (Spain)
Asunción (Paraguay)
Auckland (New Zealand)
Benghazi (Libya)
Bordeaux (France)
Boulogne (France)
Brindisi (Italy)
Brisbane (Australia)
Cagliari (Sardinia)
Cape Town (South Africa)
Djibouti (Djibouti)
Duisburg (Germany)
Flushing (The Netherlands)
Freeport (The Bahamas)
Freeport (USA)
Freetown (Sierra Leone)
Godthaab (Greenland)
Greenock (Scotland)
Hakodate (Japan)
Halmstad (Sweden)
Hamilton (Bermuda)
Hamilton (Canada)
Hay Point (Australia)
Helsinki (Finland)

Holyhead (Wales)
Hong Kong (Hong Kong)
Honolulu (Hawaii)
Istanbul (Turkey)
Kawasaki (Japan)
Kingston (Jamaica)
Klaipeda (Lithuania)
La Coruña (Spain)
La Guaira (Venezuela)
La Spezia (Italy)
Lattakia (Syria)
Limassol (Cyprus)
Limerick (Ireland)
Mannheim (Germany)
Matanzas (Cuba)
Monrovia (Liberia)
Montreal (Canada)
Mormugao (India)
Moulmein (Myanmar)
Murmansk (Russia)
Nagasaki (Japan)
New Haven (USA)
Pago Pago (Samoa)
Plymouth (England)
Portland (USA)
Port Said (Egypt)
Ramsgate (England)
Richmond (USA)
Salonica (Greece)
Salvador (Brazil)
San Diego (USA)
San Pedro (Côte d'Ivoire)
Savannah (USA)
Shanghai (China)
St Helier (Jersey)
Stockton (USA)
Surabaya (Indonesia)
Syracuse (Sicily)
Szczecin (Poland)
Takoradi (Ghana)
Tauranga (New Zealand)
Torshavn (Faroes)
Valencia (Spain)
Veracruz (Mexico)
Yokohama (Japan)
Zanzibar (Tanzania)

09 Algeciras (Spain)
Amsterdam (The Netherlands)
Anchorage (USA)
Archangel (Russia)
Baltimore (USA)
Barcelona (Spain)
Cartagena (Colombia)
Cartagena (Spain)
Cherbourg (France)
Cleveland (USA)
Constanta (Romania)
Dordrecht (The Netherlands)

Dubrovnik (Croatia)
Europoort (The Netherlands)
Famagusta (Cyprus)
Flensburg (Germany)
Fortaleza (Brazil)
Frankfurt (Germany)
Fremantle (Australia)
Galveston (USA)
Gateshead (England)
Gibraltar (Gibraltar)
Gravesend (England)
Guayaquil (Ecuador)
Hiroshima (Japan)
Kagoshima (Japan)
Kaohsiung (Taiwan)
Kirkcaldy (Scotland)
Langesund (Norway)
Las Palmas (Grand Canary)
Liverpool (England)
Long Beach (USA)
Lowestoft (England)
Maracaibo (Venezuela)
Mariehamn (Finland)
Melbourne (Australia)
Milwaukee (USA)
Mizushima (Japan)
Mogadishu (Somalia)
Newcastle (Australia)
Newcastle (England)
Nukualofa (Tonga)
Palm Beach (USA)
Paranagua (Brazil)
Phnom Penh (Cambodia)
Port Limon (Costa Rica)
Port Louis (Mauritius)
Port Sudan (Sudan)
Reykjavik (Iceland)
Rio Grande (Brazil)
Rotterdam (The Netherlands)
Santander (Spain)
Sassandra (Côte d'Ivoire)
Singapore (Singapore)
Stavanger (Norway)
St George's (Grenada)
St Nazaire (France)
Stockholm (Sweden)
Stralsund (Germany)
Sundsvall (Sweden)
Takamatsu (Japan)
Tarragona (Spain)
Toamasina (Madagascar)
Trebizond (Turkey)
Trondheim (Norway)
Tuticorin (India)
Vancouver (Canada)
Volgograd (Russia)
Walvis Bay (Namibia)
Zamboanga (Philippines)

Zeebrugge (Belgium)

10 Alexandria (Egypt)
Belize City (Belize)
Bridgetown (Barbados)
Cap Haitian (Haiti)
Casablanca (Morocco)
Charleston (USA)
Chittagong (Bangladesh)
Cienfuegos (Cuba)
Copenhagen (Denmark)
East London (South Africa)
Felixstowe (England)
Folkestone (England)
Fray Bentos (Uruguay)
Fredericia (Denmark)
Georgetown (Cayman Islands)
Georgetown (Guyana)
Gothenburg (Sweden)
Hartlepool (England)
Iskenderun (Turkey)
Kitakyushu (Japan)
Kompong Som (Cambodia)
Launceston (Australia)
Libreville (Gabon)
Los Angeles (USA)
Manzanillo (Mexico)
Marseilles (France)
Mina Qaboos (Oman)
Mina Sulman (Bahrain)
Montego Bay (Jamaica)
Montevideo (Uruguay)
New Orleans (USA)
Nouakchott (Mauritania)
Paramaribo (Suriname)
Pork Kelang (Malaysia)
Port Gentil (Gabon)
Port Kembla (Australia)
Portsmouth (England)
Port Talbot (Wales)
Providence (USA)
Sacramento (USA)
Salina Cruz (Mexico)
San Lorenzo (Argentina)
Santa Marta (Colombia)
Sevastopol (Ukraine)
Sunderland (England)
Thunder Bay (Canada)
Townsville (Australia)
Valparaíso (Chile)
Wellington (New Zealand)
Willemstad (Netherlands Antilles)
Wilmington (USA)

11 Antofagasta (Chile)
Bahia Blanca (Argentina)
Bandar Abbas (Iran)
Brazzaville (Congo)

Buenos Aires (Argentina)
Dar es Salaam (Tanzania)
Fredrikstad (Norway)
Grangemouth (Scotland)
Helsingborg (Sweden)
Livingstone (Guatemala)
Mar del Plata (Argentina)
New Plymouth (New Zealand)
Panama Canal (Panama)
Pasir Gudang (Malaysia)
Point-a-Pitre (Guadeloupe)
Pointe-Noire (Congo)
Pondicherry (India)
Port Cartier (Canada)
Port Hedland (Australia)
Port Moresby (Papua New Guinea)
Porto Alegre (Brazil)
Port of Spain (Trinidad)
Punta Arenas (Chile)
Richards Bay (South Africa)
Southampton (England)
Vlaardingen (The Netherlands)
Vladivostok (Russia)

12 Barranquilla (Colombia)
Buena Ventura (Colombia)
Fort de France (Martinique)
Jacksonville (USA)
Kota Kinabalu (Malaysia)
Kristiansand (Norway)
New Amsterdam (Guyana)
New Mangalore (India)
Novorossiysk (Russia)
Philadelphia (USA)
Ponta Delgada (Azores)
Port Adelaide (Australia)
Port-au-Prince (Haiti)
Port Harcourt (Nigeria)
Port Victoria (Seychelles)
Prince Rupert (Canada)
Puerto Cortés (Honduras)
Rio de Janeiro (Brazil)
San Francisco (USA)
San Sebastián (Spain)
Santo Domingo (Dominican Republic)
St Petersburg (Russia)

13 Coatzacoalcos (Mexico)
Frederikshavn (Denmark)
Great Yarmouth (England)
Ho Chi Minh City (Vietnam)
Middlesbrough (England)
Port Elizabeth (South Africa)
San Juan del Sur (Nicaragua)
Trois Rivières (Canada)
Visakhapatnam (India)

14 Port Georgetown (Guyana)
Santiago de Cuba (Cuba)

Portugal

position *see* **sport**

potato

Potter, Beatrix (1866–1943)

pottery

Pottery makers include:

03 Fry (Laura; 1857–1943, US)
Rie (Dame Lucie; 1902–95, Austrian)

04 Boyd (Arthur; 1920–99, Australian)
Boyd (Merric; 1888–1959, Australian)
Vyse (Charles; 1882–1971, English)
Wood (Aaron; 1717–85, English)
Wood (Enoch; 1759–1840, English)
Wood (John; 1746–97, English)
Wood (Ralph; 1715–72, English)
Wood (Ralph, Jnr; 1748–95, English)
Wyse (Henry Taylor; 1870–1951, Scottish)

05 Adams (Truda; 1890–1958, English)
Adams (William; 1745–1805, English)
Adams (William; 1748–1831, English)
Adams (William; 1772–1829, English)
Amour (Elizabeth; 1885–1945, Scottish)
Cliff (Clarice; 1899–1972, English)
Coper (Hans; 1920–81, British)
Finch (Alfred William; 1854–1930, Finnish)
Korin (Ogata; 1658–1716, Japanese)
Leach (Bernard; 1887–1979, English)
Mason (Miles; 1752–1822, English)
Moore (Bernard; 1850–1935, English)
Perry (Grayson; 1960– , English)
Spira (Rupert; 1960– , English)

06 Cardew (Michael; 1901–82, English)
Carter (Truda; 1890–1958, English)
de Waal (Edmund; 1964– , English)
Dwight (John; c.1637–1703, English)

Hamada (Shoji; 1894–1978, Japanese)
Kenzan (Ogata; 1663–1743, Japanese)
Murray (William Staite; 1881–1962, English)
Taylor (William Howson; 1876–1935, English)

07 Astbury (John; 1688–1743, English)
Britton (Alison; 1948– , English)
Doulton (Sir Henry; 1820–97, English)
Execias (fl.late 6c BC, Greek)
Exekias (fl.late 6c BC, Greek)
Forsyth (Gordon; 1879–1953, Scottish)
Fritsch (Elizabeth; 1940– , English)
Gardner (Peter; 1836–1902, Scottish)
Grotell (Maija; 1899–1973, Finnish)
Palissy (Bernard; c.1509–89, French)
Twyford (Joshua; 1640–1729, English)

08 Fujiwara (Kei; 1899–1983, Japanese)
Overbeck (Elizabeth; 1875–1936, US)
Overbeck (Hannah; 1870–1931, US)
Overbeck (Margaret; 1863–1911, US)
Overbeck (Mary; 1878–1955, US)
Robineau (Adelaide; 1865–1929, US)
Wedgwood (Josiah; 1730–95, English)
Whieldon (Thomas; 1719–95, English)
Yamamoto (Toshu; 1906–94, Japanese)

09 Kaneshige (Toyo; 1896–1967, Japanese)
Moorcroft (William; 1872–1945, English)

10 Euphronios (fl.late 6c–5c BC, Greek)

Pottery terms include:

04 kiln
raku
slip

05 delft
glaze
model

06 basalt
enamel
figure
firing
flambé
ground
jasper
lustre
sagger

07 celadon

See also **porcelain**

ceramic
crazing
faience
fairing

08 armorial
bronzing
flatback
maiolica
majolica
monogram
slip-cast

09 china clay
cloisonné
creamware
grotesque
ironstone
overglaze

porcelain
sgraffito
stoneware

10 art pottery
maker's mark
spongeware
terracotta
underglaze

11 crackleware
earthenware
scratch blue

12 blanc-de-chine

13 Staffordshire
willow pattern

15 mandarin palette

poultry

Poultry include:

03 hen	05 goose	turkey	10 guinea fowl
04 duck	06 bantam	07 chicken	

See also **chicken**; **duck**; **goose**

power station

Power stations include:

06 Huntly (New Zealand)

07 Benmore (New Zealand)

08 Bankside (England)
Dounreay (Scotland)
Sizewell (England)
Yallourn (Australia)

09 Battersea (England)
Chernobyl (Ukraine)

Dungeness (England)
Manapouri (New Zealand)
Windscale (England)

10 Sellafield (England)

11 Wallerawang (Australia)

12 Marsden Point (New Zealand)

14 Snowy Mountains (Australia)

15 Three Mile Island (USA)

prayer

Prayers include:

02 Om

05 adhan
Ardas
grace
salat
Shema

06 Amidah
Gloria
rosary
Yizkor

07 angelus

khotbah
khutbah

08 Agnus Dei
Ave Maria
Habdalah
Hail Mary
Havdalah
Kaddhish
Kol Nidre
shahadah

09 Confiteor
Our Father

10 Benedictus
Lychnapsia
Magnificat
requiescat

11 Lord's Prayer
Paternoster
Sursum Corda

12 Divine Office
Kyrie eleison
Nunc Dimittis

15 Act of Contrition

precipitation

Precipitation includes:

03 dew	rain	07 drizzle	09 rainstorm
fog	snow	08 downpour	snowflake
04 hail	05 sleet	rainfall	
mist	06 shower	snowfall	

See also **ice**; **meteorology**; **snow**; **weather**

prefix *see* **science**

presenter *see* **radio**; **television**

president

04 Bush (George; 1989–93)
Bush (George W; 2001–09)
Ford (Gerald; 1974–77)
Polk (James K; 1845–49)
Taft (William H; 1909 13)

05 Adams (John; 1797–1801)
Adams (John Quincy; 1825–29)
Buren (Martin van; 1837–41)
Grant (Ulysses S; 1869–77)
Hayes (Rutherford B; 1877–81)
Nixon (Richard M; 1969–74)
Obama (Barack; 2009–   )
Tyler (John; 1841–45)

06 Arthur (Chester A; 1881–85)
Carter (Jimmy; 1977–81)
Hoover (Herbert; 1929–33)
Monroe (James; 1817–25)
Pierce (Franklin; 1853–57)
Reagan (Ronald; 1981–89)
Taylor (Zachary; 1849–50)
Truman (Harry S; 1945–53)
Wilson (Woodrow; 1913–21)

07 Clinton (Bill; 1993–2001)
Harding (Warren G; 1921–23)
Jackson (Andrew; 1829–37)
Johnson (Andrew; 1865–69)
Johnson (Lyndon B; 1963–69)
Kennedy (John F; 1961–63)
Lincoln (Abraham; 1861–65)
Madison (James; 1809–17)

08 Buchanan (James; 1857–61)
Coolidge (Calvin; 1923–29)
Fillmore (Millard; 1850–53)
Garfield (James A; 1881)
Harrison (Benjamin; 1889–93)
Harrison (William Henry; 1841)
McKinley (William; 1897–1901)

09 Cleveland (Grover; 1885–89, 1893–97)
Jefferson (Thomas; 1801–09)
Roosevelt (Franklin D; 1933–45)
Roosevelt (Theodore; 1901–09)

10 Eisenhower (Dwight D; 1953–61)
Washington (George; 1789–97)

03 Doe (Samuel; 1951–90, Liberian)
Moi (Daniel arap; 1924–   , Kenyan)
Rau (Johannes; 1931–   , German)
Sun (Yat-sen; 1866–1925, Chinese)
Zia (Khaleda; 1945–   , Bangladeshi)

04 Amin (Idi; 1925–2003, Ugandan)
Díaz (Porfirio; 1830–1915, Mexican)
Khan (Ayub; 1907–1974, Pakistani)
Ozal (Turgut; 1927–93, Turkish)
René (France-Albert; 1935–   , Seychelles)
Rhee (Syngman; 1875–1965, Korean)
Tito (Josip Broz; 1892–1980, Yugoslav)

05 Ahmed (Shehabuddin; 1930, Bangladeshi)
Assad (Bashar al-; 1965–   , Syrian)
Assad (Hafez al-; 1928–2000, Syrian)
Banda (Hastings; 1898–1997, Malawian)
Botha (P W; 1916–2006, South African)
Havel (Václav; 1936–   , Czech)
Heuss (Theodor; 1884–1963, German)
Mbeki (Thabo; 1942–   , South African)
Menem (Carlos; 1935–   , Argentine)
Obote (Milton; 1924–   , Ugandan)
Perón (Juan; 1895–1974, Argentine)
Perón (Maria Estela Martínez de 'Isabelita';
   1931–   , Argentine)
Putin (Vladimir; 1952–   , Russian)
Ramos (Fidel; 1928–   , Philippine)
Sadat (Anwar el-; 1918–81, Egyptian)

06 Aideed (Mohammed; 1934–96, Somalian)
Aquino (Cory; 1933–   , Philippine)
Banana (Canaan; 1936–2003, Zimbabwean)
Bao Dai (1913–97, Indo-Chinese/
   Vietnamese)
Bhutto (Zulfikar; 1928–79, Pakistani)
Biswas (Abdur Rahman; 1926–   ,
   Bangladeshi)
Calles (Plutarco Elías; 1877–1945, Mexican)
Castro (Fidel; 1926–   , Cuban)
Chirac (Jacques; 1932–   , French)
Ciampi (Carlo Azeglio; 1920–   , Italian)
Gaulle (Charles de; 1890–1970, French)
Geisel (Ernesto; 1908–96, Brazilian)
Herzog (Chaim; 1918–1997, Israeli)
Juárez (Benito; 1806–72, Mexican)
Kruger (Paul; 1825–1904, South African)
Kuchma (Leonid; 1938–   , Ukrainian)
Lahoud (Émile; 1936–   , Lebanese)
Marcos (Ferdinand; 1917–89, Philippine)
Mobutu (Sese Seko; 1930–97, Zairean)
Mugabe (Robert; 1924–   , Zimbabwean)
Nasser (Gamal Abd al-; 1918–70, Egyptian)
Nathan (Sellapan Ramanathan; 1924–   ,
   Singaporean)
Ortega (Daniel; 1945–   , Nicaraguan)
Préval (René; 1943–   , Haitian)
Rahman (Ziaur; 1936–1981, Bangladeshi)
Renner (Karl; 1870–1950, Austrian)

Santos (José Eduardo dos; 1942– ,
   Angolan)
Somoza (Anastasio 1896–1956, Nicaraguan)
Somoza (Luis; 1922–1967, Nicaraguan)
Valera (Éamon de; 1882–1975, Irish)
Vargas (Getúlio; 1883–1954, Brazilian)
Walesa (Lech; 1943– , Polish)

07 Atatürk (Mustapha Kemal; 1881–1938,
   Turkish)
Batista (Fulgencio; 1901–73, Cuban)
Bolívar (Simón; 1783–1830, Colombian/
   South American)
Cardoso (Fernando Henrique; 1931– ,
   Brazilian)
de Klerk (F W; 1936– , South African)
Demirel (Süleyman; 1924– , Turkish)
Estrada (Joseph Ejercito; 1937– ,
   Philippine)
Gaddafi (Muammar; 1942– , Libyan)
Gemayel (Amin; 1942– , Lebanese)
Gromyko (Andrei; 1909–89, Soviet)
Habibie (Jusuf; 1936– , Indonesian)
Hussein (Saddam; 1937–2006, Iraqi)
Iliescu (Ion; 1930– , Romanian)
Khatami (Mohammad; 1943– , Iranian)
Mancham (James; 1939– , Seychelles)
Mandela (Nelson; 1918– , South African)
Masaryk (Thomás; 1850–1937,
   Czechoslovak)
Mubarak (Hosni; 1928– , Egyptian)
Nkrumah (Kwame; 1909–72, Ghanaian)
Parnell (Charles Stewart; 1846 91, Irish)
Sampaio (Jorge; 1939– , Portuguese)
Suharto (Thojib N J; 1921–2008, Indonesian)
Sukarno (Ahmed; 1902–70, Indonesian)
Tudjman (Franjo; 1922–99, Croatian)
Weizman (Ezer; 1924–2005, Israeli)
Yanayev (Gennady; 1937– , Russian)
Yeltsin (Boris; 1931–2007, Russian)
Zhivkov (Todor; 1911–98, Bulgarian)

08 Andropov (Yuri; 1914–84, Soviet)
Aristide (Jean-Bertrand; 1953– , Haitian)
Bani-Sadr (Abolhassan; 1935– , Iranian)
Brezhnev (Leonid; 1906–82, Soviet)
Chamorro (Violetta; 1919– , Nicaraguan)
Childers (Erskine; 1905–74, Irish)
Cosgrave (William Thomas; 1880–1965,
   Irish)
de Gaulle (Charles; 1890–1970, French)
de Valera (Éamon; 1882–1975, Irish)
Duvalier (François 'Papa Doc'; 1907–71,
   Haitian)
Duvalier (Jean-Claude 'Baby Doc'; 1951– ,
   Haitian)
Fujimori (Alberto; 1939– , Peruvian)

Galtieri (Leopoldo; 1926–2003, Argentine)
Karadžić (Radovan; 1945– , Bosnian-Serb)
Kenyatta (Jomo; c.1889–1978, Kenyan)
Khamenei (Sayed Ali; 1939– , Iranian)
Kravchuk (Leonid; 1934– , Ukrainian)
MacMahon (Patrice de; 1808–93, French)
Makarios (Cyprus Enosis; 1913–77, Cypriot)
McAleese (Mary; 1951– , Irish)
Medvedev (Dmitry Anatolyevich; 1965– ,
   Russian)
Mengistu (Haile Mariam; 1941– ,
   Ethiopian)
Museveni (Yoweri; 1944– , Ugandan)
Napoleon (I, Bonaparte; 1769–1821,
   French)
Pinochet (Augusto; 1915–2006, Chilean)
Poincaré (Raymond; 1860–1934, French)
Pompidou (Georges; 1911–74, French)
Rawlings (Jerry; 1947– , Ghanaian)
Robinson (Mary; 1944– , Irish)
Waldheim (Kurt; 1918–2007, Austrian)
Weizmann (Chaim; 1874–1952, Israeli)
Zia ul-Haq (Muhammad; 1924–88,
   Pakistani)

09 Ceaușescu (Nicolae; 1918–89, Romanian)
Chernenko (Konstantin; 1911–85, Soviet)
Gorbachev (Mikhail; 1931– , Russian)
Ho Chi Minh (1890–1969, Vietnamese)
Kim-Il Sung (1912–94, North Korean)
Kim Jong Il (1942– , North Korean)
Mao Zedong (1893–1976, Chinese)
Milošević (Slobodan; 1941–2006, Serbian)
Motlanthe (Kgalema Petrus; 1949– , South
   Africa)
Narayanan (Kocheril Raman; 1920– ,
   Indian)
Pilsudski (Józef; 1867–1935, Polish)

10 Alessandri (Arturo; 1868–1950, Chilean)
Betancourt (Rómulo; 1908–81, Venezuelan)
Hindenburg (Paul von; 1847–1934, German)
Jaruzelski (Wojciech; 1923– , Polish)
Jiang Zemin (1926– , Chinese)
Khrushchev (Nikita; 1894–1971, Soviet)
Kubitschek (Juscelino; 1902–76, Brazilian)
Mannerheim (Carl Gustav, Baron von;
   1867–1951, Finnish)
Mitterrand (François; 1916–96, French)
Najibullah (Mohammad; 1947–96, Afghan)
Rafsanjani (Hojatoleslam Ali Akbar
   Hashemi; 1934– , Iranian)
Stroessner (Alfredo; 1912–2006, Paraguayan)
Voroshilov (Kliment; 1881–1969, Soviet)
Yushchenko (Viktor; 1954– , Ukrainian)

13 Paz Estenssoro (Víctor; 1907–2001, Bolivian)

15 Giscard d'Estaing (Valéry; 1926– , French)

prey *see* **bird**

priest

04 lama (Buddhism)
papa (Greek Orthodox)
pope (Greek Orthodox)
05 bonze (Buddhism)
druid (Celtic)
magus (Ancient Persia)
mambo (voodoo)
rabbi (Judaism)
06 flamen (Ancient Rome)
Levite (Judaism)

lucumo (Etruscan)
07 Brahman (Hindu)
Pythian (Ancient Greece)
tohunga (Maori)
08 bacchant (Bacchus)
corybant (Ancient Greece)
09 bacchanal (Bacchus)
presbyter (Episcopal churches)
10 arch-flamen (Ancient Rome)

primate

03 ape
05 human
lemur
loris
pongo

06 galago
gibbon
monkey
07 gorilla
08 bushbaby

great ape
night-ape
09 catarhine
orang-utan
prosimian

10 catarrhine
chimpanzee
protohuman
11 Homo sapiens
orang-outang

See also **ape**

prime minister

04 Cook (Joseph; 1913–14, Liberal)
Holt (Harold; 1966–67, Liberal)
Page (Earle; 1939, Country)
Reid (George; 1904–05, Free Trade)
Rudd (Kevin; 2007– , Labor)
05 Bruce (Stanley; 1923–29, Nationalist)
Forde (Francis Michael; 1945, Labor)
Hawke (Bob; 1983–91, Labor)
Lyons (Joseph; 1932–39, United)
06 Barton (Edmund; 1901–03, Protectionist)
Curtin (John; 1941–45, Labor)
Deakin (Alfred; 1903–04/1905–08,
Protectionist/1909–10, Fusion)
Fadden (Arthur; 1941, Country)
Fisher (Andrew; 1908–09/1910–13/
1914–15, Labor)

Fraser (Malcolm; 1975–83, Liberal)
Gorton (John; 1968–71, Liberal)
Howard (John; 1996–2007, Liberal)
Hughes (Billy; 1915–17, National
Labor/1917–23, Nationalist)
McEwen (John; 1967–68, Country)
Watson (Chris; 1904, Labor)
07 Chifley (Ben; 1945–49, Labor)
Keating (Paul; 1991–96, Labor)
McMahon (William; 1971–72, Liberal)
Menzies (Robert; 1939–41,
United/1949–66, Liberal)
Scullin (James; 1929–32, Labor)
Whitlam (Gough; 1972–75, Labor)

04 King (William Lyon Mackenzie; 1921–
26/1926–30/1935–48, Liberal)
05 Abbot (John J C; 1891–92, Conservative)
Clark (Joseph; 1979–80, Conservative)
06 Borden (Robert; 1911–20, Conservative/
Unionist)
Bowell (Mackenzie; 1894–96, Conservative)
Harper (Stephen; 2006– , Conservative)

Martin (Paul; 2003–06, Liberal)
Tupper (Charles; 1896, Conservative)
Turner (John; 1984, Liberal)
07 Bennett (R B; 1930–35, Conservative)
Laurier (Wilfrid; 1896–1911, Liberal)
Meighen (Arthur; 1920–21, Unionist/
Conservative/1926, Conservative)
Pearson (Lester B; 1963–68, Liberal)

Trudeau (Pierre; 1968–79/1980–84, Liberal)
08 Campbell (Kim; 1993, Conservative)
Chrétien (Jean; 1993–2003, Liberal)
Mulroney (Brian; 1984–93, Conservative)
Thompson (John S D; 1892–94, Conservative)

09 Macdonald (John A; 1867–73/1878–91, Conservative)
Mackenzie (Alexander; 1873–78, Liberal)
St Laurent (Louis; 1948–57, Liberal)
11 Diefenbaker (John G; 1957–63, Conservative)

Prime ministers of New Zealand, with dates of office:

03 Key (John; 2008–   , National)
04 Bell (Francis; 1925, Reform)
Kirk (Norman Eric; 1972–74, Labour)
Nash (Walter; 1957–60, Labour)
Ward (Joseph; 1906–12/1928–30, Liberal/ National)
05 Clark (Helen; 1999–2008, Labour)
Lange (David; 1984–89, Labour)
Moore (Mike; 1990, Labour)
06 Bolger (James; 1990–97, National)
Coates (Gordon; 1925–28, Reform)
Forbes (George William; 1930–35, United)
Fraser (Peter; 1940–49, Labour)

Massey (William; 1912–25, Reform)
Palmer (Geoffrey; 1989–90, Labour)
Savage (Michael Joseph; 1935–40, Labour)
Seddon (Richard; 1893–1906, Liberal)
07 Holland (Sidney; 1949–57, National)
Muldoon (Robert; 1975–84, National)
Rowling (Wallace; 1974–75, Labour)
Shipley (Jenny; 1997–99, National)
08 Holyoake (Keith; 1957/1960–72, National)
Marshall (John Ross; 1972, National)
09 Hall-Jones (William; 1906, Liberal)
Mackenzie (Thomas; 1912, National)

Prime ministers of the United Kingdom, with dates of office:

04 Bute (John Stuart, Earl of; 1762–63, Tory)
Eden (Anthony; 1955–57, Conservative)
Grey (Charles Grey, Earl; 1830–34, Whig)
Home (Alec Douglas-Home, Earl of; 1963–64, Conservative)
Peel (Robert; 1834–35/1841–46, Conservative)
Pitt (William; 1783–1801/1804–06, Tory)
05 Blair (Tony; 1997–2007, Labour)
Brown (Gordon; 2007–   , Labour)
Derby (Edward Stanley, Earl of; 1852/1858–59/1866–68, Conservative)
Heath (Ted; 1970–74, Conservative)
Major (John; 1990–97, Conservative)
North (Frederick North, Lord; 1770–82, Tory)
06 Attlee (Clement; 1945–51, Labour)
Pelham (Henry; 1743–54, Whig)
Wilson (Harold; 1964–70/1974–76, Labour)
07 Asquith (Herbert; 1908–15, Liberal/1915–16, Coalition)
Baldwin (Stanley; 1923–24/1924–29, Conservative/1935–37, Nationalist)
Balfour (Arthur; 1902–05, Conservative)
Canning (George; 1827, Tory)
Grafton (Augustus Henry Fitzroy, Duke of; 1766–70, Whig)
Russell (John, Lord; 1846–52/1865–66, Liberal)
Walpole (Robert; 1721–42, Whig)
08 Aberdeen (George Hamilton-Gordon, Lord; 1852–55, Peelite)

Bonar Law (Andrew; 1922–23, Conservative)
Disraeli (Benjamin; 1868/1874–80, Conservative)
Goderich (Frederick John Robinson, Viscount; 1827–28, Tory)
Perceval (Spencer; 1809–12, Tory)
Portland (William Henry Cavendish Bentinck, Duke of; 1783, Coalition/ 1807–09, Tory)
Rosebery (Archibald Philip Primrose, Earl of; 1894–95, Liberal)
Thatcher (Margaret; 1979–90, Conservative)
09 Addington (Henry; 1801–04, Tory)
Callaghan (James; 1976–79, Labour)
Churchill (Winston; 1940–45, Coalition/ 1951–55, Conservative)
Gladstone (William; 1868–74/1880–85/1886/1892–94, Liberal)
Grenville (George; 1763–65, Whig)
Grenville (William Wyndham, Lord; 1806–07, Whig)
Liverpool (Robert Jenkinson, Earl of; 1812–27, Tory)
MacDonald (Ramsay; 1924/1929–31, Labour/1931–35, Nationalist)
Macmillan (Harold; 1957–63, Conservative)
Melbourne (William Lamb, Viscount; 1834/1835–41, Whig)
Newcastle (Thomas Pelham-Holles, Duke of; 1754–56/1757–62, Whig)
Salisbury (Robert Gascoyne-Cecil,

Marquess of; 1885–86/1886–92/ 1895–1902, Conservative)

Shelburne (William Petty-Fitzmaurice, Earl of; 1782–83, Whig)

10 Devonshire (William Cavendish, Duke of; 1756–57, Whig)

Palmerston (Henry John Temple, Viscount; 1855–50/1059–65, Liberal)

Rockingham (Charles Watson Wentworth, Marquess of; 1765–66/1782, Whig)

Wellington (Arthur Wellesley, Duke of; 1828–30, Tory)

Wilmington (Spencer Compton, Earl; 1742–43, Whig)

11 Chamberlain (Neville; 1937–40, Nationalist)

Douglas-Home (Alec; 1963–64, Conservative)

Lloyd George (David; 1916–22, Coalition)

17 Campbell-Bannerman (Henry; 1905–08, Liberal)

Prime ministers of other countries include:

02 Nu (U; 1907–95, Burmese)

03 Ito (Hirobumi; 1838–1909, Japanese)

04 Meir (Golda; 1898–1978, Russian/US/Israeli)

Moro (Aldo; 1916–78, Italian)

Tojo (Hideki; 1885–1948, Japanese)

05 Ahern (Bertie; 1951– , Irish)

Assad (Hafez al-; 1928–2000, Syrian)

Azaña (Manuel; 1880–1940, Spanish)

Aznar (José María; 1953– , Spanish)

Banda (Hastings; 1898–1997, Malawian)

Barak (Ehud; 1942– , Israeli)

Barre (Raymond; 1924– , French)

Begin (Menachem; 1913–92, Polish/Israeli)

Botha (Louis; 1862–1919, South African)

Botha (P W; 1916–2006, South African)

Cowen (Brian; 1960– , Irish)

Craxi (Bettino; 1934–2000, Italian)

Desai (Morarji; 1896–1995, Indian)

Faure (Edgar; 1908–88, French)

Hoxha (Enver; 1908–85, Albanian)

Juppé (Alain; 1945– , French)

Khama (Sir Seretse; 1921–80, African)

Laval (Pierre; 1883–1945, French)

Lynch (John 'Jack'; 1917–99, Irish)

Malan (Daniel; 1874–1959, South African)

Nehru (Jawaharlal; 1889–1964, Indian)

Obote (Milton; 1924–2005, Ugandan)

Pasić (Nikola; c.1846–1926, Serbian)

Peres (Shimon; 1923– , Polish/Israeli)

Prodi (Romano; 1939– , Italian)

Putin (Vladimir; 1952– , Russian)

Rabin (Yitzhak; 1922–95, Israeli)

Sadat (Anwar el-; 1918–81, Egyptian)

Singh (V P; 1931– , Indian)

Smith (Ian; 1919–2007, Rhodesian)

Smuts (Jan; 1870–1950, South African)

Spaak (Paul Henri; 1899–1972, Belgian)

06 Bhutto (Benazir; 1953–2007, Pakistani)

Bhutto (Zulfikar; 1928–79, Pakistani)

Briand (Aristide; 1862–1932, French)

Bruton (John; 1947– , Irish)

Castro (Fidel; 1926– , Cuban)

Chirac (Jacques; 1932– , French)

Ecevit (Bülent; 1925–2006, Turkish)

Fabius (Laurent; 1946– , French)

Gandhi (Indira; 1917–84, Indian)

Gandhi (Rajiv; 1944–91, Indian)

Hun Sen (1952– , Cambodian)

Jospin (Lionel; 1937– , French)

Li Peng (1928– , Chinese)

Manley (Michael; 1924–97, Jamaican)

Mugabe (Robert; 1924– , Zimbabwean)

Neguib (Mohammed; 1901–84, Egyptian)

O'Neill (Terence, Lord; 1914–90, Northern Irish)

Pétain (Philippe; 1856–1951, French)

Pol Pot (1925–98, Cambodian)

Pombal (Sebastião de Carvalho e Mello, Marques de; 1699–1782, Portuguese)

Rahman (Sheikh Mujibur; 1920–75, Bangladeshi)

Rhodes (Cecil; 1853–1902, South African)

Shamir (Yitzhak; 1915– , Israeli)

Sharif (Mian Muhammad Nawaz; 1941– , Pakistani)

Sharon (Ariel; 1928– , Israeli)

Thiers (Adolphe; 1797–1877, French)

07 Berisha (Sali; 1944– , Albanian)

Bingham (Hiram; 1875–1956, US)

Cresson (Edith; 1934– , French)

Gasperi (Alcide de; 1881–1954, Italian)

Halifax (Charles Montagu, 1st Earl of; 1661–1715, English)

Haughey (Charles; 1925–2006, Irish)

Hertzog (J B M; 1866–1942, South African)

Kosygin (Aleksei; 1904–80, Soviet)

Lubbers (Ruud; 1939– , Dutch)

Molotov (Vyacheslav; 1890–1986, Soviet)

Nkrumah (Kwame; 1909–72, Ghanaian)

Nyerere (Julius; 1922–99, Tanzanian)

Vorster (John; 1915–83, South African)

Yeltsin (Boris; 1931–2007, Russian)

08 Ben Bella (Ahmed; 1916– , Algerian)

Bismarck (Prince Otto von; 1815–98, Prusso-German)

Bulganin (Nikolai; 1895–1975, Russian)

Daladier (Édouard; 1884–1970, French)

de Gaulle (Charles; 1890–1970, French)
de Valera (Éamon; 1882–1975, Irish)
González (Felipe; 1942– , Spanish)
Kenyatta (Jomo; c.1889–1978, Kenyan)
Nakasone (Yasuhiro; 1917– , Japanese)
Poincaré (Raymond; 1860–1934, French)
Pompidou (Georges; 1911–74, French)
Quisling (Vidkun; 1887–1945, Norwegian)
Reynolds (Albert; 1932– , Irish)
Vajpayee (Atal Bihari; 1926– , Indian)
Verwoerd (Hendrik; 1901–66, Dutch/South
   African)
Zapatero (José Luis Rodríguez; 1960– ,
   Spanish)

09 Andreotti (Giulio; 1919– , Italian)
Ben-Gurion (David; 1886–1973, Polish/
   Israeli)
Hashimoto (Ryutaro; 1937–2006, Japanese)

Kim-Il Sung (1912–94, North Korean)
Kim Jong Il (1942– , North Korean)
Mussolini (Benito; 1883–1945, Italian)
Netanyahu (Binyamin; 1949– , Israeli)
Stanishev (Sergei; 1966– , Bulgarian)

10 Balkenende (Jan Peter; 1956– , Dutch)
Berlusconi (Silvio; 1936– , Italian)
Clemenceau (Georges; 1841–1929, French)
Fitzgerald (Garrett; 1926– , Irish)
Jaruzelski (Wojciech; 1923– , Polish)
Lee Kuan Yew (1923– , Singaporean)

11 Verhofstadt (Guy; 1953– , Belgian)

12 Bandaranaike (S W R D; 1899–1959,
   Ceylonese)
Chernomyrdin (Viktor; 1938– , Russian)

13 Brookeborough (Basil Brooke, Viscount;
   1888–1973, Northern Irish)

prince

03 Hal (*Henry IV Part I*, 1596/7, William
   Shakespeare)

04 Ivan (I; c.1304–41, Russian)
John (*Ivanhoe*, 1819, Sir Walter Scott)
John (of Gaunt, Duke of Lancaster;
   1340–99, English)
John (of Lancaster; *Henry IV Part I*, 1596/7,
   William Shakespeare)
York (Andrew, Duke of; 1960– , British)
York (Richard, Duke of; 1470–83, English)

05 Bulbo (*The Rose and the Ring*, 1855, W M
   Thackeray)
Canty (Tom; *The Prince and the Pauper*,
   1881, Mark Twain)
Cyrus (the Younger; 424–401 BC, Persian)
Harry (1984– , British)
Henry (1594–1612, Scottish)
Henry (*King John*, 1590/1, William
   Shakespeare)
Henry (of Wales; *Henry IV Part I*, 1596/7,
   William Shakespeare)
Madoc (fl.1150–80, Welsh)
Wales (Charles, Prince of; 1948– , British)

06 Albert (1819–61, German)
Albert (II, 1958– ; Monaco)
Andrew (1960– , British)
Aragon (*The Merchant of Venice*, 1594–5,
   William Shakespeare)
Arthur (1486–1502, English)
Arthur (*The Faerie Queene*, 1590–96, Sir
   Edmund Spenser)
Ben Hur (*Ben Hur*, 1880, Lew Wallace)
Carlos (Don; 1545–68, Spanish)
Dmitri (1583–91, Russian)

Edward (1964– , British)
Edward ('the Black Prince'; 1330–76,
   English)
Edward (*The Prince and the Pauper*, 1881,
   Mark Twain)
Egmond (Lamoraal, Graf van; 1522–68,
   Flemish)
Egmont (Lamoraal, Graf van; 1522–68,
   Flemish)
Giglio (*The Rose and the Ring*, 1855, W M
   Thackeray)
Haakon (1973– ; Norwegian)
Hamlet (*Hamlet*, 1601/2, William
   Shakespeare)
Philip (1921– , Greek)
Stuart (Charles; 1720–88, British)
Stuart (James; 1688–1766, British)
Ulrich (Crown Prince of Evarchia; *Palace
   without Chairs*, 1978, Brigid Brophy)
Wessex (Edward, Earl of; 1964– , British)

07 Amerigo (*The Golden Bowl*, 1904, Henry
   James)
Arragon (*The Merchant of Venice*, 1594/5,
   William Shakespeare)
Bedford (John of Lancaster, Duke of;
   1389–1435, English)
Charles (Prince of Wales; 1948– , British)
Charles (*The Fortunes of Nigel*, 1822, Sir
   Walter Scott)
Escalus (Prince of Verona; *Romeo and Juliet*,
   1591–96, William Shakespeare)
Manfred (Prince of Otranto; *The Castle of
   Otranto*, 1764, Horace Walpole)
Maurice (1567–1625, Nassau)
Michael (of Kent; 1942– , British)

Morocco (*The Merchant of Venice*, 1594/5,
William Shakespeare)

Orléans (Louis Philippe Joseph, Duc d';
1747–93, French)

Rainier (III; 1923–2005, Monaco)

Richard (1470–83, English)

Rothsay (David of Scotland, Duke of; *The
Fair Maid of Perth, or St Valentine's Day*,
1828, Sir Walter Scott)

Stewart (Charles; 1720–88, British)

Stewart (James; 1688–1766, British)

William (1982– , British)

William (I; the Silent; 1533–84, Dutch)

Yakimov (*The Balkan Trilogy*, 1960–65,
Olivia Manning)

08 Berthier (Alexandre; 1753–1815, French)

Bohemond (I; c.1056–1111, Antioch)

Bohemond (II; c.1108–31, Antioch)

Carloman (751–71, Frankish)

Don Pedro (*Much Ado about Nothing*,
1598/1600, William Shakespeare)

Florizel (Prince of Bohemia; *The Suicide
Club*, 1878, Robert Louis Stevenson)

Florizel (*The Winter's Tale*, 1611, William
Shakespeare)

Hans-Adam (II; 1945– ; Liechtenstein)

Pericles (*Pericles*, c.1608, William
Shakespeare)

Pyrocles (*The Countess of Pembroke's
Arcadia*, 1581–84, Sir Philip Sidney)

Queequeg (*Moby-Dick*, 1851, Herman
Melville)

Rasselas (*The History of Rasselas, Prince of
Abissinia*, 1759, Samuel Johnson)

Ulugh-Beg (1394–1449, Tatar)

Vladimir (II, Monomakh; 1053–1125, Russian)

Volscius (*The Rehearsal*, 1671, George
Villiers, 2nd Duke of Buckingham)

09 Abu al-Fida (1273–1331, Syrian)

Antipater (d.4 BC, Judean)

Balthazar (*The Spanish Tragedy*, 1592,
Thomas Kyd)

Bonaparte (Lucien; 1775–1840, Italian)

Bras-Coupé (*The Grandissimes*, 1880,
George Washington Cable)

Connaught (Arthur, Duke of; 1850–1942,
English)

Demetrius (1583–91, Russian)

Edinburgh (Philip, Duke of; 1921– , British)

Ferdinand (I; 1861–1948, Austrian)

Musidorus (*The Countess of Pembroke's
Arcadia*, 1581–84, Sir Philip Sidney)

Pretty-man (*The Rehearsal*, 1671, George
Villiers, 2nd Duke of Buckingham)

Vincentio (*The Gentleman Usher*, 1602/3,
George Chapman)

10 Anacharsis (6c BC, Scythian)

Battenberg (Alexander of; 1857–93, Austrian)

Battenberg (Henry of; 1858–96, German)

Gloucester (Henry, Duke of; 1900–74, English)

Gloucester (Humphrey, Earl of Pembroke
and Duke of; 1391–1447, English)

Gloucester (Richard, Duke of; 1944– ,
English)

Gloucester (Robert, Earl of; d.1147, English)

11 Happy Prince ('The Happy Prince', 1888,
Oscar Wilde)

14 Frederick Louis (1707–51, German)

15 Alexander Nevsky (c.1220–63, Russian)

Alexis Petrovich (1690–1718, Russian)

Bernhard Leopold (1911–2004, Dutch)

Lewis the Dauphin (*Henry V*, 1599, William
Shakespeare)

Owain ap Gruffydd (c.1109–70, Welsh)

Saxe-Coburg-Gotha (Alfred Ernest Albert,
Prince of; 1844–1900, English)

princess

Princesses include:

03 Bee (St; 7c, Irish)

04 Anne (1950– , English)

Bega (St; 7c, Irish)

Begh (St; 7c, Irish)

Ebba (St; d.683, Northumbrian)

Olga (St; c.890–968, Russian)

05 Alice (1843–78, English)

Diana (Princess of Wales; 1961–97, English)

Grace (1929–82, US)

Irene (*The Princess and the Goblin*, 1871,
George MacDonald)

Wales (Diana, Princess of; 1961–97, English)

06 Albany (Louisa Caroline, Countess of;

1752–1824, Italian)

Audrey (St; c.630–79, Anglo-Saxon)

Dympna (c.9c, Irish)

France (*Love's Labour's Lost*, c.1594,
William Shakespeare)

Lieven (Dorothea; 1784–1857, Russian)

Salome (1c AD, Judean)

07 Arsinoë (c.316–270 BC, Macedonian)

Eudocia (AD401–65, Byzantine)

Eugenie (1990– , English)

Jezebel (d.842 BC, Phoenician)

Matilda (1102–67, English)

Rosalba (*The Rose and the Ring*, 1855, W M
Thackeray)

08 Angelica (*The Rose and the Ring*, 1855, W
    M Thackeray)
    Beatrice (1988– , English)
    Berenice (1c BC, Judean)
    Berenice (c.28–c.79 AD, Judean)
    Berenice (I; fl.c.317–c.275 BC, Macedonian)
    Berenice (II; c.269–221 BC, Cyrene)
    Berenice (III; d.c.80 BC, Egyptian)
    Berenice (IV; d.55 BC, Egyptian)
    Caroline (1957– , Monacan)
    Dashkova (Yekaterina Romanovna; 1743–
    1810, Russian)
    Glorvina (Lady; *The Wild Irish Girl*, 1806,
    Lady Morgan)
    Grimaldi (Grace, of Monaco; 1929–82, US)
    Margaret (1930–2002, British)
    Victoria (1977– , Swedish)
    Volupine ('Burbank with a Baedeker;
    Bleistein with a Cigar', 1920, T S Eliot)

09 Alexandra (1936– , English)
    Bacciochi (Maria Anna Elisa; 1777–1820,
    Corsican)

    Bonaparte (Pauline; 1780–1825, Corsican)
    Charlotte (1796–1817, English)
    Katharine (Princess of France; *Henry V*,
    1599, William Shakespeare)
    Stephanie (1965– , Monacan)
    Theophano (c.955–991, Byzantine)

10 Etheldreda (St; c.630–79, Anglo-Saxon)
    Mette-Marit (1973– , Norwegian)
    Pocahontas (1595–1617, American)

11 Anna Comnena (1083–1148, Byzantine)
    Anna Comnena (*Count Robert of Paris*,
    1831, Sir Walter Scott)
    Casamassima (*The Princess Casamassima*,
    1886, Henry James)

12 Aethelthryth (St; c.630–79, Anglo-Saxon)
    Anne of Cleves (1515–57, German)

13 Anne of Denmark (1574–1619, Danish)
    Henrietta Anne (Duchesse d'Orleans;
    1644–70, English)

14 Henrietta Maria (1609–69, French)

printing

Printing methods include:

03 CTP	**11** die-stamping	thermography
05 litho	duplicating	**13** laser printing
07 etching	flexography	**14** ink-jet printing
gravure	letterpress	offset printing
08 intaglio	lithography	photoengraving
09 collotype	rotary press	screen printing
engraving	stencilling	**15** computer-to-plate
10 xerography	twin-etching	copper engraving
	12 lino blocking	

Printing terms include:

03 CTP	litho	web-fed
TLS	moiré	**07** bromide
TPS	press	carding
04 bulk	proof	compose
case	quoin	dampers
CYMK	spine	dot gain
demi	zinco	end even
laid	**06** batter	foiling
logo	coated	leading
sewn	cut-off	opacity
tint	galley	Pantone®
trim	jacket	strip in
05 bleed	mackle	woodcut
chase	matrix	**08** art paper
cloth	octavo	book wove
cover	Ozalid®	flatback
flong	quarto	foolscap
forme	spread	half-tone
	unsewn	

hardback
headband
Linotype®
logotype
misprint
Monotype®
mottling
offprint
press run
print run
sheet fed
slipcase
softback
spoilage
strike-on
tailband
thumb cut
uncoated
wood-free

09 backing-up
book-block
case cover
duodecimo
dust cover
endpapers
finishing
flexi-bind
front flap
gilt edges
half bound
hard-bound
ink spread
Intertype®
letterset
make-ready
Monophoto®

newsprint
overprint
paperback
signature
soft-bound
trim marks
UV varnish
watermark
web offset

10 back margin
collograph
compositor
dot-etching
dustjacket
feathering
imposition
impression
lamination
mechanical
perfecting
see-through
shrink-wrap
silk screen
spot colour
stereotype

11 drum printer
electrotype
French bound
letter press
line printer
Oxford bound
show through
slot binding

12 black printer
brass artwork
burst binding

flat-bed press
inking roller
keep standing
machine proof
marker ribbon
non-image area
one-piece case
planographic
quarter bound
registration

13 anodized plate
base alignment
bonded leather
composing room
cylinder press
image printing
pantone colour
printing press
process colour
reader's spread
wood engraving

14 imitation cloth
kiss impression
part-mechanical
printer's spread
relief printing
thermal printer
transparencies

15 camera-ready copy
cold composition
composition size
digital printing
marble endpapers
trimmed leaf size
trimmed page size

See also **book**; **paint**; **publishing**

prison

Prisons include:

04 Maze (Northern Ireland)
05 Fleet (England)
Hoa Lo (Vietnam)
Pozzi (Italy)
06 Albany (England)
Attica (USA)
Folsom (USA)
07 Brixton (England)
Feltham (England)
Newgate (England)
08 Alcatraz (USA)
Bastille (France)
Belmarsh (England)
Dartmoor (England)

Holloway (England)
Long Kesh (Northern Ireland)
Lubyanka (Russia/USSR)
Mountjoy (Ireland)
Saughton (Scotland)
Sing Sing (USA)
09 Barlinnie (Scotland)
Fremantle (Australia)
Parkhurst (England)
Peterhead (Scotland)
the Scrubs (England)
10 Portlaoise (Ireland)
San Quentin (USA)
Wandsworth (England)

11 Hanoi Hilton (Vietnam)	Rikers Island (USA)
Pentonville (England)	Robben Island (South Africa)
Strangeways (England)	**13** Tower of London (England)
12 Devil's Island (French Guiana)	**14** Wormwood Scrubs (England)

prize *see* **award; literature; Nobel Prize**

probe *see* **space travel**

producer *see* **director**

programme *see* **television**

programming language *see* **computer**

Prokofiev, Sergei (1891–1953)

Significant works include:

05 *Chout* (1921)

09 'Classical' (Symphony; 1918)
'Zdravitsa' (Cantata; 1939)

10 *Cinderella* (1945)
The Buffoon (1921)
The Gambler (1915–16)

11 *Le Pas d'acier* (1927)
War and Peace (1944/1952)

12 *The Steel Step* (1927)

13 *Scythian Suite* (1916)
The Fiery Angel (1919–27)

14 *Lieutenant Kijé* (1934)
Romeo and Juliet (1936)
The Prodigal Son (1929)

15 *Alexander Nevsky* (1938)
Ivan the Terrible (1945)
Peter and the Wolf (1936)

18 *The Story of a Real Man* (1948)

19 'Sinfonia Concertante' (1952)

20 *Tale of the Stone Flower* (1954)

22 *The Love for Three Oranges* (1921)

prophet

Prophets and prophetesses include:

02 Is	Ezek	Elisha	Muhammad
03 Dan	Joel	Haggai	Nehemiah
Hag	Obad	Isaiah	**09** al-Mokanna
Hos	Zeph	Nathan	Zephaniah
Isa	**05** Hosea	Samuel	Zoroaster
Jer	Jonah	St John	
Jon	Micah	**07** Ezekiel	**11** Zarathustra
Mic	Moses	Malachi	**12** the Nun of Kent
Nah	Nahum	Obadiah	**13** the Maid of Kent
Sam	**06** Daniel	**08** Jeremiah	**14** John the Baptist
04 Amos	Elijah	Mohammed	

prosody

Prosody terms include:

04 foot	**05** canto	epode	Ionic
iamb	envoy	ictus	metre

paeon	triolet	hexameter	linked verse
06 choree	tripody	macaronic	long-measure
dactyl	triseme	monometer	septenarius
dipody	trochee	monorhyme	12 alliteration
dizain	virelay	rime riche	antibacchius
laisse	08 anapaest	tetrapody	Leonine rhyme
miurus	choriamb	10 amphibrach	Pythian verse
rondel	cinquain	amphimacer	sprung rhythm
sonnet	eye rhyme	blank verse	13 abstract verse
07 ballade	Pindaric	consonance	feminine rhyme
caesura	quatrain	enjambment	heroic couplet
couplet	tribrach	galliambic	hypermetrical
distich	trimeter	heptameter	internal rhyme
elision	09 anacrusis	pentameter	14 feminine ending
pantoum	assonance	rhyme royal	masculine rhyme
pyrrhic	catalexis	tetrameter	rime suffisante
rondeau	dispondee	villanelle	15 feminine caesura
Sapphic	ditrochee	11 Alcaic verse	masculine ending
spondee	free verse	alexandrine	poulters' measure
strophe	half-rhyme	broken rhyme	

protein

Proteins include:

03 TSP	insulin	dystrophin
TVP	plasmin	factor VIII
04 zein	sericin	fibrinogen
05 actin	trypsin	huntingtin
opsin	tubulin	interferon
prion	08 aleurone	polymerase
renin	amandine	11 angiostatin
06 avidin	collagen	angiotensin
casein	Copaxone®	haemoglobin
cyclin	ferritin	hydrogenase
enzyme	globulin	interleukin
fibrin	integrin	lactalbumin
globin	lysozyme	lipoprotein
gluten	protease	myoglobulin
kinase	thrombin	phosphatase
lectin	09 fibrillin	plasminogen
leptin	hydrolase	transferrin
ligase	invertase	tropomyosin
myosin	isomerase	12 endonuclease
papain	luciferin	neurotrophin
pepsin	phaseolin	serum albumin
rennin	prolamine	13 lactoglobulin
07 albumin	protamine	14 clotting factor
elastin	sclerotin	immunoglobulin
histone	10 calmodulin	15 intrinsic factor
hordein	complement	

Proust, Marcel (1871–1922)

Significant works include:

12 *Jean Santeuil* (1927)
17 *Contre Sainte-Beuve* (1954)
18 *On Art and Literature* (1954)
19 *Pastiches et mélanges* (1919)

Pleasures and Regrets (1896)
21 *Les Plaisirs et les jours* (1896)
23 *Remembrance of Things Past* (1913–27)
24 *À la recherche du temps perdu* (1913–27)

À la recherche du temps perdu comprises:

09 *Swann's Way* (1913)
10 *La Fugitive* (1925)
11 *The Fugitive* (1925)
     The Prisoner (1923)
12 *Time Regained* (1927)
13 *La Prisonnière* (1923)
15 *Le Temps retrouvé* (1927)
16 *Sodom and Gomorrah* (1921–22)

Sodome et Gomorrhe (1921–22)
The Guermantes Way (1920)
17 *Albertine disparue* (1925)
     Du côté de chez Swann (1913)
     The Sweet Cheat Gone (1925)
18 *Le Côté de Guermantes* (1920)
19 *Within a Budding Grove* (1919)
29 *À l'ombre des jeunes filles en fleur* (1919)

Significant characters include:

05 Bloch
     Morel (Charles)
     Swann (Charles)
     Swann (Gilberte)
06 Jupien
     Leonie (Aunt)
     Marcel
     Rachel
07 Adolphe
     Charlus (Baron Palamède de 'Mémé')

     de Crécy (Odette)
     Simonet (Albertine)
08 Verdurin (Madame)
     Vinteuil (Mlle)
09 Françoise
     Saint-Loup (Robert Marquis de)
12 de Guermantes (Duchesse Oriane)
13 de Forcheville (Comte)
14 de Villeparisis (Madame)

province *see* **Canada; Ireland; New Zealand; South Africa**

pseudonym

Pseudonyms and stage names include:

03 Day (Doris: Doris Kappelhoff)
     Pop (Iggy; James Osterberg)
     Tey (Josephine; Elizabeth Mackintosh)
04 Alda (Alan; Alphonso d'Abruzzo)
     Bell (Acton; Anne Brontë)
     Bell (Currer; Charlotte Brontë)
     Bell (Ellis; Emily Brontë)
     Cage (Nicolas; Nicholas Coppola)
     Dors (Diana; Diana Fluck)
     Ford (Ford Madox; Ford Hueffer)
     Gish (Lillian Diana; Lilian de Guiche)
     Hite (Shere; Shirley Gregory)
     Holm (Sir Ian; Ian Holm Cuthbert)
     John (Sir Elton; Reginald Dwight)
     Lulu (Marie Lawrie)
     Lynn (Dame Vera; Vera Welch)

Piaf (Edith; Edith Gassion)
Reed (Lou; Louis Firbank)
Rhys (Jean; Gwen Williams)
Ross (Diana; Diane Earle)
Saki (Hector Munro)
Sand (George; Amandine Aurore Lucile
     Dupin)
West (Dame Rebecca; Cecily Andrews)
West (Nathanael; Nathan Wallenstein)
Wood (Natalie; Natasha Gurdin)
York (Susannah; Susannah Yolande-Fletcher)
05 Allen (Woody; Allen Konigsberg)
Bizet (Georges; Alexandre César Léopold
     Bizet)
Black (Cilla; Priscilla White)
Bowie (David; David Jones)

Caine (Sir Michael; Maurice Micklewhite)
Cline (Patsy; Virginia Patricia Hensley)
Dylan (Bob; Robert Zimmerman)
Eliot (George; Mary Ann Evans)
Flynn (Errol; Leslie Flynn)
Garbo (Greta; Greta Gustafsson)
Gorky (Maxim; Aleksei Maksimovich Peshkov)
Grant (Cary; Archibald Leach)
Grant (Richard E; Richard Grant Esterhuysen)
Hardy (Oliver; Norvell Hardy Junior)
Henry (O; William Porter)
Holly (Buddy; Charles Hardin)
Jason (David; David White)
Keith (Penelope; Penelope Hatfield)
Lanza (Mario; Alfredo Coccozza)
Leigh (Vivien; Vivian Hartley)
Loren (Sophia; Sofia Scicolone)
Moore (Demi; Demi Guynes)
Moore (Julianne; Julie Anne Smith)
Niven (David; James Nevins)
Queen (Ellery; Frederick Dannay)
Ryder (Winona; Winona Horowitz)
Scott (Ronnie; Ronald Schatt)
Seuss (Dr; Theodor Seuss Geisel)
Smith (Stevie; Florence Smith)
Solti (Sir Georg; Gyorgy Stern)
Stern (Daniel; Marie de Flavigny, Comtesse d'Agoult)
Sting (Gordon Sumner)
Twain (Mark; Samuel Clemens)
Wayne (John; Marion Michael Morrison)
Welch (Raquel; Raquel Tejada)

06 Bacall (Lauren; Betty Perske)
Bardot (Brigitte; Camille Javal)
Berlin (Irving; Israel Baline)
Brooks (Mel; Melvin Kaminsky)
Burton (Richard; Richard Jenkins)
Conrad (Joseph; Józef Teodor Konrad Korzeniowski)
Crosby (Bing; Harry Lillis Crosby)
Curtis (Tony; Bernard Schwartz)
Fields (Dame Gracie; Grace Stansfield)
Foster (Jodie; Alicia Foster)
France (Anatole; Anatole Thibault)
Gibbon (Lewis Grassic; James Leslie Mitchell)
Harlow (Jean; Harlean Carpentier)
Heston (Charlton; Charles Carter)
Irving (Sir Henry; John Henry Brodribb)
Jolson (Al; Asa Yoelson)
Keaton (Diane; Diane Hall)
Laurel (Stan; Arthur Stanley Jefferson)
London (Jack; John Chaney)
Lugosi (Bela; Bela Blasko)
McBain (Ed; Salvatore Albert Lombino)
Mirren (Helen; Helen Mironoff)

Monroe (Marilyn; Norma Jean Mortenson)
Morton (Jelly Roll; Ferdinand La Menthe)
Neeson (Liam; William John Neeson)
Orwell (George; Eric Blair)
Peters (Ellis; Edith Pargeter)
Rogers (Ginger; Virginia McMath)
Salten (Felix; Siegmund Salzmann)
Sapper (Herman McNeile)
Scales (Prunella; Prunella Illingworth)
Simone (Nina; Eunice Waymon)
Spacey (Kevin; Kevin Fowler)
Steele (Tommy; Thomas Hicks)
Turner (Lana; Julia Turner)
Turner (Tina; Annie Mae Bullock)
Waters (Muddy; McKinley Morganfield)
Weldon (Fay; Franklin Birkinshaw)
Wesley (Mary; Mary Siepmann)
Wonder (Stevie; Steveland Judkins)

07 Andrews (Dame Julie; Julia Wells)
Bachman (Richard; Stephen King)
Bennett (Tony; Anthony Benedetto)
Bogarde (Sir Dirk; Derek van den Bogaerde)
Bronson (Charles; Charles Buchinsky)
Carroll (Lewis; Charles Dodgson)
Deneuve (Catherine; Catherine Dorleac)
Dinesen (Isak; Baroness Karen von Blixen)
Douglas (Kirk; Issur Danielovich)
Gardner (Ava; Lucy Johnson)
Garland (Judy; Frances Gumm)
Hepburn (Audrey; Edda Van Heemstra Hepburn-Ruston)
Higgins (Jack; Harry Patterson)
Holiday (Billie; Eleanora Fagan)
Jacques (Hattie; Josephine Jacques)
Karloff (Boris; William Pratt)
Kincaid (Jamaica; Elaine Richardson)
Le Carré (John; David Cornwell)
Lindsay (Robert; Robert Lindsay Stevenson)
Lombard (Carole; Jane Peters)
Matthau (Walter; Walter Matuschanskavasky)
Mercury (Freddie; Frederick Bulsara)
Michael (George; Georgios Panayiotou)
Miranda (Carmen; Maria do Carmo Miranda da Dunha)
Molière (Jean Baptiste Poquelin)
Montand (Yves; Ivo Livi)
Novello (Ivor; David Ivor Davies)
Richard (Sir Cliff; Harry Webb)
Robbins (Harold; Francis Kane)
Russell (Lillian; Helen Leonard)
Shepard (Sam; Samuel Shepard Rogers)
Swanson (Gloria; Gloria Svensson)
Wyndham (John; John Wyndham Parkes Lucas Beynon Harris)
Wynette (Tammy; Virginia Wynette Pugh)

08 Bancroft (Anne; Anna Maria Italiano)

Coltrane (Robbie; Anthony Robert McMillan)
Coolidge (Susan; Sarah Woolsey)
Costello (Elvis; Declan McManus)
Crawford (Joan; Lucille le Sueur)
Dietrich (Marlene; Maria Magdalena von Losch)
Gershwin (George; Jacob Gershvin)
Gershwin (Ira; Israel Gershvin)
Goldberg (Whoopi; Caryn Johnson)
Hayworth (Rita; Margarita Cansino)
Kingsley (Ben; Krishna Bhanji)
MacLaine (Shirley; Shirley Maclean Beaty)
Ma Rainey (Gertrude Rainey)
Pickford (Mary; Gladys Mary Smith)
Robinson (Edward G; Emanuel Goldenberg)
Sly Stone (Sylvester Stewart)
Stanwyck (Barbara; Ruby Stevens)

Stoppard (Tom; Thomas Straussler)
Voltaire (François Marie Arouet)
Williams (Tennessee; Thomas Lanier)

09 Bernhardt (Sarah; Sara-Marie-Henriette Bernard)
Bo Diddley (Ellas Bates)
Charteris (Leslie; Leslie Bowyer-Yin)
Fairbanks (Douglas; Douglas Ullman)
Lancaster (Burt; Stephen Burton Lancaster)
Leadbelly (Huddie William Ledbetter)
Offenbach (Jacques; Jakob Eberst)
Streisand (Barbra; Barbara Rosen)
Valentino (Rudolph; Rodolfo Guglielmi)

10 Howlin' Wolf (Chester Arthur Burnett)
Washington (Dinah; Ruth Jones)
Westmacott (Mary; Agatha Christie)

11 Springfield (Dusty; Mary O'Brien)

psychiatry

Psychiatrists and psychoanalysts include:

04 Beck (Aaron; 1921– , US)
Jung (Carl; 1875–1961, Swiss)
Rank (Otto; 1884–1939, Austrian)

05 Adler (Alfred; 1870–1937, Austrian)
Clare (Anthony; 1942–2007, Irish)
Crane (Frasier; *Cheers* 1982–93/*Frasier* 1993–2004, TV sitcoms, NBC)
Freud (Anna; 1895–1982, Austrian/British)
Freud (Sigmund; 1856–1939, Austrian)
Fromm (Erich; 1900–80, German/US)
Jones (Ernest; 1879–1958, Welsh)
Klein (Melanie; 1882–1960, Austrian/British)
Lacan (Jacques; 1901–81, French)
Laing (R D; 1927–89, Scottish)
Laing (Ronald David; 1927–89, Scottish)
Meyer (Adolf; 1866–1950, Swiss/US)
Reich (Wilhelm; 1897–1957, Austrian)
Szasz (Thomas; 1920– , Hungarian/US)

06 Berger (Hans; 1873–1941, German)
Bowlby (John; 1907–90, English)
Dysart (Martin; *Equus*, 1973, Peter Shaffer)

Hitzig (Julius; 1838–1907, German)
Snyder (Solomon; 1938– , US)

07 Bleuler (Eugen; 1857–1939, Swiss)
Erikson (Erik; 1902–94, US)
Persaud (Raj; 1963– , English)

08 Halfrunt (Gag; *The Hitchhiker's Guide to the Galaxy*, 1978 et seq, Douglas Adams)
Maudsley (Henry; 1835–1918, English)
Sullivan (Harry Stack; 1892–1949, US)
Wernicke (Carl; 1848–1905, German)

09 Alexander (Franz; 1891–1964, Hungarian/US)
Alzheimer (Alois; 1864–1915, German)
Kraepelin (Emil; 1856–1926, German)
Menninger (Karl; 1893–1990, US)
Rorschach (Hermann; 1884–1922, Swiss)

11 Krafft-Ebing (Richard, von; 1840–1902, German)

13 Wagner-Jauregg (Julius; 1857–1940, Austrian)

Terms used in psychiatry include:

02 id

03 ECT
ego

04 mind

05 angst
brain
drugs

06 déjà vu
denial

psyche
shrink

07 Jungian
symptom
therapy

08 alienist
delusion
dementia
Freudian
neurosis

paranoia
superego
syndrome

09 acting out
behaviour
catharsis
cognition
diagnosis
neurology

10 abreaction

alienation
depression
11 suppression
12 psychiatrist
transference

13 conscious mind
mental illness
psychosurgery
psychotherapy
schizophrenia

14 psychoanalysis
15 bipolar disorder
personality test
unconscious mind

psychology

Branches of psychology include:

03 bio
04 para
05 child
depth
neuro
sport
06 health
social
08 abnormal

clinical
criminal
forensic
hedonics
09 cognitive
narrative
10 industrial
structural
11 educational
12 evolutionary

experimental
occupational
13 developmental
environmental
psychobiology
psychometrics
transpersonal
14 organizational
psychoanalysis
15 psychopathology

Psychology theories include:

07 atomism
Gestalt
Jungian
08 Adlerian
Freudian
Jamesian
Lacanian

09 cognitive
Pavlovian
10 attachment
functional
humanistic
Skinnerian
structural

11 behavioural
personality
13 connectionism
functionalism
structuralism
14 associationism
psychoanalytic

Psychological conditions and disorders include:

04 PTSD
06 autism
manias
07 agnosia
bulimia
phobias
08 dementia
neurosis
paranoia
09 addiction

anhedonia
Asperger's
psychosis
Tourette's
10 abreaction
Alzheimer's
blindsight
depression
dysmorphia
sociopathy
11 Huntington's

kleptomania
Munchausen's
psychopathy
12 hypochondria
13 acatamathesia
battle fatigue
schizophrenia
15 anorexia nervosa
bipolar disorder

Psychological therapies include:

03 art
05 drama
group
hypno
06 colour
psycho

07 Gestalt
08 aversion
09 cognitive
10 regression
11 behavioural

counselling
12 electroshock
13 interpersonal
person-centred
psychodynamic

Psychologists include:

04 Bain (Alexander; 1818–1903, Scottish)
Burt (Sir Cyril; 1883–1971, English)
Hall (G Stanley; 1844–1924, US)
Hebb (Donald O; 1904–85, Canadian)
King (Sir Truby; 1858–1938, New Zealand)
Mead (George Herbert; 1863–1931, US)
Ward (James; 1843–1925, English)

05 Beach (Frank; 1911–88, US)
Binet (Alfred; 1857–1911, French)
Clark (Kenneth B; 1914–2005, US)
Craik (Kenneth; 1914–45, Scottish)
Forel (Auguste; 1848–1931, Swiss)
James (William; 1842–1910, US)
Janet (Pierre; 1859–1947, French)
Kelly (George A; 1905–66, US)
Lange (Carl; 1834–1900, Danish)
Luria (Aleksandr; 1902–77, Soviet)
Pratt (J Gaither; 1910–79, US)
Rhine (Joseph Banks; 1895–1980, US)
Simon (Herbert; 1916–2001, US)
Stout (George Frederick; 1860–1944, English)
Wundt (Wilhelm; 1832–1920, German)

06 Bruner (Jerome; 1915– , US)
de Bono (Edward; 1933– , Maltese/British)
Gesell (Arnold; 1880–1961, US)
Gibson (James; 1904–79, US)
Harlow (Harry; 1905–81, US)
Kinsey (Alfred; 1894–1956, US)
Koffka (Kurt; 1886–1941, German)
Köhler (Wolfgang; 1887–1967, German)
Milner (Brenda; 1918–2008, Canadian)
Morris (Robert L; 1942–2004, US)
Murphy (Gardner; 1895–1979, US)
Piaget (Jean; 1896–1980, Swiss)
Pinker (Steven; 1954– , Canadian/US)
Terman (Lewis; 1877–1956, US)
Tolman (Edward C; 1886–1959, US)
Wallas (Graham; 1858–1932, English)

Watson (John B; 1878–1958, US)

07 Baldwin (James Mark; 1861–1934, US)
Cattell (Raymond B; 1905–98, English)
Eysenck (Hans; 1916–97, German/British)
Fechner (Gustav Theodor; 1801–87, German)
Hartley (David; 1705–57, English)
Johnson (Virginia E; 1925– , US)
Lashley (Karl Spencer; 1890–1958, US)
Meinong (Alexius von; 1853–1920, Austrian)
Milgram (Stanley; 1933–84, US)
Neisser (Ulric; 1928– , German/US)
Pringle (Mia Kellmer; 1920–83, Austrian)
Skinner (B F; 1904–90, US)
Stevens (Stanley S; 1906–73, US)

08 Bartlett (Sir Frederic C; 1886–1969, English)
Brentano (Franz; 1838–1917, German)
Gilligan (Carol; 1936– , US)
Vygotsky (Lev; 1896–1934, Soviet)

09 Broadbent (Donald; 1926–93, English)
Claparède (Édouard; 1873–1940, Swiss)
Condillac (Étienne Bonnot de; 1715–80, French)
Festinger (Leon; 1919–89, US)
Macgregor (Douglas; 1906–64, US)
McDougall (William; 1871–1938, English/US)
Sternberg (Robert J; 1949– , US)
Thorndike (Edward L; 1874–1949, US)
Thurstone (L L; 1887–1955, US)
Titchener (Edward Bradford; 1867–1927, English/US)

10 Bettelheim (Bruno; 1903–90, US)
Ebbinghaus (Hermann; 1850–1909, German)
Wertheimer (Max; 1880–1943, German)

11 Tranströmer (Tomas; 1931– , Swedish)

Terms used in psychology include:

02 id	schema	**09** anal stage
03 cue	symbol	body image
ego	**07** anxiety	catharsis
04 self	bonding	death wish
05 anima	complex	extrovert
horme	phallic	introvert
image		mechanism
imago	**08** cathexis	penis envy
limen	chunking	puerilism
	delusion	word salad
06 affect	ego ideal	
animus	fixation	**10** paragnosis
denial	illusion	perception
libido	superego	projection
		regression

repression
Zener cards
11 unconscious
12 co-dependency
cognitive map
conditioning
displacement
dissociation
preconscious

See also **therapy**

psychosexual
role reversal
subconscious
transference
13 configuration
consciousness
metacognition
primal therapy
psychosomatic

Rorschach test
14 Electra complex
identification
Oedipus complex
Phaedra complex
wish fulfilment
15 escape mechanism
externalization

public house

Public house names include:

04 Bell
Bull
Ship
Swan
05 Crown
Globe
06 Anchor
Castle
George
New Inn
Plough
07 Railway

Red Lion
08 Green Man
Nags Head
Royal Oak
Victoria
09 Black Bull
Cross Keys
King's Arms
King's Head
White Hart
White Lion
White Swan

10 Black Horse
Golden Lion
Queen's Head
Wheatsheaf
White Horse
12 Fox and Hounds
Rose and Crown
13 Hare and Hounds
Prince of Wales
14 Coach and Horses
15 George and Dragon

public transport

Public transport includes:

03 bus
cab
04 taxi
tram
tube
05 coach

ferry
metro
train
07 omnibus
railway
trolley

08 bendy-bus
10 stagecoach
trolleybus
11 park-and-ride
underground
12 light railway

See also **railway**; **ship**; **underground**

publishing

Publishers and imprints include:

02 DK
03 CUP
OUP
Pan
05 Corgi
Orion
T and F
06 Puffin
Viking
Virago
07 Berlitz

Cassell
Collins
Longman
Merriam
Methuen
Pearson
Penguin
Picador
Pimlico
Usborne
08 BBC Books
Chambers

Everyman
Flamingo
Gollancz
Ladybird
Larousse
Michelin
Palgrave
09 Allen Lane
Black Swan
Blackwell
Doubleday
Heinemann

Macmillan
Routledge
10 A and C Black
Bloomsbury
Bodley Head
Hutchinson
McGraw-Hill
Paul Hamlyn
Scholastic
Times Books
Transworld
11 Bantam Press

Bertelsmann
Fodor Guides
Rand McNally
Random House
Rough Guides
12 André Deutsch
Butterworths
Edward Arnold

Fourth Estate
Jonathan Cape
Lonely Planet
Mills and Boon
Penguin Books
Reed Elsevier
13 Allen and Unwin
AOL/Time Warner

Atlantic Books
Faber and Faber
Hachette Livre
HarperCollins
Reader's Digest
14 Canongate Books
Chambers Harrap
Chrysalis Books

Hodder Headline
Springer-Verlag
15 Chatto and Windus
Houghton Mifflin
Mitchell Beazley
Sweet and Maxwell
Thames and
Hudson

Publishing terms include:

02 em
en
PA
03 IPA
IPC
NBA
NPA
04 body
bold
copy
dupe
font
ISBN
kern
pica
rule
stet
text
typo
05 agent
blurb
caret
colon
comma
flush
folio
fount
index
point
proof
recto
roman
run-in
run on
serif
title
verso
widow
06 author
banner
byline
centre
cliché
column
delete
editor

em dash
em rule
en dash
en rule
errata
format
galley
gutter
hyphen
indent
insert
italic
margin
non-net
orphan
ragged
reader
rights
serial
series
take in
taster
07 binding
caption
cast-off
chapter
close up
concise
copyfit
drop cap
edition
excerpt
fair use
flat fee
imprint
leaders
library
literal
oblique
pen name
preface
prelims
reprint
subhead
typeset
upright
x-height

08 appendix
ascender
back flap
backlist
bad break
base line
body copy
bold face
book fair
colophon
ellipsis
endpaper
epilogue
foreword
glossary
Greeking
hackwork
headline
ligature
portrait
prepress
prologue
take back
take over
template
typeface
type spec
09 afterword
ampersand
anthology
catchword
character
clean copy
condensed
copyright
descender
duplicate
expert set
half title
justified
landscape
lower-case
paragraph
press date
pseudonym
publicist
pull quote

royalties
run-around
sans-serif
semicolon
strapline
tailpiece
title page
transpose
upper-case

10 apostrophe
back matter
bestseller
bookseller
column inch
commission
dedication
divider tab
facing page
first proof
hard hyphen
house style
journalism
journalist
large print
leader dots
manuscript
out of print

pagination
periodical
plagiarism
ragged left
review copy
royalty fee
soft hyphen
substitute
typescript
typography
undertaker
white space

11 circulation
composition
copy editing
copyfitting
front matter
ghost writer
initial caps
ragged right
running foot
running head
running text
typesetting
typographer
word spacing

12 author's proof

bastard title
bibliography
character set
contents page
divider sheet
expanded type
first edition
illustration
introduction
proofreading
public domain
specimen page

13 bestsellerdom
expert reading
hanging indent
justification
letter spacing
off-press proof
raised initial
small capitals

14 capital letters
content editing
library edition
quotation marks

15 proof correction
table of contents

See also **book**; **printing**

Puccini, Giacomo (1858–1924)

Significant works include:

05 *Edgar* (1889)
Tosca (1900)

07 *Le Villi* (1884)

08 *La Bohème* (1896)
The Cloak (1918)
Turandot (1926)

09 *Il Tabarro* (1918)

La Rondine (1917)

10 *Crisantemi* (1890)
Il Trittico (1918)
The Swallow (1917)
The Witches (1884)

12 *Manon Lescaut* (1893)
Suor Angelica (1918)

13 *Messa di Gloria* (1880)

14 *Gianni Schicchi* (1918)
Sister Angelica (1918)

15 *Madama Butterfly* (1904)

17 *Preludio sinfonico* (1876)

18 *Capriccio sinfonico* (1883)
La fanciulla del West (1910)

Significant characters include:

03 Liu
Zia (Principessa La)

04 Goro
Mimì
Pang
Ping
Pong

05 Calaf
Civry (Magda de)
Luigi
Talpa
Timur
Tinca

Tosca (Floria)

06 Altoum (Emperor)
Benoît
Minnie
Ravoir (Geronte di)
Suzuki

07 A Jailer
Colline
Edmondo
Frugola
Lastouc (Ruggero)
Lescaut
Lescaut (Manon)

Lisette
Michele
Musetta
Prunier
Rodolfo
Scarpia (Baron)
The Mole
Trouble

08 Marcello
Rinuccio
Schicchi (Gianni)
Schicchi (Lauretta)
Spoletta

The Bonze
The Tench
Turandot (Princess)
Yakuside
Yamadori (Prince)
09 Alcindoro
A Mandarin
Angelotti (Cesare)
Butterfly (Madame)

Cio-Cio-San
Des Grieux (Chevalier)
Fernandez (Rambaldo)
Giorgetta
Parpignol
Pinkerton (Kate)
Pinkerton (Lieutenant
  Benjamin)
Sacristan

Schaunard
Sciarrone
Sharpless
11 Cavaradossi (Mario)
The Rummager
14 Customs Officer
Sister Angelica

pudding *see* **cake**; **dessert**

pulse *see* **bean**

punctuation

Punctuation marks include:

04 dash	quotes	**09** backslash	**13** oblique stroke
star	**07** solidus	semicolon	
05 colon	**08** asterisk	**10** apostrophe	**14** inverted commas
comma	brackets	**11** parentheses	quotation marks
06 hyphen	ellipsis	speech marks	square brackets
period	full stop	**12** question mark	**15** exclamation mark

punishment

Punishments include:

04 fine	the cane	larruping	**11** confinement
gaol	the rack	probation	deportation
jail	**08** corporal	scourging	house arrest
05 exile	demotion	strappado	keelhauling
lines	flogging	the stocks	knee-capping
06 gating	slapping	thrashing	mastheading
hiding	smacking	torturing	penal colony
prison	spanking	**10** banishment	**12** confiscation
07 beating	the birch	cashiering	dressing-down
belting	whipping	decimation	imprisonment
borstal	**09** chain gang	defrocking	**13** horsewhipping
capital	detention	internment	incarceration
flaying	exclusion	leathering	sequestration
hitting	execution	suspension	**14** transportation
jankers	expulsion	the slipper	**15** excommunication
lashing	grounding	unfrocking	walking the plank

See also **execution**; **prison**

Purcell, Henry (c.1659–95)

Significant works include:

05 *Circe* (c.1690)	**08** *Oroonoko* (1695)
07 *Bonduca* (1695)	**09** *Abdelazer* (1695)
Oedipus (c.1692)	*Cleomenes* (1692)
Regulus (1692)	**10** *Amphitryon* (1690)

Aureng-Zebe (c.1692)
Don Quixote (1695)
Epsom Wells (1693)
King Arthur (1691)
Sophonisba (c.1685)
The Tempest (c.1695)

11 Old Bachelor (1691)

12 The Libertine (c.1692)
Tyrannic Love (1694)

13 Dido and Aeneas (1689)
The Fairy Queen (1689)
The Prophetess (1690)
The Theodosius (1680)
Timon of Athens (1694)

14 Love Triumphant (1693)
Sir Anthony Love (1690)
The Indian Queen (1695)
The Married Beau (1694)
The Wife's Excuse (1691)

15 Come, Ye Sons of Art (1694)
Female Virtuosos (1693)
Sir Barnaby Whigg (1681)
The Double Dealer (1693)
The Mock Marriage (1695)
The Rival Sisters (1695)
The Spanish Friar (1695)
The Virtuous Wife (c.1694)

16 A Fool's Preferment (1688)

The English Lawyer (1685)
The Fatal Marriage (1694)
The Indian Emperor (1691)
The Knight of Malta (1691)

17 Hail Bright Cecilia (1692)
My Heart is Inditing (1685)
Thy Word is a Lantern (c.1694)

18 Nymphs and Shepherds (c.1692)
The Canterbury Guest (1694)
The Maid's Last Prayer (1693)
The Massacre of Paris (1690)
The Richmond Heiress (1693)

19 Distressed Innocence (1694)
History of Dioclesian (1690)
The Gordian Knot Unty'd (1691)

20 Henry II, King of England (1692)
What Hope for Us Remains (1679)

21 Rule a Wife and Have a Wife (1693)

22 History of King Richard II (1681)
The Marriage-Hater Match'd (1692)

24 Arise, Ye Subterranean Winds (1695)

26 Remember Not, Lord, our Offences (1682)

28 High on a Throne of Glittering Ore (1690)

29 They that go Down to the Sea in Ships (1685)

29 The Pausanius Betrayer of His Country (1695)

purple

Shades of purple include:

04 anil	prune	heather	mulberry
plum	**06** cerise	magenta	**09** aubergine
puce	damson	purpure	**11** royal purple
puke	indigo	**08** amethyst	
05 lilac	maroon	burgundy	
mauve	violet	hyacinth	
pansy	**07** fuchsia	lavender	

See also **dye**; **pigment**

puzzle

Puzzles include:

04 maze	kakuro	tangram	Rubik's Cube®
quiz	sudoku	**08** acrostic	wordsearch
05 logic	**07** anagram	wordgame	**12** magic pyramid
rebus	cidouri	**09** crossword	
06 hitori	hangman	**10** alphametic	
jigsaw	sorites	cryptogram	

See also **crossword**; **game**

Q

qualification

queen

Parr (Catherine; 1512–48, England)
Parr (Katherine; 1512–48, England)

05 Juana (1479–1555, Castile)
Maeve (Celtic mythology, Connaught)
Maria (II; 1819–53, Portugal)
Marie (de Médicis; 1573–1642, France)
Rania (of Jordan; 1970– , Kuwaiti)
Sheba (1c BC, Sabeans)
Susan (*The Lion, the Witch and the Wardrobe*, 1950, C S Lewis)

06 Boleyn (Anne; 1501–36, England)
Esther (5c BC, Persia)
Hautia (*Mardi*, 1849, Herman Melville)
Hearts (Queen of; *Alice's Adventures in Wonderland*, 1865, Lewis Carroll)
Hecuba (Greek mythology, Troy)
Himiko (d.247 AD, Japan)
Howard (Catherine; d.1542, England)
Isabel (*Henry V*, 1599, William Shakespeare)
Louisa (1776–1810, Prussia)
Mbande (Jinga; c.1582–1663, Jaga)
Nzinga (c.1582–1663, Jaga)
Salote (1900–65, Tonga)
Silvia (1943– , Sweden)
Soraya (1932–2001, Persia)
Tamara (c.1160–1212, Georgia)
Tamora (*Titus Andronicus*, c.1589, William Shakespeare)
Videna (*Gorboduc*, 1561, Thomas Norton and Thomas Sackville)

07 Beatrix (1938– , The Netherlands)
Bonduca (*Bonduca*, 1613–14, Francis Beaumont and John Fletcher)
Eleanor (of Aquitaine; c.1122–1204, France and England)
Eleanor (of Castile; c.1245–90, England)
Jocasta (Greek mythology; Thebes)
Juliana (1909–2004, The Netherlands)
Macbeth (Lady; *Macbeth*, c.1606, William Shakespeare)
Panthea (*A King and No King*, 1611, Francis Beaumont and John Fletcher)
Phaedra (Greek mythology, Athens)
Seymour (Jane; c.1509–37, England)
Titania (*A Midsummer Night's Dream*, 1595–96, William Shakespeare)
Zenobia (3c AD, Palmyra)

08 Adelaide (1792–1849, Great Britain)
Berenice (c.280–c.246 BC, Syria)
Berenice (I; fl.c.317–c.275 BC, Egypt)
Boadicea (d.61 AD, Iceni)
Boudicca (d.61 AD, Iceni)
Caroline (of Ansbach; 1683–1737, Great Britain and Ireland)
Caroline (of Brunswick; 1768–1821, Great Britain and Ireland)
Clotilda (St; AD474–545, Franks)

Cordelia (British legend, England)
Gertrude (*Hamlet*, 1601/2, William Shakespeare)
Gloriana (*The Faerie Queene*, 1590–96, Sir Edmund Spenser)
Hermione (*The Winter's Tale*, 1611, William Shakespeare)
Isabella (*Edward II*, 1594, Christopher Marlowe)
Isabella (II; 1830–1904, Spain)
Isabella (I; of Castile; 1451–1504, Spain)
Isabella (of Angoulême; c.1188–1246, England)
Isabella (of France; 1292–1358, England)
Jane Grey (Lady; 1537–54, England)
Margaret ('Maid of Norway'; 1283–90, Scotland)
Margaret (of Angoulême; 1492–1549, Navarre)
Margaret (of Anjou; 1430–82, England)
Margaret (of Valois; 1553–1615, Navarre)
Margaret (*Richard III*, 1592/3, William Shakespeare)
Margaret (St; c.1046–93, Scotland)
Mercilla (*The Faerie Queene*, 1590–96, Sir Edmund Spenser)
Olympias (d.316 BC, Epirus)
Pasiphae (Greek mythology, Crete)
Philippa (of Hainault; c.1314–69, England)
Radigund (*The Faerie Queene*, 1590–96, Sir Edmund Spenser)
Victoria (1819–1901, Great Britain and Ireland)

09 Alexandra (1844–1925, Great Britain and Northern Ireland)
Artemisia (II; d.c.350 BC, Caria)
Bonaparte (Caroline; 1782–1839, Naples)
Brunhilde (c.534–613, Franks)
Catherine (de Médicis; 1519–89, France)
Catherine (de Valois; 1401–37, England)
Catherine (of Aragon; 1485–1536, England)
Catherine (of Braganza; 1638–1705, Great Britain and Ireland)
Christina (1626–89, Sweden)
Cleopatra (69–30 BC, Egypt)
Cleopatra (*Antony and Cleopatra*, 1606/7, William Shakespeare)
Cleopatra (*Caesar and Cleopatra*, 1898, George Bernard Shaw)
Elizabeth (1596–1662, Bohemia)
Elizabeth (1843–1916, Romania)
Elizabeth (I; 1533–1603, England and Ireland)
Elizabeth (II; 1926– , Great Britain and Northern Ireland)
Elizabeth (I; Queen of England; *Kenilworth*, 1821, Sir Walter Scott)
Elizabeth (of Portugal; St; 1271–1336, Portugal)

Elizabeth (*Richard III*, 1592/3, William Shakespeare)
Elizabeth (the Queen Mother; 1900–2002, Great Britain and Northern Ireland)
Fredegond (d.598, Franks)
Guinevere (Arthurian legend, Britain)
Hippolyta (Greek mythology, Amazons)
Maintenon (Françoise d'Aubigné, Marquise de; 1635–1719, France)
Margrethe (I; 1353–1412, Denmark, Norway and Sweden)
Margrethe (II; 1940– , Denmark)
Nefertiti (14c BC, Egypt)
Semiramis (Greek mythology, Assyria)
Tanaquill (*The Faerie Queene*, 1590–96, Sir Edmund Spenser)
Woodville (Elizabeth; c.1437–92, England)

10 Anne Boleyn (1501–36, England)
Berengaria (*The Talisman: A Tale of the Crusaders*, 1825, Sir Walter Scott)
Hatshepsut (c.1540–c.1481 BC, Egypt)
Lakshmi Bai (1835–58, Jhansi)

Marguerite (of Angoulême; 1492–1549, Navarre)
Persephone (Greek mythology, underworld)
Proserpina (Greek mythology, underworld)
Wilhelmina (of Orange-Nassau; 1880–1962, The Netherlands)

11 Beauharnais (Hortense Eugénie Cécile; 1783–1837, Holland)
Jane Seymour (c.1509–1537, England)

12 Clytemnestra (Greek mythology, Argos)
Maria Theresa (1717–80, Hungary and Bohemia)

13 Catherine Parr (1512–48, England)
Katherine Parr (1512–48, England)
Margaret Tudor (1489–1541, Scotland)

14 Henrietta Maria (1609–69, England)
Ulrika Eleonora (1688–1741, Sweden)

15 Catherine Howard (d.1542, England)
Charlotte Sophia (1744–1818, Great Britain and Ireland)
Marie Antoinette (1755–93, France)

quiz

Radio and television quiz shows and hosts include:

02 *QI* (Stephen Fry)

03 *3–2–1* (Ted Rogers)

05 *Dotto* (Robert Gladwell/Jimmy Hanley/Shaw Taylor)

06 *Gambit* (Fred Dineage)

07 *Pop Quiz* (Mike Read)
Wipeout (Paul Daniels)

08 *Bullseye* (Jim Bowen)
Mr and Mrs (Alan Taylor/Derek Batey/Julian Clary)
Quiz Ball (David Vine/Barry Davies/Stuart Hall)
Whispers (Gyles Brandreth)

09 *Brainwave* (Andy Craig)
Countdown (Richard Whiteley/Des Lynam/ Des O'Connor/Jeff Stelling)
Odd One Out (Paul Daniels)
Small Talk (Ronnie Corbett)

10 *Mastermind* (Magnus Magnusson/John Humphrys)
Masterteam (Angela Rippon/Peter Snow)
Screen Test (Michael Rodd/Brian Trueman/ Mark Curry)

11 *Call My Bluff* (Robert Robinson/Bob Holness/Fiona Bruce)
Catchphrase (Roy Walker/Nick Weir/Mark Curry)
Give Us a Clue (Michael Aspel/Michael Parkinson)
Just a Minute (Nicholas Parsons)
Mock the Week (Dara Ó Briain)
Spot the Tune (Ken Platt/Ted Ray/Jackie Rae/ Pete Murray)
The Food Quiz (Jay Rayner)
The News Quiz (Barry Norman/Barry Took/ Simon Hoggart)
What's My Line? (Eamonn Andrews/David Jacobs/Penelope Keith/Angela Rippon/ Emma Forbes)

12 *Ask the Family* (Robert Robinson)
Blockbusters (Bob Holness)
Bognor or Bust (Angus Deayton)
Face the Music (Joseph Cooper)
Fifteen to One (William G Stewart)
Going for Gold (Henry Kelly)
Lucky Numbers (Shane Richie)
Name That Tune (Tom O'Connor/Lionel Blair)
Strike It Rich (Michael Barrymore)
Take Your Pick (Michael Miles/Des O'Connor)
Telly Addicts (Noel Edmonds)
Winning Lines (Phillip Schofield)

13 *Blankety Blank* (Terry Wogan/Les Dawson/ Lily Savage)
Bob's Full House (Bob Monkhouse)
Going for a Song (Max Robertson/Michael Parkinson)

Public Opinion (Gyles Brandreth)
Strike It Lucky (Michael Barrymore)
Test the Nation (Anne Robinson & Phillip
   Schofield/Danny Wallace)
The Travel Quiz (Andi Peters)

14 *Brain of Britain* (Robert Robinson)
Criss Cross Quiz (Jeremy Hawk)
Family Fortunes (Bob Monkhouse/Max
   Bygraves/Les Dennis)
Going, Going, Gone (Andy Craig)
Quotation Marks (Vanessa Feltz)
The Weakest Link (Anne Robinson)
Wheel of Fortune (Nicky Campbell/Bradley
   Walsh/John Leslie)
Winner Takes All (Jimmy Tarbuck)

15 *Double Your Money* (Hughie Green)
The Price Is Right (Leslie Crowther)

16 *A Question of Sport* (David Vine/David
   Coleman/Sue Barker)
Celebrity Squares (Bob Monkhouse)
Cheggers Plays Pop (Keith Chegwin)
Round Britain Quiz (Nick Clarke/Louis
   Allen/Gordon Clough)

Sale of the Century (Nicholas Parsons)
Supermarket Sweep (Dale Winton)

17 *Every Second Counts* (Paul Daniels)
The $64,000 Question (Bob Monkhouse)

18 *Bruce's Price Is Right* (Bruce Forsyth)
Have I Got News for You (Angus Deayton)
Play Your Cards Right (Bruce Forsyth)

19 *I'm Sorry I Haven't a Clue* (Humphrey
   Lyttelton)
It's Only TV ... But I Like It (Jonathan Ross)
The Great British Quiz (Janice Long)
They Think It's All Over (Nick Hancock)
University Challenge (Bamber Gascoigne/
   Jeremy Paxman)

21 *Never Mind the Buzzcocks* (Mark Lamarr/
   Simon Amstell)

22 *Animal, Vegetable, Mineral?* (Glyn Daniel)

23 *Talking Telephone Numbers* (Phillip
   Schofield & Emma Forbes)

24 *Who Wants to Be a Millionaire?* (Chris
   Tarrant)

R

rabbi *see* **chief rabbi**

rabbit

Rabbits and hares include:

03 fox
lop
Rex
tan
04 jack
pika
rock
sage
05 brown
Dutch

hotot
sable
satin
swamp
water
06 Alaska
Angora
Arctic
Havana
oar-lap

Polish
silver
tapeti
Vienna
07 Argente
Belgian
Flemish
08 European
riverine
snowshoe

09 harlequin
Himalayan
10 chinchilla
cottontail
New Zealand
Van Beveren
11 black silver
English spot
Rhinelander

race

Race types include:

03 ski
04 dash
road
sack
05 cycle
horse
motor
relay
yacht
06 keirin

rowing
slalom
sprint
07 harness
hurdles
pancake
pursuit
regatta
walking
08 downhill

marathon
scramble
speedway
stock car
swimming
trotting
09 Grand Prix
greyhound
motocross
time trial

walkathon
10 cyclo-cross
Formula One
motorcycle
track event
11 egg-and-spoon
three-legged
wheelbarrow
12 cross-country
steeplechase

Races include:

02 TT
04 Oaks
05 Derby
06 Le Mans
07 St Leger
08 Boat Race
Milk Race
RAC Rally

09 Grand Prix
11 Admiral's Cup
America's Cup
Breeder's Cup
Giro d'Italia
the Classics
12 Melbourne Cup
Tour de France
13 Diamond Sculls

Grand National
Kentucky Derby
14 Greyhound Derby
London Marathon
15 Indianapolis 500
Monte Carlo Rally
New York Marathon

See also **racing: horse racing**; **racing: motor racing**

racehorse *see* **racing: horse racing**

Racine, Jean (1639–99)

Significant works include:

06 *Esther* (1689)
   Phèdre (1677)

07 *Athalie* (1691)
   Bajazet (1672)

08 *Bérénice* (1670)

09 *Iphigénie* (1675)

10 *Andromache* (1667)
   Andromaque (1667)

   Mithridate (1673)

11 *Britannicus* (1669)
   Mithridates (1673)

12 *Les Plaideurs* (1668)

16 *Alexandre le grand* (1665)

17 *La Nymphe de la Seine* (1660)

28 *La Thébaïde ou Les Frères ennemis* (1664)

Significant characters include:

04 Aman
   Nero

05 Joash

06 Aricia
   Attale
   Dandin
   Esther
   Monima

   Phèdre
   Roxane

07 Atalide
   Athalie
   Bajazet
   Leander
   Orestes
   Pyrrhus

   Theseus

08 Assureus
   Berenice
   Hermione

09 Agrippina
   Alexander
   Iphigénie
   Petit-Jean

10 Andromache
   Andromaque
   Chicanneau
   Hippolytus
   Mithridate

11 Britannicus
   Mithridates

racing: horse racing

Racehorses include:

05 Arkle
   Cigar
   Pinza

06 Nearco
   Red Rum
   Sir Ken

07 Alleged
   Dawn Run
   Eclipse

   Pharlap
   Sceptre
   Shergar
   Sir Ivor

08 Aldaniti
   Best Mate
   Corbiere
   Esha Ness
   Hyperion

   Istabraq
   Mill Reef
   Nijinsky

09 John Henry
   L'Escargot
   Oh So Sharp

10 Night Nurse
   Persian War
   See You Then

   Sun Chariot

11 Cottage Rake
   Never Say Die
   Pretty Polly

12 Dancing Brave
   Desert Orchid
   Golden Miller
   Hattons Grace

Racecourses include:

03 Ayr (Scotland)

04 York (England)

05 Ascot (England)
   Epsom (England)
   Kelso (Scotland)

07 Aintree (England)
   Chester (England)
   Curragh (Ireland)
   Newbury (England)
   Pimlico (USA)
   Sandown (England)

   Warwick (England)

08 Goodwood (England)
   Wetherby (England)

09 Chantilly (France)
   Doncaster (England)
   Leicester (England)
   Newcastle (England)
   Newmarket (England)
   Towcester (England)
   Uttoxeter (England)

10 Cheltenham (England)
   Epsom Downs (England)

   Flemington (Australia)
   Longchamps (France)
   Pontefract (England)
   The Curragh (Ireland)

11 Belmont Park (USA)
   Haydock Park (England)
   Kempton Park (England)
   Musselburgh (Scotland)
   Sandown Park (England)
   Thistledown (USA)

12 Hamilton Park (Scotland)

14 Churchill Downs (USA)

Jockeys and associated figures include:

04 Hern (Major Dick; 1921–2002, English)
   Pipe (Martin; 1945– , English)

05 Cecil (Henry; 1943– , Scottish)
   Krone (Julie; 1963– , US)

Lukas (D Wayne; 1935– , US)
McCoy (Tony; 1974– , Irish)
Moore (Ryan; 1983– , English)
Smith (Robyn; 1943– , US)
Walsh (Ruby; 1979– , Irish)

06 Arcaro (Eddie; 1916–97, US)
Archer (Fred; 1857–86, English)
Carson (Willie; 1942– , Scottish)
Eddery (Pat; 1952– , Irish)
Fallon (Kieren; 1965– , Irish)
Knight (Henrietta; 1946– , English)
Mellor (Stan; 1937– , British)
O'Brien (Aidan; 1969– , Irish)
O'Brien (Vincent; 1917– , Irish)
O'Neill (Jonjo; 1952– , Irish)
Pitman (Jenny; 1946– , English)
Stoute (Sir Michael; 1945– , Barbadian)
Winter (Fred; 1926–2004, English)

07 Cauthen (Steve; 1960– , US)
Cordero (Angel, Jnr; 1942– , Puerto Rican)
Dettori (Frankie; 1970– , Italian)

Fordham (George; 1837–87, English)
Francis (Dick; 1920– , English)
Gifford (Josh; 1941– , English)
Piggott (Lester; 1935– , English)
Sanders (Seb; 1971– , English)
Spencer (Jamie; 1980– , Irish)

08 Breasley (Scobie; 1914–2006, Australian)
Champion (Bob; 1948– , English)
Donoghue (Steve; 1884–1945, English)
Dunwoody (Richard; 1964– , Northern
  Irish)
Francome (John; 1952– , English)
Geraghty (Barry; 1979– , Irish)
Richards (Sir Gordon; 1904–86, English)

09 Scudamore (Peter; 1958– , English)
Shoemaker (Willie; 1931–2003, US)

10 Desormeaux (Kent; 1970– , US)
Fitzgerald (Mick; 1970– , Irish)
Williamson (Norman; 1969– , Irish)

11 Saint-Martin (Yves; 1941– , French)

Horse racing terms include:

03 dam
nap
net

04 colt
face
firm
foal
form
good
hand
hard
head
mare
nose
odds
rouf
sire
soft
stud
tips
trip
turf
yard

05 evens
fence
field
filly
going
heavy
neves
owner
place
silks

stake
wrist

06 bottle
carpet
chaser
faller
jockey
length
novice
odds-on
pull up
raider
sprint
stable
stayer
tic-tac
weight

07 classic
earhole
furlong
gelding
meeting
mudlark
tipster
trainer

08 ante-post
Bismarck
blinkers
handicap
hurdling
juvenile
outsider
racecard

shoulder
stallion
standard
stewards
yearling
yielding

09 favourite
group race
non-runner
pacemaker
short head
shoulders

10 all-weather
bumper race
flat racing
listed race
parade ring
stakes race

11 accumulator
connections
handicapper
hunter chase
pattern race
photo finish
Triple Crown
winning post

12 double carpet
handicap race
National Hunt
starting gate
steeplechase
thoroughbred

top of the head   **14** conditions race   stewards' enquiry

weighing room   **15** levels you devils

See also **equestrian sport; horse**

racing: motor racing

Formula One motor racing teams include:

03 BAR   Toyota   Minardi   **13** Red Bull Racing

06 Jordan   **07** Ferrari   Renault

Sauber   McLaren   **08** Williams

Formula One Grand Prix circuits include:

05 Imola (Imola, Italy; 'San Marino' GP)   Hockenheim (Hockenheim, Germany)

Monza (Monza, Italy)   Interlagos (São Paulo, Brazil)

06 Sakhir (Manama, Bahrain)   Magny-Cours (Magny-Cours, France)

Sepang (Kuala Lumpur, Malaysia)   Monte Carlo (Monte Carlo, Monaco)

Suzuka (Suzuka, Japan)   **11** Hungaroring (Budapest, Hungary)

08 Shanghai (Shanghai, China)   Nurburgring (Nurburg, Germany; 'Europe' GP)

10 Albert Park (Melbourne, Australia)   Silverstone (Silverstone, England)

Motor racing drivers, motorcyclists and associated figures include:

04 Foyt (A J, Jnr; 1935– , US)

Hill (Damon; 1960– , English)

Hill (Graham; 1929–75, English)

Hunt (James; 1947–93, English)

Ickx (Jacky; 1945– , Belgian)

Loeb (Sébastien; 1974– , French)

Moss (Sir Stirling; 1929– , English)

05 Alesi (Jean; 1964– , French)

Clark (Jim; 1936–68, Scottish)

Clark (Roger; 1939–98, English)

Hulme (Denny; 1936–94, New Zealand)

Lauda (Niki; 1949– , Austrian)

McRae (Colin; 1968–2007, Scottish)

Petty (Richard; 1937– , US)

Prost (Alain; 1955– , French)

Rossi (Valentino; 1979– , Italian)

Sainz (Carlos; 1962– , Spanish)

Senna (Ayrton; 1960–94, Brazilian)

Unser (Al; 1939– , US)

Unser (Bobby; 1934– , US)

06 Ascari (Alberto; 1918–55, Italian)

Berger (Gerhard; 1959– , Austrian)

Briggs (Barry; 1934– , New Zealand)

Button (Jensen; 1980– , English)

Doohan (Mick; 1965– , Australian)

Dunlop (Joey; 1952–2000, Northern Irish)

Fangio (Juan Manuel; 1911–95, Argentine)

Irvine (Eddie; 1965– , Northern Irish)

Lawson (Eddie; 1958– , US)

Mauger (Ivan; 1939– , New Zealand)

Piquet (Nelson; 1952– , Brazilian)

Sheene (Barry; 1950–2003, English)

Walker (Murray; 1923– , English)

07 Brabham (Sir Jack; 1926– , Australian)

Brundle (Martin; 1959– , English)

Ferrari (Enzo; 1898–1988, Italian)

Fogarty (Carl; 1965– , English)

Guthrie (Janet; 1938– , US)

Mäkinen (Tommi; 1964– , Finnish)

Mansell (Nigel; 1953– , English)

McLaren (Bruce; 1937–70, New Zealand)

Mikkola (Hannu; 1942– , Finnish)

Roberts (Kenny; 1951– , US)

Segrave (Sir Henry; 1896–1930, US/British)

Stewart (Sir Jackie; 1939– , Scottish)

Surtees (John; 1934– , English)

08 Agostini (Giacomo; 1943– , Italian)

Andretti (Mario; 1940– , Italian/US)

Campbell (Donald; 1921–67, English)

Campbell (Sir Malcolm; 1885–1948, English)

Hailwood (Mike; 1940–81, English)

Hakkinen (Mika; 1968– , Finnish)

Hamilton (Lewis; 1985– , English)

Oldfield (Barney; 1878–1946, US)

Williams (Sir Frank; 1942– , Scottish)

09 Blomqvist (Stig; 1946– , Swedish)

Chevrolet (Louis; 1878–1941, Swiss/US)

Coulthard (David; 1971– , Scottish)

Earnhardt (Dale; 1951–2001, US)

Hawthorne (Mike; c.1930–1959, English)

Kankkunen (Juha; 1959– , Finnish)

10 Ecclestone (Bernard; 1930– , English)

Fittipaldi (Emerson; 1946– , Brazilian)

Schumacher (Michael; 1969– , German)
Schumacher (Ralf; 1975– , German)

Villeneuve (Jacques; 1971– , Canadian)
12 Rickenbacker (Eddie; 1890–1973, US)

radiation

Motor racing terms include:

03 lap
off
pit
04 apex
grid
oval
pits
pole
T-car
05 apron
Armco
in lap
Nomex®
plank
shunt
06 out lap
slicks
tifosi
07 chicane
cockpit
hairpin
marshal
pace car
paddock
pit babe
pit lane

pit stop
pit wall
stagger
steward
traffic
08 diffuser
dirty air
drafting
fishtail
fuel load
lollipop
outbrake
pit board
scuderia
sidepods
straight
tyre wall
09 Brickyard
down force
monocoque
oversteer
parade lap
parc fermé
safety car
telemetry
warm-up lap
10 back marker

barge board
gravel trap
qualifying
racing line
run-off area
slipstream
team orders
understeer
11 braking zone
pit straight
shut the door
tyre blanket
victory lane
12 formation lap
ground effect
podium finish
pole position
straightaway
13 intermediates
launch control
scrutineering
start straight
stop-go penalty
superspeedway
14 finish straight
15 traction control

radiation

Radiation includes:

04 beta
hard
heat
soft
05 alpha
gamma
light
X-rays
06 cosmic

07 Hawking
visible
08 Cerenkov
gamma ray
infrared
ionizing
09 black body
10 background
insolation

microwaves
radio waves
synchroton
11 ultraviolet
12 beta particle
13 alpha particle
14 bremsstrahlung
15 electromagnetic

radio

Radio stations include:

03 LBC
XFM
04 Kiss
05 1Xtra
06 6 Music

Jazz FM
Kiss FM
Radio 1
Radio 2
Radio 3
Radio 4

08 BBC 1Xtra
Five Live
09 BBC 6 Music
BBC London
BBC Radio 1
BBC Radio 2

BBC Radio 3	Radio Five	**13** Radio Caroline
BBC Radio 4	Talksport	Radio Scotland
Capital FM	**11** Virgin Radio	**15** BBC World Service
Classic FM	**12** World Service	Radio Luxembourg

Radio shows include:

02 *PM*

04 *ITMA*

05 *Today*

07 *Midweek*
The Verb

08 *Front Row*
Money Box
Sport on 5
Whispers

09 *Loose Ends*

10 *Any Answers?*
Home Truths
The Archers
Week Ending
Woman's Hour

11 *Dead Ringers*
Just a Minute
The Food Quiz
The Goon Show
The Navy Lark
The News Quiz
You and Yours

12 *100 Best Tunes*
Any Questions?
Beyond Our Ken
Farming Today
Poetry Please
Quote … Unquote
Start the Week
Sunday Papers
The Moral Maze
Top of the Form

13 *Absolute Power*
Afternoon Play
Book at Bedtime
Book of the Week
Classic Serial
Mrs Dale's Diary

One Big Weekend
Pick of the Pops
Pick of the Week
Round the Horne
The Friday Play
The World at One
Waggoners' Walk

14 *Brain of Britain*
Changing Places
Melodies for You
Performance on 3
The Brains Trust

15 *Educating Archie*
It's That Man Again
The Saturday Play
Through the Night
Workers' Playtime

16 *Family Favourites*
Housewives' Choice
Listen with Mother
Lunchtime Concert
Round Britain Quiz
Shipping Forecast
The Food Programme
The Smith Lectures

17 *Composer of the Week*
Desert Island Discs
Letter from America
Today in Parliament
Weekend Woman's Hour

19 *I'm Sorry I Haven't a Clue*
Trevor's World of Sport

20 *The Mark Steel Lectures*
The Week in Westminster

21 *Smooth Classics at Seven*
Yesterday in Parliament

23 *Friday Night Is Music Night*
From Our Own Correspondent
I'm Sorry, I'll Read That Again

Radio presenters include:

03 Cox (Sara; 1974– , English)

04 Dunn (John; 1934–2004, Scottish)
Mayo (Simon; 1958– , English)
Peel (John; 1939–2004, English)
Ross (Jonathan; 1960– , English)
Tong (Pete; 1960– , English)

05 Clare (Anthony Ward; 1942–2007, Irish)
Cooke (Alistair; 1908–2004, English/US)
Evans (Chris; 1966– , English)
Jones (Aled; 1970– , Welsh)
Stern (Howard; 1954– , US)
Wogan (Terry; 1938– , Irish)

Young (Kirsty; 1968– , Scottish)
Young (Sir Jimmy; 1921– , English)

06 Harris (Bob; 1950– , English)
Lamacq (Steve; 1965– , English)
Lamarr (Mark; 1967– , English)
Lawley (Sue; 1946– , English)
Moyles (Chris; 1974– , English)
Murray (Jenni; 1950– , English)
Savile (Sir Jimmy; 1926– , English)
Walker (Johnnie; 1945– , English)
Whiley (Jo; 1965– , English)
Wright (Steve; 1954– , English)

07 De Manio (Jack; 1914–88, British)
Edmonds (Noel; 1948– , English)
Everett (Kenny; 1944–95, English)
Freeman (Alan 'Fluff'; 1927–2006, Australian)
Jackson (Jack; 1906–78, English)
Keillor (Garrison; 1942– , US)

See also **quiz**

Kershaw (Andy; 1959– , English)
Pickles (Wilfred; 1904–1978, English)
Plomley (Roy; 1914–85, English)
Redhead (Brian; 1929–94, English)
Tarrant (Chris; 1946– , English)

08 Anderson (Marjorie; 1913–99, English)
Campbell (Nicky; 1961– , Scottish)
Humphrys (John; 1943– , Welsh)
Metcalfe (Jean; 1923–2000, English)
Naughtie (James; 1952– , Scottish)
Westwood (Tim; 1958– , English)

09 Blackburn (Tony; 1943– , English)
MacGregor (Sue; 1941– , English)
Radcliffe (Mark; 1958– , English)

10 Gambaccini (Paul; 1949– , US)
Hardcastle (William; 1918–75, English)

11 Nightingale (Annie; 1942– , English)

railway

Railways include:

04 rack
tube
05 cable
light
metro
model
06 garden
siding

subway
07 cutting
express
freight
tramway
08 electric
elevated
main line

monorail
mountain
09 funicular
goods line
Intercity®
trunk line
10 branch line
broad gauge

feeder line
11 narrow gauge
underground
13 high-speed line
passenger line
rack-and-pinion
standard gauge
15 marshalling yard

Railway stations include:

04 Ueno (Japan)
05 Crewe (England)
Odéon (France)
Passy (France)
06 Atocha (Spain)
Egmore (India)
Euston (England)
Howrah (India)
07 Bath Spa (England)
Shibuya (Japan)
Sirkeci (Turkey)
Termini (Italy)
Varenne (France)
08 Charbagh (India)
Châtelet (France)
Concorde (France)
Mirabeau (France)
Pont-Neuf (France)
Shinjuku (Japan)
Victoria (England)
Waterloo (England)

Waverley (Scotland)
09 Carnforth (England)
Chamartin (Spain)
Haymarket (Scotland)
Ikebukuro (Japan)
Invalides (France)
Madeleine (France)
Shinagawa (Japan)
St Pancras (England)
Tuileries (France)
10 Gare de Lyon (France)
Gare du Nord (France)
Kings Cross (England)
Lime Street (England)
Marylebone (England)
Ostbahnhof (Germany)
Paddington (England)
Piccadilly (England)
Südbahnhof (Austria)
11 Hull Paragon (England)
Lille Europe (France)

Penn Station (USA)
Roma Termini (Italy)
Westbahnhof (Austria)
12 Brussels Midi (Belgium)
Charing Cross (England)
Gare St Lazare (France)
Grand Central (USA)
Hauptbahnhof (Germany)
Louvre Rivoli (France)
13 Calais Fréthun (France)
14 Cardiff Central (Wales)
Exeter St Davids (England)
Flinders Street (Australia)
Glasgow Central (Scotland)
London Victoria (England)
15 Clapham Junction (England)
Cluny La Sorbonne (France)
Fenchurch Street (England)
Gare d'Austerlitz (France)
Watford Junction (England)

Train types include:

01 Q	hover	monorail
02 up	mixed	push-pull
03 APT	paddy	**09** aerotrain
HST	steam	excursion
owl	**06** bullet	high-speed
TGV	diesel	Intercity®
way	Maglev	manriding
04 boat	**07** baggage	**10** locomotive
down	express	**12** Freightliner®
loco	freight	**13** accommodation
mail	through	**14** shuttle service
milk	**08** cable-car	**15** steam locomotive
05 goods	corridor	

Famous trains include:

03 TGV	The Ghan	**13** Indian Pacific	**15** Hogwarts Express
06 Rocket	**08** Eurostar	Orient Express	
Thomas	**09** The A-Train	Trans-Siberian	
07 Mallard	**11** Bullet Train	**14** Flying Scotsman	

Railway terms include:

01 L	halt	shunt
02 el	line	staff
Ry	loco	track
03 ABC	rail	T-rail
APT	RUCC	train
ATC	slot	truck
ATP	SPAD	trunk
bay	spur	valve
cab	stay	wagon
car	TPWS	**06** banker
cog	tube	boiler
HST	**05** aisle	branch
lie	berth	buffer
lye	bogey	bumper
rly	bogie	coaler
RMT	brake	derail
rod	brute	diesel
RPC	cabin	engine
Rwy	chair	flange
SRA	coach	fogger
Sta	coupé	fogman
TGV	crank	gantry
tie	depot	gricer
TOC	diner	hopper
van	grate	maglev
04 APEX	guard	piston
bank	local	points
crew	lorry	porter
dock	metro	Q-train
dome	Mogul	redcap
frog	rivet	reefer

saloon
siding
stoker
subway
target
tender
tunnel
up-line
waggon
Y-track

07 axle-box
ballast
banking
bay-line
booking
buckeye
bulgine
butcher
caboose
cocopan
cutting
detrain
drag-bar
drawbar
entrain
fettler
firebox
fireman
flatcar
flyover
gondola
handcar
hostler
lineman
locoman
network
off-peak
Pullman
railage
railbed
railbus
railcar
railman
roadbed
signals
sleeper
station
tank car
turnout
up-train
viaduct
whistle
yardman

08 box-wagon
Bradshaw
brakeman
brake van

bullgine
cable-car
cant-rail
carriage
catenary
choo-choo
corridor
coupling
crosstie
down-line
draw-gear
firehole
fire-tube
fly-under
horse box
junction
live-rail
loop-line
main line
manrider
monorail
motorail
motorman
overpass
owl-train
pilotman
platform
puff-puff
rack rail
railcard
railhead
railroad
roomette
side-line
smokebox
subgrade
terminus
trackage
trackbed
wagon-lit
way train

09 aerotrain
alignment
blastpipe
boat train
brakesman
buffet car
checkrail
concourse
conductor
container
couchette
crossover
cross-sill
day return
dining-car
down-train
drag-chain

fishplate
footboard
footplate
funicular
goods line
goods yard
guardrail
guard's van
Intercity®
interrail
iron horse
jerkwater
lengthman
mail-train
milk train
non-smoker
overshoot
palace-car
parlor car
plate rail
pointsman
rail-borne
rail-motor
railwoman
second man
sidetrack
signal box
signalman
slip-coach
steam pipe
tank wagon
third rail
train mile
trunk line
turntable
vestibule
wheelbase

10 baggage-car
brake block
branch line
broad-gauge
centre-rail
cog railway
cowcatcher
disentrain
draught-bar
embankment
Eurotunnel
feeder line
free on rail
goods train
griddle car
home-signal
hovertrain
lengthsman
locomotive
luggage-van
mini-buffet

mixed train
paddy train
parlour car
platelayer
Pullman car
railroader
railwayman
smokestack
steam brake
steam train
supersaver
surfaceman
switchback
tank engine
train ferry
zone-ticket

11 bay platform
block-system
bullet train
catch points
compartment
conductress
crémaillère
drawing room
gandy dancer
goods engine
lodging turn
mail-catcher
narrow-gauge
people mover
pilot engine
rack railway
railroad car
ship railway

side cutting
sleeping car
strap-hanger
throatplate
track-walker
underbridge
underground
vacuum brake
whistle stop

12 baggage-train
cable railway
coachbuilder
dormitory-car
double-header
driving wheel
engine-driver
euroterminal
express train
footplateman
Freightliner®
freight-train
light railway
loading gauge
omnibus train
permanent way
rolling stock
running board
shunting yard
slip-carriage
station house
throttle pipe
through train
ticket porter
trainspotter

13 brake cylinder
conductor rail
corridor-train
dead man's pedal
distant-signal
garden railway
level crossing
push-pull train
scenic railway
sleeping coach
standard gauge
stationmaster

14 dead man's handle
excursion train
expansion joint
footplatewoman
high-speed train
limited express
manriding train
observation car
regulator valve
saloon carriage
shuttle service
station-manager
superelevation

15 fellow traveller
marshalling yard
mountain railway
railway carriage
railway crossing
smoking carriage
steam locomotive
third-rail system

See also **London**; **underground**

rainbow

Colours of the rainbow:

03 red   **05** green   orange   yellow
04 blue   **06** indigo   violet

range *see* **mountain**

rank *see* **military**; **nobility**; **police**

Ravel, Maurice (1875–1937)

Significant works include:

06 *Boléro* (1928)

07 *Miroirs* (1906)
Mirrors (1906)
Tzigane (1924)

08 *Jeux d'eau* (1902)

09 *Fountains* (1902)

10 *Ma mère l'oye* (1910)

11 *Mother Goose* (1910)

12 *Schéhérazade* (1898)

14 *Daphnis et Chloé* (1912)

The Spanish Hour (1911)

15 Gaspard de la nuit (1909)
L'Heure espagnole (1911)
Spanish Rhapsody (1908)

16 Natural Histories (1907)

17 Phantom of the Night (1909)
The Tomb of Couperin (1917)

18 Chansons madécasses (1926)
Rhapsodie espagnole (1908)

19 Histoires Naturelles (1907)
Le Tombeau de Couperin (1917)

21 Don Quichotte à Dulcinée (1934)

22 L'enfant et les sortilèges (1925)
Pavane for a Dead Princess (1902/1911)

26 Noble and Sentimental Waltzes (1911/
1914)
The Child and the Enchantments (1925)

27 Pavane pour une infante défunte
(1902/1911)
Valses nobles et sentimentales (1911/1914)

28 Fanfare pour l'Éventail de Jeanne (1929)
Three Poems by Stéphane Mallarmé
(1914)

29 Trois poèmes de Stéphane Mallarmé
(1914)

rebellion

Rebellions include:

03 Rum (1808, Australia)

07 Fifteen (1715, Scotland)
Whiskey (1794, US)

08 Jacobite (1715/1745, Scotland)

09 Forty-Five (1745, Scotland)

See also **revolutionary**; **war**

10 The Fifteen (1715, Scotland)

11 Boxer Rising (1898–1900, China)

12 Easter Rising (1916, Ireland)
The Forty-Five (1745, Scotland)

14 Eureka Stockade (1854, Australia)

record

Recordings include:

02 CD	mono	single	videotape
EP	tape	stereo	
LP	tele	**07** digital	**11** compact disc
03 DAT	**05** album	**08** cassette	long-playing
DVD	video	MiniDisc®	**12** extended play
MP3	vinyl	**09** audiotape	magnetic tape
04 disc	**06** record	video disc	**13** video cassette

red

Shades of red include:

04 guly	damask	crimson
pink	ginger	fuchsia
rose	maroon	lobster
ruby	minium	nacarat
rust	modena	scarlet
wine	murrey	stammel
05 brick	rufous	vermeil
gules	russet	**08** beetroot
henna	Titian	blood-red
ruddy	tomato	brick-red
06 auburn	Tyrian	burgundy
cerise	**07** carmine	cardinal
cherry	carroty	chestnut
claret	cramesy	cinnabar

cramoisy
sanguine
09 carnation
solferino

vermilion
10 Chinese red
coccineous
coquelicot

terracotta
11 burnt sienna
incarnadine
sang-de-boeuf

See also **dye**; **pigment**

refining

Products and by-products of refining include:

03 tar   07 asphalt   treacle   11 golden syrup
05 sugar   bitumen   08 molasses

reformer

Reformers include:

03 Hus (Jan; c.1369–1415, Bohemian/Czech)

04 Huss (John; c.1369–1415, Bohemian/Czech)
   Knox (John; c.1513–1572, Scottish)
   Mill (John Stuart; 1806–73, English)
   Owen (Robert; 1771–1858, Welsh)

05 Perón (Evita; 1919–52, Argentine)

06 Calvin (John; 1509–64, French)
   Luther (Martin; 1483–1546, German)
   Wiclif (John; c.1329–84, English)

Wyclif (John; c.1329–84, English)

07 Stanton (Elizabeth Cady; 1815–1902)
   Wycliff (John; c.1329–84, English)
   Zwingli (Huldreich; 1484–1531, Swiss)
   Zwingli (Ulrich; 1484–1531, Swiss)

08 Wicliffe (John; c.1329–84, English)
   Wycliffe (John; c.1329–84, English)

10 Pestalozzi (Johann; 1746–1827, Swiss)

11 Wilberforce (William; 1759–1833, English)

See also **heroism**; **religion**

regiment

Army regiments include:

02 RA
   RE
   TA
03 SAS
04 REME
05 Paras
10 Black Watch
   Life Guards
   Royal Scots

11 Highlanders
   Horse Guards
   Irish Guards
   Scots Guards
   Welsh Guards
12 Army Air Corps
   Green Howards
   Rifle Brigade
   Royal Hussars
   Royal Lancers

13 Artists' Rifles
   Kings Regiment
   Light Dragoons
   Light Infantry
14 London Regiment
   Royal Engineers
15 Grenadier Guards
   Rifle Volunteers

region *see* **geography**

reindeer *see* **Christmas**

relative

Relatives include:

02 ex   mum   gran   wife
03 bro   sis   heir   05 aunty
   dad   son   nana   daddy
   mom   04 aunt   twin   mummy

nanna	sister	granddad	twin-sister
nanny	spouse	grandson	**11** first cousin
niece	**07** brother	**09** ex-husband	foster-child
uncle	grandad	godfather	goddaughter
06 auntie	grandma	godmother	grandfather
cousin	grandpa	great aunt	grandmother
ex-wife	husband	stepchild	grandparent
father	partner	**10** grandchild	half-brother
german	sibling	great uncle	stepbrother
godson	stepdad	half-sister	twin-brother
granny	stepmum	stepfather	**12** foster-parent
mother	stepson	stepmother	second cousin
nephew	**08** daughter	step-parent	stepdaughter
parent	godchild	stepsister	**13** granddaughter

See also **aunt**; **daughter**; **father**; **genealogy**; **mother**; **son**; **uncle**

religion

Religions and religious groups include:

03 Bon	Druidism	Creationism
Zen	Hasidism	Freemasonry
04 Shi'a	Hinduism	Hare Krishna
05 Amish	paganism	Lutheranism
Baha'i	Tantrism	Manichaeism
Druze	Wahhabis	Scientology
Islam	**09** Ahmadiyya	Zen Buddhism
Sunni	Cabbalism	**12** Albigensians
06 Sufism	Calvinism	Christianity
Taoism	Methodism	Confucianism
voodoo	Mithraism	Nestorianism
07 animism	Mormonism	Unitarianism
Baha'ism	occultism	**13** Church in Wales
Essenes	Parseeism	Protestantism
Jainism	shamanism	Reform Judaism
Jesuits	Shintoism	Salvation Army
Judaism	Vedantism	**14** Fundamentalism
Lamaism	Waldenses	Oxford Movement
Moonies	**10** Adventists	Pentecostalism
Opus Dei	Brahmanism	Rastafarianism
Orphism	Evangelism	Rosicrucianism
Quakers	Gnosticism	Society of Jesus
Saivism	iconoclasm	Ultramontanism
Saktism	Puritanism	Zoroastrianism
Sikhism	Soka Gakkai	**15** ancestor-worship
08 Baptists	**11** Anabaptists	Church of England
Buddhism	Anglicanism	Presbyterianism
	Catholicism	

Religious officers include:

03 nun	pope	kohen	**06** abbess
04 dean	**05** abbot	padre	bishop
guru	canon	prior	clergy
imam	elder	rabbi	curate
monk	friar	vicar	deacon

father	**07** muezzin	**09** ayatollah	archdeacon
mullah	prelate	clergyman	chancellor
parson	proctor	Dalai Lama	Pachen Lama
pastor	**08** cardinal	deaconess	
priest	chaplain	Monsignor	**11** clergywoman
rector	minister	**10** archbishop	**14** mother superior

Religious writings include:

02 NT	**07** epistle	Lotus Sutra
OT	Li Ching	Nohon Shoki
05 Bayan	Puranas	Pentateuch
Bible	Shari'ah	Svetambara
Koran	**08** Haft Wadi	Tao-te-ching
Qur'an	Halakhah	Upanishads
sutra	Ramayana	Zend-Avesta
Torah	Shu Ching	**11** Bardo Thodol
Vedas	**09** Adi Granth	Mahabharata
Zohar	Apocrypha	**12** Bhagavad Gita
06 Gemara	Chuang-tzu	Kitab al-Aqdas
gospel	Chu'un Ch'iu	Milindapanha
Granth	Decalogue	New Testament
Hadith	Digambara	Old Testament
I Ching	Hexateuch	**14** Dead Sea Scrolls
Kojiki	scripture	Mahayana Sutras
Mishna	Shih Ching	Revised Version
Talmud	Tripitaka	**15** Ten Commandments
Tantra	**10** Heptateuch	

Religious services include:

04 Mass	**09** communion	**12** confirmation
07 baptism	Eucharist	Midnight Mass
evening	**10** bar mitzvah	thanksgiving
funeral	bat mitzvah	**13** Holy Communion
morning	dedication	Holy Matrimony
wedding	**11** christening	**14** First Communion
08 evensong	Lord's Supper	morning prayers
High Mass	nuptial Mass	**15** harvest festival
marriage	remembrance	
memorial	Requiem Mass	

Religious building types include:

03 wat	gompa	pagoda	**08** gurdwara
04 fane	**06** bethel	shrine	**09** cathedral
kirk	church	temple	synagogue
shul	mandir	vihara	**10** tabernacle
05 abbey	masjid	**07** chantry	**12** meeting-house
	mosque	minster	

Religious buildings and sites include:

05 Kaaba (Saudi Arabia)	Parthenon (Greece)
08 Pantheon (Italy)	**10** Blue Mosque (Turkey)
09 Acropolis (Greece)	Erechtheum (Greece)

Harimandir (India)
Sacré Coeur (France)

11 Ajanta caves (India)
Ellora caves (India)
Erechtheion (Greece)
Great Mosque (Syria)
Great Sphinx (Egypt)
Hagia Sophia (Turkey)
Temple Mount (Israel)
Wailing Wall (Israel)
Western Wall (Israel)

12 Golden Temple (India)
Great Pyramid (Egypt)
Monte Cassino (Italy)
Temple of Hera (Italy)
Temple of Isis (Egypt)

13 Cordoba Mosque (Spain)
Dome of the Rock (Israel)
Horyuji Temple (Japan)
Kailasa Temple (India)
Mt Grace Priory (England)
Muhammad's Tomb (Saudi Arabia)
Pattan Somnath (India)
Prabhas Pattan (India)
Rila Monastery (Bulgaria)
Sistine Chapel (Vatican City)
Umayyad Mosque (Syria)
Vézelay Church (France)

14 Abu Bakar Mosque (Malaysia)

Belém Monastery (Brazil)
Certosa of Pavia (Italy)
Dilwara temples (India)
Golden Pavilion (Japan)
Great Synagogue (Israel)
Mahamuni Pagoda (Myanmar)
My Son Sanctuary (Vietnam)
Sagrada Familia (Spain)
Selimiye Mosque (Cyprus)
Suleiman Mosque (Turkey)
Temple of Amon-Ra (Egypt)
Temple of Apollo (Greece)
Temple of Athena (Greece)
Temple of Hathor (Egypt)
Temple of Heaven (China)

15 Chavín de Huantar (Peru)
Decani Monastery (Serbia)
Ggantija temples (Malta)
Ketchaoua Mosque (Algeria)
Mahabodhi Temple (India)
Maisel Synagogue (Czech Republic)
Mont-Saint-Michel (France)
Pyramid of Cheops (Egypt)
Pyramid of the Sun (Mexico)
Shwe Dagon Pagoda (Myanmar)
Shwezigon Pagoda (Myanmar)
Temple of Artemis (Turkey)
Temple of Solomon (Israel)
Temple of Somnath (India)
Thousand Temples (Indonesia)

Religious festivals and holidays include:

02 Id

03 Eid

04 Holi
Lent
Lots
Obon
Oram
Yule

05 Litha
Pesah
Purim
Vesak

06 Advent
Bakrid
Basant
Dhamma
Divali
Diwali
Easter
Imbolc
Lammas
Pesach
Sangha
Sukkot

07 Baisaki
Beltane
matsuri
New Year
Ramadan
Samhain
Shavuot
Sukkoth

08 All Souls
Baisakhi
Dipavali
Dusserah
Epiphany
Hanukkah
Id al-Adha
Id al-Fitr
Id ul-Zuha
Muharram
Passover

09 All Saints
Ascension
Candlemas
Christmas
Deepavali

Dolayatra
Durga-puja
Easter Day
Eid al-Adha
Eid al-Fitr
Mardi Gras
Navaratri
Oshogatsu
Pentecost
Up-Helly-Aa
Yom Kippur

10 All Hallows
Assumption
Good Friday
Lughnasadh
Lupercalia
Michaelmas
Palm Sunday
Ramanavami
Rathayatra
Saturnalia
Vulcanalia
Whit Sunday

11 All Souls' Day

Bacchanalia
Lakshmi-puja
Milad-un-Nabi
Panathenaea
Rosh Hashana
12 All Saints' Day
Annunciation
Ascension Day
Ash Wednesday
Christmas Day
Easter Sunday
Holy Saturday
Holy Thursday

Hoshi Matsuri
Night of Power
Ohinamatsuri
Prakash Utsav
Rosh Hashanah
Simchat Torah
Star Festival
Tango no Sekku
13 Buddha Purnima
Corpus Christi
Holy Innocents
Night of Ascent
Passion Sunday

spring equinox
Trinity Sunday
vernal equinox
14 Chinese New Year
Day of Atonement
Easter Saturday
Maundy Thursday
summer solstice
winter solstice
15 autumnal equinox
Lantern Festival
Tanabata Matsuri
Transfiguration

Religious symbols include:

02 Om

03 IHC
IHS

04 ankh
fish

yoni

05 cross
linga

06 chakra
filfot

fylfot
lingam
07 Ik Onkar
mandala
menorah

yin-yang

08 crescent
swastika

11 Christingle
star of David

Religious figures and leaders include:

03 Ali (d.661, Arab)
Fox (George; 1624–91, English)
Fry (Elizabeth; 1780–1845, English)
Hus (Jan; c.1369–1415, Bohemian)

04 Bede (St, 'the Venerable'; c.673–735, Anglo-Saxon)
Boff (Leonardo; 1938–   , Brazilian)
Eddy (Mary; 1821–1910, US)
Hick (John; 1922–   , English)
Huss (John; c.1369–1415, Bohemian)
King (Martin Luther; 1929–68, US)
Knox (John; c.1513–72, Scottish)
Küng (Hans; 1928–   , Swiss)
Mani (c.215–276 AD, Persian)
Otto (Rudolf; 1869–1937, German)
Penn (William; 1644–1718, English)
Pire (Dominique; 1910–69, Belgian)
Tutu (Desmond; 1931–   , South African)
Weil (Simone; 1909–43, French)

05 Alban (St; 3 CAD, Roman)
Amman (Jakob; c.1645–c.1730, Swiss)
Arius (c.250–336 AD, Libyan)
Askew (Anne; 1521–46, English)
Barth (Karl; 1886–1968, Swiss)
Booth (William; 1829–1912, English)
Buber (Martin; 1878–1965, Austrian/Israeli)
Keble (John; 1792–1866, English)
Lao Zi (6 c BC, Chinese)
Mahdi (al-; 1844–85, Arab)
Mbiti (John; 1931–   , Kenyan)
Moses (15–13 c BC; Bible)
Paley (William; 1743–1805, English)

Paris (Matthew; c.1200–59, English)
Smith (Joseph; 1805–44, US)
Soper (Donald, Lord; 1903–98, English)
Waite (Terry; 1939–   , English)
Young (Brigham; 1801–77, US)

06 Agatha (St; d.251 AD, Sicilian)
Anselm (St; 1033–1109, Italian)
Baxter (Richard; 1615–91, English)
Becket (St Thomas à; 1118–70, English)
Besant (Annie; 1847–1933, English)
Browne (Robert; c.1550–c.1633, English)
Buddha (Prince Siddhartha Gautama; c.560–c.480 BC, Nepali)
Bunyan (John; 1628–88, English)
Calvin (John; 1509–64, French)
Cupitt (Don; 1934–   , English)
Gandhi (Mahatma; 1869–1948, Indian)
Garvey (Marcus; 1887–1940, Jamaican)
Graham (Billy; 1918–   , US)
Hillel (1 c BC–1 c AD, Babylonian)
Hutter (Jakob; d.1536, Swiss)
Jansen (Cornelius; 1585–1638, Dutch)
Kempis (Thomas à; 1379–1471, German)
Lao-tzu (6 c BC, Chinese)
Luther (Martin; 1483–1546, German)
Mather (Cotton; 1662–1728, American)
Newman (John Henry; 1801–90, English)
Olcott (Colonel Henry Steel; 1832–1907, US)
Origen (c.185–c.254 AD, Greek)
Rahner (Karl; 1904–84, German)
Raikes (Robert; 1735–1811, English)
Ramsey (Ian; 1915–72, English)
Ridley (Nicholas; c.1500–55, English)

Rogers (John; c.1500–55, English)
Sieyès (the Abbé; 1748–1836, French)
Teresa (Mother; 1910–97, Albanian)
Tetzel (Johann; c.1465–1519, German)
Wesley (John; 1703–91, English)

07 Abelard (Peter; 1079–1142, French)
Aga Khan (III; 1877–1957, Pakistani)
Aga Khan (IV, Karim; 1936– , Pakistani)
Aquinas (St Thomas; 1225–74, Italian)
Ayeshah (c.613–678, Arab)
Brunner (Emil; 1889–1966, Swiss)
Buchman (Frank; 1878–1961, US)
Cranmer (Thomas; 1489–1556, English)
Eckhart (Johannes; c.1260–c.1327, German)
Erasmus (Desiderius; 1466–1536, Dutch)
Falwell (Jerry; 1933–2007, US)
Fénelon (François; 1651–1715, French)
Ghazali (Abu Hamid al-; 1058–1111, Persian)
Hubbard (L Ron; 1911–86, US)
Jenkins (David; 1925– , English)
Latimer (Hugh; c.1485–1555, English)
Mencius (c.372–c.298 BC, Chinese)
Müntzer (Thomas; c.1488–1525, German)
Niebuhr (Reinhold; 1892–1971, US)
Paisley (Rev. Ian; 1926– , Northern Irish)
Photius (c.820–91, Byzantine)
Ruether (Rosemary Radford; 1936– , US)
Russell (Pastor; 1852–1916, US)
Sankara (c.700–c.750, Indian)
Steiner (Rudolf; 1861–1925, Austrian)
Strauss (David; 1808–74, German)
Tillich (Paul; 1886–1965, German)
Tyndale (William; c.1494–1536, English)
Wishart (George; c.1513–46, Scottish)
Zwingli (Huldreich; 1484–1531, Swiss)

08 Agricola (Johann; 1492–1566, German)
Andrewes (Lancelot; 1555–1626, English)
Bultmann (Rudolf; 1884–1976, German)
Hamilton (Patrick; 1503–28, Scottish)
Irenaeus (St; c.130–c.200 AD, Greek)
Khomeini (Ayatollah Ruhollah; 1900–89, Iranian)
Mahavira (Vardhamana; c.540–468 BC, Indian)
Moltmann (Jürgen; 1926– , German)
Muhammad (c.570–c.632, Arab)
Muhammad (Elijah; 1897–1975, US)
Patteson (John; 1827–71, English)
Pelagius (c.360–c.420 AD, British)
Rajneesh (Bhagwan Shree; 1931–90, Indian)
Rasputin (Grigoriy; 1871–1916, Russian)
Robinson (J A T; 1919–83, English)
Selassie (Emperor Haile; 1891–1975, Ethiopian)

Williams (John; 1796–1839, English)
Williams (Roger; c.1604–83, American)
Wycliffe (John; c.1330–84, English)

09 Baha-Allah (1817–92, Persian)
Blavatsky (H P; 1831–91, Russian)
Clitherow (St Margaret; c.1556–86, English)
Confucius (551–479 BC, Chinese)
Dalai Lama (1935– , Tibetan)
Guru Nanak (1469–1539, Indian)
Gutiérrez (Gustavo; 1928– , Peruvian)
Joan of Arc (St; c.1412–31, French)
K'ung Fu-tse (551–479 BC, Chinese)
McPherson (Aimee Semple; 1890–1944, US)
Nagarjuna (c.150–c.250 AD, Indian)
Niemöller (Martin; 1892–1984, German)
Zoroaster (c.630–c.553 BC, Iranian)

10 Athanasius (St; c.296–373 AD, Greek)
Bonhoeffer (Dietrich; 1906–45, German)
Fateh Singh (Sant; 1911–72, Indian)
Huddleston (Trevor; 1913–98, English)
Huntingdon (Selina Hastings, Countess of; 1707–91, English)
Manichaeus (c.215–276 AD, Persian)
Pannenberg (Wolfhart; 1928– , German)
Savonarola (Girolamo; 1452–98, Italian)
Schweitzer (Albert; 1875–1965, German)
Swedenborg (Emmanuel; 1688–1772, Swedish)
Tertullian (c.160–220 AD, North African)
Torquemada (Tomás de; 1420–98, Spanish)
Whitefield (George; 1714–70, English)

11 Bodhidharma (6c, Indian)
Gobind Singh (1666–1708, Indian)
Jesus Christ (c.4 BC–c.30 AD, Judean)
Melanchthon (Philip; 1497–1560, German)
Wilberforce (William; 1759–1833, English)
Zarathustra (c.630–c.553 BC, Iranian)

12 John of Leyden (1509–36, Dutch)
Krishnamurti (Jiddu; 1895–1986, Indian)
Mother Teresa (of Calcutta; 1910–97, Albanian)
Tenzin Gyatso (1935– , Tibetan)

13 Muhammad Ahmed (1844–85, Arab)
Teresa of Ávila (St; 1515–82, Spanish)
William of Tyre (c.1130–85, Syrian)

14 Ignatius Loyola (St; 1491–1556, Spanish)
John of the Cross (St; 1542–91, Spanish)
Schleiermacher (Friedrich; 1768–1834, German)

15 Francis of Assisi (St; c.1181–1226, Italian)
Jesus of Nazareth (c.4 BC–c.30 AD, Judean)
Julian of Norwich (c.1342–c.1413, English)

Terms to do with religion include:

03 God
haj
Jew

04 cult
hadj
hajj
Holi
imam
kara
kesh
Magi
Mass
myth
pope
puja
Rama
saum
sect

05 Allah
Amish
Arhat
Bahai
Bible
Druze
Flood
Islam
kacha
kanga
Koran
Mahdi
Mecca
Qur'an
salah
Shiva
Sunni
Sutra
Torah
zakat

06 Babism
Brahma
chapel
church
Daoism
dharma
Diwali
Easter
Five Ks
kippah
kirpan
mandir
moksha
mosque
Nevi'im
Pesach
Ratana
sangha

Shiism
Shinto
Sufism
Taoism
temple
Tenakh
Vishnu

07 Abraham
Amoraim
apostle
atheism
Baptist
Brahman
Cluniac
deities
Gabriel
Gospels
Gurpurb
Holy Ark
Jainism
Jesuits
Jibrail
Judaism
Ketuvim
Krishna
Moonies
muezzin
nirvana
Parsees
prasada
Quakers
Ramadan
Ranters
Rig-Veda
Ringatu
Sabbath
Saivism
samsara
Shabbat
shahada
Shakers
Shingon
Sikhism
Vatican
Wahhabi
Zealots

08 Arianism
Beghards
Beguines
bhikkhus
Buddhism
cardinal
Creation
disciple
Druidism
Falashas

Gurdwara
Hanukkah
Hinduism
Id ul-Adha
Id ul-Fitr
Ismailis
Lollards
Mohammad
Muhammad
nativity
paganism
Passover
Ramayana
religion
Santería
tefillin

09 Adventism
Arya Samaj
Ascension
Bethlehem
Calvinism
Capuchins
cathedral
Christmas
Eucharist
Guru Nanak
Huguenots
Maronites
Methodism
Mithraism
Mormonism
Pharisees
Sadducees
Sephardim
Shamanism
synagogue
The Buddha
Trappists
Tripitaka
Waldenses

10 Adam and Eve
Albigenses
Anabaptism
Ashkenazim
Avatamsaka
bar mitzvah
bat mitzvah
Carmelites
Confucians
Dissenters
Dominicans
Good Friday
Holy Spirit
Mennonites
Soka Gakkai

11 agnosticism

Carthusians
Catholicism
Cistercians
Covenanters
Creationism
Crucifixion
Franciscans
Hare Krishna
Jesus Christ
Lord's Prayer
Lutheranism
Scientology
Three Jewels
Vaishnavism
Vijnanavada
Wheel of Life
Zen Buddhism

12 Augustinians
Benedictines
Christianity
Confucianism
Coptic Church
New Testament
Old Testament
Resurrection
Three Wise Men
Unitarianism
13 Nonconformism
Protestantism
Salvation Army
The Last Supper
14 Anglican Church
Armenian Church

Fundamentalism
Knights Templar
Millenarianism
Moravian Church
Orthodox Church
Rastafarianism
Society of Jesus
Zoroastrianism
15 Assemblies of God
Avatamsaka Sutra
Bhagavata-Purana
Branch Davidians
Episcopal Church
Four Noble Truths
Nestorian Church
Pentecostalists
Presbyterianism

See also **abbey**; **angel**; **apostle**; **archbishop**; **Bible**; **Buddhism**; **cardinal**; **cathedral**; **celebration**; **ceremony**; **chief rabbi**; **Christianity**; **Christmas**; **church**; **clerical vestment**; **cross**; **Dalai Lama**; **diocese**; **fast**; **Hinduism**; **Islam**; **Judaism**; **missionary**; **mythology**; **patriarch**; **plague**; **pope**; **prayer**; **priest**; **prophet**; **reformer**; **religious order**; **saint**; **Sikhism**; **theology**

religious order

Religious orders include:

04 Sufi
05 Taizé
06 Culdee
Essene
Jesuit
Loreto
Marist
07 Jesuits
Marists
Rifaite
08 Buddhist
Capuchin
Grey nuns
Minorite

Trappist
Ursuline
09 Barnabite
Capuchins
Carmelite
Dominican
Marianist
Mawlawite
mendicant
Salesians
Trappists
Ursulines
10 Bernardine
Carmelites

Carthusian
Celestines
Cistercian
Conventual
Dominicans
Franciscan
Gilbertine
Grey friars
Norbertine
Oratorians
Poor Clares
11 Augustinian
Benedictine
Black friars

Camaldolite
Carthusians
Cistercians
Franciscans
Ignorantine
Sylvestrine
White friars
12 Augustinians
Austin friars
Benedictines
13 Society of Mary
14 Knights Templar
Sisters of Mercy
Society of Jesus

Monasteries and convents include:

04 Iona (Scotland)
05 Cluny (France)
07 Mt Athos (Greece)
Shaolin (China)
08 Hilandar (Greece)
Sénanque (France)
09 Melk Abbey (Austria)
Tengboche (Nepal)
10 Douai Abbey (England)
El Escorial (Spain)
Ettal Abbey (Germany)

San Lorenzo (various)
Santa Croce (Italy)
Worth Abbey (England)
11 Ealing Abbey (England)
Glendalough (Ireland)
Lindisfarne (England)
Parkminster (England)
Simonopetra (Greece)
Val-Duchesse (Belgium)
Whitby Abbey (England)
12 Belmont Abbey (England)
Colwich Abbey (England)

Monte Cassino (Italy)
Mont St Michel (France)
St John's Abbey (USA)

13 Buckfast Abbey (England)
Donglin Temple (China)
Downside Abbey (England)
Monasterboice (Ireland)
Rievaulx Abbey (England)

Tyburn Convent (England)

14 Fountains Abbey (England)
Stanbrook Abbey (England)

15 Ampleforth Abbey (England)
Curzon Park Abbey (England)
Portsmouth Abbey (England)
St Cecilia's Abbey (England)

Monks and nuns include:

02 Fa (Hsien; fl.400 AD, Chinese)
Fa (Xian; fl.400 AD, Chinese)

03 Orm (fl.1200, English)

04 Gall (St; c.550–645, Irish)
Hume (Basil; 1923–99, English)
Rule (St; 4c AD)
Sava (St; c.1174–1235/6, Serbian)

05 Aidan (St; d.651, Irish)
Barat (St Madeleine Sophie; 1779–1865, French)
Borde (Andrew; c.1490–1549, English)
Jacob (Max; 1876–1944, French)
Ormin (fl.1200, English)
Rancé (Armand Jean de; 1626–1700, French)
Sabas (St; c.1174–1235/6, Serbian)

06 Arnulf (1040–1124, French)
Boorde (Andrew; c.1490–1549, English)
Colman (St; d.676, Irish)
Eadmer (d.c.1124, English)
Ernulf (1040–1124, French)
Gildas (St; c.493–570 AD, Roman-British)
Gyatso (Geshe Kelsang; 1931– , Tibetan)
Merton (Thomas; 1915–68, US)
Teresa (Mother; 1910–97, Albanian)
Tetzel (Johann; c.1465–1519, German)
Turgot (d.1115, Anglo-Saxon)

07 Adamnan (St; c.625–704, Irish)
Adomnan (St; c.625–704, Irish)
Arnauld (Angélique; 1624–84, French)
Arnauld (Marie-Angélique; 1591–1661, French)
Beckett (Sister Wendy; 1930– , South African/British)
Cabrini (St Francesca Xavier; 1850–1917, US)
Carpini (John of Plano; c.1182–c.1253, Italian)
Cassian (St John; c.360–c.435 AD, Romanian)

Gratian (12c, Italian)
Lydgate (John; c.1370–c.1451, English)
Mortara (Edgar; 1852–1940, Italian)
Regulus (St; 4c AD)
Schwarz (Berthold; fl.1320, German)

08 Alacoque (St Marguerite Marie; 1647–90, French)
Bonivard (François de; 1493–1570, Swiss)
Duchesne (St Rose Philippine; 1769–1852, French)
Foucauld (Charles de; 1858–1916, French)
Houedard (Dom Sylvester; 1924–92, British)
Pelagius (c.360–c.420 AD, British)
Rabelais (François; 1483 or 1494–1553, French)

09 Bonnivard (François de; 1493–1570, Swiss)
MacKillop (Mary; 1842–1909, Australian)
Skobtsova (Maria; 1891–1945, Russian)

10 Bernadette (St; 1844–79, French)
Fra Diavolo (1760–1806, Italian)
Montfaucon (Bernard de; 1655–1741, French)
Torquemada (Tomás de; 1420–98, Spanish)
Walsingham (Thomas; d.c.1422, English)
Willibrord (St; 658–739, English)

11 Bodhidharma (6c, Indian)
Ponce de León (Luis; 1527–91, Spanish)
Scholastica (St; c.480–c.543 AD, Italian)

12 Guido d'Arezzo (c.990–1050, Italian)
Mother Teresa (of Calcutta; 1910–97, Albanian)

13 The Singing Nun (Jeanne Deckers; 1933–85, Belgian)

14 Francis of Paola (St; 1416–1507, Italian)
Marianus Scotus (d.c.1088, Irish)
Peter the Hermit (c.1050–c.1115, French)

15 Bernard of Morval (12c, French)

See also **abbey**; **Buddhism**; **Christianity**; **Hinduism**; **Judaism**; **Sikhism**

reptile

Reptiles include:

04 croc
05 gator

06 caiman
cayman

garial
gavial

mugger
turtle
07 gharial
hicatee
snapper
tuatara
08 aligarta
galapago
hiccatee
See also **lizard**; **snake**

matamata
stinkpot
terrapin
tortoise
09 alligarta
alligator
crocodile
hawksbill
mud turtle
sea turtle

10 loggerhead
musk turtle
11 green turtle
leatherback
13 giant tortoise
water tortoise
14 leathery turtle
snapping turtle
15 hawksbill turtle

republic

Republics include:

03 USA
04 Chad
Cuba
Fiji
Iran
Iraq
Laos
Mali
Peru
Togo
05 Benin
Chile
China
Congo
Egypt
Gabon
Ghana
Haiti
India
Italy
Kenya
Malta
Nauru
Niger
Palau
Sudan
Syria
Yemen
06 Angola
Brazil
Cyprus
France
Greece
Guinea
Guyana
Israel
Latvia
Malawi
Mexico
Panama
Poland

Russia
Rwanda
Taiwan
Turkey
Uganda
Zambia
07 Albania
Algeria
Armenia
Austria
Belarus
Bolivia
Burundi
Croatia
Ecuador
Estonia
Finland
Georgia
Germany
Hungary
Iceland
Ireland
Lebanon
Liberia
Moldova
Myanmar
Namibia
Nigeria
Romania
Senegal
Somalia
Tunisia
Ukraine
Uruguay
Vanuatu
Vietnam
08 Botswana
Bulgaria
Cameroon
Colombia
Djibouti

Ethiopia
Honduras
Kiribati
Maldives
Mongolia
Pakistan
Paraguay
Portugal
Slovakia
Slovenia
Sri Lanka
Suriname
Tanzania
Zimbabwe
09 Argentina
Cape Verde
Costa Rica
East Timor
Guatemala
Indonesia
Lithuania
Macedonia
Mauritius
Nicaragua
San Marino
Singapore
The Gambia
Venezuela
10 Azerbaijan
Bangladesh
El Salvador
Kazakhstan
Kyrgyzstan
Madagascar
Mauritania
Mozambique
North Korea
Seychelles
South Korea
Tajikistan
Uzbekistan

0

11 Burkina Faso
Côte d'Ivoire
Philippines
Sierra Leone

South Africa
Switzerland

12 Guinea-Bissau
Turkmenistan

13 Czech Republic
Western Sahara

15 Marshall Islands

resort

Resorts include:

04 Nice (France)
Rhyl (Wales)

05 Aspen (USA)
Davos (Switzerland)

06 Cairns (Australia)
Cancún (Mexico)
Cannes (France)
St Ives (England)
St-Malo (France)
Whitby (England)

07 Funchal (Portugal)
Margate (England)
Newquay (England)
Torquay (England)
Ventnor (England)
Zermatt (Switzerland)

08 Acapulco (Mexico)
Alicante (Spain)
Aviemore (Scotland)
Benidorm (Spain)
Biarritz (France)
Chamonix (France)
Honolulu (USA)
Klosters (Switzerland)
Marbella (Spain)
Montreux (Switzerland)
Penzance (England)
Skegness (England)
St Helier (Channel Islands)
St Moritz (Switzerland)
St-Tropez (France)
Weymouth (England)

09 Albufeira (Portugal)
Blackpool (England)

See also **spa**

Galveston (USA)
Gold Coast (Australia)
Kitzbühel (Austria)
Lanzarote (Spain)
Morecambe (England)
Nantucket (USA)

10 Baden Baden (Germany)
Bondi Beach (Australia)
Costa Brava (Spain)
Eastbourne (England)
Lake Placid (USA)
Long Island (USA)
Miami Beach (USA)
Monte Carlo (Monaco)
Windermere (England)

11 Bognor Regis (England)
Bournemouth (England)
Bridlington (England)
Cleethorpes (England)
Coney Island (USA)
Costa Blanca (Spain)
Costa del Sol (Spain)
Costa Dorada (Spain)
Gran Canaria (Spain)
Grand Bahama (The Bahamas)
Palm Springs (USA)
Scarborough (England)

12 San Sebastian (Spain)
Santa Barbara (USA)
Waikiki Beach (USA)

13 Great Yarmouth (England)
Southend-on-Sea (England)

15 Martha's Vineyard (USA)
Weston-super-Mare (England)

restaurant

Restaurant types include:

04 café

05 diner
grill
NAAFI

06 bistro
buffet
chippy

pull-in

07 carvery
chipper
milk bar
taverna
tea room
tea shop

08 creperie
pizzeria
snack-bar
sushi bar
taqueria
teahouse

09 brasserie

burger bar
cafeteria
coffee bar
dining-car
grill room
trattoria
10 dining room

rotisserie
steakhouse
11 eating-house
greasy spoon
sandwich bar
self-service
12 drivethrough

Internet café
luncheonette
motorway café
13 transport café
15 fish-and-chip shop
ice-cream parlour

Restaurants include:

03 Umu (England)
04 Nahm (England)
Nobu (England)
05 Arzak (Spain)
Boyer (France)
Craft (USA)
Per Se (USA)
Spago (USA)
06 Arpège (France)
Daniel (USA)
Le Cinq (France)
Orrery (England)
Sketch (England)
St John (England)
The Ivy (England)
07 Assaggi (England)
Bukhara (India)
Capital (England)
Cote d'Or (France)
El Bulli (Spain)
Foliage (England)
Ledoyen (France)
Louis XV (Monaco)
08 Al Mahara (Dubai)
Guy Savoy (France)
Hakkasan (England)
Hibiscus (England)
La Tupina (France)
Rockpool (Australia)
Tamarind (England)
Tetsuya's (Australia)
The Cliff (Barbados)
Yauatcha (England)
09 Al Sorriso (Italy)
Aubergine (England)
Balthazar (USA)
Chez Bruce (England)
De Librije (The Netherlands)
Lameloise (France)
L'Ami Louis (France)
Le Meurice (France)
L'Escargot (England)
Mirabelle (England)
The Square (England)
Thornton's (Ireland)
Tom Aikens (England)

Troisgros (France)
Zafferano (England)
10 Club Gascon (England)
Flower Drum (Australia)
L'Ambroisie (France)
L'Arnsbourg (France)
Le Calandre (Italy)
Le Gavroche (England)
L'Espérance (France)
Michel Bras (France)
Park Heuvel (The Netherlands)
Paul Bocuse (France)
Pied à terre (England)
Roussillon (England)
Savoy Grill (England)
Taillevent (France)
The Fat Duck (England)
11 Au Crocodile (France)
Buerehiesel (France)
Chez Panisse (California)
De Karmeliet (Belgium)
Grand Vefour (France)
Jean Georges (USA)
Lucas Carton (France)
The Wolseley (England)
12 Comme Chez Soi (Belgium)
Dal Pescatore (Italy)
Dieter Muller (Germany)
Gambero Rosso (Italy)
Georges Blanc (France)
Gidleigh Park (England)
Gordon Ramsay (England)
Heinz Winkler (Germany)
Hotel de Ville (Switzerland)
Im Schiffchen (Germany)
Plaza Athénée (France)
Putney Bridge (England)
The River Café (England)
Waterside Inn (England)
13 Auberge de l'Ill (France)
Cote St Jacques (France)
Jardins de Sens (France)
Le Pont de Brent (Switzerland)
Le Tour d'Argent (France)
Martin Wishart (Scotland)
The Greenhouse (England)

14 1 Lombard Street (England)
Charlie Trotter (USA)
Ferme de mon Père (France)
Gramercy Tavern (USA)

Pierre Gagnaire (France)
15 Les Prés d'Eugénie (France)
Patrick Guilbaud (Ireland)

Fast food restaurant chains include:

03 KFC
06 Wendy's
08 Pizza Hut
Taco Bell
Wagamama
09 Harvester

McDonald's
Spud U Like
Starbucks
10 Burger King
Dairy Queen
Little Chef

Red Rooster
TGI Friday's
11 Hungry Jacks
Krispy Kreme
12 Domino's Pizza
Dunkin' Donuts

Hard Rock Café
Pizza Express
13 Baskin-Robbins
Harry Ramsden's
14 Subway Sandwich

restaurateur *see* **chef**

revolution

Revolutions include:

04 July (1830, France)
06 French (1830, France)
Orange (2004–05, Ukraine)
Velvet (1989,
Czechoslovakia)

07 October (1917, Russia)
Russian (1917, Russia)
Singing (1988, Estonia/
Latvia/Lithuania)
08 American (1775–83)

Cultural (1966–76, China)
February (1917, Russia)
Glorious (1688, Britain)
10 Industrial (18c–19c, Britain)
12 Agricultural (18c, Britain)

revolutionary

Revolutionaries, rebels and terrorists include:

02 He (Xiangning; 1880–1972, Chinese)
Ho (Hsiang-ning; 1880–1972, Chinese)
Li (Dazhao; 1888–1927, Chinese)
Li (Ta-chao; 1888–1927, Chinese)

03 Cai (Chang; 1900–90, Chinese)
Guo (Morno; 1892–1978, Chinese)
Kim (Ok-kyun; 1851–94, Korean)
Kun (Béla; 1886–c.1937, Hungarian)
Kuo (Mo-jo; 1892–1978, Chinese)
Lee (Richard Henry; 1732–94, American)
Mao (Tse-tung; 1893–1976, Chinese)
Mao (Zedong; 1893–1976, Chinese)
Qiu (Jin; 1875–1907, Chinese)
Sun (Chung-shan; 1866–1925, Chinese)
Sun (Yat-sen; 1866–1925, Chinese)
Sun (Yixian; 1866–1925, Chinese)
Sun (Zhongshan; 1866–1925, Chinese)

04 Aske (Robert; d.1537, English)
Ball (John; d.1381, English)
Biko (Steve; 1946–77, South African)
Cade (Jack; d.1450, Irish)
Chen (Duxiu; 1879–1942, Chinese)
Ch'en (Tu-hsiu; 1879–1942, Chinese)
Ch'iu (Chin; 1875–1907, Chinese)
Hong (Xiuquan; 1813–64, Chinese)
Hung (Hsiu-ch'üan; 1813–64, Chinese)
Kett (Robert; d.1549, English)

Marx (Karl; 1818–83, German)
Páez (José Antonio; 1790–1873, Venezuelan)
Peng (Pai; 1896–1929, Chinese)
Popé (c.1630–c.1690, American)
Pyat (Félix; 1810–89, French)
Song (Jiaoren; 1882–1913, Chinese)
Sung (Chiao-jen; 1882–1913, Chinese)
Ts'ai (Ch'ang; 1900–90, Chinese)

05 Allen (Ethan; 1738–89, American)
Botev (Khristo; 1848–76, Bulgarian)
Fanon (Frantz; 1925–61, French West
Indian)
Gorky (Maxim; 1868–1936, Russian)
Henry (Patrick; 1736–99, American)
Huang (Hsing; 1871–1916, Chinese)
Huang (Xing; 1871–1916, Chinese)
Jiang (Jieshi; 1887–1975, Chinese)
Kirov (Sergei; 1886–1934, Russian)
Lenin (Vladimir Ilyich; 1870–1924, Russian)
Marat (Jean Paul; 1743–93, French)
Paine (Thomas; 1737–1809, English)
Radek (Karl; 1885–1939, Russian)
Razin (Stenka; c.1630–1671, Russian)
Rykov (Aleksei; 1881–1938, Russian)
Sands (Bobby; 1954–81, Irish)
Sucre (Antonio José de; 1793–1830, South
American)

Tyler (Wat; d.1381, English)
Villa (Pancho; 1877–1923, Mexican)
06 Arafat (Yasser; 1929–2004, Palestinian)
Baader (Andreas; 1943–77, German)
Barère (Bertrand; 1755–1841, French)
Barras (Paul, Comte de; 1755–1829, French)
Cambon (Joseph; 1756–1820, French)
Carnot (Lazare; 1753–1823, French)
Castro (Fidel; 1927– , Cuban)
Clarke (Thomas; 1858–1916, Irish)
Cloots (Jean Baptiste, Baron de; 1755–94, French)
Corday (Charlotte; 1768–93, French)
Danton (Georges; 1759–94, French)
Farini (Luigi Carlo; 1812–66, Italian)
Fawkes (Guy; 1570–1606, English)
Fouché (Joseph, Duc d'Otrante; 1763–1829, French)
Frunze (Mikhail; 1885–1925, Russian)
Fuller (Margaret, Marchioness Ossoli; 1810–50, US)
Görgey (Artúr; 1818–1916, Hungarian)
Hébert (Jacques; 1757–94, French)
Kassem (Abdul Karim; 1914–63, Iraqi)
Madero (Francisco; 1873–1913, Mexican)
Misley (Enrico; 1801–63, Italian)
Moreno (Mariano; 1778–1811, Argentine)
O'Neill (Hugh, Earl of Tyrone; c.1540–1616, Irish)
Orsini (Felice; 1819–58, Italian)
Pétion (Alexandre; 1770–1818, Haitian)
Qassim (Abd al-Krim; 1914–63, Iraqi)
Stalin (Joseph; 1879–1953, Soviet)
St-Just (Louis Antoine; 1767–94, French)
Travis (William; 1809–36, American)
Zapata (Emiliano; 1879–1919, Mexican)
07 Artigas (José; 1774–1850, Spanish American)
Astorga (Nora; 1949–88, Nicaraguan)
Attucks (Crispus; c.1723–1770, American)
Bakunin (Mikhail; 1814–76, Russian)
Barnave (Antoine; 1761–93, French)
Blanqui (Auguste; 1805–81, French)
Bolívar (Simón; 1783–1830, South American)
Brissot (Jacques Pierre; 1754–93, French)
Carrier (Jean Baptiste; 1756–94, French)
Carroll (Charles; 1737–1832, American)
Catesby (Robert; 1573–1605, English)
Couthon (Georges; 1756–94, French)
Durruti (Buenaventura; 1896–1936, Spanish)
Gadsden (Christopher; 1724–1805, American)
Goldman (Emma; 1869–1940, US)
Guevara (Che; 1928–67, Argentine)
Hancock (John; 1737–93, American)
Hidalgo (Miguel; 1753–1811, Mexican)

Horváth (Mihály; 1809–78, Hungarian)
Kamenev (Lev; 1883–1936, Russian)
Kossuth (Lajos; 1802–94, Hungarian)
Laurens (Henry; 1724–92, American)
Leisler (Jacob; 1640–91, American)
Mandela (Nelson; 1918– , South African)
Meinhof (Ulrike; 1934–76, German)
Menotti (Ciro; 1798–1831, Italian)
Miranda (Francisco de; 1750–1816, Venezuelan)
Modotti (Tina; 1896–1942, Mexican)
Morelos (José; 1765–1815, Mexican)
Nechaev (Sergei; 1847–82, Russian)
Padilla (Juan de; 1490–1521, Spanish)
Padmore (George; 1902–59, Trinidadian)
Princip (Gavrilo; 1895–1918, Serbian)
Rákóczi (Francis II; 1676–1735, Hungarian)
Sandino (Augusto; 1895–1934, Nicaraguan)
Savimbi (Jonas; 1934–2002, Angolan)
Tallien (Jean Lambert; 1767–1820, French)
Trotsky (Leon; 1879–1940, Russian)
Wallace (Sir William; c.1274–1305, Scottish)
08 Abu Nidal (1937–2002, Palestinian)
Bin Laden (Osama; c.1957– , Saudi Arabian)
Bukharin (Nikolai; 1888–1938, Russian)
Cadoudal (Georges; 1771–1804, French)
Catilina (Lucius Sergius; c.108–62 BC, Roman)
Catiline (c.108–62 BC, Roman)
Grégoire (Henri; 1750–1831, French)
Hereward (fl.1070, Anglo-Saxon)
Kerensky (Aleksandr; 1881–1970, Russian)
La Farina (Giuseppe; 1815–63, Italian)
Lassalle (Ferdinand; 1825–64, German)
Lilburne (John; c.1614–1657, English)
Litvinov (Maxim; 1876–1951, Soviet)
Mirabeau (Honoré Gabriel Riqueti, Comte de; 1749–91, French)
Museveni (Yoweri Kaguta; 1944– , Ugandan)
O'Donnell (Peadar; 1893–1986, Irish)
O'Higgins (Bernardo; 1778–1842, Chilean)
Paterson (William; 1745–1806, American)
Pisacane (Carlo; 1818–57, Italian)
Proudhon (Pierre Joseph; 1809–65, French)
Santerre (Antoine Joseph; 1752–1809, French)
Stepnyak (1852–95, Russian)
Zinoviev (Grigori; 1883–1936, Russian)
09 Aguinaldo (Emilio; 1870–1964, Philippine)
Bonifacio (Andres; 1863–97, Philippine)
Chaumette (Pierre; 1763–94, French)
Chicherin (G V; 1872–1936, Russian)

Christian (Fletcher; c.1764–c.1794, English)
Garibaldi (Giuseppe; 1807–82, Italian)
Glendower (Owen; c.1350–c.1416, Welsh)
Guillotin (Joseph; 1738–1814, French)
Karavelov (Lyuben; 1835–79, Bulgarian)
Kobayashi (Takaji; 1903–33, Japanese)
Kollontai (Aleksandra; 1872–1952, Russian)
Kropotkin (Prince Peter; 1842–1921,
  Russian)
Krupskaya (Nadezhda; 1869–1939, Russian)
Lafayette (Marquis de; 1757–1834, French)
Luxemburg (Rosa; 1871–1919, German)
Nana Sahib (c.1820–1859, Indian)
Plekhanov (Georgi; 1856–1918, Russian)
Saint-Just (Louis Antoine; 1767–94, French)
Spartacus (d.71 BC, Roman)

10 Buonarroti (Filippo; 1761–1837, Italian)
Choibalsan (d.1952, Mongolian)
Christophe (Henri; 1767–1829, Haitian)
Delescluze (Charles; 1809–71, French)
Desmoulins (Camille; 1760–94, French)
Engelbrekt (c.1390–1436, Swedish)
Espronceda (José de; 1808–42, Spanish)

See also **month**; **rebellion**; **war**

Kovalskaya (Yelizaveta; 1851–1943, Russian)
Liebknecht (Karl; 1871–1919, German)
Pasvanoglu (Osman Pasha; 1758–1807,
  Balkan)
Tiradentes (1748–92, Brazilian)
Tupac Amarú (c.1742–1781, Peruvian)

11 Dzerzhinsky (Felix; 1877–1926, Russian)
Lunacharsky (Anatoli; 1875–1933, Russian)
MacDiarmada (Seán; 1884–1916, Irish)
Robespierre (Maximilien; 1758–94, French)
Tantia Topee (d.1859, Indian)
Velestinlis (Rigas; 1757–98, Greek)

13 Chiang Kai-Shek (1887–1975, Chinese)
Muhammad Ahmed (1844–85, Arab)
Paz Estenssoro (Víctor; 1907–2001, Bolivian)

14 Billaud-Varenne (Jean Nicolas; 1756–1819,
  French)
Collot d'Herbois (Jean Marie; 1751–96,
  French)
Engelbrektsson (c.1390–1436, Swedish)
García y Iñigues (Calixto; 1839–98, Cuban)

15 Hereward the Wake (fl.1070, Anglo-Saxon)

rhetoric

Rhetorical devices include:

03 pun

05 irony
trope

06 aporia
bathos
climax
simile
zeugma

07 auxesis
epigram
erotema
litotes
meiosis
paradox

08 anaphora
chiasmus
diallage
diegesis
ellipsis
epanodos
erotetic
innuendo
metaphor
metonymy
oxymoron
parabole

symploce

09 asyndeton
cataphora
dissimile
epizeuxis
euphemism
hendiadys
hypallage
hyperbole
increment
prolepsis
syllepsis
tautology

10 abscission
anastrophe
anticlimax
antithesis
apostrophe
dysphemism
enantiosis
epanaphora
epiphonema
epistrophe
metalepsis
synchrysis
synecdoche

11 anacoluthon

anadiplosis
antiphrasis
antonomasia
catachresis
enumeration
epanalepsis
hypostrophe
hypotyposis
paraleipsis
parenthesis
synchoresis
synoeciosis

12 alliteration
antimetabole
epanorthosis
onomatopoeia

13 amplification
dramatic irony
epanadiplosis
mixed metaphor
vicious circle

14 antimetathesis
double entendre
figure of speech

15 pathetic fallacy
personification

rhizome *see* bulb

rhyme

Rhymes include:

03 end
eye

04 half
head
male
near

rich
tail

05 slant
vowel

06 female
riding

tailed

08 feminine
internal

09 assonance
identical
masculine

pararhyme
rime riche

10 apocopated
cynghanedd
rhyme royal

14 rime suffisante

river

River and watercourse types include:

02 ea

03 cut
pow
sny

04 beck
burn
flow
kill
lake
lane
nala
rill
snye
wadi
wady

05 bourn

brook
canal
creek
delta
firth
fresh
frith
inlet
mouth
nalla
nulla

06 broads
influx
nallah
nullah
rapids

rillet
runnel
source
stream

07 channel
estuary
freshet
riveret
rivulet
torrent

08 affluent
brooklet
effluent
influent
waterway

09 anabranch

backwater
billabong
confluent
headwater
streamlet
tributary

10 confluence
head-stream
millstream
streamling

11 trout stream
water splash

12 distributary
embranchment

14 mountain stream

Rivers include:

02 Li (China)
Ob (Russia)
Po (Italy)

03 Ahr (Germany)
Ain (France)
Axe (England)
Bug (Ukraine/Poland)
Cam (England)
Dal (Sweden)
Dee (Scotland; England/Wales)
Don (Russia; Scotland; England)
Ems (Germany)
Esk (Scotland)
Exe (England)
Fly (Papua New Guinea)
Han (China)
Hsi (China)
Ill (Finland)
Lea (England)
Lee (England)
Lek (The Netherlands)

Lim (Albania/Serbia/Montenegro/Bosnia and
  Herzegovina)
Lot (France)
Lys (France/Belgium)
Mun (Thailand)
Mur (Austria)
Nid (Norway)
Olt (Romania)
Oti (Burkina Faso/Togo/Ghana)
Our (Belgium/Luxembourg)
Pra (Ghana)
Red (Vietnam/USA)
San (Poland)
Sau (Slovakia/Croatia/Bosnia and
  Herzegovina/Serbia)
Sil (Spain)
Taw (England)
Tay (Scotland)
Tua (Portugal)
Ume (Sweden)
Una (Croatia/Bosnia and Herzegovina)

Usk (Wales)
Váh (Slovakia)
Wey (England)
Wye (Wales/England)

04 Aare (Switzerland)
Aire (England)
Alta (Norway)
Amur (China/Russia)
Arno (Italy)
Arun (England)
Aube (France)
Aude (France)
Avon (England)
Bann (Ireland)
Beni (Bolivia)
Cher (France)
Coco (Nicaragua)
Dart (England)
Drin (Albania)
Ebbw (Wales)
Ebro (Spain)
Eden (England)
Eems (Germany)
Elbe (Czech Republic/Germany)
Enns (Austria)
Eure (France)
Gail (Austria)
Gers (France)
Gurk (Austria)
Hong (Vietnam)
Ibar (Serbia/Montenegro)
Kamp (Austria)
Kemi (Finland)
Krka (Croatia)
Kupa (Croatia)
Kymi (Finland)
Labe (Czech Republic/Germany)
Lahn (Germany)
Lech (Austria/Germany)
Leie (France/Belgium)
Lena (Russia)
Lima (Spain/Portugal)
Lule (Sweden)
Lune (England)
Maas (France/Belgium/The Netherlands)
Main (Germany)
Mino (Spain/Portugal)
Mira (Portugal)
Mole (England)
Mono (Togo)
Mürz (Austria)
Naab (Germany)
Nams (Norway)
Napa (USA)
Nene (England)
Nile (Uganda/Sudan/Egypt)
Nith (Scotland)
Oder (Czech Republic/Poland/Germany)

Odra (Czech Republic/Poland/Germany)
Ohio (USA)
Oise (Belgium/France)
Omme (Denmark)
Orne (France)
Oste (Germany)
Otra (Norway)
Ouse (England)
Oxus (Afghanistan/Turkmenistan/
  Uzbekistan)
Ping (Thailand)
Prut (Romania)
Raab (Hungary)
Rába (Hungary)
Ramu (Papua New Guinea)
Ravi (Pakistan)
Reno (Italy)
Ruhr (Germany)
Saar (France/Germany)
Sado (Portugal)
Sava (Slovakia/Croatia/Bosnia and
  Herzegovina/Serbia)
Save (Slovakia/Croatia/Bosnia and
  Herzegovina/Serbia)
Soar (England)
Spey (Scotland)
Sûre (Belgium/Luxembourg)
Svir (Russia)
Swan (Australia)
Taff (Wales)
Tajo (Spain/Portugal)
Tana (Kenya; Norway)
Tano (Ghana)
Tarn (France)
Taro (Italy)
Tees (England)
Tejo (Spain/Portugal)
Teme (Wales/England)
Test (England)
Towy (Wales)
Tyne (England)
Tywi (Wales)
Ulúa (Honduras)
Ural (Russia/Kazakhstan)
Vaal (South Africa)
Waal (The Netherlands)
Yaik (Russia/Kazakhstan)
Yalu (North Korea)
Yare (England)
Ybbs (Austria)

05 Adige (Italy)
Adour (France)
Aguán (Honduras)
Aisne (France)
Aldan (Russia)
Arges (Romania)
Argun (China/Russia)
Benue (Cameroon/Nigeria)

Black (Canada; USA)
Boyne (Ireland)
Cauca (Colombia)
Chari (Chad)
Clerf (Belgium/Luxembourg)
Clwyd (Wales)
Clyde (Scotland)
Congo (Zambia/Democratic Republic of the
  Congo)
Conwy (Wales)
Demer (Belgium)
Desna (Ukraine)
Dnepr (Russia/Ukraine)
Donau (Germany/Austria/Slovakia/Hungary/
  Croatia/Serbia/Bulgaria/Romania/Moldova)
Doubs (France)
Douro (Spain)
Drina (Bosnia and Herzegovina/Serbia)
Drôme (France)
Duero (Spain)
Eider (Germany)
Fleet (England)
Forth (Scotland)
Fulda (Germany)
Ganga (India)
Genil (Spain)
Glåma (Norway)
Gogra (China/Nepal/India)
Harut (Afghanistan)
Hugli (India)
Hunte (Germany)
Indre (France)
Indus (Pakistan)
Isère (France)
Ishim (Kazakhstan/Russia)
Iskur (Bulgaria)
Jalon (Spain)
Júcar (Spain)
Jumna (India)
Kalix (Sweden)
Körös (Hungary)
Kuban (Russia)
Lågen (Norway)
Lajta (Austria/Hungary)
Leine (Germany)
Lempa (Guatemala/El Salvador)
Liard (Canada)
Loing (France)
Loire (France)
Manas (China/Bhutan/India)
March (Serbia)
Marne (France)
Memel (Belarus/Lithuania)
Meric (Bulgaria/Greece/Turkey)
Meuse (France/Belgium/The Netherlands)
Minho (Spain/Portugal)
Mosel (France/Luxembourg/Germany)
Mulde (Germany)

Mures (Romania/Hungary)
Narew (Poland)
Negro (Argentina)
Neman (Belarus/Lithuania)
Newry (Northern Ireland)
Niger (Guinea/Mali/Niger/Nigeria)
Notec (Poland)
Onega (Russia)
Ouémé (Benin)
Ounas (Finland)
Peace (Canada)
Pearl (China)
Pecos (USA)
Perak (Malaysia)
Piave (Italy)
Plata (Argentina)
Plate (Uruguay/Argentina)
Purus (Peru/Brazil)
Rhein (Switzerland/France/Germany/The
  Netherlands)
Rhine (Switzerland/France/Germany/The
  Netherlands)
Rhône (Switzerland/France)
Rille (France)
Risle (France)
Saale (Germany)
Sabor (Portugal)
Saône (France)
Sarre (France/Germany)
Sauer (Belgium/Luxembourg)
Segre (France/Spain)
Seine (France)
Siret (Romania)
Snake (USA)
Somes (Romania)
Somme (France)
Spree (Germany)
Stour (England)
Stura (Italy)
Tagus (Spain/Portugal)
Tamar (England)
Teifi (Wales)
Thame (England)
Tiber (Italy)
Tirso (Italy)
Tisza (Hungary)
Tobol (Kazakhstan/Russia)
Traun (Austria)
Trave (Germany)
Trent (England)
Tumen (North Korea)
Turia (Spain)
Tweed (Scotland/England)
Varde (Denmark)
Volga (Russia)
Volta (Ghana)
Vouga (Portugal)
Vrbas (Bosnia and Herzegovina)

Warta (Poland)
Werra (Germany)
Weser (Germany)
Wisla (Poland)
Woleu (Gabon/Equatorial Guinea)
Xingu (Brazil)
Yonne (France)
Yukon (Canada)
Zújar (Spain)

06 Alfiós (Greece)
Allier (France)
Amazon (Peru/Brazil)
Angara (Russia)
Ariège (France)
Barrow (Ireland)
Belize (Guatemala/Belize)
Bénoué (Cameroon/Nigeria)
Brazos (USA)
Calder (England)
Chenab (India/Pakistan)
Clerve (Belgium/Luxembourg)
Clutha (New Zealand)
Coquet (England)
Creuse (France)
Danube (Germany/Austria/Slovakia/
  Hungary/Croatia/Serbia/Bulgaria/Romania/
  Moldova)
Dender (Belgium)
Dendre (Belgium)
Devoll (Albania)
Dnestr (Ukraine/Moldova)
Donets (Ukraine/Russia)
Escaut (France/Belgium/The Netherlands)
Fraser (Canada)
Gambia (Guinea/Senegal/The Gambia)
Gambie (The Gambia)
Gandak (Nepal/India)
Ganges (India)
Glomma (Norway)
Grande (Nicaragua)
Guayas (Ecuador)
Gudenå (Denmark)
Hevros (Bulgaria/Greece/Turkey)
Hudson (USA)
Humber (England)
Iijoki (Finland)
Ijoälv (Finland)
Irtysh (China/Kazakhstan/Russia)
Jantra (Bulgaria)
Jhelum (India/Pakistan)
Jordan (Syria/Israel/Jordan)
Kennet (England)
Khabur (Turkey/Syria)
Kistna (India)
Kolyma (Russia)
Lavant (Austria)
Leitha (Austria/Hungary)
Liffey (Ireland)

Litani (Lebanon)
Ljusna (Sweden)
Logone (Chad)
Marica (Bulgaria/Greece/Turkey)
Medway (England)
Mekong (China/Myanmar/Thailand/Laos/
  Cambodia/Vietnam)
Mcping (Thailand)
Mersey (England)
Moldau (Czech Republic)
Morava (Serbia)
Murray (Australia)
Mystic (USA)
Namsen (Norway)
Neckar (Germany)
Nelson (Canada)
Nidelv (Norway)
Ogooué (Congo/Gabon)
Olenëk (Russia)
Orange (Lesotho/South Africa/Namibia)
Ottawa (Canada)
Ourthe (Belgium)
Pahang (Malaysia)
Paraná (Brazil/Paraguay/Argentina)
Patuca (Honduras)
Piniós (Greece)
Pripet (Ukraine/Belarus)
Rajang (Malaysia)
Ribble (England)
Rideau (Canada)
Rovuma (Tanzania/Mozambique)
Rudall (Australia)
Ruvuma (Tanzania/Mozambique)
Salado (Argentina)
Sambre (France)
Sanaga (Cameroon)
Sarthe (France)
Sárviz (Hungary)
Segura (Spain)
Severn (England)
Seyhan (Turkey)
Struma (Bulgaria)
Sutlej (Pakistan)
Taieri (New Zealand)
Tâmega (Portugal)
Tevere (Italy)
Thames (England)
Tigris (Turkey/Iraq)
Tornio (Sweden)
Ubangi (Democratic Republic of the Congo/
  Central African Republic)
Vienne (France)
Vijosa (Albania)
Vijosë (Albania)
Vltava (Czech Republic)
Vyatka (Russia)
Wabash (USA)
Warthe (Poland)

Wharfe (England)
Wieprz (Poland)
Witham (England)
Yakima (USA)
Yamuna (India)
Yantra (Bulgaria)
Yellow (China)
Zezere (Portugal)
Zhayyq (Russia/Kazakhstan)

07 Alpheus (Greece)
Alzette (Luxembourg)
Ardèche (France)
Aveyron (France)
Biferno (Italy)
Cabriel (Spain)
Caledon (Lesotho/South Africa)
Charles (USA)
Cubango (Angola/Namibia/Botswana)
Darling (Australia)
Derwent (England)
Dnieper (Russia/Ukraine)
Dniestr (Ukraine/Moldova)
Drammen (Norway)
Durance (France)
Garonne (France)
Glommen (Norway)
Guayape (Honduras)
Hangang (South Korea)
Helmand (Afghanistan)
Hérault (France)
Hooghly (India)
Huang He (China)
Huang Ho (China)
Ilmenau (Germany)
Kavengo (Angola/Namibia/Botswana)
Kemiälv (Finland)
Kilkeel (Ireland)
Krishna (India)
Lachlan (Australia)
Limpopo (South Africa/Botswana/Zimbabwe/
  Mozambique)
Ljusnan (Sweden)
Lualaba (Democratic Republic of the
  Congo)
Madeira (Brazil)
Marañón (Peru)
Maritsa (Bulgaria/Greece/Turkey)
Mataura (New Zealand)
Mayenne (France)
Meurthe (France)
Mondego (Portugal)
Moselle (France/Luxembourg/Germany)
Motagua (Guatemala)
Narbada (India)
Narmada (India)
Neretva (Bosnia and Herzegovina)
Niagara (USA/Canada)
Nu Jiang (China/Myanmar)

Orinoco (Venezuela)
Orontes (Lebanon/Syria/Turkey)
Parrett (England)
Passaic (USA)
Pechora (Russia)
Potomac (USA)
Pripyat (Ukraine/Belarus)
Rabnitz (Austria)
Sakarya (Turkey)
Salween (China/Myanmar)
Salzach (Austria)
San Juan (Nicaragua)
Schelde (France/Belgium/The Netherlands)
Scheldt (France/Belgium/The Netherlands)
Segovia (Nicaragua)
Selenga (Mongolia)
Selenge (Mongolia)
Sénégal (Guinea/Mali/Senegal)
Shannon (Ireland)
Sittang (Myanmar)
Sorraia (Portugal)
Staaten (Australia)
Strimon (Bulgaria)
Sukhona (Russia)
Tapajós (Brazil)
Tarim He (China)
Thiamis (Greece)
Traisen (Austria)
Ucayali (Peru)
Uruguay (Brazil/Argentina/Uruguay)
Vilaine (France)
Vistula (Poland)
Voiussa (Albania)
Waikato (New Zealand)
Waveney (England)
Welland (England)
Yangtze (China)
Yenisei (Russia)
Yenisey (Russia)
Zambesi (Zambia/Angola/Botswana/
  Zimbabwe/Mozambique)
Zambezi (Zambia/Angola/Botswana/
  Zimbabwe/Mozambique)

08 Abay Wenz (Sudan)
Achelous (Greece)
Akhelóös (Greece)
Aliákmon (Greece)
Altaelva (Norway)
Amazonas (Peru/Brazil)
Amudar'ya (Afghanistan/Turkmenistan/
  Uzbekistan)
Amu Darya (Afghanistan/Turkmenistan/
  Uzbekistan)
Angerman (Sweden)
Araguaia (Brazil)
Arkansas (USA)
Berounka (Czech Republic)
Blue Nile (Sudan)

Brisbane (Australia)
Canadian (USA)
Charente (France)
Chu-Kiang (China)
Clarence (Australia; New Zealand)
Colorado (USA)
Columbia (Canada/USA)
Cuyahoga (USA)
Dalälven (Sweden)
Delaware (USA)
Dniester (Ukraine/Moldova)
Dordogne (France)
Drysdale (Australia)
Ghaghara (China/Nepal/India)
Godavari (India)
Godaveri (India)
Guadiana (Spain/Portugal)
Ialomiţa (Romania)
Kemijoki (Finland)
Kymijoki (Finland)
Mahanadi (India)
Mahaveli (Sri Lanka)
Mahaweli (Sri Lanka)
Mazaruni (Guyana)
Missouri (USA)
Okavango (Angola/Namibia/Botswana)
Orhon Gol (Mongolia)
Paraguay (Brazil/Paraguay/Argentina)
Parnaíba (Brazil)
Pisuerga (Spain)
Polochic (Guatemala)
Río Bravo (USA)
Río Negro (Argentina)
Santa Ana (USA)
Shkumbin (Albania)
Solimões (Peru/Brazil)
Syr Darya (Uzbekistan/Tajikistan/
  Kazakhstan)
Tunguska (Russia)
Vychegda (Russia)
Wanganui (New Zealand)
Zhu Jiang (China)

09 Almanzora (Spain)
Athabasca (Canada)
Churchill (Canada)
Crocodile (South Africa/Botswana/
  Zimbabwe/Mozambique)
Dangme Chu (China/Bhutan/India)
Essequibo (Guyana)
Euphrates (Turkey/Syria/Iraq)
Great Ouse (England)
Indigirka (Russia)
Irrawaddy (Myanmar)
Katherine (Australia)
Kuskokwim (USA)
Mackenzie (Canada)
Magdalena (Colombia)
Nahr el Asi (Lebanon/Syria/Turkey)

Ounasjoki (Finland)
Río Balsas (Mexico)
Rio Grande (USA)
Río Paraná (Brazil/Paraguay/Argentina)
San Carlos (Costa Rica)
Schwechat (Austria)
St Laurent (Canada)
Tennessee (USA)
Tocantins (Brazil)
Vistritsa (Greece)
White Nile (Ethiopia)
Yuan Jiang (Vietnam)

10 Albert Nile (Uganda)
Alto Paraná (Brazil/Paraguay/Argentina)
Chang Jiang (China)
Chao Phraya (Thailand)
Chateaugay (USA/Canada)
Des Plaines (USA)
Hackensack (USA)
Kizil Irmak (Turkey)
Little Ouse (England)
Rangitikei (New Zealand)
Río Uruguay (Brazil/Argentina/Uruguay)
Sacramento (USA)
San Antonio (USA)
San Joaquin (USA)
Santa Maria (USA)
Shenandoah (USA)
St Lawrence (Canada)
Usumacinta (Guatemala/Mexico)
Walla Walla (USA)

11 Assiniboine (Canada)
Bahr el Ablad (Ethiopia)
Bahr el Azraq (Sudan)
Brahmaputra (China/India/Bangladesh)
Châteauguay (USA/Canada)
Mississippi (USA)
Nyamyang Chu (China/Bhutan/India)
Río Paraguay (Paraguay)
Shatt al-Arab (Iraq)
Yellowknife (Canada)

12 Guadalquivir (Spain)
Heilong Jiang (China/Russia)
Kinabatangan (Malaysia)
Murrumbidgee (Australia)
Oranjerivier (Lesotho/South Africa/Namibia)
Río de la Plata (Uruguay/Argentina)
São Francisco (Brazil)
Saskatchewan (Canada)
Victoria Nile (Uganda)
Western Dvina (Russia/Belarus/Latvia)

13 Ångermanälven (Sweden)
Langcang Jiang (China/Myanmar/Thailand/
  Laos/Cambodia/Vietnam)
Lower Tunguska (Russia)
Mahaveli Ganga (Sri Lanka)
Mahaweli Ganga (Sri Lanka)

Northern Dvina (Russia)
Río Usumacinta (Guatemala/Mexico)

14 Northern Donets (Ukraine/Russia)
Río de las Balsas (Mexico)

Severnaya Dvina (Russia)
Zapadnaya Dvina (Russia/Belarus/Latvia)

15 Dramsvassdraget (Norway)
Severskiy Donets (Ukraine/Russia)

road

Road types include:

01 A
B
C
E

03 way

04 drag
high
lane
mews
pass
ring
side
slip
toll

05 alley
byway
close
gated
Roman
route
strip
track
trunk

06 avenue
bypass
parade
rat run
relief

strand
street
subway

07 beltway
dead end
flyover
freeway
highway
off ramp
parkway
private
through

08 alleyway
autobahn
causeway
clearway
crescent
cul-de-sac
metalled
motorway
overpass
red route
short cut
speedway
trackway
turnpike

09 autoroute
boulevard

bridleway
cart track
dirt track
esplanade
green lane
promenade
unadopted
underpass

10 autostrada
bridlepath
cloverleaf
expressway
interstate
unmetalled

11 gravel track
scenic route
single track

12 holiday route
mountain pass
superhighway
thoroughfare
unclassified

14 divided highway
gyratory system

15 dual carriageway
elevated section
European highway

Roads include:

02 A1 (England/Scotland)
M1 (England)
M2 (England)
M3 (England)
M4 (England/Wales)
M5 (England)
M6 (England)
M8 (Scotland)
M9 (Scotland)

03 M25 (England)
M40 (England)
M62 (England)

06 Big Dig (USA)

07 Route 66 (USA)
Westway (England)

08 Fern Pass (Austria)

Fosse Way (England)
Highway 1 (Australia/USA)
Silk Road (Italy–China)

09 Appian Way (Italy)
Burma Road (China/Myanmar)
Furka Pass (Switzerland)
Highway 61 (USA)
Snake Pass (England)

10 Cassian Way (Italy)
Dere Street (England/Scotland)
Flexen Pass (Austria)
Flüela Pass (Switzerland)
Gioffo Pass (Italy)
Hanger Lane (England)
Highway 401 (Canada)
Highway 407 (Canada)
Jaufen Pass (Italy)

Julier Pass (Switzerland)
Khyber Pass (Pakistan/Afghanistan)
Maloja Pass (Switzerland)
Mendel Pass (Italy)
Spluga Pass (Switzerland/Italy)
Susten Pass (Switzerland)

11 Aemilian Way (Italy)
Arlberg Pass (Austria)
Aurelian Way (Italy)
Bealach Na Ba (Scotland)
Bernina Pass (Italy/Switzerland)
Brenner Pass (Austria/Italy)
Gardena Pass (Italy)
Grimsel Pass (Switzerland)
Hume Highway (Australia)
Icknield Way (England)
Klausen Pass (Switzerland)
Mendola Pass (Italy)
Oberalp Pass (Switzerland)
Old Post Road (USA)
Oregon Trail (USA)
Salarian Way (Italy)
Simplon Pass (Switzerland/Italy)
Splügen Pass (Switzerland/Italy)
Stane Street (England)
Stelvio Pass (Italy)

12 Akeman Street (England)
Alcan Highway (Canada/USA)
Cat and Fiddle (England)
Dixie Highway (USA)
El Camino Real (USA/Mexico)
Ermine Street (England)
Flaminian Way (Italy)
King's Highway (Arabia–Mediterranean)
King's Highway (USA)
Maloggia Pass (Switzerland)
National Road (USA)

Périphérique (France)
Santa Fe Trail (USA)
Sempione Pass (Switzerland/Italy)
Sturt Highway (Australia)
Tre Croci Pass (Italy)

13 Alaska Highway (Canada/USA)
Cairnwell Pass (Scotland)
Cumberland Gap (USA)
Great West Road (England)
Lancaster Road (USA)
Mont Cenis Pass (France/Italy)
North Circular (England)
Pass of Glen Coe (Scotland)
South Circular (England)
Stuart Highway (Australia)
Uspallata Pass (Argentina/Chile)
Watling Street (England)

14 Boston Post Road (USA)
Capital Beltway (USA)
Cumberland Road (USA)
Eastern Parkway (USA)
Grand Trunk Road (India/Pakistan)
Great Ocean Road (Australia)
Great River Road (USA)
Le Périphérique (France)
Lincoln Highway (USA)
Merritt Parkway (USA)
Moncenisio Pass (France/Italy)
Pacific Highway (Australia)
St Gotthard Pass (Italy/Switzerland)
Tauernhöhe Pass (Austria)
Wilderness Road (USA)
Zirlerberg Pass (Austria)

15 Great Valley Road (USA)
Grödner Joch Pass (Italy)
Magic Roundabout (England)
Overseas Highway (USA)

See also **London**; **motoring**; **New York**; **Paris**

road sign *see* **motoring**

robber *see* **thief**

Robin Hood *see* **legend**

rock

Rocks include:		
02 aa	**05** chalk	**06** basalt
03 ore	chert	gabbro
04 coal	flint	gneiss
lava	shale	gravel
marl	slate	marble

schist
07 breccia
granite
08 dolerite
hornfels

obsidian
porphyry
09 greywacke
limestone
sandstone

10 greenstone
serpentine
11 pumice stone
12 conglomerate

Terms to do with rocks include:

05 basic
darcy
fault
07 clastic
igneous
outcrop

08 dioritic
09 schistose
siliceous
silicious
10 arenaceous
calcareous

concretion
gabbroitic
miarolitic
stratified
11 cataclastic
metamorphic

pyroclastic
sedimentary
12 argillaceous
carbonaceous
conglomerate
13 argentiferous

See also **geology; pop**

rodent

Rodents include:

03 rat
04 cavy
cony
hare
pika
vole
05 aguti
coney
coypu
mouse
06 agouti
beaver
ferret
gerbil
gopher
hog-rat
jerboa
marmot

rabbit
07 cane rat
hamster
lemming
meerkat
muskrat
ondatra
potoroo
08 black rat
brown rat
capybara
chipmunk
dormouse
hampster
hedgehog
musquash
sewer rat
squirrel
tucutuco

viscacha
water rat
09 bandicoot
groundhog
guinea pig
porcupine
water vole
woodchuck
10 chinchilla
fieldmouse
prairie dog
springhaas
springhase
11 kangaroo rat
red squirrel
spermophile
12 grey squirrel
harvest mouse

See also **rabbit**

roll *see* **bread**

Roman numeral *see* **numeral**

Romania *see* **Balkans**

Rome

The seven hills of Rome:

07 Caelian
Viminal
08 Aventine

Palatine
Quirinal
09 Esquiline

10 Capitoline

Roman emperors, with regnal dates:

03 Leo (I; AD457–74)
Leo (II; AD474)

04 Geta (AD209–12)
Nero (AD54–68)
Otho (AD69)
Zeno (AD474–91)

05 Carus (AD282–83)
Gaius (AD12–41)
Galba (AD68–69)
Nerva (AD96–98)
Titus (AD79–81)

06 Avitus (AD455–56)
Decius (AD249–51)
Gallus (AD251–53)
Julian (AD360–63)
Philip (AD244–49)
Probus (AD276–82)
Trajan (AD98–117)
Valens (AD364–78)

07 Carinus (AD283–85)
Florian (AD276)
Gordian (I; AD238)
Gordian (II; AD238)
Gordian (III; AD238–44)
Gratian (AD375–83)
Hadrian (AD117–38)
Marcian (AD450–57)
Maximin (AD235–38)
Maximus (AD238)
Severus (AD306–07)
Tacitus (AD275–76)

08 Aemilian (AD253)
Arcadius (AD395–408)
Augustus (31 BC–AD14)
Aurelian (AD270–75)
Balbinus (AD238)
Caligula (AD37–41)
Claudius (II; AD268–69)
Commodus (AD176–92)
Constans (I; AD337–50)
Domitian (AD81–96)
Galerius (AD305–11)

Honorius (AD395–423)
Licinius (AD308–24)
Macrinus (AD217–18)
Majorian (AD457–61)
Maximian (AD286–305)
Numerian (AD283–84)
Olybrius (AD472–73)
Pertinax (AD193)
Tiberius (AD14–37)
Valerian (AD253–60)

09 Anthemius (AD467–72)
Caracalla (AD198–217)
Gallienus (AD253–68)
Hostilian (AD251)
Maxentius (AD306–12)
Procopius (AD365–66)
Vespasian (AD69–79)
Vitellius (AD69)

10 Diocletian (AD284–305)
Elagabalus (AD218–22)
Magnentius (AD350–51)
Quintillus (AD269–70)
Theodosius (I; AD379–95)
Theodosius (II; AD408–50)

11 Constantine (I; AD306–37)
Constantine (II; AD337–40)
Constantius (I; AD305–06)
Constantius (II; AD337–61)
Constantius (III; AD421–23)
Julius Nepos (AD474–80)
Lucius Verus (AD161–69)
Valentinian (I; AD364–75)
Valentinian (II; AD375–92)
Valentinian (III; AD423–55)

13 Antoninus Pius (AD138–61)
Libius Severus (AD461–67)

14 Didius Julianus (AD193)
Marcus Aurelius (AD161–80)

15 Romulus Augustus (AD475–76)

16 Alexander Severus (AD222–35)
Petronius Maximus (AD455)
Septemius Severus (AD193–211)

Roman kings:

07 Romulus (753–715 BC)
12 Ancus Marcius (642–616 BC)
13 Numa Pompilius (715–673 BC)
14 Servius Tullius (578–534 BC)

15 Tullus Hostilius (673–642 BC)
17 Tarquinius Priscus (616–578 BC)
18 Tarquinius Superbus (534–509 BC)

Romans include:

04 Cato (Marcius Porcius, the Elder; 234–
149 BC, statesman, orator)

Cato (Marcius Porcius, the Younger;
95–46 BC, statesman, orator)

Livy (Titus Livius; 59 BC–AD17, historian)
Ovid (Publius Ovidius Naso; 43 BC–AD17, poet)

05 Lucan (Marcus Annaeus Lucanus; 39–65 AD, poet)
Pliny (Gaius Plinius Caecilius Secundus, the Elder; 62–c.113 AD, writer, orator)
Pliny (Gaius Plinius Secundus, the Elder; 23–79 AD, scholar)

06 Antony (Mark; c.83–30 BC, politician, soldier)
Brutus (Marcus Junius; c.85–42 BC, politician)
Cicero (Marcus Tullius; 106–43 BC, orator, statesman, man of letters)
Horace (Quintus Horatius Flaccus; 65–8 BC, poet, satirist)
Pilate (Pontius; d.c.36 AD, prefect of Judea and Samaria)
Pompey (Gnaeus Pompeius Magnus; 106–48 BC, soldier, politician)
Seneca (Lucius Annaeus; c.4 BC–c.65 AD, Stoic philosopher, statesman, tragedian)
Vergil (Publius Vergilius Maro; 70–19 BC, poet)
Virgil (Publius Vergilius Maro; 70–19 BC, poet)

07 Atticus (Titus Pomponius; 110–32 BC, intellectual, businessman, writer)
Cassius (Gaius Cassius Longinus; d.42 BC, conspirator)
Juvenal (Decimus Junius Juvenalis; c.55–c.140 AD, lawyer, satirist)
Martial (Marcus Valerius Martialis; c.40–104 AD, poet, epigrammatist)

Plautus (Titus Maccius; c.250–184 BC, comic dramatist)
Roscius (Quintus Roscius Gallus; c.134–62 BC, comic actor)
Tacitus (Publius Cornelius; c.55–120 AD, historian)
Terence (Publius Terentius Afer; c.195–159 BC, comic dramatist)

08 Agricola (Gnaeus Julius; c.63–12 BC, general, imperial administrator)
Catilina (Lucius Sergius 'Catiline'; c.108–62 BC, conspirator)
Catiline (c.108–62 BC, conspirator)
Catullus (Gaius Valerius; c.84–54 BC, poet)
Claudian (Claudius Claudianus; 340–410 AD, poet)
Gracchus (Tiberius Sempronius; 168–133 BC, statesman)
Lucretia (6c BC, matron, legendary rape victim)

09 Agrippina (the Elder; c.14 BC–AD33, noblewoman)
Agrippina (the Younger; 15–59 AD, empress, wife of Claudius, mother of Nero)
Lucretius (Titus Lucretius Carus; c.99–55 BC, poet, philosopher)
Spartacus (d.71 BC, gladiator, rebel)
Suetonius (Gaius Suetonius Tranquillus; c.69–140 AD, biographer, antiquary)

10 Coriolanus (Gaius; 5c BC, folk hero)
Quintilian (Marcus Fabius Quintilianus; c.35–c.100 AD, rhetorician)

14 Marcus Antonius (c.83–30 BC, politician, soldier)

See also **mythology**; **play**; **poetry**; **satire**; **Virgil**

roof

Roofs include:

03 hip	**05** gable	monitor	**10** imbricated
04 bell	**06** cupola	pitched	saucer dome
dome	French	**08** imperial	**12** geodesic dome
flat	lean-to	pavilion	sloped turret
helm	saddle	sawtooth	**13** conical broach
ogee	**07** gambrel	thatched	**14** gable-and-valley
span	mansard	**09** onion dome	pendentive dome

room

Rooms include:

02 WC	loo	hall	tack
03 bed	**04** ante	loft	wash
box	bath	play	work
day	cell	rest	**05** attic
den	dark	sick	board

cabin
class
cloak
court
foyer
front
games
green
guard
guest
lobby
music
porch
salon
spare
staff
state
stock
store
study
06 cellar

common
dining
engine
family
larder
living
locker
lounge
lumber
office
pantry
rumpus
saddle
strong
studio
toilet
07 boudoir
buttery
chamber
control
cubicle

drawing
en suite
fitting
kitchen
landing
laundry
lecture
library
meeting
morning
nursery
parlour
reading
seminar
sitting
smoking
utility
waiting
08 assembly
basement
chambers

changing
dressing
lavatory
scullery
workshop

09 breakfast
dormitory
mezzanine
reception
sun lounge

10 consulting
laboratory
recreation

11 kitchenette
lounge-diner

12 conservatory
kitchen-diner

15 en suite bathroom

rope

Ropes include:

03 guy
tow
04 cord
drag
head
line
stay
tack
vang
warp
05 brace

cable
lasso
noose
sheet
widdy
06 bridle
halter
hawser
hobble
lariat
runner
strand

string
tackle
tether
07 bobstay
bowline
cordage
cringle
halyard
lanyard
lashing
marline
mooring

outhaul
painter
ratline
08 buntline
clew-line
dockline
downhaul
dragline
gantline
09 hackamore

Rossini, Gioacchino (1792–1868)

Significant works include:

06 *Armida* (1817)
Otello (1816)

07 *Ermione* (1819)
Zelmira (1822)

08 *Count Ory* (1828)
Tancredi (1813)

09 *La gazetta* (1816)

10 *Le Comte Ory* (1828)
Semiramide (1823)
Sigismondo (1814)

11 *Stabat Mater* (1842)
William Tell (1829)

12 *La gazza ladra* (1817)
Mosè in Egitto (1818)

Moses in Egypt (1818)
Sins of Old Age (1863)

13 *Guillaume Tell* (1829)
La Cenerentola (1817)
La scala di seta (1812)

14 *La donna del Iago* (1819)
L'inganno felice (1812)
Matilde Shabran (1821)
Moïse et Pharaon (1827)
The Turk in Italy (1814)

15 *Bianca e Falliero* (1819)
Ciro in Babilonia (1812)
Il turco in Italia (1814)
Il viaggio a Reims (1825)
Maometto secondo (1820)

The Silken Ladder (1812)

16 Demetrio e Polibio (1812)
Eduardo e Cristinà (1819)

17 Il Signor Bruschino (1813)
Le Siège de Corinthe (1826)
L'italiana in Algeri (1813)
Ricciardo e Zoraide (1818)
The Thieving Magpie (1817)
Torvaldo e Dorliska (1815)

18 Adelaide di Borgogna (1817)
Aureliano in Palmira (1813)
Péchés de vieillesse (1863)

The Barber of Seville (1816)

19 La pietra del paragone (1812)
L'Occasione fa il Iadro (1812)

20 Il barbiere di Siviglia (1816)
L'equivoco stravagante (1811)

21 Petite Messe Solennelle (1863)

22 La cambiale di matrimonio (1810)

23 Adina, o Il califfo di Bagdad (1818)
The Italian Girl in Algiers (1813)

26 Otello, ossia Il Moro di Venezia (1816)

28 Elisabetta Regina d'Inghilterra (1815)

Round Table *see* legend

rowing

Rowers include:

04 Reed (Peter; 1981– , English)
05 Tufte (Olaf; 1976– , Norway)
06 Foster (Tim; 1970– , English)
Ivanov (Vyacheslav; 1938– , Russian)
07 Pinsent (Sir Matthew; 1970– , English)
Waddell (Rob; 1975– , New Zealand)

08 Nickalls (Guy; 1866–1935, English)
Redgrave (Sir Steve; 1962– , English)
Ridgeway (John; 1938– , English)
09 Beresford (Jack; 1899–1977, English)
Cracknell (James; 1972– , English)
Karpinnen (Pertti; 1953– , Finnish)

Rowing terms include:

03 bow
cox
rig
04 crew
easy
four
gate
keel
loom
pair
quad
rate
skeg
span
wash
05 blade
catch

coxed
drive
eight
pitch
scull
shell
stern
06 boatie
button
canvas
collar
finish
gunnel
length
puddle
rating
rigger

skying
stroke
07 bowside
coxless
give way
gunwale
regatta
row over
sculler
08 coxswain
paddling
recovery
rowlocks
09 ergometer
head races
outrigger

repechage
slide seat
stretcher
10 catch a crab
feathering
pivot point
strokeside
11 double scull
single scull
the Boat Race
toss the oars
12 missing water
shortening up
13 getting spoons
15 jumping the slide

Rowling, J K (1965–)

Significant works include:

23 Quidditch Through the Ages (2001)
The Tales of Beedle the Bard (2008)
29 Harry Potter and the Goblet of Fire (2000)
31 Harry Potter and the Deathly Hallows
(2007)

Harry Potter and the Sorcerer's Stone
(1998)
32 Harry Potter and the Half-Blood Prince (2005)
33 Fantastic Beasts and Where to Find Them
(2001)

Harry Potter and the Chamber of Secrets
(1998)

34 *Harry Potter and the Order of the Phoenix*
(2003)

Harry Potter and the Philosopher's Stone
(1997)

Harry Potter and the Prisoner of Azkaban
(1999)

Significant characters include:

05 Black (Sirius)
Snape (Professor Severus)

06 Hagrid (Rubeus)
Malfoy (Draco)
Potter (Harry)

07 Granger (Hermione)
Weasley (Fred)
Weasley (George)

Weasley (Ginny)
Weasley (Ron)

09 Voldemort (Lord)

10 Dumbledore (Professor Albus)
Longbottom (Neville)
McGonagall (Professor Minerva)

11 Crookshanks
Death Eaters

rubber

Rubber types and trees include:

03 ule

04 buna
cold
foam
hard
hule
pará
root

05 butyl
crêpe
hevea
India
Lagos
sorbo

06 Panama
sponge

07 ebonite
guayule
seringa

08 castilla
Funtumia
neoprene
Silastic®

09 camelback

vulcanite

10 caoutchouc
gum elastic
mangabeira

14 high-hysteresis

rug *see* **carpet**

Rugby League

Rugby League teams and nicknames:

04 Eels (Parramatta)
Reds (Salford City)

05 Bears (Coventry; North
Sydney)
Bulls (Bradford)
Kiwis (New Zealand)
Lions (Great Britain)
Quins (Greater London)
Storm (Melbourne)

06 Eagles (Sheffield)
Giants (Huddersfield)
Hull FC
Kumuls (Papua New
Guinea)
Rhinos (Leeds)
Sharks (Cronulla-
Sutherland)
Tigers (Castleford; Wests)

Wolves (Warrington)

07 Blue Sox (Halifax)
Broncos (Brisbane)
Cowboys (North
Queensland)
Dragons (Catalans; St
George Illawarra)
Knights (Newcastle)
Raiders (Canberra)

08 Bulldogs (Batley)
Panthers (Penrith)
Roosters (Sydney)
Warriors (Wigan)
Wildcats (Wakefield)

09 Kangaroos (Australia)
Rabbitohs (South Sydney)
Tomahawks (USA)

10 Harlequins (Greater
London)
Lionhearts (England)

11 Bravehearts (Scotland)
Leeds Rhinos
St Helens RFC

13 Bradford Bulls
Widnes Vikings
Wigan Warriors

15 Irish Wolfhounds (Boston)
Leigh Centurions
Les Chanticleers (France)
Salford City Reds

16 Warrington Wolves

18 Huddersfield Giants

24 Wakefield Trinity Wildcats

Rugby League players and associated figures include:

03 Fox (Neil; 1939– , English)

04 Roby (James; 1985– , English)

05 Bevan (Brian; 1924–91, Australian/British)

06 Boston (Billy; 1934– , Welsh)
   Hanley (Ellery; 1961– , English)
   Murphy (Alex; 1939– , English)
   Offiah (Martin; 1966– , English)

07 Edwards (Shaun; 1966– , English)
   Farrell (Andy; 1975– , English)
   Gregory (Andy; 1961– , English)
   Meninga (Mal; 1960– , Australian)
   Wellens (Paul; 1980– , English)

08 Millward (Roger; 1948– , English)
   Sullivan (Jim; 1903–77, Welsh)

Rugby League terms include:

03 try

04 back
   feed
   lock
   pack
   prop
   punt
   Test

05 dummy
   put-in
   scrum

06 centre
   hooker
   in-goal
   sin-bin
   tackle
   winger

07 dropout
   forward
   hand-off
   knock on
   offload

offside
penalty
try line

08 40/20 rule
   blood bin
   drop goal
   free-kick
   front row
   full back
   gain line
   goal line
   halfback
   handover
   open side
   scissors
   sidestep
   stand-off
   turnover

09 advantage
   blind side
   dummy half
   field goal

place kick
scrum half

10 charge down
   conversion
   five-eighth
   penalty try
   up and under
   yellow card
   zero tackle

11 forward pass
   grubber kick
   play-the-ball
   sixth tackle
   touch-in-goal

12 dead-ball line
   loose forward
   three-quarter
   video referee

13 loose-head prop

14 acting halfback

15 twenty-metre line

See also **sport**

Rugby Union

Rugby Union teams and nicknames:

04 Oaks (Romania)
   Reds (Queensland)

05 Lelos (Georgia)
   Lions (British; Irish)
   Pumas (Argentina)
   Wasps (London)

06 Eagles (USA)

07 Canucks (Canada)
   Dragons (Gwent)

08 Brumbies (Canberra)

Les Bleus (France)
Los Teros (Uruguay)
Saracens (Watford)
Waratahs (New South
   Wales)

09 All Blacks (New Zealand)
   Bath Rugby
   Wallabies (Australia)

10 Gli Azzurri (Italy)
   Gloucester
   Harlequins (Greater London)

Leeds Tykes
Sale Sharks
Springboks (South Africa)

11 London Irish

13 Brave Blossoms (Japan)

14 Cherry Blossoms (Japan)

15 Leicester Tigers

16 Newcastle Falcons

17 Northampton Saints
   Worcester Warriors

Rugby Union players and associated figures include:

04 Hare (Dusty; 1952– , English)
   Hill (Richard; 1973– , English)

John (Barry; 1945– , Welsh)
Lomu (Jonah; 1975– , New Zealand)

Sole (David; 1962– , Scottish)
Wood (Keith; 1972– , Irish)

05 Batty (Grant; 1951– , New Zealand)
Botha (Naas; 1958– , South African)
Meads (Colin; 1936– , New Zealand)
Price (Graham; 1951– , Welsh)
Rives (Jean-Pierre; 1952– , French)
Sella (Philippe; 1962– , French)

06 Andrew (Rob; 1963– , English)
Blanco (Serge; 1958– , Venezuelan/French)
Brooke (Zinzan; 1965– , New Zealand)
Calder (Finlay; 1957– , Scottish)
Cotton (Fran; 1947– , English)
Craven (Danie; 1910–93, South African)
Davies (Jonathan; 1962– , Welsh)
Gibson (Mike; 1947– , Northern Irish)
Gregan (George; 1973– , Australian)
Irvine (Andy; 1951– , Scottish)
Kirwan (John; 1964– , New Zealand)
Lynagh (Michael; 1963– , Australian)

07 Bennett (Phil; 1948– , Welsh)
Campese (David; 1962– , Australian)
Carling (Will; 1965– , English)
Duckham (David; 1946– , English)
Edwards (Gareth; 1947– , Welsh)

Guscott (Jeremy; 1965– , English)
Jeffrey (John; 1959– , Scottish)
Jenkins (Neil; 1972– , Welsh)
Johnson (Martin; 1970– , English)
McBride (Willie John; 1940– , Northern Irish)
McLaren (Bill; 1923– , Scottish)
O'Reilly (Tony; 1936– , Irish)
Pienaar (François; 1967– , South African)
Tindall (Michael; 1978– , English)
Vickery (Philip; 1976– , English)

08 Beaumont (Bill; 1952– , English)
Hastings (Gavin; 1962– , Scottish)
Richards (Dean; 1963– , English)
Slattery (Fergus; 1949– , Irish)
Williams (J P R; 1949– , Welsh)
Woodward (Sir Clive; 1956– , English)

09 Dallaglio (Lawrence; 1972– , English)
Farr-Jones (Nick; 1962– , Australian)
McGeechan (Ian; 1946– , Scottish)
Underwood (Rory; 1963– , English)
Wilkinson (Jonny; 1979– , English)

10 Rutherford (John; 1955– , Scottish)

11 Fitzpatrick (Sean; 1963– , New Zealand)

12 Starmer-Smith (Nigel; 1944– , English)

Rugby Union terms include:

03 gas
tee
try

04 back
cite
feed
hack
lock
mark
maul
pack
ping
prop
ruck

05 clear
drive
dummy
girls
Lions
loose
phase
Pumas
put-in
scrum
tight
touch
wheel

06 centre

hooker
in-goal
jumper
sevens
sin-bin
tackle
uglies
winger

07 Baa-Baas
back row
binding
box kick
dropout
flanker
fly hack
fly-half
forward
hand-off
knock on
lifting
line-out
offload
offside
penalty
recycle
restart
try line

08 blood bin

collapse
crossing
drop goal
free-kick
front row
full back
gain line
goal line
halfback
handbags
miss move
open side
scissors
scrum cap
set piece
sidestep
stand-off
turnover
Twickers

09 advantage
All Blacks
back three
blind side
breakdown
crash ball
front five
garryowen
grand slam

place kick
scrum half
second row
tap tackle
third half
tight five
touchline
twenty-two
Wallabies
10 Barbarians
charge down
conversion
pack leader
penalty try
See also **sport**

Six Nations
Springboks
tap penalty
touch judge
up and under
11 Calcutta Cup
cover tackle
forward pass
grubber kick
number eight
outside half
pushover try
ten-man rugby
triple crown

up the jumper
wing forward
12 Bledisloe Cup
dead-ball line
inside centre
loose forward
three-quarter
video referee
13 dummy scissors
loose-head prop
outside centre
tight-head prop
14 against the head
15 truck and trailer

ruler

03 aga
04 czar
duce
emir
head
khan
king
lord
rani
shah
tsar
05 begum
nawab
nizam
queen
rajah
06 Caesar

caliph
consul
Führer
kaiser
leader
mikado
prince
regent
sheikh
shogun
sultan
07 czarina
emperor
empress
monarch
pharaoh
sultana
tsarina

viceroy
08 governor
maharaja
maharani
overlord
princess
suzerain
09 commander
maharajah
maharanee
potentate
president
sovereign
10 controller
11 head of state
15 governor-general

See also **Byzantine empire; despot; Egypt; empire; governor; king; monarch; politics; president; prime minister; queen; Rome**

ruminant

Ruminants include:

02 ox
03 cow
04 goat
05 camel
sheep
06 musk ox
07 giraffe
08 antelope
cavicorn
09 pronghorn

Stomachs of ruminants include:

05 bible
rumen
06 bonnet
fardel
omasum
paunch
08 abomasum
09 king's-hood
manyplies
rennet-bag
reticulum
10 psalterium

See also **antelope; cattle; sheep**

Russia

Cities and notable towns in Russia include:

04 Omsk	**09** Archangel	Vladivostok
05 Kazan	Volgograd	**12** Ekaterinburg
06 Moscow	**11** Archangelsk	St Petersburg
Moskva	Chelyabinsk	**13** Yekaterinburg
Samara	Novosibirsk	**15** Nizhniy Novgorod
08 Novgorod	Rostov-on-Don	

Russian landmarks include:

03 Don	**08** Caucasus	**12** Palace Square
04 Neva	Mt Elbrus	Summer Garden
05 Urals	**09** Gorky Park	Summer Palace
Volga	Red Square	Winter Palace
07 Kremlin	**10** Lenin's tomb	**13** Ural Mountains
Siberia	**11** Mt Narodnaya	**14** Bolshoi Theatre
Steppes	Sheremetevo	**15** Hermitage Museum

Russians include:

05 Khant	Ostyak	**08** Siberian
White	**07** Bashkir	**09** Muscovite
06 Buryat	Cossack	**10** Volga Tatar

S

sage

sailing

Hood (Samuel, Viscount; 1724–1816, English)

Hope (*Two Years Before the Mast*, 1840, R H Dana Jnr)

Hull (Isaac; 1773–1843, US)

Jake (Congo; *Manhattan Transfer*, 1925, John Dos Passos)

Jarl (*Mardi*, 1849, Herman Melville)

King (Ernest; 1878–1956, US)

Kirk (Alan; 1888–1963, US)

Riou (Vincent; 1972– , French)

Rose (Sir Alec; 1908–91, English)

Ross (Sir James; 1800–62, Scottish)

Ross (Sir John; 1777–1856, Scottish)

Sims (W S; 1858–1936, US)

Spee (Count Maximilian von; 1861–1914, German)

Taji (*Mardi*, 1849, Herman Melville)

Toby (*Typee*, 1846, Herman Melville)

Togo (1848–1934, Japanese)

Vere (Captain Edward Fairfax; *Billy Budd, Foretopman*, 1924, Herman Melville)

Vian (Sir Philip; 1894–1968, English)

05 Acton (Sir John; 1736–1811, English)

Adams (John; c.1760–1829, English)

Adams (Will; 1564–1620, English)

Anson (George, Lord; 1697–1762, English)

Blake (Richard; *Offshore*, 1979, Penelope Fitzgerald)

Blake (Robert; 1599–1657, English)

Blake (Sir Peter; 1948–2001, New Zealand)

Bligh (Captain William; 1754–c.1817, English)

Blyth (Sir Chay; 1940– , Scottish)

Broke (Sir Philip; 1776–1841, English)

Burke (Mat; *Anna Christie*, 1922, Eugene O'Neill)

Byron (John; 1723–86, English)

Cabot (John; 1425–c.1500, Italian)

Cabot (Sebastian; 1474–1557, Venetian)

Chase (Jack; *White-Jacket*, 1850, Herman Melville)

Davis (John; c.1550–1605, English)

Davys (John; c.1550–1605, English)

Drake (Sir Francis; c.1540–96, English)

Foote (Andrew H; 1806–63, US)

Greig (Sir Samuel; 1735–88, Scottish)

Hanno (5c BC, Carthaginian)

Heijn (Piet; 1578–1629, Dutch)

Honda (Toshiaki; 1744–1821, Japanese)

Jones (John Paul; 1747–92, Scottish/American)

Joyon (Francis; 1956– , French)

Keyes (Roger, Lord; 1872–1945, English)

Leigh (Amyas; *Westward Ho!*, 1855, Charles Kingsley)

Lyons (Edmund, Lord; 1790–1858, English)

Mahan (Alfred Thayer; 1840–1914, US)

Maryk (Lieutenant Steve; *The Caine Mutiny*, 1951, Herman Wouk)

Nares (Sir George; 1831–1915, Scottish)

Parry (Sir William Edward; 1790–1855, English)

Peary (Robert; 1856–1920, US)

Perry (Commodore Matthew; 1794–1858, US)

Perry (Oliver; 1785–1819, US)

Pound (Sir Dudley; 1877–1943, English)

Ready (Masterman; *Masterman Ready*, 1842, Captain Frederick Marryat)

Scott (Sir Percy, Baronet; 1853–1924, English)

Smith (Sir Sidney; 1764–1840, English)

Stark (Harold; 1880–1972, US)

Tommo (*Typee*, 1846, Herman Melville)

Tovey (John, Lord; 1885–1971, English)

Tromp (Cornelis; 1629–91, Dutch)

Tryon (Sir George; 1832–93, English)

Viaud (Julien; 1850–1923, French)

Yonai (Mitsumasa; 1880–1948, Japanese)

06 Aubrey (Jack; *Master and Commander*, 1970, Patrick O'Brian)

Baffin (William; c.1584–1622, English)

Barrow (Sir John; 1764–1848, English)

Beatty (David, Earl; 1871–1936, English)

Behaim (Martin; 1440–1507, German)

Benbow (John; 1653–1702, English)

Bering (Vitus; 1681–1741, Danish)

Bolton (Harry; *Redburn*, 1849, Herman Melville)

Cabral (Pedro Álvarez; c.1467–c.1520, Portuguese)

Castro (João de; 1500–48, Portuguese)

Cereno (Captain Benito; *The Piazza Tales*, 1856, Herman Melville)

Claret (Captain; *White-Jacket*, 1850, Herman Melville)

Colomb (Philip; 1831–99, Scottish)

Conner (Denis; 1942– , US)

Coutts (Russell; 1962– , New Zealand)

Cuttle (Captain Ned; *Dombey and Son*, 1848, Charles Dickens)

Dönitz (Karl; 1891–1980, German)

Duncan (Adam, Viscount; 1731–1804, Scottish)

du Pont (Samuel; 1803–65, US)

Elcano (Juan Sebastian del; d.1526, Basque)

Fisher (John, Lord; 1841–1920, English)

Fraser (Bruce, Lord; 1888–1981, English)

Guzman (Don; *Westward Ho!*, 1855, Charles Kingsley)

Halsey (William F, Jnr; 1884–1959, US)

Harris (Tom; *Two Years Before the Mast*, 1840, R H Dana Jnr)

Hipper (Franz von; 1863–1932, German)

Hornby (Sir Geoffrey; 1825–95, English)

Hornby (Sir Phipps; 1785–1867, English)

Hudson (Henry; c.1550–1611, English)
Hunter (John; 1737–1821, Scottish)
Keppel (Augustus, Viscount; 1725–86, English)
Keppel (Sir Henry; 1809–1904, English)
Mapple (Father; *Moby-Dick*, 1851, Herman Melville)
Monson (Sir William; 1569–1643, English)
Morgan (Mr; *The Adventures of Roderick Random*, 1748, Tobias Smollett)
Nagano (Osami; 1880–1947, Japanese)
Napier (Sir Charles; 1786–1860, Scottish)
Nelson (Horatio, Lord; 1758–1805, English)
Nimitz (Chester; 1885–1966, US)
Osborn (Sherard; 1822–75, English)
Porter (David; 1780–1843, US)
Porter (David Dixon; 1813–91, US)
Quiros (Pedro Fernandez de; 1565–1615, Portuguese)
Raeder (Erich; 1876–1960, German)
Ralegh (Sir Walter; 1552–1618, English)
Ramsay (Sir Bertram; 1883–1945, Scottish)
Random (Roderick; *The Adventures of Roderick Random*, 1748, Tobias Smollett)
Rodney (George, Lord; c.1718–1792, English)
Rogers (Woodes; c.1679–1732, English)
Ruyter (Michiel de; 1607–76, Dutch)
Scheer (Reinhard; 1863–1928, German)
Semmes (Raphael; 1809–77, US)
Shovel (Sir Cloudesley; 1650–1707, English)
Tasman (Abel; 1603–c.1659, Dutch)
Torres (Luis de; fl.1605–13, Spanish)
Tyrone (Edmund; *Long Day's Journey Into Night*, 1956, Eugene O'Neill)
Vernon (Edward; 1684–1757, English)
Wallis (Samuel; 1728–95, English)
Wilkes (Charles; 1798–1877, US)
Winter (Jan Willem de; 1750–1812, Dutch)

07 Ainslie (Ben; 1977– , English)
Apraxin (Fyodor, Count; 1671–1728, Russian)
Barents (Willem; d.1597, Dutch)
Belcher (Sir Edward; 1799–1877, English)
Borough (Steven; 1525–84, English)
Borough (William; 1536–99, English)
Bowling (Lieutenant Tom; *The Adventures of Roderick Random*, 1748, Tobias Smollett)
Cabrera (Pedro Álvarez; c.1467–c.1520, Portuguese)
Canaris (Wilhelm; 1887–1945, German)
Cartier (Jacques; 1491–1557, French)
Dampier (William; 1652–1715, English)
Decatur (Stephen; 1779–1820, US)
Estaing (Charles Hector, Comte d'; 1729–94, French)
Exmouth (Edward Pellew, Viscount; 1757–1833, English)
Fitzroy (Robert; 1805–65, English)

Francis (Clare; 1946– , English)
Freneau (Philip; 1752–1832, US)
Gambier (James, Lord; 1756–1833, English)
Gilbert (Sir Humphrey; 1537–83, English)
Harwood (Sir Henry; 1888–1959, English)
Hawkins (Sir John; 1532–95, English)
Hawkyns (Sir John; 1532–95, English)
Kanaris (Constantine; 1790–1877, Greek)
Kolchak (Aleksandr; 1874–1920, Russian)
Leggatt (*The Secret Sharer*, 1912, Joseph Conrad)
Lingard (Captain Tom; *Almayer's Folly*, 1895, Joseph Conrad)
Lord Jim (*Lord Jim*, 1900, Joseph Conrad)
Loveday (Bob; *The Trumpet Major*, 1880, Thomas Hardy)
Marryat (Captain Frederick; 1792–1848, English)
Maturin (Stephen; *Master and Commander*, 1970, Patrick O'Brian)
Moresby (John; 1830–1922, English)
Phillip (Arthur; 1738–1814, English)
Raleigh (Sir Walter; 1552–1618, English)
Redburn (Wellingborough; *Redburn*, 1849, Herman Melville)
Selkirk (Alexander; 1676–1721, Scottish)
Sturdee (Sir F C Doveton, Baronet; 1859–1925, English)
Weddell (James; 1787–1834, English)
Zheng He (1371–1433, Chinese)

08 Alcester (Beauchamp Seymour, Lord; 1821–95, English)
Apraksin (Fyodor, Count; 1671–1728, Russian)
Beaufort (Sir Francis; 1774–1857, British)
Boscawen (Edward; 1711–61, English)
Carteret (Philip; d.1796, English)
Cochrane (Thomas, Earl of Dundonald; 1775–1860, Scottish)
Columbus (Christopher; 1451–1506, Genoese)
Cousteau (Jacques; 1910–97, French)
Dahlgren (John; 1809–70, US)
Duquesne (Abraham, Marquis of; 1610–88, French)
Elvström (Paul; 1928– , Danish)
Eriksson (Leif; fl.1000, Icelandic)
Farragut (David; 1801–70, US)
Kotzebue (Otto von; 1787–1846, Russian)
Lysander (d.395 BC, Spartan)
Magellan (Ferdinand; c.1480–1521, Portuguese)
Pitcairn (Robert; c.1745–1770, English)
Rickover (Hyman; 1900–86, Russian/US)
Sandwich (Edward Montagu, Earl of; 1625–72, English)
Saumarez (James, Lord de; 1757–1836, British)
Spruance (Raymond; 1885–1969, US)

Vespucci (Amerigo; 1451–1512, Italian/
Spanish)
Vlamingh (Willem de; fl.1690s; Dutch)
Williams (Joe; *The 42nd Parallel*, 1930, John
Dos Passos)
Yamamoto (Isoroku; 1884–1943, Japanese)

09 Beresford (Charles, Lord; 1846–1919, Irish)
Christian (Fletcher; c.1764–c.1794, English)
Duckworth (Sir John Thomas; 1748–1817,
English)
Fernández (Juan; c.1536–c.1604, Spanish)
Frobisher (Sir Martin; c.1535–94, English)
Grenville (Sir Richard; c.1541–91, English)
Hindmarsh (Sir John; c.1782–1860, English)
Hythloday (Raphael; *Utopia*, 1516, Thomas
More)
Joinville (François, Prince de; 1818–1900,
French)
Lancaster (Sir James; c.1554–1618, English)
La Pérouse (Jean François, Comte de;
1741–88, French)
MacArthur (Dame Ellen; 1977– , English)
Selacraig (Alexander; 1676–1721, Scottish)
St Vincent (John Jervis, Earl of; 1735–1823,
English)
Tourville (Anne Hilarion de Cotentin, Comte
de; 1642–1701, French)
Vancouver (George; 1757–98, English)
Verrazano (Giovanni da; c.1480–1527,
Italian)

10 Antalcidas (4c BC, Spartan)
Caracciolo (Francesco, Duca di Brienza;
1752–99, Neapolitan)
Chancellor (Richard; d.1556, English)
Chichester (Sir Francis; 1901–72, English)
Codrington (Sir Edward; 1770–1851,
English)
Codrington (Sir Henry; 1808–77, English)
Cunningham (Andrew Browne, Viscount;
1883–1963, British)
Erik the Red (10c, Norwegian)

Hatteraick (Captain Dirk; *Guy Mannering*,
1816, Sir Walter Scott)
Hornblower (Horatio; *The Happy Return*,
1937, C S Forester)
Kempenfelt (Richard; 1718–82, English)
Mountevans (Edward, Lord; 1881–1957,
English)
Poindexter (John; 1936– , US)
Shackleton (Sir Ernest; 1874–1922, Irish)
Somerville (Sir James; 1882–1949, English)
Villeneuve (Pierre de; 1763–1806, French)

11 Butterworth (Bradley; 1959– , New Zealand)
Collingwood (Cuthbert, Lord; 1750–1810,
English)
Elphinstone (George Keith, Viscount Keith;
1746–1823, Scottish)
Hobart Pasha (1822–86, English)
Mountbatten (Louis, Earl; 1900–79, English)
Mountbatten (Prince Louis; 1854–1921,
Austrian/British)
Thrasybulus (d.388 BC; Athenian)
White-Jacket (*White-Jacket*, 1850, Herman
Melville)

12 Bougainville (Louis Antoine de; 1729–1811,
French)
Knox-Johnston (Sir Robin; 1939– , English)
Nordenskjöld (Nils, Baron; 1832–1901,
Swedish)
Saint Vincent (John Jervis, Earl of; 1735–
1823, English)
Themistocles (c.523–c.458 BC, Athenian)

13 Carrero Blanco (Luis; 1903–73, Spanish)
La Bourdonnais (Bertrand François Mahé,
Comte de; 1699–1753, French)
Medina-Sidonia (Alonzo Pérez de Gusmàn,
Duque de; 1550–1619, Spanish)
Pincher Martin (*Pincher Martin*, 1956,
William Golding)

14 Dumont d'Urville (Jules; 1790–1842,
French)

Sailing terms include:

04 beat
gybe
lift
port
veer

05 abaft
fetch
lay up
lee-oh!

06 astern
leeway
upwind
yawing

07 backing
bearing
beating
bending
handing
heeling
in irons
in stays
lee helm
running
tacking

08 downwind
port tack

reaching
stepping
under way
windward

09 alongside
beam reach
knockdown
laying off
letting go
starboard
unbending

10 broad reach
casting off

close reach
fitting-out
going about
ready about!
standing on
unstepping
weathering

11 breaking out
close-hauled

See also **admiral**; **ship**

coming about
steerage way
weather helm

12 handing a sail
sail trimming
spilling wind

13 across the wind
hard on the wind
starboard tack

veer the anchor

14 bending on a sail
unbending a sail

15 fixing a position
points of sailing
sailing by the lee
sheeting in a sail
stepping the mast
taking soundings

saint

Patron saints include:

03 Ivo (lawyers)
04 Adam (gardeners)
Anne (miners)
Lucy (glassworkers/writers)
Luke (artists/butchers/doctors/glassworkers/
sculptors/surgeons)
Zita (servants)
05 Agnes (girls/virgins)
Amand (brewers/hotelkeepers)
David (Wales; poets)
James (labourers)
Louis (sculptors)
Paula (widows)
Peter (fishermen)
Vitus (actors/comedians/dancers)
06 Andrew (Scotland; fishermen)
Dismas (undertakers)
Fiacre (gardeners/taxi drivers)
George (England; soldiers)
Jerome (librarians)
Joseph (carpenters/workers)
Martha (cooks/housewives/servants/waiters)
Monica (widows)
07 Barbara (builders/miners)
Cecilia (musicians/poets/singers)
Crispin (shoemakers)
Dominic (astronomers)
Dorothy (florists)
Eligius (blacksmiths/jewellers/metalworkers)
Erasmus (sailors)
Florian (firemen)
Gabriel (messengers/postal workers/radio
workers/television workers)
Gregory (singers)
Isidore (farmers)

Leonard (prisoners)
Matthew (accountants/bookkeepers/tax
collectors)
Michael (grocers/police)
Pancras (children)
Patrick (Ireland)
08 Angelico (artists)
Genesius (actors/secretaries)
Lawrence (cooks)
Nicholas (children)
09 Apollonia (dentists)
Augustine (theologians)
Homobonus (tailors)
Honoratus (bakers)
Joan of Arc (soldiers)
John Bosco (labourers)
John of God (book trade/nurses/printers)
Sebastian (athletes/soldiers)
Wenceslas (brewers)
10 Crispinian (shoemakers)
Thomas More (lawyers)
11 Christopher (motorists/sailors/travellers)
13 Martin of Tours (soldiers)
Thomas Aquinas (philosophers/scholars/
students/theologians)
14 Albert the Great (scientists)
Francis de Sales (authors/editors/journalists)
Francis of Paola (sailors)
15 Cosmas and Damian (barbers/chemists/
doctors/surgeons)
Francis of Assisi (merchants)
Gregory the Great (musicians/teachers)
Our Lady of Loreto (aviators)
Raymond Nonnatus (midwives)

Other saints include:

03 Leo
04 Anne
Bede

Gall
Joan (of Arc)
John

John (Chrysostom)
John (of the Cross)
John (the Baptist)

Jude
Lucy
Luke
Mark
Mary
Mary (Magdalene)
Paul

05 Agnes
Aidan
Alban
Basil (the Great)
Bruno (of Cologne)
Clare
Cyril
Cyril (of Alexandria)
David
Denis
Edwin
Giles
James
Peter
Titus
Vitus

06 Albert (the Great)
Andrew
Anselm
Antony
Antony (of Padua)
Aquila
Cosmas
Damian
Edmund
Edmund (Campion)
Edward (the Martyr)
George
Helena
Hilary (of Poitiers)
Jerome
Joseph
Joseph (of Arimathea)
Justin
Martha

Martin
Monica
Oliver
Oliver (Plunket)
Oswald
Philip
Prisca
Robert
Simeon
Teresa (of Avila)
Thomas
Thomas (à Becket)
Thomas (Aquinas)
Thomas (Becket)
Thomas (More)
Ursula

07 Adamnan
Ambrose
Anthony
Anthony (of Padua)
Bernard
Bernard (of Clairvaux)
Bernard (of Menthon)
Bridget
Cecilia
Clement
Columba
Crispin
Cyprian
Dominic
Dunstan
Francis (de Sales)
Francis (of Assisi)
Francis (Romulus)
Francis (Xavier)
Gregory (of Nazianzus)
Gregory (of Tours)
Gregory (the Great)
Isidore (of Seville)
Matthew
Michael
Pancras
Patrick

Stephen
Swithin
Theresa (of Lisieux)
Timothy
Vincent (de Paul)
Wilfrid

08 Albertus (Magnus)
Barnabas
Benedict (of Nursia)
Boniface
Cuthbert
Ignatius (of Loyola)
Irenaeus
Lawrence
Margaret
Matthias
Nicholas
Polycarp
Veronica
Walpurga

09 Alexander
Alexander (Nevsky)
Augustine (of Canterbury)
Augustine (of Hippo)
Catherine
Genevieve
Kentigern
Ladislaus
Methodius
Sebastian
Valentine

10 Athanasius
Bernadette
John Fisher
Stanislaus
Wenceslaus

11 Bonaventure
Christopher

12 Justin Martyr

15 Aquila and Prisca
Cosmas and Damian

salad

Salads include:

04 herb
rice
slaw

05 fruit
Greek
green
pasta

06 Caesar

potato
tomato

07 Florida
mesclum
mesclun
Niçoise
Russian
seafood
tabouli

Waldorf

08 coleslaw
couscous

09 mixed leaf
tabbouleh
three bean

11 bulgar wheat

15 mustard and cress

Salad ingredients include:

03 egg	endive	cold meat	salad cream
ham	lovage	coleslaw	watercress
nut	potato	cucumber	**11** salad burnet
04 meat	rocket	**09** boiled egg	spring onion
tuna	tomato	corn-salad	**12** cherry tomato
05 bacon	**07** anchovy	green bean	lamb's lettuce
chard	arugula	new potato	round lettuce
cress	chicken	radicchio	**13** hard-boiled egg
olive	chicory	sweetcorn	roasted pepper
06 borage	crouton	**10** cos lettuce	salad dressing
carrot	**08** bacon bit	lollo rosso	**14** iceberg lettuce
celery	beetroot	mayonnaise	sundried tomato

Salad dressings include:

06 Caesar	Russian	mayonnaise	**14** Thousand Island
French	**09** Marie Rose	salad cream	
07 Italian	**10** blue cheese	**11** vinaigrette	

See also **lettuce**; **vegetable**

sale

Sales include:

04 boot	private	fleamarket
fair	rummage	open market
work	warrant	second-hand
06 autumn	**08** bazumble	**11** bring-and-buy
bazaar	clearing	closing-down
forced	cold call	end-of-season
garage	e-auction	on-promotion
jumble	tabletop	stocktaking
market	**09** clearance	**12** bargain offer
online	end-of-line	church bazaar
public	mail order	grand opening
spring	mid-season	of the century
summer	pre-season	special offer
winter	remainder	**13** online auction
07 auction	telesales	**14** pyramid selling
car-boot	trade show	**15** of bankrupt stock
charity	**10** exhibition	
January	exposition	

salt

Salts include:

05 azide	malate	formate	tannate
06 aurate	oleate	lactate	toluate
borate	**07** bay salt	maleate	viscose
folate	caprate	nitrate	**08** arsenite
halite	citrate	nitrite	benzoate
iodate	cyanate	oxalate	butyrate
iodide	ferrate	sorbate	caproate

chlorate
chloride
chromate
plumbate
pyruvate
rock salt
silicate
stearate
sulphate
sulphide
sulphite

tartrate
vanadate
xanthate
09 ascorbate
bath salts
carbamate
carbonate
glutamate
manganate
molybdate

periodate
phosphate
phthalate
solar salt
succinate
table salt
10 antimonite
bichromate
dichromate
Epsom salts

liver salts
salicylate
11 bicarbonate
health salts
persulphate
sal volatile
12 borosilicate
permanganate
Rochelle-salt
13 smelling salts

satellite

Planetary satellites include:

02 Io (Jupiter)

03 Mab (Uranus)
Nix (Pluto)
Pan (Saturn)
Sao (Neptune)

04 Hati (Saturn)
Kale (Jupiter)
Kari (Saturn)
Kore (Jupiter)
Leda (Jupiter)
Loge (Saturn)
Moon (Earth)
Neso (Neptune)
Puck (Uranus)
Rhea (Saturn)
Ymir (Saturn)

05 Aegir (Saturn)
Aitne (Jupiter)
Anthe (Saturn)
Aoede (Jupiter)
Arche (Jupiter)
Ariel (Uranus)
Atlas (Saturn)
Carme (Jupiter)
Carpo (Jupiter)
Cupid (Uranus)
Dione (Saturn)
Elara (Jupiter)
Greip (Saturn)
Hydra (Pluto)
Janus (Saturn)
Metis (Jupiter)
Mimas (Saturn)
Mneme (Jupiter)
Naiad (Neptune)
Narvi (Saturn)
Skoll (Saturn)
Thebe (Jupiter)
Titan (Saturn)

06 Ananke (Jupiter)
Bestla (Saturn)

Bianca (Uranus)
Charon (Pluto)
Diemos (Mars)
Europa (Jupiter)
Fenrir (Saturn)
Helene (Saturn)
Helike (Jupiter)
Ijiraq (Saturn)
Isonoe (Jupiter)
Juliet (Uranus)
Kalyke (Jupiter)
Kiviuq (Saturn)
Nereid (Neptune)
Oberon (Uranus)
Phobos (Mars)
Phoebe (Saturn)
Portia (Uranus)
Sinope (Jupiter)
Skathi (Saturn)
Sponde (Jupiter)
Surtur (Saturn)
Tarqeq (Saturn)
Tarvos (Saturn)
Tethys (Saturn)
Thrymr (Saturn)
Thyone (Jupiter)
Triton (Neptune)

07 Autonoe (Jupiter)
Belinda (Uranus)
Caliban (Uranus)
Calypso (Saturn)
Cyllene (Jupiter)
Daphnis (Saturn)
Despina (Neptune)
Erinome (Jupiter)
Erriapo (Saturn)
Euanthe (Jupiter)
Euporie (Jupiter)
Fornjot (Saturn)
Galatea (Neptune)
Himalia (Jupiter)
Iapetus (Saturn)

Iocaste (Jupiter)
Larissa (Neptune)
Methone (Saturn)
Miranda (Uranus)
Ophelia (Uranus)
Paaliaq (Saturn)
Pallene (Saturn)
Pandora (Saturn)
Perdita (Uranus)
Proteus (Neptune)
Setebos (Uranus)
Siarnaq (Saturn)
Sycorax (Uranus)
Taygete (Jupiter)
Telesto (Saturn)
Titania (Uranus)
Umbriel (Uranus)

08 Adrastea (Jupiter)
Albiorix (Saturn)
Amalthea (Jupiter)
Bebhionn (Saturn)
Callisto (Jupiter)
Chaldene (Jupiter)
Cordelia (Uranus)
Cressida (Uranus)
Erriapus (Saturn)
Eukelade (Jupiter)
Eurydome (Jupiter)
Farbauti (Saturn)
Ganymede (Jupiter)
Halimede (Neptune)
Hegemone (Jupiter)
Hermippe (Jupiter)

Hyperion (Saturn)
Jarnsaxa (Saturn)
Lysithea (Jupiter)
Margaret (Uranus)
Orthosie (Jupiter)
Pasiphae (Jupiter)
Pasithee (Jupiter)
Prospero (Uranus)
Psamathe (Neptune)
Rosalind (Uranus)
Stephano (Uranus)
Suttungr (Saturn)
Thalassa (Neptune)
Themisto (Jupiter)
Trinculo (Uranus)

09 Bergelmir (Saturn)
Desdemona (Uranus)
Enceladus (Saturn)
Ferdinand (Uranus)
Francisco (Uranus)
Harpalyke (Jupiter)
Hyrrokkin (Saturn)
Laomedeia (Neptune)
Megaclite (Jupiter)
Praxidike (Jupiter)
Thelxinoe (Jupiter)

10 Callirrhoe (Jupiter)
Epimetheus (Saturn)
Kallichore (Jupiter)
Mundilfari (Saturn)
Polydeuces (Saturn)
Prometheus (Saturn)

Man-made satellites include:

03 CAT	Rohini	**08** Explorer	Long March
04 ECHO	**07** Asterix	Inmarsat	**11** Black Knight
05 Astra	Horizon	Intelsat	
TIROS	Sputnik	Prospero	
06 Oshumi	Transit	**09** Early Bird	

satire

Satirists include:

04 Isla (José Francisco de; 1703–81, Spanish)

05 Börne (Ludwig; 1786–1838, German)
Brown (Thomas; 1663–1704, English)
Ellis (George; 1753–1815, British)
Larra (Mariano José de; 1809–37, Spanish)
Meung (Jean de; c.1250–1305, French)
Nashe (Thomas; 1567–1601, English)
Swift (Jonathan; 1667–1745, Anglo-Irish)

06 Butler (Samuel; 1612–80, English)
Giusti (Giuseppe; 1809–50, Italian)
Horace (65–8 BC, Roman)

Lucian (c.117–c.180 AD, Greek)
Pindar (Peter; 1738–1819, English)
Wolcot (John; 1738–1819, English)

07 Barclay (John; 1582–1621, Scottish)
Juvenal (c.55–c.140 AD, Roman)
Marston (John; 1576–1634, English)
Persius (AD 34–62, Roman)
Régnier (Mathurin; 1573–1613, French)

08 Apuleius (Lucius; 2c AD, Roman)
Fischart (Johann; c.1545–90, German)
Lucilius (Gaius; c.180–c.102 BC, Roman)

Rabelais (François; 1483 or 1494–1553, French)

09 Churchill (Charles; 1731–64, English)
Delavigne (Casimir; 1793–1843, French)
Junqueiro (Ablio Manuel Guerra; 1850–

1923, Portuguese)
Whitehead (Paul; 1710–74, English)

10 Mandeville (Bernard; 1670–1733, British)

12 Konstantinov (Aleko; 1863–97, Bulgarian)

sauce

Sauces include:

02 HP®

03 BBQ
jus
red
soy

04 fish
hard
mint
mole
soja
soya
wine

05 apple
bread
brown
caper
cream
curry
fudge
garum
gravy
melba
pesto
salsa

satay
shoyu
white

06 catsup
cheese
chilli
coulis
fondue
fu yung
hoisin
mornay
nam pla
oxymel
oyster
panada
reform
tamari
tartar
tomato
tommy K

07 catchup
custard
harissa
ketchup

nuoc mam
passata
rouille
sabayon
soubise
supreme
Tabasco®
tartare
velouté

08 barbecue
béchamel
bigarade
chasseur
marinara
piri-piri
salpicon
yakitori

09 béarnaise
black bean
bolognese
carbonara
chocolate
cranberry
demi-glace

espagnole
Marie Rose
remoulade
Worcester

10 avgolemono
chaudfroid
Cumberland
mayonnaise
mousseline
salad cream
salsa verde
stroganoff

11 bourguignon
buerre blanc
hollandaise
horseradish
vinaigrette

12 brandy butter
sweet-and-sour

13 crème anglaise
salad dressing
tomato ketchup

14 Worcestershire

sausage

Sausages include:

04 beef
lamb
lola
pork

05 blood
liver
Lorne
Lyons
snags
weeny
wurst

06 banger
bumbar
garlic
kishke
lolita
mumbar
polony

salami
summer
weenie
Wiener
wienie

07 Abruzzo
baloney
Bologna
boloney
cabanos
chorizo
corn dog
kabanos
klobasa
merguez
saveloy
zampone

08 cervelat

chaurice
chourico
cocktail
drisheen
kielbasa
linguica
peperoni
Toulouse

09 andouille
bierwurst
blutwurst
bockwurst
boerewors
bratwurst
chipolata
cotechino
lap cheong
loukanika

pepperoni
saucisson

10 bauerwurst
boudin noir
cervellata
Cumberland
knackwurst
knockwurst
liverwurst
mortadella

11 boudin blanc
boudin rouge
frankfurter
Wienerwurst

12 andouillette
black pudding

14 braunschweiger

saw

Saws include:

03 jig	hand	**06** coping	**08** circular
rip	**05** bench	rabbet	crosscut
04 band	chain	scroll	**09** radial-arm
fret	panel	**07** compass	**11** power-driven
hack	tenon	pruning	

scale *see* **music**

Scandinavia

Scandinavians include:

04 Dane	**05** Swede	**08** Norseman	Varangian
Finn	**06** Norman	**09** Icelander	
Lapp	Viking	Norwegian	

See also **Denmark; Finland; Norway; Sweden**

scanner

Scanners include:

02 CT	PET	SPET	flatbed
03 CAT	**04** body	**07** barcode	**10** Emi-Scanner®

scarf

Scarfs, veils and other headcloths include:

04 caul	chador	dopatta	keffiyeh
doek	cravat	dupatta	kerchief
haik	haique	foulard	mantilla
hyke	kiss-me	kufiyah	neckatee
rail	madras	modesty	puggaree
sash	rebozo	muffler	vexillum
05 curch	tippet	orarium	**09** comforter
fichu	turban	puggery	headcloth
haick	weeper	puggree	headscarf
hejab	wimple	whimple	muffettee
hijab	**07** belcher	yashmak	**10** fascinator
pagri	chaddar	**08** babushka	lambrequin
volet	chaddor	chrismal	**11** kiss-me-quick
whisk	chuddah	kaffiyeh	neckerchief
06 chadar	chuddar	kalyptra	nightingale

Schoenberg, Arnold (1874–1951)

Significant works include:

09 *Erwartung* (1924)	*Songs of Gurre* (1910)
11 *Expectation* (1924)	*The Lucky Hand* (1924)
Gurrelieder (1910)	**14** *Pierrot Lunaire* (1912)
12 *Herzgewächse* (1923)	*Verklärte Nacht* (1902)
Moses und Aron (1957)	**17** *Die Glückliche Hand* (1924)

Foliage of the Heart (1923)
Transfigured Night (1902)
Von Heute auf Morgen (1930)
18 Six Orchestral Songs (1914)
19 A Survivor From Warsaw (1948)
Four Orchestral Songs (1932)

From Today to Tomorrow (1930)
Pelleas und Melisande (1905)
20 Five Orchestral Pieces (1912)
22 Variations for Orchestra (1928)
23 Ode to Napoleon Buonaparte (1944)

school

Schools include:

03 day	Fettes	**08** Bluecoat	Winchester
04 dame	Harrow	boarding	**11** Giggleswick
Eton	public	Hogwarts	Gordonstoun
05 Rugby	**07** Loretto	**09** finishing	Marlborough
Slade	primary	secondary	Westminster
state	private	**10** Ampleforth	**12** Charterhouse
06 church	Roedean	Shrewsbury	**15** Merchant Taylors'
	St Paul's	Stonyhurst	

See also **art**; **education**; **economics**; **philosophy**; **university**

Schubert, Franz (1797–1828)

Significant works include:

05 *Bliss* (1816)
06 *Adrast* (1819)
'Tragic' (Symphony; 1816)
07 *Erl King* (1815)
'Forelle' (Piano Quintet; 1819)
08 *Erlkönig* (1815)
Fernando (1815)
Swan Song (1828)
The Diver (1813/1815)
'The Great' (Symphony; 1825)
'The Trout' (Piano Quintet; 1819)
09 *Fierabras* (1823)
Rosamunde (1823)
Seligkeit (1816)
The Pledge (c.1816)
10 *Der Taucher* (1813/1815)
Einsamkeit (1818)
Loneliness (1818)
'Unfinished' (Symphony; 1822)
11 *Hagars Klage* (1811)
'The Wanderer' (Piano Fantasy; 1822)
12 *Hagar's Lament* (1811)
The Magic Harp (1820)
The Patricide (1811)
13 *Das Marienbild* (1818)
Die Bürgschaft (c.1816)
Picture of Mary (1818)
Tantum Ergo in E (1828)

14 *Der Vatermörder* (1811)
Die Winterreise (1827)
Die Zauberharfe (1820)
Schwanengesang (1828)
Winter's Journey (1827)
15 *Four-Year Posting* (1815)
Lazarus oratorio (1820)
Shepherd's Lament (1815)
The Conspirators (1823)
The Twin Brothers (c.1820)
16 *Die Verschworenen* (1823)
17 'Death and the Maiden' (String Quartet; 1824)
Die Schöne Müllerin (1823)
Schäfers Klagelied (1815)
18 *Alfonso und Estrella* (1822/1854)
Die Zwillingsbrüder (c.1820)
19 *Gretchen am Spinnrade* (1814)
20 *Der vierjährige Posten* (1815)
21 *Claudine von Villabella* (1815)
Des Teufels Lustschloss (1815/1879)
The Friends of Salamanca (c.1815)
22 *Die Freunde von Salamanka* (c.1815)
23 *The Devil's Pleasure-Castle* (1815/1879)
26 *Gretchen at the Spinning Wheel* (1814)
27 *The Miller's Beautiful Daughter* (1823)

Schumann, Robert (1810–56)

Significant works include:

06 'Spring' (Symphony; 1841)

07 *Myrthen* (1840)
'Rhenish' (Symphony; 1850)

08 *Carnaval* (1835)
Genoveva (1850)

09 *Papillons* (1832)
Poet's Love (1840)
Song Cycle (1840)

10 *Intermezzi* (1832)

11 *Butterflies* (1832)
Liederkreis (1840)
Novelletten (1838)

12 *Bunte Blätter* (1849)
Dichterliebe (1840)
Kinderszenen (1838)
Kreisleriana (1838)

13 *Fantasy Pieces* (1837)

14 *Coloured Leaves* (1849)

15 *Phantasiestücke* (1837)

16 *Album for the Young* (1848)
Spanish Love Songs (1849)

17 *Album für die Jugend* (1848)
Woman's Love and Life (1840)

18 *Davidsbündlertänze* (1837)
Études Symphoniques (1834/1852)
Paradise and the Peri (1843)

19 *Frauenliebe und Leben* (1840)
Scenes from Childhood (1838)

21 *Das Paradies und die Peri* (1843)
Spanische Liebeslieder (1849)

24 *Dances of the League of David* (1837)

science

Sciences include:

04 agri
food
life

05 earth

06 botany

07 anatomy
biology
ecology
geology
medical
natural
physics
zoology

08 chemurgy
computer
domestic
dynamics
genetics

robotics

09 acoustics
astronomy
chemistry
dietetics
economics
materials
mechanics
pathology
political
sociology

10 biophysics
entomology
geophysics
graphology
hydraulics
metallurgy
mineralogy

morphology
physiology
psychology
toxicology
veterinary

11 aeronautics
archaeology
behavioural
climatology
cybernetics
diagnostics
electronics
engineering
linguistics
mathematics
meteorology
ornithology
ultrasonics

12 aerodynamics
agricultural
anthropology
astrophysics
biochemistry
geochemistry
geographical
macrobiotics
microbiology
pharmacology

13 environmental

14 geoarchaeology
nuclear physics
radiochemistry
thermodynamics

15 electrodynamics
space technology

Scientific concepts include:

04 area (A, a)
heat (Q)
mass (m)
time (t)
work (W)

05 force (F)
power (P)

06 energy (E)
length (l)

stress
torque (T)
volume (V, v)

07 density

08 enthalpy (H)
momentum (p)
pressure
velocity (v, u)

09 frequency (f)

impedance (Z)
reactance (X)
viscosity

10 admittance (Y)
plane angle
solid angle

11 capacitance (C)
conductance (G)
power factor (pf)

susceptance (B)
temperature (T)

12 acceleration (a)
electric flux
illumination (E)
luminous flux
magnetic flux

permeability
permittivity

13 electric force (E)
kinetic energy
moment of force (M)

14 electric charge (Q)
mass rate of flow (m, M)

self inductance (L)
surface tension

15 angular momentum (l)
electric current (I)
moment of inertia (I)
potential energy (V)
velocity of light (c)

Scientific instruments include:

06 strobe
07 coherer
vernier
08 barostat
cryostat
rheocord
rheostat
09 decoherer
heliostat
hodoscope
hydrostat
hygrostat
image tube
microtome
slide rule

telemeter
tesla coil
thyratron
zymoscope
10 centrifuge
collimator
eudiometer
heliograph
humidistat
hydrophone
hydroscope
hygrograph
iconoscope
nephograph
pantograph

radarscope
radiosonde
tachograph
teinoscope
thermostat
11 chronograph
fluoroscope
Fresnel lens
stactometer
stauroscope
stroboscope
transformer
transponder
tunnel diode
12 dephlegmator

electrosonde
Geissler tube
oscillograph
oscilloscope
spectroscope
13 dipleidoscope
phonendoscope
tachistoscope
14 absorptiometer
image converter
interferometer
torsion balance
15 electromyograph
telethermoscope

SI prefixes include:

03 exa (10^{18}; E)
04 atto (10^{-18}; a)
deca (10^1; da)
deci (10^{-1}; d)
giga (10^9; G)

kilo (10^3; k)
mega (10^6; M)
nano (10^{-9}; n)
peta (10^{15}; P)
pico (10^{-12}; p)

tera (10^{12}; T)
05 centi (10^{-2}; c)
femto (10^{-15}; f)
hecto (10^2; h)
micro (10^{-6}; μ)

milli (10^{-3}; m)
yocto (10^{-24}; y)
yotta (10^{24}; Y)
zepto (10^{-21}; z)
zetta (10^{21}; Z)

See also **acid**; **amino acid**; **anatomy**; **astronomy**; **atom**; **bacteria**; **biochemistry**; **biology**; **botany**; **chemistry**; **classification**; **electricity**; **engine**; **engineering**; **gas**; **gauge**; **genetics**; **geology**; **hydrocarbon**; **laboratory**; **law**; **measurement**; **medical**; **medicine**; **meteorology**; **oil**; **optics**; **ore**; **plastic**; **psychiatry**; **psychology**; **radiation**; **study**; **zoology**

science fiction

Science fiction works include:

03 *Air* (2004; Geoff Ryman)
RUR (1921; Karel Capek)
04 *Dune* (1965; Frank Herbert)
06 *Brasyl* (2007; Ian McDonald)
I, Robot (1950; Isaac Asimov)
N-Space (1990; Larry Niven)
Sirius (1940; Olaf Stapledon)
07 *Erewhon* (1872; Samuel Butler)
Solaris (1961; Stanislaw Lem)
10 *The Last Man* (1826; Mary Wollstonecraft Shelley)
11 *Neuromancer* (1984; William Gibson)

Off on a Comet (1877; Jules Verne)
Rainbows End (2006; Vernor Vinge)
The Naked Sun (1957; Isaac Asimov)
12 *Frankenstein* (1818; Mary Wollstonecraft Shelley)
The Lost World (1912; Arthur Conan Doyle)
13 *Brave New World* (1932; Aldous Huxley)
Childhood's End (1953; Arthur C Clarke)
Fahrenheit 451 (1953; Ray Bradbury)
The Chrysalids (1955; John Wyndham)
14 *Children of Dune* (1976; Frank Herbert)
The Kraken Wakes (1953; John Wyndham)
The Time Machine (1895; H G Wells)

15 *Last and First Men* (1930; Olaf Stapledon)
The Caves of Steel (1953; Isaac Asimov)
The Drowned World (1962; J G Ballard)
The Invisible Man (1897; H G Wells)

16 *Island of Dr Moreau* (1896; H G Wells)
The Scarlet Plague (1912; Jack London)

17 *Rushing to Paradise* (1994; J G Ballard)
The Midwich Cuckoos (1957; John Wyndham)
The War of the Worlds (1898; H G Wells)

18 *Nineteen Eighty-Four* (1949; George Orwell)
The Andromeda Strain (1968; Michael Crichton)

19 *The Day of the Triffids* (1961; John Wyndham)
When the Sleeper Wakes (1899; H G Wells)

20 *Out of the Silent Planet* (1938; C S Lewis)
The First Men in the Moon (1901; H G Wells)
The Green Hills of Earth (1951; Robert Heinlein)
The Martian Chronicles (1950; Ray Bradbury)

21 *From the Earth to the Moon* (1865; Jules Verne)
The Left Hand of Darkness (1969; Ursula Le Guin)
The Man in the High Castle (1962; Philip K Dick)

22 *Stranger in a Strange Land* (1961; Robert Heinlein)

23 *20,000 Leagues Under the Sea* (1870; Jules Verne)
The Unparalleled Invasion (1910; Jack London)

28 *Journey to the Centre of the Earth* (1864; Jules Verne)

30 *Do Androids Dream of Electric Sheep?* (1968; Philip K Dick)
The Hitchhiker's Guide to the Galaxy (1979; Douglas Adams)

33 *Frankenstein or the Modern Prometheus* (1818; Mary Wollstonecraft Shelley)
The Strange Case of Dr Jekyll and Mr Hyde (1886; Robert Louis Stevenson)

Science fiction and fantasy writers include:

04 Dick (Philip K; 1928–82, US)
Pohl (Frederik; 1919– , US)

05 Adams (Douglas; 1952–2001, English)
Banks (Iain M; 1954– , Scottish)
Capek (Karel; 1890–1938, Czech)
Hoyle (Sir Fred; 1915–2001, English)
Lewis (C S; 1898–1963, British)
Simak (Clifford D; 1904–88, US)
Smith (E E; 1890–1965, US)
Verne (Jules; 1828–1905, French)
Wells (H G; 1866–1946, English)
White (T H; 1906–64, English)

06 Aldiss (Brian; 1925– , English)
Asimov (Isaac; 1920–92, Russian/US)
Atwood (Margaret; 1939– , Canadian)
Bishop (Michael; 1945– , US)
Brooks (Terry; 1944– , US)
Clarke (Sir Arthur C; 1917–2008, English)
Gaiman (Neil; 1960– , English)
Kneale (Nigel; 1922–2006, Manx)
Le Guin (Ursula K; 1929– , US)
Orwell (George; 1903–50, English)

07 Ballard (J G; 1930– , Chinese/British)
Herbert (Frank; 1920–86, US)
Hubbard (L Ron; 1911–86, US)
Pullman (Philip; 1946– , English)
Resnick (Michael; 1942– , US)
Serling (Rod; 1924–75, US)
Tolkien (J R R; 1892–1973, South African/British)
Wyndham (John; 1903–69, English)

08 Bradbury (Ray; 1920– , US)
Crichton (Michael; 1942–2008, US)
Hamilton (Edmond; 1904–77, US)
Harrison (M John; 1945– , English)
Heinlein (Robert; 1907–88, US)
McDonald (Ian; 1960– , Northern Irish)
Moorcock (Michael; 1939– , English)
Vonnegut (Kurt; 1922–2007, US)

09 Lovecraft (H P; 1890–1937, US)
Pratchett (Terry; 1948– , English)

11 Tsiolkovsky (Konstantin; 1857–1935, Russian)

Scott, Sir Walter (1771–1832)

Significant works include:

06 *Rob Roy* (1817)
Rokeby (1813)

07 *Ivanhoe* (1819)

Marmion (1808)

08 *The Abbot* (1820)
Waverley (1814)

09 *The Pirate* (1821)
    Woodstock (1826)

10 *Kenilworth* (1821)

11 *Halidon Hill* (1822)
    Redgauntlet (1824)
    The Talisman (1825)

12 *Guy Mannering* (1815)
    St Ronan's Well (1823)
    The Antiquary (1816)
    The Betrothed (1825)
    The Monastery (1820)

13 *Macduff's Cross* (1823)
    The Black Dwarf (1816)

14 *Quentin Durward* (1823)

15 *Castle Dangerous* (1831)

16 *Anne of Geierstein* (1829)
    Peveril of the Peak (1823)
    The Highland Widow (1827)
    The Lady of the Lake (1810)

17 *A Legend of Montrose* (1819)
    History of Scotland (1829–30)

    The Lord of the Isles (1815)

18 *Count Robert of Paris* (1831)
    Harold the Dauntless (1817)
    The Fair Maid of Perth (1828)
    The Fortunes of Nigel (1822)

19 *Lives of the Novelists* (1821)
    Tales of the Crusaders (1825)

20 *The Bridal of Triermain* (1813)
    The Bride of Lammermoor (1819)
    The Heart of Midlothian (1818)

21 *The Tale of Old Mortality* (1816)

22 *The Tales of a Grandfather* (1827–30)

23 *The Lay of the Last Minstrel* (1805)

24 *Chronicles of the Canongate* (1827–28)
    Paul's Letters to His Kinfolk (1816)

27 *The Life of Napoleon Buonaparte* (1827)

29 *Minstrelsy of the Scottish Border* (1802–03)

31 *Provincial Antiquities of Scotland* (1819–26)

32 *Letters on Demonology and Witchcraft*
    (1830)

Significant characters include:

03 Lee (Alice)
    Lee (Colonel)
    Lee (Sir Henry)

04 Dods (Mistress Meg)
    Gray (Menie)
    John (Prince)
    Lyle (Annot)
    Tuck (Friar)

05 Balue (Cardinal John of)
    Binks (Sir Bingo)
    Blood (Colonel Thomas)
    Bunce (Jack)
    Deans (Davie 'Douce Davie')
    Deans ('Effie' Euphemia)
    Deans (Jeanie)
    Ewart (Nanty)
    Gurth (the Swineherd)
    James (King of England)
    Lesly (Ludovic 'le Balafre')
    Liege (Bishop of)
    Louis (King of France)
    Lovel
    Nixon (Cristal)
    Oates (Titus)
    Smith (Henry)
    Smith (Wayland)
    Troil (Brenda)
    Troil (Magnus)
    Troil (Minna)
    Wamba

06 Albany (Duke of)

Argyle (Archibald, Duke of)
Ashton (Lady)
Ashton (Lucy)
Ashton (Sir William, Lord Keeper)
Avenel (Julian)
Avenel (Mary)
Avenel (White Lady of)
Baliol (Mrs Martha Bethune)
Butler (Reuben)
de Lacy (Damian)
de Lacy (Hugo)
de Lacy (Randal)
Geddes (Joshua)
Glover (Catharine)
Glover (Simon)
Graeme (Magdalen)
Graeme (Roland)
Halcro (Claud)
Heriot (George 'Jinglin' Geordie)
Hudson (Sir Geoffrey)
James I (King of England)
Jarvie (Bailie Nicol)
Le Dain (Oliver)
Morton (Henry)
Murray (Regent)
Philip (King of France and Navarre)
Ramsay (David)
Ramsay (Margaret)
Robert (King of Scotland)
Rob Roy
Rowena (Lady)
Seyton (Catherine)

Sludge (Dickie 'Flibbertigibbet')
Tyrrel (Frank)
Ulrica (Dame Urfried)
Varney (Sir Richard)
Vernon (Diana 'Di')
Warden (Henry)
Wilson (Alison)

07 Ambrose (Father, Abbot of Kennaquhair)
Austria (Leopold, Grand Duke of)
Bertram (Harry)
Charles (King of England)
Charles (Prince)
Clement (Father)
de Clare (Lady Clare)
de Croye (Isabelle)
Dinmont (Dandie)
Durward (Quentin)
Elliott ('Hobbie' Halbert)
Eustace (Father)
Everard (Colonel Markham)
Fenella
Glossin (Gilbert)
Hartley (Dr Adam)
Ivanhoe (Wilfred of Ivanhoe)
Kenneth (Sir)
Langley (Sir Frederick)
Latimer (Darsie)
Louis XI (King of France)
MacIvor (Fergus)
MacIvor (Flora)
MacTurk (Captain Hector)
Marmion (Lord)
Mertoun (Basil)
Mertoun (Mordaunt)
Mowbray (Clara)
Mowbray (John, Laird of St Ronan's)
Oldbuck (Jonathan)
Peebles (Peter)
Peveril (Julian)
Peveril (Sir Geoffrey)
Ramorny (Sir John)
Rebecca
Richard (King of England)
Robsart (Amy)
Robsart (Sir Hugh)
Rothsay (Duke of Rothsay, Prince David of Scotland)
Sampson (Dominie Abel)
Shafton (Sir Piercie)
Tomkins (Joseph)
Wardour (Sir Arthur)
Wilfred (of Ivanhoe)

08 Bean Lean (Donald)
Berenger (Eveline)
Boniface (Abbot)
Bothwell (Sargent)
Burgundy (Charles the Bold, Duke of)

Charles I
Conachar
Cromwell (Oliver)
Dalgarno (Lord)
Dennison (Jenny)
de Wilton (Sir Ralph)
Evandale (Lord)
Fairford (Alan)
Fairford (Saunders)
Galeotti (Martius/Marti/Martivalle)
Gardiner (Colonel)
Headrigg (Cuthbert 'Cuddie')
Headrigg (Mause)
Hereward
Locksley
MacBriar (Ephraim)
M'Combich (Robin Oig)
Menteith (Lord)
Montrose (Earl of)
Musgrave (Sir Richard)
Olifaunt (Nigel, Lord Glenvarloch)
Philip II (King of France and Navarre)
Pleydell (Paulus)
Porteous (Captain John)
Richard I (Richard, Coeur-de-Lion)
Staunton (Sir George)
Steenson (Willie 'Wandering Willie')
Trapbois
Trapbois (Martha)
Waverley (Edward)
Waverley (Sir Everard)
Wildfire (Madge)
Wildrake (Roger)

09 Armstrong (Grace)
Bellenden (Edith)
Biederman (Arnold)
Brenhilda (Countess of Paris)
Briennius (Nicephorus)
Charles II
Chiffinch
Christian (Edward)
Cleveland (Captain Clement)
Cranstoun (Lord)
de la Marck (William)
Deloraine (Sir William)
Elizabeth (Queen of England)
Ellieslaw (Laird of)
Gellatley (Davie)
Hagenbach (Archibald von)
Henderson (Elias)
Leicester (Robert Dudley, Earl of)
Lochinvar
Lochleven (Lady of)
Macgregor (Rob Roy)
MacTavish ('Elspat' Elspeth)
Mannering (Colonel Guy)
Mannering (Julia)
Maugrabin (Hayraddin)

Merrilies (Meg)
Moniplies (Richie)
Ochiltree (Edie)
Pattieson (Peter)
Philipson (Arthur)
Plumdamas (Peter)
Proudfute (Oliver)
Ratcliffe (James 'Daddy Rat')
Robert III (King of Scotland)
Touchwood (Peregrine)
Wakefield (Harry)
Yellowley (Barbara 'Baby')
Yellowley (Triptolemus)

10 Berengaria (Queen)
Black Dwarf
Buckingham (George Villiers, Duke of)
Campo-Basso (Count of)
Croftangry (Chrystal)
de Beverley (Constance)
des Comines (Philip)
Dryfesdale
Elizabeth I (Queen of England)
Geierstein
Geierstein (Anne of)
Hatteraick (Captain Dirk)
Holdenough (Reverend Nehemiah)
Humgudgeon
Lowestoffe (Reginald)
Macwheeble (Bailie Duncan)
Middlemass (Richard)
Montserrat (Conrade, Marquis of)
Murdockson (Meg)
Nectabanus
Penfeather (Lady Penelope)
Quackleben (Dr Quentin)
Ravenswood (Edgar, Master of Ravenswood)
Rintherout (Jenny)
Saddletree (Bartoline)
Snailsfoot (Bryce)
Suddlechop (Benjamin)
Suddlechop (Dame Ursula/Dame Ursley)

11 Anna Comnena
Balchristie (Jenny)

Balderstone (Caleb)
Blattergowl (Mr)
Bradwardine (Baron of)
Bradwardine (Rose)
Bridgenorth (Alice)
Bridgenorth (Major)
Donnerhugel (Rudolph)
Dumbiedikes (John 'Jock' Dumbie, Laird of)
Etherington (Earl of)
Fairservice (Andrew)
Glendinning (Simon)
Glendinning (Sir Halbert)
Isaac of York
Mucklewrath (Habbakkuk)
Plantagenet (Edith)
Redgauntlet (Lilias)
The Minstrel
Tressillian (Edmund)

12 Balmawhapple (Laird of)
Bois-Guilbert (Sir Brian de)
Buonaventure (Father)
Cleishbotham (Jedediah)
Front-de-Boeuf (Sir Reginald)
Hob the Miller
Malagrowther (Sir Mungo)
Mucklebackit (Saunders)
Old Mortality
Osbaldistone ('Frank' Francis)
Osbaldistone (Rashleigh)
Osbaldistone (Sir Hildebrand)

13 Dousterswivel (Herman)
Kettledrummle (Reverend Gabriel)

14 Cedric the Saxon
Charles the Bold (Duke of Burgundy)
Mysie of the Mill
Saladin the Turk

15 Abbot of Unreason
Alexius Comnenus
Balfour of Burley (John)
Margaret of Anjou
Torquil of the Oak
Tristan l'Hermite

Scottish

Scottish clans include:

03 Gow	Shaw	Logan	Eliott
Hay	**05** Agnew	Monro	Elliot
04 Boyd	Baird	Munro	Forbes
Gunn	Boyle	Scott	Fraser
Haig	Bruce	**06** Bisset	Gordon
Home	Durie	Brodie	Graeme
Hume	Eliot	Buchan	Graham
Kerr	Grant	Dunbar	Hannay
Rose	Innes	Duncan	Hunter
Ross	Keith	Dundas	Irvine

Irving
Lamond
Lamont
Lauder
Lennox
Leslie
Macfie
Mackay
Macnab
Macrae
Moffat
Monroe
Murray
Napier
Ogilvy
Ramsay
Stuart
07 Balfour
Barclay
Burnett
Cameron
Cumming
Douglas
Erskine
Guthrie
Hopkirk
Jardine
Kennedy
Lindsay
MacBain
MacBean

MacColl
Macduff
MacEwen
MacIver
Maclean
Macleod
Macneil
Macphee
Malcolm
Maxwell
Menzies
Ogilvie
Stewart
Wallace
08 Anderson
Buchanan
Campbell
Carnegie
Cathcart
Chisholm
Crawford
Crichton
Cummings
Davidson
Drummond
Ferguson
Hamilton
Johnston
Lockhart
Macaulay
MacInnes

MacLaine
MacLaren
Macneill
Macnicol
MacQueen
Maitland
Matheson
Morrison
Oliphant
Sinclair
Stirling
Urquhart
09 Armstrong
Colquhoun
Fergusson
Henderson
Johnstone
MacAlpine
MacAndrew
MacArthur
MacCallum
Macdonald
Macdonell
Macdowall
Macduffie
Macgregor
Macintosh
Macintyre
Mackenzie
Mackinnon
MacLaurin

MacLennon
Macmillan
Macquarie
Mathieson
Nicholson
Robertson
10 Anstruther
Arbuthnott
Carmichael
Clanranald
Cunningham
MacAlister
Macdonnell
Macdougall
Macfarlane
Mackintosh
MacLachlan
Macpherson
Macquarrie
Moncrieffe
Sutherland
11 Clan Chattan
Farquharson
MacAllister
MacKendrick
MacLauchlan
MacLaughlan
Macnaughton
12 MacGillivray

Scottish boys' names include:

03 Ian
Rab
04 Doug
Euan
Ewan
Ewen
Greg
Iain

Jock
05 Angus
Arran
Blair
Calum
Clyde
Colin
Craig

Logan
Lorne
Sandy
06 Callum
Dougie
Gordon
Gregor
Hamish

Kelvin
Rabbie
Ranald
07 Cameron
Douglas
Malcolm
08 Campbell

Scottish girls' names include:

03 Rae
04 Iona
Isla
Jess

05 Ailsa
Isbel
Lorna
Morag

06 Aileen
Elspet
Ishbel
Lilias

Mhàiri
Vanora
07 Elspeth
08 Catriona

See also **football**; **monarch**; **town**; **United Kingdom**

screenwriter *see* **play**

sculpture

Sculpture types include:

04 bust	effigy	kinetic	moulding
cast	figure	telamon	**09** bas-relief
head	kouros	waxwork	death mask
herm	marble	**08** caryatid	statuette
kore	relief	Daibutsu	**10** high-relief
05 group	statue	figurine	
06 bronze	**07** carving	maquette	**11** plaster cast

Sculptures and statues include:

04 *Eros* (Alfred Gilbert; 1892–93)
Zeus (Phidias; c.430 BC)

05 *David* (Michelangelo; 1504)
Moses (Michelangelo; c.1513–15)
Pietà (Michelangelo; 1499)

06 *Balzac* (Auguste Rodin; 1898)
Hermes (Praxiteles; 4c BC)

07 *Anteros* (Alfred Gilbert; 1892–93)
Bacchus (Michelangelo; 1496–97)
Liberty (Auguste Bartholdi; 1886)
Lincoln (Daniel Chester French; 1918–22)
Perseus (Benvenuto Cellini; 1545–54)
The Kiss (Auguste Rodin; 1888–89)

08 *Mahamuni* (2c AD; Myanmar)

10 *Discobolus* (Myron; 5c BC)
Doryphorus (Myron; 5c BC)
Single Form (Dame Barbara Hepworth; 1963)

The Thinker (Auguste Rodin; 1881)

11 *Gomateswara* (983; India)
Pierced Form (Dame Barbara Hepworth; 1931)
Spear Bearer (Myron; 5c BC)
Venus de Milo (unknown; c.100 BC)

12 *Elgin Marbles* (ancient; Athens)

13 *Discus Thrower* (Myron; 5c BC)

14 *The Age of Bronze* (Auguste Rodin; 1877)
The Gates of Hell (Auguste Rodin; 1880–1917)
The Three Graces (Antonio Canova; 1814)

15 *Angel of the North* (Antony Gormley; 1998)
Buddhas of Bamian (ancient; Afghanistan)
Christ in Majesty (Sir Jacob Epstein; 1957)
Madonna and Child (Henry Moore; 1943–4)

19 *The Burghers of Calais* (Auguste Rodin; 1886–95)

Sculptors include:

03 Arp (Hans; 1887–1966, Alsatian)
Arp (Jean; 1887–1966, Alsatian)
Ray (Man; 1890–1976, US)

04 Bell (John; 1811–95, English)
Bone (Phyllis; 1896–1972, Scottish)
Boyd (Arthur; 1920–99, Australian)
Cano (Alonso; 1601–67, Spanish)
Caro (Sir Anthony; 1924– , English)
Eldh (Carl; 1873–1954, Swedish)
Gabo (Naum; 1890–1977, US)
Gill (Eric; 1882–1940, English)
King (Phillip; 1934– , British)
Mach (David; 1956– , Scottish)
Rude (François; 1784–1855, French)
Vyse (Charles; 1882–1971, English)
Zorn (Anders; 1860–1920, Swedish)

05 Akers (Benjamin Paul; 1825–61, US)
Andre (Carl; 1935– , US)
Appel (Karel; 1921–2006, Dutch)
Bacon (John; 1740–99, English)
Baily (Edward Hodges; 1788–1867, English)

Banco (Nanni di; c.1384–1421, Italian)
Banks (Thomas; 1735–1805, English)
Barye (Antoine Louis; 1796–1875, French)
Beuys (Joseph; 1921–86, German)
Boehm (Sir Joseph Edgar; 1834–90, Austrian/British)
Bosio (François Joseph, Baron; 1769–1845, French)
Boyle (Jimmy; 1944– , Scottish)
César (1921–1998, French)
Cragg (Tony; 1949– , English)
Dalou (Jules; 1838–1902, French)
Davey (Grenville; 1961– , English)
Drury (Alfred; 1857–1944, English)
Ernst (Max; 1891–1976, German)
Foley (John Henry; 1818–74, Irish)
Frink (Dame Elisabeth; 1930–93, English)
Hesse (Eva; 1936–70, German/US)
Johns (Jasper; 1930– , US)
Jones (Allen; 1937– , English)
Koons (Jeff; 1955– , US)
Leoni (Leone; 1509–90, Italian)

Manzú (Giacomo; 1908–91, Italian)
Moore (Henry; 1898–1986, English)
Myron (5 c BC, Greek)
Notke (Bernt; c.1440–1509, German)
Pilon (Germain; 1537–90, French)
Puget (Pierre; 1622–94, French)
Quinn (Marc; 1964– , English)
Rauch (Christian Daniel; 1777–1857, German)
Rodin (Auguste; 1840–1917, French)
Segal (George; 1924–2000, US)
Serra (Richard; 1939– , US)
Smith (David; 1906–65, US)
Stead (Tim; 1952–2000, English)
Story (William Wetmore; 1819–95, US)
Stoss (Veit; 1447–1533, German)
Stozz (Veit; 1447–1533, German)
Theed (William; 1804–91, English)

06 Akeley (Carl; 1864–1926, US)
Alonso (Mateo; 1878–1955, Argentine)
Ayrton (Michael; 1921–75, English)
Barton (Glenys; 1944– , English)
Butler (Reg; 1913–81, English)
Calder (Alexander; 1898–1976, US)
Canova (Antonio; 1757–1822, Italian)
Cousin (Jean; 1501–c.1590, French)
Deacon (Richard; 1949– , British)
Dobson (Frank; 1888–1963, English)
Floris (Cornelis; c.1514/1520–75, Dutch)
French (Daniel Chester; 1850–1931, US)
Gibson (John; 1790–1866, British)
Goujon (Jean; c.1510–c.1568, French)
Hanson (Duane; 1925–96, US)
Hatoum (Mona; 1952– , Lebanese/British)
Hermes (Gertrude; 1901–83, English)
Houdon (Jean Antoine; 1741–1828, French)
Jagger (Charles Sargeant; 1885–1934, English)
Kapoor (Anish; 1954– , Indian/British)
Keyser (Hendrik de; 1565–1621, Dutch)
Marini (Marino; 1901–80, Italian)
Martin (Kenneth; 1905–84, English)
Martin (Mary; 1907–69, English)
Michel (Claude; 1738–1814, French)
Milles (Carl; 1875–1955, Swedish/US)
Nauman (Bruce; 1941– , US)
Pisano (Andrea; c.1270–1349, Italian)
Pisano (Giovanni; c.1250–c.1320, Italian)
Pisano (Nicola; c.1225–c.1284, Italian)
Powers (Hiram; 1805–73, US)
Rogers (Randolph; 1825–92, US)
Schotz (Benno; 1891–1986, Estonian)
Scopas (4 c BC, Greek)
Sluter (Claus; c.1350–1405, Flemish)
Steell (Sir John; 1804–91, Scottish)
Walker (Dame Ethel; 1861–1951, Scottish)
Wright (Patience; 1725–86, American)
Wyllie (George; 1921– , Scottish)
Zorach (William; 1887–1966, Lithuanian/US)

07 Algardi (Alessandro; 1598–1654, Italian)
Álvarez (José; 1768–1827, Spanish)
Antenor (6 c BC, Greek)
Barlach (Ernst; 1870–1938, German)
Bernini (Gian Lorenzo; 1598–1680, Italian)
Bologna (Giovanni; 1524–1608, Flemish)
Bonheur (Rosa; 1822–99, French)
Borglum (Gutzon; 1867–1941, US)
Brisley (Stuart; 1933– , English)
Cellini (Benvenuto; 1500–71, Italian)
Christo (1935– , Bulgarian/US)
Claudel (Camille; 1864–1943, French)
Coustou (Guillaume; 1678–1746, French)
Coustou (Guillaume; 1716–77, French)
Coustou (Nicolas; 1658–1733, French)
da Vinci (Leonardo; 1452–1519, Italian)
Despiau (Charles; 1874–1946, French)
Duchamp (Marcel; 1887–1968, French/US)
Epstein (Sir Jacob; 1880–1959, US/British)
Flaxman (John; 1755–1826, English)
Gibbons (Grinling; 1648–1721, English)
Gilbert (Sir Alfred; 1854–1934, English)
Gormley (Antony; 1950– , English)
Hoffman (Malvina; 1887–1966, US)
Jónsson (Einar; 1874–1954, Icelandic)
Klinger (Max; 1857–1920, German)
Lambert (George; 1873–1930, Australian)
Laurens (Henri; 1885–1954, French)
Le Sueur (Hubert; c.1580–c.1670, French)
Longman (Evelyn; 1874–1954, US)
Maillol (Aristide; 1861–1944, French)
Manship (Paul; 1885–1966, US)
Millett (Kate; 1934– , US)
Noguchi (Isamu; 1904–88, US)
Orcagna (c.1308–68, Italian)
Permeke (Constant; 1886–1951, Belgian)
Pevsner (Antoine; 1886–1962, Russian/French)
Phidias (b.c.500 BC, Greek)
Pigalle (Jean Baptiste; 1714–85, French)
Quercia (Jacopo della; c.1367–1438, Italian)
Richier (Germaine; 1904–59, French)
Samaras (Lucas; 1936– , Greek/US)
Schadow (Gottfried; 1764–1850, Prussian)
Schadow (Rudolf; 1786–1822, Prussian)
Stevens (Alfred; 1818–75, English)
Turrell (James; 1943– , US)
Vischer (Peter; 1455–1529, German)
Whitney (Anne; 1821–1915, US)
Whitney (Gertrude Vanderbilt; 1875–1942, US)
Wilding (Alison; 1948– , English)
Woolner (Thomas; 1826–92, English)
Zadkine (Ossip; 1890–1967, Russian/French)

08 Aaltonen (Wäinö; 1894–1966, Finnish)
Ammanati (Bartolommeo; 1511–92, Italian)
Armitage (Kenneth; 1916–2002, English)
Armstead (Henry Hugh; 1828–1905, English)

Boccioni (Umberto; 1882–1916, Italian)
Brancusi (Constantin; 1876–1957,
 Romanian)
Carpeaux (Jean Baptiste; 1827–75, French)
Chadwick (Lynn; 1914–2003, English)
Chantrey (Sir Francis; 1781–1841, English)
Coysevox (Antoine; 1640–1720, French)
Crawford (Thomas; 1814–57, US)
Davidson (Jo; 1883–1952, US)
Falconet (Étienne Maurice; 1716–91,
 French)
Filarete (Antonio; c.1400–c.1469,
 Florentine)
Flanagan (Barry; 1941– , British)
Frampton (Sir George; 1860–1928, English)
Ghiberti (Lorenzo; 1378–1455, Italian)
Girardon (François; 1630–1715, French)
González (Julio; 1876–1942, Spanish)
Hepworth (Dame Barbara; 1903–75,
 English)
Kollwitz (Käthe; 1867–1945, German)
Lachaise (Gaston; 1882–1935, US)
Landseer (Sir Edwin; 1802–73, English)
Lipchitz (Jacques; 1891–1973, Lithuanian/
 French)
Lombardo (Pietro; c.1433–1515, Italian)
Marshall (William Calder; 1813–94, Scottish)
Nadelman (Elie; 1882–1946, Polish/US)
Nevelson (Louise; 1900–88, US)
Paolozzi (Sir Eduardo; 1924–2005, Scottish)
Pheidias (b.c.500 BC, Greek)
Rysbrack (Michael; c.1693–1770, Flemish)
Stebbins (Emma; 1815–82, US)
St-Phalle (Niki de; 1930–2002, French)
Tinguely (Jean; 1925–91, Swiss)

09 Alcamenes (5c BC, Greek)
Bartholdi (Auguste; 1834–1904, French)
Bartolini (Lorenzo; 1777–1850, Italian)
Borromini (Francesco; 1599–1667, Italian)
Bourdelle (Antoine; 1861–1929, French)
Bourgeois (Louise; 1911– , French/US)
Donatello (c.1386–1466, Florentine)
Euphranor (4c BC, Greek)
Falguière (Alexandre; 1831–1900, French)
Greenough (Horatio; 1805–52, US)
Houshiary (Shirazeh; 1955– , Iranian/
 British)
Leochares (fl.c.350–330 BC, Greek)
McWilliam (F E; 1909–92, Northern Irish)
Nollekens (Joseph; 1737–1823, English)
Oldenburg (Claes; 1929– , Swedish/US)
Rietschel (Ernst; 1804–61, German)
Roubiliac (Louis François; 1702/1705–1762,
 French)
Roubillac (Louis François; 1702/1705–1762,
 French)

See also **monument**

Sansovino (1460–1529, Italian)
Sansovino (Jacopo; 1486–1570, Italian)
Schlemmer (Oskar; 1888–1943, German)
St-Gaudens (Augustus; 1848–1907, US)
Sveinsson (Ásmundur; 1893–1982,
 Icelandic)
Whiteread (Rachel; 1963– , English)
Willumsen (J F; 1863–1958, Danish)

10 Antokolski (Mark; 1843–1902, Russian)
Archipenko (Alexander; 1880–1964, US)
Bandinelli (Baccio; 1493–1560, Italian)
Bartholomé (Albert; 1848–1928, French)
Berruguete (Alonso; c.1489–1561, Spanish)
della Robia (Luca; c.1400–82, Italian)
Giacometti (Alberto; 1901–66, Swiss)
Hildebrand (Adolf; 1847–1921, German)
Kennington (Eric; 1888–1960, English)
Marochetti (Carlo, Baron; 1805–67, Italian)
Michelozzi (Michelozzo di Bartolommeo;
 1396–1472, Italian)
Modigliani (Amedeo; 1884–1920, Italian)
Polyclitus (5c BC, Greek)
Praxiteles (4c BC, Greek)
Rossellino (Antonio; 1427–c.1479, Italian)
Rossellino (Bernardo; 1409–64, Italian)
Schwitters (Kurt; 1887–1948, German)
Torrigiano (Pietro; c.1472–1522, Italian)
Verrocchio (Andrea del; c.1435–c.1488,
 Italian)

11 Abakanowicz (Magdalena; 1930– , Polish)
della Robbia (Luca; c.1400–82, Italian)
Goldsworthy (Andy; 1956– , English)
Saint-Phalle (Niki de; 1930–2002, French)
Scheemakers (Pieter; 1691–1781, Flemish)
Thornycroft (Sir Hamo; 1850–1925, English)
Thorvaldsen (Bertel; 1770–1844, Danish)

12 Brunelleschi (1377–1446, Italian)
David d'Angers (Pierre Jean; 1789–1856,
 French)
Francheville (Pierre; 1548–1616, French)
Franqueville (Pierre; 1548–1616, French)
Jeanne-Claude (1935– , French/US)
MacGillivray (James Pittendrigh; 1856–
 1938, Scottish)
Michelangelo (1475–1564, Italian)
Saint-Gaudens (Augustus; 1848–1907, US)

13 Duchamp-Villon (Raymond; 1876–1918,
 French)
Tino di Camaino (c.1285–1337, Italian)

14 Gaudier-Brzeska (Henri; 1891–1915, French)

15 Arnolfo di Cambio (1232–1302, Italian)
Leonardo da Vinci (1452–1519, Italian)
Riemenschneider (Tilman; 1460–1531,
 German)

sea

See also **ocean**

seabird *see* **bird**

seafood

Seafood and seafood dishes include:

04	bisk		paella	08	calamari	11	clam-chowder
	clam		scampi		coquille		Dublin prawn
	crab		shrimp		crawfish		fritto misto
05	prawn		winkle		crevette		fruits de mer
	squid	07	abalone		marinara		langoustine
	sushi		lobster		zarzuela		tiger shrimp
	whelk		octopus	09	jambalaya	13	bouillabaisse
06	bisque		risotto		king prawn		Norway lobster
	mussel		scallop		surf'n'turf		prawn cocktail
	oyster		tempura	10	tiger prawn	14	Dublin Bay prawn
			toheroa				

seal

Seals include:

03	fur		ribbon		sea calf		whitecoat
04	grey		sea dog		sea lion	10	common seal
	hair		sealch		Weddell		saddleback
	harp		sealgh	08	Atlantic		sea leopard
	monk		selkie		elephant		
05	phoca		silkie		seecatch	11	sea elephant
	silky	07	harbour	09	crab-eater		
06	hooded		sea bear		Greenland		

season

Seasons include:

03	dry		silly		winter		shooting
	wet	06	autumn	07	festive	12	Indian summer
04	high		closed		holiday		
05	close		spring		monsoon		
	rainy		summer	08	breeding		

seaweed

Seaweeds include:

03	ore		laver		porphyra
	red		vraic		rockweed
04	alga		wrack		sargasso
	kelp	06	fucoid		sea wrack
	kilp		tangle		whipcord
	nori		wakame	09	carrageen
	tang	07	oarweed		coralline
	ulva		oreweed		coral weed
	ware		redware		drift-weed
05	arame		sea lace		Irish moss
	domoi		sea moss		Laminaria
	dulse		seaware		nullipore
	fucus	08	bull kelp		sargassum
	kombu		gulfweed		seabottle
					sea girdle

sea tangle
thongweed
10 badderlock
carragheen
Ceylon moss
green laver
See also **algae**

sea lettuce
sea whistle
tangleweed
11 purple laver
sea furbelow
12 bladderwrack

peacock's tail
Phaeophyceae
Rhodophyceae
13 Chlorophyceae
15 channelled wrack

sedative

Sedatives and tranquillizers include:

06 Amytal®
Ativan®
Valium®
07 codeine
Librium®
lupulin
08 diazepam
See also **drug**

Nembutal®
Rohypnol®
tetronal
thridace
09 barbitone
clozapine
lorazepam

Temazepam
10 clonazepam
11 amobarbital
deserpidine
laurel-water
scopalamine
thalidomide

12 meprobramate
methaqualone
promethazine
14 chloral hydrate
cyclobarbitone
pentobarbitone
phenobarbitone

sedge

Sedges include:

04 star
05 Carex
chufa

starr
07 bulrush
papyrus

08 clubrush
sawgrass
tiger nut

09 deergrass
13 umbrella plant
water chestnut

self-defence *see* **martial art**

Serbia *see* **Balkans**

servant

Servants include:

03 fag
04 char
chef
cook
maid
page
05 boots
carer
daily
groom
nanny
slave
valet
wench
06 au pair
barman
batman
butler

chokra
drudge
garçon
haiduk
lackey
menial
ostler
skivvy
tweeny
waiter
07 barmaid
bellboy
bellhop
cleaner
equerry
flunkey
footman
gossoon

pageboy
steward
tapsman
08 charlady
coachman
dogsbody
domestic
factotum
gardener
handmaid
henchman
home help
house boy
retainer
scullion
servitor
waitress
wet nurse

09 chauffeur
errand boy
governess
housemaid
lady's maid
major-domo
seneschal

10 chauffeuse
handmaiden

henchwoman
manservant
stewardess

11 body servant
boot-catcher
chambermaid
henchperson
housekeeper
kitchen-maid

maidservant
parlour-maid

12 domestic help
scullery maid

13 care assistant
lady-in-waiting
livery-servant

14 commissionaire

service *see* **religion**

session *see* **term**

setter *see* **crossword**

Seven Against Thebes

The Seven Greek champions who attacked Thebes:

06 Tydeus

08 Adrastus

Capaneus

09 Polynices

10 Amphiaraus
Hippomedon

13 Parthenopaeus

Seven Deadly Sins *see* sin

Seven Dwarfs *see* dwarf

seven hills *see* Rome

Seven Sages *see* sage

Seven Sisters colleges *see* university

Seven Wonders of the World *see* wonder

Shakespeare, William (1564–1616)

Shakespeare's plays:

06 *Hamlet* (1600–01)
Henry V (1598–99)

07 *Macbeth* (1606)
Othello (1603–04)

08 *King John* (1596)
King Lear (1605–06)
Pericles (1607)

09 *All Is True* (1613)
Cymbeline (1610)
Henry VIII (1613)
Richard II (1595)

10 *Coriolanus* (1608)
Richard III (1592–93)

The Tempest (1611)

11 *As You Like It* (1599–1600)
What You Will (1601)

12 *Julius Caesar* (1599)
Twelfth Night (1601)

13 *Timon of Athens* (1605)

14 *Henry IV Part One* (1596–97)
Henry IV Part Two (1597–98)
Henry VI Part One (1592)
Henry VI Part Two (1592)
Romeo and Juliet (1595)
The Winter's Tale (1609)

15 *Titus Andronicus* (1592)

16 *Henry VI Part Three* (1592)
Love's Labours Lost (1594–95)

17 *Measure for Measure* (1603)
The Comedy of Errors (1594)

18 *Antony and Cleopatra* (1606)
Troilus and Cressida (1602)

19 *Much Ado About Nothing* (1598)
The Merchant of Venice (1596–97)
The Taming of the Shrew (1593)
The Tragedy of Macbeth (1606)

20 *All's Well That Ends Well* (1604–05)
Pericles, Prince of Tyre (1607)
The Tragedy of King Lear (1605–06)

21 *A Midsummer Night's Dream* (1595)

22 *Cymbeline, King of Britain* (1610)
The Life of Henry the Fifth (1598–99)
The Life of Timon of Athens (1605)

The Merry Wives of Windsor (1597–98)
The Tragedy of Coriolanus (1608)

23 *The Two Gentlemen of Verona* (1590–91)

24 *The Tragedy of Julius Caesar* (1599)

25 *The Life and Death of King John* (1596)

26 *The History of Henry the Fourth* (1596–97)

30 *The Tragedy of Antony and Cleopatra* (1606)

31 *The Tragedy of King Richard the Third* (1592–93)

32 *The Tragedy of King Richard the Second* (1595)

33 *The Tragedy of Hamlet, Prince of Denmark* (1600–01)

34 *The Tragedy of Othello, the Moor of Venice* (1603–04)

Shakespeare's poems include:

07 *Sonnets* (1609)

14 *Venus and Adonis* (1593)

16 'A Lover's Complaint' (1609)

The Rape of Lucrece (1594)

22 'The Phoenix and the Turtle' (1601)

Significant characters in All's Well That Ends Well include:

05 Diana
Lafeu

06 France (King of)
Helena

07 Bertram

Capilet (Widow)
Lavatch
Mariana

08 Florence (Duke of)
Parolles

Reynaldo

09 Rousillon (Count of/Countess of)

Significant characters in A Midsummer Night's Dream include:

04 Moth
Puck
Snug

05 Egeus
Flute (Francis)
Snout (Tom)

06 Bottom (Nick)
Cobweb

Helena
Hermia
Oberon
Quince (Peter)
Thisbe

07 Pyramus
Theseus
Titania

08 Lysander

09 Demetrius
Hippolyta

10 Starveling (Robin)

11 Mustardseed

12 Peaseblossom

15 Robin Goodfellow

Significant characters in Antony and Cleopatra include:

04 Iras

06 Caesar (Octavius)
Pompey

07 Lepidus (Marcus Aemilius)

Octavia

08 Charmian
Pompeius (Sextus)

09 Cleopatra

Enobarbus (Domitius)

10 Mark Antony

14 Marcus Antonius

Significant characters in As You Like It include:

05 Celia
Corin
Hymen

Phebe

06 Aliena
Audrey

Le Beau
Oliver
Senior (Duke)

07 Charles
Jacques
Martext (Sir Oliver)
Orlando

Silvius
William
08 Ganymede
Rosalind

09 Frederick (Duke)
10 Touchstone

Significant characters in Coriolanus include:

06 Brutus (Junius)
07 Agrippa (Menenius)
Velutus (Sicinius)

08 Aufidius (Tullus)
Cominius
Virgilia

Volumnia
10 Coriolanus (Gaius Martius)

Significant characters in Cymbeline include:

05 Queen
06 Cadwal
Cloten
Imogen
Lucius (Caius)
Morgan

07 Filario
Giacomo
Iachimo
Pisario
08 Belarius
Leonatus (Posthumus)

Leonatus (Sicilius)
Polydore
09 Arviragus
Cornelius
Cymbeline
Guiderius

Significant characters in Hamlet include:

05 Clown
Ghost (the)
06 Hamlet
07 Horatio

Laertes
Ophelia
08 Claudius
Gertrude

Polonius
10 Fortinbras
11 Gravedigger
Rosencrantz

12 Guildenstern

Significant characters in Henry IV Part I include:

03 Hal (Prince)
04 Peto
05 Blunt (Sir Walter)
Harry (Prince)
Percy (Henry)
Percy (Lady)
Percy (Thomas)

Poins
07 Henry IV
Hotspur (Henry Percy)
08 Bardolph
Falstaff (Sir John)
Gadshill
Mortimer (Edmund)

Mortimer (Lady)
09 Glendower (Owen)
13 Prince of Wales
15 Earl of Worcester
John of Lancaster (Prince)
Mistress Quickly

Significant characters in Henry IV Part II include:

05 Harry (Prince)
Percy (Henry)
Percy (Lady)
Poins
06 Henry V

Pistol
07 Henry IV
Shallow (Justice)
08 Bardolph
Falstaff (Sir John)

13 Doll Tearsheet
14 Northumberland (Lady)
15 John of Lancaster (Prince)
Mistress Quickly

Significant characters in Henry V include:

03 Nym
04 Jamy
05 Gower
06 Chorus (the)
Henry V
Isabel

Pistol
08 Bardolph
Burgundy (Duke of)
Fluellen
Mountjoy
09 Charles VI
Katharine

Macmorris
10 Canterbury (Archbishop of)
12 King of France
13 Queen of France
15 Lewis the Dauphin
Mistress Quickly

Significant characters in Henry VI Part I include:

04 Cade (Jack)
     York (Duke of)
07 Henry VI
09 Joan of Arc
13 Joan la Pucelle
     Queen Margaret
15 Margaret of Anjou

Significant characters in Henry VI Part II include:

04 York (Duke of)
06 Edward
07 Henry VI
     Richard
08 Edward IV
11 Earl of March
13 Queen Margaret
15 Margaret of Anjou

Significant characters in Henry VI Part III include:

04 York (Duke of)
06 Edward
     George
07 Henry VI
     Richard
08 Edward IV
     Henry VII
     Richmond (Henry, Earl of)
09 Woodville (Anthony)
     Woodville (Elizabeth)
10 Earl Rivers
11 Earl of March
13 Queen Margaret
14 Duke of Clarence
     Queen Elizabeth
15 Margaret of Anjou

Significant characters in Henry VIII (All is True) include:

06 Boleyn (Anne)
     Wolsey (Cardinal Thomas)
07 Cranmer (Thomas)
09 Henry VIII
     Katherine
14 Queen of England

Significant characters in Julius Caesar include:

05 Casca
06 Brutus (Decius)
     Brutus (Marcus)
     Caesar (Julius)
     Caesar (Octavius)
     Portia
07 Cassius (Caius)
     Lepidus (Marcus Aemilius)
09 Calpurnia
10 Mark Antony
     Soothsayer
14 Marcus Antonius

Significant characters in King John include:

04 John (King)
05 Henry (Prince)
06 Arthur
     France (King of)
     Philip
07 Austria (Duke of)
     Blanche
     de Burgh (Hubert)
     Eleanor
     Lymoges
08 Brittany (Duke of/Duchess of)
     Pandulph
09 Constance
12 Falconbridge (Philip)
     Falconbridge (Robert)
14 Peter of Pomfret
15 Lewis the Dauphin

Significant characters in King Lear include:

04 Fool (the)
     Kent (Earl of)
     Lear (King)
05 Edgar
     Regan
06 Albany (Duke of)
     Edmund
     France (King of)
     Oswald
07 Goneril
08 Burgundy (Duke of)
     Cordelia
     Cornwall (Duke of)
10 Gloucester (Earl of)

Significant characters in Love's Labour's Lost include:

04 Dull
05 Boyet
     Maria
06 Armado (Don Adriano del)
     France (Princess of)
07 Berowne

Costard
Dumaine
08 Rosaline

09 Ferdinand (King)
Katharine
Nathanael (Sir)

10 Holofernes
Jaquenetta
Longaville

Significant characters in Macbeth include:

06 Banquo
Duncan (King)
Hecate

Porter (the)
07 Fleance
Macbeth

Macbeth (Lady)
Macduff
Macduff (Lady)

Malcolm
09 Donalbain
12 three witches (the)

Significant characters in Measure for Measure include:

05 Lucio
06 Angelo

Pompey
07 Claudio

08 Isabella
Marianna

09 Vincentio (Duke)

Significant characters in Much Ado About Nothing include:

04 Hero
06 Ursula
Verges
07 Claudio

Conrade
Don John
Leonato
08 Beatrice

Benedick
Borachio
Dogberry
Don Pedro

Margaret
12 Friar Francis

Significant characters in Othello include:

04 Iago
06 Bianca

Cassio
Emilia

07 Othello
08 Roderigo

09 Desdemona

Significant characters in Pericles include:

05 Cleon
06 Marina

Thaisa
07 Dionyza

08 Pericles
09 Antiochus

Helicanus
Simonides

Significant characters in Richard II include:

04 York (Duke of)
05 Bagot
Bushy
Green
Percy (Henry)

Queen (the)
07 Hotspur (Henry
Percy)
Mowbray (Thomas)
Norfolk (Duke of)

Richard (King)
08 Gardener (the)
Isabella
09 Lancaster (Duke of)
Richard II (King)

11 Bolingbroke
John of Gaunt
13 Pierce of Exton (Sir)
14 Northumberland
(Earl of)

Significant characters in Richard III include:

04 Anne (Lady)
05 Henry
March (Earl of)
06 Edward
George
07 Henry VI
Richard (Duke of York)

Richard (King)
08 Clarence (Duke of)
Edward IV
Hastings (Lord)
Henry VII
Richmond (Earl of)
09 Woodville (Anthony)
Woodville (Elizabeth)

10 Buckingham (Duke of)
Earl Rivers
Gloucester (Duke of)
Richard III
13 Queen Margaret
14 Queen Elizabeth
15 Margaret of Anjou

Significant characters in Romeo and Juliet include:

05 Nurse
Paris
Romeo

06 Juliet
Tybalt
07 Capulet

Capulet (Lady)
08 Benvolio
Mercutio

Montague
13 Friar Lawrence

Significant characters in The Comedy of Errors include:

06 Aegeon
Dromio (of Ephesus)
Dromio (of Syracuse)

07 Adriana
Aemilia
Luciana

10 Antipholus (of Ephesus)
Antipholus (of Syracuse)

Significant characters in The Merchant of Venice include:

05 Gobbo (Launcelot)
06 Portia
07 Antonio

Arragon (Prince of)
Jessica
Lorenzo

Morocco (Prince of)
Nerissa

Shylock
08 Bassanio
Gratiano

Significant characters in The Merry Wives of Windsor include:

03 Nym
04 Ford (Frank)
Ford (Mistress Alice)
Page (Anne)
Page (George)
Page (Mistress Margaret)

05 Caius (Dr)
Evans (Sir Hugh)
Robin
Rugby (John)
06 Fenton
Pistol

Simple (Peter)
07 Shallow (Justice)
Slender (Abraham)
08 Falstaff (Sir John)
15 Mistress Quickly

Significant characters in The Taming of the Shrew include:

03 Sly (Christopher)
06 Bianca
Curtis
Gremio
Grumio

Tranio
08 Lucentio
09 Biondello
Hortensio
Katharina (Kate)

Petruchio
Vincentio
11 Bartholomew
14 Baptista Minola

Significant characters in The Tempest include:

05 Ariel
06 Adrian
Alonso
07 Antonio

Caliban
Gonzalo
Miranda
Sycorax

08 Prospero
Stephano
Trinculo
09 Ferdinand

Francisco
Sebastian

Significant characters in The Winter's Tale include:

07 Camillo
Leontes
Paulina

Perdita
08 Florizel
Hermione

09 Antigonus
Autolycus
Polixenes

Significant characters in Timon of Athens include:

07 Flavius
09 Apemantus

Ventidius
10 Alcibiades

13 Timon of Athens

Significant characters in Titus Andronicus include:

05 Aaron (the Moor)
06 Tamora (Queen)
07 Lavinia

09 Bassianus
10 Andronicus (Lucius)
Andronicus (Marcus)

Andronicus (Quintus)
Andronicus (Titus)
Saturninus

Significant characters in Troilus and Cressida include:

04 Ajax
05 Helen

Paris
Priam

06 Hector
07 Calchas

Helenus
Troilus

Ulysses	Diomedes	Cassandra	**10** Andromache
08 Achilles	Pandarus	Patroclus	
Cressida	**09** Agamemnon	Thersites	

Significant characters in Twelfth Night include:

05 Belch (Sir Toby)	Viola	**07** Antonio	**09** Aguecheek (Sir
Feste	**06** Olivia	Cesario	Andrew)
Maria	Orsino	**08** Malvolio	Sebastian

Significant characters in Two Gentlemen of Verona include:

05 Julia	**06** Launce	**07** Antonio	**09** Valentine
Milan (Duke of)	Silvia	Proteus	
Speed	Thurio	**08** Eglamour (Sir)	

Terms to do with Shakespeare include:

03 act	sonnet	Bard of Avon
RSC	source	bardolatry
set	speech	blank verse
04 fame	Thames	bowdlerize
hero	troupe	chronology
line	**07** costume	dark comedy
love	couplet	First Folio
play	edition	groundling
plot	English	literature
poem	Fortune	malcontent
poet	players	manuscript
role	scholar	playwright
05 actor	tragedy	production
aside	trochee	Quarto text
clown	**08** director	**11** bear baiting
court	epilogue	Elizabethan
death	Jacobean	masterpiece
drama	King's Men	protagonist
genre	language	Rose Theatre
Greek	metaphor	Swan Theatre
Latin	New Place	**12** Globe Theatre
meter	prologue	history plays
scene	quatrain	Scottish play
stage	rhetoric	St George's Day
theme	violence	**13** acting company
witch	**09** character	collaboration
06 chorus	dramatist	Lord of Misrule
climax	Folio text	narrative poem
comedy	interlude	Shakespearean
editor	Queen's Men	Shakespearian
jester	soliloquy	**14** King's New School
masque	Stratford	revenge-tragedy
patron	universal	stage direction
plague	**10** adaptation	**15** Sweet Swan of Avon
simile		

See also **fool**

shape

Shapes include:

04 cone	hexagon	rectangle
cube	nonagon	trapezium
kite	octagon	undecagon
oval	polygon	**10** hemisphere
05 prism	pyramid	hendecagon
06 circle	rhombus	octahedron
cuboid	**08** crescent	polyhedron
oblong	cylinder	quadrangle
sector	heptagon	semicircle
sphere	pentagon	**11** pentahedron
square	quadrant	tetrahedron
07 decagon	tetragon	**13** parallelogram
diamond	triangle	quadrilateral
ellipse	**09** chiliagon	**15** scalene triangle
	dodecagon	

See also **circle**; **leaf**; **triangle**

shark

Sharks include:

03 cat	swell	leopard	porbeagle
fox	tiger	requiem	sand tiger
saw	whale	sleeper	sevengill
04 blue	zebra	soupfin	sharpnose
bull	**06** beagle	**08** blacktip	wobbegong
mako	carpet	grey reef	**10** Colclough's
05 blind	goblin	mackerel	great white
dusky	salmon	thresher	hammerhead
ghost	school	whitetip	Portuguese
lemon	sea cat	**09** angelfish	shovelhead
night	**07** basking	epaulette	**11** ragged-tooth
nurse	bramble	Greenland	smooth-hound
sagre	dogfish	man-eating	

sheep

Sheep include:

03 Rya	urial	muflon
04 Dala	**06** aoudad	Romney
Gute	Arcott	**07** Barbary
Soay	argali	bighorn
05 ammon	Awassi	burrell
ancon	Balwen	burrhel
aodad	Beltex	caracul
Jacob	bharal	Cheviot
Lleyn	burhel	Colbred
Lonck	burrel	Gotland
Masai	Dorper	karakul
Rygja	Galway	Karaman
Texel	Masham	Lincoln
Tunis	merino	mouflon

Romanov
Roussin
Ryeland
St Croix
Steigar
Suffolk
Tibetan
Vendeen

08 Columbia
Cotentin
Cotswold
Herdwick
Katahdin
Loaghtan
Meatlinc
moufflon
Ouessant
Peliquey
Polwarth
Portland
Shetland
thinhorn
Troender

09 blackface
blue sheep
Cambridge
Charmoise
Charolais
Coopworth

Dalesbred
Dall Sheep
Finn Sheep
Fuglestad
Greenland
Hebridean
Icelandic
Kerry Hill
Leicester
Llanwenog
Marco Polo
Montadale
Perendale
Rough Fell
snow sheep
Southdown
Swaledale
Teeswater
Welsh Mule
Zwartbles

10 Borderdale
Charollais
Clun Forest
Corriedale
Dorset Down
Dorset Horn
Exmoor Horn
Hill Radnor
Morada Nova
Oxford Down

Poll Dorset
Scotch Mule
Shropshire
stone sheep

11 Ile de France
Manx Loghtan
Norfolk Horn
Rambouillet
Wensleydale

12 Bleu du Marine
East Friesian
Faroe Islands
Navajo-Churro

13 Desert Bighorn
Hampshire Down
Rouge de l'Ouest
Tyrol Mountain
Welsh Halfbred
Wiltshire Horn

14 Danish Landrace
Devon Closewool
North Ronaldsay
Scotch Halfbred
Wicklow Cheviot

15 Berrichon du Cher
Border Leicester
Est A Laine Merino
Shetland-Cheviot
White Faced Marsh

ship

Ship and boat types include:

01 E
Q
U

02 MV
NS
SS
TB

03 air
ark
bum
cat
cog
cot
day
dow
fly
gig
gun
HMS
hoy
ice
jet

kit
MTB
mud
pig
row
tow
tub
tug
USS
war

04 bark
brig
buss
cock
cott
dhow
dory
falt
fire
flag
flat
fold
four

grab
HMAS
HMCS
hulk
hush
junk
keel
koff
life
long
mail
maxi
pair
pink
pont
post
pram
prau
proa
prow
punt
saic
scow

show	slave	lugger
snow	sloop	masula
surf	smack	monkey
tall	speed	mother
tilt	stake	narrow
Turk	steam	nuggar
waka	store	oomiac
well	swamp	oomiak
wind	tanka	packet
yawl	track	paddle
zulu	tramp	pedalo
	troop	pirate
05 aviso	umiak	prison
barca	wager	puffer
barge	waist	pulwar
botel	whale	puteli
butty	whiff	randan
cabin	xebec	reefer
canal	yacht	rowing
canoe	zabra	runner
casco		sailer
coble	**06** advice	saique
coper	argosy	sampan
crare	banker	sandal
dandy	barque	sanpan
dingy	bateau	school
drake	battle	schuit
ferry	bethel	schuyt
funny	bireme	settee
guard	caique	slaver
gulet	carvel	tanker
hatch	castle	tartan
horse	coaler	torpid
house	cobble	trader
jolly	cockle	turret
kayak	codder	wangan
ketch	coffin	wangun
laker	convoy	wherry
light	cooper	
liner	crayer	**07** assault
motor	cutter	Berthon
oiler	dingey	birlinn
peter	dinghy	budgero
pilot	dogger	capital
plate	dragon	caravel
power	droger	clipper
praam	dromon	coaster
prahu	drover	collier
prore	dugout	consort
razee	flying	coracle
river	galiot	corsair
rotor	galley	cruiser
saick	gay-you	currach
scout	hooker	curragh
scull	hopper	dredger
seine	jigger	drifter
shell	lateen	drogher
shore	launch	dromond
skiff	lorcha	factory

felucca
four-oar
frigate
gabbard
gabbart
galleon
galliot
Geordie
gondola
landing
liberty
lighter
lymphad
man-o'-war
mistico
mudscow
mystery
nacelle
oomiack
pair-oar
passage
patamar
pearler
pinnace
piragua
pirogue
polacca
pontoon
sailing
scooter
shallop
sharpie
sponger
steamer
tartane
torpedo
trawler
trireme
vedette
victory
wanigan
warship
weather

08 bilander
billyboy
budgerow
car ferry
corocore
corocoro
corvette
dahabieh
dispatch
eight-oar
galleass
galliass
gallivat
hospital
hoveller

Indiaman
ironclad
log-canoe
longship
mackinaw
man-of-war
masoolah
massoola
merchant
monohull
montaria
periagua
pleasure
repeater
row barge
runabout
sally-man
schooner
skipjack
smuggler
Spaniard
training
trimaran
water bus
woodskin

09 bomb-ketch
Bucentaur
catamaran
commodore
container
dahabeeah
dahabiyah
dahabiyeh
daysailer
daysailor
destroyer
firefloat
flying jib
freighter
herringer
Hollander
hydrofoil
klondiker
klondyker
lapstrake
lapstreak
leviathan
long-liner
minelayer
monoxylon
motoscafo
multihull
Norwegian
oil-burner
oil tanker
outrigger
privateer
randan gig

receiving
sallee-man
speedster
steamship
store ship
submarine
surf canoe
transport
two decker
two-master
vaporetto
well smack

10 armour-clad
bomb-vessel
brigantine
free-trader
hovercraft
icebreaker
minehunter
quadrireme
seal-fisher
tea clipper
trekschuit
triaconter
victualler
windjammer

11 bulk carrier
cockleshell
dreadnought
galley-foist
merchantman
minesweeper
motor launch
penteconter
purse-seiner
quinquereme
sallee-rover
salmon coble
side-wheeler
steam launch
steam packet
steam vessel
submersible
three-decker
three-master
victualling
wooden horse

12 cabin cruiser
deepwaterman
double-decker
East-Indiaman
line-of-battle
screw steamer
single-decker
square-rigger
stern-wheeler
tangle-netter

tramp steamer
troop carrier
13 Canadian canoe
paddle steamer
revenue cutter

roll-on roll-off
14 Flying Dutchman
ocean-greyhound
turbine steamer
15 aircraft-carrier

floating battery
logistics vessel

Ship parts include:

03 bow
box
oar
rig

04 beam
brig
brow
bunk
cant
deck
eyes
head
hold
keel
mast
port
prow
sail

05 berth
bilge
cabin
cable
chimb
chime
chine
cleat
coach
davit
hatch
hawse
stern
wheel
winch

06 anchor
bridge
buffer
dodger

fender
fo'c's'le
funnel
galley
gunnel
hawser
rigger
rudder
tiller

07 bollard
caboose
capstan
channel
counter
fardage
gangway
gun deck
gunwale
hammock
landing
quarter
rowlock
top deck
transom

08 binnacle
boat deck
boom-iron
bulkhead
bulwarks
cutwater
foot-rope
forepeak
garboard
hatchway
main deck
poop deck
porthole
wardroom

09 afterdeck
billboard
breadroom
chart room
crosstree
crow's nest
floorhead
forecabin
gangplank
goose-wing
hawsehole
hawsepipe
lower deck
radio room
stanchion
starboard
stateroom
waterline

10 boiler room
engine room
fiddlehead
figurehead
flight deck
forecastle
pilot house
stabilizer

11 boot-topping
chain locker
floor timber
paddle wheel
quarter deck

12 companionway
Plimsoll line

13 promenade deck

14 garboard strake
superstructure

15 companion ladder

Ships include:

03 *QE2*

04 *Ajax*
Argo
Hood
Nina

05 *Argus*
Maine
Pinta

06 *Beagle*
Bounty
Cathay
Oriana
Pequod
Renown

07 *Alabama*
Amistad

Belfast
Blücher
Olympic
Pelican
Potomac
Repulse
Tirpitz
Titanic

Victory

08 *Ark Royal*
Bismarck
Canberra
Fearless
Graf Spee
Intrepid
Iron Duke
Mary Rose
Royal Oak

09 *Adventure*
Aquitania
Brittania
Brittanic
Carinthia
Cutty Sark

Discovery
Endeavour
Gneisenau
Lexington
Lusitania
Mayflower
Normandie
Queen Mary
Sheffield
Téméraire
Terranova

10 *Golden Hind*
Hispaniola
Invincible
Mauretania
Prinz Eugen
Resolution

Santa Maria
Washington

11 *Dawn Treader*
Dreadnought
Illustrious
Scharnhorst

12 *Great Britain*
Great Eastern
Great Western
Marie Celeste

13 *Prince of Wales*

14 *Flying Dutchman*
Queen Elizabeth

15 *Admiral Graf Spee*
General Belgrano
Queen Elizabeth 2

Ships' crewmen and officers include:

02 AB

04 mate

06 master

purser

07 captain

steward

08 cabin-boy

ship's boy

09 first mate

10 able rating

able seaman

12 first officer

Shipping forecast areas:

04 Sole
Tyne

05 Dover
Forth
Lundy
Malin
Wight

06 Bailey

Biscay
Dogger
Faroes
Fisher
Humber
Thames
Viking

07 Fastnet

Fitzroy
Forties
Rockall
Shannon

08 Cromarty
Fair Isle
Hebrides
Irish Sea

Plymouth
Portland

09 Trafalgar

10 Finisterre

11 German Bight
North Utsire
South Utsire

16 South-East Iceland

See also **sailing**

shop

Shop types include:

01 e

02 op

03 toy

04 book
chip
farm
grog
shoe
tuck

05 baker
dairy
dress
offie
phone
stall

sweet
video

06 barber
bazaar
bookie
bottle
chippy
corner
draper
grocer
market
online
record
tailor
thrift

07 betting

butcher
charity
chemist
chipper
clothes
florist
saddler

08 boutique
hardware
jeweller
milliner
pharmacy
takeaway

09 bookmaker
drugstore
newsagent

outfitter
stationer
superette
10 candy store
chain store
electrical
fishmonger
health-food
ironmonger
mini-market
off-licence
pawnbroker

post office
radio and TV
second-hand
superstore
11 bottle store
fish and chip
five-and-dime
greengrocer
haberdasher
hairdresser
hypermarket
launderette

online store
opportunity
supermarket
tobacconist
12 cash-and-carry
confectioner
delicatessen
general store
indoor market
13 computer store
farmers' market
15 department store

Shops include:

03 BHV (France)
04 Tati (France)
05 Macy's (USA)
07 Hamleys (England)
Harrods (England)
Jenners (Scotland)
Liberty (England)
09 Century 21 (USA)
Printemps (France)
10 FAO Schwarz (USA)

Selfridge's (England)
11 Le Bon Marché (France)
12 Tiffany and Co (USA)
13 Bloomingdale's (USA)
Harvey Nichols (England/Scotland)
La Samaritaine (France)
Lord and Taylor (USA)
15 Bergdorf Goodman (USA)
Fortnum and Mason (England)
Saks Fifth Avenue (USA)

French shops include:

05 tabac
08 boutique
épicerie
09 boucherie

librairie
10 bijouterie
confiserie
fromagerie

parfumerie
pâtisserie
rôtisserie
11 boulangerie

charcuterie
12 chocolaterie
grand magasin
poissonnerie

Shopping terms include:

03 VAT
04 EPOS
mall
rail
till
05 aisle
cabas
chain
plaza
price
sales
shelf
stand
06 branch
browse
change
cheque
EFTPOS
fascia
market

markup
refund
retail
ring up
07 barcode
bargain
cashier
counter
display
dump bin
étalage
in-store
mall rat
receipt
reduced
service
spinner
tote bag
trolley
08 checkout

consumer
customer
discount
exchange
galleria
messages
precinct
price tag
purchase
salesman
sales tax
shop bell
warranty
09 brand name
debit card
dump table
guarantee
mail order
mannequin
midinette
strip mall

10 carrier bag
  channel-hop
  charge card
  credit card
  credit note
  department
  floor limit
  high street
  impulse buy
  outlet mall
  saleswoman
  shop around
  shop window

11 dump display
  fitting room
  loyalty card
  merchandise

See also **business**

salesperson
security tag
shopping bag
supermarket

12 cash register
  early closing
  hire purchase
  home delivery
  home shopping
  January sales
  opening hours
  profit margin
  shopping list
  teleshopping

13 bargain-hunter
  counter-jumper

credit voucher
outlet village
retail therapy
security guard
shop assistant
value-added tax

14 consumer rights
  counter-skipper
  sales assistant
  shopping basket
  shopping centre
  window-shopping

15 bargain basement
  express checkout
  shopping trolley
  statutory rights

short story *see* **novel**

Shostakovich, Dmitri (1906–75)

Significant works include:

03 *Nos* (1930)

07 'Babi-Yar' (Symphony; 1962)
  'October' (Symphony; 1927)
  The Bolt (1931)
  The Nose (1930)

09 'Leningrad' (Symphony; 1942)

10 'Stalingrad' (Symphony; 1943)

11 'The Year 1905' (Symphony; 1957)
  'The Year 1917' (Symphony; 1961)

12 *The Golden Age* (1930)

13 'The First of May' (Symphony; 1930)

14 *The Limpid Brook* (1935)

17 *Katerina Izmailova* (1963)

31 *Lady Macbeth of the Mtsensk District* (1934)

shotokan belt *see* **karate**

shout

Shouts and cries include:

02 io
  oi!
  yo!

03 hey
  hup
  nix

04 euoi
  evoe
  fall
  fore
  haro
  I-spy

rivo
shoo
sola

05 chevy
  chivy
  evhoe
  evohe
  havoc
  heigh
  holla
  hollo
  hooch
  huzza

06 banzai
  chivvy
  eureka
  halloa
  halloo
  harrow
  hoicks
  what ho!
  yoicks

07 glory be
  heigh-ho
  heureka
  kamerad

tally-ho
tantivy

08 alleluia
  gardyloo
  Geronimo
  harambee

09 scaldings
  stop thief!

10 halleluiah
  hallelujah
  view-halloo
  westward ho!

show *see* **quiz**; **radio**; **television**

showjumper *see* **equestrian sport**

shrub

Shrubs include:

03 ivy
04 hebe
rose
05 broom
holly
lilac
peony
yucca
06 azalea
daphne
laurel

mallow
mimosa
privet
07 arbutus
dogwood
fuchsia
heather
jasmine
phlomis
spiraea
weigela

08 berberis
buddleia
camellia
clematis
euonymus
japonica
laburnum
lavender
magnolia
musk rose
tamarisk
viburnum

wisteria
09 eucryphia
firethorn
forsythia
hydrangea
10 mock orange
witch hazel
11 cotoneaster
honeysuckle
12 rhododendron

See also **tree**

SI prefix *see* **science**

SI unit *see* **measurement**

siege

Sieges include:

04 Acre (ended 1191)
Metz (1552)
Waco (1993)
05 Alamo (1836)
Derry (1688–89)
Kuito (1992–94)
Paris (ended 1590; 1870–71)
Rouen (ended 1592)
06 Janina (1821–22)
London (1016)
Quebec (1759; 1775)
Toulon (1793)
Vienna (1529; 1683)
07 Antioch (1097–98)
Bristol (1643)
Granada (1490–92)
Lucknow (1857)
Orléans (1428–29)
08 Damascus (1148)
Limerick (1691)
Mafeking (1899–1900)
Roxburgh (1460)

Sarajevo (1992–95)
Syracuse (213–212 BC)
The Alamo (1836)
Yorktown (1781)
09 Barcelona (ended 1652; 1713–14)
Kimberley (1899–1900)
Ladysmith (1899–1900)
Leningrad (1941–44)
Silistria (1809)
Vicksburg (1863)
10 Charleston (1780)
Kut al-amara (1915–16)
Sevastopol (1854–55)
12 Tenochtitlán (1521)
14 Constantinople (1391–98; 1422; 1453)
Entebbe Airport (1976)
Iranian Embassy (1980)
Munich Olympics (1972)
15 Bourj al-Barajneh (1987)
Japanese Embassy (1996–97)
Palace of Culture (2002)

sight impairment *see* **blindness**

sign *see* **motoring; zodiac**

signal

Signals and warnings include:

03 cue
SOS

04 bell
buoy
fire
flag
gong
honk
horn
pips
toot

05 alarm
bugle
flare
knell
larum
pager
shout
siren
vigia

06 beacon
buzzer
hooter
klaxon
mayday
rocket
tattoo

tocsin
winker

07 bleeper
car horn
foghorn
go-ahead
red card
red flag
whistle

08 car alarm
drumbeat
password
red alert
red light
reveille

09 alarm-bell
fire alarm
indicator
larum-bell
Morse code
signal box
storm cone
Very light

10 alarm clock
amber light
curfew bell
green light

hand signal
heliograph
Lutine bell
smoke alarm
time signal
yellow card
yellow flag

11 bicycle bell
gale warning
smoke signal
starter's gun
storm signal
trafficator

12 burglar alarm
final warning
storm warning
warning light

13 Belisha beacon
flashing light
personal alarm
police whistle
security alarm
signal letters
traffic lights

14 distress signal
written warning

15 semaphore signal

See also **navigation**

Sikhism

Sikh groups and movements include:

05 Akali
Udasi

07 Nihangs
Nirmala

08 Namdhari

09 Nirankari

See also **religion**

sin

The Seven Deadly Sins:

04 envy
lust

05 anger

pride
sloth
wrath

06 acedia

07 accidie
avarice

08 gluttony

12 covetousness

singer

Singer types include:

03 pop

04 alto
bass

diva
folk

05 carol

mezzo
opera
tenor

06 chorus
treble

07 crooner

pop star	choirboy	choirgirl	troubadour
soloist	falsetto	chorister	**11** Heldentenor
soprano	minstrel	contralto	**12** counter-tenor
warbler	songster	precentor	mezzo-soprano
08 baritone	vocalist	sopranist	**13** basso profondo
barytone	**09** balladeer	**10** prima donna	basso profundo
castrato	chanteuse	songstress	

Singers include:

03 Day (Doris; 1924– , US)

04 Cole (Nat 'King'; 1919–65, US)
Lynn (Dame Vera; 1917– , English)
Piaf (Edith; 1915–63, French)

05 Jones (Aled; 1970– , Welsh)
Lloyd (Marie; 1870–1922, English)
Paige (Elaine; 1951– , English)

06 Atwell (Winifred; 1914–83, Trinidadian)
Bassey (Dame Shirley; 1937– , Welsh)
Church (Charlotte; 1986– , Welsh)
Crosby (Bing; 1903–77, US)
Fields (Dame Gracie; 1898–1979, English)
Jolson (Al; 1886–1950, US)
Lauder (Sir Harry; 1870–1950, Scottish)

Lillie (Beatrice; 1894–1989, Canadian)
Steele (Tommy; 1936– , English)

07 Andrews (Dame Julie; 1935– , English)
Dickson (Barbara; 1947– , Scottish)
Garland (Judy; 1922–69, US)
Jenkins (Katherine; 1980– , Welsh)
Miranda (Carmen; 1909–55, Brazilian)
Robeson (Paul; 1898–1976, US)
Secombe (Sir Harry; 1921–2001, Welsh)
Sinatra (Frank; 1915–98, US)

08 Bygraves (Max; 1922– , English)
Liberace (1919–87, US)

09 Belafonte (Harry; 1927– , US)
Chevalier (Albert; 1861–1923, English)

See also **country and western**; **folk**; **jazz**; **opera**; **pop**

skating *see* **ice skating**

skiing

Skiing events include:

05 grass	nordic	**08** combined	snowboard
mogul	slalom	downhill	**11** giant slalom
relay	sprint	halfpipe	**12** cross-country
speed	super-g	**09** classical	
06 aerial	**07** jumping	dual mogul	
alpine	pursuit	freestyle	

Skiers include:

04 Hess (Erica; 1962– , Swiss)
Vonn (Lindsey; 1984– , US)

05 Cranz (Christl; 1914–2004, Belgian)
Killy (Jean-Claude; 1943– , French)
Maier (Hermann; 1972– , Austrian)
Raich (Benjamin; 1978– , Austrian)
Tomba (Alberto; 1966– , Italian)

06 Dahlie (Bjørn; 1967– , Norwegian)
Figini (Michela; 1966– , Swiss)
Miller (Bode; 1977– , US)
Sailer (Toni; 1935– , Austrian)
Wenzel (Hanni; 1956– , German/
Liechtenstein)

07 Edwards (Eddie 'the Eagle'; 1963– , English)
Klammer (Franz; 1953– , Austrian)
Nykänen (Matti; 1963– , Finnish)
Simpson (Myrtle; 1931– , Scottish)
Svindal (Aksel Lund; 1982– , Norwegian)

08 Stenmark (Ingemar; 1956– , Swedish)
Walliser (Maria; 1963– , Swiss)

09 Schneider (Vreni; 1964– , Swiss)
Smetanina (Raisa; 1952– , Russian)

10 Girardelli (Marc; 1963– , Austrian/
Luxembourg)
Moser-Pröll (Annemarie; 1953– , Austrian)
Zurbriggen (Pirmin; 1963– , Swiss)

04 gate
05 daffy
glide
inrun
piste
split
06 basket
big air
edging
kicker
k point

outrun
p point
schuss
07 grip wax
hairpin
harries
kick wax
takeoff
08 glide wax
off-piste
start hut

table top
09 large hill
mass start
Steilhang
V-position
10 Hahnenkamm
helicopter
normal hill
11 egg position
scramble leg
spread eagle

12 starting gate
tuck position
vertical gate
13 backscratcher
critical point
herringboning
safety netting
14 outjump the hill
safety bindings
staggered start

skin

04 derm
hair
hide
pore

05 cutis
derma
06 corium
dermis

07 cuticle
papilla
09 epidermis
10 sweat gland

11 lower dermis
12 hair follicle
14 sebaceous gland

02 EB
XP
04 acne
boba
buba
rash
wart
yaws

05 favus
tinea
ulcer
06 eczema
herpes
07 anthrax
bedsore
gum rash

leprosy
rosacea
scabies
08 dandruff
melanoma
ringworm
09 keratosis
psoriasis

10 dermatitis
dermatosis
framboesia
11 prickly heat
12 athlete's foot
button scurvy

See also **hair**; **inflammation**

smell

03 hum
04 funk
fust
guff
ming
must
niff

nose
pong
reek
05 aroma
fetor
odour
scent

sniff
stink
whiff
06 miasma
stench
07 bouquet

perfume
08 malodour
mephitis
pungency
09 fragrance
redolence

02 BO
04 feet
musk
rose
05 basil
booze
ozone

smoke
spice
06 cheese
coffee
garlic
nutmeg
pepper

07 alcohol
camphor
incense
menthol
perfume
vanilla
08 bergamot
lavender

09 body odour
patchouli
pot pourri
woodsmoke
10 eucalyptus
peppermint
11 wintergreen

snake

Snakes include:

03 asp	blind	ribbon	hamadryas
boa	brown	smooth	king cobra
rat	cobra	taipan	puff adder
sea	coral	**07** diamond	river-jack
04 boma	Elaps	hognose	**10** bandy-bandy
bull	grass	langaha	bushmaster
corn	green	rattler	copperhead
file	krait		death adder
hoop	mamba	**08** anaconda	dendrophis
king	racer	cerastes	fer-de-lance
milk	tiger	colubrid	Gabon viper
naga	viper	cylinder	massasauga
Naia	water	jararaca	sidewinder
Naja	**06** carpet	jararaka	**11** constrictor
pine	dipsas	mocassin	cottonmouth
pipe	dugite	moccasin	diamondback
ring	ellops	pit viper	gaboon viper
rock	flying	ringhals	horned viper
sand	gaboon	rinkhals	massasauger
seps	garter	sucurujú	**12** carpet python
tree	gopher	water boa	**13** diamond python
whip	indigo	**09** berg-adder	water moccasin
worm	karait	boomslang	**14** boa constrictor
05 adder	python	coachwhip	river-jack viper
black	rattle	hamadryad	

See also **poison**

snooker

Snooker players include:

03 Meo (Tony; 1959– , English)

05 Davis (Fred; 1913–98, English)
Davis (Joe; 1901–78, English)
Davis (Steve; 1957– , English)
Ebdon (Peter; 1970– , English)
Virgo (John; 1946– , English)
White (Jimmy; 1962– , English)

06 Fisher (Allison; 1968– , English)
Hendry (Stephen; 1969– , Scottish)
Taylor (Dennis; 1949– , Northern Irish)

07 Doherty (Ken; 1975– , Irish)

Higgins (Alex; 1949– , Northern Irish)
Higgins (John; 1975– , Scottish)
Maguire (Stephen; 1981– , Scottish)
Parrott (John; 1964– , English)
Reardon (Ray; 1932– , Welsh)
Stevens (Matthew; 1977– , Welsh)

08 Charlton (Eddie; 1929–2004, Australian)
Thorburn (Cliff; 1948– , Canadian)
Williams (Mark; 1975– , Welsh)

09 Griffiths (Terry; 1947– , Welsh)
O'Sullivan (Ronnie; 1975– , English)

Snooker terms include:

01 D	drag	rest	break
03 bed	foul	side	chalk
cue	jaws	sink	fluke
pot	kick	spot	frame
set	kiss	stun	in-off
tip	miss	**05** angle	massé
04 ball	pack	baize	plant
butt	rail	baulk	screw

table

06 bridge
cannon
colour
double
miscue
pocket
safety
spider

See also **sport**

07 century
cue ball
cushion
English
feather
maximum
snooker
topspin

08 backspin

break-off
free ball
full ball
half ball
half-butt

09 baulk line
check side
extension
screw shot

10 object ball
push stroke
safety shot

11 half-century
running side

12 maximum break
touching ball

13 follow-through
shot to nothing

snow

Snow types and formations include:

03 red

04 corn
crud
firn
névé

See also **ice**

05 drift
flake
sleet
slush

06 powder

sludge
yellow

07 cornice
flaught

08 sastruga

09 avalanche
spindrift

Snow White *see* dwarf

soap

Soaps include:

03 Lux®

04 Dove®
hard
soft

05 glass
Pears®

sugar

06 liquid
marine
saddle
toilet
yellow

07 Castile
coal-tar
shaving
Spanish
Windsor

08 carbolic

mountain
olive-oil

09 Palmolive®

10 coconut-oil

soap opera

Soap operas include:

06 *Dallas*

07 *Dynasty*
The Bill

08 *Casualty*

See also **radio**; **television**

09 *Brookside*
Emmerdale
Holby City
Hollyoaks

River City

10 *EastEnders*
Neighbours
The Archers

11 *Home and Away*

society

Societies include:

03 BCS
BPS
CSP
ENS

04 BNES

BRCS

05 ASLEF
Royal

06 burial
choral

Dorcas

07 benefit
Camorra

08 affluent
building

friendly
Red Cross

sociology

Terms used in sociology include:

06 family
gender
07 culture
in-group
10 demography
matriarchy
patriarchy
subculture
underclass

11 dysfunction
gender roles
megalopolis
12 assimilation
primary group
13 class conflict
ethnocentrism
nuclear family

14 achieved status
ascribed status
extended family
life expectancy
secondary group
social mobility
stratification
tertiary sector
15 absolute poverty

sofa

Sofas include:

05 couch
divan
futon
squab
06 canapé
day bed
litter

lounge
settee
sunbed
07 bergère
casting
dos-à-dos
lounger

sofa bed
09 banquette
bed-settee
davenport
tête-à-tête
twoseater
10 sun lounger

11 studio couch
12 chaise-longue
chesterfield

See also **chair**

solar system *see* **planet**

soldier

Soldier types include:

02 GI
03 NCO
05 cadet
tommy
06 ensign
gunner
hussar
lancer
marine
sapper

sentry
sniper
troops
07 dragoon
fighter
officer
orderly
private
recruit
regular
terrier

trooper
warrior
08 commando
fusilier
partisan
rifleman
09 centurion
conscript
guardsman
guerrilla

irregular
mercenary
minuteman
10 cavalryman
serviceman
11 infantryman
legionnaire
paratrooper
Territorial
12 sharpshooter

Soldiers include:

02 Li (Hongzhang; 1823–1901, Chinese)

03 Chu (Te; 1886–1976, Chinese)
Chu (Teh; 1886–1976, Chinese)
Cid (El; c.1043–99, Spanish)
Lee (Charles; 1731–82, English/American)
Lee (Henry; 1756–1818, American)
Lee (Robert E; 1807–70, US)
Lin (Biao; 1908–71, Chinese)
Lin (Piao; 1908–71, Chinese)
Mac (*Rusty Bugles*, 1948, Sumner Locke

Elliott)
Odd (Sgt Fred; *Keep the Home Guard Turning*, 1943, Compton Mackenzie)
Wet (Christiaan de; 1854–1922, Boer)
Zhu (De; 1886–1976, Chinese)

04 Alba (Ferdinand Alvarez de Toledo, Duke of; 1508–82, Spanish)
Alva (Ferdinand Alvarez de Toledo, Duke of; 1508–82, Spanish)
Amin (Idi; 1925–2003, Ugandan)

Byng (Julian, Viscount; 1862–1935, English)
Cade (Jack; d.1450, Irish)
Cope (Sir John; d.1760, English)
Díaz (Porfirio; 1830–1915, Mexican)
Foch (Ferdinand; 1851–1929, French)
Gage (Thomas; 1721–87, English)
Haig (Alexander; 1924– , US)
Haig (Douglas, Earl, 1861–1928, Scottish)
Hood (John B; 1831–79, US)
Howe (William, Viscount; 1729–1814, English)
Hull (William; 1753–1825, American)
Jamy (*Henry V*, 1599, William Shakespeare)
Knox (Henry; 1750–1806, US)
Mack (Karl, Freiherr von; 1752–1828, Austrian)
Monk (George, Duke of Albemarle; 1608–70, English)
Pile (Sir Frederick, Baronet; 1884–1976, English)
Polk (Leonidas; 1806–64, US)
Rich (Brackenbury; *The Suicide Club*, 1878, Robert Louis Stevenson)
Saxe (Maurice, Comte de; 1696–1750, French)
Slim (William, Viscount; 1891–1970, English)
Tojo (Hideki; 1885–1948, Japanese)
Troy (Sgt Francis; *Far from the Madding Crowd*, 1874, Thomas Hardy)
York (Sergeant; 1887–1964, US)

05 Aidid (Mohamed Farah; c.1930–1996, Somali)
Allen (Ethan; 1738–89, American)
André (John; 1751–80, English)
Arnim (Hans Georg von; 1581–1641, German)
Arnim (Jürgen, Baron von; 1891–1971, German)
Barak (Ehud; 1942– , Israeli)
Bixio (Girolamo; 1821–73, Italian)
Botha (Louis; 1862–1919, South African)
Bowie (Jim; 1790–1836, US/Mexican)
Boyle (Roger, Earl of Orrery; 1621–79, Irish)
Bruce (Robert; 1274–1329, Scottish)
Brune (Guillaume Marie Anne; 1762–1815, French)
Cecil (Thomas, Earl of Exeter; 1542–1623, English)
Chard (John; 1847–97, English)
Cimon (c.507–c.450 BC, Athenian)
Clark (Mark; 1896–1984, US)
Cleon (d.422 BC, Athenian)
Condé (Louis I de Bourbon, Prince de; 1530–69, French)
Conté (Lansana; 1934–2008, Guinean)
Coote (Sir Eyre; 1726–83, Anglo-Irish)
Craig (Sir James; 1748–1812, British)

Crook (George; 1829–90, US)
Dayan (Moshe; 1915–81, Israeli)
Derby (James Stanley, Earl of; 1606–51, English)
Early (Jubal; 1816–94, US)
Essex (Robert Devereux, Earl of; 1591–1646, English)
Evans (Lance-Bombardier; *Events While Guarding the Bofors Gun*, 1966, John McGrath)
Ewell (Richard; 1817–72, US)
Glubb (Sir John; 1897–1986, English)
Gough (Hugh, Viscount; 1779–1869, Anglo-Irish)
Gower (*Henry V*, 1599, William Shakespeare)
Gowon (Yakubu; 1934– , Nigerian)
Grant (Ulysses S; 1822–85, US)
Guise (Claude of Lorraine, Duke of; 1496–1550, French)
Guise (Francis, Duke of; 1519–63, French)
Heros (*The Woman*, 1978, Edward Bond)
Hicks (William; 1830–83, English)
İnönü (Ismet; 1884–1973, Turkish)
Ismay (Hastings, Lord; 1887–1965, English)
Junot (Andoche, Duc d'Abrantès; 1771–1813, French)
Kluge (Günther von; 1882–1944, German)
Konev (Ivan; 1897–1973, Soviet)
Lebed (Alexander; 1950–2002, Russian)
Leese (Sir Oliver; 1894–1978, English)
Meade (George G; 1815–72, US)
Monck (George, Duke of Albemarle; 1608–70, English)
Moore (Sir Jeremy; 1928–2007, English)
Moore (Sir John; 1761–1809, Scottish)
Mosby (John S; 1833–1916, US)
Murat (Joachim; 1767–1815, French)
Nolan (Des; *Rusty Bugles*, 1948, Sumner Locke Elliott)
North (Oliver; 1943– , US)
Perón (Juan; 1895–1974, Argentine)
Pride (Thomas; d.1658, English)
Rabin (Itzhak; 1922–95, Israeli)
Rabin (Yitzhak; 1922–95, Israeli)
Sadat (Anwar el-; 1918–81, Egyptian)
San Yu (U; 1919–96, Burmese)
Sawin (Birdofredum; *The Biglow Papers*, 1848, James Russell Lowell)
Smuts (Jan; 1870–1950, South African)
Stack (Lee; d.1924, British)
Stark (John; 1728–1822, American)
Sucre (Antonio José de; 1793–1830, South American)
Sully (Maximilien de Béthune, Duc de; 1560–1641, French)
Tilly (Johann Tserklaes, Count von; 1559–1632, Bavarian)

Timur (1336–1405, Tatar)
Wayne (Anthony; 1745–96, American)
Wyatt (Sir Thomas, the Younger; c.1520–54, English)

◆6 Abacha (Sani; 1943–98, Nigerian)
Abboud (Ibrahim; 1900–83, Sudanese)
Abrams (Creighton; 1914–74, US)
Anders (Wladyslaw; 1892–1970, Polish)
Angelo (Private; *Private Angelo*, 1946, Eric Linklater)
Antony (Mark; c.83–30 BC, Roman)
Aumale (Duc d'; 1822–97, French)
Baldry (Captain Chris; *The Return of the Soldier*, 1918, Rebecca West)
Barton (David; *Strange Meeting*, 1971, Susan Hill)
Bayard (Pierre du Terrail, Chevalier de; 1476–1524, French)
Baynes (Gen; *The Adventures of Philip*, 1861–62, W M Thackeray)
Blamey (Sir Thomas; 1884–1951, Australian)
Blount (Charles, Earl of Devonshire; 1563–1606, English)
Borgia (Cesare; c.1476–1507, Italian)
Bosola (Daniel de; *The Duchess of Malfi*, 1623, John Webster)
Brooke (Sir James; 1803–68, English)
Brooks (Sgt; *Rusty Bugles*, 1948, Sumner Locke Elliott)
Browne (Sir Sam; 1824–1901, British)
Buhari (Muhammadu; 1942– , Nigerian)
Cortés (Hernán; 1485–1547, Spanish)
Cortés (Hernando; 1485–1547, Spanish)
Crerar (Harry; 1888–1965, Canadian)
Cronje (Piet; 1835–1911, South African)
Custer (George; 1839–76, US)
Davies (Christian; 1667–1739, Irish)
Dobbie (Sir William; 1879–1964, English)
Drouet (Jean Baptiste, Comte d'Erlon; 1765–1844, French)
Dufour (Guillaume Henri; 1787–1875, Swiss)
Dundee (John Graham, Viscount; c.1649–1689, Scottish)
Egmond (Lamoraal, Graf van; 1522–68, Flemish)
Egmont (Lamoraal, Graf van; 1522–68, Flemish)
Ershad (Hossain; 1930– , Bangladeshi)
Fabius (d.203 BC, Roman)
Falcon (Ken; *Rusty Bugles*, 1948, Sumner Locke Elliott)
Frunze (Mikhail; 1885–1925, Russian)
Fuller (John; 1878–1966, English)
Gatsby (Jay; *The Great Gatsby*, 1925, F Scott Fitzgerald)
Ginkel (Godert de, Earl of Athlone; 1630–1703, Dutch/British)

Giraud (Henri; 1879–1949, French)
Görgey (Artúr; 1818–1916, Hungarian)
Granby (John Manners, Marquis of; 1721–70, English)
Greene (Nathanael; 1742–86, American)
Haynau (Julius, Baron von; 1786–1853, Austrian)
Hooker (Joseph; 1814–79, US)
Howard (Oliver O; 1830–1909, US)
Howard (Thomas, Duke of Norfolk and Earl of Surrey; 1443–1524, English)
Joffre (Joseph; 1852–1931, French)
Keitel (Wilhelm; 1882–1946, German)
Lovell (Lord; *A New Way to Pay Old Debts*, 1633, Philip Massinger)
Moltke (Helmuth; 1848–1916, German)
Moltke (Helmuth, Count von; 1800–91, Prussian)
Monash (Sir John; 1865–1931, Australian)
Murphy (Audie; 1924–71, US)
Murray (Lord George; c.1700–1760, Scottish)
Napier (Robert, Lord; 1810–90, British)
Nasser (Gamal Abd al-; 1918–70, Egyptian)
Neguib (Mohammed; 1901–84, Egyptian)
Nicias (d.413 BC, Athenian)
Ojukwu (Chukwuemeka; 1933– , Nigerian)
Otford (Eric; *Rusty Bugles*, 1948, Sumner Locke Elliott)
Patton (George; 1885–1945, US)
Paulus (Friedrich; 1890–1957, German)
Pétain (Philippe; 1856–1951, French)
Pierre (*Venice Preserv'd*, 1682, Thomas Otway)
Plumer (Herbert, Viscount; 1857–1932, English)
Pompey (106–48 BC, Roman)
Powell (Colin; 1937– , US)
Procop (Andrew; c.1380–1434, Bohemian)
Prokop (Andrew; c.1380–1434, Bohemian)
Putnam (Israel; 1718–90, American)
Raglan (Fitzroy Somerset, Lord; 1788–1855, English)
Rahman (Ziaur; 1935–81, Bangladeshi)
Revere (Paul; 1735–1818, American)
Rommel (Erwin; 1891–1944, German)
Rupert (Prince; 1619–82, English)
Sevier (John; 1745–1815, US)
Sharpe (Richard; *Sharpe's Eagle*, et seq, 1981, Bernard Cornwell)
Smalls (Robert; 1839–1915, US)
Stalky (*Stalky & Co*, 1899, Rudyard Kipling)
Stuart (Jeb; 1833–64, US)
Sumter (Thomas; 1734–1832, American)
Talbot (Mary Anne; 1778–1808, English)
Talbot (Sir John, Earl Shrewsbury; c.1390–1453, English)

Turvey (*Turvey: a Military Picaresque*, 1949, Earle Birney)

Vauban (Sebastien le Prestre de; 1633–1707, French)

Waller (Sir William; c.1597–1688, English)

Wavell (Archibald, Earl; 1883–1950, English)

Wilson (Henry, Lord; 1881–1964, English)

07 Allenby (Edmund, Viscount; 1861–1936, English)

Almagro (Diego de; 1475–1538, Spanish)

Amherst (Jeffrey, Lord; 1717–97, English)

Apraxin (Stepan, Count; 1702–58, Russian)

Artigas (José; 1764–1850, Uruguayan)

Bazaine (Achille François; 1811–88, French)

Bedford (John of Lancaster, Duke of; 1389–1435, English)

Blücher (Gebhard von, Prince of Wahlstadt; 1742–1819, Prussian)

Bokassa (Jean Bédel; 1921–96, Central African Republic)

Bourbon (Charles; 1490–1527, French)

Brandon (Charles, Duke of Suffolk; 1484–1545, English)

Buckner (Simon B, Jnr; 1886–1945, US)

Budenny (Semyon; 1883–1973, Russian)

Bugeaud (Thomas; 1784–1849, French)

Bullock (John; *A Patriot's Progress*, 1930, Henry Williamson)

Cadogan (William, Earl; 1675–1726, English)

Caprivi (Leo, Graf von; 1831–99, German)

Catroux (Georges; 1877–1969, French)

Clinton (James; 1736–1812, American)

Clinton (Sir Henry; c.1738–1795, Canadian/British)

Coligny (Gaspard de, Duc; 1519–72, French)

Crillon (Louis de; 1541–1615, French)

Dalyell (Thomas; c.1615–1685, Scottish)

Dalzell (Thomas; c.1615–1685, Scottish)

Denikin (Anton; 1872–1947, Russian)

Dreyfus (Alfred; c.1859–1935, French)

Edmonds (Sarah; 1841–98, Canadian)

Enghien (Louis Antoine Henri de Bourbon, Duc d'; 1772–1804, French)

Farnese (Alessandro; 1546–92, Italian/Spanish)

Gaddafi (Muammar; 1942– , Libyan)

Gamelin (Maurice; 1872–1958, French)

Gemayel (Bashir; 1947–82, Lebanese)

Grenfel (Henry; *The Fox*, 1923, D H Lawrence)

Grouchy (Emmanuel, Marquis de; 1766–1847, French)

Hackett (Sir John; 1910–97, Australian/British)

Halleck (Henry W; 1815–72, US)

Hampton (Wade; 1818–1902, US)

Hancock (Winfield Scott; 1824–86, US)

Hunyady (János; c.1387–1456, Hungarian)

Hunyady (John; c.1387–1456, Hungarian)

Jackson (Sir W G F; 1917–99, English)

Jackson (Thomas 'Stonewall'; 1824–63, US)

Joubert (Piet; 1834–1900, Afrikaner)

Jourdan (Jean-Baptiste, Comte; 1762–1833, French)

Kérékou (Mathieu; 1933– , Benin)

Kolchak (Aleksandr; 1874–1920, Russian)

Kutuzov (Mikhail, Prince of Smolensk; 1745–1813, Russian)

Lambert (Gen; *The Virginians*, 1857–59, W M Thackeray)

Leclerc (Jacques Philippe; 1902–47, French)

Le Clerc (Jacques Philippe; 1902–47, French)

Le Fever (Lieutenant; *The Life and Opinions of Tristram Shandy*, 1759–67, Laurence Sterne)

MacTurk (Captain Hector; *St Ronan's Well*, 1823, Sir Walter Scott)

Marmont (Auguste de; 1774–1852, French)

Mastern (Cass; *All the King's Men*, 1946, Robert Penn Warren)

Metaxas (Yanni; 1870–1941, Greek)

Narváez (Ramón María; 1800–68, Spanish)

Nimeiri (Gaafar; 1930– , Sudanese)

Nivelle (Robert; 1857–1924, French)

Noriega (Manuel; 1940– , Panamanian)

Phocion (c.397–318 BC, Athenian)

Pizarro (Francisco; c.1478–1541, Spanish)

Pizarro (Gonzalo; c.1506–48, Spanish)

Prewitt (Robert E Lee; *From Here to Eternity*, 1951, James Jones)

Ptolemy (I; c.367–283 BC, Egyptian)

Qaddafi (Muammar; 1942– , Libyan)

Ritchie (Sir Neil; 1897–1983, Scottish)

Roberts (Frederick, Earl; 1832–1914, English)

Sankara (Thomas; 1950–87, Burkina Faso)

Sarrail (Maurice; 1856–1929, French)

Savimbi (Jonas; 1934–2002, Angolan)

Searing (Private Jerome; 'One of the Missing', 1888, Ambrose Bierce)

Sherman (William; 1820–91, US)

Skinner (James; 1778–1841, Indian)

Speidel (Hans; 1897–1984, German)

Spinola (Ambrogio, Marquis of Los Balbases; 1539–1630, Genoese)

St Clair (Arthur; 1736–1818, Scottish/American)

Steuben (Frederick, Baron; 1730–94, German/American)

Strozzi (Piero; 1510–58, Italian)

Suharto (Thojib N J; 1921–2008, Indonesian)

Suvorov (Aleksandr, Count; 1729–1800, Russian)

Svoboda (Ludvík; 1895–1979, Czech)
Tancred (1078–1112, Norman)
Templer (Sir Gerald; 1898–1979, English)
Turenne (Henri de la Tour d'Auvergne,
Vicomte de; 1611–75, French)
Vendôme (Louis Joseph, Duc de; 1654–
1712, French)
Villars (Claude, Duc de; 1653–1734,
French)
Warwick (Richard Neville, Earl of; 1428–71,
English)
Weygand (Maxime; 1867–1965, Belgian/
French)
Wingate (Orde; 1903–44, English)
Yolland (Lieutenant George; *Translations*,
1981, Brian Friel)
Zapolya (Stephen; d.1499, Hungarian)

08 Absolute (Captain Jack; *The Rivals*, 1775, R
B Sheridan)
Alvarado (Pedro de; c.1485–1541, Spanish)
Anderson (Robert; 1806–71, US)
Anglesey (Henry Paget, Marquis of;
1768–1854, English)
Apraksin (Stepan, Count; 1702–58, Russian)
Arminius (d.19 AD, German/Roman)
Aubusson (Pierre d'; 1423–1503, French)
Augereau (Pierre, Duc de Castiglione;
1757–1816, French)
Ayub Khan (Mohammed; 1907–74,
Pakistani)
Bamforth (*The Long and the Short and the
Tall*, 1958, Willis Hall)
Bobadill (Captain; *Every Man in his
Humour*, 1598, Ben Jonson)
Bothwell (Sgt; *Old Mortality*, 1816, Sir
Walter Scott)
Braddock (Edward; 1695–1755, Scottish)
Brusilov (Aleksei; 1856–1926, Russian)
Burgoyne (John; 1722–92, English)
Burnside (Ambrose; 1824–81, US)
Campbell (Sir Colin; 1792–1863, Scottish)
Castaños (Francisco de, Duke of Bailen;
1756–1852, Spanish)
Colleoni (Bartolommeo; 1400–75, Italian)
Cromwell (Oliver; 1599–1658, English)
Dalgetty (Captain Dugald, of Drumthwacket;
A Legend of Montrose, 1819, Sir Walter
Scott)
Eichmann (Adolf; 1906–62, Austrian)
Endicott (John; 'The Maypole of Merry
Mount', 1836, Nathaniel Hawthorne)
Fielding (Sgt; *Too True to be Good*, 1932,
George Bernard Shaw)
Fluellen (*Henry V*, 1599, William
Shakespeare)
Freyberg (Bernard, Lord; 1889–1963,
English/New Zealand)
Galliéni (Joseph; 1849–1916, French)

Galtieri (Leopoldo; 1926–2003, Argentine)
Gilligan (Joe; *Soldier's Pay*, 1926, William
Faulkner)
Ginckell (Godert de, Earl of Athlone;
1630–1703, Dutch/British)
Graziani (Rodolfo, Marchese di Neghelli;
1882–1955, Italian)
Guesclin (Bertrand du; c.1320–80, French)
Guiscard (Robert; c.1015–85, Norman)
Hamilcar (c.270–228 BC, Carthaginian)
Hamilton (James, Duke of; 1606–49,
Scottish)
Hannibal (247–182 BC, Carthaginian)
Hardinge (Henry, Viscount; 1785–1856,
English)
Harrison (Thomas; 1606–60, English)
Harrison (William Henry; 1773–1841, US)
Hastings (Francis, Marquis of; 1754–1826,
English)
Havelock (Sir Henry; 1795–1857, English)
Horrocks (Sir Brian; 1895–1985, English)
Hyder Ali (1728–82, Indian)
Ironside (William Edmund, Lord; 1880–
1959, Scottish)
Lawrence (T E; 1888–1935, Anglo-Irish)
Lucullus (c.110–57 BC, Roman)
MacMahon (Patrice de; 1808–93, French)
Manstein (Erich von; 1887–1973, German)
Marcello (*The White Devil*, 1612, John
Webster)
Marrable (Captain Walter; *The Vicar of
Bullhampton*, 1870, Anthony Trollope)
Marshall (George; 1880–1959, US)
Montcalm (Louis Joseph, Marquis de;
1712–59, French)
Montfort (Simon de, Earl of Leicester;
c.1208–65, English)
Morshead (Sir Leslie; 1889–1959,
Australian)
Museveni (Yoweri; 1944– , Ugandan)
Nicholas (Grand-Duke; 1856–1929,
Russian)
Obasanjo (Olusegun; 1937– , Nigerian)
O'Donnell (Leopoldo; 1809–67, Spanish)
Pershing (John; 1860–1948, US)
Pinochet (Augusto; 1915–2006, Chilean)
Randolph (Sir Thomas; d.1332, Scottish)
Richards (Vic; *Rusty Bugles*, 1948, Sumner
Locke Elliott)
Sanjurjo (José; 1872–1936, Spanish)
Scarlett (Sir James Yorke; 1799–1871,
English)
Sheridan (Philip; 1831–88, US)
Shrapnel (Henry; 1761–1842, English)
Sikorski (Władysław; 1881–1943, Polish)
Skorzeny (Otto; 1908–75, Austrian)
Soeharto (Thojib N J; 1921–2008,
Indonesian)

Standish (Miles; *The Courtship of Miles Standish*, 1858, Henry Wadsworth Longfellow)
Stanhope (Dennis; *Journey's End*, 1928, R C Sherriff)
Stanhope (James, Earl; 1673–1721, English)
Stilicho (Flavius; c.365–408 AD, Roman)
Stilwell (Joseph W; 1883–1946, US)
Stirling (Sir David; 1915–90, Scottish)
Sullivan (John; 1740–95, American)
Tarleton (Sir Banastre; 1754–1833, English)
Tokugawa (Ieyasu; 1543–1616, Japanese)
Valdivia (Pedro de; c.1510–59, Spanish)
Wauchope (Sir Arthur; 1874–1947, Scottish)
Williams (Leslie; *The Hostage*, 1957, Brendan Behan)
Williams (Private Ellgee; *Reflections in a Golden Eye*, 1941, Carson McCullers)
Winthrop (John; 1639–1707, Anglo-American)
Wolseley (Garnet, Viscount; 1833–1913, British)
Xenophon (c.435–c.354 BC, Greek)
Yamagata (Aritomo; 1838–1922, Japanese)
Zia ul-Haq (Mohammed; 1924–88, Pakistani)

09 Alexander (Harold, Earl; 1891–1969, Anglo-Irish)
Angoulême (Louis Antoine de Bourbon, Duc d'; 1775–1844, French)
Babangida (Ibrahim; 1941– , Nigerian)
Bellenden (Major Miles, of Charnwood; *Old Mortality*, 1816, Sir Walter Scott)
Bennigsen (Levin, Count; 1745–1826, German)
Beresford (William Carr Beresford, Viscount; 1768–1854, British)
Bonaparte (Jérôme; 1784–1860, French)
Bonaparte (Napoleon; 1769–1821, French)
Carausius (d.293 AD, Roman)
Castelnau (Noël, Vicomte de; 1851–1944, French)
Cavaignac (Louis Eugène; 1802–57, French)
Cavendish (William, Duke of Newcastle; 1592–1676, English)
Dalhousie (James Ramsay, Marquis of; 1812–60, Scottish)
Fergusson (Bernard, Lord Ballantrae; 1911–80, Scottish)
Fleetwood (Charles; c.1618–1692, English)
Garibaldi (Giuseppe; 1807–82, Italian)
Gneisenau (August, Graf von; 1760–1831, Prussian)
Gondarino (*The Woman Hater*, 1605, Francis Beaumont)
Gorchakov (Prince Mikhail; 1795–1861, Russian)
Grenville (Sir Bevil; 1596–1643, English)
Haidar Ali (1728–82, Indian)

Hideyoshi (Toyotomi; 1536–98, Japanese)
Kim-Il Sung (1912–94, North Korean)
Kitchener (Horatio, Earl; 1850–1916, British)
La Marmora (Alfonso; 1804–78, Italian)
Lismahago (Lieutenant Obadiah; *The Expedition of Humphry Clinker*, 1771, Tobias Smollett)
MacArthur (Douglas; 1880–1964, US)
Macdonald (Jacques, Duc de Tarente; 1765–1840, French)
Macdonald (Sir Hector; 1857–1903, Scottish)
Macmorris (*Henry V*, 1599, William Shakespeare)
Musharraf (Pervaiz; 1943– , Pakistani)
Napoleon I (1769–1821, French)
Oldcastle (Sir John; c.1378–1417, English)
Pausanias (5c BC, Spartan)
Pelopidas (d.364 BC, Theban)
Peniakoff (Vladimir; 1897–1951, Belgian)
Pilsudski (Józef; 1867–1935, Polish)
Rawlinson (Henry, Lord; 1864–1925, English)
Rosecrans (William S; 1819–98, US)
Rundstedt (Karl von; 1875–1953, German)
San Martin (José de; 1778–1850, Argentine)
Santa Anna (Antonio López de; 1797–1876, Mexican)
Sarsfield (Patrick, Earl of Lucan; c.1645–1693, Irish)
Schofield (John; 1831–1906, US)
Schomberg (Frederick Hermann, Duke of; 1615–90, German/French)
Sertorius (123–72 BC, Roman)
Spartacus (d.71 BC, Roman)
Trenchard (Hugh, Viscount; 1873–1956, English)
Waldstein (Albrecht von; 1583–1634, Austrian)
Worcester (Sir Thomas Percy, Earl of; 1344–1403, English)
Yahya Khan (Agha Muhammad; 1917–80, Pakistani)
Yamashita (Tomoyuki; 1885–1946, Japanese)

10 Abd-el-Kader (1807–83, Algerian)
Acheampong (Ignatius; 1931–79, Ghanaian)
Ahmed Arabi (1839–1911, Egyptian)
Alanbrooke (Alan Brooke, Lord; 1883–1963, British)
Alcibiades (c.450–404 BC, Athenian)
Amr ibn al-'As (d.664, Arab)
Auchinleck (Sir Claude; 1884–1981, English)
Bluntschli (*Arms and the Man*, 1894, George Bernard Shaw)
Clausewitz (Karl von; 1780–1831, Prussian)
Cornwallis (Charles; 1738–1805, English)
Cumberland (William Augustus, Duke of; 1721–65, English)

Enver Pasha (1881–1922, Turkish)
Falkenhayn (Erich von; 1861–1922, German)
Frundsberg (Georg von; 1473–1528, German)
Heathfield (George Augustus Eliott, Lord; 1717–90, Scottish)
Hindenburg (Paul von; 1847–1934, German)
Humgudgeon (*Woodstock*, 1826, Sir Walter Scott)
Jaruzelski (Wojciech; 1923–   , Polish)
Kellermann (François Christophe, Duc de Valmy; 1735–1820, French)
Kościuszko (Tadeusz; 1746–1817, Polish/US)
Kuropatkin (Aleksei; 1848–1925, Russian)
Longstreet (James; 1821–1904, US)
Ludendorff (Erich; 1865–1937, German)
Luxembourg (François Henri de Montmorency-Bouteville, Duc de; 1628–95, French)
Malinovsky (Rodion; 1898–1967, Russian)
Manchester (Edward Montagu, Earl of; 1602–71, English)
Mannerheim (Carl Gustav, Baron; 1867–1951, Finnish)
McNaughton (Andrew; 1887–1966, Canadian)
Montgomery (Bernard, Viscount; 1887–1976, English)
Rochambeau (Jean Baptiste Donatien de Vimeur, Comte de; 1725–1807, French)
Saint Clair (Arthur; 1736–1818, Scottish/American)
Schlieffen (Alfred, Count von; 1833–1913, Prussian)
Sébastiani (Horace, Count; 1772–1851, French)
Stroessner (Alfredo; 1912–2006, Paraguayan)
Urabi Pasha (1839–1911, Egyptian)
Voroshilov (Kliment; 1881–1969, Soviet)
Washington (George; 1732–99, US)
Wellington (Arthur Wellesley, Duke of; 1769–1852, Anglo-Irish)
William III (1650–1702, Dutch)

11 Baden-Powell (Robert, Lord; 1857–1941, English)
Cincinnatus (Lucius Quinctius; fl.460 BC, Roman)

See also **general**

Demosthenes (d.413 BC, Athenian)
Genghis Khan (c.1162–1227, Mongol)
Habyarimana (Juvenal; 1937–94, Rwandan)
Marlborough (John Churchill, Duke of; 1650–1722, English)
Mihailovich (Draza; 1893–1946, Serbian)
Montmorency (Anne, Duc de; 1493–1567, French)
Philopoemen (c.253–182 BC, Greek)
Poniatowski (Joseph; 1762–1813, Polish)
Rokossovsky (Konstantin; 1896–1968, Russian)
Scharnhorst (Gerhard von; 1755–1813, German)
Tantia Topee (d.1859, Indian)
Wallenstein (Albrecht von; 1583–1634, Austrian)
Ziaur Rahman (1935–81, Bangladeshi)

12 Aguiyi-Ironsi (Johnson; 1925–66, Nigerian)
de Chastelain (John; 1937–   , British/Canadian)
Papadopoulos (George; 1919–99, Greek)
Tukhachevsky (Mikhail; 1893–1937, Russian)
Westmoreland (William; 1914–2005, US)

13 Charles Martel (c.688–741, Frankish)
Eugène of Savoy (Prince; 1663–1736, French/Austrian)
John of Austria (Don; 1547–78, Spanish)
Komorowski-Bór (Tadeusz; 1895–1966, Polish)
Musa ibn Nosair (640–717, Arab)
Musa ibn Nusayr (640–717, Arab)
Queipo de Llano (Gonzalo; 1875–1951, Spanish)
Van Rensselaer (Stephen; 1765–1839, American)

14 Chadli Benjedid (1929–   , Algerian)
Nguyen Van Thieu (1923–2001, Vietnamese)

15 Desaix de Veygoux (Louis; 1768–1800, French)
Díaz del Castillo (Bernal; c.1492–1581, Spanish)
Eumenes of Cardia (c.360–316 BC, Macedonian)
La Tour d'Auvergne (Théophile Malo Corret de; 1743–1800, French)
Scipio Africanus (236–183 BC, Roman)

son

Sons include:

04 Abel (Bible)
Amis (Martin; 1949–   , English)
Bush (George W; 1946–   , US)

Cain (Bible)
Esau (Bible)
Pitt (William; 1759–1806, English)

05 Dumas (Alexandre; 1824–95, French)
Groan (Titus; *Gormenghast* trilogy, 1946–59, Mervyn Peake)
Harry (Prince; 1984– , English)
Isaac (Bible)
Jacob (Bible)
Milne (Christopher Robin; 1920–96, English)
Morel (Paul; *Sons and Lovers*, 1913, D H Lawrence)
Waugh (Auberon; 1939–2001, English)

06 Andrew (Prince; 1960– , English)
Edward (Prince; 1964– , English)
Gandhi (Rajiv; 1944–91, Indian)
Hamlet (*Hamlet*, 1600–01, William Shakespeare)
Joseph (Bible)

07 Absalom (Bible)
Charles (Prince; 1948– , English)
Douglas (Michael; 1944– , US)

Hotspur (*Henry IV Part I*, 1596–97, William Shakespeare)
Laertes (*Hamlet*, 1600–01, William Shakespeare)
Oedipus (Greek mythology)
Simpson (Bart; *The Simpsons*, TV show)
William (Prince; 1982– , English)

08 Benjamin (Bible)
Dimbleby (David; 1938– , English)
Dimbleby (Jonathan; 1944– , English)
Florizel (*The Winter's Tale*, 1609, William Shakespeare)
Pontifex (Ernest; *The Way of All Flesh*, 1903, Samuel Butler)

09 Dumas fils (Alexandre; 1824–95, French)

10 Duke of York (1960– , English)

11 Jesus Christ (c.6 BC–c.30 AD)

13 Prince of Wales (1948– , English)

14 Pitt the Younger (William; 1759–1806, English)

song

Song types include:

03 air	carol	melody	threnody
art	chant	number	**09** barcarole
lay	dirge	shanty	cantilena
ode	ditty	**07** calypso	dithyramb
pop	elegy	cantata	epinikion
pub	lyric	canzone	roundelay
war	plain	chanson	spiritual
04 aria	psalm	descant	**10** plainchant
bird	torch	lullaby	recitative
folk	yodel	refrain	
hymn	**06** amoret	requiem	**11** bothy ballad
lied	anthem	wassail	chansonette
lilt	ballad	**08** birdcall	rock and roll
love	chorus	canticle	**12** epithalamium
rock	gospel	canzonet	nursery rhyme
tune	jingle	madrigal	**14** Negro spiritual
05 blues	lyrics	serenade	

Songwriters include:

03 Gow (Niel; 1727–1807, Scottish)
Pop (Iggy; 1947– , US)

04 Bush (Kate; 1958– , English)
Cahn (Sammy; 1913–93, US)
Cash (Johnny; 1932–2003, US)
Hill (Joe; c.1872–1915, Swedish/US)
John (Sir Elton; 1947– , English)
Kern (Jerome; 1885–1945, US)
Reed (Lou; 1944– , US)

05 Allen (Lily; 1985– , English)
Arlen (Harold; 1905–86, US)

Berry (Chuck; 1926– , US)
Blunt (James; 1974– , English)
Brown (James; 1928–2006, US)
Brown (Nacio Herb; 1896–1954, US)
Burns (Robert; 1759–96, Scottish)
Cohan (George M; 1878–1942, US)
Davis (Miles; 1926–91, US)
Dylan (Bob; 1941– , US)
Gordy (Berry, Jnr; 1929– , US)
Holly (Buddy; 1936–59, US)
Loewe (Frederick; 1904–88, German/US)
Lover (Samuel; 1797–1868, Irish)

Melua (Ketevan (Katie); 1984– , Georgian/
   English)
Simon (Paul; 1941– , US)
Smith (Tommy; 1967– , Scottish)
Sousa (John Philip; 1854–1932, US)
Sting (1951– , English)
Styne (Jule; 1905–94, English/US)
Tormé (Mel; 1925–99, US)
Waits (Tom; 1949– , US)
Weill (Kurt; 1900–50, US)
Young (Neil; 1945– , Canadian)

06 Berlin (Irving; 1888–1989, Russian/US)
   Coward (Sir Noël; 1899–1973, English)
   Dibdin (Charles; 1745–1814, English)
   D'Urfey (Tom; 1653–1723, English)
   Foster (Stephen; 1826–64, US)
   Herman (Jerry; 1932– , US)
   Jagger (Mick; 1943– , English)
   Jensen (Adolf; 1837–79, German)
   Joplin (Scott; 1868–1917, US)
   Lennon (John; 1940–80, English)
   Lovett (Lyle; 1956– , US)
   Marley (Bob; 1945–81, Jamaican)
   McHugh (Jimmy; 1896–1969, US)
   Mercer (Johnny H; 1909–76, US)
   Morton (Jelly Roll; 1890–1941, US)
   Nairne (Lady Carolina; 1766–1845,
      Scottish)
   Nelson (Willie; 1933– , US)
   Oliver (King; 1885–1938, US)
   Parker (Charlie; 1920–55, US)
   Parton (Dolly; 1946– , US)
   Porter (Cole; 1891–1964, US)
   Seeger (Pete; 1919– , US)
   Waller (Fats; 1904–43, US)
   Warren (Harry; 1893–1981, US)

07 Boswell (Alexander, Baronet; 1775–1822,
      Scottish)
   Britten (Benjamin, Lord; 1913–76, English)
   Collins (Phil; 1951– , English)
   Dickson (Barbara; 1947– , Scottish)
   Donovan (Leitch; 1946– , Scottish)
   Dowland (John; 1563–1626, English)
   Gabriel (Peter; 1950– , English)
   Guthrie (Woody; 1912–67, US)
   Haggard (Merle; 1937– , US)

See also **musical**; **pop**

Hendrix (Jimi; 1942–70, US)
Loesser (Frank Henry; 1910–69, US)
MacColl (Ewan; 1915–89, Scottish)
Mancini (Henry; 1924–94, US)
Michael (George; 1963– , English)
Novello (Ivor; 1893–1951, Welsh)
Orbison (Roy; 1936–88, US)
Rodgers (Jimmie; 1897–1933, US)
Rodgers (Richard; 1902–79, US)
Romberg (Sigmund; 1887–1951, US)
Ulvaeus (Björn; 1945– , Swedish)

08 Coltrane (John; 1926–67, US)
   Costello (Elvis; 1955– , English)
   Gershwin (George; 1898–1937, US)
   Griffith (Nanci; 1954– , US)
   Harrison (George; 1943–2001, English)
   Jennings (Waylon; 1937–2002, US)
   Mitchell (Joni; 1943– , Canadian)
   Morrison (Van; 1945– , Northern Irish)
   Schubert (Franz; 1797–1828, Austrian)
   Schumann (Robert; 1810–56, German)
   Sondheim (Stephen; 1930– , US)
   Thompson (Richard; 1949– , English)
   Vandross (Luther; 1951–2005, US)
   Williams (Hank; 1923–53, US)

09 Andersson (Benny; 1946– , Swedish)
   Bernstein (Leonard; 1918–90, US)
   Carpenter (Mary Chapin; 1959– , US)
   Ellington (Duke; 1899–1974, US)
   Etheridge (Melissa; 1962– , US)
   Faithfull (Marianne; 1946– , English)
   Gillespie (Dizzy; 1917–93, US)
   McCartney (Sir Paul; 1942– , English)
   Winehouse (Amy; 1983– , English)

10 Carmichael (Hoagy; 1899–1981, US)
   Livingston (Jay; 1915–2001, US)
   Wainwright (Loudon, III; 1946– , US)

11 Armatrading (Joan; 1950– , West Indian/
      British)
   Lloyd-Webber (Andrew, Lord; 1948– ,
      English)
   Sainte-Marie (Buffy; 1941/42– , US)
   Springsteen (Bruce; 1949– , US)

12 Spottiswoode (Alicia Anne; 1810–1900,
      Scottish)

sound

Audible sounds include:

03		**04**			
cry	tap		chug	honk
hum		bang	clap	hoot
pip		beep	echo	moan
pop		boom	fizz	peal
sob		buzz	hiss	ping

plop	clang	swish	rustle
ring	clank	throb	scrape
roar	clash	thump	scream
sigh	click	twang	sizzle
slam	clink	whine	splash
snap	crack	whirr	squeak
thud	crash	whoop	squeal
tick	creak	**06** bubble	tinkle
ting	drone	crunch	**07** clatter
toot	grate	gurgle	crackle
wail	groan	hiccup	explode
yell	knock	jangle	grizzle
05 blare	skirl	jingle	screech
blast	slurp	murmur	squelch
bleep	smack	patter	thunder
chime	sniff	rattle	whimper
chink	snore	report	whistle
clack	snort	rumble	**08** splutter

Geographical sounds include:

03 Hoy (Scotland)
Rum (Scotland)

04 Bute (Scotland)
Calf (Isle of Man)
Crow (Scilly Isles)
Deer (Scotland)
Eigg (Scotland)
Holm (Scotland)
Iona (Scotland)
Jura (Scotland)
King (Australia)
Mull (Scotland)
Papa (Scotland)
Rock (The Bahamas)
Yell (Scotland)

05 Barra (Scotland)
Canna (Scotland)
Cross (USA)
Exuma (The Bahamas)
Gigha (Scotland)
Inner (Scotland)
Islay (Scotland)
Luing (Scotland)
Puget (USA)

See also **animal**

Sanda (Scotland)
Shuna (Scotland)
Sleat (Scotland)

06 Breton (USA)
Harris (Scotland)
Norton (USA)
Pabbay (Scotland)
Raasay (Scotland)
Ramsey (Wales)
Sanday (Scotland)
Shiant (Scotland)
Turner (The Bahamas)

07 Arisaig (Scotland)
Bardsey (Wales)
Caswell (New Zealand)
Cuillin (Scotland)
Gairsay (Scotland)
McMurdo (Antarctica)
Milford (New Zealand)
Pamlico (USA)
St Mary's (Scilly Isles)

08 Auskerry (Scotland)
Bluemull (Scotland)

Breaksea (New Zealand)
Colgrave (Scotland)
Doubtful (New Zealand)
Kotzebue (USA)
Taransay (Scotland)

09 Albemarle (USA)
Casiguran (Philippines)
Currituck (USA)
Eynhallow (Scotland)
Lancaster (Canada)
Shapinsay (Scotland)

10 Chandeleur (USA)
Cumberland (Canada)
Kilbrannan (Scotland)
King George (Australia)
Long Island (USA)
New Georgia (Solomon Islands)
Possession (USA)

11 Mississippi (USA)
Roes Welcome (Canada)

12 Prince Albert (Canada)

13 Prince William (USA)

soup

Soups include:

03 dal
pea
pho

04 cawl
crab
dhal

game
miso

05 adrak
blaff
broth
egusi

gumbo
locro
misua
rasam
snert

06 ajiaco

asapao
barley
birria
cocido
congee
fennel
guacho
harira
lentil
noodle
oxtail
pazole
posole
potage
potato
reuben
sambar
tomato
turtle
won ton
07 borscht
chicken
chowder
tarator
turbana
08 borschch
broccoli
callaloo
chirmole

consommé
ful nabed
gazpacho
halászlé
mondongo
mushroom
okroshka
sancocho
solianka
split pea
09 bird's nest
cacciucco
Clanallen
escabeche
fasolatha
pea and ham
pepperpot
picadillo
quimbombo
royal game
rozsolnyk
shark's fin
tom kha gai
white foam
10 avgolemono
caldo verde
minestrone
mock turtle
mole de olla

sauerkraut
superkanja
watercress
11 clam chowder
cock-a-leekie
cullen skink
fish chowder
French onion
gaeng som kai
gaeng som pla
Scotch broth
tom yam goong
vichyssoise
12 beef consommé
bouneschlupp
brown Windsor
chicken broth
guriltai shul
mulligatawny
seafood gumbo
13 bouillabaisse
chicken noodle
cream of tomato
lobster bisque
potato and leek
stracciatella
14 lentil and bacon
15 Queen Anne's broth

South Africa

Cities and notable towns in South Africa include:

06 Benoni
Durban
Soweto
08 Cape Town
Pretoria

09 Kimberley
Ladysmith
Polokwane
10 East London
Klerksdorp

Rustenburg
Simonstown
11 Vereeniging
12 Bloemfontein
Johannesburg

Stellenbosch
13 Port Elizabeth

South African provinces, with regional capitals:

07 Gauteng (Johannesburg)
Limpopo (Polokwane)
09 Free State (Bloemfontein)
North-West (Mmabatho)
10 Mpumalanga (Nelspruit)

11 Eastern Cape (Bisho)
Western Cape (Cape Town)
12 KwaZulu-Natal (Pietermaritzburg)
Northern Cape (Kimberley)

South African landmarks include:

05 Karoo
07 Sun City
10 Mapungubwe
11 Orange River
12 Gold Reef City

Limpopo River
Robben Island
13 Table Mountain
14 Cape of Good Hope
Crocodile River

Rhodes Memorial
The Garden Route

South America *see* **The Americas**

South-East Asia

Cities and notable towns in South-East Asia include:

03 Hué (Vietnam)

04 Cebu (Philippines)
Dili (East Timor)
Ipoh (Malaysia)
Pegu (Myanmar)
Vinh (Vietnam)

05 Ambon (Indonesia)
Dà Lat (Vietnam)
Davao (Philippines)
Hanoi (Vietnam)
Medan (Indonesia)
My Tho (Vietnam)
Pakse (Laos)

06 Can Tho (Vietnam)
Da Nang (Vietnam)
Ha Long (Vietnam)
Hat Yai (Thailand)
Iloilo (Philippines)
Malang (Indonesia)
Manila (Philippines)
Mérida (Philippines)
Padang (Indonesia)

07 Bacolod (Philippines)
Bandung (Indonesia)
Bangkok (Thailand)
Bien Hoa (Vietnam)
Henzada (Myanmar)
Jakarta (Indonesia)
Kuantan (Malaysia)
Kuching (Malaysia)
Malacca (Malaysia)
Pathein (Myanmar)
Qui Nhon (Vietnam)
Rangoon (Myanmar)
Vung Tàu (Vietnam)

08 Caloocan (Philippines)
Chon Buri (Thailand)
Haiphong (Vietnam)
Jayapura (Indonesia)
Khon Kaen (Thailand)

Mandalay (Myanmar)
Myingyan (Myanmar)
Nha Trang (Vietnam)
Pyinmana (Myanmar)
Semarang (Indonesia)
Seremban (Malaysia)
Siem Reap (Cambodia)
Songkhla (Thailand)
Surabaya (Indonesia)

09 Alor Setar (Malaysia)
Chiang Mai (Thailand)
Chiang Rai (Thailand)
Naypyidaw (Myanmar)
Palembang (Indonesia)
Phnom Penh (Cambodia)
Pontianak (Indonesia)
Putrajaya (Malaysia)
Singapore (Singapore)
Surakarta (Indonesia)
Udon Thani (Thailand)
Vientiane (Laos)

10 Battambang (Cambodia)
George Town (Malaysia)
Kâmpŏng Som (Cambodia)
Kota Baharu (Malaysia)
Mawlamyine (Myanmar)
Nonthaburi (Thailand)
Quezon City (Philippines)
Surat Thani (Thailand)
Yogyakarta (Indonesia)

11 Banjarmasin (Indonesia)
Johor Baharu (Malaysia)
Kuala Lumpur (Malaysia)

12 Kota Kinabalu (Malaysia)
Luang Prabang (Laos)
Petaling Jaya (Malaysia)
Ujung Pandang (Indonesia)

13 Ho Chi Minh City (Vietnam)
Zamboanga City (Philippines)

14 Kuala Trengganu (Malaysia)

spa

Spas include:

03 Dax (France)

04 Bath (England)

05 Baden (Germany)
Baños (Ecuador)
Epsom (England)

Sochi (Russia)
Vichy (France)

06 Aachen (Germany)
Buxton (England)
Ilkley (England)

Trebon (Czech Republic)

07 Lourdes (France)
Malvern (England)
Matlock (England)

08 Carlsbad (Czech Republic)

Shearsby (England)

09 Bad Elster (Germany)
Boston Spa (England)
Droitwich (England)
Harrogate (England)
Marienbad (Czech Republic)

Velingrad (Bulgaria)

10 Baden Baden (Germany)
Cheltenham (England)

11 Bad Dürrheim (Germany)
Scarborough (England)
Woodhall Spa (England)

12 Strathpeffer (Scotland)

13 Aix-la-Chapelle (France)
Knaresborough (England)
Leamington Spa (England)

14 Tunbridge Wells (England)

space travel

Spacecraft include:

03 Mir (Soviet space station)

06 Skylab (US space station)
Tardis (*Doctor Who* films/TV series)

07 Gemini 4 (US spacecraft)
Vostok 1 (Soviet spacecraft)
Vostok 5 (Soviet spacecraft)
Vostok 6 (Soviet spacecraft)

08 Apollo 11 (US spacecraft)
Apollo 13 (US spacecraft)
Apollo 17 (US spacecraft)
Columbia (US space shuttle)
Freedom 7 (US spacecraft)
Nostromo (*Alien* films)
Red Dwarf (*Red Dwarf* TV series)
Serenity (*Firefly* TV series)
Sputnik 1 (Soviet spacecraft)
Sputnik 2 (Soviet spacecraft)
Voskhod 1 (Soviet spacecraft)
Voskhod 2 (Soviet spacecraft)

09 Discovery (US space shuttle)
Endeavour (US space shuttle)
Galactica (*Battlestar Galactica* TV series)
Liberator (*Blake's 7* TV series)
Pioneer 10 (US spacecraft)
Shenzhou V (Chinese spacecraft)

10 Challenger (US space shuttle)
USS Voyager (*Star Trek* films/TV series)

11 Fireball XL5 (*Fireball XL5* TV series)
Heart of Gold (*The Hitchhiker's Guide to the Galaxy*, Douglas Adams, 1979)

12 SS Discovery 1 (*2001: A Space Odyssey*, Sir Arthur C Clarke, 1968)
Thunderbird 3 (*Thunderbirds* TV series)
Thunderbird 5 (*Thunderbirds* TV series)

13 Deep Space Nine (*Star Trek* TV series)
Moonbase Alpha (*Space 1999* TV series)
USS Enterprise (*Star Trek* films/TV series)

Space probes include:

04 Luna

06 Viking

07 Galileo
Mariner

Pioneer
Ulysses
Voyager

08 Magellan

09 Messenger

10 Deep Impact

15 Cassini–Huygens

Terms to do with space travel include:

03 bus
ELV
ESA
ISS
LOX
LRV
MCC

04 NASA

05 abort
flyby
orbit

06 albedo
CAPCOM
drogue
G force
hydyne

launch
module
parsec
rocket
shroud

07 booster
coolant
docking
lift-off
mission
nominal
payload
re-entry
shuttle
vidicon

08 ablation

aerozine
aimpoint
attitude
blast-off
downlink
free-fall
fuel cell
fuel tank
lunanaut
moonwalk
nose cone
sloshing

09 astronaut
cosmonaut
hydrazine
launch pad
light year

lunarnaut
spaceship
space suit
10 heat shield
pogo effect
propellant
rendezvous
spacecraft
space probe
trajectory
vomit comet
11 aerobraking
declination
inclination

lunar module
solar system
thermal tile
zero gravity
12 ascent module
launch window
liquid oxygen
lunar landing
man on the moon
microgravity
space station
13 angle of attack
ascending node
command module

descent engine
descent module
entry corridor
jet propulsion
space sickness
14 escape velocity
geosynchronous
horizon scanner
mission control
weightlessness
15 re-entry corridor
solid propellant

See also **astronaut**; **astronomy**

Spain

Cities and notable towns in Spain include:

06 Bilbao	07 Córdoba	Pamplona	10 Valladolid
Madrid	Granada	Valencia	
Málaga	Seville	Zaragoza	
Toledo	08 Alicante	09 Barcelona	

Administrative divisions of Spain, with regional capitals:

04 Jaén (Jáen)
León (León)
Lugo (Lugo)
05 Álava (Vitoria Gasteiz)
Ávila (Ávila)
Cádiz (Cádiz)
Soria (Soria)
06 Burgos (Burgos)
Cuenca (Cuenca)
Girona (Gerona; Girona)
Huelva (Huelva)
Huesca (Huesca)
Lérida (Lérida)
Madrid (Madrid)
Málaga (Málaga)
Murcia (Murcia)
Orense (Orense)
Teruel (Teruel)
Toledo (Toledo)
Zamora (Zamora)
07 Almería (Almería)
Badajoz (Badajoz)
Cáceres (Cáceres)
Córdoba (Córdoba)
Granada (Granada)
La Rioja (Logrono)

Navarra (Pamplona)
Segovia (Segovia)
Sevilla (Sevilla)
Vizcaya (Bilbao)
08 Albacete (Albacete)
Alicante (Alicante)
Asturias (Oviedo)
Baleares (Palma)
La Coruña (La Coruña)
Palencia (Palencia)
Valencia (Valencia)
Zaragoza (Zaragoza)
09 Barcelona (Barcelona)
Cantabria (Santander)
Castellón (Castellón)
Guipúzcoa (San Sebastián)
Las Palmas (Las Palmas)
Salamanca (Salamanca)
Tarragona (Tarragona)
10 Ciudad Real (Ciudad Real)
Pontevedra (Vigo)
Valladolid (Valladolid)
11 Guadalajara (Guadalajara)
19 Santa Cruz de Tenerife (Santa Cruz de Tenerife)

Spanish landmarks include:

04 Ebro	Tenerife	**11** Pico de Teide
05 Ibiza	**09** Balearics	**12** Guadalquivir
Prado	Lanzarote	**13** Canary Islands
08 Alhambra	Parc Güell	Museo del Prado
Canaries	**10** Guggenheim	**14** Sagrada Familia
Pyrenees	Montserrat	**15** Balearic Islands

spaniel

Spaniels include:

03 toy	**06** cocker	papillon	**11** King Charles
04 land	Sussex	springer	
05 field	**07** clumber	**10** Irish water	
water	**08** Blenheim	Maltese dog	

Spanish

Spanish words and expressions include:

03 olé! ('bravo!')

05 adobe (sun-dried bricks)
costa (coast)
guano (sea bird excrement)
junta (military ruling faction)
playa (beach)
tapas (savoury snacks)

06 barrio (community)
bodega (wine shop)
bolero (dance)
El Niño (southward current in the Pacific Ocean)
gaucho (South American mounted herdsman)
gitana (female Spanish gypsy)
gringo (foreigner)
hombre (man)
mañana (tomorrow; an unspecified time in the future)
pelota (racket-and-ball game)

07 chicano (Mexican or a Mexican-American)
corrida (bullfighting)
infanta (princess)
matador (bullfighter)
picador (bullfighter)
qué pasa? (what's up?)
vaquero (cowboy or cattle-driver)

See also **day**; **month**; **number**

08 compadre (companion, friend)
El Dorado (golden land or city imagined by the Spanish explorers in America)
frijoles (beans)
habanera (Cuban dance)
hacienda (house and estate)
mariachi (itinerant Mexican folk band)
nunca más (never again)
por favor (please)
toreador (bullfighter)

09 ay caramba! (expression of surprise or dismay)
bandolero (bandit)
guerrilla (person fighting an irregular war)

10 àdios amigo (goodbye, my friend)
aficionado (fan)
carabinero (frontier guard or customs officer)
peccadillo (small fault)
viva España! (long live Spain)

11 como siempre (as always)
embarcadero (wharf)

12 hasta la vista! (see you!)

13 incommunicado (deprived of the right to communicate with others)

14 mi casa es su casa (make yourself at home)

specialist *see* **medical**

spice *see* **herb**

spider

Spiders and arachnids include:

03 red

04 bird
mite
tick
wolf

05 bolas
money
water
zebra

06 diadem
epeira
katipo
mygale
violin

07 araneid
harvest
hunting
jumping
redback

08 attercop
huntsman
scorpion
trapdoor

09 funnel-web
harvester
phalangid
tarantula

10 black widow

cheesemite
harvestman
saltigrade

11 harvest mite
harvest tick

12 bird-catching
book-scorpion
money-spinner
whip scorpion

See also **poison**

spirit

Spirits include:

03 gin
kir
rum
rye

04 feni
grog
ouzo
raki
sake

05 fenny
Pimm's®
vodka

06 brandy
cognac
eggnog
geneva
grappa
kirsch
mescal
mezcal
pastis

Pernod®
poteen
Scotch
whisky

07 aquavit
Bacardi®
bitters
bourbon
Campari
dark rum
genever
pink gin
sloe gin
tequila
whiskey

08 armagnac
calvados
eau de vie
Hollands
hot toddy
sambucca

schnapps
vermouth
white rum
witblits

09 apple-jack
aqua vitae
framboise
golden rum
mirabelle
slivovitz
spiced rum

10 malt whisky
usquebaugh

11 gold tequila
Hollands gin
peach brandy

12 añejo tequila

13 peach schnapps
silver tequila

15 reposado tequila

See also **drink**; **liqueur**; **mythology**

sport

Sports include:

04 golf
judo
polo
pool

05 bowls
darts
fives
rugby

06 boules

boxing
discus
diving
futsal
hockey
karate
kung fu
luging
Nascar®
pelota

quoits
rowing
shinty
skiing
slalom
soccer
squash
tennis

07 angling
archery

camogie
cricket
croquet
curling
fencing
fishing
gliding
hunting
hurling
javelin
jogging
jujitsu
keep-fit
netball
putting
running
sailing
shot put
snooker
surfing
walking

08 aerobics
baseball
canoeing
climbing
football
handball
high-jump
hurdling
lacrosse

long-jump
marathon
pétanque
ping-pong
rounders
shooting
swimming
trotting
yachting

09 badminton
billiards
bobsleigh
decathlon
go-karting
ice-hockey
pole vault
pot-holing
sky-diving
tae kwon do
water polo
wrestling

10 basketball
drag-racing
gymnastics
ice-skating
pentathlon
skin-diving
triple-jump
volleyball

11 cycle racing
hang-gliding
horse racing
motor racing
paragliding
show-jumping
skeleton bob
table-tennis
tobogganing
water-skiing
windsurfing

12 aqua aerobics
cross-country
orienteering
pitch and putt
rock-climbing
snowboarding
speed skating
trampolining

13 roller-skating
tenpin bowling
weightlifting

14 downhill skiing
Gaelic football
mountaineering
speedway racing
stock-car racing

15 greyhound-racing

Sporting competitions include:

02 TT (motorcycle racing)
05 Ashes (cricket)
Derby (horseracing)
FA Cup (football)
06 Le Mans (motor racing)
07 Grey Cup (Canadian football)
Masters (golf/snooker)
Uber Cup (badminton)
UEFA Cup (football)
08 Rose Bowl (American football)
Ryder Cup (golf)
Speedway (motorcycle racing)
World Cup (various)
09 Grand Prix (motor racing)
Motocross (motorcycle racing)
Super Bowl (American football)
Thomas Cup (badminton)

World Bowl (American football)
10 Asian Games
Formula One (motor racing)
Solheim Cup (golf)
Stanley Cup (ice hockey)
11 Admiral's Cup (sailing)
America's Cup (sailing)
Kinnaird Cup (Eton fives)
World Series (baseball)
12 Iditarod Race (sled dog racing)
Olympic Games
Tour de France (cycling)
13 Grand National (horseracing)
Kentucky Derby (horseracing)
Leonard Trophy (bowls)
15 Paralympic Games

Sports positions include:

04 lock
slip
wing
05 cover

gully
mid-on
point
rover

06 batter
centre
goalie
hooker

libero
long on
mid-off
setter
winger

07 batsman
catcher
fine leg
flanker
fly-half
fly slip
forward
leg slip
long leg
long off
number 8
pitcher
ruckman
sweeper
torpedo

08 attacker
backstop
defender
fullback
halfback
left back
left wing
long stop
short leg
split end
third man
tight end
wing back

09 deep cover

deep point
first base
first slip
left field
left guard
leg gulley
mid-wicket
right back
right wing
ruck rover
scrum-half
short stop
square leg
third base
third slip

10 back pocket
cover point
defenceman
extra cover
goal attack
goalkeeper
goaltender
inside left
left tackle
midfielder
point guard
right field
right guard
second base
second slip
silly mid-on
silly point
wing attack

11 centre field
deep fine leg

full-forward
goal defence
goal shooter
inside right
left forward
prop forward
quarterback
right tackle
silly mid-off
wing defence

12 left half-back
power forward
right forward
short fine leg
small forward
stand-off half
wicketkeeper

13 backward point
centre-forward
deep mid-wicket
deep square leg
forward pocket
half-back flank
loosehead prop
right half-back
shooting guard
tighthead prop

14 centre half-back
deep extra cover
left corner-back
short mid-wicket

15 left half-forward
right corner-back
short extra cover

Sports equipment includes:

03 bow
cue
fly
jig
mat
net
oar
ski
tee

04 bail
bait
beam
bolt
bowl
épée
foil
gaff
hook
jack

lure
mask
mitt
nets
pins
puck
rack
reel
rest
rope
shot
wood

05 arrow
boule
brush
caman
chalk
float
rings

sabre
stump
table
trace

06 bridge
discus
fly rod
hammer
hurley
priest
spider
wicket

07 cue ball
fly reel
javelin
keep-net
netball
snorkel

08 aqualung

baseball
crossbow
football
gang-hook
golfball
golf club
ice-skate
punch-bag
ski stick
toboggan
water-ski
09 disgorger
face-guard
gum shield
punch-ball
rugby ball
sailboard
snow board
surfboard
10 basketball

cricket bat
fishing-rod
hockey ball
roller boot
skateboard
speed skate
tennis ball
trampoline
volleyball
11 balance beam
baseball bat
bowling ball
boxing glove
cricket ball
fishing-line
hockey skate
hockey stick
in-line skate
paternoster
pommel horse

racket press
rollerblade
roller-skate
shuttlecock
snooker ball
spinning rod
springboard
12 billiard ball
curling stone
golfing glove
isometric bar
parallel-bars
tennis racket
13 catcher's glove
horizontal bar
vaulting horse
14 ice-hockey stick
15 badminton racket

Sportspeople include:

03 Fox (Richard; 1960– , English, canoeing)
Lin (Ma; 1980– , Chinese, table tennis)
Nan (Wang; 1978– , Chinese, table tennis)

04 Hall (Lars; 1927–1991, Swedish, modern pentathlon)
Mota (Rosa; 1958– , Portuguese, marathon)
Ring (Christy; 1920–79, Irish, hurling)
Wood (Willie; 1938– , Scottish, bowls)

05 Barna (Viktor; 1911–72 , Hungarian, table tennis)
Howey (Kate; 1973– , English, judo)
Ngugi (John; 1962– , Kenyan, cross-country running)
Sipos (Anna; 1908–1972 , Hungarian, table tennis)
Waitz (Grete; 1953– , Norwegian, cross-country running/marathon)

06 Balczó (András; 1938– , Hungarian, modern pentathlon)
Briggs (Karen; 1963– , English, judo)
Bryant (David; 1931– , English, bowls)
Mackey (Mick; 1912–82, Irish, hurling)
Slater (Kelly; 1972– , US, surfing)
Tamura (Ryoko; 1975– , Japanese, judo)
Tergat (Paul; 1969– , Kenyan, cross-country running)

07 Allcock (Tony; 1955– , English, bowls)
Baldini (Stefano; 1971– , Italian, marathon
Fischer (Birgit; 1962– , German, canoeing)

Geesink (Anton; 1934– , Dutch, judo)
Rackard (Billy, 1930– , Irish, hurling)
Rackard (Bobby, 1927–96, Irish, hurling)
Rackard (Nicky, 1922–90, Irish, hurling)
Rodgers (Bill; 1947– , US, marathon)
Rozeanu (Angelica; 1921–2006, Romanian, table tennis)
Wanjiru (Samuel; 1986– , Kenyan, marathon)

08 Beachley (Layne; 1972– , Australian, surfing)
Bergmann (Richard; 1920–70 , Austrian, table tennis)
Douillet (David; 1969– , French, judo)
Farrelly (Bernard; 1943– , Australian, surfing)
Guoliang (Liu; 1976– , Chinese, table tennis)
Marshall (Alex; 1967– , Scottish, bowls)
Martikán (Michal; 1979– , Slovakian, canoeing)

09 Berghmans (Ingrid; 1961– , Belgian, judo)

10 Kahanamoku (Duke;1890–1968 , Hawaiian, surfing)

11 Fredriksson (Gert; 1919–2006, Swedish, canoeing)
Kristiansen (Ingrid; 1956– , Norwegian, marathon)
Mednyánszky (Mária; 1901–78 , Hungarian, table tennis)

Terms to do with sport include:

02 do
ET

gi
RU

03 air
bas

bos	juez	camán
cam	kata	casco
cue	kiai	cesta
cúl	koka	chase
dam	kote	chute
dan	lane	cinta
end	lead	court
fin	limb	dachi
gie	loop	ditch
hog	lure	dohyo
jam	mast	drive
kyo	mène	fakie
kyu	nage	field
let	nock	frame
lob	nose	green
mat	peel	grind
men	pips	guard
nut	pits	gyoji
obi	post	hit-in
rig	pull	house
tee	punt	ikkyo
tip	push	ippon
two	rack	judge
uke	rail	kayak
04 back	rest	leash
bank	rink	leave
bogu	shot	leech
boom	side	matte
bout	sire	nikyo
bull	skeg	ollie
bump	skip	pitch
butt	snap	piton
cant	spot	pivot
card	tare	place
chop	test	point
chui	tice	rails
clew	topo	raise
curl	trap	recce
dead	tube	reigi
deck	vent	resin
dojo	vert	round
draw	wake	rover
dyno	wall	sheet
faja	wire	shiai
fins	wood	shido
fire	yuko	shiko
foot	yump	skeet
foul	**05** basho	smash
gate	belay	solid
goal	belly	spare
gybe	biter	split
hack	blade	stick
hail	block	third
head	blunt	three
hook	brace	throw
iona	break	tirer
jack	broom	traps
jibe	caman	truck

tsuki
tzuki
yoshi
06 abseil
airgun
anchor
arrows
attack
barrel
batten
bisque
bounce
bowl-in
bridle
button
cannon
canopy
carpet
carrot
centre
course
cradle
crosse
dedans
double
drop in
dumper
enduro
entice
footer
freeze
grille
hajime
hakama
hammer
hazard
hot-dog
hurley
iomain
judogi
judoka
kennel
kumite
length
maiden
mallet
marker
McHawk
muzzle
noda-wa
nollie
parade
pasaka
pebble
peg out
pocket
prusik
quiver

raider
rappel
rebote
roquet
rouler
sankyo
second
seiken
sensei
shinai
slalom
street
strike
stripe
tattoo
top out
trench
trials
turkey
umpire
uphaul
upshot
upwind
uraken
wazari
yonkyo
07 aerials
armlock
banzuke
barmaid
blanket
blocker
booking
burnout
carreau
carving
chimney
chukker
coaming
cockpit
cornice
counter
cue ball
cushion
cutback
defence
English
face-off
flagman
floater
free hit
frontis
frontón
goal-hit
grommet
gutters
haragei
head pin

hog line
jai alai
judoist
jump cue
keikogi
keikoku
kendoka
kentsui
kingpin
knock in
layback
lead-out
leeward
leg rope
luffing
main nue
mawashi
McTwist
measure
offside
paddock
penalty
pin hole
plomber
pointer
push out
regatta
rikishi
ripcord
sighter
sliotar
spotter
takeout
tambour
tee-line
throw-in
toprope
topspin
toucher
trainer
waza-ari
wheelie
wipe-out
zaguero
08 aikidoka
alley-oop
ascender
ashi-tori
backhand
back line
back shot
backspin
bindings
body drop
bonspiel
bowsight
break cue
bullseye

chistera
chon-mage
co-driver
crampons
dead ball
dead draw
dead hang
dead heat
diamonds
dohyo-iri
downhaul
downwind
drop ball
drop shot
encho-sen
fall line
foot spot
forehand
foul line
free fall
free gate
free pass
funny car
glissade
goal area
griptape
half-pipe
handicap
handpass
jack high
jump shot
karateka
kata-tori
ketaguri
kick-nose
kick shot
kick-tail
kick-turn
kimarite
lollipop
low house
main wall
methanol
nearside
neck shot
pass line
pelotari
perfecta
pivoting
play line
pony goal
pro-stock
quiniela
road book
run a hoop
seoi-nage
shoot-off
shot bowl

side line
sidespin
sode-tori
sono-mama
speedway
sumotori
tail shot
third man
throw-off
traverse
trinquet
tsuppari
uchi mata
windward
yokozuna
yorikiri

09 appealing
awasewaza
baulk line
bodyboard
body-check
carabiner
cat stance
check side
choke hold
cochonnet
Croke Park
delantero
descender
dock start
duck drive
fault line
finger tab
first home
fixed rope
flatwater
free throw
galleries
goofy foot
high house
karabiner
kneeboard
koshi-nage
leech-line
longboard
makekoshi
morozashi
motocross
oicho-mage
open table
pace notes
parc fermé
passivity
penholder
penthouse
petit bois
petticoat
pivot ball

quickdraw
repêchage
Robin Hood
rover ball
rover hoop
ryote-tori
shakedown
short head
skydiving
snowcross
sore matte
speed trap
spray deck
superbike
supermoto
tai-otoshi
third home
washboard
wave board
wing balls

10 baulk lines
bouldering
centre pass
chanko nabe
classic bow
cover point
crosscourt
dead weight
double trap
draw weight
Eskimo roll
firing line
fletchings
gargu kamae
goal attack
goal circle
goal crease
goalkeeper
hailkeeper
half-strike
harai goshi
hataki-komi
head string
juji-gatame
kachikoshi
kaiten-nage
katate-tori
line player
losing cant
mono skiing
morote-tori
nose riding
object ball
petit final
pin spotter
place libre
post weight
power break

recurve bow
road racing
second home
shakehands
shomen-uchi
sideboards
spray skirt
stabilizer
static line
supercross
tachi-mochi
travelling
tsuyu-harai
whitewater
wing attack

11 anti-raiders
base jumping
boogie board
broadsiding
centreboard
combination
compound bow
court player
croquet shot
down the line
elapsed time
goal defence
goal shooter
handicapper
hanso-kumake
lag for break
natural foot
obstruction
passive play
penalty line
penalty pass
penalty shot
perfect game

photo finish
pioneer ball
quarter-pipe
Roman candle
running shot
running side
ryokata-tori
service line
service park
shroud lines
time control
udekime-nage
western grip
wing defence
yokomen-uchi

12 angle of split
back paddling
boundary line
cleek the shot
climbing wall
flying finish
free climbing
goal-area line
kesho mawashi
nitromethane
podium finish
powersliding
reaction time
referee throw
running belay
six-metre line
special stage
standing shot
starting gate
stranglehold
striker's ball
Telemark turn
trail the jack

trapshooting
trick release
upstream gate

13 airborne throw
Canadian canoe
Christmas tree
double-wake cut
expansion bolt
four-metre line
free-throw line
hare and hounds
high toss serve
neko-ashi-dachi
nine-metre line
Olympic trench
running target
scrutineering
shortmat bowls
starting boxes
step-over turns
terminal speed
waiting blocks

14 deepwater start
downstream gate
killing the ball
non-combativity
seven-metre line
shooting circle
universal joint
winning gallery

15 feathered paddle
longtrack racing
reclining dragon
seven-metre throw
third-ball attack
top fuel dragster
transverse lines
winning openings

See also **American football**; **archery**; **athletics**; **Australian rules football**; **award**; **badminton**; **baseball**; **basketball**; **boxing**; **cricket**; **cycling**; **darts**; **equestrian sport**; **exercise**; **fencing**; **football**; **golf**; **gymnastics**; **hockey**; **ice hockey**; **ice skating**; **karate**; **martial art**; **Olympic Games**; **Paralympic Games**; **race**; **racing: horse racing**; **racing: motor racing**; **rowing**; **Rugby League**; **Rugby Union**; **skiing**; **snooker**; **squash**; **stadium**; **swimming**; **tennis**; **trophy**; **volleyball**; **weightlifting**; **wrestling**

spread

Spreads include:

03 jam
04 marg
oleo
pâté
05 honey

marge
06 butter
07 Marmite®
Nutella®
08 dripping

sandwich
Vegemite®
09 butterine
lemon curd
margarine

marmalade
11 lemon cheese
12 peanut butter
13 oleomargarine

spring *see* **well**

spy

Spies, double agents and turncoats include:

03 Pym (Magnus; *A Perfect Spy*, 1986, John le Carré)

04 Blee (David Henry; 1916–2000, US)
Bond (James; *Casino Royale*, 1954, et seq, Ian Fleming)
Boyd (Belle; 1844–1900, US)
Hale (Nathan; 1755–76, American)

05 André (John; 1751–80, English)
Bazna (Elyesa; 1904–70, Albanian)
Blair (Barley; *The Spy Who Came in from the Cold*, 1963, John le Carré)
Blake (George; 1922– , Dutch/British)
Blunt (Anthony; 1907–83, English)
Fuchs (Klaus; 1911–88, German/British)
Karla (*Tinker, Tailor, Soldier, Spy*, 1974, et seq, John le Carré)
Mundy (Ted; *Absolute Friends*, 2003, John le Carré)
Sorge (Richard; 1895–1944, German/Soviet)
Wynne (Greville; 1919–90, British)

06 Arnold (Benedict; 1741–1801, American)
Cicero (1904–70, Albanian)
Haydon (Bill; *Tinker, Tailor, Soldier, Spy*, 1974, John le Carré)
Kelway (Robert; *The Heat of the Day*, 1949, Elizabeth Bowen)
Leamas (Alec; *The Spy Who Came in from the Cold*, 1963, John le Carré)

Philby (Kim; 1911–88, British)
Reilly (Sidney; 1874–1925, Russian/British)
Ricard (Marthe; 1889–1982, French)
Smiley (George; *Call for the Dead*, 1961, et seq, John le Carré)
Vidocq (Eugène François; 1775–1857, French)
Werner (Ruth; 1907–2000, German)

07 Biggles (*The Camels are Coming*, 1932, et seq, Captain W E Johns)
Burgess (Guy; 1910–63, English)
Defarge (Madame; *A Tale of Two Cities*, 1859, Charles Dickens)
Edmonds (Sarah Emma; 1841–98, Canadian)
Maclean (Donald Duart; 1913–83, English)
Nunn May (Alan; 1911–2003, British)

08 Greenhow (Rose O'Neal; 1817–64, US)
Lonsdale (Gordon; 1924–c.1970, Canadian/Russian)
Mata Hari (1876–1917, Dutch)
Westerby (Jerry; *The Honourable Schoolboy*, 1977, John le Carré)

09 Carstares (William; 1649–1715, Scottish)
Philbrick (Herbert Arthur; 1915–93, US)
Rosenberg (Ethel; 1915–53, US)
Rosenberg (Julius; 1918–53, US)

10 Cairncross (John; 1913–95, Scottish)
Litvinenko (Alexander; 1962–2006, Russian)

See also **espionage**

square

Squares include:

03 Red (Russia)
05 Times (USA)
06 Sloane (England)
07 Central (USA)
Madison (USA)
People's (China)
08 Berkeley (England)

Victoria (England/Northern Ireland)
09 Leicester (England)
Tiananmen (China)
Trafalgar (England)
10 Bloomsbury (England)
Washington (USA)
12 Covent Garden (England)

squash

Squash terms include:

01 T	**04** drop	rally	**10** service box
03 ace	nick	tight	**12** boast for nick
get	rail	**06** stroke	quarter court
let	**05** alley	volley	**13** half-court line
lob	angle	**08** telltale	
set	boast	**09** short line	
tin	not up		

stadium

Sporting stadia and venues include:

05 Ascot (horse racing)
Epsom (horse racing)
Ibrox (football)
Imola (motor racing)
Lords (cricket)
Monza (motor racing)
Texas (American football)
Troon (golf)

06 Azteca (football)
Henley (rowing)
Heysel (football)
Le Mans (motor racing)

07 Aintree (horse racing)
Anaheim (baseball)
Anfield (football)
Daytona (motor racing)
San Siro (football)
The Oval (cricket)
Wembley (football)

08 Bernabau (football)
Highbury (football)
Maracana (football)
Sandwich (golf)

09 Cresta Run (tobogganing)
Edgbaston (cricket)
Longchamp (horse racing)
Muirfield (golf)
Newmarket (horse racing)
St Andrews (golf)
The Belfry (golf)
Turnberry (golf)
Villa Park (football)
Wimbledon (tennis)

10 Brooklands (motor racing)
Carnoustie (golf)
Celtic Park (football)
Cheltenham (horse racing)
Elland Road (football)
Fairyhouse (horse racing)
Headingley (cricket/rugby)
Hockenheim (motor racing)
Interlagos (motor racing)
Monte Carlo (motor racing)
Twickenham (rugby)

11 Belmont Park (horse racing)
Brands Hatch (motor racing)
Hampden Park (football)
Murrayfield (rugby)
Old Trafford (football)
Royal Lytham (golf)
Sandown Park (horse racing)
Silverstone (motor racing)
The Crucible (snooker)
The Rose Bowl (cricket)
Trent Bridge (cricket)
Windsor Park (football)

12 Goodison Park (football)

13 Crystal Palace (athletics/football)
Lansdowne Road (rugby)
Royal Birkdale (golf)
White Hart Lane (football)

14 Churchill Downs (horse racing)
Flushing Meadow (tennis)
Stamford Bridge (football)

15 Cardiff Arms Park (rugby)

See also **football**; **golf**; **racing: motor racing**

stamp *see* **philately**

star

Stars include:

03 Dog
04 Mira
nova
Pole
Vega
05 Deneb
Dubhe
Merak
North
Spica
06 Castor

Pollux
pulsar
quasar
Sirius
07 Alphard
Antares
Canopus
Capella
falling
neutron
Polaris

08 Arcturus
Barnard's
red dwarf
red giant
shooting
09 Aldebaran
Alderamin
Fomalhaut
supernova
10 Beta Crucis
Betelgeuse

brown dwarf
supergiant
white dwarf

11 Alpha Boötis
Alpha Crucis
Delta Cephei

12 Alpha Doradus
13 Alpha Centauri
15 Proxima Centauri

See also **constellation**

star sign *see* zodiac

state *see* Australia; India; United States of America

station *see* radio; railway

stationery

Stationery items include:

03 ink
pen
pin
04 file
05 diary
label
ruler
toner
06 eraser
folder
marker
pencil
Post-it®
rubber
staple
Tipp-Ex®
07 blotter
Blu-Tack®
divider
file tab
Filofax®
memo pad
08 calendar
cash book
envelope

Jiffy bag®
notebook
scissors
stamp pad
09 card index
clipboard
desk diary
flip chart
index card
notepaper
paper clip
Sellotape®
wall chart
10 calculator
drawing pin
filing tray
floppy disk
graph paper
paper knife
ring binder
rubber band
11 account book
address book
bulldog clip
carbon paper
elastic band

rubber stamp
treasury tag
12 adhesive tape
computer disk
copying paper
pocket folder
printer label
printer paper
writing paper
13 expanding file
lever arch file
paper fastener
printer ribbon
tape dispenser
14 document folder
document wallet
manila envelope
spiral notebook
suspension file
window envelope
15 cartridge ribbon
correcting paper
correction fluid
headed notepaper
pencil-sharpener

statue *see* sculpture

stealing

Ways of stealing include:

03 bag
cly
dip
lag
mag
nap

nim
nip
rob
04 blag
crib
duff

glom
knap
lift
mill
nick
pick

pull
smug
whip
05 annex
boost
bribe

filch	finger	twitch	shoplift
heist	hijack	**07** cabbage	souvenir
hoist	pickle	purloin	**09** condiddle
miche	pilfer	snaffle	duckshove
mooch	pocket		**10** burglarize
mouch	rip off	**08** abstract	plagiarize
pinch	rustle	half-inch	run off with
purse	scrump	highjack	**11** appropriate
sneak	skrimp	knock off	pick a pocket
swipe	skrump	liberate	walk off with
06 burgle	snitch	peculate	**12** make away with
convey	thieve	scrounge	

step see **dance**

Stevenson, Robert Louis (1850–94)

Significant works include:

06 *St Ives* (1898)

08 *Catriona* (1893)
'Markheim' (1886)

09 *Kidnapped* (1886)

10 *The Ebb-Tide* (1894)
The Wrecker (1892)

11 *The Wrong Box* (1889)
'Thrawn Janet' (1881)

12 *Inland Voyage* (1878)

13 *The Black Arrow* (1888)

14 *Treasure Island* (1883)

15 *Weir of Hermiston* (1896)

16 *New Arabian Nights* (1882)
'The Beach of Falesá' (1892)

19 *Virginibus Puerisque* (1881)

21 *A Child's Garden of Verses* (1885)
The Master of Ballantrae (1889)
The Silverado Squatters (1884)

26 *Island Nights' Entertainments* (1893)

28 *Familiar Studies of Men and Books* (1882)

31 *Travels with a Donkey in the Cévennes* (1879)
The Merry Men and Other Tales and Fables
(1887)
The Strange Case of Dr Jekyll and Mr Hyde
(1886)

Significant characters include:

03 Uma

04 Case
Gunn (Ben)
Hyde (Mr Edward)
Rich (Brackenbury)
Weir (Adam)
Weir (Archie)

05 Breck (Alan)
Davis
Durie (Henry)
Durie (James)
Hyish
Innes (Frank)

06 Jekyll (Dr Henry)
McLour (Janet)
Red Fox (the)
Silver (Long John)
Soulis (Murdoch)
St Ives (Vicomte de)

07 Balfour (David)

Balfour (Ebenezer)
Elliott (Andrew 'Dand')
Elliott (Christina)
Elliott (Clement 'Clem')
Elliott (Gilbert 'Gib')
Elliott (Kirstie)
Elliott (Robert 'Rob')
Hawkins (Jim)
Herrick
Randall (Captain)
Skelton (Richard 'Dick')

08 Drummond (Catriona)
Drummond (James More)
Florizel (Prince of Bohemia)
Markheim
Tarleton

09 Mackellar (Mr)
Wiltshire (Mr)

10 Scuddamore (Silas Q)

15 James of the Glens

stick

03 lug
rod

04 cane
club
cosh
pike
pole
post

wand
whip

05 baton
billy
birch
crook
lathi
staff

stake
waddy

06 alpeen
crutch
cudgel
hockey
kierie
tripod

07 sceptre
walking
woomera

08 bludgeon

09 truncheon

10 alpenstock
knobkerrie
shillelagh

stitch *see* **embroidery**

stomach *see* **ruminant**

stone *see* **birth symbol**

storm

03 ice
sea
sun

04 dust
gale
hail
line
rain
sand

snow

05 buran
devil

06 baguio
calima
haboob
meteor
pelter
squall

07 cyclone
monsoon
Shaitan
tempest
thunder
tornado
typhoon
violent

08 blizzard

downpour
magnetic

09 bourasque
dust devil
hurricane
whirlwind

10 cloudburst
electrical

strait

03 Rae (Canada)

04 Adak (Aleutian Islands, USA)
Bass (Australia)
Cook (New Zealand)
Haro (Canada/USA)
Irbe (Estonia)
Kara (Russia)
Palk (India/Sri Lanka)
Pitt (New Zealand)
Soya (Japan)

05 Banks (Australia)
Bohai (China)
Cabot (Canada)
Canso (Canada)
Davis (Canada/Greenland)
Dease (Canada)
Dover (England)
Kerch (Ukraine)

Korea (Japan/South Korea)
Luzon (Philippines)
Menai (Wales)
Osumi (Japan)
Sunda (Indonesia)
Tatar (Russia)

06 Bering (Russia/USA)
Dundas (Australia)
Etolin (USA)
Fisher (Canada)
Hecate (Canada)
Hormuz (Iran)
Hudson (Canada)
Lombok (Indonesia)
Solent (England)
Sunday (Australia)
Tablas (Philippines)
Taiwan (Taiwan)
Tokara (Japan)

Torres (Australia/Papua New Guinea)
Vitiaz (Papua New Guinea)

07 Balabac (Malaysia/Philippines)
Chatham (USA)
Dampier (Indonesia)
Denmark (Greenland/Iceland)
Florida (USA)
Formosa (Taiwan)
Foveaux (New Zealand)
Georgia (Canada/USA)
Le Maire (Argentina)
Makasar (Indonesia)
Malacca (Malaysia)
McClure (Canada)
Messina (Italy)
Mindoro (Philippines)
Otranto (Albania/Italy)
Polillo (Philippines)
Rosario (USA)
Tsugaru (Japan)

08 Bosporus (Turkey)
Clarence (Australia)
Karimata (Indonesia)
Kattegat (Denmark/Sweden)

Mackinac (USA)
Magellan (Argentina/Chile)
Makassar (Indonesia)
Shelikof (USA)
Tsushima (Japan/South Korea)
Victoria (Canada)

09 Belle Isle (Canada)
Bonifacio (Corsica/Sardinia)
Bosphorus (Turkey)
Gibraltar (Spain)
Great Belt (Denmark)
La Pérouse (Japan)
Linapacan (Philippines)
Van Diemen (Japan)

10 Juan de Fuca (Canada/USA)
Little Belt (Denmark)

11 Dardanelles (Turkey)

12 Bougainville (Papua New Guinea)
Investigator (Australia)

13 San Bernardino (Philippines)

14 Northumberland (Canada)
Queen Charlotte (Canada)

15 Dolphin and Union (Canada)

Strauss, Richard (1864–1949)

Significant works include:

06 *Daphne* (1938)
Morgen (1894)
Salome (1905)

07 *Don Juan* (1889)
Elektra (1909)
Guntram (1894)
Macbeth (1888)
Morning (1894)

08 *Arabella* (1933)
Peace Day (1938)

09 *Capriccio* (1942)
Feuersnot (1911)
From Italy (1887)
Zueignung (1885)

10 *A Hero's Life* (1898)
Dedication (1885)
Don Quixote (1897)
Festmarsch (1881)
Fire Famine (1911)
Intermezzo (1924)

11 *Friedenstag* (1938)
Schlagobers (1922)

12 *Festive March* (1881)
Whipped Cream (1922)

13 *Four Last Songs* (1948)
Metamorphosen (1945)

14 *Alpine Symphony* (1915)
Ein Heldenleben (1898)
Josephslegende (1914)
Legend of Joseph (1914)
The Love of Danae (1952)
The Silent Woman (1935)

15 *Ariadne auf Naxos* (1912)

16 *Der Rosenkavalier* (1911)
Die Liebe der Danae (1952)
The Egyptian Helen (1928)
Tod und Verklärung (1889)

17 *Eine Alpensinfonie* (1915)

18 *Die Schweigsame Frau* (1935)
Symphonia Domestica (1904)
The Knight of the Rose (1911)

19 *Die Frau ohne Schatten* (1919)

20 *Die Aegyptische Helena* (1928)
Thus Spake Zarathustra (1896)

21 *Also sprach Zarathustra* (1896)

22 *The Woman Without a Shadow* (1919)

23 *Death and Transfiguration* (1889)

26 *Aus Italien Symphonic Fantasy* (1887)

28 *Till Eulenspiegel's Merry Pranks* (1895)

32 *Till Eulenspiegels lustige Streiche* (1895)

Stravinsky, Igor (1882–1971)

Significant works include:

04 *Agon* (1957)
   Mass (1948)
05 *Babel* (1944)
   Mavra (1922)
06 *Renard* (1922)
   Septet (1953)
   Threni (1958)
07 *Orpheus* (1948)
   Ragtime (1918)
08 *Concerto* (1924)
   Les Noces (1923)
   The Flood (1962)
09 *Fireworks* (1908)
   Introitus (1965)
   Petrushka (1911)
   Wind Octet (1923)

10 *Oedipus Rex* (1927)
   Perséphone (1934)
   Pulcinella (1920)
   Tarantella (1898)
   The Wedding (1923)
11 *Circus Polka* (1942)
   Jeu de cartes (1937)
   Le Rossignol (1914)
   The Card Game (1937)
   The Firebird (1910)
12 *Feu d'Artifice* (1908)
13 *Der Feuervogel* (1910)
   'Dumbarton Oaks'
     (Concerto; 1938)
   Faun et bergère (1907)
   Piano Rag-Music (1919)

   The Fairy's Kiss (1928)
14 *Canticum Sacrum* (1955)
   The Nightingale (1914)
15 *Abraham and Isaac* (1963)
   Apollon Musagète (1928)
   Le Baiser de la Fée (1928)
   Le roi des étoiles (1912)
   The Rite of Spring (1913)
   The Soldier's Tale (1918)
16 *Dylan Thomas Elegy* (1954)
   Requiem Canticles (1966)
   The Rake's Progress (1951)
17 *L'Histoire du soldat* (1918)
   The King of the Stars (1912)
18 *Faun and Shepherdess* (1907)
   Scherzo fantastique (1902)

street *see* **London; New York; Paris; road**

stroke *see* **swimming**

study

Subjects of study include:

02 IT
03 art
   ICT
   law
   PSE
04 PHSE
05 craft
   dance
   D and T
   drama
   music
   sport
06 botany
   design
07 anatomy
   biology
   driving
   ecology
   fashion
   fitness
   geology
   history
   physics
   pottery
   science
   zoology

08 Classics
   commerce
   eugenics
   genetics
   heraldry
   medicine
   penology
   politics
   theology
09 astrology
   astronomy
   chemistry
   cosmology
   economics
   education
   erotology
   ethnology
   forensics
   geography
   languages
   logistics
   marketing
   mechanics
   mythology
   pathology
   shorthand
   sociology

   surveying
   web design
10 humanities
   journalism
   literature
   metallurgy
   philosophy
   physiology
   psychology
   publishing
   statistics
   technology
   visual arts
11 accountancy
   agriculture
   archaeology
   calligraphy
   citizenship
   dressmaking
   electronics
   engineering
   linguistics
   mathematics
   metaphysics
   meteorology
   ornithology
   photography

the Classics
typewriting
12 anthropology
architecture
horticulture
lexicography
media studies
oceanography

pharmacology
13 gender studies
home economics
librarianship
marine studies
women's studies
14 food technology
leisure studies

natural history
social sciences
word processing
15 building studies
business studies
computer studies
creative writing
hotel management

subatomic particle *see* **atom**

sugar

Sugars include:

03 gur
04 beet
cane
date
goor
loaf
lump
milk
palm
spun
wood
05 brown
fruit

grape
icing
maple
syrup
white
06 aldose
barley
caster
castor
golden
hexose
invert
ketose
xylose

07 glucose
glycose
jaggery
lactose
maltose
mannose
pentose
refined
sucrose
treacle
08 demerara
dextrose
fructose
levulose

molasses
powdered
09 arabinose
galactose
laevulose
muscovado
raffinose
trehalose
unrefined
10 granulated
saccharose
12 crystallized
13 confectioner's

suit

Suits include:

01 g
03 cat
dry
Mao
NBC
sun
wet
04 body
Eton
jump
play

swim
zoot
05 drape
dress
noddy
pants
shell
siren
sleep
space
sweat

track
union
06 boiler
diving
flying
lounge
monkey
riding
safari
sailor
tsotsi

07 bathing
leisure
morning
penguin
trouser
08 birthday
business
pressure
skeleton
sleeping

Summer Olympics *see* Olympic Games

Summer Paralympics *see* Paralympic Games

superhero

Superheroes include:

04 Hulk (Bruce Banner; comic/TV/film)
Thor (Thor Odinson; comic)

05 Robin (Dick Grayson; comic/TV/film)
Rogue (Marie D'Ancanto; comic/film)

Storm (Ororo Munroe; comic/film)

06 Batman (Bruce Wayne; comic/TV/film)
Iceman (Bobby Drake; comic/film)
Xavier (Professor Charles; comic/film)

07 Batgirl (comic/film)
Blossom (TV)
Bubbles (TV)
Cyclops (Scott Summers; comic/film)
Elektra (comic/film)
Frozone (Lucius Best; film)
Hellboy (Anung Un Rama; comic/film)
Iron Man (Tony Stark; comic/film)
Nite Owl (Dan Dreiberg; comic/film)
Phoenix (Jean Grey; comic/film)
The Atom (Albert Pratt; comic)
The X-Men (comic/film)

08 Batwoman (Kathy Kane; comic)
Catwoman (Selina Kyle; comic/film)
Superman (Clark Kent; comic/TV/film)
The Thing (Ben Grimm; comic/film)

09 Buttercup (TV)
Daredevil (Matthew Murdock; comic/film)
Firestorm (Jason Rusch; comic)
Nighthawk (Kyle Richmond; comic)
Nightwing (comic)
Spiderman (Peter Parker; comic/film)
Supergirl (Kara Zor-El; comic/film)

Wolverine (Logan/James Howlett; comic/film)

10 Cannonball (Samuel Zachery Guthrie; comic)
Elastigirl (Helen Parr; film)
Freakazoid (TV)
Ghost Rider (John Blaze; comic/film)
Human Torch (Johnny Storm; comic/film)
Kamen Rider (TV/film)
Moon Knight (Marc Spector; comic)
Ozymandias (Adrian Veidt; comic/film)
Sailor Moon (TV/film)

11 Dr Manhattan (Dr Jonathan Osterman; comic/film)
Kim Possible (TV)
Mr Fantastic (Reed Richards; comic/film)
Wonder Woman (Princess Diana; comic/TV)

12 Black Panther (T'Challa; comic)
Mr Incredible (Robert Parr; film)
Silver Surfer (Norrin Radd; comic)

13 Captain Planet (TV)
Silk Spectre II (Laurie Juspeczyk; comic/film)

14 Captain America (Steve Rogers; comic)
Invisible Woman (Susan Storm Richards; comic/film)
Power Puff Girls (TV)
The Cheerleader (Claire Bennet; TV)

supernatural *see* **occult**

surgery

Surgery types include:

06 biopsy

07 keyhole
nose job

08 cosmesis
C-section
facelift
lobotomy
tenotomy
vagotomy

09 amniotomy
Caesarean
colectomy
colostomy
cordotomy
cystotomy
ileostomy
iridotomy
leucotomy
lipectomy
lithotomy
lobectomy
necrotomy

neurotomy
osteotomy
sex change
tubectomy
tummy tuck

10 adenectomy
autoplasty
chordotomy
cordectomy
cystectomy
cystostomy
herniotomy
iridectomy
keratotomy
laparotomy
lumpectomy
mastectomy
neurectomy
nip and tuck
ovariotomy
phlebotomy
strabotomy

thymectomy
tuboplasty
varicotomy
vitrectomy

11 angioplasty
cosmetology
craniectomy
cryosurgery
embolectomy
enterectomy
enterostomy
gastrectomy
glossectomy
hepatectomy
hysterotomy
laparoscopy
mammoplasty
nephrectomy
osteoplasty
ovariectomy
rhinoplasty
splenectomy

syringotomy
tracheotomy
uranoplasty

12 appendectomy
arthroplasty
circumcision
cluster graft
corneal graft
hysterectomy
laryngectomy
meniscectomy
microsurgery
neurosurgery
oophorectomy
patellectomy
pinealectomy

tonsilectomy
tracheoscopy
tracheostomy

13 adenoidectomy
pneumonectomy
prostatectomy
psychosurgery
salpingectomy
sigmoidectomy
stomatoplasty
sympathectomy
symphyseotomy
symphysiotomy
thoracentesis
thoracoplasty
thyroidectomy

tonsillectomy

14 appendicectomy
blepharoplasty
cholecystotomy
clitoridectomy
coronary bypass
endarterectomy
hypophysectomy
pancreatectomy
plastic surgery
staphyloplasty

15 cholecystectomy
cholecystostomy
cosmetic surgery
thoracocentesis

Surgeons include:

03 eye
04 oral
tree
05 brain

heart
house
neuro
06 dental

07 general
plastic
08 cosmetic
10 veterinary

Terms to do with surgery include:

02 op
04 CABG
seam
05 couch
curet
donor
stoma
taxis
truss
06 canula
curare
curari
domino
dossil
garrot
hobday
lancet
post-op
reduce
stitch
trepan
trocar
07 cadaver
cannula
catling
curette
forceps
garotte
heparin
myotome
operate

patient
pessary
scalpel
section
torsion
08 ablation
adhesion
bistoury
cannular
capeline
centesis
clinical
compress
cosmesis
crow-bill
curarine
écraseur
elective
garrotte
incision
incisure
invasive
operable
plastics
trephine
09 abduction
autograft
cannulate
capelline
collodion
crow's-bill
curettage

depressor
dermatome
diastasis
donor card
enucleate
operation
osteotome
piggyback
resection
retractor
tamponade
tamponage
tenaculum
10 atracurium
deligation
diorthosis
discussion
guillotine
inoperable
lithotrite
lithotrity
obstetrics
osteoclast
11 anaesthetic
arthrodesis
autoplastic
cannulation
curettement
decapsulate
exteriorize
incarnation
laparoscope

lithotripsy
lithotritor
prosthetics
trepanation
12 azathioprine
   circumcision
   cluster graft
   corneal graft
   cyclosporin A
   fenestration
   lithotripter

lithotriptor
lunar caustic
paracentesis
scarificator
short circuit
tissue-typing
trephination
13 cyclodialysis
   decompression
   herniorrhaphy
   incarceration

lithontriptor
operating room
post-operative
premedication
thoracentesis
under the knife
14 embryo transfer
   operating table
15 thoracocentesis

See also **anaesthetic; medical**

swan

Swans include:

| 04 mute | 07 Bewick's | 08 whooping | whistling |
| 05 black | whooper | 09 trumpeter | 11 black-necked |

Sweden

Cities and notable towns in Sweden include:

05 Borås	06 Kalmar	09 Gällivare	10 Gothenburg
Luleå	Kiruna	Jönköping	
Malmö	07 Uppsala	Stockholm	
Visby	08 Göteborg	Sundsvall	

Administrative divisions of Sweden, with regional capitals:

05 Skåne (Malmö)
06 Kalmar (Kalmar)
   Örebro (Örebro)
07 Dalarna (Falun)
   Gotland (Visby)
   Halland (Halmstad)
   Uppsala (Uppsala)
08 Blekinge (Karlskrona)
   Jämtland (Östersund)
   Värmland (Karlstad)
09 Gävleborg (Gävle)

Jönköping (Jönköping)
Kronoberg (Växjö)
Stockholm (Stockholm)
10 Norrbotten (Lulece)
11 Västmanland (Västeraces)
12 Östergötland (Linköping)
   Södermanland (Nyköping)
   Västerbotten (Umeå)
14 Västernorrland (Härnösand)
15 Västra Götalands (Gothenburg)

Swedish landmarks include:

05 Öland
   Sarek
06 Globen
08 Haga Park
09 Gamla Stan

Njupeskär
10 Stadshuset
   Storkyrkan
11 Fulufjället
   Lake Vättern

Royal Palace
Trollhättan
12 Örebro Castle
15 Kungliga Slottet

weet

weet

Sweets and confectionery include:

- **4** jube
  Mars®
  rock
- **5** fudge
  halva
  jelly
- **6** bonbon
  confit
  humbug
  jujube
  nougat
  tablet
  toffee
- **7** alcorza
  caramel
  fondant

- gumdrop
  lozenge
  pomfret
  praline
  truffle
  wine gum
- **08** acid drop
  bull's eye
  confetti
  lollipop
  marzipan
  noisette
  pear drop
- **09** chocolate
  jelly baby
  jelly bean

- lemon drop
  liquorice
- **10** chewing-gum
  gobstopper
  peppermint
- **11** aniseed ball
  barley sugar
  marshmallow
  toffee apple
- **12** butterscotch
  dolly mixture
- **13** Edinburgh rock
  fruit pastille
- **14** pineapple chunk
  Turkish delight

wimming

Swimming strokes include:

- **5** crawl
- **7** trudgen
- **9** back-crawl
  butterfly

- dog-paddle
  freestyle
- **10** backstroke
  front crawl

- **11** doggy-paddle
- **12** breaststroke
- **15** Australian crawl

Swimmers and divers include:

- **4** Klim (Michael; 1977– , Polish/Australian)
  Otto (Kristin; 1966– , German)
  Rice (Stephanie; 1988– , Australian)
  Rose (Murray; 1939– , Scottish/
  Australian)
  Webb (Matthew; 1848–83, English)
- **5** Crapp (Lorraine; 1938– , Australian)
  Curry (Lisa; 1962– , Australian)
  Daley (Thomas; 1994– , English)
  Ender (Kornelia; 1958– , German)
  Evans (Janet; 1971– , US)
  Gould (Shane; 1956– , Australian)
  Gross (Michael; 1964– , German)
  Jones (Leisel; 1985– , Australian)
  Lewis (Hayley; 1974– , Australian)
  Riley (Samantha; 1972– , Australian)
  Spitz (Mark; 1950– , US)
- **6** Biondi (Matt; 1965– , US)
  Davies (Sharron; 1962– , English)
  Durack (Fanny; 1891–1956, Australian)
  Ederle (Gertrude; 1906–2003, US)
  Fraser (Dawn; 1937– , Australian)
  Loader (Danyon; 1975– , New Zealand)
  O'Neill (Susie; 1973– , Australian)
  Phelps (Michael; 1985– , US)

  Thorpe (Ian; 1982– , Australian)
  Wilkie (David; 1954– , Scottish)
- **07** Goodhew (Duncan; 1957– , English)
  Hackett (Grant; 1980– , Australian)
  Perkins (Kieren; 1973– , Australian)
  Wickham (Tracey; 1962– , Australian)
- **08** Champion (Malcolm; 1883–1939, New
  Zealand)
  Charlton (Boy; 1907–75, Australian)
  de Bruijn (Inge; 1973– , Dutch)
  Louganis (Greg; 1960– , US)
  Manoudou (Laure; 1986– , French)
  Streeter (Alison; 1964– , English)
  van Wisse (Tammy; 1968– , Australian)
  Williams (Esther; 1923– , US)
- **09** Adlington (Rebecca; 1989– , English)
  Armstrong (Duncan; 1968– , Australian)
  Kellerman (Annette; 1887–1975,
  Australian)
  Klochkova (Yana; 1982– , Ukrainian)
- **11** Beaurepaire (Sir Frank; 1891–1956,
  Australian)
  Weissmuller (Johnny; 1903–84, Hungarian-
  German/US)

Swimming and diving terms include:

02 IM	layout	10 tumble turn
03 fly	length	11 dolphin kick
rip	medley	flutter kick
04 pike	07 forward	rocket split
tuck	reverse	12 combined spin
05 block	08 armstand	13 negative split
boost	backward	14 continuous spin
entry	flamingo	15 backstroke flags
scull	09 ballet leg	ballet leg double
split	eggbeater	
06 inward	elevation	

Switzerland

Cities and notable towns in Switzerland include:

04 Bern	06 Geneva	07 Lucerne	Lausanne
05 Basle	Zürich	08 Fribourg	

Administrative divisions of Switzerland, with regional capitals:

03 Uri (Altdorf)
    Zug (Zug)
04 Jura (Delémont)
    Vaud (Lausanne)
05 Berne (Berne)
06 Aargau (Aarau)
    Geneva (Genève; Geneva)
    Glarus (Glarus)
    Schwyz (Schwyz)
    St Gall (Sankt Gallen; St Gall)
    Ticino (Bellinzona)
    Valais (Sion)
    Zürich (Zürich)
07 Grisons (Coire)

    Lucerne (Luzern; Lucerne)
    Thurgau (Frauenfeld)
08 Fribourg (Fribourg)
    Obwalden (Sarnen)
09 Neuenberg (Neuchâtel)
    Nidwalden (Stans)
    Solothurn (Solothurn)
10 Basel-Stadt (Basel)
    Graubünden (Chur)
12 Schaffhausen (Schaffhausen)
15 Basel-Landschaft (Liestal)
20 Appenzell Inner-Rhoden (Appenzell)
21 Appenzell Ausser-Rhoden (Herisau)

Swiss landmarks include:

04 CERN	Lake Thun	Jungraujoch
05 Eiger	Montreux	Schloss Thun
Mönch	10 Interlaken	14 Bahnhofstrasse
	Lake Brienz	UN headquarters
06 Mt Rosa	Matterhorn	15 Bernese Oberland
08 Jungfrau	11 Fraumünster	Zürich Cathedral

sword

Swords include:

03 fox	05 bilbo	kukri
04 back	brand	saber
épée	broad	sabre
foil	court	short
simi	estoc	skean

skene
small
steel
6 espada
glaive
hanger
katana
kirpan
rapier
sweard
Toledo
waster
7 curtana
curtaxe

gladius
hunting
Morglay
shabble
spurtle
whinger
yatagan
08 claymore
curtalax
damaskin
falchion
schläger
scimitar
spadroon

whiniard
whinyard
white arm
yataghan
09 curtalaxe
damascene
damaskeen
damasquin
Excalibur
10 damasceene
12 spurtle-blade
toasting fork
toasting iron

ee also **dagger; knife**

symbol

Symbols include:

4 icon
ikon
logo
5 badge
brand
crest
motif

token
totem
06 cipher
emblem
smiley
uraeus
08 caduceus

ideogram
insignia
logogram
monogram
swastika
09 pentagram
trademark

watermark
10 coat of arms
hieroglyph
pictograph
12 yellow ribbon

See also **birth symbol; religion**

symptom *see* **disease**

T

table

03 bed
loo
tea
top
04 bird
card
desk
draw
drum
high
pier
pool
sand
side
sofa
work

05 altar
board
lunch
night
06 bureau
coffee
dining
dinner
dolmen
gaming
inking
lowboy
picnic
teapoy
toilet
vanity

07 capstan
console
counter
cricket
drawing
draw-top
dresser
gateleg
snooker
trestle
writing
08 billiard
credence
credenza
draw-leaf
dressing

drop-leaf
guéridon
mahogany
pembroke
piecrust
09 breakfast
communion
operating
refectory
10 dissecting
gate-legged
greencloth
occasional
12 council-board
13 bonheur-du-jour

03 cup
jug
mug
04 bowl
05 ashet
cruet
plate
06 goblet
saucer
teacup
teapot
tureen
07 creamer
See also **cutlery**

milk jug
platter
tumbler
08 cream jug
flatware
mazarine
rice bowl
salt mill
09 coffee cup
coffee pot
gravy boat
pasta bowl
pasta dish

pepper pot
salad bowl
sauceboat
side plate
soup plate
sugar bowl
toast rack
wineglass
10 bread plate
butter dish
cereal bowl
cruet-stand
pepper mill
salt shaker

soup tureen
11 butter plate
cheese plate
dessert bowl
dessert dish
espresso cup
serving bowl
serving dish
12 dessert plate
mazarine dish
pudding-plate
13 mazarine plate
14 serving platter

tack *see* horse

taste

03 hot
04 acid
sour
tart
05 acrid
bland

fishy
meaty
nutty
salty
sapid
sharp

spicy
sweet
tangy
06 acidic
bitter
citrus

creamy
fruity
sugary
07 insipid

peppery
piquant
pungent
savoury

08 vinegary
11 bittersweet

taxation

Taxes include:

03 GST
sur
VAT
04 PAYE
poll
toll
05 rates

tithe
06 excise
income
07 airport
council
customs
08 property

09 death duty
insurance
10 capitation
estate duty
value added
11 corporation
inheritance

12 capital gains
pay as you earn
15 capital transfer
community charge

Tchaikovsky, Pyotr Ilyich (1840–93)

Significant works include:

06 'Polish' (Symphony; 1873)
Undine (1870)
07 *Iolanta* (1891)
Mazeppa (1884)
08 *Swan Lake* (1877/1895)
10 'Mozartiana' (Suite; 1887)
'Pathétique' (Symphony; 1893)
11 *Cherevichki* (1887)
Marche Slave (1876)
The Slippers (1887)
The Voyevoda (1868)
The Year 1812 (1882)
12 *1812 Overture* (1882)
Eugene Onegin (1879)
The Oprichnik (1874)
The Sorceress (1887)
Valse-Scherzo (1877)

13 'Little Russian' (Symphony; 1873)
Slavonic March (1876)
The Nutcracker (1892)
14 *Romeo and Juliet* (1870/80)
Vakula the Smith (1876)
15 *Concert Fantasia* (1884)
Manfred Symphony (1885)
'Winter Daydreams' (Symphony; 1868)
16 *Andante and Finale* (1893)
Capriccio Italien (1880)
Pezzo capriccioso (1887)
The Maid of Orleans (1882)
The Queen of Spades (1890)
17 *Francesca da Rimini* (1876)
The Sleeping Beauty (1890)
18 *The Nutcracker Suite* (1892)
20 *Sérénade mélancolique* (1875)

tea

Teas and herbal teas include:

03 ice
04 beef
bush
chai
herb
iced
mate
mint
sage
05 Assam
black
bohea

brick
caper
China
congo
fruit
green
hyson
lemon
pekoe
senna
yerba
06 Ceylon

congou
herbal
oolong
oulong
07 cambric
instant
jasmine
lapsang
redbush
rooibos
rosehip
Russian

twankay
08 camomile
Earl Grey
Lady Grey
souchong
09 chamomile
gunpowder
10 Darjeeling
11 orange pekoe
13 decaffeinated
15 lapsang souchong

teaching

Teachers include:

04 Beck (Madame; *Villette*, 1853, Charlotte Brontë)
Eyre (Jane; *Jane Eyre*, 1847, Charlotte Brontë)
Hart (Sheba; *Notes on a Scandal*, 2003, Zoë Heller)
Howe (Joseph; *Of This Time, Of That Place*, 1943, Lionel Trilling)
King (Anna; *Only Children*, 1979, Alison Lurie)
Lamb (Michael; *Lamb*, 1980, Bernard MacLaverty)
Nunn (Sir Percy; 1870–1944, English)
Wilt (Henry; *Wilt*, 1976, Tom Sharpe)
05 Brill (Miss; *Miss Brill*, 1922, Katherine Mansfield)
Chips (Mr; *Goodbye Mr Chips*, 1934, James Hilton)

Crane (Edwina; *The Raj Quartet*, 1966–75, Paul Scott)
Crick (Tom; *Waterland*, 1983, Graham Swift)
Dixon (Jim; *Lucky Jim*, 1954, Kingsley Amis)
Doyle (Patrick; *A Disaffection*, 1989, James Kelman)
Handy (Charles Brian; 1932– , Irish)
Henri (Frances; *The Professor*, 1857, Charlotte Brontë)
Irwin (*The History Boys*, 2004, Alan Bennett)
Levin (Sam; *A New Life*, 1961, Bernard Malamud)
Lloyd (Teddy; *The Prime of Miss Jean Brodie*, 1961, Muriel Spark)
Odili (*A Man of the People*, 1966, Chinua Achebe)

Snape (Severus; *Harry Potter and the Philosopher's Stone*, 1997, et seq, J K Rowling)

06 Alcott (Bronson; 1799–1888, US)

Angelo (Albert; *Albert Angelo*, 1964, B S Johnson)

Arnold (Thomas; 1795–1842, English)

Brodie (Miss Jean; *The Prime of Miss Jean Brodie*, 1961, Muriel Spark)

Coppin (Fanny Marion Jackson; 1837–1913, US)

Cotton (George Edward Lynch; 1813–66, English)

Covett (Barbara; *Notes on a Scandal*, 2003, Zoë Heller)

Graham (Martha; 1894–1991, US)

Grimes (Captain; *Decline and Fall*, 1928, Evelyn Waugh)

Gyatso (Geshe Kelsang; 1931– , Tibetan)

Hagrid (Rubeus; *Harry Potter and the Philosopher's Stone*, 1997, et seq, J K Rowling)

Harris (Crocker; *The Browning Version*, 1948, Terence Rattigan)

Hector (*The History Boys*, 2004, Alan Bennett)

Hillel (1 c BC–1 c AD)

Hornby (A S; 1898–1978, English)

Ramsay (Dunstan; *The Deptford Trilogy*, 1983, Robertson Davies)

Solent (Wolf; *Wolf Solent*, 1929, John Cowper Powys)

07 Darling (Sir James Ralph; 1899–1995, Australian)

Eckhart (Miss; *The Golden Apples*, 1949, Eudora Welty)

Edwards (James; *Whack-o!*, 1950s, TV sitcom)

Enketei (Mira; *Amalgamemnon*, 1984, Christine Brooke-Rose)

Fischer (Marcus; *The Time of the Angels*, 1966, Iris Murdoch)

Keating (John; *Dead Poets Society*, 1989)

Krishna (*The English Teacher*, 1945, R K Narayan)

Lowther (Gordon; *The Prime of Miss Jean Brodie*, 1961, Muriel Spark)

Matthay (Tobias; 1858–1945, English)

Mr Chips (*Goodbye Mr Chips*, 1934, James Hilton)

Mulcahy (Henry; *The Groves of Academe*, 1952, Mary McCarthy)

See also **education**; **school**

Peecher (Emma; *Our Mutual Friend*, 1865, Charles Dickens)

Porpora (Nicola; 1686–1766, Italian)

Saville (Colin; *Saville*, 1976, David Storey)

Squeers (Wackford; *Nicholas Nickleby*, 1838–39, Charles Dickens)

Vaughan (Barbara; *The Mandelbaum Gate*, 1965, Muriel Spark)

Wackles (Sophy; *The Old Curiosity Shop*, 1841, Charles Dickens)

08 Bridgman (Laura Dewey; 1829–89, US)

Caldwell (George; *The Centaur*, 1963, John Updike)

Chipping (Mr; *Goodbye Mr Chips*, 1934, James Hilton)

Doubloon (Maggie; *Slouching Towards Kalamazoo*, 1983, Peter De Vries)

Lewisham (George; *Love and Mr Lewisham*, 1900, H G Wells)

Prodicus (5c, Greek)

Sullivan (Anne; 1866–1936, US)

09 Batchelor (Barbie; *The Raj Quartet*, 1966–75, Paul Scott)

Bellgrove (Professor; *Gormenghast* trilogy, 1946–59, Mervyn Peake)

Braidwood (Thomas; 1715–1806, Scottish)

Hartright (Walter; *The Woman in White*, 1860, Wilkie Collins)

Headstone (Bradley; *Our Mutual Friend*, 1865, Charles Dickens)

Strasberg (Lee; 1901–82, US)

10 Dumbledore (Albus; *Harry Potter and the Philosopher's Stone*, 1997, et seq, J K Rowling)

Leadbetter (David; 1955– , English)

Madame Beck (*Villette*, 1853, Charlotte Brontë)

Madam Hooch (*Harry Potter and the Philosopher's Stone*, 1997, et seq, J K Rowling)

McGonagall (Minerva; *Harry Potter and the Philosopher's Stone*, 1997, et seq, J K Rowling)

Protagoras (c.490–c.420 BC, Greek)

12 Pennyfeather (Paul; *Decline and Fall*, 1928, Evelyn Waugh)

Stanislavsky (1863–1938, Russian)

13 M'Choakumchild (Mr; *Hard Times*, 1854, Charles Dickens)

team *see* **American football**; **Australian rules football**; **baseball**; **basketball**; **cricket**; **football**; **Rugby League**; **Rugby Union**

teeth

Teeth include:

03 cap	tush	chisel	permanent
dog	tusk	corner	sectorial
egg	wang	cuspid	serration
eye	wolf	wisdom	**10** carnassial
gag	**05** cheek	**07** denture	first molar
gam	colt's	grinder	masticator
jaw	crown	incisor	molendinar
04 baby	false	scissor	third molar
back	first	snaggle	**11** multicuspid
buck	molar		second molar
fang	plate	**08** bicuspid	**13** first premolar
fore	store	dentures	**14** central incisor
gold	sweet	impacted	lateral incisor
milk	**06** bridge	premolar	second premolar
mill	canine	**09** milk-molar	

television

Television programme types include:

04 news	sitcom	chat show	soap opera
soap	**07** cartoon	docusoap	**11** documentary
05 anime	phone-in	game show	**12** makeover show
drama	reality	quiz show	
06 repeat	**08** bulletin	**09** panel game	

Television channels include:

02 E4	ITV1	Living TV	
FX	ITV2	Sky Arts 1	
03 ABC	ITV3	**09** al-Jazeera	
CNN	ITV4	BBC News 24	
Fox	**05** Bravo	Bloomberg	
HBO	More4	Eurosport	
MTV	Sci-Fi	Sky Movies	
NBC	Watch	Sky Sports	
QVC	**06** Sky One	**11** Nickelodeon	
S4C	The Box	**12** Adult Channel	
TCM	**07** Fantasy	Animal Planet	
VH1	Fox News	Sky Box Office	
04 BBC1	Playboy	**13** Discovery Kids	
BBC2	Sky News	Disney Channel	
BBC3	Virgin1	Extreme Sports	
BBC4	**08** BBC World	**14** Cartoon Network	
CBBC	Cbeebies	Fox Kids Network	
CNBC	Channel 4	History Channel	
Dave	Channel 9	ITV News Channel	
Five	FilmFour	**15** Paramount Comedy	
GOLD			

Television shows include:

02 *ER*	**03** *3–2–1*	*QED*
QI	*CSI*	*TW3*

04 CDUK
Chef!
Fame
GMTV
Look
M*A*S*H
NCIS
Soap
Taxi

05 Arena
Bread
Hotel
Joe 90
Kojak
LA Law
Rhoda
Shaft
Sorry!
Sykes
Tenko
The OC
Wogan
Z Cars

06 Angels
Batman
Bottom
Callan
Cheers
Dallas
DIY SOS
Hannay
Harry O
Hi-De-Hi
Lassie
Magpie
Mannix
Minder
Mr Bean
Quincy
Sharpe
Shogun
Tiswas
Trisha
Whack-o!

07 24 Hours
Airline
Airport
Bagpuss
Blake's 7
Bonanza
Cadfael
Chigley
Colditz
Columbo
Compact
Cracker
Daktari

Doctors
Dragnet
Dynasty
Flipper
Frasier
Friends
Hancock
Holiday
Horizon
Laramie
Laugh-In
Lovejoy
Maigret
McCloud
Monitor
Mr Magoo
Omnibus
Poldark
Pop Idol
Rainbow
Rawhide
Room 101
Serpico
Shelley
Spender
Taggart
The Bill
The Word
Tonight
Top Gear
Warship

08 'Allo 'Allo
Aquarius
Ask Aspel
Bad Girls
Baywatch
Benidorm
Bergerac
Casualty
Cheyenne
Clangers
Cold Feet
Dad's Army
Due South
Eldorado
Faking It
Hadleigh
Hugh and I
Lou Grant
Maverick
Mister Ed
Mr and Mrs
My Family
New Faces
NYPD Blue
On Safari
Panorama
Peep Show

Play Away
Porridge
Pot Black
Red Dwarf
Roseanne
Seinfeld
Sgt Bilko
Star Trek
Stingray
Survival
The A-Team
The Royal
The Saint
This Life
This Week
Time Team
Triangle
Trumpton
Vision On
Watchdog
Wife Swap

09 60 Minutes
Andy Pandy
Bewitched
Blind Date
Blue Peter
Brookside
Catweazle
Chronicle
Countdown
Danger Man
Danger UXB
Dark Angel
Did You See ...?
Doctor Who
Doomwatch
Dr Kildare
Emmerdale
Eurotrash
Family Guy
Father Ted
Going Live!
Happy Days
Heartbeat
Holby City
Hollyoaks
I Love Lucy
Jackanory
Jason King
Love Hurts
Miami Vice
Naked City
News at Ten
Newsnight
Newsround
Oh Brother!
Parkinson
Please Sir!

Public Eye
Real Lives
Scooby-Doo
Shameless
South Park
Strangers
TFI Friday
That's Life
The Expert
The Lovers
The Office
The X Files
Torchwood
Twin Peaks
Up Pompeii!
Whodunnit?

10 Ally McBeal
Big Brother
Blackadder
Byker Grove
Crossroads
Deputy Dawg
Dispatches
Dragon's Den
EastEnders
Elizabeth R
Full Circle
Gladiators
Grandstand
Grange Hill
Hart to Hart
Howards' Way
Jim'll Fix It
Kavanagh QC
Life on Mars
Loose Women
Masterchef
Mastermind
Miss Marple
Naked Video
Nationwide
Neighbours
On the Buses
Pebble Mill
Perry Mason
Play School
Pole to Pole
Police Five
Postman Pat
Quatermass
Rentaghost
Rising Damp
Robin's Nest
Screen Test
Secret Army
Shoestring
The Goodies
The Jetsons

The Monkees
The Sweeney
The Waltons
The Wombles
The X-Factor
Van der Valk
Wacky Races
Wagon Train
Wells Fargo
Who Do You Do?
Why Don't You?

11 Animal Magic
Bargain Hunt
Born and Bred
Butterflies
Call My Bluff
Catchphrase
Come Dancing
Comic Relief
Crackerjack
Dangerfield
Dangermouse
Daniel Boone
Dead Ringers
Falcon Crest
Fame Academy
Give Us a Clue
Ground Force
Hawaii Five-O
Home and Away
Juke Box Jury
Juliet Bravo
Just William
Life on Earth
Lost in Space
Peyton Place
Picture Book
Pie in the Sky
Rab C Nesbitt
Rock Follies
St Elsewhere
Sunset Beach
Teletubbies
The Avengers
The Brothers
The Day Today
The Fast Show
The Fugitive
The Good Life
The Invaders
The Lucy Show
The Munsters
The Prisoner
The Rag Trade
The Simpsons
The Sopranos
The Third Man
This Morning

Tom and Jerry
What's My Line?
Whirlybirds
Whistle Test
Wonder Woman
Yes, Minister

12 A Family at War
A Fine Romance
A Life of Grime
Ask the Family
As Time Goes By
Blockbusters
Candid Camera
Citizen Smith
Crimewatch UK
Dawson's Creek
dinnerladies
Face the Music
Fawlty Towers
Fifteen to One
Food and Drink
Forty Minutes
Grand Designs
Hector's House
It's a Knockout
Kaleidoscope
Knots Landing
Melrose Place
Moonlighting
Mork and Mindy
Open All Hours
Peak Practice
Play for Today
Points of View
Preston Front
Prime Suspect
Question Time
Sesame Street
Softly, Softly
Strike It Rich
Take Your Pick
Telly Addicts
Terry and June
The Champions
The Comedians
The Newcomers
The Power Game
The Sullivans
The Virginian
The Young Ones
Three of a Kind
Thunderbirds
Top of the Form
Top of the Pops
Treasure Hunt
Weekend World
Who Dares, Wins ...
Will and Grace

Working Lunch
World of Sport

13 77 Sunset Strip
A Touch of Frost
Blankety Blank
Bob the Builder
Breakfast Time
Changing Rooms
Emmerdale Farm
Family Affairs
Fantasy Island
Fortunes of War
Game for a Laugh
Going for a Song
Hamish Macbeth
Ivor the Engine
Jonathan Creek
Little Britain
Marcus Welby, MD
Match of the Day
May to December
Muffin the Mule
Pinky and Perky
Ready, Steady, Go!
Sex and the City
Silent Witness
Songs of Praise
Special Branch
Spitting Image
Steptoe and Son
Strike It Lucky
The Apprentice
The Golden Shot
The Likely Lads
The Liver Birds
The Lone Ranger
The Main Chance
The Muppet Show
The Onedin Line
The Persuaders
The Protectors
The Sky at Night
The Two Ronnies
The Woodentops
The World at War
Waiting for God
What Not to Wear
Whicker's World
World in Action

14 Animal Hospital
Ballykissangel
Cagney and Lacey
Captain Pugwash
Cash in the Attic
Charlie and Lola
Charlie's Angels
Criss Cross Quiz

Family Fortunes
Gardener's World
Gavin and Stacey
Happy Ever After
In at the Deep End
Inspector Morse
London's Burning
Murder, She Wrote
My Friend Flicka
Not Only ... But Also ...
Only When I Laugh
Property Ladder
Record Breakers
Six-Five Special
Soldier, Soldier
Surgical Spirit
Take Three Girls
The Ascent of Man
The Crystal Maze
The Flintstones
The Forsyte Saga
The Frost Report
The Golden Girls
The Good Old Days
The Lotus Eaters
The New Avengers
The Outer Limits
The Royle Family
The Weakest Link
This Is Your Life
Three Up, Two Down
Tomorrow's World
To the Manor Born
Wheel of Fortune
Winner Takes All
Worzel Gummidge

15 2 Point 4 Children
Armchair Theatre
Birds of a Feather
Camberwick Green
Challenge Anneka
Comedy Playhouse
Double Your Money
General Hospital
Hill Street Blues
It's a Square World
Just Good Friends
Late Night Line-Up
Lord Peter Wimsey
Midsomer Murders
Noel's House Party
No Place Like Home
One Man and His Dog
Ready Steady Cook
Remington Steele
Starsky and Hutch
The Addams Family
The Big Breakfast

The Flying Doctor
The Invisible Man
The Kumars at No 42
The Late Late Show
The Living Planet
The Man from UNCLE
The New Statesman
The Price is Right
The Twilight Zone
The Untouchables
The World About Us
Thirtysomething
Watch with Mother
Where the Heart Is
Wish You Were Here ...?
You've Been Framed

16 All Gas and Gaiters
All Our Yesterdays
Antiques Roadshow
A Question of Sport
Can't Cook, Won't Cook
Celebrity Squares
Coronation Street
Dalziel and Pascoe
Dixon of Dock Green
Doctor in the House
Footballers' Wives
Hancock's Half Hour
Harry Hill's TV Burp
In the Night Garden
It Ain't Half Hot Mum
Jeeves and Wooster
Love Thy Neighbour
Man about the House
Men Behaving Badly
Monarch of the Glen
Murder Most Horrid
Northern Exposure
Rag Tag and Bobtail
Sale of the Century
Sapphire and Steel
Stars in Their Eyes
Surprise, Surprise
The Dick Emery Show
The High Chaparral
The House of Eliott
The Krypton Factor
The Professionals
The Rockford Files
The South Bank Show
The Vicar of Dibley
The Wednesday Play
What the Papers Say
Within These Walls
Yes, Prime Minister

17 Alas Smith and Jones
Are You Being Served?

Auf Wiedersehen, Pet
Beggar My Neighbour
Beverly Hills 90210
Britain's Got Talent
Dr Finlay's Casebook
Drop the Dead Donkey
Every Second Counts
French and Saunders
Mission: Impossible
Nearest and Dearest
One Foot in the Grave
Opportunity Knocks
Shine On Harvey Moon
The $64,000 Question
The Dukes of Hazzard
The Generation Game
The Incredible Hulk
The Tomorrow People
Through the Keyhole
Till Death Us Do Part

18 Absolutely Fabulous
Alias Smith and Jones
A Man Called Ironside
Do Not Adjust Your Set
Goodness Gracious Me
Have I Got News for You
How to Look Good Naked
I Didn't Know You Cared
Jeux sans Frontières
Old Grey Whistle Test
Only Fools and Horses
Play Your Cards Right
Prisoner: Cell Block H
Rumpole of the Bailey
Some Mothers Do 'Ave 'Em
The Dick Van Dyke Show
The Magic Roundabout
The Partridge Family
The Phil Silvers Show
The Troubleshooters
Upstairs, Downstairs
When the Boat Comes In

19 Desperate Housewives
Goodnight Sweetheart
How Clean Is Your House?
Last of the Summer Wine
Strictly Come Dancing
Tales of the Riverbank
Thank Your Lucky Stars
The Chinese Detective
The Lenny the Lion Show
The White Heather Club
They Think It's All Over
University Challenge
Who Do You Think You
Are?
Whose Line Is It Anyway?
Xena: Warrior Princess

20 Harry Enfield and Chums
John Craven's Newsround
Keeping Up Appearances
Not the Nine O'Clock News
Tales of the Unexpected
The League of Gentlemen
Your Life in Their Hands

21 Agatha Christie's Poirot
A Very Peculiar Practice
Buffy the Vampire Slayer
Eurovision Song Contest
Ever Decreasing Circles
Multi-Coloured Swap Shop
Mystery and Imagination
Never Mind the Buzzcocks
Oh No It's Selwyn Froggitt
Skippy, the Bush Kangaroo
That Was the Week That Was
The Beverly Hillbillies

22 Around the World in 80
Days
Rowan and Martin's
Laugh-In
Television Top of the Form
The Duchess of Duke Street

The Six Million Dollar Man
The Six Wives of Henry VIII

23 It'll Be Alright on the Night
Little House on the Prairie
Not in Front of the Children
Royal Variety Performance
The Ruth Rendell Mysteries

24 Location, Location, Location
Monty Python's Flying Circus
Ramsay's Kitchen
Nightmares
Rutland Weekend Television
The Adventures of Rin-Tin-Tin
The Late, Late Breakfast
Show
The Streets of San Francisco
Who Wants to Be a
Millionaire?

25 All Creatures Great and
Small
Queer Eye for the Straight
Guy
Randall and Hopkirk
(Deceased)

26 I'm a Celebrity - Get Me out
of Here!

28 The Black and White
Minstrel Show

29 Thomas the Tank Engine
and Friends

30 The Fall and Rise of
Reginald Perrin
The Hitch-Hiker's Guide to
the Galaxy

31 Never Mind the Quality,
Feel the Width
Sunday Night at the London
Palladium
Whatever Happened to the
Likely Lads?

TV characters include:

02 C J (*The Fall And Rise Of Reginald Perrin*)

04 Best (Dave; *The Royle Family*)
Best (Denise; *The Royle Family*)
Bing (Chandler; *Friends*)
Bird (Ronald 'Budgie'; *Budgie*)
Buck (Rose; *Upstairs, Downstairs*)
Cage (John; *Ally McBeal*)
Cook (Edgar 'Egg'; *This Life*)
Fish (Richard; *Ally McBeal*)
Gale (Cathy; *The Avengers*)
Good (Barbara; *The Good Life*)
Good (Tom; *The Good Life*)
Hope (Viv; *Emmerdale*)

Hunt (Gene; *Life on Mars*)
King (Sadie; *Emmerdale*)
King (Tara; *The Avengers*)
Kirk (Captain James Tiberius; *Star Trek*)
Mike (*The Young Ones*)
Moon (Alfie; *EastEnders*)
Moon (Daphne; *Frasier*)
Mork (*Mork and Mindy*)
Neil (*The Young Ones*)
Peck (Lieutenant Templeton 'Faceman'; *The
A-Team*)
Peel (Mrs Emma; *The Avengers*)
Pike (Private Frank; *Dad's Army*)

Rick (*The Young Ones*)
Ross (Dr Doug; *ER*)
Ryan (Sam; *Silent Witness*)
Solo (Napoleon; *The Man from UNCLE*)
Sulu (Hikaru; *Star Trek*)
Tate (Kim; *Emmerdale*)
York (Charlotte; *Sex and the City*)

05 Angel (*Buffy The Vampire Slayer/Angel*)
Batty (Nora; *Last of the Summer Wine*)
Bauer (Jack; *24*)
Beale (Ian; *EastEnders*)
Bilko (Sgt Ernest G, 'Ernie'; *The Phil Silvers Show*)
Birch (Edna; *Emmerdale*)
Blake (Inspector Cyril, 'Blakey'; *On The Buses*)
Bodie (William; *The Professionals*)
Brent (David; *The Office*)
Brian (*Family Guy*)
Briss (Hilary; *The League of Gentlemen*)
Burns (Charles Montgomery 'Monty'; *The Simpsons*)
Clegg (Norman; *Last of the Summer Wine*)
Crane (Dr Frasier; *Cheers/Frasier*)
Crane (Dr Niles; *Frasier*)
Crane (Martin; *Frasier*)
Daley (Arthur; *Minder*)
Dixon (PC George; *Dixon of Dock Green*)
Doyle (Mrs; *Father Ted*)
Doyle (Raymond; *The Professionals*)
Evans (Pat; *EastEnders*)
Ewing (Bobby; *Dallas*)
Ewing (John Ross, 'J R'; *Dallas*)
Frost (DI Jack; *A Touch of Frost*)
Gates (Amber; *Footballers' Wives*)
Grant (Bobby; *Brookside*)
Grant (Sheila; *Brookside*)
Green (Rachel; *Friends*)
Jones (Lance-Corporal Jack; *Dad's Army*)
Jones (Martha; *Doctor Who*)
Jones (Miss Ruth; *Rising Damp*)
Jones (Samantha; *Sex and the City*)
Kojak (Lieutenant Theo; *Kojak*)
Lynch (Bet; *Coronation Street*)
Mayer (Susan; *Desperate Housewives*)
McCoy (Dr Leonard, 'Bones'; *Star Trek*)
McFee (Shughie; *Crossroads*)
Noble (Donna; *Doctor Who*)
Ogden (Hilda; *Coronation Street*)
Percy (*Blackadder*)
Platt (Gail; *Coronation Street*)
Polly (*Fawlty Towers*)
Regan (DI Jack; *The Sweeney*)
Roach (Megan; *Casualty*)
Rolfe (Jack; *Howard's Way*)
Royle (Antony; *The Royle Family*)
Royle (Barbara; *The Royle Family*)
Royle (Jim; *The Royle Family*)

Rudge (Olive; *On The Buses*)
Scavo (Lynette; *Desperate Housewives*)
Scott (Montgomery, 'Scotty'; *Star Trek*)
Smith (Colonel John 'Hannibal'; *The A-Team*)
Smith (Sarah Jane; *Doctor Who*)
Solis (Gabrielle; *Desperate Housewives*)
Spock (Mr; *Star Trek*)
Steed (John; *The Avengers/The New Avengers*)
Stone (Patsy; *Absolutely Fabulous*)
Tubbs (*The League of Gentlemen*)
Tyler (Rose; *Doctor Who*)
Tyler (Sam; *Life on Mars*)
Uhura (Lieutenant; *Star Trek*)
Watts (Angie; *EastEnders*)
Watts ('Dirty' Den; *EastEnders*)
Weber (Warren 'Potsie'; *Happy Days*)
Wicks (Simon 'Wicksy'; *EastEnders*)
Wilde (Danny; *The Persuaders!*)

06 Arcola (Charles 'Chachi'; *Happy Days*)
Austin (Steve; *The Six Million Dollar Man*)
Barlow (Deirdre; *Coronation Street*)
Barlow (Ken; *Coronation Street*)
Barnes (Cliff; *Dallas*)
Benton (Dr Peter; *ER*)
Bishop (Emily; *Coronation Street*)
Bishop (Harold; *Neighbours*)
B'Stard (Alan; *The New Statesman*)
Bubble (*Absolutely Fabulous*)
Bucket (Hyacinth; *Keeping Up Appearances*)
Buffay (Phoebe; *Friends*)
Butler (Stan; *On The Buses*)
Carter (Dr John; *ER*)
Carter (DS George; *The Sweeney*)
Chekov (Pavel; *Star Trek*)
Cooper (Gwen; *Torchwood*)
Cooper (Special Agent Dale; *Twin Peaks*)
Cotton (Dot; *EastEnders*)
Cowley (George; *The Professionals*)
Crilly (Father Ted; *Father Ted*)
Denton (Harvey; *The League of Gentlemen*)
Denton (Val; *The League of Gentlemen*)
Dingle (Mandy; *Emmerdale*)
Dingle (Marlon; *Emmerdale*)
Duffin (Lisa 'Duffy'; *Casualty*)
Edward (*The League of Gentlemen*)
Fawlty (Basil; *Fawlty Towers*)
Fawlty (Sybil; *Fawlty Towers*)
Ferris (Bob; *The Likely Lads*)
Forbes (Anna; *This Life*)
Fowler (Pauline; *EastEnders*)
Frazer (Private James; *Dad's Army*)
Gambit (Mike; *The New Avengers*)
Geller (Monica; *Friends*)
Geller (Ross; *Friends*)
Glover (Kathy; *Emmerdale*)
Godber (Lennie; *Porridge*)

Greene (Dr Mark; *ER*)
Hacker (Jim; *Yes Minister/Yes, Prime Minister*)
Hobbes (Miranda; *Sex and the City*)
Howard (Jan; *Howard's Way*)
Howard (Tom; *Howard's Way*)
Hudson (Mr Angus; *Upstairs, Downstairs*)
Hughes (Yosser; *Boys from the Blackstuff*)
Hunter (David; *Crossroads*)
Lurcio (*Up Pompeii*)
Mackay (Mr; *Porridge*)
Malone (Sam; *Cheers*)
Mangel (Nell; *Neighbours*)
Manuel (*Fawlty Towers*)
McBeal (Ally; *Ally McBeal*)
McCann (Terry; *Minder*)
Nassim (Milly; *This Life*)
Palmer (Laura; *Twin Peaks*)
Perrin (Reginald Iolanthe, 'Reggie'; *The Fall and Rise of Reginald Perrin*)
Purdey (*The New Avengers*)
Ramsay (Madge; *Neighbours*)
Rigsby (Rupert; *Rising Damp*)
Slater (Kat; *EastEnders*)
Sugden (Annie; *Emmerdale*)
Sugden (Jack; *Emmerdale*)
Turner (Alan; *Emmerdale*)
Turner (Tanya; *Footballers' Wives*)
Turtle (Amy; *Crossroads*)
Vassal (Elaine; *Ally McBeal*)
Vyvyan (*The Young Ones*)
Weaver (Dr Kerry; *ER*)
Wilson (Sergeant Arthur; *Dad's Army*)

07 Appleby (Sir Humphrey; *Yes Minister/Yes, Prime Minister*)
Baldwin (Mike; *Coronation Street*)
Baracus (Sgt Bosco 'B A'; *The A-Team*)
Boswell (Carol; *The Liver Birds*)
Brearly (Amos; *Emmerdale*)
Bridges (Mrs Kate; *Upstairs, Downstairs*)
Butcher (Frank; *EastEnders*)
Collier (Terry; *The Likely Lads*)
Columbo (Lieutenant; *Columbo*)
Daniels (Helen; *Neighbours*)
Garnett (Alf; *Till Death Us Do Part*)
Godfrey (Private Charles; *Dad's Army*)
Griffin (Peter; *Family Guy*)
Griffin (Stewie; *Family Guy*)
Hackett (Father Jack; *Father Ted*)
Hawkeye (Benjamin Franklin Pierce; *M*A*S*H*)
Hawkins (Benny; *Crossroads*)
Hopkirk (Marty; *Randall and Hopkirk (Deceased)*)
Jackson (Arnold; *Diff'rent Strokes*)
MacBeth (Hamish; *Hamish MacBeth*)
Maguire (Father Dougal; *Father Ted*)
Masters (Ken; *Howard's Way*)
Meldrew (Margaret; *One Foot in the Grave*)

Meldrew (Victor; *One Foot in the Grave*)
Monsoon (Edina 'Eddy'; *Absolutely Fabulous*)
Monsoon (Saffron 'Saffy'; *Absolutely Fabulous*)
Murdock (Captain H M 'Howling Mad'; *The A-Team*)
Nesbitt (Rab C; *Rab C Nesbitt*)
Pauline (*The League of Gentlemen*)
Queenie (*Blackadder*)
Randall (Jeff; *Randall and Hopkirk (Deceased)*)
Ricardo (Lucy; *I Love Lucy*)
Ricardo (Ricky; *I Love Lucy*)
Roberts (Audrey; *Coronation Street*)
Rumpole (Horace; *Rumpole of the Bailey*)
Simpson (Bart; *The Simpsons*)
Simpson (Homer; *The Simpsons*)
Simpson (Lisa; *The Simpsons*)
Simpson (Marge; *The Simpsons*)
Soprano (Tony; *The Sopranos*)
Spencer (Betty; *Some Mothers Do 'Ave 'Em*)
Spencer (Frank; *Some Mothers Do 'Ave 'Em*)
Starsky (Detective Dave; *Starsky and Hutch*)
Steptoe (Albert; *Steptoe and Son*)
Steptoe (Harold; *Steptoe and Son*)
Stewart (Miles; *This Life*)
Summers (Buffy; *Buffy The Vampire Slayer*)
The Fonz (*Happy Days*)
Tilsley (Gail; *Coronation Street*)
Trotter (Derek 'Del Boy'; *Only Fools and Horses*)
Trotter (Rodney; *Only Fools and Horses*)

08 Baldrick (*Blackadder*)
Bradshaw (Carrie; *Sex and the City*)
Corkhill (Billy; *Brookside*)
Dewhurst (Walter 'Foggy'; *Last of the Summer Wine*)
Fairhead (Charlie; *Casualty*)
Flanders (Ned; *The Simpsons*)
Fletcher (Norman Stanley; *Porridge*)
Harkness (Captain Jack; *Doctor Who/ Torchwood*)
Hathaway (Nurse Carol; *ER*)
Houlihan (Margaret 'Hotlips'; *M*A*S*H*)
Jordache (Beth; *Brookside*)
Kavanagh (James; *Kavanagh QC*)
Kuryakin (Illya; *The Man from UNCLE*)
McDonald (Steve; *Coronation Street*)
Milligan (Bruno; *Footballers' Wives*)
Mitchell (Grant; *EastEnders*)
Mitchell (Peggy; *EastEnders*)
Mitchell (Phil; *EastEnders*)
Mortimer (Meg; *Crossroads*)
Robinson (Charlene; *Neighbours*)
Robinson (Scott; *Neighbours*)
Simonite (William 'Compo'; *Last of the Summer Wine*)

Sinclair (Lord Brett; *The Persuaders!*)
Skilbeck (Dolly; *Emmerdale*)
Speakman (Norma, 'Nana'; *The Royle Family*)
Sullivan (Rita; *Coronation Street*)
Tennison (DCI Jane; *Prime Suspect*)
Tortelli (Carla; *Cheers*)
Urquhart (Francis; *House of Cards*)

09 Arkwright (Albert; *Open All Hours*)
Armstrong (Seth; *Emmerdale*)
Carpenter (Lou; *Neighbours*)
Duckworth (Jack; *Coronation Street*)
Duckworth (Vera; *Coronation Street*)
Gallagher (Frank; *Shameless*)
Granville (*Open All Hours*)
Griffiths (Josh; *Casualty*)
Hennessey (Beryl; *The Liver Birds*)
Huggy Bear (*Starsky and Hutch*)
McConnell (Mindy; *Mork and Mindy*)
Number Six (*The Prisoner*)
Partridge (Danny; *The Partridge Family*)

Partridge (Keith Douglas; *The Partridge Family*)
The Doctor (*Doctor Who*)
Tribbiani (Joey; *Friends*)
Van De Kamp (Bree; *Desperate Housewives*)

10 Blackadder (Edmund; *Blackadder*)
Cunningham (Joanie; *Happy Days*)
Cunningham (Richard 'Richie'; *Happy Days*)
Fitzgerald (Dr Eddie, 'Fitz'; *Cracker*)
Fonzarelli (Arthur 'Fonzie'; *Happy Days*)
Hutchinson (Detective Ken 'Hutch'; *Starsky and Hutch*)
Hutchinson (Sandra; *The Liver Birds*)
Lane-Pascoe (Chardonnay; *Footballers' Wives*)
Leadbetter (Jerry; *The Good Life*)
Leadbetter (Margot; *The Good Life*)
Mainwaring (Captain George; *Dad's Army*)
Penhaligon (DS Jane, 'Panhandle'; *Cracker*)

14 Krusty the Clown (*The Simpsons*)

15 Fletcher-Dervish (Piers; *The New Statesman*)

Television presenters include:

03 Ant (Anthony McPartlin; 1975– , English)
Dec (Declan Donnelly; 1975– , English)

04 Marr (Andrew; 1959– , Scottish)
Muir (Frank; 1920–98, English)
Ross (Jonathan; 1960– , English)

05 Aspel (Michael; 1933– , Welsh)
Black (Cilla; 1943– , English)
Bragg (Melvyn, Lord; 1939– , English)
Evans (Chris; 1966– , English)
Fogle (Ben; 1973– , English)
Frost (Sir David; 1939– , English)
James (Clive; 1939– , Australian)
Kelly (Lorraine; 1959– , Scottish)
Moore (Sir Patrick; 1923– , English)
Negus (Arthur; 1903–85, English)
Wogan (Terry; 1938– , Irish)

06 Carson (Johnny; 1925–2005, US)
Chiles (Adrian; 1967– , English)
McCall (Davina; 1967– , English)
Norden (Denis; 1922– , English)
Norman (Barry; 1933– , English)
Norton (Graham; 1963– , Irish)
Paxman (Jeremy; 1950– , English)
Rayner (Claire; 1931– , English)
Savile (Sir Jimmy; 1926– , English)

07 Andrews (Eamon; 1922–87, Irish)
Bellamy (David; 1933– , English)
Britton (Fern; 1957– , English)
Edmonds (Noel; 1948– , English)
Forsyth (Bruce; 1928– , English)

Kennedy (Sir Ludovic; 1919– , Scottish)
Madeley (Richard; 1956– , English)
Rantzen (Esther; 1940– , English)
Starkey (David; 1945– , English)
Tarrant (Chris; 1946– , English)
Wheldon (Sir Huw; 1916–86, Welsh)
Whicker (Alan; 1925– , English)
Winfrey (Oprah; 1954– , US)

08 Bakewell (Joan; 1933– , English)
Bleakley (Christine; 1980– , Northern Irish)
Campbell (Nicky; 1961– , Scottish)
Clarkson (Jeremy; 1960– , English)
Finnigan (Judy; 1948– , English)
Springer (Jerry; 1944– , US)
Stoppard (Miriam; 1937– , English)
Sullivan (Ed; 1902–74, US)

09 Ant and Dec (Anthony McPartlin; 1975– , English/Declan Donnelly; 1975– , English)
Magnusson (Magnus; 1929–2007, Icelandic/Scottish)
Parkinson (Michael; 1935– , English)
Schofield (Phillip; 1962– , English)
Vorderman (Carol; 1960– , English)

10 Titchmarsh (Alan; 1949– , English)

12 Attenborough (Sir David; 1926– , English)

14 Richard and Judy (Richard Madeley; 1956– , English/Judy Finnigan; 1948– , English)

See also **broadcasting**; **comedy**; **quiz**; **soap opera**

tennis

Tennis players include:

04 Ashe (Arthur; 1943–93, US)
Borg (Björn; 1956– , Swedish)
Cash (Pat; 1965– , Australian)
Graf (Steffi; 1969– , German)
Hoad (Lew; 1934–94, Australian)
King (Billie Jean; 1943– , US)
Ryan (Elizabeth; 1892–1979, US)
Wade (Virginia; 1945– , English)

05 Budge (Don; 1915–2000, US)
Bueno (Maria; 1939– , Brazilian)
Court (Margaret; 1942– , Australian)
Durie (Jo; 1960– , English)
Evert (Chris; 1954– , US)
Henin (Justine; 1982– , Belgian)
Jones (Ann; 1938– , English)
Laver (Rod; 1938– , Australian)
Lendl (Ivan; 1960– , Czech/US)
Lloyd (Chris; c.1951– , English)
Nadal (Rafael; 1986– , Spanish)
Perry (Fred; 1909–95, English/US)
Seles (Monica; 1973– , Yugoslav/US)
Stich (Michael; 1968– , German)
Vilas (Guillermo; 1952– , Argentine)

06 Agassi (Andre; 1970– , US)
Austin (Tracy; 1962– , US)
Barker (Sue; 1956– , English)
Becker (Boris; 1967– , German)
Cawley (Evonne; 1951– , Australian)
Drobny (Jaroslav; 1921–2001, Czech/British)
DuPont (Margaret; 1918– , US)
Edberg (Stefan; 1966– , Swedish)
Gibson (Althea; 1927–2003, US)
Henman (Tim; 1974– , English)
Hewitt (Lleyton; 1981– , Australian)
Hingis (Martina; 1980– , Czech/Swiss)
Hopman (Harry; 1906–85, Australian)
Kramer (Jack; 1921– , US)
Murray (Andrew; 1987– , Scottish)
Rafter (Pat; 1972– , Australian)
Tilden (Bill; 1893–1953, US)

07 Borotra (Jean; 1898–94, French)
Brookes (Sir Norman; 1877–1968, Australian)
Connors (Jimmy; 1952– , US)

Emerson (Roy; 1936– , Australian)
Federer (Roger; 1981– , Swiss)
Godfree (Kitty; 1896–1992, English)
LaCoste (Rene; 1904–96, French)
Lenglen (Suzanne; 1899–1938, French)
Maskell (Dan; 1908–92, English)
McEnroe (John; 1959– , US)
Nastase (Ilie; 1946– , Romanian)
Novotna (Jana; 1968– , Czech)
Renshaw (Willie; 1861–1904, English)
Roddick (Andrew; 1982– , US)
Sampras (Pete; 1971– , US)
Sedgman (Frank; 1927– , Australian)
Shriver (Pam; 1962– , US)
Zvereva (Natasha; 1971– , Belarus)

08 Capriati (Jennifer; 1976– , US)
Connolly (Maureen; 1934–69, US)
Djokovic (Novak; 1987– , Serbian)
Gonzales (Pancho; 1928–95, US)
Janković (Jelena; 1985– , Serbian)
Krajicek (Richard; 1971– , Dutch)
Mauresmo (Amélie; 1979– , French)
Newcombe (John; 1944– , Australian)
Rosewall (Ken; 1934– , Australian)
Rusedski (Greg; 1973– , Canadian/British)
Sabatini (Gabriela; 1970– , Argentine)
Wightman (Hazel Hotchkiss; 1886–1974, US)
Williams (Serena; 1981– , US)
Williams (Venus; 1980– , US)

09 Davenport (Lindsay; 1976– , US)
Goolagong (Evonne; 1951– , Australian)
Sharapova (Maria; 1987– , Russian)
Woodforde (Mark; 1965– , Australian)

10 Ivanisevic (Goran; 1971– , Croatian)
Kafelnikov (Yevgeny; 1974– , Russian)
Kournikova (Anna; 1981– , Russian)
Mandlikova (Hana; 1962– , Czech/Australian)
Wills Moody (Helen; 1905–98, US)
Woodbridge (Todd; 1971– , Australian)

11 Navratilova (Martina; 1956– , Czech/US)

15 Goolagong Cawley (Evonne; 1951– , Australian)

Tennis terms include:

03 ace	WTA	break	slice
ATP	**04** love	deuce	smash
let	pass	drive	**06** return
lob	tape	fault	umpire
LTA	**05** AELTC	rally	volley
set	alley	serve	winner

07 ballboy
net cord
runback

08 backhand
ballgirl
baseline
drop shot
forehand
line call
love game
midcourt
net judge

See also **sport**

overhead
overrule
set point
tie-break
wood shot

09 advantage
backcourt
baseliner
break back
foot fault
forecourt
hold serve

line judge
mini-break
shotmaker
sweet spot
tramlines
two-handed

10 break point
cross court
deuce court
match point

11 block volley

double fault
service game
service line

12 approach shot
ground stroke
mixed doubles
service court

13 second service

14 advantage court
serve and volley

Tennyson, Alfred, Lord (1809–92)

Significant works include:

04 *Maud* (1855)

06 *Becket* (1884)
Harold (1876)
Oenone (1833)
The Cup (1881)

07 *Mariana* (1830)
Ulysses (1842)

08 *The Brook* (1855)
The Daisy (1855)
Tithonus (1881)

09 *Queen Mary* (1875)
The Falcon (1879)
The Voyage (1881)
Timbuctoo (1829)

10 *In Memoriam* (1850)
St Agnes Eve (1842)
The Mermaid (1833)

11 *Edwin Morris* (1842)

The Princess (1847)

12 *Locksley Hall* (1842)
Morte d'Arthur (1842)

14 *The Lotos-Eaters* (1833)

15 *Break, Break, Break* (1842)
Idylls of the King (1859–85)

16 *The Lady of Shalott* (1833)

17 *A Dream of Fair Women* (1833)
Maud and Other Poems (1855)
Poems in Two Volumes (1842)

19 *Poems Chiefly Lyrical* (1830)

20 *Ballads and Other Poems* (1880)
The Gardener's Daughter (1842)

21 *Tiresias and Other Poems* (1885)

25 *The Holy Grail and Other Poems* (1869)

26 *The Charge of the Light Brigade* (1855)

31 *Recollections of the Arabian Nights* (1830)

tense *see* **grammar**

tent

Tents include:

03 box
mat

04 bell
dome
kata
yurt

05 bivvy

black
frame
lodge
ridge
tepee
tupik

06 big top
canopy

canvas
tunnel
wigwam

07 conical
marquee
touring
trailer
yaranga

10 single hoop
tabernacle

11 hooped bivvy

12 sloping ridge
sloping wedge

13 barrel-vaulted
crossover pole

term

terrier

territory *see* **Australia; Canada**

terrorist *see* **revolutionary**

theatre

stalls
07 balcony
catwalk
curtain
cut drop
gallery
leg drop
rostrum
the gods
upstage
08 backdrop
coulisse

trapdoor
09 backstage
cyclorama
downstage
forestage
green room
mezzanine
open stage
tormentor
10 auditorium
footlights
fourth wall

ghost light
prompt side
proscenium
11 upper circle
12 orchestra pit
13 safety curtain
14 opposite prompt
proscenium arch
revolving stage
15 proscenium doors

Theatres include:

03 Pit (England)
04 Rose (England)
Swan (England)
05 Abbey (Ireland)
Globe (England)
Lyric (England)
Savoy (England)
06 Albery (England)
Lyceum (England)
Old Vic (England)
Queen's (England)
07 Adelphi (England)
Aldwych (England)
Almeida (England)
Garrick (England)
Olivier (England)
08 Coliseum (England)
Crucible (England)
Dominion (England)
National (England)

Young Vic (England)
Ziegfeld (USA)
09 Cambridge (England)
Cottesloe (England)
Criterion (England)
Drury Lane (England)
Haymarket (England)
Lyttelton (England)
Palladium (England)
11 Comedy Store (England)
Duke of York's (England)
Moulin Rouge (France)
12 Sadler's Wells (England)
Theatre Royal (England)
13 Folies Bergère (France)
Prince of Wales (England)
The Other Place (England)
The Roundhouse (England)
14 Barbican Centre (England)
15 Donmar Warehouse (England)

Terms to do with the theatre include:

02 BS
LX
OB
OP
PS
03 act
cue
fée
fly
gel
mug
rep
run
vis
yok
04 call
cast
flat

grid
juve
loge
plot
pong
rake
tabs
wash
yock
05 actor
ad lib
angel
aside
cameo
derig
dry up
fit-up
genre

get-in
lines
lodge
props
re-rig
scene
spike
usher
06 baffle
chorus
corpse
critic
double
dry ice
Equity
flyman
fringe
get-out

make-up
miscue
places
prompt
review
script
walk-on

07 actress
costume
curtain
dresser
dry tech
matinee
pittite
preview
project
rhubarb
rigging
scenery
tableau
upstage
West End

08 audience
audition
blackout
block out
Broadway
business
coulisse
dialogue
director
duologue
entr'acte
interval
libretto
overture
pass door
play-goer
producer
ring down
thespian
wardrobe
white out

09 backlight
backstage
beginners
box office
break a leg
chaperone
curtain up
cyclorama
double act
downstage
footlight
full house
happening
limelight
monologue
periaktos
programme
rehearsal
repertory
skin money
soliloquy
soubrette
spotlight
stage crew
stage door
stage hand
stage left
usherette
visual cue

10 book-holder
dénouement
first night
followspot
fourth wall
get the bird
in the wings
piano dress
prompt book
prompt copy
prompt desk
prompt side
stagecraft
stage right

understudy
walk-around

11 bastard side
bums on seats
centre stage
curtain call
curtain time
die the death
greasepaint
house lights
iron curtain
leading lady
off-Broadway
quick change
read-through
stage fright
top one's part
wind machine

12 breeches part
breeches role
first-nighter
front of house
intermission
jeune premier
juvenile lead
monstre sacré
principal boy
prompt corner
prompt script
stage manager
travesty role

13 bastard prompt
curtain-raiser
curtain speech
grande vedette
jeune première
safety curtain

14 dress rehearsal
opposite prompt
special effects

15 genteel business
opposite bastard

See also **cinema**; **director**

theology

Theologians include:

03 Eck (Johann; 1486–1543, German)
Ela (Jean-Marc; 1936– , Cameroonian)

04 Bede (St, 'the Venerable'; c.673–735, Anglo-Saxon)
Boff (Leonardo; 1938– , Brazilian)
Cone (James H; 1938– , US)
Daly (Mary; 1928– , US)
Gore (Charles; 1853–1932, English)

Hick (John; 1922– , English)
John (St, of Damascus; c.676–c.754, Greek)
More (Henry; 1614–87, English)

05 Arius (c.250–336 AD, Libyan)
Aulén (Gustaf; 1879–1977, Swedish)
Barth (Karl; 1886–1968, Swiss)
Buber (Martin; 1878–1965, Austrian)
Colet (John; c.1467–1519, English)

Cyril (St, of Alexandria; AD376–444, Greek)
Henry (Carl F H; 1913–2003, US)
Mbiti (John S; 1931– , Kenyan)
Occam (William of; c.1285–c.1349, English)
Pusey (E B; 1800–82, English)
Rainy (Robert; 1826–1906, Scottish)
Sarpi (Pietro, Fra Paolo; 1552–1623, Italian)
Tracy (David; 1939– , US)

06 Anselm (St; 1033–1109, Italian)
Calvin (John; 1509–64, French)
Cupitt (Don; 1934– , English)
Eckart (Johannes; c.1260–1327, German)
Ferrar (Nicholas; 1592–1637, English)
Jansen (Cornelius; 1585–1638, Dutch)
Jüngel (Eberhard; 1934– , German)
Mather (Increase; 1639–1723, American)
Ockham (William of; c.1285–c.1349, English)
Origen (c.185–c.254 AD, Greek)
Pagels (Elaine; 1943– , US)
Suárez (Francisco; 1548–1617, Spanish)
Taylor (Jeremy; 1613–67, English)

07 Altizer (Thomas J J; 1927– , US)
Aquinas (St Thomas; 1225–74, Italian)
Barclay (William; 1907–78, Scottish)
Bernard (St, of Clairvaux; 1090–1153, French)
Brunner (Emil; 1889–1966, Swiss)
Eckhart (Johannes; c.1260–1327, German)
Edwards (Jonathan; 1703–58, American)
Erigena (John Scotus; c.810–c.877, Irish)
Forsyth (P T; 1848–1921, Scottish)
Ghazali (al-; 1058–1111, Islamic)
Gregory (of Nazianzus; c.330–c.389 AD, Greek)
Gregory (of Nyssa; AD331–95, Greek)
Jenkins (David E; 1925– , English)
Lombard (Peter; c.1100–1160, Italian)
Niebuhr (H Richard; 1894–1962, US)
Niebuhr (Reinhold; 1892–1971, US)
Quesnel (Pasquier; 1634–1719, French)

Ruether (Rosemary Radford; 1936– , US)
Sankara (c.700–750, Indian)
Strauss (David; 1808–74, German)
Tillich (Paul; 1886–1965, US)
William (of Auvergne; c.1180–1249, French)
William (of Auxerre; c.1140–1231, French)

08 Arminius (Jacobus; 1560–1609, Dutch)
Bulgakov (Sergei; 1871–1944, Russian)
Bultmann (Rudolf; 1884–1976, German)
Cudworth (Ralph; 1617–88, English)
Cullmann (Oscar; 1902–99, German)
Eusebius (of Caesarea; c.264–340 AD, Palestinian)
Hamilton (Patrick; 1503–28, Scottish)
Irenaeus (St; c.130–c.200 AD, Greek)
Moltmann (Jürgen; 1926– , German)
Robinson (John; 1919–83, English)
Torrance (Thomas F; 1913–2007, Scottish)

09 Gurdjieff (Georgei; c.1865–1949, Armenian)
Gutiérrez (Gustavo; 1928– , Peruvian)
Niemöller (Martin; 1892–1984, German)
Thielicke (Helmut; 1908–86, German)
Whichcote (Benjamin; 1609–83, English)

10 Athanasius (St; c.296–373 AD, Greek)
Bellarmine (St Francis; 1542–1621, Italian)
Duns Scotus (John; c.1265–1308, Scottish)
Mackintosh (H R; 1870–1936, Scottish)
Macquarrie (John; 1919–2007, Scottish)
Rosenzweig (Franz; 1886–1929, German)
Swedenborg (Emanuel; 1688–1772, Swedish)
Tertullian (c.160–c.220 AD, North African)

11 Witherspoon (John; 1723–94, American)

14 Eboussi-Boulaga (Fabien; 1934– , Cameroonian)
Rosmini-Serbati (Antonio; 1797–1855, Italian)
Schleiermacher (Friedrich; 1768–1834, German)

See also **reformer**

theory

Theories include:

03 GUT	**07** Big Bang	**11** catastrophe
TOE	quantum	**12** Grand Unified
04 game	**09** collision	Milankovitch
05 chaos	Darwinism	**14** plate tectonics
06 atomic	evolution	**15** butterfly effect
number	**10** panspermia	
string	relativity	

See also **astronomy**; **economics**; **mathematics**; **philosophy**; **physics**; **psychology**

therapy

Therapies include:

03 art
CST
ECT
HRT
LDT
sex

04 drug
play
zone

05 chemo
drama
group
music
photo
reiki

06 beauty
family
primal
retail

speech

07 Gestalt
Rolfing
shiatsu

08 aversion

09 behaviour
cognitive
herbalism

10 homeopathy
osteopathy
regression
ultrasound

11 acupressure
acupuncture
biofeedback
irradiation
moxibustion
naturopathy
reflexology

12 aromatherapy
chemotherapy
chiropractic
craniosacral
electroshock
faith healing
horticulture
hydrotherapy
hypnotherapy
occupational
radiotherapy
reminiscence

13 confrontation
dream analysis
heat treatment
physiotherapy
psychotherapy

14 electrotherapy

See also **psychology**

thief

Thieves and robbers include:

03 dip
pad

04 bung
file
prig
Tory
wire
yegg

05 crook
diver
heist
kiddy
rover
sneak

06 bandit
bulker
chummy
con man
dacoit
dakoit
dipper
hotter
ice man
latron
lifter
limmer
looter

magpie
mugger
nicker
nipper
pirate
raider
robber

07 abactor
blagger
booster
brigand
burglar
cateran
cosh boy
filcher
footpad
hoister
ladrone
land-rat
nobbler
nut-hook
pandoor
pandour
poacher
prigger
rustler
stealer
tea leaf

twoccer
whizzer
yeggman

08 cly-faker
cutpurse
hijacker
huaquero
larcener
pilferer
rapparee
river-rat
swindler

09 area-sneak
Autolycus
cracksman
embezzler
fraudster
larcenist
pick-purse
plunderer
ram-raider
sea robber

10 cat-burglar
gully-raker
highjacker
highwayman
horse-thief

land-pirate
man-stealer
pickpocket
roberdsman
robertsman
shoplifter
sneak thief
water thief

11 motor-bandit
safe-breaker
safe-cracker
snatch-purse
snow-dropper

12 appropriator
baby-snatcher
cattle-lifter

housebreaker
kleptomaniac
sheep-stealer
snow-gatherer

13 highway robber

15 resurrectionist
resurrection man

Three Graces *see* grace

Three Musketeers *see* Dumas, Alexandre

tie

Ties include:

03 bow
04 bolo
neck
05 ascot
stock

06 cravat
kipper
string
07 overlay
owrelay

soubise
08 bootlace
kerchief
09 neckcloth
solitaire

steenkirk
waterfall
10 tawdry lace
11 neckerchief

time

Time zones:

02 AT
CT
ET
MT
PT

03 AST
BST
CET
CST
EET
EST
GMT
HST
MST
PST
WET

04 AKST
CYST
HAST
WAST
WEST

08 Zulu time
10 Alaska Time
11 Central Time
Eastern Time
Pacific Time
12 Atlantic Time
Mountain Time
13 Greenwich Time
17 British Summer Time
Greenwich Mean Time

18 Alaska Standard Time
Daylight Saving Time
Hawaii Standard Time

19 British Standard Time
Central European Time
Central Standard Time
Eastern European Time
Eastern Standard Time
Pacific Standard Time
Western European Time
Western Standard Time

20 Atlantic Standard Time
Mountain Standard Time

26 Hawaii-Aleutian Standard
Time

Times and periods of time include:

02 am
pm
03 age
day
eon
era
04 dawn
dusk
fall
hour

morn
noon
week
year
05 epoch
month
night
sun-up
today
06 autumn

decade
midday
minute
moment
morrow
period
season
second
spring
summer
sunset

winter
07 bedtime
century
chiliad
daytime
evening
instant
midweek
morning
quarter
sunrise

teatime	tomorrow	nightfall	microsecond
tonight	twilight	night-time	millisecond
weekday	**09** afternoon	**10** generation	**12** quinquennium
weekend	decennium	millennium	**13** the early hours
08 eternity	fortnight	nanosecond	wee small hours
high noon	light-year	yesteryear	
lifetime	midsummer	**11** long weekend	

Terms to do with time include:

02 AD
BC

03 ago
ere
ETA
fix
now
old
TAI
UTC
yet

04 date
late
past
term
then

05 about
after
again
alarm
clock
count
dated
early
flash
jiffy
meter
metre
never
often
spell
still
tardy
tempo
watch
while

06 always
before
behind

for now
future
heyday
in time
o'clock
old hat
on time
pre-war
rhythm

07 airtime
current
delayed
diurnal
forever
history
measure
overdue
present
session
stretch

08 duration
in a flash
in a jiffy
instance
interval
juncture
mean time
on and off
on the dot
promptly
schedule
temporal

09 aforehand
aftertime
diuturnal
extra time
nocturnal
out of date
prime time

programme
sometimes
timetable

10 afterwards
beforehand
behind time
common time
frequently
in good time
injury time
now and then
on occasion
previously
punctually
repeatedly
simple time

11 at the moment
closing time
now and again
recurrently

12 apparent time
borrowed time
compound time
every so often
for the moment
occasionally
once in a while
periodically
time and again

13 again and again
for the present
in the meantime
mean solar time

14 drinking-up time
from time to time
intermittently

15 ahead of schedule
every now and then
with time to spare

See also **calendar**; **day**; **geology**; **hour**; **month**; **year**

title

Titles include:

01 M
U

02 Dr
Mr
Ms

03 bey
Dan
Dom
Don
Mrs
Pir
Rav
Reb
Rev
Rex
san
Sir
Sri
Ven

04 amir
Aunt
babu
bhai
Capt
Dame
Devi
Doña
emir
Frau
Herr
Imam
Lady
Lord
Ma'am

Miss
Prof
sama
Sant
Shri
tuan

05 baboo
begum
ghazi
hodja
khoja
Madam
Mirza
molla
padre
pasha
Rebbe
Señor
Swami
Uncle

06 Doctor
Father
khodja
kumari
Madame
Master
Milord
Mister
mollah
moolah
Mother
mullah
Regina
Señora

Signor
Sister
Tuanku

07 Bahadur
Brother
Captain
Colonel
effendi
esquire
Majesty
Signior
Signora
Signore

08 Alderman
Fräulein
Highness
memsahib
Mistress
Monsieur
Reverend
Señorita
Viscount

09 Monsignor
Professor
Signorina
Signorino
Your Grace

10 burra sahib

11 Monseigneur
Your Majesty
Your Worship

12 Mademoiselle

15 Right Honourable

See also **nobility**

toadstool *see* **mushroom**

tobacco

Tobacco and tobacco preparations include:

04 capa
chaw
chew
plug
quid
shag
weed

05 bacco
baccy

régie
snout
snuff
snush
twist

06 burley
dottle
rappee
return

sneesh

07 caporal
chewing
Latakia
nail-rod
perique
pigtail

08 bird's-eye

canaster
honeydew
short-cut
Virginia

09 broad-leaf
cavendish
flue-cured
mundungus
strip-leaf

Tobacco pipes include:

03 cob	water	dudheen	**09** chibouque
04 bong	**06** dudeen	nargile	narghilly
clay	hookah	nargily	**10** meerschaum
05 briar	kalian	**08** calabash	**12** churchwarden
brier	**07** calumet	narghile	hubble-bubble
cutty	chibouk	narghily	
hooka	chillum	nargileh	**13** woodcock's-head
peace	corncob	nargilly	

Cigarettes and cigars include:

03 cig	roach	low-tar	**08** king-size
fag	segar	manila	long-nine
tab	smoke	reefer	perfecto
04 bidi	snout	roll-up	**09** cigarillo
burn	stogy	spliff	filter tip
05 beedi	whiff	stogey	panatella
blunt	**06** beedie	stogie	**10** coffin nail
ciggy	bomber	**07** cheroot	tailor-made
claro	ciggie	high-tar	**11** cancer stick
joint	concha	manilla	corona lucis
paper	gasper	menthol	roll-your-own
	Havana	regalia	

Tolkien, J R R (1892–1973)

Significant works include:

09 *The Hobbit* (1937)

12 *Silmarillion* (1977)
The Two Towers (1954)

17 *The Lord of the Rings* (1954–55)

18 *The Return of the King* (1955)

22 *The Fellowship of the Ring* (1954)

26 *The Adventures of Tom Bombadil* (1962)

Significant characters include:

04 Took (Peregrin 'Pippin')

05 Balin
Gimli
Smaug

06 Elrond
Gamgee (Samwise 'Sam')
Gollum
Sauron
Shelob

07 Aragorn

Baggins (Bilbo)
Baggins (Frodo)
Boromir
Gandalf
Legolas
Saruman
Sméagol
Strider

08 Bombadil (Tom)
Evenstar (Lady Arwen)

09 Galadriel
Treebeard

10 Brandybuck (Meriadoc 'Merry')

11 Black Riders
Oakenshield (Thorin)
Ringwraiths (the)

14 Gandalf the Grey

15 Gandalf the White

Tolstoy, Count Leo (1828–1910)

Significant works include:

05 *Youth* (1855–57)

07 *Boyhood* (1854)
The Raid (1852)

09 *Childhood* (1852)

10 *Confession* (1879)

Hadji Murat (1911)
Sebastopol (1854–55)

11 *The Cossacks* (1861)
War and Peace (1863–69)

12 *Anna Karenina* (1874–76)

Master and Man (1894)
Resurrection (1899)
15 *Family Happiness* (1859)

17 *The Kreutzer Sonata* (1889)
21 *The Death of Ivan Ilyitch* (1886)

04 Lvov (Prince 'Arseny')
05 Levin (Konstantin Dmitrich 'Kostya')
Levin (Nicholas)
Lvova (Princess Natalie Alexandrovna)
06 Levina (Catherine Alexandrovna 'Kitty')
Rostov (Count Ilya Andreyevich)
07 Gerasim
Ilyitch (Ivan)
Ivanich (Valadimir)
Karenin (Alexey Alexandrovich)
Karenin (Sergey Alexeyich 'Seriozha')
Kuragin (Prince Anatol)
Kuragin (Prince Ippolit)
Kuragin (Prince Vasily Sergeyevich)
Rostova (Countess Natalya Ilyinichna 'Natasha')
Vronsky (Count Alexey Kirilich)
08 Bezukhov (Pyotor Kirilovich 'Pierre')
Fedorona (Praskovya)

Ivanovna (Countess Lydia)
Karenina (Anna Arkadyevna)
Kuragina (Princess Elena Vasilyevna)
Oblonsky (Prince Stepan Arkadyevich 'Stiva')
09 Bolkonsky (Prince Andrei Nikolayevich)
Bolkonsky (Prince Nikolai Andreyevich 'Nikolushka')
Tverskaya (Princess Elizabeth Fedorovna 'Betsy')
Vronskaya (Countess)
10 Nikolaevna (Mary 'Masha')
Oblonskaya (Princess Darya Alexandrovna 'Dolly')
11 Bolkonskaya (Princess Lisa)
Bolkonskaya (Princess Marya Nikolayevna)
12 Shcherbatsky (Prince Alexander)
14 Shcherbatskaya (Princess)

tool

03 awl
axe
hod
hoe
saw
04 adze
file
fork
jack
mace
pick
rake
rasp
rule
vice
05 auger
bevel
clamp
dolly
drill
level
plane
punch
snips

spade
steel
tongs
06 bodkin
chaser
chisel
dibber
gimlet
hammer
jig-saw
mallet
mortar
needle
pestle
pliers
plough
sander
scythe
shears
shovel
sickle
trowel
wrench
07 bolster

bradawl
chopper
cleaver
crowbar
forceps
fretsaw
hacksaw
handsaw
hay fork
jointer
mattock
pick-axe
pincers
scalpel
scriber
stapler
T-square
08 billhook
chainsaw
dividers
penknife
scissors
spraygun
tenon-saw
thresher

tommy bar
tweezers
09 grass-rake
jack-plane
pitchfork
plumb-line
secateurs
set-square
10 jackhammer
paper-knife
protractor
11 brace and bit
crochet hook
paper-cutter
pocket-knife
screwdriver
spirit level
12 caulking-iron
pruning-knife
sledgehammer
socket-wrench
13 pinking-shears
pruning-shears
soldering-iron

See also **agriculture**; **key**; **machinery**; **saw**

torture

Torture forms and instruments include:

03 saw
04 boot
cage
pear
rack
05 brank
irons
jougs
wheel
06 carcan
harrow
picana
shabeh
spider
stocks
turcas
07 bilboes
boiling
cat's paw
hooding
picquet
pillory
pincers
scourge
stoning

08 bootikin
branding
garrotte
knotting
pendulum
pressing
shin vice
09 bastinado
gauntlets
gridirons
picketing
scarpines
strappado
treadmill
10 brazen bull
cattle prod
impalement
iron collar
iron maiden
Judas scale
pilliwinks
spiked hare
starvation
suspension
treadwheel
11 cave of roses

forcipation
German chair
head crusher
Judas cradle
keelhauling
knee-capping
squassation
thumbscrews
wooden horse
12 ball and chain
ducking-stool
flesh tearers
scold's bridle
shrew's fiddle
skull crusher
Spanish chair
water torture
13 cat-o'-nine-tails
electric shock
heretic's forks
Spanish mantle
14 Austrian ladder
devil-on-the-neck
disembowelment
drunkard's cloak
15 confession chair

tower

Tower types include:

04 bell
fort
gate
keep
peel
05 block
minar
spire
watch
water
06 belfry
castle
church
column
donjon
pagoda
turret
07 bastion
citadel
lookout

minaret
mirador
steeple
08 barbican
bastille
fortress
high-rise
hill-fort
martello
scaffold

09 belvedere
campanile
smock mill
tower mill
10 skyscraper
stronghold
11 demi-bastion
13 fortification

Towers include:

02 CN (Canada)
03 AMP (Australia)
Sky (New Zealand)
04 Pisa (Italy)
05 Babel (Bible)
Clock (England)
Macau (China)
Sears (USA)
Seoul (South Korea)

Tokyo (Japan)
06 Big Ben (England)
Dragon (China)
Eiffel (France)
Kiev TV (Ukraine)
Riga TV (Latvia)
Tahoto (Japan)
07 Alma-Ata (Kazakhstan)
Leaning (Italy)

Olympic (Canada)
Praha TV (Czech Republic)
Yueyang (China)
08 Tashkent (Uzbekistan)
Tengwang (China)
09 Blackpool (England)
Donauturm (Austria)
Ostankino (Russia)
Tallinn TV (Estonia)
Tianjin TV (China)

10 Collserola (Spain)
Liberation (Kuwait)
11 Fernsehturm (Germany)
Space Needle (USA)
The Euromast (The Netherlands)
Yellow Crane (China)
12 Stratosphere (USA)
13 Oriental Pearl (China)
Petronas Twins (Malaysia)

town

County towns and administrative headquarters include:

03 Ayr (Ayrshire/South Ayrshire)
04 Mold (Clwyd/Flintshire)
Wick (Caithness)
York (North Yorkshire/Yorkshire)
05 Banff (Banffshire)
Cupar (Fife)
Derby (Derbyshire)
Derry (County Londonderry)
Elgin (Elginshire/Moray)
Lewes (East Sussex)
Nairn (Nairnshire)
Omagh (Tyrone)
Perth (Perthshire/Perth and Kinross)
Truro (Cornwall)
06 Armagh (County Armagh)
Brecon (Brecknockshire)
Durham (County Durham)
Exeter (Devon)
Forfar (Angus/Forfarshire)
Kendal (Westmorland)
Lanark (Lanarkshire)
London (Greater London/Middlesex)
Oakham (Rutland)
Oxford (Oxfordshire)
07 Bedford (Bedfordshire)
Belfast (County Antrim)
Bristol (Avon)
Cardiff (Glamorgan)
Chester (Cheshire)
Denbigh (Denbighshire)
Dornoch (Sutherland)
Glasgow (Lanark/Strathclyde)
Ipswich (Suffolk)
Kinross (Ross-shire)
Lerwick (Shetland/Zetland)
Lincoln (Lincolnshire)
Matlock (Derbyshire)
Morpeth (Northumberland)
Newport (Isle of Wight)
Norwich (Norfolk)
Peebles (Peeblesshire)
Preston (Lancashire)

Reading (Berkshire)
Renfrew (Renfrewshire)
Selkirk (Selkirkshire)
Swansea (West Glamorgan)
Taunton (Somerset)
Warwick (Warwickshire)
Wigtown (Wigtownshire)
08 Aberdeen (Grampian/Aberdeenshire)
Barnsley (South Yorkshire)
Beverley (Humberside/East Riding of
Yorkshire)
Cardigan (Cardiganshire)
Carlisle (Cumberland/Cumbria)
Cromarty (Cromartyshire)
Dingwall (Ross-shire)
Dumfries (Dumfriesshire/Dumfries and
Galloway)
Greenlaw (Berwickshire)
Hereford (Herefordshire)
Hertford (Hertfordshire)
Jedburgh (Roxburghshire)
Kirkwall (Orkney)
Monmouth (Monmouthshire)
Pembroke (Pembrokeshire)
Rothesay (Buteshire)
Stafford (Staffordshire)
Stirling (Stirlingshire/Stirling)
09 Aylesbury (Buckinghamshire)
Beaumaris (Anglesey)
Cambridge (Cambridgeshire)
Dolgellau (Merioneth)
Dumbarton (Dunbartonshire/
Dumbartonshire/West Dunbartonshire)
Edinburgh (Edinburghshire/Midlothian/
Lothian)
Inveraray (Argyllshire)
Inverness (Inverness-shire/Highland)
Lancaster (Lancashire)
Leicester (Leicestershire)
Liverpool (Merseyside)
Maidstone (Kent)
Newcastle (Tyne & Wear/Northumberland)

Wakefield (West Yorkshire/West Riding of
  Yorkshire)
Worcester (Hereford and Worcester/
  Worcestershire)

10 Birmingham (West Midlands)
Caernarfon (Caernarfonshire/Gwynedd)
Carmarthen (Dyfed/Carmarthenshire)
Chelmsford (Essex)
Chichester (Sussex/West Sussex)
Dorchester (Dorset)
Gloucester (Gloucestershire)
Haddington (East Lothian/Haddingtonshire)
Huntingdon (Huntingdonshire)
Linlithgow (West Lothian/Linlithgowshire)
Manchester (Greater Manchester)

Montgomery (Montgomeryshire)
Nottingham (Nottinghamshire)
Presteigne (Radnorshire)
Shrewsbury (Shropshire)
Stonehaven (Kincardineshire)
Trowbridge (Wiltshire)
Winchester (Hampshire)

11 Clackmannan (Clackmannanshire)
Downpatrick (County Down)
Enniskillen (County Fermanagh)
Northampton (Northamptonshire)

12 Kircudbright (Kircudbrightshire)

13 Middlesbrough (Cleveland)
Northallerton (North Yorkshire/North Riding
  of Yorkshire)

English towns include:

03 Ely

04 Bath
Bury
Hove
Hull
York

05 Ascot
Corby
Cowes
Crewe
Derby
Dover
Epsom
Ewell
Hythe
Leeds
Lewes
Luton
Otley
Poole
Ripon
Rugby
Truro
Wells
Wigan

06 Bexley
Bodmin
Bolton
Bootle
Boston
Buxton
Darwen
Dudley
Durham
Exeter
Harlow
Harrow
Ilkley

Jarrow
Kendal
London
Ludlow
Oakham
Oldham
Oundle
Oxford
Ramsey
Slough
St Ives
Stroud
Torbay
Warley
Whitby
Widnes
Woking
Yeovil

07 Andover
Arundel
Ashford
Bedford
Berwick
Bristol
Brixham
Burnley
Chatham
Cheddar
Chester
Crawley
Croydon
Dorking
Evesham
Exmouth
Gosport
Grimsby
Halifax
Harwich
Haworth

Helston
Horsham
Ipswich
Keswick
Lincoln
Malvern
Margate
Matlock
Morpeth
Newport
Norwich
Padstow
Preston
Reading
Redruth
Reigate
Runcorn
Salford
Stilton
Sudbury
Swindon
Taunton
Telford
Tilbury
Torquay
Walsall
Wantage
Warwick
Watford
Windsor

08 Abingdon
Barnsley
Basildon
Beverley
Bradford
Brighton
Carlisle
Coventry
Dartford

Falmouth
Grantham
Hastings
Hatfield
Hereford
Hertford
Kingston
Knowsley
Minehead
Nantwich
Newhaven
Nuneaton
Penzance
Plymouth
Ramsgate
Redditch
Richmond
Rochdale
Sandwell
Solihull
Spalding
Stafford
St Albans
Stamford
St Helens
Thetford
Westbury
Weymouth
Worthing

09 Aldeburgh
Aldershot
Ambleside
Ashbourne
Axminster
Aylesbury
Blackburn
Blackpool
Bletchley
Bracknell
Cambridge
Dartmouth
Doncaster
Gateshead
Gravesend
Greenwich
Guildford
Harrogate
King's Lynn
Lancaster
Leicester
Lichfield
Liverpool

Lowestoft
Lyme Regis
Maidstone
Morecambe
Newcastle
Newmarket
Rochester
Rotherham
Salisbury
Sheerness
Sheffield
Sherborne
Southport
St Austell
Stevenage
Stockport
Stratford
Wakefield
Worcester

10 Birkenhead
Birmingham
Bridgwater
Bromsgrove
Buckingham
Canterbury
Chelmsford
Cheltenham
Chichester
Colchester
Darlington
Dorchester
Eastbourne
Felixstowe
Folkestone
Gillingham
Gloucester
Hartlepool
Huntingdon
Kenilworth
Kensington
Launceston
Letchworth
Maidenhead
Manchester
Nottingham
Pontefract
Portsmouth
Scunthorpe
Shrewsbury
Sunderland
Tewkesbury
Warrington

Washington
Whitehaven
Winchester

11 Bognor Regis
Bournemouth
Cirencester
Cleethorpes
Farnborough
Glastonbury
High Wycombe
Northampton
Scarborough
Shaftesbury
Southampton

12 Chesterfield
Clacton-on-Sea
Great Malvern
Huddersfield
Loughborough
Macclesfield
Milton Keynes
North Shields
Peterborough
South Shields
Stoke-on-Trent
West Bromwich

13 Bury St Edmunds
Ellesmere Port
Great Yarmouth
Kidderminster
Leamington Spa
Littlehampton
Lytham St Anne's
Middlesbrough
Saffron Walden
Southend-on-Sea
West Bridgford
Wolverhampton

14 Ashby-de-la-Zouch
Bishop Auckland
Chipping Norton
Hemel Hempstead
Henley-on-Thames
Stockton-on-Tees
Tunbridge Wells

15 Ashton-under-Lyne
Barrow-in-Furness
Burton upon Trent
Sutton Coldfield
Weston-super-Mare

Northern Irish towns include:

05 Derry
Larne
Newry

Omagh
06 Antrim
Armagh

Bangor
Lurgan
07 Belfast

Lifford
Lisburn
08 Limavady

Portrush
Strabane
09 Ballymena
Banbridge
Coleraine

Cookstown
Dungannon
Portadown
10 Ballyclare
Ballymoney

11 Downpatrick
Enniskillen
Londonderry
Magherafelt
Newtownards

Portstewart
13 Carrickfergus

Scottish towns include:

03 Ayr
04 Oban
Tain
Wick
05 Alloa
Banff
Elgin
Keith
Kelso
Nairn
Perth
Scone
Troon
06 Alness
Dunbar
Dundee
Dunoon
Forfar
Girvan
Glamis
Hawick
Huntly
Irvine
Lanark
Thurso
07 Airdrie
Alloway
Braemar
Dornoch
Falkirk
Glasgow
Golspie
Gourock
Lerwick

Mallaig
Paisley
Peebles
Portree
Selkirk
08 Aberdeen
Arbroath
Banchory
Dalkeith
Dingwall
Dumfries
Dunblane
Fortrose
Giffnock
Greenock
Hamilton
Jedburgh
Kirkwall
Montrose
Stirling
Ullapool
09 Ardrossan
Callander
Clydebank
Dumbarton
Edinburgh
Inverness
Inverurie
Kingussie
Kirkcaldy
Lockerbie
Peterhead
Pitlochry
Prestwick

St Andrews
Stornoway
Stranraer
10 Coatbridge
Dalbeattie
Galashiels
Glenrothes
Kilmarnock
Kincardine
Linlithgow
Livingston
Motherwell
Newtonmore
Stonehaven
11 Blairgowrie
Campbeltown
Cowdenbeath
Crianlarich
Cumbernauld
Dunfermline
Fort William
Fraserburgh
Grangemouth
Gretna Green
Invergordon
John o'Groats
Port Glasgow
12 Auchterarder
East Kilbride
Lochgilphead
13 Castle Douglas
Kirkcudbright
Kirkintilloch
14 Grantown-on-Spey

Welsh towns include:

04 Bala
Mold
Rhyl
05 Barry
Conwy
Tenby
Tywyn
06 Bangor
Brecon
Ruthin
07 Cardiff

Cwmbrân
Denbigh
Harlech
Newport
Newtown
Swansea
Wrexham
08 Aberdare
Barmouth
Bridgend
Cardigan

Chepstow
Ebbw Vale
Hay-on-Wye
Holyhead
Lampeter
Llanelli
Monmouth
Pembroke
Pwllheli
Rhayader
St David's
Treorchy

toxin / 867 / toy

09 Aberaeron, Carnarvon, Colwyn Bay, Dolgellau, Fishguard, Llandudno, Llangefni, Pontypool, Prestatyn

Welshpool

10 Caernarfon, Caerphilly, Carmarthen, Llandovery, Llangollen, Pontypridd, Porthmadog, Port Talbot

11 Abergavenny, Abertillery, Aberystwyth, Builth Wells, Machynlleth

12 Milford Haven

13 Haverfordwest, Merthyr Tydfil

See also **Australia; Austria; Belgium; Canada; China; city; Czech Republic; Denmark; Finland; France; Germany; Greece; India; Ireland; Italy; Japan; Mexico; The Netherlands; New Zealand; Norway; Portugal; resort; Russia; Spain; Sweden; Switzerland**

toxin *see* poison

toy

Toys include:

03 gun

04 ball, bike, doll, farm, fort, game, kite, Lego®, Sega®, XBox®, yo-yo

05 slide, swing, trike

06 cap-gun, garage, go-kart, guitar, paints, pop-gun, puzzle, rattle, rocker, seesaw, tea set

07 balloon, bicycle, box-kite, crayons, Digimon®, dreidel, drum set, Frisbee®, Game Boy®, marbles, Meccano®

ocarina, Play-Doh®, Pokémon®, rag doll, sandpit, scooter, soft-toy, Turtles®

08 catapult, doll's cot, football, GameCube®, golliwog, hula-hoop, Matchbox®, model car, model kit, Nintendo®, pedal-car, Subbuteo®, train set, tricycle

09 Action Man®, aeroplane, Care Bears, doll's pram, gyroscope, playhouse, pogo stick, Sindy doll®, swingball, teddy bear, video game

10 baby-walker, Barbie doll®, doll's buggy, doll's house

fivestones, hobby-horse, kewpie doll, musical box, pantograph, peashooter, Plasticene®, Rubik's Cube®, Scalextric®, skateboard, Steiff bear, Super Mario®, toy soldier, trampoline, typewriter, Wendy house

11 baby-bouncer, glove puppet, PlayStation®, shape-sorter, spacehopper, spinning top, tiddly winks, water pistol

12 action figure, boxing-gloves, computer game, executive toy, jack-in-the-box, jigsaw puzzle, kaleidoscope, model railway, mountain bike, My Little Pony, paddling-pool, Power Rangers®, rocking-horse

skipping-rope
walkie-talkie

13 Bob the Builder®
climbing-frame
modelling clay

See also **doll**

sewing machine
Space Invaders®
Tiny-Tears doll®

14 activity centre
building-blocks

building-bricks
electronic game
Paddington Bear
Powerpuff Girls®

trace mineral *see* mineral

train *see* railway

tranquillizer *see* sedative

travel

Travel methods and forms include:

03 bus	trip	**06** aviate	mission
fly	walk	cruise	shuttle
row		flight	**09** excursion
ski	**05** cycle	outing	freewheel
	drive	paddle	hitch-hike
04 bike	jaunt	ramble	migration
hike	march	safari	orienteer
punt	motor	voyage	
ride	pilot		**10** expedition
sail	skate	**07** commute	pilgrimage
tour	steam	holiday	
trek	visit	journey	**11** exploration

See also **air travel**; **aircraft**; **aviation**; **bicycle**; **carriage**; **London**; **motoring**; **public transport**; **railway**; **road**; **sailing**; **underground**; **vehicle**

treaty

Treaties and agreements include:

03 Edo	**06** Amiens	Rapallo
INF	Berlin	Rastatt
NPT	Bruges	Tianjin
04 GATT	Harris	Trianon
Iasi	London	Wichale
Jay's	Madrid	**08** Alinagar
NATO	Passau	Brussels
Rome	Tilsit	Gulistan
05 Baden	Vienna	Kanagawa
Basic	**07** Barrier	Lausanne
Basle	Beijing	Nijmegen
CENTO	Cambrai	Rijswijk
Dover	Dresden	Tientsin
Ghent	Erzerum	Waitangi
Jassy	Kanghwa	**09** Andrusovo
Lyons	Kiakhta	Bucharest
Paris	Münster	Hay-Herrán
SEATO	Nanjing	Karlowitz
START	Neuilly	Nerchinsk
Union	Nystadt	Pressburg

St Germain
10 Adrianople
Anglo-Iraqi
Greenville
Maastricht
Magna Carta
Paris Pacts
Portsmouth
San Stefano
Tlatelolco
Versailles
Warsaw Pact
Washington
11 Campo Formio
Finkenstein
Fort Stanwix

Locarno Pact
Passarowitz
Shimonoseki
The Pyrenees
Turkmanchai
Westminster
12 Brest-Litovsk
British-Iraqi
Campoformido
Grundvertrag
Lateran Pacts
Rio de Janeiro
San Francisco
13 Anglo-Egyptian
Austrian State
Clayton-Bulwer

Hay-Pauncefote
Social Chapter
Triple Entente
14 Constantinople
Hague Agreement
Hoare-Laval Pact
Kuchuk Kainarji
Nuclear Test-Ban
Peace of Utrecht
Unkiar-Skelessi
15 Cateau-Cambrésis
Entente Cordiale
Hay-Bunau-Varilla
Munich Agreement
US-Japan Security

tree

Tree types include:

03 nut	citron	**08** hardwood	**10** ornamental
04 palm	citrus	softwood	
05 covin	forest	**09** broad-leaf	
fruit	timber	Christmas	
06 bonsai	**07** conifer	deciduous	
	dwarfed	evergreen	

Trees include:

02 ti	cola	toon
03 ash	dali	upas
bay	dhak	**05** abele
bel	dika	abies
ben	dita	ackee
box	holm	afara
elm	hule	alder
fig	ilex	apple
fir	jack	areca
gum	kina	argan
jak	kola	aspen
koa	lime	balsa
may	mako	bania
nim	neem	beech
oak	nimb	belah
sal	ombu	birch
tea	palm	bunya
ule	pear	cacao
yew	pine	carap
	plum	carob
04 acer	poon	cedar
akee	rata	ceiba
amla	rimu	china
arar	shea	ebony
bael	sorb	elder
bhel	tawa	ficus
bito	teak	genip
coco	titi	guava

hazel	acajou	mastic
hevea	almond	medlar
holly	angico	mimosa
iroko	antiar	mopane
jambu	arolla	mopani
jarul	balata	myrtle
karri	bamboo	nutmeg
kauri	banana	obeche
khaya	banian	padauk
kiaat	banyan	padouk
kokum	baobab	papaya
larch	bilian	pawpaw
lemon	bombax	peepul
lichi	bo tree	platan
lilac	cashew	pomelo
lotus	cassia	poplar
mahoe	cembra	prunus
mahua	cerris	quince
mahwa	chenar	redbud
mamee	cherry	red fir
mamey	chicha	red gum
mango	cornel	red oak
maple	damson	sallow
marri	deodar	samaan
matai	durian	sandal
mvule	durion	sapele
neemb	emblic	sapota
ngaio	feijoa	saxaul
nikau	gingko	she-oak
nyssa	ginkgo	sissoo
olive	guango	souari
opepe	gurjun	spruce
osier	illipe	tamanu
palas	illupi	titoki
palay	jambul	ti tree
panax	jarool	totara
papaw	jarrah	tupelo
peach	jujube	waboom
pecan	kamala	walnut
piñon	kamela	wicken
pipal	kamila	willow
pipul	karaka	witgat
plane	karite	zamang
quina	kermes	**07** ailanto
ramin	kowhai	apricot
raoul	laurel	avocado
roble	lebbek	Banksia
rowan	lichee	bebeeru
salix	linden	big tree
saman	litchi	bilimbi
thuja	locust	blue gum
thuya	longan	brownea
toyon	loquat	bubinga
wahoo	lucuma	buckeye
wicky	lychee	bullace
wilga	mallee	canella
zaman	mammee	catalpa
06 acacia	manuka	champac

champak
cork oak
corylus
cowtree
cumquat
cypress
davidia
dogwood
durmast
fig tree
fir tree
geebung
genipap
gum tree
hemlock
hickory
hog-plum
holm-oak
hoop-ash
jambool
jipyapa
kumquat
leechee
lentisc
lentisk
live oak
logwood
lumbang
madrona
madrone
madrono
manjack
margosa
mastich
may tree
mesquit
nut pine
oil-tree
pereira
pimento
platane
quassia
quicken
quillai
radiata
red pine
redwood
rock elm
saksaul
saouari
satsuma
sequoia
seringa
service
shittah
snow gum
soursop
sundari

talipat
talipot
tanghin
tea tree
wallaba
wax tree
wych elm
yew tree

08 basswood
bauhinia
bead tree
bean tree
bergamot
boortree
bourtree
buddleia
calabash
cecropia
chestnut
cider gum
cinchona
cinnamon
coco-palm
cocoplum
coco-tree
Cook pine
coolabah
coolibah
coolibar
coprosma
crab tree
date palm
dhak tree
dividivi
Dutch elm
euonymus
garcinia
gardenia
ghost gum
gold tree
guaiacum
hawthorn
Hibiscus
holly-oak
hornbeam
Huon pine
ironbark
ironwood
jack pine
jambolan
jelutong
kalumpit
kinakina
kingwood
lacebark
loblolly
magnolia
mahogany

mako-mako
mandarin
mangrove
manna-ash
meal-tree
mesquite
milk-tree
mulberry
neem tree
oiticica
oleaster
palm tree
pandanus
pear-tree
piassaba
piassava
pichurim
pinaster
pine tree
plantain
podocarp
pyinkado
quandang
quandong
quantong
rain tree
rambutan
rewarewa
sack tree
sapucaia
Scots fir
sebesten
shaddock
shagbark
shea tree
silky oak
simaruba
soapbark
soap tree
sourwood
swamp oak
sycamine
sycamore
sycomore
tamarack
tamarind
teak tree
tung tree
upas-tree
zizyphus

09 ailanthus
angophora
araucaria
arrowwood
Asian pear
balsam fir
berg-cedar
black bean

black butt
blackwood
bloodwood
bodhi tree
bolletrie
Brazil nut
bread tree
bulletrie
bully-tree
butternut
candlenut
carambola
casuarina
Chile pine
chincapin
chinkapin
cigar tree
clove-tree
coachwood
combretum
common ash
common oak
common yew
coral tree
cordyline
courbaril
cowdie-gum
crab apple
currajong
curry-leaf
doornboom
eaglewood
eucryphia
fever tree
flame tree
forest-oak
grapetree
greengage
hackberry
Indian fig
ivory-tree
jacaranda
jackfruit
jambolana
Judas tree
kahikatea
kapok tree
kauri-pine
kermes oak
kurrajong
lancewood
leylandii
macadamia
mahwa tree
melaleuca
mirabelle
mockernut
monkey pod

naseberry
nectarine
nikau palm
nux vomica
ohi' a lehua
paloverde
paperbark
paulownia
peach-tree
pecan tree
persimmon
pitch-tree
poinciana
prickwood
quebracho
quickbeam
quinquina
rose apple
rowan tree
royal palm
sapodilla
saskatoon
sassafras
satinwood
Scotch elm
Scotch fir
Scots pine
screw pine
silver fir
simarouba
sour-gourd
spruce fir
star anise
sterculia
stone pine
sugar pine
sweetwood
tangerine
terebinth
thorntree
tonga-bean
tonka-bean
torchwood
tulip tree
turkey oak
wagenboom
wax myrtle
whitebeam
white pine
white teak
whitewood
wild mango
winged elm
wych-hazel
zebrawood

10 afrormosia
balata tree
bitterwood

blackthorn
bottle tree
breadfruit
bullet-tree
bunya-bunya
butter-tree
buttonball
buttonwood
calamondin
candle-tree
cannonball
celery pine
cembra pine
chaste tree
chaulmugra
cheesewood
chinaberry
chinachina
chinquapin
coffee tree
corylopsis
cotton tree
cottonwood
cowdie-pine
cowrie-pine
Douglas fir
dragon tree
durmast oak
English elm
English oak
eucalyptus
fiddlewood
field maple
flindersia
gean cherry
goat willow
golden rain
grapefruit
greenheart
jippi-jappa
Joshua-tree
kaffirboom
letter-wood
lilly-pilly
locust tree
macrocarpa
manchineel
mangabeira
mangosteen
manna-larch
missel-tree
nettle-tree
noble beech
Norway pine
orange tree
pagoda-tree
paper-birch
Parana pine

pepper tree
pohutukawa
powderpuff
prickly ash
quercitron
quinaquina
red sanders
rubber tree
sandalwood
sessile oak
shillelagh
silver bell
silver tree
sneezewood
sorrel tree
sour cherry
spiceberry
spruce pine
sugar maple
tallow tree
tiger's claw
valonia oak
violet-wood
weeping elm
white birch
white cedar
wild cherry
wild cotton
witch hazel
witgatboom
wooden pear
woollybutt
ylang-ylang

11 African teak
agnus castus
Amboina pine
bastard teak
black poplar
black walnut
bottle brush
bristlecone
burning bush
chaulmoogra
Chilean pine
cluster pine
coconut palm
common alder
common beech
common hazel
common maple
copper beech
coral shower
cotoneaster
crape myrtle
dawn cypress
dipterocarp
false acacia
golden larch

honey locust
lacquer tree
leatherwood
leopard-wood
London plane
maceranduba
mammoth-tree
metasequoia
monkey bread
mountain ash
mulberry fig
Norway maple
octopus tree
Osage orange
pomegranate
pussy willow
quicken-tree
radiata pine
sandbox tree
sausage tree
saw palmetto
service tree
shittah tree
silver birch
silver maple
sitka spruce
slippery elm
sweet orange
sweet willow
sycomore fig
tonquin-bean
trumpet tree
trumpet wood
umbrella fir
varnish tree
white laurel
white poplar
white willow
wild service

12 Austrian pine
balsam poplar
benjamin-tree
calabash tree
Christ's-thorn
common walnut
Corsican pine
cucumber tree
dead rat's tree
elephant's ear
evergreen oak
golden shower
lipstick tree
liriodendron
loblolly pine
loblolly tree
longleaf pine
macadamia nut
massaranduba

masseranduba
monkey puzzle
Monterey pine
Norway spruce
red quebracho
sallow willow
serviceberry
snowdrop tree
soapbark tree
swamp cypress
tree of heaven
umbrella pine
umbrella tree
weeping birch
Wellingtonia
yellow poplar

13 angel's trumpet
autograph tree
common dogwood
common juniper
cranberry tree
European larch
hemlock spruce
horse chestnut
Japanese cedar
Japanese maple
Lawson cypress
lodgepole pine
marmalade tree
morello cherry
Moreton Bay fig
Oriental plane
paperbark tree
paper mulberry
peacock-flower
rose apple tree
sandarach tree
Siberian cedar
soapberry tree
Surinam cherry
sweet chestnut
toothache tree
weeping willow
white mulberry

14 alligator apple
cannonball-tree
Castanospermum
cedar of Lebanon
Christmas-berry
common laburnum
common mulberry
flamboyant-tree
granadilla tree
Leyland cypress
Lombardy poplar
maidenhair-tree
strawberry tree

Swiss stonepine
traveller's tree
tropical almond
turpentine tree
western hemlock
white quebracho

yellow oleander
15 beach heliotrope
bristlecone pine
candelabrum tree
common silver fir
emblic myrobalan

flamboyante-tree
gutta-percha tree
horseradish tree
small-leafed lime
Spanish chestnut
true service tree

See also **palm**; **pine**; **rubber**; **shrub**

trench *see* **ocean**

triangle

Triangles include:

05 right
07 Bermuda
eternal
Pascal's

scalene
similar
warning
09 cocked hat

congruent
isosceles
spherical
11 acute-angled

equilateral

right-angled

12 obtuse-angled

Trollope, Anthony (1815–82)

Significant works include:

09 *Orley Farm* (1861–62)
The Warden (1855)

11 *Ayala's Angel* (1880–81)
Phineas Finn (1867–68)
The Bertrams (1859)

12 *Doctor Thorne* (1858)
Phineas Redux (1873–74)

13 *The Claverings* (1866–67)

14 *The Three Clerks* (1858)

15 *An Autobiography* (1883)
Dr Wortle's School (1880)
The Belton Estate (1865–66)
The Way We Live Now (1874–75)

16 *Barchester Towers* (1857)

Can You Forgive Her? (1864–65)
Framley Parsonage (1860–61)
He Knew He Was Right (1868–69)
The Duke's Children (1879–80)
The Prime Minister (1875–76)

17 *The Palliser Novels* (1864–80)

18 *The American Senator* (1876–77)
The Eustace Diamonds (1871–73)

20 *Mr Scarborough's Family* (1882–83)

21 *The Vicar of Bullhampton* (1869–70)

24 *The Last Chronicle of Barset* (1866–67)
The Small House at Allington (1862–64)

26 *The MacDermots of Ballycloran* (1847)

Significant characters include:

04 Bold (John)
Dale (Isabella 'Bella')
Dale (Lilian 'Lily')
Fawn (Viscount Frederick)
Finn (Phineas)
Grex (Lady Mabel)
Grey (John)
Monk (Lady)

05 Eames (John)
Guest (Lady Julia de)
Guest (Lord de)
Lopez (Ferdinand)
Maule (Gerard)
Slope (Reverend Obadiah)
Tifto (Major)

Tulla (Earl of)
06 Arabin (Reverend Francis)
Bozzle (Samuel)
Burton (Florence)
Courcy (Lady Amelia de)
Crofts (Dr James)
Fisker (Hamilton K)
Lufton (Lady)
Lufton (Lord Ludovic)
Morris (Lucy)
Neroni (Signora Madeline Vesey)
Omnium (Duke of)
Petrie (Miss Wallachia)
Rowley (Emily)
Rowley (Nora)

Thorne (Dr Thomas)
Thorne (Mary)

07 Bonteen (Mr)
Brattle (Carry)
Carbury (Lady Matilda)
Carbury (Roger)
Carbury (Sir Felix)
Crawley (Grace)
Crawley (Mrs)
Crawley (Reverend Josiah)
Crosbie (Adolphus)
Daubeny (Mr)
Emilius (Reverend Joseph)
Eustace (Lady Lizzie)
Eustace (Sir Florian)
Fenwick (Reverend Frank)
Gilmore (Harry)
Goesler (Marie)
Gotobed (Elias)
Grantly (Dr Theophilus)
Grantly (Griselda)
Grantly (Major Henry)
Greenow (Mrs Arabella)
Gresham (Frank Newbold)
Gresham ('Old' Frank Newbold)
Harding (Eleanor)
Harding (Reverend Septimus)
Kennedy (Lady Laura)
Kennedy (Robert)
Lowther (Mary)
Osborne (Colonel Frederic)
Proudie (Dr)
Proudie (Mrs)
Robarts (Lucy)
Robarts (Reverend Mark)
Sowerby (Nathaniel)
Trefoil (Arabella)
Tregear (Francis Oliphant 'Frank')
Vavasor (Alice)

Vavasor (George)
Wharton (Emily)

08 Brabazon (Julia)
Chiltern (Lord Oswald Standish)
Dumbello (Lord)
Glascock (Charles)
Marrable (Captain Walter)
Melmotte (Augustus)
Melmotte (Marie)
Palliser (Adelaide)
Palliser (Lady Glencora)
Palliser (Lady Mary)
Palliser (Lord Gerald)
Palliser (Plantagenet)
Pateroff (Count)
Spalding (Caroline)
Stanbury (Aunt Jemima)
Stanbury (Hugh)
Trumbull (Farmer)

09 Boncassen (Ezekiel)
Boncassen (Isabel)
Clavering (Harry)
Demolines (Madalina)
Dunstable (Miss Martha)
Effingham (Violet)
Gordeloup (Sophie)
Greystock (Frank)
Quiverful (Mr)
Quiverful (Mrs)
Scatcherd (Sir Louis Philippe)
Scatcherd (Sir Roger)
Trevelyan (Louis)

10 Carruthers (Lord George de Bruce)
Fitzgerald (Burgo)
Flood Jones (Mary)
Nidderdale (Lord)
Trowbridge (Marquis of)

12 Chaffanbrass (Mr)
Silverbridge (Lord)

trophy

Trophies include:

05 FA Cup (football)
06 Fed Cup (tennis)
07 Auld Mug (America's Cup/sailing)
Gold Cup (horse racing)
Grey Cup (Canadian football)
Uber Cup (badminton)
08 Davis Cup (tennis)
Ryder Cup (golf)
The Ashes (cricket)
World Cup (various)
09 Aresti Cup (aerobatics)
Curtis Cup (golf)

Thomas Cup (badminton)
Walker Cup (golf)
10 Masters Cup (tennis)
Solheim Cup (golf)
Stanley Cup (ice hockey)
Winston Cup (motor racing)
11 Admiral's Cup (sailing)
America's Cup (sailing)
Eschborn Cup (race walking)
Kinnaird Cup (Eton fives)
McCarthy Cup (hurling)
12 Camanachd Cup (shinty)
Lugano Trophy (race walking)

13 Heisman trophy (American football)
   Leonard Trophy (bowls)
   Sam Maguire Cup (Gaelic football)
14 Continental Cup (ice hockey)
   Jesters' Club Cup (Rugby fives)
See also **award**

15 Champions Trophy (hockey)
   Lilienthal Medal (gliding)
   Louis Vuitton Cup (sailing)
   Nascar Nextel Cup (motor racing)
   Scotch Whisky Cup (curling)

tuber *see* **bulb**

tumour

Tumours include:

05 gumma
   myoma
   Wilm's
06 epulis
   glioma
   lipoma
   myxoma

07 adenoma
   angioma
   fibroma
   myeloma
   sarcoma
08 lymphoma
   melanoma

   teratoma
   xanthoma
09 carcinoma
   papilloma
   syphiloma
10 meningioma
11 astrocytoma

   rodent ulcer
12 glioblastoma
   mesothelioma
   osteosarcoma
13 neuroblastoma
14 retinoblastoma

See also **disease**

tunnel

Tunnels include:

03 Aki (Japan; rail)
   Box (England; rail)
05 Keijo (Japan; rail)
   Rokko (Japan; rail)
06 FATIMA (Norway; road)
   Fréjus (France/Italy; rail)
   Fucino (Italy; drainage)
   Haruna (Japan; rail)
   Hoosac (USA; rail)
   Kanmon (Japan; rail)
   Mersey (England; road)
   Moffat (USA; rail)
   Seikan (Japan; rail)
   Thames (England; pedestrian and rail)
07 Arlberg (Austria; rail)
   Cascade (USA; rail)
   Channel (England/France; rail)
   Holland (USA; road)
   Laerdal (Norway; road)
   Øresund (Denmark/Sweden; road-rail)
   Simplon (Switzerland/Italy; rail)
   Vereina (Switzerland; rail)
08 Apennine (Italy; rail)
   Flathead (USA; rail)
   Hokuriku (Japan; rail)
   Hyperion (USA; sewer)
   Lierasen (Norway; rail)
   Nakayama (Japan; rail)
   Posilipo (Italy; road)

   Tronquoy (France; canal)
09 Blackwall (England; road)
   Dayaoshan (China; rail)
   Eupalinus (Greece; water supply)
   Furka Base (Switzerland; rail)
   Mont Blanc (France/Italy; road)
   Standedge (England; canal)
10 Chesbrough (USA; water supply)
   Dai-shimizu (Japan; rail)
   Gorigamine (Japan; rail)
   Lotschberg (Switzerland; rail)
   Qinling I-II (China; rail)
   Rogers Pass (Canada; rail)
   St Gotthard (Switzerland/Italy; road and rail)
11 Kilsby Ridge (England; rail)
   Mt MacDonald (Canada; rail)
   Shin-shimizu (Japan; rail)
   Tower Subway (England; rail)
12 Detroit River (USA/Canada; rail)
   Moscow subway (Russia; rail)
13 Great Apennine (Italy; rail)
   Iwate Ichinohe (Japan; rail)
   Severomuyskiy (Russia; rail)
14 NEAT St Gotthard (Switzerland; rail)
   Romeriksporten (Norway; rail)
15 Monte Santomarco (Italy; rail)
   Orange-Fish River (South Africa; irrigation)

turncoat *see* **spy**

Twain, Mark (1835–1910)

Significant works include:

10 *Roughing It* (1872)

18 *The Innocents Abroad* (1869)

20 *Life on the Mississippi* (1883)

21 *The Mysterious Stranger* (1916)

The Prince and the Pauper (1882)

24 *The Adventures of Tom Sawyer* (1876)

27 *Adventures of Huckleberry Finn* (1885)

29 *The Man That Corrupted Hadleyburg* (1900)

Significant characters include:

03 Jim

04 Finn (Huckleberry 'Huck')
Roxy (Roxana)

05 Canty (Tom)
Polly (Aunt)
Selby (Colonel George)
Smith (Hank)

06 Edward (Prince)
Hendon (Miles)
Sawyer (Tom)
Smiley (Jim)

Wilson (David
'Pudd'nhead')

07 Brierly (Henry 'Harry')
Goodson (Barclay)
Hawkins (Clay)
Hawkins (Laura)
Hawkins (Si 'Squire')
Sellers (Colonel Beriah)
Webster (Dan'l)

08 Chambers
Driscoll (Judge York

Leicester)
Driscoll (Percy
Northumberland)
Driscoll (Tom)
Halliday (Jack)
Injun Joe
Richards (Edward)
Richards (Mary)
Thatcher (Becky)

09 Dilworthy (Senator Abner)

10 Stephenson (Howard L)

Twelve Days of Christmas *see* Christmas

twin

Twins include:

12 Jacob and Esau (Bible)
Weasley twins (*Harry Potter and the Philosopher's Stone*, 1997, et seq, J K Rowling)

14 Apollo and Diana (Roman mythology)

15 Castor and Pollux (Greek mythology)
Romulus and Remus (Roman mythology)

16 Apollo and Artemis (Greek mythology)
Thomas the Apostle (Bible)

17 Eng and Chang Bunker (1811–74, Siamese)
Mark and Steve Waugh (1965– ,
Australian)
Sebastian and Viola (*Twelfth Night*, c.1601,
William Shakespeare)

19 Hercules and Iphicles (Greek legend)
Maurice and Robin Gibb (Maurice Gibb,
1949–2003/Robin Gibb, 1949– ; English)
Ronnie and Reggie Kray (Ronald Kray,
1933–95/Reginald Kray, 1933–2000;
English)

21 Pat and Isabel O'Sullivan (*The Twins at St

Clare's*, 1941, et seq, Enid Blyton)

23 King Louis XIV and Philippe (*The Man in the Iron Mask*, Alexandre Dumas)
Tweedledum and Tweedledee (*Alice's Adventures in Wonderland*, 1865, Lewis Carroll)

24 Freelon and Francis Stanley (Francis Stanley, 1849–1918/Freelon Stanley, 1849–1940; US)

26 Jean-Felix and Auguste Piccard (Jean-Felix Piccard, 1884–1963/Auguste Piccard, 1884–1962; US)

28 Jessica and Elizabeth Wakefield (*Sweet Valley High* books, Francine Pascal)

34 Dromio of Syracuse and Dromio of Ephesus (*Comedy of Errors*, c.1594, William Shakespeare)

42 Antipholus of Syracuse and Antipholus of Ephesus (*Comedy of Errors*, c.1594, William Shakespeare)

typeface

04 Bell
bold
font
Gill

05 Arial
fount
roman
Times

06 Gothic
Impact
italic
Lucida
Modern
serif
Tahoma

07 Courier
Curlz MT
Georgia
Marlett
Verdana

08 Franklin
Garamond
Jokerman
Perpetua
Playbill
Rockwell
Webdings

09 Colonna MT
Helvetica
sans serif

Wide Latin
Wingdings

10 Courier New
Lucida Sans

11 Baskerville
Book Antiqua
Comic Sans MS
Poor Richard
Trebuchet MS

13 Century Gothic
Lucida Console
Times New Roman

14 Franklin Gothic

15 Bookman Old Style

U

umbrella

uncle

underground

underwear

Underwear includes:

03 bra

04 body
jump
slip
vest

05 bania
cimar
cymar
jupon
pants
shift
teddy
thong
tunic

06 banian
banyan
basque

briefs
corset
garter
girdle
knicks
semmit
skivvy
smalls
teddie
undies

07 chemise
drawers
G-string
hosiery
linings
panties
singlet
spencer

Y-fronts

08 bloomers
camisole
chuddies
frillies
knickers
lingerie
scanties
subucula
thermals
underset

09 brassière
crinoline
jockstrap
long johns
petticoat
stockings
union suit

wyliecoat

10 suspenders
underdress
underlinen
underpants
undershirt
underskirt

11 boxer shorts
undershorts

12 body stocking
camiknickers
combinations

13 liberty bodice
suspender-belt

14 French knickers
unmentionables

union

Unions include:

02 AU
CU
EU

03 AUT
CDU
CGT
CWU
EIS
EMU

FBU
GMB
ITU
NFU
NUJ
NUM
NUS
NUT
RFU

RMT

04 BIFU
CCCP
TGWU
UEFA
USSR
ZANU
ZAPU

05 BECTU

T and G
Unite

06 Amicus
Soviet
UNISON

07 African

08 European

See also **Africa**; **Europe**; **party**

unit *see* **measurement**; **military**

United Kingdom

Cities and notable towns in the UK include:

03 Ely

04 Bath
Hull
York

05 Derby
Derry
Leeds
Newry
Ripon
Stoke
Truro
Wells

06 Armagh
Bangor
Dundee
Durham
Exeter
London
Oxford

07 Belfast
Bristol
Cardiff
Chester
Glasgow
Lincoln

Lisburn
Newport
Norwich
Preston
Salford
Swansea

08 Aberdeen
Bradford
Carlisle
Coventry
Hereford
Plymouth
St Albans

St Davids
Stirling

09 Cambridge
Edinburgh
Inverness
Lancaster
Leicester
Lichfield
Liverpool
Newcastle
Salisbury
Sheffield
Wakefield

Worcester
10 Birmingham
Canterbury
Chichester

Gloucester
Manchester
Nottingham
Portsmouth

Sunderland
Winchester
11 Southampton
Westminster

12 Peterborough

13 Wolverhampton

15 Brighton and Hove

English counties and administrative areas:

04 Kent
York
05 Derby
Devon (Dev)
Essex (Ess)
Luton
Poole
06 Dorset (Dors)
Durham (Dur)
Halton
London
Medway
Slough
Surrey (Sur)
Torbay
07 Bristol
Cumbria (Cumb)
Norfolk
Reading
Rutland
Suffolk (Suff)
Swindon
08 Cheshire (Ches)
Cornwall (Corn)
Plymouth
Somerset (Som)
Thurrock
09 Blackpool
Hampshire (Hants)
Leicester
Wiltshire (Wilts)

Wokingham
10 Darlington
Derbyshire
East Sussex (E Suss)
Hartlepool
Lancashire (Lancs)
Merseyside
Nottingham
Portsmouth
Shropshire (Shrops)
Warrington
West Sussex
11 Bournemouth
Isle of Wight
Oxfordshire (Oxon)
Southampton
Tyne and Wear
12 Bedfordshire (Beds)
Lincolnshire (Lincs)
Milton Keynes
Peterborough
Stoke-on-Trent
Warwickshire (War)
West Midlands
13 Herefordshire
Hertfordshire (Herts)
Isles of Scilly
Middlesbrough
North Somerset
Southend-on-Sea
Staffordshire (Staffs)

West Berkshire
West Yorkshire
14 Cambridgeshire (Cambs)
Leicestershire (Leics)
Northumberland
(Northumb)
North Yorkshire
South Yorkshire
Stockton-on-Tees
Worcestershire (Worcs)
15 Bracknell Forest
Brighton and Hove
Buckinghamshire (Bucks)
Gloucestershire (Glos)
Nottinghamshire
16 Kingston upon Hull
Northamptonshire
(Northants)
Telford and Wrekin
17 Greater Manchester
North Lincolnshire
18 Redcar and Cleveland
19 Blackburn with Darwen
20 South Gloucestershire
Windsor and Maidenhead
21 East Riding of Yorkshire
North East Lincolnshire
24 Bath and North East
Somerset

Northern Irish districts:

04 Ards
Down
05 Derry
Larne
Moyle
Omagh
06 Antrim

Armagh
07 Belfast
Lisburn
08 Limavady
Strabane
09 Ballymena
Banbridge

Coleraine
Cookstown
Craigavon
Fermanagh
North Down
10 Ballymoney
11 Castlereagh

Magherafelt
12 Newtownabbey
13 Carrickfergus
14 Newry and Mourne
23 Dungannon and
South Tyrone

Scottish council areas:

04 Fife
05 Angus
Moray
06 Dundee

07 Falkirk
Glasgow
08 Aberdeen
Highland

Stirling
10 Eilean Siar
Inverclyde
Midlothian

11 East Lothian
   West Lothian
12 East Ayrshire
   Renfrewshire
   Western Isles
13 Aberdeenshire
   Argyll and Bute

North Ayrshire
Orkney Islands
South Ayrshire
15 City of Edinburgh
   Perth and Kinross
   Scottish Borders
   Shetland Islands

16 Clackmannanshire
   East Renfrewshire
   North Lanarkshire
   South Lanarkshire
18 East Dunbartonshire
   West Dunbartonshire
19 Dumfries and Galloway

Welsh council areas:

05 Conwy
   Powys
07 Cardiff
   Gwynedd
   Newport
   Swansea
   Torfaen
   Wrexham
   Ynys Mon

08 Bridgend
10 Caerphilly
   Ceredigion
   Flintshire
12 Blaenau Gwent
   Denbighshire
13 Merthyr Tydfil
   Monmouthshire

Pembrokeshire
14 Isle of Anglesey
15 Carmarthenshire
   Neath Port Talbot
   Vale of Glamorgan
16 Rhondda, Cynon, Taff

UK landmarks include:

04 Fens
   Tyne
06 Big Ben
   Exmoor
   Mersey
   Severn
   Thames
07 Avebury
   Glencoe
   Needles
   Snowdon
   St Paul's
08 Balmoral
   Bass Rock
   Ben Nevis
   Dartmoor
   Land's End
   Loch Ness
09 Cape Wrath
   Chilterns
   Cotswolds
   Helvellyn
   London Eye
   New Forest
   Offa's Dyke
   Royal Mile
   Snowdonia
   Tay Bridge
10 Beachy Head
   Cader Idris
   Holy Island

Ironbridge
Kew Gardens
Loch Lomond
Lough Earne
Lough Neagh
Stonehenge
The Gherkin
Windermere
11 Arthur's Seat
   Canary Wharf
   Forth Bridge
   Hever Castle
   Isle of Wight
   John O'Groats
   Leeds Castle
   Lizard Point
   Menai Bridge
   Old Man of Hoy
   Scafell Pike
   York Minster
12 Antonine Wall
   Brighton Pier
   Castle Howard
   Cheddar Gorge
   Forest of Dean
   Hadrian's Wall
   Hampton Court
   Humber Bridge
   Lake District
   Peak District
   Seven Sisters
   Severn Bridge

13 Arundel Castle
   Blue John Caves
   Brecon Beacons
   Bridge of Sighs
   Hatfield House
   Liver Building
   Norfolk Broads
   Robin Hood's Bay
   Royal Pavilion
   Tower of London
   Warwick Castle
   Windsor Castle
14 Blackpool Tower
   Blenheim Palace
   Giant's Causeway
   Holyrood Palace
   Inverary Castle
   Isle of Anglesey
   Sherwood Forest
   Stirling Castle
   Wells Cathedral
15 Angel of the North
   Bodleian Library
   Caledonian Canal
   Cerne Abbas Giant
   Chatsworth House
   Edinburgh Castle
   Flamborough Head
   Grand Union Canal
   Post Office Tower
   St Michael's Mount

See also **city**; **monarch**; **Prime Minister**; **town**

United Nations

United Nations members:

04 Chad
Cuba
Fiji
Iran
Iraq
Laos
Mali
Oman
Peru
Togo

05 Benin
Chile
China
Congo
Egypt
Gabon
Ghana
Haiti
India
Italy
Japan
Kenya
Libya
Malta
Nauru
Nepal
Niger
Palau
Qatar
Samoa
Spain
Sudan
Syria
Tonga
Yemen

06 Angola
Belize
Bhutan
Brazil
Canada
Cyprus
France
Greece
Guinea
Guyana
Israel
Jordan
Kuwait
Latvia
Malawi
Mexico
Monaco
Norway
Panama

Poland
Russia
Rwanda
Serbia
Sweden
Turkey
Tuvalu
Uganda
Zambia

07 Albania
Algeria
Andorra
Armenia
Austria
Bahrain
Belarus
Belgium
Bolivia
Burundi
Comoros
Croatia
Denmark
Ecuador
Eritrea
Estonia
Finland
Georgia
Germany
Grenada
Hungary
Iceland
Ireland
Jamaica
Lebanon
Lesotho
Liberia
Moldova
Morocco
Myanmar
Namibia
Nigeria
Romania
Senegal
Somalia
St Lucia
Tunisia
Ukraine
Uruguay
Vanuatu
Vietnam

08 Barbados
Botswana
Bulgaria
Cambodia

Cameroon
Colombia
Djibouti
Dominica
Ethiopia
Honduras
Kiribati
Malaysia
Maldives
Mongolia
Pakistan
Paraguay
Portugal
Slovakia
Slovenia
Sri Lanka
Suriname
Tanzania
Thailand
Zimbabwe

09 Argentina
Australia
Cape Verde
Costa Rica
East Timor
Guatemala
Indonesia
Lithuania
Macedonia
Mauritius
Nicaragua
San Marino
Singapore
Swaziland
The Gambia
Venezuela

10 Azerbaijan
Bangladesh
El Salvador
Kazakhstan
Kyrgyzstan
Luxembourg
Madagascar
Mauritania
Montenegro

Mozambique
New Zealand
North Korea
Seychelles
South Korea
Tajikistan
The Bahamas
Timor-Leste
Uzbekistan

11 Afghanistan
Burkina Faso
Côte d'Ivoire
Philippines
Saudi Arabia
Sierra Leone
South Africa
Switzerland

12 Guinea-Bissau
Turkmenistan

13 Czech Republic
Liechtenstein
United Kingdom

14 Papua New Guinea
Solomon Islands
The Netherlands

15 Marshall Islands
St Kitts and Nevis

16 Brunei Darussalam
Equatorial Guinea

17 Antigua and Barbuda
Dominican Republic
Trinidad and Tobago

18 São Tomé and Príncipe
United Arab Emirates

20 Bosnia and Herzegovina

21 United States of America

22 Central African Republic

25 St Vincent and the Grenadines

27 Federated States of Micronesia

28 Democratic Republic of the Congo

32 Democratic People's Republic of Korea

United States of America

US states, with abbreviations, state capitals and order of entry into the union:

04 Iowa (Iowa; Des Moines, 29th)
Ohio (Ohio; Columbus, 17th)
Utah (Utah; Salt Lake City, 45th)

05 Idaho (Idaho; Boise, 43rd)
Maine (Maine; Augusta, 23rd)
Texas (Tex; Austin, 28th)

06 Alaska (Alaska; Juneau, 49th)

Hawaii (Hawaii; Honolulu, 50th)
Kansas (Kans; Topeka, 34th)
Nevada (Nev; Carson City, 36th)
Oregon (Oreg; Salem, 33rd)

07 Alabama (Ala; Montgomery, 22nd)
Arizona (Ariz; Phoenix, 48th)
Florida (Fla; Tallahassee, 27th)

Georgia (Ga; Atlanta, 4th)
Indiana (Ind; Indianapolis, 19th)
Montana (Mont; Helena, 41st)
New York (NY; Albany, 11th)
Vermont (Vt; Montpelier, 14th)
Wyoming (Wyo; Cheyenne, 44th)

08 Arkansas (Ark; Little Rock, 25th)
Colorado (Colo; Denver, 38th)
Delaware (Del; Dover, 1st)
Illinois (Ill; Springfield, 21st)
Kentucky (Ky; Frankfort, 15th)
Maryland (Md; Annapolis, 7th)
Michigan (Mich; Lansing, 26th)
Missouri (Mo; Jefferson City, 24th)
Nebraska (Nebr; Lincoln, 37th)
Oklahoma (Okla; Oklahoma City, 46th)
Virginia (Va; Richmond, 10th)

09 Louisiana (La; Baton Rouge, 18th)
Minnesota (Minn; St Paul, 32nd)

New Jersey (NJ; Trenton, 3rd)
New Mexico (N Mex; Santa Fe, 47th)
Tennessee (Tenn; Nashville, 16th)
Wisconsin (Wis; Madison, 30th)

10 California (Calif; Sacramento, 31st)
Washington (Wash; Olympia, 42nd)

11 Connecticut (Conn; Hartford, 5th)
Mississippi (Miss; Jackson, 20th)
North Dakota (N Dak; Bismarck, 39th)
Rhode Island (RI; Providence, 13th)
South Dakota (S Dak; Pierre, 40th)

12 New Hampshire (NH; Concord, 9th)
Pennsylvania (Pa; Harrisburg, 2nd)
West Virginia (W Va; Charleston, 35th)

13 Massachusetts (Mass; Boston, 6th)
North Carolina (NC; Raleigh, 12th)
South Carolina (SC; Columbia, 8th)

18 District of Columbia (DC; Washington)

US state zip codes:

02 AK (Alaska)
AL (Alabama)
AR (Arkansas)
AZ (Arizona)
CA (California)
CO (Colorado)
CT (Connecticut)
DC (District of Columbia)
DE (Delaware)
FL (Florida)
GA (Georgia)
HI (Hawaii)
IA (Iowa)
ID (Idaho)
IL (Illinois)
IN (Indiana)
KS (Kansas)

KY (Kentucky)
LA (Louisiana)
MA (Massachusetts)
MD (Maryland)
ME (Maine)
MI (Michigan)
MN (Minnesota)
MO (Missouri)
MS (Mississippi)
MT (Montana)
NC (North Carolina)
ND (North Dakota)
NE (Nebraska)
NH (New Hampshire)
NJ (New Jersey)
NM (New Mexico)
NV (Nevada)

NY (New York)
OH (Ohio)
OK (Oklahoma)
OR (Oregon)
PA (Pennsylvania)
RI (Rhode Island)
SC (South Carolina)
SD (South Dakota)
TN (Tennessee)
TX (Texas)
UT (Utah)
VA (Virginia)
VT (Vermont)
WA (Washington)
WI (Wisconsin)
WV (West Virginia)
WY (Wyoming)

US state nicknames:

08 Bay State (Massachusetts)
Gem State (Idaho)

09 Beef State (Nebraska)
Corn State (Iowa)
Free State (Maryland)
Old Colony (Massachusetts)

10 Aloha State (Hawaii)
First State (Delaware)
Peach State (Georgia)
Sioux State (North Dakota)

11 Beaver State (Oregon)
Coyote State (South Dakota)
Creole State (Louisiana)
Empire State (New York)
Garden State (New Jersey)

Golden State (California)
Gopher State (Minnesota)
Little Rhody (Rhode Island)
Nutmeg State (Connecticut)
Show Me State (Missouri)
Silver State (Nevada)
Sooner State (Oklahoma)
Sunset State (Oklahoma)

12 Beehive State (Utah)
Buckeye State (Ohio)
Bullion State (Missouri)
Chinook State (Washington)
Diamond State (Delaware)
Granite State (New Hampshire)
Hawkeye State (Indiana)
Heart of Dixie (Alabama)

Hoosier State (Indiana)
Old Line State (Maryland)
Prairie State (Illinois)
Tar Heel State (North Carolina)

13 Big Sky Country (Montana)
Camellia State (Alabama)
Equality State (Wyoming)
Keystone State (Pennsylvania)
Land of Lincoln (Illinois)
Lone Star State (Texas)
Magnolia State (Mississippi)
Mainland State (Alaska)
Mountain State (West Virginia)
Old North State (North Carolina)
Palmetto State (South Carolina)
Pine Tree State (Maine)
Sunshine State (Florida/New Mexico/ South
  Carolina)
Treasure State (Montana)

14 Bluegrass State (Kentucky)

Evergreen State (Washington)
Great Lake State (Michigan)
Jayhawker State (Kansas)
North Star State (Minnesota)
Panhandle State (West Virginia)
Sagebrush State (Nevada)
Volunteer State (Tennessee)
Wolverine State (Michigan)

15 Centennial State (Colorado)
Plantation State (Rhode Island)
The Last Frontier (Alaska)

16 Flickertail State (North Dakota)
Grand Canyon State (Arizona)
Peace Garden State (North Dakota)

17 America's Dairyland (Wisconsin)
Constitution State (Connecticut)
Land of Enchantment (New Mexico)
Land of Opportunity (Arkansas)

18 Green Mountain State (Vermont)
Mother of Presidents (Virginia)

Cities and notable towns in the USA include:

02 LA
03 NYC
05 Miami
06 Boston
   Dallas
07 Chicago

Detroit
Houston
Memphis
New York
Phoenix
Seattle
08 Las Vegas

Portland
San Diego
09 Baltimore
   Milwaukee
   Nashville
10 Los Angeles
   New Orleans

Pittsburgh
San Antonio
11 New York City
12 Philadelphia
   Salt Lake City
   San Francisco
   Washington DC

US landmarks include:

05 Yukon
07 Capitol
   Rockies
08 Colorado
   Lake Erie
   Missouri
   Mt Elbert
   Mt Vernon
   Pentagon
   Yosemite
09 Graceland
   Hollywood
   Hoover Dam
   Lake Huron

Milwaukee
Mt Rainier
10 Everglades
   Great Lakes
   Joshua Tree
   Mt McKinley
   Mt Rushmore
   Mt St Helens
   Sears Tower
   White House
11 Grand Canyon
   Lake Ontario
   Liberty Bell
   Mississippi

Pearl Harbor
Space Needle
Yellowstone
12 Appalachians
   Carnegie Hall
   Lake Michigan
   Lake Superior
13 Great Salt Lake
14 Brooklyn Bridge
   Monument Valley
   Rocky Mountains
15 Lincoln Memorial
   Statue of Liberty

See also **The Americas**; **president**

university

Universities in the UK include:

03 ICL
   LSE
   UCL

04 Bath
   City
   Hull

Kent
SOAS
York

05 Aston
Derby
Essex
Keele
Leeds
Luton
Wales

06 Bolton
Brunel
Dundee
Durham
Exeter
Napier
Oxford
Surrey
Sussex
Ulster

07 Bristol
Cardiff
Glasgow
Lincoln
Paisley
Reading
Salford

Warwick

08 Aberdeen
Bradford
Brighton
Coventry
Plymouth
Stirling
Teesside

09 Cambridge
Edinburgh
Glamorgan
Greenwich
Lancaster
Leicester
Liverpool
Sheffield
St Andrews

10 Birmingham
Buckingham
De Montfort
East Anglia
East London
Heriot-Watt
Manchester

Nottingham
Portsmouth
Sunderland

11 Bournemouth
King Alfred's
Southampton
Strathclyde
Westminster

12 Huddersfield
Loughborough
Robert Gordon
Thames Valley
Wales Swansea

13 Abertay Dundee
Hertfordshire
Oxford Brookes
Royal Holloway
West of England
Wolverhampton

14 Wales Institute

15 Gloucestershire
London South Bank
Nottingham Trent
Sheffield Hallam

Ivy League universities:

04 Yale　　**07** Cornell　　**08** Columbia　　**12** Pennsylvania
05 Brown　　　　Harvard　　**09** Princeton　　**16** Dartmouth College

Seven Sisters colleges:

05 Smith　　**07** Barnard　　**09** Radcliffe　　**12** Mount Holyoke
06 Vassar　　**08** Bryn Mawr　　　　Wellesley

Universities worldwide include:

03 CIT　　**07** Caltech　　**10** California
　　MIT　　**08** Ann Arbor　　**14** Trinity College
04 CUNY　　　　Berkeley　　**15** California State
　　UCLA　　　　Sorbonne　　　　Juilliard School
06 Leiden　　　　Stanford

Terms to do with university include:

02 2:1　　LLB　　fees
　　2:2　　MCR　　gown
　　BA　　MSc　　hood
　　MA　　NUS　　pass
03 BSc　　SCR　　PGCE
　　COP　　**04** arts　　poll
　　don　　blue　　term
　　gyp　　club　　test
　　JCR　　dean　　UCAS
　　lab　　exam　　unit
　　law　　fail　　viva

05 chair
crest
essay
grace
grant
major
minor
scout
sizar
sizer
staff
study
third
tutor
union

06 agrégé
alumni
beadle
bursar
Bursch
campus
course
credit
degree
docent
fellow
finals
incept
lector
master
module
pennal
porter
reader
rector
school
sconce
senate
syndic
tenure
thesis
tosher
tripos

07 academy
alumnus
bursary
buttery
college
council
diploma
Erasmus
faculty
fresher
great go
gyp room
honours
lecture

library
live out
marshal
NUS card
procter
proctor
rag week
scholar
science
seminar
society
student
subfusc
subject
varsity

08 academic
accredit
ad eundem
bachelor
calendar
classics
clearing
cum laude
divinity
encaenia
examiner
freshman
graduate
half-blue
half term
lecturer
magister
medicine
Oxbridge
redbrick
research
semester
send down
servitor
Socrates
sorority
theology
tutorial

09 alma mater
apparitor
catalogue
commorant
doctorate
education
Ivy League
moderator
practical
principal
professor
refectory
semi-bajan
sophomore

top-up fees

10 assessment
chancellor
curriculum
department
exhibition
extramural
fellowship
fraternity
graduation
humanities
laboratory
management
non-gremial
pass degree
philosophy
praelector
prospectus
readership

11 application
certificate
convocation
double first
engineering
examination
lectureship
lower second
mathematics
mortarboard
scholarship
student loan
town and gown
tuition fees
upper second

12 access course
dissertation
exhibitioner
freshers' ball
freshers' fair
freshers' week
joint honours
long vacation
Phi Beta Kappa
postgraduate
self-catering
sport one's oak
summer school

13 academic dress
baccalaureate
honours degree
magna cum laude
matriculation
mature student
personal chair
societies fair
summa cum laude
undergraduate

14 Bachelor of Arts
graduate school
graduation ball
sandwich course

seat of learning
social sciences
vice-chancellor
15 combination room

hall of residence
higher education
modern languages

See also **college**; **education**; **institute**

utensil *see* **cookery**

V

valve

04 ball
blow
gate
side
tube
05 bleed
choke
clack
diode
heart
slide

06 escape
mitral
mixing
needle
poppet
puppet
safety
triode
ventil
07 exhaust
petcock

seacock
snifter
tetrode
08 bicuspid
bistable
cylinder
dynatron
snifting
throttle
turncock

09 air-intake
butterfly
induction
injection
magnetron
non-return
semilunar
thyratron
10 Eustachian
thermionic

See also **bicycle**; **heart**

variety *see* **fruit**; **wine**

vegetable

03 yam
04 kale
leek
okra
spud
05 chard
choko
cress
gumbo
laver
mooli
onion
swede
06 carrot
celery
chives
chocho
daikon
endive
fennel
garlic
manioc
marrow

pepper
potato
radish
rocket
sorrel
squash
tomato
turnip
07 avocado
bok choy
cabbage
cardoon
cassava
chayote
chicory
lettuce
pak choi
parsnip
pumpkin
salsify
shallot
spinach
tapioca
08 baby corn

beetroot
borecole
broccoli
capsicum
celeriac
cucumber
eggplant
finochio
kohlrabi
leaf beet
mushroom
red onion
rutabaga
zucchini
09 artichoke
asparagus
aubergine
bean shoot
calabrese
courgette
finnochio
finocchio
red pepper
sweetcorn

10 bean sprout
lollo rosso
red cabbage
swiss chard
watercress
11 cauliflower
chinese leaf
green pepper
lady's finger
spring onion
sweet potato
12 marrow-squash
savoy cabbage
summer squash
turnip greens
winter squash
yellow pepper
13 ladies' fingers
14 Brussels sprout
Chinese cabbage
globe artichoke
15 vegetable marrow

See also **lettuce**

vehicle

Vehicles include:

03 bus
cab
car
gig
HGV
van
04 bike
boat
dray
ship
sled
tank
taxi
tram
trap
Tube
05 coach
cycle
lorry
plane
sulky

train
truck
Vespa®
wagon
06 bakkie
camper
hansom
Humvee®
jinker
landau
litter
maglev
sledge
sleigh
surrey
tandem
troika
07 bicycle
caravan
dog-cart
minibus

minivan
omnibus
phaeton
Pullman
scooter
sleeper
tractor
trailer
Transit®
08 barouche
brougham
Cape cart
golf cart
monorail
rickshaw
toboggan
tricycle
wagon-lit
09 bobsleigh
buck-wagon
charabanc

motorbike
10 boneshaker
four-in-hand
juggernaut
motorcycle
post-chaise
Scotch cart
sedan-chair
service car
stagecoach
trolleybus
11 caravanette
steam-roller
12 double-decker
pantechnicon
13 fork-lift truck
penny-farthing
15 hackney-carriage

Countries with their International Vehicle Registration (IVR) codes:

04 Chad (TCH)
Cuba (C)
Fiji (FJI)
Iran (IR)
Iraq (IRQ)
Laos (LAO)
Mali (RMM)
Peru (PE)
Togo (TG)
05 Benin (DY)
Chile (RCH)
Congo (RCB)
Egypt (ET)
Gabon (G)
Ghana (GH)
Haiti (RH)
India (IND)
Italy (I)
Japan (J)
Kenya (EAK)
Libya (LAR)
Malta (M)
Nauru (NAU)
Nepal (NEP)
Niger (RN)
Qatar (Q)
Samoa (WS)
Spain (E)
Sudan (SUD)
Syria (SYR)

Yemen (YAR)
06 Belize (BZ)
Brazil (BR)
Canada (CDN)
Cyprus (CY)
France (F)
Greece (GR)
Guinea (RG)
Guyana (GUY)
Israel (IL)
Jersey (GBJ)
Jordan (HKJ)
Kuwait (KWT)
Latvia (LV)
Malawi (MW)
Mexico (MEX)
Monaco (MC)
Norway (N)
Panama (PA)
Poland (PL)
Russia (RUS)
Rwanda (RWA)
Serbia (SRB)
Sweden (S)
Taiwan (RC)
Turkey (TR)
Uganda (EAU)
Zambia (Z)
07 Albania (AL)

Algeria (DZ)
Andorra (AND)
Armenia (AM)
Austria (A)
Bahrain (BRN)
Belarus (BY)
Belgium (B)
Bolivia (BOL)
Burundi (RU)
Croatia (HR)
Denmark (DK)
Ecuador (EC)
Estonia (EST)
Finland (FIN)
Georgia (GE)
Germany (D)
Grenada (WG)
Hungary (H)
Iceland (IS)
Ireland (IRL)
Jamaica (JA)
Lebanon (RL)
Lesotho (LS)
Liberia (LB)
Moldova (MD)
Morocco (MA)
Namibia (NAM)
Nigeria (NGR)
Romania (RO)
Senegal (SN)
Somalia (SO)
St Lucia (WL)
Tunisia (TN)
Ukraine (UA)
Uruguay (ROU)
Vietnam (VN)

08 Alderney (GBA)
Barbados (BDS)
Botswana (RB)
Bulgaria (BG)
Cambodia (K)
Cameroon (CAM)
Colombia (CO)
Dominica (WD)
Ethiopia (ETH)
Guernsey (GBG)
Hong Kong (HK)
Malaysia (MAL)
Mongolia (MGL)
Pakistan (PK)
Paraguay (PY)
Portugal (P)
Slovakia (SK)
Slovenia (SLO)
Sri Lanka (CL)
Suriname (SME)
Tanzania (EAT)
Thailand (T)

Zanzibar (EAZ)
Zimbabwe (ZW)

09 Argentina (RA)
Australia (AUS)
Costa Rica (CR)
Gibraltar (GBZ)
Guatemala (GCA)
Indonesia (RI)
Isle of Man (GBM)
Lithuania (LT)
Macedonia (MK)
Mauritius (MS)
Nicaragua (NIC)
San Marino (RSM)
Singapore (SGP)
Swaziland (SD)
The Gambia (WAG)
Venezuela (YV)

10 Azerbaijan (AZ)
Bangladesh (BD)
El Salvador (ES)
Kazakhstan (KZ)
Kyrgyzstan (KS)
Luxembourg (L)
Madagascar (RM)
Mauritania (RIM)
Montenegro (MNE)
Mozambique (MOC)
New Zealand (NZ)
Seychelles (SY)
South Korea (ROK)
Tajikistan (TJ)
The Bahamas (BS)
Uzbekistan (UZ)

11 Afghanistan (AFG)
Burkina Faso (BF)
Côte d'Ivoire (CI)
Philippines (RP)
Saudi Arabia (SA)
Sierra Leone (WAL)
South Africa (ZA)
Switzerland (CH)
Vatican City (V)

12 Faroe Islands (FO)
Guinea-Bissau (RGB)
Turkmenistan (TM)

13 Czech Republic (CZ)
Liechtenstein (FL)
United Kingdom (GB)

14 Papua New Guinea (PNG)
The Netherlands (NL)

16 Brunei Darussalam (BRU)

17 Dominican Republic (DOM)
Trinidad and Tobago (TT)

18 United Arab Emirates (UAE)

19 Netherlands Antilles (NA)
20 Bosnia and Herzegovina (BIH)
21 United States of America (USA)
See also **carriage**; **motoring**

22 Central African Republic (RCA)
25 St Vincent and the Grenadines (WV)
28 Democratic Republic of the Congo (ZRE)

veil *see* **scarf**

vein

Veins include:

06 portal
    thread
07 basilic
    jugular

    organic
    precava
    saphena
08 postcava

    praecava
    varicose
    vena cava
10 innominate

15 brachiocephalic

See also **artery**

venue *see* **Olympic Games**; **Paralympic Games**; **parliament**; **stadium**

Verdi, Giuseppe (1813–1901)

Significant works include:

04 *Aïda* (1871)
06 *Alzira* (1845)
    Aroldo (1857)
    Attila (1846)
    Ernani (1844)
    Oberto (1839)
    Otello (1887)
07 *Macbeth* (1847)
    Nabucco (1842)
08 *Ave Maria* (1879–80)
    Falstaff (1893)
    Libera me (1869)
09 *Don Carlos* (1867)
    Il corsaro (1848)
    Jerusalem (1847)
    Rigoletto (1851)
    Stiffelio (1850)
10 *La traviata* (1853)
    Tantum Ergo (1836)
    The Corsair (1848)
    The Robbers (1847)
11 *A Masked Ball* (1859)
    I due foscari (1844)
    Il trovatore (1853)
    I masnadieri (1847)
    King for a Day (1840)

    Luisa Miller (1849)
    Pater Noster (1879–80)
    Pietà, Signor (1894)
    Requiem Mass (1874)
13 *Giovanna d'Arco* (1845)
    Suona la tromba (1848)
    The Two Foscari (1844)
14 *Messa da Requiem* (1874)
15 *Sicilian Vespers* (1855)
    Simon Boccanegra (1857)
    Un giorno di regno (1840)
16 *Hymn of the Nations* (1862)
    Inno delle Nazioni (1862)
    Quatro Pezzi sacri (1898)
17 *La forza del destino* (1862)
    Quattro pezzi sacri (1897–98)
    The Force of Destiny (1862)
    Un ballo in maschera (1859)
18 *Romanza senza parole* (1865)
    The Battle of Legnano (1849)
19 *Sei romanze song cycle* (1838/1845)
20 *La battaglia di Legnano* (1849)
    Les vêpres siciliennes (1855)
22 *Stornello for Album Piave* (1869)
25 *Lombards at the First Crusade* (1843)

Significant characters include:

03 Tom

04 Aïda
Anna
Ezio
Ford (Alice)
Ford (Frank)
Horn
Iago
Ines
Jorg
Lina
Mina
Page (Meg)
Ruiz
Seid
Wurm
Zuma

05 Banco
Béarn (Viscount of)
Borsa (Matteo)
Caius (Dr)
Carlo
Curra
Delil
Eboli (Princess)
Egypt (King of)
Elena
Gilda
Laura
Leone
Lerma (Count of)
Moser
Oscar
Pirro
Ramla (Emir of)
Roger
Rolla
Sofia

06 Adorno (Gabriele)
Alcade
Alvaro
Alzira
Amalia
Amelia
Annina
Aroldo
Arrigo
Arvino
Attila
Banquo
Briano
Cassio
Cuniza
Elvira
Emilia

Enrico
Ernani
Fenena
Fenton
Fiesco (Jacopo)
Gaston
Hélène
Imelda
Isaure
Kelbar (Baron)
Mantua (Duke of)
Medora
Miller
Miller (Luisa)
Oberto
Oronte
Otello
Otumbo
Ovando
Pagano
Pietro
Pisana
Pistol (Pistola)
Poggio (La Marchesa del)
Ramfis
Renato
Samuel
Sanval (Edoardo di)
Selimo
Talbot
Uldino
Ulrica
Valéry (Violetta)
Valois (Elisabetta di)
Vargas (Don Carlo di)
Walter (Count)
Zamoro

07 Abdallo
Acciano
Albiani (Paolo)
Amneris
Arminio
Ataliba
Azucena
Bervoix (Flora)
Bethune
Ceprano (Countess)
Corrado
Daniele
d'Obigny (Marchese)
Dorotea
Douphol (Baron)
Egberto
Foresto
Foscari (Francesco)
Foscari (Jacopo)

Frengel (Federico di)
Germont (Alfredo)
Germont (Giorgio)
Giacomo
Giselda
Godvino
Grenvil (Doctor)
Gulnara
Gusmano
Ismaele
La Rocca
Leonora
Macbeth
Macduff
Malcolm
Manrico
Marullo (Cavaliere)
Montano
Montova (Il Duca di)
Nabucco
Ninetta
Ostheim (Duchess of)
Quickly (Mistress)
Radamès
Raymond
Ribbing
Roberto
Rodolfo
Rodrigo
Rolando
Silvano
Stankar
Tebaldo
Trabuco

08 Amonasro
Arvidson (Mlle)
Bardolph (Bardolfo)
Belfiore (Il Cavaliere di)
Carlo VII
Delmonte
Don Carlo
Falstaff (Sir John)
Federica
Ferrando
Giovanna
Giovanni
Giuseppe
Herreros (Don Federico)
Leuthold (Raffaele di)
Lodovico
Loredano (Jacopo)
Manfredo
Melitone (Brother/Fra)
Monforte (Guido di)
Montfort (Guy de)
Montheil (Ademar de)

Nannetta
Odabella
Old Gypsy
Philip II
Rhadames
Riccardo
Roderigo
The Abbot
Thibault
Toulouse (Count of)
Viclinda
Zaccaria
09 Abigaille
Barbarigo
Calatrava (Marquis of/
Marchese di)
Contarini (Lucrezia)

Desdemona
Don Alvaro
Don Carlos
Filippo II
Francesco
Giulietta
Grenville (Dottore)
Maddalena
Monterone (Count)
Rigoletto
Stiffelio
Vaudemont (Comte)
10 Barbarossa (Federico)
Boccanegra (Simon)
Gustavo III
Letorières (Viscount
Gaston/Gastone de)

11 Count de Luna
Don Riccardo
Lady Macbeth
Preziosilla
Salinguerra (Conte de/
Conte di)
Sparafucile
12 Anckarstroem
Doge of Venice
Gomez de Silva (Don Ruy)
Massimiliano (Count)
San Bonifacio (Conte de/
Conte di)
13 High Priestess
Nabucodonosor
15 Guido di Monforte

vermin

Vermin include:

03 fox	lice	mouse	**09** cockroach
rat	mice	**06** pigeon	
04 crow	moth	rabbit	
hare	**05** louse	weevil	

See also **beetle**; **insect**; **moth**; **parasite**; **plague**; **rodent**

vessel *see* **container**; **ship**

vestment *see* **clerical vestment**

villain

Villains include:

04 Case ('The Beach of Falesá', 1892, Robert
Louis Stevenson)
Cass (Dunstan; *Silas Marner*, 1861, George
Eliot)
Hyde (Mr; *The Strange Case of Dr Jekyll
and Mr Hyde*, 1886, Robert Louis
Stevenson)
Iago (*Othello*, 1603–04, William
Shakespeare)
05 Bates (Norman; *Psycho*, 1960)
Doone (Carver; *Lorna Doone*, 1869, R D
Blackmore)
Queeg (Captain; *The Caine Mutiny*, 1951,
Herman Wouk)
Regan (*King Lear*, c.1605–06, William
Shakespeare)
06 Lecter (Dr Hannibal; *The Silence of the
Lambs*, 1988, Thomas Harris)
Oswald (*King Lear*, c.1605–06, William
Shakespeare)

Silver (Long John; *Treasure Island*, 1883,
Robert Louis Stevenson)
07 Antonio (*The Tempest*, 1611, William
Shakespeare)
Bateman (Patrick; *American Psycho*, 1991,
Bret Easton Ellis)
Blofeld (Ernst; *Thunderball*, 1961, Ian Fleming)
Goneril (*King Lear*, c.1605–06, William
Shakespeare)
08 Cornwall (Duke of; *King Lear*, c.1605–06,
William Shakespeare)
Injun Joe (*The Adventures of Tom Sawyer*,
1876, Mark Twain)
The Queen (*Snow White and the Seven
Dwarfs*, fairytale)
09 Voldemort (Lord; *Harry Potter and the
Philosopher's Stone*, 1997, et seq, J K
Rowling)
10 Darth Vader (*Star Wars*, 1977, et seq)

Goldfinger (Auric; *Goldfinger*, 1959, Ian Fleming)

Richard III (*Richard III*, 1592–93, William Shakespeare)

12 Aaron, the Moor (*Titus Andronicus*, 1592, William Shakespeare)

14 Sauron the Great (*The Lord of the Rings*, 1954–55, J R R Tolkien)

Virgil (70–19 BC)

Significant works include:

06 *Aeneid* (c.29–19 BC; twelve books)

08 *Bucolics* (37 BC; ten books)
Eclogues (37 BC; ten books)

Georgics (36–29 BC; four books)

14 *Art of Husbandry* (36–29 BC; four books)

virtue

The Virtues:

04 hope	**07** charity	**08** prudence	**10** temperance
05 faith	justice	**09** fortitude	

virus

Viruses include:

03 CDV
DNA
EBV
flu
FLV
HIV
HPV
pox
pro
RNA

04 arbo
cold
ECHO
filo
HTLV
myxo
rota

05 Ebola

flavi
hanta
irido
lenti
parvo
phage
retro
rhino

06 baculo
calici
cowpox
herpes
papova

07 oncorna
picorna
polyoma
variola

08 morbilli

Vaccinia

09 Coxsackie
influenza
papilloma

10 hepatitis A
hepatitis B
hepatitis C
Lassa fever
leaf mosaic

11 Epstein-Barr

13 bacteriophage
parainfluenza

14 human papilloma

15 canine distemper
feline leukaemia

vitamin

Vitamins include:

01 A
B
C
D
E
G
H
K
P

06 biotin
citrin

niacin

07 adermin
aneurin
retinol
thiamin

08 carotene
thiamine

09 folic acid
menadione

10 calciferol

pyridoxine
riboflavin
tocopherol

11 menaquinone
pteroic acid

12 ascorbic acid
bioflavonoid
linoleic acid

13 linolenic acid
nicotinic acid

phylloquinone
14 cyanocobalamin
dehydroretinol

ergocalciferol
phytomenadione
15 cholecalciferol

pantothenic acid
vitamin B complex

volcano

Volcanoes and extinct volcanoes include:

03 Apo (Philippines)
Awu (Indonesia)
Usu (Japan)

04 Etna (Italy)
Fuji (Japan)
Laki (Iceland)
Taal (Philippines)

05 Hekla (Iceland)
Kenya (Kenya)
Mayon (Philippines)
Pelée (Martinique)
Thera (Greece)
Thira (Greece)
Unzen (Japan)

06 Ararat (Turkey)
Erebus (Antarctica)
Hudson (Chile)
Katmai (Alaska)
Sangay (Ecuador)

07 Jurullo (Mexico)
Kilauea (USA)
Rainier (USA)
Ruapchu (New Zealand)
Surtsey (Iceland)
Tambora (Indonesia)
Vulcano (Italy)

08 Cotopaxi (Ecuador)
Krakatoa (Indonesia)
Mauna Kea (USA)
Mauna Loa (USA)
Pinatubo (Philippines)
St Helens (USA)

Tarawera (New Zealand)
Vesuvius (Italy)

09 Aconcagua (Argentina)
Coseguina (Nicaragua)
El Chichón (Mexico)
Helgafell (Iceland)
Karisimbi (Rwanda)
Lamington (Papua New Guinea)
Paricutín (Mexico)
Pichincha (Ecuador)
Santorini (Greece)
Stromboli (Italy)
Tongariro (New Zealand)

10 Bezymianny (Russia)
Chimborazo (Ecuador)
Galunggung (Java)
Lassen Peak (USA)
Tungurahua (Ecuador)

11 Kilimanjaro (Tanzania)
La Soufrière (St Vincent)
Nyamuragira (Democratic Republic of the Congo)

12 Citlaltépetl (Mexico)
Ixtaccihuatl (Mexico)
Klyuchevskoy (Russia)
Popocatèpetl (Mexico)

13 Nevado del Ruiz (Colombia)
Ojos del Salado (Argentina/Chile)
Volcán El Misti (Peru)

14 Soufrière Hills (Montserrat)

15 Haleakala Crater (USA)

See also **crust**

volleyball

Volleyball terms include:

03 ace dig	**05** block spike	setter volley	**10** attack line
04 dump kill	**06** libero screen	**08** rotation shoot set	**11** double-touch

Voltaire (1694–1778)

Significant works include:

05 *Irène* (1778)
Zadig (1747)
Zaïre (1732)

06 *Mérope* (1743)
Oedipe (1718)

07 *Candide* (1759)
Mahomet (1741)

18 *Princesse de Navarre* (1745)

20 *Philosophical Letters* (1734)
The Century of Louis XIV (1751)
Traité de métaphysique (1748)

21 *La Ligue ou Henri le Grand* (1732)
Siècle de Louis Quatorze (1751)

23 *Philosophical Dictionary* (1764)
Poem on the Lisbon Disaster (1756)

25 *Dictionnaire philosophique* (1764)
Letters on the English Nation (1734)

27 *Elements of Newton's Philosophy* (1737)

28 *Les Moeurs et l'esprit des nations* (1756)
Poème sur le désastre de Lisbonne (1756)

31 *Eléments de la philosophie de Newton*
(1738)

33 *Dictionnaire philosophique portatif* (1764)

36 *Lettres écrites de Londres sur les Anglais*
(1734)

Characters in Candide include:

06 Farmer (the)
Martin
Sailor (the)

07 Cacambo
Candide
Jacques

08 Fernando (Don)
Giroflée (Brother/Friar)
Issachar (Don)
Old woman (the)

Pangloss (Dr)
Paquette
Perigord (Abbé of)

09 Baron's son (the)
Cunégonde

10 Inquisitor (My Lord the/The Grand)
Maximilian
Parolignac (Marquis de)

11 Pococurante (Count/Lord)

12 Vanderdendur (Mynheer)

W

wading bird *see* **bird**

Wagner, Richard (1813–83)

Significant works include:

07 *Die Feen* (1888)
08 *Parsifal* (1882)
09 *Lohengrin* (1850)
 Siegfried (1876)
10 *Die Walküre* (1870)
 The Fairies (1888)
11 *The Valkyrie* (1870)
12 *Das Rheingold* (1869)
 The Rhinegold (1869)
14 *Siegfried Idyll* (1870)
15 *Das Liebesverbot* (1836)
 Götterdämmerung (1876)
16 *The Forbidden Love* (1836)
 Tristan und Isolde (1865)
 Wesendonck Lieder (1858)
17 *The Flying Dutchman* (1843)
19 *Die Novize von Palermo* (1836)

20 *Der Ring des Nibelungen* (1876)
 The Twilight of the Gods (1876)
21 *Der fliegende Holländer* (1843)
 The Ring of the Nibelungs (1876)
22 *Arrival of the Black Swans* (1861)
23 *Rienzi, Last of the Tribunes* (1842)
24 *Five Songs for a Female Voice* (1858)
26 *Rienzi, der letzte der Tribunen* (1842)
 Seven songs from Goethe's Faust (1832)
27 *Die Meistersinger von Nürnberg* (1868)
 The Mastersingers of Nuremberg (1868)
28 *Albumblatt für Frau Betty Schott* (1875)
30 *Ankunft bei den schwarzen Schwänen*
 (1861)
40 *Tannhäuser and the Song Contest on the*
 Wartburg (1845)

Significant characters include:

03 Eva
04 Elsa
 Erda
 Erik
 Froh
 Loge
 Mime
05 David
 Freia
 Irene
 Marke (King)
 Melot
 Sachs (Hans)
 Senta
 Venus
 Wotan
06 Daland
 Fafner
 Fasolt
 Fricka
 Isolde
 Kundry

 Orsini (Paolo)
 Ortrud
 Pogner (Veit)
 Rienzi (Cola)
07 Adriano
 Colonna (Stefano)
 Gunther
 Gutrune
 Hermann
 Hunding
 Kothner (Fritz)
 Tristan
 Wolfram
08 Alberich
 Amfortas
 Brangäne
 Dutchman (The)
 Gerhilde
 Klingsor
 Kurvenal
 Kurwenal
 Ortlinde

 Parsifal
 Raimondo
 Siegmund
 Stolzing (Walter von)
 Woglinde
09 Elisabeth
 Friedrich
 Grimgerde
 Gurnemanz
 Lohengrin
 Magdalena
 Magdalene
 Siegfried
 Sieglinde
 Steersman (The)
 Telramund (Frederick of/
 Federico)
 Waltraute
 Wellgunde
10 Beckmesser (Sixtus)
 Brünnhilde
 Flosshilde

Rossweisse
Tannhäuser (Heinrich)
12 Rhine-maidens

13 Elsa of Brabant
Von Eschenbach
(Wolfram)

14 Henry the Fowler (King)

wall

Wall types include:

03 dam
sea

04 dike
dyke

05 block
brick
death
fence
hedge
inner
mural

party

06 bailey
cavity
garden
paling
screen
shield

07 barrier
bulwark
curtain
divider

parapet
rampart

08 abutment
bulkhead
buttress
obstacle
palisade
stockade

09 barricade
enclosure
partition

retaining

10 embankment

11 breeze-block
load-bearing
outer bailey

13 fortification
stud partition

14 flying buttress

Walls include:

05 Great (China)

06 Berlin (Germany)

07 Wailing (Israel)

Western (Israel)

08 Antonine (Scotland)
Hadrian's (England)

war

War and warfare types include:

03 hot

04 cold
germ
holy

05 blitz
civil
jihad
total
trade
world

06 ambush
attack
battle
jungle
nerves
trench

07 assault
limited
nuclear
private

08 chemical
intifada
invasion
skirmish
struggle

09 attrition
guerrilla

10 asymmetric
biological
blitzkrieg

engagement
manoeuvres
resistance

11 bombardment

12 asymmetrical
state of siege

13 armed conflict
counter-attack

Wars include:

03 Cod

04 Boer
Gulf
Iraq
Sikh
Zulu

05 Chaco
Civil
Dutch
Great
Maori
Opium
Punic
Roses

World

06 Afghan
Balkan
Barons'
Gallic
Indian
Korean
Six-Day
Trojan
Vendée
Winter

07 Bishops'
Crimean
Italian

Mexican
Pacific
Persian
Servile
Vietnam

08 Crusades
Football
Iran-Iraq
Peasants'
Religion
Ten Years'

09 Black Hawk
Falklands
Yom Kippur

10 Devolution
Jenkins' Ear
Napoleonic
Peninsular
Queen Anne's
Seven Years'
Suez Crisis
11 Arab-Israeli
Eighty Years'
Indian Civil

King Philip's
Thirty Years'
12 English Civil
Hundred Years'
Independence
King William's
Russian Civil
Russo-Finnish
Russo-Turkish
Spanish Civil

13 American Civil
Grand Alliance
Russo-Japanese
14 Boxer Rebellion
Franco-Prussian
Indian Uprising
July Revolution
Triple Alliance
15 Easter Rebellion

See also **battle; massacre; rebellion; siege**

warning *see* **signal**

watch *see* **clock**

water

Mineral water brands include:

05 Evian®
06 Buxton®
Ty Nant®

Vittel®
Volvic®
07 Deeside®

Perrier®
08 Aqua Pura®
10 Strathmore®

13 Pennine Spring®
San Pellegrino®
14 Highland Spring®

water source *see* **well**

watercourse *see* **river**

waterfall

Waterfalls include:

05 Angel (Venezuela)
Della (Canada)
Glass (Brazil)
Pilao (Brazil)
Tysse (Norway)
06 Boyoma (Congo)
Iguaçu (Brazil/Argentina)
Krimml (Austria)
Ormeli (Norway)
Ribbon (USA)
Tugela (South Africa)
07 Mtarazi (Zimbabwe)
Niagara (Canada/USA)
Stanley (Congo)
Thukela (South Africa)
08 Cuquenán (Guyana/Venezuela)
Gavarnie (France)
Itatinga (Brazil)
Kaieteur (Guyana)
Takkakaw (Canada)

Victoria (Zambia/Zimbabwe)
Wallaman (Australia)
Yosemite (USA)
09 Churchill (Canada)
Giessbach (Norway)
Multnomah (USA)
Staubbach (Switzerland)
10 Cleve-Garth (New Zealand)
Skjeggedal (Norway)
Sutherland (New Zealand)
Wollomombi (Australia)
11 Reichenbach (Switzerland)
Trummelbach (Switzerland)
12 Cusiana River (Colombia)
Paulo Alfonso (Brazil)
Silver Strand (USA)
13 Mardalsfossen (Norway)
Tyssetrengane (Norway)
Upper Yosemite (USA)
Vestre Mardola (Norway)

weapon

Weapons include:

03 bow
gas
gun
Uzi

04 bomb
Colt®
cosh
dirk
épée
foil
Mace®
mine
pike
Scud

05 arrow
billy
bolas
CS gas
H-bomb
knife
lance
Luger®
panga
rifle
sabre
sling
spear
sword
taser
vouge

06 airgun
cannon
cudgel
dagger
Exocet®
glaive
jambok
magnum
Mauser
mortar
musket
pistol
rapier
rocket

six-gun
taiaha
tomboc

07 assegai
balista
bayonet
bazooka
bomblet
Bren gun
caltrap
caltrop
carbine
halberd
harpoon
longbow
machete
poleaxe
poniard
shotgun
sjambok
sten gun
stun gun
tear-gas
torpedo

08 air rifle
atom bomb
ballista
blowpipe
calthrop
catapult
claymore
crossbow
field gun
howitzer
landmine
nail bomb
nerve gas
nunchaku
partisan
revolver
scimitar
shuriken
stiletto
threshel

time-bomb
tomahawk
tommy-gun

09 automatic
battleaxe
boomerang
Mills bomb
smart bomb
truncheon
turret-gun

10 bowie knife
broadsword
flick-knife
gatling-gun
machine-gun
mustard gas
napalm bomb
shillelagh
six-shooter

11 Agent Orange
anti-tank gun
blunderbuss
bow and arrow
cluster-bomb
daisy-cutter
depth-charge
elephant gun
hand grenade
kalashnikov
submunition

12 binary weapon
bunker buster
flame-thrower
quarterstaff

13 Cruise missile
knuckleduster
maurikigusari
submachine-gun

14 binary munition
incendiary bomb
rocket-launcher

15 thermobaric bomb
Winchester® rifle

Terms to do with weapons include:

03 aim
cap
dog
fan
wad

04 ball

bead
bore
cock
fire
fuse
head
hilt

kick
land
load
sear
slug
vizy

05 arrow
blade
chape
chase
flint
forte
guard
mouth
point
prime
range
rifle
shaft
shell
sight
steel
stock
train
visie

06 barrel
breech
bullet
casing
charge
cocked
delope
gunner
hammer
handle
muzzle
pommel
ramrod

random
recoil
sheath
target
uncock
vizzie
volley

07 battery
caliber
calibre
chamber
chassis
dispart
quillon
rifling
tampion
tompion
trigger
warhead

08 carriage
full-cock
half-cock
kick back
pike-head
unlimber

09 bowstring
cartridge
chokebore
discharge
flechette
fléchette
foresight

hilt-guard
hindsight
proof-mark
reinforce
sword-hilt
wheel lock

10 barleycorn
basket-hilt
black Maria
cross guard
knuckle-bow
projectile
self-cocker
spear-point
spear-shaft
sword-guard

11 fingerguard
hair trigger
safety catch
self-loading

12 rubber bullet

13 ball cartridge
gauntlet-guard
percussion cap
scouring stick

14 blank cartridge
cross batteries
panoramic sight
percussion-fuse
percussion-lock

15 telescopic sight

See also **bomb**; **dagger**; **gun**; **knife**; **missile**; **sword**

weather

Weather phenomena include:

03 fog
ice
04 gale
hail
haze
mist
rain
smog
snow
thaw

wind
05 cloud
frost
sleet
slush
storm
06 breeze
deluge
shower
squall

07 chinook
cyclone
drizzle
drought
mistral
monsoon
rainbow
tempest
thunder
tornado
twister

typhoon
08 black ice
downpour
heatwave
sunshine
09 hoar frost
hurricane
lightning
snowstorm
whirlwind

See also **cloud**; **ice**; **meteorology**; **precipitation**; **snow**; **storm**; **wind**

wedding *see* **anniversary**; **marriage**

weed

Weeds include:

04 dock
moss
05 daisy
vetch
06 fat hen
oxalis
spurge
yarrow
07 bracken
ragweed
ribwort
08 bindweed
duckweed
knapweed
self-heal
09 chickweed
coltsfoot
dandelion
ground ivy

groundsel
horsetail
knotgrass
liverwort
pearlwort
snakeweed
speedwell
sun spurge
10 cinquefoil
common reed
couch grass
curled dock
deadnettle
sow thistle
thale cress
11 ground elder
meadow grass
petty spurge
salad burnet
white clover

12 annual nettle
rough hawkbit
sheep's sorrel
13 common burdock
field wood rush
large bindweed
pineapple weed
small bindweed
14 common plantain
shepherd's purse
15 broad-leaved dock
burnet saxifrage
common chickweed
creeping thistle
greater plantain
lesser celandine
perennial nettle
stemless thistle

week *see* **day**

weight division *see* boxing

weightlifting

Weightlifters include:

03 Cao (Lei; 1983– , Chinese)
04 Jang (Mi-Ran; 1983– , South Korean)
Kono (Tommy; 1930– , US)
05 Davis (John; 1921–84, US)
Vinci (Charles; 1933– , US)
06 Xiexia (Chen; 1983– , Chinese)
07 Hongmei (Qiu; 1983– , Chinese)

08 Aramanau (Andrei; 1988– , Belarussian)
Guozheng (Zhang; 1974– , Chinese)
Slivenko (Oxana; 1986– , Russian)
09 Alekseyev (Vasily; 1942– , Russian)
11 Zakharevich (Yuriy; 1963– , Russian)
Zhabotinsky (Leonid; 1938– , Soviet)
12 Suleymanoglu (Naim; 1967– , Bulgarian/Turkish)

Weightlifting terms include:

03 bar
04 jerk
05 chalk
class

clean
06 collar
no lift
snatch

07 barbell
08 good lift
press-out
10 bench press

down signal
simple grip
11 disc weights

well

Wells, springs and water sources include:

03 eye
spa
04 font

pool
05 fount
06 geyser

source
spring
supply

07 aquifer
hot well
mickery

08 artesian
    draw-well
    fountain
    pump-well
    wellhead
09 hot spring

    reservoir
    water hole
10 wellspring
11 groundwater
    mineral well
    wishing well

12 dropping-well
    watering hole
13 weeping spring

Wells, H G (1866–1946)

Significant works include:

05 *Kipps* (1905)
10 *Tono-Bungay* (1909)
11 *Ann Veronica* (1909)
    Men Like Gods (1923)
14 *The Time Machine* (1895)
15 *The Invisible Man* (1897)
17 *Love and Mr Lewisham* (1900)
    The New Machiavelli (1911)
    The War of the Worlds (1898)
    The Wonderful Visit (1895)

19 *The History of Mr Polly* (1910)
    The Island of Dr Moreau (1896)
    The Outline of History (1920)
    When the Sleeper Wakes (1899)
20 *The First Men in the Moon* (1901)
22 *The Shape of Things to Come* (1933)
23 *A Short History of the World* (1922)
    Mind at the End of Its Tether (1945)
    Mr Britling Sees It Through (1916)
25 *Experiment in Autobiography* (1934)
    The World of William Clissold (1926)

Significant characters include:

04 Eloi (the)
05 Kipps (Arthur)
    Polly (Alfred)
06 Moreau (Doctor)
07 Griffin (John)

    Stanley (Ann Veronica)
08 Britling (Mr)
    Clissold (William)
    Lewisham (George)
    Morlocks (the)
    Prendick (Edward)

09 Ponderevo (Edward)
10 Montgomery (Doctor)
12 Invisible Man (the)
13 Time Traveller (the)

Welsh

Welsh boys' names include:

03 Dai
    Huw
    Nye
    Wyn
04 Aled
    Alun
    Bryn
    Dewi
    Eryl
    Evan
    Glyn
    Ifor
    Ioan

    Owen
    Rees
    Rhys
    Siôn
05 Dylan
    Elwyn
    Emlyn
    Emrys
    Gavin
    Haydn
    Howel
    Hywel
    Idris

    Ieuan
    Lloyd
    Madoc
    Tudor
06 Dafydd
    Dilwyn
    Eirian
    Gareth
    Gwilym
    Howell
    Mervyn
    Morgan
    Rhodri

07 Aneirin
    Aneurin
    Brynmor
    Geraint
    Gwillym
    Myrddin
    Peredur
    Vaughan
08 Llewelyn
    Llywelyn
    Meredith

Welsh girls' names include:

04 Ceri
    Enid
    Gwen
    Gwyn
    Mair

    Siân
05 Carys
    Cerys
    Dilys
    Ffion

    Megan
    Nerys
    Olwen
    Olwin
    Olwyn

Rhian
06 Delyth
Eirlys
Eluned
Gaynor
Gladys
Glenda
Glenys

Glynis
Gwenda
Morgan
Olwyne
07 Bronwen
Eiluned
Gwenyth
Gwyneth

Myfanwy
08 Angharad
Morwenna
Rhiannon
09 Gwendolen
Gwenllian

See also **town**; **United Kingdom**

whale

Whales and dolphins include:

03 fin
04 blue
grey
orca
05 black
minke
pigmy
piked
pilot
right
sperm
white
06 baleen
beaked

beluga
caa'ing
finner
killer
07 bowhead
dolphin
finback
grampus
Layard's
narwhal
rorqual
toothed
08 humpback
porpoise
09 Greenland

grindhval
razorback
whalebone
10 bottlenose
humpbacked
11 bottle-nosed
false killer
12 river dolphin
strap-toothed
13 common rorqual
Risso's dolphin
sulphur-bottom
15 gangetic dolphin
harbour porpoise

wheel

Wheels include:

03 big
cog
fly
04 buff
cart
gear
idle
mill

worm
05 crown
drive
wagon
water
06 castor
charka
escape

Ferris
paddle
prayer
07 balance
driving
fortune
potter's
ratchet

08 roulette
spinning
sprocket
spur gear
steering
09 Catherine
13 spinning jenny

whisky

Whiskies include:

03 rye
04 dram
half
malt
05 blend
hooch
06 hootch
poteen
red-eye

Scotch
07 blended
Bourbon
potheen
spunkie
08 peat-reek
sour mash
09 aqua vitae
good stuff

the cratur
10 barley-bree
barley-broo
cornbrandy
corn whisky
single malt
tanglefoot
usquebaugh
11 barley-broth

mountain dew
the Auld Kirk
water of life
12 the real McCoy
13 the real Mackay
14 chain lightning
tarantula juice

white

04 ecru	**05** cream	creamy	lily-white
grey	ivory	pearly	snow-white
lily	milky	silver	**11** silver-white
opal	snowy	**08** magnolia	
whey	**06** argent	**09** champagne	

See also **pigment**

Whitman, Walt (1819–92)

08 *Drum-Taps* (1865)

12 'Song of Myself' (1881)

13 *Leaves of Grass* (1855)

16 *Sequel to Drum-Taps* (1866)

17 'O Captain! My Captain!' (1865–66)
'Pioneers! O, Pioneers!'

20 'I Sing the Body Electric'

21 *Memoranda During the War* (1875–76)

30 'Out of the Cradle Endlessly Rocking'

33 'When Lilacs Last in the Dooryard Bloom'd'
(1865–66)

wild flower *see* **flower**

Wilde, Oscar (1854–1900)

06 *Salomé* (1896)

11 *De Profundis* (1905)

14 *An Ideal Husband* (1895)

17 *The Duchess of Padua* (1891)

18 *Lady Windermere's Fan* (1892)
Vera; or The Nihilists (1883)

20 *A Woman of No Importance* (1893)

22 *Lord Arthur Savile's Crime* (1891)
The Ballad of Reading Gaol (1898)
The Picture of Dorian Gray (1891)

27 *The Happy Prince and Other Tales* (1888)
The Importance of Being Earnest (1895)

04 Gray (Dorian)

05 Prism (Miss)

06 Cardew (Cecily)
Goring (Viscount)
Salomé
Savile (Lord Arthur)
Wooton (Lord Henry)

07 Erlynne (Mrs)

08 Chiltern (Sir Robert)

Worthing (John 'Jack') [aka Ernest]

09 Arbuthnot (Gerald)
Arbuthnot (Mrs Rachel)
Bracknell (Lady)
Moncrieff (Algernon)

10 Windermere (Lady)

11 Happy Prince (the)
Illingworth (Lord)

wind

04 berg	east	**05** north
bise	föhn	trade
bora	helm	zonda

06 buster
doctor
El Niño
levant
samiel
simoom
zephyr

07 austral
chinook
cyclone
etesian

gregale
khamsin
meltemi
mistral
monsoon
pampero
sirocco

08 Favonian
libeccio
westerly
williwaw

09 harmattan
nor'wester
snow eater
southerly

10 Cape doctor
prevailing
tramontana
wet chinook
willy-willy

11 anticyclone

15 southerly buster

Literary winds include:

05 Eurus
Notus

06 Auster
Boreas

07 Aquilon
08 Argestes

Favonius
10 Euroclydon

Terms to do with the wind include:

04 calm
flaw
gale
veer

05 blore
storm

06 upwind

07 aeolian
bluster
cutting
leeward

08 downwind
forewind
headwind
landwind
light air
near gale
periodic
sidewind
tailwind
windward

09 crosswind
katabatic

10 cool change
strong gale

11 fresh breeze
light breeze
surface wind

12 gentle breeze
strong breeze
violent storm

13 following wind

14 moderate breeze

window

Windows include:

03 bay
bow

04 pane
rose
sash
shop

05 Jesse
Judas
oriel
ox-eye

06 dormer
French
lancet
louvre
Norman
oculus
rosace
screen

ticket

07 compass
guichet
lattice
lucarne
luthern
sexfoil
sliding
ventana
windock
windore
winnock

08 astragal
bull's eye
casement
fanlight
porthole
skylight

09 decorated
jut-window
mezzanine
mullioned
patio door

10 fenestella

11 lychnoscope
oeil-de-boeuf

12 double-glazed
early English
quarterlight
stained glass

13 batement light
double-glazing
perpendicular

14 Catherine wheel

15 secondary-glazed

wine

Wine-bottle sizes include:

06 flagon
magnum
08 jeroboam

rehoboam
09 balthazar
10 methuselah

salmanazar
11 Marie-Jeanne
14 nebuchadnezzar

Wine types, varieties and grapes include:

03 Dao
dry
red
sec
04 Asti
brut
Cava
fino
hock
port
rosé
Sekt
Tent
05 blush
bombo
Douro
Durif
Fitou
Gamay
house
Mâcon
Médoc
plonk
Rioja
Soave
straw
sweet
Syrah
table
Tavel
Tokay
tonic
white
06 Alsace
Barolo
Barsac
Beaune
canary
claret
grappa
Graves
Malaga
Malbec
Merlot
mulled
Muscat
Pontac

sherry
Shiraz
07 alicant
Aligoté
Amarone
Auslese
Barbera
Bunyuls
Chablis
Chianti
Cinsaut
demi-sec
Madeira
Malmsey
Margaux
Marsala
moselle
oloroso
Orvieto
Pomerol
retsina
Rhenish
sangria
vintage
Vouvray
08 Alicante
Bordeaux
Brunello
bucellas
Burgundy
Carignan
Cinsault
Dolcetto
Frascati
Garnacha
glühwein
Grenache
house red
jerepigo
Kabinett
Malvasia
Marsanne
Montilla
Muscadet
muscatel
Nebbiolo
New World
Palomino

Pauillac
Pinotage
Riesling
Rousanne
ruby port
Sancerre
Sauterne
Sémillon
Spätlese
spumante
St Julien
Sylvaner
Tinta Cão
vermouth
Viognier
09 bacharach
Bardolino
Carignane
Carmenère
champagne
Colombard
dry sherry
fortified
frizzante
Hermitage
Lambrusco
Langue d'oc
Minervois
Mourvèdre
Pinot Gris
Pinot Noir
Rhine wine
Sauternes
Scheurebe
sparkling
St-Émilion
Tarragona
tawny port
Trebbiano
Ugni Blanc
white port
Zinfandel
10 Barbaresco
Beaujolais
Chambertin
Chardonnay
Constantia
Grignolino

house white
manzanilla
Mateus Rosé
Monastrell
Muscadelle
Petit Syrah
Piesporter
Pinot Blanc
Sangiovese
Tinta Roriz
Verdicchio
vinho verde

11 alcohol-free
amontillado
Chenin Blanc
cream sherry
Niersteiner
Petite Sirah
Petit Verdot

Pinot Grigio
Portugieser
Pouilly-Fumé
Rüdesheimer
scuppernong
Steinberger
sweet sherry
Tempranillo
vintage port

12 Blanc de Noirs
Côtes du Rhône
Folle Blanche
Johannisberg
Marcobrunner
medium sherry
Pedro Ximénez
Pinot Meunier
Ruby Cabernet
Tinta Barroca

Valpolicella

13 Blanc de Blancs
Cabernet Franc
Château Lafite
Liebfraumilch
Montepulciano
Müller-Thurgau
Pouilly-Fuissé

14 Crémant d'Alsace
Crémant de Loire
Gewürztraminer
Lacryma Christi
Sauvignon Blanc

15 Crozes-Hermitage
Gewürtztraminer
Grüner Veltliner
Lachryma Christi
Touriga Nacional

Terms to do with wine include:

03 big
cru
DOC
dry
fat
hot
sec
tun

04 body
brut
DOCG
fine
full
hard
hock
lees
legs
long
marc
mull
must
nose
pipe
port
race
rack
racy
rape
ripe
rosé
sack
Sekt
soft
stum
tart
thin

VDQs
vine
vino

05 argol
clean
crisp
fresh
green
heavy
light
mirin
nutty
plonk
sharp
short
spicy
sweet
tears
vault
white
woody

06 acetic
claret
coarse
common
corked
decant
earthy
finish
flabby
flinty
fruity
grapey
grappa
hearty

honest
length
lively
magnum
mature
medium
mellow
palate
robust
severe
sherry
smooth
stalky
supple
tannin
tartar
tierce
ullage
vinous
winery
yeasty

07 acidity
balance
bouquet
breathe
chambré
château
clarity
finesse
flowery
fortify
lay down
malmsey
piquant
remuage
retsina

Rhenish
velvety
vintage
vintner
weighty

08 demijohn
generous
glühwein
grand cru
hanepoot
muscatel
noble rot
oenology
prädikat
red biddy
spritzig
spumante
vermouth
vineyard
vinosity
vin rouge
wine list
wineskin

09 character
en primeur
frizzante
malic acid
oenophile
oxidation
pétillant
Rhine wine
vin de pays
winepress
wine vault

10 aftertaste

full-bodied	vinho verde	viticulture	**14** sulphurous acid
maceration	wine cellar	**12** vin ordinaire	
madeirized	**11** viniculture	well-balanced	

Winter Olympics *see* Olympic Games

Winter Paralympics *see* Paralympic Games

witch

Witches, witch doctors and wizards include:

03 hag	mganga	conjurer	**10** besom-rider
hex	shaman	magician	reim-kennar
04 mage	voodoo	marabout	**11** enchantress
05 Hecat	wisard	night-hag	gyre-carline
lamia	zendik	**09** enchanter	medicine man
magus	**07** angekok	galdragon	necromancer
sibyl	carline	occultist	thaumaturge
weird	sangoma	pythoness	**12** Weird Sisters
06 Hecate	warlock	sorceress	**13** thaumaturgist
magian	wise man	wise woman	
	08 angekkok	witch-wife	

Witches include:

04 Nitt (Agnes; *Lords and Ladies*, 1993, et seq, Terry Pratchett)
Tick (Perspicacia; *The Wee Free Men*, 2003, et seq, Terry Pratchett)
Yoop (Mrs; *The Tin Woodman of Oz*, 1918, L Frank Baum)

05 Circe (Greek mythology)
Jadis (*The Lion, the Witch, and the Wardrobe*, 1950, et seq, C S Lewis)
Medea (Greek mythology)
Mombi (*The Marvelous Land of Oz*, 1904, L Frank Baum)
Orddu (*The Black Cauldron*, 1965, Lloyd Alexander)
Orwen (*The Black Cauldron*, 1965, Lloyd Alexander)
Owens (Gillian; *Practical Magic*, 1996, Alice Hoffman)
Owens (Sally; *Practical Magic*, 1996, Alice Hoffman)
Price (Eglantine; *Bedknobs and Broomsticks*, 1971)
Smart (Jane; *The Witches of Eastwick*, 1984, John Updike)

06 Aching (Tiffany; *The Wee Free Men*, 2003, et seq, Terry Pratchett)
Achren (*The Book of Three*, 1964, et seq, Lloyd Alexander)
Alcina (*Alcina*, 1735, G F Handel)
Aradia (mythology)

Cackle (Miss; *The Worst Witch*, 1974, et seq, Jill Murphy)
Endora (*Bewitched*, 1964–72, TV series)
Glinda (the Good Witch of the South; *The Wonderful Wizard of Oz*, 1900, et seq, L Frank Baum)
Hallow (Ethel; *The Worst Witch*, 1974, et seq, Jill Murphy)
Hecate (Greek mythology)
Hubble (Mildred; *The Worst Witch*, 1974, et seq, Jill Murphy)
Maclay (Tara; *Buffy the Vampire Slayer*, 1997–2003, TV series)
Nutter (Agnes; *Good Omens*, 1990, Neil Gaiman and Terry Pratchett)
Orgoch (*The Black Cauldron*, 1965, Lloyd Alexander)
Potter (Lily; *Harry Potter and the Philosopher's Stone*, 1997, et seq, J K Rowling)
Sprout (Pomona; *Harry Potter and the Philosopher's Stone*, 1997, et seq, J K Rowling)
Ursula (*The Little Mermaid*, 1989)
Yubaba (*Spirited Away*, 2001)
Zeniba (*Spirited Away*, 2001)

07 Blinkie (*The Scarecrow of Oz*, 1915, L Frank Baum)
de Passe (Bianca; *Bell, Book and Candle*, 1958, film)

Garlick (Magrat; *Wyrd Sisters*, 1989, et seq,
Terry Pratchett)
Granger (Hermione; *Harry Potter and the
Philosopher's Stone*, 1997, et seq, J K
Rowling)
Holroyd (Gillian; *Bell, Book and Candle*,
1950, John van Druten)
Madison (Amy; *Buffy the Vampire Slayer*,
1997–2003, TV series)
Pekkala (Serafina; *Northern Lights*, 1995, et
seq, Philip Pullman)
Repulsa (Rita; *Mighty Morphin' Power
Rangers*, 1993–96, TV series)
Sycorax (*The Tempest*, 1611, William
Shakespeare)
Weasley (Ginevra 'Ginny'; *Harry Potter and
the Philosopher's Stone*, 1997, et seq, J K
Rowling)
Weasley (Molly; *Harry Potter and the
Philosopher's Stone*, 1997, et seq, J K
Rowling)

08 Baba Yaga (Russian folklore)
Calendar (Jenny; *Buffy the Vampire Slayer*,
1997–2003, TV series)
Madam Mim (*The Sword in the Stone*, 1963)
Matthews (Paige; *Charmed*, 1998–2006, TV
series)
Nanny Ogg (*Wyrd Sisters*, 1989, et seq,
Terry Pratchett)
Rowlands (Morgan; *The Book of Shadows*,
2002, et seq, Cate Tiernan)
Spellman (Sabrina; *Sabrina, the Teenage
Witch*, 1996–2003, TV series)
Spofford (Alexandra; *The Witches of
Eastwick*, 1984, John Updike)
Stephens (Samantha; *Bewitched*,1964–72,
TV series)
Stephens (Tabitha; *Bewitched*, 1964–72, TV
series)
Wizadora (*Wizadora*, 1993–2000, TV series)

09 Aunt Clara (*Bewitched*, 1964–72, TV series)
Frau Trude (Grimm Brothers fairytale)
Gayelette (the Good Witch of the North; *The
Wonderful Wizard of Oz*, 1900, L Frank
Baum)
Halliwell (Phoebe; *Charmed*, 1998–2006,
TV series)

Halliwell (Piper; *Charmed*, 1998–2006, TV
series)
Halliwell (Prue; *Charmed*, 1998–2006, TV
series)
Hardbroom (Miss; *The Worst Witch*, 1974,
et seq, Jill Murphy)
Lestrange (Bellatrix; *Harry Potter and the
Goblet of Fire*, 2000, et seq, J K Rowling)
Moonshine (Maud; *The Worst Witch*, 1974,
et seq, Jill Murphy)
Ravenclaw (Rowena; *Harry Potter and the
Philosopher's Stone*, 1997, et seq, J K
Rowling)
Rosenburg (Willow; *Buffy the Vampire
Slayer*, 1997–2003, TV series)
Rougemont (Sukie; *The Witches of Eastwick*,
1984, John Updike)
Sanderson (Mary; *Hocus Pocus*, 1993)
Sanderson (Sarah; *Hocus Pocus*, 1993)
Sanderson (Winifred 'Winnie'; *Hocus Pocus*,
1993)

10 Hufflepuff (Helga; *Harry Potter and the
Philosopher's Stone*, 1997, et seq, J K
Rowling)
Madam Hooch (*Harry Potter and the
Philosopher's Stone*, 1997, et seq, J K
Rowling)
McGonagall (Minerva; *Harry Potter and
the Philosopher's Stone*, 1997, et seq, J K
Rowling)
Nightshade (Enid; *The Worst Witch*, 1974, et
seq, Jill Murphy)

11 Morgan Le Fay (Arthurian legend)

12 Rhea Dubativo (*The Gunslinger: The Dark
Tower I*, 1982, et seq, Stephen King)
Scarlet Witch (comic)
The Snow Queen (Hans Christian Andersen
fairytale)

13 Rhea of the Coös (*The Gunslinger: The Dark
Tower I*, 1982, et seq, Stephen King)
The White Witch (*The Lion, the Witch, and
the Wardrobe*, 1950, et seq, C S Lewis)

15 Princess Eilonwy (*The Book of Three*, 1964,
et seq, Lloyd Alexander)
The Weird Sisters (*Macbeth*, 1606, William
Shakespeare)

Terms to do with witches and wizards include:

03 hex	magic	voudou	**08** black art
04 mojo	spell	**07** cantrip	black cat
muti	wicca	gramary	cauldron
wart	**06** cackle	hag-seed	diablery
05 charm	potion	pricker	familiar
coven	Sabbat	Sabbath	gramarye
goety	voodoo	sorcery	pishogue

wizardry	witch's hat	witchcraft	thaumaturgy
09 diablerie	**10** black magic	**11** apotropaism	the black art
enchanted	broomstick	conjuration	witch-finder
occultism	divination	enchantment	**12** witching hour
the occult	necromancy	incantation	**14** Walpurgis night

See also **fairy tale**; **legend**; **Rowling, J K**; **Shakespeare, William**

wizard

Wizards include:

04 Howl (*Howl's Moving Castle*, 1986, Diana Wynne Jones)
Math (*The Mabinogion*)

05 Black (Sirius; *Harry Potter and the Prisoner of Azkaban*, 1999, et seq, J K Rowling)
Moody (Alastor 'Mad-Eye'; *Harry Potter and the Goblet of Fire*, 2000, et seq, J K Rowling)
Smith (Eskarina; *Equal Rites*, 1987, Terry Pratchett)
Snape (Severus; *Harry Potter and the Philosopher's Stone*, 1997, et seq, J K Rowling)

06 Alatar (*The Lord of the Rings*, 1954–5, J R R Tolkien)
Malfoy (Draco; *Harry Potter and the Philosopher's Stone*, 1997, et seq, J K Rowling)
Merlin (Arthurian legend)
Mordru (comic)
Potter (Harry; *Harry Potter and the Philosopher's Stone*, 1997, et seq, J K Rowling)
Zordon (*Mighty Morphin' Power Rangers*, 1993–6, TV series)

07 Calatin (Irish mythology)
Gandalf (*The Lord of the Rings*, 1954–5, J R R Tolkien)
Gwydion (*The Mabinogion*)
Saruman (*The Lord of the Rings*, 1954–5, J R R Tolkien)
Scratch (Nicholas; comic)
Weasley (Ron; *Harry Potter and the Philosopher's Stone*, 1997, et seq, J K Rowling)

08 Coriakin (*The Voyage of the Dawn Treader*, 1952, C S Lewis)
Lockhart (Gilderoy; *Harry Potter and the Chamber of Secrets*, 1998, J K Rowling)
Pallando (*The Lord of the Rings*, 1954–5, J R R Tolkien)
Prospero (*The Tempest*, 1611, William Shakespeare)
Radagast (*The Lord of the Rings*, 1954–5, J R R Tolkien)

09 Archimago (*The Faerie Queene*, 1590, Edmund Spenser)
Jack o' Kent (English folklore)
Rincewind (*The Colour of Magic*, 1985, et seq, Terry Pratchett)
Slytherin (Salazar; *Harry Potter and the Philosopher's Stone*, 1997, et seq, J K Rowling)

10 Doctor Fate (comic)
Dumbledore (Albus; *Harry Potter and the Philosopher's Stone*, 1997, et seq, J K Rowling)
Gryffindor (Godric; *Harry Potter and the Philosopher's Stone*, 1997, et seq, J K Rowling)

13 Lord Voldemort (*Harry Potter and the Philosopher's Stone*, 1997, et seq, J K Rowling)
The Wizard King (French fairytale)

15 Mustrum Ridcully (*Moving Picture*, 1990, et seq, Terry Pratchett)

Wodehouse, Sir P G (1881–1975)

Significant works include:

11 *My Man Jeeves* (1919)
12 *Quick Service* (1940)
13 *Carry On, Jeeves* (1925)
Right Ho, Jeeves (1934)

15 *The Mating Season* (1949)
20 *The Code of the Woosters* (1938) .
21 *The Man with Two Left Feet* (1916)

Significant characters include:

06 Jeeves (Reginald)	**09** Uncle Fred
Psmith (Ronald)	Aunt Agatha
07 Travers (Aunt Dahlia)	Aunt Dahlia
Wooster (Bertram Wilberforce 'Bertie')	**10** Fink-Nottle (Augustus 'Gussie')
08 Emsworth (Lord)	**15** The Oldest Member
Mulliner (Mr)	

womanizer

Womanizers and libertines include:

04 goat	**06** gay dog	Lovelace	womanizer
lech	lecher	palliard	
rake		rakehell	**10** Corinthian
roué	**07** Don Juan		lady-killer
wolf	seducer	**09** debauchee	profligate
	wastrel	ladies' man	sensualist
05 letch		libertine	
Romeo	**08** Casanova	reprobate	**11** gay deceiver
	Lothario	voluptary	philanderer

wonder

The Seven Wonders of the World:

15 Pyramids of Egypt	**23** Hanging Gardens of Babylon
16 Colossus of Rhodes	**24** Mausoleum of Halicarnassus
18 Pharos of Alexandria	Temple of Artemis at Ephesus
21 Statue of Zeus at Olympia	

wood

Woods include:

03 ash	sasa	satin	sapele
box	soft	tiger	spruce
cam	teak	torch	timber
elm	**05** alder	tulip	veneer
fir	apple	utile	walnut
nut	balsa	white	willow
oak	beech	zebra	
ply	black	**06** acacia	**07** Amboina
red	brush	bamboo	bubinga
sap	cedar	bitter	hickory
yew	drift	brazil	palmyra
04 bass	ebony	candle	quassia
cord	green	cherry	
cork	hazel	cotton	**08** amaranth
deal	heart	linden	chestnut
fire	kauri	lumber	cocobolo
hard	larch	obeche	hornbeam
iron	maple	orange	mahogany
lime	match	padauk	red lauan
pine	olive	pedauk	seasoned
pink	peach	poplar	silky oak
pulp	plane	rubber	sycamore
rose	ramin	sandal	**09** chipboard
			hardboard

jacaranda	paper birch	purple heart	yellow birch
quebracho	**11** black cherry	tulip poplar	**13** sweet chestnut
10 afrormosia	lignum vitae	white walnut	

See also **forest**

Woolf, Virginia (1882–1941)

Significant works include:

05 *Flush* (1933)

07 *Orlando* (1928)

08 *The Waves* (1931)
The Years (1937)

10 *Jacob's Room* (1922)

11 *Mrs Dalloway* (1925)
Night and Day (1919)

12 *The Voyage Out* (1915)

Three Guineas (1938)

13 *A Haunted House* (1943)

14 *A Room of One's Own* (1929)
Between the Acts (1941)

15 *To the Lighthouse* (1927)

17 *Granite and Rainbow* (1958)
The Death of the Moth (1942)

19 *The Captain's Death Bed* (1950)

Significant characters include:

05 Flush
Hewet (Terence)
Hirst (St John)
Jinny
Louis
Seton (Sally)
Susan
Walsh (Peter)

06 Denham (Ralph)

Ramsay (Mr)
Ramsay (Mrs)
Rodney (William)

07 Ambrose (Helen)
Briscoe (Lily)
Datchet (Mary)
Hilbery (Katharine)
La Trobe (Miss)
Neville

Orlando
Swithin (Mrs)
Vinrace (Rachel)

08 Dalloway (Clarissa)
Dalloway (Richard)
Flanders (Jacob)
Pargiter (Colonel Abel)
Pargiter (Eleanor)
Percival

word

Words and expressions from foreign languages include:

03 cwm (Welsh; valley or mountain hollow)
kop (Afrikaans; hill/football terrace)
obi (Japanese; sash)

04 agar (Malay; jelly used to grow bacteria
cultures)
bint (Arabic; girl)
dhow (Arabic, sailing vessel)
dojo (Japanese; place where martial arts take
place)
duma (Russian; Russian parliament)
guru (Hindi; a spiritual leader)
hajj (Arabic; the Muslim pilgrimage to
Mecca)
haka (Maori; ceremonial war dance)
jiva (Sanskrit; the soul)
khat (Arabic; narcotic shrub leaves)
luau (Hawaiian; party or feast)
veld (Afrikaans; open grassland)

05 aloha (Hawaiian; a salutation)
bagel (Yiddish; ring-shaped bread roll)
balti (Urdu; type of cuisine)
basho (Japanese; sumo wrestling

tournament)
batik (Javanese; painted form of decoration)
bhaji (Hindi; fried vegetables)
blini (Russian; stuffed pancakes)
burka (Urdu; yashmak)
cooee (Aboriginal; called to attract attention)
dacha (Russian; small country house)
dekko (Hindustani; look)
dhobi (Hindustani; washerman or
washerwoman)
dhoti (Hindustani; cloth worn by Hindu
males)
fakir (Arabic; religious mendicant)
fatwa (Arabic; ruling given on a point of
Islamic law by an expert)
haiku (Japanese; a short poem)
halal (Arabic; meat from an animal killed in
accordance with Islamic law)
jihad (Arabic; holy war against unbelievers)
kanzu (Kiswahili; a long white robe worn by
East African men)
karma (Sanskrit; the concept that actions
determine future conditions)

kayak (Inuit; covered canoe)
kippa (Hebrew; a skullcap worn by orthodox male Jews)
manga (Japanese; comic book or strip)
pasha (Turkish; officer of high rank)
pukka (Hindi; genuine, true)
samfu (Chinese; suit of jacket and trousers worn mainly by women)
wushu (Chinese; the Chinese martial arts)

06 anorak (Inuit; hooded jacket)
avatar (Sanskrit; manifestation)
banzai (Japanese; a battle cry, salute or exclamation of joy)
bonsai (Japanese; art of growing miniature trees in pots)
bunyip (Aboriginal; swamp monster)
datcha (Russian; small country house)
dim sum (Chinese; snack)
eureka (Greek; cry of triumph at a discovery)
favela (Portuguese; a shack or shanty)
fellah (Arabic; peasant)
kaftan (Turkish; long loose dress or shirt)
kirpan (Punjabi; ceremonial dagger worn by Sikhs)
kosher (Hebrew; pure or clean according to Jewish law)
kvetch (Yiddish; complain, whine)
loofah (Arabic; sponge for bathing)
muu-muu (Hawaiian; loose, brightly coloured dress)
punkah (Hindi; a large cooling fan)
salaam (Arabic; a greeting meaning 'peace')
shogun (Japanese; ruler of feudal Japan)
t'ai chi (Chinese; system of exercise and self-defence)
yakusa (Japanese; gangsters)

07 baklava (Turkish; a dessert)
basmati (Hindi; fragrant rice)
bhangra (Punjabi; folk dance/music)
biltong (Afrikaans; dried meat strips)
bortsch (Russian; soup containing beetroot)
crannog (Irish; ancient fortified settlement)
dashiki (West African; loose, brightly coloured shirt)
dervish (Turkish; a holy man)
falafel (Arabic; ball of spiced minced pulses)
ikebana (Japanese; the art of flower arrangement)
jellaba (Arabic; a loose, hooded, long-sleeved cloak)
karaoke (Japanese; singing a solo to a recorded backing)
karoshi (Japanese; death by overwork)
Kashrut (Hebrew; Jewish religious laws relating to food etc)
khamsin (Arabic; hot southerly wind)
kibbutz (Hebrew; a communal agricultural settlement in Israel)

lambada (Portuguese; a dance)
menorah (Hebrew; candelabrum)
namaste (Hindi; gesture of greeting by bringing palms together and bowing)
netsuke (Japanese; a small carved ornament)
nirvana (Sanskrit; state of enlightenment, bliss)
origami (Japanese; art of folding paper)
schlock (Yiddish; inferior, shoddy)
schmuck (Yiddish; stupid person)
tsunami (Japanese; a wave generated by movement of the Earth's surface underwater)

08 auto-da-fé (Portuguese; public declaration or carrying out of a sentence imposed on heretics)
babushka (Russian; granny)
boondock (Tagalog; remote parts of the country)
chutzpah (Yiddish; nerve to do or say outrageous things)
clarsach (Gaelic; harp)
djellaba (Arabic; a loose, hooded, long-sleeved robe)
feng-shui (Chinese; study and system of environmental harmony)
glasnost (Russian; policy of openness and forthrightness)
kamikaze (Japanese; any reckless, potentially self-destructive act)
kielbasa (Polish; highly seasoned sausage)
mazel tov (Hebrew; good luck, congratulations)
samizdat (Russian; secret printing and distribution of banned literature)
schmaltz (Yiddish; showy sentimentality)

09 apartheid (Afrikaans; enforced separation of races)
baksheesh (Persian; a gift or present of money)
balalaika (Russian; a musical instrument)
billabong (Aboriginal; backwater)
boomerang (Aboriginal; curved wooden missile)
bossa nova (Portuguese; a dance)
catamaran (Tamil; a raft, now a twin-hulled boat)
djellabah (Arabic; a loose, hooded, long-sleeved robe)
hoi polloi (Greek; the rabble)
inshallah (Arabic; if Allah wills)
maharishi (Sanskrit; a Hindu sage or spiritual leader)

10 bar mitzvah (Hebrew; religious initiation ceremony for boys)
tamagotchi (Japanese; electronic toy pet)

11 apparatchik (Russian; any bureaucratic hack)
    bath mitzvah (Hebrew; religious initiation
    ceremony for girls)

perestroika (Russian; restructuring of an
    organization)

See also **The Americas**; **French**; **German**; **Italian**; **Latin**; **Spanish**

Wordsworth, William (1770–1850)

Significant works include:

07 'Michael' (1801)

09 *Peter Bell* (1819)

10 *The Prelude* (1850)
    The Recluse (1800)

11 *The Waggoner* (1819)

12 *The Excursion* (1814)

13 *An Evening Walk* (1793)

14 *Lyrical Ballads* (1798)

17 *Poems in Two Volumes* (1807)

19 *Descriptive Sketches* (1793)

20 *The Borderers: A Tragedy* (1796)

21 *The White Doe of Rylstone* (1815)
    'Upon Westminster Bridge' (1801)

27 'Ode: Intimations of Immortality' (1807)

29 'Lines Written Above Tintern Abbey' (1798)

World Heritage site

World Heritage sites include:

03 Bam (Iran)

04 Bath (England)
    Graz (Austria)
    Lima (Peru)
    Pisa (Italy)
    Riga (Latvia)
    Troy (Turkey)

05 Aksum (Ethiopia)
    Berne (Switzerland)
    Bosra (Syria)
    Cuzco (Peru)
    Delos (Greece)
    Kandy (Sri Lanka)
    Lyons (France)
    Paris (France)
    Petra (Jordan)
    Quito (Ecuador)
    Siena (Italy)
    Sucre (Bolivia)

06 Aleppo (Syria)
    Amazon (Brazil)
    Angkor (Cambodia)
    Assisi (Italy)
    Brugge (Belgium)
    Cyrene (Libya)
    Delphi (Greece)
    Kracow (Poland)
    Naples (Italy)
    Oporto (Portugal)
    Potosi (Bolivia)
    Prague (Czech Republic)
    Puebla (Mexico)
    Sintra (Portugal)
    Thebes (Egypt)

    Toledo (Spain)
    Venice (Italy)
    Verona (Italy)
    Vienna (Austria)
    Warsaw (Poland)

07 Abu Mena (Egypt)
    Avignon (France)
    Caracas (Venezuela)
    Caserta (Italy)
    Cordoba (Spain)
    Holy See (Vatican City)
    Kremlin (Russia)
    Olympia (Greece)
    Pompeii (Italy)
    St Kilda (Scotland)
    Vicenza (Italy)

08 Agra Fort (India)
    Alhambra (Spain)
    Brasilia (Brazil)
    Budapest (Hungary)
    Damascus (Syria)
    Florence (Italy)
    Istanbul (Turkey)
    Pyrénées (France/Spain)
    Salzburg (Austria)
    Shark Bay (Australia)
    Taj Mahal (India)
    Timbuktu (Mali)
    Valletta (Malta)
    Yosemite (USA)

09 Acropolis (Greece)
    Agrigento (Italy)
    Auschwitz (Poland)
    Ayutthaya (Thailand)

Dubrovnik (Croatia)
Galapagos (Ecuador)
Jerusalem (Israel)
Mesa Verde (USA)
New Lanark (Scotland)
Purnululu (Australia)
Red Square (Russia)

10 Everglades (USA)
Herculaneum (Italy)
Lake Baikal (Russia)
Lake Malawi (Malawi)
Luxembourg (Luxembourg)
Mexico City (Mexico)
Safranbolu (Turkey)
Stonehenge (England)
The Rockies (Canada)
Versailles (France)

11 Ajanta Caves (India)
Ancient Nara (Japan)
Danube Delta (Romania)
Ellora Caves (India)
Grand Canyon (USA)
Kilimanjaro (Tanzania)
Leptis Magna (Libya)
Machu Picchu (Peru)
Medina of Fez (Morocco)
Parque Güell (Spain)

Quedlinburg (Germany)
Vatican City (Holy See)
Yellowstone (USA)

12 Altamira Cave (Spain)
Ancient Kyoto (Japan)
Anuradhapura (Sri Lanka)
Fraser Island (Australia)
Hadrian's Wall (England)
Hué Monuments (Vietnam)
Koguryo Tombs (North Korea)
Los Glaciares (Argentina)
Robben Island (South Africa)
Santo Domingo (Dominican Republic)
The Great Wall (China)

13 Bamiyan Valley (Afghanistan)
Tower of London (England)

14 Blenheim Palace (England)
Elephanta Caves (India)
Giant's Causeway (Northern Ireland)
Rocky Mountains (Canada)

15 Aachen Cathedral (Germany)
Amiens Cathedral (France)
Classical Weimar (Germany)
Ironbridge Gorge (England)
Kasbah of Algiers (Algeria)
Kathmandu Valley (Nepal)
Statue of Liberty (USA)

worm

Worms include:

03	eel		hook		leech	**07**	annelid
	lug		tape		round		bristle
	pin	**05**	arrow	**06**	peanut	**08**	sea mouse
	rag		earth		ribbon	**10**	blood fluke
04	flat		fluke		thread		liver fluke

wrestling

Wrestling holds and throws include:

03	hug		hip-lock		full nelson	
04	lock	**08**	arm throw		hammerlock	
06	grovet		body lock	**11**	backbreaker	
	nelson		headlock		scissor hold	
	souple		scissors	**12**	cross-buttock	
	suplex	**09**	ankle lace		scissors hold	
07	bear hug		body throw		stranglehold	
	buttock	**10**	Boston crab	**14**	grand amplitude	

Wrestling terms include:

03	mat		fall	**05**	judge
	pin		hold	**06**	action
04	bout		open		bridge

souple
07 default
referee
08 arm throw
body lock
chairman
exposing
reversal
takedown

09 ankle lace
body throw
bridge out
freestyle
grapevine
gut wrench
passivity
10 arm control
Greco-Roman

13 central circle
cross-body ride
passivity zone
14 danger position
grand amplitude
protection area
15 double-leg tackle
single leg tackle
technical points

writing

Writings include:

03 ode
04 blog
book
epic
news
play
poem
tale
05 diary
drama
essay
fable
lyric
novel
paper
story
study
06 annals
column
letter
memoir
record
report
review
satire

script
sketch
sonnet
thesis
weblog
07 account
apology
article
epistle
feature
fiction
history
journal
novella
parable
profile
08 apologia
critique
treatise
yearbook
09 biography
chronicle
criticism
discourse
editorial

life story
monograph
narrative
statement
technical
10 commentary
journalism
literature
non-fiction
propaganda
scientific
travelogue
11 confessions
copywriting
documentary
12 dissertation
13 autobiography
legal document
14 correspondence
15 advertising copy
curriculum vitae
newspaper column

Writing instruments include:

03 pen
04 Biro®
reed
05 quill
06 crayon
dip pen
pencil
stylus
07 cane pen
08 brailler

CD marker
steel pen
09 ballpoint
eraser pen
ink pencil
marker pen
10 felt-tip pen
lead-pencil
typewriter
11 board marker

fountain pen
highlighter
12 cartridge pen
writing brush
13 laundry marker
Roman metal pen
word-processor
14 calligraphy pen
coloured pencil
15 permanent marker

Writers include:

04 bard
hack
poet
05 clerk
06 author
editor
fabler
penman
pen-pal
rhymer
scribe
07 copyist
diarist
08 annalist
composer
essayist

lyricist
novelist
penwoman
reporter
satirist
09 columnist
dramatist
historian
pen-friend
penpusher
scribbler
sonneteer
web author
10 biographer
chronicler
copywriter
journalist

librettist
playwright
11 contributor
ghost writer
storyteller
12 leader-writer
poet laureate
scriptwriter
stenographer
13 calligraphist
correspondent
court reporter
fiction writer
lexicographer
14 autobiographer
15 technical writer

See also **alphabet**; **Austen, Jane**; **Blyton, Enid**; **Brontë, Anne**; **Brontë, Charlotte**; **Brontë, Emily**; **Carroll, Lewis**; **Chaucer, Geoffrey**; **Christie, Dame Agatha**; **Defoe, Daniel**; **Dickens, Charles**; **Dostoevsky, Fyodor**; **Doyle, Sir Arthur Conan**; **Dumas, Alexandre**; **Eliot, George**; **fable**; **Hardy, Thomas**; **Hemingway, Ernest**; **James, Henry**; **Joyce, James**; **Kipling, Rudyard**; **Lawrence, D H**; **Morrison, Toni**; **Murdoch, Dame Iris**; **Nobel Prize**; **non-fiction**; **novel**; **Orwell, George**; **poetry**; **Potter, Beatrix**; **Proust, Marcel**; **religion**; **Rowling, J K**; **science fiction**; **Scott, Sir Walter**; **Stevenson, Robert Louis**; **Tolkien, J R R**; **Tolstoy, Count Leo**; **Trollope, Anthony**; **Twain, Mark**; **Voltaire**; **Wells, H G**; **Wodehouse, Sir P G**; **Woolf, Virginia**; **Zola, Émile**

XYZ

year

Yeats, W B (1865–1939)

yellow

yoga

Yoga types include:

03 Dru		Kaula	**07** Iyengar		Shadanga
04 Agni		Kriya		Kripalu	**09** Ghatastha
Japa		Nidra		Samkhya	Kundalini
Laya	**06** Abhava			Samputa	Pashupata
Maha		Bhakti		Tantric	Patanjala
Nada		Bikram		Vinyasa	Patanjali
Raja		Buddhi	**08** Adhyatma		Sivananda
Vini		Mantra		Ashtanga	**12** Yoga-Darshana
05 Hatha		Sahaja		Asparsha	**13** Hiranyagarbha
Jñāna		Taraka		Ayurveda	
Karma		Yantra		Saptanga	

Yoga terms and positions include:

02 om
03 Bow
Cat
04 anga
Boat
Easy
Fish
Hero
Lion
Plow
Tree
yama
yogi
05 Angle
asana
Camel
Child
Cobra
Crane
Eagle
Lotus
mudra
mukti
prana
Staff
Wheel
yogin
06 asanas
Bridge
chakra
Corpse
dhyana
Lizard
Locust
mantra

Monkey
niyama
Pigeon
Prayer
Secret
shakti
siddha
siddhi
Throne
07 Compass
Cow Face
dharana
Diamond
drishti
Firefly
Garland
Goddess
Peacock
Pendant
Pyramid
samadhi
Warrior
08 chin lock
Cobbler's
Cockerel
ekāgrata
Half Moon
Mountain
Palm Tree
Powerful
Scorpion
Tortoise
Triangle
09 alignment
Crocodile

Dog and Cat
Happy Baby
Headstand
One-legged
pranayama
Side Crane
Side Plank
10 Flying Crow
Head to Knee
meditation
pratyahara
Salutation
shatkarmas
tongue lock
11 Raised Hands
Thunderbolt
yogic flying
yogi toe lock
12 Accomplished
Awkward Chair
Forearm Stand
13 abdominal lock
Cat-Cow Stretch
Legs up the Wall
Shoulder stand
Sun Salutation
Wind-releasing
14 Hand-foot-big toe
King of the Dance
Reclined Big Toe
Sleeping Vishnu
15 Four Limbed Staff
Turned Side-Angle
Upward Facing Dog

York *see* **archbishop**

young *see* **animal**

zip code *see* **United States of America**

zodiac

Signs of the zodiac:

03 Leo (Lion; 24 Jul-23 Aug; fire)
05 Aries (Ram; 21 Mar-20 Apr; fire)
    Libra (Balance; 24 Sep-22 Oct; air)
    Virgo (Virgin; 24 Aug-23 Sep; earth)
06 Cancer (Crab; 22 Jun-23 Jul; water)
    Gemini (Twins; 21 May-21 Jun; air)
See also **astrology**

    Pisces (Fishes; 20 Feb-20 Mar; water)
    Taurus (Bull; 21 Apr-20 May; earth)
07 Scorpio (Scorpion; 23 Oct-22 Nov; water)
08 Aquarius (Water Bearer; 21 Jan-19 Feb; air)
09 Capricorn (Goat; 23 Dec-20 Jan; earth)
11 Sagittarius (Archer; 23 Nov-22 Dec; fire)

Zola, Émile (1840–1902)

Significant works include:

04 *Rome* (1896)
05 *Paris* (1898)
06 *Vérité* (1903)
07 '*J'accuse*' (1898)
    Lourdes (1894)
    Travail (1901)

09 *Fécondité* (1899)
13 *Thérèse Raquin* (1867)
14 *Les Trois Villes* (1894–98)
17 *Les Rougon-Macquart* (1871–93)
18 *Les Quatre Évangiles* (1899–1903)
19 *Le roman experimental* (1880)

Les Rougon-Macquart comprises:

04 *Nana* (1880)
06 *Le Rêve* (1888)
07 *La Curée* (1872)
    L'Argent (1891)
    La Terre (1887)
    L'Oeuvre (1886)
08 *Germinal* (1885)
09 *La Débâcle* (1892)
10 *L'Assommoir* (1877)
    Pot-Bouille (1882)

13 *La Bête humaine* (1890)
    La Joie de vivre (1884)
    Une Page d'amour (1878)
15 *Le Docteur Pascal* (1893)
    Le Ventre de Paris (1873)
17 *Au Bonheur des dames* (1883)
18 *La Fortune des Rougon* (1871)
20 *La Conquête de Plassans* (1874)
    La Faute de l'Abbé Mouret (1875)
25 *Son Excellence Eugène Rougon* (1876)

Significant characters include:

04 Dide (Aunt)
05 Baudu (Denise)
    Hugon (Georges)
    Hugon (Philippe)
    Maheu (Toussaint)
    Puech (Félicité)
    Quenu
    Quenu (Pauline)
    Weiss
06 Buteau
    Chaval

Fouque (Adélaïde)
Mouret
Mouret (Désirée)
Mouret (François)
Mouret (Hélène)
Mouret (Octave)
Mouret (Serge)
Mouret (Silvère)
Pascal (Le Docteur)
Rougon
Rougon (Angélique)

Rougon (Aristide)
Rougon (Charles)
Rougon (Clotilde)
Rougon (Eugène)
Rougon (Marthe)
Rougon (Maxime)
Rougon (Pascal)
Rougon (Pierre)
Rougon (Sidonie)
Rougon (Victor)
Sandoz (Pierre)

07 Coupeau
  Coupeau (Anna 'Nana')
  Coupeau (Louis 'Louiset')
  Deleuze (Caroline)
  Hedouin (Mme)
  Lantier (Auguste)
  Lantier (Claude)
  Lantier (Étienne)
  Lantier (Jacques)
  Lantier (Jacques-Louis)
  Laurent
  Levaque
  Mareuil (Louise de)
  Racquin (Camille)
  Racquin (Laurent)

Racquin (Mme)
Racquin (Thérèse)
Rambaud
Steiner
Vineuil (Colonel de)

08 Fauchéry (Léon)
  Gavaudan (Joséphine)
  Macquart
  Macquart (Antoine)
  Macquart (Gervaise)
  Macquart (Jean)
  Macquart (Lisa)
  Macquart (Ursule)
  Sicardot
  Sicardot (Angèle)

09 Bordenave
  Catherine
  Chavaille (Rosalie)
  Grandjean
  Grandjean (Jeanne)
  Souvarine

10 Hallegrain (Christine)
  Hautecoeur (Angélique de)
  Hautecoeur (Felicien VII de)
  Vandeuvres (Comte Xavier de)

14 Angélique Marie
  Béraud du Châtel (Renée)

15 Beulin d'Orchères (Véronique)

zoology

Branches of zoology include:

07 ecology
  zoonomy
  zootaxy
08 cetology
  oecology
09 acarology
  hippology
  mammalogy
  ophiology
  therology
10 autecology

conchology
embryology
entomology
limacology
malacology
morphology
nematology
11 arachnology
  herpetology
  ichthyology
  insectology
  myrmecology

ornithology
12 gnotobiology
  parasitology
  protozoology
  zoopathology
13 helminthology
  neuroethology
  palaeozoology
  zoophysiology
14 archaeozoology
15 lepidopterology

Zoologists include:

03 Pye (John David; 1932– , English)
04 Gray (John Edward; 1800–75, English)
  Gray (Sir James; 1891–1975, English)
  Mayr (Ernst Walter; 1904–2005, German/US)
  Owen (Sir Richard; 1804–92, English)
  Savi (Paolo; 1798–1871, Italian)
05 Blyth (Edward; 1810–73, English)
  Ewart (James Cossar; 1851–1933, Scottish)
  Fabre (Jean Henri; 1823–1915, French)
  Hinde (Robert Aubrey; 1923– , English)
  Hyman (Libbie Henrietta; 1888–1969, US)
  Krebs (Sir John; 1945– , English)
  Yonge (Charles Maurice; 1899–1986, English)
06 Darwin (Charles; 1809–82, English)
  de Beer (Sir Gavin; 1899–1972, English)
  Flower (Sir William Henry; 1831–99, English)
  Fossey (Dian; 1932–85, US)
  Frisch (Karl von; 1886–1982, Austrian)
  Hooker (Sir Joseph; 1817–1911, English)

Kinsey (Alfred; 1894–1956, US)
Lorenz (Konrad; 1903–89, Austrian)
Morris (Desmond; 1928– , English)
Newton (Alfred; 1829–1907, English)
Osborn (Henry Fairfield; 1857–1935, US)
Rensch (Bernhard; 1900–90, German)
Sloane (Sir Hans; 1660–1753, British)
Thorpe (William Homan; 1902–86, English)
Wilson (Edmund Beecher; 1856–1939, US)

07 Agassiz (Alexander; 1835–1910, US)
  Agassiz (Louis; 1807–73, US)
  Audubon (John James; 1785–1851, US)
  Dawkins (Richard; 1941– , British)
  Durrell (Gerald; 1925–95, English)
  Griffin (Donald; 1915–2003, US)
  Hediger (Heini; 1908–1992, Swiss)
  Hertwig (Oscar; 1849–1922, German)
  Mantell (Gideon; 1790–1852, English)
  Medawar (Sir Peter; 1915–87, British)
  Merriam (Clinton Hart; 1885–1942, US)
  Rüppell (Eduard; 1794–1884, German)

Siebold (Karl Theodor Ernst von; 1804–65, German)
Spemann (Hans; 1869–1941, German)
Wallace (Alfred Russel; 1823–1913, English)
08 Brünnich (Morten Thrane; 1737–1827, Danish)
Hamilton (William Donald; 1936–2000, English)
Jennings (Herbert Spencer; 1868–1947, US)
Kammerer (Paul; 1880–1926, Austrian)
Leuckart (Karl Georg Friedrich Rudolf; 1822–98, German)
Linnaeus (Carolus; 1707–78, Swedish)
Mitchell (Sir Peter Chalmers; 1864–1945, Scottish)
Schultze (Max Johann Sigismund; 1825–74, German)
Thompson (John Vaughan; 1779–1847, English)
Thompson (Sir D'Arcy; 1860–1948, Scottish)

09 Aristotle (384–322 BC, Greek)
Lankester (Sir Edwin; 1847–1929, English)
Schaudinn (Fritz; 1871–1906, German)
Southwood (Sir Richard; 1931–2005, English)
Tinbergen (Nikolaas; 1907–88, Dutch)
Zuckerman (Solly, Lord; 1904–93, South African/British)
10 Kettlewell (Henry Bernard David; 1907–79, English)
Rothschild (Lionel Walter, Lord; 1868–1937, English)
Rothschild (Dame Miriam; 1908–2005, English)
Steenstrup (Johannes Iapetus Smith; 1813–97, Danish)
Williamson (William Crawford; 1816–95, English)
12 Attenborough (Sir David; 1926– , English)
Wynne-Edwards (Vero; 1906–97, English)

Terms used in zoology include:

04 host
05 biped
   clade
   morph
06 aliped
   atocia
07 habitat
   mimicry
   oestrus
08 gastrula
   holotype

   monogamy
   ommateum
   parasite
   polygamy
   ungulate
09 anoestrus
   didelphic
   oviparous
   quadruped
   refection
   taligrade

10 alloparent
   camouflage
   gressorial
   nucivorous
   omnivorous
   prehensile
   viviparous
11 aestivation
   artiodactyl
   carnivorous
   granivorous

   herbivorous
   hibernation
   iteroparous
   multiparous
   noctilucent
   plantigrade
12 carpophagous
   exteroceptor
13 hermaphrodite
14 autocoprophagy
   startle colours

See also **classification**